The New International Dictionary of New Testament Theology

The New International Dictionary of

Companion Volume

THE NEW INTERNATIONAL
DICTIONARY OF THE CHRISTIAN CHURCH

New Testament Theology

Colin Brown
GENERAL EDITOR

Translated, with additions and revisions, from the German
THEOLOGISCHES BEGRIFFSLEXIKON
ZUM NEUEN TESTAMENT

Edited by Lothar Coenen, Erich Beyreuther *and* Hans Bietenhard

ZONDERVAN PUBLISHING HOUSE
OF THE ZONDERVAN CORPORATION
GRAND RAPIDS, MICHIGAN 49506

THE NEW INTERNATIONAL DICTIONARY OF NEW TESTAMENT THEOLOGY
Originally published in German under the title,
THEOLOGISCHES BEGRIFFSLEXIKON ZUM NEUEN TESTAMENT

© 1967, 1969, 1971 by Theologischer Verlag Rolf Brockhaus, Wuppertal.
English Language edition copyright © 1975, The Zondervan Corporation
Grand Rapids, Michigan, U.S.A. and The Paternoster Press, Ltd. Exeter,
Devon, U.K.

Second printing 1979

Library of Congress Cataloging in Publication Data
Main entry under title:

The new international dictionary of New Testament
 theology.

 "Translated, with additions and revisions, from the
German Theologisches Begriffslexikon zum Neuen Testament,
edited by Lothar Coenen, Erich Beyreuther and Hans
Bietenhard."
 "Companion volume: The new international dictionary
of the Christian Church."
 Includes bibliographical references and indexes.
 1. Bible. N.T.—Theology—Dictionaries. 2. Bible.
N.T.—Dictionaries. I. Brown, Colin.
BS2397.N48 230'.03 75-38895

ISBN 0-310-21890-X

Printed in the United States of America

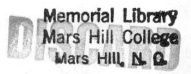
Contents

Preface

BURY YOURSELF IN A DICTIONARY AND COME UP IN THE PRESENCE OF GOD. THIS improbable-sounding piece of advice of the late Sir Edwyn Hoskyns contains a wisdom born of experience. At first sight a dictionary may appear to contain nothing but a mass of antiquarian information. But to those who know where and how to look, the forbidding mass of material is not a barrier between the individual and real life but a bridge to a richer appreciation of it. It is when we ask, "What is the writer getting at?", "Why did he say this?", "Why did he put it like that?", "What lies behind that remark?", that we begin to see things in a new light.

A theological dictionary is not a collection of prepackaged sermons or an anthology of predigested devotion. It is more like an invitation to join in the collective enterprise of quarrying and building. (The picture itself is not without affinities with the apostle Paul's picture in 1 Cor. 3:10 ff. of Christian work as a collective building enterprise.) It is as one quarries among the mass of data and tries to build something out of it that the data become alive. What was perhaps previously flat and featureless takes on new perspective and meaning. One can go even further. The great revivals of the Christian church have come about when some individual here and there has been grasped by something that his predecessors and contemporaries have taken for granted without stopping to ask why it should be so. Perhaps the greatest need for the church in the last quarter of the twentieth century is for men to stop, to ask themselves this question as they study the Bible, and then to translate their answers into action.

Two things characterise this enterprise. On the one hand, one has to do it for oneself. There is no substitute for individual initiative. On the other hand, it is a co-operative endeavour. One cannot do without the work of others in unearthing facts and bringing to light insights which would otherwise be lost. But paradoxically enough, it is only when others have done this kind of work that one can see the truth in it for oneself.

At all its stages *The New International Dictionary of New Testament Theology* is a collective enterprise. The original German work on which it is based was the product of ten years of teamwork, shared by university professors, college lecturers and others engaged in various branches of teaching and pastoral work. The extensive new material which will be included in all three volumes is the work of scholars on both sides of the Atlantic. The draft translation was prepared by a team of translators which included Professor G. H. Boobyer, the Rev. Dr. Colin Brown, Mr. H. L. Ellison, the Rev. M. C. Freeman, the late Rev. Dr. George Ogg, Mr. John D. Manton, the Rev. Philip J. Seddon, the Rev. David Sharp and Dr. A. J. M. Wedderburn.

A special debt of gratitude is owed to Professor F. F. Bruce, Rylands Professor of Biblical Criticism and Exegesis in the University of Manchester. Professor Bruce has read the articles in both typescript and proof, and has made many valuable comments and suggestions. Thanks are also due to the Rev. A. C. Thiselton of the Department of Biblical Studies in the University of Sheffield for reading the bibliographies and making numerous suggestions. The bibliographies have also benefited from the comments of his colleagues at Sheffield, Mr. D. J. A. Clines and the Rev. Wesley Carr. Mr. Michael Sadgrove has shouldered the heavy burden of proof-reading in the course of his doctoral studies at Oxford. The indexes have been compiled by the Rev. Norman Hillyer whose vigilant scholarship has also contributed to the correction of the proofs.

Finally, the editor would like to record his appreciation of the happy co-operation at all stages of the work with the editor of the German edition, Dr. Lothar Coenen, and the German publishers, the Theologischer Verlag Rolf Brockhaus of Wuppertal and for their kind agreement to the features incorporated in the English edition.

Scripture quotations in this Dictionary from the Revised Standard Version of the Bible are used by permission of the owners of the copyright, the Department of Christian Education of the National Council of the Churches of Christ in the United States of America.

Introduction

SINCE ITS FIRST APPEARANCE IN 1965 THE *Theologisches Begriffslexikon zum Neuen Testament* has established itself as a standard work of reference among theologians, ministers, students and all who are concerned with a closer understanding of the teaching of the Bible. It offers its readers a concise discussion of the meaning and use of the key terms of the New Testament against their background in the ancient world and the Old Testament, combining an awareness of the progress of modern scholarship with a sensitivity to the message of Scripture. The work had its origin in a double conviction. On the one hand, theology at its deepest level is concerned with the revelation of God – the God who has revealed himself in Scripture. On the other hand, this revelation came to man over a period of many hundreds of years. It was expressed in ancient languages, employing the thought-forms of bygone civilizations. In order to understand the meaning and significance of Scripture, it is necessary to understand the meaning and use of its language against the background of its history and social structures.

Some fifty years ago Karl Barth compared Calvin as an interpreter with the exegetes of his own day in the following terms:

> How energetically Calvin, having first established what stands in the text, sets himself to re-think the whole material and to wrestle with it, till the walls which separate the sixteenth century from the first become transparent! Paul speaks, and the man of the sixteenth century hears. The conversation between the original record and the reader moves round the subject-matter, until a distinction between yesterday and to-day becomes impossible. If a man persuades himself that Calvin's method can be dismissed with the old-fashioned motto, "The Compulsion of Inspiration," he betrays himself as one who has never worked upon the interpretation of Scripture (*The Epistle to the Romans*, ET 1933, 7).

Whether Calvin, Barth (or, for that matter, anyone else) consistently attained this ideal is less important than the points that Barth makes. The goal of biblical study – like that of expository preaching – is an understanding of the text which enables its message to speak directly to the reader or hearer in his contemporary situation. In this process there are two main stages characterized by the terms exegesis and hermeneutics. The latter – and it is on this that Barth focuses his attention – is concerned with reflecting on words and events from the past and interpreting their significance for us today. But before this may come about there must be the prior stage of exegesis, the elucidation of words, phrases, clauses and sentences, as their authors intended them to be understood and as they would have been understood by their original hearers. It is the exegesis of biblical terminology that is the primary concern of the present dictionary.

9

In their fulfilment of this task the authors of the individual articles have endeavoured not simply to analyse, classify and catalogue the most important words that occur in the New Testament. They have also sought to trace the meaning and use of words in secular Greek, the Septuagint and other versions of the Old Testament used by the early church in the New Testament period, comparing them with the Hebrew of the Old Testament. They have also taken into account the use of words in the Dead Sea Scrolls and writers like Philo and Josephus. Finally, the New Testament writings themselves are examined individually in order to ascertain the precise shade of meaning which each work attaches to the words used.

In using a work of this kind there is always a danger of what James Barr has called "illegitimate totality transfer" (*The Semantics of Biblical Language*, 1961, 218). This arises when the various meanings of a word in different contexts are run together and then presumed to be present on each and every occasion that the word is used. To quote Barr's own example, the word *ekklēsia* (church) may in various contexts mean "the Body of Christ," "the first instalment of the Kingdom of God," and "the Bride of Christ." It would be illegitimate to presume without further indication that in any given passage the word *ekklēsia* must bear all or even any of these meanings. To answer this question, one has to ask whether the author is acquainted with a particular meaning and whether the context indicates that this was his intention. Similarly, it is illegitimate to apply without more ado the meaning of a word in secular Greek or even the Septuagint to the New Testament, unless there be some indication that the word is used in the same sense.

Heed must also be given to Barr's warnings about etymologies. To know the derivation of a word is no infallible guide to its meaning. Barr observes: "The main point is that the etymology of a word is not a statement about its meaning but about its history; it is only as a historical statement that it can be responsibly asserted, and it is quite wrong to suppose that the etymology of a word is necessarily a guide either to its 'proper' meaning in a later period or to its actual meaning in that period" (op. cit., 109). Words have histories as well as etymologies. The meaning of any given word in any given context depends at least as much upon the place and use of the word in that context as upon any supposed derivation.

General Structure

The entire work is divided into articles under English titles, arranged in alphabetical order. These in turn contain one or more studies of the relevant terms in New Testament Greek which have been grouped under key words. Thus, the article on *Baptism, Wash* is divided into separate studies under the key Greek words *baptizō*, *louō* and *niptō*. For the sake of easy reference the key Greek word is placed in a box at the head of the appropriate study thus: | βαπτίζω |. In each case there follow the principal forms of the associated Greek words and their cognates which are given in both Greek letters and transliteration together with their basic dictionary equivalents.

Each article is divided into three main sections denoted by the letters CL indicating discussion of the word in classical and secular Greek, OT in Old Testament usage, and NT dealing with New Testament usage. They are arranged as follows:

10

CL Discussion of the word in secular Greek. Uses of the word are illustrated by references to classical literature, inscriptions and papyri. But in view of the expressly theological interest of the dictionary discussion here is kept to a minimum.

OT Discussion of the word in the Old Testament. The language of the church of the New Testament era was Greek, and the Old Testament Scriptures used by the church were largely the Greek translation of the Hebrew known as the Septuagint (LXX). The discussion is therefore based on the terms as they occur in the LXX and other Greek versions. But throughout these are compared with the corresponding Hebrew words of the Hebrew Masoretic text. (On these terms see the *Glossary of Technical Terms*.) This second section also includes discussion of terms in rabbinic writers, Philo and Josephus, and the discoveries at Qumran. In some instances comparison with the New Testament reveals close affinity of thought; in others there is a wide gulf between it and other religious thought.

NT Discussion of the word in the New Testament, noting statistical occurrences of the word, its uses in relation to its background, and the specific emphases of individual writers and writings.

The same method of study is followed for each separate key Greek word, except occasionally where the word may not occur or be relevant in either secular Greek (as in the case of certain proper names) or the Old Testament. Bibliographies are appended to all major articles.

Scope

The dictionary is expressly theological in intention. Historical, geographical and archaeological information, appropriate in a general dictionary of the Bible, is here included only in so far as it is theologically relevant. The main emphasis falls on the elucidation of terms. For this reason the dictionary does not attempt to summarize the theology of Paul, John, or the Synoptic Gospels, or to trace influences upon individual writers as subjects in themselves. Nevertheless, attention is paid to the distinctive outlook of any given writer in relation to particular terms. A number of proper names have been included in so far as they have a special theological significance in the New Testament.

Transliteration

The dictionary is designed for use both by the student of Greek and by those who have no prior grounding in ancient languages. For this reason all Greek and Hebrew words are given in transliteration. Greek words are given in Greek letters with the appropriate transliteration and translation at the head of each key Greek word. Thereafter only the transliterations are given. Hebrew words are given in transliteration only. A key to the transliterations is given on p. 47.

Features of the English Edition

The translation has been edited to meet the needs of English readers. This has involved a certain amount of re-writing and re-phrasing for the sake of clarity. The relative merits of different translations of Biblical passages have been discussed in English instead of German versions, and quotations have been taken from the English translations of published works. Where appropriate, references to important works relating to matters under discussion have been inserted.

A major difference that will be immediately apparent to those who compare the present work with the German original is the complete reorganization of the order of the articles. The German original had its articles arranged according to the alphabetical order of the German titles. Each article has been given an English title set in alphabetical order. This means that the present volume contains articles from all three volumes of the German original, and also that articles which appeared in the first volume of the German are distributed throughout all three volumes of the English edition. In assigning titles to the articles, it was decided not to restrict the title to a single key word, but to include in it those words which would indicate the general contents of the article concerned.

This English edition contains some 70 major articles which did not appear in the original German version. Other articles have been extended to include important new sections and other material which likewise have not previously been published. The *Glossary of Technical Terms* has been extensively enlarged. As the work proceeds, it is the publishers' intention to include further new material which is being prepared for inclusion in the new revised German edition.

The bibliographies appended to each article have been extensively revised and enlarged. The majority are divided into two sections. The first contains a list of books and articles in English, including translations of works listed in the original German bibliography. The second section is devoted to works in other languages. This contains titles listed in the original bibliography and also other works, including important works published since the article was written. The purpose is twofold. On the one hand, it offers English readers a conspectus of relevant literature in English. By separating the two sections, they will be able to see at a glance which works are relevant to their particular needs. On the other hand, it was decided to include titles not available in English translation in order to meet the needs of the more specialist student.

Certain articles in the German original contained homiletical sections which were directed to the pastoral situation in Germany and on the continent of Europe. They included references to discussions and literature which were significant in a continental setting but which are less so outside that context. In view of the different situation in the English-speaking world, it was decided with the agreement of the German publishers not to include these sections in the present edition.

Biblical References

Quotations from the Bible in English have normally been taken from the Revised Standard Version which is quoted by kind permission of the Division of Christian Education of the National Council of the Churches of Christ in the United States of America. However, translations of other versions are also given at certain points where the sources are specifically stated. In certain Old Testament passages where the LXX reference differs from that of the Hebrew Masoretic Text and the English versions the variant reference is given in brackets.

Statistical and Lexical Information

Statistical and lexical information has been drawn from the following sources: R. Morgenthaler, *Statistik des neutestamentlichen Wortschatzes*, 1958; E. Hatch and H. A. Redpath, *A Concordance to the Septuagint and the Other Greek Versions of the Old Testament*, I–III, (1897) 1954; K. G. Kuhn, *Konkordanz zu den Qumrantexten*, 1960; W. F. Moulton and A. S. Geden, *A Concordance to the Greek Testament*, (1897) 1963[4]; A. Schmöller, *Handkonkordanz zum griechischen Neuen Testament*, 1968[14]; S. Mandelkern, *Veteris Testamenti Concordantiae*, I–II, (1896) 1955; F. Brown, S. R. Driver and C. A. Briggs, *A Hebrew-English Lexicon of the Old Testament, with an Appendix containing the Biblical Aramaic*, (1907) 1955; L. Koehler and W. Baumgartner, *Lexicon in Veteris Testamenti Libros*, 1958[2]; H. G. Liddell and R. Scott, *A Greek-English Lexicon* revised by H. S. Jones, 1940[9]; and W. F. Arndt and F. W. Gingrich, *A Greek-English Lexicon of the New Testament and Other Early Christian Literature*, 1957.

Indexes

Separate indexes are provided to Volumes I and II, and indexes to the complete work in Volume III. A great many words are dealt with which are not included under the main headings in the Table of Articles, so the indexes should be consulted for full details.

Table of Articles in Volume I

16

21

Contributors

Editors and Advisors

Editor of the English edition   .   .   **Colin Brown**

General Editor of the German edition   **Lothar Coenen**

Greek philology, philosophy and
classical background .   .   .   .   **Gerhard Fries**

Old Testament and Septuagint   .   .   .   **Horst Seebass**

Qumran   .   .   .   .   .   **Reinhard Deichgräber**

Rabbinics .   .   .   .   .   .   **Hans Bietenhard**

New Testament philology and theology **Hans Bietenhard**

Church history and historical
theology .   .   .   .   **Erich Beyreuther**

Bibliographical consultant to the
German edition   .   .   .   .   **Werner Georg Kümmel**

Contributors to Volume I

In the following list the author's work is denoted by the Greek words which follow
the title.

Ernst Achilles, Superintendent, Göttingen
    Evil, *kakos, ponēros*
Gervais T. D. Angel, M.A., Dean of Studies, Trinity College, Bristol
    Bag, Box, *ballantion, glōssokomon, pēra*; Bitter, *pikros, pikrainō, parapikrainō;* Black,
    White, Red, *melas, leukos, pyrros;* Broad, Wide, *platos;* Exhort, Warn, Console,
    Rebuke, *epitimaō*
Hugo Aust, Steinfeld
    Curse, Insult, Fool, *anathema* (part)
Joyce G. Baldwin, B.A., B.D., Dean of Women, Trinity College, Bristol
    Cherub, *cheroub;* Fullness, Abound, Multitude, Fulfil, Make Room, Give Way,
    gemō, chortazō
Heinrich Baltensweiler, Dr. theol., Professor, Basel
    Discipline, Prudence, Immorality, Prostitute, *enkrateia*; Eunuch, *eunouchos*
Karl Heinz Bartels, Dr. theol., Niederbieber
    First, Firstborn, *prōtos, prōtotokos*

Wolfgang Bauder, Cologne
Animal, *thērion;* Disciple, Follow, Imitate, After, *mimeomai, opisō;* Fall, Fall Away, *aphistēmi, pipto;* Fullness, Abound, Multitude, Fulfil, Make Room, Give Way, *plēthos*
Gerhard Bauer, Starnberg
Birth, Beget, Bear, etc., *tiktō*
G. R. Beasley-Murray, M.A., B.D., M.Th., Ph.D., D.D. Professor, Southern Baptist Theological Seminary, Louisville
Abomination of Desolation, *to bdelygma tēs erēmōseōs;* Baptism, Wash, *baptizō, louō, niptō;* Blood, Sprinkle, Strangled, *rhantizō*
Oswald Becker, Bonn
Covenant, Guarantee, Mediator, *engyos, mesitēs;* Faith, Persuade, Belief, Unbelief, *peithomai*
Ulrich Becker, Dr. theol., Professor, Hanover
Blessing, Blessed, Happy, *makarios;* Book, Read, Letter, *biblos*
Ulrich Becker, Osterwald ü. Wunstorf
Conversion, Penitence, Repentance, Proselyte, *prosēlytos*
Roger T. Beckwith, M.A., Warden of Latimer House, Oxford
Baptism, Wash: Infant Baptism, its Background and Theology
Erich Beyreuther, Dr. theol., Professor, Feldkirchen, Munich
Desire, Lust, Pleasure, *hēdonē*
Hans Bietenhard, Dr. theol., Professor, Steffisburg
Accuser, Accuse, *katēgoros;* Amen, Hallelujah, Hosanna, *amēn;* Angel, Messenger etc., *angelos;* Beginning, Origin etc., *archē;* Blood, Sprinkle, Strangled, *pniktos;* Demon, Air, Cast Out, *aēr, daimonion, ekballō;* Dragon, Serpent etc., *drakōn, ophis;* Elijah, *Hēlias;* Enemy, Enmity, Hate, *echthros;* Fire, Burn, *pyr;* Foreign, Alien, Dispersion, Stranger, *allotrios, xenos, parepidēmos, paroikos*
Christian Blendinger, Nuremberg
Disciple, Follow, Imitate, After, *akoloutheō*
Jürgen Blunck, Solingen
Book, Read, Letter, *anaginōskō;* Firm, Foundation, Certainty, Confirm, *themelios;* Freedom, *eleutheria*
Egon Brandenburger, Dr. theol., Professor, Bethel
Cross, Wood, Tree, *stauros*
Theodor Brandt, Bad Salzuflen
Fullness, Abound etc., *perisseuō*
Georg Braumann, Dr. theol., Billerbeck
Advocate, Paraclete, Helper, *paraklētos;* Child, Boy, Servant, Son, Adoption, *nēpios, pais, teknon, hyios;* Comfort, Encouragement, *paramytheomai;* Exhort etc., *parakaleō;* Form, Substance, *eidos, morphē, schēma*
Colin Brown, M.A., B.D., Ph.D., Lecturer, Trinity College, Bristol
Adam, Eve, *Heua;* Animal: types of animal in the NT; Bird, *peteinon;* Birth, Beget, Bear, Become, Miscarriage etc., *ektrōma* (part); Child, Boy, Servant, Son, Adoption, *pais* (part), *hyios* (part); Conscience, *syneidēsis* (part); Cross, Wood, Tree, *stauros* (part); Cry, *boaō;* Destroy, Perish, Ruin, *olethros* (part); Empty, Vain, *kenos* (part); Firm, Foundation Certainty, Confirm, *asphaleia;* Fruit, Fig, Thorn, Thistle, *skolops;* Glossary of Technical Terms (part); Apostle, *apostolos* (part)
Wilhelm Brunotte, Dr. theol., Hameln
Anoint, *aleiphō*
Philip J. Budd, B.A., M.Litt., Lecturer, Trinity College, Bristol
Abraham, Sarah, Hagar, Isaac, *Sarra, Hagar, Isaak;* Angel, Messenger, Gabriel,

Michael, *Gabriēl, Michaēl;* Bethlehem, *Bēthleem;* Command, Order, *keleuō;* Danger, Risk, Peril, *kindyneuō, chalepos;* Deaf, Dumb, *kōphos;* Dragon, Serpent, Scorpion, Sting, *skorpios, kentron;* Dream, *onar;* Drunken, Sober, *methyō, nēphō;* Dry Up, Wither, *xērainō*

D. A. Carson, M.A., research student, Cambridge
Brother, Neighbour, Friend, *hetairos;* Cry, *krazō;* Cunning, *panourgia;* Escape, Flee, *pheugō;* Flow, *rheō*

Lothar Coenen, Dr. theol., Wuppertal
Bishop, Presbyter, Elder, *episkopos, presbyteros;* Call, *kaleō;* Church, Synagogue, *ekklēsia;* Death, Kill, Sleep, *apokteinō, katheudō, nekros;* Elect, Choose, *eklegomai*

Karl Dahn, Frankfurt
Fight, *thriambeuō* (part)

Günter Dulon, Hamburg
Determine, Appoint, Present, *horizō*

James D. G. Dunn, M.A., B.D., Ph.D., Lecturer, Nottingham
Caesar, Consul, Governor, *Kaisar, hēgemōn, hypatos*

Johannes Eichler, Frankfurt
Fellowship, Have, Share, Participate, *echō*

Erich von Eicken, Dr. theol., Marburg
Apostle, *apostellō* (part)

Margaret Embry, B.A., B.D., Lecturer, Trinity College, Bristol
Beat, Chastise, Scourge, *mastigoō*

Hans-Helmut Esser, Dr. theol., Professor, Horstmar bei Münster
Command, Order, *dogma, entolē;* Creation, Foundation, Creature, Maker, *katabolē, ktisis*

Ulrich Falkenroth, Dr. theol., Braunschweig
Brother, Neighbour, Friend, *plēsion*

David H. Field, M.A., Tutor, Oak Hill College, London
Busybody, Meddle, *periergazomai;* Buy, Sell, Market, *agorazō, pōleō;* Conceive, Apprehend, *syllambanō;* Earth, Land, World, *agros, chous;* Ecstasy etc., *ekplēssō;* Envy, *phthoneō*

Günter Finkenrath, Burscheid-Hilgen
Avarice, Greed, Love of Money, *philargyria;* Book, Read, Letter, *epistolē*

Otto Flender, Villigst
Earth, Land, World, *oikoumenē*

Dieter Fürst, Bayreuth
Confess, *homologeō*

Burkhard Gärtner, Hamburg
Distinguish, Doubt, *diakrinō*

Jürgen Goetzmann, Essen
Care, Anxiety, *merimna;* Conversion, Penitence, Repentance, Proselyte, *metanoia*

Friedrich Graber, Riehen, Basel
All, Many, *pas, polloi;* Blind, *typhlos*

Joachim Guhrt, Bentheim
Birth, Beget, Bear, Become etc., *ginomai, palingenesia;* Covenant, Guarantee, Mediator, *diathēkē;* Desire, Lust, Pleasure, *oregomai;* Earth, Land, World, *kosmos*

Walther Günther, Dr. theol., Stuttgart
Brother, Neighbour, Friend, *adelphos;* Fight, etc., *nikaō*

Hans-Cristoph Hahn, Bad Boll
Anger, Wrath, *orgē;* Boast, *kauchēma;* Circumcision, *peritemnō;* Conscience, *syneidēsis* (part); Darkness, Night, *nyx, skotos;* Destroy, Perish, Ruin, *apōleia, olethros*

27

Günther Harder, D. theol., Dr. jur., Professor, Berlin
Form, Substance, *hypostasis*

Colin J. Hemer, M.A., Ph.D., Cambridge
Bury, Grave, Tomb, *thaptō;* Cold, Hot, Lukewarm, *psychros;* Crown, Sceptre, Rod, *stephanos, rhabdos*

Robert Hensel, Dr. theol., Bad Bergzabern
Fruit, Fig, Thorn, Thistle, *karpos*

Otfried Hofius, Dr.theol., Professor, Paderborn
Father, *abba, patēr*

Paul Jacobs, Dr. theol., Professor, Münster
Foreknowledge, Providence, Predestination, *proginōskō, pronoeō, prohoraō, prohorizō, protithēmi* (part)

Erwin Kauder, Kassel
Antichrist, *antichristos*

Kenneth A. Kitchen, B.A., Ph.D., Reader, Liverpool
Egypt, Egyptian, *Aigyptos*

Hartmut Krienke, Wuppertal
Foreknowledge, Providence, Predestination, *proginōskō, pronoeō, prohoraō, prohorizō, protithēmi* (part)

Fritz Laubach, Dr. theol., Hamburg
Blood, Sprinkle, Strangled, *haima;* Conversion, Penitence, Repentance, Proselyte, *epistrephō, metamelomai*

Helgo Lindner, Tübingen
Apostle, *apostellō* (part)

Hans-Georg Link, Dr. theol., Cologne
Blessing, Blessed, Happy, *eulogia;* Burden, Heavy, Labour, *kopos* (part); Deny, *arneomai* (part); Empty, Vain, *kenos* (part); Fight, Prize, Triumph, Victory, *thriambeuō* (part)

I. Howard Marshall, M.A., B.D., Ph.D., Senior Lecturer, Aberdeen
Council, Sanhedrin, *symbouleuō, synedrion;* Creation, Foundation, Creature, Maker, *dēmiourgos;* Divorce, *apostasion*

Reinhold Mayer, Dr. theol, Wis. Rat., Tübingen
Feast, Passover, *heortē*

Wichmann von Meding, Winsen/Aller
Bind, *deō* (part)

Friedemann Merkel, Dr. theol., Professor, Münster
Bread, Daily, Manna, *artos, manna;* Destroy, Perish, Ruin, *phtheirō*

Otto Michel, Dr. theol., Professor, Tübingen
Faith, Persuade, Belief, Unbelief, *pistis*

Robert Morgenthaler, Dr. theol., Professor, Muri bei Bern
Earth, Land, World, *gē*

J. A. Motyer, M.A., B.D., Principal, Trinity College, Bristol
Akeldama, *Akeldamach;* Amen, Hallelujah, Hosanna, *hallēlouia, hōsanna;* Birth, Beget etc., *eugenēs;* Body, section on parts of the body; Courage, Boldness, *tolmaō;* David, *Dauid;* Fish, *ichthys;* Fruit, Fig, Thorn, Thistle, *sykē, tribolos, akantha*

Dietrich Müller, Marburg
Anoint, *chriō;* Apostle, *apostellō* (part); Bind, *deō* (part); Curse, Insult, Fool, *anathema* (part); Disciple, Follow, Imitate, After, *mathētēs*

Hermann Müller, Dr. phil., Hilchenbach
Birth, Beget, Bear, Become, Miscarriage etc., *ektrōma* (part)

Wilhelm Mundle, Lic. theol., Professor, Marburg
Bread, Daily, Manna, *epiousios;* Burden, Heavy, Labour, *baros;* Come, *erchomai, katantaō;* Comfort, Encouragement, *tharseō;* Command, Order, *parangellō;* Curse, Insult, Fool, *kakologeō, kataraomai;* Ecstasy, Astonishment etc., *ekstasis;* Fear, Awe, *phobos*

Karlfried Munzer, Gauting
Determine, Appoint, Present, *paristēmi*

Gerhard Nordholt, Dr. theol., Leer
Elect, Choose, *haireomai*

James I. Packer, M.A., D.Phil., Associate Principal, Trinity College, Bristol
Abolish, Nullify, Reject, *katargeō, atheteō, exoutheneō;* Accuser, Accuse. *enkaleō;* Carpenter, Builder, Workman, Craftsman, Trade, *tektōn;* Defile, *miainō,* Despise, *kataphroneō, oligōreō;* Destroy, Perish, Ruin, *exaleiphō;* Determine, Appoint, Present, *tassō, tithēmi, prothesmia, cheirotoneō, lagchanō;* Dirt, Filth, Refuse, *rhypos, skybalon, koprion;* Firm, Foundation, Certainty, Confirm, *kyroō*

Horst Reisser, Ilten
Discipline, Prudence, Immorality, Prostitute, *porneuō*

Karl Heinrich Ringwald, Tübingen
Birth, Beget, Bear etc., *gennaō;* Fight, Prize, Triumph, Victory, *agōn, brabeion*

Friedrich Samuel Rothenberg, Korbach
Fast, *nēsteuō;* Foreign, Alien, Dispersion, Stranger, *diaspora*

Bernd Schaller, Dr. theol., Göttingen
Feast, Passover, *pascha*

Johannes Schattenmann, Dr. theol., Ottobrun
Ecstasy, Astonishment, Distraction, Horror, Madness, *mainomai;* Fellowship, Have, Share, Participate, *koinōnia*

Reinier Schippers, Dr. theol., Professor, Amsterdam
Age, Stature, Maturity, *hēlikia;* Fullness, Abound, Multitude, Fulfil etc., *plēroō*

Peter Schmidt, Frankenthal
Determine, Appoint, Present, *procheirizō;* Fullness, Abound, Multitude, Fulfil, Make Room, Give Way, *chōreō*

Walter Schmithals, Dr. theol., Professor, Berlin
Death, Kill, Sleep, *thanatos*

Walter Schneider, Hanover
Come, *mellō*

Hans Schönweiss, Dr. theol., Stuttgart
Anger, Wrath, *thymos;* Desire, Lust, Pleasure, *epithymia;* Firm, Foundation, Certainty, Confirm, *bebaios*

Hans Georg Schütz, Dr. theol., Dortmund
Body, Member, Limb, *melos*

Horst Seebass, Dr. theol., Münster
Abraham, Sarah, Hagar, Isaac, *Abraam;* Adam, Eve, *Adam;* Babylon, *Babylōn;* Enemy, Enmity, Hate, *miseō;* Flesh, *sarx* (part)

Manfred Seitz, Dr. theol., Professor, Erlangen
Burden, Heavy, Labour, *kopos*

Friedel Selter, Rheinkamp-Repelen
Avarice, Greed, Love of Money, *pleonexia;* Exhort, Warn, Console, Rebuke, *noutheteō*

Burghard Siede, Coburg
Cross, Wood, Tree, *xylon*

Siegfried Solle, Darmstadt
    Fire, Burn, *kauma*
Theo Sorg, Stuttgart
    Curse, Insult, Fool, *rhaka*
Anthony C. Thiselton, B.D., M.Th., Lecturer, Sheffield
    Explain, Interpret, Tell, Narrative, *exēgeomai, epilyō, hermēneuō;* Flesh, *sarx* (part)
Erich Tiedtke, Frankfurt
    Deny, *arneomai* (part); Empty, Vain, *kenos* (part), *mataios;* Face, *prosōpon*
Herwart Vorländer, Dr. phil., Professor, Ludwigsburg
    Forgiveness, *aphiēmi*
Horst Weigelt, Dr. theol., Privatdozent, Erlangen
    Clothe, Naked, Dress, Garment, Cloth, *gymnos, dyō, himation*
Siegfried Wibbing, Dr. theol., Professor, Mainz
    Belly, Stomach, *koilia;* Body, Member, Limb, *sōma;* Determine, Appoint, Present, *kathistēmi;* Discipline, Prudence, Immorality, Prostitute, *sōphrosynē*

Abbreviations

1. Old Testament

Gen.	Genesis	Ezr.	Ezra	Dan.	Daniel
Exod.	Exodus	Neh.	Nehemiah	Hos.	Hosea
Lev.	Leviticus	Est.	Esther	Joel	
Num.	Numbers	Job		Amos	
Deut.	Deuteronomy	Ps. (Pss.)	Psalms	Obad.	Obadiah
Jos.	Joshua	Prov.	Proverbs	Jon.	Jonah
Jdg.	Judges	Eccl.	Ecclesiastes	Mic.	Micah
Ruth		Cant.	Song of Solomon	Nah.	Nahum
1 Sam.	1 Samuel		(Canticles)	Hab.	Habakkuk
2 Sam.	2 Samuel	Isa.	Isaiah	Zeph.	Zephaniah
1 Ki.	1 Kings	Jer.	Jeremiah	Hag.	Haggai
2 Ki.	2 Kings	Lam.	Lamentations of	Zech.	Zechariah
1 Chr.	1 Chronicles		Jeremiah	Mal.	Malachi
2 Chr.	2 Chronicles	Ezek.	Ezekiel		

2. New Testament

Matt.	Matthew	Phil.	Philippians	Jas.	James
Mk.	Mark	Col.	Colossians	1 Pet.	1 Peter
Lk.	Luke	1 Thess.	1 Thessalonians	2 Pet.	2 Peter
Jn.	John	2 Thess.	2 Thessalonians	1 Jn.	1 John
Acts	Acts of the Apostles	1 Tim.	1 Timothy	2 Jn.	2 John
Rom.	Romans	2 Tim.	2 Timothy	3 Jn.	3 John
1 Cor.	1 Corinthians	Tit.	Titus	Jude	
2 Cor.	2 Corinthians	Phlm.	Philemon	Rev.	The Revelation to
Gal.	Galatians	Heb.	Hebrews		John (Apocalypse)
Eph.	Ephesians				

3. Old Testament Apocrypha and Pseudepigrapha

Ad.Dan.	Additions to Daniel (Apocrypha, found in LXX, Theod., Vulg.):
	Prayer of Azariah (LXX Dan. 3:25–45)
	Song of the Three Children (LXX Dan. 3:52–90)
	Susanna (appended to Dan. 12)
	Bel and the Dragon (appended to Dan. 12)
Ad.Est.	Additions to Esther (Apocrypha)
Aristeas	Letter of Aristeas (Pseudepigrapha)
Ass.Mos.	The Assumption of Moses (Pseudepigrapha)
Bar.	1 Baruch (Apocrypha). The Epistle of Jeremy appears at the conclusion of the Book of Baruch (Bar. 6)
1 Esd.	1 Esdras (in LXX and Eng. versions; 3 Esd. in Vulg.) (Apocrypha)
2 Esd.	2 Esdras, or 4 Ezra, or Apocalypse of Ezra (Pseudepigrapha)

31

Eth.Enoch	Ethiopic Book of Enoch, or 1 Enoch (Pseudepigrapha)
Gr.Bar.	Greek Book of Baruch, or 3 Baruch (Pseudepigrapha)
Gr.Enoch	Greek Book of Enoch (Pseudepigrapha)
Heb.Enoch	Hebrew Book of Enoch, or 3 Enoch (Pseudepigrapha)
Jub.	The Book of Jubilees (Pseudepigrapha)
Jud.	Judith (Apocrypha)
Life Adam	The Life of Adam and Eve (Pseudepigrapha)
1, 2, 3, 4 Macc.	1, 2, 3 Maccabees (Apocrypha), 4 Maccabees (Pseudepigrapha)
Man.	Prayer of Manasses (Apocrypha)
Mart.Isa.	The Martyrdom of Isaiah (Pseudepigrapha)
Pirke	Pirke Aboth (Pseudepigrapha)
Pss.Sol.	The Psalms of Solomon (Pseudepigrapha)
Sib.	The Sibylline Oracles (Pseudepigrapha)
Sir.	The Book of Sirach, or Ecclesiasticus (Apocrypha)
Sl.Enoch	Slavonic Book of Enoch, or Book of the Secrets of Enoch, or 2 Enoch (Pseudepigrapha)
Story	The Story of Ahikar (Pseudepigrapha)
Syr.Bar.	Syriac Apocalypse of Baruch, or 2 Baruch (Pseudepigrapha)
Test.Abr.	Testament of Abraham (Pseudepigrapha)
Test.XII	Testaments of the Twelve Patriarchs (Pseudepigrapha)
Test.Ash.	Testament of Asher
Test.Ben.	Testament of Benjamin
Test.Dan	Testament of Dan
Test.Gad	Testament of Gad
Test.Iss.	Testament of Issachar
Test.Jos.	Testament of Joseph
Test.Jud.	Testament of Judah
Test.Lev.	Testament of Levi
Test.Naph.	Testament of Naphtali
Test.Reub.	Testament of Reuben
Test.Sim.	Testament of Simeon
Test.Zeb.	Testament of Zebulun
Tob.	Tobit (Apocrypha)
Wis.	Wisdom of Solomon (Apocrypha)

4. Qumran Writings, Dead Sea Scrolls

CD	Damascus Document
1QS	Community Rule, or Manual of Discipline
1QSa	Messianic Rule (originally included in the same scroll as 1QS)
1QSb	The Blessings (originally included in the same scroll as 1QS)
1QH	Hymns, Hodayot
1QM	War Scroll
1QpHab	Commentary on Habbakuk
1QGenAp	Genesis Apocryphon
1Q14	Commentary on Micah
1Q22	Words of Moses
1Q27	Book of Mysteries
1Q34	Collection of Liturgical Prayers
4QEx^a	Exodus Fragment
4QpHos	Commentary on Hosea
4QpIsa	Commentary on Isaiah
4QpNah	Commentary on Nahum
4QpPs37	Commentary on Ps.37
4Qflor	Florilegium
4Qpatr	Blessings of the Patriarchs

32

4Qtest   Testimonies
11QMelchizedek   Melchizedek Scroll

See further K. G. Kuhn, ed., *Konkordanz zu den Qumrantexten*, 1960. Where possible, translations of passages from Qumran have been collated with the ET of G. Vermes, *The Dead Sea Scrolls in English*, 1962.

5.   Classical and Hellenistic Writers and Sources

Aesch.	Aeschylus (525/4–456 B.C.)
Ag.	*Agamemnon*
Cho.	*Choephori*
Eum.	*Eumenides*
Pers.	*Persae*
PV	*Prometheus Vinctus*
Sept.	*Septem contra Thebas*
Supp.	*Supplices*
Apoll.Rhod.	Apollonius Rhodius (3rd cent. B.C.)
Argon.	*Argonautica*
Appian	Appian of Alexandria (2nd cent. B.C.)
Bell.Civ.	*Bella Civilia Romana*
Apul.	Apuleius (2nd cent. A.D.)
Apol.	*Apologia*
Asclep.	*Asclepius*
De deo Soc.	*De deo Socratico*
De dog.Plat.	*De dogmate Platonis*
Flor.	*Florida*
Met.	*Metamorphoses*
Aratus	Aratus (*c.* 315–*c.* 240 B.C.)
Phaen.	*Phaenomena*
Progn.	*Prognostica*
Aristid.	Aelius Aristides (*c.* A.D. 117/129–81)
Aristoph.	Aristophanes (*c.* 450–385 B.C.)
Aristot.	Aristotle (384–322 B.C.)
An.	*De Anima*
An.Post.	*Analytica Posteriora*
An.Pr.	*Analytica Priora*
Ath.Pol.	*Athēnaiōn Politeia*
Cael.	*De Caelo*
Cat.	*Categoriae*
Div.Somn.	*De Divinatione per Somnia*
Eth.Eud.	*Ethica Eudemia*
Eth.Nic.	*Ethica Nicomachea*
Fr.	*Fragmenta*
Gen.An.	*De Generatione Animalium*
Gen.Corr.	*De Generatione et Corruptione*
Hist.An.	*Historia Animalium*
Int.	*De Interpretatione*
Mem.	*De Memoria*
Met.	*Metaphysica*
Part.An.	*De Partibus Animalium*
Phys.	*Physica*
Poet.	*Poetica*
Pol.	*Politica*
Rhet.	*Rhetorica*
Sens.	*De Sensu*
Soph.El.	*Sophistici Elenchi*

33

Top.	*Topica*
Artem.	Artemidorus Daldianus (late 2nd cent. A.D.)
Ascl.	Asclepius (Hermetic writing of 2nd–3rd cents. A.D.)
Bacchyl.	Bacchylides (5th cent. B.C.)
BGU	*Berliner Griechische Urkunden (Ägyptische Urkunden aus den Kgl. Museen zu Berlin),* 1895–
Cicero	Marcus Tullius Cicero (106–43 B.C.)
Arch.	*Pro Archia*
De Or.	*De Oratore*
Div.	*De Divinatione*
Fat.	*De Fato*
Fin.	*De Finibus*
Leg.	*De Legibus*
Nat.D.	*De Natura Deorum*
Rep.	*De Republica*
CIG	*Corpus Inscriptionum Graecarum,* ed. A. Boeckh, 1828–1877
CII	*Corpus Inscriptionum Iudaicarum,* ed. J.-B. Frey, 1936–
CIL	*Corpus Inscriptionum Latinarum,* 1863–
CIS	*Corpus Inscriptionum Semiticarum,* 1881–
Corp.Herm.	*Corpus Hermeticum* (anonymous Hell. writings of 2nd–3rd cents. A.D.)
CPR	*Corpus Papyrorum Raineri Archiducis Austriae,* ed. C. Wessely, 1895
Dem.	Demosthenes (384–22 B.C.)
De Cor.	*De Corona*
Lept.	*Against Leptines*
Meid.	*Against Meidias*
Democ.	Democritus (5th–4th cent. B.C.)
Diels-Kranz	*Die Fragmente der Vorsokratiker,* I–III, ed. H. Diels, W. Kranz, 1952[6]
Dio Cass	Cassius Dio Cocceianus (2nd–3rd cents. A.D.)
Dio Chrys.	Dio Cocceianus, later called Chrysostomos (*c.* A.D. 40–after 112)
Diod.Sic.	Diodorus Siculus (end of 1st cent. B.C.)
Diog.Laert.	Diogenes Laertius (3rd cent. A.D.)
Dion.Hal.	Dionysius of Halicarnassus (fl. 30 B.C.)
Emp.	Empedocles (*c.* 493–*c.* 433 B.C.)
Epict.	Epictetus (*c.* A.D. 55–*c.* 135)
Epim.	Epimenides (fl. 500 B.C.)
Eur.	Euripides (*c.* 485–*c.* 406 B.C.)
Bacch.	*Bacchae*
El.	*Electra*
Iph.Aul.	*Iphigenia Aulidensis*
Iph.Taur.	*Iphigenia Taurica*
Or.	*Orestes*
Phoen.	*Phoenissae*
FGH	*Fragmente der griechischen Historiker,* ed. F. Jacoby, 1923–
Hdt.	Herodotus (*c.* 484–*c.*425 B.C.)
Heracl.	Heraclitus (*c.* 535–475 B.C.)
Hesiod	Hesiod (fl. 700 B.C.)
Theog.	*Theogony*
Works	*Works and Days*
Homer	Homer (8th–7th cents. B.C.)
Il.	*Iliad*
Od.	*Odyssey*
IG	*Inscriptiones Graecae,* ed. Preussische Akademie der Wissenschaften zu Berlin, 1873–
Isoc.	Isocrates (436–338 B.C.)
Areop.	*Areopagiticus*
Bus.	*Busiris*
Paneg.	*Panegyricus*

34

Josephus	Flavius Josephus (*c.* A.D. 37–97)
Ant.	*Antiquitates Judaicae* (*Jewish Antiquities*)
Ap.	*Contra Apionem* (*Against Apion*)
Life	*Life of Flavius Josephus* (*Vita*)
War	*The Jewish War* (*Bellum Judaicum*)
M.Ant.	Marcus Aurelius Antoninus (A.D. 121–180)
Menand.	Menander (*c.* 342–293/89 B.C.)
Epit.	*Epitrepontes*
Her.	*Heros*
Pk.	*Perikeiromene*
Sam.	*Samia*
OGI	*Orientis Graeci Inscriptiones Selectae*, ed. W. Dittenberger, 1903–5
Parm.	Parmenides (*c.* 500 B.C.)
Paus.	Pausanias (fl. A.D. 150)
P.Fay.	B. P. Grenfell, A. S. Hunt, D. G. Hogarth, *Fayûm Towns and their Papyri*, 1900
Philo	Philo of Alexandria (*c.* 50 B.C.–A.D. 45), also known as Philo Judaeus
Abr.	*De Abrahamo*
Aet.Mund.	*De Aeternitate Mundi*
Agric.	*De Agricultura*
Conf.Ling.	*De Confusione Linguarum*
Congr.	*De Congressu Eruditionis Gratia*
Decal.	*De Decalogo*
Det.Pot.Ins.	*Quod Deterius Potiori Insidiari Soleat*
Deus Imm.	*Quod Deus Sit Immutabilis*
Ebr.	*De Ebrietate*
Exsec.	*De Exsecrationibus*
Flacc.	*In Flaccum*
Fug.	*De Fuga et Inventione*
Gig.	*De Gigantibus*
Jos.	*De Josepho*
Leg.All.	*Legum Allegoriae*
Leg.Gai.	*Legatio ad Gaium*
Migr.Abr.	*De Migratione Abrahami*
Mut.Nom.	*De Mutatione Nominum*
Omn.Prob.Lib.	*Quod Omnis Probus Liber Sit*
Op.Mund.	*De Opificio Mundi*
Plant.	*De Plantatione*
Post.C.	*De Posteritate Caini*
Praem.	*De Praemiis et Poenis*
Quaest. in Exod.	*Quaestiones in Exodum*
Quaest. in Gen.	*Quaestiones in Genesin*
Rer.Div.Her.	*Quis Rerum Divinarum Heres Sit*
Sacr.	*De Sacrificiis Abelis et Caini*
Sobr.	*De Sobrietate*
Som.	*De Somniis*
Spec.Leg.	*De Specialibus Legibus*
Virt.	*De Virtutibus*
Vit.Cont.	*De Vita Contemplativa*
Vit.Mos.	*De Vita Mosis*
Philostr.	Flavius Philostratus (*c.* A.D. 170–244/9)
Imag.	*Imagines*
VA	*Vita Apollonii*
VS	*Vita Sophistarum*
Pindar	Pindar (518–438 B.C.)
Isth.	*Isthmian Odes*
Nem.	*Nemean Odes*

Ol.	*Olympian Odes*
Pyth.	*Pythian Odes*
Plato	Plato (*c.* 427–347 B.C.)
Alc.	*Alcibiades*
Ap. or *Apol.*	*Apologia*
Chrm.	*Charmides*
Cra.	*Cratylus*
Cri.	*Crito*
Criti.	*Critias*
Epin.	*Epinomis*
Euthyphr.	*Euthyphro*
Grg.	*Gorgias*
Hipparch.	*Hipparchus*
Hp.Mi.	*Hippias Minor*
Lach.	*Laches*
Leg.	*Leges*
Menex.	*Menexenus*
Phd.	*Phaedo*
Phdr.	*Phaedrus*
Phlb.	*Philebus*
Prm.	*Parmenides*
Prt.	*Protagoras*
Resp. or *Rep.*	*Respublica* (*The Republic*)
Soph.	*Sophista*
Symp.	*Symposium*
Tht. or *Theaet*	*Theaetetus*
Tim.	*Timaeus*
Pliny	Pliny the Elder, Gaius Plinius Secundus (A.D. 23/24–79)
Nat.Hist.	*Naturalis Historia* (*Natural History*)
Pliny	Pliny the Younger, Gaius Plinius Caecilius Secundus (*c.* A.D. 61–*c.* 112)
Epp.	*Epistolae* (*Letters*)
Plut.	Plutarch (*c.* A.D. 46–120)
Mor.	*Moralia*
Vit.	*Vitae Parallelae*
Polyb.	Polybius (*c.* 200–after 118 B.C.)
P.Oxy.	*Oxyrhynchus Papyri*, ed. B. P. Grenfell, A. S. Hunt *et al.*, 1898–
Ps.Arist.	Pseudo-Aristotle
Mund.	*De Mundo*
Oec.	*Oeconomica*
Prob.	*Problems*
P.Teb.	*Tebtunis Papyri*, ed. B. P. Grenfell, A. S. Hunt, J. G. Smyly, E. J. Goodspeed 1902–
Pythagoras	Pythagoras (6th–5th cent. B.C.) and followers
Epp.	*Epistolae* (*Letters*)
SIG	*Sylloge Inscriptionum Graecarum*, ed. W. Dittenberger, 1915–24[3]
Soph.	Sophocles (*c.* 496–406 B.C.)
Aj.	*Ajax*
Ant.	*Antigone*
El.	*Electra*
Fr.	*Fragments*
OC	*Oedipus Coloneus*
OT	*Oedipus Tyrannus*
Phil.	*Philoctetes*
Trach.	*Trachiniae*
Stob.	Iohannis Stobaeus (5th cent. A.D.)
Ecl.	*Eklogai* (*Eclogues*)
Anth.	*Anthologion* (*Anthology*)

Strabo	Strabo (*c.* 63 B.C.–after A.D. 21)
Geog.	Geography
Hist.Sk.	Historical Sketches
SVF	Stoicorum Veterum Fragmenta, ed. J. von Arnim, 1903
Tacitus, *Ann.*	Cornelius Tacitus (*c.* A.D. 55–120), *Annals*
Thuc.	Thucydides (*c.* 460–*c.* 396 B.C.)
History	History of the Peloponnesian War
Xen.	Xenophon (*c.* 430–354 B.C.)
Ages.	Agesilaus
Anab.	Anabasis
Ap.	Apologia Socratis
Cyn.	Cynegeticus
Cyr.	Cyropaedia
Hell.	Hellenica (Greek History)
Mem.	Memorabilia
Oec.	Oeconomicus
Symp.	Symposium
Vect.	De Vectigalibus

6. New Testament Apocrypha and Early Christian Writers

Act.And.	Acts of Andrew
Act.Jn.	Acts of John
Act.Paul	Acts of Paul
Act.Paul and Thecla	Acts of Paul and Thecla
Act.Pet.	Acts of Peter
Act.Thom.	Acts of Thomas
Apc.Abr.	Apocalypse of Abraham
Apc.El.	Apocalypse of Elijah
Apc.Mos.	Apocalypse of Moses
Apc.Pet.	Apocalypse of Peter
Apoc.Jn.	Apocryphon of John
Asc.Isa.	Ascension of Isaiah
Aug.	Augustine (A.D. 354–430)
Conf.	Confessiones (Confessions)
De civ.	De civitate Dei (The City of God)
De cons.	De consensu evangelistarum (On the Agreement of the Evangelists)
De doct.	De doctrina christiana (On Christian Learning)
De haer.	De haeresibus (Against Heresies)
De spir.	De spiritu et littera (On the Spirit and the Letter)
De trin.	De trinitate (On the Trinity)
Enchir.	Enchiridion ad Laurentium sive de fide, spe et caritate (Handbook for Laurentius concerning Faith, Hope and Love)
En. in Pss.	Enarrationes in Psalmos (Discourses on the Psalms)
Quest.ev.	Quaestiones evangeliorum (Questions on the Gospels)
Retract.	Retractationes (Retractations)
Tract. in Ioan.	Tractatus in Ioannis evangelium (Tracts on the Gospel of John)
Tract. in ep.Ioan.	Tractatus in epistolam Ioannis I (Tracts on the First Epistle of John)
Barn.	Letter of Barnabas
1, 2 Clem.	1 and 2 Clement
Clem.Alex.	Clement of Alexandria (*c.* 150–213)
Exc.Theod.	Excerpta ex Theodoto
Strom.	Stromateis
Did.	Didache
Ep.Apost.	Epistola Apostolorum

37

Ep.Diog.	Epistle to Diognetus
Ep.Laodiceans	Epistle to the Laodiceans
Epiph.	Epiphanius (*c.* 315–403)
. Haer.	*Haereses* (*Refutation of all Heresies* or *Panarion* (Medicine Box))
Euseb.	Eusebius of Caesarea (*c.* 260–*c.* 340)
Hist.Eccl. or *HE*	*Historia Ecclesiastica* (*Ecclesiastical History*)
Praep.ev.	*Praeparatio evangelica* (*Gospel Preparation*)
Gos.Eb.	Gospel of the Ebionites
Gos.Egy.	Gospel of the Egyptians
Gos.Heb.	Gospel of the Hebrews
Gos.Mar.	Gospel of Mary
Gos.Naz.	Gospel of the Nazaraeans
Gos.Pet.	Gospel of Peter
Gos.Phil.	Gospel of Philip
Gos.T.	Gospel of Truth
Gos.Thom.	Gospel of Thomas
Hermas	Hermas (2nd cent.)
Com. or *Man.*	*Commandments* or *Mandates*
Sim.	*Similitudes*
Vis.	*Visions*
	These constitute the three parts of the *Shepherd* of Hermas
Hippol.	Hippolytus (*c.* 170–*c.* 236)
Haer.	*Refutatio omnium haeresium* (*Refutation of all Heresies*)
Ign.	Ignatius of Antioch (*c.* 35–*c.* 110)
Eph.	*Letter to the Ephesians*
Mag.	*Letter to the Magnesians*
Phil.	*Letter to the Philadelphians*
Pol.	*Letter to Polycarp*
Rom.	*Letter to the Romans*
Smy.	*Letter to the Smyrnaeans*
Trall.	*Letter to the Trallians*
Iren.	Irenaeus of Lyons (*c.* 140–202)
Epid.	*Epideixis tou apostolikou kērygmatos* (*Demonstration of Apostolic Preaching*)
Haer.	*Adversus haereses* (*Against the Heresies*)
Justin	Justin Martyr (*c.* 100–*c.* 165)
Apol.I, II	*Apology, I, II*
Dial.	*Dialogue with Trypho*
Mart.Poly.	Martyrdom of Polycarp
Od.Sol.	Odes of Solomon
Origen	Origen (*c.* 185–*c.* 254)
Contra Cels.	*Contra Celsum* (*Against Celsus*)
De prin.	*De principiis* or *Peri archōn* (*On the Principal Doctrines*)
Hex.	*Hexapla*
Hom.	*Homilies*
Schol.	*Scholia*
Pistis Soph.	Pistis Sophia
Polycarp	Polycarp, *To the Philippians*
Prot.	Protevangelium (Book of James)
Soph.J.C.	Sophia Jesus Christi
Tert.	Tertullian (*c.* 160–*c.* 220)
Adv.Herm.	*Adversus Hermogenem* (*Against Hermogenes*)
Adv.Marc.	*Adversus Marcionem* (*Against Marcion*)
Adv.Prax.	*Adversus Praxean* (*Against Praxeas*)
Adv.Val.	*Adversus Valentinianos* (*Against the Valentinians*)
Apol.	*Apologeticum* (*Apology*)
De an.	*De anima* (*On the Soul*)

De car.	*De carne Christi (On the Flesh of Christ)*
De praesc.	*De praescriptione haereticorum (On the Proscription of Heretics)*

7. Rabbinic Writings

The following are the Tractates of *The Mishnah* (ET, H. Danby, 1933) in the order in which they occur:

First Division: Zeraim (Seeds)

Berakoth (Benedictions)
Peah (Gleanings)
Demai (Produce not certainly tithed)
Kilaim (Diverse Kinds)
Shebiith (The Seventh Year)
Terumoth (Heave-offerings)

Maaseroth (Tithes)
Maaser Sheni (Second Tithe)
Hallah (Dough-offering)
Orlah (The Fruit of Young Trees)
Bikkurim (First-fruits)

Second Division: Moed (Set Feasts)

Shabbath (The Sabbath)
Erubin (The Fusion of Sabbath Limits)
Pesahim (Feast of the Passover)
Shekalim (The Shekel Dues)
Yoma (The Day of Atonement)
Sukkah (The Feast of Tabernacles)

Yom Tob or Betzah (Festival Days)
Rosh ha-Shanah (Feast of the New Year)
Taanith (Days of Fasting)
Megillah (The Scroll of Esther)
Moed Katan (Mid-Festival Days)
Hagigah (The Festal Offering)

Third Division: Nashim (Women)

Yebamoth (Sisters-in-law)
Ketuboth (Marriage Deeds)
Nedarim (Vows)
Nazir (The Nazirite-vow)

Sotah (The Suspected Adulteress)
Gittin (Bills of Divorce)
Kiddushin (Betrothals)

Fourth Division: Nezekin (Damages)

Baba Kamma (The First Gate)
Baba Metzia (The Middle Gate)
Baba Bathra (The Last Gate)
Sanhedrin (The Sanhedrin)
Makkoth (Stripes)
Shebuoth (Oaths)

Eduyoth (Testimonies)
Abodah Zarah (Idolatry)
Aboth (The Fathers) or Pirke Aboth (Chapters of the Fathers)
Horayoth (Instructions)

Fifth Division: Kodashim (Hallowed Things)

Zebahim (Animal-offerings)
Menahoth (Meal-offerings)
Hullin (Animals killed for food)
Bekhoroth (Firstlings)
Arakhin (Vows of Valuation)
Temurah (The Substituted Offering)

Kerithoth (Extirpation)
Meilah (Sacrilege)
Tamid (The Daily Whole-offering)
Middoth (Measurements)
Kinnim (The Bird-offerings)

Sixth Division: Tohoroth (Cleannesses)

Kelim (Vessels)
Oholoth (Tents)
Negaim (Leprosy-signs)
Parah (The Red Heifer)
Tohoroth (Cleannesses)
Mikwaoth (Immersion-pools)

Niddah (The Menstruant)
Makshirin (Predisposers)
Zabim (They that suffer a flux)
Tebul Yom (He that immersed himself that day)
Yadaim (Hands)
Uktzin (Stalks)

Mishnah passages are referred to by chapter and section: e.g. Ber. 4:1. The abbreviations used follow the initial letters of the individual tractates.

Tosefta references are prefixed by T. and followed by a reference to the edition of M. S. Zuckermandel (1880–82), giving page and line: e.g. T. Ber. 4:1.

Referenece to the Babylonian Talmud are to folio and side: e.g. Ber. 59a. References to the Jerusalem Talmud are prefixed by T. J. The numbers refer to chapter, section, folio, column and line: e.g. T.J.Ber. 1:4:27d:6.

Other abbreviations:

Ab.R.N.	Aboth de Rabbi Nathan
Mek.	Mekilta (a Midrash on the Book of Exodus compiled by Rabbi Ishmael, c. 60–c. 140)
P.B.	Prayer Book (*The Authorized Daily Prayer Book*, ed. S. Singer, many editions)
Pes.K.	Pesikta de-rab Kahana (Midrash of 6th cent. named after a Babylonian–Palestinian scholar of the 3rd cent.)
Pes.R.	Pesikta Rabbati (homiletic midrash)
R.	Rabbah (great; 6th cent. midrash on Pentateuch and Megilloth; e.g. Gen.R., Genesis Rabbah)
Tan.d.b.El.	Tanna debe Eliyyahu (medieval ethical midrash probably from Italy)
Tanh.	Tanhuma (homilies collected by Rabbi Tanhuma, c. A.D. 400 and those collected in his name)
Tanh.B.	*Midrasch Tanchuma*, I–III (IV), ed. S. Buber, 1885
Tg.	Targum
Tg.O.	Targum of Onkelos (translation of the Pentateuch into Aram. by Onkelos, a proselyte to Judaism, in the 1st cent. A.D.)
Tg.J.I.	Targum Pseudo-Jonathan (Targum of the Pentateuch representing a Babylonian version of the Palestinian tradition in its most developed form)

See the *Glossary of Technical Terms* for further elucidation of rabbinic terms.

8. Reference Works and Journals

AnBib	*Analecta Biblica*
ANET	*Ancient Near Eastern Texts*, ed. J. B. Pritchard, 1955[2]
Arndt	W. F. Arndt and F. W. Gingrich, *A Greek–English Lexicon of the New Testament and Other Early Christian Literature*, 1957 (translation and adaptation of W. Bauer, *Griechisch-deutsches Wörterbuch zu den Schriften des Neuen Testaments und der übrigen urchristlichen Literatur*, 1952[4])
ARW	*Archiv für Religionswissenschaft*
ASTI	*Annual of the Swedish Theological Institute*
ATD	*Das Alte Testament Deutsch*, ed. V. Herntrich and A. Weiser
AThANT	*Abhandlungen zur Theologie des Alten und Neuen Testaments*
AzTh	*Arbeiten zur Theologie*
BA	*The Biblical Archaeologist*
Barth, *CD*	K. Barth, *Church Dogmatics*, 1936– (ET of *Kirchliche Dogmatik*)
BASOR	*Bulletin of the American Schools of Oriental Research*
BDB	F. Brown, S. R. Driver, and C. A. Briggs, *A Hebrew–English Lexicon of the Old Testament, with an Appendix containing the Biblical Aramaic*, (1907) 1955
BEvTh	*Beiträge zur evangelischen Theologie*
BFBS	Η ΚΑΙΝΗ ΔΙΑΘΗΚΗ (British and Foreign Bible Society), ed. G. D. Kilpatrick, 1958[2]
BFChTh	*Beiträge zur Förderung christlicher Theologie*
BHHW	*Biblisch-historisches Handwörterbuch*, ed. B. Reicke and L. Rost, I–III, 1962–
BHTh	*Beiträge zur historischen Theologie*
Bib	*Biblica*

BJRL	*Bulletin of the John Rylands Library*
BKAT	*Biblisches Kommentar: Altes Testament,* ed. M. Noth
BNTC	*Black's New Testament Commentaries*
BSOAS	*Bulletin of the School of Oriental and African Studies*
BSt	*Biblische Studien*
BuK	*Bibel und Kirche*
BuL	*Bibel und Liturgie*
BWANT	*Beiträge zur Wissenschaft vom Alten und Neuen Testament*
BZ	*Biblische Zeitschrift*
BZAW	*Beihefte zur Zeitschrift für die alttestamentliche Wissenschaft*
BZNW	*Beihefte zur Zeitschrift für die neutestamentliche Wissenschaft*
CBQ	*Catholic Biblical Quarterly*
Charles	R. H. Charles, ed., *Apocrypha and Pseudepigrapha of the Old Testament,* I–II (1913) 1963
CNT	*Commentaires du Nouveau Testament*
DAC	*Dictionary of the Apostolic Church,* I–II, ed. J. Hastings, 1915–18
Dalman	G. H. Dalman
Grammatik	*Grammatik des jüdisch-palästinischen Aramäisch,* 1905[2]
AHTTM	*Aramäisch-neuhebräisches Handwörterbuch zu Targum, Talmud und Midrasch,* (1938) 1967
Jesus	*Jesus–Jeshua,* ET 1929
Words	*The Words of Jesus,* ET 1902
DBT	*Dictionary of Biblical Theology,* ed. X. Leon-Dufour, (1967) 1972[2]
DCG	*Dictionary of Christ and the Gospels,* I–II, ed. J. Hastings, 1906–8
DTh	*Deutsche Theologie*
EBT	*Encyclopedia of Biblical Theology,* I–III, ed. Johannes B. Bauer, 1970
EKL	*Evangelisches Kirchenlexikon,* I–III, ed. H. Brunotte and O. Weber, 1962[2]
EMZ	*Evangelische Missionszeitschrift*
EQ	*Evangelical Quarterly*
ERE	*Encyclopaedia of Religion and Ethics,* I–XIII, ed. J. Hastings, 1908–26
EvKomm	*Evangelische Kommentare*
EvTh	*Evangelische Theologie*
ExpT	*Expository Times*
FRLANT	*Forschungen zur Religion und Literatur des Alten und Neuen Testaments*
Funk	R. Funk, *A Greek Grammar of the New Testament and Other Early Christian Literature* (A revised edition of F. Blass and A. Debrunner, *Grammatik des neutestamentlichen Griechisch,* 1954 incorporating supplementary notes by A. Debrunner), 1961
HADOT	G. Fohrer, *Hebrew and Aramaic Dictionary of the Old Testament,* 1973
Hatch–Redpath	E. Hatch and H. A. Redpath, *A Concordance to the Septuagint and the Other Greek Versions of the Old Testament,* I–III (1897) 1954
HDB	*A Dictionary of the Bible,* I–V, ed. J. Hastings, 1898–1904
Henn.–Schn.	E. Hennecke and W. Schneemelcher, *Neutestamentliche Apokryphen,* I–II, ET ed. R. McL. Wilson, *New Testament Apocrypha,* 1963–65
HNT	*Handbuch zum Neuen Testament*
HTR	*Harvard Theological Review*
IB	*The Interpreter's Bible,* I–XII, ed. G. A. Buttrick *et al.,* 1952–57
ICC	*The International Critical Commentary,* ed. S. R. Driver, A. Plummer, C. A. Briggs, 1895–
IDB	*The Interpreter's Dictionary of the Bible,* I–IV, ed. G. A. Buttrick *et al.,* 1962
IKZ	*Internationale Kirchliche Zeitschrift*
JE	*Jewish Encyclopedia,* I–XII, ed. I. Singer *et al.,* 1901–6
JES	*Journal of Ecumenical Studies*
JBL	*Journal of Biblical Literature*
JNES	*Journal of Near Eastern Studies*
JQR	*Jewish Quarterly Review*

JR	*Journal of Religion*
JSS	*Journal of Semitic Studies*
JTS	*Journal of Theological Studies*
KEK	*Kritisch-exegetischer Kommentar über das Neue Testament*, founded by H. A. W. Meyer, 1832
KidZ	*Kirche in der Zeit*
Koehler-Baumgartner	L. Koehler and W. Baumgartner, *Lexicon in Veteris Testamenti Libros*, 1958²
KuD	*Kerygma und Dogma*
Lampe	G. W. H. Lampe, *A Patristic Greek Lexicon*, 5 fascicles, 1960–68
Liddell–Scott	H. G. Liddell and R. Scott, *A Greek–English Lexicon*, revised by H. S. Jones, 1940⁹
LTK	*Lexikon für Theologie und Kirche*, founded by M. Buchberger, ed. J. Höfer and K. Rahner, I–X, 1964²
Mandelkern	S. Mandelkern, *Veteris Testamenti Concordantiae* I–II, (1896) 1955
Metzger	B. M. Metzger, *A Textual Commentary on the Greek New Testament*, 1971
ML	C. G. Montefiore and H. Loewe, *A Rabbinic Anthology*, (1938) 1963
MNTC	*The Moffatt New Testament Commentaries*
Moore, *Judaism*	G. F. Moore, *Judaism in the First Centuries of the Christian Era*, I–III, 1927–30
Morgenthaler	R. Morgenthaler, *Statistik des neutestamentlichen Wortschatzes*, 1958
Moule	C. F. D. Moule, *An Idiom-Book of New Testament Greek*, 1963²
Moulton, *Grammar*	J. H. Moulton, *A Grammar of New Testament Greek*, I, 1908; II ed. W. F. Howard, 1929; III by N. Turner, 1963
Moulton–Milligan	J. H. Moulton and G. Milligan, *The Vocabulary of the Greek Testament Illustrated from the Papyri and Other Non-Literary Sources*, 1930
MPG	J. P. Migne, ed., *Patrologia Graeca*, 162 vols., 1857–66
MPL	J. P. Migne, ed., *Patrologia Latina*, 221 vols., 1844–64
MPTh	*Monatsschrift für Pastoraltheologie*
NBCR	*The New Bible Commentary Revised*, ed. D. Guthrie and J. A. Motyer
NBD	*The New Bible Dictionary*, ed. J. D. Douglas et al., 1962
NIDCC	*New International Dictionary of the Christian Church*, ed. J. D. Douglas, 1974
NLC	*The New London Commentary on the New Testament* also called *The New International Commentary on The New Testament*
NovT	*Novum Testamentum*
NTAbh	*Neutestamentliche Abhandlungen*
NTD	*Das Neue Testament Deutsch*, ed. P. Althaus and J. Behm, 1932–, P. Althaus and G. Friedrich, 1956–
NTS	*New Testament Studies*
Nu	*Numen*
NWDB	*The New Westminster Dictionary of the Bible*, ed. H. S. Gehman, 1970
OCD	*The Oxford Classical Dictionary*, ed. M. Cary et al., 1949, 1970² ed. N. G. L. Hammond and H. H. Scullard
ODCC	*The Oxford Dictionary of the Christian Church*, ed. F. L. Cross (1957), rev. F. L. Cross and E. A. Livingstone, 1974
OTS	*Oudtestamentische Studiën*
Pauly-Wissowa	A. F. Pauly, G. Wissowa et al., eds., *Real-Encyclopädie der klassischen Altertumswissenschaft*, 1893–
RAC	*Reallexikon für die Antike und Christentum*, ed. T. Klausner et al., 1941–
RB	*Revue Biblique*
RE	*Realencyclopädie für protestantische Theologie und Kirche*, founded by J. J. Herzog, ed. 3 by A. Hauck, I–XXIV, 1896–1913
RGG³	*Die Religion in Geschichte und Gegenwart: Handwörterbuch für Theologie und Religionswissenschaft*, ed. K. Galling et al., I–VII, 1957–65³
RHR	*Revue de l'Histoire des Religions*
RSR	*Recherches de Science Religieuse*

Sacramentum Mundi	*Sacramentum Mundi: An Encyclopedia of Theology*, I–VI, ed. K. Rahner et al., 1968–1970
Sacramentum Verbi	American title of *EBT*
SAH	*Sitzungsberichte der Heidelberger Akademie der Wissenschaften* (*phil.-hist. Klasse*), 1910–
SB	H. L. Strack and P. Billerbeck, *Kommentar zum Neuen Testament aus Talmud und Midrasch*, I–VI, 1926–61
SBT	*Studies in Biblical Theology*
Schürer	E. Schürer, *A History of the Jewish People in the Time of Jesus Christ*, I, 1–2, II. 1–3, 1885–90; Vol. I revised by G. Vermes, F. Miller and M. Black, 1973
SJT	*Scottish Journal of Theology*
SNT	*Die Schriften des Neuen Testaments*, ed. J. Weiss, 1906–, W. Bousset and W. Heitmüller, 1916–
SThZ	*Schweizerische Theologische Zeitschrift*
StTh	*Studia Theologica*
StudEv	*Studia Evangelica*
StUNT	*Studien zur Umwelt des Neuen Testaments*
TB	*Tyndale Bulletin*
TC	*Tyndale Commentary*
TDOT	*Theological Dictionary of the Old Testament*, I–, ed. G. J. Botterweck and H. Ringgren, Eng. tr. of *TWAT*, 1974–
TDNT	*Theological Dictionary of the New Testament*, I–IX ed. G. Kittel, ET by G. W. Bromiley of *TWNT*, 1964–74
THAT	*Theologisches Handwörterbuch zum Alten Testament*, ed. E. Jenni and C. Westermann, I–II, 1971–
ThB	*Theologische Bücherei*
ThBl	*Theologische Blätter*
ThEH	*Theologische Existenz Heute*
TheolStud	*Theologische Studien*
ThF	*Theologische Forschung*
ThG	*Theologische Glaube*
ThQ	*Theologische Quartalschrift*
ThR	*Theologische Rundschau*
ThStKr	*Theologische Studien und Kritiken*
ThV	*Theologia Viatorum*
ThZ	*Theologische Zeitschrift der theologischen Fakultät der Universität Basel*
TLZ	*Theologische Literaturzeitung*
TNTC	*Tyndale New Testament Commentaries*
TS	*Texts and Studies*
TU	*Texte und Untersuchungen zur Geschichte der altchristlicher Literatur*
Turner, *Insights*	N. Turner, *Grammatical Insights into the New Testament*, 1965
TWAT	*Theologisches Wörterbuch zum Alten Testament*, ed. G. J. Botterweck,
TWBB	*A Theological Word Book of the Bible*, ed. A. Richardson, 1950 H. Ringgren et al., 1970–
TWNT	*Theologisches Wörterbuch zum Neuen Testament*, ed. G. Kittel and G. Friedrich, 1933–74
UBS	The Greek New Testament (United Bible Societies edition), ed. K. Aland et al., 1966
Vermes, *Scrolls*	G. Vermes, *The Dead Sea Scrolls in English*, 1962
VT	*Vetus Testamentum*
WMANT	*Wissenschaftliche Monographien zum Alten und Neuen Testament*
WTJ	*Westminster Theological Journal*
WuD	*Wort und Dienst, Jahrbuch der theologischen Hochschule Bethel*
WUNT	*Wissenschaftliche Untersuchungen zum Neuen Testament*
WZ . . .	*Wissenschaftliche Zeitschrift* (followed by the name of the relevant university)

ZAW	Zeitschrift für alttestamentliche Wissenschaft
ZDMG	Zeitschrift der Deutschen Morgenländischen Gesellschaft
ZEE	Zeitschrift für evangelische Ethik
ZEK	Zeitschrift für evangelisches Kirchenrecht
ZKT	Zeitschrift für katholische Theologie
ZNW	Zeitschrift für die neutestamentliche Wissenschaft und die Kunde der älteren Kirche
ZPEB	The Zondervan Pictorial Encyclopedia of the Bible, ed. M. C. Tenney, I-V, 1975
ZPT	Zeitschrift für praktische Theologie
ZRGG	Zeitschrift für Religions- und Geistesgeschichte
ZSTh	Zeitschrift für systematische Theologie
ZTK	Zeitschrift für Theologie und Kirche
ZWT	Zeitschrift für wissenschaftliche Theologie

9. General Abbreviations

(a).	In a bibliography denotes works in English
(b).	In a bibliography denotes works in other languages
acc.	accusative(s)
Accad.	Accadian
act.	active
A.D.	Anno Domini
adj.	adjective
ad loc.	ad locum (Lat.), at the place referred to, on the relevant passage
adv.	adverb
Aleph	Codex Sinaiticus
aor.	aorist
Apc.	Apocalypse
Apoc.	Apocrypha
Arab.	Arabic
Aram.	Aramaic
Arm.	Armenian
art./Art.	article/Article
Ass.	Assyrian
ASV	American Standard Version (1901)
Att.	Attic
AV	Authorized Version (1611)
b.	bar/ben (Aram./Heb.), son of
Bab.	Babylonian
B.C.	before Christ
c.	circa (Lat.), about, approximately
cent.	century
ch(s).	chapter(s)
cl.	classical
Comm(s).	commentary/ies
dat.	dative
ed.	edited by, edition
[Ed.]	Editor, denoting an insertion by the editor
Eng.	English
ET	English translation
et al.	et alii (Lat.), and other persons/things
EV(V)	English Version(s)
f(f).	and the verse(s) following, and the chapter(s) following
fem.	feminine
Festschr.	Festschrift (Ger.), volume in honour of someone
fig.	figurative(ly)
fl.	floruit (Lat.), flourished
frag.	fragment(s)
fut.	future
gen.	genitive
Ger.	German
Gk.	Greek
Heb.	Hebrew
Hel.	Hellenistic
hiph.	hiphil
hith.	hithpael
hoph.	hophal
ibid.	ibidem (Lat.) in the same work/place
idem	the same
i.e.	id est (Lat.), that is
imp.	imperfect
ind.	indicative
infin.	infinitive
intrans.	intransitive(ly)
Introd.	Introduction
JB	The Jerusalem Bible (1966)
Jud.	Judaism
K	Kethib (the Heb. consonantal text)
KJV	King James Version (AV)
Knox	R. A. Knox's translation of the Bible (NT 1945, OT 1949)
Lat.	Latin
lit.	literal(ly)
loc.cit.	loco citato (Lat.), in the place already quoted
LXX	Septuagint(al)
masc.	masculine

mg.	margin	RV	Revised Version (NT 1881, OT 1885)
mid.	middle voice		
Moffatt	J. Moffatt *A New Translation of the Bible*, 1936[2]	sc.	scilicet (Lat.), namely
		sect./§	section
MS(S)	manuscript(s)	Sem.	Semitic
MT	Masoretic text	seq.	sequens (Lat.) and the following verse(s) or chapters
n(n).	note(s)		
NEB	The New English Bible (NT 1961, OT 1970)	Ser.	Series
		sing.	singular
neut.	neuter	sub.	substantive, noun
niph.	niphal	subj.	subjunctive
NT	New Testament	Suppl.	Supplementary volume
obj.	object	s.v.	sub verbo (Lat.), under the relevant word
op.cit.	opere citato (Lat.), in the work quoted		
		Symm.	Symmachus' Gk. translation of the OT
OT	Old Testament		
par.	parallel, and parallel(s)	TEV	Today's English Version, 1946
part.	participle	Theod.	Theodotion's Gk. translation of the OT
pass.	passive		
Pent.	Pentateuch	[Tr.]	translator's note follows
perf.	perfect	TR	Textus Receptus
Phillips	J. B. Phillips, *The New Testament in Modern English*, 1958	trans.	transitive(ly)
		tx.	text
plur.	plural	v.	von (in Ger. names)
plup.	pluperfect	v(v).	verse(s)
prep.	preposition	vid.inf.	vide infra (Lat.), see below
pres.	present	vid.sup.	vide supra (Lat.), see above
pron.	pronoun	viz.	videlicet (Lat.), namely
pseud.	pseudonym or pseudonymous	v.l.	varia lectio (Lat.), variant reading
Q	Qere (the rabbinic reading of the OT text). In gospel criticism Q also stands for the German *Quelle*, or source, thought to be behind the sayings of Jesus common to Matt. and Lk.	voc.	vocative
		vol.	volume
		vs.	versus (Lat.), against
		Vulg.	Vulgate
		Weymouth	R. F. Weymouth, *The New Testament in Modern Speech*, 1903
R.	Rabbi		
Rab.	Rabbinic	†	Hapax legomenon, the sole instance of a term
ref(f).	reference(s)		
reflex.	reflexive(ly)	→	See article indicated
RSV	Revised Standard Version (1952)	*	Form of word conjectured and not found in any extant literature

45

Transliteration

Hebrew, Greek and Arabic words have been transliterated in accordance with the following system.

Hebrew

א	=	'	ד	=	$\underline{d}$	י	=	y	ס = s	ר = r

א = ' ד = $\underline{d}$ י = y ס = s ר = r
ב = b ה = h כ = k ע = ' שׂ = $\acute{s}$
כ = $\underline{b}$ ו = w כ = $\underline{k}$ פ = p שׁ = $\check{s}$
ג = g ז = z ל = l פ = $\bar{p}$ ת = t
ג = $\bar{g}$ ח = ḥ מ = m צ = ṣ ת = $\underline{t}$
ד = d ט = ṭ נ = n ק = q

Long Vowels

(ה)ָ = $\hat{a}$ (h)   ָ = $\bar{a}$

ֵי = $\hat{e}$ ֵ = $\bar{e}$

ִי = $\hat{i}$

וֹ = $\hat{o}$ ֹ = $\bar{o}$

וּ = $\hat{u}$

Short Vowels

ַ = a

ֶ = e

ִ = i

ָ = o

ֻ = u

Very Short Vowels

ֲ = ^{a}

ֱ = ^{e}

ְ = ^{e} (if vocal)

ֳ = ^{o}

Greek

α = a   κ = k   τ = t   γγ = ng
β = b   λ = l   υ = y   γκ = nk
γ = g   μ = m   φ = ph   γξ = nx
δ = d   ν = n   χ = ch   γχ = nch
ε = e   ξ = x   ψ = ps   αυ = au
ζ = z   ο = o   ω = $\bar{o}$ ευ = eu
η = $\bar{e}$ π = p   ῥ = rh   ου = ou
θ = th   ρ = r   ʽ = h   υι = yi
ι = i   σ, ς = s

Arabic

ا = '   خ = ḫ   ش = $\check{s}$ غ = ġ   ن = n
ب = b   د = d   ص = ṣ   ف = f   ه = h
ت = t   ذ = $\underline{d}$ ض = ḍ   ق = ḳ   و = w
ث = t   ر = r   ط = ṭ   ك = k   ى = y
ج = ğ   ز = z   ظ = ẓ   ل = l   ة = t
ح = h   س = s   ع = '   م = m

Glossary of Technical Terms

Hans-Georg Link
Supplementary material by **Colin Brown**

→ in this Glossary indicates a cross-reference to another entry in the Glossary.

Allegory (Gk. *allēgoria;* Lat. *allegoria*, allegory, lit. speaking otherwise than one seems to speak). The figurative representation or interpretation of one thing under the image of another. In theology it denotes a method of interpreting Scripture which sees in the text a meaning other than the apparently intended or historical one. The technique is found in pre-Christian literature, and was practised by the Alexandrian Jew, Philo (*c.* 20 B.C.–*c.* A.D. 50) to interpret the Law in terms of the Hellenistic philosophy of his day. It was taken over by the Christian Platonic theologians of Alexandria, Clement (*c.* 150–*c.* 215) and Origen (*c.* 185–*c.* 254). The latter sought to follow a threefold method of interpretation, seeing in most passages a literal, a moral and a spiritual meaning. Thus the story of the blind men at Jericho (Matt. 20:29–34) is not only literally true. According to the moral meaning, our eyes must be likewise opened by the Word of God and we must come out of our Jericho. According to the spiritual meaning, the two beggars represent Israel and Judah, whilst Jericho is the world. Traces of allegory have been detected in the NT in Gal. 4:21–26; 1 Cor. 9:8 ff.; and Heb. 7:2, though some regard these passages as examples of → typology. The validity of any instance of allegory or typology turns on whether there are genuine similarities between the passage in its original intention and its spiritual interpretation. Otherwise allegorical interpretation reads into the text meanings which cannot be supported, at the expense of the intended meaning.

Amoraim → Tannaim

Analogy (Gk. *analogia*, right relationship, proportion, agreement; Lat. *analogia*, resemblance, agreement). In general analogy denotes a similitude of relations. But in theology it is found with a variety of meanings. (1) In logic it means reasoning from parallel cases. (2) Thomas Aquinas (*c.* 1225–74) held that words applied to God have an analogical meaning. They cannot be applied strictly literally to God, for this would make God identical with man. Thus, when we call God "our Father", he is not a human being who lives in time and space and who has brought children into the world by natural procreation. But there is an analogy between human fatherhood at its best and God's fatherhood, in that there is a resemblance between the two. Without analogy it would be impossible to speak about God. (3) Philosophers of history use the word analogy in a quite different sense. Following Ernst Troeltsch (1865–1923), they use analogy as a criterion for understanding and interpreting accounts of the past. Troeltsch himself believed that before we can accept an account as historical we must be able to show that it bears analogies to events as we experience them. But others have objected that this is too restrictive, as it predetermines what is possible by the historian's own experience of life. They maintain that at best analogy can only help to show what features are common to the account and

49

the historian's experience of life and what are not. (4) In Rom. 12:6 the expression *kata tēn analogian tēs pisteōs* means "in agreement with (or 'in proportion to') the faith." The context indicates that Paul is speaking about the use of gifts. (5) In reformed theology "the analogy of faith" is used to indicate the procedure of interpreting difficult passages of scripture in the light of passages where the meaning is clear.

Anthropomorphism (Gk. *anthrōpos*, man; *morphē*, form). The metaphorical use of human characteristics in speaking about God. The entire ancient world including the Bible represented deity in human terms (e.g. "the Lord smelled the pleasing odor", Gn. 8:21; the earth is God's "footstool", Matt. 5:35). The anthropomorphic way of speaking subsequently declined under the influence of abstract philosophical thought. But → Analogy (2).

Apocalyptic (Gk. *apokalypsis*, uncovering, disclosure, revelation) is used of revelations of the end of the world which are mostly bound up with a particular interpretation of the world's destiny and the cosmic history of mankind. An apocalypse is a work which contains "revelations" about the end of the world and its portents. The Book of Daniel and the Isaiah Apocalypse (chs. 24–27) in the OT and the Revelation to John in the NT are classed as apocalypses. There were numerous apocalypses in Judaism about the time of Jesus. The most important were the Books of Enoch, 4 Ezra and Baruch (→ Pseudepigrapha).

The term apocalyptist is given to writers of apocalyptic writings which are usually pseudonymous. Such authors lay claim to hidden knowledge of the end of the world through revelation which enables them to pronounce on contemporary questions. The adj. "apocalyptic" is applied to thought and speculations on the theme of the revelation of the end of the world.
→ Chiliasm, → Eschatology, → Parousia

Apocrypha (Gk. *apokryptō*, hide, conceal; *apokryphos*, pl. *-a*, hidden, secret). Originally obscure, secret writings which were not read aloud in public worship. Later, as the → canon became more fixed, the term apocrypha acquired a deprecatory sense, denoting works which were rejected as uncanonical. The use of the adj. "apocryphal" to denote the books now so designated (mainly, the books in the → LXX but not the → MT) originated with Jerome (AD *c.* 342–420; *Prologus Galeatus* to the Books of Samuel). These are the books which, as he says in his Prologue to the Books of Solomon, the church reads "for the edification of the people, not to confirm the authority of ecclesiastical dogmas." In common with Luther, Article VI of the Church of England set the apocryphal books of the OT on a lower level than Scripture, insisting that no doctrine should be founded on them, but allowed that they were profitable to read.

The OT apocrypha were mainly written in Gk. Although they occur in the → LXX and the → Vulgate, they were never part of the canonical Heb. OT. They include: 1 Esdras, 1–3 Maccabees, Tobit, Judith, Sirach, Wisdom of Solomon, 1 Baruch, Epistle of Jeremy, Prayer of Manasses, Prayer of Azariah and the Song of the Three Children, Bel and the Dragon, and additions to Esther. → Pseudepigrapha. Some of the apocryphal books were originally written in Heb.: 1 Macc., Sirach, Tobit (of which both Heb. and Aram. fragments have been found at Qumran), and most probably the Song of the Three Children.

NT apocrypha are early Christian writings which in their titles at least resemble those of the canonical NT. They include Gospels, Acts, Epistles and Apocalypses which sometimes claim authority for themselves by falsely claiming apostolic authorship. Some of the Gospels, like those according to the Hebrews, the Egyptians and that of Peter may occasionally embody trustworthy traditions. But those of Philip, Thomas, Marcion and the Twelve Apostles were intended to support heretical, especially → Gnostic views.

50

Another group sought to satisfy curiosity about aspects of Jesus' life, especially his childhood and passion. The most important apocryphal Acts are those of Peter, Paul, Andrew, John and Thomas which are all probably late second century. The Epistles include one to the Laodiceans attributed to Paul and a correspondence between Seneca and Paul. The writings of the → Apostolic Fathers do not properly belong to the Apocrypha.

Apology (Gk. *apologeomai*, speak in defence, answer; *apologia*, speech in defence, answer). The word is used in 1 Pet. 3:15 of the defence or reply which the Christian should be ready to give of his hope to outsiders and opponents. Whereas the word apology denotes a particular defence of the Christian faith, apologetics is the working out and presentation of intellectual, scientific and philosophical arguments which may underlie such an apology. In the early church Apologists like Aristides, Justin Martyr, Tertullian and Origen raised the apology to the status of a distinct genre of theological literature.

Apostasy (Gk. *apostasia*, rebellion, abandonment, apostasy; from *apo*, away, and *histēmi*, stand). The deliberate repudiation of belief once formerly held. An apostate is one who thus abandons Christianity. In the post-NT church apostasy, murder and adultery were regarded for a time as unpardonable sins. Later it become pardonable only after great (in some cases, lifelong) public penance.

Apostolic Fathers. A title given since the 17th century to the writers of the age immediately after the NT period. They include Clement of Rome, Ignatius of Antioch, Hermas, Polycarp, Papias, and the authors of the Epistle of Barnabas, the Epistle to Diognetus, 2 Clement and the Didache.

Aramaic. The Semitic language which was in common use in Palestine in the time of Jesus and which he himself almost certainly spoke. It was a sister-language of Hebrew which in later OT times had increasingly ousted classical Hebrew as the principal spoken language of the people. A few sections of the OT are written in Aramaic (Ezra 4:8–6:18; 7:12–26; Dan. 2:4–7:28; Jer. 10:11). Hebrew became increasingly the language of the learned, and to make the Scriptures accessible to ordinary people Aramaic paraphrases known as → Targums were produced.

Authenticity. The distinction between authentic and inauthentic is used in literary criticism to distinguish original parts of a passage or source from later additions and in discussion of whether a writing is to be attributed to the author whose name is associated with it. It does not necessarily imply a value-judgment on the historicity or general worth of the work concerned.

Baraitha (Aram. lit., outside, external, i.e. outside the → Mishnah). A → tannaitic tradition not incorporated in the Mishnah, or a collection of such.

Canon (Gk. *kanōn*, measuring rod, bar, standard, rule). The term is found in Gal. 6:16 for "rule", and in the 2nd century the expression "rule of faith" (Lat. *regula fidei*) came to denote the standard of revealed truth, the basic articles of faith constituting the essential Christian confession.

The words canon and canonical which had already been used by Origen (*c.* 135–*c.*254) came into general use in the 4th century with the technical meaning of the books which were received by the church as the rule of the Christian faith. The last of the books belonging to the OT canon was written several centuries B.C., but for pious Jews the question of the canon was closed about the end of the 1st century A.D. Many scholars hold that at the Synod of Jamnia (*c.* A.D. 100), a city which had been the seat of the great Sanhedrin

51

since the destruction of Jerusalem in A.D. 70, the content of the OT was discussed and, as the → Mishnah may suggest, the extent of the canon finally settled. However, other scholars question whether there was actually such a synod. The core of the NT canon (the Four Gospels and the 13 Epistles of Paul) had come to be accepted in the church *c*. 130. But doubts persisted in some quarters about some books especially Hebrews, Jude, 2 and 3 John and Revelation, whilst some accounts and collections of books included the Epistle of Barnabas and the Shepherd of Hermas (→ Apostolic Fathers). Athanasius' Festal Letter for 367 is the earliest exact witness to the canon as we have it today. The canon was recognized by synods at Hippo and Carthage in the late 4th century. But there was no general council of the early church which authorized the canon.

Captivity. After the death of Solomon (931 B.C.) the kingdom was divided into two, Israel consisting of the northern tribes with important shrines at Dan and Bethel and the capital subsequently at Samaria, and Judah consisting of the southern tribes of Judah and Benjamin with Jerusalem as the capital. The kingdom of Israel came to an end in the 8th century B.C., when Samaria fell to the Assyrians in 722. The Assyrians took large numbers of the population captive and replaced them by immigrants. → Samaritans. The kingdom of Judah fell to the invading Babylonians in the 6th century B.C. who now dominated the Middle East. Jerusalem fell in 597 and was destroyed in 581. Large deportations of the population followed. Following the fall of Babylon to Cyrus of Persia (539–530), Jews were encouraged to return from exile. But the monarchy was not restored. The final collapse of Israel is recorded in 2 Ki. 15–17 and that of Judah in 2 Ki. 23–25 (cf. 2 Chron. 36). Jeremiah and Ezekiel prophesied during the latter period, and Daniel is set against the exilic background. Isa. 40–66 consists of prophesies from an exilic or post-exilic standpoint. Ezra and Nehemiah describe events of the return. The prophecies of Haggai and Zechariah belong to this period.

Casuistry (Lat. *casus*, fall, occasion, mishap, case). Originally a term of disparagement, coined in the 18th century. In law and ethics it signifies the attempt to resolve, formulate and judge possible courses of action in accordance with a predetermined system. If one believes that one possesses a comprehensive system of ethical values, it is possible to aim at regulative prescriptions for every action. Thus freedom of personal, responsible action is extensively limited. Religious casuistry is worked out with particular thoroughness in Jewish and Catholic moral theology.

Catholic Epistles (Gk. *katholikos*, general, universal). The seven general NT letters which are called not after their addressees but after their authors: 1 and 2 Peter, 1, 2 and 3 John, James and Jude. In contrast with the letters of Paul, the Catholic letters do not quite so presuppose concrete situations in particular churches. Their purpose is to give general instruction, and they are addressed to a wider circle of readers.

Charisma (Gk. *charis*, grace, favour; *charisma*, gift, a favour bestowed). A gift given by grace, an endowment bestowed by the Holy Spirit. A charismatic is a person who has or claims to have special, spiritual gifts. The adj. charismatic is applied to actions or behaviour performed in the power of a special, divine enabling.

Chiliasm (Gk. *chilioi*, a thousand). The theory based upon a literal interpretation of Rev. 20:1–5 that Christ will return to earth and reign for a thousand years before the final consummation of all things. A chiliast is one who holds this view. These terms tend to be applied to movements and people in the early church. In more recent times this belief has been denoted by the Lat. word *millennium*, meaning a period of 1000 years. Three rival schools of interpretation have emerged. *Premillennialists* hold that the second coming of Christ will precede the millennium. Some go so far as to say that various OT prophecies about the restoration of Israel and the temple will be fulfilled in the millennial age. *Postmillennialists* hold that the return of Christ will follow the millennium which may be expected during or at the close of the gospel age. *Amillennialists* hold that the period of a thousand years mentioned in Rev. 20 is to be taken symbolically and that it applies to the present gospel age. Satan deceives the nations no more in that the gospel is now proclaimed to the nations. He is bound, in the sense that the strong man of Matt. 12:29 and Mk. 3:27 is bound, by Christ, and his goods, those held captive by him, are now being plundered. Whereas others see various dispensations and more than one resurrection, amillennialists hold that the various → eschatological events of the → parousia will come together.

Christology (Gk. *chriō*, anoint; *christos*, anointed one, Christ). (1) As an adj. used as a noun, the anointed one, the Christ, the Messiah. The Gk. word *christos* is a translation of the Heb. word *māšíah*, Messiah or anointed one. (2) Christ is more properly a title rather than a name. Christology originally meant the doctrine of the person and work of Christ. Later a distinction was drawn between christology as the doctrine of the person of Christ and → soteriology as the doctrine of the redemptive work of Christ. Sometimes the distinction is drawn between Christocentric (centred on Christ) and christological (pertaining to Christ or the concept of the Christ or Messiah).

Chronicler. The name given to the anonymous author or group of writers who composed 1 and 2 Chronicles. In the Heb. canon they form a single book. The division into two goes back to the → LXX where they are treated as a sequel to Samuel and Kings. Originally the work formed a continuous whole with the books of Ezra and Nehemiah. The term Chronicles was introduced by Jerome (c. 342–420). The first part of the work (1 and 2 Chron.) depicts Israel's history from Adam to the Exile. In the centre stand Kings David and Solomon. The second part (Ezra and Nehemiah) gives an account of the return of the Jews from exile to Jerusalem, the rebuilding of the Temple and city walls, and the public reading of the Law. In contrast to the → Deuteronomic standpoint, the Chronicler (like the → priestly tradition) is particularly interested in cultic institutions and ritual. He sees the commencement of Temple worship as the focal point of Israel's history, and sees the cult with its worship of God, feasts, priests and singers as the underlying support of Israel's existence. The writings are dated between the 4th and 3rd centuries B.C.
→ Captivity, → Deuteronomy, → Priestly Writing

Codex (pl. codices; Lat. *codex* or *caudex*, tree trunk, book). The term was used of the wooden leaves, smeared over with wax for writing. It later came to be used for books of leaves laid over one another, as distinct from *volumina* which were rolls or scrolls. The Codex Sinaiticus and the Codex Vaticanus are important manuscripts of the NT.

Conquest. The term refers to the conquest of Canaan (c. 1240 B.C.) which followed Israel's exodus from Egypt under the leadership of Moses and the period of wanderings in the Sinai desert. Gen. 12:1–3 tells of the original promise to Abraham. The account of the entry into Canaan, the subjugation of the opposing tribes and early life under judges is given in the books of Joshua, Judges and Ruth. 1 Samuel tells of the appointment of the first king of Israel, Saul.

Cosmology, Cosmogony, Cosmic (Gk. *kosmos*, world). Cosmology is that branch of → metaphysics which deals with the universe as an ordered whole. A cosmogony is a doctrine or myth about the origin of the universe. Cosmic means pertaining to the universe, esp. as distinguished from the earth.

53

Dead Sea Scrolls → Qumran.

Decalogue (Gk. *deka*, ten; *logos*, word; lit. the ten words). The Ten Commandments (Exod. 20:1–17; cf. 34; Deut. 5:6–21.

Demythologization (Ger. *Entmythologisierung*). In the 19th century several writers, but above all D. F. Strauss in his *Life of Jesus* (1835–6), claimed the presence of mythical elements in the NT. Liberal writers were inclined to dismiss certain stories as myth but insisted that these could be detached from the main historical outline. In the 20th century, however, R. Bultmann (1884–) has argued that the whole thought-world of the NT is mythological with its alleged three-decker universe of heaven, earth and hell, angels and demons, heavenly redeemer, sacramentalism etc. Bultmann holds that these myths are drawn from Jewish → apocalyptic and → gnosticism. As such, they are obsolete and offensive to modern man. What is therefore needed is to demythologize the Christian → kerygma, not to remove all offence but to remove the obsolete stumbling-blocks so as to allow the real offence of the preaching of the cross and resurrection to make its full impact. For it is the latter which enables man to be liberated from the life of the flesh and give him the possibility of understanding his existence.

The debate provoked by Bultmann has been one of the most violent of modern times. Some of his followers accuse him of not going far enough by refusing to demythologize the concepts of God, the cross and the resurrection. Opponents have argued that he dissolves the gospel in → existentialist philosophy, that his reading into the NT of gnostic themes is anachronistic, and that he is mistaken in his analysis of myth.
→ Existentialism

Determinism (Lat. *determinare*, enclose within boundaries, limit, prescribe, determine). In general, the doctrine that every event is causally produced by impersonal, material factors or by some superhuman power. In → ethics this means that the human will is never free to make its own choices, but is always controlled by external or internal factors. The opposite is indeterminism. The case for free will rests on the fact that it is a presupposition of our everyday thinking and acting. Such freedom is never unlimited, but is always circumscribed by environment, past acts of the agent, and personal traits. Nevertheless, upholders of free will claim that it would be senseless to talk of responsibility and ethics if there is no range of freedom with the possibility to think or act otherwise.

Deutero-Isaiah (Gk. *deuteros*, second). The designation given by scholars who separate Isa. 40–55 from the previous chapters and attribute them to an anonymous author who lived during the exile (→ Captivity). He is distinguished from Isaiah of Jerusalem who lived during the 8th century BC and was called to prophetic office in the year of King Uzziah's death (739; Isa. 6:1). Deutero-Isaiah is thought to have lived in the latter part of the Babylonian exile (597/587–538 B.C.) and was a prophet proclaiming a message of salvation between 550 and 538. At the time the Babylonian empire was in decline and faced collapse before the Persian King Cyrus who was awaited as the deliverer of suppressed, captive peoples. Deutero-Isaiah proclaimed the imminent return of the exiles of Israel as the beginning of the era of salvation which would embrace the whole creation.

Some scholars treat the last eleven chapters of Isaiah as a separate work (Isa. 56–66), holding that they were written by a later prophet. They are designated Trito-Isaiah (Third Isaiah), even when they are not held to be the work of a single author.

Deuteronomy (Gk. *deuteros*, second; *nomos*, law). The title given to the fifth book of the → Pentateuch which arose through the → LXX mistranslation of Deut. 17:18 of the Heb. *mišnê hattôrâh* ("copy of the law") by the Gk. *deuteronomion* ("repetition of the law").

Deuteronomy takes the form of an address by Moses to the Israelites before the crossing of the Jordan and the → conquest of Canaan. It is regarded by some scholars to have received its final form about the time of Josiah's reform of Israelite worship (c. 621 B.C.; cf. 2 Ki. 22 f.). Scholars who regard the book as the work of an unknown group of authors refer to the latter as the Deuteronomic School. Scholars have discerned a distinctive style and diction in Deut. Its stress is laid on the fact that → Yahweh is the only true God. His love for his chosen people is unbounded. Hence, Israel must love him in return. The work is presented as an authentic compilation of the beliefs and statutes of Israel to which nothing should be added or taken away. It insists that Yahweh is to be worshipped only in one place, the sanctuary.

The term Deuteronomic is applied not only to the theological outlook of the book Deut., but to the whole historical work from Deut. 1:1 to 2 Ki. 25:30, covering the time of Moses, the → conquest, the age of the judges to the end of the monarchy. The final author of this historical material is sometimes called the Deuteronomist. He is envisaged by critical scholars to have collected and sifted ancient sources, interpreting this material by inserting speeches and observations. He is thought to have composed the work during the exile in the shadow of the catastrophe of 587 B.C. Consequently, he presents the history of Israel as the story of the progressive turning away from Yahweh.

The distinction is sometimes drawn between Deuteronomic (pertaining to the book Deut. and its outlook) and Deuteronomistic (denoting the general outlook on history associated with these writings with their strong Zion theology).
→ Chronicler, → Captivity

Deutero-Pauline Writings (Gk. *deuteros*, second). A collective term applied to those letters which are generally attributed to Paul but which some scholars attribute to unknown authors who desired to make use of the name and authority of the apostle. The letters in question are Ephesians, Colossians and 2 Thessalonians, but not the → Pastoral Epistles.

Diaspora, Dispersion (Gk. *diaspeirō*, scatter; *diaspora*, scattering, dispersion). The dispersion of the Jews which had its beginnings in the deportations by the Assyrians and Babylonians (722 and 597 B.C.; → Captivity). It later spread throughout the Roman Empire to Egypt, Asia Minor, Greece and Italy. The term refers generally to Jews living outside Palestine. Some of the first Christian preaching was addressed to them (cf. Jas. 1:1 and 1 Pet. 1:1 which may refer to → Jewish Christians).
→ Septuagint

Didache (Gk. *didachē*, teaching). (1) The instructional element in early Christian teaching, as contrasted with → kerygma or preaching. (2) The title of an early Christian manual on morals and practice dating from the 2nd century.

Docetism (Gk. *dokeō*, seem, appear). The doctrine that Christ had only an apparent body during his earthly life and consequently only appeared to suffer on the cross. Docetism denies the historical reality of Jesus' life and regards the physical body, like matter, as contrary to the spirit (→ Dualism). In the early church docetism was maintained chiefly by → Gnostics and theologians influenced by them (Valentinus, Marcion in the 2nd century). But it was soon rejected as false teaching.
→ Gnosis, Gnosticism

Dualism (Lat. *dualis*, containing two; *duo*, two). Any doctrine which asserts that there are two ultimate powers or principles. The → Gnostics were dualists in that they held that matter and spirit were two ultimately opposing realms. Dualism may also denote the doctrine that good and evil are the product of two equally ultimate first causes.

55

Ecclesiology (Gk. *ekklēsia*, assembly, church). (1) The doctrine of the church and its structure; (2) the science which treats matters connected with churches, esp. architecture and decoration.

Ellipsis (Gk. *elleipsis*, falling short, defect, ellipse). In grammar and rhetoric the omission of a word or thought necessary to complete the construction or sense of an expression. The latter must be determined from the context. An elliptical expression is one which omits a thought or word in this way.

Elohist, "E" (Heb. *'elōhîm*, God; it is a plu. form and can also mean gods). Elohist is the name given to the author of one of the conjectured sources of the → Pentateuch, whose style is thought to be characterized by his extensive use of the name Elohim for God together with the occasional use of → Yahweh, but only after Exod. 3:14 f. The so-called Elohistic source (or "E") is thought to begin with Gen. 15 and describes the → patriarchal period and the time of Moses up to the entry into Canaan, but without the prologue depicting pre-history. The passages assigned to "E" are characterized by features common to the 8th century prophets which has led to the conjecture of an 8th century date.

Empiricism (Gk. *empeiria*, experience; *empeirikos*, experienced). A British philosophical movement of the 17th and 18th centuries. In contrast to the rationalists who sought to erect philosophical systems by means of reasoning on the basis of allegedly self-evident truths, the empiricists stressed the role of experience in knowledge. They claimed that we have no ideas at all other than those derived from experience which comes to us through our senses. The leading figures in the movement were John Locke (1632–1704), George Berkeley (1685–1753) and David Hume (1711–76).

The adj. empirical denotes that which is known by the senses. Thus, empirical evidence is evidence which may be perceived by the senses.

Eschatology (Gk. *eschaton*, last, end; *logos*, word). Traditionally the doctrine of the last things: the end of the world, the second coming of Christ, the resurrection of the dead, the last judgment, and the creation of the new heaven and earth. The term itself first came to be used extensively in the 19th century, but the underlying ideas are connected with → apocalyptic. In contemporary theology the term is frequently used with a somewhat different meaning. In contrast to apocalyptic with its theme of unveiling the hidden events of the end of the world and the last things, stress is laid on present hope, expectations and promises about what may happen. In its widest sense eschatology can mean simply being open to the future, being prepared for what may befall us. C. H. Dodd (1884–1973) spoke of a realized eschatology, claiming that certain passages in Paul, Jn. and Heb. transform the literalism of earlier apocalyptic imagery and stress the new and present realities wrought by Christ. Statements about the end of history already accomplished by Christ, the future hope of Christians and the end of the world may all be termed eschatological, according to the broader or narrower concept of eschatology.

Ethics (Gk. *ēthos*, character). The science of morals. It involves: (1) questions of what is right and wrong, good and bad, or how we ought to behave (normative ethics); (2) the study of the answers given to such questions by particular societies (descriptive or comparative ethics); (3) the investigation of the nature or logical character of moral concepts in the light of the meaning and use of moral language (moral philosophy or philosophical ethics).

Etymology (Gk. *etymos*, true; *logos*, word, account). The branch of linguistics which investigates the origin and derivation of words, or the origin or derivation itself of a word.

56

Until the advent of modern philology the derivation of words was often a matter of guesswork. The Ger. term *Volksetymologie*, or popular etymology, denotes an etymological explanation which has arisen through popular misunderstanding. Recent discussions have stressed that in determining the meaning of a word, usage and context play as great, if not a more important, part than etymology. Moreover, the derivation and meaning of a word at one stage in its history may not be decisive for its meaning at another stage.

Exegesis (Gk. *exēgeomai*, explain, interpret, tell, report, describe; *exēgēsis*, narrative, description, explanation, interpretation). Exegesis means interpretative explanation; an exegete is one who so explains. The task of exegesis is to explain the meaning of a text as the author would have it understood. The theological exegesis of biblical texts follows the general, scholarly method of interpreting ancient texts. It involves the following disciplines: → textual criticism, translation, → literary criticism, the investigation of literary → genre, → form-criticism, the comparative study of literature and religions, word studies, investigation of historical background, → redaction criticism. Exegesis is not confined to the explanation of words. Its goal is to discern the subject-matter lying behind the words. → Hermeneutics, → Historical Criticism

Exile → Captivity

Existentialism (Ger. *Existenzphilosophie*). A philosophy which sprang up in Germany after the First World War and subsequently had considerable influence on European philosophy and Protestant theology especially in the realm of → hermeneutics. Its beginnings may be traced back to the rejection of → metaphysics by Kierkegaard and Nietzsche in the 19th century. Existentialism endeavours to explore the structure and meaning of human existence without metaphysical presuppositions. R. Bultmann's → demythologized restatement of the Christian → kerygma consciously draws upon the existentialism of Martin Heidegger (1889–). He regards the biblical picture of fallen man, redeemed by the atoning sacrifice of the Son of God on the cross as mythological, in so far as it states the Christian message in the imagery of the mythological thought-world. In his restatement he sees sin as the inauthentic existence of man striving to secure his well being by grasping after the tangible. Authentic human existence is to be attained by faith, i.e. by response to the preaching of the cross and resurrection which liberates man from the pursuit of the tangible and enables him to be open to the future.

Exodus (Gk. *exodos*, going out). The second book of the → Pentateuch which derives its name from the → LXX description of the chief event recorded in it, Israel's going out of Egypt. The event has been dated *c.* 1280 B.C., and the route of the exodus has been the subject of considerable investigation. Since the 19th century many OT scholars see behind the book various sources which they identify as → J, → E, and → P.

Form-Criticism (Ger. *Formgeschichte*, lit. form history). The exegetical technique of studying literary forms in the Bible, in order to determine characteristic features and regular patterns in passages which distinguish them from other forms of literature. It concentrates on the smallest literary units in the biblical texts (e.g. parables, miracle stories, sayings of Jesus), genres or forms which received their initial form through oral tradition before they were incorporated into larger literary contexts, and perhaps thereby modified. Form-criticism investigates literary → genres, the historical context (→ Sitz im Leben), the processes of oral transmission and editorial adaptation.
→ Logia, → Redaction, → Tradition

57

Gemara (*gēmārā'* from an Aram. root meaning repeat or a Heb. root meaning complete). The discussions of the rabbis in Palestine and Babylonia on the → Mishnah which together with the Mishnah constitute the → Talmud.

Gemeinde (Ger. community). The term is used in Ger. for the community or local church as distinct from the church at large (Ger. *Kirche*). *Gemeindetheologie* (lit. community theology) has become a technical term to designate the particular theology or theological emphases of a local church.

Genre (cf. Ger. *Gattung*). A literary species characterized by identifying features common to its constituent passages. In → form-criticism scholars proceed on the assumption that many biblical texts were not the work of a single author, but consist of units which were initially handed on by oral tradition. Certain regular patterns or rules have been discerned. It is important for understanding a genre to examine its historical context (→ Sitz im Leben), i.e. the situation which it presupposes, the speaker, his intentions, hearers, and the entire character of the text.

The following are important genres in the OT: songs or psalms, proverbs, narratives, legends, priestly oracles, cultic rites and formulas, divine utterances, sermons and credal formulas. In the NT there are sayings of Jesus (→ Logia), parables, miracle stories, passion narratives, credal formulas, Christ-hymns and sermons.

Gentile (Lat. *gentilis* from *gens*, nation). A non-Jew. The expression arose from the Jewish practice of speaking of non-Jews as the nations (Heb. *gôyîm*) which were outside the covenant relationship between Yahweh and Israel.

Geschichte → Historie

Gnosticism (Gk. *gnōsis*, knowledge). The term given to various religious movements which make redemption and man's liberation dependent upon knowledge of the nature, origin and goal of the world and human life as well as of the heavenly regions. Gnosticism was a → syncretistic form of religion which drew elements from Judaism, eastern religions and Christianity, it flourished in the 2nd century A.D. and continued until the 4th century. Some scholars, especially in Germany, trace its beginnings to the 1st century B.C. and claim to see its influence on the church and Christian thought in NT times. Others, however, think that it is anachronistic to speak of gnosticism proper in the NT period.

The gnostic belief system included a theological → dualism of creation and redemption, theories of the world's emanation from the divine spirit, insistence upon the need of liberation from the material world, and the spirit's need to return to its original, heavenly home, the physical efficacy of the sacraments as the medicines of immortality (*pharmaka athanasias*). Christian gnosticism tried to detach faith from its historical basis by denying the reality of the incarnation of Christ (→ docetism), and relaxed the necessity of obedience. Adherents to gnosticism are termed gnostics.

Haggadah (Heb. *haggadâh*, narrative). Jewish biblical interpretation of a non-legal or narrative character which was directed at furthering inner piety and religious devotion. As such, it supplemented → Halachah.

Hagiographa (Gk. *hagiographa*, holy writings). The Writings, the third division of the Heb. Bible. In contrast with the other two (the Law and the Prophets), it is a miscellaneous collection of eleven books. In the printed Heb. Bible they occur in the following order: (1) three large poetic books (Pss., Prov., Ruth); (2) five scrolls (Megilloth) which were

58

read in the synagogues at the great feasts (Song of Solomon, Ruth, Lam., Eccl., Est.); (3) a book of late prophecy (Dan.); (4) two books of post-exilic history (Ezr.-Neh. and Chr.). English versions which follow the Gk. set the books in a different order and do not preserve this division as a unity.

Halachah (Heb. *hᵃlāḵâh*, that by which one walks, cf. Exod. 18:20). The body of postbiblical Jewish legal decisions based on the Law. It arose out of the pious wish to apply the Law to every aspect of life. At first it was handed on orally. It gave rise to the → Mishnah and forms the bulk of the → Talmud, the remainder consisting of → Haggadah.

Hasmonaean → Maccabees

Haustafel (Ger., pl. -n, lit. household table). A list of ethical injunctions. The word has now become a technical term in NT criticism. It originated from Luther's Ger. tr. of the Bible which headed two such lists (Eph. 5:21–6:9; Col. 3:18–4:11) by the word. The term *Gemeindetafel* (lit. community table; → Gemeinde) is sometimes used in the more inclusive sense of rules within the church and rules for conduct towards those outside. It is applied to such passages as 1 Tim. 2:1–15; 5:1–21; 6:1 f.; 1 Pet. 2:13–3:7.

Heilsgeschichte (Ger. salvation history). The term focuses on the thought that the unifying theme of Scripture is the history of God's saving acts, first in Israel under the old covenant and then in Christ who brings about a new covenant relationship between God and man. This in turn points to the → Parousia and the culmination of history. Salvation history is seen as the key to the meaning and course of secular history.

The idea, though not the term, goes back to Irenaeus (*c.* 130–*c.* 200) and Augustine (354–430). It has been revived in 20th century theology especially by Protestant theologians who wish to stress that Christianity is based on faith in a God who acts in history, rather than on an attenuated philosophy of religion or on a → demythologized existential → kerygma which is concerned with man's self-understanding. A leading exponent is Oscar Cullmann (1902–).

Hellenism (Gk. *Hellēn*, Greek). A term given to designate the period of Gk. culture from Alexander the Great (356–323 B.C.) to the beginning of the Roman Empire under Augustus (31 B.C.), i.e. to approximately the beginning of the Christian era. Hellenism decisively influenced both the intellectual and the historical development of late antiquity. Its influence continued through the Middle Ages and the Renaissance. It is characterized by the mutual interpenetration of Gk. and oriental culture (→ mystery religions) the extensive mingling of populations, the idea of the inhabited world (*oikoumenē*), the common use of Gk. as the world language (→ Koine), the ascendency of philosophy over poetry (→ Stoicism, → Scepticism), and → syncretism in religion in which a monotheistic tendency is discernible.

Hermeneutics (Gk. *hermēneuō*, interpret, explain; *hermēneia*, interpretation, explanation). The science of the interpretation of written texts in accordance with scientifically formulated rules and principles. Schleiermacher defined hermeneutics as "the doctrine of the art of understanding." It involves the study of language, tradition, historical setting, intention, the original readers, the universe of discourse and the subject matter of the text. In its broadest sense hermeneutics can be understood as the methodological basis of the human sciences. Biblical hermeneutics has to do with the interpretation of biblical texts in the light of the various techniques and branches of → exegesis. Theological hermeneutics seeks to translate, interpret and make comprehensible the message of the Bible in the contemporary situation. See further the article on *Explain*, art. *hermēneuō*.

Hermetic Literature. A collection of Gk. and Lat. writings ascribed to Hermes Trismegistus (Hermes the Thrice-Greatest), a designation of the Egyptian God, Thoth, the father and protector of knowledge. The writings date from the middle of the 1st to the end of the 3rd centuries A.D. Much of them deal with astronomy and alchemy. The *Corpus Hermeticum*, consists of some 17 theological and philosophical treatises, the first and most important of which bears the title *Poimandres*. Like the other works, it is → syncretistic and → gnostic in outlook. It has affinities with the NT in its description of the divine as light and life and its doctrine of the → Logos as active in creation. It may have been written within a generation after Jn., but the influence of the NT on these writings is thought to be negligible.

Historical Criticism (Gk. *krinō*, separate, distinguish, decide, judge). A branch of → exegesis which examines biblical texts in the light of scientific methods and criteria for the investigation of history. According to Ernst Troeltsch (1865–1923) whose approach has set guidelines for much Ger. thinking on the subject, historical criticism involves: (1) The historian must be independent and autonomous. He must critically scrutinize all traditions, though approaching his material with sympathetic understanding. Moreover, in the realm of history only probable judgments are possible. (2) The sense of probability depends upon the historian's capacity to discern → analogy between events here and now and events of the past. Where there is no analogy the alleged event is questionable. (3) The principle of correlation that all historical happening is knit together in a permanent correlation. Any one event is causally related to the rest. This has given rise to a closed view of the world in which everything is interpreted in terms of finite natural and historical causes and in which no supernatural events or actions of God are admitted. More recently W. Pannenberg and others have argued that this approach requires restatement and modification, for it prejudges the issue by imposing upon data the limitations of the historian's experience and thus does not allow historical data to speak for itself.

Historical criticism is not of itself hostile to the text of the Bible. Rather, it claims its justification on the grounds that, since the Bible bears witness to what happened in history, it is important to see it in historical perspective.
→ Literary criticism

Historicism. A term which is given a variety of meanings, but often it is used in the sense that every person, event, institution, or idea is capable of being explained entirely in terms of their historical antecedents. It is thus a form of relativism which refuses absolute significance to anything, insisting that nothing must be taken at face value, but rather as the produce of the historical forces acting upon it.

Historie and Geschichte. The Ger. language uses two words for history, together with their corresponding adj. *historisch* and *geschichtlich*. The less common *Historie* is used in contemporary theology to denote that which is public and verifiable according to generally accepted standards of history writing. *Geschichte* refers to the significance of a historical fact for the believer which is not open in the same way to historical verification. The term *der historische Jesus* (the historical Jesus) thus refers to the Jesus that can be known in the light of critical research. The terms *der Christus des Glaubens* (the Christ of faith) or *der geschichtliche Christus* (the historic Christ) refer to Christ as seen by the eyes of faith. The distinction is illustrated by the title of Martin Kähler's work *Der sogenannte historische Jesus und der geschichtliche biblische Christus* (1892), E.T. *The So-called Historical Jesus and the Historic Biblical Christ* (1964).

History of Religions. A branch of the study of religions. But whereas comparative theology is concerned with the systematic and comparative study of the beliefs of different religions,

60

the history of religions is concerned with the development and history of particular religions in their origin, evolution, phases and changes.

The study of the history of religions is an empirical science which employs the appropriate techniques of historical criticism and the philological interpretation of texts. At the turn of the present century the history of religions school sought to set the study of the Bible in the context of the wider history of religions in order to understand better the characteristics of biblical religion.

Holiness Code, "H". The collection of Mosaic legislation in Lev. 17–26 and designated "H". Its subjects include sacrifice, marriage laws, penalties, the priesthood, the sacred calendar. According to certain critical views, it is post-Deuteronomic and was drawn up some time after the fall of Jerusalem in 586 B.C.
→ Pentateuch, → Deuteronomy, → J, → Elohist, → Priestly Writing

Hypothesis (Gk. *hypothesis*, proposal, suggestion, supposition). A conjectured explanation which has not yet been verified but which has been devised as a means towards scientific understanding. A hypothesis seeks to explain, and thus goes beyond the purely descriptive. It suggests reasons which as such are only apparent. A hypothesis represents a preliminary step towards a theory which offers a rationally more comprehensive and better grounded explanation. Hypothetical assertions operate on the level of conjecture and appearance.

Israel (Heb. *yiśrā'ēl*, God strives). (1) The name given to Jacob after his night of wrestling (Gen. 32:28; cf. 35:10; Hos. 12:3 f.). (2) The Hebrew nation which traced its descent back to Israel through his twelve sons (Gen. 34:7; 32:32; 49:16, 28). (3) The name was appropriated by the ten northern tribes which broke away from the southern kingdom of Judah after the death of Solomon (c. 933 B.C.) and which were carried away to Assyria (c. 721 B.C.; → Captivity). (4) In the NT the church is described as the new "Israel of God" (Gal. 6:16), as it now inherits the privileges of ancient Israel as the covenant people of God.

J → Yahwist

Jewish Christian. Churches in the NT and → patristic periods whose members were converts from Judaism, in contrast to the → gentile churches whose members were drawn from → Hellenistic, → syncretistic religion. There was a tendency in Jewish Christian churches to retain Jewish ritual laws with regard to circumcision and commandments relating to food. But as Jewish Christians joined the gentile churches this began to decline, especially in view of Paul's opposition to → Judaizers and his teaching that the ritual law is superseded in Christ. With the destruction of Jerusalem by the Romans in A.D. 70 the main centre of Jewish Christianity disappeared.

Judah (Heb. *yᵉhûḏāh*). (1) The fourth son of Jacob by Leah (Gen. 29:35, where the name is explained as meaning "praised"; cf. 49:8 which contains a play on this meaning; other → etymologies have also been suggested). (2) Gen. describes how the tribe of Judah is descended from him (Gen. 38) and how it is promised a position of leadership (49:8–12). In the → conquest of Canaan Judah was allotted territory in the south (Jos. 15). After the death of Saul, David was made king over Judah (2 Sam. 2:4), perhaps ruling over a dual kingdom which included the rest of → Israel (2 Sam. 5:1–5). (3) After the death of Solomon, the ten northern tribes formed the kingdom of Israel (1 Ki. 12), leaving Judah together with Benjamin as the southern kingdom with Jerusalem as its capital and focal point of worship. Judah survived the advances of Assyria, but large portions of its population were deported by the Babylonians (2 Ki. 23–25; Jer. 52; c. 597–c. 538 B.C.; → Captivity). The return from exile brought about a restoration of Judah but without the monarchy (cf. Ezr.–Neh.). Judah came increasingly under Hellenistic influence, especially under the pressure of the Syrian Seleucid empire. Although this was withstood under the → Maccabees, the land came under the sway of the Romans in the 1st century B.C. who destroyed Jerusalem in AD 70 and with it the last vestiges of independence. With the crushing of Bar Kochba's revolt in A.D. 135 Judah ceased to be a Jewish land. The name remained in the form of Jew as the title for the adherents of the Mosaic law, irrespective of which tribe they came from. (4) After the Babylonian exile Judah became a favourite name among Jews.

Judaizers (→ Judah). The name given to militant → Jewish Christians who insisted upon retention of the Jewish Law in the church not only by converted Jews but by → gentile converts as well. They insisted upon circumcision and the distinction between clean and unclean meat. The issues they raised were debated and rejected by the Jerusalem council (Acts 15) and they figure prominently in Gal.

Kerygma (Gk. *kērygma*, proclamation, announcement, preaching). The proclamation or preaching of the Christian message. In the NT kerygma can refer to the content, event and office of proclamation. In contrast to teaching (→ *didachē*) which expresses the revelation of Christ conceptually and logically in doctrines, the emphasis of the kerygma falls on public proclamation and the promise and claims of the saving event.

In modern times the somewhat unfortunate distinction has been drawn between a theology of the saving events which lays emphasis on facts and a kerygmatic theology which stresses the relation between the word spoken in address and the response of faith. The NT does not draw this sharp distinction.

Koine (Gk. *koinē*, common, ordinary). The common every-day language of the → Hellenistic period. The NT writings were written in Koine Gk. rather than in classical (Attic) Gk.

Law → Torah

Libertinism (Lat. *libertas*, freedom, liberty). Commonly used to describe the attitude of freethinkers, frequently in a deprecatory sense. In ethics it denotes the attitude and practice of unlimited moral freedom which rejects all restraints, standards and conventions.

Literary Criticism (Lat. *littera*, letter). A branch of → exegesis, concerned with the sources of biblical writings, especially those books which are thought to be based upon several sources (such as the → Pentateuch and the Gospels). It seeks to distinguish between the original literary components of a text and later additions. The ability of the exegete to resolve literary questions enables him to set a piece of work in its historical context in the world of the OT or the NT.

Logia (Gk. *logion*, oracle, saying). A saying. The term is used esp. of the sayings of Jesus. Since the later 19th century students of → synoptic criticism have favoured the suggestion that Mk. was the earliest gospel and that both Matt. and Lk. made use of it in writing their own gospels. Mk. contains mainly narrative material. To explain the sayings and teaching material common to Matt. and Lk. scholars have suggested the existence of a sayings source referred to as Q (possibly so-named after the Ger. *Quelle*, source). This source does not exist as such in manuscript form in the way that (e.g.) Mk. does, but is posited from the material common to Matt. and Lk. The exact extent of the alleged source cannot be determined with any certainty. In form it is thought to consist mainly of sayings and discourses with little narrative. The chief purpose of such a source would be to give Jesus' proclamation of the Kingdom of God and the Son of Man. A secondary theme would be the presentation of Jesus' authority in word and deed. It is not thought to contain references to the → passion. The source is thought to be older than Mk. and was written in Aramaic. The church connected with Q has been identified with the primitive Palestinian community of the first decade after the death of Jesus.

Logos (Gk. *logos*, word, reason). The notion of the Logos figured in Gk. philosophy from Heraclitus (*c*. 500 B.C.) who understood it as the universal reason which permeates and governs the world. It was taken over by the → Stoics in this sense. The → Hellenistic Jewish thinker, Philo (*c*. 20 B.C.–*c*. A.D. 50), regarded it less as an immanent power than as an intermediary agent. Logos is also the → LXX translation for Heb. *dābār* (word). In the NT the technical use of the term is confined to Jn. 1:1 ff.; 1 Jn. 1:1; Rev. 19:13 (cf. Heb. 1:2; 4:12). The 2nd century → Apologists developed logos christologies which presented belief in Jesus Christ in terms of the divine logos in creation.

LXX → Septuagint

Maccabees. (Gk. *Makkabaios*, hammerer or extinguisher). The Jewish family which played a prominent part in freeing Judea from the Syrian Seleucid empire in the 2nd century B.C. The Maccabean revolt prevented the advance of → Hellenism which had threatened the destruction of Judaism. It began in 168 B.C. when an aged priest Mattathias killed an apostate Jew who was about to offer sacrifice on an idolatrous altar in the town of Modia. The Maccabees are also known as Hasmonaeans, as Mattathias was reputed to be descended from Hasmon. The four books of Maccabees are named after the hero of the first two, Judas Maccabaeus. The first three are included in the → Apocrypha.

Masoretic Text, frequently abbreviated as *MT* (Heb. *māsōreṭ*, tradition). The Heb. text of the OT, so-called because in its present form it is based on the "masora" or body of traditional information compiled by the Masoretes. The latter were Jewish scholars of the 10th and earlier centuries A.D. The most important feature of their work was to provide a system of pointing (strokes and dots indicating vowels) for the unpointed text. The original unpointed text consisted of consonants only, and the reader was left to supply the vowels for himself. The Masoretes provided points to preserve the pronunciation of ancient Heb. and to provide a definitive version of the text. Although the OT was originally written in Heb., the questions therefore arise, whether the MT represents faithfully the original text, and whether in some cases where there is a difference of reading the Gk. → LXX is not sometimes to be preferred.

Megilloth → Hagiographa

Memra (Aram. *mêmrā'*, word) is used in Jewish lit. for the divine creative → logos, manifesting God's power in the world and the human mind and mediating between God and man. It possibly underlies Jn. 1. It was sometimes used in the → Targums instead of → Yahweh, to avoid → anthropomorphism.
→ Art. *Word*

Messianic Titles (Heb. *māšîaḥ*, anointed one). Titles and ascriptions given in the OT to the expected Messiah and adopted by the Christian church in its proclamation of Jesus as the Messiah who has come. They include: Messiah, Christ (Gk. *christos*, anointed one, a tr. of *māšîaḥ*), Son of David, Son of God, Son of Man, King of the Jews.

Metaphysics (Gk. *meta ta physika*, beyond or behind [the books on] physics). The terms referred originally to the order of works by the Gk. philosopher, Aristotle, in the library of Andronicus Rhodius who placed works on "first philosophy" dealing with principles and ultimate causes behind those on nature. This original use of the term was gradually changed in meaning, so that metaphysics came to be understood as that branch of philosophy which deals with the principles and conditions of all beings which lie behind physical nature.

This is the commonly accepted meaning today. However, through the changed historical understanding of the principles of being, the understanding of metaphysics has correspondingly changed in the course of history. Following Kant's devastating criticism of metaphysics in his *Critique of Pure Reason* (1781), the possibility of metaphysics has been radically questioned in the 19th and 20th centuries. Nevertheless, philosophy has not been able to dispense entirely with metaphysical presuppositions.

→ Ontology, → Empiricism, → Existentialism

Midrash (Heb. *dāraš*, search out, investigate; *miḏrāš*, investigation). A Jewish method of → exegesis which sought to discover deeper meanings in the text beyond the literal one. Since the text was of divine origin, every detail was significant. Midrash → halachah was concerned with the Law and midrash → haggadah was concerned with the non-legal parts of scripture. Tradition traces midrash back to Ezra as the first of the scribes (*sôp̄erîm*) who began this type of exposition. The earliest collections of midrashim date from the 2nd century A.D.

→ Rabbinism, → Mishnah, → Talmud

Millennium → Chiliasm

Mishnah (Heb. *šānâh*, repeat; *mišnâh*, repetition, instruction). Originally the oral, repeated teaching of the Law in contrast to the written Law. The word became a technical term for the orally transmitted case law, which developed over and above the → Torah and which ultimately became normative in post-exilic Judaism. The Mishnah provides the foundation for the Babylonian and Palestinian → Talmud. It is divided into 6 sections or Sedarim, comprising 63 tractates.

→ Rabbinism, → Haggadah, → Halachah → Midrash

Mystery Religions (Gk. *mystērion*, mystery). The secret cults of the Hellenistic period which were open only to initiates, who were granted redemption and access to the eternal world of the divine being. Among the most important mystery cults were the Gk. cult of Dionysus (Bacchus), the mysteries of Isis and Serapis which originated in Egypt, the Syrian Adonis cult, the worship of the mother god Cybele and Attis in Asia Minor, and the mysteries of the light god Mithras from Persia. The mystery gods were originally nature divinities whose death and return to life mirrored the change of the seasons. Through the cult the initiate participates in the fate of the deity. Since the mystery cults made no exclusive claim on their adherents, one could be initiated into several cults in order to gain as much divine, life-giving power as possible.

Ontology (Gk. *ōn*, being). A philosophical term coined in the 17th century meaning: (1) the doctrine of being in general (Ger. *Sein*); (2) the doctrine of beings, that which is, the things that are (Ger. *das Seiende;* Gk. *ta onta*). Sometimes a distinction is drawn between ontological and ontic. Whereas the former is concerned with being, the latter is concerned with beings. Anything that exists in any way is ontic. Ontology is concerned with the knowledge of the structure of being both of man and of the world. It is a branch of → metaphysics. It goes back to the earliest Gk. thinkers, the pre-Socratic philosophers whose doctrine of the origin (*archē*) of things was the first answer to the question of being. In the course of the history of philosophy various highly different ontological systems

have been developed, including those of Plato (427–347 B.C.), Aristotle (384–322 B.C.), the scholasticism of Thomas Aquinas (1225–74), and Christian Wolff (1697–1754). In the 20th century Martin Heidegger sought to give a new basis to ontology in his seminal work *Being and Time* (1927), which developed an analysis of human existence in terms of an existential-ontology. Whereas Catholic neo-scholasticism of the 19th century endeavoured to revive Thomistic ontology, Protestant theology since A. B. Ritschl (1822–89) has seriously questioned the usefulness of ontology.
→ Existentialism

Paraenesis (Gk. *paraineō*, advise, recommend, urge, exhort). Exhortation. Passages with a strong exhortatory content in both OT and NT are termed paraenetic. The proclamation of Christ (→ kerygma) and paraenesis are related to each other as gift and task, indicative and imperative, and in the realm of theological reflection as dogmatics and ethics. The promise of the gospel is the foundation and presupposition of the claims of paraenesis (cf. Rom. 1–11 with 12–15).

Parousia (Gk. *parousia*, presence, coming). The coming or presence of a person or God in order to help. In Christian language the parousia means the coming of Christ at the end-time for the general resurrection, last judgment and the creation of the new heaven and earth.
→ Apocalyptic, → Eschatology

Pastoral Epistles (Lat. *pastor*, shepherd). A term given to 1 and 2 Tim. and Titus, as these letters are concerned with pastoral questions, being addressed to leaders of churches and containing directions and exhortations for the leadership of Christian churches. In modern times it has been debated whether the author was the apostle Paul (as the letters themselves indicate) or whether he was an anonymous author of slightly later times making use of the authority of Paul.

Patriarch (Gk. *patēr*, father; *archē*, beginning). The father of the tribe or nation, in particular Abraham, his son Isaac and grandson, Jacob (→ Israel) and the 12 sons of Jacob (Gen. 12–50; cf. Acts 7:8 f., Heb. 7:4), to whom the nation of Israel is traced in scripture. The patriarchal age begins *c.* 2100 B.C. Genealogies of antediluvian patriarchs are given in Gen. 5. King David is called a patriarch in Acts 2:29.

Pentateuch (Gk. *hē pentateuchos biblos*, the five-part book). The technical term for the first 5 books of the Bible (Gen., Exod., Lev., Num., Deut.), traditionally ascribed to Moses and forming the first part of the OT → canon with the name → Torah (Law). The division of the Torah into 5 books is not original. However, the translators of the → LXX found the division already made and gave the books individual names: Genesis (beginning, after the opening words of the creation account in ch. 1), Exodus (after the → exodus, the chief event recorded), Leviticus (Lat., relating to the Levites), Numbers (on account of the two enumerations of the people which it records) and → Deuteronomy.
→ Elohist, → Yahwist, → Holiness Code, → Priestly Writing, → Deuteronomy

Pericope (Gk. *perikopē*, section; *perikoptō*, cut off). A biblical passage, especially one appointed to be read aloud in public worship. The term was already used in the early church in the sense of a proof passage for a dogmatic utterance. In contemporary exegesis it is used to denote a passage or section of the text.

Pesher (Aram. *pᵉšar* [emphatic state, *pišrā'*] solution, interpretation). A type of exegesis found in the → Qumran scrolls, which took earlier prophecy as being directly concerned with themselves. The word is placed after almost every prophetic statement cited and may be translated as "the interpretation of this is . . .", "this refers to . . .", or "this means . . ."

Platonic. Pertaining to the doctrines or person of Plato (427–*c.* 347 B.C.) who taught that the world that we see with our eyes and touch with our bodies is only a world of transitory shadows. It is a copy of the eternal world of spiritual Forms or Ideas to which men may attain by detached, intellectual contemplation. He held that man was an immortal soul in a material body. When the body dies, the soul is preserved. His view was bound up with the thought of a premundane fall and the transmigration of souls as a means of purification through successive forms of existence.

Neo-Platonism was developed by Plotinus (A.D. *c.* 205–69) and others, teaching that behind all existence there is an ultimate One in which the distinction between thought and reality is overcome. The One is reached by a way of negation culminating in mystical experience.

Pneumatology (Gk. *pneuma*, breath, wind, spirit). The doctrine of the person and work of the Holy Spirit. Pneumatological refers to statements involving the Holy Spirit.

Pre-existence of Christ (Lat. *prae-existentia*). The existence of Christ as a divine being with God the Father prior to his incarnation and earthly life (cf. Jn. 1:1–12). The idea of pre-existence is also found in pre- and non-Christian religions.

Priestly Writing, designated P in → Pentateuchal criticism. Since J. Wellhausen (1844–1918), P has been thought by many scholars to represent the most recent stratum of the Pentateuch. The designation rests upon the supposed source's interest in cultic and ritual institutions and priestly ordinances. These are described partly in narratives and partly in accounts of varying length (e.g. of the erection of the tabernacle, Exod. 25–31).

The source is thought to begin with Gen. 1:1 and end with Deut. 34:9 and contain (parallel with → J) a primeval creation narrative and a history of the times of the patriarchs, and Moses up to the → conquest of Canaan. The characteristics of the source are thought to be a formal style, avoidance of → anthropomorphisms, and interest in genealogies, numbers, the cult and the priesthood. It is thought to have originated in priestly circles, living in the Babylonian → diaspora in the 6th century B.C.

Prophets (Gk. *prophētēs*, lit. one who speaks forth). (1) The Prophets was the designation of a section of the OT canon (→ Torah, → Hagiographa). It consisted of the Former Prophets (Jos., Jdg., 1 and 2 Sam., 1 and 2 Ki.), the Latter Prophets (Isa, Jer., Ezek., and the 12 Minor Prophets – Hos., Joel, Amos, Obad., Jonah., Mic., Nah., Hab., Zeph., Hag., Zech., Mal.).

(2) The term prophet could also be used in a wide sense to Moses and the expected prophet like him (Deut. 18:15 ff.), David (Acts 2:29 f.), and Jesus (Matt. 8:28; Jn. 4:19). Prophets are also mentioned in the early church (1 Cor. 12:29 ff.; Eph. 4:11), though the continued use of the term need not imply identity of function.
→ Art. Prophet

Pseudepigrapha (Gk. either *pseudos*, falsehood, or *pseudēs*, false; *epigraphē*, address, title). Post-canonical Jewish writings which were published with a false title or name (as the lit. translation of the title suggests). In the broadest sense, they include the entire uncanonical writings written between 200 B.C. and A.D. 100. They thus constitute a bridge between the OT and the NT. The distinction between apocrypha and pseudepigrapha is not clear cut, as pseudonymous works occur in the → apocrypha. The most important pseudepigrapha are: the Books of Enoch, the Testaments of the Twelve Patriarchs, the Assumption of Moses, the Pss. of Solomon, 4 Ezra and 4 Macc.

Q → Logia

Qumran. The name of the site of Khirbet-Qumran (ruin of Qumran) on the north-west shore of the Dead Sea, near to which between 1947 and 1956 eleven caves were discovered, containing numerous manuscripts, commonly referred to as the Dead Sea Scrolls. The manuscripts are apparently the remains of the library of the Jewish Essene sect which had its monastic-like community at Khirbet-Qumran between the 2nd century B.C. and the 1st century A.D. The Dead Sea Scrolls contain biblical manuscripts (e.g. Isa.), commentaries on various passages from the OT, the most extensive being one on Hab., parts of the apocrypha and pseudepigrapha, and various unique texts dealing with the community's life and beliefs, including the Community Rule, the Damascus Rule, the Messianic Rule, the War Rule, Hymns and various fragments which are uniquely informative on aspects of Judaism about the time of Jesus.
→ Pesher

Rabbinism (Heb. *rabbi*, my master). Rabbinic theology began to emerge about the beginning of the Christian era, and it subsequently became normative for the life of the Jewish community to the present day. As scribes and teachers of the Jewish schools, the rabbis had the task of expounding the Jewish scriptures, especially the → Torah or Law, of regulating the life of Jewish communities in the light of the → Talmud, and, particularly in the earlier period, of judging legal matters. The schools of Hillel and Shammai about the time of Jesus, Rabbi Akiba and his pupil Rabbi Meir in the 1st and 2nd centuries A.D., the Karaites in the 8th century, and the Chassidim in the 18th are particularly well known. The aim of rabbinism was to bring about obedience to God's commandments consistently and → casuistically through a multitude of comprehensive laws and the exposition of the Torah.
→ Mishnah, → Talmud, → Halachah, → Haggadah, → Midrash, → Synagogue → Tanna

Redaction (Lat. *redigo*, bring back, get together). The revision or adaptation of one or more sources to form a single work. Many scholars hold that the → Pentateuch and other writings show evidence of this process. The person who has collected such sources and set them in order with perhaps some theological comment is termed the editor or redactor. Since about 1945 → form-criticism which is largely concerned with pre-literary forms has been supplemented by redaction-criticism (Ger. *Redaktionsgeschichte*, lit. history of redaction). The latter attempts to determine the characteristics and outlook of the redactor in the light of the general structure, train of thoughts and theology of a text, and so assess the character of a text in the light of its treatment of sources.

Samaritan. (1) Samaria was the capital of the northern kingdom of → Israel. It also gave its name to the surrounding territory. It was founded in *c.* 880 B.C. and fell to the Assyrians in *c.* 722 B.C. (2 Ki. 18:9 ff.). (2) Samaria came to be used as the name of the territory west of the Jordan, bounded by Galilee in the north and Judea in the south. After the mass deportation in *c.* 721, the remaining Israelites formed the core of a new community which continued to worship Yahweh, but were also influenced by other cults. There was deep hostility between the Samaritans and the Jews who returned from → captivity in Babylon in the 6th century. This was evident in NT times (Lk. 10:29–37; 17:16–13; Jn. 4:1–42). (3) The Samaritans possessed the Law → (Torah), but not the → Prophets. The Samaritan → Pentateuch which dates from pre-Christian times differs slightly from the Jewish version. One difference is the name of the Samaritan holy mountain, Mt. Gerizim, for Mt. Ebal in Deut. 27:4.

Sayings and Sayings Source → Logia

Semantics (Gk. *sēmantikos*, significant). The branch of philology which deals with the meaning of words and their sense-development. The adj. semantic means relating to significance or meaning.

Semitic (Heb. *šēm*, Shem). A Semite is lit. one descended from the peoples mentioned in Gen. as descended from Shem, the son of Noah. They include the Hebrews, Aramaeans, Arabs, and Assyrians. The Semitic languages include Hebrew, Aramaic, Ethiopic, Akkadian, Ugaritic and Arabic. In most semitic languages the writing is from right to left, though in this they are not unique. Gk. was originally so written, as was Etruscan and the oldest extant Lat. inscription. Cuneiform writing after *c.* 2500 B.C., on the other hand, was regularly from left to right.

Septuagint (Lat. *septuaginta*, seventy). The Gk. translation of the OT and most of the → apocrypha which according to Jewish legend was translated by seventy (or seventy-two) Jewish scholars of the → Diaspora at Alexandria in the 3rd century B.C. (cf. *Letter of Aristeas*). Hence it is commonly designated by the Roman numeral LXX. In fact, the OT was translated into Gk. over a period of time by various translators, beginning with the → Pentateuch in the 3rd and 2nd centuries B.C. The purpose was to help Jews of the dispersion to read the scriptures in familiar language. Numerous alterations and changes of meaning in relation to the Heb. occurred. But in point of time the LXX is earlier than the Heb. → Masoretic Text, and sometimes its readings are to be preferred. In the early church the LXX was the normative form of the OT.

Sitz im Leben (Ger. lit. seat in life). The life-setting or original historical context of an incident or saying. It is a technical term of → form-critical exegesis, coined by the OT scholar Hermann Gunkel (1862–1932), referring to the situation, speaker, hearers, social and personal background, and attitude presupposed by a given biblical passage.
→ Form-criticism, → Genre

Soteriology (Gk. *sōtēria*, deliverance, salvation). The doctrine of the saving work of Christ, Statements relating to soteriology are termed soteriological.

Source Criticism. A branch of OT and NT → exegesis, concerned with the investigation of sources or strata behind the existing texts. This is practised not only in the → Pentateuch → and Synoptic Gospels but in historical books like 1 and 2 Sam, 1 and 2 Ki. It seeks to discover the role of → redactors in the production of the final text, the different sources or strata in order to determine and assess the characteristics and pecularities of a text against its historical background.
→ Authenticity, → Literary criticism

Stoicism (Gk. *stoa*, porch, hall, the painted corridor on the north side of the market place at Athens). A Hellenistic philosophical school, founded at Athens by Zeno of Citium (Cyprus), so called after the place where he taught. It survived into the 3rd century A.D. The history of Stoicism falls into three periods: the Old Stoa (*c.* 300–150 B.C.), the Middle Stoa (*c.* 150 B.C.–A.D. 50), and the Later Stoa (*c.* A.D. 50–250). Its best-known representatives are Zeno (335–264 B.C.), Seneca (*c.* 4 B.C.–A.D. 65), and the Emperor Marcus Aurelius (A.D. 128–80). Stoic philosophy lays stress on → ethics. Its ideal is embodied by the wise man, the citizen of the world, the true cosmopolitan, who lives in harmony with nature and reason, masters his affections, bears suffering with "Stoic" calmness (*ataraxia*), and finds the greatest happiness in virtue. For many in the ancient world Stoicism provided a bridge to Christianity.

Synagogue (Gk. *synagōgē*, assembly, place of meeting, synagogue). (1) The meeting place of the Jewish community, used chiefly for worship and instruction in the → Torah, apparently originating after the exile in the 6th century B.C. (→ captivity); (2) the Jewish community gathered there for worship.

Syncretism (Gk. *synkerannymi*, mix together). The merging and synthesis into a unity of different religions, together with their beliefs and practices. Today syncretism is used particularly to denote the religious world and the historical amalgamation of cults in the declining ancient world in the period known as → Hellenism.

Synoptic Gospels. (Gk. *synopsis*, general view; *synopsizō*, bring together in a general view). The first three Gospels, Matt., Mk., and Lk. show extensive agreement in general outline and in the contents of numerous individual sections. Their text can be printed in three parallel columns in a synopsis in order to present their agreements and differences.

Talmud (Heb. *lāmaḏ*, learn; *talmîḏ*, pupil, scholar; *talmûḏ*, teaching). Jewish compilation embodying the → Mishnah, which was regarded as the codified exposition of the → Torah and pious practice, and the → Gemara or collection of explanations by later generations of rabbis (the Amoraim). The Jerusalem Talmud which contains the discussions of the Palestinian rabbis and was completed *c*. A.D. 400 survives only in incomplete form. The more recent Babylonian Talmud is considerably more extensive and important in Jewish estimation. It was completed *c*. A.D. 500. The term Talmudic Judaism denotes the strict body of Judaism which upholds the tenets of the Talmud in contrast to liberal Judaism. → Rabbinism, → Halachah, → Haggadah

Tannaim (Heb. *tanna'îm*, teachers). A name given to the doctors of the → Mishnah, dating from the rival schools of Shammai and Hillel (*c*. A.D. 10). The period of their greatest activity was between A.D. 70 and 200. Some 120 known teachers are so called. After the Mishnah had been published *c*. 220, the → rabbis are known as Amoraim (Heb. *'ªmōrā'îm*, speakers, interpreters), because from then on they were commentators on the Mishnah. Later on the word *tanna* was used of one who had successfully learned the tradition.

Targum (Heb. *targēm*, interpret; *targûm*, interpretation). The translation and paraphrases of the OT into Aramaic. In the post-exilic period Heb. was increasingly pushed out by Aramaic as the common and literary language. Consequently, the Heb. scripture readings in worship were accompanied by translations and expositions in Aramaic. The various written Targums originated from this oral practice. A characteristic feature is the combination of explanatory interpretation and translation.

Teleology (Gk. *telos*, goal, end). The theory of the meaning, goal and purpose of the world. It is the counterpart of cosmology which is concerned with the universe and causality The latter looks back to the ultimate cause of the world, whilst teleology looks forward to its goal or purpose. Teleological means adapted for a purpose, directed towards a goal.

Textual Criticism. A branch of → exegesis which takes account of the fact that the biblical texts have come to us in numerous manuscripts or → codices. Often they differ from each other in detail. The task of textual criticism is to study the extant texts in the light of different versions or variant readings, taking account of parts which have been spoilt or are in some way defective and which can only partially be translated. Its aim is to reconstruct the original reading of the manuscript in accordance with scientifically formulated principles. The practice of textual criticism requires knowledge of different manuscripts and their families, knowledge of manuscript writing, and of the characteristics of Heb. and Gk.

Textus Receptus. Lat. for "Received Text". It takes its name from a phrase in the preface to the Elzevir edition (1633) and is substantially the Gk. text of Erasmus (1516) and the Complutensian Polyglot (1522). Erasmus's Gk. text of the NT was the basis of the reformed translations of the NT in Ger. and English including the AV or KJV (1611). It continued to be the standard text of the Gk. NT until the later 19th century. But it is now recognized to be largely Byzantine in character and based on a limited number of manuscripts most of which were relatively late. It has been superseded by the text of Westcott and Hort which provided the basis of the RV (1881) and other more recent texts which are based on earlier manuscripts employing the techniques of → textual criticism.

Theism, Deism (Gk. *theos*, God; Lat. *deus*, God). (1) Theism is the belief that the ultimate ground of all things is a single, supreme reality which is the source of everything other than itself but does not depend on them for its existence. This reality is complete, perfect and personal, and consequently is worthy of unqualified worship. Orthodox Christianity is thus theistic. It sees God as both immanent, i.e. present in the world and → transcendent. (2) Deism was originally a philosophical movement in Britain in the 17th and 18th centuries which sought to establish a natural theology independent of the Christian revelation. It regarded the essential truth of Christianity as no more than a republication of the religion of nature and on this basis criticized the historical veracity of the Bible. Sceptical deists contributed considerably to the rise of biblical criticism. In modern parlance, however, deism is often divorced from its historical background and means belief in a transcendent God who no longer has any dealings with the universe he created.

Theologoumenon (Gk. *theologeō*, speak of God or divine things; *theologoumenon* is the pres. pass. participle). Lit. that which is said about God or divine things. As a technical term it denotes a theological thought or saying.

Torah (Heb. *tōrâh*, instruction, doctrine, law). The word is thought to come from the Heb. root meaning to throw, the torah being the decision obtained by the priest through casting the sacred lot. Torah came to be used predominantly for instruction in the will of God (e.g. Jer. 18:18) and written collections of priestly decisions (e.g. Hos. 8:12). It was used of individual laws as well as of the → Pentateuch containing the Mosaic legislation. It thus became the designation for the first part of the OT → canon. The Eng. term Law is used as a synonym for the Torah, but it is only an approximate designation as the Pentateuch contains more than legislation.

Tosefta (Heb., supplement). A collection of early Jewish tradition, contemporary with, but not included in the → Mishnah. Like the Mishnah, it has six main divisions containing tractates. It contains more → Haggadah than the Mishnah.

Tradition (Lat. *traditio*, delivery, surrender, tradition). Tradition is a fundamental process in every culture and all forms of spiritual life. It applies to words, customs, usages, ritual, ordinances, laws and attitudes. Both the process and the content of tradition are expressions of the historical past as it affects the present. As a technical term, tradition often denotes the oral transmission of biblical material prior to its fixation in writing (→ tradition history). Apostolic tradition denotes the tradition of words, views and practices which may be traced back to the apostles and which came to be regarded as authoritative in the course of history.

Tradition History (Ger. *Überlieferungsgeschichte*). The branch of → exegesis concerned with the formation of biblical texts through oral tradition up to being finally committed to writing. It investigates the origin, growth and background of material in its pre-literary form. On this basis scholars have tried to distinguish original material from later additions. Valuation of this method differs widely. Some scholars regard it as a branch of scientific criticism, while others regard it as highly subjective speculation.

Transcendence (Lat. *transcendere*, climb over, step over, surmount). The distinction between immanence and transcendence belongs to the distinction between this world and the next, the conditioned and the unconditioned, the physical and the spiritual, the objective and the non-objective, the realm of tangible existence and its unobservable ground. The term transcendence denotes the unconditioned ground which lies beyond and behind the realm of the directly observable world of objects. Orthodox Christian theology understands the relation between God and the world in terms of immanence and transcendence. In so far as God is present and operative in the world, he may be said to be immanent, but in so far as he is over and above it he is transcendent.
→ Theism, Deism

Typology (Gk. *typos*, trace, image, form, figure, example, pattern). The scheme of thought which sees historical persons, events and institutions as "types" or patterns of subsequent greater persons, events and institutions. Typology plays an important part in the Christian interpretation of the OT, in identifying statements which originally belonged to a particular historical situation and applying them to Jesus and the church. A presupposition underlying the typological interpretation of the OT is the → analogy between the old and new covenants which are based on the same God and his covenant relation with his people. Already in the NT Paul understands Adam as the antitype of Christ (Rom. 5:14) and Israel as the antitype of the Christian church (1 Cor. 10:6).
→ Allegory

Variant Readings. These occur when different manuscripts of the same text present different forms of wording.
→ Textual criticism

Version. (1) Different forms of a statement; (2) different accounts of an event; (3) different renderings of a translated text; (4) different translations of the Bible.

Vulgate (Lat. *vulgare*, make known, publish). The name of the Latin translation of the Bible prepared by Jerome at the request of Pope Damasus (A.D. 382). The Vulgate gradually replaced the other Latin translations in use in the early church, like the Old Latin (Vetus Latina). At the Council of Trent (1546) it received canonical authority in the Roman Catholic Church.

Yahweh (Heb. YHWH). One of the names of God (Exod. 17:15). Out of reverence for the divine name the practice had grown up by *c.* 300 B.C. of not pronouncing it, and the circumlocution 'adōnai (my lord) was uttered instead. When the vowel points were added to Heb. (→ Masoretic text), the vowels for 'adōnai were added to the consonants of YHWH. This gave rise to the mistaken form Jehovah in the AV. The → LXX translators substituted "Lord" (*kyrios*) for the tetragram YHWH wherever they found it. The original pronunciation is thought to have been Yahweh.

Yahwist (derived from the tetragram YHWH). The designation of a hypothetical author of one of the conjectured sources of the → Pentateuch. The source is designated "J" (cf. Jehovah or Yahweh). In contrast to the → Elohist, the Yahwist used the name Yahweh for God from the beginning. J is thought to begin with Gen. 2:4b with the creation narrative and contains the primeval history of the fall, Cain and Abel, Noah and the flood, the genealogies of the nations and the tower of Babel. It is thought to give an account of the patriarchs and the time of Moses up to the conquest of Canaan. These passages represent a collection of narratives, developing the theme of promise and fulfilment, expressed in Yahweh's promise to Abraham of the promised land. J is thought to be dated in the 10th century B.C. originating in Judah.

Zealot (Gk. *zēlōtēs*). Members of a political, messianic, radical group in Judaism which split off from the Pharisaic movement. The zealots did not wish to wait patiently for the advent of the messiah, but strove to force the fulfilment of the messianic promise by the sword. Zealot groups began by living off plunder in the desert, but steadily grew in influence and significance in Palestine until in A.D. 66 they led a revolt against the Roman rule. It led to the destruction of Jerusalem by Titus in A.D. 70. The movement continued in Palestine until the final catastrophe in A.D. 135.

Abolish, Nullify, Reject

| καταργέω | καταργέω (*katargeō*), abolish, nullify. |

CL Derived from *argos*, meaning inactive, idle, unused, useless, *katargeō* is a late
 word which in secular Gk. means to render inactive, put out of use, cancel,
bring to nothing, do away with. It is used in a wide range of contexts.

OT It only appears in the LXX in 2 Esdr. [Heb. Ezra] 4:21, 23; 5:5; 6:8, where it
 signifies hindering or interrupting the rebuilding of the temple.

NT Of its 27 occurrences in the NT, one is in a parable (the non-fruiting fig tree of
 Lk. 13:7 "cumbers" the ground in the sense of making it unproductive); the rest
are in theological contexts, all but one being in Paul, who uses the word mainly to
express the following:

1. God's putting out of action through the cross and the *parousia* destructive
powers which threaten man's spiritual well-being. These include (a) world-rulers
(1 Cor. 2:6: possibly human, but more likely demonic); (b) the law which set Jew
and Gentile at enmity and made both guilty before God (Eph. 2:15, cf. Rom. 7:2,
"discharged from the law of the husband"); (c) the body of sin (Rom. 6:6: Paul
means "our sinful self", "the sin-dominated nature that was ours in Adam"); (d) the
"man of sin" (2 Thess. 2:8); (e) all forces hostile to Christ at present (1 Cor. 15:24),
including death, already brought to nothing in principle through Jesus' resurrection
(1 Cor. 15:26; cf. 2 Tim. 1:10). The writer to the Hebrews adds (f) the devil (Heb.
2:14).

2. God's removing and displacing what is transient to make way for better and
abiding things. Already displaced through the coming of the new order in Christ is
the "glory", such as it was, of the Mosaic dispensation (2 Cor. 3:7, 11, 13), and the
"veil" which was on Jewish hearts like Paul's (2 Cor. 3:14). Being displaced, as
God's plan goes forward, are "things that are (sc., something)" in this world –
though grammatically neuter, the phrase denotes people (1 Cor. 1:28). Due for dis-
placement through the changes which the *parousia* will bring are (a) the belly and
food (1 Cor. 6:13: our present bodies will be changed), and (b) prophecies and
conceptual knowledge (*gnōsis*), which, being at best modes of partial and indirect
apprehension, will be left behind, as a grown man abandons childish things, when
we apprehend God directly by sight (1 Cor. 13:8, 10, 11).

3. Man's attempts, witting or unwitting, to contradict and cancel those principles and powers of divine working which bring salvation. To preach justification
by circumcision, and to seek justification by works of law, is not only to cancel the
offence of the cross (Gal. 5:11), but also to be "severed" (cancelled, discharged)
from Christ and his grace (Gal. 5:4). But as faith does not cancel the law (Rom.
3:31), nor the law the promise (Gal. 3:17), nor Israel's unbelief God's faithfulness
(Rom. 3:3), so the gospel of grace will stand, despite man's efforts to nullify it, and
in the end it will triumph.

Though *katargeō* is elusive in translation (AV renders it in 17 different ways, RV
in 13), its basic meaning of rendering something inoperative is clear and constant.

ἀθετέω

ἀθετέω (*atheteō*), set at naught, reject.

CL In classical Gk. *atheteō* means to set aside a treaty or promise, to break faith, and in general to deny, disprove and do away with what has been laid down.

OT In the LXX *atheteō* renders a wide range of Hebrew words. It is frequently used for breaking faith with God and man, and for profanely disregarding and abusing something holy (e.g. God's sacrifice, 1 Sam. [1 Ki.] 2:17; God's law, Ezek. 22:26).

NT In the NT, apart from one reference to promise-breaking (Mk. 6:26), one to setting aside a will (Gal. 3:15), and one to God exploding the pretensions of this world's wisdom (1 Cor. 1:19, citing Is. 29:14, though not in the LXX version, which has *apolō* for *athetēsō*), the word is used for acts of irreligion – rejecting God (1 Thess. 4:8), his command (Mk. 7:9), his purpose (Lk. 7:30), Jesus Christ (Mk. 10:16, Jn. 12:48), God's grace (Gal. 2:21), Moses' law (Heb. 10:28), one's first faith (1 Tim. 5:12), and "dominion" (Jude 8) – probably the authority of Christ in his ministers.

ἐξουδενέω

ἐξουδενέω (-όω), ἐξουθενέω (-όω) (*exoudeneō* (-oō), *exoutheneō* (-oō)) reject with contempt.

CL & OT A post-classical Gk. word, used in both its forms for several Heb. words in the LXX, but always with the same precise meaning. It is an emphatic word.

NT In its 13 NT occurrences, its meaning is as above. Christ is the object of contempt in Mk. 9:12, and the despised "stone" in Acts 4:11 (citing Ps. 118:22, but not from the LXX, which has *apedokimasan* [cf. Mk. 8:31; Lk. 17:25]).
→ Despise   *J. I. Packer*

G. Delling, *katargeō*, *TDNT* I 452 ff.; R. Macpherson, "Despise", *DCG* I 453 f.

Abomination of Desolation

τὸ βδέλυγμα τῆς ἐρημώσεως

τὸ βδέλυγμα τῆς ἐρημώσεως (*to bdelygma tēs erēmōseōs*), the abomination of desolation.

CL & OT The phrase *to bdelygma tēs erēmōseōs* occurs in Mk. 13:14 and its parallel Matt. 24:15. It is taken from the LXX of Dan. 12:11 and appears with slight variations in Dan. 9:27, 11:31 and 1 Macc. 1:54 ff. In Dan. the Heb. expression which it translates (*šiqqûṣ šōmēm*) appears to signify "the abomination which causes (spiritual) desolation", i.e. it creates either a horror in the mind of the beholders or an objective condition of spiritual devastation. In the OT an abomination denotes chiefly something which is abominable to God, especially objects offensive in the light of the ceremonial law, hence it frequently describes idolatrous objects (*šiqqûṣ* is synonymous with *tōʿēḇāh*, and in Ezek. 5:11 both terms refer to detestable and abominable idols; for a vivid narrative illustrating the horror caused by worshipping "abominations" see Ezek. 8). E. Nestle (in an article in *ZATW* 1884) demonstrated that the phrase "abomination of desolation" originated as a typical Jewish term of contempt for a heathen deity. The title "Lord of Heaven" (*baʿal šāmayim*, frequently pronounced *ba'al šāmēm*) was given to Zeus as chief of the gods. When the Jews were asked to acknowledge Zeus under such terms they described him not as *ba'al šāmēm* but *šiqqûṣ šōmēm*, i.e. not "Lord of heaven" but "an abomination which desolates". The situation is narrated in I Macc. 1:54 ff., which tells how Antiochus Epiphanes (175–164 B.C.) caused a pagan altar to be erected on the great altar in the Jerusalem temple, and this pagan altar is described as "the abomination of desolation". There is evidence to suggest that with the altar was placed an image of Zeus (of whom Antiochus viewed himself as representative), which naturally intensified the horror of the sacrifices commanded (cf. C.C. Torrey, *Documents of the Primitive Church*, 26). By this means the temple of God was turned into a heathen temple. The command to render such worship, in Jerusalem and beyond, led to the Maccabaean revolt and to the writing of the prophecies of Daniel.

NT In Mk. 13:14 the desolating abomination is referred to as well known, without explanation. Many exegetes, observing that "abomination" is neut. in gender, but the participle "standing where it ought not" is masc., have concluded that the abomination is the → Antichrist, who steps into the place reserved for God (cf. 2 Thess. 2:4). If the term "Antichrist" be extended to mean a power which sets itself against God it could be employed in this context, but the later developed doctrine, such as appears in Rev. 13 and 17, should not be read into Mk. 13:14. To Jesus the term "abomination" would probably connote idolatry of some sort. It is to be observed that Luke paraphrases his words by the expression "Jerusalem surrounded by armies" (Lk. 21:20). It is possible that that is closer to the intention of Jesus than is commonly recognized, for the Roman armies were notorious for the idolatrous images affixed to their ensigns, which were set in the ground at night and accorded worship. By agreement with the Jews these ensigns were never brought into the Roman fortress in Jerusalem. If the time should come when the ensigns were set in the holy place, that could only be as a result of brute force and it would entail war to the death. The "abomination" would thus bring about the desecration of the city and sanctuary and would lead to destructive warfare, so bringing to pass the fulfillment of the prophecy of Jesus in Mk. 13:2. Such an interpretation is in harmony with the meaning of the phrase in Dan., and it accords with other teaching of Jesus wherein disaster for his nation and for Jerusalem is anticipated (cf. Matt. 23:35 ff; Lk. 13:1 ff.; 19:41 ff.; 23:28 ff.). The use of the expression "abomination of desolation" for the desecration and ultimate destruction of the temple and city indicates that Jesus viewed such an event in the light of the Day of the Lord, as the OT prophets before him and above all Daniel in his references to the abomination.

G. R. Beasley-Murray

(a). G. R. Beasley-Murray, *Jesus and the Future*, 1954, *passim*; G. R. Beasley-Murray, *A Commentary on Mark Thirteen*, 1957, 54–72; D. Daube, *The New Testament and Rabbinic Judaism*, 1956, 418–37; C. H. Dodd, *More New Testament Studies*, 1968, 69–83; W. Foerster *TDNT* I 598 ff.; S. B. Frost, *IDB* I, 13 f.; L. Gaston, *No Stone on Another: Studies in the Significance of the Fall of Jerusalem in the Synoptic Gospels*, 1970; G. Kittel, *TDNT* II 660; W. G. Kümmel, *Prophecy and Fulfilment*, 1957, 95–103; A. L. Moore, *The Parousia in the New Testament*, 1966; V. Taylor, *St. Mark*, 1952, 511–15; C. C. Torrey, *Documents of the Primitive Church*, 1941, 26.
(b). F. Busch, *Zum Verständnis der synoptischen Eschatologie; Markus 13 neu untersucht*, 1938; E. Nestle, *ZATW* (1884), 4, 248; SB I 945, 951.

Abraham, Sarah, Hagar, Isaac

'Αβραάμ	'Αβραάμ (*Abraam*), Abraham.

OT The name derived either from the Babylonian *Abam-rāmā*, he loves the Father, i.e. God, or from the Aram. lengthening of the Canaanite name *Âb-rām*, the Father, i.e. God, is exalted. The popular etymology of the Heb. *'aḇrāhām* (Gen. 17:4 f.) makes the name signify "father of a multitude".

1. The tradition of Gen. 11:27–25:11(18) depicts Abraham as the first of the so-called patriarchs, the ancestor of the later people of Israel. Admittedly, he continues to have the second place in the OT behind the patriarch Jacob, as is already indicated by the name Israel which Jacob received and which was applied to the nation (→ Israel, arts. *Israēl*, *Iakōb*). But a profound and far-reaching significance was attached to Abraham.

(a) Abraham stands for the extreme prophetic experience of Israel. He is not only called a → prophet (Gen. 20:7; cf. 15:13–16) and as such was wrested from all personal security (20:13). He was also tested as a prophet (22:1), to see whether in his person the people of God would esteem God enough to be willing to offer human sacrifice. Abraham held to the word of his God almost to the point of killing his only son. God then released him and the people of Israel, because he loves faithfulness and not sacrifice.

(b) Abraham was the recipient of a promise of land which steadily grew despite the extremely scanty beginnings. His life constantly appeared threatened by the lack of a son and heir (15:2 ff.), and the latter was only born when Sarah was past the age of child-bearing (18:1–15). But this stands in contrast with the promise of the land which was extended from its simplest form (12:8, Shechem), through 13:14–17 (Hebron) to the kingdom of → David (15:18). In the panoramic perspective of the Pentateuch the theme of the land is not brought to fulfilment, but looks towards fulfilment with the dying → Moses (Deut. 34). In so far as the land was never merely a physical possession, but was constantly seen as a spiritual heritage (representing freedom, peace and well-being in and with God), later Israel remained profoundly conscious of the fact that it still looked for the ultimate fulfilment of the promise to Abraham.

(c) The making of the → covenant in Gen. 17 develops this theme and ensures that the land promised as a *possession* to Abraham and his posterity is not understood in a nationalistic way as personal property, but as the place of worship appropriate to the creator of the world (Gen. 1). In Gen. 17 the message is formulated which enabled Israel to survive even the terrible situation of the national collapse and the far from glorious period of reconstruction under Persian rule. The people of God received the commission amidst the world powers to serve the creator in a way commensurate with his being.

(d) This insight was decisively influenced by the age-old declaration that Abraham was called, so that "the families of the earth wish blessing for themselves in his name" (12:3). It stands in the context of the promise of the land which looks forward to the kingdom of David (15:18), relating these words with their ring of power politics to an anti-nationalistic perspective. Mankind, including Israel and the patriarchs, had fallen prey to the desire to be like God (3:5), to the mysterious couching of sin before the door of the heart (4:7), and to the need to establish a name for oneself in a single kingdom (11:1–9). But the Lord of the world made a new beginning with Abraham, the man who unconditionally remained true to the promise (of the land) despite the extremely meagre fulfilment, so that the prospect of blessing for the families of the earth does not fail on account of the meagre fulfilment in the time of the OT.

Alongside the instances where Abraham is mentioned in Gen., there is the particularly important and oft-repeated expression especially in Deut. "the land that Yahweh has sworn to your fathers, Abraham, Isaac and Jacob" (cf. Deut. 1:8; 6:10; 9:5, 27; 29:13; 30:20; 34:4). For amid the despair of the exile it denotes the fixed point on which election depended: a solemnly attested promise of God which made it possible for the Israelites after the loss of the land and in the anxiety of being remote from God (Isa. 63:15–64:11; cf. especially the complaint of 63:16!) to accept their sin as sin, because they understood God as the one who is dependable. Furthermore, there is the prophetic word from God, highly apt at the time of the exile, that calls Abraham "my friend" (Isa. 41:8; cf. Ps. 105:6; 2 Chr. 20:7). Thus Abraham is the forefather to whom the promise was the basis of his life (Gen. 15:6); God counted this to him as righteousness.

2. The special position of Abraham, already foreshadowed in this development, reached its highest expression in Judaism. There the belief is found that because of Abraham's → election all who confess themselves as his have a place in the coming kingdom of God, even though their sins have been many (SB I on Matt. 3:9). Rab. Judaism saw Abraham's life as a series of acts of obedience. According to it, Abraham had kept the whole → law. By contrast, Hel. Judaism, especially Philo, stressed his trust in God's promises, especially those about the final judgment and the kingdom of God, and attributed the beginnings of belief in a world to come to his time (SB III 194, 197; cf. Syr. Bar. 57:2). Jewish legends relate that he was the first to recognize monotheism, and as the first → proselyte Abraham also served as a missionary (*TDNT* I 8).

NT 1. Since Abraham was the ancestor of Israel, the descent of Jesus from Abraham became of great importance for the proclamation of Jesus as the Messiah. It underlined the continuity in God's saving activity both for his people and the world (cf. the genealogy in Matt. 1:1–17). Lk.'s genealogy (Lk. 3:23–38) mentions Abraham in v. 34, but stresses the descent from the first man → Adam.

2. (a) For the Jews in general it was a special title of honour to be known as "children of Abraham" (Matt. 3:9; Lk. 3:8), for according to the popular belief, Abraham's merits guaranteed Israel a share in the kingdom of God. John the Baptist attacked this idea, as Luther attacked indulgences. To be descended from Abraham was in itself of no value. Only he who sets his heart and mind on the coming kingdom of God, brings forth the true → fruit of repentance (→ conversion), and by → baptism anticipates the final judgment has any right to hope for a place in the kingdom. God can raise up from stones children for Abraham. That is why Jesus considered it so important to search for the lost sheep of Israel. He healed a daughter of Abraham who had been excluded from the community, the woman with an issue of blood (Lk. 8:43–48), and caused salvation to come to the house of Zacchaeus as a son of Abraham, although he had been living outside the → Law (Lk. 19:9).

When Luke records that the apostles addressed their hearers as descendants of Abraham and mentions the God of Abraham, Isaac and Jacob, he intends his readers to understand how aware the apostles were of their loyalty to the faith of their ancestors and how strenuously they had sought to win Jesus' people despite their unwillingness (Acts 3:12 f., 25; 13:26).

The incident in Matt. 8:11 f. and Lk. 13:28 f. in which Jesus threatens "the sons of the kingdom" with being cast out into darkness, may have as its background the belief that Abraham was the first proselyte and the greatest maker of proselytes (see above OT 2). But it does not follow that he will be surrounded in the kingdom of God only by his physical and national heirs. There will also be those of his own type, i.e. proselytes.

(b) "Abraham's bosom" (Lk. 16:22) means the pouch (*ḥēq*) above the girdle made by pulling up the garment slightly. This picture is relatively seldom found in Rab. writings (SB II 226). It may refer to special care, as that of a mother loving her child which she carries in the folds of her dress over her breast, or to the place of honour at table beside Abraham. When one reclined at table, one's head came approximately to the level of one's neighbour's chest (Jn. 13:23, SB II ad loc.).

Judaism frequently expected intercession by Abraham who lives with God (Lk. 16:22 ff.). The same is true of Isaac and Jacob (→ Advocate). But this was not without conditions, as Jesus' parable indicates. Intercession by those who already have eternal life for those who still await death is basic to the idea of the invocation of saints. The Jewish belief that those who have lived with God, e.g. the patriarchs, must remain alive after death was shared by Jesus, who justified it by saying that where God is there also must be → life (cf. Mk. 12:26 f.; Matt. 22:32; Lk. 20:37 f.). He who lives with God can die but cannot cease to live. It is from this angle that we must understand the → resurrection of Jesus.

3. When Paul explains the importance of Abraham, he is concerned above all with justification (→ righteousness) by faith. His exposition both in Gal. 3:6 ff. and Rom. 4:1–13 is not a deductive proof in the strict sense. Paul's method is the opposite. In the light of the revelation of Christ he recognizes that Scripture had long before spoken of it.

(a) The details of the apostle's arguments about Abraham were partly determined by the ideas of his Judaizing opponents, who maintained that the → Law was the definitive revelation which brought salvation. It followed that Abraham must have lived by it, even before it had been revealed at Sinai. By contrast Paul maintained in Gal. that anyone who wishes to live by the → works of the Law (Gal. 3:10) is under a curse, since it implies that men must earn their salvation by them. By so doing, such a person does not permit God to be the God who alone can give man that which is good without qualification and save him (Rom. 7; cf. Gen. 3). As Paul sees it, Scripture shows clearly that Abraham was justified not by works of the Law but by faith (Rom. 4:3; Gal. 3:6; cf. Gen. 15:6). Scripture even foresaw the placing on an equal footing of the lawless pagan and the pious Jew through faith (Gal. 3:6–9), because faith excludes every basis for human honour, even the precedence of the Jew. The Law did not have the function of making Abraham's blessing inoperative. It was given to reveal that sin, in the last analysis, is directed against God and not against men. Thus it prepared men for the recognition that their only hope is in God (Gal. 3:24), and that Jesus is the promised offspring of Abraham (3:16 f.). By abrogating the Law, God opened to all the possibility of living by faith and so sharing the heritage of Abraham in all its fullness.

(b) In Rom. 4 these thoughts are expressed with even greater clarity. What has Abraham found? Was it something to → boast about? Not in God's presence, for it was faith that was reckoned to him for righteousness (vv. 1–3). A man cannot earn wages from God. Blessed is only he against whom the Lord does not reckon sin (vv. 4–8; cf. Ps. 32:1 f.). Following the methods of Rab argument, Paul now maintains that this blessing does not result from → circumcision, which Judaism regarded as a sign of the fulfilment of the Law and of turning away from transgression (vv. 9–12). Abraham was after all justified before he was circumcised. Circumcision was simply a → seal of the righteousness by faith reckoned to the Gentile Abraham. Hence Abraham is the father of the believers who come from the Gentiles (v. 16). It will not be to the glory of Israel, as in Jewish expectation, that Abraham will be the father of nations and the inheritor of the world (v. 13).

In conclusion, Paul adds another example of Abraham's faith (vv. 18–22). Just as we are dead before God and have nothing to hope for, so Abraham's and Sarah's procreative power was dead. But trust in God created and creates new life. The point of comparison is the deadness, the lack of any prerequisite conditions, not the willingness to yield oneself. That is probably the reason why the story of the sacrifice of Isaac which was popular in Judaism as an example of obedience is not mentioned here. Rom. 9:7; 11:1, 16 ff. and 2 Cor. 11:22 fit easily into this fundamental Pauline scheme of interpretation.

Paul's view of obedience in faith was not always readily accepted in the primitive church. Jas. 2:14–26 pointedly shows that Pauline concepts were misused even by Christians. For some only the relationship of the soul to God was important. The deeds of our transient bodies which belong to a fallen world were considered to be relatively unimportant. Against such a view it was necessary to stress that faith expresses itself in works, and that faith will be judged, as with Abraham, by its works, i.e. by the way it works itself out in life.

4. This false security with which Jews and Judaizers alike deluded themselves by appealing to Abraham (see above OT 2) contributed in great measure to this attitude. The way in which it hindered faith in Jesus is the background to the discussion about Abraham in Jn. 8:30–40, 48–59. The first section (vv. 30–40) makes it clear that the newly found faith of the Jews was not genuine but only superficial, for they were not doing the works of Abraham (vv. 39 f.). Abraham relied solely on God's liberating → word, but they wished to silence that word when it stood before them incarnate in Jesus. They thought that descent from Abraham guaranteed their freedom, whereas in fact only Jesus and holding fast to his word can give them true freedom.

The second section of the discussion (vv. 48–59) begins with the Jews' suggestion that Jesus was demon-possessed, when he proclaimed his word, or rather, proclaimed himself as God's word. For when Jesus promised eternal life to those who kept his word (v. 51), he was, according to Jewish ideas, blaspheming God. Only God's word can guarantee eternal life, but Jesus was a mortal man like Abraham and the prophets who have died (v. 52). However, Jesus is greater than Abraham in the sense of being more than human, for according to Jewish ideas the Messiah and Moses were greater than Abraham. God has given him authority to grant eternal life. Jesus said that Abraham had called himself happy in that he should see the day of God's word (Jesus). He saw it and rejoiced (v. 56). There is ample evidence for Jewish speculations that at the time of the making of the covenant (Gen. 15:12–21) Abraham saw the main lines of Israel's future (SB II, ad loc.). Then comes the vital sentence, "Before Abraham was, → *I am*" (v. 58). The Word of God was, is, and ever will be. Hence Jesus is truly eternal, but Abraham lived and died.

5. The descendants of Abraham in Heb. 2:16 are presumably all who live by faith as did Abraham, i.e. not only Jews but all who believe in Christ (so Westcott and Montefiore, ad loc.). In Heb. 6:13, as in Jewish tradition, Abraham is presented as a model of the believing patience and perseverance which obtain the promise. This trait is also stressed in 11:8–12, 17–19. Salvation, however, does not come from Abraham and his descendants (7:2, 4 ff.). They are, and remain its recipients. Abraham recognized one greater than himself, → Melchizedek. In the same way, the Levitical priesthood is only temporary, for they too, as descendants of Abraham, gave tithes to Melchizedek. Hence the one who has been proclaimed a priest for ever after the order of Melchizedek must be greater. *H. Seebass*

| Σάρρα | Σάρρα (*Sarra*), Sarah. |

OT This is the personal name of the wife of Abraham and mother of Isaac (Heb. *śārâh*). In Gen. 17:15 her name is changed from Sarai to Sarah, and all subsequent references conform to this. No explanation or reason for the change is offered, and it may be that Sarah is merely a modernization of the old Semitic feminine form. The name is generally understood to mean princess, but there may be a connection with the root *śārâh* (to strive), the root underlying the name Israel.

In the Genesis traditions Sarah emerges as the beautiful wife who is all but lost to a foreign ruler (Gen. 12:10–20; 20:1–17, the resolute adversary of Hagar and her offspring (Gen. 16:1–14; 21:8–21), and the mother of Isaac (Gen. 18:1–15 [J]; 21:1–7 [E]). All three stories are part of a narrative complex which traces the somewhat tortuous course by which the promise of Gen. 12:1–3 moved towards its fulfilment. To later Jews Sarah could therefore be appreciated, along with Abraham, as the rock from which Israel was hewn (Isa. 51:2).

NT Sarah has a place in two important Pauline arguments. In his theology of justification her barrenness is the context in which Abraham's justifying faith is demonstrated (Rom. 4:19). Secondly the conception of Isaac as the heir of promise over against Ishmael is cited as evidence of the free sovereignty of God's electing purpose (Rom. 9:9; cf. also the argument of Gal. 4:21–31).

The authors of Hebrews and 1 Peter treat Sarah as a model of faith (Heb. 11:11) and submission (1 Pet. 3:6), though the originality of the allusion to Sarah in Heb. 11:11 is debated (for discussion cf. F. F. Bruce, *The Epistle to the Hebrews*, 1964). The present text clearly affirms hers as the faith that accepts the unseen as real, and takes nothing to be impossible. In 1 Pet. 3:6 her obedient attitude to her husband is set out as the pattern which Christian wives should follow. This tendency to see her as the ideal wife is not uncommon in later Judaism (cf. e.g. Philo, *Abr*. 42–44). *P. J. Budd*

| `Ἀγάρ` | `Ἀγάρ` (*Hagar*), Hagar (Heb. *hāgār*). |

OT Hagar was Abraham's concubine, and the mother of Ishmael. The name
probably means emigrant or fugitive. The only substantial Hagar stories are
those preserved in Gen. 16:1–16; 21:8–21. Both recount the hostility of Sarah, the
expulsion of Hagar, and Ishmael's ultimate home in the wilderness. These stories
reflect the conviction that Israel was related to the warlike Bedouin peoples of
Palestine, and seek both to explain the connection and give the reason for the
Ishmaelites' wild way of life. Their status as children of the slave-concubine is
clearly inferior.

NT In the NT Paul, in rabbinic fashion, makes allegorical use of this inferiority to
urge the superiority of the new Covenant (Gal. 4:21–31). Hagar and her son
represent the bondage of the old Jewish dispensation, which is in stark contrast to
the new freedom experienced by those for whom Isaac, as son of the free woman,
is the allegorical prototype. The textual difficulty in Gal. 4:25 makes little difference
to the sense. The Hagar of the allegory represents Sinai, because Sinai is in Arabia
where Hagar lived.   *P. J. Budd*

| `Ἰσαάκ` | `Ἰσαάκ` (*Isaak*), Isaac (Heb. *yiṣḥāq*). |

OT The son of Abraham's old age, whose name means "he laughs". The traditions
supply several popular etymologies (Gen. 18:12–15 [J]; 21:6 [E]; 21:9 [E];
17:17–19 [P]).

In the Genesis narratives Isaac is a less colourful individual than the other
Patriarchs, but in the theological development of the tradition has an important
place as the child of promise. His birth (Gen. 21:1–7) is the first step towards the
fulfilment of the promise of Gen. 12:1–3, and a refutation of the human impatience
which produced Ishmael. The questions of faith in the promise and obedience to the
God of the promise underlie the challenge of Isaac's sacrifice (Gen. 22:1–19). The
remaining Isaac narratives trace the next steps in the development of the promise,
the marriage to Rebekah (Gen. 24:62–67) and the births of Esau and Jacob (Gen.
25:19–28). The success that attends him is viewed as a mark of God's special blessing (Gen. 26:12–13, 29). The deception practised by Jacob (Gen. 27) explains how
and why the promise moves through the younger son's descendants. In Amos 7:9,
16 Isaac is a synonym for the nation Israel.

NT In the NT Isaac occurs in genealogies (Matt. 1:2; Lk. 3:34) and in formal
conjunction with other Patriarchs (Matt. 8:11; 22:32; Mk. 12:26; Lk. 13:28;
20:37; Acts 3:13; 7:8, 32). Like Sarah he figures in the Pauline argument for the
freedom of God's electing purpose (Rom. 9:7, 10), and like Hagar in the allegorical
proof that Christians are the children of promise (Gal. 4:28). The Letter to the
Hebrews follows the theological pattern of the Genesis traditions seeing Isaac as
heir to the promise (11:9), the testing ground for Abraham's faith (11:17–18), and
the hander on of the blessings of the promise to the next generation (11:20). The
Letter of James uses the sacrifice of Isaac to prove the necessity of → works
(obedience) as well as → faith (belief) (2:21). The submission and obedience of
Isaac may be implicit in these texts; it is explicit in some later Jewish texts (cf. e.g.
Test. Lev. 18:1–14). The tendency to see in the sacrifice of Isaac a type of Christ's

81

death is essentially a feature of later Christian interpretation (e.g. Barn. 7:3; Clement of Alexandria, *Stromateis* 2, 5; Irenaeus, *Heresies* 4, 4).   P. J. Budd

(a). On Abraham: W. F. Albright, "The Names *Shaddai* and *Abram*," *JBL* 54, 1935, 193–203; and *The Biblical Period from Abraham to Ezra*, (1949) 1963, 1–9; C. K. Barrett, *From First Adam to Last*, 1962, 22–45; K. Barth, *CD*, II, 2, 213ff.; J. Bright, *A History of Israel*, (1960) 1972², 68–102; R. Clements, *Abraham and David: Genesis 15 and its Meaning for Israelite Tradition*, 1967; B. Gemser, "Questions concerning the Religion of the Patriarchs" in A. van Selms and A. S. van der Woude, *Adhuc Loquitur: Collected Essays of Dr. B. Gemser*, 1968, 30–61; C. H. Gordon, "The Patriarchal Narratives," *JNES* 12, 1954, 56–59; and "Abraham of Ur" in *Studies Presented to G. R. Driver*, 1963, 77–84; A. T. Hanson, "Abraham the Justified Sinner," in *Studies in Paul's Technique and Theology*, 1974, 52–66, cf. also 67–84; M. Haran, "The Religion of the Patriarchs: An Attempt at a Synthesis," *ASTI* 4, 1965, 30–55; R. K. Harrison, *IOT*, 560–65; L. Hicks, "Abraham," *IDB* I 14–21; J. Jeremias, *Abraham, TDNT* I 8 f.; E. Käsemann, "The Faith of Abraham in Romans 4", in *Perspectives on Paul*, 1971, 79–100; K. A. Kitchen, *Ancient Orient and Old Testament*, 1966, 35–56; H. H. Rowley, "Recent Discoveries and the Patriarchal Age," *BJRL* 32, 1949, 1–38; L. A. Snijders, "Genesis XV: The Covenant with Abram," *OTS* 12, 1958, 261–79; R. de Vaux, "Method in the Study of Early Hebrew History," in J. P. Hyatt, *The Bible in Modern Scholarship*, 1965, 15–29; D. J. Wiseman, *NBD* 5 ff.; and *The Word of God for Abraham and To-day*, 1959. Commentaries on *Genesis* (see especially on chapters 11–26) by U. Cassuto, II 1964; D. Kidner, 1967; G. von Rad (1961) 1963 rev.; and E. A. Speiser, 1964. Commentaries on *John* (see 8:33–58) by B. F. Westcott, 1881; and C. K. Barrett, 1960. Commentaries on *Romans* (see 4:1–25) by C. K. Barrett, 1957; J. Murray, 1959; F. F. Bruce, 1969. Commentaries on *Galatians* (see 3:16 ff.) by E. D. Burton, 1920; and J. B. Lightfoot, 1865. Commentaries on *Hebrews* (see 6:13 ff.; 7:4–10; 11:8–19) by B. F. Westcott, 1903; F. F. Bruce, 1964; and H. W. Montefiore, 1964.

(b). A. Alt, *Der Gott der Väter*, 1929; F. M. T. Böhl, "Das Zeitalter Abrahams," *Der Alte Orient* 29, 1930, 1–56; reprinted in *Opera Minora*, 1953, 26–49; A. George, "Le Sacrifice d'Abraham", *Mélanges Vaganay*, 1948, 99–110; J. Hoftijzer, *Die Verheissungen an die Drei Erzväter*, 1956; R. Martin-Achard, *Actualité d'Abraham*, 1969; O. Schmitz, "Abraham im Spätjudentum und im Christentum" in *Festschrift für A. Schlatter*, 1922, 99–123; N. S. Schneider, "Patriarchennamen in zeitgenössischen Keilschrifturkunden," *Biblica* 33, 1952, 516–22; H. Seebass, "Zu Genesis 15," *WuD* Neue Folge, 7, 1963, 132–49; R. de Vaux, "Les patriarches hébreux et les découvertes modernes," *RB* 53, 1946, 321–48; 55, 1948, 321–47; 56, 1949, 5–36; A. Weiser, "Abraham," *RGG*³ I 68–71; W. Zimmerli, "Sinaibund und Abrahambund," *Gottes Offenbarung: Gesemmelte Aufsätze*, 1963, 205–16; R. Kilian, *Die vorpriesterlichen Abrahamsüberlieferungen literarkritisch und traditionsgeschichtlich untersucht*, 1966. Commentaries: O. Michel, *Der Brief an die Römer*, *KEK* IV, 1966¹³; and *Der Brief an die Hebräer*, *KEK* XIII, 1966¹².

On Sarah, Hagar and Isaac: H. J. Schoeps, "The Sacrifice of Isaac in Paul's Theology," *JBL* 65, 1946, 385–92; E. A. Speiser, "The Wife-Sister Motif in the Patriarchal Narratives," *Biblical and Other Studies*, I, 1963, 15–28; M. Noth, *A History of Pentateuchal Traditions*, 1972, 102–115; B. Haensler, "Nochmals zu Röm. 4, 19," *BZ* 14, 1916–17, 164–69; H. Reventlow, *Opfere deinen Sohn* (*Gen. 22*), 1968; R. Kilian, *Isaaks Opferung*, Stuttgarter Bibelstudien 44.

On patriarchal religion: T. C. Vriezen, *The Religion of Ancient Israel*, 1967, 103–23; H. Ringgren, *Israelite Religion*, 1966; H. Weidmann, *Die Patriarchen und ihre Religion im Licht der Forschung seit Julius Wellhausen*, 1968; F. M. Cross, "Yahweh and the God of the Patriarchs," *HTR* 55, 1962, 225–59.

On the patriarchs and history: J. van Seters, "The Problem of Childlessness in Near Eastern Law and the Patriarchs of Israel," *JBL* 87, 1968, 401–8; J. C. L. Gibson, "Light from Mari on the Patriarchs," *JSS* 7, 1962, 44–62; G. Wallis, "Die Tradition von den drei Ahnvätern," *ZAW* 81, 1969, 19–40; B. Mazar, "The Historical Background of Genesis," *JNES* 28, 1969, 73–83; J. M. Holt, *The Patriarchs of Israel*, 1964.

Accuser, Accuse

κατήγορος

κατήγορος (*katēgoros*), accuser; κατήγωρ (*katēgōr*), accuser; κατηγορέω (*katēgoreō*), accuse; κατηγορία (*katēgoria*), accusation.

CL & OT *katēgoros* means speaking against someone, accusing. As a noun, it means "accuser". A loanword (Arndt, 424), it entered Mishnaic Heb. as *qaṭēgôr* (SB I 141) or *qāṭēgôr* (Dalman), and by analogy the verb *katēgoreō* appears as *qiṭrēg*. "He that commits one transgression gets for himself one accuser" (Aboth 4:11). More especially → Satan is the accuser. In the Talmud (Bab. B. 16a) R. Simon b. Lakish said, "Satan and the evil impulse and the angel of death are one." An earlier anonymous tanna taught that Satan comes down to earth and leads astray; he ascends to heaven and accuses, awakens wrath, and takes away the soul. This cannot be regarded as typical Rab. teaching. The biblical foundation for this teaching is above all Job 1 f. Satan as *katēgôr* is concerned especially with Israel, but he also accuses individual persons. He acts particularly when a man accuses himself, runs into danger, or lives carelessly. In the heavenly court he can appear when he wants to, and he is turned away only on the merits of the case. Michael is his opponent, for he acts as defending counsel (*sᵉnēgôr*; Gk. *synēgoros*).

NT Rev. 12:10 is clearly based on Jewish concepts, and only here in the NT is Satan called *katēgôr*, as in the Rab. writings. He is said to accuse the children of God continually, "day and night". After the exaltation of Jesus Christ, he is cast out of heaven (Rev. 12:7 ff.). The same picture of the fall of Satan, but without the use of *katēgoros*, is found in Lk. 10:18, Jn. 12:31, and Rom. 8:33 f. Jesus Christ, the intercessor, replaces the accuser. In other NT passages accuser refers to human accusers before earthly tribunals, as in the case of Paul's enemies before the Roman procurators (Acts 23:30, 35; 25:16, 18).

katēgoreō is derived from *katēgoros* and means to be an accuser, to accuse, betray, make known, affirm, assert. The enemies of Jesus spied on him, to see whether he would heal on the → Sabbath, so that they might accuse him of a breach of the Sabbath before the local → sanhedrin (Mk. 3:2; Lk. 6:7). The chief priests accused Jesus before Pilate (Mk. 15:3 f.; Lk. 23:10, 14). The word appears more frequently in Acts because of the repeated accounts of attacks on Paul (22:30; 24:2; 25:5; 28:19). He defended himself by pointing out that his accusers could not prove their accusations (24:13, 19; cf. 25:5, 11, 16). He appealed to → Caesar, but not because he wanted to accuse the Jews (Acts 28:19). Satan as *katēgôr* is the one who accuses (*katēgorōn*) in Rev. 12:10.

The vb. is used also in a non-legal sense: "their conflicting thoughts accuse or perhaps excuse them" (Rom. 2:15).

Jn. 5:45 refers to the last → judgment. It is not Jesus who will accuse the Jews who do not believe, but Moses, because he who does not believe in Jesus refuses also to believe in the Torah of Moses. The Torah bears witness to Jesus (5.46). Rab. tradition could say of Moses that he accused the sinful people before God (Exod. R. 47:14).

katēgoria is derived from *katēgoros* and means an accusation in the legal sense. Pilate asked the chief priests what accusation they brought against Jesus (Jn. 18:29). Timothy was instructed not to accept an accusation against an elder unless there were two or three witnesses (1 Tim. 5:19; cf. Deut. 19:15). One of the conditions that a candidate for eldership must fulfil is that his children are not open to the accusation of being profligate or insubordinate (Tit. 1:6). *H. Bietenhard*
→ Satan, → Judgment

| ἐγκαλέω | ἐγκαλέω (*enkaleō*), accuse; ἔγκλημα (*enklēma*), accusation, charge. |

CL & OT Deriving from *kaleō*, "call", *enkaleō* in secular Gk. means first to demand as one's due (to "call for" or "call in"), and then to make a claim or bring an accusation against someone, usually in a context of actual or threatened legal proceedings. *enklēma* corresponds to this developed meaning, and signifies a claim, charge or indictment. The canonical LXX uses *enkaleō* 3 times, each time for a different Heb. word, but does not use *enklēma* at all.

NT In the NT, Lk. uses *enkaleō* in its regular classical sense, actively with the dative of the person accused and passively with the genitive, with or without *peri*, for the matter of the accusation, these being the standard classical constructions (Acts 19:38, 40; 23:28, 29; 26:2, 7). The only theological use of the word is in Rom. 8:33, where Paul dispels apprehensions lest Satan or some other should succeed in impeaching God's elect at judgment day. *enklēma* is used of the charge against Paul in Acts 23:29; 25:16. *J. I. Packer*

F. Büchsel, *katēgoros*, *TDNT* III 636 f.; A. Deissmann, *Light from the Ancient East*, 1927, 93 f.; Commentaries on *Revelation* by H. B. Swete (1906), I. T. Beckwith (1919), R. H. Charles (ICC, 1920), G. B. Caird (Black, 1966), and G. E. Ladd (1972) on Rev. 12:1–10.

Adam, Eve

| Ἀδάμ | Ἀδάμ (*Adam*), Adam. |

OT Adam (probably but not certainly from the common Sem. root *'dm*, [to be red], thus the red blooded one (?) cf. Akkad. *adamatu*, blood; Heb. *'ᵃdāmâh*, the red arable soil in contrast to the lighter coloured desert) is a collective term for mankind, people. A single person is called *ben-'ādām* (lit. son of man). *'ādām* is the ordinary Heb. word for man.

Adam, as a proper name, is found in the OT only in Gen. 4:25; 5:2–5; 1 Chron. 1:1; Sir. 49:16; possibly also in Gen. 2:20; 3:17, 21. Only Gen. 2 f. is of importance for the use of Adam in the NT. For its other uses → Man. The purpose of Gen. 2 f. is to tell how, in spite of the goodness of God's creation, man experienced → evil (misfortune, illness, death, etc.).

When God created heaven and earth, he formed man out of the earth and breathed the breath of life into him. Ps. 104:30, 29 takes up these statements: "When thou sendest forth thy breath, they are created, and thou renewest the face of the ground. When thou takest away their breath, they die and return to their dust." Hence man is entirely dependent on God. Without God's sustenance he is only a pile of earth. To give man an understanding of his true nature, God brought him the animals to be named, which had been made for man. In naming them, man realized that they could not be a real partner for him. This prepared him for the creation of → woman as his partner. Man is really man only when he is with other human beings. This occurs above all in the mutual relationship of husband and wife. Man was allotted a place to live in, a garden containing the tree of life, where uninterrupted life with God was to be found. There was also the tree of the knowledge of good and evil. The fact that man was not allowed to approach it and take of its fruit suggests that though evil existed, God desired at first to spare him the knowledge of all that it involved, for only God himself could overcome it. Then the cleverest of the animals attacked man at his most vulnerable spot. It suggested to him that God was leaving him foolish and ignorant, so that God might not lose his unique authority. The result of man's transgression (→ Sin, *parabasis*) was not that God was no longer God, but that man experienced evil. He did so first subjectively in his experience of shame (3:7), and then objectively through → death and God's → curse. Evil affected the relationship of man and beast (3:15 → enmity), woman and childbirth, man's labour and his personal relationships (3:16). God did not wish evil for man. Man reached out for it, so that he might know like God. But he is not God, and he cannot endure evil. He remains man, but he has crossed the boundary to an existence which is ultimately impossible, striving to deny his creatureliness.

Rab. Judaism faced the question of how Adam's → guilt and that of humanity were linked. On the one hand, it saw death as our doom for Adam's sin. On the other hand, it tried to explain why death should be the punishment for each individual's sin, but it could find no satisfactory answer (SB III 227 ff.).

Although Rab. Judaism did not recognize the first Adam as a type of the second (SB III 477 f.), Philo used the two creation stories to distinguish between the first created heavenly man (Gen. 1:27) and the later created earthly man (Gen. 2:7). The former is considered to be the true and spiritual man; the latter to be transient. In the former he sees the "idea" of man's spirituality, which, from the philosophical angle, alone can have permanence, while the earth-born man with his corporeality belongs to the world of appearance and transience (cf. W. D. Davies, *Paul and Rabbinic Judaism*, 1955, ch. 3; C. K. Barrett, 1 *Corinthians*, BNTC, 374 f.; *From First Adam to Last*, 1962, 7 f.)

NT 1. Philo's concept cannot be found in the NT, but in Pauline theology Adam as a type is important (see 3 below). The name Adam is found 9 times. Jude 14, quoting Eth. Enoch 1:9, mentions Enoch as the seventh from Adam the first man. In Lk. 3:38 Adam is mentioned last in the genealogy as son of God. This may be related to Acts 17:28 ("In him we live, move and have our being"), where a Hellenistic poet is quoted ("For we are indeed his offspring", Aratus *Phairomena* 5). By referring to a Hellenistic belief, Luke wishes to affirm that Adam, and with him the whole human race, is of divine origin. When in contrast to Matthew, he goes back beyond Abraham and traces Jesus' genealogy to Adam, his purpose is probably to show that Jesus is the Revealer for all mankind and not only for Jews. Jesus reveals what was intended by Adam, as the representative of mankind. This is also shown by the fact that, of all the people mentioned in the long genealogy, Jesus is the only one after Adam who is said to be of divine origin (Lk. 1:34 f.).

2. 1 Tim. 2:13 ff. deals with a very different question in saying that Adam was formed first, then Eve; and Adam was not deceived, but the woman was deceived and became a transgressor. Rab. belief held that that which was first created, i.e. Adam, was of greater value (SB III 645 f.). The second clause may be related to a Jewish belief that Eve was deceived sexually by Satan. It is in this sense that Adam

is said not to have been deceived. ([Tr.] There are good grounds for regarding the idea of Eve's sexual defilement by the serpent as later; SB I 694 f. gives the earlier beliefs. Moreover, Paul is only following then Gen. story which depicts Eve as the one who succumbed to the blandishments of the serpent.)

3. In Rom. 5:12–21; 1 Cor. 15:20–22, 45–49 Paul sets out the contrast between the old and the new age (→ Time), between man under → sin and under the salvation of God, by a typological parallelism of Adam and Christ, where Adam is the type and Christ the antitype (→ Image, *typos*).

(a) When (according to Gen. 3), the transgression of God's commandment brought about a loss of trust in both God and fellow-man, an inevitable consequence had occurred. Paul refers to it in Rom. 5:12: "Sin came into the world through one man" (→ Sin, Art. *hamartia*). The thought is not that of the transmission of sin by physical inheritance, but the creation of a situation of mutual mistrust which no one can avoid. Hence sin permeates the whole of humanity.

(b) Death is now not the natural result of sin but God's judgment on it (Rom. 6:23; see above OT). Hence death came through sin to all men (Rom. 5:12), or put more briefly, "As in Adam all die" (1 Cor. 15:22).

(c) Before the giving of the → Law man did not sin as Adam did (Rom. 5:14). This was a special era. In contrast to Adam and to men under the Law they had no express commandment. They died because they had sinned, but there was no exact book-keeping. Sin takes on the explicit character of transgression and disobedience directed against God in the light of the Law (Rom. 7:7 ff.). Sin becomes "sinful beyond measure" and fully recognizable in its nature. To that extent Adam typifies fallen man before God.

(d) Adam is also a type of that which is to come, the age to come, the kingdom of God (Rom. 5:14). The sentence, "For as in Adam all die, so also in Christ shall all be made alive" (1 Cor. 15:22; cf. Rom. 5:14 ff.) means that mankind which has lost its real life through sin is typified by Adam. The Risen One is the personal agent of new life, for he represents the beginning of the general → resurrection of the dead (1 Cor. 15:20). In Jewish thought this was linked with the beginning of the new → creation, the forgiveness of sins (cf. 1 Cor. 15:17, "If Christ has not been raised . . . you are still in your sins"; Rom. 4:25, "Who was . . . raised for our justification"). This creates for all the possibility of being freed from the compulsion to sin, the root of which is mistrust of God. The Risen One is the beginning of a new humanity, for he accepted the validity of God's sentence of judgment, allowing God to be God. He put his trust in him alone, and expected from him nothing but what was good. In so doing, he undid man's basic sin, that of Adam, which was mistrust of God's goodness (Gen. 3).

(e) When Paul speaks of Jesus as Adam's antitype, he used the idea of "the second man" (1 Cor. 14:45 ff.), a term which may be borrowed from gnosticism. ([Ed.] On the other hand, gnosticism may have derived it from Christian thought.) The term suggests the true, original man who came into the world to impart the saving truth by which he himself lived. Whatever personalities Judaism may have expected in the last days, Jesus as the Risen One exceeded all expectations, for in his individual person he represented the general resurrection, and with it the advent of the kingdom of God, the new creation and the forgiveness of sins (1 Cor. 15:18; Col. 1:18). These conceptions were not as familiar to the Greeks as to the

Palestinian Jews. Consequently Paul may have used this picture to express to the Greeks and the Hellenistic world the message proclaimed to the Palestinian Christian of the resurrection, the advent of the kingdom of God and the forgiveness of sins. The Greek could conceive of salvation only as the truth, the "idea", which lies behind the world and which has been obscured by the transitory, vain world of appearances. Therefore, only the original man can bring about the true being of man, for he incorporates the original purpose of God for mankind. But this true man, Paul says, is not Adam but Christ. As the original man revealed in the resurrection, Jesus can make the new creation a reality for the Greeks.

4. We should note that Paul corrects Gnostic mythology at this point, by insisting on the corporeality of the resurrection body. It shows the world unknown to us as God's good creation. Resurrection does not mean that the spiritual element in man is now with God. It is not the fact that we exist in → "flesh" as transient beings that makes us sinners, but that we live "according to the flesh". That is, we allow ourselves to be determined by that which is transitory in our lives. Hence, resurrection is not without a body. The Risen One was recognized as the one who he was (his → *sōma*, lit. body, means the man himself). Nevertheless this *sōma* cannot be described by any terms at our disposal. The corporeality given to man at the Creation is not that given at the resurrection. The original man is not merely the simple original picture of mankind. The concept is eschatological. The Risen One brings us a new and for us unknown existence with God (1 Cor. 15:44b ff.). Hence the new creation is more than a mere restoration of the original; it brings into being something new and until now unknown. *H. Seebass*

→ Image, → Man

| *Eὔα* | *Eὔa (Heua)*, Eve. |

ot Gen. 3:20 derives the name Eve (Heb. *ḥawwâh*) from the fact that she was the "mother of all living" (*'ēm kol-ḥai*). Midrashic exegesis connected the name with the Aram. *ḥiwyā'*, serpent, a view which has been revived in recent times. Koehler-Baumgartner (280 f.) mention 9 explanations of the etymology of the name given to Adam's wife. The first creation narrative tells of the creation of man and woman together in the → image of God (Gen. 1:27). In the second narrative (Gen. 2:18–25 → woman was formed from man to be his helper. In Gen. 3 it is the woman who heeds the blandishments of the serpent and eats the forbidden → fruit before giving some to her husband. It is only after the → fall that the name Eve is mentioned. She is mentioned as the mother of Cain (Gen. 4:1) and Abel, but not elsewhere in the OT. In inter-testamental literature she is mentioned in Tob 8:6; Sib. 1:29; Philo, *Leg. All.*, 2, 81; Josephus, *Antiquities*, 1, 49.

nt Eve is mentioned by name in 1 Tim. 2:13 and 2 Cor. 11:3. The former passage alludes to Gen. 2 f. in support of Paul's argument why he permits "no woman to teach or to have authority over men" (v. 12). For the Gen. story depicts Adam being formed first and the woman (not Adam) being deceived. For Paul the story is symbolic of the role of the sexes in life in general and that of the church. In 2 Cor. 11:2 the deception of Eve by the serpent (→ Dragon, Serpent) is seen as an

example of how Christians may be led astray. It was only in post-biblical literature that Eve was seen as a type of Mary (e.g. Iren., *Haer.*, 3, 22, 4; 5, 19, 1; cf. H. Graef, *Mary: A History of Doctrine and Devotion*, I–II, 1963–65).   *C. Brown*
→ Woman

(a). C. K. Barrett, *From First Adam to Last*, 1962; K. Barth, *Christ and Adam: Man and Humanity in Romans 5*, 1956; M. Black, "The Pauline Doctrine of the Second Adam," *SJT* 7, 1954, 170–79; F. H. Borsch, *The Son of Man in Myth and History*, 1967; and *The Christian and Gnostic Son of Man*, 1970; R. Bultmann, "Adam and Christ according to Romans 5," in W. Klassen and G. F. Snyder, eds., *Current Issues in New Testament Interpretation*, 1962; B. S. Childs, "Adam," *IDB* I 42 ff.; and "Eve" ibid. II 181 f.; and *Myth and Reality in the Old Testament*, 1960; O. Cullmann, *The Christology of the New Testament*, 1963², 137 ff.; J. Daniélou, *From Shadows to Reality: Studies in the Typology of the Fathers*, 1960, 11–65; W. D. Davies, *Paul and Rabbinic Judaism*, 1948, 36 ff.; J. D. G. Dunn, "I Corinthians 15:45—Last Adam, Life-giving Spirit"; and M. E. Thrall, "Christ Crucified or Second Adam," in B. Lindars and S. S. Smalley, eds., *Christ and Spirit in the New Testament*, (Moule Festschrift) 1973, 127–42, 142–56; W. Eichrodt, *Theology of the Old Testament*, II, 1969, 118 ff.; J. de Fraine, *Adam and the Family of Man*, 1965; J. G. Gibbs, *Creation and Redemption: a Study in Pauline Theology*, 1971; J. Hick, *Evil and the God of Love*, 1966; M. D. Hooker, "Adam in Romans I," *NTS* 6, 1959–60, 297–306; J. Jeremias, *'Adam, TDNT* I 141 ff.; E. Käsemann, "On Paul's Anthropology," in *Perspectives on Paul*, 1971, 1–31; T. C. Mitchell and J. Murray, "Adam," *NBD* 13 f.; J. Murray, *The Imputation of Adam's Sin*, 1959; W. Mork, *The Biblical Meaning of Man*, 1967; R. Prins, "The Image of God in Adam and the Restoration of Man in Jesus Christ," *SJT* 25, 1972, 32 ff.; E. K. V. Pearce, *Who Was Adam?*, 1969; B. Ramm, *A Christian View of Science and Scripture*, 1955, 221 ff.; O. Schilling, "Adam," *EBT* I, 6–9; R. Scroggs, *The Last Adam: A study of Pauline Anthropology*, 1966; D. Somerville, *St. Paul's Concept of Christ, or the Doctrine of the Second Adam*, 1897; W. D. Stacey, *The Pauline View of Man*, 1956; G. Widengren, "Early Hebrew Myths and their Interpretation," in S. H. Hooke, ed., *Myth, Ritual and Kingship*, 1958; N. P. Williams, *The Ideas of the Fall and of Original Sin*, 1917. Commentaries on Genesis by U. Cassuto, I, 1961; D. Kidner, 1967; G. von Rad, 1961; and E. A. Speiser, 1964. Commentaries on *Romans* by C. K. Barrett, 1957; F. F. Bruce, 1969; J. Murray, 1959.

(b). X. Le Bachelet, "Adam", *DTC* I, 1, 509–19; E. Brandenburger, *Adam und Christus: Exegetisch-religionsgeschichtliche Untersuchung zu Römer 5, 12–21*, 1962; J. Cambier, "Péchés des hommes et péché d'Adam en Rom. V. 12," *NTS* 11, 1965, 217–55; H. Gressmann, "Mythische Reste in der Paradieserzählung," *ARW* 10, 1907, 358 ff.; and "Die Paradiessage," in *Festgabe von Fachgenossen und Freunden A. von Harnack*, 1921; J. Jervell, *Imago Dei: Gen. 1, 26 f. im Spätjudentum, in der Gnosis und in den Paulinischen Briefen*, 1960; E. Jüngel, "Das Gesetz zwischen Adam und Christus," *ZTK* 60, 1963, 42–74; L. Ligier, *Péché d'Adam et Péché du Monde*, 1960; O. Michel, *Der Brief an die Römer*, KEK IV, 1966¹³; B. Reinach, "La Naissance d'Eve," *RHR* 78, 1918, 185 ff.; H. Renckens, *Urgeschichte und Heilsgeschichte*, 1959; H. Tuerck, *Pandora und Eva*, 1931; T. C. Vriezen, *Onderzoek naar de Paradijsvoorstelling bij de oude semietische Volken*, 1937, 130 ff.; C. Westermann, *'ādām, THAT* I 42–58.

Advocate, Paraclete, Helper

παράκλητος

παράκλητος (*paraklētos*), helper, intercessor, advocate, paraclete.

CL *paraklētos* is a cognate of the vb. *parakaleō*, the meanings of which in cl. Gk. range from call in, send for, summon, to exhort, encourage, comfort, console. The noun *paraklētos* is derived from the verbal adj. and means called [to one's aid]. It is first found in a legal context in the court of justice, meaning legal assistant, advocate (Demosthenes, 19, 1; cf. Lycurgus, *Frag.* 102). "There is no instance of *paraklētos*, like its Lat. equivalent *advocatus*, being used as a tt. for the professional legal advisor or defender of an accused person in the same sense as *syndikos* or *synēgoros*. But the use of *paraklētos* for representative is to be understood in the light of legal assistance in court, the pleading of another's case, Dion. Hal. Ant. Rom., XI, 37, 1" (J. Behm, *TDNT* V 801). The existence of the Lat. legal term *advocatus* may have led early Christian writers to use it to translate *paraklētos* (cf. Tert., *Adv. Prax.*, 9; Cyprian, *Ep.* 55, 18; Novatian, *De trinitate*, 28, 29; Augustine, *Tract. in Ioan.*, 94; cf. Arndt, 623). In the history of religions numerous religions have helpers. In the Mandaean writings dating from the 2nd and 3rd centuries A.D. there are several helpers, including Yawar (means helper) which has some features in common with the Johannine *paraklētos* (*TDNT* V 808).

OT Job's "comforters" are called *paraklētores* (plur. in Job 16:2 LXX; Aquila and Theodotion have *paraklētoi*). The Heb. is *menaḥamîm*. It is significantly the only instance of the word in the LXX. The question may be asked whether there is a correspondence between the "comforters" and Satan (cf. Job 1:6 ff.; 2:11 f. → Accuse). They are ostensibly friends who come to admonish Job but are unable to do so. Philo used the word in the sense of intercessor (*Jos.*, 239; *Vit. Mos.*, 2,134; *Spec. Leg.*, 1) and adviser, helper (*Op. Mund.*, 23; 165). Josephus used only the compounds *aparaklētos* and *dysparaklētos* (*War*, 6,190; *Ant.*, 16,151) in a similar sense to Philo. The word was transliterated in Rab. Jud. as *peraqlēṭ* and other similar forms. It was used as a loanword in the sense of advocate, counsel, defender, especially of man before God (SB II 560 ff.; *TDNT* V 802). There is no known corresponding word in Qumran literature. Only later did the meaning of "comforter" penetrate early Christian literature through its connection with *parakaleō* (→ Exhort, art. *parakaleō*).

NT The etymology of *paraklētos* suggests that it was used originally in the passive sense of one called in to help. But the passages in which it occurs in the NT show that this is alien to its meaning there. The *paraklētos* is not called in but sent (Jn. 14:26; 15:26; 16:17), given and received (Jn. 14:16 f.). He does not merely put in a good word, but brings active help. The sense of helper and intercessor is suitable in all occurrences of the word (Arndt, 624; cf. E. J. Goodspeed, *Problems of New Testament Translation*, 1945, 110 f.). 1 Jn. 2:1 f. gives the term a soteriological character in calling "Jesus Christ the righteous" our "advocate" (*paraklētos*) and "propitiation" (*hilasmos*) "for the sins of the whole world" (→ Reconciliation, art. *hilaskomai*).

The descriptions of the *paraklētos* in Jn. go beyond the task of an intercessor. He will "convince the world of sin and of righteousness and of judgment" (16:8 RSV, cf. vv. 9 ff. → Guilt, art. *elenchō*). He will "teach you all things, and bring to your remembrance all that I have said to you" (14:26). Although the world will not know the *paraklētos*, the disciples "know him, for he dwells with you, and will be in you" (14:17). He will "bear witness" to Jesus (15:26). All this indicates that his role is to continue the revealing work of Jesus. The Spirit of truth "will guide you into all the truth; for he will not speak on his own authority, but whatever he hears he will speak, and he will declare to you the things that are to come. He will glorify me, for he will take what is mine and declare it to you" (16:13 f.). The purpose is not to satisfy curiosity about the future, but to continue the work of the historical Jesus in the Christ proclaimed by the church.

The paraclete-sayings lead to a stage in early christian history which Luke treats in his description of the bestowal of the → Spirit (Acts 1, 2 and 10). The Spirit honours Jesus and gives prominence to the time of Jesus. On the other hand, the church has the gift of the Spirit, and to that extent stands in continuity with Jesus and his time that is now past. But this is far removed from the Roman Catholic idea that the Paraclete is bound to an institutional teaching office whose work is to expound the apostolic tradition preserved in the church.

A further question arises out of the fact that the word *paraklētos* in the NT denotes both a person and a power. In Jn. the *paraklētos* is the successor of Jesus who is himself called *paraklētos* (Jn. 14:16; 1 Jn. 2:1). But he is also termed "the → Spirit of → truth" (*to pneuma tēs alētheias*, Jn. 14:17; 15:26; 16:13) and "the Holy Spirit" (Jn. 14:26). This leads O. Betz to the conjecture of a being behind which stands a heavenly power (see bibliography). Hence, the question arises whether the *paraklētos* refers to a particular person, perhaps "a prophetic teacher who preserves, develops and completes the revelation of Jesus" (Betz), or is even the evangelist himself (H. Sasse, see bibliography). However, the identification of the *paraklētos* with the Spirit is for Bultmann the decisive factor in assessing the traditional understanding of the teaching of the evangelists. This militates against identifying him with a particular person.

The sole exception is Jesus himself who together with the Spirit is called *paraklētos* (Jn. 14:16; 1 Jn. 2:1). This restriction of the title to Jesus and the Spirit requires a theological interpretation of the term which is at the same time polemical. They alone – and not the multitude of non-Christian revealers and helpers – are the sole and real paracletes. This accounts for the repeated and stressed connection with the Father. The term is a variable concept which cannot be reduced to a single interpretation. On the one hand, it is Jesus who sends the *paraklētos* from the Father (Jn. 15:26). On the other hand, the Father sends the *paraklētos* at the request of Jesus (14:16, 26). According to Jn. 14:26, Jesus himself is a *paraklētos* who is distinct from the other *paraklētos* whom the Father will send in his name.

It is striking that the term *paraklētos* is only found in the Johannine writings, and apart from 1 Jn. 2:1 it occurs only in the discourses (Jn. 14:16, 26; 15:26; 16:7; cf. 16:12 ff.). To that extent the paraclete-sayings belong to the questions raised by the Fourth Gospel and in particular by its discourses. The term is not found in Paul or the Synoptics. Rom. 8:26, 34 (cf. Heb. 7:25) does not form an exact parallel in style or teaching. Such considerations have led critics to question whether there are any traditions apart from Jn. which trace the idea or the teaching back to the historical Jesus. The suggestion has also been made that Jn. was influenced by extraneous thought-forms in the composition of these sayings. Their interpretation will depend on whatever weight may be given to critical considerations and other factors in the history of religions. ([Ed.] The question may, however, be asked whether the other evangelists do not express aspects of Jn's paraclete teaching in other ways. Matt., in particular, speaks of the continued presence and help of Christ in a way which does not involve his physical presence (Matt. 18:20). It is linked with the Father and the Holy Spirit (Matt. 28:19 f.; Lk. 24:48 f.; cf. Matt. 11:27; Lk. 10:22). As such, it is not known to the world generally but only to those to whom the revelation is given. Moreover, Jesus promised the assistance of the Holy Spirit in enabling them speak under trial (Matt. 10:20; Mk. 13:11; cf.

Lk. 21:15). Although they themselves are being judged, the implication is that their witness will convict their adversaries. Matt. and Lk. speak of a commitment of Jesus to his followers in such a way that those who receive them receive him and him who sent him (Matt. 10:40; Lk. 10:16; cf. Jn. 13:20). Moreover, this presence of Jesus in those who are his forms the basis of the conviction of the nations in judgment (Matt. 25:31–46). This gives rise to the suggestion that what in Matt. and Lk. is depicted as the continuing presence and work of Jesus in the post-resurrection church is depicted by Jn. as the activity of the *paraklētos* of Jesus.)

([Ed.] The translation of the word *paraklētos* into English presents obvious difficulties. The word "advocate" reflects the early Christian Lat. equivalent with all its legal connotations, as does the RSV "Counsellor", though the latter may also have overtones of giving advice. Whilst this may well fit Jn 16:7 ff. and 1 Jn. 2:1 (where RSV also has "advocate"), the legal connotation seems to be absent from the other passages. The same applies to N. H. Snaith's suggestion of "convincer" (see bibliography). The translation "comforter" which goes back to Wycliffe is weak and misleading, unless one reads into it an etymological sense (Lat. *con* with; *fortis* strong). J. G. Davies (see bibliography) has, however, argued that comforter is the original meaning on the basis of the connection between *paraklētos* and *parakaleō* in the LXX where it means comfort or console. He sees this idea foremost in such passages as Isa. 33:7–10; 35:2–7; 61:1 f.; 66:10–19 [cf. 66:14 with Jn. 16:22]; Ezek. 31:15 ff. However, these passages are not particularly associated with the *paraklētos* in the NT, and the idea of "comforter" does not seem to be particularly appropriate in the *paraklētos*-passages. This leaves either the loanword "paraclete" or "helper". Paraclete has the advantage and disadvantage of being neutral and meaningless, unless the Gk. background is known. Helper is an active word and thus does not convey the passive sense of the Gk. etymology, i.e. someone called in. Nevertheless, it is the one English word which is both meaningful and fits all the passages in which *paraklētos* occurs in the NT.) G. Braumann
→ Spirit, Holy Spirit

(a). Arndt, 623 f.; C. K. Barrett, "The Holy Spirit in the Fourth Gospel," *JTS* New Series 1, 1950, 1–15; idem, *The Holy Spirit and the Gospel Tradition*, 1947; idem, *The Gospel According to St. John*, 1955; J. Behm, *paraklētos*, *TDNT* V, 800–14; R. E. Brown, "The Paraclete in the Fourth Gospel," *NTS* 13, 1966–67, 113–32; F. D. Bruner, *A Theology of the Holy Spirit*, 1971; R. Bultmann, *The Gospel of John*, 1971; J. G. Davies, "The Primary Meaning of *paraklētos*." *JTS* New Series 4, 1953, 35–8; A. Deissmann, *Light from the Ancient East*, 1911², 339 f.; J. D. G. Dunn, *Baptism in the Holy Spirit*, 1970; W. F. Howard, *Christianity According to St. John*, 1943, 71–80; G. Johnston, *The Spirit-Paraclete in the Gospel of John*, 1970; A. R. C. Leaney, "The Johannine Paraclete and the Qumran Scrolls", in J. H. Charlesworth, ed., *John and Qumran*, 1972, 38–61; L. Morris, *The Gospel According to John*, 1971, 662–66; O. Schmitz and G. Stählin, *parakaleō, paraklēsis*, *TDNT* V 773–79; H. N. Snaith, *ExpT*, 57, 1945–46, 47–50; H. B. Swete, *The Holy Spirit in the New Testament*, 1903.
(b). E. Bammel, "Jesus und der Paraklet in Johannes 16," in B. Lindars and S. S. Smalley, eds., *Christ and Spirit in the New Testament* (Moule Festschrift), 1973, 199–218; O. Betz, *Der Paraklet: Fürsprecher im häretischen Spätjudentum, im Johannes-Evangelium und in neu gefundenen gnostischen Schriften*, 1963; G. Bornkamm, "Der Paraklet im Johannesevangelium" in *Festschrift für Rudolf Bultmann*, 1949, 12–35; J. Jeremias, *Heiligengräber in Jesu Umwelt*, 1958, 133 ff.; N. Johansson, *Parakletoi: Vorstellungen von Fürsprechern für die Menschen vor Gott in der alttestamentlichen Religion, im Spätjudentum und im Urchristentum*, 1940; G. W. Locher, "Der Geist als Paraklet," *EvTh* 26, 1966, 565 ff.; W. Michaelis, "Zur Herkunft des Johanneischen Paraklet-Titels," *Coniectanea Neotestamentica*, 11, 1947, 147–62; S. Mowinckel, "Die Vorstellungen des Spätjudentums

vom heiligen Geist als Fürsprecher und der Johanneische Paraklet," *ZNW* 32, 1933, 97–130; F. Mussner, "Die johanneischen Parakletsprüche und die apostolische Tradition," *Biblische Zeitschrift* 5, 1961, 56–70; S. Schulz, *Untersuchungen zur Menschensohn-Christologie im Johannesevangelium*, 1957; H. Windisch, "Die fünf Parakletsprüche" in *Festgabe für Adolf Jülicher*, 1927, 110–37.

Age, Stature, Maturity

| ἡλικία | ἡλικία (*hēlikia*), age, life-span, stature.

CL Originally *hēlikia* meant (1) the relative age in life of the person mentioned (Homer, *Il*. 22, 419) hence it could be applied to any age; (2) the years of discretion as an expression of manliness (*en hēlikia*, come of age); (3) a generation (Hdt. onwards) as a measure of time. Finally from the second meaning we get (4) height, size of body (Dem. onwards). Only (1) and (2) can be clearly found in the papyri, and no example of (4) has yet been discovered in them.

OT In the LXX *hēlikia* is probably found only with the first two meanings (*c*. 20 times) and that mostly in 2, 3, 4 Macc., in other words, in late writings of the Hellenistic period. It is found once as a translation of the Heb. *qômâh*, stature (Ezek. 13:18). Philo used the word mostly of age.

In Judaism, as in antiquity generally, there was great respect for the older men (Lev. 19:32), because they had wisdom and understanding (Job. 15:10, Sir. 6:34 f.; 25:4 ff.). There is nothing surprising in the fact that the elders accordingly exercised a leading role among the people from the first.

NT In the NT *hēlikia* doubtless means stature in Lk. 19:3. But normally it has the first two meanings (e.g. Heb. 11:11, age; Jn. 9:21, 23, maturity). The three following points are of importance:

1. Man cannot influence the physical age he attains; it is a gift of the creator. Hence in Matt. 6:27 and Lk. 12:25 *hēlikia* should not be translated height or stature (AV, RV tx, RSV mg) but age or span of life (RV mg, RSV tx). With all his worrying man is not even able to lengthen his life by a trifling measure of time. This saying is found also in P. Oxy. 655 fragment 1b., but is missing in Gos. Thom., logion 6.

2. Lk. 2:52 says that Jesus "increased in wisdom and in stature" (RSV mg "in years"). The references to Jesus' growth in 1:80 and 2:40 have caused many to think here of "stature". Nevertheless the verb "increase" (*prokoptō*, i.e. make progress) makes it probable that *hēlikia* is used here in the fig. sense of growing up to maturity, to full manhood (G. Stählin, *TDNT* VI 712 ff.).

3. The word is also found in a metaphorical sense in Eph. 4:13, "to the measure of maturity (*hēlikia*) of the fulness of Christ." Maturity is that through which the grown man – *anēr teleios* (v. 13), RSV "mature manhood" – is to be distinguished from the child, the minor (*nēpios*, v. 14), who is tossed about and easily influenced. The measure of the maturity implies a goal that has been set (as under 2). But here it is not for the individual believer but the church, which is built up as the body of Christ (v. 12). Each member contributes his measure of effectiveness (v. 16)

according to the measure of the grace given to each (v. 7). The goal, however, is that they should all arrive at the unity of faith and knowledge of the Son of God (v. 13a) (→ Fullness, Art. *pleroō*). For only then will the whole body be like a grown man (v. 13). We may, therefore, see the meaning of stature or size here in *hēlikia*, but that of mature manhood is to be preferred (→ Goal). *R. Schippers* → Old, → Time

J. Schneider, ἡλικία, *TDNT* II 941 ff.; Moulton-Milligan, 279; E. K. Simpson, *Words Worth Weighing in the Greek New Testament*, 1946, 24 f.

Akeldama

> 'Ακελδαμάχ

'Ακελδαμάχ (*Akeldamach*), Akeldama. There are also the *v.l. Akeldaimach, Akeldama, Akeldamak,* and *Achelda-mach.*

This place name is found only in Acts 1:19 where it refers to a field which Judas purchased with the thirty pieces of silver and where (so it is implied, though not precisely stated) he subsequently committed suicide. It can well be identified with the field purchased by the priestly authorities (Matt. 27:3–10), the two being linked by the popular designation of the place as *chōrion* (Matt. 27:8; in Acts 1:19, *agros*) *haimatos* (of → blood). Tradition associates the site with a cemetery used up to the 17th century for the burial of pilgrims at the east end and on the south slope of Hinnom.

Problems surround every aspect of this matter.

1. The acquisition of the field. Matthew's account (27:7) says that the priests used the returned silver to make the purchase; Acts 1:18 makes Judas the purchaser. Since Matt. 27:3 associates Judas' contribution with the condemnation of Jesus, and records that he took immediate steps to relieve himself of the accursed money, we ought to understand Acts as merely intending to make a direct link between that which was paid to Judas, and was therefore his money, and the purchase of the field. In this regard, the priests were but his agents.

2. The OT background. Behind Matt. 27:9 there is a complex of OT passages, certainly including Jer. 32:7–9 and Zech. 11:12, 13 and possibly the potter-allusions in Jer. 18, 19 also. In returning the money, Judas did what Zechariah did; in buying the field, the priests did what Jeremiah did.

3. The name. The wealth of variants reveals a real element of uncertainty concerning the Aramaic background to the name. The most likely is *ḥ°qēl d°ma'*, consonant with the interpretative comment in Matt. and Acts, "the field of blood", but "field of sleep" has been seriously canvassed and would accord aptly with the use of the plot for burials, along the line of the well-established → death/sleep metaphor.

4. The relation of Akeldama to the death of Judas. Matt. explains that the name "field of blood" arose from the use of blood money in its purchase. Acts does not absolutely require more than this; it does not specify that Judas' suicide took place there; at most it offers the circumstance of his death as additional justification for such a repellent nomenclature. Recognizing the possibility of foreshortening in

93

narrative forms, we need not assume that Judas' suicide followed at once on the return of the money (Matt. 27:5), though it may well have done. In any event it became notorious through the grim details as recorded in Acts. The expression *prēnēs genomenos* is usually taken as "falling headlong"; i.e. subsequent to hanging (Matt. 27:5), the body fell – before or after death, maybe in the actual death throes of the unfortunate man. There is a possibility, however, that *prēnēs* could be traced to *pimprēmi*, "to burn with fever, to swell up." This would provide an even more suitable introduction to *elakēsen mesos* (Acts 1:18): *lakaō* is hapax legomenon in NT. It is related classically to *lēkeō* and thence to *laskō*, to shout, (of animals) to scream, (later) to crack, burst. *J. A. Motyer*
→ Blood

(a). Arndt, 29; K. W. Clark, "Akeldama," *IDB* I 73 f.; Funk § 39, 3; B. Gärtner, *StTh* 8, 1954, 16–20; R. H. Gundry, *The Use of the Old Testament in St. Matthew's Gospel*, 1967, 122 ff.; J. Jeremias, *Jerusalem in the Time of Jesus*, 1969, 138 ff.; B. Lindars, *New Testament Apologetic*, 1961, 102, 109, 116–122, 263 f.; K. Stendahl, *The School of St. Matthew*, 1968[2], 120–27; commentaries on Acts by F. F. Bruce, 1952[2], and E. Haenchen, 1971; A. B. Gordon, "The Fate of Judas according to Acts 1:18", *EQ* 44, 1971, 97–100.
(b). SB I 1029 ff.; J. Sickenberger, "Judas als Stifter des Blutackers," *BZ* 18, 1929, 69 ff.

All, Many

Statements which apply to the totality of a group may be made from two different standpoints. On the one hand, stress may be laid on the group as a whole. In this case Gk. uses *pas*, or its plur. *pantes*. The sing., like *holos*, can also mean "whole", a meaning also borne occasionally by *polloi*. On the other hand, stress may be laid on each of the many individuals or parts which make up the totality. In this case, we find either *hekastos* (used 81 times in the NT, but only once in plur.) and often the strengthened form *heis hekastos* (→ One) or *pas*, one of the commonest words in the NT. *pas* and *hekastos* are used with unusual frequency in 1 Cor.

πᾶς

πᾶς (*pas*), each, all, the whole; ἅπας (*hapas*), all, the whole.

pas as an adj. in the sing. (a) without art., means each; (b) before a noun with art., all (e.g. *pasa hē Ioudaia*, all Judea (Matt. 3:5); (c) between the art. and noun, the whole, all (e.g. *ho pas nomos* (Gal. 5:14), the whole law). Here the sum total as opposed to the parts, the complete as opposed to the separated portions is stressed. *pas* in the plur. means all. *pas* as a noun means each, everyone; linked with *tis* it means any. *to pan* means all, the whole, also the main point. *en panti* means in each matter, in every respect, in all. The neut. plur. *panta* means all, *ta panta*, all this (2 Cor. 4:15), all things (Rom. 11:36; Col. 1:16 f., and frequently); in secular Gk. *ta panta* also means the all, the universe. *hapas* is a strengthened form of *pas*, often used with the same but sometimes with an intensive meaning, the whole, all, everybody.

1. In the NT, as in the OT, *pas* together with *hapas* is one of the commonest words. The concept expresses a collective totality. → *polloi* (see below) often bears a similar meaning. Often it may be translated by "each thing". The Israelite was not permitted to sum up the world by a unifying concept like cosmos, for God alone is

94

one. The → world remained a plurality showing many differences and is unified only by the creative sovereignty of God over it. The NT never approaches pantheism, though references to → powers, → demons and → magic might occasionally give the contrary impression. Its understanding is based on the OT, as 1 Cor. 8:6 shows: "For us there is one God, the Father, from whom are all things (*ta panta*) and for whom we exist, and one Lord, Jesus Christ, through whom are all things and through whom we exist." All comes from God and returns to him. God is the beginning and the end, origin and goal, and as such he has made himself known in his son. That is why the Christian is in no uncertainty about the outcome of his faith.

2. Paul expresses the same point in Rom. 11:36: "For from him and through him and to him are all things (*ta panta*)." This corresponds to the OT declaration of Isa. 44:24: "I am the Lord, who made all things." This witness to the uniqueness and universality of God is fully aware of the first commandment and rejects every power that claims to have shared in God's work of → creation. This is not contradicted by the claim that through Jesus Christ all things were made (1 Cor. 8:6), in heaven and on earth, visible and invisible (Col. 1:15 f.). For as "God's image" (→ Image, art. *eikōn*) Christ is God himself in his relationship with the world. He is the executor of God's will (Col. 1:19 f.). All beings exist because he exists, live because he lives, and are under God's rule because he rules them (Col. 1:16 ff.; Jn. 1:3). He who separates himself from the Son cuts himself off from the root of his life. He who is in complete fellowship with Christ shares in his complete creation ("All are yours", 1 Cor. 3:22; cf. Col. 2:9).

3. The exaltation of the Son confirms that all authority (→ Might) has been given to him (Matt. 28:18). His office as ruler embraces the fullness and majesty of God. Hence, he has authority in heaven, and on earth there is nothing that has power apart from him (Jn. 1:3; Col. 1:15 ff.; cf. Matt. 11:27).

Our Lord's power over all was not there merely to comfort the disciples. They were to proclaim it in all the world to every creature (Matt. 28:18 ff.; Mk. 16:15; Col. 1:23). It gives motive and success to the apostolic preaching, to mission and evangelism. The church is to reach its fulfilment in Christ (Eph. 1:22; Col. 3:11). The whole creation is to recognize and acknowledge Christ as Lord (Phil. 2:9 ff.). If all authority had not been given him, the proclamation of the gospel would be a fruitless venture, condemned in advance to futility. But what his emissaries bring is fellowship with him who is lord of all and who accomplishes his work through the Son and his Spirit (Matt. 28:18 ff.) He lifts men from striving after security for their own existence and raises them to participate in the work of the creation.

F. Graber

| πολλοί | πολλοί (*polloi*), many, the many. |

CL *hoi polloi* (plur. of *polys*) has in secular Gk. the meaning of the most, the majority, great multitude.

OT In the LXX it often represents the Heb. *rabbîm*, which tends to mean "all".
Hence the Gk. use of the word draws a distinction between the many (but not all) and the rest, a majority as contrasted with a minority. But Heb. use, and hence

that of the Gk. of the LXX is capable of an inclusive meaning denoting the many individuals in a totality. A possible residue may not be considered (cf. Deut. 7:1; 5:6; 28:12; Isa. 52:14 f.; Ezek. 39:27).

If we omit its collective use (much water, long time, etc.), *rabbîm* in the OT is used almost always with *'ammîm* or *gôyîm* of non-Israelite peoples. Many peoples stream to Zion to come under God's protection and enter his service (Isa. 2:2 ff.); the Servant of God bears the sins of the many (Isa. 53, → Son, art. *pais theou*).

This summarizing use of *rabbîm* is also found in the Qumran texts, though in another context. The message of the Teacher of Righteousness, the founder of the Qumran community, is for the congregation, the many (1QH 4:27). In the Manual of Discipline "the many" are the whole body of full members.

NT In the NT the interpretation depends on grammatical position. Three usages may be distinguished.

1. As a noun with the art. *hoi polloi* is twice used differentiatingly with the meaning of "the most"; Matt. 24:12, "And because wickedness is multiplied, most men's love will grow cold"; and 2 Cor. 2:17, "For we are not as the many, corrupting the word of God" (RV).

Elsewhere in the NT *hoi polloi* may have the summarizing meaning of the OT, e.g. Mk. 6:2 (Lk. 4:22, the parallel passage has "all"), "the large congregation who heard him" (NEB); Mk. 9:26, "most of them said" (RSV – but in fact "all of them said"); Rom. 5:15, "For if the wrong doing of that one man brought death upon so many" (NEB), i.e. "all".

In the section Rom. 5:15–21 "the many" in the sense of all are contrasted with the one who puts an end to the dominating power of sin and death. Through Adam we see what Christ achieves. As through one man sin and death came to all, so also through one individual man, Jesus, righteousness and life was brought to all. That *hoi polloi* has here a summarizing meaning can be seen from the context. To translate "most men had to die" would be meaningless. The meaning is indicated in v. 15 by the parallels in v. 12 and 1 Cor. 15:22 which have *pantes* meaning all, and in v. 19 by v. 18 with its *pantes* (cf. also 11:32). Besides all this, the section has clear references to Isa. 53:11 f., which makes an interpretation in the Heb. sense the more likely. Paul contrasts here the totality of the descendants of Adam with the totality of believers. He leaves it an open question whether the totality of believers will ever include the whole of mankind.

Rom. 12:5 and 1 Cor. 10:17a speak of the many (*hoi polloi*) as being one → body in Christ, referring to all the members of the church (cf. *pantes* in 1 Cor. 12:13; 10:17b). In Heb. 12:15 reference to "the many" suggests that the whole congregation might be defiled through the bitterness of some.

2. As a noun without the art. The question arises whether *polloi* without the art. or used as an adj., is used with a summarizing meaning in the sense of all, or whether it should be translated as "many". The question is important in cases like Matt. 22:14, "Many are called, but few are chosen"; Mk. 10:45 (Matt. 20:28), "The Son of man also came . . . to give his life as a ransom for many"; Mk. 14:24 (Matt. 26:28), "This is my blood of the covenant, which is poured out for many"; Heb. 9:28, "Christ having been offered once to bear the sins of many". J. Jeremias (*TDNT* VI 543 ff.) assumes the summarizing meaning of *polloi* in these passages.

It may be doubted whether this is so in Matt. 22:14. When the called (*klētoi*) and the chosen (*eklektoi*) are contrasted, we are not concerned with the suspension of the normal exclusive understanding of "called" (→ Call). We have here a dialectical usage. The many who have come together to hear the word of God are in fact called, but their mere belonging to the congregation is no guarantee that they are the chosen for the world to come. Thus in Matt. 22:14 the "many" means a majority in contrast with the "few", a minority who have fellowship with God. The saying is parallel with 7:21 ff. In it "we see the strictness with which Matthew consistently judges the Christian community" (J. Schniewind, *NTD* II 1954⁷, 221, 3; cf. A. Schlatter, *Matthäus*, 1959⁵, 641). The present writer agrees with Jeremias when he finds a summarizing meaning in Mk. 10:45 (Matt. 20:28); 14:24 (Matt. 26:28); Heb. 9:28, for all these passages look to Isa. 53, and a stronger Semitic sense may be assumed. In this case "the many" of Isa. 53 means all the nations of the world. Jesus, the Servant of God, gives his life as a ransom for all men and sheds his blood as a reconciliation for the whole world (cf. *hoi polloi* in Heb. 12:15).

3. As an adj. In Rom. 5:16 and Lk. 7:47 *polloi* is linked with sins and transgressions. In Rom. 5 a summarizing meaning may be deduced from the context. God's free gift of grace covers not only the majority of transgressions but all of them in bringing justification. The Gk. of Lk. 7:47 says lit.: "her sins, the many, are forgiven". This implies the totality: "all her sins – and they are many – are forgiven her."

F. Graber

(a). Arndt, 636–39, 694 ff.; J. Jeremias, *polloi*, *TDNT* VI 536 ff.; and *The Eucharistic Words of Jesus*, 1955, 148 ff.; B. Reicke and G. Bertram, *pas*, *TDNT* V 886 ff.; P. Kaufmann, "The One and the Many: Corporate Personality in the Old Testament and Paul," *Worship* 42, 1968, 546–58; commentary on *Mark* by V. Taylor, 1952, on 10:45 and 14:24; commentaries on *Romans* by K. Barth, 1933, A. Nygren, 1952, and C. K. Barrett, 1957, on 5:12–19; commentary on *1 Corinthians* by C. K. Barrett, 1968, on 15:22–28; commentary on *2 Corinthians* by P. E. Hughes, 1962, on 5:14 f.; commentaries on *The Pastoral Epistles* by E. K. Simpson, 1954, and J. N. D. Kelly, 1963, on 1 Tim. 2:4 ff.; H. L. Ellison, "Paul and the Law – 'All Things to all Men'" in W. W. Gasque and R. P. Martin, eds., *Apostolic History and the Gospel*, 1970, 195–202.
(b). J. Jeremias, "Das Lösegeld für Viele," *Judaica* 3, 4, 1948, 249 ff.; W. Michaelis, *Versöhnung des Alles*, 1950; F. Mussner, *Christus, das All und die Kirche*, 1968; G. Sauer, *kōl*, *THAT* I 828 f.; A. Schlatter, *Der Evangelist Matthäus*, 1959⁵, 641.

Amen, Hallelujah, Hosanna

ἀμήν

ἀμήν (*amēn*), amen.

 OT 1. Amen is a transliteration of the Heb. '*āmēn*, derived from '*āman*, (niph.) show oneself firm, dependable, be durable, last; (hiph.) know oneself to be secure, have faith, and so it means certain, true.

The word was used some 25 times in the OT on solemn occasions to confirm a curse or adjuration by identifying oneself with it, to accept a blessing, or to associate oneself with a doxology. To say "Amen" confirms a statement by someone else. In Num. 5:22 the woman suspected of adultery confirmed the priest's adjuration with a double amen. In Deut. 27:15–26 a twelvefold confirmation is given to the curses pronounced against certain transgressors of the Law. In Jer. 11:5 the prophet agreed with God's threat of a curse on those who did not keep the covenant terms by saying "Amen". In Neh. 5:3 the people likewise confirmed their promise under the threat of a curse by Nehemiah. Since God himself is a witness of such confirmation, he is called in Isa. 65:16 "the God of the Amen" (LXX *theos alēthinos*; RSV "the God of truth"). The doxologies at the end of the first four books of the Pss. (41:13 (14); 72:19; 89:52 (53); 106:48) are closed by Amen. Neh. 8:6 and 1 Chr. 16:36 show it to be the people's expression of response. Through "amen" that which has been said is affirmed as certain, positive, valid and binding. A human commission which needs God's help to be carried out is confirmed by "amen" (1 Ki. 1:36). As a confirmation by the speaker (or writer) of his own words, amen has been found only once in the OT period, in a letter (an *ostrakon*) from the end of the 7th cent. B.C., written by Metzad Chashavyahu, where he says, "Amen, there is no mistake on my part."

LXX transliterates the Heb. *'āmēn* 8 times; in Jer. 28:6 (LXX 35:6) it is translated by *alēthōs*; it is rendered 17 times by *genoito* (so may it be). This latter makes it an expression of hope and desire, and no longer a confirmation of what is; the obligation conveyed by "amen" is also obscured (H. Schlier, *TDNT* I 336).

2. In Rab. sources "amen" is found only as a confirmatory and emphatic answer to what has been said by another. R. Jose b. Chanina (*c.* A.D. 270) said, "Amen contains an oath, the acceptance of words, and the confirmation of words." Anyone saying amen to a prayer or doxology made it his own. Anyone saying amen to an adjuration, blessing or curse made it binding on himself. Hence it was inferred that the adjuration of the woman suspected of adultery to which she had to answer Amen (Num. 5:11–31), had to be in a language she understood (Sifre Num. 12 on Num. 5:19). The Jew had to say amen to any doxology he heard. He who says amen properly will be richly rewarded by God. Amen is seldom found at the end of a prayer. In the worship of the Synagogue, but not of the Temple, the congregation answered "amen" to the doxologies pronounced by the leader of the worship and also to the three sections of the Aaronic blessing (Num. 6:24 ff.), which had to be modified to a prayer if spoken by a layman.

When someone joined the Qumran community, the priests repeated doxologies to God's glory and blessed all the men who belonged to God's portion, while the Levites cursed all the men who belonged to Belial's portion. All those entering the covenant answered these doxologies, blessings and curses with a double amen (1QS 1:20; 2:10, 18; cf. Deut. 27:15–62).

NT Amen is found some 126 times in the NT (including 31 times in Matt., 13 in Mk., 6 in Lk., 50 in Jn., 14 in Paul, 8 in Rev.). In the Gospels amen is found only in the mouth of Jesus, generally in the phrase, "Amen, I say to you...." Sometimes Luke translates amen by *alēthōs* ("truly", 9:27; 12:24; 21:3); *ep'alētheias* ("in truth" 4:25); *plēn* ("howbeit" 22:21). John has a double amen 25 times either for liturgical reasons or because amen was regarded as an exclamation capable of being doubled and hence strengthened. Strikingly, and obviously characteristic of his way of speaking, Jesus used the Heb. amen to confirm the words he spoke in Aram., although there were Aram. phrases that he could have used instead. (The nearest to Jesus' manner of speech was the Bab.-Aram. *hēmānûṭā'*, in good faith.)

Jesus' unusual way of expressing himself remained preserved in the older gospels, because of the wish to preserve and transmit his words faithfully.

There is no evidence from the time of Jesus that others confirmed their words with an amen, though it was possible earlier. The sayings of Jesus introduced by amen often show primitive traits, eschatological pronouncements (Matt. 10:23; 19:28; 24:34; 25:40), and a sharp contrast with Pharisaism (Matt 6:2, 5, 16; 8:10). ([Tr.] The contrast here is rather with standard Judaism or its exaggeration.) By introducing his words with amen Jesus labelled them as certain and reliable. He stood by them and made them binding on himself and his hearers. They are an expression of his majesty and authority.

Amen appears in the other NT writings at the close of prayers and doxologies, strengthening and confirming them (Rom. 1:25; 9:5; 11:36, 16:27; Gal. 1:5; Eph. 3:21; Phil. 4:20; Heb. 13:21). Prayer and praise have their place in worship. Anyone hearing a thanksgiving in a service answers it with amen. Hence it must be expressed in a language he understands (1 Cor. 14:16; cf. the reference to Sifre Num. 12 under OT 2 above). In the Epistles it is assumed that the congregation will answer with amen (Rev. 1:7; Rom. 15:33; Gal. 6:18). In Rev. 7:12 amen stands before and after a doxology, linked with Hallelujah in Rev. 19:4, and with "even so" in Rev. 1:7. In Rev. 22:20 the church answers a divine "surely" with its amen and so endorses the promise. When Rev. 3:14 calls Christ himself the Amen and affirms that he is "the faithful and true witness" (cf. Ps. 89:37, 38), which is virtually a translation of amen, it is taking up Isa. 65:16 (LXX). In 2 Cor. 1:20 Paul sees all the promises of God fulfilled and guaranteed in him.   *H. Bietenhard*

| ἀλληλουϊά | ἀλληλουϊά (*hallēlouia*), hallelujah. |

OT Though Jewish tradition attempts to cast doubt, there is no good reason for refusing the eminently reasonable explanation that "Hallelujah" is composed of two elements: the 2nd pers. pl. masc, imperative piel of the root *hālal*, which in the piel means "to praise", and the abbreviated form of the divine Name *yâh* (on *yâh* cf. e.g. Ps. 68:18). The verb is used widely of secular (e.g. Gen. 12:15) and religious (e.g. Jdg. 16:24) praise, and in its usage combines the notions of admiration, adulation and rejoicing. The fact that *halᵉlû-yâh* is followed (e.g. Ps. 148:1) immediately by *halᵉlû-'eth-yahweh* suggests that from early days it had become a cultic cry, a recognized shout of praise in its own right (cf. its use in 1 Chr. 16:36, etc.). It is only thus used in LXX (the opening verses of Pss. 104–106; 110–118; 134; 135; 145–150), i.e. not as a translation but as a transliteration, *hallēlouia* with -*ē*-. On the lengthened -*ē*- see E. Kautzsch, *Gesenius' Hebrew Grammar*, revised by A. E. Cowley, (1910) 1949, 97. The LXX spelling may reflect liturgical lengthening for emphasis while the Temple choir still functioned. Praise is offered to Yahweh for his words in creation (e.g. 104), the deliverance of the Exodus and his patience in the wilderness days (105, 106), his universal rule through the → Melchizedek priest-king (110), his eschatological purpose to make the whole world at the end what his chosen people are now (145 ff.).

NT Use is confined to Rev. 19:1, 3, 4, 6, and reflects the "cultic cry" usage of LXX.

The heavenly host praise the Lord for his victory over the "great harlot", ascribing to him salvation, glory and power. *J. A. Motyer*

ὡσαννά

ὡσαννά (*hōsanna*), hosanna, transliteration from Aram. *hôša' nā'* (Heb., *hôšî'âh nā'*), meaning "O, save".

OT The precise OT equivalent to the NT cultic shout "Hosanna" is to be found in the *hôšî'âh nā'* of Ps. 118:25. Here LXX does not view it as a cultic cry of the "hallelujah" type, and produces the translation *sōson*. There is general agreement that we should find in Ps. 118 a liturgy for the Feast of Tabernacles, but beyond that interpretations vary as to who the "coming one" of v. 26 is. The view that it is the Jerusalem pilgrim who is so "blessed" by the welcoming priests (see, e.g. *IDB* II, s.v. Hosanna) is singularly unimpressive. The whole movement of the Psalm, and certainly its exalted tone of spiritual elation, is better suited if we imagine the Davidic king, in his role as the → Melchizedek priest, leading his people in procession to Yahweh's house (cf. *NBCR*). In this context the cry "O, Save" would indicate an imploring cry to Yahweh to bring to reality that which the liturgy has depicted. Judaism later followed out this thought by making the great cry focus on the expectation of the messianic king.

NT By NT times Hosanna had become a full "cultic cry", exactly as is reflected in in LXX use of → *hallēlouia*. The Greek of Matt. 21:9; Mk. 11:9; Jn. 12:13 transliterates but does not translate. The sight of Jesus fulfilling the kingly prophecy of Zech. 9:9, coupled with the strewing and waving of branches reminiscent of the ceremonial fronds which had come to characterize the → Feast of Tabernacles, prompted the shout appropriate to that occasion and, all unwittingly, they greeted the true → David with the Davidic welcome. All the NT "hosanna" verses above centre their thought on the "son of David", the "kingdom of David" and the "King of Israel". *J. A. Motyer*

On Amen: (a). Arndt, 45; F. F. Bruce, *Commentary on Corinthians*, 1969, on 2 Cor. 1:20; G. Dalman, *The Words of Jesus*, 1902, 226 ff.; and *Jesus–Jeshua*, 1929, 30; D. Daube, *The New Testament and Rabbinic Judaism*, 1956, 288–93; J. Hempel, *IDB* I 105; H. W. Hogg, "Amen", *JQR* 9, 1897, 1–23; J. Jeremias, "Characteristics of the Ipsissima Vox Jesu" in *The Prayers of Jesus*, 1967, 108–15; M. G. Kline, "Abram's Amen," *WTJ* 31, 1968, 1–11; C. F. D. Moule, *The Phenomenon of the New Testament*, 1967, 67 f.; H. Schlier, *amēn*, *TDNT* I 335 ff.; S. Talmon, "Amen as an Introductory Formula," (on Jer. 15:11 LXX), *Textus* 15, 1970, 124–9.
(b). K. Berger, *Die Amen-Worte Jesu. Eine Untersuchung zum Problem der Legitimation in apokalyptischen Rede*, BZNW 39, 1970; J. C. C. van Dorssen, *De Derivata van de Stam* amn *in het hebreeusch van het Oude Testament*, 1951; A. R. Hulst, "Het Woord 'Amen' in het Oude Testament," *Kerk en Eredienst*, 8, 1953, 50–68; A. Jepsen, *'āman*, *TWAT* I, 1971 313–48; A. Stuiber, *RAC* I 153–59; E. Pfeiffer, "Der alttestamentliche Hintergrund der liturgischen Formel 'Amen'," *KuD* 4, 1958, 129–41; W. C. van Unnik, "Reisepläne und Amen-Sagen," in *Studia Paulina in Honorem J. de Zwaan*, 1953, 215 ff.; C. Westermann, *Der Segen in der Bibel und im Handeln der Kirche*, 1968; H. Wildberger, *'mn*, *THAT* I 177–210.
On Hallelujah: (a). Arndt, 38; J. Hempel, "Hallelujah," *IDB* II 514 f.
(b). E. Lohse, "Halleluja," *RGG³* III 38; T. Nöldeke, "Halleluja," *BZAW* 33, 1918, 376–80.
On Hosanna: Arndt, 907; F. C. Burkitt, *JTS* 17, 1916, 139–49; F. D. Coggan, *ExpT* 52, 1940–41, 76f.; J. Hempel, "Hosanna," *IDB* II 648; J. S. Kennard, " 'Hosanna' and the Purpose of Jesus," *JBL* 67, 1948, 171–76; E. Lohse, *hōsanna*, *TDNT* IX 682 ff.

Angel, Messenger, Gabriel, Michael

ἄγγελος

ἄγγελος (angelos), angel, messenger; ἀρχάγγελος (archangelos), archangel; ἰσάγγελος (isangelos), like an angel.

CL Gk. uses angelos for the messenger, the ambassador in human affairs, who speaks and acts in the place of the one who has sent him. He is under the protection of the gods and is inviolate. In Homer it is used especially of the messenger of the gods, i.e. Hermes, who is also an angelos as the one who escorts souls to Hades (→ Hell). Later, gods of the underworld are also mentioned in this capacity.

OT 1. There are two contrasting views of angels in the OT. (a) There are angels who are heavenly beings, members of Yahweh's court, who serve and praise him (Job. 1:6; cf. Isa. 6:2 f.). But in the older books they play no such special part. Historically this concept is associated with the Canaanite background. But Yahweh remained the sole creating power in nature and history, and angels never became autonomous or had cults dedicated to them in Israel. God's court also included other heavenly beings, especially in post-exilic writings. They are not always explicitly called angels, but "holy ones", "strong ones", "heroes", "sons of God" (perhaps better translated "heavenly beings"). Sometimes they appear in warlike contexts (e.g. Gen. 32:1 f. (2f.); Jos. 5:13 ff.). They witnessed the creation of the world (Job. 38:7), but as created beings they are not without fault (Job 4:18; 15:15). Yet they can be mediators of revelation (Zech. 1:9, 11 ff.; 2:2–5 (2:6–9); Ezek. 40:3). Also mentioned are "destroying angels" (Ps. 78:49), "the destroyer" (Exod. 12:23), and "ministers of death" (Job 33:22 NEB). Special kinds of angels are the cherubim, who show traits of both men and animals (Gen. 3:24; Ezek. 1:5–12; 10:19–22; 11:22; Ps. 18:10(11)), and the seraphim who have 6 wings (Isa. 5:2).

After the exile belief in angels greatly increased. This may well be explained by Israel's greater contact with other religions and increasing stress on Yahweh's transcendence, without any diminution in his activity in the world. This may have been a factor in the growth of belief in intermediate beings (cf. Job. 5:1; 15:15; Ps. 89:5, 7(6, 8); Zech. 14:5). In Dan. they appear as powerful intermediate beings with personal names, archangels, watchers, and angels of the nations. Many millions surround God's throne (Dan. 4:13, 17 (10, 14); 7:10; 8:16; 9:21; 10:5 f.; 12:1).

(b) We should distinguish these from the angel of Yahweh. He is a heavenly being given a particular task by Yahweh, behind whom the angel's personality entirely disappears. Hence it is wrong for the one to whom the angel has appeared to try and fathom his nature (→ Name) (cf. Jdg. 13:17 f.). The angel of Yahweh appears almost always to help either Israel or an individual. He is virtually a hypostatic appearance of Yahweh, the personified help of God for Israel (Exod. 14:19; Num. 22:22; Jdg. 6:11–24; 2 Ki. 1:3 f.). Only in 2 Sam. 24:16 f. do we find him in opposition to Israel. Sometimes we cannot distinguish between Yahweh and his angel. When the reference is to Yahweh without regard to man, "Yahweh" is used. Where man observes him, the expression "the angel of Yahweh" is used. This preserves Yahweh's transcendence (e.g. Gen. 18; Exod. 23:20–23). Because Yahweh's holiness could have destroyed Israel, only his angel was to go with the people.

2. In later Judaism popular belief in angels greatly increased. It was not hindered by the rabbis, but was rejected by the Sadducees (cf. Acts 23:8). Provided that

they were not regarded as independent and no angel cult formed, belief in angels was considered to be an extension of OT piety. Angels represented Yahweh's omniscience and omnipresence, formed his court and attendants, and were his messengers. They were linked with the stars, elements, natural phenomena and powers, which they ruled as God's representatives. The individual had his guardian angel. National guardians were set over the peoples, including Michael over Israel (Dan. 10:13, 21). There were 4, 6 or 7 archangels. Other groups of angels included powers, dominions, thrones, lords, authorities, serving angels. Angelology was highly developed in Eth. Enoch with speculations on an angelic fall (6–16; 19–21; cf. Gen. 6:1–6). Angels also mediate God's secrets to men in time and space in Heb. Enoch.

In the scrolls of the Qumran community angels are a feature of a cosmic dualism. God has created two kingdoms, light and darkness, and each has a prince (*śar*) or angel set over it (→ Demon, art. *daimōn*). Under these princes are all men and also other angelic beings, which are also called princes (1QS 2:20; CD 5:18; 1QM 13:10) or spirits (*rûḥôt*, 1QS 3:18 ff., 25). The angels of light are often called "sons of heaven" (1QS 4:22; 1QH Frag. 2:10), and "sons of God" (1QH Frag. 2:3). They are special servants of God (1QH 5:21) and members of his council (1QH 6:13). Israel's God and "the angel of his truth" (in 1QM 17:7 f., he is equated with Michael) help all the "sons of light" (1QS 3:24 f.). The converted man enters "the everlasting host" in God's presence (1QH 11:13), and "the angel of opposition" yields before him (CD 16:5). But "the disobedient Heavenly Watchers" have fallen (CD 2:18; cf. 1Q GenAp. 2:1, 16). God has judged the angels (1QH 10:34 f.; 1QM 14:15). In the last days "the war of the heavenly warriors shall scourge the earth" (1QH 3:36), when God, with his angels who are in the camp of the sons of light (1QM 7:6; cf. 10:11 f.; 12:7 f., 9; 15:14), will fight against the sons of darkness (1QM 1:10 f.). We meet Michael, Gabriel, Raphael, Sariel as angelic names. But the consciousness is never lost that the godly man is always shielded by God's care and concern in the various angelic forms.

Philo often sees the Logos (→ Word) behind the angels mentioned in the OT. Otherwise angels and → demons are manifestations and powers of the universe. In Josephus *angelos* is used both for angel and messenger. When he makes angels take a part in the giving of the Law (*Ant.*, 15, 5, 3), he is following Jewish tradition. He mentions that the Essenes speculated about angels (cf. *War* 2, 8, 7).

NT *angelos* is found 175 times in the NT (51 times in the Synoptics, 21 in Acts, 67 in Rev.). It is used of men only 6 times (Lk. 7:24; 9:52; Jas. 2:25; and Matt. 11:10, Mk. 1:2, Lk. 7:27, quoting Mal. 3:1). In 2 Cor. 12:7 *angelos Satana* may personify a disease. In general the Jewish concepts of the OT are taken over. Angels are representatives of the heavenly world and God's messengers. When they appear, the supernatural world breaks into this one. Because God is present in Jesus, his way on earth is accompanied by angels (Matt. 1:20; 2:13, 19; 28:2, 5; Mk. 1:13; Lk. 1:19; 2:9, 13; 22:43; Jn. 1:51; cf. Acts 1:10). At his coming again they will be at his side (Matt. 13:49; 16:27; 25:31, 2 Thess. 1:7). As Son of God, Jesus stands indisputably above the angels (Mk. 13:27; Heb. 1:4–14; Phil. 2:9 ff.).

The concept of the guardian angel occurs in Matt. 18:10 as an expression of the love of God for the "little ones" (cf. Acts 12:15). According to 1 Cor. 11:10 angels watch over decorum. Angels are mediators of God's judgment (Acts 12:23). They act on behalf of the apostles (Acts 5:19; 12:7–10), and make God's will known to them (Acts 8:26; 10:3–8; 27:27 f.).

For Paul the fact of Christ dominates the thought of angels (Eph. 1:20 f.; Phil. 2:9 ff.). The apostle with his commission given him by the Lord is superior to the word of an angel (Gal. 1:8). Love is better than the tongues of angels (1 Cor. 13:1). No creature or elemental angel can separate us from the love of God (Rom. 8:38; cf. Gal. 4:3 and above OT 2). Paul attacked Gnostic veneration of angels because it obscured the recognition of Christ's unique position as mediator (Col. 1:15 ff.; 2:18; cf. Rev. 19:10; 22:8 f.). But he recognized various categories of angels (Rom. 8:38 f.; 1 Cor. 15:24; Eph. 1:21; Col. 1:16). Angels took part in the giving of the Law at Sinai (Gal. 3:19; cf. Acts 7:53; Heb. 2:2). They take an interest in the fate of men (Lk. 15:10) and the apostles (1 Cor. 4:9). They carry the soul to Paradise (Lk. 16:22). Angels surround God's throne and fill the heavenly world with songs of praise (Rev. 5:11; 7:11). They mediate revelation and give visions (Rev. 1:1; 10:1 ff.; 8 f.; 14:6 ff.; 17:1). They carry out God's judgments (Rev. 7:1; 8:2 f.; 9:1, 13; 11:15; 12:7 ff.; 14:15, 17 ff.; 15:1, 6 f.; 18:1 f.; 19:17; 20:1 ff.). On the other hand, Satan also has angels (Matt. 25:41; 2 Cor. 12:7). 1 Pet. 3:19 f., 2 Pet. 2:4 and Jude 6 speak of the fall of the angels.

Probably "the angels of the churches" (Rev. 1:20; 2:1 etc.) are really angels and not pastors.

archangelos (archangel) is found in the NT only in 1 Thess. 4:16 and Jude 9. The concept, however, may also be found in Rev. 8:2, 7 f., 10, 12; 9:1, 13; 11:15. The only names given are Gabriel (Lk. 1:19) and Michael (Jude 9; Rev. 12:7).

isangelos, like an angel, is found only in Lk. 20:36 (cf. Matt. 22:30; Mk. 12:25). The word describes the condition of those who have been raised from the dead, who are no longer subject to the natural conditions of earthly life, including marriage.

H. Bietenhard

| Γαβριήλ | Γαβριήλ (*Gabriēl*), Heb. *gabrî'ēl*, Gabriel. |

OT The name comes from the root *geber* (man or strong) together with '*ēl* (God).

This suggests two meanings: man of God, or God is strong. In the OT Gabriel appears only in Daniel, and there as a heavenly messenger who makes his appearance as a man (Dan. 8:16, 9:21). His functions are to reveal the future by interpreting a vision (8:17), and to give understanding and wisdom to Daniel himself (9:22).

Other late Jewish texts display much greater interest in Gabriel. His position of eminence in the presence of God is stressed (Eth. Enoch 9:1; 20:7; 40:3; Sl. Enoch 21:3). Particularly noteworthy is his position at God's left hand (Sl. Enoch 24:1), and his authority over all powers (Eth. Enoch 40:9). His functions extend beyond those in Daniel to intercession (Eth. Enoch 9:1; 40:6; Sl. Enoch 21:3) and destruction of the wicked (Eth. Enoch 9:9–10; 54:6). The Qumran Covenanters showed similar interest in angels, and Gabriel is one of the four angelic names written on the shields of the Sons of Light as they go out into battle (1 QM 9:14–16). The

Targums introduce Gabriel into the Biblical narratives as the one who leads Joseph to his brothers (Gen. 37:15), who buries Moses (Deut. 34:6), and who destroys Sennacherib's army (2 Chr. 32:21).

NT In the NT Gabriel appears only in the Lukan birth narrative. There he is the angelic messenger announcing the births of John (1:11–20) and Jesus (1:26–38). As the one who comes from the immediate presence of God he brings reassurance to Mary of her standing in God's sight (1:30). *P. J. Budd*

| $M\iota\chi\alpha\acute{\eta}\lambda$ | $M\iota\chi\alpha\acute{\eta}\lambda$ (*Michaēl*), Heb. *mî̱kā'ēl*, Michael. |

OT The name probably means "who is like God?". The Michael who is to be found in the NT appears in the OT only in Daniel. Like Gabriel, he is a celestial being, but he has special responsibilities as the champion of Israel against the rival angel of the Persians (Dan. 10:13, 20), and he leads the heavenly armies against all supernatural forces of evil in the last great battle (12:1).

This military patronage is frequently attested in other late Jewish writings (cf. Jub. 1:29; 2:1; Eth. Enoch 20:5; Test. Levi 5:6), and his name as protector of Israel is also on the shields of one division of the Sons of Light (1QM 9:14–16). Michael also has an intercessory role (Test. Dan. 6:2). It was further believed of Michael that he was the recording angel (Asc. Isa. 9:22–23). He was therefore the intermediary between God and Moses at Sinai (Jub. 1:27; 22:1; Asc. Isa. 11:21; Targ. Exod. 24:1).

NT In the NT Michael appears on two occasions. In Jude 9 there is reference to a dispute between Michael and the devil concerning the body of Moses. Origen believed this to be recorded in the Assumption of Moses, but the story does not appear in the extant but incomplete texts of this work. Later rabbinic literature seems to be aware of the story (cf. e.g. Deut. Rabbah 10:11). In Rev. 12:7 the theme of Dan. 12:1 is taken up, presenting Michael as the vanquisher of the primordial dragon, identified as Satan and representing the supernatural forces of evil. *P. J. Budd*

(a). Arndt, 7 f.; K. Barth, *CD* III, 2, 477–531; G. A. Barton, "Demons and Spirits (Hebrew)," *ERE* IV 594 ff.; and "The Origin of the Names of Angels and Demons in the extra-Canonical Apocryphal Literature to 10 A.D.," *JBL* 31, 1912, 156 ff.; B. M. Bellas, *Mal'ak Yahweh*, 1931; G. B. Caird, *Principalities and Powers*, 1956; L. S. Chafer, "Angelology," *Bibliotheca Sacra* 98, 1941, 389–420; 99, 1942, 5–25; G. Cooke, "The Sons of (the) God(s)," *ZAW* 76, 1964, 22 ff.; O. Cullmann, "On the Most Recent Discussion of the *exousiai* in Rom. 13:1," Excursus to *The State in the New Testament*, 1957, 94 ff.; R. Davidson, *A Dictionary of Angels*, 1967; G. Delling, *archē*, *TDNT* I 482 ff.; and *stoicheion*, *TDNT* VII 670 ff.; G. H. Dix, "The Seven Archangels and the Seven Spirits," *JTS* 28, 1927, 233–50; J. A. Fitzmyer, "A Feature of Qumran Angelology and the Angels of 1 Cor. 11:10," in J. Murphy–O'Connor, ed., *Paul and Qumran*, 1968, 31–47; W. Foerster, *exousia*, *TDNT* II 562 ff.; T. H. Gaster, "Angels," *IDB* I 128–34; W. Grundmann, *dynamis*, *TDNT* II 284 ff.; W. Grundmann, G. von Rad and G. Kittel, *angelos*, *TDNT* I 74–87; G. Heidt, *Angelology in the Old Testament*, 1949; L. Jung, *Fallen Angels in Jewish, Christian and Mohammedan Thought*, 1926; C. Kaplan, "Angels in the Book of Enoch," *Anglican Theological Review* 12, 1930, 423–37; H. B. Kuhn, "The Angelology of the Non-Canonical Jewish Apocalypses," *JBL* 67, 1948, 217–32; E. Langton, *The Ministries of the Angelic Powers according to the Old Testament and Later Jewish Literature*, 1937; and *The Angel Teaching of the New Testament*,

1937; J. Y. Lee, "Interpreting the Demonic Powers in Pauline Thought," *NovT* 12, 1970, 54 ff.; R. Leivestad, *Christ the Conqueror*, 1954; H. Loewe, "Demons and Spirits (Jewish)," *ERE* IV 612 ff.; R. N. Longenecker, *The Christology of Early Jewish Christianity*, 1970, 26–32; G. H. C. Macgregor, "Principalities and Powers: the Cosmic Background to Paul's Thought," *NTS* 1, 1954, 17–28; W. Manson, "Principalities and Powers: the Spiritual Background of the Work of Jesus in the Synoptic Gospels," *Bulletin of the Studiorum Novi Testamenti Societas*, 1952; J. Michl, "Angel," *EBT* 1 20–28; G. Miller, "*hoi archontes tou aiōnos toutou* – A New Look," *JBL* 91, 1972, 522 ff.; C. D. Morrison, *The Powers that Be: Earthly Rulers and Demonic Powers in Romans 13:1–7*, 1960; M. Noth, "The Holy Angel of the Most High", *The Laws in the Pentateuch and Studies*, 1966, 215 ff.; E. Peterson, *The Angels and the Liturgy*, 1964; O. Procksch, *hagios, TDNT* I 88 ff.; H. Schlier, *Principalities and Powers in the New Testament*, 1961; and "The Angels according to the New Testament," *The Relevance of the New Testament*, 1967; J. S. Stewart, "On a Neglected Emphasis in NT Theology," *SJT* 4, 1951, 292 ff.; M. Takahashi, "An Oriental's Approach to the Problem of Angelology," *ZAW* 78, 1966, 343 ff.; Y. Yadin, *The Scroll of the War of the Sons of Light against the Sons of Darkness*, 1962, 229–42; A. L. Williams, "The Cult of Angels at Colossae," *JTS* 10, 1909, 413 ff.

(b). M. Allard, "L'annonce à Marie et les annonces de naissances miraculeuses de l'Ancien Testament," *Nouvelle Revue Théologique* 78, 1956, 730–33; E. Bertholet *Mystère et Ministère des Anges*, 1967; H. Bietenhard, *Die himmlische Welt im Urchristentum und Spätjudentum*, 1951; J. Blinzler, "Lexikalisches zu dem Terminus *ta stoicheia tou kosmou* bei Paulus," *Studiorum Paulinorum Congressus Internationalis Catholicus 1961*, II, 429 ff.; H. von Campenhausen, 'Zur Auslegung von Röm. 13. Die dämonische Deutung des *exousia*-Begriffes," *Festschrift für A. Bertholet*, ed. W. Baumgartner et al., 1950, 97 ff.; J. Daniélou, *Les Anges et leur Mission d'après les Pères de l'Église*, 1952; G. Dehn, "Engel und Obrigkeit: ein Beitrag zum Verständnis von Röm. 13:1–7," *Theologische Aufsätze für Karl Barth*, ed. E. Wolf, 1936, 90 ff.; F. Dexinger, *Sturz der Gottessöhne oder Engel vor der Sintflut*, 1966; O. Everling, *Die paulinische Angelologie und Dämonologie*, 1888; A. Feuillet, "Les 'chefs de ce siècle' et la sagesse divine d'après I Cor. 2:6–8," *Studia Paulinorum Congressus Internationalis Catholicus 1961*, I, 383 ff.; R. Ficker, *mal'āk*, *THAT* I 900–8; R. M. Grant, "Les êtres intermédiaires dans le Judaisme tardif," *Le Origini dello Gnosticismo*, ed. U. Bianchi et al., 1967, 141 ff.; H. Gross, "Der Engel im Alten Testament," *ARW* 6, 1, 1959, 28–42; W. Herrmann, "Die Göttersöhne," *ZRGG* 12, 1960, 242–51; G. Kurze, *Der Engels- und Teufelsglaube des Apostels Paulus*, 1915; W. Michaelis, *Zur Engelchristologie im Urchristentum*, 1942; J. Michl, *Die Engelvorstellungen in der Apokalypse des hl. Johannes*, 1937; F. Nötscher, *Geist und Geister in den Texten von Qumran*, 1957, 305–15; O. Opham, *Die Engel*, 1956; B. Otzen, "Die neugefundenen hebräischen Sektenschriften und die Testamente der zwölf Patriarchen," *StTh* 7, 1953–54, 125–57; F. Prat, "Le triomphe du Christ sur les principautés et les puissances," *Recherches Scientifiques Religieuses* 3, 1912, 210 ff.; J. Rybinski, *Der Mal'ak Jahwe*, 1930; H. Ringgren, "Engel," *RGG*³ II 1301 ff.; K. L. Schmidt, "Die Natur- und Geistkräfte im paulinischen Erkennen und Glauben," *Eranos-Jahrbuch* 14, 87-143; J. Schniewind, "Die Archonten dieses Äons. 1. Kor. 2. 6–8," *Nachgelassene Reden und Aufsätze*, 1951, 104 ff.; E. Schweizer, "Die 'Elemente der Welt', Gal. 4, 3:9; Kol. 2, 8, 20," *Verborum Veritas. Festschrift für Gustav Stählin zum 70. Geburtstag*, ed. O. Böcher and K. Haacker, 1970, 245 ff.; C. Spicq, *L'Épître aux Hébreux*, II, 50–61; F. Stier, *Gott und sein Engel im Alten Testament*, 1934; A. Vacant et al. "Anges," *DTC* I 1189–1272; P. Volz, *Die Eschatologie der jüdischen Gemeinde im neutestamentlichen Zeitalter*, 1934²; A. Winkelhofer, *Die Welt der Engel*, 1958; M. Ziegler, *Engel und Dämon im Lichte der Bibel*, 1957.

Anger, Wrath

θυμός

θυμός (*thymos*), passion, anger, wrath, rage; θυμόομαι (*thymoomai*), pass. become angry; ἐνθυμέομαι (*enthymeomai*), reflect, consider; ἐνθύμησις (*enthymēsis*), thought, reflection, idea.

CL *thymos* (the root *thym* is cognate with Lat. *fumus*, smoke, steam), occurs from Hom. onwards, meaning (a) breath, life (Homer, *Il*, 6, 17; 5, 852), (b) spirit, strength (*Od.*, 10, 78; *Il.* 17, 744), (c) soul as shown by feelings and passions, including desire and appetite (*Il.*, 4, 263), anger (*Il*, 9, 496, 598), the heart as the seat of emotions (*Il*, 14, 156; 7, 189) and the mind as the seat of thought (*Il.*, 1, 193; 4, 163). Cognates include *enthymeomai* (Thuc. onwards), lay to heart, ponder and *enthymēsis* (Eur., Thuc.), consideration, esteem. For *epithymeō* and *epithymia* → Desire, Lust.

OT There is virtually no distinction in the LXX between *thymos* and → *orgē*. Both terms appear for the same numerous Heb. equivalents (especially *ḥēmâh*, *'ap̄*) and are used synonymously. For *thymos* in the LXX (used *c.* 200 times) → *orgē*, anger, indignation, wrath.

NT *thymos* occurs only 18 times in the NT: twice in the Lucan writings, 5 times in Paul, once in Heb. and 10 times in Rev. The NT usage is connected with that of later secular Gk.; *thymos* in the NT means anger, wrath, rage.

1. In Heb., and the Lucan and Pauline writings (apart from Rom. 2:8) *thymos* refers to human anger. It has the same meaning, whether used in sing. or plur. The plur. may denote outbursts of anger or even passions. As in the LXX it often stands alongside *orgē*, without any perceptible distinction of meaning (e.g. Col. 3:8; Eph. 4:31). It stands in between words like *eris* (wrangling, quarrelling), *zēlos* (jealousy), *eritheia* (selfish ambition, contentiousness), in 2 Cor. 12:20 and Gal. 5:20. It is mentioned together with *pikria* (bitterness) in Eph. 4:31. These are dangers into which even the church might fall. On the other hand, men could be filled with rage at the teaching of Jesus (Lk. 4:28) and Paul (Acts 19:28).

All this has its origin in the → "flesh", and the "old nature" (Gal. 5:19 f.; Eph. 4:31; Col. 3:8 f.). It can only be overcome in the power of the Spirit who renews the heart (Eph. 4:23; Gal. 5:16, 18, 22, 25), and creates a new nature (Eph. 4:24).

2. In Rom. 2:8 *thymos* is used along with *orgē* without differentiation to express divine anger. It is used absolutely without mention of the name of God. The divine anger will be revealed at the final judgment (v. 5) in those whose heart is hardened and impenitent, and who do not obey the truth (v. 8), but do evil (v. 9). It will bring distress and despair.

In Rev. *thymos* denotes almost exclusively divine anger (e.g. 15:1, 7; 16:1). The picture of the wine of God's anger (*oinos tou thymou*) is a striking expression of the divine judgment (14:10; 16:19; 19:15) which man must, as it were, drink. It brings eternal ruin. The expression is from the OT (cf. Jer. 25:15–28). The expressions "the winepress of God's anger" (14:19) and "the bowls of God's anger" (15:7; 16:1) are also similar. Even when the wine of anger of Babylon's passion of fornication (*thymos tēs porneias*) is spoken of (14:8; 18:3), the thought of God's anger and judgment still stands in the background.

3. Of the vbs. derived from *thymos*, *thymoomai* occurs in the NT only in Matt. 2:16 meaning to become angry, and *enthymeomai* only in Matt. 1:20 and 9:4 for weighing up, reflecting, considering, thinking. The noun *enthymēsis* accordingly means in the NT consideration, reflection, thought. But it is always in the negative sense of bad or foolish thoughts (Matt. 9:4; 12:25; Acts 17:29; Heb. 4:12). Except in Acts 17:29 the contexts suggest hidden, secret thoughts which a man prefers to keep to himself and not to reveal, but which God in his omniscience perceives and brings to light.   *H. Schönweiss*

| ὀργή | ὀργή (orgē), anger, indignation, wrath; ὀργίζω (orgizō), be, become, or make angry; ὀργίλος (orgilos), inclined to |

anger; παροργίζω (parorgizō) enrage, make angry; παροργισμός (parorgismos), anger; παροξύνω (paroxynō), provoke to anger, παροξυσμός (paroxysmos), sharp disagreement, ardent incitement.

CL *orgē* is a cognate of *orgaō* (be puffed up, swell, be excited) and means (a) a natural impulse, temperament, disposition, mood, (b) anger, wrath (Hdt., 3, 25; Thuc., 4, 122). Where *orgē* has a gen., it indicates the subject of the anger or the object or occasion of the anger. The object of the anger is usually designated by the prepositions *eis, pros* or *epi* with the acc., meaning towards or against.

orgizō in the act. means to anger, in the pass. to be or to become angry. *orgilos*, a related adj., means inclined to anger, passionate, irritable. The vb. *parorgizō*, a derivation of *orgizō*, is only found in later secular Gk. and means to provoke to anger. The related noun *parorgismos* equally only attested in late Gk means provocation, anger.

1. The post-Homeric word *orgē* orig. means natural impulse, temper, temperament, nature, heart (cf. Hdt. VI, 128). *orgē* is thus initially still a neutral word. In the tragedians (e.g. Aesch., *Ag.*, 414 ff.; Soph., *Ant.*, 875; *El.*, 221 f.) the use of the word is increasingly limited to denote "the most striking manifestation of powerful inner passion, *thymos*" (H. Kleinknecht, *TDNT* V 384). *thymos* thus denotes "the wrath which boils up, *orgē* the wrath which breaks forth" (H. Cremer, cf. *TDNT* V 409, 383). The aim of the anger can be either to take vengeance or to exact → punishment. Thus in Dem., *Orationes*, 24, 118, *orgē* appears as the attitude which is particularly appropriate for a judge. It is positively evaluated as being in the service of → righteousness. For the rest, however, anger is mainly seen as a character defect, which man should strive to lay aside. For anger as the expression of unrestrained passion stands in contradiction to → reason, *gnōmē* (decision on the basis of knowledge), and *logos* (→ Word) and conflicts with the image of the wise man. It is an *amēchanon kakon*, an evil which runs out of control. One cannot make amends for its consequences (Eur., *Medea* 446 f.). It "necessarily leads to other *kaka*", evils (cf. H. Kleinknecht, *TDNT* V 384).

2. *orgē*, however, is also one of the most prominent characteristics of the Gk. divinities. The idea of wrathful gods is one of the basic factors of the majority of religions. (Mazdaism is an exception.) In earlier times the words *cholos* (anger, gall), *kotos* (grudge) and *mēnis* (anger) were used instead of *orgē*. Their anger was directed either against their own kind (e.g. Hom. *Il.*, 8, 407) or against human beings (e.g. Hom., *Il.*, 5, 177 f.; 24, 606). It was provoked as a rule by violation of one of the fundamental demands of life, morals or law. "By it order is restored, assertion made good and destiny achieved. Hence the wrath of the gods is not just blind rage. It is seeing anger, and even in regard to man, *via negationis*, it confers dignity on him by marking him out or putting him in the limits set for him, thus making him what he is" (H. Kleinknecht, *TDNT* V 385). For man, on the other hand there is the possibility, particularly within the framework of the cult, of counteracting the anger of the gods by means of → prayer, vows, → sacrifice and expiatory rites (→ Reconciliation).

3. In the Roman world the idea of wrathful gods and their punitive judgments,

affecting individuals in sickness, suffering and natural catastrophes, is even more strongly historicized. Again and again the great historical writers, Tacitus (e.g. *Historia*, 4, 26, 84; *Ann*. 16, 16) and Livy (e.g. *Hist*. 5, 14, 3 and 22, 9, 1) allude to divine anger as the effective cause of historical incidents. Vergil in his *Aeneid* depicts how the origin of Rome was affected by the wrath of the gods, especially Juno, and how this was eventually appeased by cultic actions (*rite preces*).

4. If in Gk. philosophy *orgē* was at first a neutral or even positive quantity, people came increasingly to reject this idea. Among the Stoics *orgē* was a reprehensible passion (*pathos*), which befitted neither rational human beings nor gods. In particular, the thought of the impassibility of the gods also determines Philo's conception of God.

OT 1. (a) The OT speaks of God's anger and also human anger very frequently.

The following Heb. words are mostly used: *'ap* (*c*. 210 times), which first designates the nose (Isa. 2:22), then its trembling and snorting and thence the reason for this, anger (Job. 4:9); *ḥēmâh* (*c*. 115 times), heat, poison, venom, rage (used of the spirit, Ezek. 3:14), and rage, anger (Gen. 27:44; Prov. 21:4); *ḥārôn*, burning in combination with *'ap* (33 times; only for the anger of God); *'ebrâh* (24 times), excess, arrogance, anger, fury; *qeṣep* (28 times), wrath; *za'am* (22 times), curse and *rōgez*, thunder, agitation, wrath (Hab. 3:2). In addition, vbs. are used to denote anger which are mostly cognate with the above nouns. For all these words the LXX has as a rule either → *thymos* or *orgē*, used synonymously.

(b) In the earlier strata of the OT the *orgē* word-group or *thymos* appear to be used to designate a human reaction in a neutral or even a positive sense. Zebul's anger (Jdg. 9:30) is to be recognized as thoroughly justified. Still more legitimate appears David's anger with the rich man in Nathan's fable (2 Sam. 12:5) and Nehemiah's anger at grievances in Jerusalem (Neh. 5:6). Moses' indignation at the sin of the people dancing round the golden calf is even presented as a holy anger in which Moses places himself on the side of God (Exod. 32:19; cf. Exod. 16:20; 1 Sam. 11:6; Jer. 6:11; Job 32:2 f.). But expecially in the later writings of the OT, outbursts of anger are depicted as a vice (cf. Ps. 37:8 f.; Job 36:13) and rejected (cf. Gen. 49:7 where anger is cursed). It is not only cruel (Prov. 27:4), but leads to quarrelling and wrangling (Prov. 30:33). It disunites men (1 Sam. 20:30) and can lead to bloody acts (Gen. 49:6). By his anger a man shows himself to be unwise (Prov. 29:8); for anger is a mark of fools (Prov. 12:16; 27:3). A man should avoid it at all costs (Job 36:18).

(c) The role of the divine anger in the OT is of much greater significance. Yahweh is repeatedly said to be a jealous and angry God. His anger can be presented in quite drastic terms (Isa. 30:27 f.; 13:13; Jer. 30:23 f.; Ps. 2:5). Man's encounter with the holy could be dangerous (Gen. 32:25 ff.; Exod. 4:24 ff.; 19:9 ff.; Isa. 6:5); for the anger of Yahweh is to be appraised as an expression of his holiness and righteousness. It points to the living personal nature of God whose ways are beyond man (Gen. 32:23 ff.; Exod. 4:24; 1 Sam. 26:19; 2 Sam. 16:10 ff.; 24:1). But it is also surrounded by the experience of the divine covenant will in righteousness and love (W. Eichrodt, *RGG*³, IV 1930). This anger is provoked by the behaviour of individuals (Exod. 4:14; Num. 12:9; Deut. 29:18 ff.; 2 Sam. 6:7; 2 Chr. 19:2; 25:15; cf. Sir. 47:20 ff.; Man. 9 f.). But more often it is provoked by apostasy, unfaithfulness and violation of God's law on the part of the covenant people Israel (Num. 25:3; 32:10; Deut. 29:25 ff.; Jdg. 2:14, 20; Ps. 78:21). The prophets, especially Amos, Hosea, Isaiah and Micah "spoke of the divine wrath as a fact, and designated as its proper object their contemporaries' whole way of life, their social and economic attitudes, their political behaviour and, in particular, their cultic practice" (G. von Rad, *Old Testament Theology*, 1965. II, 179). God's people often offend him. "His anger is always a lawful reaction to the violation of a law or to opposition against his historically-determined activity, in which he not only requites the violation or opposition, but also wills to effect the restoration and maintenance of the order set between himself and man." (S. Platn, *Die Furcht Gottes*, 105)

Within the framework of covenant theology the wrath of God can be seen as an expression of rejected and wounded love. This is the deepest root of the concept of wrath, and in this light one can understand the overwhelming force of the message. It is Yahweh's wounded love which awakens his wrath (J. Fichtner, *TDNT* V, 403). But Yahweh's anger can equally be directed against the nations (Isa. 10:25; 13:3; Jer. 50:13; Ezek. 30:15; Mic. 5:14). It comes over all who desert him (Ezr. 8:22) or who are literally godless (Wis. 11:90; Sir. 5:7). It does not overtake men without prior warning (Exod. 22:23 f.; 32:10; Deut. 6:13 ff.). Those "who did not wish to hear" (Mic. 5:15; cf. Jer. 42:18; Lam. 3:42 f.), who did not walk in accord with the divine ordinances (Ezek. 9:8–10; 22:31) are punished. Upon the disobedient God pours out his wrath (Jer. 7:20). He passes judgment on the wicked and on whole nations, sending sword, hunger and pestilence (Ezek. 6:11 ff.), trampling under foot (Isa. 63:6; Hab. 3:12), annihilation (Deut. 29:22), devastation (Jer. 25:37 f.), depopulation (Jer. 50:13), scattering (Lam. 4:16) and burning of the land (Isa. 9:18 f.; 30:27). He treads the nations in his winepress (Isa. 63:1 ff.) and gives them the cup of his fury to drink (Isa. 51:17; cf. Jer. 25:15 f.). Hosea 13:11 appears to reckon even the monarchy to be a gift of the divine wrath (cf. 1 Sam. 8).

But God's anger does not have to last for ever. The "moment" of anger is spoken of repeatedly (cf. Ps. 30:6; Isa. 26:20; 54:7 f.; Wis. 18:20). Behind the divine anger there often already shines grounds for → hope (cf. 2 Sam. 24:16; Isa. 40:2; 51:22; 54:8–10; Hos. 14:4). Such hope is nourished on observation of history in which God's saving will prevails again and again (Ps. 78:38; 103:6–13). Man is able to hold to this hope if he humbles himself (cf. 2 Chr. 12:12; 32:26), turns to God in penitent prayer (Exod. 32:12, 14; 2 Sam. 12:13; Ps. 6:2; 27:9; Dan. 9:15 f.; Hab. 3:2) and reaffirms the covenant in obedience (Num. 25:6–11; Jos 7; cf. Jon. 3:7–10). If that happens, then God's anger has fulfilled its task and has brought about restoration (Jer. 4:4; 36:7; Isa. 42:25).

2. In later Judaism and Qumran some passages are concerned with justified anger, anger directed against sinners (e.g. 1QS 10: 19). But the negative judgment on anger as a vice which is incompatible with wisdom is forcefully exemplified (Wis. 10:3; Sir. 27:30; 1QS 4:10). Women (Sir. 25:21), the rich (Sir. 28:10), and rulers (Sir. 47:20 ff.; 2 Macc. 14:27; CD 8: 3; 19: 15 f.; cf. Matt. 2:16) appear as particularly susceptible to anger. In every case anger and rage are "an abomination" which the godless pursue (Sir. 27:30). But God's wrath is directed against the godless and pagans (Wis. 11:9; 19:1; Sir. 5:7; 16:7; Man. 5; cf. the calling down of God's anger on an apostate member of Qumran, 1QS 2:15). This must be seen

and taken as seriously as his compassion (Sir. 16:12). It is an admonition to genuine repentance (Sir. 5:7 ff.; cf. Zeph. 2:3). In later Judaism, in particular, besides the idea of the wrath of God at work within history (Sir.; CD 1:5f.; 21; 3:8), there is the thought of an ultimate day of wrath when God will sit in judgment (Jub. 24:28; 30; Eth. Enoch 62:12; cf. 1QM 4:1; Ezek. 7:19; Dan. 8:19; Zeph. 2:2f.; Prov. 11:4; 1QS 5:12). This day is presented in strong apocalyptic colours, as "a day of ruin and devastation, a day of → darkness and gloom" (Zeph. 1:15), as a day of "the burning anger of the Lord" (Zeph. 2:2; cf. 1QH 3:28). On this day the righteous and unrighteous will be divided according to the way they have → walked (Ezek. 7:3). God will accept those who turn to him in penitence. But his → righteous anger will destroy the others (1QS 4:12; 1QH 3:25 ff.; 15:17, 1QM 3:9).

NT In the NT the noun *orgē* occurs 36 times (21 times in the Pauline writings, 6 times in Rev., and only occasionally in the Gospels) and relates both to human and divine anger. *orgizomai*, to be angry, is found 8 times, but like *orgilos*, angry (only in Tit. 1:7) and *paroxynomai*, to become angry (Acts 17:16; 1 Cor. 13:5) only of human anger. The same is true of *parorgizō*, make angry (Rom. 10:19; Eph. 6:4) and the nouns *parorgismos*, anger (Eph. 4:26) and *paroxysmos* stirring up, provoking, disagreement (Acts 15:39), ardent or affectionate incitement (Heb. 10:24).

1. In the NT *orgē* denotes, on the one hand, a human passion. It is largely used synonymously with → *thymos*. A slight shift of emphasis may be seen in the fact that *thymos* is preferred for depictions of sudden outbursts of anger (Lk. 4:28; Acts 19:28), whereas in *orgē* there is an occasional element of deliberate thought. But this does not prevent both *thymos* and *orgē* from being condemned as vices, in some cases in the same breath (Eph. 4:31; Col. 3:8).

If the anger of the king in the parable of the wedding feast (Matt. 22:7; cf. Lk. 14:21) is justified, the anger of the elder brother in the parable of the Prodigal Son (Lk. 15:28) is certainly not. A prohibition of anger directed against one's brother is clearly expressed in the Sermon on the Mount (Matt. 5:22). Most of the rest of the NT statements concerning human anger move within the lines thus laid down. Thus, in Eph. 6:4 fathers are enjoined not to provoke their children to anger (*parorgizein*). Jas. 1:19 f. lays down the general rule: "Let every man be quick to hear, slow to speak, slow to anger, for the anger of man does not work the righteousness of God." But where a man has become angry (whether for good or bad reasons), he is not to let the sun set on his anger (*parorgismos*), and so give opportunity to the devil (Eph. 4:26). Prayer is incompatible with anger (1 Tim. 2:8).

From this standpoint it is understandable why anger is repeatedly named in lists of sins (Eph. 4:31; Col. 3:8; Tit. 1:7). In Eph. and Col. anger (*orgē*) is expressly reckoned among the things on account of which God's wrath "will come upon the sons of disobedience" (Eph. 5:6; cf. Col. 3:6). The context of both passages contrasts anger and other wrong attitudes with the life of faith. In Eph. 4:32 there is the injunction: "Be kind to one another, tenderhearted, forgiving one another, as God in Christ forgave you." Love in contrast to anger, wrath, malice, slander and foul talk, is the life-style which the Christian should adopt (Col. 3:14; cf. 3:8). Being *orgilos* ("quick-tempered", Tit. 1:7 RSV) is a characteristic which unfits a man for being a → bishop (*episkopos*).

110

2. However, in a few places human anger is not evaluated negatively. Eph. 4:26, quoting Ps. 4:5, may be paraphrased: "You may be angry, only do not sin." The anger of the king with those who refused his invitation (Matt. 22:7; cf. Lk. 14:21), and even more clearly that of the king with the unforgiving servant (Matt. 18:34) may thus appear thoroughly justified. "For if anger is ruled out *a limine*, what is said about God's wrath has to be explained away. Conversely, when this is taken seriously, a limited anger has to be accepted in the human sphere too" (G. Stählin, *TDNT* V 419). Yet it has to be asked whether in these cases anger is not to be understood as participation by men in the anger of God. The mention of Jesus' anger (Mk. 3:5) and angry behaviour suggest this possibility, even if the words themselves do not always occur (e.g. against Peter, Matt. 16:23; Mk. 8:33; the Pharisees, Matt. 23; or where God's honour is insulted, Matt. 21:12; Mk. 11:15 ff.; Lk. 19:45 f.; Jn. 2:14 ff.). Paul can even regard the ruler of the secular state as "the servant of God to execute his wrath on the wrongdoer" (Rom. 13:4). But otherwise believers are never to avenge themselves, "but leave it to the wrath of God; for it is written, 'Vengeance is mine, I will repay, says the Lord'" (Rom 12:19; cf. Lev. 19:18; Deut. 32:35; Heb. 10:30). It is naturally not a case of sharing in God's nature, but of the discharge of a service in which God can use pagans like Assyria and Cyrus (Isa. 10:5; 44:28; 45:1) and even satanic powers, as in Job 1, 2 and Rev. 13:7 ff.; 20:7 ff.

3. (a) As in the OT so also in the NT the *orgē* word-group serves to illustrate the character of God. The future wrathful judgment of God plays an important role in the preaching of John the Baptist (Matt. 3:7; cf. Mk. 1:3–8; Lk. 3:2–17; Jn. 1:6 ff.; 19–28). Only he who repents (→ Conversion, art. *metanoia*) will be able to escape the wrath; merely appealing to being children of Abraham does not suffice. But the proclamation of Jesus also contains this urgent reference to the days of wrath which will come over Israel and bring great distress (Lk. 21:23; cf. Matt. 22:7 et pass.; Jn. 3:36).

(b) This thought of the future wrath of God is unfolded on a massive scale in Rev., which speaks of the anger of the nations (Rev. 11:18), and of the anger of the → Dragon, a power opposed to God (Rev. 12:17). "This is the great eschatological wrath which opposes the wrath of God. It is described with colours taken from the Psalter. The drama of revelation can thus be understood in large measure as a battle between two *orgai*" (G. Stählin, *TDNT* V 439). The wrath of God (for which the term → *thymos* is also used, e.g. Rev. 15:1) will finally introduce the judgment, in which God will reward those who fear his name. But those who → destroy the earth will be brought to destruction (Rev. 11:18; cf. 6:16 which speaks of the judicial "anger of the Lamb"). The descriptions of the judgment include the pictures of the rod of iron and "the wine press of the fury of the wrath of God the Almighty" (Rev. 19:15; cf. 14:19; Ps. 2:9; Joel 3:13; Isa. 63:1 f.), and the "cup of his anger" (Rev. 14:10; cf. Jer. 25:15; 51:7), from which those who worship the beast and also Babylon must drink (Rev. 16:19; cf. 17:4; 18:3).

4. While attention is thus forcibly drawn to the awful wrath of God in the future, it is viewed in Pauline theology on the horizon of an eschatology which is already being realized in the course of history from the time of the coming of Jesus Christ. The decisive significance of Jesus Christ for men in the face of the *orgē theou* is described clearly and impressively. By nature, as a child of this world-age, man

111

stands under the wrath of God (Eph. 2:3; cf. Rom. 1:18–3:20). It does not merely await him on the day of judgment (cf. Jn. 3:36), although Paul can also speak of it as a future event (Rom. 2:5; cf. Eph. 5:6; Col. 3:6).

The wrath of God is first directed against unrighteousness, transgression of the law, irreverence (→ Godliness, art. *sebomai*), and disdain of the Creator (Rom. 1:18, 21 ff.). Secondly, however, the anger of God is also aroused by the attitude of the so-called pious man, who through his observance of the Law allows himself to be driven into a feeling of his own self-esteem which finds expression in an unfitting → boasting. But no man is able to satisfy the Law. Therefore the Law brings wrath (Rom. 4:15). For it is man's transgression of the Law – which becomes clear when the Law is radically understood – that is the ground of the righteous anger of God. The lost situation of man, both Jew and pagan, who is a prisoner in sin and therefore stands under the anger of God, has now been revealed by God through the sending of Jesus Christ. That is the central statement of Rom. 1:18. In him God shows the world his righteousness (*dikaiosynē*), which embraces both his wrath (*orgē*) and also his grace (*charis*) and compassion (*eleos* → Mercy). In the words of G. Bornkamm: "Because he lets his 'righteousness' be made known, all the 'wickedness' of men also comes to light. In that he lets it be said to the world that in its sin it is subject to the 'wrath' of God, that there is no righteousness in it and that he alone in the dispute in which it entered with him (3.4), at the same time he lets the world be told that he has disclosed this 'righteousness' of his to believers" ("The Revelation of God's Wrath (Romans 1–3)," in *Early Christian Experience*, 1969, 64).

Through the two aspects of this revelation man is placed in a situation which inescapably demands a decision. On the one hand, he may persist as a "vessel of wrath" (Rom. 9:22) in the realm of the *orgē theou*, the wrath of God, as – to Paul's sorrow – does the greater part of the Jews of his time (1 Thess. 2:16; cf. Rom. 9:22). (In the light of the context and the quotations of Deut. 32:21 (cf. Isa. 65:1) in Rom. 10:19, O. Michel observes: "In his wrath God hides himself from Israel, coming out on the side of a foreign people", *Der Brief an die Römer*, KEK 1957[11], 263.) On the other hand, he may turn to Jesus Christ and allow him to save him from the wrath of God in the realm of the love of God (Rom. 5:8 f.; 1 Thess. 1:10). Ignatius put this realisation in the shape of a formula: "We must either fear his future wrath or love his present grace – one of the two!" (Ign., Eph. 11:1; cf. *TDNT*, V 446). It is thus clear that the coming of Jesus Christ does not simply mean "cheap grace" for all. "God continues to be the Judge, and Christian faith in the grace of God does not consist in the conviction that God's wrath does not exist or that there is no threateningly impending judgment (II Cor. 5:10), but in the conviction of being rescued from God's wrath" (R. Bultmann, *Theology of the New Testament*, I 1952, 288). If God has destined us to be "vessels of mercy" (Rom. 9:23) "to obtain salvation" (1 Thess. 5:9), the offer of salvation requires acceptance. "If there is deliverance from eternal wrath in Christ alone, then everything depends on whether a man rejects Christ or appropriates, or more correctly, lets himself be appropriated to, what Christ is and brings" (G. Stählin, *TDNT*, V 446). This comes about through → faith. Only he who believes in the Son need no longer fear the → judgment of God, for it is only to him that the promise of eternal → life is given. In both Jn. and Paul, eternal life describes the contrast

112

between → destruction, the fruit of the divine anger, and compassion, the fruit of the divine → mercy (Jn. 3:36; Rom. 2:7). *H. C. Hahn*

(a). K. Barth, *CD* IV, 1, 211–83 et passim; G. C. Berkouwer, *The Providence of God*, 1952; *The Work of Christ*, 1970; *Sin*, 1971; G. Bornkamm, "The Revelation of God's Wrath (Romans 1–3)," *Early Christian Experience*, 1969, 47–70; F. Büchsel, *thymos*, *TDNT* III 167–72; R. Bultmann, *Theology of the New Testament*, I, 1950, 288–92; C. H. Dodd, *The Epistle to the Romans*, 1932, 18 ff.; W. Eichrodt, *Theology of the Old Testament*, I, 1960, 258–59; S. Erlandsson "The Wrath of YHWH", *TB* 23, 1972, 111–16; A. T. Hanson, *The Wrath of the Lamb*, 1957; J. Hick, *Evil and the God of Love*, 1966; D. Hill, *Greek Words and Hebrew Meanings*, 1967, 23–162; H. Kleinknecht, O. Grether, J. Fichtner, G. Stählin, E. Sjöberg, *orgē*, *TDNT* V 382–447; G. H. C. Macgregor, "The Concept of the Wrath of God in the New Testament," *NTS* 7, 1960–61, 101 ff.; L. Morris, *The Apostolic Preaching of the Cross*, 1965³; A. W. Pink, *The Sovereignty of God*, 1961; A. Ritschl, *The Christian Doctrine of Justification and Reconciliation*, III, 1900; A. Stöger, "Wrath," *EBT* III 1006–11; R. V. G. Tasker, *The Biblical Doctrine of the Wrath of God*, 1957.
(b). C. V. Gablenz and L. Pinomaa, "Zorn Gottes," *EKL* III 1919 ff.; N. J. Hein, W. Eichrodt, H. Conzelmann and H. Baudt, "Zorn Gottes," *RGG*³ VI 1929 ff.; A. von Jüchen, *Der Zorn Gottes*, 1948; A. Ritschl, *De Ira Dei*, 1859; G. Schrenk, *Unser Glaube an den Zorn Gottes nach dem Römerbrief*, 1944.
→ Literature under Cross, Curse, Death, Judgment, Law, Punishment, Reconciliation, Sacrifice, Sin.

Animal

θηρίον

θηρίον (*thērion*), wild animal, beast.

CL *thērion* (a diminutive form of *thēr*, cf. Lat. *ferus*) means a wild animal, occasionally an animal kept at pasture, and generally an animal. Early on (Plato onwards) it came to be used metaphorically as a derogatory term for people of a "bestial" type: beast, monster. Nero was called a beast of prey which eats up everything (Philostr. *VA* IV 38).

OT In the O.T *thērion* is used to render the Heb. *ḥayyâh* in the sense of "the not domesticated, in the open country living, in most cases big and dangerous animal" (Koehler–Baumgartner, 293; cf. the division of the animal kingdom into different kinds, Gen. 1:24 f.; Ps. 148:10; Hos. 4:3). The *thērion* is man's enemy (Gen. 3:14 f.; 9:2, 5; 37:20). In warnings of God's judgment the ravages of wild beasts are listed along with other troubles (Lev. 26:22; Deut. 32:24; Jer. 12:9; 15:3; Ezek. 5:17; 14:21). The devouring of human corpses by beasts is regarded as the height of shame, and as evidence of being forsaken by God (Gen. 40:19; 2 Sam. 21:10). Not until the era of salvation to come will the harmony between man and beast, which existed in Paradise, be restored (Lev. 26:6; Isa. 35:9; Ezek. 34:25; Hos. 2:20).

In Dan. 7 *thērion* refers to world powers, which are seen as supernatural, beast-like figures. They arise from the chaos which is hostile to God (→ Water), and represent the sort of political powers, hostile to man, with which the Jewish people has had to deal throughout the centuries. The coming of the Son of Man puts an end to them. Dan. 4:13–33; 5:21 depicts the fall of Nebuchadnezzar as a descent from the height of human pride to the depths of an animal existence.

NT 1. The NT follows the OT, in that *thērion* is found in lists of living creatures (Acts 11:6; Jas. 3:7), in a catalogue of plagues (Rev. 6:8), and as a description of the national characteristics of the Cretans (Tit. 1:12). In Mk. 1:13 the wild beasts emphasize the horror and human desolation of the wilderness; possibly they are also intended as an allusion to the Messianic return of the Paradise era, with its state of peace between man and beast.

2. 38 of the 45 instances of the word in the NT are found in Rev., particularly in chs. 6–19. The beast and the false prophet representing powers opposed to God, join with the → dragon to form the Satanic trinity (16:13). From their mouths issue three foul demonic spirits like frogs who assemble the world rulers for Armageddon (→ War). The beast in 11:7 combines the characteristics of all four beasts in Dan. 7, dreadfully intensified. It originates in the realm of chaos (11:7; 13:1), is given authority by the "dragon" (13:2, 4), has the attributes of beasts of prey (11:7), and executes its claims to total power with ruthless force (13:7 f., 15). As the → Antichrist the beastly monster caricatures the → Lamb (with its wound, 13:3, 14, cf. 5:6; its horns, 13:1, cf. 5:6; world dominion, 13:2, cf. 5:5; and worship, 13:4, cf. 5:8 ff.). It also apes the title of God (17:8, 11; cf. 1:4). The "other" beast (13:11), otherwise called the false prophet (16:13; 19:20; 20:10), furthers the plans of the first beast by its propaganda, working miracles (13:13), erecting an → image (*eikōn*, 13:14), and branding people with a mark (*charagma*, 13:16 f.). Though to outward appearances a lamb, it speaks like a dragon (13:11; cf. Matt. 7:15).

The final victory over these beastly powers will belong to Christ and his church (15:2; 19:19 f.). The imagery is not intended to refer to the first-century historical situation alone, but to indicate that every generation is simultaneously threatened by these powers   *W. Bauder*

Animals in the NT

The word *ktēnos* is also used in the NT for an animal, particularly a domesticated animal, a pet, a pack animal, or an animal used for riding. It is used in the latter sense of the Good Samaritan's beast (Lk. 10:34) and Paul's mount, when he was taken under escort to Felix (Acts 23:34). It probably means cattle in Rev. 18:13. It seems to refer to animals generally in 1 Cor. 15:39, where Paul is speaking of different kinds of flesh in the course of his argument that the resurrection body has its own peculiar nature and that we ought not to think of it as being identical with our present bodies.

It has been estimated that animals are mentioned some 3,000 times in the Bible. In the NT they feature as part and parcel of everyday life and also serve to illustrate by their characteristic features moral and religious truths. In the ancient world the goat (*tragos*) seems to have been kept chiefly as a milk-producer. Its tough, strong-smelling meat was not so edible as that of the kid (*eriphos* or *eriphion*) which was eaten on festive occasions (Jdg. 6:19; Lk. 15:29). Skins of both sheep and goats were used for bottles (Mk. 2:22), and goat skins were used for clothing for those in reduced circumstances (Heb. 11:37). The he-goat is mentioned as a sacrificial animal, especially in connection with the annual Day of Atonement rites (Heb. 9:12 f.; 19; 10:4; cf. Lev. 16). Here the high priest took two goats, slaying one together with a bull as a sin offering and sprinkling their → blood on the mercy seat on entering the holy place in the tabernacle and on the altar of incense to cleanse the people of Israel from their sin. After this he confessed the iniquities of Israel over the live goat, laying his hands upon its head, before letting it go in the wilderness. One of the main arguments of Heb. is that such sacrifices cannot ultimately take away sins (10:4). Rather, they foreshadow Christ who has entered the sanctuary, offering his own blood once and for all (9:23–28; cf. 10:1).

In Matt. 25:32 sheep (→ Lamb, Sheep) and goats are mentioned together in a mixed flock, representing the nations standing before the king in judgment. The practice of keeping mixed flocks is still current among Arabs. To the stranger the sheep and the goats may be scarcely distinguishable in colour and shape, but their owner knows which are which (G. S. Cansdale *Animals of Bible Lands*, 1970, 48). They are separated in the evening, the goats needing to be kept warm at night, while the sheep which are more valuable prefer the open air. J. Jeremias has suggested that the white colour of the sheep is a symbol of righteousness which contrasts with the black of the goats (*The Parables of Jesus*, 1963², 206). But there is no mention of colour in the parable. If Cansdale is right, the parable teaches that just as there is no obvious, outward identifying mark of Christ as he encounters men *incognito* through his needy brethren, so there is also no obvious, outward mark to identify those who are righteous before God. The parable puts the question: "By what criterion will the heathen (v. 32) be judged?" (J. Jeremias, op. cit., 209). It gives the answer that the righteous will show their righteousness (albeit unawares) by their service to Christ in the person of his brethren in need. The unrighteous will be oblivious to the day of opportunity, just as the Jews were when confronted by Jesus. The parable suggests that Jews and Gentiles are alike outwardly. The decisive difference between men depends on their inner righteousness which finds expression in their outward acts.

In addition to the detailed legislation for the → sacrifice of sheep and cattle (see esp. Lev. 1–9, 16; cf. Exod. 12:21 ff.; 24:6 ff.), there was also considerable humanitarian concern for animals in the OT. The sabbath rest extended to the ox and the ass (Exod. 20:10; 23; 12; Deut. 5:14). The straying ox had to be returned to safety (Exod. 23:4 f.; Deut. 22:1), and the fallen ox was to be helped to its feet again (Deut. 22:4). There was a ban on oxen and asses ploughing together (Deut. 22:10). On the other hand, dangerous animals were to be restrained and even slaughtered and their owners made liable to penalties (Exod. 21 and 22). Jesus endorsed this humanitarian attitude towards animals but extended it to apply to man as well. For whereas many could accept the need to water and tend sheep and cattle (Gk. *bous*) on the → sabbath, they failed to see that caring applied all the more in the case of man (Matt. 12:11; Lk. 13:15; 14:5). There were, of course, in these instances the overtones of material advantage in caring for animals on the sabbath, whereas there was no such material advantage in caring for one's fellow man. The injunction not to muzzle the ox as it treads out the corn was seen by Paul as the expression of a principle that those who labour are entitled to support from the benefits of their work (1 Cor. 9:9; 2 Tim. 5:18; cf. Deut. 25:4). Thus Christian workers are entitled to support from those who benefit from their toil. This again is an instance of extending to men a principle that could be seen to be self-evident in the case of animals.

Other words for cattle in the NT include *damalis*, he fer, the ashes of which were used in the rite of cleansing (Heb. 9:13; cf. Num. 9:9, 17 f.). This is contrasted with "the blood of Christ, who through the eternal Spirit offered himself without blemish to God" and who thus purifies the → "conscience from dead works to serve the living God" (Heb. 9:14). *thremma* denotes a domesticated animal, including sheep and goats (Moulton-Milligan, 292) and is used of Jacob's cattle drinking from the well of Samaria (Jn. 4:12; cf. Gen. 33:19; 48:22). *moschos* is the calf or young bull sacrificed on the Day of Atonement (Heb. 9:12, 19; see above discussion of the goats in the Day of Atonement rites). The fatted calf (*ho moschos ho siteutos*) was preserved for special feasts and brought out on the return of the prodigal son (Lk. 15:23; 27, 30; cf. Jud. 6:25a, 28a). It appears as an apocalyptic animal, as one of the four living creatures around the throne together with the lion, the man and the eagle (Rev. 4:7; cf. Ezek. 1:10). Later Christian writers identified these creatures with the four evangelists. Irenaeus identified the man with Matthew, the eagle with Mark, the ox with Luke and the lion with John (*Haer.* 1, 11, 8). Augustine attributed the lion to Matthew, the man to Mark, the ox to Luke and the eagle to John (*De cons.* 1, 6). But this is an allegorical reading into the text of a meaning not originally intended. The vision symbolizes the whole created order in its service and praise to God. The different figures suggest the most powerful wild beast (the lion), the mightiest domestic animal (the ox), the most indomitable of the birds (the eagle), and the most intelligent creature (the man). The word *tauros* means a bull, used as a sacrificial animal (Acts 14:13; Heb. 9:13; 10:4) and in banquets where it is mentioned together with *sitista*, fatted cattle or calves (Matt. 22:4).

The camel (*kamēlos*) is mentioned in various connections in the NT. John the Baptist wore clothes of camel's hair (Matt. 3:4; Mk. 1:6). It was the cheapest, coarsest and simplest material available. But the chief reason for John's garb was that it was the traditional dress of the prophet (C. H. H. Scobie, *John the Baptist*, 1964, 128; cf. Zech. 13:4; 1 Ki. 19:19; 2 Ki. 2:13 f.). The saying that it is easier for a camel to pass through the eye of a needle than for a rich man to enter the kingdom of God illustrates the impossible by comparing the largest animal with the smallest opening (Matt. 19:24; Mk. 10:25; Lk. 18:25). Since the early centuries attempts have been made to mitigate the contrast or provide an explanation by suggesting that there was a narrow gate in the walls of Jerusalem through which a man or a camel might pass in emergency. But they could only do so by removing all encumbrances. There is, however, no known evidence for such a gate and it seems preferable to take the saying as an example of deliberate hyperbole like the sayings about the beam and the splinter (Matt. 7:3; Lk. 6:41), and straining out a gnat and swallowing a camel (Matt. 23:24). A later rabbinic parallel spoke of the impossibility of an elephant passing through the eye of a needle (Ber. 55b; cf. SB I 828; V. Taylor, *The Gospel According to St. Mark*, 1952, 431; M.-J. Lagrange, *Évangile selon Saint Marc*, 1942[6], 269 ff.). To strain out a gnat (*kōnōps*) and swallow a camel draws attention to the fatal danger of being over-zealous in small matters and oblivious to important ones. In Matt. 23:23 f. it is applied to the scribes and Pharisees who are scrupulous about tithing even herbs at the expense of neglecting "the weightier matters of the law, justice and mercy and faith" (cf. Lev. 27:30; Mic. 6:8). The AV "strain at" is either a misprint or an archaism for "strain out" (Arndt, 199). The hapaxlegomenon *kōnōps* which is usually translated as "gnat" has been suggested as a word for a certain worm found in wine (Arndt, 463).

All four evangelists say that Jesus rode into Jerusalem on a *pōlos* (Matt. 21:2,

7; Mk .11:2, 4 f., 7; Lk. 19:30, 33, 35; Jn. 12:15). The word generally means the colt of a horse that is old enough to use. But in our literature it refers to an ass's foal, a young donkey. The evangelists see the action as the fulfilment of the prophecy of Zech. 9:9. In early Israel even the nobility rode on donkeys (Jdg. 5:10; 10:4; 12:14; 2 Sam. 17:23; 19:26), but the situation was changed after David with the widespread introduction of the horse (1 Ki. 10:25–29; 2 Ki. 9:18 ff.). A merchant or humble traveller might still ride a donkey in Jesus' day, but a conquering king might be expected to ride a charger or enter the city marching at the head of his troops. Jesus' action not only appears as the fulfilment of prophecy but as an indication of the sort of king he was, ruling in humility (cf. L. Morris, *The Gospel According to John*, 1971, 586 f.; J. G. Baldwin, *Haggai, Zechariah, Malachi*, 1972, 164 ff.). John describes the animal as an *onarion*, lit, a little donkey, but often used as a diminutive in form only for *onos*, donkey (cf. Lk. 13:15; 14:5 TR; Matt. 21:2; Jn. 12:14). (See also W. Bauer, "The 'Colt' of Palm Sunday", *JBL* 72, 1953, 220–9.)

Numerous critics have seen in Matt's reference to two animals (an ass [*onos*] and a colt [*pōlos*]; 21:2, 7) a mistaken understanding of a Heb. parallelism in Zech. 9:9. On the other hand, it would be natural for the young animal to be tethered by its parent. Both Mk. 11:2 and Lk. 19:30 (but not Matt.) observe that no one had yet sat on the animal. This suggests the conjecture that the old animal was brought to calm the young animal amid the crowds.

The pig (*choiros*) was an unclean animal (Lev. 11:7; Isa. 65:4; 66:3; Ps. 79(80): 14; cf. SB I 448 ff., 492 f.). In general, the rule was a safe one in view of the fact that it is now known that pork is only safe when fully cooked (cf. Cansdale, op. cit., 99). But references to pigs in the NT suggest that their use for food was more widespread than the law allowed. The reaction of the Gadarenes at the loss of their pigs (Matt. 8:30–34) is an ironic comment on their values. In begging Jesus to go, they showed that they preferred their unclean animals to the presence of the Son of God and the healing of the demoniacs. The utter degradation of the prodigal son is shown by his employment in looking after unclean animals and in his desire to eat the pods that the pigs ate (Lk. 15:15 f.).

Pigs and dogs feature in two NT sayings. "Do not give dogs what is holy; and do not throw your pearls before swine, lest they trample them underfoot and turn to attack you" (Matt. 7:6). The words were quoted by Did. 9 in forbidding the admission of the unbaptized to the Lord's Supper and by Tertullian who blamed heretics for admitting them (*De praesc.* 41). The word dog (*kyōn*) was used by Jews in the 1st cent. A.D. to designate the heathen (cf. Matt. 15:26; Mk. 7:27 f.). The usage seems to have been adapted by the church to designate the Jews themselves who were outside the church and attacked it (Phil. 3:2 f.; Rev. 22:16). In Deut. 23:18 "the wages of a dog" refers to the wages of a male prostitute. 2 Pet. 2:22 applies to those who have turned back "the true proverb, The dog turns back to his own vomit, and the sow (*hys*) is washed only to wallow in the mire" (cf. Prov. 26:11). The reference to the dogs licking the sores of Lazarus (Lk. 16:21) recalls the fact that dogs in Egypt and Palestine were mainly scavengers which were not welcomed as household pets. The Syro-Phoenician woman's reply to Jesus that the little dogs (*kynaria*) eat the children's crumbs under the table (Matt. 15:27; Mk. 7:28) emphasizes the gulf between herself and the true Jew.

The horse (*hippos*) is mentioned in Jas. 3:3. Just as the bit guides the horse and the rudder the ship, the tongue which is likewise relatively small plays a determinative part in human life for both good and ill. The remaining references to horses all occur in Rev., representing forces before which men are powerless. In the vision of the seals (6:2–8) the four horses recall those of Zech. 1:8; 6:1–8, but the OT imagery is transformed (cf. R. H. Charles, *The Revelation of St. John*, I, 1920, 160–71). The rider of the white horse has a bow and is given a crown and goes out conquering and to conquer (6:2). In view of 19:11, this rider represents Christ in the present age. But the other horses and riders represent destructive powers. The rider of the red horse is permitted to take peace from the earth so that men slay one another. He is given a great sword (6:4). The rider of the black horse carries a balance. A voice cries: "A quart of wheat for a denarius, and three quarts of barley for a denarius; but do not harm oil and wine!" (6:6). The thought here is that the necessities of life are being sold at famine prices, while luxury commodities are available for those who can afford them (cf. R. H. Charles, op. cit., I, 166 ff.). The rider of the pale horse is → Death and Hades (6:8). They are given power over a fourth part of the earth to kill with the sword, famine, pestilence and wild beasts. The fact that the power of none of the latter three is absolute and final is indicative that they will continue throughout the present age, but they will not be able to extinguish life altogether.

The horses in Rev. 9:7, 9, 17, 19 have an apocalyptic aspect, representing the ultimate in destructive power. They are like locusts (9:3, 7). By contrast, he who is called "Faithful and True" and judges in righteousness and makes war (19:11) sits upon a white horse, followed by the armies of heaven also on white horses (19:14). Together they will bring about the final overthrow of evil (19:17–21).

Like the horse, the lion (*leōn*) also symbolizes the powers of evil and the powers of Christ. Heb. 11:33 possibly alludes to Dan. 7. 2 Tim. 4:17 ("So I was rescued from the lion's mouth") may be taken both lit. and fig. The lion appears in apocalyptic imagery in Rev. 4:7 (cf. Ezek. 1:10); 9:8, 17; 10:3; 13:2 in both good and bad senses. The devil is compared with a roaring lion seeking whom he may devour in 1 Pet. 5:8. On the other hand, John is urged: "Weep not; lo, the Lion of the tribe of Judah, the Root of David, has conquered, so that he can open the scroll and its seven seals" (Rev. 5:5; cf. Gen. 49:9). When, however, John looks, the lion is in fact a lamb, "standing as though it has been slain, with seven horns and seven eyes, which are the seven spirits of God sent out into all the earth" (5:6).

Like the dog, the fox (*alōpēx*), the wolf (*lykos*), and the bear (*arkos*) have negative connotations. Jesus called Herod a fox (Lk. 13:32). In the context of rabbinic thought the fox could suggest both slyness and inconsequentiality (SB II 200 f.; D. Daube, *The New Testament and Rabbinic Judaism*, 1956, 191). Jesus' reminder to the disciples that foxes have holes but the Son of man has nowhere to lay his head (Matt. 8:20; Lk. 9:58) graphically expresses the utter demands made on him as Son of man and consequently upon those who would follow him. Whereas the foxes have somewhere to call their own in this world, Jesus has nowhere. False prophets are called "ravenous wolves" who come in sheep's clothing (Matt. 7:15; cf. 10:16; Lk. 10:3; Jn. 10:12; Acts 20:29; Ezek. 22:27; Zeph. 3:3; cf. G. W. H. Lampe, " 'Grievous Wolves' (Acts 20:29)", in B. Lindars and S. S. Smalley, eds., *Christ and Spirit in the New Testament*, 1973, 253–69). They call for even more

118

caution than dogs and pigs, for whereas the latter may be left alone wolves are hostile and marauding. The reference to sheep's clothing may be an allusion to the prophet's mantle as a sign of authority (cf. Matt. 3:4; Zech. 13:4). But outward signs and claims to authority are no guarantee of good intention or divine authority. The description of the apocalyptic beast (*thērion*), which is in league with the dragon and is like a leopard (*pardalis*) with feet like a bear's and a mouth like a lion's, is drawn from the OT (Rev. 13:2; cf. Dan. 7:1–8; Hos. 13:7). It has been identified with various Roman emperors such as Nero and Caligula, especially in view of the latter's recovery from a dangerous illness (cf. Rev. 13:2; R. H. Charles, op. cit., I, 349). It is followed by another beast which exercises all the authority of the first, making the earth and its inhabitants worship the first beast (13:12), performing signs and wonders and claiming absolute authority. The → number of this beast, 666 or 616 (13:18) suggests a Heb. cryptogram for Nero *redivivus* (cf. Charles, op. cit., I. 364–8). The beasts, therefore, present an image of secular power exalting itself against God and tyrannizing mankind.

The destructive power of the locust (*akris*) has already been alluded to (cf. Rev. 9:7 ff.; Exod. 10; 2 Chron. 7:13; Joel 2:25; Amos. 4:9). They were also used for food (Lev. 11:20 ff.; Matt. 3:4). The ravages of the moth (*sēs*) graphically depict the transitoriness of earthly wealth (Matt. 6:19 f.; Lk. 12:33; Jas. 5:3).

→ Bird, → Dragon, → Fish, → Lamb, Sheep   *C. Brown*

(a). G. S. Cansdale, *Animals of Bible Lands*, 1970; W. Foerster, Art. *thērion*, *TDNT* III 133 ff.; D. L. Harrison, *The Mammals of Arabia*, I, 1964; II, 1968.
(b). E. Fascher, "Jesus und die Tiere", *TLZ*, 90, 1965, 561 ff.; H. Wohlstein, "Zur Tier-Dämonologie der Bibel", *ZDMG*, 84, 1963–64, 483 ff.

Anoint

In ancient thought, various kinds of anointing oil (*elaion*) can penetrate deep into the body and impart strength, health, beauty and even joy. The idea of anointing thus gained at an early period a symbolic and religious meaning, over and above its normal use in cosmetics and medicine. Anointing in the literal, non-figurative sense is expressed in the NT by *aleiphō*, while *chriō* and *chrisma* are used exclusively in a religious and symbolic sense.

ἀλείφω

ἀλείφω, aleiphō, anoint.

CL 1. *aleiphō* occurs as early as Mycenaean Gk., and denotes the process by which soft fat (*myron*, ointment), or oil (*elaion*), is smeared upon or poured over a person or object.

2. In the ancient East, anointing gained a special significance in very early times. Anointing bowls and vessels are among the prehistoric finds in Egypt. Early on, the cleansing and strength-giving properties of ointments and oils were applied not only for purposes of purification, bodily hygiene and beautification, but also to the treatment of wounds and curing of diseases. The actual healing properties cannot be disentangled from the magical conceptions associated with anointing. Every ailment was associated with the power of gods or demons.

Anointing acquired a further significance, which may be traced to these magical ideas, when practised at the institution of an official or a vassal king in Egypt, or a priest in Babylon. Here the action indicates obligation and honour, and also protection for the one who is anointed (→ art. *chriō*). Holy trees, idols and even weapons were anointed. By this means they could be invested with special powers (→ art. *chriō* OT). Further uses of anointing are: to set a purchaser and a seller free of obligations; to free a female slave; and to release a bride from her parental home at her wedding.

OT 1. Anointing in the OT is very close in its uses and in its significance to practices outside Israel. In the LXX *aleiphō* is normally used of anointing in the lit. sense (Heb. equivalents *sûḵ* and *ṭûaḥ*): anointing for the care of the body, or for beauty's sake (Ruth 3:3; 2 Chr. 28:15; Dan. 10:3; Jdg. 16:8). It is omitted during a period of mourning (2 Sam. 14:2; cf. 12:20). Anointing by a host is a mark of care and honour for his guest (Ps. 23:5). In Ezek. 13:10–16 *aleiphō* is used in the sense of "to daub" (with whitewash). Only very occasionally is it synonymous with *chriō*, for Heb. *māšaḥ*, which signifies anointing in the symbolic sense (cf. Gen. 31:13 of the anointing of a pillar; Exod. 40:15 and Num. 3:3 of anointing to the priesthood (→ *chriō* OT)). There are a number of OT references to anointing practices where neither *aleiphō* nor *chriō* are used: for medicinal purposes (Isa. 1:6; Jer. 51:8), to express joy, (Isa. 61:3); and to honour the dead (Gen. 50:2; 2 Chr. 16:14).

2. Judaism retains the varied uses of anointing.

NT In the NT *aleiphō* occurs only 8 times (in all four gospels and in Jas.). In contrast with the more important word *chriō*, it refers consistently to the physical action of anointing, performed exclusively on people: for care of the body (Matt. 6:17); as a mark of honour to a guest (Lk. 7:38, 46; Jn. 11:2; 12:3); to honour the dead (Mk. 16:1); and to heal the sick (Mk. 6:13; Jas. 5:14). Ointments used are olive oil, or the more expensive myrrh, and balsam.

The physical action of anointing the body presents no particular problems. Its theological significance in the NT cannot, however, be reduced to a single pattern. Three ideas may be distinguished.

1. In the Sermon on the Mount (Matt. 6:17), Jesus commands all who fast in order to pray, not to stop anointing themselves. This is seen as a normal expense for personal hygiene and a general expression of joy, which should be continued during the fast. Only what is done secretly before God and not before men, and can be offered joyfully, has true worth.

2. The background of Lk. 7:38 ff. is the Jewish custom of anointing the head of a guest. Jesus here exposes the Pharisee who failed to show him this honour and who now has to watch Jesus receive it at the hands of a humble woman whom the Pharisee would regard as one of the lost. Here anointing becomes an expression of faith, and its omission an expression of unbelief. The case is similar in Jn. 12:3, where the anointing of Jesus by Mary is interpreted as an anticipation of the anointing (or honouring) of his body at death.

3. Where anointing with oil is performed on sick persons (Mk. 6:13; Jas. 5:14), we are reminded of the anointing of the sick elsewhere in the ancient world. It may be that in the NT medicinal properties were attributed to the anointing,

though these are not emphasized. Probably passages like Mk. 6:13 and Jas. 5:14 have their background rather in the practice of exorcism. Anointing is a symbolic act by which demons are cast out. The healings performed by the disciples or elders of the church were accompanied by anointing, and took place in the context of preaching and prayer. Healing, and therefore anointing also, came to be seen as a visible sign of the beginning of God's reign. The quasi-magical misunderstanding of anointing is, however, held firmly in check, especially in Jas. 5:13 ff., by the importance attached to accompanying prayer.   W. Brunotte

| χρίω |

χρίω, chriō, anoint; χρίσμα (chrisma), anointing, unction.

CL chriō (Homer onwards), touch the surface lightly, anoint, to paint. chrisma (Xenophon; earlier chrima) meant originally paint, whitewash, oil or salve used in anointing; and later (beginning with LXX) also the action of painting, smearing anointing (the latter exclusively, in NT). For non-biblical practices of anointing → aleiphō.

OT chriō occurs some 60 times in the LXX. Apart from two instances (Deut. 28:40; Ezek. 16:9, Heb, sûk), it always stands for the Heb. māšaḥ, to smear, anoint with oil or ointment. Unlike aleiphō, chriō is used basically in the symbolic ritual sense (except at Deut. 28:40 and Amos 6:6). Likewise chrisma (and chrisis which does not occur in the NT) is used consistently of ritual anointing (Exod. 30:25; 40:9 etc.).

1. (a) From the petty states of the Canaanites in the region of Syria and Palestine, Israel adopted the institution of the monarchy, and with it probably also the anointing of kings (Jdg. 9:8, 15; 1 Sam. 9:16; 10:1; 15:1, 17; 16:3, 12 f.). The OT tradition concerning the anointing of the king is not, however, uniform. In one place the anointing could be performed by the "elders of Israel" on the basis of a contract between the king and these representatives of the twelve tribes (2 Sam. 5:1–12). Elsewhere it is said to have taken place at the direct command of Yahweh, by the hand of a prophet (1 Sam. 9:16 etc.). In M. Noth's view monarchy in Israel had numerous historical roots and practices (The Laws of the Pentateuch and other Studies, 240 ff.). It does not follow, however, that we can distinguish a secular anointing (by the representatives of the people) and a sacred anointing which took place "before Yahweh" (at the hands of a prophet). We should rather conclude that, regardless of whether it was Yahweh or the people who "made" the king, the anointing of the king very soon became a sacred act forming part of the ceremony of enthronement, which took place in a holy place "before Yahweh". It is significant that, "the elevation of a person by the elders to be king originally had as its prerequisite a declaration of the divine will concerning the person who was to be the future king" (M. Noth, op. cit., 16).

The anointing gave the new king the legal right to rule over Israel. It was done from a special vessel, a horn which was kept in the temple (1 Ki. 1:39; cf. 1 Sam. 10:1; 16:1, 13), using olive oil mixed with spices (myrrh, cinnamon, calamus, etc.), which was poured over the king's head with an appointed form of words (2 Ki. 9:3, 6). The anointing formed the first part of the coronation ceremony in the temple

121

(2 Ki. 11:12; cf. the anointing of Solomon, 1 Ki. 1:33 ff., which took place at the spring of Gihon, probably a holy place). It was followed by the acclamation by the people, "Long live the king!" (2 Ki. 11:12), and finally the ascent of the throne in the royal palace (2 Ki. 11:19).

(b) The anointing signified communication of *kābôd*, the gift of authority, strength and honour (cf. Ps. 45:7), as in → blessing. Through the anointing the king became the bearer of special authority. In Ps. 45:7 f. the Psalmist sings of the robes of the anointed one, fragrant with myrrh and aloes. Through the anointing, the royal office radiates joy and fragrance (cf. H.-J. Kraus, *Psalmen*, I 336). The kind of anointing mentioned in Ps. 45, cannot be determined with certainty. "It is quite within the realms of possibility, that the royal wedding was preceded by a ceremonial repetition of the enthronement of the heir of David, at the royal feast of Zion" (H. J. Kraus, ibid.).

The sons of David were certainly regarded as David's successors to the throne (2 Sam. 7), as Yahweh's anointed, without having in every instance been symbolically anointed by a prophet. The anointing of Yahweh is sometimes coupled with the gift of the Spirit and Yahweh's special protection (1 Sam. 16:13; 24:6–11; 26:9–23; 2 Sam. 1:14 ff.; 19:21 f.; 23:1 f.; Isa. 11:2; cf. E. Kutsch, *RGG*³ V 1331). The anointed one stood in direct contact with God, and was regarded as inviolate.

2. M. Noth, G. von Rad and others think that anointing of priests came in later than that of the kings, and was practised after the exile, when, with the disappearance of the monarchy, certain cultic functions which before the exile had been performed by the king were given to the High Priest (→ Priest).

The High Priest was anointed (Exod. 29:7) and later the other priests (Exod. 40:15). This anointing took place during the 7-day-long consecration of the priests, after the preparation of the sacrifice (Exod. 29:1–3), the ritual cleansing (Exod. 29:4) and the enrobing (Exod. 29:5 f.) at the entrance of the sanctuary (Exod. 29:7; cf. 28:41; 29:29; 40:13; Lev. 4:3). The anointing made the priests sacrosanct. It separated them from the sphere of the unclean (Exod. 30:29). This same process of desecularization and sanctification could also apply to objects. The tabernacle (Exod. 40:9; Lev. 8:10; Num. 7:1), the altar (Exod. 29:26; 40:10), the vessels used in the sanctuary, and the ark (Exod. 30:26; Num. 7:1) could also be anointed.

3. In passages like Isa. 61:1 and Ezek. 16:9, the anointing is to be understood metaphorically, since in Israel ritual anointing was only available to kings and priests. Isa. 61:1 should be seen as the testimony of the prophet, who is here speaking of his charismatic endowment with authority. In the NT (Lk. 4:18) this text is applied to Jesus: he has been anointed by God to be the promised prophet.

NT In the NT *chriō* (apart from the form *christos* → Jesus Christ) is found only 5 times, and *chrisma* only 3 (all in 1 Jn.). Both words are used exclusively in a figurative sense, corresponding to their use in the LXX. Anointing is a metaphor for the bestowal of the Holy Spirit, special power, or a divine commission.

1. On 4 occasions we read of the anointing of Jesus by God (Lk. 4:18 quoting Isa. 61:1; Acts 4:27; 10:38; Heb. 1:9 quoting Ps. 45:7). All these texts indicate that a special endowment by the → Holy Spirit with supernatural power (cf. especially Acts 10:38). This anointing by the Holy Spirit (Lk. 4:18; Acts 4:27: 10:38) probably recalls what happened at Jesus' → baptism. At baptism Jesus received

the royal and priestly anointing which made him the *Christos*, the Messiah. Jesus of Nazareth was thereby declared the instrument of the gospel of the peace of God. According to Luke 4:18, Jesus read out the Isaiah passage in order to proclaim that the period which begins with him is the period of salvation. In Acts 4:27, Luke sees Psalm 2 (which has just been cited) as fulfilled in Jesus "whom thou didst anoint" *hon echrisas*, as the Christ.

Heb. 1:9 does not refer to baptism when it speaks of anointing, but to the ceremonial act of enthronement in heaven (cf. 1:3, 4). On account of (*dia*) his obedience and his endurance of suffering (Heb. 2:9), Jesus has been anointed and elevated (→ Height, art. *hypsos*) at his ascension to the rank of eschatological ruler (1:8) and high priest (5:9 f.). The anointing mentioned in the OT quotation underlines once again the theme of Heb. 1:5 ff. (cf. Pss. 2:7; 45:6 f.; 2 Sam. 7:14). The official bestowal of the rank of son, king and high priest signifies "as in Phil. 2:9, an increase in authority as compared with the earthly history of Jesus" (E. Käsemann, *Das Wandernde Gottesvolk*, 59).

2. The remaining instances refer to the anointing of Christians (the word *Christianos* is found in the NT only at Acts 11:26; 26 28, 1 Pet 4:16; → Jesus Christ, art. *christianos*). Some exegetes suggest the existence of an act of anointing before → baptism, as part of the baptismal ceremony. It is quite possible that *chrisas hēmas theos* (lit. "God having anointed us", RSV "commissioned") in 2 Cor. 1:21 and *chrisma* ("anointing") in 1 Jn. 2:20, 27 are references to baptism (see 1 above). But there is no evidence of anointing as an independent sacramental rite within the baptismal ceremony. R. Bultmann believes that: "In using this designation 'unction' John apparently has adopted a term of some Gnostic mystery-cult, against which he turns the barbs of his remarks in their own language" (*Theology of the NT*, II 88).

For Jn. the *chrisma* is the → Spirit of Truth who gives Christians the power of understanding, so that they do not need any other teacher (1 Jn. 2:27). Through their anointing they have received the Spirit, who brings to mind what Jesus has said (cf. Jn. 14:26; 15:26; 16:13 f.). The anointing of the Spirit is the power which works in the believer through the divine authoritative word. In following and abiding in Jesus (1 Jn. 2:28) and through the power of the preached word as it works in the church, the believer is given a share in the Messianic anointing of Jesus. He receives the Holy Spirit, who is able to discern the spirits (1 Jn. 4:1 ff.; 2:18).

It is difficult to determine the meaning of *chriō* in 2 Cor. 1:21 Is it baptism? Or is it a kind of adoption in faith, on the pattern of the Israelite anointing of kings? Or is it a reference to election? Verse 22 mentions the gift of the Spirit. Those exegetes are probably right who regard the three verbs (establish, anoint, seal) as three different aspects of what happens in baptism. By their spiritual anointing, Christians are made rightful members of the covenant of promise. It is possible that Paul's language here, like that of Heb. 1:9, implies a reference to a term in the Gnostic mysteries, from which he thus dissociates himself. It is not man's own choice and decision that leads him through a mystic anointing to higher knowledge of the other world and to the way of redemption. It is the decision made by God for man in Christ Jesus, which operates through faith. This is how he becomes the anointed one. *D. Müller*

123

(a) M. de Jonge, "The Word 'Anointed' in the Time of Jesus," *NovT* 8, 1966, 132–42; T. Fawcett, *Hebrew Myth and Christian Gospel*, 1973, 283–87; G. W. H. Lampe, *The Seal of the Spirit*, (1951) 1967²; W. Michaelis, *myron, TDNT* IV 800 f.; C. R. North, "The Religious Aspects of Hebrew Kingship," *ZAW* 50, 1932, 8–38; M. Noth, *The Laws in the Pentateuch and Other Studies*, 1966, 1–107, 145–78, 229–49; H. Schlier, *aleiphō, TDNT* I 229–32; S. Szikszai, "Anoint," *IDB* I 138 f. (b) H. Bardtke, "Salbung," *EKL* III 776 f.; G. Dalman, *Arbeit und Sitte in Palästina* IV, 1935, 201 ff.; E. Käsemann, *Das wandernde Gottesvolk, FRLANT* Neue Folge, 37, (1939) 1961⁴, 59 f.; H.-J. Kraus, *Psalmen*, I, (1960) 1966³, 336; E. Kutsch, G. Delling, C. A. Bouman, "Salbung," *RGG*³ V 1330 ff.; E. Kutsch, *Salbung als Rechtsakt im alten Testament und im alten Orient, BZAW* 87, 1963; D. Lys, "L'Onction dans la Bible," *Études Théologiques et Religieuses* 29, 1954, 3 ff.; F. J. Schierse, "Verheissung und Heilsvollendung," *TheolStud.* 1, 9, 1955, 112 ff.; R. Schnackenburg, *Die Johannesbriefe*, 1965², 152 f.; H. Weinel, "*mšḥ* und seine Derivate," *ZAW* 18, 1898, 1–82; J. Wellhausen, "Zwei Rechtsriten bei den Hebräern," *Archiv für Religionswissenschaft* 7, 1904, 33–41.

Antichrist

| ἀντίχριστος |

ἀντίχριστος (*Antichristos*), Antichrist; ψευδόχριστος (*pseudochristos*), false Christ.

The words *antichristos* and *pseudochristos* are first found in the second half of the 1st cent. A.D., and are creations of Christian literature.

The prep. *anti* originally meant "in the place" of and then "against". It indicates a fundamental, dualistic opposition of a kind familiar in Hellenism. Both contemporary with the NT and later we find the expression *antitheos*, anti-God (originally "like the gods" in Homer's *Iliad*). On the other hand, the compound with *pseudo*, found about 70 times in Gk., gives the word the ethical connotation of being false or deceptive.

OT The real background of the word is to be found in Jewish apocalyptic. This is the literature of a movement specially interested in calculating and describing the end of this age, the coming of the Messiah (→ Jesus Christ, art. *Christos*) and the setting up of the → Kingdom of God. Dan. 7–12 is the earliest expression of this literature which was very influential and widespread. Although it does not form a true unity, apocalyptic brings together eschatological expectations of Jewish prophecy (e.g. Isa. 26; 35; Jer. 5:1 ff.; Ezek. 37–48), elements from Babylonian and Persian dualistic mythology (→ Evil, *kakos* OT 2), classical theories about the ages (→ Time, art. *aiōn*) and explanations and veiled judgments on contemporary political events. Dating is difficult, and the visions and pictures of the course of history often remain obscure for us. Examples of pre-Christian apocalyptic writings are the Testament of the Twelve Patriarchs and most of the Ethiopian Book of Enoch; 2 Esdras and the Syriac Apc. of Baruch are approximately contemporary with the NT.

Regular features of this literature are the birth-pangs of the Messiah, the dissolution of the old age and the transition to the new age with all its terrors including plagues, diseases, wars, tyranny, miscarriages, earthquakes, and signs in the sun, moon and stars (e.g. 2 Esd. 5:50 ff.; 5:8; 6:21; Eth. Enoch 80:4 ff.; 99). Man's apostasy will increase, and all the powers of evil will arm themselves under the leadership of → Satan against God and his people. Satan is often called Beliar

(Sib. 3:63 ff.; Mart. Isa. 3:11; cf. 2 Cor. 6:15), Sammael (Mart. Isa. 2:1), or Mastema. Their personification and climax is the enemy of the people of God (e.g. Pss. Sol. 2:29(25) ff. ("the Dragon", perhaps Pompey); 8:16(5) ff. (God uses him as an instrument of punishment); 17:13(11) ("the godless one"); Sib. 3:63 ff. (Beliar does mighty signs including raising the dead, and leads many astray), 388 ff. (the man in the purple garment who causes much bloodshed). He is the rival of the Messiah (→ Jesus Christ, *Christos*) who is either the forerunner or central figure of the Kingdom of God. The greater the → tribulation the more fervently the Messiah was awaited by the godly.

The typical example of such personification is King Antiochus IV Epiphanes (the manifested god) of Syria (175–164 B.C.). Some scholars see him in Dan. 8:23 ff., depicted in more than human stature. His desecration of the Jerusalem temple by an altar to Zeus and the sacrifice there of a pig was considered to be an → "abomination of desolation", and his reign to be the breaking in of the anti-God. In Ass. Mos. 6 ff. traits of his personality have clearly been united with those of Herod the Great to form an anti-God figure. Such traits were also seen in Caligula, the Roman emperor (A.D. 37–41), who wished to erect a statue of himself in the temple at Jerusalem.

All these factors formed the expectation and concept of the Antichrist, who appears sometimes as tyrant, sometimes as false prophet. He is always in league with Satan, and may be no more than his mask. In the last analysis our constructions of the picture of Antichrist are based on inferences from Rev. 13 and similar passages, which in general are neither clear nor unambiguous.

NT If we based our thoughts only on the NT, one thing is certain. All that is said of the Antichrist is essentially negative in relation to the picture of the Christ (→ Jesus Christ, → Redemption). It gives the dark background against which his victory and his kingdom shine out the more brightly. The actual word is found only 5 times in 1 and 2 Jn. The outlines of the Antichrist are also to be found unmistakably in Mk. 13 par. (Matt. 24; Lk. 21), 2 Thess. 2:3 ff. and in Rev. They may also play a part in the story of Jesus' temptation (Matt. 4:1–11 par.).

(a) Mk. 13 par. speaks of "the abomination of desolation" (cf. Dan. 9:27; 12:11). It is personified, for the construction is masc. (RSV renders "the desolating sacrilege"). Also mentioned are false prophets (*pseudoprophētai*, → Prophet) and those who falsely claim to be the Christ (*pseudochristoi* – they say "I am He"). These may all apply to Antichrist, the deceiver, and opponent of God in all his disguises and masks. No distinction need really be made between sing. and plur.

(b) 2 Thess. 2:3 f. speaks of the man of sin (RSV tx "lawlessness", *anomia*; mg "sin", *hamartia*), the son of perdition, the opposer, who exalts himself above (RSV "against") every so-called god or object of worship, who claims to be God and takes his seat in the temple of God. This is the Antichrist, but Jesus will annihilate him with the breath of his mouth. It remains undecided whether the term "Antichrist" was unknown to Paul or whether he is deliberately writing with reserve.

(c) Rev. gives the fullest picture of the Antichrist and his war against the church of God. Here too the name is missing, but everything said in ch. 13 about the two beasts clearly contains the traits of a personified power opposed to God, which is in

125

fact a blasphemous parody of the Christ. We must interpret the number of the beast (v. 18) in terms of contemporary history with the help of the numerical symbolism then prevalent (→ Number). It cannot be decided with certainty today to whom the number 666, or possibly 616, refers. It may be Nero, or Domitian, regarded as Nero returned to life, or just the Empire. The details of the figure include traits from Dan. 7:7 ff., and comparative history suggests parallels with Babylonian and Persian mythology. But on an eschatological interpretation every one is no doubt intended who deceives and persecutes the church and blasphemes the Christ. In both cases the conqueror is Christ.

(d) In the Johannine Epistles (1 Jn. 2:18, 22 f.; 4:3; 2 Jn. 7) teachers of false doctrines are called antichrists. Both the sing. and plur. are used in 1 Jn. 2:18, otherwise only the sing. (see above (a)). No clear details are given of the doctrine. It is clear that they were claiming special fellowship with and love for God (cf. 1 Jn. 1:5 f.; 2:4 f.; 5:1 f.). But they denied that Jesus is the Christ and that he had become man (4:2 f.). The impression is also given that, convinced that they enjoyed special fellowship with God, they did not take sin very seriously (cf. 3:6 ff.). Here the deception does not come from outside but from inside the church. Members of the church had become servants of the Antichrist. Even though they had separated from the church, the danger had not disappeared.   *E. Kauder*

(a). G. C. Berkouwer, *The Return of Christ*, 1972, 260–90; W. Bousset and A. H. Keane, *The Antichrist Legend*, 1896; F. C. Grant, *Ancient Judaism and the New Testament*, 1960; G. V. Jones, *Christology and Myth in the New Testament*, 1956, 202–33; J. Michl, "Antichrist," *EBT* I 28–32; A. L. Moore, *The Parousia in the New Testament*, 1966; D. S. Russell, *The Method and Message of Jewish Apocalyptic*, 1964, 276–80; E. Stauffer, *New Testament Theology*, 1955, 213 ff.; G. Vos, *The Pauline Eschatology*, 1961², 94–135. Commentaries on the Johannine Epistles by B. F. Westcott, 1902⁴; C. H. Dodd, 1946; F. F. Bruce, 1970; R. Bultmann, 1973; and on *Thessalonians* by L. Morris, 1956.
(b). P. Althaus, *Die letzten Dinge*, 1955, 282–97; O. Betz, "Der Katechon," *NTS* 9, 1962–63, 276–91; W. Bousset and H. Gressmann, *Die Religion des Judentums im späthellenistischen Zeitalter*, 1926³; J. Jeremias, *Der Antichrist in Geschichte und Gegenwart*, 1930; E. Lohmeyer, *RAC* I 450–57; V. Maag, "Der Antichrist als Symbol des Bösen" in *Das Böse*, 1961; F. Mussner, "Das Buch Judith und die neutestamentliche Antichristidee," *Trierer theologische Zeitschrift* 72, 1963, 242 ff.; B. Rigaux, *L'Antéchrist et l'opposition au royaume messianique dans l'Ancien et le Nouveau Testament*, 1932; H. Schlier, "Vom Antichristen: Zum 13. Kapital der Offenbarung Johannes" in *Theologische Aufsätze Karl Barth zum 50. Geburtstag*, 1936, 110 ff., reprinted in *Die Zeit der Kirche*, 1958², 16–29; J. Schmid, "Der Antichrist und die hemmende Macht," *Theologische Quartalschrift* 129, 1949, 323–43; L. Sirard, "La Parousie de l'Antéchrist: 2 Thess. 2:3–9," *Studiorum Paulinorum Congressus II*, 1963, 89–100.

Apostle

ἀποστέλλω

ἀποστέλλω (*apostellō*), send; ἐξαποστέλλω (*exapostellō*), send out; πέμπω (*pempō*), send; ἀπόστολος (*apostolos*), envoy, ambassador, apostle.

CL 1. *apostellō* (Soph. onwards), a compound of *stellō*, put up, make ready, and the prep. *apo*, from, away, back, means send (both persons and things), send away, chase away, send off. Where delegation for a particular purpose is involved, the cause for sending is often particularly stressed.

Since the envoy has full powers and is the personal representative of the one sending him, a close connection is established between the sender and the recipient (cf. the formula from the 3rd cent. B.C., "the envoys (*apestalmenoi*) of the king"). This is particularly stressed by the use of *apostellō*, while *pempō*, send, which is much commoner in secular Gk., stresses the mere fact of sending. In popular Stoic philosophy the idea of the envoy's authority to represent his master acquires a religious significance. A Cynic peripatetic teacher considered himself to be an envoy and an example sent by Zeus (Epict.). Hence *apostellō* also occurs as a technical term denoting divine authorization.

2. *apostolos* is derived from *apostellō* first as a verbal adj. and then as a noun. It is first found in maritime language, where it means a cargo ship, or the fleet sent out (Dem.). Later it denoted a commander of a naval expedition, or a band of colonists sent overseas. In the papyri it can mean an invoice, or even a passport (cf. K. H. Rengstorf, *TDNT* I 408). Only in two passages in Hdt. does *apostolos* mean envoy or emissary as a *single* person. The normal terms are *angelos* (→ Angel) or *kēryx* (→ Proclamation). Josephus uses the word for a group sent on a mission (the Jews sent to Rome, *Ant.*, 17, 11, 1 (300)). All its usages have two ideas in common: (a) an express commission, and (b) being sent overseas. Thus the root meaning in the case of the noun is narrowed down.

It was probably only later in gnostic circles that *apostolos* came to convey the oriental concept of emissaries as mediators of divine revelation. There, according to the system in question it could be used in the sing. for a heavenly saviour, or in the plur. for a number of saving persons or "spiritual men".

 OT The LXX uses *apostellō* and *exapostellō* some 700 times. They are used almost exclusively to render *šālaḥ*, stretch out, send (the root meaning is to let loose, cf. Lat. *mittere*), which is translated only 5 times by *pempō*. (The latter occurs 26 times in the LXX altogether.) The translators rightly realized that the Heb. verb does not describe the sending (which could be the meaning of *pempō*) so much as its essential purpose, the authorization of the messenger (cf. Jos. 1:16; 1 Ki. 5:9(23); 20:9 (RV); 21:11; 2 Ki. 19:4; Jer. 34:3 (LXX 27:3)). Furthermore the noun *apostolos* is found only in 1 Ki. 14:6, where it translates *šālûaḥ*, the pass. part. of *šālaḥ*. Here there is no question of sending, but of the commissioning and empowering of the prophet Ahijah with a hard message for Jeroboam's wife, who was coming to consult him. Hence two conclusions may be drawn:

(a) The LXX, following the Heb. text, uses *apostellō* and its cognates to denote not the institutional appointment of someone to an office, but the authorization of him to fulfil a particular function or a task which is normally clearly defined. This explains why the vb. rather than the noun is used almost exclusively.

(b) If the sending is linked with a task in the use of *apostellō*, it follows that attention is always focused on one who sends. In other words, the stress falls on the one who gives his authority to the one whom he sends and whom he takes into his service. In the story of Isaiah's call the messenger is not even named (Isa. 6:8).

2. The common Jewish legal institution of the *šāliah* (the Aram. pass. part. of *šālaḥ*) has become important for NT exegesis. Rab. Judaism in the time of Jesus clearly recognized the function of the representative or proxy derived from the old Sem. law concerning messengers. It is expressed briefly in the principle found in the

127

Mishnah, "A man's agent (*šālûaḥ*) is like himself" (Ber. 5:5 *et al.*). Hence the messenger becomes the proxy of the one who has given him the commission (cf. 1 Sam. 25:40 f.; 2 Sam. 10:4, 6). Irrespective of the personality of the messenger or of the one who commissioned him, irrespective even of the commission, the expression *šālîaḥ* means a person acting with full authority for another (cf. W. Schmithals *The Office of Apostle in the Early Church*, 103). According to Rab. writings a *šālîaḥ* could act as a representative in a betrothal. The leader in synagogue prayer was the *šālîaḥ* of the community. Rabbis were sent as representatives of the Sanhedrin for inspections and collections, at home and in the diaspora.

These representatives were not missionaries. Jud. does not know of mission in the sense of officially sending missionaries. So *šālîaḥ* could not be used of those trying to win others for Judaism. Strangely enough, the name *šālîaḥ* is not applied to the prophets in spite of Isa. 6:8, though to have done so would have been an easy deduction from their position as messengers. Certain great men of the past, (e.g. Moses, Elijah, Ezekiel) are called God's *šᵉlûḥîm* (plur.) because of the mighty acts performed through them.

What has been said of the use of *apostellō* in the LXX applies equally to the *šālîaḥ*. The term does not denote a continuing office, important in itself, but the exercise of a function limited in scope and duration by a definite commission, and terminating on its completion.

NT A. *apostellō* is used 131 times in NT; 119 of the cases are found fairly evenly divided among the Gospels and Acts. Luke uses the compound *exapostellō* 11 times out of the 13 occurrences. In Lk. 1:53; 20:10 f. it has the force of send away, allow to go. In the 7 examples in Acts it means the same as *apostellō*. By contrast, *pempō* occurs as a virtual synonym especially in Jn. (32 times) but also in Lk. and Acts (10 or 11) times. These are writings more independent than Matt. and Mk. of the Sem. originals, including LXX (where *pempō* is used only 26 times). John's use of the two words side by side without any obvious difference is not to be put down merely to contemporary Hel. usage. It may be that he wished to stress the purely functional aspects of the term in contrast to the institutional concepts already being attached to *apostolos* (see below), and also to underline more strongly the authority of the → Lord who sends (cf. Jn. 4:34; 7:16; 14:24 with 5:36; 7:29; 17:21, 25). *E. von Eicken, H. Lindner*

B. 1. In contrast to the LXX, the frequent occurrence of the noun *apostolos* is something new. It is found 6 times in Lk., 28 in Acts, 34 in Paul, once in Heb., 3 times in Peter, once in Jude, 3 times in Rev. Matt., Mk., Jn. use it once each. In striking contrast with classical Gk., *apostolos* is used in the NT only in the general sense of messenger, and particularly as the fixed designation of a definite office, the primitive apostolate.

(a) With the exceptions of Lk. 11:49, Acts 14:14, Luke applies *apostolos* expressly to the Twelve. They had been called by the historical Jesus to their office (Lk. 6:13; cf. 1:17). They had been with him throughout his ministry from the time of John's baptism. The risen Lord had met them in various appearances (Lk. 24:36 ff.; Acts 1:3). And so they had the best possible knowledge of what Jesus had said. Before the ascension they had received the promise of the → Spirit (Acts 1:4) and the command to evangelize (Acts 1:8). By the event of Pentecost (Acts 2) they were made bearers of the Spirit, the great authorities of early Christianity who, based on Jerusalem, guarded the true tradition which went back to the historical Jesus.

According to Luke, there could be no other independent authorities beside the Apostles. They had to make or confirm every important decision (cf. Acts 15). They commissioned the Seven (6:6), though the idea of apostolic succession can hardly be based on this passage (→ Serve). They arranged the tasks in the local church (15:2 ff.), and began the mission to the Gentiles (10:1-16). So for Luke *apostolos* becomes the equivalent of membership of the Twelve. Except in 14:14, which he may have taken from another source, Luke never calls Paul an apostle. He clearly did not fulfil the preconditions for the office of an apostle which were fulfilled by the Twelve. According to Luke's account, the gap left in the circle of the Twelve by Judas' betrayal was closed by the election of Matthias (1:16-28).

(b) It is therefore remarkable that such a fundamental concept as *apostolos* should appear only once in each of the other three gospels. Jn. 13:16 cannot be understood of an office, for here it obviously means no more than messenger (cf. K. H. Rengstorf, *TDNT* I 421; R. Bultmann, *The Gospel of John*, 1971, 477 n. 4). In Matt. 10:2 the term is found at the head of the list of the Twelve before they are sent out, and in Mk. 6:30 they are called by this name when they return, their task accomplished. Both remind us of the *šālîaḥ* concept (see also ot 2). Otherwise these three gospels do not use the expression "apostle" for the Twelve.

(c) The Pauline epistles are regarded by many to have been written before Luke–Acts, and so are regarded as the oldest source of information about the technical use of *apostolos* in the NT. The following features and assumptions emerge from Paul's understanding of the office of apostle in his debates with his opponents:

(i) The → call and commissioning to lifelong service of an apostle is not through men but "through Jesus Christ and God the Father" (Gal. 1:1; cf. Rom. 1:5; 1 Cor. 1:1; 2 Cor. 1:1). It comes about through meeting with the risen Lord (1 Cor. 15:7; Gal. 1:16), who himself gives his apostle the message of the gospel (1 Cor. 11:23; 2 Cor. 4:6; Gal. 1:12). The apostle delivers the → gospel to men as Christ's "ambassador" (2 Cor. 5:20). "The service of the apostle makes it clear that the local church is not a law unto itself but under law to Christ" (E. Schweizer, *Das Leben des Herrn in der Gemeinde und ihren Diensten*, 1946, 70).

(ii) In contrast with the Jewish *šālîaḥ*, the call to the Christian apostleship is bound with the duty of mission among the Gentiles (→ People; Rom. 11:13; Gal. 2:8; cf. Rom. 10:15; 1 Cor. 1:17). Presumably the apostles were originally sent out two by two (Gal. 2:1, 9; cf. Mk. 6:7; Lk. 10:1; Acts 15:36-40). Special signs and wonders attended their work (Rom. 15:19; 2 Cor. 12:12). Their task was primarily to preach and not to baptize (1 Cor. 1:17).

(iii) Suffering is an inescapable part of the apostle's service (1 Cor. 4:9-13; 15:30 ff.; 2 Cor. 4:7-12; 11:23-29).

(iv) Like the prophets, the apostle has a special insight into the mystery (→ Secret) of Christ (1 Cor. 4:1; Eph. 3:1-6).

(v) Paul gives no suggestion that the apostle's special position (e.g. as an example, 1 Cor. 4:16; Phil. 3:17, etc.), exalts him above the church and distinguishes him from the others with spiritual gifts (1 Cor. 12:25-28; cf. Eph. 4:11; Rom. 1:11 f.). His spiritual gifts are there to fulfil definite functions in the church (→ Grace).

"The apostle knows that he also is a member of the local church" (Schweizer, ibid.). His authority is not derived from some special quality in him (2 Cor. 3:5), but from the gospel itself in its truth and power to convict (Rom. 15:18; 2 Cor. 4:2). That is why Paul takes pains to make it clear when he is giving his own opinion (1 Cor. 7:10, 12).

(vi) Paul met the risen Lord as last of the apostles (1 Cor. 15:8); if we are to take "last of all" absolutely, then there was no possibility of continuing the apostolate by calling others to it.

It is no longer clear whom Paul reckoned as apostles. He certainly belonged to their number. This is affirmed 14 times in the Pauline letters. So too did Peter (Gal. 1:18 f.), Junias, Andronicus (Rom. 16:7), and Barnabas (cf. Acts 14:14 with Gal. 2:1, 9, 13). Some doubt whether he considered James, the Lord's brother, to be an apostle, as the *ei mē* (except) of Gal. 1:19 is ambiguous. It is uncertain if he included Silvanus (2 Cor. 1:19; 1 Thess. 1:1; 2 Thess. 1:1). At any rate Paul never applies the title of apostle to the Twelve as a definite group. To interpret 1 Cor. 15:7 and Gal. 1:17, 19 as referring unambiguously to the Twelve is possible only by presupposing Lukan language. When Paul calls Titus, Epaphroditus and others "apostles of the churches" in 2 Cor. 8:23 (cf. Phil. 2:25), he is clearly not using *apostolos* as a technical term for a member of the Christian apostolate but rather as "messenger" (so AV, RV, RSV; NEB renders "delegates" in the former case). In other words, we cannot be certain whether the characteristics Paul attributed to the apostles are necessarily applicable to the NT apostle as such, or whether Paul considered the Twelve to be apostles and how numerous the apostles were in Paul's day.

(d) Light is thrown on the question whether we can equate the Twelve with the apostles by the fact that only in Rev. 21:14 are they expressly so called in the other NT writings. In 1 Tim. 1:1; 2:7; 2 Tim. 1:1; 2:11; Tit. 1:1; Eph. 1:1; Col. 1:1; 1 Pet. 1:1 and 2 Pet. 1:1 *apostolos* refers to the writer. In Heb. 3:1 the title is given to Jesus.

(e) It is clear then that, apart from the general meaning of messenger or envoy, two differing concepts lie behind the NT use of "apostle". We must ask the questions: Where did the idea and institution of Christian apostleship come from? When did the Twelve begin to bear the name "apostle"? What is the relation between their apostleship and that of Paul? What was the origin of the differing concepts of Paul and Luke? If the circle of apostles in the time of Paul was obviously wider than that of the Twelve, and possibly did not include it, how was the title attributed and even confined to them? These questions may not be answered by questioning the textual accuracy of our sources or by a false harmonization, which may involve the elimination of certain passages.

2. NT scholars have attempted to trace the sources of the Christian concept of apostleship and the reasons for its varied forms by using the results of investigations in the history of religion, and in the historic background and development of the period. Some typical attempts at a solution may be mentioned.

(a) For a long time scholarship has been dominated by the view best expounded by K. H. Rengstorf. This maintains that both linguistically and functionally Christian apostleship was derived from the Jewish institution of the *šālîaḥ*. It is firmly linked with the history of the earthly Jesus by passages like Mk. 6:7–13 par.; 9:28–32; Matt. 10:40 ff.; and Lk. 10:16.

130

After a period for hearing and learning Jesus appointed his disciples as apostles (who included more than the Twelve) by sending them out and setting them to active work (Matt. 10:1–5; Mk. 6:7–11; Lk. 9:10; cf. *TDNT* I 424 ff.). In other words the apostolate was originally not an office but a commission "in the sense of the authorization which is limited in time and space, and which is conditioned materially rather than personally, as in the Jewish concept of *šāliaḥ*" (loc cit., 427) This commission was renewed, but modified, by the risen Lord, for the apostles were now called to an authoritative position (i) as Spirit-empowered witnesses of the resurrection, (ii) for their whole life, (iii) with a missionary responsibility. Through this the apostolate received the character of an office, but we can no longer determine the size of the apostolic circle, though the Twelve were its chief members.

A special position was occupied by Paul, who had been neither one of the disciples nor one of the earliest Christians. Since he saw his equality with the Twelve doubted, Paul felt compelled "to establish his apostolate in a way which saved him from a verdict of inferiority and at the same time proved to be of basic importance for the whole conception and claim of the early Christian apostolate" (loc. cit. 437). In spite of this, he consciously desired to remain with the primitive tradition about Jesus (1 Cor. 11:23–26; 15:1–7; etc.), which "constitutes the unity" between him and the original apostles, however many the differences between them (Acts 15:12; cf. Gal. 2:9 and especially 1 Cor. 15:11; cf. Rengstorf, loc. cit., 437). Paul was probably the first to link the apostolate with a meeting with the glorified Christ and to link it with the consciousness of being sent possessed by the OT prophets. It is he who shows us the classical picture of the apostle (loc. cit., 439).

(b) A weighty argument against this view nevertheless continued to be heard. It is impossible to prove exegetically from our texts, except Luke, that Jesus transmitted the office of apostle to the Twelve, either during his earthly activity, or immediately after his resurrection. A. v. Harnack had argued that the title of apostle was reserved for the Twelve first by Paul's opponents, and Paul had then included himself in that circle, thus fixing his own status (*Die Lehre der Zwölf Apostel*, 1884, 116). This was expanded by a group of scholars, including A. Fridrichsen, E. Lohse and J. Munck, who asked whether the concept of "apostle" had not first been attributed to the originally non-apostolic Twelve during the Pauline controversies (cf. G. Klein, *Die Zwölf Apostel*, 53). The original title of "apostle" had been given to the missionaries and travelling preachers sent out by the churches, especially the primitive church in Jerusalem, and not to the Twelve, who remained in Jerusalem as eschatological "pillars" (cf. Gal. 2:9), and with the exception of Peter (1 Cor. 9:5) never thought of missionary activity, but confined their preaching to Israel (E. Lohse, "Ursprung und Prägung des christlichen Apostolats", *ThZ* 9, 1953, 264 f.). Paul did not have this authorization as *šāliaḥ* from the primitive church; in the face of remonstrances he had to base his apostolate Jesus Christ himself. He recognized, however, that the Twelve, especially Peter had it in the same way. "The result was that 'apostle' acquired a well-defined meaning and was confined to the Twelve and Paul. Only they were in a true sense apostles of Jesus Christ. Thanks to Paul the old concept of the Twelve (*dōdeka*) receded, and in the Gentile church 'apostle' took its place" (E. Lohse, loc. cit., 269). Luke finally carried back the result of this development into his description of the life of Jesus and of the first apostolic age. Quite logically he omits Paul from the list of apostles. The gap in the circle was filled by Matthias before Paul began his career as the great world missionary.

The question has rightly been asked whether Gal. 2:7 and 1:18 f. will permit this hypothesis (cf. G. Klein, *Die Zwölf Apostel*, 1961, 54 ff.). It would follow, e.g., that the "other apostles" of 1 Cor. 9:5 would simply be "delegates of the churches" amongst whom Paul – against the run of his argument – would have numbered himself as an "authorized itinerant preacher" (Lohse). It is far more likely that Paul was using an already common meaning of "apostle" and not coining a new one for his argument. The same inference may be drawn from his formula "an apostle of Jesus Christ" in the superscription of many of his letters (1–2 Cor., Gal., Eph., Col.).

(c) It is not surprising that scholars have looked for other solutions of the problem. H. v. Campenhausen considers that the origins of the apostolate in the primitive church elude research, but the Twelve were probably instituted by the historical Jesus ("Der urchristliche Apostolatsbegriff", *StTh* 1, 1948, 96–130; *Ecclesiastical Authority and Spiritual Power in the Church in the First Three Centuries*, 1969, 12–29). Paul, for whom we have first-hand information, did not consider himself to be essentially an exception. He was an apostle like the rest. For him "the apostles – and he is deliberately using an existing term – are the foundation-laying preachers of the Gospel, missionaries and church founders possessing the full authority of Christ and belong to a bigger circle in no way confined to the Twelve" (*StTh* 1, 127). Paul did not create a new concept of apostleship, and the limitation to the Twelve occurred after his death.

Luke took over a picture of the apostles conditioned by the disappearance of "living members of 'the apostolic generation' " (ibid., 117) and an idealized concept of the Twelve (in some cases because of the influence of old rivalries). He considered the Twelve to have been "above all the authoritative witnesses of the life and resurrection of Jesus, and moreover the initiators, first teachers and leaders of the whole Church" (ibid., 127).

This view too was inadequate to answer all the problems. If the Twelve "as a whole" could hardly have been considered "apostles from the first", how are we to understand their commissioning by the historical Jesus? And if their commissioning as apostles goes back to the historical Jesus, then surely an "idealization" of them cannot have caused the apostolate to have been restricted to them in the eyes of the first post-apostolic generation. In addition von Campenhausen acknowledges that some survivors of "the apostolic generation" must have long continued, so "such a restriction cannot have been due to a reaction to a lack of living apostles" (cf. Klein, op. cit., 62). We must also ask whether we should generally speak of a limitation of the apostolic circle or rather of a transference of the title of apostle to the Twelve (cf. W. Schmithals, *The Office of Apostle in the Early Church*, 266). In addition we must ask whether Paul coined the formula "apostle of Jesus Christ", or whether he took it over and was responsible for its becoming a technical term.

(d) The work of G. Klein and W. Schmithals to some extent questions the whole basis of earlier studies. They claim that a relationship between the Christian office of apostle and the institution of the *šālîaḥ* is unprovable. The earliest use of *šālîaḥ* in Heb. texts in such a sense is in A.D. 140 or later. Furthermore, the term is purely juridical, limited in time, and never applied to missionaries or OT prophets. But apostleship has a religious connotation, is eschatological in character and life-long, and the missionary charge cannot be separated from it. The *šālîah* expects his message to be received because of his authorization, but the legitimacy of the apostle is proved by his message. Apart from the fact that both are sent, *šālîah* and apostle have nothing in common (Schmithals, op. cit., 96–110; Klein, op. cit., 26 ff.).

According to Schmithals, there is only one notion of apostleship to be found in Paul, but it was not invented by him (op. cit., 22 ff.). It derived from Jewish or Jewish-Gnostic circles as a title for redeemer figures or heavenly emissaries (op. cit., 114–192). These featured in Mesopotamian speculative thought which gnosticism took over. Jewish-Christian gnosticism and the church's apostolate both originate in the region of Syria. Schmithals claims that the characteristic features of apostle-ship in the church correspond to those of gnosticism. The idea spread from the missionary centre at Antioch to the Gentile church at large. In both gnosticism and the church the emissary does not come from the community (op. cit., 198). In both cases mission is entrusted to the apostle (op. cit., 200). The apostle in the church is "called" by the exalted Christ; "the relationship of the genuine Gnostic to Christ is one of identity of being" (op. cit., 204). Since for the gnostic apostle Christ himself is the gospel, Paul's claim to have received his apostleship "not from man, nor through men, but through Jesus Christ and God the Father" (Gal. 1:1; cf. 2 Cor. 12:1) is readily comprehensible (op. cit., 206 ff.).

Schmithals also claims that the terminology indicates gnostic origin: "for *apostolos* and *apostellein* belong to the most characteristic and most original technical expressions of Gnosticism in general, and can only have been given by Gnosticism to Christianity, but never by Christianity to Gnosticism" (op. cit., 230). At all events, the first Christian missionaries who came from the region of Syria were called apostles. Peter soon came to be so called because of his missionary work. The title was then quite naturally extended to others among the Twelve, as tradition increasingly identified them with the leadership of the Gentile mission (op. cit., 231–271). However, Paul who came into direct contact with gnosticism only relatively late did not realize his dependence on gnosticism.

Schmithals's argument fails, however, to explain why, when the title of apostle came to be applied to the Twelve, all the others who had previously been called apostles lost their status (cf. G. Klein, op. cit., 64). Nor does his exegesis explain passages like Gal. 1:17 and 1 Cor. 15:7 with their evidence of apostles in the primi-tive church at Jerusalem (op. cit., 64 ff.). Moreover, in gnosticism the apostle is the pneumatic or spiritual man (op. cit., 175 ff.). How then could this description of the gnostic in general give rise to the idea of apostleship in the church which was much more than a mere term for a function? (cf. G. Klein, op. cit., 63, n. 277).

Schmithals holds that the use of "apostle" to designate the Twelve did not result from the controversies between Paul and the Jerusalem church, but arose in the late post-apostolic age (op. cit., 277–288). The institution of apostleship in general goes back not to the historical Jesus, but to the exalted Lord. G. Klein goes further. He considers the idea of the Twelve as apostles to be the tendentious invention of Luke to help in the struggle against gnosticism, by making the Twelve the only legitimate bearers of the divine message, commissioned and sent out by Jesus. He wrote at the beginning of the 2nd cent., and knew of the Pauline epistles but did not

133

use them. By witholding from Paul the title of apostle, he put him on a lower level. To deprive the gnostics of the Pauline epistles and to maintain the church's tradition, Luke transferred apostleship to the Twelve, subordinated Paul to them and erased all traces of a wider circle of apostles. Thus he identified the circle of disciples with that of the Twelve, and read this back into the life of Jesus (op. cit., 190 ff.; cf. Schmithals, op. cit., 265–278).

E. Haenchen's criticism is justified, that Klein's theory stands or falls with the proof that no one before or contemporaneously with Luke amalgamated the Twelve and the "apostles" into the combination of the "Twelve Apostles" (*The Acts of the Apostles*, 1971, 123 ff.). Klein has to reinterpret or dub as later interpolations all these passages which are older than the date he attributes to Luke and which connect apostleship with the Twelve (e.g. Rev. 21:14; 1 and 2 Pet., cf. 1 Clem.; Barn.). In many cases this is impossible. It is easier to believe that Luke was already familiar with a tradition that gave such a standing to the Twelve, and which existed independently of the Pauline tradition (cf. also Schmithals, op. cit., 263).

3. We are forced by the perplexing multitude of attempts at a solution to the conclusion that the darkness that lies over the beginnings of the primitive Christian apostolate can no longer be illuminated with certainty. In any case, if we take the growth of the canon seriously, we shall have to recognize that the concepts of the apostolate vary in the various NT writings. However we try to understand these various conceptions in their historical setting, we cannot avoid hypotheses. That does not free us from the duty of choosing the most probable of these, and of constantly checking and questioning it anew.

We may take it as incontrovertible that the missionary commission was an essential part of the primitive Christian apostolate. If we bear in mind, however, that the twelve disciples were tied to Jerusalem by their eschatological role as representatives of the twelve tribes of Israel, it is unlikely that Jesus himself, either before or immediately after his resurrection, appointed them as apostles in the sense in which that office was later understood. It is also hardly credible that a circle of disciples with such authority derived from their Lord himself should have lost its precedence already by the time of the Apostolic Council, so that one was soon no longer certain who the Twelve were. Finally how could Mark, Matthew and, circumstances permitting, John also have concealed without apparent reason the fact that Jesus had appointed a circle of twelve apostles?

The present writer considers that the investigations of Schmithals and Klein make it impossible to take in the institution of the *šālîaḥ* as the basis of apostleship in the church. This does not mean that every influence from that quarter is to be excluded. Strangely enough, overtones of the *šālîaḥ* occur particularly in passages, where *apostolos* is not used in a technical sense (e.g. Jn. 13:16). In Matt. 10:2 and Mk. 6:30 the later technical term is applied to the disciples as representatives of Jesus.

We consider that NT scholarship has not sufficiently considered the meaning of the vb. *apostellō* as a starting point for a solution. Already in secular Gk. "to send" was used as a technical term for a divine authorization, and its sub. was used, admittedly very rarely, with the meaning "messenger". Since the Hellenistic churches could not be assumed to have an understanding for the concept of the *šālîaḥ*, the Gentile Christians would understand apostle in exactly this sense. If we consider too that the LXX uses this term for the mission of the prophets, we shall ask ourselves whether OT prophecy cannot serve as a positive basis for the special concept of apostleship in the primitive church. If that is so, the primitive church chose, as it so often did, an unfamiliar word, seldom used in the secular language, with little ready-made content, in order to fill it with one expressing its own conceptions. Missionaries specially called by the Lord bore this title. It was soon applied to Peter, the only disciple, at least known to us, active in missionary work. Paul was included in this circle because of his special meeting with the risen Lord. We can no longer establish, even hypothetically, how numerous the circle was in Paul's day. It is through Paul's controversy with his gnostic opponents that we know the general features of this apostleship.

After the time of Paul, when the Twelve became more and more regarded as the only legitimate bearers of the message of Jesus as the Christ, and the conviction became general that they had been the initiators of the mission to the Gentiles, the title of apostle was gradually transferred to the whole circle of the Twelve. It may possibly have been through Luke that the title of apostle was finally confined to the Twelve, in the more restricted technical sense, indicating their role as guarantors of the legitimate tradition.

Whether things happened like this or in some other way, one thing is certain. The NT never betrays any understanding of the apostolate as an institutionalized church office, capable of being passed on. The varied statements make it clear that the adoption and transformation of the concept of apostleship by the primitive church had an important and possibly decisive influence in preventing the disintegration of the witness to Christ and maintaining the continuity of its tradition down to the time when the canon of the NT was fixed (→ Rule). It was due to the office of the apostolate that the link between the Crucified and the Exalted, between the earthly Jesus and the Christ of the proclamation, was preserved.

D. Müller

Note on Apostleship in Luke–Acts

The above article reflects the tendency in German scholarship to see a sharp distinction between the picture in Luke–Acts and that in the Pauline writings and other gospels. English-speaking scholars, whilst recognizing Luke's special interests, are on the whole less inclined to see a conflict of attitudes over apostleship and the Twelve (cf. A. M. Farrer in K. E. Kirk, ed., *The Apostolic Ministry*, (1946) 1957[2], 119–41; E. M. B. Green, *Called to Serve*, 1964, 11–32; L. Morris, *Ministers of God*, 1964, 39–61; A. Ehrhardt, *The Apostolic Succession*, 1953, 11–34; M. H. Shepherd, *IDB*, I 171 f.).

The omission to make explicit reference to the "Twelve" as such at the Jerusalem Council in Acts 15 may be due to the author's taking their identity for granted in the light of his previous identification of the twelve disciples with apostles (Lk. 6:12–16; Acts 1:13–26). The fact that in the council's decision-making they are accorded no special pre-eminence does not compel the conclusion that they did not exist. It is consonant with the non-authoritarian, collegiate character of church leadership which Acts consistently depicts (1:13–26; 6:2 ff.; 8:14 ff.; 11:1 ff.; 13:1–4). It is, moreover, consonant with the teaching of the gospels and epistles on → humility and → service.

It can hardly be said that Acts plays down the call and commissioning of Paul which it records no less than three times (9:1–19; 22:1–21; 26:2–18). We would hardly expect Paul to be given the title of apostle at his conversion. Nevertheless, the Lord reveals to Ananias that Paul is "a chosen instrument of mine to carry my name before the Gentiles and kings and the sons of Israel" (9:15), and Luke's account of Paul's words contain the vbs. *exapostellō* ("Depart; for I will send you far away to the Gentiles," 22:21) and *apostellō* ("I have appeared to you for this purpose to appoint you to serve and bear witness to the things in which you have seen me and to those in which I will appear to you, delivering you from the people and from the Gentiles – to whom I send you," 26:16 f.). In encountering the risen Christ on the Damascus road, Paul fulfilled a basic qualification for apostleship, that of being "a witness to his resurrection" (Acts 1:22). He did not fulfil the other condition, that of being a follower of Jesus in his earthly ministry. In short, the picture that Acts paints is not that Paul was not an apostle, but that he was an apostle extraordinary which is consonant with Paul's own account (1 Cor. 9:1 ff.; 15:5–9; Gal. 1:12–17). Whilst Acts presents the Jerusalem apostles as a closely-knit body working separately from Paul (e.g. 8:14; 9:27; 15:2; 16:4), it does speak of Paul and Barnabas as apostles (14:4, 14).

The difference of emphasis between Luke and the other evangelists is also less sharp than may appear at first sight. *apostolos* occurs in Matt. 10:2 (=Lk. 6:13) and Mk. 6:30 (=Lk. 9:10). Luke uses the term on only 5 more occasions of which 11:49 may simply mean one sent by God and the other occasions are patently synonyms for the disciples (17:5 (cf. 17:1); 9:10; 22:14; 24:10). The use of the term in all four gospels appears to be by the application of a term familiar at the time of writing but which was not necessarily current at the time when the incidents described happened. All four gospels give accounts of the call of the disciples (Matt. 10:2–4; Mk. 3:16–19; Lk. 6:14 ff. (cf. Acts 1:13); and Jn. 1:35–43). In all four (but especially Matt.) the disciples are called the → Twelve. During the earthly ministry of Jesus they figure as learners (→ Disciple). And in all four they are sent as → witnesses to the risen Christ (Matt. 28:16–20; Mk. 16:7 (cf. 3:14); Lk. 24:46 ff. (cf. Acts 1:8); Jn. 20:21 ff., 30 f.; 21:15 ff., 24).   *C. Brown*

→ Bishop, Presbyter, Elder, → Disciple, → Number, → Serve

(a). K. Barth, *CD* II, 2, 431–49; IV, 1, 714–25; C. K. Barrett, *The Signs of an Apostle*, 1970 and *The Second Epistle to the Corinthians*, 1973; R. E. Brown, K. P. Donfried and J. Reumann, eds., *Peter in the New Testament*, 1973; F. F. Bruce, *The Acts of the Apostles*, 1952²; H. von Campenhausen, *Ecclesiastical Authority and Spiritual Power in the First Three Centuries*, 1969; O. Cullmann *Peter: Disciple, Apostle, Martyr*, 1962²; A. Ehrhardt, *The Apostolic Succession in the First Two Centuries of the Church*, 1953; *The Acts of the Apostles*, 1969; and *The Apostolic Ministry*, 1958; A. Fridrichsen, *The Apostle and his Message*, 1947; S. Freyne, *The Twelve: Disciples and Apostles. A Study in the Theology of the First Three Gospels*, 1968; L. Goppelt, *Apostolic and Post-Apostolic Times*, 1970; E. M. B. Green, *Called to Serve*, 1964; E. Haenchen, *The Acts of the Apostles*, 1971; A. T. Hanson, *The Pioneer Ministry*, 1961; O. Karrer, *Peter and the Church: An Examination of Cullmann's Thesis*, 1963; J. A. Kirk, "Apostleship since Rengstorf: Towards a Synthesis", *NTS* 21, 1974-75, 249-64; K. E. Kirk, ed., *The Apostolic Ministry* (1946) 1957²; K. Lake, "The Twelve and the Apostles", in F. J. Foakes-Jackson and K. Lake, eds., *The Beginnings of Christianity* Pt. 1, vol. 5, 1933, 37–59; T. M. Lindsay, *The Church and the Ministry in the Early Centuries*, 1902; T. W. Manson, *The Church's Ministry*, 1948; and *Ministry and Priesthood: Christ's and Ours*, 1958; H. Mosbech, "*Apostolos* in the New Testament," *StTh* 2, 1949–50, 166–200; J. Munck, *Paul and the Salvation of Mankind*, 1959, 11–68; and "Paul, the Apostles, and the Twelve," *StTh* 3, 1950–51,

96–110; D. W. O'Connor, *Peter in Rome: The Literary, Liturgical, and Archaeological Evidence*, 1969; L. Morris, *Ministers of God*, 1964; P. M. Peterson, *Andrew, Brother of Simon Peter*, 1963; K. H. Rengstorf, *apostolos*, *TDNT* I 407–45; and *Apostolate and Ministry: The New Testament Doctrine of the Office of Ministry*, 1969; B. Rigaux, *Letters of St. Paul*, 1968, 40–67; M. H. Shepherd, "Apostle," *IDB* I, 170 ff.; R. Schnackenburg, "Apostles Before and During Paul's Time," in W. W. Gasque and R. P. Martin, eds., *Apostolic History and the Gospel*, 1970, 287–303; W. Schmithals, *The Office of Apostle in the Early Church*, 1971; E. Schweizer, *Church Order in the New Testament*, 1961; and *Lordship and Discipleship*, 1960; J. Weiss, *Earliest Christianity*, II, (1937) 1959, 673–87.

(b). O. Betz, *Nachfolge und Nachahmung Jesu Christi im Neuen Testament*,1957; P. Bläser, "Zum Problem des urchristlichen Apostolats," *Unio Christianorum*, 1962, 92–107; H. von Campenhausen, "Der urchristliche Apostelbegriff; *StTh* I, 1948–49, 96–130; J. Dupont, "Le nom d'apôtres a-t-il été donné aux Douze par Jésus?", *L'Orient Syrien* 1, 1956, 266–90 and 425–44; P. Gaechter, *Petrus und seine Zeit*, 1958; B. Gerhardsson, *Die Boten Gottes und die Apostel Christi*, 1962; M. Hengel, *Nachfolge und Charisma: Eine exegetisch-religionsgeschichtliche Studie zu Mt. 8:21 ff. und Jesu Ruf in die Nachfolge*, 1968; K. Heussi, *Die römische Petrustradition in kritischer Sicht*, 1955; H. Kahlefeld, *Der Jünger: Eine Auslegung der Rede Lk. 6, 20–49*, 1966³; E. Käsemann, *Die Legitimität des Apostels*, 1942; G. Klein, *Die zwölf Apostel: Ursprung und Gehalt einer Idee*, *FRLANT* 59, 1961; E. M. Kredel, "Der Apostelbegriff in der neueren Exegese," *ZKT* 78, 1956, 169–93 and 257–305; and "Apostel," in H. Fries, ed., *Handbuch theologischer Grundbegriffe*, I, 1962, 61–7; E. Lohse, "Ursprung und Prägung des christlichen Apostolats," *ThZ* 9, 1953, 259–75; W. Maurer, "Paulus als der Apostel der Völker," *EvTh* 19, 1959, 28 ff.; W. Nagel, "Paulus als der Apostel der Völker," *EvTh* 19, 1959, 28 ff.; K. H. Rengstorf, ed., *Das Paulusbild in der neueren Deutschen Forschung*, 1969²; H. Riesenfeld, "Apostel," *RGG*³ 1497 ff.; A. Schulz, *Nachfolge und Nachahmen: Studien über das Verhältnis der neuttestamentlichen Jüngerschaft zur urchristlichen Vorbildethik*, 1962.

Avarice, Greed, Love of Money

| $\pi\lambda\varepsilon o\nu\varepsilon\xi\acute{\iota}\alpha$ |

$\pi\lambda\varepsilon o\nu\varepsilon\xi\acute{\iota}\alpha$ (*pleonexia*), greediness, insatiableness, avarice, covetousness; $\pi\lambda\varepsilon o\nu\varepsilon\kappa\tau\acute{\varepsilon}\omega$ (*pleonekteō*), take advantage of, outwit, defraud, cheat; $\pi\lambda\varepsilon o\nu\acute{\varepsilon}\kappa\tau\eta\varsigma$ (*pleonektēs*), one who is greedy, a covetous person.

CL Etymologically the words connected with *pleonexia* are related to *pleon* (more) and *echō* (have). Gk. writers did not confine their use of these words merely to the desire for more material possessions. In the earliest instance of it, *pleonexia* denotes immoral lust for power (Herodotus, 7, 149). In Thucydides (3, 82) it is, together with *philotimia* (ambition), the decisive force in human action and the progress of history. In Plato *pleonekteō* means both to surpass someone in a just action and also to defraud. The noun is used by Plato and Aristotle always negatively in the sense of desire and covetousness, including sexual desire. There is no room for *pleonexia* in a just society. The Cynics and Stoics repudiated all desire, for possessions of any kind meant attachment to what is empty.

OT In the LXX the word group occurs only occasionally. It appears chiefly in the denunciations and warnings of the prophets about dishonest gain and the enrichment by violence of the politically powerful (Jer. 22:17; Ezek. 22:27; Hab. 2:9). In 2 Macc. 4:50 *pleonexia* refers to coveting gain by bribery. The emphasis thus falls on the ungodly and thoroughly bad character of covetousness. For that reason the person praying in Ps. 119 asks to be preserved from *pleonexia* (v. 36 LXX).

137

NT 1. In the NT the words of this group are found only in Paul, apart from the use of *pleonexia* in Mk. 7:22; Lk. 12:15; and 2 Pet. 2:3, 14. The action denoted by them is always judged negatively, and except in 2 Cor. 2:11 it always appears to be directed towards material gain. Thus *pleonekteō* (2 Cor. 7:2; 12:17 f.; 1 Thess. 4:6; 2 Cor. 2:11) means to take advantage of, wrong, defraud, or cheat. *pleonektēs* (1 Cor. 5:10 f.; 6:10; Eph. 5:5) means a greedy person, someone who is covetous. *pleonexia* (in the passages cited above and Rom. 1:29; 2 Cor. 9:5; Eph. 4:19; 5:3; Col. 3:5; 1 Thess. 2:5) means greed, avarice, covetousness, insatiableness.

2. In the catalogues of vices *pleonexia* is a mark of a life which lacks knowledge of God (Rom. 1:29; 1 Cor. 6:10 f.), faith and obedience (1 Cor. 5:10 f.; Eph. 5:3). Where the bond between creature and creator is severed, human society falls into disorder. The man who no longer has his goal and fulfilment in God seeks fulfilment in himself, his possessions and acquisitiveness. Ultimately he makes himself into an idol that strives to subject everything to itself. For that reason Col. 3:5 identifies covetousness with idolatry (*eidōlolatria;* → Image, art. *eidōlon*). In Matt. 6:24 and Lk. 16:13 Mammon (→ Possessions, art. *mamōnas*,) wealth itself, is an idol which holds in its sway the man who seems to control it. 1 Thess. 4:6 lays down the rule that no one should "transgress, and wrong his brother in the matter" (RSV; "defraud his brother in business" RSV mg.; *to mē hyperbainein kai pleonektein en tō pragmati ton adelphon autou*). It is not clear whether this general rule refers to sexual relations outside marriage (as the previous vv. suggest) or whether it refers to business conduct (cf. RSV mg.).

3. For Christians there can be no association with men of this sort in the church (1 Cor. 5:11). By their *pleonexia* they exclude themselves from it and ultimately from the → Kingdom of God (1 Cor. 6:10; Eph. 5:5; → Possessions, arts. *ploutos* and *chrēma*). Like immorality and impurity, covetousness must be strictly kept out of the life of the church (Eph. 5:5). (The latter verse is not to be understood in a narrow literal sense, cf. H. Schlier, *Der Brief an die Epheser*, 1957, 233.) Col. 3:5 urges its readers to "Put to death what is earthly in you: immorality, impurity, passion, evil desire, and covetousness which is idolatry." This recalls Matt. 5:29 f. and urges that the physical nature enslaved in sin be subjected to the rule of the new spiritual life, with its transforming liberating power revealed in Christ (Col. 3:3 f.; → Flesh, → Spirit).

4. According to 2 Pet., false teachers are characterized by their greed for material gain (2:3, 14). Similarly, Paul's opponents are "peddlers of God's word" (2 Cor. 2:17 RSV, *kapēleuontes ton logon tou theou*). Against this Paul can point out that as a rule he earned his keep with his own hands (Phil. 4:15; 1 Thess. 2:9). Even in Corinth it could not be argued that he and his co-workers had desired to enrich themselves by their service (2 Cor. 7:2; 12:17). But with regard to the collection for Jerusalem, Paul could ask in urgent terms for a liberal gift (2 Cor. 8f.).

F. Selter

φιλαργυρία

φιλαργυρία (*philargyria*), love of money, avarice, miserliness.

In 1 Tim. 6:10 *philargyria* (lit. love of money) is described as "the root of all evils" (*rhiza pantōn tōn kakōn*).→ Evil, art. *kakos*. The saying sounds exaggerated. It may, however, be seen against the background of an ancient proverb which expresses a pagan philosophical judgment on all material things. Democritus and others described the love of money as the "metropolis" of all evil (Diog. Laert., 6, 50). But what is said in this text comes of experience. The dream of wealth and happiness can gain a demonic hold over a man or a nation.

The proverb gets its point in its biblical context through its application to man's relationship with God. Selfish amassing of material possessions has its prototype in man's grasping after the forbidden fruit in the garden of Eden. It is an indication that life, limited as it is by time, circumstance and the vital interests of others, is no longer accepted thankfully from the hand of God. Love of money erects a selfish dividing wall against God and our neighbours. It drives the man who is possessed by it into utter isolation. Thus striving after wealth is the germ of total alienation from God.   *G. Finkenrath*

→ Possessions

(a). G. Delling, *pleonektēs, pleonekteō, pleonexia*, TDNT VI 266–74.
(b). E. Klaar, *pleonexia, pleonektēs, pleonektein, ThZ* 10, 1954, 395 ff.; S. Lyonnet, " 'Tu ne convoiteras pas' (Rom. vii 7)," in *Neotestamentica et Patristica* (O. Cullmann Festschrift), 1962, 157–65; H. Schlier, *Der Brief an die Epheser*, 1957; W. Schrage, *Die konkreten Einzelgebote der paulinischen Paränese: Ein Beitrag zur neutestamentlichen Ethik*, 1961.

Babylon

| Βαβυλών |

Βαβυλών (*Babylōn*), Babylon; Heb. *Bābel*, Babel, Babylon.

CL 1. We do not know when Babylon was founded. The earliest known reference is from the time of Sarkali-sharri of Accad (*c.* 2500–2290 B.C.). It is to Kadingir or Bâb-ilim, Gate of God, which may possibly be the popular etymology of a pre-Semitic name Babila. The name of Bab. *ziggurat* E-temen-an-ki, the House of the Foundation of Heaven and Earth, may be compared with the name Beth-el, the House of God, given to the holy stone of Bethel (Gen. 28:17). [*Tr.* But the suggestion that what Jacob saw was a *ziggurat* and not a ladder (v. 12) has little support.] The Gk. form expresses the later variation Bab-ilani, Gate of the Gods.

2. Until the time of Hammurapi (or Hammurabi), probably 1728–1686 B.C. ([Tr.] or 1792–1750 B.C.) the town had little historical importance. Hammurapi was responsible for making it the cultural leader of the Near East. This lasted until the Hel. period. This was partially due to making Marduk the city god of Babylon, and so the head of the Sumerian-Accad. pantheon of some 1300 deities. It brought all the religious traditions into one system. He made of Babylon a world power and the successor of the world power of the Accad. kings Sargon and Naramsin (probably 24th cent. B.C.), even though this did not last long. Babylon developed, independently of Greece, scientific knowledge, the major developments of which were in mythology, philology, medicine, mathematics and (1st cent.) astronomy (cf. Dan. 1:4, 17). Babylon did not regain political power until the time of the Chaldean kings (625–539 B.C.), the most important of whom was Nebuchadnezzar or Nebuchadrezzar II (605–562 B.C.). Its immense riches came from its far-reaching commercial traffic. Among the Greeks and Romans it was proverbial for its trade and magnificence.

OT Babylon is mentioned in the OT only in 1. the Yahwistic prehistory (Gen. 10:8–12; 11:1–9); and 2. in the history of the decline and fall of the kingdom of Judah and of the exile.

1. (a) Gen. 10:8–12 traces back the concept of world dominion to Babylon: Babylon, Erech, Accad, Kalneh (instead of the latter unidentified town RSV has "all of them"). After that, dominion passed to Assyria: Ashur, Nineveh, Rehoboth-Ir, Kalach (or Calah, today Nimrūd). Gen. 10:9 describes Nimrod as "a mighty hunter before the Lord". In the Assyrian pantheon he may well be regarded as Ninurtu, god of Kalach, and of the chase and war.

(b) In Gen. 11:1–9 the architecture of the giant temple of Babylon is stigmatized as the expression of human. pride that wishes to storm heaven. God himself

140

prevented its completion. This conception is doubtless linked with the fact that E-temen-an-ki, 295 feet long, broad and high – in the ancient world only the three main pyramids were higher – was in all probability begun at a very early, and certainly pre-Israelite date, but was completed only under Nebuchadrezzar II. Both references in Gen. show an anti-Babylonian note.

2. As a result of the exile we find four types of statement:

(a) The king of Babylon is Yahweh's instrument for the destruction of Judah and its allies (Jer. 25:9; 27:6 f.). He bears Yahweh's sword in his world conquest (Ezek. 30:24 f.). Judah will be destroyed because of its harlotry with Assyria and Babylon, in view of the introduction of their cults when on friendly terms with them (Ezek. 23:11–32). Ezek. objects above all to political alliances, which in themselves he regards as apostasy.

(b) Towards the end of the exile the downfall of Babylon and the deliverance of the exiles was proclaimed (Isa. 47; 48:12–16a, 20–22; 21:1–10; Jer. 50; 51). In this connection the total desolation of Babylon in war was expected.

(c) It is highly significant that Isa. 13 expects the eradication of sinners and the destruction of tyranny to coincide with the destruction of Babylon, and 14:1–23 mocks Babylon as a fallen power, the end of which will bring a period of peace and salvation to all peoples. Here Babylon appears as a type of the power, which opens to evil men every possibility in the world. When it falls, they perish. An apparently earlier poem (14:4–21) is here applied to Babylon. It dealt with a fallen world-ruler who tried to force his way even into the assembly of the gods. The intention was to unveil the real nature of the lofty Babylonian religion by looking at it from the viewpoint of its political and human activity. As the later chapters of Isa. show, the polemic against Babylon exceeded in seriousness anything that had gone before.

(d) Contrary to expectation, Babylon was not destroyed, and the freeing of the exiles did not mark the opening of a new era of salvation. The apocalyptic writer of Dan. 2 and 7 used a tradition of four world powers which eliminated one another. In its original form it probably had Assyria including Babylon, Media, Persia, Greece. The destruction of the last of them would be followed by a final kingdom of salvation.

NT 1. The mention of Babylon in Acts 7:43 picks up OT threads. The Babylonian exile appears as in Jer. and Ezek. as punishment for Israel's idolatry since the conquest of Canaan. According to Matt. 1:11, 17 (in the genealogy of Jesus), the second phase of Israel's history ended with the exile. After the passing of the foreseen time – fourteen generations as in the period from Abraham to David – its removal and the fulfilment of all promises was to be expected. In the framework of the genealogy this serves to prove that Jesus is the Messiah.

1 Pet. 5:13 is rather to be understood against the background of contemporary Jewish parallels. In all probability we should see Rome behind the phrase "She who is at Babylon", for in the whole of ancient tradition only the apostle Thomas is linked with Babylon. The significance of this name, which is probably more than a mere disguise, will then be: as the Jews once lived in exile in Babylon, so the Christians now live in the world, as exiles; they are strangers in the Dispersion (1 Pet. 1:1), attacked with hate by a totalitarian world that seeks to have its own way (cf. 4:12 ff.; 5:8 f.).

2. The most important ocurrence of the name is in Rev. 14:8; 16:19; 17:1–19:10, in the apocalyptic delineation of Babylon the great (cf. Dan. 4:30 (MT 27)), which links up with Isa. 13 and 14. Here Babylon is the type of worldly power in rebellion against God and the antitype of the heavenly Jerusalem (21:1–22:5). John wants to show that the great shifts of nations and power which are recorded as history have a deeper historical significance. In the last analysis history consists in the great struggle of worldly power against the rule of Christ. As Christ is killed and passes on his way through death to resurrection and redemption, the powers of this world continually manifest their might, riches and abominations. But in the end they will be conquered by the impotent, slaughtered Lamb on the throne. Hence Babylon the great has some of the features of historic Babylon. She sits "upon many waters" (17:1) and has seven hills like Rome (cf. 17:4, 9). She wears a fillet with a name, as worn by Roman harlots (17:5). The description of the woman riding on the beast (17:3 f.) recalls pictures of oriental gods and goddesses. Perhaps one should think of Cybele, the Magna Mater, worshipped in Rome since 204 B.C., with her orgiastic cult. This would explain "mother of harlots", the epitome of harlotry (K. G. Kuhn, *TDNT* I 515)) as well as other homes of abomination (e.g. Tyre; cf. Ezek. 27, 28). Similarly one may also find traits of contemporary powers.

H. Seebass

(a). J. A. Brinkman, *A Political History of Post-Kassite Babylonia, 1158–722* B.C., 1968; A. Champder, *Babylon*, 1958; G. Contenau, *Everyday Life in Babylonia and Assyria*, 1954; O. Cullmann, *The State in the New Testament*, 1956, 71–85; S. Erlandsson, *The Burden of Babylon*, 1970; S. H. Hooke, *Babylonian and Assyrian Religion*, 1962; T. Jacobsen and P. S. Minear, "Babylon," *IDB* I 334–38; K. G. Kuhn, *Babylōn, TDNT* I 514–17; A. L. Oppenheim, *Mesopotamia: Portrait of a Dead Civilization*, 1964; A. Parrot, *Babylon and the Old Testament*, 1958; H. W. Saggs, *The Greatness that was Babylon: A Survey of the Civilization of the Tigris-Euphrates Valley*, 1962; D. J. Wiseman, "Babylon," "Babylonia," *NBD* 116–28; and *Chronicles of the Chaldaean Kings*, 1956, commentaries on *1 Peter* by J. N. D. Kelly, 1969; E. G. Selwyn, 1947²; commentaries on *Revelation* by H. B. Swete, 1906; I. T. Beckwith 1919; R. H. Charles, 1920; G. B. Caird, 1966; G. E. Ladd, 1972.
(b) H. Schlier, *Die Zeit der Kirche*, 1956, 265 ff.; C. Spicq, *Les épîtres de S. Pierre*, 1966; E. Unger, *Die heilige Stadt*, 1931; and "Babylon," *Reallexikon der Assyriologie*, 1932, 330–69.

Bag, Box

βαλλάντιον

βαλλάντιον (*ballantion* or *balantion*, cf. Funk § 11.2), purse.

CL & OT *ballantion* is found in secular Gk. (Pseudo-Simonides to Plutarch), the LXX (Job 14:17; Prov. 1:14; Tob. 1:14; 8:2; Sir. 18:33), and Philo, meaning a bag for holding coins.

NT In the NT it is found only in Lk. 10:4; 12:33; 22:35 f. Jesus charged the Seventy not to take a *ballantion*, as he warned the Twelve against taking money in their belts (*zōnē*, Matt. 10:9; Mk. 6:8). Luke is commending poverty here (10:4) as elsewhere (e.g. 12:13 ff.), perhaps as a demonstration of trust in God on an urgent mission (cf. Lk. 22:35 with Matt. 6:32).

γλωσσόκομον

γλωσσόκομον (*glōssokomon*), box, chest, money-box.

CL & OT *glōssokomon* is a vernacular form of *glōssokomeion* (from *glōssa*, tongue, and *komeō*, take care of). It is found in secular Gk. from the 2nd cent. B.C. to the 2nd cent. A.D., and meant originally a case for keeping reeds or tongues of musical instruments, but then generally a case for books, a corpse, etc., a money-box (Plutarch and papyri). It is used of the ark (2 Sam. [LXX Ki.] 6:11) and of a chest (2 Chron. 24:8, 10 f.).

NT In the NT it is found only in Jn. 12:6 and 13:29 for the money-box from which Jesus and the Twelve paid their expenses. Both passages mention the fact that it was Judas who kept this box, and the former that he was in the habit of misappropriating funds.

| πήρα | *πήρα* (*pēra*), knapsack, traveller's bag.

CL & OT *pēra* is found in secular Gk. from Homer to the Gk. inscriptions from Syria c. 2nd cent. A.D. It is used of a shoulder bag for carrying provisions and small animals, a beggar's bag, the Cynic itinerant preacher's bag, and the shepherd's bag (Josephus, *Ant.*, 6, 185). It occurs in the LXX only in Jud. 10:5; 13:10, 15.

NT *pēra* is found only in the synoptic gospels (Matt. 10:10; Mk. 6:8; Lk. 9:3; 10:4; 22:25, 36). A. Deissmann identifies the article with the beggar's collecting bag, and sees Matt. 10:10 as a prohibition to the disciples to beg. But W. Michaelis denies the association with begging on the grounds that *pēra* did not normally mean a beggar's bag. He identifies it with the traveller's bag, and sees the passage as a call to the disciples to rely on God's generous provision without the encumbrance of heavy stores. J. Schniewind suggests that the disciples are to appear before men in the same attire as before God, for those who fasted and prayed did so barefoot and without a staff (*Das Evangelium nach Matthäus*, 1956, ad loc.).

The references to *pēra*, like those to *ballantion* and *glōssokomon*, all suggest that the followers of Jesus should not seek → money or → possessions for their own sake, but should put God's service first in their lives and trust in him to supply their material needs. → also Bread, art. *epiousios*. *G. T. D. Angel*

Arndt, 130, 161, 662; A. Deissmann, *Light from the Ancient East*, 1911², 108 ff.; J. N. Geldenhuys, *Luke*, 1950, 300; D. Hill, *The Gospel of Matthew*, 1972, 186; W. Michaelis, *pēra*, *TDNT* VI 119 ff.; Moulton–Milligan, 52, 128; K. H. Rengstorf, *ballantion*, *TDNT* I 526.

Baptism, Wash

Baptism belongs to the general group of practices connected with washing (→ Water). Hence, besides the key words *baptō/baptizō* which indicate (mostly total) immersion, attention must be paid to the actions described by the words *louō* and *niptō*, namely complete and partial washings. Apart from the literal meaning of purifying (→ Pure), there was already before the NT period a figurative use of the term. At first it meant the provision of cultic purity, and then in the NT it was extended to express the complete renewal of human existence.

| βαπτίζω | βάπτω (baptō), dip; βαπτίζω (baptizō), dip, immerse, submerge, baptize; βαπτισμός (baptismos), dipping, washing; βάπτισμα (baptisma) baptism. |

CL In secular Greek *baptō* means (a) dip, (b) dip into a dye, and so dye, and (c) draw (water). *baptizō* is an intensive form of *baptō* and means (a) dip, and (b) cause to perish (as by drowning a man or sinking a ship).

While there is some evidence that *baptō* was occasionally used in secular Greek of a ritual bath, there is none to show that *baptizō* was so employed (perhaps because of its association with the idea of perishing). Far commoner words for religious ablutions were *louō*, wash (the whole body) and *niptō*, wash or rinse (members of the body) and *rhainō*, sprinkle (→ Blood, Art. *rhantizō*).

OT 1. In the LXX *baptō* usually translates the OT Heb. *ṭābal*, dip (13 times; on 3 occasions *baptō* represents other vbs.). *baptizō* occurs only 4 times: in Isa. 21:4 it is used metaphorically of destruction, but in 2 Ki. 5:14 it is used in the mid. of Naaman's sevenfold immersion in the Jordan (the only passages as equivalent for Heb. *ṭābal*). This is significant, because in this case there is no suggestion of Naaman's destruction. The use of *baptizō* in the story of Naaman may have been decisive for its later use in the mid. to signify taking a ritual bath for cleansing (so J. Ysebaert, *Greek Baptismal Terminology*, 1962, 27 f.). The vb. has this meaning in Sir. 34(31): 25; Jud. 12:7. Despite assertions to the contrary, it seems that *baptizō*, both in Jewish and Christian contexts, normally meant "immerse", and that even when it became a technical term for baptism, the thought of immersion remains. The use of the term for cleansing vessels (as in Lev. 6:28 Aquila [cf. 6:21]; cf. *baptismos* in Mk. 7:4) does not prove the contrary, since vessels were normally cleansed by immersing them in water. The metaphorical uses of the term in the NT appear to take this for granted, e.g. the prophecy that the Messiah will baptise in Spirit and fire as a liquid (Matt. 3:11), the "baptism" of the Israelites in the cloud and the sea (1 Cor. 10:2), and in the idea of Jesus' death as a baptism (Mk. 10:38 f. *baptisma*; Lk. 12:50; cf. Ysebaert, op. cit., 41 ff.). The Pauline representation of baptism as burial and resurrection with Christ is consonant with this view, even if it does not demand it.

2. The Jewish "baptizing sects" do not appear to have used *ṭābal* and *baptizō* for their lustrations. This holds good even of the Qumran Sect. In the Dead Sea Scrolls the common term is *rāḥaṣ* (Gk. *louō*), bathe; *nāzâh* (Gk. *rhantizō*), sprinkle, also occurs twice, although the adherents of the Sect actually immersed themselves for purification. It is unlikely that the latter term was retained with the former in view of the stress laid by the Sect on inward as well as outward cleansing and the conjunction of these where repentance (→ Conversion) and ablution were united. (Note the common association of sprinkling and cleansing from sin in the OT, e.g. Num. 19:18 f.; Ps. 51:7 (50:9); Ezek. 36:25.) It is disputed whether the lustrations of the Sectaries should in any sense be classed with baptism, seeing that the lustrations were perpetually repeated and baptism is received but once; nevertheless there is much in favour of regarding the first lustration of a novice as having the character of initiation into full membership of the Community (see especially 1QS 2:25–3:12). In any case, it is of importance to observe that the lustrations of

Qumran had a more than purely ceremonial significance. Where they were accompanied by penitence and submission to the will of God, they were viewed as effective for the cleansing of moral impurity. Josephus attests that in his day the Essenes (of whom the Qumran Sectaries were at least forerunners) were assisted in their divinations by "using several sorts of purifications", and those among them who were married subjected their brides to special lustrations with a view to early conception and child-birth (*War*, 2, 8, 12 f. (159 f.)). If these practices were developments of earlier views, there must nevertheless have been sacramental elements in the earlier stages from which they developed.

3. A Gentile convert to Judaism at the beginning of the Christian era was required to receive → circumcision, to undergo a ritual bath and to offer sacrifice. For this so-called "proselyte baptism" the Heb. and Aram. texts employ the term *ṭābal*. The few references to it in Gk. literature employ *baptō* but not *baptizō*. This may be accidental, but it is consonant with the avoidance by Gk. writers of *baptizō* when describing the rites of purification.

The extent to which the practice and understanding of proselyte baptism influenced the baptism of John and early Christian baptism is a much debated question. The earliest references to proselyte baptism belong to the latter half of the 1st cent. A.D. While they indicate the probability of its being a pre-Christian institution, the uncertainty they manifest as to the significance of the rite and especially its relation to circumcision, suggest that its adoption was gradual and that its interpretation was still evolving during the 1st cent. A.D.

In assessing the significance of proselyte baptism, it is essential to note the importance attached by the Jews to circumcision. The oft-quoted saying in Yeb. 2:29, "One who has become a proselyte is like a child newly born" (Soncino Talmud ed., 22a), should be compared with that in Pes. 91b, "One who separates himself from his uncircumcision is like one who separates himself from the grave." The decisive turn from heathenism is taken in circumcision; the bath fits the newly made Jew to enter upon his first act of worship, i.e. sacrifice. If it be legitimate to infer from these sayings, that conversion from heathenism to Judaism was viewed as an entry upon life from the dead and that this was the source for the Christian doctrine of the new life of a convert to Christ, it should be observed that in Judaism the concept is only secondarily associated with proselyte baptism, and that the Christian understanding of baptism in terms of dying and rising is determined by its character as a baptism to the Messiah who died and rose, and thereby inaugurated the "age to come". In Christian baptism the emphasis falls on the redemptive action of the Messiah and the convert's relation to him.

NT 1. *Philology and statistics give the following picture for the NT. baptō* occurs only 4 times (twice in Jn. 13:26, and also in Lk. 16:24 and Rev. 19:13), and only with the meaning "dip". *baptizō* is a technical term for baptism, and in all the Gospels it occurs chiefly in the account of John's baptism, in particular that of Jesus. But while in Matt. it occurs outside ch. 3 only at 28:19 (the command to baptize), its use in the other Gospels is more widespread. Nevertheless, it refers almost entirely to John's baptism. It is only in the Synoptics that John is described as the *baptistēs* (used as a noun, Matt. 7 times, Mk. twice, Lk. 3 times). On the other hand, in Acts *baptizō* is almost always used of Christian baptism (13 out of 21 passages;

145

3 refer to John's baptism). Apart from this, the vb. occurs only twice more in Rom. 6:3, 9 times in 1 Cor. (especially 1:13–17) and in Gal. 3:27. Of the substantival forms *baptismos* occurs only once in Mk. and twice in Heb., and *baptisma* occurs 4 times each in Mk. and Lk., 6 times in Acts and twice in Matt., referring to John's baptism. Only in Rom. 6:4; Eph. 4:5; Col. 2:12 and 1 Pet. 3:21 is it used of Christian baptism. Furthermore, it is striking how these words are never found in 1 and 2 Thess., the Pastoral and Catholic Epistles and Rev., with the exception of Heb. 6:2; 9:10; 1 Pet. 3:21. John's baptism is universally described by the vb. *baptizō*; this is also true of Christian baptism throughout the NT.

2. *The baptism of John.* John administered a "repentance-baptism for the forgiveness of sins" (Mk. 1:4) in anticipation of the baptism of Spirit and fire that the Messiah would exercise (Matt. 3:11). Isa. 4:2–5 and Mal. 3:1–6 suggest that this Messianic baptism was symbolic of a universal judgment that would refine the people of God and fit them for the → Kingdom, but consume the wicked that they should not participate in it. The baptism of John had, therefore, two focal points: it marked the "turn" (repentance means → conversion) of a Jew to God, associating him with the penitent people and assuring him of forgiveness and cleansing, and it anticipated the Messianic baptism with Spirit and fire, assuring him a place in the Kingdom (cf. G. R. Beasley-Murray, *Baptism in the NT*, 1962, 31 ff.). It is a plausible conjecture that the lustrations of Jewish groups like the Essenes suggested to John a means whereby the OT predictions of cleansing in the last times, prior to the great Messianic purgation, should be fulfilled, and that the rite was viewed by him in a manner comparable to the acts of prophetic symbolism performed by the prophets who were before him.

3. *Jesus' baptism and the command to baptize.* Christian baptism is rooted in the redemptive action of Jesus. His submission to the baptism of John (Mk. 1:9) demonstrated and effected his solidarity with sinful men. The divine response of an opened heaven and voice of approval showed it to be the initiation of the movement of salvation, and gave promise of the revelation of the Kingdom in the completed action of the Messiah. The authorization of baptism during the ministry of Jesus (Jn. 4:1 ff.) was provisional. The command to baptize falls of necessity in the resurrection era, when redemption has been achieved, universal authority accorded to the risen Lord, and the mission of the church to the world begun (Matt. 28:18 ff.).

4. *The early church.* (a) Baptism seems to have accompanied the → proclamation of the gospel from the beginning of the church's mission (Acts 2). Luke's understanding of Christian baptism appears in Acts 2:38. Baptism is conversion-baptism; it is administered "in the name of Jesus Christ", i.e. in relation to Jesus Christ and with the use of his name, so that the baptized calls on the name of Christ (Acts 22:16) even as the name is called over him, signifying to whom he belongs (cf. Jas. 2:7); it is "for the forgiveness of sins" and with a view to the gift of the Holy Spirit. Variations from this norm (notably Acts 8:14 ff.; 10:44 f.; 19:1 ff.) reflect the variety of circumstances and of experiences of the Spirit in a period of transition.

(b) For Paul's interpretation of baptism Gal. 3:27 is significant. Baptism is "to Christ" (a shorthand expression for "in the name of Christ"); it relates the believer to Christ in such a way that he is "in Christ" (cf. v. 26). From this basic view flow the other features of baptism that appear in Paul. Baptism "to Christ" is baptism "to his death" (Rom. 6:3 ff.); it relates the believer to Christ's redemptive action, so that Christ's death on Golgotha was his death, and it entails an end ("death") to the life of estrangement from God and the beginning of life in Christ. Baptism to Christ is baptism to the → church, for to be in Christ is to be a member of the body of Christ (Gal. 3:27 ff.; 1 Cor. 12:13). Baptism to Christ is baptism in the Spirit of Christ ("We were all immersed in one Spirit . . . and were all saturated in (the outpouring of) one Spirit", 1 Cor. 12:13), for the Spirit and Christ are inseparable (Rom. 8:9 f.; 2 Cor. 3:17). Baptism to Christ is for life after the pattern of Christ's dying to sin and rising for righteousness ("We were buried with him through baptism . . . that we might walk in a new life", Rom. 6:4; see further the baptismal ethics of Col. 3:3–13). Baptism to Christ is for life in the kingdom to be revealed in the day of Christ (2 Cor. 1:22; Eph. 1:13; 4:30). The latter passages strictly refer not to baptism but to the baptism of the Spirit with which baptism in water is associated in the apostolic writings (cf. the alleged utterance of Thecla when about to die, "In the name of Jesus Christ I baptize myself for the last day!" Act. Paul 3:34 [Henn.–Schn., II, 262]).

This eschatological relation of baptism made possible the adoption by the church of the custom, apparently reflected in 1 Cor. 15:29, of baptizing the living for the dead, that the latter might share in the kingdom of God. The practice could hardly be reconciled with the Pauline proclamation, and was cited by Paul as part of his polemic: people who deny the resurrection of the dead ought not to get baptized for the dead! Baptism to Christ is subordinate to the gospel of Christ (1 Cor. 1:17). Paul as an apostle usually left it to others to administer (1 Cor. 1:14 ff.). This is not to minimize baptism, but to clarify its function. It is an embodiment of the gospel of grace and the supreme occasion for confessing it, hence the climactic point of the restoration of relations between God and the repentant sinner. Many of the confessional declarations in the epistles are thought to have originated as baptismal confessions (e.g. Rom. 10:9; Phil. 2:6–11; Eph. 4:4–6; Col. 1:13–20), and from such beginnings the later creeds of Christendom developed.

(c) The relation between "washing" and the → "Word" is reflected in Eph. 5:26; cf. 4:5. In harmony with this 1 Pet. 3:21 defines baptism as "an appeal to God for a clear conscience" or "an answer to God from a clear conscience" (the interpretation is uncertain). On either view it is the occasion of the baptized addressing himself to God in response to the gospel. And in this context the power of the resurrection is known ("Baptism saves . . . through the resurrection of Jesus Christ").

In Tit. 3:5 and Jn. 3:5 baptism is associated with regeneration (→ Birth). In both passages the operation of the Spirit is to the fore. In the former (a baptismal hymn?) the pertinent clause should be rendered, "He saved us through the washing characterised by the regeneration and renewal wrought by the Holy Spirit" (cf. M. Dibelius-H. Conzelmann, HNT, XIII, 111 f.). The latter passage affirms the necessity of a "new beginning" from God ("from above") through submission to baptism and through the recreative work of the Holy Spirit. The Christian reader knows that while these two things were for Nicodemus separated as present demand and future hope, through the lifting up of Jesus on the cross (vv. 14 f.) and the sending of the Holy Spirit (v. 8, cf. 7:39) the two "baptisms" have been brought together.

147

(d) In the light of this apostolic teaching, modern confessional watchwords about baptism like "declarative", "symbolic", "self-operative" etc. are inadequate. In Acts and the epistles baptism appears as a divine-human event, even as the "turning" to God, with which it is invariably associated, is a divine-human event. Both elements are given due weight – the divine and the human. Since baptism signifies union with Christ (Gal. 3:27), all that Christ wrought for man in his redeeming acts and bestows by virtue of them is conjoined with baptism in the apostolic writings. This includes union with Christ (→ Fellowship) in his death and resurrection (Rom. 6:1 ff.; Col. 2:11 f.), → forgiveness of sins and cleansing from sins (Acts 2:38; 22:16), bestowal of the Spirit (Acts 2:38; 1 Cor. 12:13), membership in the body of Christ (1 Cor. 12:13; Gal. 3:27), renewal by the Spirit (Tit. 3:5), the promise of the kingdom of God (Jn. 3:5). Rightly to estimate this teaching requires the recognition that in the apostolic writings these benefits of Christ and his saving grace are given to → faith. In particular this is true of union with Christ (Eph. 3:17), participation in his death and resurrection (Gal. 2:20; 5:24; Col. 2:12), forgiveness and cleansing (1 Jn. 1:9), the gift of the Spirit (Gal. 3:2, 14), renewal by the Spirit (Jn. 1:13), life in the kingdom of God (Jn. 20:31). This coincidence of divine action for faith and in baptism presumes that God's gracious giving to faith belongs to the context of baptism, and that his gift in baptism is to faith. This coincidence of divine action for faith and in baptism comes to expression in the definition of baptism in 1 Pet. 3:21, where baptism appears as a trysting place for the Redeemer and the penitent, who addresses him on the basis of the gospel.

A word of caution is, however, required. The Acts of the Apostles show that all statements about the action of God in baptism must make allowance for the divine freedom in bestowing salvation and the Spirit. This is illustrated even in the initial sending of the Spirit to the church, for at Pentecost the Spirit was outpoured on a company of men and women who had not received *Christian* baptism (i.e. baptism in the name of Jesus), and we do not know how many of them had received any other baptism. The complicated phenomena regarding baptism and the Spirit in the stories of the Samaritan believers (Acts 8:14 ff.), Cornelius and his company (10:44 ff.) and the Ephesian "disciples" (19:1 ff.) doubtless were not solitary in the primitive church. They illustrate that life is more complex than formulations of doctrine, and that God is able to meet every variation from the norm. That holds good of the church of all ages, from the apostolic to our own.

5. *Infant baptism.* The belief that the apostles commanded the baptism of infants as well as of responsible persons is attested as early as Origen (3rd cent. A.D.), and apart from some notable exceptions it became the unquestioned conviction of Christendom until the present century. The rise of the critical study of the Bible caused a widespread change of opinion, so that by 1940 the majority of NT scholars (as distinct from systematic theologians) were agreed that in the apostolic age baptism was administered to believers only. In recent years this view has been contested, above all by J. Jeremias, O. Cullmann and in the Reports of the Church of Scotland on Baptism. It is maintained that the traditional arguments for the apostolic institution of infant baptism are vindicated alike by sound theology and by modern biblical and archaeological research. For example, the conviction that household baptisms (Acts 11:14; 16:33; 18:8) included infants is strengthened by

the contention that the term *oikos* (→ house) had gained an almost technical significance among Jews and had especial reference to little children. The terminology of Jewish proselyte baptism is believed to be employed in 1 Cor. 7:14, with the presumption that Jewish customs related to the baptism of young children of proselytes were accepted by the primitive church. The saying of Jesus concerning little children and the kingdom of God (Mk. 10:14) has been given form-critical evaluation: the story is said to reflect the *Sitz-im-Leben* of a church seeking to answer the question, "Should we baptize our children?" and the answer is implied, "Yes, bring them to baptism as they were once brought to Jesus." This conclusion is supported by the belief that the command, "Do not forbid them", reflects an early liturgical use of the term in baptism. (→ Hinder, art. *kōlyō*.)

The reformed view of the one → covenant with its continuing sacraments, stressing the close relation between → circumcision and baptism, is supported by typological exegesis, hinted at in 1 Cor. 10:1 ff. (where baptism is seen as symbolized by the passing through the Red Sea), and evidence from early Christian burial inscriptions is adduced as proof of the baptism of infants in the earliest church.

These views have met with differing reactions. Some, like Kurt Aland, consider the rise of infant baptism to be not earlier than the close of the 2nd cent. A.D. (cf. K. Aland, *Did the Early Church Baptize Infants?*, 1963). The present writer believes that infant baptism is excluded from the horizon of the apostolic writers, not alone by its apparent lack of mention in their writings, but by their equation of the gift of baptism with the gift of faith. In the NT it is not merely a "blessing" that is given to the baptized, but Christ and his full salvation, so that A. Schlatter could rightly affirm: "There is no gift or power which the apostolic documents do not ascribe to baptism" (*Theologie des NT*, II, 495). This is comprehensible only in a milieu where baptism and conversion are inseparable, as in the primitive church (cf. Acts 2:41; 16:33), so that the effect of the one may be predicated of the other. Where it is believed that the instinct of the church has been right in administering baptism to infants as well as to those of riper years, the present writer would contend that there must be recognized a modification of baptismal doctrine and provision must be made at a later stage in life for an occasion for confession of faith. This has been a subject of discussion in various churches of the reformation, including the Church of England (see its reports *Confirmation Today*, 1944; *The Theology of Christian Initiation*, 1948; *Baptism Today*, 1949; *Baptism and Confirmation Today*, 1955; *Baptism and Confirmation*, 1959).

6. The nouns *baptismos*, *baptisma* and *baptistēs*. (a) *baptismos*, dipping, immersion, has in classical literature the connotation of perishing, like the vb. *baptizō*. In Mk. 7:4 it represents Jewish ritual cleansing (by immersion) of vessels, and in Heb. 9:10 it refers to the purification of persons. Presumably this reflects the Jewish usage of the term. Among Greek-speaking Jews it was probably used for proselyte baptism, since Josephus employs it for John's baptism. In Heb. 6:2 "instruction about washings" (*baptismoi*) appears to concern the contrast between Christian baptism and all other religious washings, including the OT ablutions and every kind of initiatory bath, Jewish and pagan, known to the readers.

(b) *baptisma* appears for the first time in the NT. No instance of its occurrence in pagan and Jewish literature has yet been found. In view of the fact that its earliest employment is for the baptism of John, it could conceivably have been

149

coined by John's disciples. More plausibly, it is a Christian innovation, and was applied by Christian writers to John's baptism in the conviction that the latter should be bracketed with Christianity rather than with Judaism. It is often affirmed that *baptismos* denotes the act of immersion and *baptisma* includes the result (e.g. A. Oepke, *TDNT* I 545). Of this there is no evidence. It is more likely that *baptisma* was formed on the analogy of its Heb. equivalent *ṭebîlâh*. Apart from the general preference of Jewish Christians for Gk. terms phonetically similar to Heb. equivalents, it may well have been adopted by them to express their consciousness that Christian baptism was a new thing in the world, differing from all Jewish and pagan purificatory rites (so Ysebaert, *op. cit.*, 52).

(c) *ho baptistēs* is the surname given in the Synoptic Gospels to John the Baptizer (e.g. Matt. 3:1). It draws attention to the characteristic element in his ministry, namely the demand for repentance-baptism, and still more to the novelty of administering baptism to others, instead of leaving them to baptize themselves, as happened with all OT ablutions and in Jewish proselyte baptism.

7. The importance attached to baptism in the NT, above all in the Pauline exposition of its relation to union with Christ and participation in his death and resurrection, has led some scholars to the conviction that this interpretation stems directly from the Hellenistic Mystery Religions. R. Reitzenstein indeed was prepared to ascribe such influence even to the baptism of John (*Die Vorgeschichte der christlichen Taufe*, 1929, 279). A dependence of the forerunner and of the early church on the Mystery Religions, however, is very difficult to substantiate and is highly unlikely. Christian baptism is firmly set within the tradition of Jewish cultic acts of cleansing, above all in the activity of John, and its interpretation is rooted in the apostolic gospel (cf. I Corinthians 15:3 f, "Christ *died* for our sins . . . was *buried* . . . has been *raised* . . . ", with Romans 6:3 f, "We were baptized to his *death* . . . *buried* with him . . . that as Christ was *raised* we should walk . . . "). The language used of baptism in Paul's writings flows from his basic understanding of redemption in and through Christ. Some of the most significant elements of his doctrine of salvation are absent from the Mystery Religions (e.g. the nature of Christ's death as for sin; the ethical implications of the believer's baptism to sin; the dying and rising *with* Christ; the once-for-all event of Christ's death and resurrection; the insistence on faith in relation to baptism). It is, moreover, of great importance to note that the links that have been observed between Paul's teaching and the practices of the Mystery Religions belong to later developments within those religions which did not take place till the Christian faith had been proclaimed throughout the ancient world. For a detailed discussion of the issues see G. Wagner, *Pauline Baptism and the Pagan Mysteries*, 1967.   *G. R. Beasley-Murray*

λούω

λούω (*louō*), wash; ἀπολούω (*apolouō*), wash, wash away; λουτρόν (*loutron*), bath, washing.

CL In Gk. literature *louō* means wash, (mid.) wash oneself, take a bath; generally it indicates washing the whole body, in contrast to *niptō* which is used for washing parts of the body, and *plynō* which is used of inanimate objects, especially clothes. *apolouō* is a strengthened form of *louō*, having the same meaning but

150

stressing the removal of dirt. The sub. *loutron* means the place where one has a bath, the bath-house, or the water for a bath, or simply the bath.

Washing for ritual purification was common among ancient peoples of the Orient. The common term for cleansing was *louō*; *apolouō* rarely appears in this connection; *rhainō* and its cognates are employed for aspersion. The origin of religious lustrations lies in animistic religion, when men believed that certain waters were impregnated with the power of deity, and that this power was communicated to persons and objects plunged in them. Recourse was had to such washing to safeguard a person, when approaching a deity in view of the power of holiness to destroy a man, and to seek protection on those occasions, when men are peculiarly exposed to demonic assault, above all in circumstances connected with birth and death. When the nature of religious belief changed, the lustrations were, in measure, spiritualized and extended in their application. Thus, washing was required before prayer, in preparation for initiation into religious cults, after bloodshed in war, manslaughter and crimes of any kind (see J. Ysebaert, *Greek Baptismal Terminology*, 1962, 15 ff.).

OT 1. Similar phenomena, relating both to ideas and terminology of cleansing, may be traced in the OT, though all has been sublimated. When Aaron enters the Most Holy Sanctuary on the Day of Atonement he has to bathe his body in water and put on "holy garments" (Lev. 16:4), offer a sacrifice (v. 6), and burn incense in the sanctuary "that the cloud of incense may cover the mercy seat which is upon the testimony, lest he die" (v. 13). This washing prior to the High Priest's appearing "before the Lord" is thus part of the conditions under which he may approach the divine holiness and live.

The processes of birth, sickness and death all entail ritual uncleanness. Purification by washing in water is required after sexual intercourse (Lev. 15), menstruation and birth (Lev. 15), after contact with leprosy (Lev. 13, 14) and with death (Num. 5:1 ff.; 19:11 ff.). The conviction of Israel's exclusive relationship with Yahweh possibly lent to these rites a polemic aspect. If Israel's neighbours resorted to magical rites to secure the aid of the gods in the critical moments of life, the answer of Israel's priests to these, as to all worship of foreign gods and contact with animals sacred to idolatrous cults, was to urge cleansing from them all and to be exclusively devoted to the Lord (cf. W. Eichrodt, *Theology of the OT*, I, 1961, 166). The more painstakingly scrupulous they were in their observance of these ritual washings on the one hand, the more obvious it becomes, on the other, that in addition to these they cherished the hope of a radical purging by God in the last days. He himself would sprinkle water on his people, and give them a new heart and a new spirit (Ezek. 36:25); he would open up a fountain to purify them from sin and uncleanness (Zech. 13:1), and he would purge them with fire and fuller's bleach (Mal. 3:1 ff.).

In the LXX these words occur most often in the Pentateuch: *louō* occurs only c. 45 times, particularly in Lev., and almost always represents the Heb. *rāḥaṣ*; it is used generally of ritual purification. *rhantizō* and its derivatives are used of sprinkling (Num. 19:13; Ps. 51:7 (50:9) → Blood). On *niptō* see below. It is worth noting that Josephus prefers the compound *apolouō* for ritual washing (e.g. *Ant.* 11, 5, 6 (163)). He always uses it, when he is talking about the Essenes' lustrations. *louō*, on the other hand, only appears in this context, when he describes the ritual bath of Banus the Eremite (*Life*, 2(7)). *loutron* only occurs twice in the LXX, referring to animals' bathing (Cant. 4:2; 6:6) and in Sir. 34:25, referring to a ritual washing. Josephus uses it in *War*, II, 8, 13 (161) of a bath that married Essenes take with their wives to aid conception.

2. The Qumran Sect regularly employs *rāḥaṣ* (Gk. *louō*) for its ritual washing, rather than *ṭābal* (→ *baptō/baptizō*). It also uses *nāzâh* (Gk. *rhantizō* → Blood) "sprinkle", although the "washing" apparently involves immersion (cf. e.g. 1QS 3:8 f.: "It is by humiliating himself under all God's ordinances that his flesh can be cleansed, by sprinkling (*nāzâh*) with water for impurity and by sanctifying himself with water of purity"). This preference for terms indicative of washing and sprinkling is probably due to their long association in Israel's religious history with cleansing from sin and defilement. The Sectaries laid great stress on the necessity for repentance, if the ritual bath was to be efficacious for religious cleansing (cf. 1QS 3:4 f.: a man who persists in the stubbornness of his heart "cannot be cleared by mere ceremonies of atonement, nor cleansed by any waters of ablution, nor sanctified by immersion in lakes or rivers, nor purified by any bath. . . . Unclean, unclean he remains so long as he rejects the government of God and refuses the discipline of communion with him").

NT 1. (a) *louō* occurs only 5 times in the NT. In Acts 16:33 it has a purely non-religious meaning, but in Jn. 13:10 it relates to washing for purification and entails a contrast between washing the entire body (*louō*) and rinsing individual limbs (*niptō*). Despite claims often made, it is improbable that any reference to Christian baptism is intended in this passage.

(b) It is otherwise with Heb. 10:22. Christians have their "hearts sprinkled (*rhantizō*) from an evil conscience" and "bodies washed (*louō*) with pure water." We are not to interpret this as a contrast between internal cleansing by the blood of Christ's sacrifice and external cleansing by baptism. If the sprinkling and the washing do not both refer to cleansing waters, as in Ezek. 36:25 and the Qumran writings, the cleansing blood of Christ is thought of as effective in baptism, even as the cleansing power of baptism is the shed → blood of Christ. It is the doctrine of Rom. 6:1 ff. expressed in terms of sacrifice (→ Priest NT).

(c) In Acts 22:16 *apolousai* indubitably relates to baptism. The similarity of language in 1 Cor. 6:11 indicates that it, too, has in view the cleansing of sins in baptism. Observe also the aor. tense of the verbs, pointing to a single occasion of washing, sanctification and justification. "In the name of the Lord Jesus" reflects the use of the → Name in baptismal formulae. "In the Spirit of our God" links the action of the → Spirit with baptism as in 1 Cor. 12:13; Acts 2:38 etc.

Some MSS of Rev. 1:5 read *lousanti* ("to him who has washed us from our sins") instead of *lysanti* ("to him who has redeemed us from our sins"). It may be a scribal error arising out of the similarity of the two words in Gk., but it has perhaps also been influenced by Rev. 7:14 (although there the Greek has *plynō*).

The admittedly infrequent use of *louō* and its cognates in the NT instead of the common term *baptizō* has its analogy and sufficient explanation in the Qumran writings. The traditional association of these terms with cleansing through ablution emphasizes the symbolism of washing away sins in baptism.

152

2. *loutron* in literary Gk. signifies the place where a bath is taken, whether the house for bathing, water for bathing, or simply the bath. The occurrence in the LXX is rare (see above, OT 1.). In appears twice in the NT in contexts which apparently relate to baptism: Eph. 5:26; Tit. 3:5. In both passages it denotes the act rather than the place of washing. Eph. 5:26 may allude to the ceremonial bath taken by a bride in preparation for marriage (→ *baptizō* OT 2; cf. A. Oepke, *TDNT*, IV, 296 f.). For the bride of Christ (→ Marriage, art *nymphē*), the counterpart to this bath is baptism, in which the members of the → body are cleansed "by the washing of water by the Word". In the enactment of this rite the word of the gospel is enshrined and it is expressed in the confession ' Jesus is Lord" (Rom. 10:9) given on that occasion.

In Tit. 3:5 baptism is defined as the "washing (*loutron*) for the regeneration and and renewal that the Spirit effects." Observe that it is not the washing that effects renewal. The washing is the occasion when the Spirit creatively works in the individual, just as he made the community of disciples the Body of Christ at Pentecost (Acts 2:33) and at the end will produce a new creation (Matt. 19:28).

G. R. Beasley-Murray

νίπτω	*νίπτω* (*niptō*), wash.

CL In Gk. literature *niptō* means "wash", when the object is part of the body, in contrast with *louō*, when the whole body is the object; *plynō*, wash things, especially clothes; and *rhainō*, sprinkle. In religious contexts *niptō* is commonly used of the ceremonial washing of hands, e.g. before prayer or sacrifice.

OT A similar use of *niptō* appears in the LXX, both in a secular sense (e.g. Gen. 18:4) and for religious washings (note especially the laver provided for priests for use in the performance of their duties, Ex. 30:17 ff.). Philo often mentions religious cleansing of the body, though he prefers the compound term *ekniptō*. His manifest preference for expressions denoting partial ablution indicates a greater interest in these forms of ritual washing than in the kind of ritual bathing that was customary among the Essenes. This accords with the extension of ritual washings among the Jews in late Judaism. The prescriptions relating to priests washing their hands amidst religious duties was extended to a demand that Jews generally rinse their hands before meals, a custom that some attributed to Solomon but others to Hillel and Shammai (SB I 695).

NT Reference to this custom is made in the NT by the evangelist (Mk. 7:3). The disciples of Jesus were criticized by Pharisees for eating with unwashed (*aniptos*), i.e. ceremonially unclean, hands (Mk. 7:2). In their defence Jesus not only rejects the tradition that included the custom (vv. 5ff.), but denies some fundamental presuppositions concerning uncleanness which it involves (vv. 14 ff.).

The narrative of the foot-washing (Jn. 13) may contain a reference to current Jewish teaching on purification: "He who has bathed does not need to wash but is completely clean" (v. 10), i.e. he who has taken a complete bath (*louō*) does not need lesser ritual washings before a meal (*niptō*). The insertion of "except for his feet" after "wash" is almost certainly due to a later scribe, who did not understand that the action of Jesus in washing the feet of the disciples represented a complete bath (*louō*). If v. 7 hints that more is involved in the act than a lesson in humility (vv. 13 ff.) and that it cannot be understood until after the crucifixion, it is likely that we are to interpret it as an acted parable of the Lord's humiliation unto death, rather than an exposition of the unrepeatability of baptism, or of the complete cleansing given in baptism (*louō*) as compared with the repeated cleansing in the eucharist (*niptō*). It is enough to draw a secondary lesson from the incident without multiplying refinements. *G. R. Beasley-Murray*

Infant Baptism: Its Background and Theology

The question whether infant baptism was practised in apostolic times, and certain related issues (the connection between baptism and circumcision, and the antiquity of Jewish proselyte baptism), have received some degree of attention in the earlier parts of this article, but deserve to be developed further because of their important theological and practical implications.

The first explicit reference to infant baptism in Christian history is that made by Irenaeus, about A.D. 180, who speaks of "all who through Christ are born again to God, infants and children and boys and youths and old men" (*Adv. Haer.*, 2, 22, 4 [2, 33, 2]), "born again to God" being a technical phrase meaning baptism, well attested in other parts of Irenaeus's writings. How much weight one gives to earlier implicit references which paedo-baptists believe they find in Fathers such as Justin Martyr and Polycarp, and in the New Testament itself, depends chiefly upon the conformity of infant baptism, first, with the historical background of the apostolic church in Judaism, and, secondly, with biblical theology as the New Testament writers understand it.

1. *The Jewish Background.* There are three important Jewish ceremonies which are linked with Christian baptism at its source and which could create a presumption for or against its being administered originally to infants as well as adults.

(a) The first of these is *circumcision*, which was administered only to males, but to infant males as well as adults. Circumcision is linked with baptism by the fact that both are divinely instituted initiation rites; by the fact that a ritual washing or baptism for proselytes had apparently been added to circumcision before the time of our Lord; by Paul's words in Col. 2:11 f.; and by the significance of the two practices – for circumcision is given three meanings by the Old Testament which the New Testament gives to baptism, repentance (Deut. 10:16; Jer. 4:4), regeneration (Deut. 30:6) and cleansing (Isa. 52:1; Ezek. 44:7), and Paul adds a fourth such meaning, justification by faith (Rom. 4:11). A final link is that both are covenanting rites. This is explicit in the case of circumcision (Gen. 17:10–14; Acts 7:8), but appears also to be the case with baptism, since spiritual regeneration and remission of sins, which are fundamental to the idea of baptism (Jn. 3:5; Acts 2:38; 22:16; Eph. 5:26; Col. 2:12 f.; Tit. 3:5–7; Heb. 10:22), are the characteristic graces of the new covenant (Matt. 26:28; 2 Cor. 3:6; Heb. 8:6–13; 10:15–18).

(b) The second Jewish ceremony linked with Christian baptism is *proselyte baptism*. The link is partly through circumcision, to which proselyte baptism had

154

been added, and partly through the similarity of the two rites. The earliest Jewish references to proselyte baptism are Greek Testament of Levi 14:6 "The daughters of the gentiles shall ye take to wife, purifying them with unlawful purifications"; Sibylline Oracles 4:165–67 "Bathe the whole body in ever-flowing streams, and reach your hands to heaven, praying forgiveness for these things that ye have done"; and Mishnah, Pesahim 8:8 "The school of Shammai say, If a man became a proselyte on the day before passover he may immerse himself and consume his passover offering in the evening; and the school of Hillel say, He that separates himself from his uncircumcision is as one that separates himself from a grave" (i.e. he remains unclean for a week). The most important facts to notice here are, first, that proselyte baptism is basically a lustration for the unclean; secondly, that since uncleanness may befall anybody, it is not just a religious duty of adult males, like so many of the religious duties of Judaism, but also of females; and thirdly, that it is spiritualized to refer to cleansing from moral impurity as well. There are various uncertainties about the dates of these passages, but they probably range from the first or second century B.C. (Testament of Levi) to the late second century A.D. (Mishnah), with the fourth book of the Sibylline Oracles in between, in the late first century A.D. Attempts have recently been made to revive the view that the Greek Testaments of the Twelve Patriarchs (to which the Testament of Levi belongs) is a Christian work, and not a Jewish work with later interpolations, but these attempts have met with heavy criticism. The work is a Greek paraphrase of Aramaic writings discovered at Qumran, having links with the Dead Sea Scrolls and the Book of Jubilees, the last of which emphatically shares its concern about mixed marriages. As regards the Mishnah, its date in the second century A.D. does not alter the fact that it is recording a first-century controversy. Now, though the first explicit mention of a child receiving proselyte baptism is fairly late (see J. Jeremias, *Infant Baptism in the First Four Centuries*, 1960, 37–40), the first explicit mention of a woman receiving it is remarkably early, in the Testament of Levi. And since Gentile women were required to be cleansed from impurity in this way, not simply Gentile men, the implication is that Gentile children were too. If the parents had not hitherto observed the laws of ceremonial cleanness, certainly the children had not done so, and the liability of children to contract uncleanness is plainly stated in the Mishnah (Tohoroth 3:6; Zabim 2:1). Consequently, as soon as a lustration of this kind was judged necessary for proselytes, it was judged necessary for them all, without distinction. Like circumcision, it would be given to infants as well as adults, but unlike circumcision it would be given to females as well as males. In the latter respect, proselyte baptism approaches more closely to Christian baptism than circumcision does; but, on the other hand, there is one respect in which circumcision comes closer than proselyte baptism does. For, whereas proselyte baptism was only given to a converted family in the first generation (see Jeremias, op. cit., 46 f.), since after that they would observe the laws of ceremonial purity like other Jews, with Christian baptism it has been different: this, like circumcision, has traditionally been administered to each generation afresh.

(c) The third Jewish ceremony linked with Christian baptism is *the baptism of John*. The link here is uniquely close, since John's mission was to prepare Israel to receive Christ, who was himself baptized by John and found many of his disciples

155

among John's followers. Moreover, John's baptism, like Christian baptism, was a baptism of repentance for the remission of sins, anticipating the coming baptism with the Holy Spirit. Now, in the view of some, John's baptism marked a decisive break with Judaism, in that it laid emphasis on the necessity for personal repentance and forgiveness in the same way that Christian baptism does, and so was not a ceremony suitable for administration to infants. But how far was this emphasis on personal repentance and forgiveness something really new? We have seen above how in the Sibylline Oracles (late first century) *proselyte* baptism is reinterpreted ethically to express repentance and forgiveness, and the clearest evidence for the administration of proselyte baptism to infants comes after this reinterpretation, not before. John was probably already acquainted with the reinterpretation. Certainly, it is proselyte baptism which appears to be the immediate antecedent of John's baptism, since in both cases the baptism has initiatory significance and is received once for all, not whenever occasion arose (as with the Old Testament lustrations) or every day (as with the lustrations of the Essenes). There was some difference in the mode of administration between John's baptism and proselyte baptism, since the latter, in the case of adult males, was self-administered, whereas the prophet John seems always to have administered his baptism himself; but the real difference was that John's baptism was for Jews not Gentiles, thus emphasizing that there was need for repentance on the part of Jews as well. Even so, John's innovation must not be exaggerated. The Old Testament prophets, in whose succession John stood, had regularly preached repentance to the Jews; and though proselyte baptism was not given to Jews, circumcision was; and circumcision, like proselyte baptism, signified repentance and cleansing (see section (a)), and was the basic rite of initiation to which proselyte baptism had been added. Thus, it was only in terms of contemporary Judaism, not in terms of the Old Testament, that John's preaching of repentance to Jews was new; and it was only in terms of proselyte baptism, not in terms of initiation ceremonies as a whole, that his administration of a baptism of repentance to Jews was new. Nor is there any evidence that John addressed his message of repentance simply to individuals, not to the nation, or thought of his ministry as a prolonged one, in which the baptism of infants could be deferred until they grew up. On the contrary, it was to the nation, including for example Herod the Tetrarch, that he directed his challenge (Mk. 6:17–20), and his message was an urgent one, which warned of imminent judgment on those who did not respond (Matt. 3:1, 10, 12; Lk. 3:9, 17). Consequently, the likelihood that his baptism would have diverged from Jewish practice by dealing with people as individuals not as households, and by deferring for years the baptism of infants, does not seem to be great. It is true that the gospels and Josephus are silent about the baptism of infants by John (or, indeed, of women), but this more probably means that he conformed to existing custom than that he altered it. If proselyte baptism, though symbolizing repentance, was given to infant Gentiles, and if circumcision, though symbolizing repentance, was given to infant Jews, the expectation would be that John's baptism of repentance would follow these precedents, and one would not expect to see the matter alluded to unless it did otherwise.

2. *New Testament Theology*. Having said all this, the fact remains that the force of Jewish example was only one of the influences at work in the New Testament

church. An even more potent influence was the Christian gospel. Any Jewish custom which conflicted with the gospel would have been strongly opposed. So it is now necessary to consider whether the baptism of infants is in accordance with New Testament theology. The relevant themes of this theology appear to lie in the following broad areas:

(a) *Grace and Faith.* Those who maintain that John the Baptist's emphasis on personal repentance and forgiveness sharply differentiated his baptism from earlier Jewish practice hold that the same is true of Christian baptism, which is likewise associated with repentance and forgiveness, and also with faith (Acts 2:38; 19:4 f.; 22:16; Gal. 3:26 f.; Eph. 5:26; Col. 2:12 f.; Heb. 10:22). We have already seen reason, from what we know of proselyte baptism, to question such an inference. The new feature of the Baptist's ministry was not, probably, that he stressed repentance and forgiveness, but that he did so in the case of Jews. With regard to Christian baptism, however, even this difference does not exist, since from an early stage (and in idea, probably, from the beginning) it was given not only to Jews but to Gentiles. Its relation to proselyte baptism, therefore, was even closer than in the case of John's baptism, and if proselyte baptism was given to infants, one would expect the same to be true of Christian baptism, provided that theological considerations permitted it.

One of these theological considerations is the faith with which Christian baptism is associated. It is argued that only in believers' baptism can faith regularly accompany the rite with which it is associated. It is some answer to this to say that circumcision and proselyte baptism were likewise associated with *repentance*, which nevertheless could not accompany the rite when it was administered to infants, but could only follow it. Another answer is that faith is a human counterpart of divine grace. The human activity of faith is bound up, in New Testament teaching, with → grace, → salvation and → justification. Each of these are divine activities, freely initiated by God. Faith relates to them as a response or a means (Acts 15:7–11; Rom. 3:21–30; 4:3, 5, 11, 16, 19–25; Gal. 2:16; 3:6, 8; Eph. 2:5–8). If, therefore, it is a good argument that the baptism of our children should be deferred until faith can accompany it, in order to stress the importance of the human response (and that the New Testament church must have acted accordingly), there is at least an equally strong case for holding that the baptism of children should precede the advent of faith, in order to stress the still greater importance of the divine initiative. In the New Testament period the latter emphasis would have been particularly appropriate in view of the conflict with the doctrine of justification by works, put forward by the Judaizers.

(b) *The Efficacy of the Sacraments.* To argue in this way is not to assume that the New Testament sacraments are the exact equivalents of the Jewish ceremonies preceding them, and were neatly substituted for their antecedents on the Day of Pentecost. Such an assumption would be both historically and doctrinally untrue. In Jewish Christianity there was apparently a long period of overlap, in which those zealous for the right to continue practising the Mosaic Law observed not only baptism and the Lord's Supper but also circumcision and the passover. In discussion with Jewish Christians, therefore, it would have been both offensive and unconvincing if Paul had argued that baptism had replaced circumcision, and he does not do this either at the Jerusalem council in Acts 15 or in his controversy with the Judaizers in the Epistle to the Galatians. He does indeed point to the parallel between baptism and circumcision in Col. 2:11 f., but in doing so he makes a marked difference between the two, speaking of baptism as "a circumcision not made with hands", i.e. as a rite which fulfils what circumcision foreshadowed. Even John's baptism is seen to fall short of Christian baptism in one significant particular, that it is a baptism of water and not the coming baptism of the Spirit (Mk. 1:8; Jn. 1:33; Acts 1:5; 11:16), whereas, when the baptism of the Spirit actually comes at Pentecost, Peter immediately relates it to Christian baptism (Acts 1:5; 2:38). There are other effects of baptism too which manifestly belong to the new era, namely, the putting on of Christ and the sharing in his death and resurrection (Rom. 6:3–11; Gal. 3:27; Col. 2:12), and though effects like forgiveness and salvation are more timeless, the fact that they have now been brought into clear relation with Christ and his redeeming work makes it meaningful for the first time to speak of a ceremony as actually conferring them.

Despite these differences between baptism and its antecedents, the many points of correspondence between them which were pointed out in section 1 remain important, and the superiority of baptism must not be exaggerated. Though the New Testament normally speaks of baptism as conferring benefits which the Jewish ceremonies only symbolized or foreshadowed, these benefits are not tied to baptism in any mechanical way, as is shown particularly by the fact that the same benefits which are attributed to baptism are attributed also to the preaching of the gospel, and to faith in Christ, which is the outcome of such preaching (Jn. 17:20; Acts 15:7; Rom. 10:17; Eph. 1:13). Thus, on the one hand, regeneration is said to come through baptism (Jn. 3:5; Tit. 3:5), while on the other hand it is said to come through the preaching of the word and through faith (Jn. 1:12 f.; Jas. 1:18; 1 Pet. 1:23–25). Similarly the gift of the Spirit comes through baptism (Acts 2:38) but also through faith (Gal. 3:2, 14; Eph. 1:13), and the same is true of salvation (Tit. 3:5; 1 Pet. 3:21; contrast Eph. 2:8) and of forgiveness, the cleansing of the heart and justification (Acts 2:38; 22:16; Tit. 3:5–7; Heb. 10:22; contrast Acts 13:38 f.; 15:9; Rom. 3:22 ff.; Gal. 2:16 ff.). It will be noticed that passages of both kinds are found in the same New Testament book, and in four places both means of receiving the same benefit are mentioned together (Acts 19:4 f.; Gal. 3:26 f.; Eph. 5:26; Col. 2:12 f.). Now, if two means are needed for the reception of the same benefit, its reception cannot be synchronized with them both, however, closely together they may come. In the New Testament, baptism and faith do normally come very close together: the Acts of the Apostles shows adults being baptized as soon as they profess conversion, with no catechumenate in between. Even so, the preaching which issued in faith must have preceded the confession of that faith in baptism; and there are two instances in Acts where the gift of the Spirit, though one of the benefits of baptism (Acts 2:38), is explicitly stated to have been delayed after baptism or conferred before baptism (Acts 8:15–17; 10:44–48). But if baptism is only one of the means by which the benefits it symbolizes are received, and if, though it may be said to confer those benefits, it does not necessarily confer them at once, the gap is *ipso facto* narrowed between this rite and other rites, like circumcision and proselyte baptism, which symbolize similar benefits but are *not* said to confer them. There is no more reason why baptism, conferring regeneration, forgiveness and justification but not necessarily at once, should be withheld from infants, than there is why circumcision and proselyte baptism, merely symbolizing the same benefits, should be withheld, which we know they are not. Even circumcision and proselyte baptism had a proleptic aspect, in that they symbolized the infant's future repentance. So, all things considered the fact that, if baptism is administered to infants, its efficacy must be partly proleptic, does not seem to be any reason for believing that the New Testament church would have judged infants to be unsuitable candidates for the rite.

(c) *The Covenant and its Heirs.* It was noted in section 1(a) that baptism, like circumcision, appears to be a covenanting rite. The Bible speaks of three great covenants between God and his people, the covenant with Abraham, the covenant of Sinai and the new covenant. The church, with which the new covenant is made, is not a completely fresh, Gentile community, but has a Jewish nucleus; and Paul emphasizes in Rom. 9–11 that there is only one people of God, the elect and believing, who primarily belong to Abraham's natural seed, but are found also among those many Gentiles who have been "ingrafted" into that seed since the coming of Christ. To each of his covenants God attached obligatory external rites, notably the initiatory rite of circumcision, to which baptism has since succeeded. Thus, membership of the covenant people consists in three things: (i) election and faith, (ii) birth or ingrafting, and (iii) circumcision or baptism.

Because the first two covenants were made not merely with one generation but with many, circumcision was commanded to be given not just to the head of the household but to its whole male membership, including the infant children, and to each new generation of infant children thereafter (Gen. 17:9–14). Similarly, when a Gentile convert joined the community, not just he but "all his males" had to be circumcised (Exod. 12:48). Later, when the rite of proselyte baptism was added to circumcision, this too was given to the children along with the parent; but as it was a rite for both sexes, not just one, the problem for the first time arose, what was to be done if a husband was converted without his wife or a wife without her husband. Many wives did in fact become proselytes without their husbands around the beginning of the Christian era, and one such is mentioned in the New Testament (Acts 16:1–3; 2 Tim. 1:5; 3:15; *Jewish Encyclopaedia*, art. "Proselyte"). The answer given to the problem, as is clear from the Mishnah was that either partner might receive the initiation rites without the other, and that even if it was the wife, the children might receive the rites with her (Yebamoth 11:2; Ketuboth 4:3; 9:9). The only case in which the children would not be included would be where a pagan husband allowed his wife to be initiated but not his children.

The New Testament extends these conceptions to the Christian church. The church is the continuation of Abraham's natural seed, with Gentile converts adopted in (Rom. 11:1–32). The divine promise accompanying initiation (now by baptism) is "to you and to your children" (Acts 2:38 f.). The children are sanctified by the converted parent, whether father or mother (1 Cor. 7:14). Converts are initiated (now by baptism) not simply as individuals but as households (Acts 16:15, 31–34; 18:8; 1 Cor. 1:16). In all this, infant baptism seems clearly to be implied. The usual objections are readily answered. Jn. 1:13 simply expresses the principle of election, which is given its due place in these contexts as well (Acts 2:39; Rom. 9:6–29; 11:5, 7). Matt. 10:34–37 speaks of division in families, but so does 1 Cor. 7:14. 1 Cor. 7:14 does not imply that the unbelieving parent may be baptized, if the children may; it is the children that Paul argues from, and the unbelieving parent is sanctified only in so far as their sanctity involves it, not in himself. A comparison between Acts 18:8 and 1 Cor. 1:14 does not show that Crispus and his household were baptized apart from each other – rather that Crispus was one of the few among Paul's many converts whom he baptized with his own hands, whereas his household were baptized (doubtless on the same occasion) by Paul's assistants Silas and Timothy. Paul was evidently in the habit of delegating the task of baptizing, as our Lord and Peter had also done (Jn. 4:1 f.; Acts 10:48).

(d) *The Kingdom and the Church.* Jesus' act of receiving and blessing little children (or, as Luke says, *brephē*, infants) is chiefly relevant because of the words with which he accompanied it: "Of such is the kingdom of God. Whosoever shall not receive the kingdom of God as a little child, he shall in no wise enter therein" (Mk. 10:13–16; Lk. 18:15–17). Jn. 3:5 attributes to Jesus the declaration: "Truly, truly, I say to you, unless one is born of water and the Spirit, he cannot enter the kingdom of God" (RSV). Although some commentators see in this a contrast between natural and spiritual birth (cf. L. Morris, *John*, 1972, 215 ff.), most see in it a reference to baptism and spiritual regeneration. In Acts 8:12 one responds to the preaching of the kingdom of God by being baptized.

In his saying on little children, Jesus was speaking not only of them themselves, but also of adults with a childlike attitude; yet it can hardly be denied that little children themselves are included. To enter the kingdom of God implies joining the church, and it is noteworthy that in Ephesians and Colossians children are among the groups in the church which are addressed (Eph. 6:1–3; Col. 3:20). Presumably, as in Judaism, they belong to the community both by birth and by initiation. The objection that if children had been baptized as infants they would also have been admitted to communion as infants lacks substance. Infant communion is a less ancient practice, without a background in Judaism, and open to various objections from the New Testament.   *R. T. Beckwith*
→ Circumcision, → Conversion, → Covenant, → Faith, → Holy Spirit

(a). K. Aland, *Did the Early Church Baptize Infants?* 1963; K. Barth *The Teaching of the Church Regarding Baptism*, 1948; and *CD* IV, 4 Fragment; G. R. Beasley-Murray, *Baptism in the New Testament*, (1962) 1972; and *Baptism Today and Tomorrow*, 1966; G. Bornkamm, "Baptism and New Life in Paul (Romans 6)", *Early Christian Experience*, 1969, 71–86; G. W. Bromiley, *Baptism and the Anglican Reformers*, 1953; and *Sacramental Teaching and Practice in the Reformed Churches* 1957; N. Cryer, *By What Rite?*, 1969; O. Cullmann, *Baptism in the New Testament*, 1950; J. G. Davies, *The Spirit, the Church and the Sacraments*, 1954; J. D. G. Dunn, *Baptism in the Holy Spirit*, 1971; and "Spirit-Baptism and Pentecostalism," *SJT* 23, 1970, 397–407; W. F. Flemington, *The New Testament Doctrine of Baptism*, 1948; A. Gilmore, ed., *Christian Baptism*, 1959; W. Goode, *The Doctrine of the Church of England as to the Effects of Baptism in the Case of Infants*, 1850²; F. Hauck, *niptō*, *TDNT* IV 946 ff.; J. Jeremias, *Infant Baptism in the First Four Centuries*, 1960; and *The Origins of Infant Baptism*, 1963; G. W. H. Lampe, *The Seal of the Spirit*, 1967²; P. C. Marcel, *Biblical Doctrine of Infant Baptism*, 1953; J. B. Mozley, *A Review of the Baptismal Controversy*, 1862; H. G. Marsh, *The Origin and Significance of New Testament Baptism*, 1941; W. E. Moore, "One Baptism," *NTS* 10, 1963–64, 504–16; J. Murray, *Christian Baptism*, 1952; A. Oepke, *baptō* etc., *TDNT* I 529–46; and *louō*, *TDNT* IV 295–307; R. Schnackenburg, *Baptism in the Thought of St. Paul*, 1964; G. Wagner, *Pauline Baptism and the Pagan Mysteries*, 1967; G. Wainwright, *Christian Initiation*, 1969; R. E. O. White, *The Biblical Doctrine of Initiation*, 1960; J. Ysebaert, *Greek Baptismal Terminology*, 1962. H. Thyen, "*baptisma metanoias eis aphesin hamartiōn*", in J. M. Robinson, *The Future of our Religious Past, Essays in Honour of Rudolf Bultmann*, 1971, 131–68.
(b). SB I 695 ff.; F. J. Leenhardt, *Le Baptême Chrétien, son origine, sa signification*, 1946; H.

Schlier, "Zur kirchlichen Lehre von der Taufe," *TLZ* 72, 1947, 321 ff.; P. Althaus, "Was ist die Taufe? Zur Antwort an Karl Barth," *TLZ* 74, 1949, 705 ff.; J. Schneider, *Die Taufe im Neuen Testament*, 1952; E. Barnikol, "Das Fehlen der Taufe in den Quellen der Apostelgeschichte und in den Urgemeinden der Hebräer und Hellenisten," *Wissenschaftliche Zeitschrift der Martin-Luther Universität Halle-Wittenberg*, 1956–57, 593 ff.; E. Klaar, "Zum paulinischen Taufverständnis," *ZNW* 49, 1958, 278 ff.; M. Barth, *Die Taufe, ein Sakrament*, 1952; M. Barth, W. Andersen, J. Beckmann, G. F. Vicedom, "Taufe," *EKL* III 1283 ff.; H. Mentz, *Taufe und Kirche in ihrem ursprünglichen Zusammenhang*, 1960; G. Delling, *Die Zueignung des Heils in der Taufe*, 1961; J. Gnilka, "Die essenischen Taufbäder und die Johannestaufe," *Revue de Qumran* 3, 1961, 185 ff.; R. Bijlsma, *Die Taufe in Familie und Gemeinde*, *Theologische Existenz Heute* 103, 1962; G. Braumann, *Vorpaulinische christliche Taufverkündigung bei Paulus*, *BZWANT* 4, Heft 2, 1962; H. Diem, *Die Taufverkündigung und Taufordnung*, *Theologische Existenz Heute* 98, 1962; C. M. Edsman *et al.*, "Taufe," *RGG*[3] VI 626 ff.; W. Lohrmann, *Glaube und Taufe in den Bekenntnisschriften der evangelisch-lutherischen Kirche*, 1962; C. H. Ratschow, "Waschungen," *RGG*[3] VI 1954 ff.; M. Rissi, "Die Taufe für die Toten," *AThANT* 42, 9162, 3 ff.; H. Braun, "Die Täufertaufe und die qumranischen Waschungen," in *Theologia Viatorum*, IX 1963; J. Gnilka, "Der Täufer Johannes und der Ursprung der christlichen Taufe," *Bibel und Leben* 4, 1963, 39 ff.; A. Strobel, "Säuglings- und Kindertaufe in der ältesten Kirche," in O. Perels, ed. *Begründung und Gebrauch der heiligen Taufe*, 1963, 7 ff.; P. Weigandt, "Zur sogenannten Oikosformel," *NovT* 6, 1963, 49 ff.; W. Michaelis, "Lukas und die Anfänge der Kindertaufe," in *Apophoreta*, Festschrift für Ernst Haenchen, 1946, 194 ff.; G. Delling, "Zur Taufe von 'Häusern' im Urchristentum," *NovT* 7, 1964–65, 285 ff.; G. Braumann, "Leidenskelch und Todestaufe (Mk. 10, 38 f.)," *ZNW* 56, 1965, 178 ff.; G. Friedrich, "Ein Tauflied hellenistischer Judenchristen (1 Thess. 1, 9 f.)," *ThZ* 21, 1965, 502 ff.; W. Jetter, *Taufgeleit*, 1965; E. Lohse, "Taufe und Rechtfertigung bei Paulus," *KuD* 11, 1965, 309 ff.; G. Walther, "Übergreifende Heiligkeit und Kindertaufe im Neuen Testament," *EvTh* 25, 1965, 668 ff.; W. Bieder, *Die Verheissung der Taufe im Neuen Testament*, 1966; L. L. Fazekaš, "Taufe als Tod in Rom. 6, 3 ff.," *ThZ* 22, 1966, 307 ff.; G. Walther, "Ein Beitrag zur Diskussion über die Kindertaufe," *Theologische Versuche*, 1966, 46 ff.; N. Gäumann, *Taufe und Ethik. Studien zu Röm. 6*, *BEvTh* 47, 1967; F. Mussner, "Zur paulinischen Tauflehre in Röm. 6, 1–6," in *Praesentia Salutis, Gesammelte Studien zu Fragen und Themen des Neuen Testaments*, 1967, 189 ff.; E. Schott, *Taufe und Rechtfertigung in kontroverstheologischer Sicht*, 1967; W. Wilkens, "Wassertaufe und Geistempfang bei Lukas," *ThZ* 23, 1967, 26 ff.; G. Bauer *et al.*, "Taufverkündigung und Taufpraxis," *Praktische Theologie* 57, 1968, 353 f.; J. Beckmann, "Ist die Taufe ein Sakrament?" *Ev.Komm.* 1, 1968, 330 ff.; J. Fangmeier, "Darbringung und Taufe," in *Wort und Gemeinde*, E. Thurneysen zum 80. Geburtstag, 1968, 460 ff.; D. Hoch, *Kindertaufe in der Volkskirche*, *TheolStud* 94, 1968; W. Jetter, *Was wird aus der Kirche?* 1968, 198 ff.; E. Jüngel, *Karl Barths Lehre von der Taufe*, *TheolStud* 98, 1968; *Kindertaufe Pflicht oder Verpflichtung? Beiträge zur Information und Diskussion*, 1968; J. Seim, "Schrift, Bekenntnis und Taufe," *Praktische Theologie* 57, 1968, 546 ff.; "Einheit in der Taufe: ein ökumenisches Ziel. Gespräch mit L. Vischer," *Ev.Komm.* 2, 1969, 587 ff.; H. Falcke, "Katechumenatstaufe," *EvTh* 29, 1969, 477 ff.; M. Ferel, *Gepredigte Taufe. Eine homiletische Untersuchung zur Taufpredigt bei Luther*, 1969; "Kindertaufe oder Erwachsenentaufe, eine falsche Alternative. Bericht über die Taufdiskussion in den Evangelischen Kirche Deutschlands," *Ev.Komm* 2, 1969, 559 ff.; K. F. Müller and W. Blankenburg, eds., *Leiturgia V: Der Taufgottesdienst*, 1969; E. Schlink, *Die Lehre von der Taufe*, 1969; G. Fitzer, "Taufe-Gemeinschaft – Mission," in O. Böcher and K. Haacker, eds., *Verborum Veritas*, Festschrift für G. Stählin, 1970, 263 ff.; F. von Lilienfeld, "Evangelisch-orthodoxer Dialog über die Taufe," *Ev.Komm.* 3, 1970, 43 ff.

Beat, Chastise, Scourge

μαστιγόω

κολαφίζω (kolaphizō), beat; δέρω (derō), beat; μάστιξ (mastix), whip, lash, scourging, torment; μαστιγόω (mastigoō), whip, flog, scourge, chastise; μαστίζω (mastizō), strike with a whip, scourge; πατάσσω (patassō), strike, hit; πληγή (plēgē), blow, stroke, wound; ῥάβδος (rhabdos), rod, staff, stick; ῥαβδίζω (rhabdizō), beat with a rod; ῥαπίζω

161

(*rhapizō*), strike; ῥάπισμα (*rhapisma*), a blow (with a club, rod, or whip); ὑπωπιάζω (*hypōpiazō*), strike under the eye, treat roughly, maltreat; φραγέλλιον (*phragellion*), whip, lash; φραγελλόω (*phragelloō*), flog, scourge.

CL In secular Gk. a variety of words denote physical violence, often distinguished, as in English, by the manner in which the violence is inflicted. Of those which later occur in the NT, *derō* originally had the meaning "flay" or "skin", but from Aristoph. onwards it was a general word for "beat". *rhapizō* denotes beating with a stick or rod, generally as a punishment for minor offences by slaves or children, though *rhabdos* does not only mean a stick to beat with. *mastizō* and *mastigoō* refer to a much more severe form of punishment and are later applied to the Roman punishment of scourging which accompanied capital offences, together with the Lat. loan words *phragellion* and *phragelloō* (cf. Lat. *flagellum, flagellare*, the noun and the vb. respectively meaning "whip", "scourge"). *rhapizō* indicates striking with the hand. *hypōpiazō* seems to derive from the world of boxing, lit. strike under the eye, give a black eye (Arist., Plut.), hence, treat roughly, maltreat.

Besides their lit. sense, several of these terms have a fig. meaning. In classical tragedy *plēgē* is a misfortune sent by a god. The fig. sense of *mastix* is found as early as Homer, but it loses its religious significance after Aeschylus.

OT The most frequent of the above words in the LXX are *plēgē, patassō* and *mastigoō*. Besides their lit. usage, they are all regularly applied figuratively to the plagues and sorrows inflicted by God both on the nations and on his own people. *plēgē* is used of the plagues on Egypt (Exod. 11:1; 12:13) and of the servant who is *anthrōpos en plēgē* ("a man struck down with misfortune", Arndt, 674; Isa. 53:3 cf. also v. 4). Gen. 8:21 uses the fut. of *patassō*: "I will never again smite every living creature." Ps. 39(38):11 pleads, "Remove thy stroke (*mastix* in plur.) from me." *rhabdos* is used with a variety of meanings: the shepherd's staff (Mic. 7:14), Aaron's rod (Num. 17), the ruler's sceptre (Ps. 45:6), the stick as a means of punishment (Exod. 21:20). *derō* is rare and is found only in the sense of flay (Lev. 1:6).

NT 1. These various words are used in a lit. sense in the NT.
(a) *derō* (Lk. 22:63), *phragelloō* (Matt. 27:26; Mk. 15:15) and *mastigoō* (Jn. 19:1) are used to describe the treatment received by Jesus in the passion events. They are all used in connection with the Roman punishment of scourging. In addition Jesus was also struck by the soldiers (*rhapizō*, Matt. 26:67; *rhapisma*, Mk. 14:65; Jn. 19:3; Matt. and Mk. also have *kolaphizō*). C. Schneider points out that Lk. 23:16 has the weaker *paideusas* (chastise), whereas Matt. 27:26 and Mk. 15:15 have *phragelloō* (scourge). He sees it as an instance of Luke's softening of the passion story (*TDNT* IV 517), suggesting also that Pilate's aim was to impose scourging without crucifixion. However, it may be noted that Luke's euphemistic word occurs in the context of Pilate's own suggestion, whereas *phragelloō* of Matt. and Mk. and the *mastigoō* of Jn. 19:1 are part of the evangelists' description of what happened.

mastigoō occurs in the passion predictions (Matt. 20:19; Mk. 10:34; Lk. 18:33; but *not* Matt. 17:23; Mk. 9:31). In addition to the passion predictions, Jesus' parabolic teaching shows that he anticipated such treatment of himself (Matt.

162

21:35; Mk. 12:3, 5; Lk. 20:10 f. all contain references to beating, *derō*). J. Jeremias holds that Jesus, together with many contemporaries, regarded martyrdom as part of the prophet's office. Would Jesus have expected a better fate for himself? (*New Testament Theology*, I 280; cf. Matt. 23:35 par.; Lk. 13:33). This attitude to the prophet's calling makes such sayings perfectly credible.

(b) Several passages refer to Jewish punishment inflicted in the synagogue. The disciples are warned to expect scourging (*mastigoō*, Matt. 10:17; 23:34) and beating (*derō*, Mk. 13:9). Acts 5:40 and 22:19 describe instances of beating by Jewish authorities, the latter at the hands of Paul before his conversion. In 2 Cor. 11:24 Paul recalls how he himself received five times "forty save one" (where the omission of the plur. *plēgas* is idiomatic). Such punishment is referred to in Deut. 25:1–3 and Jos., *Ant.* 4, 8, 21. The example of those who were scourged for their faith is held up by Heb. 11:36.

(c) Punishment by civil magistrates is also mentioned, perhaps sometimes as a mode of examination under torture (Acts 16:23, 33, *plēgē*; 16:37, *derō*; 22:24, *mastix*; 2 Cor. 11:23, *plēgē*; Acts 16:22; 2 Cor. 11:25, *rhabdizō*).

2. Some of these words are used in a fig. sense to describe acts of God.

(a) God corrects and chastises (*mastigoō*) his own people for their good (Heb. 12:6; cf. Prov. 3:12). The believer is encouraged by Paul to forestall this by imposing self-discipline. He treats his own body roughly (*hypōpiazō*) and subdues it, lest having preached to others he should himself be disqualified or be found unfit (*adokimos*) (1 Cor. 9:27; cf. 11:30 f.).

(b) In Mk. 3:10; 5:29 and Lk. 7:21 *mastix* is used of a bodily illness in the sense of torment, suffering or affliction. It reflects a contemporary belief that illness was a chastisement from God, though Jesus denied that there was a necessary connection between sickness and sin (Jn. 9:3).

(c) At the crucifixion the shepherd himself is smitten (*patassō*) by God (Matt. 26:31; cf. Zech. 13:7 and Isa. 53:3 f.), and thus shoulders God's judgment on all men. The hapax legomenon *mōlōps* is used to express the paradox: by his wound(s) you have been healed (1 Pet. 2:24).

(d) God inflicts judgment on all men who have rebelled against him with the intention of leading them back to repentance. The word *plēgē*, used to translate plague in Exod., is repeatedly used in Rev. The plagues are manifestations of God's → wrath. Where they fail to evoke a response of repentance, they finally destroy (Rev. 9:20 f.; 11:6; 15:1).

(e) *kolaphizō*, lit. strike with the fist, beat, cuff, is used lit. in Matt. 26:67; Mk. 14:65; and generally in 1 Cor. 4:11 and 1 Pet. 2:20. In 2 Cor. 12:7 it is used fig. of the "thorn in the flesh, a messenger of Satan", sent "to beat me, to keep me from being too elated." In view of the reference to flesh, this is widely taken to be a physical affliction. Numerous theories have been put forward, including epilepsy, hysteria, periodic depressions, headaches, severe eye trouble, malaria, leprosy, and a speech impediment (cf. Arndt, 442). Gal. 4:15 and 6:11 (cf. 6:17) might support the theory of serious eye trouble. However, in response to Paul's prayer three times for the removal of affliction the reply is given, "My grace is sufficient for you, for my power is made perfect in weakness" (2 Cor. 12:9).

(f) *rhabdos* is used several times to denote divine majesty, rule and power, particularly in connection with the final overthrow of evil (→ Crown, Sceptre).

163

This absolute authority has been entrusted to the Son (Heb. 1:8; cf. Ps. 45:6; Rev. 2:27; 12:5; 19:15; cf. Ps. 2:9). The one who will smite (*patassō*) the nations and rule them with a rod of iron (Rev. 19:15) is the → lamb who was himself slain (Rev. 5:8; 12:11; 19:7, 9, 13).   *E. M. Embry*

→ Teach, art. *paideuō*, → Torment, art. *kolaphizō*, → Fight

C. Schneider, *mastigoō*, *TDNT* IV 515–19; *mōlōps*, *TDNT* IV 829; *rhabdos*, *TDNT* VI 966–71; A. N. Sherwin-White, *Roman Society and Roman Law in the New Testament*, 1963, 25–8, 71–76.

Beginning, Origin, Rule, Ruler, Originator

ἀρχή

ἀρχή (*archē*), beginning, cause; ἄρχω (*archō*), to begin, to rule; ἄρχων (*archōn*), ruler, prince; ἀρχηγός (*archēgos*), ruler, leader; ἀρχαῖος (*archaios*), old, ancient.

CL 1. *archē* (Homer onwards) is an important term in Gk. philosophy. It means (a) beginning, start, (b) starting point, original beginning, (c) the first cause, (d) power, authority, rule. The vb. *archō* commonly means (a) to be the first, to begin in the sense that one is the first, the one who does something before others, (b) to begin by doing something in contrast to what one does later, (c) as leader to be first, to rule. Its part. *archōn* means ruler, commander, prince. *archēgos* has a similar meaning, only that in the former there is more stress on the power needed for commanding. The adj. *archaios* denotes that which has been from the beginning or from early times; hence old, ancient.

2. *archē* developed a special meaning in Gk. philosophy: (a) It denotes the point at which something new begins in time, the end of which can be seen from the first. When one spoke of the beginning (*archē*), the end (*telos*) was also in view. Since the beginning comes out of the infinite, so the end will also lose itself in it.

(b) It is the starting point, the cause, the first cause of all that is, the basic principle of all, e.g. for Thales, water; for Anaximander, infinity; for Anaximenes, air. Gradually *archē* developed its meaning from the underlying cause to the underlying laws, which determine the development and progress of the cosmos.

(c) For the Stoics God (*theos*) and matter (*hylē*) were *archai*.   *D. Müller*

OT The LXX uses this word group to translate over 30 Heb. words, though many occur only once or twice. The following meanings may be noted:

1. The vb. *archō* is most commonly used as a rendering of *ḥālal* in the hiph. (e.g. Gen. 6:1; Jdg. 10:18), or of *yā'al* in the hiph. (e.g. Gen. 18:27; Deut. 1:5). Both indicate the beginning of an action which is concerned with the overcoming of difficulties or customs. The usage is purely linguistic and no theological colouring should be seen in it. Also the noun *archē* is used for the beginning of a process (Heb. *tᵉḥillâh*; e.g. Gen. 41:21; Dan. 9:21).

2. The concept of a beginning in time which is dominant in the vb. can be seen in an even more specialized sense in the noun *archē*, when it is used to translate *'ōlām*, a distant time (only Jos. 24:2; Isa. 63:16, 19) or *qeḏem*, antiquity, of old (e.g. Hab. 1:12; Ps. 74[73]:1[2]; Mic. 5:2[1]). So used, it does not mean only the distant past in time (*qeḏem* meant originally the beginning, and so East), but the state that once was, the beginning of a nation or of the world (→ Time, *aiōn*; →

Creation). Used in this sense, the meaning of *archē* stretches from the previous condition that can be remembered back over the original condition into the past before time (Isa. 37:26). The adj. *archaios*, old, has more or less the same range of meaning (→ Age, Old, art. *palai*). In Ps. 139(138):5 the *archaia*, the earlier, are contrasted with the *eschata*, the last, so as to paraphrase *ta panta*, the whole. (In MT and in Eng. it is "behind and before".)

3. The meaning of foremost or highest rank is found alongside the temporal meaning. This comes from its rendering of Heb. *rô'š*, head, with its wide range of nuances, and its derivatives *ri'šōn*, first or earlier, and *rē'šît*, beginning, first part, product. The use of *archē* for these is often quite mechanical, thus forcing it to take on a wide range of meanings (e.g. Jer. 22:6 "the summit" (of Lebanon); Num. 1:2 "the number" (of names); Gen. 2:10 (four) "rivers"). It is used as a paraphrase (in Amos 6:1; Num. 14:20, "the first" (of the nations); Exod. 12:2, "the beginning" (of months); 1 Ki. 21(20):9, 11, set Naboth "on high" i.e. give him the most important place in the gathering; Gen. 40:20, "lifted up the head", i.e. restored to a position of power; → First, art. *prōtos*). The connotations of beginning and of the highest rank come together in certain passages, e.g Ps. 111(110):10, where the fear of the Lord is the *archē tēs sophias* ("beginning of wisdom"). Here *archē* is the principle which governs the components of beginning, progress and result of the whole.

4. From the Heb. *rô'š* it takes on the meaning of "command" or the "military unit" command (Jdg. 9:34; 1 Sam. 11:11). The element of "ruling" is particularly clear, when it used to render *memšālâh*, rule, dominion (Gen. 1:16; Jer. 34:1 (LXX 41:1); Mic. 4:8). This is even more frequent with *archō*, when it is used 15 times for the Heb. *māšal*, rule (e.g. Gen. 1:18; Jdg. 9:2; Deut. 15:6; → Lord).

5. This lies behind the relatively unambiguous use of *archōn* (450 times) and *archēgos* (23 times). Both are used relatively often, particularly by the Chronicler, and in Deut., Jos., Num., and Jdg., for the Heb. *rô'š* meaning a political or military leader, and also a head of a family (e.g. Num. 25:4; 30:1(2); 1 Chr. 8:6, 28; Neh. 11:3, 16 f.). *archōn* is used to render *śar*, holder of authority and power, leader, nobleman, ruler (e.g. Gen. 12:15; Jdg. 8:3; Amos 1 15), and in Num. and Ezek. *nāśî*, head (of a tribe), patriarch (e.g. Num. 2:3, 5, 7; Ezek. 9:27), while *archēgos* is used for the elected charismatic leader in time of need (Heb. *qāṣîn*, Jdg. 11:6). *archēgos* refers more to the actual exercise of power and *archōn* more to the authority behind it. Hence its meaning extends from the one able to exercise influence to the leader of the people, to officials and even to the celestial beings (Dan. 10:13) who represent the nations in the world of spirits and who in great measure are hostile to God's people. This too is called an *archē* (Dan. 7:27).

L. Coenen

NT When the NT uses the word-group, it implies, as does secular Gk., a certain priority, both of time and of standing and prestige. In other words, the NT uses the concepts in much the same way as secular Gk. We find them used especially to denote a first point in time and to indicate an area of authority.

1. *archē* which is used 55 times in NT (18 times in the Johannine writings) means:

(a) *Beginning, commencement* (Mk. 1:1; the beginning of the Gospel; 13:8, the beginning of the sufferings of closing age; Heb. 3:14, the beginning of confidence or

165

faith; Acts 10:11, the beginning, i.e. corner, of a cloth). In Jn. 8:25 *tēn archēn* means "at all" (cf. RSV mg.). In Heb. 5:12; 6:1 *archē* carries the meaning of "groundwork", "elementary teaching". Christ is exalted above → time, and so has neither beginning nor end (Heb. 7:3). The phrases *ap' archēs* and *ex archēs* denote the first point in time, its occasion being determined from the context: "the beginning" of Jesus' activity (Lk. 1:2; Jn. 15:27; 16:4); Jesus knew "from the beginning" whether someone believed (Jn. 6:64); Paul's life "from the beginning" was among his own nation (Acts 26:4). John points to what the church had "from the beginning" i.e. the same gospel, the same Word of God, and no new commandment (1 Jn. 2:7). It was to abide in them (2:24); it is the message of love (3:11; 2 Jn. 5) which is effective through activity based on the will of God (2 Jn. 6).

The interpretation of 2 Thess. 2:13 is not quite certain. Does it mean that the → election of the readers was from the moment of their birth or from eternity? The devil was a murderer and liar "from the beginning" and has nothing to do with the truth. Hence his children can perform only their father's desires (Jn. 8:44; cf. 1 Jn. 3:8, the devil sins from the beginning). Monogamy goes back to the beginning of creation (Gen. 1:27; Matt. 19:4, 8; Mk. 10:6). Mk. 13:19 and 2 Pet. 3:4 look back to the beginning of the world. Acts 11:15 thinks of the first days of the church in Jerusalem, and Phil. 4:15 of the beginning of Paul's missionary activity.

(b) *Absolute beginning*. Jn. 1:1 implies something before time, i.e. not a beginning within time, but an absolute beginning, which can be affirmed only of God, of whom no temporal categories can be predicated. The Logos (→ Word) is in the strictest sense pre-existent before the → world and so before → time which begins with the world. Such is also the sense in 1 Jn. 1:1; 2:3 f. The former reference with the subject in the neut. makes the intention even clearer.

(c) *First Cause*. It is a controversial point of exegesis whether this meaning of *archē* may be assumed in Col. 1:18. Is it to be included with the cosmological statements about Christ which precede it, or should a full stop be placed after *synestēken* (hold together, v. 17) as in RSV and so begin a new chain of thought? If the former course is adopted the meaning "first cause" would seem to be indicated. In the latter case the word would take on a meaning like *aparchē*, first-fruits (→ Sacrifice). Christ is the first-fruits and the first-born from the dead. In this respect Rev. 3:14; 21:6; 22:13 are also uncertain. It is possible that Christ is here being called the First Cause of → creation, but it may be equally possible that his existence before time is meant. In this case we shall include these verses under (b) with Jn. 1:1 and 1 Jn. 1:1.

(d) *archē* has the meaning of *power, authorities, rulers* in Lk. 12:11; 20:20; Tit. 3:1, where it is linked with *exousia*, authority, and refers to the civil or religious (Jewish) authorities. The first reference states that persecution may come to the disciples from the heads of the synagogue communities. In Lk. 20:20 it is the Roman procurator in Palestine (Judea and Samaria) that is meant. Tit. 3:1 calls for obedience to the civil powers and the authorities in general.

(e) In some NT passages *archē* means an *angelic power*. As in ·early Rab. Judaism, the world or nature, and all its manifestations and powers are regarded as being under the control of → angels and are guided by them. Various categories or classes of angels are recognized, but the NT sees no importance in working out their grades, whether as individuals or as hierarchies. Nor does the NT introduce us to any special functions which the *archai* exercise in contrast with the *dynameis* and the *exousiai*. This is in strong contrast to certain inter-testamental Jewish writings and primitive Christian extra-canonical ones dependent on them. Col. 1:16 is fundamental in this connection. The supernatural, heavenly beings and powers, of whom the *archai* form part, have been created through Christ and for him. Accordingly, Christ's reconciling act embraces the whole cosmos (Col. 1:20). At the present time too Christ is the head of every *archē* and *exousia* (Col. 2:10; cf. Phil. 2:10 f.). He is the ruler of the world, both in nature and history and → Lord and → head of the whole cosmos. These rulers and authorities brought him to the → cross without recognizing him (1 Cor. 2:8). But on the cross Christ disarmed these powers, robbing them of their → might (Col. 2:14 f.). By the → resurrection Christ was exalted to God's right hand above all lords, authorities, powers (*archai*), rulers and every name which can be named.

It is a striking thought that the mystery (→ Secret) of the call of the Gentiles to Christian faith should be made known to the principalities and powers in the heavenly places through the church (Eph. 3:10). The mystery of the call of the Gentiles has a cosmic meaning which reaches out into the spiritual world. This is true also of the church's → proclamation. In Eph. 6:12 the *archai* are part of the evil world of spirits ruled by the devil against which Christians have to fight. In Rom. 8:38 the *archai*, alongside angels and powers, denote a special category of heavenly or supernatural beings which are at work at the present time but cannot separate the believer from the love of God. In the events of the end-period, which bring about the establishment of God's → kingdom, Christ will destroy every *archē, dynamis*, and *exousia* (1 Cor. 15:24).

2. *archō* is found 85 times in the NT. In the act. it means to be the first, rule (Mk. 10:42; Rom. 15:12); in the mid. begin, commence. Very often *archō* probably translates the Aram. *šᵉrā'* (haph.) which serves as a formal introduction to a speech or action (e.g. he began to say . . .). It is often almost superfluous, and can be omitted in the Eng. translation without affecting the meaning (e.g. Matt. 4:17; 11:7, 20; 26:22; Mk. 6:7; Lk. 3:8; 15:14; Jn. 13:5; Acts 1:1; 11:4, 15). It is retained in the RSV, but see the usage in other modern translations. Sometimes it serves to separate a new action from the previous one (e.g. Matt. 26:37; Lk. 4:21; 7:15, 38, 49).

It has its full meaning in Lk. 3:23, Jesus was about thirty years old, when he began his work. Similarly it marks a temporal beginning in Matt. 16:21; and a literal beginning in Lk. 24:27, where the Risen One began his explanation of the Scriptures with Moses and the Prophets. In Jn. 8:9 the eldest went first. In 1 Pet. 4:17 judgment comes first to the household of God and then to the others. *arxamenos* may denote the place where an action begins; the word of repentance and good news had its beginnings in Galilee (Lk. 23:5; Acts 10:37).

3. *archaios* (that which has been since days of old, old) occurs 9 times in the NT. The people of an older generation, the generation in Israel which received the Word, is called *hoi archaioi*, the men of old, ancestors (Matt. 5:21; cf. v. 27 in some MSS). Some thought that Jesus was one of the old prophets, one of those who had lived in OT times and who had come back to life (Lk. 9:8, 19). Mnason of Cyprus was an *archaios mathētēs*, a disciple who had known Jesus for a long time and so also one from the first days of the church (Acts 21:15). There is an element of

167

hyperbole in Acts 15:7 "from days of old" (RSV "in the early days" gives a weakened rendering). God had decided the matter under debate, the preaching of the gospel to the Gentiles, and had called Peter to do it long before. The "ancient world" (2 Pet. 2:5) is the world before the flood. Satan is "the ancient serpent" – alluding to the Eden story (Gen. 3:1, 14 f.) – who was active at the beginning of the world and of human history (Rev. 12:9; 20:2). He who is in Christ, he who believes in Christ in virtue of the gift of the Holy Spirit (Rom. 8:4, 9 f.), is a → new → creation in whom the "old", the earthly nature, and with it the sinful existence lived before Christ, have passed away (2 Cor. 5:17).

4. *archēgos* is found only 4 times in the NT and is applied only to Jesus. It means:

(a) *Leader, ruler, prince*. Peter's phrase is paradoxical, when he accuses the Jews of having chosen a murderer and of having killed "the Prince of life" (RSV "Author", Acts 3:15). The expression here can mean that Jesus brings men to life, and also that Jesus Christ is the author of life (cf. Jn. 1:4). God raised up Jesus, who had been murdered on the cross, and exalted him to his right hand as *archēgos* (Acts 5:31), i.e. "as leader" (and Saviour). The expression should be taken as a parallel to Acts 2:36: God has made him *Kyrios* (→ Lord) and Christ.

(b) *Author, founder*. Heb. 2:10 speaks solemnly of Christ as *archēgos tēs sōtērias*: Jesus is pioneer and author of salvation (cf. Heb. 5:10; 6:20). "The way, the work and the image of the Christ determine the 'salvation' of man" (O. Michel, *Der Hebräerbrief, KEK* XIII, 75). Because Christ has himself reached the goal, he is not only author but also perfecter of salvation (Heb. 12:2).

5. *archōn* also means:

(a) *Ruler, lord, prince*, and is found 37 times with this meaning in the NT. Only in Rev. 1:5 is it used of Christ, where referring to Ps. 89:27(88:28), he is called the *archōn* of the kings of the earth (cf. Rev. 19:16; Phil. 2:11, *kyrios*, → Lord). Otherwise, the *archontes* are those that rule over the nations and oppress them (Matt. 20:25; Mk. 10:42). In Acts 4:25 f., Ps. 2:1 f. is quoted and applied to the co-operation of Herod and Pilate, both *archontes*, at the crucifixion of Jesus.

(b) *Authorities, chief men, those in charge*. It is used in this sense especially of the synagogue authorities (e.g. Matt. 9:18, 23; Lk. 8:41; 12:58; 18:18), the lay members of the Sanhedrin (e.g. Lk. 23:13, 35; 24:20; Jn. 3:1), members of the highest Jewish authorities in general (Jn. 7:26, 48; 12:42; Acts 3:17; 4:5, 8; 13:27) and the high priest (Acts 23:5). Exod. 2:14 is quoted in Acts 7:27: the Israelite refused to recognize Moses as his ruler, or as one set in authority over him. The *archōn* of the Pharisees (Lk. 14:1) would have been a leading Pharisee (but cf. RSV "a ruler who belonged to the Pharisees"). In Acts 14:5 Jewish and Gentile authorities are noted as being hostile to the apostle. Paul and Silas were dragged before the magistrates of Philippi (Acts 16:19). In his teaching about the state Paul says that the authorities (*archontes*) are not a cause of fear to those who do good (Rom. 13:3).

(c) In addition evil spirits are called *archōn* (→ Demon, art. *daimōn*). The Pharisees accused Jesus of driving out demons by the power of the *archōn* of the demons, meaning Beelzebul as the *diabolos* (Matt. 9:34; 10:25; 12:24; Mk. 3:22; Lk. 11:15). Satan is prince (*archōn*) of this world, who has been judged (Jn. 16:11), and cast out of heaven through the death and exaltation of Jesus (Jn. 12:31). He tries in vain to get hold of Jesus and to destroy him (Jn. 14:30). The whole of the present world is under *archontes* who are on their way to destruction (1 Cor. 2:6). They have a

wisdom which contrasts with the wisdom of God, which Paul proclaims in a mystery. It is these *archontes* who crucified Christ (1 Cor. 2:8). The *archōn* of the kingdom of the air (Eph. 2:2) is → Satan.   *H. Bietenhard*
→ Caesar, Consul, Governor, → Creation

(a). G. B. Caird, *Principalities and Powers*, 1956; G. Delling, *archō, archē* etc. *TDNT* I 478–89; A. Ehrhardt, *The Beginning: A Study in the Greek Philosophical Approach to the Concept of Creation from Anaximander to St. John*, 1968; Moulton–Milligan, 81. Commentaries on *John* by B. F. Westcott, 1880; C. K. Barrett, 1955; R. Schnackenburg, 1968; R. E. Brown, 1966; L. Morris, 1971, on 1:1 f. Commentaries on *Colossians* by J. B. Lightfoot, 1879; C. F. D. Moule, 1957; F. F. Bruce, 1957; E. Lohse, 1971, on 1:15–18.
(b). J. C. M. van Winden, *In den beginne. Vroechristelijke exegese van de term beginne in Gen. 1.1*, 1967.

Belly

κοιλία

κοιλία (*koilia*), belly.

CL & OT The basic meaning of *koilia* is a hollow or cavity. In Gk. it is found with the meanings (1) belly, abdomen, bowels, stomach; (2) the abdomen as the site of the sexual organs, the womb; (3) the LXX and Rab. literature use it also metaphorically for the inner man, as a synonym for *kardia* → Heart.

NT Hence in the NT it means (1) belly, stomach (Lk. 15:16 some MSS) and, in OT quotation (Matt. 12:40 = Jon. 1:17(2:1), Rev. 10:9f. = Ezek. 3:3); (2) the womb (Lk. 2:15, 41, 42; 2:21; 11:27, Acts 3:2); (3) the inner man (only in Jn. 7:38).

In Mk. 7:14–23 and Matt. 15:10–20 evil is said to come out of the heart (*kardia*) of man (v. 21). That which enters a man from outside, enters his stomach (v. 19). Thus in contrast with Rab. Judaism, food cannot make a man unclean. The stomach is mortal like the → body. Paul too argued with his opponents against a false evaluation of stomach and food (1 Cor. 6:13). The linking of stomach and food shows that every effort to give man's food a religious value and make it subject to all kinds of ideologies is theologically improper and therefore to be rejected. Paul uses the word metaphorically in Rom. 16:18 and Phil. 3:19 ("their god is the belly"). He rejects not merely gluttonous and sexual excess, but also undue estimation of physical life (→ Flesh).

Only Jn. 7:38 uses *koilia* of the inner man, as a synonym of *kardia*, as in the LXX. Powers are promised to those who believe, which flow from the inner man and can be given only by the Holy Spirit.   *S. Wibbing*
→ Avarice, → Desire

(a). J. Behm, *koilia, TDNT* III 786–89; R. Bultmann, *The Gospel of John*, 1971, 303 f.
(b). G. Friedrich, *Der Brief an die Philipper*, NTD VIII, 1962, 121; E. Lohmeyer, *Der Brief an die Philipper*, KEK IX, 1953[10], 143 ff.; O. Michel, *Der Brief an die Römer*, KEK IV, 1955[10], 346 f.

Bethlehem

Βηθλέεμ

βηθλέεμ (*Bēthleem*), Bethlehem.

OT This is the modern Beit Lahm, a town in the Judaean hill country, some five
    miles south-west of Jerusalem. The Heb. *bêṯ leḥem* means "house of bread",
but the name more probably derives from "house of Laḥama" (a goddess). Eph-
rath was probably the surrounding district, hence the distinctive form "Bethlehem
Ephrathah" (Mic. 5:2). Another Bethlehem was part of Zebulun (Jos. 19:15), and
was situated some seven miles north-west of Nazareth in NT Galilee. It was
probably the home of Ibzan the Judge (Jdg. 12:8–10). The NT allusions are always
to the Judaean town.

Prior to the monarchy Israel's hold on this part of the Judaean hills was insecure
as the Philistine incursion of 2 Sam. 23:14 shows. Nevertheless there were
probably early Israelite settlements there. In one of the Amarna letters the prince
of Jerusalem remarks that Bit-lahmi (probably Judaean Bethlehem) had been taken
over by Apiru. Israelite tribal tradition remembered the town as the birth place of
the Levite who ultimately founded the sanctuary at Dan (Jdg. 17:7), and also of
the concubine whose death foments an inter-tribal war (Jdg. 19:1). Asahel was
buried at Bethlehem (2 Sam. 2:32), and Elhanan, one of David's mighty men, was
born there (2 Sam. 23:24). Two texts link the town with Rachel's burial place
(Gen. 35:19; 48:7; cf. 1 Sam. 10:2). It seems likely that Bethlehem remained one
of the smaller Judaean towns, though according to the Chronicler, it was rebuilt
or fortified by Rehoboam (2 Chr. 11:6). The post-exilic lists of exiles indicate a
relatively small community (Ezr. 2:21; Neh. 7:26).

Bethlehem's permanent theological significance rests exclusively in its claim to be
David's birth place (1 Sam. 16:4; 17:12; 17:15; 20:6; 20:28). This claim is integral
to the stories of Ruth, which link both her and her family with Bethlehem (1:22),
and also with David himself (4:12). With the development of an eschatological
theology, in which a Davidic → Messiah was central, it was naturally believed that
Bethlehem would be his place of origin. In extant intertestamental literature the
Judaean origins of a Messiah are regularly affirmed, though Bethlehem itself does
not figure with any prominence. This sparsity of evidence is probably accidental,
and it seems reasonable to suppose that the town was important in later Jewish
expectation (cf. Jn. 7:42).

The crucial text for NT theology is clearly Mic. 5:2, one of the foundation stones
for Christian messianic interpretation. The main stress in this text is on the contrast
between the numerical insignificance of Bethlehem's population and its theological
importance as the place from which, like David of old, Israel's ideal ruler will come.

NT In Matthew's Gospel Bethlehem is identified as the birth place of Jesus (2:1),
   and as the place to which the magi are therefore directed (2:5; 2:8). His main
purpose here is to show the fulfilment of Micah's prophecy, and his quotation of
Mic. 5:2 follows the MT closely, though he does omit the last two lines of the
verse. In thus neglecting material which might have given him opportunity to
affirm the pre-existence of Jesus he clearly wishes to concentrate solely on Jesus'
messianic role. This quotation is just one element in a substantial network of OT
texts which are interpreted and elaborated in the special Matthaean material of
chapters 1–2. Herod's massacre of the infants at Bethlehem (2:17–18) is likewise
associated with Jer. 31:15. In the context of Matthaean theology as a whole the
birth at Bethlehem conveys the fact of Jesus as Messiah.

In Luke this specialized Jewish interest is absent. Though he draws no explicit theological conclusion from Jesus' birth at Bethlehem, Luke adheres firmly to this particular tradition (2:15). The description of the census (2:1–3) is the Evangelist's means of showing how Jesus, a Galilean, came to be born at Bethlehem.

P. J. Budd

→ Messiah, → Fullness, art. *plēroō*

C. Kopp, *The Holy Places of the Gospels*, 1963, 1–47; R. H. Gundry, *The Use of the Old Testament in St. Matthew's Gospel*, 1967, 91 ff., 205–34; R. Laurentin, *Structure et Théologie de Luc I–II*, 1964; W. M. Ramsay, *Was Christ Born at Bethlehem?* 1892[2].

Bind

δέω

δέω (*deō*) bind, tie.

CL & OT *deō* (pre-Homeric), bind, fasten to, fetter. In the LXX it is used mainly for Heb. '*āsar*, but only in the lit. meaning of binding with a thread or rope and not the figurative sense of binding with an oath. A tied thread can be a sign of recognition (Gen. 38:28), but *deō* is used chiefly for tying up animals (2 Ki. 7:10), or the binding and fettering of men (so frequently in Jdg. 15 f.). Love can be said metaphorically to bind (Cant. 7:5, (6), RSV "is held captive").

NT In the NT as in the LXX, *deō* is frequently used literally, of tying up or securing an animal (Mk. 11:2 par.) or binding a man (Matt. 14:3 par; Acts 9:2). In Col. 4:3 Paul's being bound (RSV, NEB "in prison") is an expression of the mystery of Christ, a sign that even in the greatest affliction God's power is at work (cf. 2 Tim. 2:9). *deō* is used symbolically in Acts 20:22, where Paul sees his plans and travels bound by the Spirit of God. This binding controls his actions like a command which he cannot avoid. It is also symbolic in Rom. 7:2 and 1 Cor. 7:27, 39, where it is used for the binding of husband and wife to each other. The binding in Matt. 16:19 and 18:18 recalls the Heb. '*āsar* which denotes both teaching authority (to determine what is forbidden) and disciplinary power (to place under a ban). "Binding and loosing" was a technical term in Rab. Jud. for the authority of the rabbis in teaching and discipline. The passages in Matt. are concerned with the judicial function to be exercised by Peter, or the disciples. This did not lie in a personal authority given to him or to them, divorced from the Gospel. It lies rather in the nature of the Word of God itself as it is proclaimed. Wherever the message entrusted to the disciples is rejected, it inevitably binds people to their unforgiven guilt to await the coming judgment (cf. Jn. 12:47 f.). This is where the authority given to the disciples by virtue of their message is fundamentally different from the authority claimed by Rab. casuistry. Consequently the messengers themselves do not know in the last analysis who has been loosed and who has been bound by their message, for this rests alone with the divine Judge. In Matt. 13:30, the harvest is a picture of the judgment and the binding of the weeds symbolizes condemnation (cf. also Matt. 22:13 f.). Binding should not be confused with mistaken efforts to create a pure Messianic community here and now by separating out sinners. The best illustration of Matt. 16:19 and 18:18 is probably Matt. 10:12–15 (J. Jeremias,

171

The Parables of Jesus, 1963², 216 f.). This is not the act of pronouncing a human judgment on actions that are regarded with disfavour (as in Rab. thought), but of handing the matter over to God and letting him pass judgment.

W. von Meding, D. Müller

(a). J. B. Bauer, "Binding and Loosing," *EBT* I 67; F. Büchsel, *deō, TDNT* II 60 f., H. von Campenhausen, *Ecclesiastical Authority and Spiritual Power in the First Three Centuries of the Church*, 1969; C. H. Dodd, *NTS* 2, 1955–56, 85 f.; A. M. Honeyman, *JBL* 71, 1952, 11–18; J. Jeremias, *kleis, TDNT* III 744–53; and *The Parables of Jesus*, 1963², 216 f.; E. Käsemann, "Ministry and Community in the New Testament," in *Essays on New Testament Themes*, 1964, 63–94; E. Schweizer, *Church Order in the New Testament*, 1961, 21 ff., 56 ff., 82 f.; H. J. Schoeps, "The Expository Character of the Aqedath Isaac," *Paul*, 1961, 141–49.
(b). P. Boccaccio, *Biblica* 33, 1952, 173–90; G. Lambert, "Lier – Délier," *Vivre et Penser* 3, 1943–44, 91–103; O. Michel, *RAC* II 374–80; "Echtheitsfragen und Deutungen der Primatsstelle Mt. 16, 18 f. in der deutschen protestantischen Theologie der Letzten 30 Jahre," *NTAbh* 21, 1961, 3 f.; SB I 738–47; H. Thyen, "Schlüsselgewalt," *RGG³* V 1449 f.
→ Apostle for works on Peter's role in the early church.

Bird

πετεινόν

πετεινόν (*peteinon*), bird.

CL The adj. *peteinos* means able to fly, winged. In its neut. form *peteinon* it means a bird. It is connected with the vbs. *petomai* (Homer onwards), fly, and *petannymi* and its cognates, spread out. In the Graeco-Roman world some birds were held as sacred. They could also represent the deity and be used for omens (*OCD*, 154, 169, 356 f.). But this did not obtain in Israel or the church.

OT In the creation narrative birds are described by the expression *kol-'ôp kānāp*, every winged bird (Gen. 1:21; cf. Ps. 78:27). The term *ṣippôr kānāp*, winged birds, occurs in Deut. 4:17 and Ps. 148:10. *'ôp* is also used of insects (Lev. 11:20 f.; Deut. 14:19).

The OT distinguishes between clean and unclean birds (Lev. 11:13–19; Deut. 14:11–20). Generally speaking, the latter are birds of prey. In post-biblical times the Mishnah proffered the following clarification: "Any bird that seizes food in its claws is unclean; and any that has an extra talon and a craw and the skin of whose stomach can be stripped off, is clean" (Hullin 3:6). Numerous references to hunters, fowlers and traps suggest that birds were eaten for food (Lev. 17:13; Job 18:8 ff.; Ps. 124:7; Prov. 6:5; Jer. 5:27; Hos. 7:12; Amos 3:5). Doves and pigeons were offered in sacrifice (Lev. 1:14 ff.; 14; cf. Gen. 8:20). On the birth of a child the mother was to offer a lamb for a burnt offering and a young pigeon or a turtledove for a sin offering to make atonement, but in cases of poverty two turtledoves or two young pigeons, one for a burnt offering and the other for a sin offering (Lev. 12:6 ff.). The fact that the parents of Jesus offered the latter is an indication of their poverty (Lk. 2:24).

Numerous species of birds are mentioned in the OT (for details see the works listed in the bibliography). In many cases precise identification is difficult in view of the fact that strict classification is a relatively modern science. The *rāḥām* of Lev. 11:18 and Deut. 14:17 is now thought to be the Egyptian vulture. *nešer* is probably a general term which includes all large birds of prey, but particularly the eagle and the vulture. Here, as with → animals in both the OT and the NT,

172

characteristics and behaviour are used to illustrate religious and moral truth. Referring to the exodus from Egypt, Moses is charged to remind the people how Yahweh bore them "on eagles' wings" and brought them to himself (Exod. 19:4; cf. Ps. 103:5; Deut. 32:11; Jer. 49:22; Obad. 4). "They who wait for the Lord shall renew their strength, they shall mount up with wings like eagles, they shall run and not be weary, they shall walk and not faint" (Isa. 40:31). The order here of soaring, running and walking might at first sight suggest an anticlimax. But in the context of the promised release from captivity and exile, the prophecy indicates the exhilaration of release (as in Exod. 19:4) followed by the promised sustenance throughout the long pilgrim, homeward journey.

The eagle also appears as one of the four living creatures in Ezek. 1:10 (cf. Rev. 4:7, → Animal) and in contexts of judgment (Deut. 28:49; Hab. 1:8; Jer. 49:16; cf. Hos. 8:1; Lam. 4:19). The behaviour of the eagle or griffon-vulture (Job 39:27–30) whose ways are far beyond man's comprehension or control are not beyond God's. It presents a picture of the unfathomable wisdom of God. Birds and animals present a contrast with Israel. For whereas they know their ways, Israel has turned away from his (Jer. 8:7; cf. Isa. 1:3).

Birds can depict desolation (Ps. 102:6 f.; Isa. 34:11; Zeph. 2:14). But they can also be the object of God's care (Job 38:41; Pss. 84:3; 147:9). The flitting of the sparrow and swallow illustrates the ineffectuality of a causeless curse under the providence of God (Prov. 26:2). Birds may also serve man (Gen. 8:6–12). Elijah subsisted for a time on the food of the ravens (1 Ki. 17:4 ff.). Flocks of quails providentially provided Israel with food in the exodus wanderings (Exod. 16:13; Num. 11:31 f.; Ps. 105:40).

NT As in the OT, birds illustrate the workings of divine providence. Apart from the reference to Peter's denial of Jesus three times before cock crow (Matt. 26:34, 75; Mk. 14:30, 72; Lk. 22:34, 61; Jn. 18:27), virtually all the other allusions to birds have a theological significance. Jesus urged the disciples not to be anxious even about the necessities of life. God provides for the birds who know nothing of anxious toil. Are not his children of more value than they? (Matt. 6:26; Lk. 12:24). The thought is taken a step further with the reminder to would-be followers that foxes (→ Animal) have holes and birds have nests, but the Son of Man has nowhere to lay his head (Matt. 8:20; Lk. 9:58). It is a summons to utter trust and abandonment to the providence of the Father. The question: "Are not two sparrows (strouthion) sold for a penny? And not one of them will fall to the ground without your Father's will" (Matt. 10:29; cf. Lk. 12:6) underlines the stark realities of the situation. The birds were not sold as pets but as food for the poor (cf. A. Deissmann, Light from the Ancient East, 1927, 272 ff.). The saying follows a warning not to fear those who kill the body and can do no more, but to fear him who has power to kill and to cast into → hell. The saying, therefore, does not promise being spared from suffering and → death. But it gives assurance of God's love and providential ordering in life and death. It expresses tersely and poignantly what Paul expressed in his exultant celebration of God's providence in Rom. 8:28–39.

Birds feature in the parables of the sower and the mustard seed. In the former they depict the activity of the devil in removing the seed of the word which is not

173

understood (Matt. 13:4, 19; Mk. 4:4, 15; Lk. 8:5, 12). In the latter, the fact that birds can make nests in the branches of what once was a tiny seed that they might so easily have consumed emphasizes the sureness of the growth of the kingdom from apparently insignificant beginnings (Matt. 13:32; Mk. 4:32; Lk. 13:19).

One of the most striking sayings in the gospels is Matt. 23:37 ff.: "O Jerusalem, Jerusalem, killing the prophets and stoning those who are sent to you! How often would I have gathered your children together as a hen (*ornis*) gathers her brood (*nossia*) under her wings (*pterygas*) and you would not! Behold, your house is forsaken and desolate. For I tell you, you will not see me again, until you say, 'Blessed be he who comes in the name of the Lord' " (cf. Lk. 13:34 f.; the saying is widely attributed to Q). The EVV usually have "hen", but *ornis* is a general word for bird. The imagery may be suggested by Ps. 84(83):3, where the Psalmist sees birds and their young finding sanctuary in God's house and sees this as a picture of man's true well-being, and by the reference to wings in Ps. 57:1 (56:2) (cf. SB I 943) and Ps. 91:4.

In view of the fact that the synoptics do not record a repeated ministry of Jesus in Jerusalem, and the fact that the saying appears detached from any particular context in Lk. it has been suggested that the saying may be regarded as an utterance of the risen Christ (cf. E. E. Ellis, *The Gospel of Luke*, 1966, 190; W. Grundmann, *Das Evangelium nach Lukas*, 1959, ad loc.). The words are reminiscent of Stephen (Acts 6:3, 13 f.; 7:47–58). The "I" would then include the disciples like the "me" in Acts 9:4. But the conjecture is unnecessary. For the saying fits the context of Jesus' earthly ministry. Matt. locates it at the climax of Jesus' public confrontation with the scribes and the Pharisees in the temple (cf. 21:23; 22:23; 24:1). In particular, Jesus is addressing the crowds commenting on the scribes and Pharisees after a series of arguments with them (cf. 23:1). Far from being a source of light and refuge, the religious leaders have been foremost in misleading the people and persecuting the men of God – both in the past and in Jesus' own day. The reference to → Jerusalem need not imply repeated visits, but rather Jesus' concern for Jerusalem as the focal point of Judaism, centred on the temple which should have been the true sanctuary of God for the people. The saying actually implies that Jesus himself is the true sanctuary and thus he assumes the role of both the temple and Yahweh as the refuge of the people.

The saying may be applied to Jesus' earthly ministry. But the context in Matt. may also suggest a wider application. For it follows the denunciation of these who build the tombs of the prophets and upon whom will come the blood of the righteous from Abel to Zechariah (Matt. 23:29–36; cf. Lk. 11:45–52). The first person sing. of v. 37 might be identified with that of v. 34. In Lk. 11:49, the parallel to v. 34, the one who sends prophets and apostles whom men kill is called the → Wisdom of God who may be identified with Jesus (cf. 1 Cor. 1:24; Col. 2:3). In other words, Jesus' desire to protect the children of Jerusalem in his earthly ministry is but the climax of the same divine desire throughout history. The sayings in both Matt. and Lk. make it clear that the day of opportunity is irrevocably lost. Judgment involving the desolation of the house of Israel is now inevitable. At the same time it will vindicate Jesus whose messianic return will then be welcomed (Matt. 23:39; Lk. 13:35; cf. Ps. 118:26; SB I, 849 f., 876).

It would be more natural to identify the *aetoi* gathered over the body in Matt. 24:28 and Lk. 17:37 with vultures rather than eagles (cf. G. S. Cansdale, *Animals of Bible Lands*, 1970, 142). But the eagle is a symbol of might and judgment (Hab. 1:8; cf. Job 39:30; Prov. 30:17 → above OT). There may also be a hint in this cryptic saying of the standards of the Roman legions through which the judgment on Jerusalem and the vindication of Christ was effected in A.D. 70. (On the interpretation of the apocalyptic language in this passage see J. M. Kik, *Matthew Twenty-Four*, 1948.) Whatever the particular nuances in this verse, it clearly indicates that the coming of Christ will not be secret but will be obvious to all (cf. Matt. 24:23–7; Lk. 17:23 ff.), and it will be in judgment.

On the offering of Jesus' parents (Lk. 2:24; cf. Matt. 21:12; Mk. 11:15; Jn. 2:14, 16) see above OT. From the viewpoint of ancient science the dove (*peristera*) has no bile, and it became a symbol of virtues for the early Christians (Arndt, 657; W. Bauer, *Das Leben Jesu*, 1909, 117). This finds expression in the saying: "Be wise as serpents and innocent as doves" (Matt. 10:16). At the baptism of Jesus the → Holy Spirit appeared "as a dove" (Matt. 3:16; Mk. 1:10; Lk. 3:22; Jn. 1:32). The symbolism here may have various facets. It may recall the Spirit of God brooding on the waters (cf. Gen. 1:2; Hagigah 15a), suggesting the guiding presence of the Creator Spirit in the new creative work about to begin through Christ (cf. 2 Cor. 4:6 and Jn. 1:1 ff. for passages which link the work of Christ with that of creation). In late Jewish literature the dove symbolized the Spirit of God (Targ. Cant. 2:12) and also the community of Israel (Hos. 7:11; cf. SB I 123 ff.). This may suggest the idea of the recreation of Israel through the one who has been baptized and on whom the Spirit of God rests. In Philo it is a symbol of wisdom. "The coming of the Spirit of God – whose activity in the present time was denied by the rabbis, though they expected a great outpouring in the eschatological Messianic age – upon Jesus indicates his endowment with power, wisdom and holiness for the fulfilment of the Messianic ministry (cf. Ps. Sol. 17:37; 1 Enoch 49:3; Test. Levi 18:6 ff.)" (D. Hill, *The Gospel of Matthew*, 1972, 97; see further W. Telfer, "The Form of a Dove," *JTS* 29, 1928, 238–42; H. Gressmann, "Die Sage von der Taufe Jesu und der vorderorientalischen Taubengöttin," *Archiv für Religionswissenschaft* 20, 1920–21, 1–40, 323–59; F. Sühling, *Die Taube als religiöses Symbol im christlichen Altertum*, 1930; H. Greeven, *peristera*, *TDNT* VI, 63–72; L. E. Keck, "The Spirit and the Dove," *NTS* 17, 1970, 41–67).

Peter's vision of a great sheet containing all kinds of animals, reptiles and birds (Acts 10:12; 11:6) which he was commanded to kill and eat, symbolized that God now accepted what was hitherto unclean (see above OT). The way was open to receive Gentiles into the fellowship of the church, as they had already received the Holy Spirit.

Rom. 1:23 (cf. Acts 17:29) recalls the Second Commandment (Exod. 20:4; Deut. 5:8). The visual representation of God in animal and bird images shows the misguided nature of heathen religion. Jas. 3:7 compares the tongue with birds and animals that can be domesticated. The tongue cannot be tamed. On Rev. 4:7 → OT above and → Animal. The eagle also appears in Rev. 8:17 announcing woes to those on earth. *C. Brown*

→ Animal, → Dragon, → Fish

G. S. Cansdale, *Animals of Bible Lands*, 1970, 140–93; G. R. Driver, "Birds in the Old Testament",

PEQ 86, 1954, 5 ff.; 87, 1955, 129 ff.; "Once Again: Birds in the Bible", *PEQ*, 90, 1958, 50 ff.; W. S. McCullough, *IDB* I, 459 f.; A. Parmelee, *All the Birds of the Bible*, 1960.

Birth, Beget, Bear, Become, Miscarriage, Regeneration, Well-born

These words all have to do with birth, both literally and metaphorically. *tiktō* means to bring forth or bear. The more frequently used *gennaō* means both to bear and to beget. It is used of the birth of Jesus and, with the prefix *ana-* in Jn., of the renewal of man in rebirth by the Holy Spirit. *palingenesia* means regeneration both of an individual and of the world order. *ginomai* originally meant to be born, but in the NT this meaning has faded and the vb. is used with the general meaning of become, take place, be. The nouns *genea* (race, generation) and *genesis* (birth, origin, genealogy) are derived from it (for *genea* → Generation). *ektrōma* means miscarriage.

γεννάω

γεννάω (*gennaō*), beget, become the father of, bear; ἀναγεννάω (*anagennaō*), cause to be born again, bear again.

CL *gennaō* is a causal form of *ginomai* (Liddell-Scott, 344). Cf. the back-formation *genna*, origin, race, birth. It belongs to the same root *gen-* which appears in various Lat. words like *genus* (race), Old High German *Kind* (child) and various derivatives via Lat. such as pregnant, malignant (cf. Lat. (*g*)*nascor*, to be born; *natus*, born, birth; *natura*, birth, nature; *naevus*, birth mark, mole).

Like → *tiktō* and *teknoō*, *gennaō* is used of begetting by the father and bearing by the mother as in the Heb. equivalents, the LXX and the NT. This is certainly the case in later Gk. literature (Apollodorus, Lucian, Plutarch). In the secular world of NT times *gennaō* has the meaning of *come into being* as well as *produce* in a metaphorical or vague general sense (cf. 2 Tim. 2:23 of quarrels; Gal. 4:24 of the covenants).

The compound *anagennaō* has the meaning of cause to be born again. The frequently assumed derivation of the expression from the mystery religions is improbable, for the vb. has so far only been traced to a single late passage in which Sallustius (4th cent. A.D.) speaks of initiates as *hōsper anagennōmenōn* (as born again, *De deis et mundo* 4; cf. G. Wagner, *Pauline Baptism and the Pagan Mysteries*, 1967, 235). In the Hel. period the idea of the *renatus* (Lat. one born again) occurs in the cults of Mithras and Isis (cf. F. Büchsel, *TDNT* I 673; cf. Apuleius, *Metamorphoses*, II, 21). G. Wagner observes: "The assertion that Paul is dependent on the mystery religions because he shares the idea of rebirth with them is misleading, not only because this idea is not at all frequent in the mystery religions and never occurs in the first century A.D., but also because Paul never uses the term" (op. cit., 270).

OT In the LXX OT *gennaō* is used chiefly for Heb. *yālad* (bear, bring forth, mostly in hiph.). Occasionally it translates *hārāh* (conceive, become pregnant). In addition to the lit. usages, there is the fig. in Job 38:28; "Has the rain a father, or who has begotten (Heb. *hôlîḏ*; Gk. *ho tetokōs*) the drops of dew?"

1. The words → father and son (→ Child) are sometimes used in an address as a sign of trust or affection (1 Sam. 3:16; 24:12; 2 Ki. 2:12). Unlike the NT (→ NT, 2), *gennaō* is never used in such contexts. Neither is it used in those passages which speak of Israel as God's firstborn (Exod. 4:22; 23:4; → First), or God as the father and the Israelites as his sons. The absence of this vb. in this connection indicates a marked contrast between Israel and the surrounding culture. The OT sharply dissociates itself from the procreation myths. Israel is Yahweh's people not by natural procreation but by → election.

2. Two passages in the Pss. speak of the begetting of the king-messiah by God (Heb. *yālaḏ*, Gk. *gennaō*). "I will tell of the decree of the Lord: He said to me, 'You are my son, today I have begotten you' " (Ps. 2:7). "Before [the creation of] the morning star I begat thee" (Ps. 110:3 LXX; but cf. the Heb. MT "From the womb of the dawn the dew of thy youth comes to thee").

The idea that the king as the earthly representative of the deity was the "son of God" was current in the ancient East. Scholars have seen remarkable parallels in Egypt and Mesopotamia which lead them to think that Israel has clearly drawn on them. G. von Rad sees the rite in 2 Sam. 7 and the Pss. as almost copies of the rites of the Egyptian court which had long been conventionalized (*Old Testament Theology*, I, 1962, 40). But Israel had refashioned the idea in the light of its belief in Yahweh. The Egyptians had the mythological idea that Pharaoh was the physical son of the God Amun. The OT idea comes nearer to the Mesopotamian ritual in which the king who has been installed by the gods is a chosen servant (op. cit., 320). But the sonship of the Israelite king rests neither upon physical begetting nor upon the thought that through the act of enthronement the king somehow physically entered the sphere of the divine. M. Noth comments: "Possibly as a deliberate reaction to this ancient oriental conception, the formula of adoption is used to describe the relationship; the God-King relationship has no foundation in Being and the King is not divine, but he is declared to be a son when he ascends the throne – by a manifestation of the divine will. Probably when the heirs of David acceded to power the formula of adoption was solemnly pronounced (Ps. ii, 7, and perhaps also Ps. cx, 3). This means that the relationship was confirmed, on a historical basis, at each new accession" (*The History of Israel*, 1958, 223). The word "today" (Ps. 2:7) also points to sonship by adoption. (See further A. A. Anderson, *The Book of Psalms*, I, 1972, 67 ff.; K. A. Kitchen, *Ancient Orient and the Old Testament*, 1966, 106–11; G. von Rad, "The Royal Ritual in Judah" in *The Problem of the Hexateuch and Other Essays*, 1966, 225 ff.) The connection of the Psalm passages with the prophecy of Nathan (2 Sam. 7) is extensive. They have their basis in the declaration "which the prophet Nathan made to David and his dynasty for all time" (H.-J. Kraus, *Die Psalmen*, 1960, I, 20 f.).

The line of christological interpretation in the NT starts here (cf. Matt. 22:43 f.; Mk. 12:36 f.; Lk. 20:42 f.; Acts 4:25; 13:33; 1 Cor. 15:25; Heb. 1:5, 13; Rev. 2:27). The absence of physical procreation is shown by the reference to the "seed of David" (Heb. *zera'*) which is used in the sing. collectively of David's posterity. The tension between human parentage and the role of God which appears in accounts of Jesus' birth and descent (Matt. 1:16; cf. vv. 1, 6, 20; Lk. 1:33b, 35b; cf.

3:23–38) is already present in the OT view of kingship. The son-passages of Isa. 7 and 9 do not use *gennaō*. Apart from an apocryphal passage (Sir. prologue 28 *v.l.*), *anagennaō* does not occur in the LXX.

3. In Palestinian Judaism the thought of God begetting occurs only in connection with messianic expectation. It is remarkable that in all the voluminous rab. literature there is only one reference which applies Ps. 2:7 to the Messiah (Suk. 52a). This silence is apparently due to the rabbis' opposition to the Christian church which had applied Ps. 2 to Jesus' sonship. However, the Dead Sea Scrolls relate Nathan's prophecy (especially 2 Sam. 7:14a) to the "seed of David" (4Qflor. 1:10 ff. and perhaps 1QSa. 2:11). But there is no thought of the Messiah as God's son in a physical sense in the ancient synagogue, nor is there of pre-existence (SB IV, 1 452–65). The thought of Ps. 2:7 is taken up in Pss. Sol. 17:23 . But significantly the begetting of the Messiah is not.

4. In Hel. Jud. Philo used *gennaō* of God in describing his work as creator (*Leg. All.* 3, 219). The logos (→ Word), animals and plants are begotten by God (*Conf. Ling.* 63; *Mut. Nom.* 63; cf. *Migr. Abr.* 35). But Philo did not apply the idea to the relation of God to the devout. Philo's use of the word contrasts with the Nicene Creed in the 4th cent. which used *gennaō* of the Father's begetting the Son but *ktizō* (create) of the world.

"In the Mysteries ideas and processes from sex life play an important part . . . . On the other hand, there seems to be no reference to the birth of an initiate through a goddess or to his begetting by a god. In pre-Christian times, at least, the real thought is that of adoption" (F. Büchsel, *TDNT* I 669).

anagennaō does not occur in Philo. But in Josephus it is quite common and is, e.g., applied to fruit. The noun *anagennēsis* (new birth) is used by Philo to express the Stoic doctrine of world renewal after the universal conflagration (*ekpyrōsis*, cf. *Aet. Mund.* 8). He usually calls this → *palingenesia* (rebirth, regeneration cf. *Aet. Mund.* 9). *anagennēsis* was not necessarily a Stoic term (F. Büchsel, *TDNT* I 673). *anagennaō* was a quite common vb. in NT times and was not confined to the mystery cults.

NT *gennaō* occurs 97 times in the NT, including 45 times in Matt. and 28 times in the Johannine literature. However, there is no particular emphasis in its use in the NT. Other terms that are used are → *tiktō* (bring forth, bear), *apokyeō* (give birth, bear, in the NT only fig. Jas. 1:15, 18), *ōdinō* (suffer birth pangs, Gal. 4:19; Rev. 12:2; → Lament, art. *lypeō*); cf. also *palingenesia*, regeneration; *anakainōsis*, renewal. The actual meaning of *gennaō* must be determined by the context in both its active and passive forms, as it is used both of the father and the mother as in cl. Gk. (cf. Matt. 1:3, 5 f.; 2:1, 4; 19:12; Lk. 1:13; Jn. 9:34; 16:21; Gal. 4:23). It is, however, used in a fig. or extended sense as follows:

1. Various passages apply the term to God himself who is said to have begotten someone.

(a) Ps. 2:7 is quoted by Acts 13:33 and Heb. 1:5; 5:5. Significantly the passages in Heb. relate it to Ps. 110 and 2 Sam. 7:14. Jesus Christ is seen as the true → Son and God's → King. He has fulfilled what the Israelite kings left unfulfilled. For as the crucified and risen One, he has assumed the office of the Lord's anointed as the truly anointed One. Strikingly, the NT does not apply Ps. 2:7 to the birth narratives

178

of Jesus. Wherever Ps. 2 is quoted in the NT, a physical, sexual begetting is utterly precluded. Acts 13:33 applies the words "this day have I begotten thee" to the → resurrection of Jesus. On the other hand, the variant reading in the Western Text of Lk. 3:22 (Codex Bezae, the Old Lat. versions, Justin and Origen) quotes the words of Ps. 2:7 and applies them to Jesus at his baptism. It is not easy to determine the precise significance of "today" in Heb 1:5 and 5:5. H. Strathmann thinks that it refers to the baptism of Jesus and that the second half of Ps. 2:7 was quoted in Heb. simply because it formed part of the text (J. Jeremias and H. Strathmann, *Die Briefe an Timotheus und Titus; Der Brief an die Hebräer*, NTD 9, 1963[8], 78 f.). E. Käsemann identifies it with the confirmation of sonship through a heavenly proclamation after the exaltation (*Das Wandernde Gottesvolk*, 58 ff.). However the word "today" may be understood, it s clear that the begetting by God goes beyond the OT understanding of adoption. The passages are concerned with the declaration and proclamation of what the Son already is. Jesus' sonship denotes the mystery of the incarnation of God. Jesus is the last Adam [*ho eschatos Adam*, 1 Cor. 15:45). "The idea that this generation must be thought of either in the sense of adoption or in that of the Virgin Birth rests on a misconception of the early Christian belief in Christ and understanding of Scripture, and especially of the basic significance of the resurrection of Jesus and the resultant beginning of the new *aiōn*, in short of the eschatological impulse in early Christian thinking" (F. Büchsel, *TDNT* I 670).

(b) The Johannine writings use the expression *gennēthēnai ek* (to be begotten of) to describe the origin of the believer. The phrase may be compared with (*ex*)-*erchesthai ek* (come [forth] from, cf. Jn. 8:42 where Jesus is speaking of himself) and *einai ek* (be from, cf. Acts 5:39 of events, and Jn. 3:10 of men). The believer knows that his true existence does not belong to this world; his beginning and end are in God through Jesus Christ. In the dialogue with Nicodemus the references to being born (*gennēthēnai*) mean that man must receive a new origin. He must exchange his old nature for a new and be born again (Jn. 3:3, 5, 6, 7, 8; cf R. Bultmann, *The Gospel of John*, 1971, ad loc.). The idea of being "born again" expresses the same essential idea as being born "of God" (*ek tou theou*, 1 Jn. 3:9; cf. 2:29; 4:7) and being born "from above" (*anōthen*, Jn. 3:7, cf. 8:23). Jn. describes this as an act of God: "But to all who received him, who believed in his name he gave power to become children of God; who were born, not of blood nor of the will of the flesh nor of the will of man, but of God" (Jn. 1:12 f.). To the human mind such rebirth is necessarily absurd (Jn. 3:4), for it is beyond man's capacity. But Jn. attributes this to the work of the → Spirit (3:5–8). Only the believer who has been born of the Spirit comprehends his origin and is thus able to see the → Kingdom of God (3:5; cf. Matt. 19:28).

A number of scholars are of the opinion that the expression *anōthen gennēthēnai* (to be born from above) is derived from gnosticism. *anōthen* (from above) is not only applied to rebirth (Jn. 3:3, 7) but to the power given to Pilate from above (Jn. 19:11). Jesus compared himself who is from above (*anō*) with his adversaries who are from below (*katō*) (Jn. 8:23). But *anōthen* can also mean "again". This birth is also described as being of water (*ex hydatos*) and the Spirit (Jn. 3:5). But in Jn. 1 and 1 Jn. there is no reference to water or baptism. Both Jn. and Paul appear to regard baptism as something secondary and less important (Jn. 4:2; 1 Cor. 1:14–

17). The questions have not received sufficient attention whether water in Jn. 3:5 does not refer to creation (Gen. 1:2), and whether washing does not follow birth (as in human birth). It is only with Justin and Irenaeus in the 2nd cent. that rebirth became a synonym for → baptism (→ Water, art. *hydōr*). ([Ed.] On the question of the possibility of a gnostic background to the NT see E. Yamauchi, *Pre-Christian Gnosticism*, 1973.)

2. Paul uses *gennaō* in 1 Cor. 4:15 and Phlm. 10 of his relationship with his converts. He could even speak of being in labour (*ōdinō*) or suffering birth pangs until Christ is formed in them (Gal. 4:19). The same thoughts lie behind those passages which speak of his "son" in the faith (1 Cor. 4:17; 1 Tim. 1:2; 2 Tim. 2:1; cf. 1 Pet. 5:13).

Rabbinic Judaism spoke in a similar way of winning proselytes (→ Conversion, art. *prosēlytos*). The command to be fruitful (Gen. 1:28; 9:7) was sometimes taken to mean that the Israelite had to win others to his faith. The idea of new birth through conversion to Judaism was common among the rabbis (SB III 339 f. on 1 Cor. 4:14 f.). "When a man teaches the son of another the Torah, the Scriptures treat him as if he had begotten him" (San. 19b; cf. 99b). "A proselyte who has been converted is like a child who has just been born" (Yeb. 22a). K. H. Rengstorf sees in the rab. attitude a sense of standing beside God as a creator *ex nihilo* (*TDNT* I 666). Paul's language in the passages discussed seems to have taken over and adopted Jewish ideas.

3. The vb. *anagennaō* occurs only in 1 Pet. 1:3 and 23 in the form of a participle where it means "born anew". Its meaning is similar to *gennēthēnai* in Jn. 3:3 f. (see above, and *palingenesia* below). "The NT did not 'take over' the concepts of rebirth and begetting from the mystery religions, as the old history of religions school assumed; it developed it out of its own fundamental concerns and under the stimulus of the hellenistic and Jewish world around it. The oldest NT passage (1 Pet. 1:3, 23) stands in close connection with the tradition of the OT and Judaism which saw the holy people of God as strangers (1 Pet. 1:1–2:10)" (L. Goppelt, *RGG*³ VI 1697). Through the gospel that has been preached, the word of the living God (1:23), believers have been born anew, i.e. they have been called by God into new life. This new life is summed up as *elpis zōsa* (living → hope, 1:3) and *agapē* (→ love, 1:22). New birth is not in the NT something that a man can take up and dispose of as he pleases. It is only possible by God's "great mercy" (1:5) and power (1:5). "In the resurrection of Jesus God has had mercy on us in an omnipotent, regal and free way, so that he removed once and for all in Jesus Christ the whole reality of death. He has crossed out and overthrown our claim that our life is real life. He has brought another new, abiding and unspotted life so near to our life that we can grasp the new and let go of the old" (H.-J. Iwand, *Predigt-Meditationen*, 344). The believer possesses his life in hope. On the one hand, his existence stands under the indicative: "we have been born anew to a living hope through the resurrection of Jesus from the dead" (1:3). On the other hand, he stands under the imperative: "set your hope fully upon the grace that is coming to you at the revelation of Jesus Christ" (1:13). He does this as one born anew realizing moment by moment the separation from the old aeon that has been overcome. The decisive factor which makes rebirth possible is God's act in the resurrection of Jesus Christ.

A. Ringwald

γίνομαι

γίνομαι (*ginomai*), be begotten, be born, become, come about, happen; ἀπογίνομαι (*apoginomai*), die; γένεσις (*genesis*), birth, origin.

CL & OT 1. *ginomai* is an Ionic and secondary form of *gignomai* which became common from the 4th cent. B.C. It has several shades of meaning: come into being, be produced (of things), take place (of events), become.

2. In the LXX, in addition to its ordinary use, it also occurs as a substitute for forms of *einai* (to be). The construction *kai egeneto ... kai* (and it happened ... and Gen. 4:8 and often) renders a Heb. construction that is strange in Gk. *(wayᵉhî ... wa*, and it came to pass that ...). See Funk § 442(5); Moulton, *Grammar*, III 334 f.

3. *apoginomai* is a compound using the prefix *apo* (from), and means to go away, cease, depart, i.e. die. It does not occur in the LXX.

4. *genesis* (origin, birth) is a cognate of *ginomai*. It occurs in the LXX as the title of Genesis and mostly as the equivalent of *tôlēḏôṯ* (generations, Gen. 2:4; 5:1 etc.) and to a lesser extent of *môleḏeṯ* (kindred, Gen. 31:13; 32:9).

NT 1. *ginomai* is used in the NT in a variety of connections.

(a) It means to be born (Gal. 4:4); grow (of fruit, Matt. 21:19); arise, happen, be (of various occurrences, Matt. 8:26; Acts 6:1; 12:18); to be made, be done (Jn. 1:3; Matt. 11:21); to become something (Mk. 1:17); to come (Gal. 3:14). *ginomai* is sometimes used with a verbal adj. to denote a passive: "they did not confess it lest" *aposynagōgoi genōntai* (lit. become ones put out of the synagogue, cf. RSV "be put out of the synagogue", Jn. 12:42; cf. Acts 12:23). It is frequently used in Lk. and Acts in the construction *kai egeneto de ...* followed by *kai* and a finite vb. (and it happened that ...; and it came to pass that ...). The pleonastic *egeneto* used without *kai* (and) is preferred by Lk. (e.g. Lk. 5:1; 9:28; cf. Funk § 442(5)). Paul also uses the defensive negation *mē genoito* (lit. let it not become, by no means! e.g. Rom. 3:4; 6:3; cf. Funk §§ 384, 440(2); Moulton, *Grammar*, III, 118–22).

(b) *ginomai* may also stand for *einai* (to be, e.g. Matt. 10:16; Mk. 4:22). With the gen. it denotes origin or membership (Lk. 20:14; 2 Pet. 1:20; cf. Funk § 162(7)). With the dat. of the person it denotes belonging to (Rom. 11:5; cf. Funk § 189). 1 Cor. 16:10 is an example of its use with an adv. and prep. *hina aphobōs genētai pros hymas* (that he may be at ease with you).

(c) *ginomai* has no special religious or theological meaning.

2. *apoginomai* occurs only in 1 Pet. 2:24: "who his own self bare our sins in his body on the tree, that having died (*apogenomenoi*) to sin we might live (*zēsōmen*) to righteousness." It thus stands in contrast to living. It denotes the change that has come about in the life of the believer through the saving act of Christ through his death and resurrection which makes a rebirth possible (→ *gennaō*, NT 3 on *anagennaō*; cf. Rom. 6:8, 11).

3. *genesis* means birth in Matt. 1:18 and Lk. 1:14. It also means created life or being. It is used in this sense in Jas. 1:23: "he is like a man who observes his natural face in a mirror" (RSV). The Gk. has *prosōpon tēs geneseōs autou* which more lit. means "the face of his created life [or natural being]." Two other passages require closer examination.

(a) Matt. begins his gospel with the words *biblos geneseōs Iēsou Christou hyiou Daueid hyiou Abraam* which RSV translates as "The book of the genealogy of

181

Jesus Christ, the son of David, the son of Abraham." The formula goes back to an OT model, where it introduces, or is appended to, a genealogy or family register (Gen. 2:4 of the heavens and earth; 5:1 of Adam; 11:10 of Shem) or a family story (6:9 of Noah; 37:2 of the family of Jacob). The genealogies and family stories often overlap. Some expositors (e.g. Zahn) hold that Matt. 1:1 is to be understood as "The Book of the history of Jesus Christ" and so is the title of the whole gospel. Others (like Lohmeyer and Michaelis) take it to be the title of the family register which follows in Matt. 1:2–27. In favour of the latter view is the fact that the genealogy follows immediately. If it is not the title of the genealogy, one would expect some kind of introduction to it in v. 2. Moreover, the birth narrative is itself introduced separately with its own introduction in v. 18: "Now the birth of Jesus Christ took place in this way." (See further Arndt, 154.)

(b) Jas. 3:6 contains the expression *trochos tēs geneseōs* which has been variously translated as "wheel of life", "wheel of birth" (RSV mg.), "cycle of nature" (RSV). The passage describes the tongue as "an unrighteous world", capable of "staining the whole body" and "setting on fire the cycle of nature." Comparative study in the history of religions has seen in this expression a parallel to Orphic teaching. The term denotes the idea of the perpetual recurrence of nature, and Jewish circles probably adopted the expression. "Doubtless they did not take over the original technical meaning. The term had probably lost its Orphic character and had become a current phrase for the ups and downs of life, perhaps as today the term 'struggle for existence' which belongs to the evolutionary theory of Darwin is generally applied to social conditions rather than to particular aspects of biology" (M. Dibelius, *Der Brief des Jakobus*, revised by H. Greeven, KEK 15, 1964[11], 183).

J. Guhrt

| ἔκτρωμα | ἔκτρωμα (ektrōma), miscarriage. |

CL & OT *ektrōma* is connected with the vb. *ektitrōskō*, to have a miscarriage, and is derived from *trōō*, wound, injure, damage. It is found in secular Gk. from Aristotle onwards, especially in medical language denoting a premature still birth. It occurs in the LXX in contexts which suggest that an untimely still birth would have been preferable to life (Job 3:16; Eccl. 6:3), and of the appearance of an aborted foetus (Num. 12:12).

NT In the NT the word occurs only in 1 Cor. 15:8 where Paul describes his encounter with the risen Christ: "Last of all, as to one untimely born (*tō ektrōmati*), he appeared also to me." Attention must be paid to the definite art. (*tō*) in this disputed passage. It is not to be taken as the equivalent of inverted commas or the indefinite *tini*. Its function is to draw attention to this birth as something singular and even shocking. It is softened only by the addition of the word "as" (*hōsperei*). The words "also to me" stand at the end in a place of emphasis and contrast Paul with the other disciples in his reprobate hatred of Christ.

The interpretation of Calvin and J. Weiss is to be rejected which sees the point of the comparison in *ektrōma* with the suddenness or violence of Paul's conversion. So too the view of Lange which saw in it a reference to the comparative lateness of

182

Paul's call or his inadequate preparation compared with the other apostles, and that of Wettstein which saw in it a reference to Paul's diminutive stature. Harnack's conjecture is unnecessary that Paul here is using a word which was applied to him in a derogatory manner. Rather, v. 9 is decisive for the interpretation. Here Paul alludes to his unworthiness to be called an "apostle" (a title of honour), because he formerly persecuted the church. If *ektrōma* is thus understood, not as premature birth, but as still birth, the significance of Paul's choice of the word lies in his joyful gratitude that God has chosen him to be an apostle despite his utterly reprobate life as a former persecutor. *H. Müller*

It may also be noted that the rabbis could speak of grown men in this way (SB III 471, 496), and that Ign., *Rom.* 9:2 probably alludes to this passage but without defining *ektrōma*. Several scholars agree with Harnack that it was probably a term of abuse (A. Harnack, *Sitzungsberichte der Preussischen Akademie der Wissenschaften zu Berlin*, 1922, 72; A. Fridrichsen, "Paulus abortivus", in *Symbolae philologicae O. A. Danielsson dicatae*, 1932, 79 ff.; J. Schneider, *TDNT* II 465 ff.; J. Munck, "Paulus tamquam abortivus" in A. J. B. Higgins ed., *New Testament Essays: Studies in Memory of T. W. Manson*, 1959, 180–93; G. Björck, "Nochmals Paulus abortivus", *Coniectanea Neotestamentica 3*, 1938, 3 ff.; T. Boman, "Paulus abortivus. (1 Kor. 15, 8)", *Studia Theologica 18. I,* 1964, 46–50; C. K. Barrett, *A Commentary on the First Epistle to the Corinthians*, 1968, 344; F. F. Bruce, *1 and 2 Corinthians*, 1971, 142; cf. H. Conzelmann, *Der erste Brief an die Korinther*, KEK 5, 1969, 306). It might refer to his physique or infirmities to which there are numerous allusions in his writings (1 Cor. 2:3; 4:10; 2 Cor. 11:30; 12:7 ff.). It might contain a hint that Paul was still too much influenced by the law and was not as spiritual as his opponents in Corinth (cf. 1 Cor. 2). There may be in it the suggestion that Paul is still an embryo believer; he has not had the same period of gestation as the other apostles. These suggestions are not necessarily mutually exclusive. But they have also to be understood in the context of the argument. The preceding verses are concerned with the proof of the resurrection of Jesus based upon his appearances to the apostles and others. Referring to his encounter with Christ on the Damascus road, Paul writes; "Last of all, as to the *ektrōma*, he appeared also to me" (1 Cor. 15:8; cf. 9:1; Gal. 1:16; Acts 9:3–6; 22:4–16; 26:9–18). The thought of the appearance of Christ to him leads immediately to the thought of his apostleship (v. 9). Paul's apostleship was questioned by some (1 Cor. 9:1). It could have been queried for a variety of reasons. Paul was a former persecutor of the church. Moreover, he lacked the two qualifications which were laid down when the other apostles considered a replacement for Judas. He had not been a disciple of Jesus in his earthly ministry and he was not a witness like them of Jesus' resurrection (Acts 1:21 f.). Against this, Paul claimed to have his apostleship directly from the risen Lord whom he had seen (cf. the above references). Admittedly, he had not known the earthly Jesus and his encounter had happened after the ascension. Nevertheless, Paul insisted that he had encountered the risen Christ and received his apostleship directly from him. As such, the description of him as the aborted one is triply apt. As a person he was not as acceptable as others. He was premature in the sense that he had not served the period of discipleship like the Twelve and had become an apostle at his conversion, having been a persecutor of the church

183

right up to that point. But above all, he had encountered Christ as "one untimely born" (RSV) some time after the resurrection appearances to the others had ceased.   *C. Brown*

| *παλιγγενεσία* |

παλιγγενεσία (*palingenesia*), rebirth, regeneration.

CL *palingenesia* is a compound noun from *palin* (again) and *genesis* (birth, origin).

In every day speech it denotes various kinds of renewal: the return or restoration of something, return to former circumstances, termination of captivity, restoration to health following a birth or illness. "The original notion was not that of human birth... on the basis of sexual conception" (F. Büchsel, *TDNT* I 686, n. 2).

1. Among the Stoics it was a concept used in a cosmic context. The cosmos would periodically perish through a world-conflagration (*ekpyrōsis*) and then arise anew in a rebirth (*palingenesia*) (M. Ant. 11, 1; Philo, *Aet. Mund.* 89 ff.). But the cosmos did not attain to a new mode of being or quality through the rebirth; the world that has passed away was there once again. Plutarch used the word in describing the myths of Dionysus and Osiris and also in an individual sense in describing the rebirth of souls (used as a synonym for *anabiōsis*, reanimation) (*De Ei apud Delphos* 9; *De Iside et Osiride* 35; cf. F. Büchsel, *TDNT* I 687). *palingenesia* was also used to express the rebirth of individuals in a new cosmic age. It thus denotes a human occurrence as well as a cosmic event.

2. In the mystery religions of the Hel. period the idea of rebirth occupied a large place. However, it cannot be established what role the word played there. All the mystery religions know of a deity who died and awoke to new life. In the cultic rites this was not taught as a doctrine, but represented in a dramatic way in which the initiate (*mystēs*) took part thus sharing in the life-giving and renewing power of their deity. Rebirth is a renewal to a higher, divine existence. The old history of religions school tried to relate rebirth in Tit. 3:5 to the influence of the mystery religions. But in view of the very different doctrine and the late attestation of rebirth in the mystery religions the connection is very much disputed. However, it cannot be denied that NT language at this point presents certain parallels to the mystery religions. (→ Baptism; cf. also G. Wagner, *Pauline Baptism and the Pagan Mysteries*, 1967).

OT 1. *palingenesia* (like → *anagennaō*) does not occur in the LXX. The nearest is the verbal form *heōs palin genōmai* which is a free rendering of Job 14:14 ("If a man die, shall he live again?" RSV). There is no thought here of the rebirth of an individual in a new age, as in the NT. There is, however, the thought of eschatological renewal in Ezek. 11:19: "And I will give them one heart, and put a new spirit within them; I will take the stony heart out of their flesh and give them a heart of flesh" (RSV). God will put his law within them and write it on their hearts (Jer. 31:33; cf. Isa. 60:31; Jer. 24:7; 31:18; Ezek. 36:26 f.). This change and renewal is proclaimed as a future blessing of salvation which the Lord himself will bring about. The people are not themselves capable of such a change (Gen. 6:5; 8:21; Jer. 13:23). Therefore the man of faith prays to his God: "Create in me a clean heart, O God, and put a new and right spirit within me" (Ps. 51:10). Cf. also the

184

promise of a restoration of Israel (Ezek. 36:24 f.; Isa. 11:1 ff.; Ezek. 37:25 f.; Mic. 4:6 f.), of a new covenant (Jer. 31:31 f.; Ezek. 34:25), of a new Jerusalem (Zech. 14:10 f., 16), the creation of a new heaven and a new earth (Isa. 65:17; 66:2). This gives rise to the suggestion that the NT idea of rebirth or regeneration has its roots in the OT prophecy of restoration and renewal in the messianic age.

2. In Hel. Jud. *palingenesia* occurs frequently. Philo used it to denote the renewal of the world after the flood and also of individuals (*Vit. Mos.* 2, 65; *Post. C.* 124; *Cher.* 114). Josephus describes the revival of Israelite national life after the exile as the *palingenesia* of the land (*Ant.* 11, 66; but cf. *Ap.* 2, 218 on the resurrection). Jewish thought, influenced by the OT, gave the word a different meaning from that of the Stoics. The world's new existence is not simply a return of the old. Regeneration is unique, and does not occur in cycles.

NT In the NT *palingenesia* occurs only in 2 places.

1. "Jesus said to them, 'Truly, I say to you, in the new world (*palingenesia*) ["regeneration" AV; "when all is made new" JB], when the Son of man shall sit on his glorious throne, you who have followed me will also sit on twelve thrones, judging the twelve tribes of Israel'" (Matt. 19:28 RSV). The parallel in Lk. 22:28 omits the reference to the *palingenesia*. In Matt. it is an eschatological term denoting the renewal of the world. It will take place when the Son of man appears in shining splendour as judge. Both the title of majesty → "Son of man" and the reference to judgment connect the regeneration with the end-time (cf. Rev. 21:1–5). Similarity with Stoic language is only superficial. The new earth belongs to another order and is qualitatively different. J. Schniewind, however, offers a different interpretation: "Since the whole tenor of our saying points to the early church, one may conjecture that regeneration here denotes the new life style of the new man which participates in God's reign" (*Das Evangelium nach Matthäus*, NTD 2, 1969, 207).

(b) Tit. 3:5 declares: "He saved us, not because of deeds done by us in righteousness, but in virtue of his own mercy, by the washing of regeneration (*palingenesias*) and renewal (*anakainōseōs*) in the Holy Spirit." It denotes a saving act of God, performed on man and in man, but not by man. The "goodness and loving kindness of God our Saviour appeared" in Jesus (v. 4). Corresponding to this, the saving of man comes about through "the washing of regeneration and renewal in the Holy Spirit". The picture suggests baptism (cf. Eph. 5:26). In baptism the believer receives the Holy Spirit (cf. Acts 2:38). (On the relation of baptism to regeneration and faith see the discussion in the articles on Baptism.) The washing and the reception of the Spirit are here seen as a unity. Regeneration comes about through water and the Spirit (cf. Jn. 3:5). The born again person lives in the hope that in the righteousness of God that has been promised to him he will be an heir and participator of future life. In this renewal a new life style opposed to his former one (v. 3) is made possible. For regeneration includes a basic reorientation of moral life. On the connection between the rite of baptism and the reality of this new life → baptism and → faith.

2. *anakainousthai* (renew, Col. 3:10; 2 Cor. 4:16) and *anakainōsis* (renewal, Rom. 12:2; Tit. 3:5) also occur alongside of *palingenesia* and the corresponding vb. → *anagennaō*. Although these words are comparatively rare, the ideas which they signify are common to the whole NT. Thus Paul declares: "If any one is in Christ,

185

he is a new creation" (2 Cor. 5:17). He also speaks of baptism symbolizing being in Christ (Rom. 6:3; cf. Gal. 3:27). See also the NT use of → gennaō.

In the NT regeneration is not understood in a materialistic or magical fashion as in the mystery cults, as if it could be effected by lustrations and blood ceremonies. Baptism does not effect regeneration by its mere performance. Tit. 3:5 testifies to the fact that "washing" is effected only by the Holy Spirit. Regeneration does not bring sinless perfection but leads to daily renunciation of irreligion and worldly passions and to sober, upright, godly living in this world (Tit. 2:12).

Matt. 19:28 draws attention to the eschatological and cosmic dimensions of regeneration. As the salvation which comes to man it must be understood in a wider framework. Even though Matt. 19:28 and Tit. 3:5 present two different perspectives, a connection between them may be seen. The individual man who is by nature dead and enters new life only by the working of the Holy Spirit is not the only final goal of salvation history. The NT is bounded by the horizon of the new → creation (2 Cor. 5:17; 2 Pet. 3:13; Rev. 21:5) and the restoration of all things (Acts 3:21). With regeneration the reality of this salvation enters this world and human existence. The reborn man is directed towards the universal work of salvation.

It must, however, be stressed that the picture of regeneration in the NT is never presented as more than an illustration of the saving event. It is not seen as more important than other concepts such as being "in Christ" and "putting on Christ."

J. Guhrt

τίκτω

τίκτω (*tiktō*), bring forth, bear, give birth to, produce.

CL *tiktō* is formed from the reduplicated root *tek-*, and is attested from Hom. *Od.* 4, 86 onwards. It has the following meanings: (1) beget (of the father), bear, give birth to (of the mother); (2) bear young, breed (of animals); (3) bear, produce (of the earth); (3) generate, engender, produce (metaphorically).

OT In the LXX *tiktō* occurs some 215 times and stands almost exclusively for Heb. *yālaḏ* (bear). It occurs only once for *hārâh* (conceive, become pregnant, Hos. 2:5(7)) and *mālaṭ* (normally "save" but "give birth" in Isa. 66:7). Secular Gk. usage was generally preserved in the LXX, except that the word was used predominantly of the woman. Male begetting is expressed almost exclusively by → gennaō. In the first instance the word denotes the physical act of labour or travail which comes as something over which one has no control (Isa. 13:8; 26:17 f.). It is the result of prior conception (*gennaō*). On Isa. 7:14; cf. Matt. 1:23 → God, art. *Emmanouēl*; → Woman, art. *parthenos*. *tiktō* can be applied to animals as well as humans (Gen. 30:39). It may even be applied to seed that sprouts from the earth (Isa. 55:10). This sense is found in Philo but no longer in the strict biblical sense, since his language inclines towards a deification of nature when it speaks of the earth as the *gēs tēs panta tiktousēs* (the earth which bears all things, *Op. Mund.* 132).

tiktō is also used in a metaphorical, though somewhat negative, sense in the LXX in speaking of the nation (Num. 11:12; Isa. 66:8), and of bearing mischief (Ps. 7:15; Isa. 59:4). The picture here is of a hidden, irresistible power breaking out of a person. *tiktō* is never used of the Lord himself, the Lord of all events. But *gennaō* is used of the Lord, again as the equivalent of Heb. *yālaḏ* (Ps. 2:7; Deut. 32:18).

186

NT 1. In the NT *tiktō* occurs chiefly in the Matthaean and Lukan birth narratives of Jesus and John the Baptist. It occurs in Rev. 12:2, 5 in the heavenly vision of the birth by a woman of a child who is appointed to be Lord and Redeemer of the world who is immediately caught up to God from the power of the dragon. *gennaō* is also used occasionally in the same sense. But it is striking that *gennaō* is used more in a general sense, e.g. in the announcement to Elizabeth and Mary of the impending birth of their sons (Lk. 1:13, 35) and the report of Jesus' birth (Matt. 1:16), whereas *tiktō* expresses more the physical reality of giving birth (Lk. 2:6 f., 11). It is the more drastic word, and is used in passages which bring home the reality of labour (Jn. 16:21; Rev. 12:3), or the shame of the woman who cannot give birth because she is barren (Gal. 4:27). *tiktō* expresses the element of travail, danger and the stark realities of childbirth. It is not used in the general sense of being born (Gal. 4:4) or in the sense of spiritual rebirth.

This is also connected with the fact that *tiktō* in the NT is used exclusively of the woman. 1 Tim. 2:15 reinterprets the judgment pronounced on Eve about pain in child-bearing (Gen. 3:16). This does not mean that woman is eternally condemned. "Woman will be saved through bearing children (*dia tēs teknogonias*), if she continues in faith and love and holiness, with modesty." Widows should marry and bear children (*teknogoneō*) thus giving the enemy no opportunity to revile the church (1 Tim. 5:14). Widows should not be enrolled under the age of sixty, and among other things they should be known for having brought up children (*teknotropheō*, 1 Tim. 5:10).

2. *tiktō* occurs only rarely in a metaphorical sense: of the earth bearing useful plants (Heb. 6:5), and of the desire that gives birth to sin (Jas. 1:15). In these two cases *tiktō* expresses the necessary connection between conception and birth. Where there is rain, there is fruit. Where there is desire, there is sin. Where there is sin, there is death. Jas. 1:15, 18 also contain the word *apokyeō* (bring forth) which is likewise used in a metaphorical sense. It expresses the end-result, in the one case of desire and in the other case of God's will. "Then desire when it has conceived (*syllabousa*) gives birth to (*tiktei*) sin; and sin when it is full-grown brings forth (*apokyei*) death" (Jas. 1:15). "Of his own will he brought us forth (*apekyēsen*) by the word of truth that we should be a kind of first fruits of his creatures" (Jas. 1:18).

→ Generation, art. *genea*.   G. Bauer

| εὐγενής | εὐγενής (*eugenēs*) well-born, noble in descent or character; νόθος (*nothos*) born out of wedlock, unable to register a valid claim to ancestry. |

CL From Homer onwards, *eugenēs* possessed the meaning of "well-born", "of noble descent", but it extended its meaning, esp. in Gk. tragedy (e.g. Soph., Ant., 38) to mean "noble-minded". It is also used of things: animals of good pedigree (Soph., El., 25), and (later) plants of good stock. It even extends to nobility of bearing and appearance (Eur., *Helena* 10).

nothos strictly means "born out of wedlock", but in Athenian writers it was used where one parent was not a citizen (e.g. Plut., *Themistocles*, 1, *nothos pros mētros*, illegitimate on the mother's side). It had the general derivative meaning of "spurious, counterfeit" both of people and things.

OT The LXX uses *eugenēs* only once, of Job (1:3) where it means "well-favoured" especially in this world's goods, corresponding to MT *gāḏôl*, in the sense of "wealthiest". *nothos* is unexemplified in LXX.

NT The NT reflects classical usage in its sparing examples of *eugenēs*. It is most easily understood as "high-born" in Lk. 19:12, and certainly so in 1 Cor. 1:26 where it forms a third category with "wise" and "influential" *kata sarka* ("as this world reckons such things"). Acts 17:11 uses it of the Jews at Beroea who were more "well-disposed" to the truth, more "right minded" in that they "received the word" with complete alacrity of mind (*prothymia*) and tested what they heard by Scripture.

nothos only occurs at Heb. 12:8 where it means not "born out of wedlock" but "unable to make an accredited claim" to sonship of God. *J. A. Motyer*

(a). T. Boslooper, *The Virgin Birth*, 1962; F. Büchsel, *ginomai . . . palingenesia*, *TDNT* I 681–89; F. Büchsel and K. H. Rengstorf, *gennaō . . . anagennaō*, *TDNT* I 665–75; H. von Campenhausen, *The Virgin Birth in the Theology of the Early Church*, 1964; J. Daniélou, *The Infancy Narratives*, 1967; E. M. B. Green, *The Meaning of Salvation*, 1965; A. T. Hanson, "Birth with Promise," *Studies in Paul's Technique and Theology*, 1974, 52–66; M. D. Johnson, *The Purpose of the Biblical Genealogies*, 1969; J. G. Machen, *The Virgin Birth of Christ*, 1930; L. Morris, *The Gospel according to John*, 1972, 208–50; J. Orr, *The Virgin Birth of Christ*, 1914[3]; J. Schneider, *ektrōma*, *TDNT* II 465 ff.

(b). G. Bolsinger, "Die Ahnenreihe Christi nach Mt. und Lk.," *BuK* 12, 1957, 112 ff.; W. Bousset, *Die Briefe: Die Johanneischen Schriften*, *SNT* II, 1908[2], 147 ff.; W. Dantine, "Der Mensch zwischen Wiedergeburt und Geburt," *KuD* 11, 1965, 220 ff.; J. Dey, "*Palingenesia*. Ein Beitrag zur Klärung der religionsgeschichtlichen Bedeutung von Tit. 3, 5," *Neutestamentliche Abhandlungen* 17/5, 1937; M. Dibelius, *Der Brief des Jakobus*, *KEK* 15, 1964[11], 183; A. von Harnack, "Die Terminologie der Wiedergeburt und verwandter Erlebnisse in der älteren Kirche," *TU* 42, 3, 1918, 97 ff.; C. F, Kling, *Die Korintherbriefe*, *Theologisch-homiletisches Bibelwerk*, *Neues Testament*, Teil 7, 1861, 226 f.; A. Lindenmeyer, *Regeneratio. Das neumachende Handeln Gottes am Menschen und an der Welt*, 1943; A. Schlatter, *Paulus, der Bote Jesu*, 1934, 400 ff.; J. Schniewind, *Das Evangelium nach Matthäus*, *NTD* II, 1964[11]; W. Schweitzer, *Gotteskindschaft, Wiedergeburt und Erneuerung im Neuen Testament und seiner Umwelt*, 1944 (dissertation); E. Sjöberg, "Wiedergeburt und Neuschöpfung," *StTh* 4, 1951–52, 44 ff.

Bishop, Presbyter, Elder

The following article brings together the entries on *episkopos* and *presbyteros* which were both offices in the early church. There is evidence to suggest that they overlapped in function, and that the two titles may have been different terms for what was essentially the same office.

ἐπίσκοπος

ἐπίσκοπος (*episkopos*), overseer, guardian, bishop; ἐπισκέπτομαι (*episkeptomai*), view, inspect, visit, afflict; ἐπισκοπέω (*episkopeō*), take care, oversee, care for; ἐπισκοπή (*episkopē*), visitation, affliction, position or office as an overseer or bishop.

CL 1. This group of words is formed from the root *skep-* with the prefix *epi* and denotes the activity of looking at or paying attention to a person or thing. *skopeō* (→ Goal, *skopos*) suggests the continuing recurring character of such action, while *episkeptomai* suggests an act that is complete in itself. The verbs can mean to observe, review (Xen., *Anab.*, 2, 3, 2), superintend (Plato, *Rep.*, 6, 506 B), watch over, scrutinize (Xen., *Mem.* I 6, 4) and also inspect, examine (Xen., *Mem.*, 3, 2, 10). The group is distinguished from the group formed from the root *ep-opt-*, which is very similar in meaning but relatively less used. The latter means first merely looking at, and then also guarding. *episkopeō* and cognates stress active and responsible care for that which has been seen.

2. *epopteuō* (Homer, onwards) look at; *epoptēs* (from Pindar, 5th cent. B.C.) is used as an epithet for the gods (Zeus, Poseidon, Apollo), for men knew that they were under their watchful eyes. In the language of the mystery religions the highest grades of the initiates, who had seen the holiest, bore this title. So *epopteuō* came to be associated with the highest human good fortune.

3. *episkopos* (from Homer on), overseer, is used first of all to describe a deity (e.g. Artemis in Elis) as the one who keeps watch over a country or people, and in particular over the keeping of treaties and the markets (Homer, *Il.*, 22, 255, together with *martys* → Witness; Soph., *Antigone* 1148). Already in *Il.*, 10, 38 and 24, 729 (Hector), however, the title was also given to men who had a responsible position in the state. This was later extended to religious communities. The title was given to officials (with minor judicial functions) sent from Athens to dependent states to ensure order or to fix their constitutions. In Rhodes they are mentioned together with councillors, treasurers, secretaries and military strategists, but the context does not allow us to determine their exact functions. Syrian records use the title for members of a committee of control for building or a board of trustees. In cultic groups organized according to Gk. laws concerning organizations, the *episkopoi* were those members responsible for external relationships, rather like churchwardens or trustees.

ot 1. (a) In the LXX this word group is mostly used for variants of the root *pāqaḏ*. This originally meant to take care of. In the Qal it means to look for, investigate (1 Sam. 14:17, RSV "see"), visit (Jdg. 15:1), inspect (Num. 1:44). Occasionally it represents *bāqar*, investigate closely. *episkopeō* is used only five times for various Heb. words. *episkeptomai* is found some 150 times, of which 48 are in Num., especially in chs. 1–4, where it is used of the reviewing of tribes and families (e.g. 2:4; 3:39, in the part. form; RSV: numbered). Since this was for the purpose of service, the verb gained the meaning "appoint for supervision, commission" (cf. the prayer in Num. 27:16).

(b) A second meaning emerges in the LXX. *episkeptomai* is used for God's loving watching over and solicitious care for the land (Deut. 11:12), his elect people (Ruth 1:6; Zeph. 2:7; Ps. 80:14 (15)), and individuals, e.g. Sarah (Gen.21:1). This is an expression of God's loyalty to the covenant and his → mercy. It includes the meaning of visit, afflict and punish (Exod. 32:34; 10:12), for since God has seen, he must judge men to bring them to repentance. The relevant passages are mostly in the prophets, especially in Jeremiah's message of judgment.

(c) Occasionally *episkeptomai* is found in its Hel. meaning of blissful beholding (Pss. 27:4(5); 106:5).

(d) The LXX coined the sub. *episkepsis* and *episkopē* to represent *p^equddâh* or *p^eqûḏâh*, the number of those who had been mustered as a result of the action

(Num. 1:21, 23, 25); appointment to a duty, and so the order of service (1 Chr. 24:3); and the visitation of God in judgment, either in the course of history or in the Day of Yahweh, as it ends all human activity (cf. Jer. 11:23; 23:12; Job 7:18).

2. *episkopos* might be expected to represent Heb. *pāqîd*, overseer, officer, governor, but this is so only in 2 Chr. 24:11; Neh. 11:9, 14, 22; 12:42. The other eleven instances have no uniform meaning. *episkopos* is used only once of God (Job 20:29 where it represents *'ēl*, "the heritage decreed for him by God" RSV). In certain cases (e.g. Jdg. 9:28; Num. 31:14) particular persons in a position of authority are *episkopoi*, but sometimes it denotes the exercise of power as well as those who exercise it (e.g. Isa. 60:17). In any case, the examples do not permit any direct connection to be drawn between the OT and the later office of *episkopos*, or bishop. For the various offices in Israel and their relationship to one another → *presbyteros*.

3. We are more likely to find the later office of bishop foreshadowed in the *mᵉbaqqēr*, overseer (of the community), found in the Damascus Rule and the Community Rule of Qumran (e.g. 1 QS 6:12, 20), who is probably the same as the *pāqîd* (1QS 6:14). This *mᵉbaqqēr* was one who knew the law, but was not a priest. He had entrusted to him all important decisions about "the camp" and full members. He shows clear monarchical traits, for he had to decide who was to be received into the community. He could inflict punishments. Together with the judges, he controlled the community's welfare funds and had to give his approval to all legal and commercial dealings of members with outsiders (CD 13:6 f.; 14:9–12). At the same time his office, following OT analogies, is compared with that of a shepherd: "He shall love them as a father loves his children, and shall carry them in all their distress like a shepherd his sheep. He shall loosen all the fetters which bind them" (CD 13:9). It is instructive for our understanding of the figure of the overseer that all these functions were later clearly transferred to the leader of the priests, who is the determinative figure in 1QS, while the non-priestly overseer has been reduced to the role of an administrator (1QS 6:14, 20). The independent dignity of the president of the *'ēḏâh*, the congregation as a meeting of full members, which showed its independence by its integration and subordination of the priests, was presumably transferred gradually to the priestly president. This foreshadows the emergence of the priestly bishop. ([Tr.] This interpretation assumes that the Damascus Document is earlier than the Manual of Discipline; there is no agreement on this point but weighty opinion reverses the order suggested, cf. Millar Burrows, *More Light on the Dead Sea Scrolls*, pp. 254 ff.)

NT 1. The word-group is markedly less common in the NT than in the LXX, and appears only in a few books. *episkopeō* is found only in Heb. 12:15 and possibly 1 Pet. 5:2 (omitted in some MSS. and the RSV, but not NEB). In the former passage it is used to describe the effort Christians are urged to make to see that all remain in divine grace. "See to it that no one fails to obtain the grace of God" (RSV). "Episcopal" supervision is the duty of the fellowship and not of a special priestly order. *episkeptomai*, which is so common in the LXX, is found only 11 times (7 in Lk.–Acts; and Matt. 25:36, 43; Heb. 2:6; Jas. 1:27). *episkopē* is found 4 times: Lk. 19:24 and 1 Pet. 2:12 (for the day or moment of visitation, or confrontation with the Lord in judgment or salvation); Acts 1:20 (a quotation from the LXX); 1 Tim. 3:1 (as a title of the apostolic or episcopal office). Though *episkopos* was to become so important, it is found only 5 times, four being for the leader of the community (Acts 20:28; Phil. 1:1; 1 Tim. 3:2; Tit. 1:7), whereas 1 Pet. 2:25 refers to Christ as the guardian of souls.

2. (a) Apart from Acts 6:3, where it describes selection by the church of men to serve (RSV "pick out") *episkeptomai* is used in the Lukan writings and in Heb. 2:6 (Ps. 8:4 (5)) for the loving and seeking care of God. He has chosen out of all the nations the one people (Acts 15:14), which he has visited in blessing (Lk. 7:16) and redeemed (Lk. 1:68) (→ Redemption, art. *lytrōsis*). His mercy moves him to visit this people as "the day-spring from on high"; thus the gracious birth of the Baptist is praised as an opportunity for forgiveness and salvation. In Heb. 2:6 the writer expresses his wonder that God should create and care for man.

(b) *episkeptomai* is used in Acts 7:23 of Moses, and in Acts 15:36 of Paul and Barnabas as they return to care for their converts. It is similarly used in Jas. 1:27; service to God is shown above all in caring for widows and orphans. This meaning is vividly expressed in Matt. 25:36, 43. In the person of every sufferer and prisoner the Lord himself stands before men. As we meet him, we make a decision that leads to salvation or condemnation, depending on whether we see him and make his needs our concern or whether we look past him (→ Brother, → Love).

(c) Both groups of examples stress the same loving care and seeing with a heart that is moved to action. The OT meaning of visitation for punishment is completely lacking, or rather, it is replaced by other terms (→ Judgment → Punishment). God's visitation took place once for all on the → cross.

3. (a) Earlier uses of *episkopos* reach their climax in 1 Pet. 2:25, where Jesus Christ is described as "the Shepherd (*poimēn*) and Guardian (*episkopos*) of your souls" (RSV). As a title of the exalted Christ, it sums up everything expressed by the term in the OT, Jud., and Gk. religious thought. It is no accident but the expression of a conscious insight, that *episkopos* is here linked with *poimēn*. The two thoughts are already connected in the OT (Num. 27:17) and again in the NT (Acts 20:28). Oversight means loving care and concern, a responsibility willingly shouldered; it must never be used for personal aggrandisement. Its meaning is to be seen in Christ's selfless service which was moved by concern for the salvation of men.

(b) It is highly significant that, as the growing band of disciples became a church, they apparently hesitated to apply the title of *episkopos* to designate an office. OT and secular Gk. usage did not stand in the way of this, but Gk. usage may have had materialistic overtones and OT associations may have been too reminiscent of authoritarian oversight. Its application to oversight in the church is to be seen in the context of the application of all Christ's work to the church. In other words, titles of offices in the NT are essentially titles that apply to Christ in the first instance.

The need for pastoral oversight to keep the church in the → way of faith was originally a duty binding on all members, as it apparently still was in Heb. 12:15. But early on oversight became the task of a special office. The change may be seen in Acts 20:28. The passage focuses on the duties of the hearers to the church. But already these hearers are a clearly defined group, though the title of *episkopos* is not yet an explicitly defined designation. No doubt, it is to be distinguished from that of → apostle and → prophet, and perhaps too from that of teacher (→ Teach, Art. *didaskō*), for bishops were linked with a particular place and church. But at first

191

it was probably synonymous at least with that of → shepherd (*poimēn*) and → elder (*presbyteros*) and the ideas associated with them. The use of *diakonos* (→ Serve) was also not yet fixed.

(e) *episkopē* (RSV "office of a bishop") is first used in 1 Tim. 3:1 to designate a defined office to which one could aspire. It is striking how, now that the office has come into being, attention shifts from its duties to the personal qualities that are needed for it: personal discipline, a well-ordered family (there is no question of celibacy here!), gifts of teaching and personal relationships, and a good name in the non-Christian world around. There is nothing in this picture to contradict Acts 20:28 and Phil. 1:1, which show several bishops at work in a single, local church. Reference to the qualities required in a bishop (sing.) in Tit. 1:7 offers little support for the theory of monarchical episcopacy with a single bishop supervising all other office holders. This system triumphed in the 2nd and 3rd centuries, partly because of individuals with outstanding gifts and partly because of the need for tighter organization.

(d) The development of the episcopal office marks the transition from the missionary era of the church with its charismatic gifts to an institution with a permanent character. Once the apostles had died out and the teachers and prophets become more rare, it was felt that the expanding church needed a form which would ensure continuity. Monepiscopacy triumphed over shared, collegiate ministry. But the fact that it presented merely *one* possible solution is abundantly shown by counter-movements in the church's history. On the relation of the various offices and duties to each other → *presbyteros*.   *L. Coenen*

πρεσβύτερος

πρεσβεύω (*presbeuō*), be older, be an ambassador, rule; πρεσβύτερος (*presbyteros*), older, elder, presbyter; πρεσβυτέριον (*presbyterion*), council of elders, rank of elder or presbyter; πρεσβύτης (*presbytēs*), old man; πρεσβεία (*presbeia*), embassy, ambassador; προίστημι (*prohistēmi*), be at the head of, rule, be concerned about; κυβέρνησις (*kybernēsis*), administration.

CL 1. (a) The comparative *presbyteros*, elder, and the superlative *presbytatos*, eldest, are found as early as Homer, but the positive *presbys*, old, appears first in Pindar as a poetical variant of *presbytēs*, old man (common stem *presb-*, old, cf. Latin *prisc-*). The group of words probably first signified older in comparison with others; then, of greater importance (cf. *ta tou theou*, things divine, in contrast with *ta tōn anthrōpōn*, things human, Hdt. 5, 63), or "I consider nothing more important (*presbyteron*) than prudence" (Eur., *Fragment* 959). Finally, it meant more honoured. In the order of society the elders receive respect and authority on the ground of their experience and wisdom (cf. Arist., *Ethica Eudemia* 1215a 23, *hoi sophoi kai presbyteroi*, the wise and elder men). There is no disparaging note, in the sense of feeble, weak, or old-fashioned (cf. *palaios* → old).

(b) This meaning of greater respect, usually combined with greater age, determines the use of the other words from this root. Thus the noun *presbytēs* (Aesch. onwards) denotes age, rank, or the old or older man, who is no longer a *neaniskos* (young man) and is probably over 50 years old. The feminine *presbytis* (Aesch. also onwards) means old woman.

192

(c) From Hdt., 7, 2 and Soph., *Oedipus Coloneus*, 1422, the vb. *presbeuō* means to be older or eldest; then to take the first place (Soph., *Antigone*, 720). Corresponding to this, *presbeia* means first the rights of dignity of an elder (Aesch., *Persae* 4); then generally, rank or dignity (Plato, *Republic* 505b).

(d) Hence the words from this root come to be used also for institutional functions in society, for which the wisdom of age is regarded as a prerequisite. *presbeuō* is used for the activity of an ambassador, who represents the people who send him and negotiates for them (Hdt., 5, 93 mid., to negotiate through envoys). *presbeia* means embassy, ambassador, ambassadors (*presbeutēs*, Thuc. 5, 4, has also the same meaning). In the Dorian world the pre-eminence that went with age led not only to a representative function abroad, but also to an advisory one within the political community. Hence, the vb. can mean command; and *presbyteros* can be the title of an office of state. In Sparta this title is given to the presidents of the colleges of ephors (*IG* 2² 6,552.11), the *nomophylakōn* (ib. 555b, 19), and the *synarchias*, assembly of magistrates. Outside Sparta, however, the term did not have an institutional significance in Greece. It retained its meaning of seniority as contrasted with youth.

In Egypt, however, the plur. *presbyteroi* appears as the title for members of a committee, e.g. of associations (*P. Teb.* 13, 5) or guilds, and also of religious bodies, and for the annually elected agents of village councils, who had judicial and administrative duties.

2. *prohistēmi* (used once in Homer (*Il.* 4, 156), but no further examples before the 5th century) to set before or over someone or something; pass. 2 aor., perf. and plup. act., to come forward, be set over, rule (e.g. Hdt., 1, 69). It is used to refer, especially in the participial form *prohistamenos*, to the functions of leadership in an army, a state, or a party (Hdt., 1, 59; 3, 82; Plato, *Laches* 197d). A position of this sort involves the task of guarding and responsibility for (Hdt., 9, 107) and protection of those over whom one is placed (*P. Fay.* 13, 5). Thus the vb. can express the meanings of support, care for, and even concern oneself with.

3. The vb. *kybernaō*, is probably derived from language used by sailors in the Mediterranean region and is related to the Lat. *gubernare*, govern, guide (Homer, *Od.* 3, 283). It was originally used of the action of a helmsman (*kybernētēs*, Homer, *Il.* 19, 43; Hdt. 2, 164). Later Plato (*Phaedrus* 247c) used the noun metaphorically in the sense of a leading statesman, and *kybernēsis*, government, of his activity (*Republic* 488b). It is comparable with the modern expression "ship of state". From Pindar onwards divine guidance and rule are described by cognate words of this group.

OT 1. In the LXX words derived from the root *presb-* have 3 main areas of meaning:

(a) As the equivalent of Heb. *zāqēn* (originally, bearded; one who has attained legal majority; then, old man), they have the sense of *older in years*, as contrasted with younger. *presbytēs* occurs some 30 times in this sense (e.g. Eli, the old man, I Sam. 2:22); the old and young contrasted in a list of those to be exiled (Isa. 20:4). *presbeion* denotes advanced age, and the right of the eldest as firstborn (Ps. 71:18; Gen. 43:33). While *presbytēs* occurs almost exclusively with this meaning (occasionally for other Heb. words, or without a Heb. equivalent), *zāqēn* is even more frequently rendered by the comparative *presbyteros* (in 50 cases out of a total of

193

some 150). It occurs in Gen. (in 18:11 and elsewhere for the age of Abraham and Sarah; 19:4 ff. for the old man Lot), Pss., Wisdom literature, and in 1 and 2 Ki.

(b) For an *elder, the elders* (mostly plur.; only rarely in sing.), as a group of men within a tribe, family, people, or community of settlers, whose rôle is variously to be understood, according to the historical circumstances (for details, see 4 below). The only pre-Christian example of *presbyterion* (*Sus.* 50 (Theodotion)) denotes the honour of the elder's status (cf. J. Jeremias, *ZNW* 48, 1957, 132).

(c) *presbeutēs* and *presbys* are used in some instances in the classical sense of ambassador, negotiator, spokesman. There are no examples of the vb. *presbeuō*. In 2 Chr. 32:31 *presbeutēs* renders *lîṣ* in hiph., act as spokesman (5 further examples are found in 1 Macc.). In Num. 21:21; 22:5; and Deut. 2:26 *presbys* renders *mal'āk̲*, and in Isa. 57:9 *ṣîr*, both meaning envoy. Further examples without Heb. equivalents occur in Isa. and I Macc. On the whole, therefore, this meaning is noticeably rare, a fact which may well be at least partially accounted for by the difference between Gk. ideas and the *šālîaḥ* concept of the Jews (→ Apostle OT).

2. *prohistēmi* occurs only 8 times, always without Heb. equivalent and meaning to be head of a household (2 Sam. 13:17; Am. 6:10), to govern the people (1 Macc. 5:19), and even to take trouble (Isa. 43:24).

3. *kybernaō* and *kybernēsis* are found only in a few places in the Wisdom literature, and in Prov. have the meaning of the Heb. *taḥbûlôt*, wise counsel. *kybernēsis* is a function of rulers (Prov. 1:5; 11:14). But *kybernaō* is also used of the wily plans of the wicked (Prov. 12:5). *kybernētēs* (Heb. *ḥōbēl*) is used in Ezek. 27:8, 27 f. for pilot.

4. There is no theological significance in age except in the case of the rights of the → firstborn. Nor is age important in an ambassador. Although their rôle was in origin neither religious nor cultic but socio-political, the existence of elders *as an institution* was of considerable significance in the life of Israel and the Jewish synagogue community, as it was among other peoples of the ancient world (cf. the elders of Egypt in Gen. 50:7). The institution was already established when Israel became a people. It is assumed in every strand of OT tradition (cf. G. Bornkamm, *TDNT* VI 655).

Elders are an established part of the patriarchal clan and tribal system, where an authority which was scarcely challenged, though variously qualified, belonged to the heads of families. M. Noth regards the elders of Israel as the real leaders of the people in the departure from Egypt, their actual role having been obscured in the tradition by the towering figure of Moses (*A History of the Pentateuchal Traditions*, 1972, 175–88).

The stages of development in the interpretation of elders may be traced in the different strands of the OT:

(a) Evidence of the earliest concept may be present in the Yahwistic section, Exod. 12:21–27. When all the elders of Israel (LXX translates this by *gerousia*, council of elders) are called together and given instructions about the Passover celebrations in their *mišpāḥôt* (families, clans), the passage is referring to those who have authority over these communities which are joined by consanguinity (LXX *syngeneia*, kinsfolk).

(b) In Exod. 12 the expression used is "elders of Israel", suggesting that the families are already seen as constituent parts of the people as a whole. In the rest of the writings of the Pentateuch the elders are seen as *representatives of all Israel*, who stand as the first and so representative eye- and ear-witnesses of the event. Moses is told to inform them of Yahweh's resolve to deliver his people, and they are to be witnesses of his plea at Pharaoh's court (Exod. 3:16, 18 4:29; LXX again has *gerousia*). They see the miracle of the spring at Horeb (Exod. 17:5). They take part in the feast with Jethro (Exod. 18:13). To them God's offer of the covenant at Sinai is made ("the whole people" Exod. 19:7 f.; LXX *v.l.* introduce *presbyteroi* at Exod. 34:30, 32 as well). They are witnesses of the punishment of Dathan and Abiram (Num. 16:25). The title "elder" is given to a considerable number of men, as is clear from the fact that Moses twice chooses out 70 "*of* the elders of Israel" to form what is in a sense a body representative of the representatives. This occurs when the Sinai covenant is ratified (Exod. 24:1), and when the murmuring of the people is about to be answered by the gift of quails and manna (Num. 11:16 ff.). This tradition was understood in Judaism (and also in Christian thought) to imply that the originally ethnic office of elder now took on a new function by divine commission. This is its proper one within the framework of the Mosaic covenant (cf. Exod. 18:13 ff. and Deut. 1:9 ff., though the men there assigned juridical duties are not described as elders). This understanding of the office, with its responsibility for judicial decisions and the honour that went with it, doubtless lay behind Isa. 24:23. It was later seen as a type of the rab. ordination, as is clear from the number 70 in the constitution of the Sanhedrin (see below (f)).

(c) In contrast to this understanding of the office, which was designed for the wandering people of God as a whole, the settlement brought to the fore another aspect. This represents an obvious modification of the first, and reflects the sociological change which had taken place. Since the individual's life was now more strongly influenced by the community living in settlement around him, the elders now appear as the *men who control the local communities*, a kind of patrician class like that found among the Canaanites (cf. Jos. 20:4; 1 Sam. 16:4; Jdg. 11:5 ff.; Ruth 4:2 ff.; 1 Sam. 30:26 ff.). The responsibility of the elders for judicial, political and military decisions within the towns applied, according to the tradition, not only in Israelite towns but also in foreign ones like Gibeon (Jos. 9:11), Succoth (Jdg. 8:14, 16), and Shechem (Jdg. 9:2 – the 70 sons of Jerubbaal). In all these places the same aristocratic, patriarchal, social structure is found.

Meanwhile the title of "elder" continued to be applied to the ruling class of the individual tribes (cf. 2 Sam. 19:11) and of Israel as a whole. The elders make the decision to send the ark against the Philistines (1 Sam. 4:3). It is they who demand the introduction of the monarchy (1 Sam. 8:4 ff.). How much the kings were dependent on their goodwill is demonstrated by Saul's pleas to Samuel (1 Sam. 15:30), David's ascent of the throne (2 Sam. 3:17; 5:3), Absalom's threat to it (2 Sam. 17:4, 15; 19:12), the role of the elders as kingmakers in Rehoboam's time (1 Ki. 12:6 ff.; 2 Chr. 10:6 ff.), Ahab's consultation of them in a time of danger, and his attempt to manipulate them (I Ki. 20:7 f.; 21:8, 11). Finally, they appear as representatives of the whole people at Solomon's dedication of the temple (1 Ki. 8; 2 Chr. 5), along with the heads of the tribes and families. Their critical, occasionally conspiratorial, attitude towards the monarchy is doubtless due not least to the threat to their influence posed by the formation of a royal civil service and the growth of dynastic power.

195

(d) The result of this development can be seen in Deut. Now that they were squeezed out of the position of leadership in the state as a whole, there remained the elders' authority in the local community, which consisted mainly in the judicial functions assigned to them. Their task – together with the judges, who were probably permanent officials (cf. Deut. 21:2; 25:8) – was to make sure that the requirements of the Mosaic law were kept. According to Deut. 13:9, this task was shared with the priests. Their relation to these judges is just as obscure. So too is the question whether the officials (*šōṭᵉrîm*), mentioned in Deut. 1:15, along with the commanders of thousands and of hundreds (curiously given military titles), are to be regarded as elders, in the sense of members of the *gerousia*. The old representative system has been superseded by a new constitutional system. The term has been retained but the function altered. The practical effect is to give the institution its character as the guardian of the traditions handed down in the law and local customs.

(e) How deeply rooted was the position of the elders is demonstrated by what happened after the end of the monarchy and the exile of large portions of the population. It was the elders who once again appeared as guardians and representatives of the Jewish community both in exile (Jer. 29:1) and in the homeland (Ezek. 8:1ff.; cf. also the elders of the land who in Jer. 26:17 speak on behalf of the prophet). But there was also a change which took place during this period. The clans were superseded by influential families, and individual families thus gained a position of eminence among the people as a whole. The heads of these appear now as an aristocratic ruling class (cf. Ezr. 8:1 ff.). The Heb. expression *śîḇ* for these heads of families (cf. Ezr. 6:14) is likewise translated *presbyteros* in the LXX. Although we can recognize in Ezr. 10:14 the continuation of the Deuteronomic rank of elder of state, the emphasis has shifted to the aristocratic upper class. At the table of the governor Nehemiah there is a daily gathering of 150 notables, who are without any recognizable legal function, but certainly not without influence.

(f) At the end of the 3rd or beginning of the 2nd cent. B.C. under the Seleucid king Antiochus III, we have evidence of the existence of a *council of elders* consisting of 70 (or 71) members, the Sanhedrin (cf. Josephus, *Ant.* 12, 2, 5 ff.). At first, on the analogy of the Gk. *gerousia* and the Rom. *senatus*, the members generally are spoken of as *presbyteroi*. But the word is used more and more to distinguish the lay members, who probably came from the patrician families of Jerusalem, from those drawn from the priestly families on the one hand and (after *c.* 70 B.C.) from the ranks of the scribes on the other. The NT probably records accurately the historical situation, when it portrays these elders as standing for the most part on the side of the Sadducean priestly aristocracy, yet having less influence than any of the other members (the evangelists name them mostly at the end of lists). The scribes, who were increasingly taking over the actual leadership, were mainly orthodox Pharisees.

(g) After the destruction of Jerusalem (A.D. 70), the term *zāqēn* is given a new significance. The newly constituted *Sanhedrin of Jamnia*, whose function is restricted to the exposition and application of the Law, consists solely of scribes. Consequently the term "elder" comes to be used as a title of honour for outstanding theologians. It implies, if not membership of the council, as least ordination (cf. San. 11:1–4). At the same time the presidents of the Jewish synagogues, in which the old structure of the local communities persists, are also called *presbyteroi* (cf.

196

the elders of Bethulia, Jud. 6:16, 21). They have leadership and the duty of preserving the traditional order with disciplinary powers. In addition to Lk. 7:3, there is inscriptional evidence of this. From about the 2nd cent. A.D. the word loses its functional significance in the Jewish communities and is replaced by other expressions, chiefly Gk. ones, in the Diaspora. But it is still found frequently as a title of honour for patrician families.

5. In the Qumran community the title "elder" is still retained, but without designating a particular office. In 1QM 13:1 they are named along with priests and Levites in the description of the battle order; here the heads of families are probably intended. In CD 9:4 and 1QS 6:8, however, elders take their place in the seating and order of rank behind the priests. They are second to them in responsibility for instruction and judicial decisions, in providing knowledge of the correct behaviour required by the law.

NT 1. (a) In the NT *presbyteros* (65 examples, see below 2) is also so dominant among the derivatives of this root, that the others need only be mentioned in passing. *presbeia* occurs only in parables (Lk. 14:32; 19:14) in the sense of a political delegation, embassy. The vb. *presbeuō* is used twice by Paul. In 2 Cor. 5:20 it expresses the official character of the message of reconciliation which he brings: *hyper Christou oun presbeuomen hōs tou theou parakalountos di* hēmōn ("we are ambassadors for Christ, God making his appeal through us," to accept the reconciliation which has been effected). Eph. 6:20 carries the same meaning. *presbytēs* and *presbytis* (Lk. 1:18; Tit. 2:2 f.; Phlm. 9) refer simply to length, or greater length, of life and mean old man and woman respectively. *presbyterion* is used in Lk. 22:26 and Acts 22:5 for the Jewish Sanhedrin (see above OT, 2 (f)). Otherwise it is only found in 1 Tim. 4:14, where it means office of elder, which is conferred by laying on of hands (→ Hand). It is not stated who conducts the ordination. J. Jeremias, loc. cit., 132, takes *tou presbyteriou* as a genitive of purpose i.e. "for the presbyterate"; as against Dibelius, *HNT* 13 ad loc. and E. Lohse, *Die Ordination*, 82, who see here a Christian body of elders conferring ordination.

(b) *prohistēmi* is found only in the writings of Paul and the Pastorals. 1 Thess. 5:12 has the participle in the plur. for those who labour in the church and who are *prohistamenous hymōn en Kyriō* (are over you in the Lord). They help others to live rightly and therefore deserve special esteem and love. The reference here seems to be to a group exercising leadership in the church. The present writer believes that there were as yet no institutionalized or precisely differentiated offices in the church known to Paul. He was influenced by the pattern of the charismatic community: "Whoever is filled with zeal, whoever does not shirk hard work, proves himself thereby to be one who can lead the way for others" (H. Greeven, *ZNW*, 44, 34, cf. 32). This is confirmed by the list of gifts in Rom. 12:8, where the *prohistamenos* is characterized by *spoudē* (zeal). The *prohistamenos* is here listed alongside the *didaskōn* (he who teaches), the *parakalōn* (he who exhorts), the *eleōn* (he who does acts of mercy). All of these words are participles which suggest an activity rather than an office. Tit. 3:8, 14 have the infinitive of the vb. *prohistasthai* with *kalōn ergōn* (good works) in the Gk. sense of taking trouble over good works (see above CL, 2). Behind 1 Tim. 3:4, 5, 12, where the participle is used with *tou idiou oikou* (his own house), there is the picture of the patriarchal head of the household or father of the family. If he is capable of fulfilling this rôle well, he fulfils a vital qualification for being leader in the church. This is the qualification for the offices of bishop (*episkopos*) and deacon (*diakonos* → Serve), though their rôles are not as yet unambiguously defined. The context makes it probable that in one church there would be several *episkopoi*, just as there were a number of *diakonoi*. But the definition of the episcopal office is not clear, and its relation to the *presbyteroi* cannot be determined with certainty. In 1 Tim. 5:17 the participle *prohestōtes* is closely linked with *presbyteroi*. The passage refers to presiding elders (cf. the excursus by M. Dibelius on 1 Tim. 3:7 in *HNT* 13). In any case, by the time of the Pastoral Epistles the charismatic structure of the earlier Pauline church, whose functions are described grammatically by the use of participles, has given way to an organized system of offices for which substantives are used. Dibelius sees in this combination of the participle with *presbyteroi* a combination of offices, and understands the "honour" due to them in the sense of an honorarium for this honorary work (cf. Did. 13).

(c) *kybernēsis* (administrator, lit. administration) is used only at 1 Cor. 12:28 in a list beginning with apostles, prophets and teachers, and then progressing to various charismatic gifts. (The vb. *kybernaō* is totally lacking.) The first three differ from the rest by being numbered, but it is unlikely that any basic contrast is intended. The position of *kybernēseis* after the gifts of healing and giving help, and before those of tongues, suggests that the word is a term for a mediating function of keeping order within the whole life of the church. Dibelius thinks it unlikely that either the conduct of worship or administrative duties are involved. *kybernētēs* occurs only at Acts 27:11 and Rev. 18:17 in the sense of helmsman.

2. *presbyteros* is found in the NT in three senses. In the synoptic gospels, and at the beginning and end of Acts, the sub. is used of the lay members of the Sanhedrin (see below (a)). In the central portion of Acts, the Pastoral Epistles, Jas. 5:14, and the salutations in 2 and 3 Jn., the Christian elder is meant (see below (b)). Finally in Rev., it denotes heavenly beings (see below (c)), although it remains an open question whether they surround the divine throne as representatives of the heavenly or of the earthly church (cf. E. Lohmeyer, *HNT* 16 on Rev. 4:4). In Acts 2:17 (the quotation from Joel 2:28) the old as opposed to the young are meant. So too in 1 Tim. 5:2; Heb. 11:2; 1 Pet. 5:1, 5; Lk. 15:25; and Jn. 8:9. Apart from Jn. 8:9, which did not form part of the original text, the word is completely lacking in the Fourth Gospel. It does not appear in the Pauline epistles apart from the Pastorals.

(a) The *Jewish elders* have their place within the synoptic tradition only in the prediction of the passion and the passion narratives. The reference is to the lay members of the Sanhedrin, drawn from the patrician families particularly of Jerusalem. It lists their almost regular position after the "high priests" (*archiereis*), members of the priestly aristocracy (→ Priest), and shows their close association with and dependence on the latter. The only place – and this may be significant – where they head the list of the groups belonging to the High Council is the first passion prediction (Mk. 8:31 par.). This may be significant because their title marks them out as representatives of the Law, under which Jesus must be put to death. In the account of the events of the passion, however, it is the priestly members of the Sanhedrin that appear as the real agents and instigators (→ Cross, art. *stauros*, NT, 1(a)).

198

In Mk. 7:3, 5 (par. Matt. 15:2) the reference is not to elders as holders of office, but to the *paradosis tōn presbyterōn* (the tradition of the elders, i.e. of earlier scribes). *presbyteros* is thus understood as a title of honour for the ordained *grammateus* (scribe). Note that the questioners are scribes and Pharisees!

It will be noticed that Matthew in particular emphasizes the close association of chief priests and elders (*archiereis kai presbyteroi*), omitting in most cases mention of the *grammateis* (scribes). In Mark if anything the contrary tendency may be observed (cf. Matt. 26:3 with Mk. 14:1; Matt. 27:12, 20, 41 with Mk. 15:3, 11, 31). Luke has retained a list of all three only at Lk. 20:1 (par. Matt. 21:23; Mk. 11:27). Once (Lk. 22:66, par. Matt. 27:1, Mk. 15:1) he introduces the collective description *to presbyterion tou laou* ("the assembly of the elders of the people" RSV); cf. also Acts 22:5. This is hardly a matter of differing terminology. The choice of terms enables us rather to draw conclusions as to the viewpoint of each evangelist. Mark wishes to underline the part played by the scribes in the passion of Jesus, while Matthew places the emphasis more heavily on to the representatives of all Israel. He is the only one to use the expression *presbyteroi tou laou*, elders of the people (21:23; 26:3, 47; 27:1). Where, however, the gospel is intended more for non-Jewish readers (as with Luke), such distinctions are less evident, or disappear completely. John speaks merely of "the Jews" as the opponents of Jesus (→ Israel).

Only at Lk. 7:3 does the other type of *presbyteros* occur in the gospels. Here elders, in the sense of members of the presiding body of the local synagogue, approach Jesus on behalf of a Roman officer.

(b) Luke is the first not only to use the term *Christianoi* for the members of a Christian church (Acts 11:26), but also to introduce the expression *presbyteroi* in the same context to describe the men who exercised leadership in the Christian church at Jerusalem on the Jewish synagogue pattern (Acts 11:30; cf. 21:18). On the analogy of the Sanhedrin this presupposes a *gerousia*, council of elders, in which the leading rôle is played by the *apostoloi* (→ Apostles). Both are mentioned together in Acts 15:2, 4, 6, 22 f. and 16:4. By adopting this term, Luke enabled the continuity between the Old Covenant and the New to find expression in the structure of the church. He uses the term in describing the Pauline churches (cf. the travel narrative, Acts 14:23, and the mention of elders from Ephesus, Acts 20:17). By the time of the composition of Acts it is clear that the Pauline churches of Asia Minor had adopted the "presbyterian" system of government.

In the description of the offices in 1 Tim. 5:17, 19 and Tit. 1:5 *presbyteros* has become the title of honour for members of a body which cares for the members and the life of the church. Mention of them in 1 Tim. 4:14 in conferring the gift of prophecy suggests the collegiate character of their working. From this body those who "preside" in the strict sense (see above NT 1 (b)), and the preachers and teachers, are drawn (1 Tim. 5:17). Here we find the root of the present-day Presbyterian system.

Tit. 1:5, 7 makes it probable that the terms *presbyteros* and *episkopos* (bishop) are interchangeable (cf. Acts 20:17, 28). Besides meeting general personal and moral requirements, they have the special tasks of exhorting, and refuting objectors. In other words, they continue the juridical role of elders in the synagogue in the form of a presiding group. The same collegiate pattern forms the background of Jas. 5:14. Here too the reference is to the prominent members of local churches.

199

It remains to be added that in the Pastoral Epistles this local order still retains the collegiate form. But already there are tendencies towards the establishment of a body of clergy and the first hints of the emergence of monarchical heads over several churches. These appear in the shape of the apostle's disciples, Timothy and Titus. The latter appoints the elders in the individual churches in the apostle's name (Tit. 1:5; cf. Acts 14:23). H. Schlier sees in this the beginnings of the principle of succession, resulting, as in Judaism, in the rank of presbyter being given even in the ancient church only to the → priests who now fulfil the rôle of the scribes (*Die Zeit der Kirche*, 146). R. Sohm regards 1 Clem. as the beginning of church law, for it upholds with great vigour the rank and rights of the "office" over against the recalcitrant church. Not until the Reformation in Western Europe does the old *gerousia* principle of a body of worthy men reappear, and then the process, which is so familiar in the history of the Jewish and Christian office of elders, repeats itself for a third time.

The writer of 2 and 3 Jn. calls himself *presbyteros* (v. 1 in both cases). R. Bultmann takes this to signify not so much membership of a local body of elders, as a title of honour for a bearer and deliverer of the apostolic tradition (*KEK* 14, 7, 95). This would mean not an office-holder in the institutional sense, but rather a man valued and respected widely in the churches of the day, in a similar way to the early prophets and teachers. His authority would lie solely in the importance of what he said, in the power of truth and of the Spirit (cf. H. von Campenhausen, *Ecclesiastical Authority and Spiritual Power in the First Three Centuries*, 1969, 76–123).

(c) Finally *presbyteroi* are mentioned 12 times in the visions of Rev., always as a group of 24 men (2 x 12; first mentioned Rev. 4:4 ff.; cf. 7:11). They wear white clothes, and are crowned. They sit around the throne of the Almighty, separated from it only by the four heavenly creatures. They are thereby marked out as the bearers of high heavenly office. They are the ones who utter the praises of God for his saving acts in history (Rev. 4:10 f.; 5:6 ff.; 11:16 ff.), or are present when his praises are sung (Rev. 14:3). Occasionally one of them comes forward to say something (Rev. 5:5; 7:13; cf. the testimony of Peter and the other disciples in Matt. 16:15 ff.).

Although these visions suggest the idea of a heavenly counterpart of the office of elders in the earthly churches, so elevating it to a higher plane, it is not possible to verify this suggestion. The number 24 and the grouping around the throne may carry echoes of astronomical notions. But this does not mean any more than that these elders are to be seen as belonging to heaven and so to God. It is more probable that the image and the number are derived from the leaders of the 24 divisions of Jewish priests (1 Chr. 24:7 ff.), or of the temple singers (1 Chr. 25:9 ff.), who were called "elders" in later Judaism (cf. E. Lohmeyer *HNT* 16 on Rev. 4:4; A. Satake, "Gemeindeordnung", *WMANT* XXI, 147 ff.). They may represent the twelve patriarchs and the twelve apostles whose names are written on the gates and foundations of the holy city (Rev. 21:12 ff.) or a combination of these and other ideas (G. B. Caird, *A Commentary on the Revelation of St. John the Divine*, 63 f.).
→ Apostle, → Church, → Serve   *L. Coenen*

(a). H. W. Beyer, *episkeptomai* etc., *TDNT* III 599–622; G. Bornkamm, *presbys* etc., *TDNT* VI 651–83; C. Brown, "Ministry in the New Testament," in J. C. Porthouse, ed., *Ministry in the*

Seventies, 1970, 10–22; R. E. Brown, *Priest and Bishop: Biblical Reflections*, 1971; P. Burke, "The Monarchical Episcopate at the End of the First Century", *JES* 7, 1970, 499–518; H. von Campenhausen, *Ecclesiastical Authority and Spiritual Power in the First Three Centuries of the Church*, 1969; K. M. Carey, ed., *The Historic Episcopate*, 1954; W. D. Davies, "Light on the Ministry from the New Testament," *Christian Origins and Judaism*, 1962, 231–45; A. Ehrhardt, *The Apostolic Succession in the First Two Centuries of The Church*, 1953; and *The Apostolic Ministry*, 1958; E. M. B. Green, *Called to Serve*, 1964; A. T. Hanson, *The Pioneer Ministry*, 1961; A. E. Harvey, "Elders", *JTS* New Series 25, 1974, 318–32; A. G. Hebert, *Apostle and Bishop*, 1963; K. E. Kirk, ed., *The Apostolic Ministry*, 1957²; H. Küng, *Structures of the Church*, 1964; *The Church*, 1967; and *Why Priests?* 1972; T. M. Lindsay, *The Church and the Ministry in the Early Centuries*, 1902; T. W. Manson, *The Church's Ministry*, 1948; and *Ministry and Priesthood: Christ's and Ours*, 1958; D. P. Meyer, *The Episcopal Ministry and the Apostolic Succession in Recent Anglican Theology*, 1968; L. Morris, *Ministers of God*, 1964; B. Reicke, *prohistēmi*, *TDNT* VI 700–3; K. H. Rengstorf, *Apostolate and Ministry: The New Testament Doctrine of the Office of the Ministry*, 1969; E. Schillebeeckx, "The Catholic Understanding of Office in the Church," *Theological Studies* 30, 1969, 567–87; E. Schweizer, *Lordship and Discipleship*, 1960; and *Church Order in the New Testament*, 1961; W. Telfer, *The Office of a Bishop*, 1962.
(b). J. Benzinger, "Älteste in Israel," *RE* I 224 ff.; U. Brockhaus, *Charisma und Amt: Die paulinische Charismenlehre auf dem Hintergrund der frühchristlichen Gemeindefunktionen*, 1972; J. Brosch, *Charisma und Ämter in der Urkirche*, 1951; H. Brunotte, "Neue Literatur zur Bischofsfrage," *ZEK* 13, 1967–68, 282–98; G. Friedrich, "Bischof," *BHHW* I 254 f.; H. Greeven, "Propheten, Lehrer und Vorsteher bei Paulus," *ZNW* 44, 1952–53, 1 ff.; M. Horn, *Amt und Bischofsamt. Ein Überblick über das Verständnis des Amtes in der ev.-luth. Theologie der Gegenwart*, 1964; J. Jeremias, "Presbyterion,' ausserchristlich bezeugt," *ZNW* 48, 1957, 127 ff.; E. Lohse, *Die Ordination im Spätjudentum und im Neuen Testament*, 1951; W. Michaelis, *Das Ältesteamt*, 1953; W. Nauck, "Probleme des frühchristlichen Amtsverständnisses (1 Petr. 5, 2 f.)," *ZNW* 48, 1957, 201 ff.; F. Nötscher, "Vorchristliche Typen urchristlicher Ämter?" in *Die Kirche und ihre Ämter*, 1960, 315 ff.; K. Rahner and J. Ratzinger, *Episkopat und Primat*, 1961; B. Reicke, "Die Verfassung der Urgemeinde im Lichte jüdischer Dokumente," *ThZ* 10, 1954, 95 ff.; L. Rost, *Die Vorstufen von Kirche und Synagoge im Alten Testament*, *BWANT*, 4. Folge 24, 1938; H. Schlier, "Die Ordnung der Kirche nach den Pastoralbriefen," in *Die Zeit der Kirche*, 1956, 129 ff.; K. L. Schmidt, "Amt und Ämter," *ThZ* 1, 1945, 309 ff.; R. Schnackenburg, "Episkopos und Hirtenamt in Apg. 20, 28," in *Episcopus: Studien über das Bischofsamt*, (Festschrift Faulhaber) 1949, 66 ff.; R. Stockmeyer, "Gemeinde und Bischofsamt in der alten Kirche," *ThQ* 149, 1969, 133–46; K. Weiss, "Paulus, Priester der Kultgemeinde," *TLZ* 79, 1954, 355–64; H. D. Wendland, "Geist, Recht und Amt in der Urkirche," *Archiv für evangelisches Kirchenrecht* 2, 1938, 289–300.

Bitter

πικρός

πικρός (*pikros*), bitter; πικρῶς (*pikrōs*), bitterly.

CL & OT Found in secular Gk. from Homer onwards, *pikros* means lit. pointed, sharp, pungent, bitter tasting, and in a transferred sense painful, angry, relentless, embittered. It occurs some 40 times in the LXX, occasionally lit. (e.g. Exod. 15:23; Jer. 23:15), but mostly in a transferred sense (e.g. Ruth 1:20; Hab. 1:6). The adv. *pikrōs* occurs 9 times (e.g. Isa. 22:4; 33:7). The adj. and the adv. occur in both Philo and Josephus.

NT The adj. *pikros* is found only at Jas. 3:11 (bitter water as a symbol of the evil that issues from the tongue; the same spring cannot pour forth fresh water and bitter or brackish) and Jas. 3:14 (of bitter jealousy). In both passages Jas. shows that such conduct is utterly incompatible with the Christian profession and must be done away with. The adv. *pikrōs* is found only at Matt. 26:75 and the par. Lk.

201

22:61, where Peter acknowledged his denial and "wept bitterly." "The weeping was violent and uncontrolled, expressing utter despair at the denial" (W. Michaelis, *TDNT* VI 124).

πικρία

πικρία (*pikria*), bitterness.

CL & OT *pikria* is rare in secular Gk., though it is found from Demosthenes and Aristotle onwards, meaning bitterness of taste or temper, and the hardness of times. It occurs about 30 times in the LXX: of the place-name Marah (Num. 33:8 f.; cf. Exod. 15:23); metaphorically in Deut. 32:32; Lam. 3:15, 19; Prov. 5:4; and of God in Isa. 28:21, 28. It regularly denotes the bitterness associated with grief, disappointment, hate and anger. Philo and Josephus use the noun in the same sense as the LXX, though Josephus rarely.

NT In Heb. 12:15 ("root of bitterness" = Deut. 29:18 LXX) bitterness is associated with anger as in the OT (cf. Deut. 32:32). Rom. 3:14 (quoting Ps. 10:7, 9:28) associates it with cursing in the course of an argument which shows that both Jews and Gentiles are "under the power of sin" (Rom. 3:9). In Acts 8:23 Peter accused Simon Magus of being "in the gall of bitterness and in the bond of iniquity" after he tried to purchase the Holy Spirit. The latter phrase reflects Isa. 58:6, and the former the connection made in the OT between bitterness, gall, wormwood and poison (Deut. 29:18; Lam. 3:15, 19; Prov. 5:4; cf. Amos 6:12). Unrighteous actions and desires produce bitterness. *pikria* (bitterness, perhaps including animosity, anger, resentment, harshness) comes first in a list of vices which the Christian is called upon to put away (Eph. 4:31).

πικραίνω

πικραίνω (*pikrainō*), make bitter, embitter.

CL & OT In secular Gk. from Hippocrates onwards, meaning lit. to make to taste bitter and in a transferred sense to affect harshly; in the pass. to be angry, to be embittered. It is found in the LXX some 12 times (e.g. Job 27:2; Ruth 1:13; Exod. 16:20, be angry, enraged). It is never used of God.

NT Husbands are not to be bitter, ill-disposed or harsh towards their wives (Col. 3:19). In Rev. 8:11 it means to make water bitter through wormwood (cf. Deut. 29:18; Jer. 9:15; 23:15; Lam. 3:15, 19; Amos 5:7; 6:12; Prov. 5:4). It describes one of the afflictions of mankind in the vision of the angels and trumpets. It also occurs in Rev. 10:9 f. of the scroll which the angel commanded John to eat which was sweet in his mouth but made his stomach bitter. The image suggests the anguish caused him by his prophetic message. The unpalatable message contrasts with the bitterness which afflicts men through the wormwood described earlier which contains the implication that it is brought about by their own evil.

παραπικραίνω

παραπικραίνω (*parapikrainō*), embitter, make angry, provoke; also used like an intransitive, to be disobedient, be rebellious, rebel.

CL & OT *parapikrainō* is not found before the LXX, where it is used over 40 times with the above meanings (e.g. Jer. 32[39]:29; 44[51]:3, 8 of provoking God's anger; and of being disobedient and rebellious in Deut. 31:27; Pss. 68[67]:6; 106 [105]:7; Ezek. 3:9; 12:9).

NT In the NT it is found only at Heb. 3:16 which is dependent on the LXX of Ps. 95[94]:7–11. The noun *parapikrasmos*, rebellion, occurs in Heb. 3:8, 15 (both from Ps. 95[94]:8). It is used in the OT to refer to the Exodus rebellion (cf. Exod. 15:23; 17:7; Num. 14; 20:2–5). The author of Heb. cites the Ps. as a warning against disobedience, urging believers: "Today, when you hear his voice, do not harden your hearts as in the rebellion." *G. T. D. Angel*

Arndt, 626, 663; Moulton-Milligan, 512; W. Michaelis, *pikros* etc. *TDNT*, VI 122–27.

Black, White, Red

μέλας

μέλας (*melas*), black.

CL & OT *melas* is found in secular Gk. from Homer to the 3rd cent. A.D., meaning dark, black, and in a transferred sense sinister, malignant, enigmatic. It occurs in the LXX (Cant. 1:5; Zech. 6:2 etc. for *šāḥōr*), Philo and Josephus who uses *melas* metaphorically as the sign of a stranger, of mourning (as also the Talmud) and of personal misfortune.

NT The neut. *to melan* is used for ink at 2 Cor. 3:3; 2 Jn. 12; 3 Jn. 13.

melas is contrasted with → *leukos*, white, in Matt. 5:36: "And do not swear by your head, for you cannot make one hair white or black." There is perhaps here a complex of ideas. Swearing was sometimes made by the → head (cf. also Mishnah Sanh. 3:2) and in some instances the vow was symbolized by not cutting the hair (Exod. 20:25; Num. 19:2; Deut. 15:19; Jdg. 13:5; 16:17 ff.; Acts 18:18; 21;24). Several times disciples are assured that the hairs of their heads are all numbered, and thus will not perish (Matt. 10:30; Lk. 12:7; 21:18; Acts 27:34). Man has no control over the course of time; his vows cannot turn the clock back by turning his white hair again to the black of his youth. Nevertheless, the disciple can trust in the → father's providential care that nothing will befall him without the father's will.

At Rev. 6:5 the rider of a black horse holds a balance, while a voice quotes high prices for food, probably a sign of famine sent as judgment. The apocalyptic image is derived from the four horses in Zech. 6:2 which represent the universal lordship of God. (On this passage see W. D. McHardy, "The Horses in Zechariah" in *In Memoriam Paul Kahle* [*Beihefte zur Zeitschrift für die alttestamentliche Wissenschaft*] 1968, 174–79; and J. G. Baldwin, *Haggai, Zechariah, Malachi*, 1972, 138 ff.) In Rev. 6:12 the sun becomes "black as sackloth", the colour indicating mourning, as often in Jewish literature in the setting of → judgment (cf. Joel 2:31). The darkening of the sun is a recurrent eschatological symbol of the day of the Lord's coming in judgment which the NT takes over from the OT (Isa. 13:10; 50:3; Ezek. 32:7; Joel 2:10, 31; Amos 8:9; Ass. Mos. 10:5; Matt. 24:29; Mk. 13:24; Lk. 23:45; Acts

2:20; Rev. 6:12; 9:2; cf. R. H. Charles, *The Revelation of St. John* [ICC], I, 1920, 180; → Darkness, → Present, art. *hēmera*).

Later Christian literature called the devil "the black one" (e.g. Barn. 4:9; 20:1).

| λευκός | λευκός (*leukos*), white. |

CL & OT In secular Gk. from Homer onwards *leukos* means light, fair, bright, clear, white. In the LXX it means the colour white (Gen. 49:12; Isa. 1:18; Zech. 1:8; chiefly for *lāḇān*), though white here may include half-yellow. It is used of clear speech in Isa. 32:4. White was the colour of the priest's linen clothing symbolizing purity (Schürer, II, 1, 276 ff.; W. Michaelis, *TDNT* IV 242 f.; cf. Exod. 28:40–43; 39:27 ff.; Ezek. 44:17 ff.; Josephus, *Ant.*, 3, 7, 1 ff.). White symbolizes the state of being purified from the defilement of sin (Ps. 51:7; Isa. 1:18; Dan. 11:35; 12:10). It is the colour of God himself (Dan. 7:9). But it is also used in the diagnosis of leprosy (Lev. 13 where about half the references occur). Both Philo and Josephus saw symbolic implications in the colour (cf. *TDNT* IV 243 f.). The latter mentions that the Essenes went clothed in white (*War*, 2, 123). From the 1st cent. A.D. onwards the dead were buried in white linen (*TDNT* IV 244 f.). This may be connected with the imagery of the garments of glory worn by the saints in their transfigured state (Eth. En. 62:14 ff.; Sl. Enoch 22:8).

NT *leukos* occurs only in the Gospels, Acts and Rev. It is used of the yellowish white, ripe corn ready for harvest (Jn. 4:35), in a context which suggests that the eschatological harvest is at hand and that the disciples are now being sent out as reapers (cf. Matt. 9:37). (See further R. E. Brown, *The Gospel according to John* (*i–xii*), 1966, 173 f. L. Morris, however, finds puzzling the application of white to crops and suggests that it may be a metaphorical reference to the white garments of the crowds, *The Gospel according to John*, 1971, 297.)

White is an eschatological colour in various other contexts, especially in the description of garments. In the transfiguration of Jesus, his garments appeared brilliantly white (Matt. 17:2; Mk. 9:3; Lk. 9:29; → Form, art. *morphē*). So too was the appearance of the angels at the tomb (Matt. 28:3; Mk. 16:5; cf. Jn. 20:12; Lk. 24:4), and of the two men who addressed the disciples after Jesus had ascended (Acts 1:10). White is also the colour of the garments of the saints in the after-life (Rev. 3:4 f., 18; 4:4; 6:11; 7:9, 13; 19:14). In the first instance, white is associated with eschatological and transcendent existence, and not with Godhead as such. However, the throne of God is white (Rev. 20:11), and in an earlier vision John has seen "one like a son of man" seated upon a white cloud wearing a golden → crown and bearing a sharp sickle (Rev. 14:14). In his first vision the glorified Christ appeared with white hair like wool and snow (Rev. 1:14), associating the Risen Christ with the "ancient of days" (Dan. 7:9) whose raiment was white as snow and hair white as wool, showing that for John "Christ is equal to God in essence and appearance" (W. Michaelis, *TDNT* IV 247, quoting J. Behm, *Apokalypse* [NTD], ad loc.). Perhaps there is also the implicit thought in Rev. that since white is the colour symbolic of God himself, the white garments of the saints symbolize the holiness and purity that only God bestows. In keeping with this, the glorified

Christ who comes in judgment is seen riding a white horse (Rev. 6:2; 19:11) and the armies of heaven who follow him are clad in "fine linen, white and pure" riding "white horses" (Rev. 19:14). However, the horse which symbolizes death which is followed by Hades is a pale (*chlōros*) horse (Rev. 6:8; cf. R. H. Charles, op. cit., I, 168 f.; → *melas* NT).

In the letter to the church at Pergamum those who overcome are promised "hidden manna" (→ Bread, art. *manna*) and "a white stone, with a new name written on the stone which no one knows except him who receives it" (Rev. 2:17). Various images may lie behind this. The white stone was used by jurors to signify acquittal (Ovid, *Metamorphoses*, 15, 41). It was regarded as a mark of felicity (Pliny, *Epistulae*, 6, 11, 3). In a certain royal assembly possession of a stone entitled one to free entertainment, and there was a rabbinic tradition that precious stones fell along with the manna (R. H. Charles, op. cit., I, 66). The tribes of Israel were represented by precious stones in the high priest's breastplate (Exod. 28:15-21). Perhaps John is combining some of these ideas with that of → confessing the → name of Christ as → Lord and the implied corollary of being owned by God (cf. Matt. 10:32; Mk. 8:38; Lk. 12:8; Rom. 10:9 ff.; 1 Cor. 12:3; Phil. 2:11).

What has been said above stands in contrast with the vb. *koniaō*, whitewash, which is used of the tombs which were whitewashed annually before the Passover, lest pilgrims inadvertently tread on them and so became → defiled (Matt. 23:27; cf. Lk. 11:44; SB I 936 f.). The whitewashing appears to have served both as a warning and as an embellishment. Jesus denounced the scribes and Pharisees as hypocrites, "for you are like whitewashed tombs, which outwardly appear beautiful, but within they are full of dead men's bones and all uncleanness" (Matt. 23:27). Similarly, Paul denounced Ananias as a "whitewashed wall" (Acts 23:3, perhaps combining the idea of a tomb built into a wall and that of the whitewashed fragile wall in Ezek. 13:10 ff.).

| πυρρός | πυρρός (*pyrros*), red (as fire). |

CL & OT *pyrros* is connected with *pyr*, → fire, and *pyroō*, burn. It is attested in secular Gk. from Aeschylus onwards, and can mean red, yellow, yellow-grey, tawny. The LXX uses *pyrros* for *'ādōm* (Gen. 25:30; Num. 19:2; 2 Ki. 3:22; Cant. 5:10). Red horses figure in the vision of Zech. 1:8 and 6:2 (→ *melas*), the red symbolizing the east.

NT The word occurs only at Rev. 6:4 and 12:3, though *Pyrros*, Pyrrhus, occurs as a proper name in Acts 20:4. The rider of the red horse (6:4) is a war-monger, the colour signifying slaughter. Most commentators interpret the four riders as agents of destruction, sent out or simply permitted by God. The red dragon (12:3) denotes → Satan, but recalls the evil Leviathan (Isa. 27:1), associated with Egyptian power (Ezek. 29:3). The colour might stand for bloodthirstiness (12:4), or for evil, as does scarlet (*kokkinos*, 17:3; cf. Isa. 1:18). Purple (*porphyros*, 17:4) symbolizes wealth and luxury (18:16; cf. Lk. 16:19). The noun *porphyra* meant originally the purple shell-fish (murex), then the dye obtained from it, and finally cloth, clothing (cf. Acts 16:14). It is used of the garment which the Roman soldiers put on Jesus (Mk. 15:17, 20; Jn. 19:2, 5) mocking him as King of the Jews. *G. T. D. Angel*

205

Arndt, 441, 473, 501, 700, 738; F. Lang, *pyrros*, *TDNT* VI 952; Liddell–Scott, 1042, 1095 f., 1559; W. Michaelis, *leukos* and *melas*, *TDNT* IV 241–50, 549 ff.; O. Michel, *kokkinos*, *TDNT* III 812 ff.; Moulton–Milligan, 395; M. Rissi, *The Future of the World*, 1972, 19, 91; and commentaries on *Revelation* on the passages cited, by R. H. Charles (ICC), I–II, 1920; A. Farrer, 1964; G. B. Caird, 1966; L. Morris, 1969; G. E. Ladd, 1972; G. R. Beasley-Murray, 1974.

Blessing, Blessed, Happy

εὐλογία

εὐλογέω (*eulogeō*), speak good of, praise, bless; εὐλογία (*eulogia*), fine speaking, praise, blessing; εὐλογητός (*eulogētos*), praised, blessed; ἐνευλογέω (*eneulogeō*), bless; ἀσπάζομαι (*aspazomai*), greet; ἀσπασμός (*aspasmos*), greeting.

CL 1. The vb. *eulogeō* is found in Gk. literature from the tragedians onwards. It is compounded from the adv. *eu*, well, and the root *log*-, speak (→ Word), and means to speak well. (Its opposite is *kakologeō*, speak badly.) Correspondingly the noun *eulogia* (attested from Pindar onwards) means speaking well. The verbal adj. *eulogētos* corresponds to the perf. part. pass. *eulogēmenos* and means a person or thing which is favourably spoken of and thus praised. The intensive compound form *eneulogeō* or *eneulogeomai* is not found in secular Gk. literature.

(a) Applied to *form*, speaking well (*eulogia*) refers to its aesthetic appeal, the attractive presentation of what one is saying (cf. *TDNT* II 754). In *Rep.*, 3, 400de Plato names *eulogia* alongside *euharmostia* (harmony), *euschēmosynē* (good deportment), and *eurhythmia* (symmetry) as consequences of *euēthia* (good morals or good character). In Lucian (*Lexiphanes* 1) and Aesop (ed. Halm 274, 274b: *eulogos*) the concept takes on the negative sense of a well-composed, but false, attractiveness of speech (so also Rom. 16:18).

(b) Applied to its *content*, speaking well (*eulogia*) expresses praise and extolling. This praise can be of things (e.g. a city, Aesch. *Agamemnon*, 580; distinguished deeds, Isoc., 6, 105), or persons (e.g. fathers, Aristoph., *Knights*, 565; women, Aristoph., *Ecclesiazusae*, 454). Occasionally it is used of the praise of the gods (objective gen.) (e.g. Pan in *CIG*, III p. 1190, no. 4705b 2; and Isis, ibid. no. 4705c 3). In such a context *eulogeō* comes close to the meaning of *eucharisteō*, thank (→ Thank, Art. *eucharistia*). Only once (Eur., *Suppliants* 927) are the gods the subject of *eulogein*. The gods consider men in their good deeds. This reflects the rôle of the gods as protecting and endowing men, which is not altogether unknown in Gk. religion (cf. Aesch., *Eumenides*, 997 ff.). Yet one cannot ascribe to the Gk. gods a specific activity of blessing. *eulogeō* first comes to mean bless in the LXX.

2. H. Windisch thinks that the basic meaning of *aspazomai* is that of embracing as in the mutual greeting of two good friends (*TDNT* I 497). Its etymology is obscure, and it is found from Homer onwards. It is also possible that its basic meaning is to speak or say. Like *phileō* (→ Love), *aspazomai* originally expressed liking and welcoming, respect and love for persons and things (Xen., *Cyropaedia*, 1, 4, 1; *Anabasis*, 7, 1, 8; Plato, *Apology* 29d, *Symp.* 209B; Eur., *Ion* 587). Later its application was limited to the act of greeting, as opposed to the word of greeting (cf. *chaire*, hail!). It included offering one's hand, embracing, kissing (*philēma*) and

206

genuflexion (→ Prayer, Art. *proskyneō*) (Plut., *Titus.* 11; *Agesilaus*, 11; *Phocion*, 27; Josephus, *Ant.* 11, 8, 5 (331)). Correspondingly, the sub. *aspasmos* means first embrace, love (Plato, *Laws*, 11, 919e), then greeting, visit (Epict., *Diss.*, 4, 4, 3, 37). Written greetings are uncommon in the pre-Christian era, but they were more frequent in the Oriental world (cf. Amarna and Elephantine Letters).

ot In the LXX these words are very common (in al. 640 occurrences, 450 in the case of *eulogeō*). Most often they represent forms of the root *bārak* (bless). Here *eulogeō* comes to mean bless and is no longer contrasted with *kakologeō* (see above cl 1), but with *kataraomai* (curse). This group of words occurs in almost all OT and apocryphal texts, but it is particularly common in Gen., Deut., Pss. and Tob. The descriptions of blessing in the OT have to some extent developed a peculiar "language of blessing" (C. Westermann, *Der Segen in der Bibel und im Handeln der Kirche*, 1968, 33). It is, therefore, necessary for the understanding of the OT concept of blessing to deal not only with cases of the *bārak* and *eulogeō* groups of words but also with texts which describe the blessing in their own way without using this terminology.

1. The concept of blessing has its origins in pre-Israelite times and is connected with magical concepts from which blessing could originally be distinguished only with difficulty (cf. G. van der Leeuw, *Religion in Essence and Manifestation*, 1964², §59). This is implied even in the etymological links of the Heb. *bārak* with the Ugaritic root *brk* and the Akkad. word *karābu*. Basically *bārak* means endow with beneficial power. This meaning involves both the process of endowing and the condition of being endowed. Hence blessing originally involved a self-contained beneficial force which one could transmit to another and which stood in contrast to the destructive power of cursing (→ Curse, Art. *kataraomai*).

2. In the OT one can find elements of such pre-Israelite ideas and customs of blessing which were common particularly in the ancient religions of the Near East. Blessing features strongly in the stories of the patriarchs in Gen. 12–36.

(a) The performance of a blessing involves a → word invested with power and an action ratifying it. The oldest formula of blessing is a promise in the indicative: Blessed are you! (*bārûk 'attâh*; LXX *eulogētos [sy ei*, e.g. Gen. 26:29). The actions that accompanied this pronouncement have a symbolic significance. Through physical contact they confer beneficial power by the laying on of hands. This is by the right hand (Gen. 48:13 ff.), or at least by the raising of the hands or the arms (Exod. 17:11), kissing or embracing (Gen. 48:10), and the touching of clothes (2 Ki. 2:13 f.), staffs (2 Ki. 4:29), or placing the hand under the thigh (Gen. 24:9; 47:29). The one who was to bestow the blessing fortified for bestowing it by eating a special food (Gen. 27:4).

(b) The imparted blessing works unconditionally and irrevocably. It is permanent and can neither be revoked nor rendered ineffective (Gen. 27:33; 2 Sam. 7:29).

(c) The blessing does not have its original setting in the sacral context of the cult, but in that of the family bonds of kinship.

(d) There are correspondingly different occasions for blessing. The most frequent form of expression is a greeting at meeting and parting (Gen. 47:7 ff.). A blessing was imparted particularly at the climactic points in life: at birth (Ruth 4:13 f.; cf. Lk. 2:34), marriage (Gen. 24:60) and death (Gen. 48:1 ff.; 49:28 ff.). In this connection it is important to note the blessing of the heir, by which the head of the family conveyed his power before his death chiefly to his first-born son, and thus passed it on to the next generation (Gen. 27:1 ff.; 48:1 ff.).

(e) Basically anyone is entitled to impart a blessing or a curse. But some men were specially endowed with a power to bless and curse, e.g., the seer Balaam (Num. 22), charismatic leaders like Joshua (Jos. 6), Melchizedek Gen. 14:18 ff.), and later also prophets and priests.

(f) In earlier times blessing had a mutual character. Not only did the mighty bestow a blessing on their inferiors (e.g. Melchizedek on Abraham in Gen. 14:18 ff.), but also the inferiors on the mighty (e.g. Jacob on Pharaoh in Gen. 47:7-10). Men reply to the blessings of a deity by blessing him, i.e. by recognizing his power in praise. Hence *bārak* means, on the one hand, bless (subject: God) and, on the other, praise (subject: men).

(g) The nature of the blessing is that of the conferring and transference of beneficial power, which produces fertility in men (Gen. 24:34-36) and in livestock and lands (Gen. 30:25 ff.). Blessing works vertically in the continued growth of succeeding generations (expressed in the genealogies of Gen. 5 and 11:10 ff.). Horizontally it effects peace, security from enemies, good fortune and well-being for a tribe or group (expressed most comprehensively in the concept *šālôm*, well-being.

(h) This original concept of a blessing, which precedes both the emergence of cult and theological reflection appears most clearly in Jacob's plot to steal the blessing in Gen. 27.

3. (a) The story of Balaam (Num. 22-24) combines the pre-Israelite phenomenon of the blessing with the power of Yahweh, the God of Israel. Balak, king of Moab, apprehensive of an invasion of the Israelites into his land, called on the pagan charismatic soothsayer Balaam to help by checking the threatening foe with a → curse (Num. 22:1-6). The point of the story is that Yahweh, the God of Israel, shows himself to be master of the power to pronounce blessing. Balaam is deprived of his own innate powers of control and may only bless, instead of curse, at Yahweh's command (Num. 22:12, 31, 38; 23:3-5). In this transference of all the power of blessing to Yahweh, blessing has lost its magical quality. The visible contacts conveying the power are reduced to actions in which Yahweh is understood as the real agent of blessing.

(b) The pronouncements of the blessing (Num. 23:7-10, 18-24; 24:3-9, 15-24) in the story of Balaam have their true home in the formal pronouncements of blessing and cursing (cf. Gen. 9:26; 49; Num. 22-24; Deut. 33; Gen. 3:14 f.; 4:11; Lev. 26; Deut. 28). Blessing belongs to the language of the seer. It differs from the prophetic promise of salvation in the way it depicts salvation. It portrays the earthly well-being of the people or the land. Thus Num. 24:5 f. declares: "How fair are your tents, Jacob, your encampments, Israel. Like valleys that stretch afar, like gardens beside a river, like oaks that the Lord (MT *YHWH*) has planted, like cedar trees beside the waters."

(c) The decisive switch from the prehistoric, unhistorical concept of the blessing within the tribe to the historical understanding of the blessing in the context of the history of Israel occurs in the Yahwistic prologue to the story of the patriarchs in Gen. 12:1-3. The text is divided into a three-fold command (v. 1) and a six-fold promise, each part linked by *waw* (and; vv. 2–3). The command contains the demand that Abraham depart from his land, his tribe and his family. He is to break off his settled way of life, in order to travel on towards a vaguely indicated destination. It is a striking feature of the formulation of the promise, that in these programmatic promises the root *bārak* occurs 5 times, each time in a different form, as the key word. As distinct from the immediate transference of power in pre-Israelite times, the Yahwist has made the blessing into an object of Yahweh's → promise. He has given the previous unhistorical procedure of blessing a future perspective: the blessing is promised for future times.

The Yahwist takes up the tradition of the promise of a son or a posterity in the patriarchal stories (cf. Gen. 26:34–36; 26:24). Here the son is not named as the blessing promised to Abraham, as he is in Gen. 15:4; 18:10. The blessing is the great nation and the great name which this nation obtained later as in the time of the empire of David and Solomon (v. 2; cf. 2 Sam. 7:9). The blessing is seen as a promise realized in the history of Israel. " 'Blessing' becomes the key word of the great history of Israel from Abraham's departure up to the Davidic empire" (H. W. Wolff, *Gesammelte Studien*, ThB 22, 1964, 356).

The sixth clause, formulated with a constative perf., is the most comprehensive: "all tribes of the earth can obtain blessing in you" (v. 3b; cf. 13:18; 28:14; the niph. of *bārak* is to be translated as mid., not pass.). This sentence is to be understood in the context of the primal history which embraces all mankind (Gen. 1–11), which mentions 5 instances of the curse on mankind (Gen. 3:14, 17; 4:11; 5:29; 9:25). In contrast to this history of the curse, Gen. 12:3b sets before "all tribes of the earth" a history of blessing. It includes liberation from vain toil (Gen. 3:17), care-fraught wandering (Gen. 4:11 f.), base servitude (Gen. 9:25) and the destructive chaos of the nations (Gen. 11:1 ff.). Thus in Gen. 12:1–3 the Yahwist spans the histories of patriarchs, nation and mankind with his promise of blessing.

4. (a) After Israel's settlement in Canaan a lengthy struggle began over whether the Canaanite fertility gods, the Baalim, or Yahweh, the God of promises who brought Israel out of Egypt, was to be honoured as bestower of blessing. The fierceness of this clash is especially apparent in the accounts of the prophet Elijah (1 Ki. 17–19). The story of God's judgment on Carmel (1 Ki. 18) symbolizes the victory of Yahweh who causes fire to fall from heaven over the powerless deity, Baal (cf. G. von Rad, *Old Testament Theology*, II, 1967, 16 f.) The story of drought and rain (1 Ki. 17:1; 18:1, 2a, 16 f., 41–46) transfers Baal's powers of fertility and blessing to Yahweh, who is now seen as Lord of the land. His continued activity in bestowing blessing in the promised land of Canaan adds a new element to his actions in history.

(b) This understanding of blessing is expressed in Deuteronomy. Here the whole nation receives the gifts of civilized society – fertility of body, of cattle, of field, political unity and harmony with neighbouring peoples – as blessings from Yahweh's hand. "Blessed are you in the city, and blessed in the field. Blessed is the fruit of your body, the fruit of your land and the fruit of your cattle . . . . The Lord will cause your enemies who rise up against you to be defeated by you" (Deut. 28:3–7; cf. 7:13–16). Yahweh's blessing is understood in Deut. in this-wordly, secular terms. G. von Rad speaks of a "material view of salvation, which . . . extends even to the kneading-trough of the individual household (Deut. 28:5)" (op. cit. I, 1962, 229).

In contrast to the concept of blessing in Gen. 12, 15, 26, Deuteronomy does not speak of blessing in the form of an unconditional promise, but in the form of conditional sentences. "*If* (MT *'im*; LXX *ean*) you now listen carefully to the voice of Yahweh, your God . . . then all these blessings will come upon you" (Deut. 28:1 f.; cf. vv. 15 f.). Being thus bound to the obedience of the nation, the blessing is an element in the → covenant between Yahweh and Israel. As Yahweh fulfils his covenant obligations in blessing, so Israel is bound to keep the covenant. The reverse side of this conditional blessing under the covenant is the curse that attends Israel's failure to keep its obligations. That is the significance of the command of Deut. 11:29 to set the blessing on Mount Gerizim and the curse on Mount Ebal. The two possibilities, between which Israel must choose (Deut. 30:19), are developed at length in ch. 28: vv. 1–14, the blessing; and vv. 15–68, the curse. By drawing blessing into the covenant, Deut. unites the polarity of blessing and cursing with that of salvation and judgment (→ Redemption, art. *sōzō* OT; → Judgment, art. *krima* OT; cf. C. Westermann, *Der Segen*, 51 f.).

(c) Besides Yahweh, the real bestower of blessing, there are also in Israel individual people or groups who mediate blessing: → kings, → prophets and → priests. The role of the king in mediating blessing is never so prominent in Israel as, e.g., in Egypt. But the promise given by Nathan (2 Sam. 7:16) shows that at any rate the Davidic kingship conveys blessing. The first temple at Jerusalem is consecrated with a two-fold act of blessing by Solomon before and after the prayer of consecration (1 Ki. 8:14, 54). The extent to which the king was seen as bringing blessing is particularly clear in the messianic texts which speak of a new king who will bring his nation the blessings of well-being and peace (cf. Isa. 9:6 f.; 11:1 ff.). Part of the task of the early prophets was to intercede for Yahweh's blessing on the nation (1 Ki. 18:41 ff., Elijah; 2 Ki. 6:24 ff., Elisha; Amos 7:1 ff.; Jer. 14). The later literary prophets proclaimed well-being in the form of a future activity of Yahweh in salvation and blessing. Like the apocalyptic writers, they portrayed this blessing promised for the future as an earthly salvation in the language of blessing (see above 3 (b)). It is seen as a messianic kingdom of peace (Isa. 11; Zech. 9:9 f.), a quiet and prosperous life (Mic. 4:3 f.; Zech. 9:17), prosperity and a great banquet (Isa. 55:1 ff.; 25:6), the destruction of enemies (Isa. 27:1), lasting peace (Isa. 26:12) and universal well-being (Isa. 65:17–25).

5. (a) Blessing also plays an important part in Israelite worship. That is apparent in the consecration of Solomon's temple (1 Ki. 8:14, 54; see above 4 (c)). The temple as the holy precinct is the true place for the mediation of blessing to the nation and the land. The blessing was bestowed at the close of worship on the members of the cultic community as they returned to their houses, that it might be realized in their daily lives (cf. the Pss. of blessing: 65; 115:12–15; 128; 129:8; 132 etc.). The community responded to the blessing that it had received by blessing Yahweh in their turn, in the cry of adoration, "Praised be Yahweh" (MT *bārûk YHWH;* LXX *eulogētos kyrios*). This formula occurs especially frequently in the Pss. of praise (Pss. 18:47; 28:6; 31:21(22); 66:20; 68:19(20); 119:12; 124:6; etc.; cf. also the doxologies of Pss. 41:13(14); 72:18(19); 89:52(53); 106:48). Probably the blessing was also pronounced on certain cultic occasions (e.g. the presentation of the first-fruits, Deut. 26:1 ff.) and over individuals (cf. Pss. 91; 121).

(b) The theology of blessing in the so-called priestly tradition presupposes the
210

institutions of the cult. The bestowal of blessing is a privilege of the Levitical →
priests. Lev. 9:22 f. tells of the first pronouncement of the priestly blessing at the
end of the first service of sacrifice in the holy tent. It is confirmed by the appearance
of Yahweh's glory. Num. 6:24–26 records the wording of the priestly, Aaronic
blessing, to be pronounced at the end of every act of worship: "May Yahweh bless
you, and keep you; may Yahweh let his face shine upon you, and may he be gracious to you; may Yahweh lift up his countenance towards you, and may he set
well-being upon you." This rhythmic blessing falls into three parts, each of which
describes Yahweh's blessing and its content with different words, so rendering it
more impressive. The process of his blessing is described as a shining or lifting up
of his → face (MT *pānîm*; LXX *prosōpon*). *pānîm* means that side of Yahweh's
nature which is turned towards men (cf. the *kᵉḇôḏ YHWH*, Yahweh's glory). If
Yahweh does not hide that side of himself that is turned towards men, but lifts it
up; if he does not darken it in wrath, but lets it shine; then Yahweh's blessing
means his welcoming disposition towards men. The content of the blessing is
described by the concepts of protection, grace and – most comprehensively – well-
being (Heb. *šālôm*, → Peace OT). The blessing is received by the community of the
Israelites gathered for worship, who are addressed as a single person (v. 23). The
six verbs of the blessing are in the cohortative imperfect, i.e. in the form of a desire
for blessing and not a promise in the indicative. Thus Yahweh's freedom over against
cultic blessing is safeguarded. The priests can simply pray for his blessing; but they
cannot dispense it. Nevertheless, Yahweh's promise attends the priests' act of
blessing: "If they thus set my name upon the Israelites, I myself will bless them"
(v. 27).

(c) While the concept of blessing in Num. 6 has a sacral, priestly, cultic character,
related to the cultic community, the blessing pronounced in Gen. 1:22, 28 embraces
all creation, men and other creatures. "Be fruitful, increase, fill the earth and
subject it to yourselves" (Gen. 1:28). Gen. 2:3 does not only sanctify the seventh
day for the cultic community, but primarily blesses it for all men. C. Westermann
deduces from the common and contrasting elements in Gen. 1 and Num. 6 that
"the blessing given in worship . . . is in fact meant for all mankind; and the blessing
pronounced upon the community gathering for sacred worship is that intended for
all mankind and indeed for all living things" (op. cit., 61).

6. (a) Even the occasionally thoroughly secular sayings collected in the OT
Wisdom literature are indirectly related with blessing. Here Yahweh's blessing is
expressed in the shrewd advice which a wise man can give in secular matters (details
in Westermann, op. cit., 40 ff.).

(b) The dramatic dialogues of the Book of Job also discuss the question of
Yahweh's action in bestowing and withdrawing his blessing. The argument shows
that the mechanical application of the theology of blessing of Deut., that
blessing and cursing are entirely dependent on obedience or disobedience (cf. 4 (b)),
upheld by Job's "friends", with all their merciless implications, is not the complete answer. For it does not square with the reality of Job's sufferings (cf. also
Ps. 73 and the scepticism of the Preacher in Eccl.). Here the OT theology of blessing
reaches its limits. Yahweh's blessing is no longer primarily experienced in the present.
As in apocalyptic, it is awaited in the promised *eschaton*.

(c) The original forms of the blessings are preserved in the Book of Tobit which echoes the stories of the patriarchs: the blessing of children by their parents, especially at their departure (Tob. 5:16; 7:7; 9:6; 10:12), and in greetings (Tob. 7:6; 10:12).

(d) In Rab. Jud. pronouncements of blessing and praise are widespread. The first tractate of the Mishnah is called $b^e r\bar{a}\underline{k}\hat{o}\underline{t}$. Praises are introduced with the formula "Praised be the Lord", and extol Yahweh for his deeds and gifts. The rabbis knew of appropriate praises for all the most widely varied situations of daily and cultic life (cf. SB IV 616 ff., 627 ff.). We should remember here the blessing that Jews pronounced at table before and after a meal. Ber. 35a says: "It is forbidden to a man to enjoy anything of this world without a benediction, and if anyone enjoys anything of this world without a benediction, he commits sacrilege" (for details cf. H. W. Beyer, *TDNT* II 759 ff.).

(e) The texts of the Qumran community include hymns of praise, some of which begin with the formula "Praised are you, Lord" (the Qumran Thanksgiving Hymns or Hodayot, 1QH). The extant fragments of the Blessings Scroll (1QSb) contain blessings for priests and other persons. The Community Rule quotes a (gnostic?) version of the Aaronic blessing: "May He (Yahweh) bless you with all good and protect you from all evil and illuminate your heart with the understanding of life and be gracious to you with everlasting knowledge, and may He lift up his gracious countenance towards you for your eternal well-being" (1QS 2:2–4).

NT Compared with the fundamental significance of blessing in the OT, the NT gives less prominence to both the concept and the act. The group of words associated with the root *eulog-* occurs altogether 68 times in the NT. The vb. *eulogeō* accounts for 41 occurrences; *eneulogeō* 2 (Acts. 3:25; Gal. 3:8); *kateulogeō* 1 (Mk. 10:16); the noun *eulogia* 16; and the verbal adj. *eulogētos* 8. Comparatively speaking, this group is most frequent in Lk., the major Pauline epistles and Heb. But Jn. uses the vb. only once (12:13) in an OT quotation. In the shorter Pauline epistles, the Pastorals, the Johannine and the Catholic epistles, 2 Pet., Jude, the group does not occur at all.

1. The formal and aesthetic sense of *eulogia* found in classical Gk. is only alluded to in a deprecatory fashion in Rom. 16:18: "They (Paul's opponents) do not serve our Lord Jesus Christ, but their own belly and they deceive the hearts of the unsuspecting with their skill of speech (*chrēstologia*) and pleasing eloquence (*eulogia*)."

2. Far more often (40 times out of 68) the root has the meaning praise, extol. The adj. *eulogētos* means only blessed, praised. This usage derives, on the one hand, from the basically secular Gk. meaning, to speak well of someone (see above CL 1 (b)), and, on the other hand, from the LXX translation of the OT form of praise of God, "Blessed, i.e. praised, by Yahweh" (see above OT 5 (a)).

(a) The NT also uses this root to express its praise of God. In this context it takes on a doxological character. As in late Judaism (Ber. 7:3; Eth. Enoch 77:1), God is called the "praised (*eulogētos*) One" (Mk. 14:61). Zechariah's hymn (Lk. 1:68, the *Benedictus*) and some letters (2 Cor. 1:3; Eph. 1:3; 1 Pet. 1:3) begin with the formula "Praised be God (the Lord)" (*eulogētos (kyrios) ho theos*). The relationship of greeting and praise of God is particularly clear here (cf. the formula of greeting still practised in S. Germany, "Grüss (dich) Gott", "God greet you").

Another form of doxology occurs as a short interjection of praise (*eulogia*) in Paul's letters (Rom. 1:25b; 9:5; 2 Cor. 11:31). It is expanded as a hymn in Rev. (5:12, 13b; 7:12 → Song, Art. *hymnos*).

(b) The greeting of a superior was expressed not by the doxological adj. *eulogētos* but by the perf. part. pass. of the more versatile vb. *eulogeō: eulogēmenos*. This expresses not only praise and greeting, but recognition that God has blessed the person concerned. Jesus is greeted with the cry of *eulogēmenos*, praised, blessed, welcome (Mk. 11:9 par.; Matt. 23:39 par.; cf. Ps. 118:26). This form of greeting also welcomes the coming of God's kingdom, initiated by God with the Messiah's coming (Mk. 11:10). It is applied to Mary, the mother of the Messiah (Lk. 1:42).

(c) The Jewish custom of offering praise on various occasions in everyday life and in worship (see above OT 6 (d)) is also attested in the NT writings (Lk. 1:64; 2:28 f., the *Nunc Dimittis*; 2:34; 24:53; 1 Cor. 14:16; Jas. 3:9 f.). According to the synoptic accounts, Jesus followed the practice of the Jewish paterfamilias in pronouncing a blessing as a prayer at table before and after meals (Mk. 6:41 par., the feeding of the 5000; 8:7, the feeding of the 4000; 14:22 f. par., Jesus' last meal with his disciples, → Lord's Supper NT 4 (b); Lk. 24:30, table fellowship with the risen Christ). As the parallelism of *eulogeō* and *eucharisteō* (→ Thank, Art. *eucharistia*) in Mk. 8:6 f.; 14:22 f. and Matt. 26:26 f. shows, the blessing at meals gives thanks to the Creator for his material gifts. (See above OT 4 (b); cf. also 1 Cor. 10:16, SB IV 627 ff. on the cup of blessing and → Lord's Supper NT 4 (d). On the whole of sect. 2 cf. W. Schenk, *Der Segen im NT*, 1967, 97–130).

3. Where this word group occurs with the special sense of bless or blessing (28 times out of 60), the NT understanding of this concept is oriented more towards the theology of blessing in the OT than towards that of late Judaism. The picture presented by the NT corresponds to the statistical evidence (see above NT introduction). In contrast to the OT (see above OT 3(c), 4(b), 5(b)), the NT presents no special theology of blessing. It refers to it incidentally as something familiar to its readers, though it is by no means unimportant.

(a) In the Synoptic Gospels the idea of blessing is significant in three pericopes: (i) the blessing of the children, (ii) Jesus' commissioning of the Twelve, and (iii) the departure of the risen Jesus from his followers.

(i) In laying his hands on the → children and blessing them (Mk. 10:13–16 par.), Jesus did nothing unusual. On the contrary, he acted just as a Jewish father or rabbi would (cf. SB I 807 f.). The important point to note is that for Mk., Jesus' activity is not limited to adults. It also includes children, and so embraces man at all stages of life. The kingdom of God, with which this pericope is principally concerned (v. 15), is "man's bodily and creaturely existence positively co-ordinated with Jesus' activity" (so C. Westermann, op. cit., 83; as against W. Schenk, op. cit., 72, who understands Jesus' blessing "as clearly intercession").

(ii) The context of the commissioning in Matt. 10:1–16 shows that the instructions to greet houses (v. 12 *aspasasthe*) refers to the greeting of blessing (cf. v. 13 *eirēnē*, Heb. *šālôm*, well-being). As in Jesus' own ministry, the disciples have a twofold task: (1) preaching, and (2) healing (vv. 7–8a). They are sent out as evangelists and bearers of blessing. Matt. holds that the disciples' commission – like Jesus'

213

own mission – involves not only announcing the kingdom of God, but also compassion for the creaturely suffering of the world and action directed towards man's earthly well-being. Acts also shows particularly clearly the complementary activities of the apostles in proclaiming salvation by word and deed (cf. Peter's healing and preaching in Acts 3). There blessing does not reach its fullness until the spasmodic missionary preaching has given way to the regular building up of churches (see above OT 4 (a)). This new situation, which is so unlike the unsettled conditions of Jesus' life and that of the disciples and apostles (particularly Paul), is not yet present in most of the NT. It is, therefore, not surprising that blessing is not so often spoken of in the NT as in the OT.

(iii) Neither the priestly blessing (so Schenk, op. cit., 58) nor the blessing of the heir in the stories of the patriarchs lies behind the risen Christ's benediction in Lk. 24:50 f. Rather it is the custom of blessing given at departure (see above OT 2 (d), 6 (c)). The departing Lord shares with his church the power of his blessing through which he remains bound to it. Its content is the presence of the exalted Lord with his church, as Matt. expressly says at the corresponding point in his account: "I am with you always" (Matt. 28:20; cf. Gen. 26:3).

(b) Of all the NT writers Paul used the concept of blessing the most deliberately and gave it its new decisive christological form (cf. OT 3 (c) above).

(i) In Gal. 3:8 Paul cites Gen. 12:3b: "All nations shall be blessed in you" (i.e. all nations of the earth; cf. the LXX translation which Paul uses here). Paul gives the quotation a new interpretation corresponding to his christological train of thought. The fulfilment of the blessing promised to Abraham is now seen as God's redeeming act in Christ. The gift of the blessing is no longer that of a great nation or of the fruitfulness of the land, but the promised → Spirit of Christ (v. 14). The common ground between the quotation from Gen. 12:3 and its Pauline interpretation lies in the fact that both the promised blessing and its fulfilment in Christ should reach all nations of the earth (vv. 8, 14). In Gal. 3:8–14 Paul so interprets the relation of blessing and curse that, through Christ's taking to himself once and for all the curse of the Law in his death (v. 13; → Cross, art. *xylon* NT), the believers of all nations now receive the blessing of God's redeeming activity in Christ (v. 14; cf. Eph. 1:3; Acts 3:25 f.).

(ii) The phrase *eulogia Christou* (Rom. 15:29) does mean not an act of blessing but the effect of the preaching of Christ in the church. It means that Paul is certain that his coming to Rome will further the growth of the community.

(iii) The connection between blessing and gifts (cf. Gen. 33:11) is shown especially in 2 Cor. 9:5 f. Paul calls the collection which he has been making for the community at Jerusalem a *eulogia*. The context shows that *eulogia* means a generous gift (as opposed to *pleonexia*, stinginess). The Corinthian church should contribute ungrudgingly (*ep' eulogias* as opposed to *pheidomenōs*, grudgingly), so that through this gift God's blessing may be given tangible expression in the Jerusalem church.

(c) The Letter to the Hebrews makes fullest use of the OT concept of blessing found in the stories of the patriarchs, e.g. in 6:7 f. (see above OT 2). It frequently alludes to or paraphrases OT benedictions: 6:14 (Abraham, cf. Gen. 22:16 f.); 7:1–7 (Melchizedek, cf. Gen. 14:18–20); 11:20 (Isaac, cf. Gen. 27:27 ff.); 11:21 (Jacob, cf. Gen. 48:15 f.); 12:27 (Esau, cf. Gen. 27:30 ff.). The book's purpose in telling of these examples is stated in 6:12: "so that you may imitate the example of those

214

who through faith and patient endurance inherit the promises." Sometimes these passages contain formulas like "to inherit blessing" (Heb. 12:17; cf. 1 Pet. 3:9) and "to inherit promises" (Heb. 6:12, 15). The parallelism of blessing and promise shows that blessing here means not present, but eschatological well-being (cf. also Matt. 25:34 and Isa. 65:23b; see above OT 4 (c)).

(d) Finally, there are the paraenetic texts on blessing: Lk. 6:27 f.; Rom. 12:14; 1 Cor. 4:12; 1 Pet. 3:9. Here Jesus' disciples are exhorted to meet the curses, persecutions, abuse or reproaches of enemies with the opposite, blessing. Blessing here means simply a friendly disposition towards enemies. The commandment to love one's enemies replaces the *ius talionis* (this is especially clear in 1 Pet. 3:9). What Paul formulated christologically is here developed in paraenesis The opposition of blessing and cursing is abolished. Since Christ has taken the curse upon himself (Gal. 3:13; see above (b) (i)), Christians can only be exhorted to bless without reserve (Rom. 12:14). "Christ's church and individual Christians need curse no one any more, for Christ's work avails also for his enemies" (Westermann, op. cit., 90).

H.-G. Link

μακάριος

μακάριος (*makarios*), blessed, fortunate, happy; μακαρίζω (*makarizō*), call or consider blessed, happy; μακαρισμός (*makarismos*), blessing.

CL 1. *makarios*, originally a parallel form to *makar*, is first attested in Pindar and means free from daily cares and worries. In poetic language it describes the condition of the gods and those who share their happy existence. In the 4th cent. B.C. it gradually lost this meaning, and became a word in common use, like our "happy", and was therefore avoided by poets (cf. Plato, *Meno*, 71a).

2. It is important to note that it most frequently occurs in the formalized language of *makarismos* (blessing) in the formula *makarios hos(tis)* ... happy is he who ... (e.g. Pindar, *Pyth.*, 5, 46; only rarely in the 2nd person). Hence a person can be congratulated on a happy event. "In content beatitudes, which are common in both poetry and prose throughout the centuries, reflect the sorrows and afflictions, the aspirations and ideals, of the Greeks" (F. Hauck, *TDNT* IV 363). Parents are congratulated on their children (Aristoph., *Wasps*, 1512), the well-to-do on their wealth (Bacchyl., 5, 50), the wise on their knowledge (Plato, *Laws*, 2, 660e), the pious on their inward well-being (Eur., *Frag.* 256, ed. Nauck 434), initiates on their experience of God (Homeric Hymn to Demeter 480) and (in funerary inscriptions) the dead on their escape from the vanity of things (Aesch., *Persians* 712).

3. The different Gk. concepts of happiness also recur in the use of the vb. *makarizō* (Homer, *Od.* onwards) and the sub. *makarismos* (Plato, *Rep.* 591e onwards). The latter first occurs as a technical term in the sense of pronouncing blessed in Aristotle (*Rhet.*, A9 1367b 33).

OT 1. In the LXX *makarios* and *makarizō* generally translate the Heb. *'ešer*, happiness, well-being, *'āšar*, pronounce happy, or *'ašrê*, well-being to .... The meaning of these words is also determined by the dominant aspirations and ideas of happiness.

Stylized blessings do not occur in the early strata of the OT (as in early eastern literature in general). They are found first in the wisdom literature, "praising the prudent man, in a participial or relative clause" (K. Koch, *The Growth of the Biblical Tradition*, 1969, 17). This is irrespective of whether the reference is to earthly blessings (Sir. 25:8; Gen. 30:13; Ps. 127:5), prosperity (Job. 29:10 f.), a wise life (Prov. 3:13; Sir. 14:20), or fulfilling God's commandment (Pss. 1:1; 41:1(2); 119:1). Those psalms that have been influenced by the wisdom tradition pronounce him blessed who trusts in God. "Blessed are all those who put their trust in him" (Pss. 2:12; 34:8(9); cf. 84:12(13); Isa. 30:18). "Blessed is he whose sin has been forgiven" (Ps. 32:1 f.). The connection between religious happiness consisting in Yahweh's favour and earthly happiness through the Creator's gifts is basic in wisdom literature. Yahweh himself is, however, never called *makarios*. This formula always solemnly ascribes well-being to a man. It is quite different from a benediction (→ *eulogia*) which is an authoritative and efficacious word. It is indicative of this distinction that in an age when blessing was a priestly prerogative (Sir. 50:20) laymen had recourse to *makarismos*.

2. In the later Israelite period (e.g. Sir. 25:7–10) more elaborate pronouncements of this sort and even whole series of them are found, especially in apocalyptic texts (Dan. 12:12; Tob. 13:14 f.). Pronouncements of blessedness are often supplemented by a contrasting series of woes (Sl. Enoch 52:1 ff.; cf. Eth. Enoch 103:5). In substance these pronouncements have the force of an eschatological consolation (as Eth. Enoch 58:2 shows: "Blessed are you righteous elect! For glorious shall your lot be"). "No longer is it a general matter of trust in God, but belief in the coming of the end of the world, in the eschatological hope" (Koch, op. cit., 17).

3. In Hel. Judaism Hellenistic influence showed itself clearly in the use of the word *makarios*, especially in Philo. According to him, only the deity attains to blessedness. He alone is blessed (*monos makarios*, *Sacr.* 101). Men share in this only in so far as the divine → nature penetrates the creation. On the other hand, Rab. Judaism latched on to the OT usage: "Happy are you and those who bore you! Happy are my eyes that they have seen a thing!" cried R. Johanan b. Zakkai to his pupils (Hag. 14b). Eschatological blessedness is alien to him.

NT 1. In the NT the vb. *makarizō* occurs only twice (Lk. 1:48; Jas. 5:11), and the noun *makarismos* only 3 times (Gal. 4:15; Rom. 4:6, 9; both these Pauline passages suggest use of the word in a formula). On the other hand *makarios* is relatively more frequent, generally in the context of pronouncing someone or something blessed. Of 50 instances 13 and 15 are in Matt. and Lk. respectively, 7 in Paul, only 2 each in Jn., 1 Pet. and Jas., and 7 in Rev.

2. Stylistically the NT pronouncements follow the tradition of those in apocalyptic, including the setting of them in series noted above. Corresponding to the Heb. *'ašrê*, the eschatological pronouncements in Jesus' preaching and the gospel records are made in the 3rd person. Almost uniformly they are furnished with a reason or a description of the bliss ascribed (Lk. 1:45 etc.). "Blessed are the spiritually poor; for the kingdom of heaven is theirs" (Matt. 5:3 etc.). Contrasting woes are explicitly set against the ascriptions of blessing in Lk. 6:20 ff. and implicitly in the visions of Rev. 14:13; 16:15; 19:9 (cf. also Lk. 6:5 Codex D). They occur predominantly in the Synoptics and in Rev., but apparently not in those strata of early Christianity

that came under Hel. influence. In pronouncing blessed the man who does not condemn himself in his decisions (Rom. 14:22) and in calling the unmarried more blessed (1 Cor. 7:40), Paul aligns himself stylistically more with the pronouncements of the wisdom tradition. A clearly Gk. or Hel. usage is found in 1 Tim. 1:11 and 6:15, where God himself is pronounced blessed (cf. also Tit. 2:13 and Philo).

3. The pronouncements of the Sermon on the Mount dominate the NT scene (Matt. 5:3–10 par. in the introd. to the so-called Sermon on the Plain in Lk. 6:20 ff.). There the 3rd person in Matt. 5:3–10 over against 5:11 f. and Lk. 6 corresponds to the general usage. The contents of the pronouncements parallel those of apocalyptic as well as their style. "Previously the Beatitudes were seen as a vehicle for setting out the virtues ordained by God for man, but now it is quite clear that phrases such as 'poor in spirit', 'those that mourn', 'are meek', hunger and thirst after righteousness' are merely different aspects of an attitude to the world nearing its close, an attitude of lasting patience and hope. It s not the virtues which are important so much as the promise of salvation conveyed by the 'blessed' at the beginning as well as by the motive clause in the second half of each line" (Koch, op. cit., 8). The eschatological pronouncements are distinguishable from the apocalyptic by their paradoxical statements (the kingdom belongs to the poor in spirit, the powerless, the sorrowful), and by the fact that this kingdom of God is bound up with the life and message of Jesus. They are an example of what is meant in Matt. 11:5: the message of joy is brought to the poor. The salvation that is announced here depends on the coming kingdom of God, which in turn is inseparable from him who brings it.

Present and future are thus related to one another in these pronouncements. This is clearest in Lk.'s version of them in 6:20 ff. where the word "now" is inserted in v. 21 underlining this relationship. "Blessed are you who hunger now, for you will be satisfied." All the benefits praised in Hellenism and the OT are now eclipsed. "The predominating estimation of the kingdom of God carries with it a reversal of all customary evaluations" (Hauck, *TDNT* IV 368). Hence the pronouncement also applies to all those who share the experience of the arrival of the kingdom of God (Matt. 13:16 f.), who face this encounter in the right way (Lk. 1:45; Matt. 16:17; Jn. 20:29), and are not offended at it (Matt. 11:6). They act according to what they have heard and seen (Lk. 14:14; Jn. 13:17) and remain steadfast and faithful on the watch (Lk. 12:37 f.; Matt. 24:46; Jas. 1:12; Rev. 16:15). Although the pronouncements in the NT are so varied, their futuristic character is not to be understood in the sense of consolation and subsequent recompense The promised future always involves a radical alteration of the present. *U. Becker*

(a). J. M. Allegro, "A Possible Mesopotamian Background to the Joseph Blessing of Gen. XLIX," *ZAW* 64, 1952, 249–51; H. W. Beyer, *eulogeō*, *TDNT* II 754–65; D. Daube, *Studies in Biblical Law*, 1947; S. A. Blank, "The Curse, Blasphemy, the Spell and the Oath," *Hebrew Union College Annual* 23, 1950–51, 73–95; W. J. Harrelson, "Blessings and Cursings," *IDB* 1 446 ff.; J. Jeremias, *The Eucharistic Words of Jesus*, 1966²; G. van der Leeuw, *Religion in its Essence and Manifestation*, 1964², 408–12; A. Murtonen, "The Use and Meaning of the Words *lebārek* and *berākâh* in the Old Testament," *VT* 9, 1959, 158–77, 330; S. Mowinckel, "Psalms of Blessing and Cursing," *The Psalms in Israel's Worship*, II, 1962, 44–52; H. Mowvley, "The Concept and Content of 'Blessing' in the OT," *The Bible Translator* 16, 1965, 74–80; J. Pedersen, *Israel: Its Life and Culture*, I–II, 1926, 162 ff., 182–212; G. von Rad, *Old Testament Theology*, I, 1963, II, 1965; J. Scharbert, "Blessing," *EBT* I 69–75; A. C. Thiselton, "The Supposed Power of Words in the Biblical Writings," *JTS* n.s.

25, 1974, 283–99; H. Windisch, *aspazomai, TDNT* I 496–502; G. P. Wiles, *Paul's Intercessory Prayers: The Significance of Intercessory Prayer Passages in the Letters of Paul*, 1974, 108–55: R. E. Brown, "The Beatitudes according to Luke", *New Testament Essays*, 1967, 265–71; W. D. Davies, *The Setting of the Sermon on the Mount*, 1964; and *The Sermon on the Mount*, 1966; C. H. Dodd, "The Beatitudes: a form-critical Study", *More New Testament Studies*, 1968, 1–10.

(b). A. Alt, "Das Gottesurteil auf dem Karmel," in *Kleine Schriften zur Geschichte des Volkes Israel*, II (1953) 1964³, 135 ff.; J.–P. Audet, "Esquisse historique du genre littéraire de la 'bénédiction' juive et de l'eucharistie chrétienne," *RB* 65, 1958, 371–99; E. J. Bickermann, "Bénédiction et prière," *RB* 69, 1962, 524–32; C. Brockelmann, *Hebräische Syntax* 1956; L. Brun, *Segen und Fluch im Urchristentum*, 1932; O. Eissfeldt, "Jahwe und Baal," *Kleine Schriften*, I, 1962, 1 ff.; S. Herrmann, "Die Königsnovelle in Ägypten und Israel," *WZ* Leipzig, 1953–54, 33 ff.; J. Hempel, "Die israelitischen Anschauungen von Segen und Fluch im Lichte altorientalischer Parallele," *Zeitschrift der deutschen morgenländischen Gesellschaft*, Neue Folge 4, 1925, 20–110; F. Horst, "Segen und Segenshandlungen in der Bibel," *EvTh* 7, 1947–48, 23–37 (*Gottes Recht, ThB* 12, 1961, 188 ff.); H. Junker, "Segen als heilsgeschichtliches Motivwort," *Sacra Pagina*, 1959, 548–58; C. A. Keller and G. Wehmeier, "*brk*," *THAT* I 353–76; E. Klessmann, "Was heisst Segen nach der heiligen Schrift?" *MPTh* 48, 1959, 26 ff.; B. Landsberger, "Das 'gute Wort'" *Festschrift B. Meissner*, 1929, 294–321; S. Morenz, F. Horst and H. Köster, "Segen und Fluch," *RGG*³ V 1648 ff.; S. Mowinckel, *Religion und Kultus*, 1953, 64 ff.; J. Scharbert, *Solidarität in Segen und Fluch im Alten Testament und in seiner Umwelt*, I, *Väterfluch und Vätersegen*, Bonner Biblische Beiträge 14, 1958; " 'Fluchen' und 'Segen' im Alten Testament," *Biblica* 39, 1958, 1–26; and *bārak, bᵉrākâh, TWAT* 1 808–41; W. Schenk, *Der Segen im Neuen Testament*, 1967; J. Schreiner, "Segen, für die Völker," *BZ* 6, 1962, 1–31; E. Schweizer, "Formgeschichtliches zu den Seligpreisungen Jesu," *NTS* 19, 1973, 121–26; G. Strecker, "Die Makarismen der Bergpredigt", *NTS* 17, 1971, 233–54; C. Westermann, *Der Segen in der Bibel und im Handeln der Kirche*, 1968; C. Westermann, U. Luck and O. Brodde, "Segen und Fluch," *EKL* III 916 ff.; H. W. Wolff, "Das Kerygma des Jahwisten," *EvTh* 24, 1964, 73 ff.; G. Wehmeier, *Der Segen im Alten Testament. Eine Semasiologische Untersuchung der Wurzel brk*, 1970.

Blind

τυφλός

τυφλός (*typhlos*), blind.

CL *typhlos* (Homer onwards) means blind. It is used lit. of men and animals, and fig. of the other senses and the mind. It may even be applied to dark, obscure things, and also to rivers and harbours choked with mud. The barbaric custom of blinding for revenge or punishment is well attested.

OT 1. *typhlos* in the LXX represents Heb. *'iwwēr*. Blindness has always been relatively common in the Near East. The brightness of the sun, dust and dirt all encourage inflammation of the eyes, which may lead to blindness. The helplessness of the blind was proverbial (Deut. 28:29; Isa. 59:10; Lam. 4:14). They were the weakest and most needy among the people (cf. 2 Sam. 5:6 ff.). Consequently they were under the special protection of the law (Lev. 19:14; Deut. 27:18), and are expressly mentioned in the promise of release from bondage (Jer. 31:8). The pious Israelite helped the blind (Job 29:15).

Fish-gall was used as a cure for blindness in the apocryphal story of Tobias (Tob. 6:5, 9; 11:12 ff.). One knew, however, that there was little hope of a cure, for that was one of the miracles of the last days (Isa. 29:18; 35:5; cf. Matt. 11:5).

The proper functioning of the senses is a gift from God. It depends on him entirely whether a man sees or is blind (Exod. 4:11). Only in Deut. 28:28 f., in the

218

context of the great curse on those who do not obey the law, is blindness mentioned as a punishment in the OT. In contrast to the Babylonian penal law (cf. 2 Ki. 25:7), blinding was not a punishment in Israel.

Blindness was a cultic blemish. The blind could not function as priests (Lev. 21:18), and blind animals might not be offered as sacrifices (Lev. 22:22; Deut. 15:21).

In the LXX blindness is also used metaphorically. Bribes make one blind (Exod. 23:8; Deut. 16:19), so that one no longer sees the injustice. God can blind the disobedient, so that he no longer sees what is right and true (Isa. 6:10; 29:9f.).

2. For late Jud. blindness was regarded as God's punishment for human sin because it prevented study of the Law (cf. SB II 193, 196). "And any judge that takes a bribe and perverts judgment shall not die in old age before his eyes wax dim" (Peah 8:9). The benediction on seeing a blind man was "Blessed be the truthful Judge," which implies that the blindness was a just judgment by God either on the man's own sins, or on those of his parents working themselves out in their children (cf. Jn. 9:2; Exod. 20:5; Deut. 5:9; R. Bultmann, *The Gospel of John*, 1971, 330 ff.). Precedent for this was sought in Deut. 28:15 ff. The Qumran community excluded the blind and others with physical defects from their membership (cf. 1QSa 2:5 ff.; 1QM 7:4 f.). This is probably based on Lev. 21:18 ff., though the official justification of the rule is that "the angels of holiness are with their congregation."

NT The view of blindness changes in the NT.

1. Jesus received the blind into his fellowship and so gave them a share in the kingdom of God. In contrast to the rule of Qumran, he told the man who had invited him to a meal that he should invite the poor and blind (Lk. 14:13, 21). ([Tr.] There was no discrimination against the blind in the synagogue.)

2. The many cases where Jesus healed the blind were messianic signs (Matt. 9:27–31; 12:22; 15:30; 21:14; Mk. 8:22–25; 10:46–52 par.; Lk. 7:21). When John the Baptist grew doubtful and sent disciples to question him, Jesus answered, "The blind receive their sight" (Matt. 11:5), pointing him to Isa. 29:18; 35:5. Jesus' appearance and ministry means that the promised time of redemption has become a present reality. The new age, in which there would be no more blindness, had broken in.

When he healed the man born blind (Jn. 9:1 ff.), Jesus rejected the question that seemed so obvious to late Jud., as to who was responsible for the blindness with which he had been born. He changed it from "Why is this man blind?" to "What is the purpose of his blindness?" No longer is man's sin the ultimate cause of suffering. God's redemptive work is the ultimate factor. "It was not that this man sinned, or his parents, but that the works of God might be manifest in him" (Jn. 9:3). Again this leads to the question of the authority, task and significance of Jesus. God's work is done in this man and at the same time God reveals Jesus as the light of the world through the work. "God made the truth of divine pardon visible, when he turned a destroyed, imprisoned life into a healed and freed life" (A. Schlatter, *Der Evangelist Johannes*, ad. loc.).

3. Acts 13:11 tells of a man temporarily blinded as the result of a curse. The story makes clear the superiority of the Christian servant over the heathen magician. The latter's failure shows the power of God over magic and traffic with demons.

4. Blindness is used metaphorically in Matt. 15:14, where Jesus calls the Pharisees blind guides of the blind. He is referring, as does Paul in Rom. 2:19, to the assumption of the Jews versed in the Law that they were *hodēgoi typhlōn* (guides of the blind), and so were entitled to use the phrase as a title of honour. They considered that they were the only authoritative interpreters of the Law, and as such they were the only legitimate leaders and guides of the "blind" heathen. As bringers of light, they offered them truth and understanding. Jesus felt no sympathy for the Pharisees in their blindness, but rather condemned them, because it showed that they had become hardened (cf. also Matt. 23:16 f., 19, 26; 16:4). The parallel to Matt. 15:14 in Lk. 6:39 is angled rather differently. Since it is linked with teaching on judging, it may be interpreted: How can you exalt yourself as a judge, since you are blind and have no standard to judge by?   *F. Graber*

→ Deaf, Dumb, → Heal, → Miracle, Wonder, Sign

(a). F. Dunbar, *Emotions and Bodily Changes*, 1954[4], 553–68; B. L. Gordon, "Ophthalmology in the Bible and in the Talmud," *Archives of Ophthalmology* 9, 1933, 751 ff.; R. K. Harrison, "Blind," *IDB* I 448 f.; H. van der Loos, *The Miracles of Jesus*, 1965, 415–34; W. Schrage, *typhlos*, *TDNT* VIII 270–94; R. E. D. Clarke, "Men as Trees Walking", *Faith and Thought* 93, 1963, 88–94. (b). A. Esser, "Das Antlitz der Blindheit in der Antike," *Janus. Revue internationale de l'histoire des science, de la medicine, de la pharmacie et la technique*, Supplement 4, 2, 1961; W. Herrmann, "Das Wunder in der evangelischen Botschaft. Zur Interpretation der Begriffe blind und taub im Alten Testament und Neuen Testament," *Aufsätze und Vorträge zur Theologie und Religionswissenschaft* 20, 1961; A. Schlatter, *Der Evangelist Johannes*, 1960[3] on Jn. 9; H. Stoebe, "Blind,' *BHHW* I 257 f.

Blood, Sprinkle, Strangled

haima, blood, is important for NT christology and soteriology and is one of the main concepts of the Bible. This art. also deals with two other terms which are not immediately connected with *haima*, but which have theological associations: *rhantizō*, sprinkle (→ Pure); and *pnigō*, strangle, and more especially *pnikton*, that which has been strangled without blood letting.

αἷμα

αἷμα (*haima*), blood.

CL Already in Homer *haima* is used physiologically as the bearer of life and the life force. It is prerequisite for the maintenance of life both of man and beast, for it is physically and organically necessary to them. In Homer *haima* metaphorically denotes lineage. Since blood is the seat of life, "shedding blood" was used already at an early date as a synonym for "kill" (Aesch., *Eumenides* 653).

In secular usage *haima* was used for the blood of both men and beasts. It gained special importance in cultic usage, for it was the most important element in human sacrifice, and then in animal sacrifice which took its place. Greeks and Romans had blood sacrifices for the dead; originally the blood was poured over the dead, then later onto the funeral pyre, and finally into the grave and on the grave mound (*Il.*, 23, 34; cf. *Od.* 11, 35 f., 50, 96). Blood guilt had to be atoned for by blood. Since Orestes had shed his mother's blood, the Erinyes wished to drink his blood

(Aesch., *Eumenides*, 261 ff.). But human blood could be replaced by animal blood, and Orestes was purified by the blood of a young pig (Aesch., *Eumenides* 28 ff.).

Sacrificial blood was regarded as having strengthening and cleansing power (Heraclit., Frag. B5; Diels, I, 78). Various blood rituals involving the drinking or sprinkling of blood, often including human blood, were employed especially in magical rites to bring rain, welfare, love or harm. The drinking of blood, especially that of a killed enemy (Hdt., 4, 64, 1), brought strength and gave the gift of prophecy (Pausanias, 2, 24, 1). In a blood covenant human blood was collected in drops in a cup and drunk in wine by all participants.

OT For the OT, as in the classical world, blood was the seat of life. The "soul", i.e.
life, life force, is in the blood (Gen. 9:4; Lev. 17:11, 14; Deut. 12:23). God is the sole Lord of all life. He is sovereign over the blood and life of men (Ezek. 18:4). Hence he avenges the shedding of innocent blood (Gen. 9:5; cf. Jer. 51:35 f.). Animal blood also belongs to God. It is holy, and the consumption of blood is forbidden on pain of death (Lev. 3:17; 7:26 f.; 17:10, 14; Deut. 12:23; 1 Sam. 14:32 ff.). Lev. 17:8, 10, 13, 15 stress that these laws apply not merely to Israelites but also to "strangers", the heathen resident aliens. In the OT the blood of the sacrificial animals is given back to God, being poured out at the base of the altar. It was used for sprinkling the altar (Exod. 29:16; Lev. 3:2), the high priest (Exod. 29:21), and also the temple veil (Lev. 4:6; Num. 19:4. The power of the sacrificial blood is atoning (Lev. 16:6, 15 ff.), purifying (Lev. 14), and sanctifying (Exod. 29:30 f.). It belongs to the making of the covenant (Exod. 24:6 ff.). Blood removed sin in sacrifices of purification, sin and guilt, especially on the great Day of Atonement (Lev. 16). It purified the priests, the people and the temple, and renewed the covenant (2 Chr. 29:23 f.). Blood put on the doorposts protected the first-born from death (Exod. 12:22 f.).

Late Jud. (Eth. Enoch, Aristeas, Philo, Josephus, Test. XII) understood the concept of blood as in the OT. The idea of the holiness of blood especially lives on (Jub. 6:7, 12 ff.; Josephus, *Ant.*, 3, 11, 2 (260)). The expression *sarx kai haima*, flesh and blood, is a typical description of man in this period. It designates both the individual and the species "in his creatureliness and his distinction from God" (J. Behm *TDNT* I, 172; cf. Sir. 14:18; 17:31; Gr. Enoch 15:4).

NT *haima* is found 97 times in the NT (apart from the *v.l.* in the TR of Acts 17:26
and Col. 1:14 inserted here from the par. Eph. 1:7). There are 21 instances in Heb. and 19 in Rev. It is used (a) for human blood, both lit. (Mk. 5:25; Lk. 13:1; Jn. 19:34) and fig. i.e. shed blood (Matt. 23:35); (b) in the combination *sarx kai haima*, flesh and blood, 6 times; (c) for the blood of animals in general (Acts 15:20, 29, where the decree of the Jerusalem council is based on Lev. 17), and in particular for the blood of sacrificial animals (12 times in Heb. recalling the OT); (d) theologically most important, for the blood of Christ, where it is linked directly 25 times with the saving significance of the death of Jesus; (e) 9 times as an apocalyptic sign.

1. *haima*, as human blood (Jn. 19:34), like animal blood, is the bearer of life, and is so used in Jn. 1:13 (only here in plur.). This was also the use in Acts 17:26 (but only in the TR, D and some other MSS). When used of human blood, it often refers to a person's violent death in which other people are guiltily involved. It is

thus a fig. expression for the destruction of human life (Rom. 3:15). This idea of the destruction of life is to be understood in Heb. 12:4, "You have not yet resisted to the point of shedding your blood." In the same way the blood of Jesus can refer to his violent death of which Judas (Matt. 27:4), Pilate (Matt. 27:24) and Israel (Matt. 27:25; Acts 5:28) are guilty. Expressions like *timē haimatos*, the price of blood, blood money (Matt. 27:6) and *agros haimatos*, the field bought with blood money (Matt. 27:8) express this fig. use.

God alone is the Lord of all life. He alone controls the blood and life of man. Hence he avenges innocent human blood that has been shed (Gen. 9:5). This is particularly true of the blood of the martyrs, the prophets and righteous men (Matt. 23:30, 35; Lk. 11:50 f.), and the saints and witnesses to Jesus (Rev. 6:10 f.; 16:6 f.; 17:6; 18:24; 19:2) who lost their lives for the sake of the truth of the word of God. Hence blood can denote the whole existence of a man in God's sight, for which each individual will have to give account to God, but in which his fellow men may have a guilty involvement. When Paul said, "Your blood be upon your heads" (Acts 18:6) and "I am innocent of the blood of all of you" (Acts 20:26), he was looking back to Ezek. 3:17 ff. He meant that he had fulfilled his task of proclaiming the gospel to his hearers, and that they were now solely answerable to God for their life both now and in eternity.

2. Blood is a necessary part of the human body and is used in the expression *sarx kai haima*, flesh and blood, to express man's slavery to sin and death. In the NT the expression is used to characterize man's weakness and transitoriness. He is the slave of death. Fear of death (Heb. 2:14 f.) is an important sign of his fallen state as creature, as flesh and blood. In his natural state man cannot share God's glory; for flesh and blood cannot inherit the kingdom of God (1 Cor. 15:50). "His old existence must fall away; God must begin a new creation, if the kingdom of God is to come" (K. Heim, *Gemeinde der Auferstandenen*, 1949, 237 f.).

The severe limitations of human knowledge are bound up with man's incapacity due to sin. Only God has infinite powers of knowledge and revelation. Hence true knowledge of God is possible only by God's own self-revelation. "Flesh and blood has not revealed this to you, but my Father who is in heaven" (Matt. 16:17). For the NT this means the final abandonment of all effort to base the divine revelation on human authority (Gal. 1:16). The Christian is engaged in a battle of faith with hostile powers which are not flesh and blood (Eph. 6:12). Hence in his struggle he cannot find weapons in his own psychological or moral powers, but must turn to God for aid.

3. The blood of sacrifice and the blood of Christ. The NT took over from the OT the concept of sacrificial blood as operative in covenant making and reconciliation. Heb. 9:7, 12 f., 18–22, 25; 10:4; 11:28; 13:11 mention the sacrificial blood of animals. They link up with the types of the OT and point to the superiority of the blood of Christ, the NT antitype. For his death has a reconciling significance. The power of the sacrificial blood of Christ brings forgiveness and sanctification. It establishes peace with God and is the foundation of the new fellowship with God. In practice the sacrifice was carried out by the *haimatekchysia*, the shedding of blood. This concept is found in the NT only in Heb. 9:22, and cannot be found in non-Christian usage. In the context of Heb. 9:19 ff., it refers primarily to the making of the covenant at Sinai (Exod. 24:5–8) and specifically to the killing of the sacrificial

222

animal. ([Tr.] The Talmud (Yoma 5a, Men. 93b, Zeb. 6a) contains the statement, "There is no atonement apart from blood.") Probably the term is intended to include the pouring out of the blood at the base of the altar (Exod. 29:12; Lev. 4:7, 18, 25, 30, 34; 8:15; 9:9), the throwing of the blood against the altar (Exod. 24:6; Lev. 1:5, 11; 9:12), and the throwing of it on the people of Israel (Exod. 24:8; Heb. 9:19). The context shows that in Heb. 11:28 the *proschysis tou haimatos*, the pouring (or sprinkling) of the blood refers solely to the Passover sacrifice (Exod. 12:7, 13, 22 f.).

"When the author of Hebrews says, 'Without the shedding of blood there is no forgiveness of sins', the killing of the animal is for him the decisive factor in the carrying out of the sacrifice. Surrender of life is the essential prerequisite for the granting of forgiveness" (E. Riggenbach, Comm., ad. loc.). The OT gave typological expression to the power of the blood to remove sin and save, making it a fundamental element of every cultic sacrifice for atonement. The NT sees in the death of Christ the ultimate significance and fulfilment of this idea.

The blood of Jesus Christ (1 Pet. 1:2), the blood of Jesus (Heb. 10:19; 1 Jn. 1:7), the blood of Christ (1 Cor. 10:16; Eph. 2:13; Heb. 9:14), the blood of the Lord (1 Cor. 11:27), the blood of the Lamb (Rev. 7:14; 12:11), occupies a central position in NT thought. It derives its meaning particularly from the sacrifices of the Day of Atonement (Lev. 16). It is sacrificial blood that Christ in perfect obedience to God (Rom. 5:19; Phil. 2:8; Heb. 5:8) presented in giving himself on the cross (Heb. 9:12 ff.). In his suffering and death Jesus offered the true sacrifice for the removal of sins. In place of all the sacrifices that had been brought by men, he brought the perfect sacrifice of his life. His sacrifice is the carrying out of the reconciliation of man with God (cf. K. Barth, *CD* IV 1, 283–357).

By his blood Christ ransomed and freed the church, the new people of God, from the power of the devil and all evil powers (Acts 20:28; Eph. 1:7; 1 Pet. 1:18 f.; Rev. 5:9). Christ's sacrificial blood justifies all who appropriate for themselves his sacrificial death (Rom. 3:25; 5:19). The blood cleanses the members of the church from their sins. God blots out the entire guilt of the person who confesses his sins to him in faithful trust (1 Jn. 1:7–10; Rev. 1:5; 7:14). Because the blood of Christ avails for his church, it is again possible to have a clear conscience before God (Heb. 9:14; 10:22; 13:18). In the OT → reconciliation (atonement) and purification (→ Pure) were two different actions, though connected in character. Reconciliation resulted from the bringing of the sacrificial blood into the Holy of Holies once a year on the Day of Atonement. Purification could be achieved at any time in the year outside the Holy of Holies. Both are given in the NT in the salvation through the blood of Christ (cf. G. Menken, *Homilien*, 110 f.).

In the blood lies the power for sanctification (Heb. 13:12) and the conquest of all powers at enmity with God (Rev. 12:11). A transforming and renewing power flows from the atoning death of Jesus into the life of those who have accepted redemption in faith. Christ's blood makes possible life in God's presence; it gives access to God (Heb. 10:19; Eph. 2:13, 18). An expression of the fact that the atoning power of the blood has been appropriated by a man is assurance of faith, glad confidence in prayer and a changed life (1 Pet. 1:13 ff.). As the blood of the covenant (Matt. 26:28; Mk. 14:24; Lk. 22:20 [not in the best MSS]; 1 Cor. 11:25; Heb. 10:29; 13:20), it is the basis of the new divine order. By its connection with the covenant ceremony at Sinai (Exod. 24:8, Heb. *dam ha-bᵉrît*, blood of the covenant; cf. Heb. 9:18 ff.) the blood of Christ serves as guarantee that the promise of the New Covenant (Jer. 31:31–34) is fulfilled in the NT church. Col. 1:20 (cf. 2:13 ff.) speaks of the cosmic significance of Jesus Christ's sacrificial death. The blood makes peace both on earth and in heaven.

Blood is sometimes used fig. for the atoning work of Christ (Rev. 19:13; Jn. 6:53–56), the part being used for the whole saving act and work of Jesus (Eph. 1:7). In most of the passages that have been cited one cannot, however, simply substitute the death of Christ for the blood of Christ. "The blood of Christ means more than this. It stresses the close links between the death of Jesus and both his life and his triumph in his resurrection and exaltation" (H. J. Iwand *RGG*³ I 1330). The blood means the application of the death of Jesus to the individual. This is clearly indicated in the phrase "the sprinkled blood" (Heb. 12:24). It is a phrase that also links with the OT sacrificial cultus. The reconciling and purifying power of the sacrificial death was appropriated by the one who had brought the sacrifice by the sprinkling of the blood. In the OT community this was carried out visibly with the blood of an animal. In the NT church it is an invisible spiritual reality through the blood of Jesus (1 Pet. 1:2; Heb. 9:13 f.; 10:22). As the believer appropriates the blood of Jesus, the power of his sacrificial death becomes his in all its effects.

4. Blood as an apocalyptic sign. Blood, and its colour, red, symbolically express the eschatological terrors on earth and in heaven in the last days. Here too there are direct links with the OT. The NT takes over from Joel the prophecy of the change in the moon's colour (Joel 2:31 (MT 3:4); Acts 2:20; Rev. 6:12). Similarly blood and fire are used as a picture of war (Joel 2:30 (MT 3:3); Acts 2:19; Rev. 8:7). The change of water to blood refers to eschatological catastrophes (Exod. 7:17 ff.; Rev. 8:9; 11:6; 16:3 f.). The blood of grapes, in the OT a metaphorical expression for wine (Gen. 49:11; Deut. 32:14), becomes a picture of the great judgment on the nations (Rev. 14:19 f.; cf. Isa. 63:2 f.), when God will destroy all powers opposed to Christ at the end of history. *F. Laubach*

→ Akeldama, → Cross, → Feast, → Forgiveness, → Guilt, → Pure, → Reconciliation, → Redemption, → Sacrifice, → Sin

---

ῥαντίζω	ῥαντίζω (*rhantizō*), sprinkle; ῥαντισμός (*rhantismos*), sprinkling.

CL *rhantizō* is an alternative form of *rhainō*, sprinkle. In secular Gk. it is rare and late; in the LXX it is infrequent; but it is the only form found in the NT. As aspersion, it is distinguished from *niptō*, rinse part of a body; *louō*, wash the whole body; and *baptō/baptizō* immerse (→ Baptism, Wash). In Gk. literature the predominant use of the term is profane, but sprinkling for religious cleansing is attested (e.g. Plato, *Cratylus*, 405ab).

OT 1. In the OT the vb. and its cognates appear mainly in the religious sense. Oil, mixed with blood of sacrifice, is sprinkled on Aaron and his sons for consecration (Exod. 29:21), but sprinkling is chiefly for cleansing, whether by the blood of sacrifice or by water. On the Day of Atonement the sanctuary and its sacred objects were annually cleansed by the sprinkling of the blood of a bull and of a goat offered as sin offerings (Lev. 16:11–19). The sprinkling of the people of Israel with the "blood of the covenant" at the making of the Sinaitic covenant (Ex. 24:8) had a different purpose, namely to bring Israel into a unity of fellowship with Yahweh and seal the covenant then made. Sprinkling was performed especially for cleansing from defilement incurred through contact with leprosy (Lev. 14:6 f., 51) and with the dead (Num. 19). In Ps. 51:7 (50:9) the ceremony of cleansing of the leper and his house provides the inspiration for the symbolic language of inner cleansing by sprinkling. As a leper is cleansed by blood sprinkled from a sprig of hyssop and by water, so the self-confessed sinner seeks in prayer spiritual cleansing from God. In Ezek. 36:25 sprinkling with water symbolizes an eschatological cleansing in the last times which is tantamount to a new creation. Alongside "the restoration of Israel (v. 24), the gift of a new heart of flesh (v. 26) and the gift of the Spirit (v. 27), the cleansing sprinkling carried out by God himself is an act of eschatological recreation of the people of God" (C.-H. Hunzinger, *TDNT* VI 980).

2. In the Qumran literature sprinkling (*nāzâh*) appears with washing (*rāḥaṣ*) as a term for the lustrations of the community, although these lustrations entailed immersion of the body. The employment of this term was doubtless due to its long association with cleansing from defilement, and indicates the effect rather than the mode of the lustrations. The Sectaries also awaited an eschatological cleansing at the end of the times, expressed under the symbolism of sprinkling. "He will cleanse him of all his wicked deeds with the spirit of holiness; like purifying waters He will shed upon him the spirit of truth (to cleanse him) of all abomination and falsehood. And he shall be plunged into the spirit of purification that he may instruct the upright in the knowledge of the Most High and teach the wisdom of the sons of heaven to the perfect of way" (1QS 4:21 f.; Vermes, *Scrolls*, 77 f.).

NT The NT (Mk. 7:3 f.) reflects current Jewish ritual purification. Jews wash their hands (*niptō*) before eating and sprinkle themselves (*rhantizō*) with water when they return from the market place. (A variant reading replaces *rhantizō* with the vb. *baptizō*, but the former is to be preferred.) The sprinkling is not upon objects bought in the market but persons who may have contracted defilement in mixing with others.

Hebrews frequently recalls the OT sprinkling with blood of → sacrifice, in order to show the superior power of the blood of Christ to cleanse (e.g. 9:13 ff., 18 ff.). In Heb. 10:22 cleansing by sprinkling (of Christ's sacrificial blood?) is set in parallelism with washing with pure water: "Let us draw near with a true heart in full assurance of faith, with our hearts sprinkled clean from an evil conscience and our bodies washed with pure water." "For it is impossible that the blood of bulls and goats should take away sins" (Heb. 10:4). The cleansing power of Christ's sacrifice is known in baptism, even as the believer becomes one with Christ in his dying and rising (cf. Rom. 6:1 ff.).

The noun *rhantismos*, sprinkling, has not been found outside the Bible. Its occurrence in Heb. 12:24 is instructive, for though it is set in parallelism with Abel's blood, the latter was not sprinkled. The phrase "blood of sprinkling" was therefore a current formula. In contrast to the cry of Abel's blood for vengeance (Gen. 4:10), the sprinkled blood of Christ assures forgiveness.

G. R. Beasley-Murray

πνικτός

πνικτός (*pniktos*), strangled; ἀποπνίγω (*apopnigō*), strangle; πνίγω (*pnigō*), strangle; συμπνίγω (*sympnigō*), strangle.

CL & OT *pnigō* (etymology uncertain) means to strangle, choke, cause choking or vomiting, harass, frighten. In the pass. it means drown. The compounds *apopnigō* and *sympnigō* have the same meaning. The verbal adj. *pniktos*, strangled, is found only with the meaning steamed, stewed, outside the NT. In the LXX this group of words is rare (1 Ki. 16:14 f.; Nah. 2:12). *pniktos* does not occur.

NT 1. In the story of the demoniac at Gerassa the herd of pigs is said to have drowned in the lake (*epnigonto*, Mk. 5:13; *apepnigē*, Lk. 8:33). In the parable of the sower thorns choked the seed (*synepnixan* Mk. 4:7; *apepnixan* Matt. 13:7, Lk. 8:7). We find the same usage in the explanation of the parable. The unforgiving servant choked his fellow-servant to force him to pay his debt (Matt. 18:28). In Lk. 8:42 we are told hyperbolically that the multitude choked Jesus (NEB "He could hardly breathe for the crowds").

2. The adj. *pniktos* is of theological importance in Acts 15:20, 29; 21:25. The context is a command about food, which the Jewish Christians imposed on the Gentile Christians, and which is closely linked to the prohibition against eating blood. The command goes back to Lev. 17:13 f. and Deut. 12:16, 23. An animal should be so slaughtered that its blood, in which is its life, should be allowed to pour out. If the animal is killed in any other way, it has been "strangled". The rabbis extended and intensified the OT regulations. The question raised by the passage here is whether only such meat was being forbidden as in the OT, where the blood was still present, or whether the details of the rabbinic regulations were to be followed. The reason behind the prohibition was possibly that among the heathen animals were often killed by being strangled especially in the sacrificial cultus. It may be that such customs are here being forbidden. It should be noted that there is some doubt about the text. A few authorities omit the word, which could be a secondary addition to the other three. *H. Bietenhard*

(a). J. Behm, *haima*, TDNT I 172–77; H. Bietenhard, *pniktos*, TDNT VI 455–58; J. Denney, *The Death of Christ*, ed. R. V. G. Tasker, 1951, 34 ff., 96 ff., 149–54; C.-H. Hunzinger, *rhantizō*, TDNT VI 976–84; S. Lyonnet and L. Sabourin, *Sin, Redemption and Sacrifice. A Biblical and Patristic Study*, 1970; L. Morris, "The Biblical Use of the Term 'Blood'," *JTS* N. S. 3, 1952, 216–27; *NTS* N.S. 6, 1955, 77–82; *The Apostolic Preaching of the Cross*, 1965[3], 112–28; and *The Cross in the New Testament*, n.d., 218 f., 357 ff.; J. Scharbert, "Blood," *EBT* I 75–79; H. Schlier, *Principalities and Powers in the New Testament*, 1961; A. M. Stibbs, *The Meaning of the Word "Blood" in Scripture*, 1947; V. Taylor, *The Atonement in New Testament Teaching*, 1940, 92–95; and *Jesus and His Sacrifice*, 1937, 125–39; B. F. Westcott, *The Epistles of St. John*, 1902[4], 34–37; J. Ysebaert, *Greek Baptismal Terminology*, 1962; J. Schmid, "Blood of Christ," *EBT* I 79 ff.
(b). E. Bischoff, *Das Blut im jüdischen Schrifttum und Brauch*, 1929; W. Brandt, *Die jüdischen Baptismen*, 1910; S. Eitrem, *Opferritus und Voropfern der Griechen und Römer*, 1915; A. J. Fernandes, *Caetano da Cruz, Sanguis Christi*, 1959; G. Gerleman, *dām*, *THAT* I 448–51; H. Gottlob, *To haima mou tēs diathēkēs*, *StTh* 14, 1960, 115 ff.; E. Mühlhaupt and K. Galling, "Blut," *RGG*[3] I 1327 ff.; W. Nauck and H. J. Iwand, "Blut Christi," *RGG*[3] I 1329 ff.; E. Riggenbach, *Kommentar zum Hebräerbrief*, 1922[3]; O. Schmitz, *Die Opferanschauung des späteren Judentums und die Opferaussagen des Neuen Testaments*, 1910; A. Thales, *Sein Blut über uns und unsere Kinder. Eine Untersuchung zu* Mt. 27, 24, 25, 1969; J. Vetter, *Das heilige Blut*, 1958[14]; J. Waszink, *RAC* II 1327 ff.
→ literature under Baptism

Boast

καύχημα

καύχημα (*kauchēma*), boast, pride, object of boasting; καύχησις (*kauchēsis*), boasting; καυχάομαι (*kauchaomai*), boast; ἐγκαυχάομαι (*enkauchaomai*), to boast; κατακαυχάομαι (*katakauchaomai*), boast against, exult over, triumph over.

CL 1. In classical Gk. the vb. *kauchaomai* is found from Sappho onwards. Homer uses instead *euchomai*, pray, ask, wish. The traged ans and orators use *aucheō*, boast, plume oneself. Intrans. *kauchaomai* means to boast, vaunt oneself, be proud. With the preps. *en, epi, peri, hyper, eis*, or *kata*, it means to boast of a person or thing. The trans. form also occurs. The compound vb. *enkauchaomai* has the same meaning. *katakauchaomai* is used particularly with reference to the situation of an object, and may be translated to vaunt oneself against someone, to treat someone in a derogatory or contemptuous manner.

kauchēma (Pindar) refers to the subject of boasting, to the words used by the boaster, and occasionally also to the act of boasting, although for the latter (especially in the NT) the noun *kauchēsis* is more frequently found. *kauchēsis* (Epicurus) can likewise on occasion be used to denote the subject of boasting.

2. Although the ancient Greeks recognize legitimate pride in oneself (e.g. Homer, *Il.*, 6, 208), there is a clear appreciation of the distinction between this and unwarranted bragging, which was pilloried by the satirists and others. Plutarch also attacked ostentation in an essay on *Self-praise without Envy*.

OT 1. The OT also recognizes legitimate pride, e.g. of children in their fathers (Prov. 17:6, Heb. *tip'eret*, beauty, distinction), or of old men in their grey hair (Prov. 16:31). Boasting, on the other hand, is regarded as reprehensible (1 Ki. 20:11, Heb. *hithallēl*, to boast; Prov. 25:14; 27:1), and as the expression of sheer folly and ungodliness (Ps. 52:1; 94:4). The theological basis for the rejection of all self-praise lies in the fact that the man who boasts has his attention focused on himself, and no longer looks up to God, the creator and redeemer. He trusts in himself instead of having confidence in God, praising his grace and faithfulness (Jer. 9:23 f.; cf. 1 Sam. 2:10 LXX).

Boasting in God and his acts is spoken of in a good sense in the OT (Ps. 5:11; 32:11; 89:16 f.; 1 Chr. 16:28 f.; 29:11; Deut. 33:29; Jer. 7:14). Such boasting comprises the elements of "confidence, joy and thanksgiving, and the paradox is that the one who glories thus looks away from himself, so that his glorying is a confession of God" (R. Bultmann, *TDNT* III 647). In the LXX, *kauchēma* and the associated words are also used to translate this sense of the Heb. *hithallēl*.

2. In Judaism this group of words has more or less the same meaning as in the OT, except that the → Law is added to the list of things which are truly worthy of praise, and in which the God-fearing man may rejoice (Sir. 39:8). In Rab. theology this idea is further developed. Praise of Abraham is represented as having its basis in his fulfilment of the Law (SB III 187). At the same time, however, there are warnings against arrogance and spiritual pride, and exhortations to humility. Furthermore, suffering is introduced as a ground for boasting, as it is received by the believer at God's hand (SB II 274 ff.).

3. Philo unequivocally rejects self-praise, but the group of words considered

here is not used to any significant extent. Instead, Philo uses terms like *philautia*, self-love; *alazoneia*, bragging; *kenodoxia*, vainglory, to describe the *mega kakon*, great evil, of self-praise, which is the exact opposite of *eusebeia*, godliness (cf. *Spec. Leg.* 1, 333; 4, 170; *Leg. All.* 1, 52).

NT In the NT the vb. *kauchaomai* occurs 37 times and the equivalent *enkauchaomai* once. *katakauchaomai* is found 4 times (in Jas. 2:13 with the meaning, "mercy triumphs over judgment"). The nouns *kauchēma* and *kauchēsis* each occur 11 times. Apart, however, from 5 instances in Jas. and one in Heb., words of this group are found only in the Pauline writings.

Paul uses the words to clarify and strongly emphasize an idea which is central to his doctrine of justification. This is the teaching that man's original sin consists in glorifying himself and not giving God his due. Like *ergon* (→ Work) and *nomos* (→ Law), *kauchaomai* occurs with particular frequency in polemical passages. Just as Paul attacks the Jewish doctrine of justification by works, so he opposes the closely related habit of human self-praise, based on fulfilment of the Law. The emptiness of such *kauchēsis* is revealed by the rhetorical question in Rom. 3:27: "What then becomes of boasting?" Through the "law of faith" all human glory is made of no account.

This is shown clearly in Eph. 2:8 f.: "For by grace you have been saved, through faith; and this is not your own doing, it is the gift of God – not because of works, lest any man should boast." A. Schlatter comments: "All is given to us in Christ, in order that we may not use God's grace to build up our own self-glorification." The worthlessness of human boasting, when based on the law, is similarly exposed in the context of Rom. 2:23 (cf. also Rom. 4:2, where Abraham's works give him nothing about which to boast before God). Contary to Jud. ideas, Paul also rejects the glory attached to proselytizing (Gal. 6:13). He attacks just as strongly the self-confidence of the Greeks, who boast of their *sophia* (wisdom, 1 Cor. 1:29 and context; cf. also 1 Cor. 3:21). All these forms of boasting in the flesh (*kauchaomai kata sarka*, 2 Cor. 11:18, is practically synonymous with *pepoithenai en sarki*, Phil. 3:3 f.) include such things as the arrogant attitude of Gentile Christians to the non-Christian Jews (Rom. 11:17 f.), and false bragging (1 Cor. 4:7; cf. Jas. 3:14; 2 Cor. 5:12; 12:6). They come into the category of evil, i.e. unjustified, boasting (*kauchēsis ponēra*, Jas. 4:16, cf. 1 Cor. 5:6). And they conflict with the one appropriate form of boasting, cited from Jer. 9:24 in 1 Cor. 1:31: "Let him who boasts, boast of the Lord" (cf. 2 Cor. 10:17 f.).

For Christians, this is the only fitting form of *kauchēsis*: to boast of God through Jesus Christ (Rom. 5:11; cf. Phil. 3:3); or, as Gal. 6:14 puts it, to glory in the → cross of our Lord (*en tō staurō tou kyriou*). This glorying "has (thus) as its object something before which all self-praise disappears" (K. L. Schmidt, *Theol. Stud.* 11/12, 98). The Christian's *kauchēsis* can include glorying in the acts of God to which the apostles bear witness, and also in those which are brought about in the course of apostolic ministry. In this sense Paul, for instance, can boast of the *exousia* (authority → Might) which has been given to him (2 Cor. 10:8; cf. Rom. 15:17) in contrast to the false apostles (2 Cor. 11:12 ff.). He also boasts of individual churches in which he considers that the fruits of faith can be seen (1 Cor. 15:31; 2 Cor. 1:14; 7:4, 14; 8:24; 2. Thess. 1:4; cf. his "workmanship" → Work,

228

art. *ergon*, 1 Cor. 9:1). In the context of Christ's return, he can describe the Thessalonians as his "crown of boasting" (1 Thess. 2:19; for the phrase cf. Ezek. 16:12; Prov. 16:31). He writes that the Philippians will be his *kauchēma* "on the day of Christ" (Phil. 2:16; cf. 1:26). He will have no one deprive him of this apostolic ground for boasting (1 Cor. 9:15). Naturally Paul knows exactly where the limit comes (cf. 2 Cor. 11:16 ff.). A Christian can really only boast of his weakness, because it is here that God's strength becomes apparent (2 Cor. 11:30; 12:5, 9; cf. Rom. 5:3). If he boasts of his own behaviour (2 Cor. 1:12; cf. Gal. 6:4; Jas. 3:14), he should do so only in so far as his life is lived in dependence on God and in responsibility to him. For in the last analysis the Christian can never boast about himself (1 Cor. 9:16), but only of his Lord. Where the Lord cannot be seen as the foundation and content of the *kauchēma*, boasting remains "in the flesh" and therefore sinful. However, it is vital in the face of every difficulty "to hold firm to the end our confidence and pride in our hope" (Heb. 3:6; cf. Rom. 5:2).

H. C. Hahn

(a). Arndt, 426 f.; J. Bligh, *Galatians*, 1969, 490–93; R. Bultmann, *Theology of the New Testament*, I, 1952, 239–46; "Christ the End of the Law," *Essays*, 1955, 36–66; and *TDNT* III 645–54; E. A. Judge, "Paul's Boasting in Relation to Contemporary Professional Practice," *Australian Biblical Review* 16, 1968, 37–50.
(b). M. Carrez, "La confiance en l'homme et la confiance en soi selon l'apôtre Paul," *Revue d'Historie et Philosophie Religieuses* 44, 1964, 191 ff.; K. L. Schmidt, "Ein Gang durch den Galaterbrief," *ThSt* 11/12, 1942, 98 ff.; G. Sanchez Bosch, *Sentido y teologia de kauchaomai en las Ep. de S. Pablo*, 1968.

Body, Member, Limb

Men frequently glorify the body on account of its beauty or strength. Alternatively, they look down on it as the prison house of the → soul. For while the body passes away, the immaterial, immortal soul goes on. By contrast, the NT idea of the *sōma* refers to the whole man, mostly in the sense of man as he stands before God. The → flesh, on the other hand, signifies the sphere of human life on earth and has negative overtones, in so far as man bases his existence on it. *sōma* is also used in the general biological sense of the body, and even in the sense of corpse. The NT can describe man as a *sōma* (body). But it can equally describe him as a *psychē* (→ soul).

The body was also used in antiquity in a figurative and corporate sense in mythology and for groups of people. In this connection *melos* (member, limb) denotes a part of the group or whole. It is used in theological contexts to show the functions of members in relation to the whole. At the same time their action reveals something of the corporate personality.

| μέλος | μέλος (*melos*), member, part, limb. |

CL 1. *to melos* means: (a) limb; (b) musical member, phrase, hence song (*Hymni Homerici* 19, 16), music to which a song is set (Aristot., *Poet.* 1450ᵃ 14), melody (Theognis, 761); (c) in the plur., body.

2. In Hom., *Il.*, 7, 131 and other early writers like Hesiod and Pindar the word occurs only in the plur., although it has the singular meaning of body. In the pre-Socratic writers the plur. has the meaning, members. It is used in the sing. by Aristotle as a member of a body. It is also used of the members of a city (cf. Dion. Hal. 6, 86, 1; Epictetus, *Dissertationes*, 2, 5, 26). It stands out clearly in the fable of Menenius Agrippa of the rebellion of the members of the body against the stomach. The city (*polis*) is understood as an organism, the existence of which depends on the willing incorporation of the citizens in the whole. (Here the thought of the *polis* is the primary one; not that of the living organism which is a secondary interpretation.) In the Hellenistic mystery religions and gnosticism the idea of the body and its members has a religious and speculative application in → creation mythology (→ Myth) but more especially in gnostic → redemption myth. The redeemed are thought of as lost members of the redeemer's body which have now been found. (For examples of gnostic teaching see R. M. Grant, *Gnosticism: An Anthology*, 1961; and for discussion of their relation to the NT see E. Yamauchi, *Pre-Christian Gnosticism*, 1973, 27 ff., 163–69.)

OT 1. *melos* occurs some 28 times in the LXX, but only 11 times in the canonical books. It renders the Heb. *nēṭaḥ* (piece of meat, carcass), in particular the dismembered parts of the sacrifice (Exod. 29:17). In Jdg. 19:29 it is used of the dismembered body of the Levite's concubine.

Since the word is not used of the limbs of a living human body, there is no thought of the body and its members either in a theological or a sociological sense. On the other hand, the OT shows an interest in the function of the individual parts of the body. → Heart, → Hear, → See, → Head, → Blood, → Flesh. The heart (Heb. *lēḇ*, *lēḇāḇ*; Gk. *kardia*) is mentioned some 851 times, but rarely if ever does it refer to the physical organ. It is more associated with man's thoughts and feelings, similarly to the way in which we today associate the heart with our emotions (Isa. 6:10; Hos. 7:2). The lower parts of the body, such as the liver and kidneys (Heb. *kāḇēḏ*, the "heavy" organ) are regarded as the emotional centre of man (Lam. 2:11. The RSV translation of "heart" is a modern idiomatic rendering; cf. Gen. 49:6; Pss. 16:9; 30:12, where RSV has "spirit" or "soul"). The brain is not mentioned at all in the OT. The appropriate faculty is sometimes designated by the organ (e.g. the ear, Exod. 15:26; Ps. 5:1; the eye, Eccles. 4:8; cf. Ps. 34:15).

2. Philo combined Jewish functional thinking with Gk. philosophical organic thinking which he applied ontologically to the idea of unity (*Spec.Leg.* 1, 199). The dismembered parts of the sacrificed animal have an ontological significance. The apologetic intention is clear. The physiological fact derived from the OT which saw the part in relation to the whole conceals the philosophical principle that the parts receive their function from the whole and that their function is essential to the existence of the whole.

3. Josephus applied the picture of the mutual dependence of the members to the political situation in the Jewish war (*War* 4, 406). When the chief city is ill, the other parts of the land also fall ill.

4. In rab. literature the number of members of the human body serves to illustrate the totality and universality of the → Law. The body was reckoned to have 248 members, corresponding to the 248 positive commands of the Torah (Ber. 8b,

60 ff.; there were 365 negative commands or prohibitions corresponding to the number of days in the year; cf. *TDNT* IV 559). On the other hand, rab. theologians related their observations on the function of the individual members to assessments of their worth and mutual relations. Thus → "evil inclination" (→ Desire, art. *hēdonē*) can take possession of individual members in order to gain dominance over the whole.

NT Most instances of *melos* in the NT occur in Rom. and 1 Cor. (Rom. 6:13, 19; 7:5, 23; 12:4 f.; 1 Cor. 6:15; 12:12 ff.). It also occurs in the plur. in Eph. 4:25; 5:30; Col. 3:5; Jas. 3:5 [sing.]; 3:6; 4:1. It occurs only twice in the synoptic gospels in two parallel sayings of Jesus in the Sermon on the Mount (Matt. 5:29 f.).

1. "If your right eye cause you to sin, pluck it out and throw it away; it is better to lose one of your members (*melōn*) than that your whole body be thrown into hell (Gehenna, Gk. *geennan*). And if your right hand causes you to sin, cut it off and throw it away; it is better that you lose one of your members (*melōn*) than that your whole body go into hell (Gehenna, Gk. *geennan*)" (Matt. 5:29f.). Jesus clearly did not intend the sayings to be taken literally. They apply to the evil functions of which the eye and the hand are instruments. It is these that are to cease. It is not the eye and the hand, but the lustful look and the malicious act that are to be cut out. This means that man's evil will must be rooted out if his body (i.e. the whole person) is to be saved in the judgment. There is no trace here of the Gk. idea of perfection as the complete number of the members in their entirety. Rather, the whole body (*holon to sōma*) is saved from judgment only by having a part rooted out.

In the same eschatological sharpening and clarity, Jas. 3:5 ff. describes the tongue as a little member that destroys like a devouring fire. Jas. 4:1 shows that the passions can arise from all the members of the body. Moreover, these passions can destroy the common life of the Christian church.

2. In describing the new life of the Christian in Rom. 6, Paul writes: "Do not yield your members to sin as instruments of wickedness, but yield yourselves to God as men who have been brought from death to life, and your members to God as instruments of righteousness" (6:13). "For just as you once yielded your members to impurity and to greater and greater iniquity, so now yield your members to righteousness for sanctification" (6:19). The test of whether a man has this new life is whether he practises righteousness in his relationships in the world. At the same time this reveals the tension between what he desires to do as a Christian and the sinful nature which still remains with him. "For I delight in the law of God, in my inmost self, but I see in my members another law at war with the law of my mind and making me captive to the law of sin which dwells in my members" (Rom. 7:22 f., cf. 5). The tension remains as long as his existence on earth. "So then, I of myself serve the law of God with my mind, but with my flesh I serve the law of sin" (7:25).

The thought of the members of the body as instruments is renewed in Col. 3:5 and 1 Cor. 6:15. The former declares: "Put to death therefore the members that are on the earth: immorality, impurity, passion, evil desire, and covetousness which is idolatry." The latter passage precludes prostitution for the Christian. "Do you not know that your bodies are members of Christ? Shall I therefore take

231

the members of Christ and make them members of a prostitute?" In so far as a man is a believer, his members are the members of Christ. To have sexual relations with a prostitute is to become one body (*hen sōma*) with her (v. 16). Thus the members of Christ would become the members of a prostitute.

3. Rom. 12 and 1 Cor. 12 teach that the church is the body of Christ in both reality and function. It is made a reality by the presence of the Holy Spirit whose gifts are enjoyed and practised by numerous individuals. But taken by themselves in isolation they are without significance. They have significance only in relation to the whole fellowship. "To each is given the manifestation of the Spirit for the common good" (1 Cor. 12:7). It is significant that in this extended sense of members (i.e. individual believers as members of the body of Christ), Paul's great concern is with the well-being of the body, the church as a whole. The same is true of Eph. 4:25 ("Therefore, putting away falsehood, let everyone speak the truth with his neighbour, for we are members one of another") and Eph. 5:30 (where Paul exhorts husbands to love their wives "because we are members of his body").

H. G. Schütz

| σῶμα | σῶμα (*sōma*), body.

CL The original meaning of *sōma* is not clear. It first appears in Hom. meaning a dead body of a man or animal, a corpse or carcass. It retained this meaning into the 5th cent., when it began to be used in the sense of torso, the whole body and by extension the whole person (Hdt. 2, 66, 4; cf. E. Schweizer, *TDNT* VII 1025 ff.). In the pre-Socratic writers it has the meaning of element, figure, corresponding to the basic sense of the bodily. As the idea developed of the → soul alongside of the body, the body came to be regarded as a chain or grave, that which is mortal as distinct from the immortal soul. These ideas were further developed in Plato. The body is only the abode of the pre-existent soul. Death frees the soul from the body (*Phdr.*, 64c, 67a; *Grg.* 524b). The picture of the body was also applied to the cosmos. The latter is ruled and directed by the divine soul. Zeus conceals everything in himself and lets it all proceed from himself (*Orphicorum Fragmenta* 21a). Similarly man can be represented as a microcosm (Dem., *Frag.* 34; Diels-Kranz II, 153, 8, 12 f.). By contrast, Aristotle held that the body is primarily that by which the soul becomes something particular. The bond between body and soul is thus indissoluble (*An.*, 2, 1 f.). Aristotle also used the *sōma* in the sense of an organism to explain the character of the state (*Pol.*, 1, 2; 5, 2; cf. E. Schweizer, *TDNT* VII 1032).

The Stoics continued to maintain the traditional dichotomy of body and soul. Strictly speaking, Epictetus drew a distinction between the soul and the → flesh, rather than the body. The soul is the animating principle, whose seat can be the head just as much as the heart (Cleanthes, cf. *TDNT* VII 1033). The soul permeates the whole body and conveys its sense impressions. But the basic idea of wholeness in *sōma* remained decisive. Even the Stoic philosopher-emperor, Marcus Aurelius, could say of the tripartite conception of man: "There are three parts of which thou art composed: body, *pneuma* [spirit, soul] and *nous* [mind, reason]" (cf. M. Pohlenz, *Die Stoa*, 1948, I, 342). The further development of these thoughts together with neo-Platonic ideas in general led to a devaluation of the body as opposed to the soul (cf. *TDNT* VII 1042 f.).

OT 1. There is no Heb. equivalent in the OT corresponding to the Gk. idea of *sōma*. In the LXX *sōma* is used to denote the range of ideas conveyed by the Heb. *bāśār*, → flesh, signifying man in his individual corporeality. This is distinct from *sarx*, flesh, denoting man or even humanity in their creatureliness. *sōma* can mean corpse (1 Sam. 31:10, 12), dead body (Deut. 21:23; Isa. 5:25) and even back (1 Ki. 14:9; Isa. 38:17). But the basic meaning is the body in the sense of the whole person (cf. Lev. 15:11, 16, 19; 16:4; 19:28 and often). *sōma* in the OT has virtually the sense of person, though this is not to be confused with personality. "There is no sense of his standing at a distance from himself or regarding his corporeality as something which can finally be parted from him" (E. Schweizer, *TDNT* VII 1048). Even angels have *sōmata* (Ezek. 1:11, 23; Dan. 10:6). *sōma*, then, does not suggest an earthly sphere in contrast to a heavenly. Nor is there an anthropological dualism in the OT canon which would oppose the soul or mind to the body as something of higher value.

2. Depreciation of the body as the seat of passion first occurs in Sir. 23:16 ff.; 47:19. The books of the Maccabees reflect Hel. influence in the distinction drawn between soul and body. A good soul and an undefiled body belong together (Wis. 8:20). But the dominant thought is that of the soul as the particular gift of God. Hence, the body can be given up in persecution. Even though the relationship of body and soul is here seen in relation to God, the Gk. dichotomy of the mortal body and the immortal soul is also present (Wis. 9:15).

3. These ideas were further developed in the Jewish background literature of the NT period. In Test. XII *sōma* is seen particularly in relation to sex. Through → desire (art. *hēdonē*) of the body fornication arises (Test. Jud. 14:3; → Discipline, art. *porneuō*). The significance of death stands out all the more sharply in the light of the connection between body and soul. For death separates body and soul. The body remains on earth and the soul is taken up to heaven (2 Esd. 60). This notion, influenced by Hel., stood over against Jewish thinking which approximated more closely to the OT. There the body representing the whole person comes under → judgment and is raised from the dead (→ Resurrection). It is a question of man as a whole person. This found expression in the Qumran literature and its notions of judgment (cf. H. Ringgren, *The Faith of Qumran*, 1963, 94 ff., 144 ff., 152 ff.). Rab. literature confirms the double aspect of the concept of body which was common in the NT period (cf. R. Meyer, *TDNT* VII 117 f.). On the one hand, there is the sense of body or person, and on the other hand there is the distinction drawn between body and soul, spirit or mind.

4. The notion of the body played a central part in gnosticism (→ knowledge, art. *ginōskō*). Man's inner self must be set free from the material world of the flesh and the human body. This comes about through → redemption. The idea of the redemption of the individual was applied to the cosmos. The idea occurs of the redeeming body of the original man which is applied to the body of Christ in the developed gnostic systems. There could hardly have been a developed pre-Christian system of gnostic mythology, but there are a series of themes which may be present in the NT. ([Ed.] For gnostic writings see R. M. Grant, *Gnosticism: An Anthology*,

233

1961; W. Foerster, *Gnosis: A Selection of Gnostic Texts*, I, 1972; II, 1974. H. Jonas, *The Gnostic Religion*, 1958, and R. M. Grant, *Gnosticism and Early Christianity*, 1959, are among those who see gnostic themes adapted and taken up in the NT. R. M. Wilson, *The Gnostic Problem*, 1958, and *Gnosis and the New Testament*, 1968, prefers to speak of an incipient gnosticism rather than gnosticism proper. E. Yamauchi, *Pre-Christian Gnosticism*, 1973, has provided substantial arguments to show that many of the features which Bultmann, Reitzenstein and other German scholars believed were derived from gnosticism by Christianity were, in fact, derived from Christianity by gnosticism. The gnostic texts upon which the arguments depend are post-Christian.)

NT 1. (a) *sōma* in the NT reflects the wide range of meaning which it had in Gk. generally as well as in OT thought. It means corpse in Matt. 27:52; Lk. 17:37 and often, and is used of the body of Jesus in Matt. 27:58; Mk. 15:43; Lk. 23:52; 23:55; Jn. 19:31. The thought that a dead body can be raised to life (Matt. 27:52) stands behind the expression "temple of his body (*naos tou sōmatos autou*)" (Jn. 2:21). This is the only instance in the Johannine writings where *sōma* does not mean dead body or slave (cf. Rev. 18:13).

(b) The physical aspect of the body is uppermost in Mk. 5:29 ("she felt in her body that she was healed of her disease") and Jas. 2:16 ("without giving them the things needed for the body"). Matt. 6:22 speaks of the eye as the lamp of the body (cf. 5:29). Matt. 6:25 speaks of the body as being more than clothing. These passages in Matt. point beyond the body as a mere physical organism to the *sōma* as signifying the self (cf. E. Schweizer, *TDNT* VII 1058).

(c) Heb. 10:10 contrasts "the offering of the body of Jesus Christ once for all" with the temple sacrifices. The passage takes up the thought of Ps. 40:6 ff. Heb. 10:5, "Sacrifices and offerings thou hast not desired, but a body thou hast prepared for me," appears to be an interpretative gloss on Ps. 40:6 ("Sacrifice and offering thou dost not desire; but ears thou hast dug for me"). ([Ed.] On the Ps. see A. A. Anderson, *The Book of Psalms*, I, 1972, 316 ff. F. F. Bruce regards the translation in Heb. 10:5 as an interpretative paraphrase. He suggests that the digging or hollowing out of the ears is taken in this (LXX) translation of the Ps. as using the part of the body to suggest the whole [*The Epistle to the Hebrews*, 1964, 232]. The Ps. stresses the obedience of the speaker in hearing God's law and doing his will. Heb. extends the idea by applying the words to Christ who did this by offering his body [10:5; cf. 10:10].) The precise reference of body in this passage does not seem to be paralleled elsewhere, except possibly for 1 Pet. 2:24 ("He himself bore our sins in his body on the tree, that we might die to sin and live to righteousness"). Body in these passages denotes not only Jesus' physical body but the total giving of himself in death. It thus contrasts with the merely physical bodies of animals in the sacrificial system.

2. (a) In Paul *sōma* has a specialized meaning in the sense of person. Human existence – even in the sphere of the *pneuma* (spirit) – is a bodily, somatic existence. It is un-Pauline to think of the body merely as a figure or form. Passages like Rom. 6:12 ("Let not sin therefore reign in your mortal bodies, to make you obey their passions") and Rom. 12:1 ("present your bodies a living sacrifice") clearly show that the *sōma* is not merely an outer form but the whole person (cf. R. Bultmann,

234

Theology of the New Testament, I, 1952, 192). There is in Paul a series of passages in which *sōma* is understood in the general physical sense of body (e.g. 1 Cor. 5:3; 7:34). In only one passage (1 Thess. 5:23) does Paul follow current (liturgical?) language and speak of man in a tripartite way: "May your spirit [*pneuma*] and soul [*psyche*] and body [*sōma*] be kept sound and blameless at the coming of our Lord Jesus Christ." Rom. 12:4 f. and 1 Cor. 12:12–26 take up the picture of the relation of the body to its members (→ *melos;* 2. (d) below; → Church). The "marks of Jesus" (*ta stigmata tou Iēsou*) which Paul bears in his body are to be understood as scars from wounds received in the service of Jesus (Gal. 6:17; cf. 2 Cor. 12:24 ff. and perhaps Gal. 2:20. (There may also be an implicit contrast between these marks and the marks left by circumcision. The main purpose of Gal. is to refute the claims of the circumcision party which had got a strong hold over the churches in Galatia [Ed.].)

In 1 Cor. 9:27 Paul writes: "I pommel my body and subdue it, lest after preaching to others I myself should be disqualified" (RSV). ([Ed.] Here the thought seems to be similar to what is said elsewhere about the members → *melos* NT 1. and 2.; → Beat NT; cf. F. F. Bruce, *1 and 2 Corinthians*, 1971, 89 f.; C. K. Barrett, *A Commentary on the First Epistle to the Corinthians*, 1968, 218.) In the same letter Paul can say, "If I give away all I have, and if I deliver my body to be burned, but have not love, I gain nothing." The reading "to be burned" is a better one than "that I may glory" (cf. Metzger, 563 f.). ([Ed.] Martyrdom by fire was not known before Nero (cf. Tacitus, *Ann.*, 15, 44), though similar language is used of the martyrs under Antiochus (2 Macc. 7:37; 4 Macc. 18:3; cf. Dan. 3:6). In Judaism death by burning was reserved for those who had intercourse with a woman and her daughter and for the adulterous priest (Sanhedrin 9:1). Paul seems to have had in mind the most painful form of self-immolation which would be worthless without love, cf. Barrett, op. cit., 302 f.; Bruce, op. cit., 125 f.)

The body is mentioned in connection with sex in Rom. 4:19 (Abraham's body was "as good as dead") and 1 Cor. 7:4 (the wife and the husband rule over each other's body). But the warnings against unchastity (Rom. 1:24; 1 Cor. 6:13–20) show that there is a wider significance here than the merely physical. Bodily acts affect not only the individual act of sin but the whole person to his innermost being. This is underlined by Paul's questions: "Do you not know that your bodies are members of Christ? . . . . Do you not know that your body is a temple of the Holy Spirit within you which you have from God? . . . . So glorify God in your body" (1 Cor. 6:15, 19 f.).

(b) The body is not something external to man which, as it were, is added to his essential self or soul. "Man does not *have* a *sōma;* he *is sōma*" (R. Bultmann, op. cit., I, 194). *sōma* denotes man as a whole, man as a person. *sōma* can be understood as man as the object of an action and man as the subject of an action. He has a relationship with himself. This is shown, e.g., by 1 Cor. 9:27 where Paul speaks of treating his body roughly and subjecting it. This does not simply mean treating his body roughly, but treating himself roughly. Similarly, 1 Cor. 13:3 shows how one can immolate oneself. One can sacrifice oneself in the service of God by presenting the body "as a living sacrifice, holy and acceptable to God" (Rom. 12:1).

Only in one place is the *sōma* mentioned as the subject of an action in Paul. "If by the Spirit you put to death the deeds of the body you will live" (Rom. 8:13). The deeds of the body (which in the context are identified with living according to the flesh, Rom. 8:12, cf. 5 ff.) suggest action by the body. Body here is equivalent to the self, the human "I" in its sinfulness. The same thought emerges from the relation of the body and desire. The Christian should not be led by the desires of the body (Rom. 6:12) which can be dominated by the power of sin. The desires of the body and the desires of the flesh are synonymous (Gal. 5:16 ff., 24).

Paul's understanding of *sōma* as "I", as a "person", as distinct from the *sarx* (flesh) is illustrated by Rom. 7:14 ff. "I am carnal (*sarkinos*), sold under sin" (v.14). The body is open to the two possibilities of desire and obedience. In this sense there is no difference between "body of sin" (Rom. 6:6) and "sinful flesh" (Rom. 8:3). When Paul cries: "Who will deliver me from this body of death?" (Rom. 7:24), he is thinking of the shattered character of human existence as it finds expression in the body. He sees in his existence the powers of sin, the flesh and spirit which can mean either destruction or life. Man's bodily existence does not in itself denote something either good or bad. Rather the body is the concrete sphere of existence in which man's relationship with God is realized.

(c) In this light, it is understandable why Paul in 1 Cor. 15 stresses the → resurrection of the body as against his Corinthian opponents. Paul's understanding of resurrection is influenced by Jewish anthropology. Man's life is thinkable only in a body. Thus any division of man into soul and body along the lines of Gk. anthropology is precluded (cf. also 2 Cor. 5:1–10). In this discourse on resurrection Paul sets in opposition an earthly or "physical body" (v. 44 RSV, *sōma psychikon*) and a "spiritual body" (*sōma pneumatikon*). These are the two possibilities before man. The former represents his earthly existence and the latter his post-resurrection life. The images are represented in spatio-temporal terms, though naturally a spiritual body cannot be conceived in terms of matter. Paul's aim is to express what is man's essential being. It is characterized by existence in a body, again using the terminology of space and time. The body in the sense of the "I", the "person", will survive death through the creative act of God. "But God gives it a body as he has chosen, and to each kind of seed its own body. . . . So it is with the resurrection of the dead. What is sown is perishable, what is raised is imperishable. . . . It is sown a physical body, it is raised a spiritual body" (1 Cor. 15:38, 42, 44). The continuity between the earthly body and the heavenly body does not rest upon a transformation. If that were the case, Paul would have stressed the temporal aspect of his concept of the "spiritual body" (v. 44). The thought would then be of a body consisting of a substance *pneuma*. But Paul is not concerned with the description of a spiritual substance of which the heavenly *sōma* is constituted. His concern is with the fact that God determines this *sōma* through the Spirit as a power of God (cf. v. 50). Thus after the resurrection this *sōma* is no longer subject to sin and death. It is no longer a divided self. This also emerges from the understanding of faith, hope and love which Paul develops in 1 Cor. 13:13. Man's earthly existence is characterized by paradoxical contradictions (1 Cor. 13:3). The one thing that is not contradictory or fragmentary in this life is love which is complete now and in the life to come. It is with these concepts that Paul describes the continuity between the earthly body and the heavenly. It shows that man's personhood is not something that is at his disposal. It is not founded upon himself. It remains a gift.

(d) Over and above this, *sōma* has a specific meaning in Paul which no longer

236

refers to an individual but to a group. He speaks of the *sōma Christou*, the body of Christ (1 Cor. 12:27; Rom. 12:5; Eph. 4:12 and often). Paul takes up the picture of the body to express the essential character of the Christian church. In 1 Cor. 12:12–30 his exposition takes up the Gk. thought of the organism (cf. vv. 14–26), basing the necessity of the different functions of the members upon the unity of the body. But the essential character is not based on the Gk. image. The several members do not constitute the whole. Rather it is the task of the members that highlights their corporate nature in their diverse functions. The body constitutes the unity, and in this sense it can be described as the body of Christ. It is based on Christ himself. "For just as the body is one and has many members, and all the members of the body, though many, are one body, so it is with Christ. For by one Spirit we were all baptized into one body" (1 Cor. 12:12 f.).

The act of incorporation through → baptism does not mean that the body of Christ is the issue of a community that constitutes itself and grows by a rite of initiation. Rather, the description of the church as the body of Christ means that Christ constitutes the existence of the individual as a member of his body. The bestowal of the Spirit is connected with baptism (1 Cor. 12:13). The church has an eschatological character. It exists by the promise of God in Christ for the future.

The → Lord's Supper is rooted in the concept of the body as a community (Mk. 14:22–25; Matt. 26:26–29; Lk. 22:19 f.; cf. 1 Cor. 10:16 f.; 11:23–26). Paul admittedly refers to pagan practices in his account, but it is the death of Christ that gives the Lord's Supper its meaning. His death is the decisive saving act "for you" (1 Cor. 11:24) and is proclaimed as such by the Lord's Supper (1 Cor 11:26). In the centre stand not the elements or substance of bread and wine but the action of the fellowship as the body of Christ in the knowledge that it is dependent upon his blessing and subject to his Lordship. To be guilty of the body and blood of the Lord (v. 27) signifies an act of one brother against another. The giving of Christ's body in death is the decisive enactment of God's promise to man. It is the authentic sign of his church which understands itself as the body of Christ. The proclamation of Christ's body as given for us in death and the picture of the body of Christ as the church are given in an irreversible sequence.

(e) Col. and Eph. develop a picture of the body of Christ which is distinct from that in the other Pauline epistles. The Col. understanding of the body of Christ is presented in the hymn in Col. 1:15–20. The section shows indications of adaptation. In my opinion "the church" (v. 18a) is an interpretative insertion by the author into an already existing hymn. In the original form of the hymn the body of Christ was the → world. There are affinities with gnostic motifs which occur in the later gnostic systems which present the body of the original man as the expression of the world. The cosmic dimension of Christ's saving act is particularly clear. The world, the cosmos, is to be understood as the body of Christ. ([Ed.] Cf. E. Lohse, *Colossians and Philemon*, 1971, 50–55. Whether or not "the church" is to be regarded as an insertion into the text of an already existing hymn, the passage clearly regards Christ's person and work as having cosmic significance. "For in him all the fullness of God was pleased to dwell, and through him to reconcile to himself all things, whether on earth or in heaven, making peace by the blood of the cross" [Col. 1:19 f.]. But this is not unique. See further Eph. 1:22 f.: "he has put all things under his

237

feet and has made him the head of all things for the church which is his body, the fulness of him who fills all in all." The cosmic significance of Christ is also expressed in Rom. 11:36 which immediately precedes the exposition of the idea of being "one body in Christ" [12:5], and in 1 Cor. 15:24–28 which speaks of Christ delivering the kingdom to the Father that God may be all in all.)

If men were threatened by cosmic powers, a redemption was here offered them which held good even in the face of these powers. "The whole realm of being is related to him as the mediator of the Lordship of God" (H. Conzelmann in H. W. Beyer *et al.*, *Die Kleineren Briefe*, *NTD* 8, 1962, 137). "In opposition to an emotional enthusiastic understanding of the body of Christ which regards the whole universe as already reconciled physically in Christ the Pauline view is upheld that talk about the body of Christ is a summons to obedience and to service for the new Lord" (E. Schweizer, *TDNT* VII 1077).

The thought of Christ as the head of the world is rightly maintained in this connection by the reference to the church in v. 18. His body is the church in which this obedience is proclaimed for realization in the world. If the symbolic ideas here are rightly interpreted, it is clear that the church and the world are not two great fixed entities set in permanent opposition. The church signifies the recognition and realization of real possibilities in the world under the Lordship of Christ, the freedom of faith to live in the world.

In contrast to Col., the concept of the body as the church of Christ is clear in Eph. from the beginning. Christ is the → head (*kephalē*) of the body of the church (4:15 f.). Neither the Gk. nor the general concept of the body as an organism fit exactly here. The passage speaks of the believers growing up "in every way into him who is the head, into Christ, from whom the whole body, joined and knit together by every joint with which it is supplied, when each part is working properly, makes bodily growth and upbuilds itself in love" (4:15 f. RSV). These ideas of the body are stamped by motifs which are to be found in later gnostic writings. It is clear that Eph. is attacking gnostic-type ideas within and without the church. "Children" (→ *nēpioi*) are the hesitant and misguided who are carried about by every wind of doctrine (v. 14). They were perhaps gnostics who boasted of their knowledge, but are not more precisely described.

The picture of the body as the church is again taken up not only in defence but to provide a definitive understanding of the church for the situation after Paul. Paul's teaching of unity in multiplicity in 1 Cor. 12 is now put forward stressing the head. For headship implies both lordship and promise. The church is held and sustained by Christ. In order to preserve it from false teaching and schisms, it is presented not with an institutional form, but with the reflection that the head and the body are mutually related in love and truth. "Two possibilities stand opposed to each other: existence in the body, that is in unity and love, and isolated existence apart. . . . There is unity in the church in speaking and doing what is commanded – the practice of love in the sphere of truth. And there is the arbitrary assertion of subjective opinions in all their deceptive attraction" (H. Conzelmann, op. cit., 79). Thus the church has its place in the world. It does not stand over against it; it is set in it. "The body of Christ is precisely the Church in which Christ moves out into the world. The preaching of the Gospel by the Church is the answer to cosmic anxiety" (E. Schweizer, *TDNT* VII 1080). *S. Wibbing*

238

Parts of the Body

Rooted in *ankos*, a "bend", "hollow", *ankalē* is the "bent arm" and classically a metaphor for anything which enfolds, e.g., an "arm" of the sea. In the LXX only 1 Ki. 3:20 of mother's arms nursing a baby and Prov. 5:20 of man embraced by his mistress. In NT only Lk. 2:28 (cf. *enankalizomai*, Mk. 9:36; 10:16) of baby or child held in arms.

Classically, *pous* means the "foot" of man, animals or things (e.g. hill); as idiom of proximity or direction, e.g. *para podos* "at once", *para podi* "at hand"; measure of length in space or poetry. In LXX the foot of man, animals, things (e.g. table, Exod. 25:26), idols, Seraphim; anthropomorphically, of God (Exod. 24:10); but chiefly in at least forty metaphorical usages wherein a person is depicted as enjoying, suffering, doing or refusing that wherein his foot is the most notably used member: e.g. rest (Gen. 18:4), restlessness (Dt. 28:65), victory (Jos. 10:24), calamity (Deut. 32:15); the position of the follower (Jdg. 4:10), the organ expressive of reverence (Ex. 3:5), consecration (Ex. 29:20 – the consecration of life's activity), etc.

The NT matches the balance of LXX usage, mainly offering metaphor: separation (Matt. 10:14), straying (Matt. 18:8), devotion, submission, supplication (Mk. 5:22; Lk. 8:35; 10:39), service offered in love (Jn. 13:5; 1 Tim. 5:10), triumph (Rom. 3:15). To cut off the foot is a severely debilitating act but one which expresses the urgency of Jesus' message (Matt. 18:8; Mk. 9:45; but cf. Matt. 4:6). The pierced feet of Jesus are seen as evidence of the reality of the resurrection (Lk. 24:39 f.). To shake off the dust from one's feet (Matt. 10:14; Mk. 6:11; Lk. 9:5; Acts 13:51) is a gesture of breaking off all connection, performed in those places which have rejected the gospel. But to wash the feet of others is a menial service which is performed as an act of love by both followers of Jesus (Lk. 7:38–46; Jn. 11:2; 12:3; cf. 1 Tim. 5:10) and Jesus himself (Jn. 13:5–14). Perhaps significantly it is women who perform this act. In the case of Jesus' washing the disciples' feet, the action symbolizes both the cleansing that Jesus gives to the sinner and the humility and care that disciples should have for each other in following the example of their master. The prophetic announcement of the saving presence of God of Isa. 52:7 ("How beautiful upon the mountains are the feet of him who brings good tidings, who publishes peace, who brings good tidings of good, who publishes salvation, who says to Zion, 'Your God reigns' ") is seen as being fulfilled by those who preach the gospel (Acts 10:36; Rom. 10:15; Eph. 6:15). Similarly, the OT idea of having one's enemies under one's feet is interpreted christologically in the NT (Ps. 45:7; Heb. 2:8; Ps. 110:1; Matt. 22:44; cf. 5:35; Mk. 12:36; Lk. 20:23; Acts 2:35; 7:49; Heb. 1:13; 10:13; but cf. Jas. 2:3; 1 Cor. 15:25, 27; Rom. 16:20). See also the descriptions of Rev. 1:15, 17; 2:18; 3:9; 10:1; 11:11; 12:1; 13:2; 19:10; 22:8.

osphys means "loins, lower body", by synecdoche "body", classically, the loins, lower body, of man, sacrificial victims and animals (Xen.). The LXX uses loins in the general sense of "body" (e.g. Gen. 37:34), but more particularly the "body" as the source of offspring (Gen. 35:11) and, within the body, the loins as a seat of strong emotion: pain (Isa. 21:3), fear (Dan. 5:6). Against this background it develops vivid metaphors: the girt loins (Exod. 12:1), the expression for personal strength or capacity (1 Ki. 12:10); mourning (Isa. 32:11), immobilization (Ezek. 29:7). That which is worn on the loins declares personal commitment and character (Isa. 11:5; cf. 1 Ki. 2:5).

In the NT both the physical (e.g. Matt. 3:4) and metaphorical (e.g. Lk. 12:35; Eph. 6:14) aspects are exemplified. The development of the metaphor to using the physical to describe the mental (1 Pet. 1:13) is a new feature, as is also the extension of the thought of the loins as the source of offspring (Acts 2:30; Heb. 7:5) to become a means of describing the solidarity of offspring with their ancestor and their involvement in his actions (Heb. 7:10).

kolpos means "bosom", by synecdoche "person"; especially with connotations of love, close relationship etc. It is related to *kolpoō*, to swell out (e.g. as sail in wind). Hence *kolpos* as the human "bosom", the "bosom" of a garment, of the sea (originally referring to sea-goddess), bay, valley.

The LXX concentrates on metaphorical usages save in Exod. 4:6 (of garment), Ruth 4:16; 1 Ki. 3:20; 17:19 (of nurse or mother with child). It specifies tender relationships (Deut. 13:6; 2 Sam. 12:3; Num. 11:12; Isa. 49:22); the self (Ps. 34 [35]:13; Prov. 6:27), strong personal emotion (Eccl. 7:10), inactivity (Ps. 73[74]:11), the heart (Job 23:12), vengeance personally suffered (Ps. 78[79]:12).

The NT exemplifies the classical use in "bay" (Acts 27:39), and reflects Ps. 78[79]: 12 in Lk. 6:38. The general notion of tender relationship (Jn. 13:23) is given two specific adaptations, first as descriptive of the intimate oneness, yet distinctiveness, of the Father and the Son in their mutual love (Jn. 1:18), and secondly, of the tender love awaiting God's people after death, their rest in "Abraham's bosom" (Lk. 16:22, 23). In our Lord's parable the emphasis rests not on the condition on which this blessing is granted but on the nature of the blessing itself: bliss, recompense, eternal separation from all that is evil, a richness which cannot be forfeited, for the gulf which separates also encloses. This specific idea of eternal distinctions after death is no more than barely incipient in the OT and began to emerge with clarity from Enoch (*c.* 110 B.C., cf. Eth. En. 22) onwards becoming specific in 1st cent. A.D. Jewish literature (cf. SB II 226, 227; IV 1018, 1019; R. Meyer, *kolpos*, *TDNT* III 824 ff.).

mastos and *mazos* mean "breast," by synecdoche the upper body; classically the breast, both of men and women; rarely the udder of animals; and metaphorically a hill or cup-shaped object.

In LXX it is used only of women (general, e.g. Cant. 1:13 etc., specifically mothers, e.g. Job 3:12) and metaphorically of Jerusalem (Isa. 66:11), family blessings (Gen. 49:25), sorrow (Isa. 32:13), adultery (Hos. 2:2). It is used of animals in Lam. 4:3. The NT exemplifies only the physical use: mother's breast (Lk. 11:27; 23:29), upper body (Rev. 1:13, where one reading is *mazos*, the only example of this word in NT).

osteon means "bone", by synecdoche, a living or dead body; in cl. Gk. the "bone/ bones" of the living or the dead; metaphorically the rocks, as constituting the bony structure of the earth; a fruit stone. The LXX uses the word likewise of the dead (e.g. Gen. 50:25) and the living (e.g. Eccl. 11:5); also the bones of the Passover lamb (Exod. 12:46), and metaphorically for determination (Prov. 25:15, cf. Eng. "backbone"). Coupled with → flesh (Job 2:5) and → heart (Isa. 66:14) bones express the totality of physical existence. Bones are the seat of health (lost by sin, Ps. 37:4 [38:3], enjoyed through godliness, Prov. 3:8), vitality (Job 20:11), are broken by divine judgment (Ps. 50:10 [51:8]; Isa. 38:13), especially the seat of pain (Job 30:17 etc.). Once (Job 7:15) "bones" stands for the self. With "flesh", "bone" is metaphorical for kinship (cf. Gen. 2:23; 2 Sam. 5:1. NT usage (apart from Mt. 23:27; Heb. 11:22, in each case "dead body") focuses on Christ: his identity with the Passover lamb (Jn. 19:36), the reality of his resurrection body and person (Lk. 24:39, and in *v.l.* of A, B and other manuscripts), the kinship between Christians and Christ (Eph. 5:30).

haphē means joint, junction, binding. It is connected with *haptō*, "to fasten, bind, engage in, kindle", hence *haphē*, a kindling, touching, grasp, joint, junction. The LXX only uses the word in the sense of "blow or stroke", of punishment (2 Sam. 7:14), assault (Deut. 17:8), and of the "plague" of "leprosy" (Lev. 13 passim, etc.). In the NT the word only appears in the sense of "joint", the point of "binding" or "junction", or even "that which effects the binding" with reference to the metaphor of Christians as a "body" under Christ as the "head" (Eph. 4:16; Col. 2:19).

harmos, joint. In cl. Gk. *harmozō* means to joint or dovetail together, primarily of joiner's work, then metaphorically of arranging, fitting together, harmonizing. *harmos* is thus primarily a joint in masonry, etc. and only derivatively the "shoulder-joint". Absent from the LXX, the sole occurrence in NT is Heb. 4:12 where the scrutinizing power of "the word of God" is illustrated by the fact that it penetrates to the "most critical parts of the physical framework of man" (B. F. Westcott, *Hebrews*, 1892, ad loc.).

trachēlos, neck, in cl. Gk. of the "neck" or "throat" of man, animals and things (e.g. gourd, mid-part of mast). It occurs in the LXX, of human and animal anatomy (Gen. 27:16; Jdg. 8:21), but chiefly in metaphorical and idiomatic usage: of burdens borne (Gen. 27:40), greeting (Gen. 33:14), stubbornness (Deut. 10:16; Isa. 48:4); expressive of victory (Jos. 10:24), personal effort (Neh. 3:5); a point at which life can be gravely endangered (Is. 30:28; Hab. 3:13) or mortally wounded (Ezek. 21:29); when ornaments are worn, especially the metaphorical "wearing" of truth, etc. (Prov. 3:3). The NT reflects LXX usage in its metaphorical aspects. The neck is the place of peril to the life (Matt. 18:6; esp. Rom. 16:4); burdens are borne (Acts 15:10); connected with greeting (Lk. 15:20) and sorrow at parting (Acts 20:37).

pterna (cf. *pternismos*), "heel". Classical use covers the heel of a person or shoe, and the lower part of anything. In the LXX, the anatomical use is exemplified in Gen. 25:26; 49:17. In addition, the heel is the place of non-mortal injury (Gen. 3:15), aggravating opposition (Jos. 13:23), and lurking danger whether of a physical (e.g. Ps. 55:7 [56:6]) or moral (Ps. 48:5 [49:5]) foe. The NT quotes LXX Ps. 40:10 (41:9) (*pternismos*) at Jn. 13:18, where the "lifting up of the heel" symbolizes base treachery.   *J. A. Motyer*

(a). J. Barr, *The Semantics of Biblical Language*, 1961, 35 ff; E. Best, *One Body in Christ: A Study in the Relationship of the Church to Christ in the Epistles of the Apostle Paul*, 1955; R. Bultmann, *Theology of the New Testament*, I, 1952. 192–203; M E. Dahl, *The Resurrection of the Body: A Study of 1 Corinthians 15*, 1962; W. Eichrodt, *Theology of the Old Testament*, II 1967, 118–50; H. Grobel, "*sōma* as 'Self, Person' in the Septuagint," in *Neutestamentliche Studien für Rudolf Bultmann*, BZNW 21, 1954, 54 ff.; J. Horst, *melos, TDNT* IV 555–68; G. Howard, "The Head/Body Metaphors of Ephesians", *NTS* 20, 1974, 350 ff; R. Jewett, *Paul's Anthropological Terms: A Study of their Use in Conflict Settings*, 1971, 201–304, 456 ff.; E. Käsemann, "On Paul's Anthropology" and "The Theological Problem Presented by the Motif of the Body of Christ," in *Perspectives on Paul*, 1971, 1–31, 102–37; R. Kempthorne, "Incest and the Body of Christ: A Study of I Corinthians vi, 12–20," *NTS* 14, 1967–68, 568–74; W. L. Knox, "Parallels to the NT

Use of *Sōma*", *JTS* 39, 1938, 243–46; W. G. Kümmel, *Man in the New Testament*, 1963; E. Lohse, *Colossians and Philemon*, 1971; R. J. McKelvey, *The New Temple*, 1969; E. Mersch, *The Whole Christ: The Historical Development of the Doctrine of the Mystical Body in Scripture and Tradition*, 1938; J. R. Nelson, *The Realm of Redemption*, 1963[6], 67–104; G. Owen, *Body and Soul: A Study of the Christian View of Man*, 1961; W. Pesch, "Body," *EBT* I 81–4; J. R. Porter, "The Legal Aspects of the Concept of 'Corporate Personality' in the Old Testament," *VT* 15, 1965, 361 ff.; A. E. J. Rawlinson, "Corpus Christi," in G. K. A. Bell and A. Deissmann, *Mysterium Christi*, 1930, 225–46; B. Reicke, "Body and Soul in the New Testament," *StTh* 19, 1965, 200–12; J. A. T. Robinson, *The Body*, 1952; E. Schweizer, *Lordship and Discipleship*, 1960, 119–25; E. Schweizer and F. Baumgärtel, *sōma* etc. *TDNT* VII 1024–94; O. J. F. Seitz, *One Body and One Spirit: A Study of the Church in the New Testament*, 1960; W. D. Stacey, "Man as a Soul," *ExpT* 72, 1960–1, 349 f.; "St. Paul and the Soul," *ExpT* 66, 1954–55, 274–77; and *The Pauline View of Man in Relation to its Judaic and Hellenistic Backgrounds*, 1956; A. J. M. Wedderburn, "The Body of Christ and Related Concepts in I Corinthians", *SJT* 24, 1971, 74–96; D. E. H. Whiteley, *The Theology of St. Paul*, 1964, 190–99; H. W. Wolff, *Anthropology of the Old Testament*, 1974.

(b). P. Bonnard, "L'Eglise corps du Christ dans le Paulinisme," *Revue de Theologie et de Philosophie* 3, 1958, 268–82; H. Clavier, "Brèves remarques sur la notion de *sōma pneumatikon*", in W. D. Davies and D. Daube, eds., *The Background of the New Testament and its Eschatology. In Honour of Charles Harold Dodd*, 1956, 342–62; C. Colpe, "Zur Leib-Christi-Vorstellung im Epheserbrief," in *Judentum, Urchristentum, Kirche, BZNW* 26, 1960, 172 ff.; and *Die Religionsgeschichtliche Schule: Darstellung und Kritik ihres Bildes vom gnostischen Erlösermythus, FRLANT* Neue Folge 60, 1961; H. Conzelmann, *Der Brief an die Epheser, der Brief an die Kolosser*, NTD 8, 1961[9]; L. Deimel, *Leib Christi, Sinn und Grenzen einer Deutung des innerkirchlichen Lebens*, 1940; E. Dhorme, *L'Emploi métaphorique des Noms de Corps en Hébreu et en Akkadien*, 1923; W. Goossens, *L'Église Corps du Christ d'après S. Paul*, 1949; W. Gutbrod, *Die paulinische Anthropologie*, 1934; E. Hartmann, "Leib und Seele," *RGG*[3] IV 287–91; D. Haugg, *Wir Sind Dein Leib*, 1937; J. Havet, "Christ collectif ou Christ individuel en I Cor. 12, 12?" *Ephemerides Theologicae Lovanienses* 23, 1947, 499–520; and "La doctrine paulinienne du 'Corps du Christ', Essai de Mise au Point," in A. Descamps, B. Rigaux, H. Riesenfeld and L. Cerfaux, eds., *Littérature et Théologie Pauliniennes*, 1960, 184–216; H. Hegermann, "Zur Ableitung der Leib-Christi-Vorstellung," *TLZ* 85, 1960, 839 ff.; J. Jervell, *Imago Dei*, 1960; E. Käsemann, *Leib und Leib Christi*, 1933; and "Das Interpretation des Epheserbriefes," *Exegetische Versuche und Besinnungen*, II, 1964, 253 ff.; H. Koller, "*sōma* bei Homer," *Glotta* 37, 1958, 278 ff.; W. Kütemeyer, "Leib und Seele," *EKL* II 1062 ff.; L. Malevez, "L'Église Corps du Christ," *Revue des Science Philosophiques et Théologiques* 32, 1944, 27–94; J. J. Meuzelaar, *Der Leib des Messias. Eine exegetische Studie über den Gedanken vom Leib Christi in den Paulusbriefen*, 1961; A. Oepke, "Leib Christi oder Volk Gottes bei Paulus," *TLZ* 79, 1954, 363 ff.; E. Percy, *Der Leib Christi in den paulinischen Homologumena und Antilegomena*, Lunds Universitets Årsskrift 38, 1, 1942; A. Plack, *Die Gesellschaft und das Böse*, 1967, 199–216; P. Pokorny, "*Sōma Christou* im Epheserbrief," *EvTh* 20, 1960, 456 ff.; J. Reuss, "Die Kirche als Leib Christi und die Herkunft dieser Vorstellung beim Apostel Paulus," *BZ* 2, 1958, 103–27; O. Sander, "Leib-Seele-Dualismus im Alten Testament?" *ZAW* 77, 1965, 329 ff.; H. Schlier, "Corpus Christi," *RAC* III 437 ff.; *Der Brief an die Epheser*, 1963[5], excursus on *to sōma tou Christou*, 90 ff.; T. Schmid, *Der Leib Christi*, 1919; E. Schweizer, "Abendmahl im Neuen Testament", *RGG*[3] I 10–21; "Die Kirche als Leib Christi in den paulinischen Homologumena," *TLZ* 86, 1961, 161–74; "Zur Trichotomie des pneumatikon vom psychikon in I Kor. 2, 14; 15, 44; Jak. 3, 15; Jud. 19," *TZ* 9, 1953, 76 f.; J. N. Sevenster, "Die Anthropologie des Neuen Testaments," *Anthropologie Religieuse*, 1955, 166–77; T. Soiron, *Die Kirche als der Leib Christi*, 1951; A. Wikenhauser, *Die Kirche als der mystische Leib Christi nach dem Apostel Paulus*, 1949.

→ also literature under Church, Man, Resurrection.

Book, Read, Letter

The book (*biblos*) and the letter (*epistolē*) are the normal means by which ideas are recorded, so that they may be accessible to others, when the author is not present, especially after his death. Both book and letter are ntended to be read or read aloud (*anaginōskō*).

| βίβλος | βίβλος (*biblos*), book; βιβλίον (*biblion*), book.

CL *biblos* is derived from an older form *byblos*, the Sem. g*ᵉbal*, Gubla. It originally meant the papyrus plant, or its fibrous stem, which was exported to Greece through the port of Byblos in Syria where the plant was prepared.

It is found from Aesch. onwards not merely in its basic meaning of papyrus, but also for any material used in writing, e.g. a clay tablet, leather, parchment, and even for what has been written on it. Finally it came to mean a scroll, book, writing, then deed, letter, order. In Koine Gk. *biblos* is often replaced by its diminutive *biblion*.

In secular Gk. these words increasingly came to denote an ancient, holy book (cf. the magical books in Acts 19:19). Josephus and Philo followed this use and called the Pent., the Torah, or the whole OT, *hierai bibloi*, holy books. The Eng. word Bible comes from the plural *ta biblia*, via the Lat.

OT In the LXX *biblos*, or more commonly *biblion*, is a translation of Heb. *sēper*, and its meaning is fixed by OT usage.

1. It is used for anything that has been written (e.g. a scroll, book, writing, letter). Examples are a war diary (Exod. 17:14; cf. Num. 21:14), a law-book (Deut. 17:18; cf. Exod. 24:7), a private letter (2 Sam. 11:14), a divorce document (Deut. 24:1, 3; cf. Mk. 10:4), a land register (Jos. 18:9), various chronicles of the kings (1 Ki. 15:31). There is a religious connotation only in so far as Yahweh is a witness of that which has been written, and watches over their fulilment especially in cases of contracts (→ Covenant).

2. In the sing. it is used for individual OT writings (Tob. 1:1; 1 Chr. 27:24), in the plur. for groups of writings in the OT (Dan. 9:2; I Macc. 12:9). Important in this connection is the use of these two words in the sing. for the book of the Law, the Torah. This usage springs undoubtedly from the fact that the Torah was written on a special scroll. Since this scroll of the Torah contains God's holy will, *biblion* became in the LXX a solemn expression for the Book of the Law (Deut. 28:58; Jos. 1:8). We find here the roots of the later church usage, "the Bible."

Originally various later books stood beside the Torah and the other OT writings, but already by the end of the first cent. A.D. the canon was closed (→ Rule). 2 Esd. 14:42–47 mentions 94 books of which 24 were available to all, i.e. they were canonical, but 70 were hidden. This gave rise to the problem of canonical and apocryphal writings.

3. Various "books" are frequently mentioned in Jewish writings, especially apocalyptic. The idea goes back to the OT. The book is here a picture of God's eternal purposes for the future of his people, his world or his creatures. There is the book of the divine world-plan (cf. Ezek. 2:8 ff.), the book of life (cf. Exod. 32:32 f.; Isa. 4:3; Dan. 12:1; Jub. 19:9), the book of human history (a term found already in the surrounding nations and also in Pss. 139:16; 56:3 (9)), and the book of judgment (Dan. 7:10; Isa. 65:6; Eth. Enoch 81:4; 89:61–64). These books are always an expression of the sovereign will and work of God in history. There are no books of fate.

243

NT 1. (a) The NT follows the practice of the LXX in using *biblion* (34 times) more frequently than *biblos* (10 times). Particularly noticeable are the 23 occurrences of *biblion* in Rev. alone (only 11 times in the rest of the NT). In contrast to secular Gk., no difference of meaning can be found between the two forms.

(b) OT usage reappears in Matt. 1:1, "the book of the genealogy" (cf. Gen. 5:1); and Matt. 19:7; Mk. 10:4, "a certificate of divorce" (cf. Deut. 24:1, 3). *biblos* and *biblion* are used for the Torah (Gal. 3:10; Heb. 9:19), or for other books of the OT canon (cf. Lk. 3:4 (Isa.); 4:17 ("and he was given the book of the prophet Isaiah"); Mk. 12:26 (Pent.); Acts 7:42 (Amos), Lk. 20:42 and Acts 1:20 (Pss.). The writer of the Fourth Gospel also calls his work a *biblion* (Jn. 20:30; 21:25). Book is used in a special way in Rev.: the book in which all is to be written (1:11); the book sealed with 7 seals contains the plan for the world in the last days (5:1 ff.); the book of life, in which are found the names of those that are to enter eternal life, while those who are not in it will not be able to withstand the temptation to worship the beast (13:8; cf. Phil. 4:3); and the book of judgment (20:12). While it is the language of apocalyptic that appears here, it has been given a new force and significance (cf. H. Bietenhard, *WUNT* 2, 231–254).

2. All the books of the Bible contain a message which awakens and demands faith. Only where this message is believed are they rightly read and understood (Jn. 20:30 f.). But when John speaks of his book in this connection, he is not necessarily using the word with any theological significance.

It is otherwise in Rev. Just as in Jewish apocalyptic, the *biblion* is "the book of the sacredly established divine decrees concerning the future of the world and the community" (G. Schrenk, *TDNT* I 619). In Jewish apocalyptic, however, books are attributed to some pious man of God in the past, who received a secret revelation, hidden and sealed for a later time and for a select circle of people. In Rev., on the contrary, the seer John passes on a prophetic message under his own name to the contemporary churches known to him. It is intended to provide comfort and warning (cf. 2 Esd. 14:42–47; Dan. 12:4, 9; Rev. 1:11). The message here is about the events of the last time until the return of Christ, who will triumph at the last over every power opposed to God as the crucified and exalted One.

Rev. 5:1 ff. speaks of a scroll like that in Ezek. 2:9 f. It is a scroll written on both sides and sealed with 7 seals, presumably a deed and probably a will. Here too the book contains God's eschatological plan. It is sealed, i.e. withdrawn from all human knowledge, and yet it is already there. The history of God's dealings with the world is already decided. Only One, the crucified and exalted Christ, is worthy to break the seals and to make God's plans a reality and to fulfil them. Confession of Christ is decisive for the concept of history in Rev.

The end time is the time of judgment. In this context Rev. takes up once more the pictures of the book of life and of the books of judgment (20:12). The names of those who will be preserved in judgment are contained in the book of life (cf. Lk. 10:20; Phil. 4:3). They are the conquerors (Rev. 3:5), or those who have been predestined from the foundation of the world (Rev. 17:8). That does not mean that predestination makes the call to obedience unnecessary, for a name can be blotted out of the book of life. Human victory and divine predestination are here linked, just as are faith as a gift and as a personal decision.

U. Becker

| ἀναγινώσκω |

ἀναγινώσκω (*anaginōskō*), read; ἀνάγνωσις (*anagnōsis*), reading.

CL *anaginōskō* is a compound derived from *ginōskō* a late variant of *gignōskō*, recognize, know (→ knowledge, art. *ginōskō*). Originally it had only an intensive or restrictive force, to know exactly, or know again, acknowledge. Then it came to mean generally read, read aloud. There is no essential difference, for in the classical world anyone reading for himself alone always did so aloud. In legal orations *anaginōskō* was frequently used as a call to the court secretary, whose duty it was to read the documents in the case. Similarly *anagnōsis* occasionally meant recognizing, but normally reading, or reading aloud, especially in meetings or before a court.

OT The cultic reading aloud of the divine commandments and legal requirements was an early practice at the great Israelite festivals (Exod. 24:7; cf. Jos. 24:25). It is probable that the main incidents in Israel's history were recounted (Exod. 15:1–18; Jdg. 5) or even reproduced dramatically (cf. Ps. 68:24–27 (25–28)). Jeremiah substituted a reading of his oracles for the prophetic sermon he was not allowed to give (Jer. 36:5 ff.). Ezra's reading of the Law had to be supplemented by a Levitical explanation (Neh. 8:8). There was also private reading of and meditation on the Scriptures. This was, of course, restricted to those who were able to read, but they were urged to do it (Deut. 17:18 ff.; cf. Isa. 30:8; Ps. 1:2).

In late Jud. the reading of the Law was an unquestioned part of every service (cf. the synagogue inscription found in Jerusalem: *synagōgēn eis anagnōsin nomou*, the synagogue is for the reading of the Law). This was the right of every member of the congregation (Lk. 4:16 f.)., but was early on linked to a lectionary, at least for the Torah. ([Tr.] In spite of opinions to the contrary there were no regular readings in the Temple. In the synagogue there is a reading from the Pent. on sabbaths, all festivals, the New Moon, fast days, Mondays and Thursdays, with a reading from the Prophets on sabbaths, festivals and fasts. No fixed lectionary existed in the 1st cent. A.D.) In this connection it should be noted that already in the LXX Yahweh's command to the prophets to proclaim the word (Jer. 3:12; 11:6, etc.) was translated by *anaginōskō*, thereby implying reading in a service. It was usual to read also on special occasions, e.g. before battle (2 Macc. 8:23).

NT In the NT *anaginōskō* is found only with the meaning of read, read aloud. It is found 32 times, 14 in the Synoptics, 7 in Acts, 9 in the Pauline epistles and once in Jn. and Rev. *anagnōsis*, reading, is found 3 times. Normally, reading the OT is meant. It is always so in the Synoptics, and also in Acts 8:28 and Gal. 4:21 *v.l.* It refers to the reading in the synagogue service in Lk. 4:16; Acts 13:15, 27; 15:21; and 2 Cor. 3:14 f. It is used also for the reading of a letter (Acts 15:31; 2 Cor. 1:13; 3:2), especially in a service (1 Thess. 5:27; Col. 4:16).

Jesus considered that an intensive reading of Scripture is a pre-requisite for theological discussion, as indeed for all knowledge of God. Hence the frequent reproach, "Have you never read?" (Mk. 2:25; 12:10; etc.). Fundamentally Jesus agreed with Jud. But with the Jews, as Paul argued in 2 Cor. 3:14 ff. expounding the OT, there is a veil over their minds. They do not understand the Scriptures aright, for the reading takes place without conversion to Christ (v. 16), and so without the

245

Spirit (v. 17). Without the illumination of the Spirit a man does not understand the Scriptures (1 Cor. 2:14). The study of the Scriptures must be linked with prayer for the illumination of the Holy Spirit. Then the Scriptures become a witness of Christ to him (cf. Jn. 5:39 → Scripture, art. *graphē*).

The epistles of the NT were from the first intended to be read in Christian services (1 Thess. 5:27). They were not confined to the local church to which they were addressed (Col. 4:16). As was the case with Jeremiah, this reading had to replace the apostolic preaching, on which all later preaching is based. In this way the reading of the epistles ranked equally with the reading of the OT in the services.

J. Blunck

| ἐπιστολή | ἐπιστολή (*epistolē*), letter; ἐπιστέλλω (*epistellō*), inform, or instruct by letter, write. |

CL 1. *epistellō*, send, announce, order through the passing on of a message or commission, generally in writing. Hence, that which is transmitted, originally a military or administrative order, is called *epistolē*, i.e. normally a letter.

With the spread of Hel. culture a whole range of letters was developed, from private letters of an intimate nature, open letters (e.g. the didactic letters of the Epicurean philosophers), to artistic epistles, which were aesthetic treatises in letter form. Travelling philosophers and their pupils were accustomed to carry letters of recommendation (Diog. Laert., 7, 1, 3; 7, 8, 87).

2. In contrast to oriental examples, Gk. letters began according to a fixed scheme with a sentence: the sender (nom.) to the recipient (dat.), greetings (*chairein*). The words "says" or "conveys" are understood (Funk, § 480). The letter ends with a short farewell greeting.

OT The Heb. equivalent of *epistellein* in the LXX is *šālaḥ*, send; those of *epistolē*, include *sēper*, *miktāb* and especially later *'iggeret*, from Ass. *egirtu*, official document.

1. Pre-exilic letters are only briefly quoted in the OT. They are rulers' letters to other rulers or to their subjects. They involve conspiracy (2 Sam. 11:14 f.; 1 Ki. 21:9 f.; 2 Ki. 10:1–6), mockery (2 Ki. 19:10–13, par.), homage (2 Ki. 20:12, par.). There is also a prophetic oracle in letter-form (2 Chr. 21:12–15). Naaman carried a letter of recommendation (2 Ki. 5:6).

A wider range of epistolary literature appears in the later writings of the OT. Because of the occupation of the land after the Exile there had to be political correspondence with the foreign rulers (cf. Ezr. 4:7–6:12; Ad. Est. 13:1–6; 1 Macc. 10:3, 7, 17–20; 11:29–37; 12:5–23, etc.). The diaspora resulted in religious letters and instructions being sent to those in exile. The earliest known example is Jer. 29:4–23. In the later OT writings and the apocryphal books we can trace the development of the letter as an art-form (e.g. Dan. 4:1–37 (MT 3:31–4:34); 2 Macc. 1:1–9; 1:10–2:18; Ep. Jer.; Od. Sol. 23:5).

2. In letters following the oriental pattern the introduction is normally: sender to recipient, May your salvation increase! The body of the letter begins: "And now . . ." (*we'attâh*).

246

NT *epistolē*, letter, occurs 24 times in the NT; and *epistellō*, write, 3 times. Of the 27 books of the NT 21 are clearly letters. In addition, epistolary style as a literary form can be found in Rev. 1:1; Acts 1:1; 15:23–29; 23:26–30; and Lk. 1:3 f.

1. It is no accident that most early Christian writings took the form of occasional literature. Imminent expectation of the parousia may have contributed to this. On the other hand, the problems of the missionary churches, which found themselves in constant tension with their political and religious surroundings, needed answers and explanations (cf. 1 Cor. and Rom. 13). Moreover, after a lengthy absence the missionary found it necessary to remind his converts of his message, to reaffirm and to develop it (cf. the many examples in 2 Cor.). Some thought there was but little time to the parousia (2 Thess. 2:2 f., 15).

Two further factors influenced the development of the NT epistle. There was the conflict about tradition and doctrine in the fight against heresy, especially incipient gnosticism (→ Knowledge); and there was the increasing need felt for church order (→ Church, → Bishop). Besides collections of Paul's letters (cf. 2 Pet. 3:16; such a collection of a number of letters to the same congregation is possibly to be found in 2 Cor.), some have suggested that other authors, following a widespread literary convention in the ancient world and feeling themselves to be responsible for the tradition which they guarded, generally wrote under the name of one of the apostles (e.g. the so-called Deutero-Paulines, 2 Pet.) It is maintained that these letters are kept general in tone, that they teach by appealing to the apostolic tradition or to "the doctrine of Christ" (2 Jn. 9), and warn with authority. Epistles played a decisive role in carrying the young church through a period of outward and inward danger. The extent of this practice of pseudonymity in the NT is much disputed.

2. It was Paul who gave the NT letters their original form and set the pattern for others. He was not motivated by any stylistic reasons but by the Christian message he had to give in them. The standard Gk. preface (cf. Acts 15:23; 23:26; Jas. 1:1) was expanded. *chairein* was replaced by an explicit greeting according to the oriental pattern, e.g. *charis hymin*, grace be with you. The formulation of the expanded preface often prepares for the contents of the letter (cf. 1 Cor. 1:1 ff.; Rom. 1:1–7; Gal. 1:1–5). The preface is followed by thanksgiving, prayer and an assurance of remembrance (1 Thess. 1:2–10; Phil. :3–11; Rom. 1:8–12). When necessary, this changes to blame and warning (Gal. :6–9). Equally the short fare-well greeting becomes a full prayer for blessing. Paul dictated his letters (Rom. 16:22). He often penned the closing sentences himself as a guarantee of authenticity (1 Cor. 16:21; Gal. 6:11; Phlm. 19).

3. All the Pauline letters are letters in the true sense of the word. They arose from actual situations and are written for particular circles of readers (cf. 1 Cor. 16:5–9). They are often answers to questions raised by the church, especially 1 Cor. They are also influenced by the official and authoritative connotation inherent in *epistolē* and *epistellō* (see CL, OT and examples in Acts). They are moulded throughout by the *kerygma* and Paul's apostolic office. Hence, they are all public, official letters; they were designed to be read in church services and to be passed on (1 Thess. 5:27). But Philemon is probably an exception to this rule.

epistolē is only once found in a metaphorical sense (2 Cor. 3:2 f.), but this instance is of great importance. When one thinks of the technique of dictating a letter at that time – slow writing on rough papyrus with thick ink, while the thought

247

of the one dictating outran the scribe – the passage suggests that in this section two pictures are here being interwoven, one derived from what had already been written, and the other from what had formed itself in the author's mind (cf. 1 Cor. 3:9).

The former picture, "you are our letter," refers back to the practice of his enemies just mentioned (travelling prophets claiming to be Christians but propagating their particular views, referred to scornfully by Paul as "so many" in 2:17 and "some" in 3:1). They obtained letters of recommendation from the churches to establish their *hikanotēs*, sufficiency, ability (3:5), so that they might be paid accordingly (2:17). *hikanotēs*, ability, refers presumably to their ability to make an imposing appearance, and to attract by their oratory and the wonder and thrill of their message (cf. 1 Cor. 1:26–29; 2:1 f.). Paul rejected them brusquely. His ability was from God, and that was only for service (3:6). The local → church itself in its spiritual and historical existence is his letter of recommendation, composed by the exalted Lord and written "with the spirit of the living God," with the freedom experienced and lived out under the lordship of Christ (3:17). Paul was only the secretary (3:3), through whose weak help a church had come into existence and lived, and the miracle of a new creation had come into being (5:17).

This introduces the second picture: the letter is "written on our (NEB; RSV "your") heart . . . not on tablets of stone, but on tablets of human hearts" (3:2 f.). Looking back to Ezek. 11:19 and Jer. 31:31–34, Paul prepares for the theme of the section immediately following: the letter (the Old Covenant apart from the Spirit) and the Spirit (the New Covenant in the Spirit). The church's attestation of the New Covenant lies in its spiritual existence, in which the Gospel of the cross puts an end to all self-glorification and unbridled speculation. In it the Crucified and Exalted One is alone Lord and awaited as the coming Judge (1 Cor. 2:2; 2 Cor. 5:10, 15). 2 Cor. 3:2 f. is concerned with what Calvin called the *testimonium Spiritus Sancti internum* (the inner testimony of the Holy Spirit) (cf. 1 Cor. 2:15 ff.). If one reads the letter, that is, the church, unspiritually, then one merely establishes the external fact of its existence. In fighting the fight of faith, the church is deprived of all tangible security and proof. It is a conflict between life and death, salvation and destruction (2:15 f.). Paul's polemic gained its seriousness and its clarity from his realization of this fact.   G. Finkenrath

→ Teach, → Scripture, → Proclamation, → Witness, → Word

On *biblos*: (a). J. B. Bauer, "Book," *EBT* I 84 ff.; F. W. Beare, "Bible," *IDB* I 407; F. F. Bruce, *The Books and the Parchments*, 1963³; F. F. Bruce and E. G. Rupp, eds., *Holy Book and Holy Tradition*, 1968; *The Cambridge History of the Bible*, I, ed. P. R. Ackroyd and C. F. Evans, 1970; II, ed. G. W. H. Lampe, 1969; III, ed. S. L. Greenslade, 1963; F. G. Kenyon, *Books and Readers in Ancient Greece and Rome*, 1951²; and *Our Bible and the Ancient Manuscripts*, rev. A. W. Adams, 1958; C. H. Roberts, *The Codex*, 1954; G. Schrenk, *biblos, biblion*, *TDNT* I 615–20.
(b). H. Bietenhard, *Die himmlische Welt im Urchristentum und Spätjudentum*, *WUNT* 2, 1951; P. Glaue, *Die Vorlesung heiliger Schriften im Gottesdienst*, 1907; C. F. G. Heinrici, *Der literarische Charakter der neutestamentlichen Schriften*, 1908; F. Maass, A. Jepsen, R. Meyer and W. G. Kümmel, "Bibel," *RGG³* I 1123–41; E. Norden, *Die antike Kunstprosa vom VI. Jahrhundert vor Christi bis zur Zeit der Renaissance*, 1898, especially 492–510; H. Stoeve and E. Nestle, "Bibelkanon," *EKL* I 448 ff.
On *anaginōskō*: R. Bultmann, *anaginōskō*, *TDNT* I 343 f.; F. X. J. Exler, *The Form of the Ancient Greek Letter: A Study in Greek Epistolography*, 1923.
On *epistolē*: (a) K. Aland, "The Problem of Anonymity and Pseudonymity in Christian Literature in the First Two Centuries", *JTS* New Series 12, 1961, 39–49 (reprinted in *The Authority and*

Integrity of the New Testament SPCK Theological Collections 4, 1965, 1–13); L. G. Champion, *Benedictions and Doxologies in the Epistles of Paul*, Dissertation Heidelberg, 1934; A. Deissmann, *Bible Studies*, 1901, 1–59; and *Light from the Ancient East*, 1911², 143–246; D. Guthrie, "The Development of the Idea of Canonical Pseudepigrapha in New Testament Criticism", *Vox Evangelica* 1, 1962, 43–59 (reprinted in *The Authority and Integrity of the New Testament*, 1965 14–39); and *New Testament Introduction*, 1970³, 671–84; W. G. Kümmel, *Introduction to the New Testament*, 1966, 176 ff.; W. M. Ramsay, *The Letters to the Seven Churches*, 1905; J. T. Sanders, "The Transition from Opening Epistolary Thanksgiving to Body in the Letters of the Pauline Corpus," *JBL* 81, 1962, 348 ff.; P. Schubert, "Form and Function of the Pauline Letter," *JR* 19, 1939, 367–77; O. J. F. Seitz, "Letters," *IDB* III 113 ff.; P. Schubert, *Form and Function of the Pauline Thanksgivings*, *BZNW* 20, 1939.
(b). G. Beer, *Zur israelitisch-jüdischen Briefliteratur*, 1913; C. J. Bjerkelund, *Parakalō. Form, Funktion und Sinn der Parakalō-Sätze in den paulinischen Briefen*, 1967; A. Brunot, *La Génie Littéraire de S. Paul*, 1955; E. Fascher, "Briefliteratur," *RGG³* I 1412 ff.; D. Georgi, *Die Gegner des Paulus im 2. Korintherbrief, Studien zu religiösen Propaganda in der Spätantike*, 1964, 246 ff.; E. Käsemann, "Die Legitimität des Apostels. Eine Untersuchung zu 2 Kor. 10–13," *ZNW* 41, 1942, 58 ff.; W. G. Kümmel, "Paulusbriefe," *RGG³* V 197 f.; E. Lohmeyer, "Briefliche Grussüberschriften," *Probleme paulinischer Theologie*, 1955, 7 ff.; A. Meyer, "Religiöse Pseudepigraphie als etisch-psychologisches Problem", *ZNW* 35, 1936, 262 ff.; B. Olsson, *Papyrusbriefe aus der frühesten Römerzeit*, 1925; K. H. Rengstorf, *epistellō*, TDNT VII 593 ff.; O. Roller, *Das Formular der paulinischen Briefe*, *BWANT* 4. Folge, 6, 1933; J. Schneider, *RAC* II 564 ff.; A. Sint, *Pseudonymität im Altertum*, 1960; W. Straub, *Die Bildersprache des Apostels Paulus*, 1937, 82 f.; J. Sykutris, "Epistolographie," Pauly-Wissowa, Suppl. V 186–220; P. Wendland, *Die urchristlichen Literaturformen*, 1912² (*Handbuch* I, 3, 342 ff.); S. Witkowski, *Epistulae Privatae Graecae*, 1906.

Bread, Daily, Manna

The following arts. deal not only with *artos*, bread, but also with *epiousios*, daily, found only in the Lord's Prayer, and *manna*. The latter looks back to the wilderness wanderings, but has a spiritual significance in the NT. The two nouns denote both food for the body and that which sustains spiritual life.

ἄρτος

ἄρτος (*artos*), bread, loaf.

CL The etymology of the word is uncertain. Even before Homer *artos* was used for bread baked from various kinds of flour. Together with meat it was the most important form of food.

OT Bread was the chief food of Israel. Originally it was made from barley flour mixed with broad beans, lentils, etc., for Palestine was a poor country. Later wheat bread became more common, but only the better off could afford it. Barley bread remained the food of the poor. Bread is used of food in general in 1 Sam. 20:34. ([Tr.] the Arabic equivalent of Heb. *lehem*, bread, means meat.) Both forms of bread were made from ground grains to which leaven had normally been added. The bread was baked on a griddle (Lev. 2:5), or in clay ovens, more or less cylindrically shaped (Hos. 7:4, 6 f.). The flat loaves were about half an inch thick and could be as much as twenty inches in diameter. There was generally a hole in the middle to make it easier to pull them apart for eating, for bread was never cut. Bread was not merely the basic food. It was also served in eating other foods, e.g. meat or fish, which were wrapped in it and so eaten.

249

When there was an unexpected guest (Gen. 19:3), or when people were busy as at harvest time (Ruth 2:14), bread was baked from unleavened dough, or the grain was simply eaten roasted. Because the latter kept almost indefinitely, it was taken on sudden journeys (cf. 1 Sam. 17:17). The use of unleavened bread in this connection is linked especially with the Exodus from Egypt (Exod. 12:8, 11, 34, 39). The festival of Unleavened Bread (*maṣṣôt*) in Exod. 12:14–20; 13:3–10 is derived from this. Its observance meant the cultic representation of the divine rescue from Egypt year by year.

In the Israelite sacrificial system flour or bread found a place as gifts in the cereal offering (*minḥâh*, cf. Lev. 2) which was pre-Mosaic in its origin. The twelve loaves of "the Bread of the Presence" (AV, RV "shewbread") were placed on a special table in the sanctuary (Exod. 25:30; 1 Chr. 28:16). They were of unleavened bread and were placed as an offering before "the Presence" of Yahweh.

In the early rabbinic period, when guests were present, the head of the house took the loaf from the table in front of him and pronounced the blessing, "Blessed be the Lord, our God, the King of the universe, who has caused bread to spring out of the earth". The guests answered, "Amen". The host then gave a piece of bread to each of the guests, and then ate first himself. Jesus, who was firmly rooted in Jewish tradition, used this blessing, as is suggested both in the accounts of the feeding of the five and four thousand (Mk. 6:41 par.; 8:6 par.) and of the Last Supper (→ Lord's Supper).

NT Since bread was the main item of food in biblical lands in NT times, it was often used as a synonym for food and the support of life in general quite apart from its lit. meaning. The prodigal son in the far country remembers that his father's paid servants "have bread enough and to spare," i.e. "have more food than they can eat" (NEB, Lk. 15:17). Hence, to eat bread means to have a meal (cf. Isa. 65:25). To break one's bread for the hungry means to feed and care for him (Isa. 58:7, 10). Not to eat another's bread without paying means working with one's own hands, so as not to be a burden to others (2 Thess. 3:8). To eat no bread and drink no wine means living as an ascetic (Lk. 7:33). The fourth petition of the Lord's Prayer (Matt. 6:11) is concerned with "all things that be needful both for our souls and bodies" (Prayer Book Catechism). "He who shall eat bread in the kingdom of God" (Lk. 14:15) will share in the festival meal of rejoicing in heaven. In quoting Deut. 8:3, "Man does not live by bread alone," Jesus was referring to material things in general, to which he opposed the life-sustaining power of the word of God (Matt. 4:4).

The stories of the miraculous feeding of the five thousand (Matt. 14:13–21 par.) and of the four thousand (Matt. 15:32–39 par.), where with a few loaves and a couple of fishes many were fed, are found in six accounts. They show that Jesus as the Messianic Lord gives the true bread of life. In Jn. the story of the feeding and Jesus' walking on the lake is followed by the revelation of Jesus as the bread of life. Behind the concept of the bread of life lies the ancient and wide-spread desire for a food which imparts everlasting life. This explains the request, "Lord, give us this bread always" (Jn. 6:34). Jesus' answer was: I am what you are asking for. He who wants to share in this eternal life must know that Jesus himself is the bread and that he will give it to those who come to him. In saying this, he opposes all those who claim to be or to have the bread of life. There is only one possibility through which life

250

is given to the world. "The bread of God is the Revealer, who comes from heaven and gives life to the world" (R. Bultmann, *The Gospel of John*, 228). In this way the question about the meaning and goal of life finds its answer.

For all passages about bread in the Last Supper (Mk. 14:22 par.; Acts 2:42; 1 Cor. 10:16; 11:23) → Lord's Supper. *F. Merkel*

| ἐπιούσιος | ἐπιούσιος (*epiousios*), daily. |

epiousios, daily, is linked with *artos* in the fourth petition of the Lord's Prayer. Apart from Matt. 6:11 and Lk. 11:3 it is found only once in a papyrus of the fifth cent. A.D., where its meaning is far from certain. Otherwise it is unknown to secular Gk. and the LXX, though in the latter there is the presumably related *epiousa*. Hence the translation and interpretation of the term has been a matter of controversy from early times, but the rendering "daily" is found already in Tertullian (2nd cent. A.D.). Four possibilities emerge from the long debate.

1. The term is derived from *hē epiousa hēmera*, the next day (cf. Acts 7:26), *epiousa* being the part. of *epeimi*, approach. Jerome (c. A.D. 380) claims to have seen in the Gos. Heb. the word *māhār* in its version of the prayer, the next day, tomorrow. In that case *epiousios artos* would mean bread for tomorrow. Matt. 6:34 would seem to contradict this: "do not worry about tomorrow." But the use of *epiousa hēmera* in Prov. 27:1 shows that it does not necessarily mean tomorrow, but can indicate the coming day in general, which could be today. Hence a number render Matt. 6:11 and Lk. 11:3 bread for the coming day (e.g. F. V. Filson (*BNTC*), J. Schniewind, K. H. Rengstorf (*NTD*)). One should remember, however, that there is no certainty that the Gos. Heb. is necessarily original. It may be secondary retranslation. ([Tr.] RV mg., RSV mg., NEB mg., all have "our bread for the coming day", or "the morrow").

2. Origen suggested that we should understand it as *epi tēn ousian*, (the bread) necessary for existence. Since Origen's mother tongue was Gk. we cannot deny the linguistic possibility of his interpretation. It can be supported by reference to Prov. 30:8, and it reminds us of Exod. 16:4. The Israelites were to gather only so much manna as they needed for the day (cf. SB I 420 f). So also the disciples should pray daily (Lk. 11:3) for the bread needed for life. Among those accepting this meaning are Phillips and SB.

3. Some have taken the first interpretation and have tried to reinterpret it in terms of the final consummation. The morrow which Jesus had in mind is not the next day, but the great morning of the final fulfilment (cf. J. Jeremias, *The Prayers of Jesus*, 1967, 98–104). It is the day when Jesus with his disciples will eat the bread of life, the heavenly manna, in eternity (Lk. 22:30; Matt. 26:29; Rev. 2:17). The disciples were to pray for this bread. The church Fathers similarly linked the fourth petition with the Christ who imparts himself in the Lord's Supper as "the bread of life" (Jn. 6:35) ([Trs.] so Jerome with his rendering "*supersubstantialis*"). Although these gifts for salvation may be included in the fourth petition, in the light of Matt. 6:25–33 we cannot doubt that Jesus was thinking first of all of earthly bread.

251

4. K. G. Kuhn believes that the translator chose the unknown *epiousios* to bring out a special stress in the Aram. (*Achtzehngebet und Vaterunser und der Reim, WUNT* 1, 1950). A reconstruction of the original text suggests that the word was *l^eyômā*'. This had a double meaning which could be expressed in Gk. only by combining two terms (*artos*) *epiousios* (our bread) in so far as it is needed for the day, and *sēmeron*, for today. Then the daily prayer for bread sufficing for the day would not merely be a constant reminder to the disciples of God's fatherly faithfulness. It would also remind them that in the new age, which had already begun and whose consummation could be expected at any time, prayer for provision for a longer period could no longer concern the disciples. (A full discussion with bibliography will be found in Arndt, pp. 296 f.)   *W. Mundle*

| μάννα | μάννα (*manna*), manna.

ot Heb. *mān* is a pre-Israelite name for the sap which is sucked from the manna-tamarisk in the Sinai desert in the rainy season by a kind of scale insect which drops in the form of small, very sweet, little balls to the ground. It is there collected by ants, but melts and disperses in the heat of the midday sun. That it was this phenomenon that the Israelites met in the desert as a helping miracle from God has been considered certain since Josephus (*Ant.*, 3, 1, 6) and Origen. It is also supported by the Gk. *manna*, crumb, and modern scientific investigations (cf. F. S. Bodenheimer, "The Manna of Sinai", *BA* 10, 1947, 1.)

Exod. 16:15 offers a Heb. etymological explanation of the name, expressing the amazement of the people: *mān hû'*, what is it? Our information comes from several sources. In Num. 11:4–9 the people grow tired of it, and quails are sent, but in Exod. 16 both come on the same day. According to this (v. 35) Israel lived on it for 40 years. This does not imply that this was the people's sole source of food, for we are told that they brought their flocks and herds with them out of Egypt (cf. Exod. 12:38). In addition they would find other food in oases (Exod. 15:27) and from defeated enemies (Num. 31:25–41). But this is no diminution of the OT's feeling for the miracle of the food received which had kept Israel from perishing of hunger.

Exod. 16 and Num. 11 are concerned only with the actual food. Deut. 8:3 uses the memory of the miraculous food to stress that "man does not live by bread alone, but . . . by everything that proceeds out of the mouth of the Lord" (cf. Matt. 4:4 par.). The concept was increasingly spiritualized. We can see this in Ps. 78:24 f., where the *mān* is called the grain of heaven and the bread of the angels, and where it is used together with God's other gracious acts to his people as symbolic of divine salvation.

In Jewish apocalyptic and haggadic literature (SB II 481 f.) manna plays a considerable part. On the one hand, it is linked with the tradition that the Messiah will bring back the ark and its contents, which had been hidden by the prophet Jeremiah (2 Macc. 2:4 ff.). Rab. tradition based on deduction from Exod. 16:33 included the pot of manna along with the tables of the law (cf. Heb. 9:4). On the other hand, manna is the heavenly bread which will come down from heaven to feed the believers who experience this age (Apc. Bar. Syr. 29:8). ([Trs.] In a tradition at least as old as A.D. 300 the Messiah would parallel Moses in various respects including the giving of manna (SB II 481).)

NT Both concepts probably lie behind Rev. 2:17. "To him who conquers – and has not eaten food sacrificed to idols (2:14) – I will give some of the hidden manna." He will be saved and live. Preservation of manna in the tabernacle is mentioned in Heb. 9:4 (cf. Exod. 16:32 ff.).

In Jn. 6:31–34 the Jews refer to the belief that the miracle of the manna will be repeated in the Messianic age. The "second" redeemer, the Messiah, must do the same act as the "first" redeemer, Moses (see above OT). Jesus rejected this parallelism by pointing out that it was not Moses, but God himself, who had given the bread in the wilderness.

In Jn. 6:49–51a the manna of the wilderness wanderings is contrasted with the true bread from heaven. The manna had not kept those who had eaten it from dying. True bread from heaven is that which alone can impart eternal life. This can be found only in the one who says of himself, "I am the living bread which came down from heaven" (Jn. 6:51). That which had been said of the bread from heaven had become a reality in the Revealer, Jesus Christ.   *F. Merkel*

→ Hunger, art. *esthiō*, → Life, → Lord's Supper

(a). Arndt, 110, 296 f. (extensive references to literature on *epiousios*), 491 f.; H. F. Beck, "Bread of Presence," *IDB* I 464; J. Behm, *artos*, *TDNT* I 477 f.; F. Bodenheimer, "The Manna of Sinai," *BA* 10, 1947, 1 ff.; P. Borgen, *Bread from Heaven: On the Midrashic Exposition of the Manna pericope in the Homilies of Philo and the Gospel of John*, 1965; E. E. Brown, *The Gospel according to John (i-xii)*, 1966, 260–304; R. Bultmann, *The Gospel according to John*, 1971, 218–37; W. Foerster, *epiousios*, *TDNT* II 590–99; J. Jeremias, *The Prayers of Jesus*, 1967, 98–104; H. J. Held, "Matthew as Interpreter of the Miracle Stories," in G. Bornkamm, G. Barth and H. J. Held, *Tradition and Interpretation in Matthew*, 1963, 165–299; J. P. Hyatt, *Exodus*, 1971; E Lohmeyer, *The Lord's Prayer*, 1965, 134–59; W. Lüthi, *The Lord's Prayer*, 1961, 37–45; B. M. Metzger, "How many times does *epiousios* occur outside the Lord's Prayer?" in *Historical and Literary Studies*, 1968, 64 ff.; R. Meyer, *manna*, *TDNT* IV 462–66; J. L. Mihelic, "Manna," *IDB* III 259 f.; L. Morris, *The Gospel according to John*, 1971, 361–81; M. Noth, *Exodus*, 1962; J. F Ross, "Bread," *IDB* I 461–64; G. Vermes, " 'He is the Bread': Targum Neofiti Exodus 16:15," in E. E. Ellis and M. Wilcox, *Neotestamentica et Semitica: Studies in Honour of Matthew Black*, 1969, 256–63.
(b). F. Bodenheimer and O. Theodor, *Ergebnisse der Sinaiexpedition 1927*, 1929; J. Feliks, "Manna," *BHHW* II 1141 ff.; G. Friedrich, "Die beiden Erzählungen von der Speisung in Mk. 6, 30–44; 8, 1–9," *ThZ* 20, 1964, 10 ff.; F. Hauck, *artos epiousios*, *ZNW* 33, 1934, 199 ff.; H. Kaiser, *Der heutige Stand der Manna-Frage*, 1924, 99 ff.; J. Knackstedt, "Die beiden Brotvermehrungen im Evangelium," *NTS* 1, 1963–64, 309 ff.; K. G. Kuhn, *Achtzehngebet und Vaterunser und der Reim*, 1950, 35 ff.; J. Rogge, "Brot," *BHHW* I 274; H. Schürmann, *Das Gebet des Herrn*, 1958, 63 ff.

Broad, Wide

πλάτος

πλάτος (*platos*), breadth, width; πλατύνω (*platynō*), make broad, enlarge, open out; πλατύς (*platys*), broad, wide.

CL & OT *platos* is found in secular Gk. from Herodotus to the 2nd cent A.D., the LXX, Philo and Josephus. The vb. *platynō* occurs in secular Gk. from Xenophon to Plut. and Epictetus, the LXX, and Josephus, and means lit. to widen; pass. to grow wide, be opened; and in a transferred sense to open (the heart) and to expand (the understanding). *platys*, wide or level, occurs in secular Gk. from Homer onwards, the LXX, Philo and Josephus. In an extended sense it can mean widespread, strong (oaths), brackish or flat (of the sea).

NT *platos* occurs only at Eph. 3:18; Rev. 20:9; and 21:16. In Eph. 3:18 "breadth," together with length, height and depth, represents the universe of experience known in God. This conception is found also in Stoicism, later gnosticism and in magical formulae (cf. K. Preisendanz, *Papyri Graecae Magicae*, 4, 970, 978: "Let there be light, width, depth, length, height, dawn"). "It may refer to the cross of Christ, symbol of that love, seen as stretching out towards all points of the universe" (J. L. Houlden, *Paul's Letters from Prison*, 1970, 304). Rev. 21:16 simply means "breadth." At Rev. 20:9, RSV translates "the broad earth", lit. "the breadth of the earth." This phrase, as used in Dan. 12:2 LXX ("dust of the earth"), denotes the place of the dead awaiting everlasting life or everlasting contempt. Its use in Rev. is contested. It may mean that there is enough room for large armies or for Satan (cf. Arndt, 672). However, M. Rissi sees it as "the middle of the world . . . which is the place of the church of the millennium", though without specific geographical reference (*The Future of the World: An Exegetical Study of Revelation 19:11–22:15*, 1972, 35).

platynō in Matt. 23:5 ("They do all their deeds to be seen by men; for they make their phylacteries broad and their fringes long" RSV) may refer to ostentatious wearing of wider straps (D. Hill, *Matthew*, 1972, 310), or to larger leather cases containing texts (cf. Exod. 13:16). In using the words "open out" at 2 Cor. 6:11, 16, Paul is demonstrating, and appealing for, a show of generous, expansive affection. The words, but not the sense, are taken from Ps. 119(118):32 (cf. C. K. Barrett, *The Second Epistle to the Corinthians*, 1973, 191).

platys is found only at Matt. 7:13 (in the fem. form) where it refers either to a road (some manuscripts omit "gate") and thus means wide or level, or to a gate (most manuscripts) and means wide. For the road to destruction see Ps. 1:6; Prov. 13:15; 14:12; Sir. 21:10; cf. also Sl. Enoch 30:15; → Destroy. The saying graphically states the cruciality of response and the need of the hearer to separate from the masses who follow the easy way which leads to destruction.   *G. T. D. Angel*

Brother, Neighbour, Friend

The first two terms in this article denote those who stand in an immediate blood, or human, relationship to us. *adelphos*, brother, was originally a term denoting family relationships, but early on it became a synonym for *plēsios*, neighbour, with its much wider meaning. *hetairos* means comrade, companion, friend.

ἀδελφός

ἀδελφός (*adelphos*), brother; ἀδελφή (*adelphē*), sister; ἀδελφότης (*adelphotēs*), brotherhood; φιλάδελφος, (*philadelphos*), loving one's brother or sister; φιλαδελφία (*philadelphia*), love for brother, or sister, Philadelphia; ψευδάδελφος (*pseudadelphos*), false brother.

CL *adelphos* is compounded from *delphys*, the womb, and the copulative *a*, and hence means one born from the same womb. It was originally used for brother in the physical sense, while *adelphē* was a lit. sister. The masc. plural could cover all the children of a family.

Nevertheless, it came to signify all near relatives, e.g. nephew, brother-in-law, etc. The adj., identical in form, meant also related, similar, of one mind. Presumably the wider meanings of the adj. led to a widening of the meaning of the noun.

In Gk. literature *adelphos* is used for a physical brother or close relation, and metaphorically for companion, friend, fellow-man. In addressing letters, it was also applied to a fellow-official or a fellow-member of a society.

It would seem that the use of *adelphos* for a "brother" in faith was first introduced under Eastern influence. The term was widely used in the Baal cults. The successors of Alexander the Great granted the title brother as a mark of honour. In the Mithras cult the initiates were called "brothers". At the head of its priests was the *pater fratrum*, the father of the brothers. Stoic philosophy, with its deeper sense of brotherhood, calls for special mention. Brotherhood is here to be understood from the standpoint of a universal humanity. Brothers are those who live together according to the world-reason. From the standpoint of the monism of the spirit (Plotinus), everything in the world can become *adelphoi*.

OT 1. *adelphoi* is used for the Heb. *'āh*; *plēsion*, neighbour, represents *rēc'*. *adelphos* is used first of all for a physical brother, and *adelphē* for a physical sister (Gen. 4:8 ff.; 12:13; 44:20). Gen. 29:12 ff. indicates that it could be applied to other relatives as well.

Examples also occur of brother being used for fellow Israelites. We can explain relationship in the people being valued as much as relationship through blood by remembering that Jacob's sons were also ancestors of the tribes. The OT genealogies often refer to tribal relationships, though the terminology of blood relationship is generally used. In Exod. 2:11 Moses' fellow Hebrews are called brothers (RSV "his people"; cf. Gen. 16:12; Deut. 2:4). In Gen. 19:7 Lot calls the Sodomites brothers. Hosea uses the terms son and brother in his picture of God's relationship to his people (1:10–2:1 (2:1–3)). Here we see the transference of brother from physical to spiritual relationship. When used only in a religious sense, the thought of physical relationship disappears. Deut 15:1 ff. demands love for the poor brother. Here brother and neighbour become synonymous. In Ps. 22:22 brothers are in parallelism with the congregation of Israel. In the command to love (Lev. 19:17 f.) brother and neighbour are used interchangeably. The difference between *plēsion* and *adelphos* in the OT is that the latter also includes blood relationship. In the religious use there is hardly any difference. *plēsion* is a more colourless term and can be translated simply "the other" (cf. 1 Sam. 15:28; 28:17).

2. This usage also occurs in some late Jewish writings. In the Qumran texts love for the brother or the neighbour is constantly demanded. But these terms refer only to members of the Qumran community which considered itself the true Israel. They could hate all others.

The rabbis distinguished between brother and neighbour. National and religious community were no longer considered one as in the OT. Brother was the adherent to Judaism in contrast to the stranger living in the land who did not belong to the people of God. The full proselyte was also a brother. By contrast the neighbour was the inhabitant who was a non-Israelite (cf. SB I 276).

255

NT In the NT *adelphos* means literally a brother, *adelphē* a sister. But it is frequently impossible to establish whether they do not represent another close relationship, though the interpretation of full blood relationship is the more likely. This is particularly the case with the statements about the brothers and sisters of Jesus (Mk. 6:3 par.; 3:31–35 par.).

The assertion of the virginity of Mary both before and after the birth of Jesus was early on taken to mean that the brothers and sisters of Jesus mentioned in the NT were simply close relatives. Gk., Heb. and Aram. linguistic usage would allow such an interpretation. But in no case in the NT can *adelphos* be interpreted with certainty in this sense.

To this day the Orthodox churches understand the brothers and sisters of Jesus as children of Joseph by an earlier marriage. Roman Catholic interpretation tries to prove that they were male and female cousins of Jesus. This interpretation goes back to the ante-Nicene Church, but Tertullian could still speak of later children of Joseph and Mary. (Cf. H. von Soden, *TDNT* I 145; *LTK*² II 714 ff.; J. B. Bauer, *EBT* I 86 ff.)

The gospels indicate that Jesus had a number of brothers and sisters who, according to Mk. 3:31–35 and Jn. 7:5, did not recognize his mission, or did so only later (cf. Acts 1:14; 1 Cor. 9:5). According to Gal. 1:19 (cf. 1 Cor. 15:7), James, the brother of the Lord, belonged to the circle of the → apostles.

2. The use of brother for fellow Israelites in the OT is taken up in the NT. Christians are the new people of God (2 Cor. 6:16 ff.; 1 Pet. 2:9 f.; Heb. 8:8–12; cf. also Rom. 9–11). Hence the term brother was applied to fellow Christians. The decision of the apostolic council explicitly applied the term to Gentile Christians (Acts 15:23).

The NT uses the terminology of the family of God far more commonly than that of the people of God. God is the Father. Through faith in Jesus Christ Christians become his sons and daughters (cf. Rom. 8:14; 2 Cor. 6:18; Gal. 3:26 → Child, art. *hyios*). They are also called his children (Rom. 8:16 f.; Jn. 1:12 f. → Child, art. *teknon*). All this makes intelligible the use of *adelphos* as a title for a brother in the faith. The children of God are his household (Gal. 6:10; Eph. 2:19).

The coming of Jesus underlines the sharp distinction between relationship to God and relationship by birth. The birth narratives show this by their reserve in their statements about paternity. Joseph as father slips into the background behind the fatherhood of God. The conflict also becomes clear in the story of the twelve-year-old Jesus in the Temple (Lk. 2:41–51). Later Jesus himself pointed up the tension (Mk. 3:31–35 par.; 3:3 ff. par.; 13:12 f. par.). He demanded that one should leave one's natural family for the new community. This applied to the disciples as well as to Jesus himself (Mk. 10:28 ff. par.; Lk. 14:26; cf. Rom. 8:12–17).

Jesus is the only-begotten, first-born, beloved Son of God. But he is also the first-born brother of Christians (Rom. 8:29), "the first-born of all creation" (Col. 1:15; cf. 1:18), and "the first-born of the dead" (Rev. 1:5).

In his humiliation the Son of God became the brother of believers (Heb. 2:11 f.). In this sense Jesus can speak of his disciples as his brothers (Mk. 3:33 ff. par., etc.). Yet this designation of Jesus as brother occurs only in passages where his humiliation is stressed (cf. Heb. 2:17). Even as brother he always remains the Lord. So

Paul calls himself the *doulos*, slave of Christ, and the *adelphoi* he entitles *syndouloi*, fellow slaves (Col. 1:7; 4:7).

3. Rom. 8:29 makes it clear that this new standing as brothers has been made possible by the first-born of the brothers, Jesus Christ, who died for them all. Because he became our brother, we are brothers among ourselves. The ruling principle in this brotherhood is *agapē* (→ love; cf. esp. 1 Jn.). When Paul addresses Christians as *adelphoi* (plur.), he prefers to add *agapētoi*, beloved (1 Cor. 15:58; Phil. 4:1). The use of *adelphoi* for brother in faith is also common in other religions. The specific Christian understanding of brotherhood is expressed by linking it with *agapē*. The spiritual community is based on the love of God, which creates a new reality from God among men.

Love as typified in natural relationships is sometimes expressed by *philia* (→ Love). *philia* is found in the vocabulary of the NT in Jas. 4:4 (love of the world) and in compound terms like *philadelphos*, loving the brethren (1 Pet. 3:8), and *philadelphia*, love of the brethren (Rom. 12:10). It has been attracted to the superior concept of *agapē* and, applied to love among men, has become a synonym of it. The same is true of the concept *adelphotēs*, brotherhood (1 Pet. 2:17; 5:9). Philadelphia is one of the seven churches in Rev. (1:11; 3:7). It is praised for its patient endurance.

The love demanded for one's brother involves willingness to share the fate of Jesus Christ even in a martyr's death (1 Jn. 3:16; cf. Jn. 15:13 with 1 Cor. 8:11).

Linguistic usage in Acts does not necessarily have this theological colouring, as it is clearly related to Jewish practice. Since the apostolic preaching began in the synagogue, the hearers addressed as brothers are fellow Jews (cf. Acts 13:26). It should be noted that Paul does not use the word when speaking to a Gentile audience (Acts 17:22). In the introduction to the epistles this Jewish custom was applied to the Christian community. Paul can casually mention his fellow Israelites as *adelphoi kata sarka*, brothers according to the flesh, just as in 1 Cor. 10:18 he mentions Israel *kata sarka*, according to the flesh in contrast to the Israel *tou theou*, of God (Gal. 6:16). (The RSV and NEB rendering of 1 Cor. 10:18 lay no stress on *kata sarka*.) The professing Christian who does not follow the commandments, especially the commandment to love, in his dealings with his brother is still walking in the dark (1 Jn. 2:9). A "so-called" brother is mentioned by Paul in 1 Cor. 5:11 (NEB). Anyone spreading false teaching or accepting it is a *pseudadelphos*, false brother (Gal. 2:3; 2 Cor. 11:26). By his actions he excludes himself from fellowship with God, and no longer belongs to the family of God.

4. It is to be noted that the NT demands love for the brother and love for the neighbour equally. This means that the two terms are considered synonymous as far as their claim upon us is concerned. John uses only *adelphos*.

But we can make a distinction with regard to the object of love. Those passages which demand love for one's neighbour (→ *plēsion*) almost all look directly or indirectly to Lev. 19:18. This presumes that love is to extend beyond the circle of those to whom one is linked by physical or spiritual relationship, i.e. the *adelphia*. There are also cases where *adelphos* refers to more than those who are strictly included in the term. But the use of *plēsion* opens up a much wider sphere. We see in the parable of the Good Samaritan (Lk. 10:29–37) Jesus' *reductio ad absurdum* of the Rab. discussion about who one's neighbour is. Anyone in need is always our

257

neighbour. Since in Matt. 5:43–48 the command to love is extended to include one's enemies, any limits one may give to *adelphos* are completely transcended. The scope of human love is as wide as the scope of God's salvation, which comes to men as a new creation for all, and in its cosmic dimension embraces all things (cf. Matt. 28:18; Col. 1:16 ff.; 3:11). *W. Günther*

→ *plēsion*, → Love, art. *agapē*

ὁ πλησίον

ὁ πλησίον (*ho plēsion*), the neighbour.

CL *plēsios* (from Homer onwards) is connected with *pelas* (near) and *pelazō* (approach, bring near) and means near, nearby. Derivatives are (a) the noun *ho plēsion*, the one standing near, neighbour, fellow man, the nearest, and the rather vague term, the other; (b) the prep. *plēsion* with the gen. (Josephus uses it also with the dat.), nearby (Jn. 4:5).

OT In the vast majority of cases *plēsion* in the LXX represents *rēaʻ* or its derivatives (in five cases it renders *ʼāḥ*) the root of which *rāʻâh* probably means to have to do with another. Hence, it can represent every form of human relationship. In Jdg. 14:20 it means "act as best man." *ʼāḥ* clearly means one related by blood, and *gēr* the stranger living in my neighbourhood. *rēaʻ* means one belonging to my surroundings and life, without any reference to blood relationship or nationality. He is the one with whom I have to do. He is my neighbour (Exod. 11:2), friend (2 Sam. 13:3), fellow (Exod. 2:13; Acts 7:27), fellow man (Prov. 6:1, "another man," NEB), and simply "another" (Hos. 3:1, NEB), all of whom are in practice living in God's covenant.

The appearance of *rēaʻ* in legal texts is also ambiguous. In the law of love (Lev. 19:18) only members of the covenant people are under consideration, as in the law of holiness as a whole. The stranger is not mentioned until vv. 33 f. This suggests that the concept *rēaʻ* passed through the same development as the Law in the history of Israel. At first it meant in practice only those incorporated in the covenant people. But later it came to mean simply one's fellow men. By choosing *plēsion* the LXX arrayed itself with the wider interpretation and was supported by many streams in Hel. Jud. In stricter circles only the Jew and the full proselyte were included under *plēsion*, and in the Qumran community it was confined to its members.

NT The NT does not follow the Qumran usage, but clearly adopts the wider meaning of the LXX. This is seen esp. in Matt. 5:43 ff. and Lk. 10:29–37, which are basic for the interpretation of the command to love. Jesus did not agree with the restriction of Lev. 19:18 to the brother and friend. He demanded the inclusion of even the enemy. However, he gave no wider commandment, but placed the law of love under the gospel. Moreover, the statement "Anyone in need is always my neighbour" is subordinate to the statement "My neighbour is the one who shows me mercy" (cf. Lk. 10:37). As Karl Barth has said, "My neighbour is my fellow-man acting towards me as a benefactor" (CD, I, 2, 420; cf. the whole section, pp. 416–420). In his important theological exposition Barth stresses that the question as to whom I am to love is foolish, because the Samaritan, the former enemy, becomes my neighbour by his compassionate treatment of me and so challenges me to act in love (v. 37). In other words, the experience of being loved comes before the challenge, the encouragement before the claim, and the gospel before the commandment. For Jesus himself is the key to the parable. The phrase "he had compassion on him" (v. 33b → Mercy, art. *sp'anchna*) which in the gospels is applied elsewhere only to Jesus, indicates that Luke saw the figure of Jesus shining through that of the Samaritan. The early church interpreted the parable allegorically of Jesus (cf. C. H. Dodd, *The Parables of the Kingdom* 1936², 11 ff.; W. Monselewski, *Der barmherziger Samariter*, 1967).

The NT combines the two OT commandments of love to God (Deut. 6:5; 10:12) and of love to one's neighbour (Lev. 19:18) into a double commandment (Lk. 10:25 –37; Matt. 22:37 ff. par.; cf. Rom. 13:9; Gal. 5:14; Jas. 2:8). It sees them embodied together in him. Christ awakens love for him in us bruised and miserable men. His call to "Go and do likewise" demands action which is capable of awakening love in my neighbour. This is the meaning given by the gospel to the popular concept of love for one's neighbour. Christ meets me in the other person, whether he is brother or enemy, neighbour or godless, helper or beggar. He gives me his love and fills me with it, so that it flows over to the other. This moves love to my neighbour out of the dangerous region of new legalism, or proud charity, and puts it under the sway of love, which both takes and gives. It opens up a wide sphere of Christian action (Eph. 4:25 ff.) and creates new fellowship and new service of God (Mk. 12:28 ff.; cf. Hos. 6:6).   *U Falkenroth*

ἑταῖρος

ἑταῖρος (*hetairos*), comrade, companion, friend.

CL The noun *hetairos* means "one who is linked to another" in some fashion
   determined only by the context. The link may be military (Homer, Theopompus), religious (*Orientis Graecae Inscriptiones* 573.1), political (Lysias, Thucydides), or simply the bond of friendship or companionship (Plutarch, Philo). It is often used of peers or in reference to inferiors, e.g. pupils are associated by virtue of sharing one teacher (Aristotle, Xenophon, Epictetus), or soldiers are linked together and addressed by a superior officer (Josephus). It does not apply to the superior alone. Metaphorically *hetairos* can be applied to things: wind (Homer), empty-headed ill-will (Pindar), laughter (Plutarch).

OT In the LXX *hetairos* commonly translates Heb. *rēaʻ* (friend, fellow) and its
   cognates, but twice represents *ḥāḇēr* (associate, companion: Cant. 1:7; 8:13). The word is more common in the other Greek translations of the OT, where it occasionally replaces the words *plēsion*, *philos*, and *adelphos* found in the LXX. Philo uses the term of friends and companions, while Josephus applies it not only to soldiers and junior officials, but also to bad company.

In later Judaism, although *ḥāḇēr* continued to mean "friend", "associate", it came to be applied in the Jerusalem Talmud to the qualified teachers who for some reason had not yet been ordained as official rabbis. In Qumran literature, the same Heb. word group refers to anyone in the community, or to the community itself, but not, apparently, in a technical manner.

NT Except for the weakly attested *v.l.* of Matt. 11:16, *hetairos* is found only
   three times in the NT, all three occurrences being in Matt., and all three in the

vocative *hetaire* (20:13; 22:12; 26:50). In each case, the person speaking is addressing an inferior who has insulted him in some way, but the words are without malice. Moreover, the speaker and the person addressed are bound in some sort of relationship, and it is that binding relationship which has suffered an egotistical disregard of what it means. In the two parables the speaker has the last word; in the climactic incident Jesus suffers at the hands of his betrayer, yet nevertheless the impression is unfailingly transmitted that this event still leaves Jesus in control of his destiny (cf. Matt. 26:53; Jn. 10:17 f.). D. A. Carson

(a). Arndt, 15 f., 314, 678 f.; K. Barth, *CD* I, 2, 417 ff.; J. B. Bauer, "Brother," *EBT* I 88 ff.; F. Beck, "Neighbour," *IDB* III 534 f.; H. Greeven and J. Fichtner, *plēsion*, *TDNT* VI 311–15; J. Jeremias, *The Parables of Jesus*, 1963²; G. Johnston, "Brotherhood," "Brotherly Love," *IDB* I 468 f.; J. Ratzinger, *Christian Brotherhood*, 1966; K. H. Rengstorf, *hetairos*, *TDNT* II 699 ff.; H. von Soden, *adelphos*, *TDNT* I 144 ff.; H. Thielicke, *The Waiting Father*, 1960, 158–69; and *Theological Ethics*, I, 1966.

(b). R. Bultmann, "Das christliche Gebot der Nächstenliebe," *Glauben und Verstehen*, I, 1933, 229 ff.; J. Fichtner, "Der Begriff des 'Nächsten' im Alten Testament mit einem Ausblick auf Spätjudentum und Neues Testament," *WuD* Neue Folge 4, 1955, 23–52 (*Gottes Weisheit*, 1965, 88–114); D. J. Georgacas, *Glotta* 36, 1957, 106 ff.; H. Gollwitzer, *Der barmherziger Samariter*, *BSt* 34, 1959; E. P. Groenewald, "Die Christelike Broederskap volgens die Heilige Skrif," *Arcana Revelata*, 1951, 23–32; E. Jenni, *'aḥ*, *THAT* I 98–104; J. Manek, "Mit wem identifiziert sich Jesus? Eine exegetische Rekonstruktion ad Matt. 25:31–46," in B. Lindars and S. Smalley, eds., *Christ and Spirit in the New Testament; In Honour of C. F. D. Moule*, 1973, 15–25; O. Michel, "Das Gebot der Nächstenliebe in der Verkündigung Jesu," *Zur sozialen Entscheidung*, 1947, 53 ff.; W. Monselewski, *Der barmherzige Samariter*, 1967; C. H. Ratschow, "Agape, Nächstenliebe und Bruderliebe", *ZSTh* 21, 150–52; K. H. Schelkle, *RAC* II 631–40; J. Souček, "Der Bruder und der Nächste," *Hören und Handeln* (Wolf Festschrift), 1962; C. Spicq, "La charité fraternelle selon 1 Thess. 4:9," *Festschrift A. Robert*, 1957, 507–11.
→ Literature under Command and Love

Burden, Heavy, Labour

A burden can be both a heavy load and a metaphor for trouble. The Gk. language has four basic words for different kinds of burdens and encumbrances. *baros* means a weight or physical burden, something heavy. *phortos* and *phortion* denote a burden in the sense of a load, something carried. *ponos* denotes labour, toil, and hence pain, distress, affliction. *kopos* was early used in the sense of a stroke. It came to mean trouble, difficulty, work, labour, toil. The use of these words in the NT in a figurative sense points not so much to the psychological overtones associated with them but to the hope of an eschatological conquest of the burdens of life.

| βάρος |

βάρος (*baros*), weight, burden; βαρύς (*barys*), heavy, burdensome, weighty, important, fierce; βαρέω (*bareō*), to load, burden, weigh down; βαρύτιμος (*barytimos*), very expensive or precious; βαρύνω (*barynō*), weigh down; φορτίον (*phortion*), burden, load; φόρτος (*phortos*), burden, cargo; φορτίζω (*phortizō*), to burden, load.

CL *baros* in cl. Gk. and Hel. usage means a weight, heaviness, a burden. *phortos* and its diminutive *phortion* both mean a load or burden carried by an animal or a man, and hence also cargo. These words came to be used interchangeably. The adj. *barys*, heavy, virtually corresponds to the range of meaning of the noun. The vb. *bareō* means to load, burden, weigh down.

ot In the LXX *baros* (Heb. *kāḇôḏ*) and *bareō* (Heb. *kāḇēḏ*; Exod. 7:14; 2 Macc. 13:9) occur only rarely. *barys* (Heb. *kāḇēḏ*) is more frequent. The adv. *bareōs* in conjunction with *akouō* (to hear) denotes being heavy of hearing (Isa. 6:10; cf. Matt. 13:15; Acts 18:27). Isaiah is called to prophesy and make the heart of the people fat, their ears heavy and their eyes shut, "lest they see with their eyes, and hear with their ears, and understand with their hearts, and turn again and be healed." See also the use of this prophecy in Mk. 4:12 and Jn. 12:39 ff.

nt 1. (a) *baros* is used in Matt. 20:12 of the burden of daily toil. The Jerusalem council desired to lay no greater burden on the Gentile Christians than that they should abstain from meat sacrificed to idols, from blood, from what had been strangled, and from unchastity (Acts 15:28 f.). Teaching in Rev. 2:24 is also described as a burden. 2 Cor. 1:8 and 5:4 speak of being burdened (*bareisthai*; RSV "crushed" 1:8) by persecution on the one hand and the general human condition on the other. *bareisthai* is used of the eyes weighted with sleep (Matt. 26:43; Lk. 9:32), of being weighed down with dissipation and drunkenness (Lk 21:34), and of the church being burdened by unnecessary financial demands (1 Tim. 5:16).

(b) While *bareō* is used in the NT only in the passive, compounds are used in the active: *epibareō* (2 Cor. 2:5; 1 Thess. 2:9; 2 Thess. 3:8) and *katabareō* (2 Cor. 12:16). Both mean to burden. *barynō* which has the same meaning in secular Gk. and is frequent in the LXX is found in the NT only as a *v.l.* (Lk. 21:34; Acts 3:14; 28:27; 2 Cor. 5:4). The burdens mentioned in 2 Cor. 1:8 and 5:4 are overcome by confidence in God who raises the dead and by hope of ultimate triumph. "For this slight momentary affliction is preparing for us an eternal weight of glory (*baros tēs doxēs*) beyond all comparison" (2 Cor. 4:17). Paul's use of the word may be influenced by the fact that weight and → glory in Heb. come from the same root *kbd*. In Gal. 6:2 Paul encourages his readers to bear one another's burdens. They ought to come to the aid of one another, if overtaken by a fault. The joint bearing of suffering is not excluded. Such joint bearing does not do away with the personal responsibility of Christians. Consequently, everyone has also to bear his own load (*phortion*, v. 5) before God. In 1 Thess. 2:7 *baros* denotes the weight of authority which Paul might have exerted at Thessalonica, had he so wished. It also denotes the financial burden which he spared them by toiling to support himself (1 Thess. 2:9).

2. (a) The adj. *barys* occurs only 6 times in the NT. In Acts 20:29 false teachers who break into the church are described as "weighty", i.e. fierce or savage, wolves of whom the church must beware. In Acts 25:7 the Jews brought weighty charges against Paul. On the other hand, Paul's opponents at Corinth sneered at his weighty (*bareiai*) letters (2 Cor. 10:10).

(b) Both the burden of suffering and the burden of the Law figure in the teaching of Jesus, the latter especially in his discussions with the scribes and Pharisees. Matt. 23:4 and Lk. 11:46 speak of the heavy burdens which the hypocrites lay upon men without themselves touching them with a finger. They stress the multiplicity of external commandments and leave out of consideration "the weightier matters (*ta barytera*) of the law, justice and mercy and faith" (Matt. 23:23). Here Jesus endorses the early prophetic demand of Mic. 6:8.

261

Compared with the yoke of the interpreters of the law under which Judaism stood, Jesus' yoke (*zygos* → Slave) is easy and his burden (*phortion*) light. For that reason he can call to himself all those who labour and are heavy-laden (*pephortismenoi*) (Matt. 11:28 ff.). There are commandments also for Jesus' disciples. But these commandments are not heavy, for Jesus is jointly yoked with those who heed this call. In the words of 1 Jn. 5:3, "his commandments are not burdensome (*bareiai*)." For the commandments are the enactment of love.   *W. Mundle*

κόπος

κόπος (*kopos*), trouble, difficulty, work, labour, toil; κοπιάω (*kopiaō*), become weary, tired, work hard, toil; πόνος (*ponos*), hard labour, toil, pain, distress, affliction; μόχθος (*mochthos*), labour, exertion, hardship.

CL 1. *kopos* means a striking, beating (Liddell–Scott, 978). It also denotes in the tragic poets striking the breast in lamentation. It then came to denote the physical consequences of a stroke, weariness, depression (cf. Aesch., *Supp.* 206; Plato, *Leg.* 537b). Thus everything that leads to work, exertion, toil, pain and hardship can be called *kopos*. The same applies to the vb. *kopiaō*. It denotes not only the activity of exertion and toil (Aesop, *Fables* 391p) and the process of becoming tired (Aristophanes; Jos., *War* 6, 142; Philo, *Cher.* 41), but also the consequent fatigue and exhaustion.

2. *ponos* is frequently found from Homer onwards as a synonym for *kopos*. *ponos* in Homer denotes physical exertion in war (*ponos machēs*, *Il.* 16, 586; 17, 718). More generally it means work and daily toil (Plato, *Soph.* 230a). In Xenophon it means pain (*Mem.* 2, 2, 5). *ponos* was a favourite term of the Stoics (Epict., *Dissertationes*, 1, 2, 15; 1, 7, 30; 2, 1, 10 and 13 f. and often). It occurs 4 times in the NT (3 times in Rev.). The vb. *poneō* (Pindar onwards) meaning to toil does not occur in the NT. Occasionally from Hesiod onwards *mochthos* is mentioned alongside *kopos* (in the NT only 3 times in Paul).

OT The LXX uses *kopos* chiefly to translate the Heb. '*āmāl*, labour (Ps. 72(73):5), toil (Eccles. 1:3; 2:18–22 translates Heb. '*āmāl* by Gk. *mochthos*), adversity (Jdg. 10:16), trouble (Ps. 10:7, 14; 94:20; Job 5:6 f.). *kopiaō* frequently renders the Heb. *yāḡa'* to grow weary (Isa. 40:28, 30), be weary of (Isa. 43:22), labour (Isa. 49:4; Job 20:18). The ideas are found mostly in later writings, in the later chapters of Isa., the Pss., Job, Sir. and Eccles. They are not spiritualized as in Philo, but give expression to the sober reality of pessimism and resignation. "What does a man gain by all the toil (*mochthos*) at which he toils under the sun?" (Eccles. 1:3; cf. 2:18 ff.). Even the Servant of the Lord laments his toil: "I have laboured in vain, I have spent my strength for nothing and vanity" (Isa. 49:4). The growth of eschatological hope is understandable against this background. Man shall no longer toil in vain (Isa. 65:23). In general the toil of life will be overcome (Jer. 33:24). To those returning from exile Isa. 40:30 f. gives the promise: "Even the youths shall faint and be weary (*kopiaō*), and young men shall fall exhausted; but they who wait for the Lord shall renew their strength (*ischys*), they shall mount up with wings like eagles, they shall run and not be weary, they shall walk and not faint" (→ Bird OT).

NT In the NT *kopos* occurs less than 40 times. It is not common in the gospels, but is frequent in Paul. The following usages may be noted:

1. *kopiaō* is used in the general sense of to labour or toil in everyday work (cf. Matt. 6:28; Lk. 5:5; Rom. 16:6; 1 Cor. 3:8 *kopos*). Jn. 4:38 and 2 Tim. 2:6 refer to labouring in the fields and harvesting, used as a picture of work in the kingdom of God. Work (*kopos*) in Rev. 2:2 and 14:13 has an eschatological significance. It refers to work here and now which has eternal significance but which one day will be over.

2. It also denotes weariness. As was common in the ancient world, Jn. 4:6 speaks of weariness through the exertions of a journey. The church at Ephesus is praised for having borne much persecution without however having become weary (Rev. 2:3). Matt. 11:28 is to be understood eschatologically. Jesus offers those who are are exhausted by the claims of the law an enduring → rest from their toil.

3. Paul uses work in his own particular sense of work in the Lord. *kopos* and *kopiaō* describe his own manual labour (1 Cor. 4:12; 1 Thess. 2:9). He practised this in the context of his missionary calling, to make himself financially independent of the churches. There is therefore a close connection between this and the missionary work to which he was commissioned by God. This missionary activity is likewise designated from time to time by *kopos* and *kopiaō*. For Paul it meant a heavy burden and even blows (2 Cor. 6:5; 11:23, 27), together with the risk of it proving fruitless (Gal. 4:11). On the other hand, it meant the joy of encouragement (1 Cor. 15:10; Phil. 2:16). Its goal was to present every man complete in Christ before God (Col. 1:29; cf. 1 Tim. 4:10).

Other missionaries laboured together with Paul (Rom. 16:12; 1 Cor. 16:16; 1 Thess. 5:12). They laboured "in preaching and teaching" (1 Tim. 5:17) with the same goal and methods. It was a labour of love (1 Thess. 1:3).

M. Seitz, H.-G. Link

(a). Arndt, 133, 444; F. Hauck, *kopos, TDNT* III 827–30; C. Schrenk, *baros, TDNT* I 553–61.
(b). A. von Harnack, "*kopos* im frühchristlichen Sprachgebrauch," *ZNW* 27, 1928, 1 ff.; E. Lohmeyer, *Der Brief an die Kolosser und an Philemon, KEK* 9, 2, 1964¹², 89; SB I 608 ff., II 728, III 577; C. Westermann, *kbd, THAT* I 794–812.

Bury, Grave, Tomb,

| θάπτω |

θάπτω (*thaptō*), bury; τάφος (*taphos*), tomb; ταφή (*taphē*), burial; ἐνταφιάζω (*entaphiazō*), prepare for burial; ἐνταφιασμός (*entaphiasmos*), laying out for burial; μνῆμα (*mnēma*), μνημεῖον (*mnēmeion*), memorial, tomb.

CL (a) *thaptō* in pagan Greek is properly to "honour with funeral rites", whatever the manner of disposal of the dead. Thus the word is used with *hypo chthonos* (under the ground) in Homer, *Od.* 11, 52, and with *pyri* (with fire) in Plutarch, *Mor.* 286 f.

(b) *taphos* and cognates derive from the root of *thaptō*. *taphos* is always "funeral-rites" in Homer, later a regular word for "tomb"; *taphē* is "burial", "funeral", or is used of the place of burial, for a cinerary urn (Sophocles) or even of a "mummy"

263

in the Egyptian papyri. Both words may be used in connection with either inhumation or cremation.

(c) *entaphiazō* and *entaphiasmos* are both relatively rare, and both are applied specifically to instances of inhumation or of embalming, the cognate *entaphiastēs* being an "embalmer" in the papyri.

(d) The Gk. language is rich in other words for "tomb", some euphemistic, others specialized but often used with little significant distinction. Thus *tymbos*, properly a "mound" or "barrow", is used generally for any form of grave. So too *mnēma* and *mnēmeion*, from *mnaomai* (be mindful of).

(e) Both burial and cremation were widespread practices at various dates and places in antiquity. The Homeric heroes were burnt, though their Mycenaean prototypes had been buried. In Greece and Rome alike both modes had a long subsequent history. In the NT period cremation had become almost universal among the Romans (cf. Tacitus, *Ann.* 16, 6), but inhumation again became prevalent from the 2nd century. In the Semitic East burial was always predominant. In Asia Minor the tomb was conceived as the eternal house of the dead.

It is questionable how far religious significance should necessarily be attached to differences in the manner of disposal of the dead, though in some cases, as in Egypt, preservation of the body was seen as all-important, as indispensable to the after-life. Otherwise the emphasis was often more upon the proper care and guardianship of the tomb as a cultic place.

OT 1. (a) OT usage is here open to fairly easy classification. Three words are freely used for "tomb": *taphos*, *mnēma*, and *mnēmeion*. Their distribution varies widely in different sections of the LXX, but all three render the Heb. *qeber* (tomb) and *qᵉbûrâh* (tomb, burial) indiscriminately, apparently according to the preferences of different translators.

(b) *taphē* usually renders the same two Heb. words, and is often likewise for "tomb", sometimes rather "burial". In Gen. 50:2, 3, 26 *entaphiazō*, *taphē* and *thaptō* are successively used to render derivatives of the different Heb. root *ḥānaṭ* (to spice, embalm) in speaking of the embalming of Jacob and of Joseph in Egypt.

(c) In some 60 places English versions use "grave" to represent Gk. *hadēs* (Heb. *šᵉʾôl*, the place of the dead). → death, hell.

(d) *thaptō* (Heb. *qābar*) is otherwise to "bury" throughout the LXX. Inhumation or placing in caves or rock-sepulchres was universal Jewish practice at all periods. Tombs were commonly the communal possession of a family (Gen. 23:4 etc.); there the dead was "gathered to his people" (Gen. 25:8 etc.). The cremation of Saul and his sons (1 Sam. 31:12) was exceptional, and such treatment might be regarded as a shameful abuse (Amos 2:1) or as a solemn punishment (Jos. 7:25). The law required burial of the executed criminal the same day (Deut. 21:23), and the same care was taken to bury enemies slain in battle (1 Ki. 11:15 etc.). To be denied burial was a shameful indignity (Deut. 28:26; 1 Ki. 13:22).

2. The practices of later Judaism were closely based upon the OT and early custom. It was common in the NT period to practise secondary burial, placing the bones in "ossuaries" which were stored in extended family sepulchres, sometimes in niches called *kôkîm* (Lat. *loculi*). Scrupulous care was taken to let none be unburied (Josephus, *contra Apionem* 2, 29, 211 etc.). Rabbinic interpretation of

Deut. 21:23 (Sanhedrin 46b etc.) insisted that burial must be completed if possible on the day of death.

NT (a) In the NT the same three Gk words are used for "tomb" as in the LXX.

mnēmeion occurs 42 times, *mnēma* and *taphos* 7 times each. All alike are used both of the tomb of Jesus and of other tombs, and are variably rendered "grave", "tomb" or "sepulchre" in AV. Matt. accounts for 6 of the occurrences of *taphos*: Jn. has *mnēmeion* exclusively. No significance should be attached to these variations.

(b) In Matt. 23:27 Jesus likens the scribes and Pharisees to "whited sepulchres" (*taphoi kekoniamenoi*; cf. Lk. 11:44). It was the custom to chalk graves on 15th Adar, lest those inadvertently walking over them incur pollution before the Passover (cf. Jn. 11:55; 18:28). In Matt. 23:29–31=Lk. 20:47–48 Jesus alludes further to the scrupulosity of the Pharisees in embellishing the tombs of prophets whom their forebears had rejected and killed. The effective contrast is between their fastidious outward observance of cleanliness and the evil of their inward motives (cf. Rom. 3:13, citing Ps. 5:9, and perhaps also Acts 23:3).

(c) Several NT passages illustrate contemporary practice and feeling about burial. The duty of burial fell upon the family or closest associates of the deceased (Matt. 8:21–22=Lk. 9:59–60; Matt. 14:12; Mk. 6:29). It was carried out with the utmost possible speed (Acts 5:5 ff., presumably by young men of the Christian community). It was deemed a good work to make special provision for the burial of strangers, though with money tainted for other purposes (Matt. 27:8). And in Rev. 11:9 the two witnesses are subjected by their enemies to the final indignity of lying dead and unburied for three days and a half. The fullest accounts of funeral practice are contained in the narratives of Lazarus (John 11) and of Jesus himself.

(d) The raising of Lazarus is important but not without difficulty. Jesus' deliberate delay in answering the summons for his help (Jn. 11:6) has the result that Lazarus had been four days in the tomb at Jesus' arrival (Jn. 11:17). The lapse of time is significant. It was the custom for mourners to visit the dead for the first three days (Semaḥoth 47a), after which interval the progress of decomposition was thought to be irreversible (cf. SB II 544 f.). Hence the action of Jesus demonstrated his absolute mastery over death. The episode is a critical point in Jn., which polarized reactions to Jesus and pointed forward to his own resurrection.

(e) The action of Joseph of Arimathea in initiating the burial of Jesus was an act both of obedience to the Jewish Law and of devotion to one whom he had feared to acknowledge in his life. Deut. 21:22–23 instructs that a man hanged on a tree shall not remain all night there, but be buried the same day, that the land be not defiled, for he is accursed.

Nicodemus brought an enormous quantity of myrrh and aloes for the burial (Jn. 19:39). This evidently accorded with usual practice (cf. Jn. 11:44), except that the sheer quantity of spices represented a costly act of devotion to Jesus, resembling that of Mary (Jn. 12:2–11). Jesus there applied her gift to the theme of his "burial" (*entaphiasmos*, Jn. 12:7), and similar words occur also in the Synoptic parallels (*entaphiasmos*, Mk. 14:8; *entaphiazō*, Matt. 26:12). The Gospel tradition, both Synoptic and Johannine, seems to insist that these acts had a significance which merited their inclusion. We may compare the significant gift of myrrh to the baby Jesus (Matt. 2:11): this was early seen as symbolizing burial and the expectation of resurrection. The Jews did not embalm like the Egyptians, but myrrh and the other aromatic spices represented the preservation of the body, and this to the Jewish mind was the prerequisite of resurrection. Thus Mary and Nicodemus had performed acts more significant than they understood.

(f) The burial of Jesus plays a part in the primitive Christian preaching. Paul stresses it in 1 Cor. 15:4. It was the authentication both of his death and resurrection, both of them foreshadowed in the scriptures. Ps. 16:10 is an important text in the speeches presented in Acts. The words "neither wilt thou suffer thine Holy One to see corruption" were applicable to the risen Christ, but not to David, whose body had seen decay (Acts 13:35–37) and whose tomb remained to that day (Acts 2:27 ff.). The focal burial text, Deut. 21:22–23, likewise recurs but in a new and startling application which avers the treatment of the sin-bearing Jesus as under its curse (cf. Acts 5:30; 10:39; 13:29; Gal. 3:13; 1 Pet. 2:24).

This emphasis on the burial contrasts with a disinterest in the actual tomb. The discovery of the empty tomb is described in all four Gospels, but the subject is not mentioned in 1 Cor. 15, the earliest surviving testimony to the resurrection. That same chapter however insists strongly on the relevance of eye-witness testimony. Paul's argument is that the literal and theological aspects of the resurrection are inseparable. The truth of the fact that Christ is risen cannot be divorced from an event to whose objectivity such testimony was relevant. The paucity of reference to the empty tomb may be explained by the indications that its emptiness was not in dispute; indeed the notoriety of the fact is presupposed in the following narratives.

(g) Matt. 27:52–53 is a notorious difficulty. The point is apparently to show the resurrection of Christ as the prototype of that of the saints.

(h) In Rom. 6:4 and Col. 2:12 burial (*synthaptomai*, be buried with) is used as a figure of baptism. The disciple is represented as identified with his Master in death, burial and risen life. *C. J. Hemer*

H. von Campenhausen, "The Events of Easter and the Empty Tomb", *Tradition and Life in the Church*, 1968, 42–89; K. Kohler, *JE* (1901–6), III 432–437; T. Nicol, *HDB* I 331–333; A. D. Nock, "Cremation and Burial in the Roman Empire", *HTR* 25, 1932, 321–359; reprinted in Nock, *Essays on Religion and the Ancient World*, ed. Z. Stewart (1972); J. Spencer Kennard, "The Burial of Jesus", *JBL* 74, 1955, 227–238; J. M. C. Toynbee, *Death and Burial in the Roman World*, 1971.

Busybody, Meddle

περιεργάζομαι	περιεργάζομαι (*periergazomai*), meddle, be a busybody; περίεργος (*periergos*). meddlesome, a busybody.

CL *periergazomai* is compounded from the prep. *peri* (around, beyond) and the vb. *ergazomai* (work). Its primary meaning is to do superfluous work. In secular Gk. it is sometimes found in a good sense, to investigate thoroughly; but more often it has a bad connotation, to take more pains than necessary, be a busybody. The derived adj. is used similarly to mean either of an enquiring mind, curious (and hence magical; cf. Lat. *curiosus*); or, in a bad sense, officious, meddlesome.

OT In the LXX *periergazomai* only appears in two alternative readings preserved in Origen's *Hexapla*, where it means seek diligently (2 Sam. 11:3; Eccl. 7:30).

periergos does not feature in biblical literature, but Jewish writers preserve both vb. and adj. in their more usual bad sense of meddle and busybody.

NT *periergazomai* is used once in the NT, in 2 Thess. 3:11, where there is a deliberate word-play on *ergazomai*. Paul condemns those whose only business is to be a busybody. The adj. *periergos* occurs twice: once in 1 Tim. 5:13 to describe young women on the church widows' register who become busybodies (as well as idlers and gossips) through having nothing constructive to do; and once in Acts 19:19 with the semi-technical sense of magic arts (cf. CL above).   *D. H. Field*

Buy, Sell, Market

ἀγοράζω

ἀγορά (*agora*), market; ἀγοραῖος (*agoraios*), frequenting the market; ἀγοράζω (*agorazō*), buy; ἐξαγοράζω (*exagorazō*), redeem.

CL Originally any place of public assembly, the *agora* became identified in classical times with the market-place, a centre of community life which was regularly used for political meetings, judicial hearings, and especially for trade. The derived adj. *agoraios* (lit. belonging to the *agora*) is occasionally found in a good sense to describe those who do their business in the market-place (especially advocates in law-suits), but it is applied much more frequently to loafers who hang around the *agora* looking for excitement or trouble. *agorazō*, the vb. (lit., frequent the *agora*), came to mean "buy in the market-place", and thence "buy" in general. In Hellenistic times it was also in common use as a term for buying slaves, which is significant for its NT usage, although the practice of sacral manumission is not clearly linked with *agorazō*. The intensive form *exagorazō* could be applied to the redeeming of slaves (e.g. by Diodorus Siculus in the first century B.C.).

OT In the LXX *agora* is used, by metonymy, to describe the trading activity of Tyre (Ezek. 27:12–22). It is also the place where a girl seeks her lover (Cant. 3:2); and the "shut doors of the *agora*" are used by Eccl. 12:4 as a figure for deafness. Where the vb. *agorazō* is used, the reference is normally to commercial purchase (e.g. Gen. 41:57; Neh. 10:31). Just once, in Lev. 27:19, it translates Heb. *gā'al*, "redeem", but the object here is a field, not a person. The idea of sacral manumission was not a Jewish one. Dan. 2:8 preserves an interesting use of *exagorazō*, where the Chaldaeans attempt to evade their fate by "buying time".

NT The *agora* features several times in the Gospel narrative, and twice more in Acts. It serves as a place for children to play (Matt. 11:16 par.), an employment exchange (Matt. 20:3), a centre of public life where the Pharisees love to be conspicuous (Mk. 12:38 par.), and one focal point of Jesus' healing ministry (Mk. 6:56). Paul found himself on trial in the Philippi *agora* (Acts 16:19), and seized evangelistic opportunities among the crowds in the *agora* at Athens (Acts 17:17). In Acts 17:5 there is a reference to the *agoraioi*, the market-place rabble-rousers; and the adjective *agoraios* reappears in Acts 19:38 in its semi-technical sense of "court-sessions" (*agoraioi hēmerai*).

The verb *agorazō* is found twenty-five times in the NT with its usual commercial

267

meaning, mostly in the Gospels (e.g. Matt. 13:44; Lk. 22:36), but on five other occasions it describes the "buying" of Christians. This clearly reflects the contemporary terminology of the slave-market (see under CL above). In 1 Cor. 6:19; 7:23 (cf. Rev. 14:3) the main point of emphasis is not the freedom of the redeemed (as with other redemption terminology, e.g. → *apolytrōsis*), but their new status as slaves of God, bought with a price to do his will. Hence the sheer effrontery of heretics who "deny the Master who bought them" (2 Pet. 2:1). The price Christ paid for his people is spelled out in Rev. 5:9 ("by thy blood").

exagorazō is also used with this special sense of "redeem" in Gal. 3:13; 4:4, where the idea of escape from the consequences of breaking God's law is added. The intensive form of the verb occurs twice more in Paul's epistles to express the rather different idea of "redeeming the time (*kairos*)" (Eph. 5:16; Col. 4:5). In this context it probably means to "buy up intensively"; i.e., to snap up every opportunity that comes.

πωλέω	πωλέω (*pōleō*), sell; πιπράσκω (*pipraskō*), sell; ἐμπορεύομαι (*emporeuomai*), trade.

CL In secular Gk., *pōleō* and *pipraskō* appear without very much distinction as normal trading terms for "sell". Both could also be used in a bad sense to mean "betray" or "sell for a bribe". *pipraskō* was the word normally used for selling captives or slaves. *emporeuomai* began as a general term for "travel", but by later classical times its meaning was restricted to "travel on business", "trade". It could be used figuratively (e.g. "trade in philosophy"), and in Hellenistic Gk. it sometimes had a bad connotation (e.g. "trade on the forgetfulness of the judges").

OT In the LXX *pōleō* is used for selling either things or people (e.g. Gen. 41:56; Ex. 21:8). *pipraskō* is also found in both senses (especially in the law-codes of Lev. and Deut. to translate the Heb. *mākar*); and it could also be applied figuratively to express the consequences of sin (so God "sells" his people – Isa. 48:10; 50:1, and the individual can "sell himself" to do what is evil – 1 Ki. 20:20; 2 Ki. 17:17; cf. 1 Macc. 1:15). *emporeuomai* normally means "trade" in the LXX (i.e., in the commercial sense, e.g. Gen. 42:34; Amos 8:6). Once it is used figuratively of trading in wisdom (Prov. 3:14).

NT Both *pōleō* and *pipraskō* are regularly employed in the NT as commercial terms for selling commodities (though by no means always for personal gain – cf. Mk. 10:21 par.; Lk. 12:33; Acts 4:34). Only *pipraskō* is used of selling a person – once literally in a Gospel parable (Matt. 18:25), and once figuratively in Rom. 7:14 ("sold under sin"). *emporeuomai* occurs twice in the NT: in Jas. 4:13 it keeps its usual meaning of "engage in trade", but in 2 Pet. 2:3 it is used figuratively, and in a bad sense, to convey the idea of exploitation.   *D. H. Field*

F. Büchsel, *agorazō, exagorazō, TDNT* I 124–28; L. Morris, *The Apostolic Preaching of the Cross*, 1965³, 53–9; H. Preisker, *pipraskō, TDNT* VII 160.

Caesar, Consul, Governor

| _Καῖσαρ_ | _Καῖσαρ_ (_Kaisar_), Caesar, emperor. |

CL "Caesar" was originally a proper name, the family name of the Julian family,
esp. of Julius Caeser, but also of Augustus (so Lk. 2:1). It developed a titular
significance and became equivalent to "the Emperor", in which sense it occurs
frequently in literature, inscriptions and papyri – e.g. "the Emperor's freedman",
"N. the Emperor's slave", "the Caesars". The titular usage appears in all the other
NT refs.: Lk. 3:1; 23:2; Acts 25:21; 26:32; 27:24; 28:19; Phil. 4 22; and below
(→ NT).

OT The only refs. in Jewish literature up to and including 1st century A.D. are
several historical refs. to Julius Caesar and Augustus in Josephus.

NT Insofar as _Kaisar_ functions as a theological concept within the NT it denotes
the legitimate power of political authority. Thus it is important for Luke that
Paul can affirm his innocence not only in respect of the Jewish law and temple, but
also with respect to Caesar (Acts 25:8); so too Paul is wholly justified in appealing
to this civil power for protection against what amounts to religious persecution
(Acts 25:11).

It is possible however for the authority of Caesar to be opposed to the authority
of God in a _false antithesis_. Thus Acts 17:1–9, where it would appear that in Thessalonica a section of the Jewish community who had achieved a satisfactory balance
between their religious and secular obligations felt this equilibrium to be threatened
by the strong eschatological challenge of the Christian gospel (cf. 2 Thess. 2:5). That
which was a threat to their own peace and established way of life they accused of
being a threat to the law and order of society at large. The claims of the exalted and
soon coming Jesus upon personal life and relationships in his gospel were so far-
reaching that they could be misrepresented as the claims of an earthly tyrant, and
Jesus portrayed as a rival to Caesar (Acts 17:7).

The problem of possible conflict between the authority of God and that of
Caesar must have been a very real one for the early Christians and is specifically
tackled in the apophthegm (pronouncement story) preserved in Mk. 12:13–17. The
question put to Jesus concerned the poll-tax which had been levied on the inhabitants of Judea, Samaria and Idumea since A.D. 6. As tribute money to a victorious
conqueror and occupying power the tax was a focus for intense national and religious feeling on the part of the Jews. The Zealots in particular were vehement and
implacable in their hostility; God they affirmed was "their only ruler and king"

(Josephus, *Ant*. 18, 1, 6). The question whether it was lawful or permitted to pay the tax to Caesar or not was therefore well chosen to trap Jesus on the horns of a dilemma: either deny the authority of Caesar (rebellion) or deny the full authority of God (treason and blasphemy). Jesus' reply makes it clear that in his view the antithesis was false: political and divine authority need not necessarily conflict. The payment of tax is a legitimate obligation within the network of human relationships. As such it did not conflict with the higher and all-embracing authority of God, any more, we may say, than human love between two people need conflict with love to God. To pose Caesar and God as mutually exclusive authorities is to make all human relationships antithetical to divine authority, for all relationships involve obligation and responsibility of one kind or another. Jesus did not sanction such an either-or. Man can live within human relationships of authority and obligation and still "pay to God what is due to God".

There is however the possibility of real conflict between obligation to Caesar and obligation to God. Loyalty to Caesar can become an excuse for evading higher obligation to the truth (Jn. 18:38; 19:12–16). Whoever limits his motives and aims to friendship with Caesar shuts himself off from an answer to the question, "What is truth?" Whoever affirms loyalty only to Caesar is thereby self-condemned (cf. Jn. 16:8–11).

ἡγεμών

ἡγεμών (*hēgemōn*), in Greek generally leader, commander, chief; in particular it can refer to the emperor or a provincial governor (Strabo), and frequently the prefect of Egypt. Similarly NT (Matt. 10:18; Mk. 13:9; Lk. 21:12; 1 Pet. 2:14), particularly the procurators in Judea – Pilate (Matt. 27:2, 11, 14 f., 21, 27; 28:14; Lk. 20:20), Felix (Acts 23:24, 26, 33; 24:1, 10), and Festus (Acts 26:30). In Matt. 2:6 more generally "ruler". In 1 Pet. 2:13 f. the same attitude to political authority (→ NT above) is expressed more explicitly and forcibly.

ὕπατος

ὕπατος (*hypatos*), consul (e.g. Polybius). ἀνθύπατος (*anthypatos*) proconsul (frequently in inscriptions and papyri); so Acts 13:7 f., 12; 18:12; 19:38. In Acts 18:12–17 and 19:35–41 Luke shows the civil power exercising its legitimate authority in the manner appropriate to it. Consul was the title of the two chief magistrates of the Roman Republic. Holders of the office were of senatorial rank, and served for one year in Rome before going to administer in the provinces as proconsuls. The office was somewhat modified in the Empire, when even children could be given the title. It survived in the West until A.D. 534.   *J. D. G. Dunn*

→ Authority, → King, → Lord

(a). Arndt, 68, 343 f., 396; J. D. M. Derrett, "Render to Caesar . . .", *Law in the New Testament*, 1970, 313–38; *OCD*, 286, 881 f.; B. Reicke, *The New Testament Era*, 1968; A. N. Sherwin–White, *Roman Society and Roman Law in the New Testament*, (1963) 1965; E. Stauffer, *Christ and the Caesars*, 1955.
(b). L. Hahn, *Rom und Romanismus im griechisch.-römischen Osten*, 1906; W. Liebenam, *Beiträge zur Verwaltungsgeschichte des römischen Reiches*, I, 1896.

Call

| καλέω |

καλέω (*kaleō*), call; κλῆσις (*klēsis*), call, invitation; κλητός (*klētos*), called, invited; ἐπικαλέομαι (*epikaleomai*), call, appeal to; προσκαλέομαι (*proskaleomai*), summon.

CL 1. *kaleō*, in contrast to *keleuō*, urge on, command, means to speak to another either immediately or mediately, in order to bring him nearer, either physically or in a personal relationship. This leads to the following meanings in classical Gk.:

(a) Invite, e.g. into a house, to a feast (Homer, *Od.*, 10, 231). The part. *klētos* in such contexts means invited, welcomed, a guest (Homer *Od.*, 17, 386). Where the invitation conferred special honour, the word came to mean chosen (Homer, *Il.*, 9, 165). The noun *klēsis* means the act of inviting (Xen., *Symp.*, 1, 7; Plut., *Pericles*, 7, 5) and more often an official summons by a recognized authority (e.g. military or the city assembly), and so means calling together or calling to oneself (Homer, *Od.*, 1, 90; 8, 43).

(b) Hence *kaleomai*, occasionally *epikaleomai*, and correspondingly *klēsis*, are used for the summoning of one's adversary or of witnesses before a court of law (Dem., 19, 211; Xen., *Hell.*, 1, 7, 13). Very early, except in capital charges, they were replaced by the technical terms *proskaleomai* (Xen., *Hell.*, 1, 7, 12) and *prosklēsis* (Dem., 43, 15 f.).

(c) It also means name, either when a man is being addressed (Homer, *Il.*, 1, 402) or when a name is bestowed. When it is a question of a nickname *epikaleō* is normally used (Hdt., 8, 44). *kaloumenos* (already in Hdt., 6, 61) with the name of people or places means called, so called. Since the → name was considered an expression of a man's character, the pass. *kaleisthai* was used as a virtual synonym of *einai* to be (e.g. Homer, *Od.*, 313).

2. The compound *epikaleō*, usually in the mid., normally has the meaning of invoking (but see above 1 (b)). It is used either (a) of the worship of the gods (Hdt. onwards; cf. 2, 39; also Plato, *Tim.*, 27c; Polyb., 15, 1, 13) or (b) in legal language of appealing, lodging an appeal, e.g. with a ruler, an official (Plut., *Marcellus* 2, 4) or the people (Plut., *Tiberius Gracchus*, 16, 1, 832b).

3. In classical Gk. *kaleō* and *klēsis* are only seldom used of a divine call. This comes rather from the mystery religions (e.g. that of Isis), the influence of the LXX, and specially the NT use. From these *kaleō* takes on the ideas of claiming (Herm., 119 B III, 10 f.) and commissioning (*CPR* 18, 9). In contrast to such a personal call, the Stoic understood *klēsis* impersonally to mean the demand made on him by a critical position to maintain the truth and power of his principles (cf. Epict., *Dissertations*, 1, 29, 49).

4. Since Gk. society did not know the biblical concept of calling, it did not share our concept of vocation. An individual's activity in the working society was called *ergon* (→ work), *ponos* (→ burden), *epangelia*, assent (→ Promise), *pragma*, deed (→ Work), *technē*, art, *schesis*, situation, condition, or *taxis*, order. Though a general term for manual labour was sought, the consciousness of vocation remained confined to priests and to some extent to those who devoted themselves to intellectual and administrative tasks.

5. The following compounds are treated under other headings: *parakaleō* → Exhort; *paraklētos* → Advocate; and *ekklēsia* → Church.

271

ot With minor exceptions *kaleō* (*c.* 300 times), *epikaleō* (*c.* 150 times), and *proskaleomai* (11 times) are used in the LXX to render various forms of the Heb. *qārā'*. The latter is only seldom translated by other words (e.g. *krazō*, shout). In the translation of the MT *klēsis* is used only in Jer. 31:6 (LXX 38:6) as a verbal noun. It is also found in 3 Macc. 5:14 for an invitation regarded as an action, and in Jud. 12:10 of the meal to which a person is invited. *klētoi* and the part. *keklēmenoi* are used for those invited, the guests. The combination *klētē hagia* represents the Heb. expression *miqrā'-qōḏeš*, holy assembly, i.e. the worshipping congregation at festivals (Exod. 12:16; Num. 28:25; and 11 times in Lev. 23:2–37). The phrase is particularly used with reference to their calendar. For further treatment see under *ekklēsia* and *synagōgē* (→ Church).

1. (a) *kaleō* is found very often in the sense of naming, whether of things (e.g. Gen. 1:5, 8 f., day, night, heaven, earth; Gen. 2:19, the animals), or of persons (e.g. Gen. 25:26, Jacob; Gen. 29:32–35; 30:6–24, Jacob's sons), of a city (e.g. 2 Sam. 5:9, the city of David), or of qualities (in Isa. 35:8 a way and in Exod. 12:16 a day are called holy; cf. Isa. 56:7 where the Temple is called a "house of prayer"). When the Jewish people are called "the priests of the Lord" (Isa. 61:6), or "sons of the living God" (Hos. 1:10 (MT 2:1)), this is equivalent to calling God's servants by "a different name" (Isa. 65:15), which implies a new existence.

(b) *epikaleō* is sometimes used with the act. sense of naming (e.g. Num. 21:3). The phrase "Thy name is called (*epikeklētai*) over us" (Jer. 7:14; cf. 14:9) implies a special degree of possession and protection.

2. Taken all in all, *epikaleō* is the most important term in the LXX for calling on and worshipping, and has the special characteristic of open confession (e.g. Gen. 4:26; 33:20) ([Tr.] the LXX interpretation)). Where a cry of need is involved, *krazō* may be used. The worship is addressed to God, or the God of Israel (used with the acc.: 1 Chr. 4:10), or to the Lord (1 Ki. 17:21) or above all it is to the name of God (Gen. 13:4; Deut. 14:23 f.; Isa. 64:7; Jer. 10:25 – in all such cases the accusative is used). Frequently we find the Semitism *en* (*tō*) *onomati*, Heb. *bᵉšēm* ("in the name" e.g. 1 Ki. 18:24 ff.). This may have been influenced by the idea that the worshipper comes under the name of God as in a strong tower (cf. Prov. 18:10). Since according to Deut., God wills to be worshipped at a specified place chosen by him, the LXX can even render the Heb. *šāḵan*, dwell, by *epikaleisthai* (Exod. 29:45 f.; Deut. 12:11; 16:2, 6, 11). The purpose of the revelation and manifestation of the presence of God is that men should turn to him in worship. They should answer his call in the way he expects. The legal sense (see above cl 2) is not found. The vb. is used in Deut. 15:2 for the proclamation of the year of release, but in Isa. 61:2 and Jer. 34:17 (LXX 41:17) *kaleō* is used.

3. (a) Above all *kaleō* and the few examples of *proskaleō* describe the call of the higher in rank to individuals or groups, e.g. parents to children (Gen. 24:58), rulers to subjects (Exod. 1:18; Jdg. 12:1), and Moses to the elders (Exod. 12:21; 19:7). Such a call was always a command, never a mere invitation (Job 13:22). This call expects that men should → hear and answer. Hence it is not despotic compulsion. Men can refuse to obey the call of God (Isa. 65:12; Jer. 13:10); they can refuse to hear it (Isa. 50:2; Jer. 7:13) or seek to avoid it (Exod. 3:11; 4:1, 10, 13; Jer. 1:6). By contrast, God's commanding call creates order in the universe. He calls the

272

stars (Isa. 40:26), and causes events to happen in history. He calls hunger (Psa. 105(104):16) and the sword (Jer. 25:29 (LXX 32:29)).

(b) Before a man can answer, he must realize that the call he has heard comes from God. How little he is prepared for this, even in the sanctuary, how hard it is for him to distinguish it from all other voices is shown dramatically in the story of Samuel's call (in 1 Sam. 3:4–10 *kaleō* appears 11 times). Just because God's call creates a claim on a man, he can hardly avoid conflict with the claims of earthly rulers (cf. Elijah (2 Ki. 1:3, 9) and Moses (Exod. 3:4; 5:2)). The call will often lead to → suffering for God's sake. This shows that fundamentally it is only bringing to light the → election which long preceded it. It is significant that in the later chapters of Isa., specially in the Servant Songs (→ Son, Art. *pais theou*) we have the profoundest use of *kaleō* in the sense of service and dedication, linked with an exceptionally frequent appearance of *eklegomai*, choose. It is the elect one (Isa. 41:8; 43:10) whom God calls in → righteousness (Isa. 42:6) and by name (Isa. 43:1; 45:3). He is a type of all who have been called from the beginnings of humanity (Isa. 41:2, 4).

4. Our word-group does not occur in the accounts of the call of the judges (Jdg. 6:13) and the prophets' accounts of their calls (cf. Isa. 6:1–8; 40:6 ff.; Jer. 1:4–9; Ezek. 2:1 ff.). This is because the call is not characterized by the use of certain phraseology but by its content and form. God speaks to a man to whom in his → foreknowledge he wishes to entrust a task. It may be prophetic or political (cf. Cyrus (Isa. 48:14 f.)), and it may be defined at once or later. God's → Word demands a decision from the one addressed. God's call is the means by which he makes men who are entirely unqualified into instruments of his will.

5. Within Judaism only the men of Qumran seem to have had a special sense of call. While statements about → election play a considerable part there, the call of God is mentioned only in 1 QM 14:5. In 1QM 16:1 God calls a sword on the nations. But the expression "the called of God" is found a number of times. In CD 4:4 it is used as an equivalent of the "the elect of Israel". In 1QM 2:7 and 1QSa 2:11, 13 it is a title of the prominent men of the council of the community. In 1QM 3:2 it is used of the trumpets calling for a gathering, and in 1 QM 4:10 of one of the standards on the battlefield.

NT In the NT *kaleō* is found 148 times (43 times in Lk 18 in Acts; 29 in Paul; and 26 in Matt.). *epikaleomai* is found 30 times, 20 of these being in Acts. *proskaleomai* occurs 29 times, 4 in Lk., 9 in Acts and Mk. Though *klēsis* is found 11 times, it does not occur in the Gospels and Acts. *klētos* with 10 occurrences is found only once in Matt. These two words are essentially Pauline. It is noticeable that Jn. uses *kaleō* only twice, and that the word-group occurs only rarely in the Catholic Epistles and Rev.

The relatively frequent use of the word-group by Luke is due to his cultured Gk. He is the only NT writer to use compounds which occur only in superior Koine (e.g. *eiskaleō*, invite, *metakaleomai*, have brought to oneself). The usages mentioned already under CL 1, 2 occur in him. Contrasted with these are the specifically theological uses of *kaleō*, *klēsis* and *klētos* by Paul (see below 3).

1. (a) In the NT too *kaleō* means the giving of a name or nickname (Matt. 1:21; Jn. 1:42), the use of a title when addressing someone (Matt. 23:7 f.), or the attribution

273

of a particular rank (Lk. 6:46, Lord; Matt. 23:9, Father; Lk. 22:25, benefactor). The part. *kaloumenos*, called (Lk. 6:15; 19:29; Rev. 16:16), sometimes does not really need translation (cf. Lk. 8:2; Acts 10:1; 15:37 (so NEB)). Of special importance are the cases where God gives a name. By conferring the names Jesus (Lk. 1:31) and John (Lk. 1:13) he expresses, as in the OT, his control over their lives.

(b) More frequently than in classical Gk. and even than in the LXX there lies concealed behind the pass. *kaleomai*, be named, be called, an expression of the character and existence of a person or thing. This is perhaps seen most clearly in Paul's remark that he is "unfit to be called an apostle" (1 Cor. 15:9). Frequently in such expressions OT ideas have been taken over, as in Mk. 11:17 par., where the Temple is called "a house of prayer", quoting Isa. 56:7. This usage is particularly important in Lk. 1:32, 35, where Jesus is called the Son of the Most High, i.e. the Son of God. Consequently, his followers will be called sons of God (Matt. 5:9; Rom. 9:26) and children of God (1 Jn. 3:1). The new → name is here clearly an expression for the new existence granted by an act of God.

2. (a) We meet the meaning "invite" for *kaleō* principally in the parables of the great banquet (Lk. 14:16–25), where it occurs 9 times, and the marriage feast (Matt. 22:2–10), where it occurs 5 times. It is also used in Jn. 2:2 and Rev. 19:9 of inviting to a wedding and of those invited to the Lamb's marriage feast. With the exception of Jn. 2:2 there is a hint of privilege and command in these passages. Probably this is how we should understand "I came not to call the righteous, but sinners" (Matt. 9:13; Mk. 2:17; Lk. 5:32) on the lips of Jesus. These parables make it clear that, when a man ignores the divine invitation, he not only misses an opportunity, but may be squandering his life and hope.

(b) The note of command in the verb is seen even more clearly in the passages where rulers or officials call their subordinates: Herod (Matt. 2:7), the owner of the vineyard (Matt. 20:8); cf. also Mk. 3:31; Lk. 19:13; see above OT 3 f.). As a result, it would have been natural to use it as a special term for the call of the disciples. In fact, it occurs only in Matt. 4:21 and Mk. 1:20. In the other narratives we have the story and the words spoken, but no definite term is used to introduce them. In the Gospels the narrative does not necessarily include interpretation and technical language. This comes to the fore in Paul.

(c) It is striking that *proskaleomai* (found only in Matt., Lk., Acts and Jas. 5:14) is likewise not used for such a call. It is used of a commanding call to an individual (Matt. 18:2; Mk. 15:44) or to an existing, fairly well defined group like the disciples (Matt. 10:1; Mk. 6:7; 12:43; Acts 6:2) or the people (Matt. 15:10; Mk. 7:14). The statement, "He . . . called to him those whom he desired" (Mk. 3:13), is no exception, for the Twelve were obviously already envisaged by Jesus. In Acts 13:2 the vb. indicates the heavenly call to Paul and Barnabas, which is to be realized in their earthly commissioning. We should see in Acts 16:10 a heavenly directive to Paul and his companions which was communicated by a vision. Furthermore, the use of the part. *proskalesamenos* may suggest that the Synoptic writers saw in the call only a means to an end, and their attention was fixed on the event set in motion by it. It is the spoken → word which determines → discipleship.

(d) The statement, "For many are called, but few are chosen" (Matt. 22:14), reflects on the relationship between God's call and election. It shows that, at least

274

from the standpoint of human response, the circle of the called and of the elect cannot be taken as necessarily coinciding (→ Election).

3. (a) Paul uses the words *kaleō* (29 times), *klēsis* (8 times) and *klētos* (7 times) almost always with the sense of divine calling. Exceptions are 1 Cor. 15:9 (see above NT 1 (b)), 1 Cor. 10:27 (invite), and three quotations from the LXX: Rom. 9:7 (Gen. 21:12); Rom. 9:25 (Hos. 2:23(25)); and Rom. 9:26 (Hos. 1:10 (MT 2:1)). *proskaleomai* is not found in the Pauline writings. This usage is continued in the Pastorals and is taken over by Heb., and 1 and 2 Pet.

Paul understands calling as the process by which God calls those, whom he has already elected and appointed, out of their bondage to this world, so that he may justify and sanctify them (Rom. 8:29 f.), and bring them into his service. This means that the call is part of God's work of reconciliation and peace (1 Cor. 7:15). It reaches a man only through the love of Christ directed towards him and seeking him (Gal. 1:6, 15). When Paul says that God's decision is not dependent on works but solely on him who calls (Rom. 9:11), he is stressing the unfettered choice of God, which is not influenced by human preconditions. It alone brings men to faith and is able to preserve them in it. Paul's language stresses this divine initiative in its participial constructions (cf. 1 Thess. 2:12 *kalountos*, "who calls"; Gal. 1:6 *kalesantos*, "who called"; cf. also 1 Pet. 1:15 *ton kalesanta*, "who called"). In addition, Rom. 4:17 shows that God's call means a new existence, equivalent to a new → creation.

(b) God's call is mediated by the message of the Gospel (2 Thess. 2:14) which comes through the witness of men. It brings the one called both into fellowship with Christ (1 Cor. 1:9) and at the same time into fellowship with the other members of his → body. Since the call is "in the one body" (Col. 3:15, *en heni sōmati*) it is equivalent to entering the → Kingdom of God. For while God's call (*klēsis*) is addressed to the individual, it never concerns him alone. The use of the word always indicates either that the call comes from God (Rom. 11:29; Phil. 3:14) or that one is brought into fellowship with the church as a whole (1 Cor. 1:26; Eph. 4:1). Baptism is both a visible sign of the call and of the obligation of the believer to live a life worthy of his call (Eph. 4:1; 1 Thess. 2:12).

(c) Paul addresses church members as *klētoi*, called ones (Rom. 1:6 f.; 8:28; and 1 Cor. 1:2, 24). In Rom. 1:7 and 1 Cor. 1:2 he addresses the *klētoi hagioi*, those called as saints. He desires to stress that both the existence of the church and individual membership in it are based solely on the will and work of God. 1 Cor. 1:26 shows how Paul saw this calling as dependent on God and how it involves the church. The Corinthians are to consider their calling. They will realize what they once were, and with what sort of people God has joined them in his church. 1 Cor. 7:15–24 makes it clear that the call does not necessarily change the Christian's social status. So far as the law is concerned, it does not free the slave from his master, or force the believer to change his occupation. The change in relationships is reached not by revolution, but by a change in the inner attitude. In 1 Cor. 7:20 *klēsis* presents some difficulty. The literal rendering 'calling' (AV) can be misunderstood as vocation, a meaning that cannot be legitimately attributed to Paul ([Tr.] the renderings "condition" (RV, NEB), "state" (RSV) are lexically questionable. It is more likely that Paul has in mind a particular place or station (perhaps even in the church?)).

(d) In rare cases Paul can use *klētos* of a personal commission. When in Rom. 1:1 and 1 Cor. 1:1 he declares himself to be *klētos apostolos* (called to be an apostle, RSV), he is stressing that he owed his office as → apostle to a special call by God.

4. The use of the word-group in 1 Pet. is essentially Pauline. Peter stresses in 1:15 and 5:10 that the call comes from God, and that God has a purpose in his call (2:21; 3:9, "for to this you have been called"). Those called by him are to bear witness to the One who had called them out of darkness (2:9) by following the example of Christ even in suffering (2:21), so that they may inherit a blessing (3:9; cf. 2 Pet. 1:3 f.).

Pauline influence may be seen also in Heb. 3:1 and 9:15 which speak of the heavenly call and the promised inheritance for those called.

5. *epikaleomai* (in the NT only in the mid. and pass.) is used in much the same way. In the expression "the name (of God) is called over (us)" (Jas. 2:7; Acts 15:17 quoting Amos 9:12, *epikaleitai . . . epi*) both God's assumption of power over a person and his simultaneous expression of care for him are brought out. The RSV renders both passages: "are called by". Similarly in Acts 4:36 and 12:12 it is used like a synonym for *kaleō* and means "called". It is used of Paul's appeal to Caesar 6 times in Acts 25–28 (but nowhere else in the legal sense of appeal). In addition, it is frequently used of calling on God or his name (cf. Acts 7:59 ([Tr.] RSV inadequately, "he prayed"); 9:14; Rom. 10:12 ff.; 1 Cor. 1:2). It normally carries with it the thought of confessing God within the church. 2 Cor. 1:23 is an exception, for here God is being called on as a witness. Such expressions are based on OT language for the invocation of Yahweh. When they are used in the NT for the disciples' approach to Jesus (cf. 1 Cor. 1:2; Acts 22:16), it is a recognition of him as God's presence, as Son and Messiah. *L. Coenen*

(a). Arndt, 399 f.; J. Jeremias, *New Testament Theology*, I, 1971, 49–56; G. Molin, "Vocation," *EBT* III 954–58; M. Noth, "Office and Vocation in the Old Testament," *The Laws in the Pentateuch and Other Studies*, 1966, 229–49; H. H. Rowley, *The Biblical Doctrine of Election*, 1952; K. L. Schmidt, *kaleō*, *TDNT* III 487–536.

(b). W. Bieder, *Die Berufung im Neuen Testament*, 1961; J. Daumoser, *Berufung und Erwählung*, 1955; E. Engel, *Die Berufungstheologie des Apostels Paulus*, 1939; J. Hempel, "Berufung und Bekehrung," *Festschrift* G. Beer, 1935, 41–61; G. Mensching, J. Fichtner and O. Michel, "Berufung," *RGG³* I 1083–88; F. Müller, "Berufung und Erwählung," *ZSTh* 24, 1955, 38–71.

Care, Anxiety

$\mu \acute{\epsilon} \rho \iota \mu \nu a$

$\mu \acute{\epsilon} \rho \iota \mu \nu a$ (*merimna*), care; $\mu \epsilon \rho \iota \mu \nu \acute{a} \omega$ (*merimnaō*), care, be anxious; $\pi \rho o \mu \epsilon \rho \iota \mu \nu \acute{a} \omega$ (*promerimnaō*), be anxious beforehand; $\mu \acute{\epsilon} \lambda \omega$ (*melō*), be concerned, be worried about.

CL This group of words is frequent in classical Gk. literature. The noun *merimna* is found from Hesiod onwards (*Works* 178), and the vb. *merimnaō* since Soph. (*Oedipus the King* 1124). Both words have the same range of meaning as the Ger. *Sorge* and *sorgen* (noun and vb. meaning care) and the Eng. *care*. Thus *merimna* can mean both care in the sense of an anxious fear and also caring for, providing for, and *merimnaō* can mean being anxious, worried, and care, take responsibility for someone or something. In keeping with this meaning, the words are usually

276

concerned with objects in the future (cf. the compound *promerimnaō*, be anxious beforehand, which occurs only in the NT in Mk. 13:11).

Besides *merimna* and *merimnaō* there appear in Gk. literature the words *phrontis*, worrying, anxiety (not in the NT), and *phrontizō*, think of, be mindful of, care for (only Tit. 3:8).

melei, it concerns someone about . . . , is the 3rd person sing. of *melō*, be concerned about. It is usually used impersonally, but is occasionally personal. It is attested since Homer and expresses interest and concern.

ot 1. In the LXX these words appear relatively infrequently and have the same range as in classical Gk. The noun *merimna* (12 times; in Ps. 55(54):22(23) it represents the Heb. *yᵉhāḇ*, burden; otherwise it has no Heb. equivalent) means anxious care (e.g. Job. 11:18 with *phrontis*, apprehension; Dan. 11:26; 1 Macc. 6:10). The vb. *merimnaō* (9 times for different Heb. verbs) means be anxious (2 Sam. 7:10; 1 Chr. 17:9) or be troubled (e.g. because of sin: Ps. 38(37):18(19)). The same word is used in a weaker sense in Exod. 5:9, be concerned for, think of.

The wisdom literature uses the vb. and the noun in the positive sense of caring, providing (e.g. Prov. 14:23; 17:12). However, in this literary genre *merimna* can mean anxious care (e.g. Sir. 30:24; 42:9).

2. In Philo and Josephus, as already in the Stoa, *phrontis* is used for worry, care, instead of *merimna*, and *phrontizō*, be mindful of, care for, instead of *merimnaō*. Their range of meaning is the same.

nt In the NT the noun *merimna*, care, only occurs 6 times in the Synoptics, once in Paul and once in 1 Pet. The vb. *merimnaō*, be anxious, care for, occurs only in Matt. (6 times), Lk. (5 times) and Paul (5 times in 1 Cor., 2 times in Phil.).

Like the OT, the NT understands care chiefly as the natural reaction of man to poverty, hunger and other troubles which befall him in his daily life. Oppressed by the burdens laid upon him, man imagines himself delivered to a fate before which he stands powerless. By his care man tries to protect himself as best he can from what confronts him.

1. The most comprehensive summary of the NT's witness on the matter of worry is to be found in the Sermon on the Mount (Matt. 6:25–34) or the Sermon on the Plain (Lk. 12:22–31). It is directed against that error which denies God's care and love by supposing that man can secure his own future by temporarily securing what he needs for his livelihood. Worrying is foolish because life is more than food (Matt. 6:25), and because he who worries cannot secure his life (Matt. 6:27).

If *hēlikia* (→ Age, Old, Stature) should be translated as stature, length of body, not length of life, then the folly of worry is emphasized by this *reductio ad absurdum*. For if something so completely unimportant as bodily size cannot be guaranteed by man's worry, how much less can life itself.

We can take the saying of Matt. 6:34 in the same ironic sense. It comes from the discourses of the wisdom tradition and has Jewish and Gentile parallels (cf. Comms. ad loc.). This disciple who adds tomorrow's cares to today's is acting in an absurd way and is put to shame by secular wisdom which has long recognized the fact. But worry is not only foolish but also God-less (→ Wisdom, Folly), because it impugns God's care for men. God who feeds the birds of the air and decks the transitory flowers of the field with beauty, will do "much more" for his creature, man (Matt. 6:26, 30). For he is the Father who knows all that his children need (Matt. 6:32). He who forgets that and, in the weakness of his faith, gives way to worry is acting like a Gentile (Matt. 6:32 → Possessions, particularly the art. *mamōnas*).

By contrast, the knowledge that the → kingdom of God is dawning liberates man from anxiety and worry. He who welcomes this kingdom of God and the → righteousness proclaimed in it with zeal and trust, finds by experience that all that is needful for his life is given to him by God's provision (Matt. 6:33). In God's kingdom all men's needs are put in their rightful place, because the Father's love provides alike things great and small, daily needs and special ones (e.g. the ability to witness faithfully under persecution, Matt. 10:19 par.).

It may be asked whether or not Jewish traditions of belief in providence (→ Foreknowledge) have been adapted or made more radical. It used to be held that the action of the righteous guaranteed God's provision (cf. Ps. 55:22(23)). It is now firmly stated that, if one gives one's undivided attention to the kingdom of God, it is superfluous to make anxious provision to secure one's life. This is stated with the help of various ideas drawn from the OT background, sometimes by the idea of God as → Father as in the Sermon on the Mount and the parallels, and sometimes by the OT belief in providence as in 1 Pet. 5:7 (cf. Ps. 55:22(23)). Because God is concerned (*melei*) about man and cares for him, man can unload his cares on to God.

2. Luke's picture of Mary and Martha (Lk. 10:38–42) exhibits the same contrast of attitudes as the Sermon on the Mount. The "many things" over which man worries, in order to secure the necessities of life, are contrasted with the "one thing" that is necessary. That is the question concerning the purpose of life, which Mary sees to be answered in Jesus' teaching. Worry is contrasted with zeal for God's kingdom.

In the same way the parable of the sower sees the word as imperilled by cares (Mk. 4:19 par.). Lk. 21:34 warns against being weighed down by *merimnai* (plur.), cares, qualified by the adj. *biōtikai*, belonging to life, daily, and so the cares for the needs of daily life.

3. *merimna*, care, and *merimnaō*, care for, can also be given a positive sense, as that caring for others that God entrusts to men. Hence Paul sees himself as one who must care for all the churches (2 Cor. 11:28). God has fashioned the church like a body so that "the members might care each alike for the other" (1 Cor. 12:25). Timothy is commended to the church in Philippi as one who will care for their interests like no one else (Phil. 2:20). Hence Paul can regard a care of this nature as a part of *ta Iēsou Christou zētein*, seeking what belongs to Jesus Christ, that is, of involvement in the affairs of Jesus Christ (Phil. 2:21).

1 Cor. 7:32 ff. shows that Paul is aware of the dangers in caring about other people. Because he desires the members of the church to be without worries (*amerimnous*), he recommends the unmarried not to marry in future in view of the eschatological situation (vv. 29, 31) and the married to live to the Lord in the freedom opened up by the concept *hōs mē*, as if not (1 Cor. 7:29).

In the exhortation of Phil. 4:6 ("Worry about nothing . . .) *merimnaō* is used with the same meaning as elsewhere in the NT, anxious care. The reason for this freedom from care lies in the Lord's proximity (v. 5) and in the church's privilege

of being able to present all their requests in → prayer to God with thanksgiving
(→ Thank).   *J. Goetzmann*

R. Bultmann, *merimnaō*, *TDNT* IV 589–93; and *Theology of the New Testament*, I, 1952, 239–46; H. Riesenfeld, "Vom Schätzesammeln und Sorgen – ein Thema urchristlicher Paränese. Zu Mt. vi 19–34," in *Neotestamentica et Patristica. Eine Freundesgabe Herrn Professor Dr. Oscar Cullmann zu seinem 60. Geburtstag überreicht*, 1962, 47–58.

Carpenter, Builder, Workman, Craftsman, Trade

τέκτων

τέκτων (*tektōn*), builder; ἀρχιτέκτων (*architektōn*), masterbuilder; τεχνίτης (*technitēs*), craftsman; τέχνη (*technē*), art, skill, trade.

CL In secular Gk. *tektōn* means a craftsman or builder in wood, stone or metal; *architektōn* means a head builder, masterbuilder, contractor, or director of works; *technitēs* means a craftsman, artisan or designer; and *technē* means an art, craft, trade, or professional skill.

OT In the LXX all these words appear in their classical meaning. *tektōn* usually renders *ḥārāš*. It is noteworthy that, unlike the more intellectual and aristocratic societies of Greece and Rome, the Jews had a high regard for manual work and a deep respect for those who did it well, whose ability was sometimes at any rate seen as a gift of God's spirit (Exod. 35:30 ff.).

NT In the NT, usage is as follows:

(a) *tektōn* appears only in the identification of Jesus by the people of Nazareth as "the carpenter" (Mk. 6:3), "the carpenter's son" (Matt. 13:55). Though "carpenter" is the common rendering here, *tektōn* could equally mean "mason" or "smith" (as indeed some of the Fathers took it); or it could mean that Joseph and Jesus were builders, so that both carpentry and masonry would have been among their skills.

(b) *architektōn* appears once, in Paul's description of himself as a "wise masterbuilder" (the phrase is lifted from the LXX of Isa. 3:3) who laid the foundation of the Corinthian church. Paul identifies this foundation with Christ – Christ, that is, as set forth in the doctrine Paul had preached, the doctrine of the givenness of reconciliation through the cross and the new community created thereby. This was the doctrine that had produced the Corinthian church (1 Cor. 3:10 ff.).

(c) *technitēs* bears its ordinary secular sense in Acts 19:24, 38; Rev. 18:22. In Heb. 11:10, however, the word is applied to God, as the craftsman who has built the heavenly city for which his people hope.

(d) *technē* has its ordinary secular sense in Acts 17:29, 18:3 (where Paul and Aquila are identified as "tent-makers" or "leather-workers" by trade), and Rev. 18:22.   *J. I. Packer*

→ Creation, art. *dēmiourgos*

Cherub

χερούβ

χερούβ (*cheroub*); plur. varies between χερουβείμ (*cheroubeim*), χερουβείν (*cheroubein*), χερουβίμ (*cheroubim*), χερουβίν (*cheroubin*).

279

CL The word does not occur in secular Gk, but is a transliteration of the Heb. or Aram., hence the variety of plur. endings.

OT The Heb. word is $k^e r\hat{u}\underline{b}$ (pl. $k^e r\hat{u}\underline{b}\hat{i}m$ or $k^e ru\underline{b}\hat{i}m$), a winged heavenly messenger sometimes associated with the seraph or burning one (Isa. 6:2–6). Cherubim guard the way to the tree of life (Gen. 3:24) and either support or flank the throne of God (Pss. 80:1; 99:1; Isa. 37:16). Their swiftness in flight is likened to the wind (2 Sam. 22:11; Ps. 18:10). Two wooden replicas of cherubim, gold covered and with wings outspread, were placed over the cover or "mercy seat" of the ark of the covenant, protecting the holy things and forming a pedestal for the throne of Yahweh (Exod. 23:17–21; 37:7–9; cf. Num. 7:89). Cherubim also adorned the inmost curtains of the tabernacle and the "veil" which separated off the most holy place (Exod. 26:1, 31), and symbolized the heavenly hosts of the Lord God of hosts (1 Sam. 4:4; 2 Sam. 6:2; Ki. 19:15; 1 Chr. 13:6). In Solomon's temple emphasis is laid on the size of the cherubim, whose wings span the width of the sanctuary (1 Ki. 6:23–28; 2 Chr. 3:10–13).

Among the prophets only Ezekiel mentions the word. The golden cherubim on which had rested the glory of the God of Israel were deserted (Ezek. 9:3), and he was to be found among living cherubim who carried out his every wish (Ezek. 10, cf. Ezek. 1:5 ff.), having moved the place of his throne away from the Temple. In Ezekiel cherubim also guard the presence of God (Ezek. 28:14–16 RSV).

Later Judaism meditated much on Ezekiel's chariot throne, but speculation was discouraged by the Rabbis, and liturgical use of Ezekiel's chapters on the chariot was forbidden in the Mishnah. In the Qumran scrolls one fragment "The Divine Throne-Chariot" describes the cherubim as uttering blessings, and accompanied by a still small voice (cf. 1 Ki. 19:12) as they moved their wings. A similar interest in the heavenly throne is found in Eth. Enoch (14:11, 18; 20:7).

NT In the New Testament the word occurs only in Heb. 9:5; the phrase *cherubim of glory* is used in a description of the Holy of holies. The book of the Revelation, without using the word, describes in terms reminiscent of both cherubim and seraphim (Rev. 4:6–8) the living creatures who worship the One on the throne.

Cherubim are specifically associated with God's throne, whether in heaven or in its earthly counterpart. They stand guard, support the throne and act as swift messengers of the Lord of hosts, whom they worship. *J. G. Baldwin*
→Angel

P. Dhorme and L. H. Vincent, "Les Chérubins", *RB*, 35, 1926, 328–358; 481–495; T. H. Gaster, art. "Angel", *IDB* I 131 f.; R. K. Harrison, art. "Cherubim," *NBD*, 208 f.

Child, Boy, Servant, Son, Adoption

The word child may be understood both lit. and fig. (e.g. as a child of a particular age or society). The following article discusses a number of related terms. *teknon* (cf. *tiktō*, to bear, → Birth) means child as the offspring of his parents and forefathers. With regard to age, a distinction is made between *paidion*, the baby or little child (cf. *brephos*, baby, infant) and *pais*, the child between 7 and 14 years old. *pais* also suggests the child's lowly position in society and his ancient function as a slave.

It can therefore also mean servant or slave. *nēpios*, infant, minor, carries the overtones of helplessness, inexperience and simplicity. It can also suggest foolishness. While *pais* and *teknon* can refer to either boy or girl, the son (*hyios*) is distinguished from the daughter (*thygatēr*). *hyios* is frequently used in fig. senses, either to denote teacher-pupil relationship or membership of a particular group (cf. also *teknon*). On the christological titles Son of God (*hyios* (*tou*) *theou*) or Servant of God (*pais tou theou*) see the respective arts. under Son of God.

νήπιος

νήπιος (*nēpios*), infant, minor.

CL *nēpios* denotes an infant, child or minor in cl. Gk. The word can be used in metaphorical sense, e.g. of young seedlings (Theophrastus, *Historia Plantarum*, 8, 1, 7). Furthermore, the characteristics of the foolish and inexperienced child may be so to the fore that the meaning of child recedes in favour of foolish, inexperienced (cf. Sophocles, *Electra*, 145 f.). Gk. philosophers who wanted to communicate to men true knowledge of the world and the life of reason dismissed with biting sarcasm the unperceptive man with no experience of life as *nēpios*, a fool (cf. Hesiod, *Works*, 130, 286 ff.; Epictetus, *Dissertations*, 3, 24, 53). Lucian mocked Christians as foolish children (*de morte Peregrini*, 11), for calling themselves *paides* (→ *pais*).

OT Heb. has no exact equivalent of Gk. *nēpios*. The LXX uses *nēpios*, with the meaning of child, to translate 4 different Heb. words: *yônēq*, baby, suckling (Isa. 11:8; in LXX frequently rendered by *thēlazōn*); *'elāl* or *'ôlēl*, little child (1 Sam. 15:3; in LXX sometimes *brephos*); *ṭap*, little child (Ezek. 9:6) and *na'ar*, boy (Prov. 23:13). In these contexts the most important characteristics of the *nēpios* are the weakness, helplessness and submission of the child over against the adult (cf. Lam. 1:5). Hos. 11:1 represents the origins of Israel (i.e. the exodus from Egypt; cf. also 2:17) as the people's youth (*nēpios*, *na'ar*). By contrast with the period of apostasy in Canaan, Israel followed Yahweh with undivided loyalty.

In addition to the words mentioned above, the LXX also translates *peṭi*, simple man, by *nēpios* (Ps. 19:8). Whereas the wisdom lit. reproaches the *nēpios* for being simple, i.e. dull and foolish (Prov. 1:32; cf. also 1:22 Aquila), *nēpios* in the Pss. denotes the man of simple faith (e.g. Pss. 116:6; 119:130) who stands under God's protection and pays attention to his instruction (cf. Paul's use of *mōros*, foolish [1 Cor. 4:10] → Wisdom, Folly).

NT In the NT *nēpios* occurs particularly in Paul, otherwise only in Matt., Lk. and once each in Eph. and Heb.

1. (a) In Matt. 21:16, Ps. 8:2(3) is quoted in the account of the cleansing of the Temple (Matt. 21:10–17). Jesus answers the indignation of the chief priests and scribes at the Hosanna of the children with the question, "Have you never read, 'Out of the mouths of babes and sucklings thou hast brought perfect praise'?" The quotation had undisputed authority for his opponents, so that their accusations immediately lost all substance. Clearly *nēpios* (v. 16) and the parallel *thēlazontōn*, sucklings, is linked with *paidas* (v. 15), but without any particular weight being attached to this connection. What is important is that the cry Hosanna (vv. 9, 15) is justified. The ground is thus knocked from beneath the feet of Jesus' accusers.

(b) The saying in Matt. 11:25 and Lk. 10:21 is widely attributed to the Q source, and may bear traces of Aram. (cf. SB I 606 f.). Both evangelists place it after the woes pronounced on Chorazin, Bethsaida and Capernaum, and Lk. mentions the mission of the seventy. The wording is identical in both versions: "I thank thee, Father, Lord of heaven and earth, that thou hast hidden these things from the wise and understanding and revealed them to babes; yea, Father, for such was thy gracious will." In both cases it is followed by the saying about the Son's unique mediation of the knowledge of the Father. *nēpioi* draws a contrast with the wise and understanding, and refers either to children, who by comparison with adults are considered as a rule immature and unwise (cf. 1 Cor. 14:20), or generally to the simple, without any emphasis being laid on the age of the "children".

2. (a) 1 Cor. 13:11 refers to the child/adult contrast. Paul uses this opposition to distinguish one age (*arti*, now) from the other (*tote*, then, v. 12). Just as the man now thinks differently from the child, so his knowledge in the age to come will be transformed. But faith, hope, and especially love hold good now (*nyni*) and will abide in the age to come (v. 13). In Rom. 2:20 the child/adult contrast is applied to the teacher/pupil relationship. The Jew, who has the law, is conscious of being in the role of the teacher, who instructs the *nēpios*, who does not have the law. But his failure to see his own hypocrisy in the light of the law undermines this role and brings dishonour to God (vv. 22–24).

In 1 Cor. 3:1 the spiritual is contrasted with the fleshly and the childish. The "not yet" and the additional "in Christ" with *nēpios* stand in contrast to the development that has begun, as the further metaphor of milk and solid food indicates. So what is at issue here is not a pre-Christian stage in contrast to the Christian life, but Christian life which has begun but still needs to develop. The Hel. mystery cults may well stand in the background (but cf. H. Schlier, *gala*, *TDNT* I 646), in which the devotee achieves ever higher stages of perfection by means of many ceremonies. The difference between Paul and the mystery cults, however, lies in the fact that he is not referring to pagan sacramental meals but to the Christian message. Accordingly, childishness is not a closed stage, but only a transitional phase (thus also Heb. 5:13 f.). The Hel. mystery cults may also provide the background to Eph. 4:14: "so that we may no longer be *nēpioi*, tossed to and fro and carried about with every wind of doctrine, by the cunning of men, by their crafty deceitful wiles." It is a question of growing (v. 15) and becoming complete (v. 13). Here again it is not a matter of distinguishing between Christians and non-Christians, but of Christians, who are as easily led astray as immature children, growing up into complete Christians.

(b) There are two readings of 1 Thess. 2:7: (a) *ēpioi* (we were *gentle* in your company); (b) *nēpioi* (babes). The preceding word ends with *n*, and it seems likely that this *n* has been doubled by mistake in copying. Moreover the interpretation of the second reading leads to difficulties. For in v. 7b it is not himself but the Thessalonians whom Paul likens to "children"; he and his colleagues were like a nurse (*trophos*). Paul's argument in Gal. 4:3 is different from that of the other passages. Here he uses legal and temporal categories. The pre-Christian period, i.e. the time before Jesus' coming on earth (v. 4) was the *nēpios*-period of the immature and slaves. The *nēpioi* were held in bondage as slaves by the *nomos* (→ Law) and the *stoicheia*, the elemental powers (→ Law). But Christ has come to redeem those under the law that they might receive adoption as sons (*hyiothesia*, v 5 → Son). The two periods stand in clearly marked contrast.   G. Braumann

| *pais* |

παῖς (*pais*), child, young man, son, servant; *παιδίον* (*paidion*), very young child, infant; *παιδάριον* (*paidarion*) little boy, child, youth; *βρέφος* (*brephos*), unborn child, embryo, baby, infant.

CL 1. *pais* (from Homer onwards; connected with the root *pou* or *pau*, few, little, cf. Lat. *pauper*, *paulus*) means child (mostly masc.) as son, but also a daughter in relation to descent (Homer, *Il.* 2, 205). In relation to age it denotes a child in years (Homer, *Od.* 4, 665), a boy between 7 and 14 years, as distinct from the little child or the youth (cf. Hippocrates, *De Hebdomadibus* 5). Socially it means a servant or slave (Aesch., *Cho.* 653 f.), fem. *paidiskē*, maid, servant girl, female slave. → Son of God, art. *pais theou*.

2. *paidion* (from Homer onwards), a diminutive of *pais*, denotes a little child up to 7 years (Hdt. 2, 119), the newborn child (Hdt. 1, 110). It may also refer to a young slave, male or female.

3. *paidarion* (from Aristoph. onwards), likewise a diminutive of *pais*, generally means, like *paidion*, a little child (cf. Plato, *Symp.* 207d). But it can mean a young man (cf. Tob. 6:2 f.), a young servant or slave (Xenoph., *Agesilaus* I 21; Aristoph., *Plutus* 823, 843).

4. *brephos* (from Homer onwards) denotes the unborn child, the embryo (Homer, *Il.* 23, 266), the newborn child, the baby and the little child (from Pindar on).

OT 1. In the LXX *pais* occurs some 500 times and stands for 10 different Heb. words, particularly often for *'ebed*, slave, servant, subordinate (341 times; → Slave, art. *doulos*; → Son of God, art. *pais theou*, for Servant of the Lord). But since it also renders Heb. *na'ar*, youth (e.g. Prov. 1:4), *bēn*, son (e.g. Prov. 4:1), the use of *pais* in its breadth of meaning is not to be distinguished from secular Gk. (see above CL, 1).

2. Heb. equivalents for *paidion* include *yeled* (boy, 35 times), *na'ar* (youth 27 times), *bēn* (son, 19 times), *ṭap̄* (child, 7 times); for *paidarion* predominantly *na'ar* (youth). *paidion* or *paidarion*, in the LXX as in secular Gk., denote the baby (Gen. 21:7), the little child (Gen. 21:14), the lad (Gen. 22:5, 12) and the young man (Jdg. 8:14). They are frequently used to emphasize the serving capacity of young people, as companion (Gen. 22:5), messenger (Jdg. 7:10), arms bearer (Jdg. 9:54; 1 Sam. 14:1) or servant (Neh. 13:19; Ruth 2:5 f.).

NT 1. Passages attributed to the Q source use both *pais* and *paidion*. The centurion's servant is called a *pais* (Matt. 8:6, 13; Lk. 7:7) and the children in the market place are *paidia* (Matt. 11:16; Lk. 7:32). Matt. also uses *pais* of Herod's servants (14:2) and *paidion* (Matt. 14:21; 15:38) in the great feedings. The number of those filled excluded women and children. Mk. has only *paidion* and does not use *brephos* or *pais*, e.g. Mk. 5:39 (cf. Matt. 9:24, *korasion*, girl); 7:28; 9:24. Lk. is the only evangelist to use *brephos*, chiefly in the infancy narratives, of the unborn child (Lk. 1:41, 44), and the newborn baby (Lk. 2:12, 16; Acts 7:19). In using *brephos* instead of *paidion* in Lk. 18:15 (though not 16 f.; cf. Matt. 19:13 ff.; Mk. 10:13 ff.) Lk. was perhaps thinking especially of babies. But *pais* also occurs in Lk. 2:43 of the 12 year old Jesus; 8:51, 54 of a girl; 12:45 and 15:26 of servants. So too does *paidion* (Lk .1:59, the child at the circumcision; 11:7, children in the parable of the friend at midnight). Jn. also uses both *pais* (only Jn. 4:51), *paidion* (4:49) and *hyios* (son, 4:50) of the same child. He uses *paidion* of the newborn child (16:21) and, in addition, *paidarion* (Jn. 6:9 the only NT occurrence of the word) of the lad with five loaves and two small fishes.

In 1 Cor. 14:20 Paul warns against being childish ("do not be children"). Thus the picture of the child is here used negatively (contrast Mk. 10:15). Otherwise the word group occurs in Paul only in Gal. 4:22 f., 30 f. in the comparison of the bondage of Judaism with Sarah's maid or female slave (*paidiskē*; cf. Gen. 16:15; 21:2, 9–12). Heb. uses *paidion* 3 times (2:13, 14; 11:23). Apart from the Lk. passages referred to, *brephos* occurs only in 2 Tim. 3:15 (*apo brephous*, from childhood) and 1 Pet. 2:2 ("Like newborn babes, long for the pure spiritual milk, that by it you may grow up to salvation"). The latter passage speaks of newborn children (*brephē*) in a metaphorical sense. It may be understood against the background of the Hel. mystery cults (→ *hyios* OT, 2c and → *teknon* NT, on the Johannine understanding of child of God). *G. Braumann*

2. In the above passages no special theological significance attaches to *pais* and *paidion*. They have the same range of meaning as in ordinary language. But in three groups of passages children are related to the kingdom.

(a) Matt. 19:13 ff.; Mk. 10:13–16; and Lk. 18:15 ff. relate the incident of Jesus' blessing the children despite the protests of the disciples. The reluctance of the disciples to allow adults to bring children to Jesus has been ascribed to the disciples' concern that Jesus was tired. But perhaps there was also the implication that children (Matt. and Mk. *paidia;* Lk. *brephē*) were too young to make a responsible commitment. Certainly they would not be of the age of becoming Bar Mitzwah at 13 and able to take on themselves the yoke of the Law (cf. J. Bowman, *The Gospel of Mark: The New Christian Jewish Passover Haggadah*, 1965, 211). Jesus replies: "Let the children come to me, do not hinder them; for to such (*toiouton*) belongs the kingdom of God. Truly, I say to you, whoever does not receive the kingdom of God like a child shall not enter it" (Mk. 10:14 f.; cf. Matt. 19:14; 18:3; Lk. 18:17). Mk. adds: "And he took them in his arms and blessed them, laying his hands upon them" (10:16; cf. Matt. 19:15). The term *such* may suggest "these and other (literal) children" or "these and others who, though not literally children, share the characteristics of children" (D. E. Nineham, *Saint Mark*, 1969, 267 f.). On the role of children in the divine order see Ps. 8:2; Matt. 11:25; 21:15 f. But Mk. 10:15 suggests that the second interpretation is appropriate. In this case, Jesus' pronouncement reverses the apparent understanding of the disciples. Instead of insisting that men should be mature enough to make a responsible commitment, Jesus is saying that there is a sense in which the reverse is true. The reason why the kingdom belongs to children is not because of any subjective qualities that they may have; it lies in their objective helplessness (C. E. B. Cranfield, *The Gospel According to Saint Mark*, 1959, 324; cf. E. Schweizer, *The Good News According to Mark*, 1970, 206 f. who points out that Jesus is not speaking of their sinlessness or purity and that the child is not a symbol for the ascetic as in Gos. Thom. 22). The saying is paralleled in Jn. 3 by the discourse with Nicodemus comparing entry into the kingdom with rebirth. Some have seen implications of infant baptism in this story

284

(cf. O. Cullmann, *Baptism in the New Testament*, 1950, 71 ff.; A. Richardson, *An Introduction to the Theology of the New Testament*, 1958, 360 f.). On the evidence for the practice of baptism after the NT period see J. Jeremias, *Infant Baptism in the First Four Centuries*, 1960; K. Aland, *Did the Early Church Baptize Infants?*, 1963; and J. Jeremias, *The Origins of Infant Baptism: A Further Study in Reply to Kurt Aland*, 1963. With regard to the present passage, there is no solid evidence for inferring that Jesus or the early church linked the event with baptism. On the other hand, Jesus' categorical statement that the kingdom belongs to such implies that they may be full members of the church and thus fit subjects to receive the sacrament of incorporation.

(b) A similar saying occurs in Matt. 18:3 f. in the course of the dispute among the disciples as to who would be the greatest in the kingdom. Jesus set a child (*paidion*) in their midst and said: "Truly, I say to you, unless you turn (*straphēte*) and become like children (*hōs ta paidia*) you will never enter the kingdom of heaven. Whoever humbles himself like this child, he is the greatest in the kingdom of heaven." Neither of the parallel accounts in Mk. 9:33–37 and Lk. 9:46 ff. contains this saying. This has led to the suggestion that it is a doublet taken from the passages discussed under (a). But there the thought is of receiving the kingdom as a little child; here it is of becoming like little children and entering the kingdom, leading to the thought of humbling oneself "like this child." On humility in Matt. see 5:3; 20:26; 23:11.

(c) The saying which immediately follows in Matt. 23:12 is paralleled and amplified by Mk. 9:37 and Lk. 18:17. In Mk.'s version it reads: "Whoever receives one such child in my name receives me; and whoever receives me, receives not me but him who sent me." This underlines again the role that children have in their own right in the kingdom of God and at the same time the responsibility of the church in acting upon this. But it is also related to a theme which finds recurrent expression in the gospels: Jesus is present (albeit *incognito*) in those who are his. This is said of appointed witnesses to Christ (Matt. 10:40; Lk. 10:16; Jn. 13:20), of children (in the present passage), of those in need (Matt. 25:35–45; cf. Mk. 9:41), and of those in prayer and service (Matt. 18:20; cf. Jn. 15:4 ff.). These passages carry with them the corollary that those who maltreat the representatives of Christ (perhaps not even realizing the significance of their actions) bear a terrible responsibility.

C. Brown

τέκνον

τέκνον (*teknon*), child; τεκνίον (*teknion*), little child.

CL & OT *teknon*, attested from Homer on, denotes the child in relation to his parents and forefathers (*tiktein*, beget, bear; cf. LXX *teknopoiein*, bear a child, Gen. 11:30 etc.; NT *teknogonia*, bearing of children, 1 Tim. 2:15; *teknogonein*, bear or beget children, 1 Tim. 5:14 f.). *teknon* denotes both the child still unborn (Gen. 3:17; 17:16) and the elder son (Gen. 27:13). It does not distinguish sex, although in the LXX *teknon* (representing 11 Heb. words) frequently translates *bēn*. In addition to the broader meaning, descendant (Gen. 30:1), the word is also used metaphorically, as an intimate form of address (Gen. 43:29) or to denote a pupil in his relationship to his master (1 Sam. 3:16; 26:17). In Ps. 34:11 wisdom calls to men:

285

"Come, O children, listen to me." *teknion*, diminutive of *teknon*, is a nursery term (A. Oepke, *TDNT* V 639) and denotes the little child. It does not occur in the LXX.

NT 1. All the strands of the synoptic tradition contain the word *teknon*. It occurs in the description of the relationship of parents to their children as a picture of our relationship with God (Matt. 7:11; Lk. 11:13), in Jesus' lament over Jerusalem (Matt. 23:37; Lk. 13:3; → Bird), and in the sense of descendant (Matt. 3:9; Lk. 3:8; cf. also Jn. 8:39; Rom. 9:7 f.; Gal. 4:31). All these passages common to Matt. and Lk. are widely attributed to Q. Mk. speaks of children with respect to their relationship to their parents (Mk. 13:12; Matt. 10:21). Jesus used the word as a form of address (Mk. 2:5; Matt. 9:2; Mk. 10:24). In the material peculiar to Matt. it refers both to children and to family relationships regardless of age (Matt. 18:25; 21:28; 27:25). The same is true of the material peculiar to Lk. 15:31, cf. 23:28; Acts 2:39; 7:5; 13:33; 21:5). As a form of address, "child" is used in Lk. 16:25, expressing intimate or group relationship (cf. wisdom's children in Lk. 7:35).

There are several references in the epistle to parent-child relationships. The obedience of children to their parents (Eph. 6:1; Col. 3:20) should be reciprocated by the kindness of parents towards their children (Eph. 6:4; Col. 3:21; cf. 1 Thess. 2:7). The parent's task includes warning; hence Paul also warns the church (1 Thess. 2:11). He compares his flock to children (1 Cor. 4:14; 2 Cor. 6:13; Gal. 4:19). Paul also saw his relationship to Timothy as a father-child relationship (1 Cor. 4:17; Phil. 2:22). The Pastoral Epistles lay great stress on orderly family relationships (1 Tim. 3:4, 12; Tit. 1:6; cf. also 1 Tim. 5:4). Timothy and Titus are addressed as Paul's children in the faith (1 Tim. 1:2; 2 Tim. 1:2; 2:1; Tit. 1:4).

teknion, little child, is used only in the Johannine writings, and then only as a form of address to the disciples or the church (Jn. 13:33; 1 Jn. 2:1, 12, 28; 3:7, 18; 4:4; 5:21; → *pais*).

teknon can, however, also describe membership of a particular group: 1 Pet. 4:14 (the obedient); Eph. 2:3 (those who have fallen under the wrath of God); Eph. 5:8 (of light); 2 Pet. 2:14 (those who stand under a curse); cf. also 2 Jn. 1, 4, 13; 3 Jn. 4. Arndt regards most of these as Hebraisms together with the expression children of wisdom (i.e. those who attach themselves to her and are led by her, Matt. 11:19 *v.l.*; Lk. 7:35) and the designation of the inhabitants of a city as its *tekna* (Joel 2:23; Zech. 9:13; 1 Macc. 1:38; Matt. 23:37; Lk. 13:34; 19:44; Gal. 4:25).

2. Traditions which are independent of each other speak of children of God. Paul's starting point is the promise that those who belong to Israel stand under God's blessing (Rom. 9:4 f.; Gal. 4:21 f.). But who belongs to Israel? Not the natural descendants of Abraham (Rom. 9:6 f.; Gal. 4:23), but those who believe, for whom the promise is valid (Rom. 9:8; Gal. 4:23, 28). "It is men of faith who are sons of Abraham" (Gal. 3:7). There is a contrast between → flesh and → spirit (Gal. 4:29; Rom. 8:13). It is not a question, therefore, of a natural relationship as children to God, but of a legal acceptance by adoption of believers as children of God and heirs of the promise. The gift which establishes the relationship (*hyiothesia*, cf. art. *hyios* below) is the → Spirit, who cries Abba, Father, leads into freedom, and engenders the hope of sonship (Rom. 8:13–17, 19–23; cf. Gal. 4:5 f.).

Paul sees the question in the light of salvation history and does not distinguish between child and son. Some scholars believe that Jn. uses the language of the Hel.

mystery religions, which saw being children of God realistically in terms of begetting and birth, as a new being mediated by initiation. The child of God is born of God (Jn. 1:12 f.; 1 Jn. 2:29; 3:2). Children of God (not sons of God) and children of the devil stand opposed (1 Jn. 3:10). Love for God and love for the brethren characterize the children of God (1 Jn. 4:21; → hyios NT, 2(a)). Jn. uses hyios (son) of Jesus Christ the only begotten Son of God (3:16; 20:31), but tekna of men who receive him and so become children of God (see above passages).

In Eph. 5:1 the church is called to be mimētai tou theou, imitators of God, and as such are hōs tekna agapēta, as beloved children. This expresses the call to discipleship. The → disciple stands in a child-father relationship to God. Discipleship may, however, entail, under certain circumstances, the abandonment of all by the disciple, even his children (Mk. 10:29 f.; cf. Lk. 14:26).

The horror of the end is depicted, among other things, in terms of the father set against the child and the child against the parents (Mk. 13:12; Matt. 10:21; cf. Lk. 21:16).

3. Thus the NT has not developed a theology of the child. Children are referred to in passing as a matter of course, and their role discussed accordingly. Where the documents deal with Jesus' encounters with children, we can find neither a sentimental love of children nor an ideology of childhood innocence. G. Braumann

---

| υἱός | υἱός (hyios), son; υἱοθεσία (hyiothesia), adoption. |

CL 1. hyios, attested from Mycenean Gk. onwards, denotes the son in the widest sense, as both the son of human parents (Homer, Il., 5, 159) and the offspring of animals and plants. Further, hyios can mean descendant in general (Homer, Il., 2, 727) with no reference to the immediate forebears, e.g. it can stand for grandson. The idea of family relationship can recede completely and give way to one of relationship of interest: the teacher-pupil relationship can be represented by the father–son relationship. Closely connected with this is the fact that membership of a particular group can be expressed by the word son (Homer: sons of the Achaians). Finally hyios with the gen. (cf. Heb. ben in the construct) can denote that certain things and concepts are dependent upon one another and belong together (e.g. sons of light, of darkness, etc.).

2. The attitude of Gk. antiquity towards the child underwent various changes. In the closely knit and ordered society of the city-state children (above all sons) were the pride of the family. They were a welcome help at work and inherited the honour and the duties of their father. On the other hand, deformed children, especially girls, were just not reared at Sparta and other places. Later generations with an individualistic outlook on life manifested a tendency to limit the number of children. In the early period of the arts the theme of children had no role at all. In the classical period the "children" of Niobe were represented as adult figures. From the 3rd cent. B.C. there began an increasing preference for the idyll of childlikeness, a tendency which had its origin in the sphere of playfulness and privacy, and from there was transferred to the child (details in A. Oepke, TDNT V 640 f.).

3. hyiothesia occurs seldom (never in the LXX). It is a technical legal term and means adoption, the accepting of a child as one's own.

OT 1. (a) In the OT the child and especially the son (in the LXX, above all to translate *bēn*, ca. 4800 times) was seen as the gift of God (Gen. 1:28; Deut. 28:4–11; Isa. 54:1; Ps. 128:3), although the burden of pregnancy and the pain of childbirth were understood in Gen. 3:16 as God's punishment. To have no children was reckoned a disadvantage, a disgrace (Gen. 30:1 f.; 1 Sam. 1:11), and a sign of a lack of blessing (Gen. 33:5). One was proud of one's sons, because they were a help and a support (Ps. 127:3 ff.). This did not exclude the fact that children needed upbringing (→ discipline) and that parents must exercise their responsibility towards their children (Deut. 6:7). Correspondingly, children must respect their parents and elders (Exod. 20:12). For violence against father and mother on the part of children the death penalty was prescribed (Exod. 21:15). Corporal punishment was taken for granted (Prov. 22:15). The idea of the original innocence of children, which is widespread among us, was foreign to the OT (Jer. 6:11; 44:7). Children were unwise and helpless. They were introduced to the customs and rites of religion from an early age (Exod. 12:26; 1 Sam. 1:4). In Rab. Judaism we find authorities who speak with the greatest respect of children (SB I 781). On the other hand, it was permissible for children to be sold (SB I 798). They were blessed by their parents (SB I 807 f.) and by the righteous (SB II 138).

2. (a) The motif of God's son or sons is a frequent one in the OT (→ Son of God). Israel and the Israelites, in particular the righteous, are called the children of God. Israel is "my firstborn son" (Exod. 4:22; cf. Isa. 1:2). The idea of the son of God, in dependence on Egyptian traditions, has a place in particular in the royal psalms (cf. Ps. 2:7 etc.). The son, however, is not understood here as lit. begotten but as elected (cf. A Weiser, *The Psalms*, 1962, 113 f.; → Height, art. *hypsoō*).

(b) In Judaism there is the idea of the children of God based not on nature but on God's election and man's action. Whoever acts righteously is a son of God (Wis. 2:18; cf. Matt. 5:9; Hos. 1:10 ff.; MT 2:1 ff.). This operates, however, within Judaism. The Hel. mystery religions, on the other hand, thought of this relationship as transmitted naturally or sacramentally by means of initiation ceremonies. What was sought was not a close relationship and fellowship with the godhead, but substantial interchange with and participation in it.

3. The Qumran documents speak of sons in a wide variety of phrases: the sons of light and of darkness, the sons of righteousness and unrighteousness, of truth and corruption, of Belial, of God's good pleasure (IQH 4:32; cf. Lk. 2:14), of heaven (1QS 4:22), of grace (1QH 7:20), of the world (CD 20:34), of iniquity (1QH 6:30), and of mischief (1QH 5:25).

NT 1. Apart from 1 Cor., Phil., Col., the Pastorals, 2 Pet. and the letters of Jn., *hyios* occurs in every strand and document of the NT, sometimes very frequently (on Mk. and Jn. → Son of God).

(a) *hyios* can denote the relationship of the son (→ First, art. *prōtotokos*) to his father (Mk. 10:46), to his mother (Matt. 2:20) or to both (Lk. 1:13), or to his physical ancestors (Matt. 1:20, son of David; Lk. 19:9, son of Abraham). From this arises the more general meaning of descendant (Matt. 23:31).

(b) *hyios* is used metaphorically to denote membership of a particular group of people: Acts 3:25 speaks of the sons of the prophets and of the covenant; Acts 23:6 of a son of the Pharisees. Sons of men and son of man denote membership of the human race (Mk. 3:28; Eph. 3:5; Heb. 2:6). Participation in a greater whole is expressed in this way, so that it is possible to talk about sons of the resurrection (Lk. 20:36), of the kingdom (Matt. 8:12; 13:38), of light (Lk. 16:8; Jn. 12:36; 1 Thess. 5:5), of encouragement (Acts 4:36), of the evil one (Matt. 13:38), of hell (Matt. 23:15), of this age (Lk. 16:8; 20:34), of destruction (Jn. 17:12; 2 Thess. 2:3), of the devil (Acts 13:10), of disobedience (Eph. 2:2; 5:6), of thunder (Mk. 3:17).

(c) The allegory of the weeds among the wheat contains the contrast between the "sons of the kingdom" and "the sons of the evil one" (Matt. 13:38). Just as in the field the grain grows up with the weeds and the two are not separated until the harvest, so, according to Matt., the church is a mixed body until the day of judgment. Only then does a separation take place (Matt. 13:40 ff.).

(d) The parent–child relationship is set in a new light by Jesus' call to discipleship. On the one hand, ties of blood pale into insignificance in the light of the call (Matt. 10:37; Lk. 14:26 f.) and in the events of the end may even be transformed into enmity (Mk. 13:12). On the other hand, they regain the significance they had lost at the hands of the Pharisees (Mk. 7:9–13). In the later epistles the handling of children became a theme in its own right. Children have their place in the directions about social and family relationships (Col. 3:20 f.; Eph. 6:1 ff.).

2. (a) Of special theological significance are those passages which speak of God's sons (*hyioi theou*) and of the relationship of sonship to God (cf. *hyiothesia* 5 times in Paul). The fact that the phrase occurs both in Paul and in documents which are independent of Paul suggests the possibility of early, primitive Christian traditions existing before Paul, however one sees a background for them in the OT or in the history of religions (cf. SB I 219 f.). This suggestion finds support in so far as it is possible to demonstrate a context for the preaching of sonship to God in the early church. With regard to Rom. 8:14 f. O. Michel has commented: "Sonship . . . expresses the freedom of the baptized Christian, who needs to recognize no other tie but the will of God; it expresses the realization that God has committed himself to man; and it expresses the trust which grows out of his fatherhood" (*Der Brief an die Römer*, KEK 1965[13], 197). In Gal. 4:5 Paul speaks of receiving adoption as sons. This is linked with → baptism in Gal. 3:26 f. (cf. O. Michel, op. cit., 196; H. Schlier, *Der Brief an die Galater*, KEK, 1966[13], 172). But baptism in the NT is never treated as a rite separable from → faith (cf. Gal. 2:20; 3:5 ff, 23 ff.; Rom. 6:3 ff.; cf. 1:17; 4:1–5:1).

Paul takes the idea a stage further in that he understands sonship not just as a present condition (like his predecessors) but also as the goal of hope, still to be fulfilled (Rom. 8:23; cf. also Jas. 1:18; 1 Pet. 1:23). Thus the concept takes on a peculiar double aspect. "On the one hand, it is a thing of the future, a longed-for goal (Rom. 8:23: [*hyiothesian apekdechomenoi*] we wait for adoption as sons); on the other hand, it is a present thing, as is attested by the fact that in the Spirit – that eschatological gift – we cry 'Abba!' (Rom. 8:15 f.; Gal. 4:6 f.)" (R. Bultmann, *Theology of the New Testament*, I, 1952, 278). Moreover, Paul places the preaching of sonship within his own framework of salvation history. From the fact that one belongs to Christ by being among "those of faith" (*hoi ek pisteōs*), he concludes that one belongs to the sons of Abraham (Gal. 3:7, 29). Belonging to them guarantees salvation. But if this recalls the question of descent from Abraham, the question that it raises for Paul is the question of inheritance (Gal. 4:1 ff.). Christians have entered into the inheritance, because they are heirs of Christ and of God (Gal. 4:4 ff.; Rom. 8:17).   *G. Braumann*

(b) Peacemakers are promised, in the seventh beatitude, that they will be called sons of God (Matt. 5:9; cf. Rom. 9:26). "To be called a son of God is the highest honour and the richest gift of grace. The words 'shall be called' indicate that it all depends upon God's verdict. . . . A man cannot make himself a son of God; he has to be given the name by which he becomes a son" (A. Schlatter, *Der Evangelist Matthäus*, 1959⁵, 140; cf. Deut. 14:1; Hos. 2:1). The beatitude is all the more significant in view of the fact that at various crucial points in Matt. Jesus is called → the Son of God either explicitly or by implication. These include the baptism, temptation, Peter's confession, the transfiguration, crucifixion and sending out of the disciples (Matt. 2:15; 3:17; 4:3, 6 f.; 8:9, 29; 11:25 ff.; 14:33; 16:16; 17:6; 21:37 f.; 26:63; 27:40, 43, 54; 28:19). Against this background, there is the double implication in the beatitude (1) that Israel as such is not the son of God but only those in Israel who are peacemakers, and (2) that men may become through being → disciples of Jesus what he is in himself.

Matt.'s use of Hos. 11:1 ("Out of Egypt have I called my son", cf. Matt. 2:15) reinforces this conclusion. Matt. sees the return of the holy family from Egypt as a → fulfilment of this prophecy. As a fulfilment, this is not to be understood in the sense of a prediction that has come off. For Hosea is clearly talking about the exodus and not about the infant Jesus coming from Egypt. It is, however, fulfilment in the deeper sense that Jesus, and not the nation of Israel, is the true son of God, and that the original event that Hosea spoke about and which the Jews regarded as one of the great events of history was in fact only a foreshadowing of an apparently insignificant event which would turn out to be the most significant event for mankind.

(c) Lk. 20:36 speaks of "sons of the resurrection" (cf. Mk. 12:25 f.; Matt. 22:30 f.). The expression is a Hebraism which had acclimatized itself in Gk. (M.-J. Lagrange, *L'Évangile selon Saint Luc*, 1941⁵, 516; A. Deissmann, *Bible Studies*, 1903², 162 f.). There are, however, several NT passages which make the metaphor explicit by relating resurrection and rebirth. Matt. 19:28 speaks of the regeneration (*palingenesia*) suggesting a cosmic event. The only other use of this word relates it to baptism and personal renewal as a present reality (Tit. 3:5). 1 Pet. 1:3 speaks of being "born anew to a living hope through the resurrection of Jesus Christ from the dead." Here there is an element of realization in the present, and the resurrection in this instance is Christ's and not ours, but it has a future aspect (cf. 1:4, 23; 3:21 f.; 5:10; cf. Col. 3:1–4). The discussion of Jesus with Nicodemus on rebirth in Jn. 3 is usually taken to refer to present spiritual experiences, but it may well have overtones of the connection between resurrection, rebirth and sonship. For that which is born of the flesh cannot enter the kingdom of God, but only that which is born of the Spirit (Jn. 3:5; cf. 1 Cor. 15:50). Sonship is connected with rebirth in Jn. 1:12 f. (where the Gk. word is *tekna*). But Jn. prefers to keep the term Son of God for Jesus (20:31; cf. 17:1 ff.) and his stress falls on the present reality of new life (cf. 3:16–21; 15:7 ff.).   *C. Brown*
→ Son of God, Servant of God, Son of Man, Son of David

290

(a). G. Bertram, *nēpios*, *TDNT* IV 912–23; J. Jeremias, *The Parables of Jesus*, 1963²; and *New Testament Theology*, I, 1971, 178–202; F. Lyall, "Roman Law in the Writings of Paul—Adoption", *JBL* 88, 1969, 458–66; Moore, *Judaism* II 131–35; A. Oepke, *pais*, *TDNT* V 636–54; E. Schweizer *et al.*, *hyios*, *TDNT* VIII 334–400.
(b). G. Delling, "Lexikalisches zu *teknon*. Ein Nachtrag zur Exegese von 1 Kor. 7, 14," in *Festschrift* for E. Barnikol, 1964, 35 ff.; W. Grundmann, *Die Gotteskindschaft in der Geschichte Jesu und ihre religionsgeschichtlichen Voraussetzungen*, 1938; O. Michel, " 'Diese Kleinen', eine Jünger-bezeichnung Jesu," *ThStKr* 108, 1937–38, 401–15; H. Schlier, *Der Brief an die Galater*, KEK 7, 1965¹³; J. Weiss, *Der erste Korintherbrief*, KEK 5, 1910.
→ Literature under Baptism, Conversion, Son

Church, Synagogue

ἐκκλησία

ἐκκλησία (*ekklēsia*), assembly, meeting, congregation, church; συνάγω (*synagō*), gather; συναγωγή (*synagōge*), assembly, synagogue.

CL 1. (a) *ekklēsia*, derived via *ek-kaleō*, which was used for the summons to the army to assemble, from *kaleō*, to call (→ Call). It is attested from Eur. and Hdt. onwards (5th cent. B.C.), and denotes in the usage of antiquity the popular assembly of the competent full citizens of the *polis*, city. It reached its greatest importance in the 5th cent. and met at regular intervals (in Athens about 30–40 times a year, elsewhere less frequently) and also in cases of urgency as an extra-ordinary *ekklēsia*. Its sphere of competence included decisions on suggested changes in the law (which could only be effected by the council of the 400), on appointments to official positions and – at least in its heyday – on every important question of internal and external policy (contracts, treaties, war and peace, finance). To these was added in special cases (e.g. treason) the task of sitting in judgment, which as a rule fell to regular courts. The *ekklēsia* opened with prayers and sacrifices to the gods of the city. It was bound by the existing laws. Every citizen had the right to speak and to propose matters for discussion, but a proposition could only be dealt with if there was an expert opinion on the matter (Aristot., *Ath. Pol.* 45). A decision was only valid if it won a certain number of votes. Authorization to participate, and the methods of summoning the assembly and of voting – by show of hands in Athens (Aristot., *Ath.Pol.*, 45), by acclaim (Thuc., 1, 87), by ballot sheets or stones (Xen. *Hell.*, 1, 7, 9) – were strictly regulated, as was the control of the assembly, which originally lay with the president of the Prytaneis and from the 4th cent. B.C. with a college of nine.

(b) Thus *ekklēsia*, centuries before the translation of the OT and the time of the NT, was clearly characterized as a political phenomenon, repeated according to certain rules and within a certain framework. It was the assembly of full citizens, functionally rooted in the constitution of the democracy, an assembly in which fundamental political and judical decisions were taken. The scope of its competence varied in the different states. Only occasionally were other terms used for this organ of government by the people (e.g. *halia*, *agora*). What is noteworthy, however, is that the word *ekklēsia*, throughout the Gk. and Hel. areas, always retained its reference to the assembly of the *polis*. In only three exceptional cases was it used

291

for the business meeting of a cultic guild (cf. H. Lietzmann, *An die Korinther*, HNT 9, 4). Otherwise it was never used for guilds or religious fellowships. These were referred to by such expressions as *thiasos*, cultic assembly to worship a god; *eranos*, lit. contract of partnership, but in this context a fellowship which held particular → feasts (*heortē*), to which each participant contributed; *koinon*, lit. that which is in common (→ Fellowship, art. *koinos*); or *synodos*, which meant a group following the same → way, i.e. the same teaching. Significantly, however, none of these words found its way into the NT. The same is true, moreover, of the derivatives of the nouns, the vbs. *ekklēsiazō*, trans. to assemble, and *exekklēsiazomai*, intrans. to gather together, which only occur in the LXX a few times.

2. In contrast to *ekklēsia*, which had become a technical term by an early date, the other word which is important to us in this context, *synagōgē* (derived from *synagō*, bring together, and attested from the 5th cent. B.C. onwards), exhibited from the first a wide breadth of usage. It denoted quite generally, in the trans. sense, the collecting or bringing together of things (books, letters, possessions, fruit at harvest time), and also of troops and people. Nevertheless, the word found its specialized and most clearly defined meaning in the activities of the guilds. Here it was used (above all from the 2nd cent. B.C. onwards, and now intrans.) for the regular, mostly festive assembly, linked with a meal and sacrifice, of the guilds which are almost without exception to be understood as cultic fellowships. It can also denote their normal business meeting, and the guild itself but only rarely, late, and to all appearances only in non-cultic contexts (the contexts are those of profession or interest). It is impossible to find in classical Gk. absolutely clear attestation of the fact that *synagōgē*, progressing from the nature of the activity to its scene, was used to denote the place of assembly. This probably originated within Judaism (see below OT 3 (b); relevant material in W. Schrage, *TDNT* VII 806 ff.).

OT 1. (a) In the translation of the LXX the Gk. word *ekklēsia* occurs about 100 times, of which 22 are in the Apocrypha and a further 3 have no Heb. equivalent. It represents exclusively the Heb. *qāhāl* (including once each for four derivatives of the root). On the other hand, it is striking that the Heb. word is not always rendered by *ekklēsia*. In Gen., Lev. and Num., for example, *qāhāl* is translated 21 times by *synagōgē*, and of the 15 passages in Ezek. *ekklēsia* appears only in Ezek. 32:23 and never in the five passages in Jer. Instead, *synagōgē*, along with *ochlos*, crowd (e.g. Jer. 31:8; Ezek. 16:40; 17:17) or *plēthos*, multitude (Exod. 12:6; 2 Chr. 31:18) are used.

(b) By contrast, *synagōgē* appears (225 times, of which 34 have no Heb. equivalent) with only isolated exceptions for Heb. *'ēḏâh*, for which, practically speaking, there is no other important translation. The exceptions are Num. 4:34 *dēmos*, people; 16:40 (MT. 17:5) *episystasis*, uprising, tumult; Ps. 1:5 *boulē*, assembly. In nine passages the Heb. word is not translated directly, but has fallen out as the result of tautology. But while *qāhāl* could clearly be rendered by both Gk. words, *'ēḏâh* was never translated by *ekklēsia*. It seems, therefore, that *synagōgē* was capable of expressing the sense of both Heb. terms, whereas *ekklēsia* could only be used with a specific meaning (cf. on this point CL 2).

2. (a) *qāhāl*, probably related to *qôl*, voice, means a summons to an assembly and the act of assembling and is perhaps most accurately translated as mustering. Verbal

forms derived from the noun occur, each 19 times, in the hiph. (to summon an assembly, e.g. Exod. 35:1; Num. 20:8; 1 Chr. 15:3) and in the niph. (to assemble, e.g. Lev. 8:4; Jer. 26:9). In these cases, especially in the Pentateuch, it is frequently the '*ēḏâh* (see under b) which assembles (e.g. Lev. 8:3; Num. 17:7; Jos. 18:1; Jdg. 20:1), or the '*ām*, the people (e.g. Exod. 32:1; Deut. 4:10), (the house of) Israel (1 Chr. 13:5), Judah (1 Ki. 12:21), the elders (1 Ki. 8:1), or the princes (1 Chr. 28:1). This breadth of usage clearly indicates that the decisive meaning of the word is to be determined from the noun and not from the vb.

Who, then, is addressed as the *qāhāl*, denoted by it, and belongs to it? In the earliest strata of the OT the word is rare and stands primarily for the summons to war of all the men capable of bearing arms (Gen. 49:6; Num. 22:4; verbal form in 2 Sam. 20:14; 1 Ki. 12:21). To a certain extent, these represent the people (the '*ām*), but occasionally the word stands for the whole congregation of the people (Num. 16:33). In Deut. *qāhāl* means above all the congregation gathered to conclude the covenant at Sinai (Deut. 9:10; 10:4). It is qualified by being linked to the name of Yahweh (cf. especially Deut. 23:2 ff.). The word stands here for the people which Yahweh has summoned, which is bound by the rules he has given (→ Commandment; → Law), and whose participation in Yahweh's → Covenant is only maintained by obedience. Thus *qāhāl* had also a religious element alongside that of a special, solemn assembly. In the subsequent period (the stratum of the deuteronomic history) the word admittedly lost once again its strictly religious character (e.g. 1 Ki. 8:65; 12:3 ff.) and came to mean simply the special, general assembly of the people, including women and probably even children in Jer. 44:15 and in the post-exilic passages (Ezr. 10:1; Neh. 8:2). In Ezek., where the word occurs as many as 15 times (it is more frequent only in Chr.: 30 times), it is used once again quite without religious significance for the mustering of the army, troops, and even refers to nations other than Israel (Ezek. 17:17, Egypt; 27:27, Tyre; 32:22, Assyria). It is understandable that the LXX translates it throughout, not by *ekklēsia*, but by *synagōgē* or *ochlos*.

In 19 passages from Gen. to Num the word is used only quantitatively for the great multitude (of the peoples in Gen. 28:3; 35:11). But it can also give solemn emphasis to the special character of the one people dedicated to Yahweh (e.g. Num. 16:3; 20:6). The characteristic word for the congregation, however, is '*ēḏâh* (see below). In Chr., where with 30 occurrences *qāhāl* is most frequent, it appears both in a representative sense for the assembly of the leaders of Israel summoned by the king to take decisions, which may be religious (the bringing up of the ark 1 Chr. 13:2, 4) or political (1 Chr. 29:10), and also for the crowd gathered for sacrifice and worship (e.g. 2 Chr. 20:5, 14; 30:2, 4). This crowd (gathered in the temple) is also designated *qāhāl* in the Pss. (e.g. 22:23; 89:6 "or the holy ones"; 149:1 "of the faithful"). But there is also a *qāhāl* of the evil-doers (Ps. 26:5). Thus, from the point of view of meaning, *qāhāl* extends from call-up for military service, via meeting political consultation or judicial hearing, to assembly for worship.

(b) It is quite different in the case of '*ēḏâh*, which occurs above all in the Pentateuch (123 out of 147 occurrences, of which 81 are in Num. alone), the prophets (only at Jer. 6:18 and Hos. 7:12), and 10 times in Pss. This word is related to the root *yā'aḏ*, to appoint. It implies "the announcement of a resolution or decision, the carrying out of which is so bound up with a particular place or an appointed time

293

or a given situation, that any departure from the determining or conditioning factors is equivalent to a failure to carry out the command" (L. Rost, *Die Vorstufen von Synagoge und Kirche im Alten Testament*, 1938, 6). It is not difficult to recognize that the significance of this root agrees very closely with the deuteronomistic use of *qāhāl*. The reference to time is clear in Exod. 9:5 and 1 Sam. 13:8, 11 which have a word derived from the stem, *môʿēd*, appointed time, assembly, and appointed festival.

The *ʿēdâh*, mostly without further qualification but sometimes with the addition of "of Israel" (e.g. Exod. 12:3; Num. 16:9) or "of the sons of Israel" (e.g. Exod. 16:9; Num. 1:2; Lev. 4:13; 27 times), can be defined as the expression coined for the people (*ʿām*) gathered before the *ʿōhel môʿēd*, the tent of meeting (Exod. 33:7 ff.). The people were the people of the → covenant and thus of the → Law, represented by their menfolk. In the wilderness narratives this *ʿēdâh* is divided up into tribes, clans and families, led by elders, heads and princes. The word expresses a concept of corporateness, in which the stress falls not on the total of individuals, on the crowd, but on the unity of the fellowship. The *ʿēdâh*, the congregation, appears to have been constituted with the command to leave Egypt and celebrate the Passover. The first occurrence in our present text is Exod. 12:3. (Exod. 12:6 has *qᵉhal ʿᵃdat yiśrāʾēl*, "assembled community of Israel" NEB, a combination of the two words). At this point → Israel comes into view as a congregation. It is Israel that travels through the wilderness, that rebels, that experiences God's help (Exod. 16:1 ff. Num. 20:1 ff.). But Israel is also the witness of the revelation of God and receiver of God's commandments (Exod. 34:31 f.; 35:1). Israel offers sacrifices (Lev. 4:13 ff.), and can become guilty through the sin of individuals (Lev. 10:6). But Israel also keeps corporate watch over the ordering of the covenant to the point of carrying out sentence (the stoning of the blasphemer, Lev. 24:14, 16; of the Sabbath breaker, Num. 15:35 f.). In preserving Israel's purity the → priests play an important role as representatives and mediators to God (cf. the sin offering for the sins of the congregation through the priests, Lev. 4:13 ff.; the consecration and offering of Aaron, Lev. 8:3 ff.; 9:5 ff.; Num. 15:22; and the commissioning and consecration of the Levites, Num. 3:7; 8:9, 20).

But *ʿēdâh* does not only mean the community centred in the cult or the law (Num. 35:12, 24). In the sense of *ʿām* it also represents the community as a people. It is the *ʿēdâh* which receives and deplores the report of the spies (Num. 13:26; 14:1 ff.). It is to the *ʿēdâh* that troops returning from battle (Num. 31:12 ff.) and the leaders of the people (Jos. 9:18 ff.) have to justify themselves. In the disputes with individual tribes it represents Israel as a whole (e.g. Num. 32:2, 4; Jos. 22:12 ff.). Nevertheless the *ʿēdâh* itself does not wage war, but appoints forces to do it (Num. 31:3 ff.). Otherwise, however, the word in practice covers the people as a community in all its functions, of which even the most secular was not without some connection with the law and the sanctuary. On the other hand, the *ʿēdâh* is not bound to a particular land or to a particular place. The generation of the wilderness did not yet have one, and the generation of the exile had it no longer. The tent and the ark are the symbols and source of that obedience to the law which so strongly characterizes the post-exilic community. It is for this reason that, in contrast to *qāhāl*, *ʿēdâh* never refers to any people other than Israel and clearly needs no other special qualification: only four times is the name of Yahweh added. The passages with the personal suffix for the 'ēḏâh of Korah in Num. 16:5 merely serve to underline the illegitimacy of the claims made by this group. The 'ēḏâh is always the whole and admits of no sectarianism.

(c) If one compares the use of the two Heb. words, it becomes clear, from the passages in which both occur in the same context (e.g Exod. 12:1 ff.; 16:1 ff.; Num. 14:1 ff.; 20:1 ff.; 1 Ki. 12:1 ff.) that 'ēḏâh is the unambiguous and permanent term for the covenant community as a whole. On the other hand, qāhāl is the ceremonial expression for the assembly that results from the covenant, for the Sinai community and, in the deuteronomistic sense, for the community in its present form. It can also stand for the regular assembly of the people on secular (Num. 10:7; 1 Ki. 12:3) or religious occasions (Ps. 22:26), as well as for a gathering crowd (Num. 14:5; 17:12).

3. (a) This conclusion is reflected in the translations. What we have already established for the LXX (OT 1(a)) can also be seen in the Targums, the Aram. translations of the MT. 'ēḏâh is rendered almost consistently by k°ništā', assembly, even when the reference is not to the actual assembly but to the constant entity (with the exception of the ten passages in Pss., 2 Chr. 5:6, Job 15:34). qāhāl appears mostly as a loan word, q°hillā' (80 times), but is also rendered by k°ništā' (15 times, especially in Gen. and Pss.) and mašrîṯā', camp, troop (Jer., Ezek. for enemy armies). Rost concludes, "that Judaism at the time of the Targums associated itself not with the qāhāl but with the 'ēḏâh. The strictly regulated common life of the 'ēḏâh as the priests had expounded it ... was their model, ... not the qāhāl with its basically less determinate form as the occasional response to the summons to action. There is always something indefinable about the qāhāl; for it embraces only those who have heard the call and are following it. 'ēḏâh, on the other hand, is the permanent community into which one was born and in which one possessed, if one was a man, certain rights and duties in an exactly determined and defined measure. The dynamic of the summons to the community was replaced by the rigidity of the community of birth, which could be regulated by laws" (op. cit., 103).

This naturally gives rise to a whole series of questions in view of the thesis that the Christians took over directly the Jewish concept of the qāhāl and expressed it by ekklēsia. This is all the more acute when one takes into account the utterly unspecific use of the word in the prophets, which does not point in the direction one would expect, even though the term was no doubt available to them as a contrast to 'ēḏâh which is almost completely absent.

(b) If the translation of the LXX (OT 1 (a)) agrees essentially with that of the Targums, this permits the inference that in the Gk. speaking dispersion, that is the Jews who were later known as the Hellenists, the total Jewish community as determined by the law and the temple was denoted synagōgē in the sense of 'ēḏâh (e.g. Num. 8:9; Lev. 4:13; 10:3; Exod. 12:19).

Where ekklēsia is used in the LXX for qāhāl, it indicates the assembly of the people or a judicial assembly (e.g. Deut. 9:10; 23:3 ff.; Jdg. 21:5, 8; Mic. 2:5), the political body (e.g., the returned exiles Ezr. 10:8, 12; Neh. 8:2, 17). It also indicates, especially in the Chronicler, the assembly of the people for worship (e.g. 2 Chr. 6:3 at the consecration of the temple; 30:2, 4, 13, 17 at Hezekiah's Passover; cf. also Joel 2:16 and several times in the Pss., e.g. 21 (MT 22):22; 88(89):6). Nevertheless, even in these instances (even though, unlike Deut. 23:2, 3, 4, 9, Mic. 2:5, and

295

Jdg. 20:2, the gen. *kyriou*, of the Lord, or *tou theou*, of God, is not added) *ekklēsia* is only used where it is a question of the people as God's assembly, characterized by having answered Yahweh's call. Admittedly the word is used especially where the historic greatness of Israel is implied, and avoided where it could perhaps suggest to the Gk. reader merely a political claim on the part of the contemporary Jewish community (in the sense of the Gk. *ekklēsia*, see above, CL). Perhaps that is why, in the legal passages regulating the life of the community, *qāhāl* is translated by *synagōgē* (cf. L. Rost, op. cit., 127 ff.).

synagōgē, on the other hand, apart from its general use as assembly, place of assembly, harvest (Gen. 1:9; Exod. 34:22; Lev. 11:36; all for neither *qāhāl* nor *'ēḏâh*) and the mustering of troops (Ezek. 38:4, 7 etc. for *qāhāl*), was clearly used to denote the religiously defined community of Yahweh. It took over none of the usual Gk. terms for cultic assemblies (see above, CL), but was a word without previous associations. Hence we can understand why in the Pentateuch (with the exception of Deut. 5:22) *qāhāl* was also translated by *synagōgē*. This choice of word could give expression to the fact that the present community had been given the Law or the laws which were regularly read in public worship. Thus *synagōgē* is at the same time a reminder of the great events of salvation history and of the promises to → Israel (Num. 14:7 ff.). The term also acquired eschatological significance from its context (Isa. 56:8; Ezek. 37:10; cf. W. Schrage, *ZThK*, 60, 1963, 184 ff.).

4. The Qumran texts agree with the usage described above under 2. *qāhāl* occurs only seldom, and then for the summoned assembly of the community (CD 11:22; 12:6; 1QM 14:5; 1QSa 2:4), or in the sense of levy (1QM 4:10; *qᵉhal 'ēl*, God's levy). *qᵉhillā'* also occasionally means the mustering for the eschatological battle (1QM 1:10). *'ēḏâh*, on the other hand, serves both as a designation for the "congregation of unity" (e.g. 1QSa 2:21), and throughout 1QSa for the congregation of the remnant of Israel (who "keep his covenant in the midst of iniquity" 1QSa 1:3 f.) in its branches and duties (e.g. 1QSa. 1:9, 13; 2:5, 1QM 2:5; 3:4). In addition it appears in the representative sense of the elect (1QSa 2:7 f.: the congregation of the men of renown). But alongside the "holy congregation" (1QSa 1:9; cf. 1QM 12:7) or the "congregation of his elect" (4QpPs. 37 2:5; 3:5) we read in the Qumran documents also of the congregation of Belial (1QH 2:2), of wickedness (1QM 15:9), of scoffers (in Jerusalem: 4QpIsaᵇ on Isa. 5:24–25), of vanity (1QH 7:34) or raised by the prophets of deceit (1QpHab 10:10), all *'ēḏâh*. This reflects the struggle between the true and false congregations (→ Israel), which cannot be decided on the basis of names but only by obedience to Yahweh. It remains to be demonstrated whether in the Qumran texts *'ēḏâh* (perhaps directly influenced by *qāhāl*) is definitely moving in the direction of an elect → remnant, marked by special obedience and by expectation of the Messiah.

NT 1. (a) It is striking that Jesus' followers did not describe their meetings and the community represented by them as a *synagōgē* (with the single exception of Jas. 2:2). For the word would have been natural for a group which sprang from Jewish roots and which at least in the beginning counted itself a part of Judaism (→ Israel NT). *synagōgē* occurs in the NT, apart from the Jas. passage and Rev. 2:9; 3:9 (see below), only in the gospels (Matt. 9 times; Mk. 8 times; Lk. 15 times, Jn. twice) and Acts (19 times). It describes either the meeting place of the local

Jewish community or this congregation itself, representing the total number of Jews. Since the assembly most often took place in the synagogue building, the word carries both meanings. (Exceptions are Lk. 7:5 and Acts 18:7, where only the building is meant; and perhaps Lk. 20:46; 21:12 Acts 18:19, 24:12.) Acts 13:5; 14:1; 17:1, 10 have the explicit addition, *tōn Ioudaiōn*, of the Jews. Acts 6:9 mentions that Stephen's opponents came from the Synagogue of the Freedmen (as it was called), the Cyrenians and the Alexandrians. ([Ed.] Opinions differ as to the number of synagogues indicated by this verse. It may be as many as five, those of the Libertini, Cyrenaeans, Alexandrians, Cilicians and Asians, cf. F. F. Bruce, *The Acts of the Apostles*, 1952[2], 156.) There were in Jerusalem several synagogues, no doubt formed according to the country of origin of the members. In general there is no special qualification (except in Lk. 4:44, the synagogues of Judea), because the place is named in the context, or synagogue is in the plur. (in Matt. 7 out of 9 times; in Lk. and Acts 14 out of 34, in Mk. 3 out of 8). Rev. 2:9 and 3:9 have a special significance. Here the Jewish assembly as a whole is described with the sharpest differentiation as *synagōgē tou Satana*, a synagogue of Satan. Their claim to be a congregation of God, the true Israel, is disputed and the title claimed for the Christians.

It is from the tension recognizable in the polemic of Rev., Jn. and Acts 6, even though it is concealed in the present text (cf. E. Haenchen, *Acts*, ad loc.), that we can infer why the Christian church consciously avoided *synagōgē* as a term to describe itself. The name synagogue which was originally a technical term for the Jewish assembly came to be regarded in time as the "symbol of the Jewish religion of law and tradition" (W. Schrage, *ZThK* 60, 1963, 196 ff.). Once the → Law of Moses had effectively taken central place in its life, liturgy and institution (cf. the ref. to Moses' seat in Matt. 23:2), the idea of the synagogue must have seemed so rigid to the Christian that he separated from it in favour of a reformed Christian assembly. It was no doubt also felt that a word with such connotations could not be used to describe a fellowship and an event, at the centre of which was the proclamation of a gospel of freedom from law and of salvation available only through → faith in Jesus Christ. Furthermore, there were probably semantic reasons which made *ekklēsia* seem more suitable as a rendering of Heb. *qāhāl* (see below (b)).

On the other hand, the vb. *synagō* occurs not only in its general meaning of gather (things, troops, fruit etc.), but particularly in Isa., Jer. and Ezek. also in eschatological contexts with the meaning of gathering the people of God (e.g. Isa. 11:12; 43:5; 60:22; Jer. 31 (LXX 38):8; Ezek. 37:21) from among nations (cf. Isa. 66:18). It appears in the NT a few times, no longer in its general sense but with a clearly eschatological meaning. In Mk. especially (2:2; 4:1; 5:21; 6:30; 7:1; cf. Matt. 13:2) it expresses the coming of people to Jesus as the salvation of God. In Acts 4:31; 15:6, 30; 20:7f. it denotes the coming together of the congregation. In Matt. 12:30 par.; chap. 25 (especially v. 32) and in Jn. 11:52; 16:6 it is used for the eschatological gathering of the people of God. Alongside these passages it is used conventionally for the meeting of the Jewish council (e.g. Matt. 26:3, 57; Lk. 22:66; Acts 4:5).

(b) What is immediately striking about *ekklēsia* is that, with the exception of Matt. 16:18 and 18:17, the word is entirely absent from the gospels. The fact that Luke, on the other hand, uses the word 23 times in Acts suggests the conclusion

297

that he, at least, consciously avoided using it for a group that belonged to the period of Jesus' earthly activity. By far the majority of occurrences of the word appears in Paul's letters (46 out of a total of 114; including 9 in Eph. and 4 in Col.), above all in 1 Cor. (22 times). It is Paul in particular who shaped this concept, which in Eph. and Col. was further developed in a specifically cosmic sense. The term does not appear in 1 and 2 Pet., 2 Tim. and Tit. There are only isolated instances in Jas. and Heb., and it is used only in the third of the Johannine letters. However, Rev. employs it 20 times. The fact that it occurs not only in the sing. but also frequently in the plur. (in Paul 20 times; in Rev. 13 and in Acts twice) will require particular attention.

2. *The primitive community.* The absence of the word *ekklēsia* from all the gospels (with the exception of Matt. 16:18; 18:17) cannot be explained by saying that at the time of their writing the concept was not in current use, since the gospels received their literary form contemporary with or later than the Pauline letters. Nevertheless, one can say with certainty that all the early Christian writers use *ekklēsia* only for those fellowships which come into being after the crucifixion and → resurrection of Jesus (cf. O. Cullmann, *The Early Church*, 1956, 118 ff.). It is not used for the period of the historical Jesus or to describe the → disciples who gathered around him. W. G. Kümmel has shown that the philological findings exactly correspond with the historical. In all probability Jesus himself called together the Twelve (→ Apostle), but did not found the *ekklēsia* as such in his own lifetime, not even through the institution of the → Lord's Supper ("Kirchenbegriff", *Symbolae Biblicae Upsalienses*, I 1943, 32 f., 36). This by itself would not settle the question whether he intended the church to come into being.

But equally clearly a consciousness of the church arose as early as the primitive Christian community. Its roots lie in the fact that some of the disciples became witnesses of resurrection appearances. They thus became commissioned bearers of the news that the time of salvation had dawned. The concept of the church in the primitive community is characterized by consciousness of being in the eschatological situation created by the resurrection appearances (cf. 1 Cor. 15:3 ff.). It is a situation in which one is already experiencing the signs of the end. The primitive Christian *ekklēsia* understood itself as the herald of the Lordship of Christ, which was approaching with the imminently expected parousia and was already being realized in their midst (cf. Cullmann, op. cit., especially 126 ff.). But the church was also aware that it was still part of this age, and was therefore not identical with the *basileia*, the → kingdom of God (Cullmann, op. cit., 120 ff.; Kümmel, op. cit., 22).

3. *Paul.* When he speaks of the church, which he does in individual letters with different emphasis, Paul's starting point is the → proclamation of Christ. When men receive it in faith Christ becomes present and real in their experience. The *ekklēsia* appears as the event in which God fulfils his → election through his personal → call (Rom. 8:29 f.). For this reason he can speak of the *klētoi*, the called, when he means the Christian community (e.g. Rom. 1:6 f.; 1 Cor. 1:2). For the same reason he addresses his early letters to Thessalonica to the *ekklēsia* of the Thessalonians *en theō patri*, in God the Father (1 Thess. 1:1 f.; 2 Thess. 1:1 f.), a formula which links the idea of the church as event with that of the local church. It is not difficult to recognize the basic idea of the OT *qāhāl*. But the *ekklēsia* of the Thessalonians also introduces to the Gk. mind the claim that the call of God, which

has gone out through the apostle and other preachers in the form of the offer of reconciliation (cf. 2 Cor. 5:19 f.), has brought together this assembly. It represents for this place God's new creation, the eschatological order of salvation and thus the → people of God. (Note: *laos*, people, is rare in Paul, and is only used of → Israel in OT quotations.)

It is not only the church's origin which lies with God. The *ekklēsia* can only be understood in relation to the Lord, as the *ekklēsia tou theou*, the congregation of God (1 Cor. 1:2; 11:16, 22; 2 Cor. 1:1; Gal. 1:13; 1 Thess. 2:14; 2 Thess. 1:4). Only Gal. 1:22 and Rom. 16:16 have the qualifying *en Christō*, in Christ, or *tou Christou*, of Christ. The adj. "Christian" is as yet unknown, and would in any case proclaim a sense of ownership which is only present in the experience of being received.

(b) The fact that *ekklēsia* has the nature of an event does not, however, exclude the factor of continuity. However little this happening can be commanded by men, it nevertheless expresses itself in permanent forms and institutions. Where the *ekklēsia* is an event, the institution of the *ekklēsia* comes into being and will continue to do so in the expectation that Lord will continue to make his presence real. Coming together (*synagō* as in the LXX) must be reckoned an essential element in *ekklēsia* (cf. 1 Cor. 11:18). Hence the *ekklēsia* can be thought of in purely concrete terms, and any spiritualizing in the dogmatic sense of an invisible church (*ecclesia invisibilis*) is still unthinkable for Paul.

([Ed.] The idea of the invisible church is found in Augustine, *City of God*; Wycliffe, *De ecclesia;* Luther, *Preface to Revelation;* Calvin, *Institutes* IV 1 7; and many other writers (see edition of Calvin's *Institutes*, ed. J. T. NcNeill, 1960, II 1022). The thought that is uppermost is not to minimize the importance of church membership, but to recognize the possibility of hypocrisy and deceit. In the last analysis, those who belong to God are visible to God alone. Membership of the true church is a fact which is not visible to man. The idea recalls the statement of 2 Tim. 2:19: "The Lord knows who are his." It extends to the church what Paul says of Israel, that they are not all Israel who belong to Israel, but only "the children of the promise" (Rom. 9:6 f.). It recognizes the danger, which church members are warned against, of reaping corruption through sowing to the flesh (Gal. 3:7; cf. Rom. 8:12 f.). Paul recognized the need for discipline in his own life lest he should become a castaway (1 Cor. 10:27; cf. Phil. 2:12, 19). The possibility of church members falling away is one of the great themes of Heb. (cf. 2:3; 3:7–4:14; 6:1–12; 10:26–39; 12:12–28). It is also suggested by the parables of the weeds (Matt. 13:24–43) and the sheep and the goats (Matt. 25:31–46) and the example of Judas (Matt. 10:4; 26:14, 25, 47 ff.; 27:3; Mk. 14:10, 43; Lk. 6:16; 22:3, 47; Jn. 13:2; 17:12; 18:22 ff.; Acts 1:17 ff., 25).)

The *ekklēsia* has its location, existence and being within definable geographical limits. The apostle thus writes of the *ekklēsia tē ousē en Korinthō*, the church which is in Corinth (1 Cor. 1:2; 2 Cor. 1:2), indicating both that it belongs to the people of the place and that it has a new and different quality. This is also true when he speaks of the *ekklēsia Thessalonikeōn* (1 Thess. 1:1). Whoever is drawn into the *ekklēsia* and belongs to it, lives in the sphere of power of the new → creation (2 Cor. 5:17) through the word of Christ. But he is not removed from his position in the social order. He remains a Thessalonian, an Israelite or a Roman, a slave or a freeman (cf. 1 Cor. 7:17 ff.). The new citizenship (*politeuma* Phil. 3:20) does not mean loss of citizenship, although naturally deprivation of rights can result. It creates a new relationship alongside the old, opening up a new dimension in the midst of this world. The differences still exist in Christ, but they lose the divisive power which prevents unity and fellowship (cf. Gal. 3:27 ff.). Therefore, there are churches in particular places and among particular peoples, but not to the exclusion of others. Those who are counted among the "saints", as Paul, taking over the OT terminology for the people of God, calls the members of the *ekklēsia* (1 Cor. 1:2; Phil. 1:1; Rom. 1:7; → Holy, art. *hagios*), are those whom the Lord calls, to whom he gives → faith and whose belonging to the new life is indicated by → baptism (Rom. 6:3 ff.).

(c) Paul expressed his understanding of the Christian community in a word which best characterizes his concept of the church. He speaks of the *ekklēsia* as the → body (*sōma*, cf. Rom. 12:1 ff.; 1 Cor. 12:12–27). The metaphor of building, which he also uses (words from the group *oikodomeō*, to build, → house; e.g. 1 Cor. 3:9; 10:23), does not form a contrast to this, but expresses the same truth. The fact that the Christian community is the body, and the body of Christ at that (1 Cor. 12:27), immediately takes up the spatial idea. It is "the realm of blessing in which the crucified Lord and the realm of dominion in which the risen Lord continues to work" (E. Schweizer, *Church Order in the New Testament*, 7b, 92). But this also expresses the idea that belonging to Christ means becoming like a limb, part of an organism in which each part has its own special function. Each is assigned a particular → gift (*charisma;* → Grace, art. *charis* NT, 4) to be exercised in mutual giving and receiving, for specific tasks within the fellowship itself or in fulfilment of its commission to those outside. There is no gradation according to importance. Instead, the concept shows a remarkable breadth in the way it embraces gifts of leadership and organization, as well as healing, speaking in tongues and the discernment of spirits (1 Cor. 12:14 ff.; Rom. 12:4 ff.). They are all manifestations of the working of the one → Spirit, i.e. of the presence of the exalted Lord in this his body, through which the salvation event becomes contemporary, and the congregation becomes an eschatological reality. Their development and orderly growth requires Christian community life (1 Cor. 14:33). But Paul clearly did not intend to secure this by means of a rigid system of offices. The exercise of the gifts must be thought of concretely. Paul always understands *ekklēsia* as the living, assembled congregation. This is expressed particularly in 1 Cor. 14 (vv. 4 f., 12, 19, 23, 28). It is only in the meeting and living together of the members that → love, described in 1 Cor. 13 as the supreme gift, can be made real, just as it is only in this way that the other God-given gifts can be recognized and acknowledged. (This is also the way to understand election and commissioning.) The situation at Corinth appears to be prior to the general adoption of institutionalized offices like those of the → bishop and → elder mentioned in Phil. 1:1, Acts and the Pastoral Epistles. But even in 1 Tim. 3:15 the congregation itself is accorded greater intrinsic value than the office-holders for it is the congregation that is the *oikos theou*, the house of God.

(d) The fact that the *ekklēsia* in the full sense exists in several places at once arises out of the concreteness of Paul's concept. For it points to the present manifestation of the expected rule of the crucified Christ. (*basileia* → kingdom, is spoken of as already present in 1 Thess. 2:12; 2 Thess. 1:5; Rom. 14:17; and 1 Cor. 4:20

out of nine occurrences in Paul. In the other five instances it is qualified as future being linked with the fut. of *klēronomeō*, to inherit.) It is for this reason that *ekklēsia* occurs so frequently in the plur. (20 out of 50 instances), whether it refers to the different congregations in an area like Judea (Gal. 1:22), Galatia (Gal. 1:2; 1 Cor. 16:1), Macedonia (2 Cor. 8:1) or Asia (1 Cor. 16:19), or to a number of churches, or to all of them (e.g. Rom. 16:1; 1 Cor. 7:17; 14:33 f.; 2 Thess. 1:4). The fact that small groups in individual houses are called *ekklēsia* (Phlm. 2; 1 Cor. 16:19; Rom. 16:5; cf. also Col. 4:15) indicates that neither the significance of the place nor the numerical size of the assembly determines the use of the term. What counts is the presence of Christ among them (cf. Gal. 3:1) and faith nourished by him. Wherever possible there were several house churches in the same place. Some doctrines of the church have inferred that individual churches arose as a response to the witness of the apostles, and that the Pauline churches are to be included here, since Paul was counted as an apostle because of his call. But the church does not have its basis in a historic succession but in the fact that Christ continually reveals himself and commissions new messengers (cf. 1 Cor. 3:4–10). Hence the collections for Jerusalem (2 Cor. 8:19; 1 Cor. 16:1) should not be seen as an expression of respect for the superiority of the Jerusalem church, but as an expression of fellowship under the one Lord.

(e) The *ekklēsia* is always described and ordered in terms of its particular, local form. Neither the pattern of its life nor the gifts that determine that particular pattern need be uniform. Nevertheless, there is a sense in which there is *one* *ekklēsia*. Characteristically, the passages which make this clear are in particular those in which Paul recalls the time when he still persecuted the church (1 Cor. 15:9; Gal. 1:13; Phil. 3:6). It is one because the Lord of the church is one. → Baptism seals the relationship with Christ, and in the → Lord's Supper the fellowship of those in Christ experience their corporate nature (cf. the exposition of *sōma* in 1 Cor. 11:29 with reference to the congregation!). These are particular events, tied to particular places, and yet at the same time they are related to the body of Christ in its totality. Therefore, despite differences of detail, there can exist not only the one faith but beyond that common rules and even ordinances (1 Cor. 7:17; 11:16; 16:1), laid down and enforced by the authority of the apostle.

(f) A particular emphasis is added to Paul's statements about the church by the letters to the Colossians and Ephesians. The description, already used in 1 Cor. 12 and Rom. 12 of the mutual relations of the members in terms of the *sōma*, is further developed in terms of the relationship of the members to the → head (*kephalē*, Col. 1:18). If in the process (as some Ger. scholars think), Col. has taken up elements of Valentinian Gnosticism, it is only to emphasize the cosmic dimension of the atoning work of Christ. Whoever has been rescued by the Father out of the realm of the powers of → darkness (*ek tēs exousias tou skotous*) and transferred into the → *basileia* of the Son, finds himself now in this → body (Col. 1:13). He shares in *apolytrōsis* (→ redemption) and in the → forgiveness of sins, and has therefore entered the peace which Christ has created (Col. 1:20; cf. Eph. 2:12 ff.). The → reconciliation achieved by Christ in his death and announced by his messengers is the beginning of the *ekklēsia*, in terms both of chronology and of relative significance. The members of Christ's body are drawn into his being (cf. already Phil. 2:4 ff.), specifically now by the way of → suffering (Col. 1:24). The *sōma* of the *ekklēsia* thus becomes a way of describing the sphere towards which Christ's Lordship is directed. From the point of view of the *sōma*-idea, *ekklēsia* and *basileia* are practically identical.

Eph. develops this thought in the assertion that through the *ekklēsia* the wisdom of God is made known even to the cosmic powers (Eph. 3:10; 4:8 ff.). They have lost their influence (Col. 2:14 f., 20). For Christ, who in any case stands over them, has reconciled heaven and earth (Col. 1:15 ff.; Eph. 1:20 f.).

Although in Col. 4:15 f. it is still the local or house church that is called the *ekklēsia*, the emphasis in Eph. falls on the mystical unity of the body in its cosmic aspect (especially Eph. 4:3 ff.). It is no longer seen only from the standpoint of the different functions in an organism. Taking up the ancient idea of primal man, it serves as a picture of growth "to mature manhood" (Col. 2:19; Eph. 4:13). A sharp contrast is now made between the → head and the body; the Lord stands over against his church which is completely dependent upon him. It is no accident that the relationship is spoken of in Eph. 5:25–27 in terms of the relationship of husband and wife. The concept also takes on an organizational aspect. It is related to the role of offices, clearly underlining the significance of the apostolic tradition and displaying institutional and hierarchical features (cf. Eph. 4:11). What was earlier to be the concern of the whole congregation is now the responsibility of specific officials: to equip the saints to carry out their duty (Eph. 4:12, *pros katartismon*, a medical term referring to the setting of a fracture).

4. *Matthew and Luke.* (a) From the context, *ekklēsia* in Matt. 18:17 is to be understood as the number of those living and meeting in one place, who understand themselves be to the true → Israel because of their allegiance to the Messiah Jesus, upholding the → Law (Matt. 18:16; cf. Deut. 19:15; Num. 35:30). Matt. is interested in tracing the outlines of an order for the new community. This suggests that *ekklēsia* is used here in the sense of '*ēḏâh* synagogue. The passage may have assumed a polemical character directed against assemblies with antinomian tendencies.

The interpretation of Matt. 16:18 is more difficult. For one thing, one cannot with certainty determine the Heb. or Aram. equivalent; and for another, the context does not enable one to decide whether the fut. *oikodomēsō*, I will build, refers to Jesus' lifetime or to the period after his death. Moreover, the role ascribed to Peter cannot be determined conclusively from what we know about the early church. There were others also numbered among the pillars, Gal. 2:9; cf. also the opposition in Acts 11:1 ff. Apart from this the question whether Jesus envisaged the foundation of a church in his lifetime is bound up with the question whether he already thought of himself as Messiah (→ Jesus Christ, art. *Christos* NT 5). However much the *qāhāl*, and therefore the *ekklēsia*, belongs to the Messiah as the messianic community, there is a good deal in favour of the view that the fut. refers to the period after Jesus' death, and very little in favour of idea of the foundation of a church before this. It is clearly impossible to interpret this saying in Matt. as meaning that Jesus spoke of a church coming into being at that moment.

It seems indisputable that, if *ekklēsia* here represents an idea of late Judaism, it has taken over the content of *qāhāl*, and is probably to be understood as the eschatological assembly of the true people of God. On the analogy of the claim of remnant groups representing the whole (cf. OT, 4) the word then stood for an

302

eschatologically determined special synagogue, in which the true Israel was present. The statement that "the powers of death (Gk.: the gates of Hades) shall not prevail against it" has its foundation in the fact that this community is linked to the risen Christ as victor over death. This again indicates the period of the primitive church.

(b) For Luke the period of the church is a particular segment of salvation history, between the resurrection and the parousia. This follows directly from the use he makes of the word. While *ekklēsia* is completely absent from his gospel, he uses the term in Acts 16 times from 5:11 onwards (but not in chap. 2).

5. In *Acts*, as in Paul, *ekklēsia* indicates first of all the Christians living and meeting in a particular place: the primitive community in Jerusalem (Acts 5:11; 8:1; 11:22; 12:1, 5), the church at Antioch (Acts 13:1), and other places which Paul visited in order to appoint elders, or as a pastor to give encouragement (Acts 14:23; plur. 15:41; 16:5). Acts 20:28 characterizes the *ekklēsia* as the *ekklēsia tou theou*, the church of God, an idea which may be understood throughout. It becomes this through the → Spirit, who incorporates individual members into the church. It is the Spirit who moves the church, equips it (Acts 1:5, 8; 2:4 ff.; cf. 4:31 ff.), and for whose sake it is attacked and persecuted (7:55 ff.).

In the Acts too the *ekklēsia* is ultimately one. Admittedly, it appears only as it gathers in particular places (cf. 14:27). But it always implies the totality. As in the OT (cf. 7:38, which refers to Israel in the wilderness period), the *ekklēsia* is those who follow the call of God, come together (cf. the *synagein* of 14:27) and yet even when their meeting is over still retain their quality of *ekklēsia*. It is one throughout the whole world and yet is at the same time fully present in every individual assembly. The sing. and plur. are qualitatively identical. Therefore Luke can speak in the sing. equally of the church at large (Acts 8:3) and of the *ekklēsia* "throughout all Judea and Galilee and Samaria" (9:31). The use of the word in Acts 19:32, 39 f. for the riotous assembly in Ephesus demonstrates that Luke is at the same time fully aware of the Gk. sense of the word.

6. *The Johannine writings*. (a) The word *ekklēsia* is absent from John's Gospel. Jn. focuses attention on the fact that in this world of death and unbelief which cannot recognize the Lord (Jn. 1:10; 14:17), people can still experience the → birth from above (Jn. 3:3 ff.; cf. 1:12 f.) and pass from death to → life. Unlike Acts, with its households and local groups, it is always individuals who come to this → faith and → knowledge, and have to prove them. It is consistent with Jn.'s picture of the victorious Christ, in which everything is already completed and in the past, that for the → disciple (*mathētēs*) the Christ-relationship achieves absolute precedence.

The application to Jesus of Jewish concepts for the eschatological people of God (vine Jn. 15:1 ff.; shepherd and flock Jn. 10; door of the cosmic house Jn. 10:7–9) shows him to be the one revealer and fulfiller. Jn. draws attention to the unbridgeable gulf between faith and unbelief, and the recognition that God alone can bring a person to Jesus (Jn. 6:44; 17:2). The emphasis on the individual as a → witness is filled out by the command to mutual → love (Jn. 13:34 f.; in Jn. it is never directed to those outside), without any organizational forms and terms, however, coming into view. The disciples' authorization to → forgive sins (Jn. 20:23) is not (as in Matt. 16:18; 18:17) directly connected with the idea of the church. It seems rather that in the light of the unique authority of Jesus every

303

human institution fades into the background. Allegiance has long ago been determined by God (Jn. 10, especially vv. 26 ff.; 17:6; cf. 18:37, who are of the truth). Even coming together in unity can only be his work (Jn. 17:21, which certainly does not refer only to ecumenical church fellowship).

(b) In Revelation, on the other hand, *ekklēsia*, as in Acts, means the congregation which has grown up, exists and meets in a particular place. Until 22:16 all the references occur in the letters of chs. 2 and 3 or in the vision of the seven lampstands that precedes them in ch. 1 (vv. 4, 11, 20 always of the seven *ekklēsiai* in Asia). Each of these letters is addressed to the angel of the *ekklēsia* in a given place (*tēs en . . . ekklēsias*, 2:1, 8, 12, 18; 3:1, 7, 14).

It is striking that in all these passages some important MSS link the geographical name grammatically by the dat. of the *tō* with the angel, to the angel, the one . . . etc. This suggests that he should be understood not only as guardian angel and messenger, but at the same time as the embodiment of the essential characteristics of the congregation, and therefore distinct from the historical reality (cf. E. Lohmeyer, HNT 16, excursus on 1:20). Here then we have an apocalyptic exaggeration of the idea of the congregation, the meaning of which might be to assure the historical congregations, which were facing temptation and according to the text of the letters were by no means characterized by faith, obedience and holiness, that the decisions about their enduring or passing would be made at the throne of God itself (cf. Matt. 16:18).

The identical concluding statement in each letter makes what has been said with reference to the particular local church binding for all other *ekklēsiai*. This is also true of the reference to the churches at the end of the book (22:16). The only difference is that here the exalted Jesus is speaking to the churches, whereas there it is the Spirit. The three passages in 3 Jn. (vv. 6, 9, 10) all refer to a particular local Christian assembly.

7. *James and Hebrews*. Jas. 5:14, which deals with the elders of the *ekklēsia*, uses the word in the purely technical sense for a local congregation clearly organized on the pattern of a Jewish synagogue, whereas Heb. 2:12 cites Ps. 22:22 (Heb. *qāhāl*) and means the cultic festival gathering.

Heb. 12:23 is different. Here the word occurs in a series of eschatological terms taken from Jewish tradition (mount Zion, city of the living God, heavenly Jerusalem) and is qualified as *ekklēsia prōtotokōn apogegrammenōn en ouranois*, the congregation of the first-born who are written in heaven. The context indicates that entrance into this "congregation" is understood as entering into fellowship with "just men made perfect" and with "Jesus, the mediator of a new covenant," made possible by the crucifixion ("sprinkled → blood"). It is not here a question of the description of a group (perhaps even definable in terms of organization), but of the characterization of the eschatological event (the service of worship, which is indicated also by *panēgyris*, festival gathering; cf. O. Michel, Comm. ad loc.). It uses OT terminology (even though *ekklēsia* is not an established expression for such a gathering), and an apocalyptic title of honour (Michel, ad loc.) for "the wandering people of God" of the new covenant (E. Käsemann).

8. There remains the question of other terms used to denote the Christian community, particularly in writings from which *ekklēsia* is absent or where it is rare.

(a) In the gospels one is struck above all by the term *mathētēs*, → disciple, which penetrated Rabbinic Jud. from the Hel. philosophic schools, but remained unknown to the LXX. It occurs predominantly in the plur. (exceptions: Matt. 10:25 f.; Lk. 14:26 f., 33; and 14 passages in Jn. 18–21). The word originally denoted those who were devoted to the → teaching of a master and were committed to passing it on. In the NT a disciple is also a → witness. The term occurs most frequently in Matt. (68 times; cf. Mk. 44 times) and in Jn. (58 times) and is typical of their understanding of the Christian community. It is striking that Lk. uses the word only up to the scene in Gethsemane (22:45) and then not again until Acts (from ch. 6; 24 times in each). If one excludes the passages in the sing. and reflects on the fact that the word does not occur outside the gospels and Acts, its use indicates a stratum of tradition in which the corporate concepts for the Christian community had not yet been formulated. It belongs to the period of the first gathering of people around the earthly Jesus, and in Acts around the exalted Jesus, thought of as present in the → Spirit.

(b) It is different with the plur. *hoi hagioi*, the saints, which occur 4 times in Acts (ch. 9 and 26:10, always in narratives about Paul), but 38 times in Paul for the members of the churches especially in the introductions to letters. The saints are also called the elect (Rom. 1:7; 1 Cor. 1:2; → Election), those who have been sanctified by God. The word indicates the true Israel, and was probably first used for the original congregation in Jerusalem (1 Cor. 16:1; Acts 9:13), and then for Christians in general. Of individuals → Holy.

(c) This conviction led in 1 Pet. to the use of a whole series of Jewish expressions shaped by the OT. The letter is addressed to the *eklektoi parepidēmoi*, elect strangers (1:1; → Election; → Foreign), who are to be *hagioi*, saints (1:15) and are already *pistous eis theon*, believers in God (1:21). They are described as *genos eklekton*, a chosen race, → (Generation), *basileion hierateuma*, a royal priesthood (→ Priest), *laos eis peripoiēsin*, a peculiar people (all 1 Pet. 2:9). This reflects the language of the LXX. What the author wishes to underline is the fact that the Christian community is nothing new; it is to be understood as the fulfilment of the promises and hopes given to Israel. In this it is not dissimilar to the Qumran community's understanding of itself, except that the Qumran idea of the → remnant has become in 1 Pet. absorbed in the idea of the church. The emphasis, meanwhile, rests on the unity of those who, as pilgrims (1 Pet. 1:1 f.) and in suffering (1 Pet. 2:21 ff.; 4:12 ff.; 5:8 f.), come together as living stones in a spiritual → house (2:5 ff. the metaphor of building expresses growth). They serve one another (4:10) with different gifts as a witness to the grace of God which is being revealed in them. In the process, the OT order of elders from the *qāhāl* seems to have been taken over (cf. 5:1 ff.). In all this, according to the eschatological terminology of shepherd and flock, Christ stands at the head as chief shepherd, i.e. as Messiah.

(d) The members of the congregation are also called *adelphoi*, → brothers. The term occurs most frequently in Paul (73 times as an address and a further 23 times), and also in Acts, the Johannine letters, Jas. and Heb. This form of address corresponds both to Jewish usage and to that of the ancient religious societies. The derived term *adelphotēs*, brotherhood, occurs only in 1 Pet. 2:17; 5:9.

L. Coenen

(a). C. K. Barrett, "The New Testament Doctrine of Church and State," *New Testament Essays*, 1972, 1–19; K. Barth, *CD* IV, 1, 643–739, IV, 2, 614–726, IV, 3, 681–901, and IV, 4 *Fragment;* E.

Best, One Body in Christ, 1955; M. Black, *The Scrolls and Christian Origins*, 1961; J. Blauw, *The Missionary Nature of the Church: A Survey of the Biblical Theology of Mission*, 1962; E. Brunner, *The Misunderstanding of the Church*, 1952; and *Dogmatics* III, *The Christian Doctrine of the Church, Faith, and the Consummation*, 1962; L. Cerfaux, *The Church in the Theology of St. Paul*, 1959; and *The Christian in the Theology of St. Paul*, 1967; R. E. Clements, *God and Temple*, 1965; A. Cole, *The Body of Christ: A New Testament Image of the Church*, 1964; Y. M. J. Congar *The Mystery of the Temple*, 1962; A. Correll, *Consummatum Est: Eschatology and Church in the Gospel of John*, 1959; O. Cullmann, *The Early Church*, 1956; N. A. Dahl, "Christ, Creation and the Church," in D. Daube and W. D. Davies, eds., *The Background of the New Testament and its Eschatology* (Studies in Honour of C. H. Dodd), 1956, 422–43; F. W. Dillistone, *The Structure of the Divine Society*, 1951; F. G. Downing, *The Church and Jesus: A Study in History, Philosophy and Theology*, 1968; C. W. Dugmore, *The Influence of the Synagogue upon the Divine Office*, (1944) 1964; A. Ehrhardt, "The Birth of the Synagogue and R. Akiba" in *The Framework of the New Testament Stories*, 1964, 103–31; R. N. Flew, *Jesus and his Church*, 1943[2]; B. Gärtner, *The Temple and the Community in Qumran and the New Testament*, 1965; F. Hahn, *Mission in the New Testament*, 1965; S. Hanson, *The Unity of the Church in the New Testament: Colossians and Ephesians*, 1946; F. J. A. Hort, *The Christian Ecclesia*, 1897; E. Käsemann, "Ministry and Community in the New Testament," *Essays on New Testament Themes*, 1964, 63–94; "Unity and Multiplicity in the New Testament Doctrine of the Church", *New Testament Problems of Today*, 1969, 252 ff; "Paul and Early Catholicism", ibid., 236 ff.; J. Knox, *The Early Church and the Coming Great Church*, 1955; W. L. Knox, *St. Paul and the Church of Jerusalem*, 1925; and *St. Paul and the Church of the Gentiles*, 1939; H. Küng, *Structures of the Church*, 1965; and *The Church*, 1967; J.-L. Leuba, *The New Testament Pattern*, 1953; E. Lohmeyer, *The Lord of the Temple*, 1961; R. J. McKelvey, *The New Temple: The Church in the New Testament*, 1969; J. P. Martin, "The Church in Matthew", *Interpretation* 29, 1975, 41–56; P. H. Menoud, "Church, Life and Organization of," *IDB* I 617–20; E. Mersch, *The Whole Christ: The Historical Development of the Doctrine of the Mystical Body in Scripture and Tradition*, 1938; and *Theology of the Mystical Body*, 1951; P. S. Minear, *Images of the Church in the New Testament*, 1961; "Church, Idea of," *IDB* I 607–17; and "Ontology and Ecclesiology in the Apocalypse," *NTS* 12, 1965–66, 89 ff.; R. J. Nelson, *The Realm of Redemption: Studies in the Doctrine of the Church in Contemporary Protestant Theology*, 1964[7]; L. Newbigin, *The Household of God*, 1953; A. Nygren, *Christ and his Church*, 1957; C. O'Grady, *The Church in the Theology of Karl Barth*, 1968; and *The Church in Catholic Theology: Dialogue with Karl Barth*, 1969; B. Reicke, "The Constitution of the Primitive Church in the Light of Jewish Documents," in K. Stendahl, ed., *The Scrolls and the New Testament*, 1958, 143–56; J. A. T. Robinson, *The Body: A Study in Pauline Theology*, 1952; A. Schlatter, *The Church in the New Testament Period*, 1955; H. Schlier, "The Unity of the Church according to the New Testament", *The Relevance of the New Testament*, 1967, 193 ff.; K. L. Schmidt, *kaleō . . . ekklēsia*, *TDNT* III 487–536; R. Schnackenburg, *The Church in the New Testament*, 1965; E. Schweizer, *Lordship and Discipleship*, 1960; *Church Order in the New Testament*, 1961; and "The Concept of the Church in the Gospel and Epistles of St. John," in A. J. B. Higgins, ed., *New Testament Essays: Studies in Memory of T. W. Manson*, 1959, 230–45; R. A. Stewart, "The Synagogue", *EQ* 43, 1971, 41–56; J. Swetman, "The Greater and More Perfect Tent: A Contribution to the Discussion of Hebrews ix. 11," *Biblica* 47, 1966, 91–106; L. S. Thornton, *The Common Life in the Body of Christ*, 1941; and *Christ and the Church*, 1956; T. F. Torrance, *Royal Priesthood*, 1955; *Kingdom and Church*, 1956; and *Conflict and Agreement in the Church*, I–II, 1959–60; V. Warnach, "Church", *EBT* I, 101–16; C. Westermann, "God and His People; The Church in the Old Testament", *Interpretation* 17, 1963, 259–70; D. E. H. Whiteley, *The Theology of St. Paul*, 1964, 186–204; C. W. Williams, *The Church* (New Directions in Theology Today IV), 1969; J. E. Yates, *The Spirit and the Kingdom*, 1963.

(b). H. Beintker, "Wort, Geist, Kirche. Zur Frage der peneumatischen Leiblichkeit der Kirche," *KuD* 11, 1965, 277 ff.; H. Berkhof, *Die Katholizität der Kirche*, 1964; W. Bieder, *Ekklesia und Polis im Neuen Testament und in der Alten Kirche*, 1941; G. Bornkamm, "Herrenmahl und Kirche bei Paulus," *ZThK* 53, 956, 312 ff.; N. A. Dahl, *Das Volk Gottes: Eine Untersuchung zum Kirchenbewusstsein des Urchristentums*, (1941) 1963[2]; G. Delling, "Merkmale der Kirche nach dem Neuen Testament," *NTS* 13, 1966–67, 217 ff.; L. Fendt, *Die Existenz der Kirche Jesu Christi*, 1949; G. Gloege, "Reich Gottes und Kirche im Neuen Testament," *Neutestamentliche Forschung*, 2, 4, 1929; H. Greeven, "Kirche und Parusie Christi," *KuD* 10, 1964, 113 ff.; H. Honecker, *Kirche als Gestalt und Ereignis*, 1963; W. Jetter, *Was wird aus der Kirche?* 1968; E. Käsemann, *Das wandernde*

Gottesvolk, 1938; R. Köbert, *qhl (pal.-aram.)-laos-ekklēsia*, *Biblica* 46, 1965, 464 ff.; W. G. Kümmel, *Kirchenbegriff und Geschichtsbewusstsein in der Urgemeinde und bei Jesus*, Symbolae Biblicae Upsalienses I, 1943; "Jesus und die Anfänge der Kirche," *StTh* 7, 1953, 1–27; E. Lohse, "Christusherrschaft und Kirche im Kolosserbrief," *NTS* 11, 1964-5, 203 ff.; P. E. Menoud, *L'Église naissante et le Judaisme*, 1952; O. Michel, *Das Zeugnis des Neuen Testaments von der Gemeinde*, 1949; O. Moe, "Urchristentum und Kirche," *TLZ* 76, 1951, 705 ff.; A. Nygren, A. Fridrichsen et al., *Ein Buch von der Kirche*, 1951; A. Oepke, *Das neue Gottesvolk*, 1950; and "Leib Christ oder Volk Gottes bei Paulus," *TLZ* 79, 1954, 363 ff.; J. Ridderbos *et al., De Apostolische Kerk*, 1954; J. Roloff, *Apostolat, Verkündigung, Kirche*, 1965; L. Rost, *Die Vorstufen von Kirche und Synagoge im Alten Testament*, 1938; A. Satake, *Die Gemeindeordnung in der Johannesapokalypse*, Wissenschaftliche Monographien zum Alten und Neuen Testament 21, 1966; H. Schlier, *Christus und die Kirche im Epheserbrief*, 1930; H. M. Schenke, *Der Gott "Mensch" in der Gnosis. Ein religionsgeschichtlicher Beitrag zur Diskussion über die paulinische Anschauung von der Kirche als Leib Christi*, 1962; J. Schneider, *Die Gemeinde nach dem Neuen Testament*, 1955; W. Schrage, " 'Ekklesia' und 'Synagoge'–zum Ursprung des urchristlichen Kirchenbegriffs," *ZTK* 60, 1963, 178 ff.; E. Schweizer, "Die Kirche als Leib Christi in den paulinischen Homologumena," *TLZ* 86, 1961, 161 ff. (*Neotestamentica*, 1963, 272 ff.); and "Die Kirche als Leib Christi in den paulinischen Antilegomena," *TLZ* 1961, 241 ff. (*Neotestamentica*, 1963, 293 ff.); K. Skydsgaard, "Vom Geheimnis der Kirche, *KuD* 10, 1964, 137 ff.; K. Stendahl, "Kirche II. Im Urchristentum," *RGG*³ III 1297 ff.; H. E. Weber, "Theologisches Verständnis der Kirche," *TLZ* 73, 1948, 449 ff.; O. Weber, *Versammelte Gemeinde. Beitrag zum Gespräch über Kirche und Gottesdienst*, 1949; G. Wehrung, "Die Kirche als Herrenleib," *TLZ* 75, 1950, 79 ff.

→ Literature under Apostle, Bishop, Body, Disciple, Serve

Circumcision

περιτέμνω

περιτέμνω (*peritemnō*), circumcise; περιτομή (*peritomē*), circumcision; ἀπερίτμητος (*aperitmētos*), uncircumcised; κατατομή (*katatomē*), mutilation; ἀκροβυστία (*akrobystia*), foreskin, uncircumcision, hence Gentiles.

CL The compound vb. *peritemnō* means lit. cut round. In Homer it is used fig., meaning rob, i.e. cut off for oneself. Later in secular Gk. literature from Herodotus, 2, 36, 3; 2, 104, 2 onwards it is used as the technical term for the separation (*incisio*) or removal (*circumcisio*) of the male prepuce (*akrobystia*). In the case of female circumcision, it is also used for the removal of the clitoris.

The corresponding sub. *peritomē* is first found in the 2nd cent. B.C. It seems always to have been used as the technical term for circumcision.

aperitmētos used as an adj. means unmutilated, uncircumcised. The vb. *orthotomeō* (from *orthos*, *temnō*), handle correctly, apportion aright, has moved further away from the basic meaning of the root. The later Gk. noun *katatomē*, mutilation, is nearer to it.

In secular Gk. this word-group with its religious associations is used only in the talking about foreign peoples, especially Egyptians, for the Greeks did not practise circumcision, although it was widely used in the Near East.

OT The word-group is of great theological importance in the OT. where it is used exclusively to designate circumcision as a cultic practice. In the LXX it represents mostly the Heb. root *mûl* and occasionally other terms used for circumcising and circumcision, e.g. *kāraṭ*.

1. (a) The origins of circumcision are a matter of debate among scholars. In Exod. 4:24 ff. and Jos. 5:2–7 there are possible indications of a ransom ceremony connected with marriage, or a puberty ritual. In this connection circumcision played an important role among other West-Semitic peoples, and it is found as far away as amongst the Malaysian and Polynesian tribes. Theologically circumcision first gained importance through its connection with faith in Yahweh, and through its obligatory role in Judaism as a token of membership of the covenant. In the passages mentioned above R. Meyer suggests that, "the ancient rite carried out with stone knives . . . is traced back to a command of Yahweh but not associated with the intrinsically close concept of the covenant" (*TDNT* VI 76). Circumcision is first described in Gen. 17:1–14 where it is commanded by Yahweh as the sign and seal of his → covenant with Abraham. Many scholars believe that circumcision became important in Judaism during the exile. G. von Rad sums up the view as follows: "Because of the abolition of the great cultic regulations, the feasts, sacrifice, etc., which were binding on the national community, the individual and the family were suddenly summoned to decision. Each family with all its members, each of them personally, was bound to Yahweh's offer, and since the Babylonians (like all eastern Semites) did not practise circumcision, the observance of this custom was a *status confessionis* for the exiles; i.e. it became a question of their witness of Yahweh and his guidance of history" (*Genesis*, 1963², 196). Hence circumcision was an important distinguishing mark of the covenant for Judaism. "Circumcision is the sign that Israel belongs to the covenant with God . . . it is the guarantee of the blessing promised in the covenant" (O. Michel, *Der Brief an die Römer*, 1963¹², 90).

Circumcision was evidently not practised among adults at certain periods in Israel's history (Jos. 5:2–7). But its mandatory use is clearly reflected by the ordinances in Gen. 17:12; Gen. 21:4; and Lev. 12:3. "He that is eight days among you shall be circumcised; every male throughout your generations." Not merely the children of Jewish parents, but also slaves, whether born in the house or bought, were to be circumcised (Gen. 17:12 f.). Obviously this applied also to the foreigner who came to believe in Yahweh (cf. Exod. 12:48). Only those who were circumcised might eat the Passover meal (Exod. 12:43–48). "No foreigner, uncircumcised in heart and flesh . . . shall enter my sanctuary" (Ezek. 44:9). Anyone refusing circumcision was regarded as in breach of the covenant; he was to be cut off from his people (Gen. 17:14).

(b) Beside the lit., physical meaning of circumcision the OT knows a spiritualized sense. It was not sufficient to be physically circumcised. Only the man who lets his heart be circumcised, i.e. who humbles himself before God, who accepts the punishment of his iniquity (Lev. 26:41 RV; who makes amends for his iniquity, RSV) and so repledges his loyalty to the covenant, is really circumcised "to the Lord" (Jer. 4:4; cf. 9:25; Ezek. 44:9). The recognition that physical circumcision could in some circumstances cause false confidence led to the use of this deepened meaning of the concept as a call to Israel to repent: "Circumcise therefore the foreskin of your heart, and be no longer stubborn" (Deut. 10:16). The thought is present in the prophets (cf. Jer. 4:4; Ezek. 44:7). Paul's thought coincides with this understanding of circumcision as a new non-cultic, but complete surrender to God, at many points.

2. (a) In the troubles of the Hel. and Roman periods circumcision appears above all as a confessional sign. In his attack on the Jewish religion Antiochus IV Epiphanes (176–163 B.C.) threatened circumcision and castration with the same penalty as murder (1 Macc. 1:48 ff.). So to did Hadrian (A.D. 117–138) later. Jewish women preferred death to abandoning "the holy law of God" by refusing to have their children circumcised (1 Macc. 1:60 f.). Circumcision belonged so inseparably to the traditional religion, that under no condition could it be abandoned. This is shown by the fact that for the Jews apostasy, renunciation of faith and breach of the covenant were mostly expressed by the so-called *epispasmos*, the surgical replacement of the foreskin. Just as they held fast to circumcision themselves so they demanded it of the heathen who happened to live within Israelite territory (cf. already Gen. 34:13–17). Josephus (*Ant.* 13, 9, 1 (257)) tells us that the Hasmonean John Hyrcanus I carried through compulsory Judaizing in Idumea, when he had conquered it, and this was marked by general circumcision.

(b) In spite of every criticism by Greeks and Romans, who considered circumcision to be barbaric, indecent and even a perversion, and although it hindered the spread of Judaism, the rite was continued unimpaired. Philo defended it, maintaining, that it was proper for a priestly people, and that it was in any case hygienically necessary (*Spec. Leg.* I, 1–11).

(c) The prophetic spiritual interpretation of circumcision is found again among the Essenes of Qumran (cf. 1QS 5:5; 1QH 18:20). But in the post-Christian period in Pharisaic-Rabbinic nomism "the purely physical understanding of circumcision was exclusively assessed" (R. Meyer, *TDNT* VI 79). Here physical circumcision is "a precondition, sign and seal of participation in the covenant which God made with Abraham" (Meyer, loc. cit., 80; cf. Jub. 15; Shab. 137b.). ([Tr.] The implied difference between Qumran and the later rabbis is almost certainly invalid. The former will have enforced the rite physically; the latter were writing in exile, which gave the rite increased importance.)

NT The vb. *peritemnō*, circumcise, is found 17 times in the NT; 9 times in Paul, 5 times in Acts, twice in Lk, and once in Jn. The noun *peritomē* is found 36 times, 31 of which are in Paul. It can mean three things: (a) circumcision itself, (b) the fact of being circumcised (e.g. Phil. 3:5), (c) the Jews (e.g. Tit. 1:10). The adj. *aperitmētos*, uncircumcised (Acts 7:51), the sub. *katatomē*, mutilation (Phil. 3:2) and the vb. *orthotomeō*, cut straight (2 Tim. 2:15), are found once each. The opposite of *peritomē*, i.e. *akrobystia*, occurs 20 times in the NT, apart from Acts 11:3 always in Paul. Like *peritomē*, it is found with three meanings: (a) the foreskin, (b) the fact of being uncircumcised (e.g. Rom. 4:10), (c) the Gentiles (e.g. Rom. 3:30).

1. The Gospels mention circumcision only in its physical meaning and without any special theological stress. Lk. 1:59 and 2:21 tell of the naming of John the Baptist and of Jesus on the occasion of their circumcision on the eighth day after birth in accordance with Jewish law (cf. Acts 7 8; Phil. 3:5). Jn. 7:22 f. also assumes the Jewish custom and its position in the law of Moses, in order to throw

309

doubt on the rabbinic concepts of how the Sabbath was to be hallowed. The contradiction lay in the fact that, when the eighth day fell on the Sabbath, circumcision so far from profaning it was actually commanded (cf. Shab. 132a). Yet they were angry with Jesus that he had "made a man's whole body well".

2. The word statistics given above show that the word-group is important chiefly in the Pauline epistles and Acts, where it illustrates the tension between Paul and the circumcision party. In the early Christian communities there was a tension between *hoi ek peritomēs pistoi*, the believers from among the circumcised, i.e. the Jewish Christians (Acts 10:45; cf. Acts 11:2; Rom. 3:30; Gal. 2:12; Col. 4:11; Tit. 1:10), and *hoi legomenoi akrobystia*, those called uncircumcision, i.e. the Gentile Christians (Eph. 2:11; cf. Acts 11:3; Rom. 4:10; 1 Cor. 7:18). These two groups, associated respectively with Peter and Paul, constantly clashed, because the Jewish Christians insisted that circumcision was necessary for salvation: "Unless you are circumcised according to the custom of Moses, you cannot be saved" (Acts 15:1; cf. Acts 15:5, where circumcision and the keeping of the Law are linked).

James and the elders of the Jerusalem church remonstrated with Paul, the apostle of the Gentiles, because they had heard rumours that he had taught that not merely Gentile Christians but also Jewish Christians were free from the law of circumcision (Acts 21:21). After all Paul made → freedom from the → law through the death and resurrection of Christ a central point in his proclamation, and his rejection of Jewish zeal for the Law is clearly stated. Paul stressed that the gospel for the uncircumcised (*to euangelion tēs akrobystias*) had been entrusted to him, even as that for the Jews (*tēs peritomēs*) had been to Peter (Gal. 2:7). This clearly implied freedom from the law of circumcision. This had been granted him at the Apostolic Council (Acts 15:19 f.; cf. Gal. 2:6 ff.), and it had included his fellow-workers like Titus (Gal. 2:3).

Some scholars have doubted whether the account of Timothy's circumcision by Paul, as a concession to the Jews (Acts 16:3; contrast Gal. 6:12 ff.), really represents the historical facts. In its favour is the fact that according to Jewish law Timothy was a Jew and so should have been circumcised (cf. SB II 741), and so Paul was only making good an oversight ([Ed.] It is also consistent with Paul's claim to "have become all things to all men, that I might by all means save some" (1 Cor. 9:22). This included becoming as a Jew, in order to win Jews, to those under the law "becoming as one under the law – though not being myself under the law – that I might win those under the law" (v. 20). It also may explain Paul's conduct in Acts 21:17–26.)

If Paul "had no small dissension and debate" with the Jewish Christians about circumcision (Acts 15:2), we may be sure that he was not concerned merely with a cultic act. The issue was linked with the whole question of → Law and freedom. ([Tr.] For both Jew and Jewish Christian it was axiomatic that acceptance of circumcision involved the obligation to keep the Law.) That is why he was so intransigent, and why he took Peter's vacillation so seriously (Gal. 2:11–14; cf. Paul's criticism of those who advocated circumcision out of fear of man in Gal. 6:12 f.). The Jewish belief was that circumcision gave the one who had received it an indelible characteristic that could not be lost. It made him a member of the covenant → people once and for all. Using Jewish arguments, Paul took up an

310

extreme position on the relationship of circumcision and the Law, stressing that only for those who did the will of God without reserve was circumcision a true sign of the covenant. Breaking the Law meant that circumcision becomes uncircumcision (Rom. 2:25; cf. also his sarcastic use of "mutilation" in Phil. 3:2 in his attack on false teachers). To keep the Law complete y by his own unaided power is impossible for a man. Life must be lived by → grace revealed in Christ. "Christ is the end of the law" (Rom. 10:4; cf. also Gal. 3).

For the church, therefore, circumcision can never have the importance it has in Judaism. For Paul, "We are the true circumcision, who worship God in spirit, and glory in Christ Jesus, and put no confidence in the flesh" (Phil. 3:3; cf. 3:5; Gal. 6:13 f.). In Rom. 3:1 f. Paul speaks of a relative value attached to circumcision because of the promises connected with it. But it is only to stress that the fulfilment of the promises is solely dependent on → faith, irrespective of circumcision. For God "will justify the circumcised on the ground of their faith and the uncircumcised through their faith" (Rom. 3:30).

Rom. 4:7–12 shows clearly that from the standpoint of eternity it is immaterial whether or not a man is circumcised. There Paul calls → Abraham as his chief witness for his concept of the equal value of Jewish Christian and Gentile Christian faith. He is equally "father" of both groups. "He received circumcision as a sign or seal of the → righteousness which he had by faith while he was still uncircumcised. The purpose was to make him the father of all who believe without being circumcised and who thus have righteousness reckoned to them, and likewise the father of the circumcised who are not merely circumcised but also follow the example of the faith which our father Abraham had before he was circumcised" (Rom. 4:11 f.). If in Rom. 15:8 Paul can warn the Gentiles against pride by pointing out that, historically speaking, Christ "became a servant to the circumcised" for the sake of God's trustworthiness and faithfulness (Rom. 15:8), it has to be understood in the context of Rom. 11:17–24 (cf. 15:5 ff.).

Fundamentally neither circumcision nor uncircumcision have any decisive value in God's sight. The decisive question is how man reacts to the total claim of God. He may reject it, as to Paul's grief many circumcised did, or he may put his faith in him and allow this faith to become effective through love (cf. 1 Cor. 7:19; Gal. 5:6; 6:15; Col. 3:11). Theologically the question of circumcision turns on whether one is circumcised in heart through the → Spirit (Rom. 2 29; cf. Acts 7:51), and is not merely the true Jew, but also the new man through the Gospel. How this bursts the bounds of the Law of Moses is shown by Paul's pointed claim, "We are the true circumcision, who worship God in spirit, and glory in Christ Jesus, and put no confidence in the flesh" (Phil. 3:3). Jesus Christ has made circumcision and uncircumcision one (Eph. 2:14 ff.), a new creation (Gal. 6:15).

This new man, however, is put on in the act of — Baptism which is depicted in Col. 2:11 f. as spiritual circumcision. When the old man is thus put off and the new man put on, old contrasts are suspended by a new reality. In the future there is neither Greek nor Jew, neither circumcision nor uncircumcision, but "Christ is all, and in all" (Col. 3:9 ff.; cf. H. Schlier, KEK 7, 208). *H. C. Hahn*

(a). W. Eichrodt, *Theology of the Old Testament*, I, 1961, 57, 133 f., 420; II, 1967, 252, 288, 466, 471; J. P. Hyatt, *IDB* I 629 ff.; D. Jacobson, *The Social Background of the Old Testament*,

1942, 300–310; K. Kohler *et al.*, "Circumcision," *JE* IV 92–102; W. Kornfeld, "Circumcision," *EBT* I 116 ff.; R. Meyer, *peritemnō*, *TDNT* VI 72–84; Moore, *Judaism* (see index); J. B. Payne, *The Theology of the Older Testament*, 1962, 391 ff.; R. de Vaux, *Ancient Israel*, 1961, 46 ff.; G. Vermes, "Baptism and Jewish Exegesis: New Light from Ancient Sources," *NTS* 4, 1957–8, 308–19; Commentaries on *Genesis* by D. Kidner (1967), G. von Rad (1963²), E. A. Speiser (1964); on *Acts* by F. F. Bruce (1951) and E. Haenchen (1971); on *Romans* by C. K. Barrett (1965, *BNTC*), F. F. Bruce (1963), J. Murray, I–II (1960–65); M. Black (1973); on *Galatians* by J. B. Lightfoot (1865, reprint 1967) and J. Bligh (1969).

(b). F. R. Lehmann, "Bemerkungen zu einer neuen Begründung der Beschneidung," *Sociologus* 7, 1957, 57–74; F. R. Lehmann and K. Galling, "Beschneidung," *RGG*³ I 1090 f.; O. Michel, *Der Brief an die Römer*, KEK 5, 1959⁹, 98 f.; H. Sahlin, *Die Beschneidung Christi*, Symbolae Biblicae Upsalienses 12, 1950; H. Schlier, *Der Brief an die Galater*, KEK 7, 1951¹¹.

Clothe, Naked, Dress, Garment, Cloth

In Gk. dressing and undressing are expressed by various modifications of the root *dyō*. There are a number of terms in the NT for different articles of clothing, the commonest being *himation*. *esthēs* is used for a specially valuable garment, e.g. a shining, white one, twice in the Lukan writings, and 3 times in John. *stolē*, which represents the long outer garment and which may indicate its wearer's social standing, occurs 5 times in Rev., and twice each in Lk. and Mk. In the LXX *stolē* is used especially for the priestly garment. In Mk. 12:38 it is the garment of the scribes, and in Rev. that of the glorified martyrs. *gymnos*, naked, has always a negative connotation.

γυμνός

γυμνός (*gymnos*), naked; γυμνάζω (*gymnazō*), exercise, train; γυμνασία (*gymnasia*), exercise; γυμνότης (*gymnotēs*), nakedness.

CL 1. *gymnazō* is found in secular Gk. from Aesch. onwards. As a trans. vb. it means to train someone or oneself; when intrans. it means do gymnastics. Since athletics were carried out naked, we can easily understand why the vb. was developed from *gymnos* (Homer onwards), naked (lit.), undressed, robbed of one's clothes (Appian), without an outer garment (Hesiod), poorly dressed (Dem.), and (fig.) unveiled, bare. The closely linked sub. *gymnotēs*, seldom used in secular Gk., means (lit.) nakedness, bareness, (fig.) bareness, bitter need; *gymnasia* means exercise.

2. In Gk. philosophy *gymnos* and *gymnotēs* are used to describe the state of the soul, when it is separated from the body (Plato). In later classical religion the concept of the body as the garment of the soul is widespread. *gymnasia* is used fig. for debate (Plato).

OT 1. In the LXX *gymnos* is found in the sense of extreme helplessness (Isa. 58:7; Ezek. 16:22). This helps us to understand the fig. use in Job 26:6. Even the realm of the dead cannot hide itself from God but is manifest to him in its complete helplessness. *gymnotēs*, nakedness, is found only in Deut. 28:48.

2. In late Jud. too *gymnos* is found with a double meaning. It is so used by

Josephus and especially Philo. In parts of Jewish apocalyptic it becomes a major concept with the meaning uncovered, without a covering for the body.

NT 1. The NT use of *gymnos* and its group is the same as in secular Gk.:

(a) It is found 16 times and varies in meaning from completely naked (Mk. 14:52) to forcibly stripped (Acts 19:16) and inadequately dressed (Matt. 25:36, 38, 43 f.). In Jn. 21:7 the meaning is somewhat different. RSV renders well "he was stripped for work", for a boat-man worked without his outer garment on. Peter put his outer garment on, so as not to stand *gymnos* before Jesus. The fig. use, unveiled, disclosed, revealed, made clear, is found in Heb. 4:13; 1 Cor. 15:37; 2 Cor. 5:3; Rev. 3:17; and 16:15 (cf. NT, 2).

(b) *gymnotēs* in a material context meaning nakedness, bareness, bitter need, extreme poverty, is found in Rom. 8:35 and 2 Cor. 11:27. It can be extended to mean spiritual poverty in an unfavourable sense (Rev. 3:18).

(c) *gymnazō*, train, is used only metaphorically in the NT in 1 Tim. 4:7; Heb. 5:14; 12:11; and 2 Pet. 2:14.

(d) *gymnasia* is found only in 1 Tim. 4:8 with the meaning of training, exercise. Paul is not attacking Gk. athletics, but a mistaken asceticism, as is shown by the context.

2. Of this word-group *gymnos* is the only one that has theological importance in some of the passages where it is found.

(a) No one can hide himself from the word of God (Heb. 4:13). It completely lays bare, and nothing can be hidden.

(b) In 1 Cor. 15:37 Paul compares the "naked grain" (NEB), which is sown in the earth, with the plant that emerges from it. Formerly men were less concerned with the biological process that lies behind the development from "naked grain" to full-grown plant. They wondered rather at the miracle of God's creation of a new plant after the old had died in the ground. Paul saw a type of the → resurrection of the dead in creation. Just as new plant-life springs up from the naked grain, so God causes the resurrection → body to come into being through the death of the earthly body. The continuity between the old and the new body is historical rather than material.

(c) In 2 Cor. 5:3 *gymnos* is used meaning without a body covering. The theological interpretation is difficult and there are 3 possibilities:

(i) Paul assumes that between death and the coming of Christ there is an intermediate state marked out by "nakedness", i.e. by existence without a body. Paul would gladly have avoided this state by being alive at the time of the Parousia. For it means that the redeemed then living will have the heavenly body put on over the old one (*ependyesthai*; → *dyō*, below). Paul shrank from → death because it would mean his being "unclothed".

(ii) *gymnos* may express the fate of the unredeemed. The damned do not receive a body of glory. This concept is found later in the Samaritan liturgy.

(iii) Modern German scholars for the most part assume that Paul is combatting gnostic concepts in Corinth. The gnostics denied that they had, or even wanted, "a heavenly habitation" (2 Cor. 5:2 NEB; cf. Corp. Herm.). The gnostics' goal was being unclothed (*ekdyō;* → *dyō*) of every form of body; the rising up of the naked ego freed from the body (cf. R. Bultmann, *Theology of the NT*, I, 202). The

313

Christian cannot desire bodilessness as the goal of → redemption, for it would rob him of communion with God. Paul longed for the new heavenly dress, so that the unclothing, i.e. death, should not end in his being naked, in his bodilessness, but in a new existence in a God-given body.

(d) *gymnos* can mean inner poverty as in Rev. 3:17 and 16:15. ([Tr.] In the latter case the reference is to the custom in the Jerusalem temple of setting on fire the clothes of Levitical sentries found asleep at their posts (Middoth 1:2).) The same is true of *gymnotēs* in Rev. 3:18. *H. Weigelt*

δύω

δύω/δύνω (*dyō/dynō*), set, dress; ἐκδύω (*ekdyō*), undress; ἀπεκδύομαι (*apekdyomai*), undress, strip; ἀπέκδυσις (*apekdysis*), laying aside; ἐνδύω (*endyō*), dress, clothe; ἐπενδύομαι (*ependyomai*) put on over; ἀποτίθημι (*apotithēmi*), put off; ἀπόθεσις (*apothesis*), putting off, removal.

CL 1. *dyō* occurs in secular Gk. only in Theophr. with a trans. meaning to sink.

From Homer onwards *dyō*, *dynō* and *dyomai* are frequently found used intrans. of the going down or sinking of the sun; fig. they mean put on, die, arm oneself, e.g. with strength.

2. The compound *ekdyō* (Homer onwards) means (trans.) undress; (intrans.) undress oneself, rid oneself of, extract oneself from, escape. Artemidorus uses it metaphorically of the laying aside of the covering of the body.

3. *apekdyō*, undress, disarm, and its noun *apekdysis*, laying aside, are not found earlier than the NT.

4. *endyō* (Homer onwards) means (trans.) dress, clothe; it takes an acc. of the thing (Homer), or a double acc. of the person and thing (Aristoph.). Intrans. it is used lit. (Homer) meaning dress oneself, put on, e.g. a garment, weapon, and fig. meaning assume qualities, virtues (e.g. take courage, Aristoph.), later also assume the part of a person (e.g. play the role of Tarquin, Dionysius of Halicarnassus).

5. The double compound *ependyomai* is found with the meaning put on over (Hdt. onwards).

OT In the LXX and late Jud. this word-group is used essentially as in secular Gk., though the words listed under CL 3 and 5 are not found in the LXX.

1. *dynō* is used lit. in Gen. 28:11; and fig. in Jon. 2:5(6).

2. *ekdyō* is used trans. in Gen. 37:23; Hos. 2:3(5); and intrans. in Isa. 32:11 and Prov. 11:8.

3. *endyō* for the Heb. *lāḇaš* is used lit. in Gen. 3:21 and fig. in Job 29:14 (righteousness), Isa. 52:1 (strength), Ps. 132:16 (salvation), 1 Macc. 14:9 (glory), Job 8:22 (shame), Ezek. 7:27 (despair).

4. *ependyō* is found only in later Jewish and Gnostic writers.

NT 1. *dynō* is found only in Mk. 1:32 and Lk. 4:40, both times of the setting of the sun.

2. The meaning of *ekdyō* (4 times in the Synoptics and once in 2 Cor.) is the same as in secular Gk.

(a) The lit. meaning is found in Matt. 27:28, 31; Mk. 15:20 and Lk. 10:30, each time in the sense of stripping a person of his clothes.

(b) The fig. meaning is found in 2 Cor. 5:4. Paul uses it without an obj. in the sense of undressing oneself, losing the garment of the body: "not that we would be unclothed". Three general lines of interpretation may be traced:

(i) Paul longed for Christ's return before his death, because death would bring with it an intermediate, bodiless state (→ gymnos), an existence in nakedness. So Paul did not wish to lose his garment, his → body, through → death, but desired to be further clothed at the Parousia. His longing for deliverance (Rom. 8:23; 2 Cor. 5:6) is one of the arguments against this interpretation.

(ii) Paul did not want to lose the garment of his body, because its loss is the fate of the unbelievers, who would lose their earthly body in death, whether before or during the Parousia, and would receive no heavenly body, as would believers. A major argument against this is that Paul was looking forward to fellowship with Christ in the intermediate period (Phil. 1:23).

(iii) Paul was combatting a Gnostic group in Corinth. The Gnostics longed to be freed of the covering of the body (→ gymnos). This interpretation is supported by the fact that Paul is not stressing being unclothed, but being further clothed. So Paul is contrasting the ideal of the Gnostics of not being clothed with the being further clothed with the new body.

Like *ekdyomai* we find *apotithēmi* used fig. in the NT for the laying aside of carnal qualities (Rom. 13:12; Eph. 4:25), even one's whole being in so far as it lies under the power of the former age. "Put off your old nature" (Eph. 4:22; cf. Col. 3:9) so as to "put on the new nature" (Eph. 4:24; Col. 3:10; Gal. 3:27, cf. Rom. 6:4 f.). In 1 Pet. 3:21 *apothesis* is used for the removal of dirt, and in 2 Pet. 1:14 for the putting off of the earthly body, i.e. death.

3. (a) *apekdyō* is found in Col. 2:15 and 3:9. In the latter the obj. is a thing: "you have put off the old nature". The use of the double compound is probably to stress that it is a complete putting off and putting away, which makes a falling back into the former manner of life impossible. In Col. 2:15 it has the force of undressing, rendering powerless. It is actually a mid., lay aside something for oneself. Hence Ambrose and Augustine understood it to mean the laying aside of the flesh. Gk. expositors, including Origen, take it as having an act. force. They were correct, for in Koine Gk. the mid. could be used as an act. God has "undressed" the principalities and powers (→ Beginning). Behind the picture lies an oriental custom. When the possessor of high office was deposed, he had to put off his robes of office. In the same way God stripped the principalities and powers of their honours and gave their power to the one to whom it alone belonged, Christ. In other words, the background of Col. 2:15 is not the battlefield, for which there are no parallels, but the royal court.

(b) *apekdysis* occurs only in Col. 2:11, where it is used metaphorically. Paul uses it to describe the true → circumcision, "a circumcision made without hands", "the circumcision of Christ". It consists of the putting off of the body of-flesh, which the Christian experiences in → baptism, and baptism is being buried with Christ (Col. 2:12). In this case the double compound may have been used polemically against the inadequacy of Jewish circumcision.

4. *endyō* is used 28 times in the NT (10 times in the Synoptics, once in Acts, 14 times in the Pauline writings, 3 times in Rev.). Alongside its lit. meaning (Matt. 27:31) it is often used fig.

(a) With the acc. of the thing put on: the spiritual armour (1 Thess. 5:8; Eph. 6:11; Rom. 13:12), Christian virtues (Col. 3:12), the spiritual, resurrection body (1 Cor. 15:53).

(b) With the acc. of the person: put on Christ (Gal. 3:27; Rom. 13:14). This is done both by → baptism and by → faith. Faith and baptism stand here in paradoxical tension, as though inseparably linked. Were we to regard this purely formally, Paul's linguistic usage would suggest an approximation to the rituals of the mystery religions. In them the initiates sought to identify themselves with the gods by putting on their ritual garments or masks. In fact, however, Paul is concerned with a new relationship of the personality with Christ. For him putting on Christ means the beginning of sharing Christ's nature. He writes also of the putting on of the new man (Eph. 4:24; Col. 3:10). For Paul the new man is identical with Christ.

(c) It is used absolutely in 2 Cor. 5:3: "In the hope of being thus clothed" (NEB). Paul did not desire to be freed from having a body, but wished to put on a new body which is spiritual. We hear an anti-gnostic note, for the Gnostics longed to be freed from the garment of the body, to have → gymnotēs, nakedness. This being clothed upon will take place at the Parousia.

5. *ependyomai* is found only in 2 Cor. 5:2, 4. In contrast to the Gnostics, Paul longs to have his heavenly body put on over his present one (see above NT 2 (b) and → gymnos). The mid. is used with a pass. sense. *H. Weigelt*

ἱμάτιον

ἱμάτιον (himation), garment.

CL The form *himation* is technically a diminutive of *heima* from *hennymi*, dress.

It is found from Hdt. onwards meaning a dress, garment, article of clothing. In secular Gk. it is not found with a fig. sense until a very late date, e.g. "the walls are the garments of the city" (Eustath.).

OT In the LXX *himation* is used for the Heb. *beged*, meaning both the outer garment and the clothes as a whole. Clothes could be torn as a mark of sorrow (Jdg. 11:35) or anger (2 Ki. 5:7; [Tr.] though the king's action is not necessarily to be interpreted as anger.) Because of the personal significance of clothing, it is easy to see that a garment can become a symbol of the transient (Isa. 50:9; 51:6, 8) and also of God's salvation and protection (Isa. 61:10; cf. Gen. 3:21).

In the Rab. writings it is used as a metaphor for repentance, the fulfilling of the commandments, good works, study of the Torah, which one wraps oneself in as a garment or armour. In Enoch (Eth. and Sl.) the garment is used as a symbol of salvation. In the Hel. mystery cults the garments had religious functions. The Gnostics sometimes used *himation* as a symbol for life.

NT *himation* is used 60 times in the NT, 41 being in the Gospels. It is used lit. for clothing in general (cf. Matt. 27:31; Acts 9:39), and more especially for the outer garment (cf. Matt. 9:20 f.; Jn. 19:2). It is also used fig. or parabolically (cf. Matt. 22:11 f.; Mk. 2:21; Heb. 1:11). The NT reflects both the usage of secular Gk. and also the fig. use of the LXX and contemporary Jewish writers.

The word has theological importance especially in the following cases:

1. Where clothes are involved in actions giving a special emphasis to what has been said:

(a) Men tear their garments as a sign of sorrow, when they hear blasphemy (Matt. 26:65; Acts 14:14). Paul shook out his garments (Acts 18:6). This should be linked with Neh. 5:13. It shows that he no longer felt any responsibility for the hardened Jews of Corinth.

(b) In Mk. 11:7 f. the multitude took their garments to use them as a saddle on the donkey and a carpet on the road of the divine rider in his triumph. By this symbolic action Jesus was proclaimed king at his entry into Jerusalem. Jesus' kingship was mocked by the purple robe which the soldiers put on him (Jn. 19:2, 5).

2. It is used fig. and parabolically:

(a) In Mk. 2:21 f. par. and Heb. 1:11, quoting Ps. 102:25(26) ff., *himation* as the "world-garment" is a symbol standing for the universe. According to the parable in Mk. 2, it is meaningless to use new cloth to patch old rags. "The old world's age has run out; it is compared to the old garment which is no longer worth patching with new cloth; the New Age has arrived" (J. Jeremias, *The Parables of Jesus*[2], 1963, 118).

(b) The garment is the symbol of the righteousness promised by God (Matt. 22:11 ff.). In the parable of the marriage feast the *himation*, the wedding garment, is a metaphor for forgiveness and the promised righteousness (cf. Isa. 61:10: "He has clothed me with the garments of salvation, he has covered me with the robe of righteousness"). Being clothed with this garment is hence a symbol of belonging to the community of the redeemed. In Rev. this eschatological dress takes the form of → white garments (Rev. 3:4, 5, 18), the → white robes washed in the blood of the Lamb (Rev. 7:14 *stolē*). White (*leukos*) was an eschatological colour.

H. Weigelt

(a). L. Bellinger, "Cloth", *IDB* I 650–55; J. Jeremias, *The Parables of Jesus*, 1963[2], 187 ff.; A. Oepke, *gymnos*, *TDNT* I 773–76; and *dyō TDNT* II 318–21; J. N. Sevenster, "Some Remarks on the *gymnos* in II Cor. v. 3," in J. N. Sevenster and W. C. van Unnik, eds., *Studia Paulina in honorem J. de Zwaan*, 1953, 202 ff.; W. Schmithals, *Gnosticism in Corinth*, 1971.
(b). R. Bultmann, *Exegetische Probleme des 2. Korintherbriefes*, Symbolae Biblicae Upsalienses, 1947, 1 ff.; W. Michaelis, "Das hochzeitliche Kleid," in *Die Gleichnisse Jesus*, 1956; E. Percy, *Die Probleme der Kolosser- und Epheserbriefe*, 1946; E. Peterson, "Theologie des Kleides," in *Marginalien zur Theologie*, 1956, 41 ff.; W. Straub, *Die Bildersprache des Apostels Paulus*, 1937.

Cold, Hot, Lukewarm

ψυχρός

ψυχρός (*psychros*), cold; ζεστός (*zestos*), boiling, hot; χλιαρός (*chliaros*), lukewarm; θέρμη (*thermē*), heat.

CL (a) The adjective *psychros* and the noun *psychos* (cold) derive from *psychō* (blow, breathe; make cold). In secular Greek these words are commonly used of literal cold, often of liquids, the neuter adjective *psychron* sometimes standing *per se* for "cold water" (Theognis, Herodotus), but also metaphorically, to mean "ineffectual" (Herodotus) or "insipid" (Aristophanes), or of persons, "cold-hearted" (Xenophon, Aristotle).

(b) *zestos*, like the verb *zeō* (boil, seethe), is usually literal, but may be applied figuratively to the passions of men. *zeō* is used thus in Sophocles and Plato.

(c) *chliaros* (cf. *chliō*, luxuriate, revel, and the Homeric *liaros*, warm, gentle) refers mostly to liquids or to food (Herodotus etc.).

(d) *thermos* (hot), *thermē* (heat) and cognates are very common in both literal and metaphorical senses, and are the usual antithesis of *psychros* and cognates. Unlike most of the words under discussion, *thermos* is freely predicated of persons and actions in the sense "hot", "passionate".

OT In the LXX *chliaros* never occurs, and derivatives of *zeō* are rare and never figurative. *psychos* (Heb. *qôr*, cold) and the *thermē* group (Heb. root *ḥāmam*, to be warm) are freely used of temperature. The latter group is also occasionally figurative: in particular, *thermainō* (to warm), used commonly of fire, may be applied to the heart (Deut. 19:6; Ps. 39:3; Hos. 7:7). Such metaphors are, however, found sparingly in the Greek, being avoided, for instance, in the rendering of Hebrew idiom where it speaks of God's "hot" displeasure (Deut. 9:19; Ps. 6:1; 38:1).

NT (a) *Primary Meanings*. In Matt. 10:42 the neuter adjective *psychron* is used alone of "cold water". *psychos* appears at Jn. 18:18, Acts 28:2, and 2 Cor. 11:27, always of temperature.

The otherwise common word *thermos* is absent from the NT, but *thermē* (once) and *thermainō* (6 times) are used in two of the above passages where Paul and Peter respectively warm themselves at the fire (Acts 28:2; Mk. 14:54, 67; and Jn. 18:18 ff.). To be "warmed and filled" with food and clothing are the fundamental necessities of the destitute (Jas. 2:16; cf. 1 Tim. 6:8), and James insists on a practical faith which will supply them to a brother in need.

(b) *Metaphorical Meanings*. The verbal forms *psychō* and *zeō* are applied to spiritual fervour (of love growing cold, Matt. 24:12; "fervent in spirit", Acts 18:25; Rom. 12:11).

(c) The principal NT interest of the word-group attaches to the only occurrences not thus far noted. Some aspects of the association of the three words *chliaros*, *psychros* and *zestos* in Rev. 3:15–16 are unique in surviving Greek literature. Here all three are used metaphorically and absolutely of personal character. The passage has usually been understood to refer to levels of spiritual fervour, as in (b) above, and this assumption accords with the exhortation in Rev. 3:19 (*zēleue*, be zealous): it would be natural to urge earnest endeavour upon the half-hearted.

The common interpretation is however open to question. The modern sense of *chliarotēs* (lukewarmness) is not apparently attested before Athanasius and Nilus. And the passage presents "cold" and "hot" indifferently as though both were desirable conditions: indeed, "cold" twice precedes "hot". It is not a matter of saying "it is better to be hot or *even* cold, better *even* stony indifference than half-hearted support".

Rudwick and Green have argued convincingly that the present usage is a bold image referring to the water-supply of Laodicea, which was derived from an artificial pipeline bringing water which was literally lukewarm and so impure as to have an emetic effect (cf. *emesai*, to spue out). The remains of the aqueduct survive and the hypothesis may be verified from the deposits still encrusting the pipes. It is notable that the words "hot" and "cold" are singularly applicable to the waters of the two neighbouring and rival cities, Hierapolis and Colossae (cf. Col. 4:13). The *hot* water which produces the celebrated petrified cascades of Hierapolis (Pamukkale) was medicinal, being used for the eyes by local people even today (cf. Rev. 3:18b); the *cold* perennial stream at Colossae made that city the earliest natural settlement of the valley, though later overtaken by the positional advantage and commerce of Laodicea.

A similar collocation (*psychos, chliaros, thermos, zeō*) is used by Herodotus of spring waters (4:181), and Strabo applies *zestos* to hot springs of the Laodicea district. The whole word-group is used more often of water than of anything else. The imagery here is to be explained in vividly concrete terms.

Lukewarmness should probably be taken as denoting "ineffectiveness", the inadequacy of human effort as a substitute for diverse manifestations of God's giving. The central thought of the letter is that effective service hinges upon response to Christ, not upon human endeavour. The Laodicean Christians are characterized as those whose wealth and self-sufficiency prompted them to work by their own resources rather than recognize their need of Christ, just as their city had recently recovered from an earthquake disaster "by its own resources" (Tacitus, *Ann.* 14,27). The point is reinforced by a series of images derived from notable industries and achievements of their city. They were "rich and had need of nothing" – but they must do their business with Christ if they are to obtain the real spiritual goods. In a city which sold eye-ointments the church is spiritually blind: Christ alone can supply it with vision. The same thought runs through the references to "gold" and "white raiment": Laodicea was a great banking centre which had amassed wealth from trade in the wool of black sheep.

The appeal of Christ to the individual for admission into the inward fellowship of the heart (Rev. 3:20) may be set against this collocation of images. The message of the other letters "is essentially didactic, the Laodicean is kerygmatic; whereas the call to repentance in the others is admonitory . . . , here it is promissory" (Rudwick and Green). Cf. also Origen's application of "lukewarm" to the unregenerate man (*De Principiis* 3,4,3). *C. J. Hemer*

W. M. Ramsay, *Cities and Bishoprics of Phrygia*, I, 1895, esp. 48–9, 85–6; W. M. Ramsay, *The Letters to the Seven Churches*, 1904, 413–30; M. J. S. Rudwick and E. M. B. Green, "The Laodicean Lukewarmness", *ExpT* 69, 1957–8, 176–8; P. Wood, "Local Knowledge in the Letters of the Apocalypse", *ExpT* 73, 1961–2, 263–4.

Come

The words discussed below have all to do with movement with regard both to place and time. *erchomai* (come) is capable of a wide variety of meanings through the addition of various prefixes. The verbs formed from the root *anta* (against) focus attention on arrival at the goal, reaching the destination, and attaining what one set out for. Apart from their broad, general usage, these words have a special significance in connection with the saving acts of God in the world. This is expressed in spatial terms when we speak of the coming and second coming of Christ. At the same time, this language has a temporal aspect. → also Present and → Goal.

| ἔρχομαι | ἔρχομαι (*erchomai*), come, appear; ἔλευσις (*eleusis*), coming, advent; εἰσέρχομαι (*eiserchomai*), come in, enter; ἀπέρχομαι (*aperchomai*), go away, depart; παρεισέρχομαι (*pareiserchomai*), come in, step in; περιέρχομαι (*perierchomai*), wander; προέρχομαι (*proerchomai*), go forward, advance, proceed; προσέρχομαι (*proserchomai*), go to, approach, accede to; συνέρχομαι (*synerchomai*), come together, assemble; διέρχομαι (*dierchomai*), go through, come through; ἐξέρχομαι (*exerchomai*), go out, come out, get out; ἐπέρχομαι (*eperchomai*), come, come along, approach; παρέρχομαι (*parerchomai*), go by, pass by, pass; ἥκω (*hēkō*), have come, be present.

CL & OT *erchomai*, with the Hel. fut. *eleusomai*, aor. *ēlthon* and *ēltha*, perf. *elēlytha*, occurs in secular Gk. from the time of Homer and also in the LXX. It means to come or go, mostly in the lit. sense. The direction of movement is determined by prepositions like *apo* (from), *eis* (into, to), *ek* (out of). It is used metaphorically in a temporal sense: *erchontai hēmerai*, days are coming (1 Sam. 2:31; 2 Ki. 20:17 and often); and also of destruction which comes upon men (Prov. 1:26; 6:15). The rare noun *eleusis* is formed from the fut. *eleusomai* and has been traced to Dionysius of Halicarnassus (fl. 30 B.C.). It denotes arrival. But in the NT it is used only in Acts 7:52 of the coming of Jesus (cf. G. D. Kilpatrick, "Acts vii, 52, *eleusis*", *JTS* 46, 1945, 136 ff.) and in Lk. 21:7 *v.l.* and 23:42 *v.l.* of the second coming of Christ. (Both these variant readings are in the Codex Bezae, cf. Metzger, 181.) *hēkō* is used virtually as a synonym for *erchomai*. It meant originally the state of having come. Hence, in the Hel. period the conjugation is often perfect: *hēka* (fut. *hēxō*, aor. *hēxa*). The original perfect sense is not always to the fore. The use of these two words in the LXX and the NT passes over into each other. This also applies to the metaphorical use of *hēkō* (cf. Isa. 47:11; Ezek. 7:10, 12).

Greek Hellenistic piety could speak in terms of the divinity coming to men and men coming to God. The prayer summons *elthe*, come (cf. Ps. 80:2 (79:3)), is found in ancient prayer texts and magical papyri (cf. J. Schneider, *TDNT* II 927). But apart from the formal similarity, there is no connection between pagan and biblical worship.

In the LXX the words are used mainly in their original, literal sense. But in the light of its purpose, coming may have a religious significance. A man comes to sacrifice (1 Sam. 16:2, 5), and to worship and praise God before the sanctuary (Lev. 12:4; 1 Ki. 8:42; Ps. 100:2, 4). The heathen also go into the house of their god (2 Chron. 32:21). The composite *eiserchomai* is also used to denote such coming

In a metaphorical sense, prayer and supplication (2 Chron. 30:27; Ps. 88:3; 119:170) and man's cries (Exod. 3:9; Ps. 102:2) are said to come before God. References to the coming of the Gentiles to Israel and thus to God are bound up with messianic expectation (Isa. 60:5 f.; 66:18; Jer. 16:19; Hag. 2:7). OT writers frequently mention God's coming in judgment. The days of judgment are already spoken of by Hosea (9:7). The day of Yahweh (→ Present, art. *hēmera*) features prominently in prophecy (cf. Joel 2:31; Zech. 14:1; Mal. 4:5; Ps. 96:13; 98:9). But God comes not only as → judge, but as deliverer (Isa. 35:4; Ps. 50:3 f., 15; Zech. 14:5 ff.). He comes as the saviour who feeds his flock, the redeemer who takes away the sin of Jacob, and the bringer of → light to → Jerusalem (Isa. 40:10 f. 59:20; 60:1; → Redemption). The → hope of God's coming is bound up with messianic expectation. The Messiah (→ Jesus Christ, art. *christos*) will come as the king of peace (Zech. 9:9), and the one who has been blessed in the → name of the Lord (Ps. 118:26). Dan. 7:13 speaks of the coming of "one like a → son of man." In the first instance, this is related to the → kingdom given to "the saints of the Most High" (vv. 22, 27). But because a kingdom cannot be thought of without a king, the son of man here was identified with the Messiah ever in pre-Christian times (cf. Eth. En. 46:3 f.; 48:2). The Qumran writings indicate a lively expectation of the coming Messiah or Messiahs (1QS 9:11; 1 QM 9:7 f.; CD 12:23; 20:1; cf. F. F. Bruce, *The Teacher of Righteousness in the Qumran Texts,* 1957; H. Ringgren, *The Faith of Qumran,* 1963, 167–98). On rabbinic messianic expectation see SB IV 2, 872 ff.; J. Klausner, *The Messianic Idea in Israel,* 1955, 427 ff., 440 ff.; S. Mowinckel, *He That Cometh,* 1956; G. Scholem, *The Messianic Idea in Judaism,* 1971, 1–36.

NT 1. The NT use of *erchomai* and *hēkō* follows secular Gk. usage. The original, spatial meaning is dominant. But it merges into a religious meaning. Coming to Jesus (Jn. 1:39, 47) leads to → discipleship. There are the same overtones in the coming of the wise men from the East (Matt. 2:2) which is also symbolic of the coming of the heathen. It points to their entry into the → kingdom of God (Matt. 8:11; Rom. 11:25). The metaphorical sense of events coming in time also occurs, especially in eschatology: the days or hour are coming when . . . (Matt. 9:15; Mk. 2:20; Jn. 2:4 and often); the fullness of time comes (Gal. 4:4), as does the message of faith (Gal. 3:23, 25), wrath (Eph. 5:6), and judgment (Rev. 18:10).

2. The addition of various prefixes to *erchomai* to form compounds gives a wide range of meaning. Usage here generally agrees with secular Gk. and the LXX.

(a) *aperchomai* means to go away literally (Gen. 18:33; Mk. 1:35; 6:46; 14:39 where Jesus "went away and prayed"). *apēlthon opisō* is used of the sons of Zebedee who followed Jesus (Mk. 1:20; cf. Job 21:33). It is a Hebraistic construction (Funk § 193(1)). The use of *opisō* (after) reflects the LXX rendering of Heb. *'aḥᵃrê* (after) (Moulton, *Grammar,* III, 277). *aperchomai* is also used in the opposite sense of going away from Jesus (Jn. 6:66; Jude 7). It is used metaphorically in the sense of pass away (of woes in Rev. 9:12; 11:4; and of "the first earth" and "the former things" in Rev. 21:1, 4).

(b) *dierchomai* means to go through or come through (1 Macc. 3:8; Acts 14:24 etc.). It is used of death coming to all men (Rom. 5:12) and of Jesus as the great high priest passing through the heavens (Heb. 4:14).

(c) *eiserchomai,* come in, enter, is used of the entry of the Israelites into the promised land (Num. 14:30; 15:2 etc.), and of the Lord's entry into his temple (Ps. 24:7, 9). In the NT it is used lit. of entering the temple or synagogue (Lk. 1:9; 4:16). *syneiserchomai* means to enter with, and is used of Jesus entering the boat with his disciples and of Peter entering the court of the high priest with Jesus (Jn. 6:22; 18:15). It is used metaphorically of entering the kingdom, → life and → rest (Matt. 18:3; Heb. 3:11, 18).

(d) *exerchomai,* go out, come out, get out, is used in both the LXX and the NT mostly in a lit. sense (e.g. Gen. 4:16; Matt. 14:14). But it is also used metaphorically of the coming forth of the Messiah (Isa. 11:1; Mic. 5:2; Matt. 2:6), and of the law and righteousness which proceed from the mouth of God (Isa. 2:3; 45:23; 51:4).

In the NT it is also applied to news (Matt. 9:26 and often), the emperor's decree (Lk. 2:1), the word of God (1 Cor. 14:36 "Did the word of God originate with you?" RSV), demons (Mk. 1:25 f.), and the thoughts of the heart (Matt. 15:18 f.). In Johannine language it is used of Jesus' coming forth from God (Jn. 8:42; 13:3 etc., cf. Mk. 1:38).

(e) *eperchomai*, come, come along, approach, is an intensive form of *erchomai*. It is used lit. (Acts 14:19), in a hostile sense (Lk. 11:22), and temporally in a neutral sense of the coming ages (Eph. 2:7). It denotes the coming of an imminent evil (Gen. 42:21; Lk. 21:26, 35; Jas. 5:1 and often) and of the coming of the Spirit (Isa. 32:15 *v.l.*; Lk. 1:35; Acts 1:8).

(f) *parerchomai*, go by, pass by, pass, is used locally (Gen. 18:3; Mk. 6:48; Lk. 18:37) and of time (Mk. 14:35). It also has the meanings of come by (Lk. 12:37), and pass away (of time Sir. 42:19; 1 Pet. 4:3; of wealth, heaven and earth Wis. 5:9; Matt. 5:18; 24:35), and transgress (commands, Isa. 24:5; Lk. 15:29).

(g) *pareiserchomai* is found in Polybius in the 2nd cent. B.C., but is rare. It means to come in or step in, and is used of the coming in of the law (Rom. 5:20) which has a subordinate purpose in God's plan of salvation, and of false brothers who have slipped into the church at Jerusalem (Gal. 2:4).

(h) *perierchomai*, wander (Jos. 6:6, 10). It is used of Jewish itinerant exorcists (Acts 19:13), the circuit made by Paul around the coast of Sicily (Acts 28:13), of the going around from house to house of young widows (1 Tim. 5:13), and of the roaming around of the persecuted witnesses to the faith (Heb. 11:37).

(i) *proerchomai*, go forward, advance, proceed (Gen. 33:3, 14; Acts 20:5; 2 Cor. 9:5). It is used in a metaphorical sense of the precursor of Christ (Lk. 1:17; cf. *v.l. proseleusetai*).

(j) *proserchomai*, go to, approach, accede to, is used mostly lit. in the LXX and NT (e.g. Gen. 42:24; Matt. 5:1). It is used in a cultic context of the people (Ex. 16:9) and the priest (Lev. 9:7 f.) before God. It is chiefly used in the LXX for the Heb. *qārab* (approach, come near). This usage continues in the Qumran writings. In the NT Heb. 4:16 speaks of drawing near to the throne of grace (cf. Ezek. 44:16). Heb. 10:22 and 11:6 speak of the believer's drawing near to God in a way which far exceeds the prerogative of the high priest. In a more general sense Sir. 6:18 f. refers to drawing near to wisdom, and 1 Tim. 6:3 of acceding to, or agreeing with "sound words."

(k) *synerchomai*, come together, assemble (Exod. 32:26; Mk. 3:20; 1 Cor. 11:17 ff.; 14:23, 26, of a crowd or the local church); come with, accompany (Tob. 12:1; Lk. 23:55; Acts 1:21); and come together in the sense of sexual union (Wis. 7:2; Matt. 1:18; 1 Cor. 7:5).

3. (a) The idea of coming has a fundamental theological significance in relation to the coming of Christ, and the coming of God and his → kingdom. The statements about his having come in all the gospels indicates Jesus' messianic self-consciousness. The synoptic gospels present Jesus as having come to preach the → gospel, not to destroy the → Law but to fulfil it, to call sinners to → repentance, not to bring peace but a sword and to cast fire upon the earth (Mk. 1:38 f.; Matt. 5:17; 9:13; Mk. 2:17; Lk. 5:32; 12:49). The Son of man has come to give his life a ransom for many, and to seek and to save the lost (Matt. 20:28; Mk. 10:45; Lk. 19:10).

Rudolf Bultmann regards the "I-Sayings" of Jesus in the gospels as inauthentic (*The History of the Synoptic Tradition*, 1968², 150–166). He sees them as the invention of the early church which put them into the mouth of Jesus. But this does not explain how this belief arose, if Jesus did not have such an awareness of his calling (→ I am).

Jn. bears witness to Jesus as the → light of the world (Jn. 1:9; 3:19; 8:12) who came to give to those who belong to him → life in all its fullness (Jn. 10:10). He did not come to judge the world, but to save it and to bear witness to the → truth (Jn. 12:46 f.; 18:37). He has come in the name of the Father. He has come from God and has returned to him (Jn. 5:43; 8:42; 16:28).

John the Baptist went before him (Lk. 1:17). He too has "come", and is indeed the → Elijah who is to come again (Mal. 4:5; Matt. 11:14, 18; 17:10; Mk. 9:11). John pointed to one mightier than himself who would come (Matt. 3:11; Mk. 1:7; Lk. 3:16). Jn. lays special stress on the preparatory significance of the Baptist. He is not himself the light, but has come to bear witness to the light. Jesus is the Lord who was before him, even though he came after him (Mk. 1:7; Jn. 1:7, 15, 27). (See further C. H. H. Scobie, *John the Baptist*, 1964, 62–79.)

(b) The coming of Jesus in the → flesh (1 Jn. 4:2) gave rise to the doubt which even the imprisoned John entertained: "Are you he who is to come, or shall we look for another?" (Matt. 11:3 RSV). The people at Jerusalem greeted the saviour king who came to them with Ps. 118:25 f. (Matt. 21:9; Mk. 11:9 f.; Lk. 19:38). But his death on the → cross set a question mark against Jesus' messianic claims (Matt. 27:42; Mk. 15:31; Lk. 23:35; Jn. 19:19 ff.). Through his resurrection Jesus is "designated Son of God in power" (Rom. 1:4 RSV). This power will also be manifested in the world. Therefore, the certainty that Jesus will come again in power and glory belongs to the Easter message. In the synoptic gospels this faith in the coming of Christ is formulated in terms of the messianic interpretation of Dan. 7:13. The Son of man will come in the clouds of heaven (Matt. 24:30; Mk. 13:26; Lk. 21:27; and Matt. 26:64; Mk. 14:62; Lk. 22:69). Christ will come as → judge (Matt. 16:27; 25:31; 2 Cor. 5:10; Rom. 2:6; 14:10). It makes no material difference if God is also spoken of as judge (Matt. 10:32 f.; Mk. 8:38; Lk. 9:26; Rev. 3:5; 2 Tim. 2:12). The strength of this hope which fills the whole NT is shown by the prayer-cry *maranatha* (1 Cor. 16:22) which was an early Aram. expression meaning "Our Lord, come!" It is reflected in the prayer at the end of Rev.: "Come, Lord Jesus!" (22:20; → Present, art. *maranatha*).

Prayer for the coming of the Lord is bound up with prayer for the coming of the → kingdom of God (Matt. 6:10; Lk. 11:2). The coming of the Messiah is not to be separated from the coming of the kingdom (Matt. 16:28; Lk. 22:29 f.). False → prophets, messiahs and even the → Antichrist will precede the coming of Christ (Mk. 13:22 f.; Matt. 24:24; 1 Jn. 2:18; 2 Thess. 2:3 ff.). The day and hour of this coming is known neither by the angels in heaven, nor even the Son, but only the Father; it is not granted the disciples to know (Mk. 13:32; Matt. 24:36; Acts 1:7). The Lord will come suddenly like a thief in the night (Matt. 24:42 f.; Lk. 12:39; 1 Thess. 5:2). Therefore, the disciples must be awake (Matt. 24:44; 25:13). Although the timing of this coming is never laid down in the NT, the hope that it will be soon is not precluded (Rev. 22:20). It is always imminent.

(c) The Fourth Gospel sees Easter and Pentecost in the light of the coming of

323

Jesus and → the Spirit. In departing, Jesus does not leave his disciples as orphans, but returns to them as the living one. He will reveal himself to those who love him. The Father and the Son will come to them and will make their home with them (Jn. 14:16 ff.). Jesus promises help in the coming of the *paraklētos* (Jn. 14:16, 26; 15:26; 16:7; cf. 16:12 ff.; 1 Jn. 2:1; → Advocate, Paraclete). He has the task of bearing witness to Jesus. As the Spirit of truth he will lead the disciples into all → truth. This does not mean, as some have supposed, the abandonment of the early church's hope for the future. The thought of the last judgment and resurrection is firmly held by Jn. and is indissolubly linked with the person of Jesus (5:25, 29; 6:39, 44, 54; 11:25 f.). Jn. stresses the close connection between the saving presence of Christ who has already come and the future. This finds classic expression in the statement "the hour is coming and now is" (4:23; 5:25).

(d) Men are now called to come to this → Lord who has come and who will come. Jesus refers to this in the parable of the great supper (Matt. 22:1–14; Lk. 14:16–24). But the invitation results in a refusal to come. The same picture comes in Jn. 5:40; 7:37. Clearly it is not a matter of physical presence or the expression of interest. The gospels are concerned with following Jesus (Mk. 1:20; Matt. 10:38; Lk. 14:27; Matt. 16:24; Mk. 8:34; Lk. 9:23; → Disciple, arts. *akoloutheō* and *opisō*). In Jn.'s terminology *akoloutheō* (follow) and *pisteuō* (believe) stand close together (→ Faith). The fact that Christ has already come is the basis of man's access to him. But in the last analysis man's response to this invitation is the work of God's grace (Jn. 6:37, 44). *W. Mundle*

| καταντάω |

καταντάω (*katantaō*), come to, arrive at; ἀπαντάω (*apantaō*), meet; ὑπαντάω (*hypantaō*), meet; ἀπάντησις (*apantēsis*), meeting; ὑπάντησις (*hypantēsis*), meeting, coming to meet.

CL *katantaō* is found in secular Gk. from Polybius (2nd cent. B.C.). It meant originally to come to, and denotes movement towards a goal, primarily a place such as a town. In a metaphorical sense it denotes the attainment of an objective, or conversely something which comes to us.

OT Use of the word in the LXX is restricted to 4 passages in 2 Macc. and 2 Sam. 3:29. But these reflect important shades of meaning. It is used lit. in the sense of coming to Jerusalem or Tyre (2 Macc. 4:21, 44). It is used metaphorically of attaining to the status of high priest and of men reaching the full measure of sin (2 Macc. 4:24; 6:14). In 2 Sam. 3:29 it translates the Heb. *ḥûl* (lit. "turn upon"), and is used of Yahweh requiting blood guilt on the head of Joab.

NT 1. In the NT the word occurs only in Acts (9 times) and Paul (4 times). In Acts it is used almost exclusively in the lit. physical sense of arrive at (in the case of Paul and the places he arrived at on his missionary journeys, cf. Acts 16:1; 18:19, 24). It occurs once in a metaphorical sense. In his address to Agrippa, Paul declared that the twelve tribes of Israel hope to *attain* the promise made by God to their forefathers, as they earnestly worship day and night, and that this was the theme of his preaching.

324

2. This expression is related to Paul's usage which is always metaphorical. The ultimate goal of the Christian life is to attain to the resurrection of the dead (Phil. 3:11). Eph. 4:13 speaks of all Christians attaining to the unity of faith and the knowledge of the Son of God. Bound up with the attainment of this goal is the maturity, firm faith, and growth in love which unite the church with Christ its head (Eph. 4:14 ff.).

Paul also speaks of a movement from God to man. 1 Cor. 10:11 speaks of us "upon whom the end of the ages has come." Heb. 9:26 contains a similar expression: "at the end of the ages" (→ Time, art. *aiōn*) Christ has appeared to put away sin by the sacrifice of himself. The movement is directed by God towards its end; with us it has now attained its goal. The thought also contains the certainty that, with Christ who inaugurates the end of the ages, a new world era and order of things has begun. Admittedly this is apparent only to the believer. Nevertheless, the form of this → world is passing away (1 Cor. 7:31). This movement that comes from God is also to be seen in the fact that the Word of God has reached the churches (1 Cor. 14:36), and that it is spread abroad by them. This → word is the apostolic message which reaches its goal in the churches as they receive it as the Word of God (1 Thess. 2:13).

3. Alongside *katantaō*, the NT has two other verbs which are related in both form and sense. *apantaō* (Mk. 14:13; Lk. 17:12) and *hypantaō* (Matt. 8:28; Lk. 8:27) both mean meet, and the related nouns *apantēsis* (Acts 28:15; 1 Thess. 4:17) and *hypantēsis* (Matt. 8:34; 25:1) mean meeting. The words occur in secular Gk. and the LXX always in a spatial sense. This is also true of *synantaō*, meet (Lk. 9:37; Acts 10:25; Heb. 7:1, 10). It is used in Acts 20:22 in the sense of befall.

The use of *apantēsis* in 1 Thess. 4:17 is noteworthy. The ancient expression for the civic welcome of an important visitor or the triumphal entry of a new ruler into the capital city and thus to his reign is applied to Christ. "Then we who are alive, who are left, shall be caught up together with them in the clouds to meet the Lord (*eis apantēsin tou Kyriou*) in the air; and so we shall always be with the Lord." The same thoughts occur in the parable of the ten virgins. The virgins leave to meet the bridegroom (*eis apantēsin tou nymphiou*), i.e. the Lord, to whom they wish to give a festive reception (Matt. 25:1). (See E. Peterson, "Die Einholung des Kyrios", *ZSTh* 7, 1929–30, 682 ff.; and *TDNT* I 380 f.)   W. Mundle

---

μέλλω

μέλλω (*mellō*), to be about to, to be on the point of, be destined to, intend, propose, have in mind; μέλλων (*mellōn*), is a participle used in the sense of to come, future.

CL *mellō* (imp. *emellon*; Attic form *ēmellon*) is found from Homer onwards. It is commonly used with a following infinitive, or absolutely as a participle. The action indicated by the infinitive is modified by *mellō*, making it dependent upon the intentions of the subject. Thus *mellō* means "I am able to, I can." More frequent is its use in cl. Gk. with a future infinitive: "I am in the act of, I am about to, I intend to." Often it simply means "I shall." When the action is seen as compelled by the gods, fate or some law, *mellō* means especially in the imp. "to have to." It denotes something inevitable and determined. But it may be weakened by conjecture or probability. In that case it means "I may well." When the action in question is delayed by reflection so long that it never comes about, *mellō* means to hesitate.

The participle *mellōn* means future, what is about to come. In Aeschylus, Euripides and Plato, *ho mellōn chronos* (lit. the time to come) means the future. Similarly, the noun *to mellon* means the future, and *ta mellonta* means future things.

OT In the LXX *mellō* is often used with a present infinitive, especially in 2 Macc., 4 Macc., Wis., Job and 6 times in Isa. Mostly it is used as the equivalent of the imperfect future form of the Heb. vb. In Job 3:8 it stands for *ha'ªṭîḏîm*, i.e. those who are *ready* to rouse up Leviathan. In Job 19:25 *mellō* translates Heb. *'aḥªrôn*, "last", which EVV translate adverbially as "at last." In both cases the Heb. is difficult. See further E. Dhorme, *A Commentary on the Book of Job*, 1967, 29, 282 f.; H. H. Rowley, *Job*, 1970, 45, 173. Some LXX manuscripts of Isa. 9:6(5) add *patēr tou mellontos aiōnos* (father of the age to come). This is the only instance in the LXX of *ho aiōn ho mellōn* (the age to come). Later it was of great significance in Jewish apocalyptic in such works as 4 Esd. and Apoc. Bar. (→ Time, art. *aiōn*. Cf. D. S. Russell, *The Method and Message of Jewish Apocalyptic*, 1964, 223 f., 266 ff.).

NT 1. In the NT *mellō* has all the meanings that it has in Gk. literature. It means to intend, to have in mind in Matt. 2:13; Lk. 10:1; 19:4; Jn. 6:6, 15; 7:35; Acts 5:35; 20:3, 7, 13; 23:15; 27:30; 2 Pet. 1:12; Heb. 8:5. It occurs frequently with the present infinitive (84 times) and occasionally with the aorist infinitive with the sense of "to be about to", "to be on the point of" (Matt. 24:6; Lk. 7:2; 19:11; 21:7; Jn. 4:47; Acts 3:3; 12:6; 16:27; 18:14; Rev. 3:2; 10:4, 7; 12:4 f.). The participle formed from *mellō* is used both as an adj. and as a noun in the sense of future (Lk. 13:9; 2 Pet. 2:6; Rom. 8:38; 1 Cor. 3:22; 1 Tim. 6:19; Heb. 11:20). *ti melleis* (Acts 22:16) means "Why do you hesitate?"

2. *mellō* means must, to have to, be certain to, in the context of events which happen according to the will and decree of God and which are thus necessary, certain and inevitable. It occurs in statements about the saving work of Christ, especially his suffering and death. Thus, "he began to tell them what *was to* happen to him" (Mk. 10:32); "the Son of man *is to* be delivered into the hands of men" (Matt. 17:22; cf. 17:12; 20:22; Lk. 9:31, 44; 24:21; Jn. 7:39; 11:51; 12:33; 14:22; 18:32; Acts 26:23). It is used in connection with Judas' betrayal (Lk. 22:23; Jn. 6:71; 12:4). It occurs in the context of God's action in grace and judgment (Mk. 13:4; Acts 17:31; Rom. 4:24; 8:13; Gal. 3:23; 1 Thess. 3:4; 1 Tim. 1:16; Heb. 1:14; 10:27; 11:8; Rev. 1:19; 3:10). With this may be included prophetic utterances made with divine certainty (Acts 11:28; 24:15; 26:22).

3. Participial forms of *mellō* are used both as adjs. and nouns in the sense of coming, future (as in NT 1.). In this sense, it is incorporated in an important NT eschatological formula, which has taken over the thought of late Judaism and Hel. apocalyptic. The basic apocalyptic doctrine of the two ages (→ Time, art. *aiōn*) provides the foundation for the NT doctrine of the → kingdom of God. The present age which is passing away has been broken into by the age to come (*mellōn aiōn*). The coming world (*hē oikoumenē hē mellousa*, Heb. 2:5; cf. Eph. 1:21) is alone the realm of Christ. Here in the present world, believers have no abiding (*menousa*) city; they seek the future (*mellousa*) one (Heb. 13:14). This future city

has firm foundations (Heb. 11:10), and has been prepared by God for the patriarchs (Heb. 11:16). It is the heavenly city (Heb. 11:16; 12:22), our home and the promised rest (Heb. 3:11, 18; 4:3 ff.). It is our refuge from death and judgment. This new world is described in terms of future glory (*tēn mellousan doxan*, Rom. 8:18; cf. 1 Pet. 5:1). It is already present with God and is ready to be revealed. In the light of it, the inevitable sufferings of the present age are to be counted as nothing. But he who is afraid to suffer and lives according to the → flesh must die (*mellete apothnēskein*, Rom. 8:13). This is the inevitable outcome of the coming judgment and wrath (Matt. 3:7; Acts 24:25). Christ is the coming Son of man (Matt. 16:27) and judge (2 Tim. 4:1). In the age to come there is no → forgiveness of blasphemy against the Spirit (Matt. 12:32; cf. Mk. 3:29). Godliness is of value as it holds promise for the present → life and the life to come (1 Tim. 4:8). It is possible to taste the powers of the age to come (Heb. 6:5). Christ is the "high priest of the good things that are to come" (Heb. 9:11 *v.l.* which is very strongly attested [cf. Metzger, 668]; it is the marginal reading in RSV, the text having "the good things that have come"). These good things of the new age have been secured for the believer by Christ's death. The → law has only the shadow of the good things to come (Heb. 10:1). Regulations are "only a shadow of what is to come; but the substance belongs to Christ" (Col. 2:17 RSV). This reality is the → body of Christ, the coming one (cf. E. Lohmeyer, *Die Briefe an die Kolosser und an Philemon*, KEK 9, 2 1964[12], 122 f.). As the one to come who inaugurates the new world. Christ is seen as the antitype of → Adam in Rom. 5:14.   *W. Schneider*

(a). Arndt, 310 f., 345, 416, 501 f.; O. Michel, *katantaō*, *TDNT* III 623–26; S. Mowinckel, *He That Cometh*, 1956; J. Schneider, *erchomai*, *TDNT* II 666–84; and *hēkō*, *TDNT* II 926 ff.
(b). H. Conzelmann, "Eschatologie im Urchristentum," *RGG*[3] II 665 ff.; A. von Harnack, "Ich bin gekommen," *ZTK* 22, 1912, 1 ff.; S. Herrmann, *Die prophetischen Heilserwartungen im Alten Testament*, 1965; E. Jenni, *bō'*, *THAT* I 264–69; E. Lohmeyer, *Die Briefe an die Kolosser und an Philemon*, KEK 9, 2, 1964[12]; W. Mundle, *Der Glaube an Christus und der historische Zweifel*, 1950, 24 ff.; R. Prenter, "Eschatologie im NT und Urchristentum," *EKL* I 115; R. Schnackenburg, "Eschatologie," *LTK* III 1088 ff.
→ Literature under Present

Comfort, Encouragement

θαρσέω

θαρρέω (*tharreō*), θαρσέω (*tharseō*), be of good courage, take heart.

CL *tharseō* (Homer), like the Attic form *tharreō* (from 5th-4th cent. B.C.), means, to be of good courage, take heart, have confidence. In later Gk. both forms are found side by side. The imperative form *tharsei, tharseite*, take heart, is common in classical Gk. usage. A famous example is the exhortation from a pagan mystery rite recorded by Firmicus Maternus (4th cent. A.D.), *tharreite mystai*, "Take heart, initiates!"

OT The dominant form in the LXX is *tharseō; tharreō* (e.g. Prov. 1:21; Dan. 6:16 (17)) is less frequent. Only in Prov. 31:11 is it used to render the Heb. *bāṭaḥ*, to trust (not in a religious sense, but of trusting one's wife). Otherwise it is consistently used for *yārē'* in the prohibition, "fear not". Whether it is Moses' exhortation to the

327

people overcome with fear (Exod. 14:13; 20:20), Elijah's words of comfort to the widow in Zarephath threatened with death by starvation (1 Ki. 17:13), or prophetic encouragement to the nation or to Jerusalem (Zeph. 3:16; Hag. 2:5; Zech. 8:13, 15), comfort and encouragement arise from overcoming → fear and are based on confident → hope in God's help and promises.

NT In the NT the form *tharseō* appears 3 (possibly 2) times in Matt. and Mk., and once each in Jn. and Acts. *tharreō* occurs 5 times in 2 Cor. and in Heb. 13:6.

1. In Mk. 10:49 the companions of blind Bartimaeus address him with the expression, *tharsei*, take heart. He may take heart because Jesus is calling him and offering him help. Elsewhere the imperative is found only in the mouth of Jesus. The paralytic whose sin Jesus forgives is to be of good cheer (Matt. 9:2), as is the woman with an issue of blood whom he heals (Matt. 9:22; cf. Lk. 8:48 *v.l.*). When the disciples are frightened by his appearance on the lake, the word of comfort is strengthened by the addition of *mē phobeisthe*, → fear not (Matt. 14:27). In the farewell discourses of the Fourth Gospel, Jesus commands the disciples, whom he is leaving behind in a world full of tribulation: "Be of good cheer, I have overcome the world" (Jn. 16:33). In Acts 23:11 a similar word of comfort is given by the risen Lord to the apostle in prison.

2. In 2 Cor. 7:16 Paul uses the word *tharrō* to express the confidence which he has in the Corinthian church. But in 10:1, 2 the same word is used of the boldness with which he is determined to face those who oppose him in Corinth (→ Openness). In 2 Cor. 5:6, 8 he uses *tharrountes* and *tharroumen* to speak of the confidence which fills his heart. In his life of suffering he is supported by the assurance that he has an eternal home with the Lord → faith, art. *peithomai*). The letter to the Hebrews exhorts its readers to a similar confidence, as they face the necessity of holding out in a pagan environment which is hostile towards them (Heb. 13:6).

W. Mundle

παραμυθέομαι

παραμυθέομαι (*paramytheomai*), encourage, cheer up, console; παραμυθία (*paramythia*), encouragement, comfort, consolation; παραμύθιον (*paramythion*), encouragement, consolation, alleviation.

CL *paramytheomai* (Homer) has the more general meaning of to speak to someone, in a positive, benevolent way (Plato, *Phaedo* 83a; philosophy comforts the soul and seeks to release it). But it also means to encourage or exhort (Homer, *Il.* 9, 417: "the others too I would kindly exhort to sail home"), and to comfort, soothe, address cheering words to (Plato, *Phaedo* 70b: "But surely it requires a great deal of argument and many proofs to show that when a man is dead his soul yet exists and has any force or intelligence," B. Jowett, *The Dialogues of Plato*, 1973 ed., 453). *paramythion*, encouragement, exhortation, assuagement, is attested from Soph. onwards. Commenting on Phil. 2:1, E. Lohmeyer cites Papyri Florentini III 339, 19, "Write to me . . . concerning your health, that I may have some consolation (*paramythion*)", and from an epitaph from the time of Hadrian the words, "Father's and mother's . . . comfort (*paramythion*)" (*Die Briefe an die Philipper, Kolosser und an Philemon*, KEK 1956[11], 83).

328

ot In Heb. there is no term equivalent to *paramytheomai*. The LXX uses the word in the sense of comfort, console, encourage. "And he exhorted (*parekalei*) his men not to fear the attack . . . and encouraged (*paramythoumenos*) them from the law and the prophets" (2 Macc. 15:8 f.). "If they die young, they will have no hope and no consolation (*paramythion*) in the day of judgment" (Wis. 3:18). In the OT there is mention of various kinds of comfort (*paraklēsis*) and comforting (*parakaleō*, → Exhort, Warn), but not with the sentimental overtones which the word has acquired in our language. Isa. 57:17 f. speaks first of God's anger and punishment; but then God alters his plan and brings healing and comfort. The word of God has life-giving power, and thus brings comfort in affliction (Ps. 119:50). A faithful friend is described as an elixir of life (Sir. 6:16).

In Rab. Judaism the "consolation of Israel" is a blanket term for the fulfilment of Messianic expectation (cf. Lk. 2:25 → *paraklēsin tou Israēl*; SB II 124), while to comfort those who mourn is one of the works of love which earn merit (SB II 544; IV, 1 592 ff.).

nt The first example of the use of *paramytheisthai* in early Christian literature is in 1 Thess. 2:12, where it is used, as at 5:14, in conjunction with *parakalein*, to exhort (cf. also v. 3). Paul reminds his readers ("for you know", v. 11) that when he visited Thessalonica (v. 1), he exhorted and encouraged them. He also indicates the content of this encouragement in the words: "to lead a life worthy of God, who calls you into his own kingdom and glory" (v. 12). The term → kingdom (*basileia*) belongs to the very earliest language of the → church. Paul undertook the task of encouraging the people in this way with complete devotion ("Like a father with his children", v. 11) and person to person ("each one of you", v. 11). In 1 Thess. 5:14 the apostle urges the brethren (i.e. the whole church and not just their leaders) in Thessalonica, to encourage (*paramytheisthe*) the faint-hearted.

Encouragement is an expression of love. Together with participation in the Spirit and heartfelt sympathy, it forms one of the foundations of church life as lived out in the sphere of Christ (Phil. 2:1). This applies also to the special circumstances at Corinth. There it is the → prophets (or more exactly, those who exercise the gift of prophecy) who build up, encourage and console the church. "He who prophesies speaks to men for their upbuilding (*oikodomēn*) and encouragement (*paraklēsin*) and consolation (*paramythian*)" (1 Cor. 14:3 f.). Such prophets did not have any right of office which was binding for other churches (cf. 1 Thess. 5:14, where it is "brothers" rather than prophets who exercise this ministry). To sum up, giving comfort is part of the apostle's missionary activity and also of the life of the young church. It is extended in a personal way both to individuals and to the church. It builds and establishes them, gives strength to the faint-hearted, and is an expression of love in the sphere of Christ.

In Jn. 11:19, 31 *paramytheomai* is a technical term for the expression of sympathy. Mk. 5:38 and Lk. 7:12 record instances of weeping for the dead (cf. Moed Katan 3:7 ff.; T. B. Moed Katan 23a; T. J. Moed Katan 3:82b:28; SB IV 596).

G. Braumann

→ Advocate, art. *paraklētos*, → Exhort, Warn, Console, arts. *noutheteō, parakaleō*
→ Openness, Boldness, Frankness

W. Grundmann, *tharreō TDNT* III 25 ff.; G. Stählin, *paramytheomai, TDNT* V 816–23.

Command, Order

This article deals with the following words: *dogma* (decree, ordinance, decision, command, doctrine, dogma), *entolē* (command, order), and the vb. *parangellō* (to give orders, command, instruct, direct).

δόγμα	δόγμα (*dogma*), decree, ordinance, decision, command, doctrine, dogma; δογματίζω (*dogmatizō*), decree, ordain.

CL The word *dogma* stems from the vb. *dokeō* (think, suppose, imagine, conclude), and means opinion, conclusion, belief. From the noun comes the intensive vb. *dogmatizō* (lay down as an opinion, order, decree).

It occurs only 3 times in the pre-Socratic writers and always in connection with Pythagoras. From Xenophon onwards in the fourth cent. B.C. it has the following meanings: (1) opinion (in ordinary speech); (2) a doctrine (in philosophy, e.g. Epicurus, *De rerum natura*, 14, 1, 15 and 28); (3) a decree of God (in religious writers); (4) a decree, ordinance, edict (in official language, with the emphasis on public promulgation). (See Arndt, 200.)

OT 1. The following are found in the later writings of the LXX: (1) *dogma* in the sense of a public decree, edict or ordinance (Est. 4:8; Dan. 2:13; 4 Macc. 4:23), and the corresponding vb. *dogmatizō* (Dan. 2:13; Est. 3:9; 2 Macc. 10:8); (2) *dogma* in the sense of a divine ordinance of the Mosaic law (3 Macc. 1:3); and (3) *dogmatizō* meaning to make a decision in the community (2 Macc. 15:36).

2. In the late Judaism of the first cent. A.D., Philo and Josephus understood the Mosaic law as a system of holy tenets, the *dogmata* of a divine philosophy. As the most exalted of all systems, it was superior to the doctrines of the rest of ancient philosophy (Philo, *Leg. All.*, 1, 54 f.; *Spec. Leg.*, 1, 269; *Gig.* 52; Josephus, *War*, 2, 42; *Ap.*, 1, 42; cf. G. Kittel, *TDNT* II 231).

NT 1. (a) *dogma* has the meaning of CL (4) in the writings of Lk. It is used of the decree of Caesar Augustus concerning the enrollment (Lk. 2:1). The Jews at Thessalonica accused Jason before the civil authorities of aiding and abetting Paul and Silas in "acting against the decrees of Caesar" (Acts 17:7). It also occurs in some manuscripts at Heb. 11:23.

(b) In Acts 16:4 the decisions of the Jerusalem council that were to be enforced in the mission churches are called *dogmata* (cf. 2 Macc. 15:36 in OT 1 above).

(c) Eph. 2:15 uses the pl. *dogmata* to denote the individual statutes of the commandments (*entolōn*) of the Mosaic Law. Col. 2:14 uses the word to denote the "legal demands" (RSV) levelled against us which God has nailed to the cross. Hence, Col. 2:20 forbids the church to allow statutes, rules or regulations regarding food and cleanliness to be imposed upon it (cf. v. 21). Here the vb. *dogmatizō* is translated by RSV: "Why do you submit to regulations?"

2. Where *dogma* is used in a general, secular sense as an official, public decree, it has only indirect theological significance. The parents of Moses were witnesses to the faith in that they fearlessly disregarded Pharaoh's command (*dogma*) that children should be put to death (Heb. 11:23 in some manuscripts; the better attested reading is however *diatagma*, edict). Caesar's edict is seen by Lk. 2:1 ff. to serve God's plan of salvation, in bringing about the birth of the Messiah at → Bethlehem.

The Jewish opponents of the Christian mission complained that the Christians were guilty of treason by contravening Caesar's edicts (Acts 17:7; cf. E. Haenchen, *The Acts of the Apostles*, 1971, 508). The contexts of these passages show the impotence of all the *dogmata* of the mighty ones on earth in the face of the saving works of God.

3. With the death of Christ, the → law with all its commandments and ordinances "is removed from the world as a factor in salvation" (M. Dibelius, *An die Kolosser, Epheser, An Philemon*, HNT 12 revised by H. Greeven, 1953³, 70 on Eph. 2:15; cf. 2.14 and 2:20 ff. on the regulations of "the elemental spirits" → Law, art. *stoicheia*).

4. The use of *dogma* is, therefore, all the more surprising when used in a positive sense (cf. above OT) for teaching that is binding on the whole church. Acts 16:4 lays the foundation for the idea of dogma as an ecclesiastical decree, requiring intellectual assent. It runs the risk of turning the gospel of Christ into legalism. On the other hand, the pressure from the Judaizers forced the Jerusalem council to take a stance in defining their attitude. The *dogmata* of the council were in fact decrees proclaiming liberty within a defined area rather than a series of tight restrictions.

H. H. Esser

ἐντολή

ἐντολή (*entolē*), command, commandment, order; ἐντέλλομαι (*entellomai*) to command, give orders, order.

CL The noun *entolē* (injunction, order, command) is connected with the deponent mid. vb. *entellomai* (enjoin, command, either a person or an order). The vb. is also used either absolutely, or with acc. and infin. act. or infin. pass. *entolē* has replaced the perf. pass. participle used as a noun *ta entetalmena*, lit. what has been commanded. The vb. and the noun occur from the 5th cent. in Aeschylus, Pindar and Herodotus to denote chiefly the instructions given by a person of high social standing to a subordinate. The plur. of the noun is common in the expression *entolas dounai*, to give instructions.

This secular use is dominant. But at an early date (Aeschylus and Pindar) these words were also used of the commands of God, in a way similar to the royal or imperial decrees (→ *dogma*). Most examples of this are found in inscriptions and papyri. In the 4th cent. A.D. the words came to be used as technical terms in connection with the power of attorney.

OT 1. The vb. is found approximately 400 times in the LXX, of which 39 instances are without a Heb. equivalent. The noun occurs 244 times (46 times without a Heb. equivalent). The occurrence of both is concentrated in the Pentateuch (where more than half the instances of the vb. are to be found) and especially in Deut. The Deuteronomic literature and the historical writings dependent on it often exhibit words of this group (see 2. below). For the rest, the vb. is frequent in Jer. and the noun in the Pss.

2. (a) Among the Heb. equivalents rendered by *entolē* and *entellomai* the most common are the words derived from the root *ṣwh* (the vb. *ṣiwwâh* 344 times; the noun *miṣwâh* 159 times).

ṣiwwâh means to order, direct, summon a person or thing to a place or task. Yahweh appoints a king over his people (2 Sam. 13:14; 16:21). He gives his angels

331

charge over those whom he protects (Ps. 91[90]:11; the same idea is also translated by *apostellō*, send → Apostle, cf. Isa. 10:6; Exod. 4:28). He summons help for Israel (Ps. 44:5 [LXX 43:4]). He commands things to be done (Gen. 32:18). Alternatively, when the vb. is linked with a negative, he forbids (Gen. 2:16; 18:1). On God's commands see also Gen. 6:22; Exod. 7:2; Deut. 1:3.

miṣwâh is also used of a human command, but mostly of divine commands. In the Pentateuch it is reserved for the latter. There especially such formulae occur as: the command (or commandment) of Yahweh, the command of my (or our) God, his command, his commands, these commands, the command. When God speaks, the expression "my commands" occurs. The Pss. especially speak frequently of "your commands." These expressions imply that the command of God is something known. The noun means: commission, command, single commandment, commandments in general (in this case mostly in the plur. with *phylassesthai*, to keep), ordinance (Neh. 13:5 [LXX 2 Esd. 23:5]), obligation (Neh. 1:32 [LXX 2 Esd. 20:33]).

(b) Among the less common equivalents the root *pqd* (24 times) is the most frequent. The vb. *pāqaḏ* is translated by *entellesthai* 6 times. In the qal it means to entrust something to someone (2 Chron. 36:23) and to call to account, to punish (wickedness, Isa. 13:11). In the piel it means to muster (a host, Isa. 13:4). In all these cases the subject is God. In the niphal it means to get lost, to be missing (1 Sam. [LXX 1 Ki.] 25:7; in v. 15 it is used in the qal in the sense of miss).

The noun *piqqûḏîm* (pl.) occurs 18 times as an equivalent, and is used as a technical term for the precepts or commandments of God (cf. Pss. 103[102]:18; 111 [110]:7; and 119[118] where it comes 21 times in the formula "thy commandments"). However, on 5 occasions the LXX translates the word by the Gk. *dikaiōmata* (Ps. 119[118]27, 56, 93, 94, 141; → Righteousness).

(c) The root *dbr* is translated by *entolē* and *entellomai* 10 times. It is the common word for speak, and it means command in the Heb. of 6 of these instances. It is always Yahweh or his representative who is thus commanding (Moses, Deut. 18:14; Joshua, Jos. 4:12). What he thus speaks is a particular command: Exod. 7:13 23:22; Jos. 4:12 (a plan of battle); 11:23; 1 Ki. (LXX 3 Ki.) 13:17; Jer. 19:15; Exod. 34:32 (a collection of commandments); Deut. 28:14 (a collection of blessings and cursings); Ps. 119(118):57, 139 (the claim of God to thorough obedience).

(d) The equivalent *ḥōq, ḥuqqâh* (mostly in the plur.) merits special attention. It means lit. what is established, engraved (in stone), carved, fixed in writing, and therefore a statute (→ Law, art. *stoicheia*). It is often used in Deuteronomic theology for the unaltered handing on of the tradition that is necessary for life: the instruction of children in the confession (Deut. 6:24); instructions for feasts (Deut. 16:12); the laws regulating life of Israel at the renewal of the covenant (Deut. 28:15); David's testament to Solomon (1 Sam. [3 Ki.] 2:3); the prophetic designation of Jeroboam as king (1 Ki. 11:38). In this tradition these statutes are handed down and experienced. God's → covenant, the → law, justice, commandments and ordinances are thus realized. This may be seen in God's answer to the prayer of Solomon (1 Ki. 3:14). The underlying relationship of God to his people is determined by the commandments proclaimed to them and their obedience in return. This applies even when national unity is lost, as with the end of the northern kingdom and the exile in Babylon. The newly proclaimed commandment was essential for the ordering of the life of the community that returned after the exile (Neh. 8 ff.). Disregard of the divine statutes brings the punishment of Yahweh (1 Ki. [3 Ki.] 11:11). But future observance of the rules of life opens up Yahweh's forgiveness of earlier trespasses and a new grant of life to the penitent sinner (Ezek. 18:21 f.).

(e) *entolē* is rarely used for Heb. *tôrâh* (→ law). In such cases it has the secondary sense of the summary of God's commandments and thus the normative law of God for Israel (2 Ki. 21:8, where the stem *entel-* occurs 3 times; 2 Chron. 30:16). It occurs in the phrase "all the words of the law" (Deut. 17:19), where it is parallel to the expression "these commandments" (Heb. *ḥuqqîm*, Gk. *dikaiōmata*).

3. In the Qumran literature the Heb. words discussed under section 2 occur some 235 times: *ṣiwwâh* (26 times), *miṣwâh* (25 times), *pāqaḏ* (33 times), *pequddâh* (14 times), *piqqûḏîm* (once), *dibbēr* (as a vb. 5 times, as a noun 12 times), *ḥōq* (50 times, of which 16 are in the sing.; it is often used absolutely), *ḥāqaq* (twice), *ḥuqqâh* (3 times), *tôrâh* (63 times in the sense of 2 (e), mostly used absolutely, otherwise as the "law of Moses"). This linguistic usage strengthens the contention that the Qumran sect was concerned with the literal, scriptural keeping of the commandments of the Pentateuch and the prophets (cf. 1QS 1:3). This differentiated them from the more lax attitude of the Jerusalem priesthood. The following stereotyped formulae occur: "as he [God] has commanded" (1QS 1:3, 17; 5:1, 8, 22; and often); "what I have commanded you", "what I command you this day" (1QS 1:3; 4:6, 9 and often); all "that thou hast commanded" (1QH 15:11, 18 f.). The substance of the Mosaic law is presupposed in these summary formulae and in the terms commandment and law, used absolutely. It was preserved through constant learning and remembrance in daily living. Observance of this normative pattern for life is decisive in determining whether someone belongs to the children of light. It is also decisive in whether one will stand in the impending last → judgment (see 1QM as a whole). From this standpoint the predilection for the *pqd* word-group is understandable. Its meaning encompasses a whole concept of history. It denotes the mustering of the men who belong to the sect (1QM 2:4; 12:8 and often; CD 10:2 and often), the keeping of the commandments (1QS 5:22), the commandments themselves (CD 20:2), and God's calling to account of the response that men have given to the commandment of God (CD 8:3 and often). This is more than simply God's visiting (→ Bishop, art. *episkopos* NT). On the appropriate form of action see above 2 (b).

There is only occasional reference to the necessity of actualizing in the historical present the eternal commandments of God (1Q22 2:8; 1QS 9:12 ff.). In the latter reference the rules of the sect express the particular form of the divine commandments through the teacher and instructor. Since the rules of the community are understood as the logical interpretation of the Mosaic law, the term *ḥōq* (commandment) is occasionally used to denote these rules (e.g. 1QS 9:12 ff.; 1QSa 1:5; CD 12:20). The use of ethical terms to describe creation ordinances indicates that the dualism of light and darkness was adapted to express faith in creation and the covenant (cf. CD 2:21; 1QM 10:12; 1QH 1:10; 12:5). In short, the use of these terms in the Qumran literature reflects a rigid reduplication of the law (see above 2 (a) and (d)).

333

4. In the strictly regulated life of the Qumran community the supervision of moral behaviour appears to have been ensured. On the other hand, the Judaism of the synagogues suffered from an atomistic ethic which fragmented everything into nothing but individual demands and individual acts (G. Schrenk, *TDNT* II 547: SB I 814 ff.; IV, 1 3–19, 490–500). The OT apocrypha and pseudepigrapha maintained the usage and sense of the OT and LXX (cf. Test. Lev. 14:2, 6; Test. Jud. 14:6; 16:3 f.; Ass. Mos. 12:10; Test. Dan. 5:1; Test. Ben. 10:3 f.). Josephus probably assimilated his ideas of *entolē* to Roman thinking and used it in a legal rather than a theological sense (*Ant.* 1, 43; 7, 338, 342; 8, 94, 120, 337). Philo exhibits a Stoic antipathy towards the necessity of concrete commands, for the man who controls his knowledge and natural inclinations has no need of them (*Spec. Leg.* 1,300; *Rer. Div. Her.* 8; *Praem.* 79, 101; *Som.* 2, 175; cf. G. Schrenk, *TDNT* II 546 f.).

Judaism at the time of Jesus thus lived in a tension. On the one hand, there was the search for comprehensive basic commandments, the obligation of the halachah (the transmission in a kind of catechism of ethical rules) to observe a casuistical system. On the other hand, there was the attempt to distinguish between the important and the less important commandments (cf. SB I 903, 907; II 87 f.; III 543; 4 Macc. 5:20; the two great commandments consisting of Deut. 6:5 and Lev. 19:18 discussed in Mk. 12:29 f.; Matt. 22:34–40; Lk. 20:39 f.; 10:25–28). Test. Iss. 5:2 contains the exhortation: "But love the Lord and your neighbour. Have compassion on the poor and weak." However, scholars are divided over whether the work is Jewish (2nd cent. B.C.; cf. Charles, II, 289 f.) or Christian (c. A.D. 200; cf. M. de Jonge, *The Testament of the Twelve Patriarchs*, 1953). The theological problem in Judaism lay in the lack of an authoritative, prophetic message which could apply the law in terms of commandments which were valid for the contemporary situation.

NT In the NT the noun occurs 68 times and the vb. 14 times. These are concentrated chiefly in the Johannine writings including Rev. (34 times; 14 times in Jn. where the vb. occurs only 3 times) and in Paul (14 times, the noun only, of which Rom. has 7 instances). In the syn. gospels Matt. uses the noun 6 times and the vb. 4 times; Mk. the noun 8 times and the vb. twice; Lk. the noun 5 times and the vb. once. The remaining instances are divided between Acts (3 instances), Heb. (6 instances) and 2 Pet. (2 instances).

1. According to the syn. gospels, Jesus' teaching entered without reserve into the divisive discussion of the commandments (see above OT 4). Jesus refused to participate in casuistry or set up a hierarchical scale which would distinguish between the least, and therefore dispensable commandments (*entolē* as an individual commandment, Matt. 5:19) and a great commandment in the sense of an an omni-comprehensive, unified law. The latter is reflected in the expressions *megalē en tō nomō* (lit. "great in the law", Matt. 22:36); *prōtē* (first, Matt. 22:38; Mk. 12:28); *meizōn toutōn* (greater than these, Mk. 12:31). He refused to play off the command to love God against the command to love men (see the above passages, cf. Lk. 10:25 ff. though the word *entolē* is not actually used here). He also refused to allow a clear commandment of God to be rendered void by man-made ordinances under the pretext of a supposed love of God which had priority. He

denounced these human statutes as "your tradition" (*tēn paradosin hymōn*, Matt. 15:3; Mk. 7:9) and "the tradition of men" (*tēn paradosin tōn anthrōpōn*, Mk. 7:8). Instead of this, Jesus taught that love of God and love of man were inseparable. Beside the first great commandment, there is a "second like it. . . . On these two commandments depend all the law and the prophets" (Matt. 22:39 f.). "There is no other commandment greater than these" (Mk. 12:31). By relating the commandment to its original sense of an offer of life springing from the love of God, it is possible both to love God and one's neighbour in gratitude.

This is shown by numerous examples in the teaching of Jesus. The rich young ruler was challenged to surrender all his goods to the poor in order to live without reserve by the daily care of God as he followed Jesus (Matt. 19:16–30; Mk. 10:17–31; Lk. 18:18–30). God's original ordinance of monogamous marriage was designed to further the joy of marriage, rather than sanction a casuistical approach to divorce (Matt. 19:7; Mk. 10:3, 5; cf. Deut. 24:1). Both the context and the parable of the Good Samaritan (Lk. 10:25–37) show Jesus' loving attitude to his legalistic opponent. They show how, through encounter with the love of God, the shattered unity of love for God and love for one's neighbour is restored (cf. Lk. 10:27, 29). Through response to the loving commandment of God (10:37, cf. 33 ff.), love for God grasps the God-giving opportunities to serve and love one's fellow man (→ Mercy, Compassion).

Jesus brought word and action into a unity. He stands in contrast to his opponents who burdened men with commandments (Matt. 23:4; cf. Lk. 11:46; Matt. 11:28 ff.; where *phortion*, → burden, is a picture of the oppressive burden of the commandments, cf. Arndt, 873). Jesus displayed a prophetic and regal authority over the commandment. He showed this in the antitheses of the Sermon on the Mount (Matt. 5:21–48) and his attitude to the → sabbath (Mk. 2 23–27). He did not set aside the law. Rather, he rose above the discussion of the commandments and the bondage into which men get when they administer them, by turning our eyes to the giver of the law (Matt. 5:48; cf. 5:17). The doing of the law is no longer a problem in the presence of God revealed by Jesus.

Jesus fulfilled utterly and completely the commandment of God to abandon self for mankind (Matt. 26:39; Mk. 14:36; Lk. 22:42; cf. Phil. 2:8; Jn 19:30). Hence, the Johannine writings can rightly speak of a "new commandment" (*kainē entolē*, Jn. 13:34 and often, see under 3). The missionary command can speak of doing all that Jesus commanded (Matt. 28:20; cf. Acts 1:2, 8). Paul could speak of serving the law of God in the power of the Spirit in gratitude to God through Christ (Rom. 7:25; cf. 7:1–24; Rom. 8:2; see below 2 (a)).

The remaining synoptic passages containing *entolē* and *entellesthai* are less significant theologically and have the meanings outlined under OT. The parents of John the Baptist walked "in all the commandments and ordinances" (Lk. 1:6). The women among the followers of Jesus rested on the sabbath "according to the commandment" (Lk. 23:56). In the temptation narratives the devil quoted Ps. 91[90]:11: "He shall give his angels charge over you" (*enteleitai . . . peri* with the gen., Matt. 4:6; Lk. 4:10 adds "to guard you"). Jesus commanded (*eneteilato*) his disciples not to speak about his transfiguration (Matt. 17:9). Mk who lays great stress on the messianic secret used the stronger term *diesteilato* (charged, Mk. 9:9).

335

2.(a) The rabbis taught that the → law was the best means appointed by God to subdue evil inclination (SB III 237). In contrast, Paul developed the sharpest antithesis to this in the central section of Rom. (7:7 ff.). For Paul, the Spirit of God is the only power that subdues evil inclination (O. Michel, *Der Brief an die Römer*, KEK, 4 1963[12], 147, 180; cf. above 1). Using the first person singular the apostle testifies to the revelatory function of the law in history in unveiling the power of sin. Although the law is holy (Rom. 7:12) it results in bringing about → desire which brings in its train sin and death (7:10; cf. G. Bornkamm, *Early Christian Experience*, 1969, 87–104). Law (*nomos*) and commandment (*entolē*) are identified in the whole passage Rom. 7:7–13. The intention is to express the force of the law concretely in the commandment, so that "the *nomos* becomes acute through the *entolē*" (G. Schrenk, *TDNT* II 550). The word commandment does not denote the creation ordinance, for it is the tenth commandment of the Decalogue that is quoted (Exod. 20:17; Deut. 5:21). Moreover, it is intensified by omitting the object. The fateful, compulsive plunge from desire to sin, to eschatological death is, however, depicted ontologically by the story of the fall (Gen. 3; cf. S. Lyonnet, see bibliography). Paul twice uses the formula: "sin, finding opportunity [*aphormēn labousa*] in the commandment" (7:8, 11). Thus sin works all kinds of covetousness (7:8), and deceives and kills through the commandment by making use of it (cf. O. Michel, op. cit., 173). The commandment has even provoked the virulence of sin and brought to life its death-dealing power through which the self that succumbs to it perishes (7:9 f.). However, the commandment is holy, just and good (7:12). This is not only because it corresponds to God (= good), is given for life (7:10) and represents God's rights (= just). It is also holy in that it is set apart for the service of God and thus fights on the side of the Spirit (cf. 7:14 "the law is spiritual" [*pneumatikos*]). Its service is ultimately beneficial, because its leads man to see his powerlessness before sin and the hopeless and fatal character of his struggle. As one set under the law, he is obliged to carry it on by himself against the personal might of sin (7:24). But the law also drives him to the saving power of the gospel of Jesus Christ (7:25; 8:1 ff.; cf. O. Michel, op. cit., 179 ff.). The teaching of Paul, the servant of the risen Christ, is thus in line with the teaching of Jesus (see above 1). The apostle also removes exhortation from the burden of the law and presents it in the context of the Christ-event, as God's saving will here and now. Nowhere is this basic theme of Pauline preaching found in a more pregnant form than in the confessional formula: he has abolished "in his flesh the law of commandments and ordinances" (Eph. 2:15). The accumulation of synonyms *ton nomon tōn entolōn en dogmasin* graphically describes how they were all swept away by Christ. Similarly, Tit. 1:14 exhorts not to give heed "to Jewish myths or to commands of men who reject the truth" (cf. Mk. 7:8 f. par.).

There is no basic contradiction when Paul, like Jesus (cf. Matt. 19:17), urges men to keep "the commandments of God" (*tērēsis entolōn theou*, 1 Cor. 7:19). Gal. 5:6 and 6:15 have the same premise (neither circumcision counts for anything nor uncircumcision, but . . .). These passages show that faith which works through love (Gal. 5:6) and the new creation (Gal. 6:15) provides the presupposition for keeping the commandments. On this basis, 1 Cor. 7:19 repudiates Christian libertinism (see below, 3 and 4). Eph. 6:2 endorses the Fifth Commandment to "Honour your father and mother" (cf. Exod. 20:12). Rom. 13:9 sees the command "You shall love your neighbour as yourself" (Lev. 19:8) as a summary of all the individual commands of the second table of the Decalogue. Both these passages stand in close conjunction with apostolic exhortation. The imperative is grounded in the preceding indicative that has already been expounded.

On several occasions Paul uses *entolē* to denote the directions that he gives in his authority as an apostle. Col. 4:10 speaks about the instructions concerning Barnabas (cf. Acts 17:15). 1 Cor. 14:37 stresses that what he is writing is a command of the Lord, and thus will be recognized by those who are spiritual. Timothy is charged to keep the commandment unstained (1 Tim. 6:14; cf. 6:20).

(b) In agreement with Paul (see above on Eph. 2:15), Heb. systematically expounds the theme of the superiority of the heavenly, royal high-priesthood of Christ over the levitical priesthood. It shows how "a former commandment is set aside [*athetēsis*, a legal technical term] because of its weakness and uselessness" (Heb. 7:18). It is superseded by a better hope (Heb. 7:19; cf. Rom. 7:7–10). In the same way, Heb. 7:16 speaks of the setting aside of the "law of fleshly commandment" (*nomon entolēs sarkinēs*), i.e. the commandment bound to what is transitory, by the power of "an indestructible life" (*dynamin zōēs akatalytou*). The remaining passages deal with OT references (7:5; 9:19 f.). *eneteilato* in Heb. 11:22 is used of Joseph's giving directions for his bones.

3. (a) In Jn. *entolē* and the plur. *entolai* and the vb. *entellomai* are used virtually exclusively in relation to the only Son, the revealer. Jn. 11:57 is an exception. Here the chief priests and Pharisees gave police instructions (*entolas*) that they should be informed of Jesus' whereabouts. Otherwise, the words occur only in the discourses which are presented as the utterances of the Son. There is no basic significance in the frequent oscillation between the sing. and plur. of the noun. Just as the Father's commands to Jesus (15:10) constitute one command (12:49 f.), so he speaks now of his commands (15:10; 14:15, 21) and now of his command (13:34; 15:12). His commands are really only one command, the command to love (15:12). "The new *entolē* of Jesus to His disciples is the command to love. It is given its deepest basis in Jn. 13:34. The new factor is not the law of love as such, nor a new degree of love, but its christological foundation. They are to love one another as those who are loved by Jesus. . . . The *entolai*, always summed up in the one command of love, do not imply a Jewish multiplicity of ordinances, but the radiating of the one *entolē* out into the manifoldness of the obedient life" (G. Schrenk, *TDNT* II 553 f.). The expressions "keep [*tērein*] the commandments" (Jn. 14:15; 15:10), "have [*echein*] the commandments" (14:21), "keep the word [*logon*]" (8:51 f., 55; 14:23; 15:20; 17:6), and "keep the words [*logous*]" (14:24) are also interchangeable, because the word of the Son is the source of the command.

The basic relationship established by the commandment is that of the Father to the Son (10:18; 14:31; 15:10; 12:49 f.). There is no conflict between the authority given to the Son and his free decision and active obedience (cf. 10:18 with 10:17; 14:31). Nor is there a conflict here with the words and actions of the Son (12:49; cf. above, 1). The command of the Father is eternal life (12:50), not because anyone could fulfil it and thus gain eternal life, but because the fulfilment of this command by the Son means eternal life for the world. Through keeping the Father's commands, the Son loves the Father (14:31). The Son remains in the love of the Father, i.e. in the love with which the Father loves him (15:10). This love is not a mystical or purely

337

inner-trinitarian love; it is active in history (3:16). It means the giving of the Son through the Father and the self-giving of the Son for the disciples (14:9; 15:12 ff.). For Jn. the disciples represent the whole eschatological community (10:16; 17:20ff. and often).

The historical expression of the Son's love does not end with the person who is loved. Rather, it provides the basis, conditions and possibility of extending this love through the loved one. "A new commandment I give to you, that you love one another; even as I have loved you, that you also love one another" (13:34, on *kathōs*, as, see Arndt, 392; cf. also R. Bultmann, *The Gospel of John*, 1971, 382, 492, 525, 536). This love is to be practised. It is therefore the one new commandment (cf. also 15:12). Here again *kathōs* is the conjunction which gives both the reason and the manner of love. The vb. *entellomai* is connected with friendship and love in 15:12 and 17. The unique ground of all this is the Son's act of love which has introduced a new era. Historically and ethically this commandment is by no means new (see above OT and NT 1). The love of the disciples should have its ground and norm in the love of Jesus which they have received (cf. R. Bultmann, op. cit., 542, on 15:12). It excludes all legalism and also all antinomianism that might try to evade with gnostic arrogance the logical consequences of this single imperative (13:35; cf. 1 Cor. 7:3 f., 19: Lk. 10:25 ff.; Rom. 13:9). At the same time as the disciples love one another they also love the Son, and vice versa (14:21; cf. 14:15). To abide in the Son's commandments is to abide in his love, just as his own abiding in the Father's commandment means to abide in the Father's love (15:10 see above 1). He who has and keeps the Son's commandments loves the Son, and will be loved by the Father. Likewise the Son will love him and will reveal himself as the exalted one to him (14:21).

(b) The use of the terms in the Johannine epistles is essentially the same as in Jn. The plur. (1 Jn. 2:3 f.; 3:22, 24; 5:2 f.; 2 Jn. 6) alternates with the sing. (1 Jn. 2:7 f.; 3:24; 2 Jn. 4 ff.). Keeping the commandment or commandments is equated with keeping the word (1 Jn. 2:4 f., 7). However, there are significant formal differences which are also significant for interpretation. In the letters it is no longer the Son himself who proclaims the commandment. Instead, there are discussions and meditations on the commandment of God or Jesus. In contrast with the gospel, the discussion is often about the "commandment of God" or "the Father", giving the impression that the writer is thinking simply of the command to love in the gospel. The OT commandments do not come into view. This indicates a distance in time from the gospel (1 Jn. 3:21 ff.; 5:2 f.; 2 Jn. 4). The apologetic situation of the author and the recipients of his letters suggests a conflict with antinomian docetism which evidently disputed both the person of Christ and the need for spiritual believers to submit to an ethic binding on all (cf. 1 Jn. 1:1–10; on the background see D. Guthrie, *New Testament Introduction*, 1962, II, 191–94). This necessitates further explanation of the commandment. "And this is his commandment, that we should believe in the name of his Son Jesus Christ and love one another, just as he has commanded us" (1 Jn. 3:23; cf. Gal. 5:6; 1 Cor. 7:19). The idea of the commandment can also be given a new meaning. God's timing (*kairos*) adds a new perspective. "Yet I am writing to you a new commandment, which is true in him and in you, because the darkness is passing away and the true light is already shining" (1 Jn. 2:8). On the other hand, the commandment to love preached in the mission field of the churches (the "new commandment" of Jn., cf. 3 (a) above) is now the "old commandment." "Beloved, I am writing you no new commandment, but an old commandment which you had from the beginning; the old commandment is the word which you have heard" (1 Jn. 2:7; cf. 2 Jn. 5 f.). Here the word → old (*palaia*) means known of old, of long standing, as opposed to the enthusiastic new doctrine of the docetic gnostics. This long known commandment is so deep-rooted that the author speaks of it without using the art. (1 Jn. 3:23; 2 Jn. 4, 6). This commandment which has been long observed in the churches provides the ground for certainty that all prayers are answered by God (1 Jn. 3:22). 1 Jn. 4:21 formulates the twofold commandment of the OT and the synoptics (cf. Mk. 12:28 ff., see above 1) as a single command which comes from "him": "And this commandment we have from him, that he who loves God should love his brother also." Again the stress falls on brotherly love. But there is also a corollary. "By this we know that we love the children of God, when we love God and obey his commandments" (1 Jn. 5:2). Overtones of Jesus' invitation in Matt. 11:28 ff. and the certainty of victory in 1 Jn. 2:8 may be heard in 1 Jn. 5:3 f. The fulfilment of the commandment on the part of God and also on the part of the man equipped for it is assured.

(c) In the same certainty of victory, Rev. testifies to present opposition (12:17, in the demand for the worship of images), patience and final victory (12:14; 22:14, where some manuscripts read "do his commandments"). This is the lot of those who keep God's commandments and bear witness to Jesus. Never again in the Johannine teaching are the commandments spoken of without Jesus being named (G. Schrenk, *TDNT* II 555).

4. 2 Pet. attacks libertine groups in the churches he addresses even more strongly than 1 and 2 Jn. These opponents have turned back "from the holy commandment delivered to them" (2:21). This refers to the entire Christian teaching, above all in ethical practice which is described in the same verse as "the way of righteousness" (cf. Prov. 21:16; Job 24:13; Matt. 21:32). The sole defence against libertinism is to recall OT prophecy and "the commandment of the Lord and Saviour through your apostles" (3:2). In both passages the way is prepared to understand Jesus as the proclaimer of a new law and Christian doctrine as the summary of it.

5. Finally, the exhortatory passages of the Apostolic Fathers present a picture of a new legalism. The scheme of a two ways doctrine (especially in Barn. 19 ff.; cf. Hermas, *Com.*) promises eternal punishment to those who do not hear or keep the commandments of Christ (2 Clem. 4:5, an unknown word of the Lord; 6:7). (The expression "God's commandments" [Barn. 4:11; 1 Clem. 50:5] is less common.) But those who keep the commandments are promised eternal life (2 Clem. 8:4; Hermas, *Vis.* 3, 5, 3; Hermas, *Com.* 8, 12; Hermas, *Sim.* 10, 3, 9, the command of the angel of repentance; cf. *Vis.* 5, 5 ff.). Ignatius exhorted the church to be subject to the bishop and to the commandment (absolutely, *Trall.* 13:2). He praised them because they were united in the commandments of Christ (*Rom.* preamble), and were "adorned with the commandments of Jesus Christ" (*Eph.* 9:2). The instructions of the Sermon on the Mount were understood as the "commandment and ordinances [*parangelmata*] of the Lord" (1 Clem. 13:3). The almost exclusive use of the plur. shows how far they were removed in understanding from the Johannine *one* commandment (see above, 3).   *H. H. Esser*

| παραγγέλλω | παραγγέλλω (*parangellō*), order, give orders, command, instruct, direct; παραγγελία (*parangelia*), order, command, precept, advice. |

CL *parangellō* means to order or command (someone or with the infin. of the vb.).
Originally it meant passing on a command. *parangelia* means order or instruction in secular Gk. and is found from about the 5th and 4th cents. B.C. The words were used by persons of different kinds of authority, including military commands, the instructions of the philosophers (Epictetus), and even a god (in Plato). The essential element is that someone is put under an obligation.

OT The noun does not occur in the LXX. 1 Sam. 22:14 has *parangelma* which has the same meaning. The vb. is common in the LXX for Heb. *šāma'* in the piel and hiphil, meaning to cause to hear, assemble, proclaim, summon. It is used of the military proclamations of kings and generals (1 Sam. 15:4; 23:8; 1 Macc. 5:58 and often), the command of Joshua and Cyrus (Jos. 6:7; 2 Chron. 36:22) etc. In prophetic teaching it is used of the call to war against Babylon (Jer. 27[MT50]:29; 28[MT51]:27). The instructions of Daniel and Judas Maccabaeus also had a religious character (Dan. 2:18; 2 Macc. 13:10). Nebuchadnezzar's command to worship the image of his cult was opposed to God (Dan. 3:4).

NT 1. Both words are used in the NT in a general, secular sense. Both the noun and the vb. occur in the account of the command of the authorities at Philippi to put Paul and Silas into prison (Acts 16:23 f.). The tribune Claudius Lysias issued orders to protect Paul from assassination (Acts 23:22, 30). The high priests commanded the apostles not to speak and teach in the name of Jesus (Acts 4:18; 5:28, 40). The emphatic semitic construction *parangelia parēngeilamen* (5:28, "we strictly charged" RSV) underlines the seriousness of the command. (Cf. M. Wilcox, *The Semitisms of Acts*, 1965, 151, who sees the construction as a reflection of the Heb. infinitive absolute construction. The construction is found some 200 times in the LXX.) In the early church there were Jewish Christians who were Pharisees who said that it was necessary to circumcise Gentile Christians and "charge them to keep the law" (Acts 15:5).

2. In the gospels only the vb. is used, and that in a few passages in the synoptics which refer exclusively to the commands of Jesus. In the feeding of the four thousand, Jesus commanded the crowd to sit down on the ground (Matt. 15:35; Mk. 8:6). Jesus commanded silence of the leper who had been healed and the parents of Jairus's daughter (Lk. 5:14; 8:56). The disciples received the same order at the confession of Christ (Lk. 9:21). The statements in Matt. 10:5 and Mk. 6:8 refer to the instructions that the Lord gave to the disciples when he sent them out. Jesus commanded the unclean spirit to leave the demoniac (Lk. 8:9). Paul gave the same rebuke "in the name of Jesus" to the spirit of divination in a girl (Acts 16:18). The risen Christ gave the disciples the command not to leave Jerusalem before Pentecost (Acts 1:4). The authority of Jesus continued in the apostolic preaching which stood under the command of Jesus and through which God commands men to repent (Acts 10:42; 17:30).

3. The letters of the apostles present the same picture. Paul based his prohibition of divorce on the word of the Lord (1 Cor. 7:10). Here he distinguished between

the authority of Jesus and his own. He wanted to show that the commands which he gave "of the Lord" were absolutely binding for the church (1 Cor. 7:25; cf. 1 Thess. 4:2). Apostolic authority lay behind the directions for the behaviour of women in worship, the exhortations to Christians to behave respectably in the eyes of the pagan world, to work in peace and to eat their own bread (1 Cor. 11:17; 1 Thess. 4:11; 2 Thess. 3:12). Regardless of whether it is in the form of written or oral instruction, the apostle expected that the church would comply with them. They were even to keep away from any brother who did not walk according to the apostolic commands (2 Thess. 3:4, 6, 10 ff.). Paul commanded (*parangellō*) Timothy to "keep the commandment [*entolēn*] unstained and free from reproach until the appearing of our Lord Jesus Christ" (1 Tim. 6:14). "The aim of our charge [*parangelia*] is love that issues from a pure heart and a good conscience and sincere faith" (1 Tim. 1:5). Timothy is therefore charged to wage a good warfare (1:18), and to "charge certain persons not to teach any different doctrine" (1:3). The apostolic instructions apply to certain individual groups, including "widows" (5:7) and the rich (6:17). The solemn appeal to God and Christ makes clear the nature of authority behind the apostolic commands (6:13 f.). *W. Mundle*
→ Exhort, Warn, Console, → Law, → Love

κελεύω	κελεύω (*keleuō*), command, order; κέλευσμα (*keleusma*), signal, cry of command.

CL & OT The verb *keleuō* occurs widely in classical Greek from Homer onwards.
It is generally used of verbal orders emanating from a person of superior rank or status. The word is also attested in Philo (*Leg. All.* 2; 28) and Josephus (*Ant.* 11, 28; 20, 132). In the LXX its use is confined to books from the Apocrypha. Here it can be used of a Levitical command (1 Esd. 9:53), of a master's instructions (Tob. 8:18), of an army officer's command (Jud. 2:15; 12:1; 2 Macc. 5:12; 13:12; 14:31), of royal directives (2 Macc. 1:20; 7:5; 9:7; 14:27), of a prophet's word (2 Macc. 1:4), and of God's command (2 Macc. 15:4).

NT In the NT the use of *keleuō* is confined very largely to Matthew and Acts. There are eighteen occurrences in Acts, eight in Matthew, and one in Luke. In Acts the word is used only of orders given by human authorities: of the Sanhedrin (4:15), the Ethiopian eunuch (8:38), Gamaliel (5:34), Herod (12:19), the magistrates (16:22), the tribune (21:33; 22:24; 22:30; 23:10), the High Priest (23:3), Felix (23:35; 24:8), Festus (25:6; 25:17; 25:21; 25:23) and the centurion (27:43). The word is not used for commands issued by God or members of the church. In these cases *entellomai* or *parangellō* is used (Acts 13:47; 10:42; 15:5; 16:18; 17:30).
In Matthew *keleuō* is again used of orders given by human authorities: of Pilate (27:58; 27:64) and Herod (14:9) (cf. also the master in the parable of 18:25). On a few occasions however the word is used of orders given by Jesus. It occurs in his command to cross over and escape the crowds (8:18), and in the two feeding miracles where it expresses Jesus' order to the crowds to be seated (14:19; 15:35). Luke's solitary use of the word is also a command of Jesus to the effect that the blind man be brought to him (Lk. 18:40). Mark prefers to use such words as *eipon, entellomai, epitassō* and *parangellō*.

The word *keleusma* occurs in classical Greek from Herodotus and Aeschylus onwards. Here it is often used of the command of a god. The word can also mean signal, summons, and can even be a word of encouragement to animals (Plato) or rowers (Aeschylus). Sometimes *keleusma* is simply a cry. Its meaning is therefore fairly wide, ranging from specific commands to terse orders and inarticulate cries. All of these senses are attested in Josephus (*Ant.* 17, 140, 199; 19:110; *War* 2, 549) and Philo (*Praem.* 117; *Abr.* 116). In the LXX *keleusma* occurs only in Prov. 30:27, where it refers to the orderly march of locusts at one command. In the NT *keleusma* is to be found only in 1 Thess. 4:16 where it denotes a shout of command at the onset of the parousia, together with a call of the archangel and a trumpet sound. It is not clear who gives this *keleusma* – God, Christ or the archangel. The context suggests that the specific purpose of the shout is to awaken the dead, but it is probably also meant to intimate the end of all things in general.   *P. J. Budd*

(a). A. Alt, "The Origins of Israelite Law," in *Essays on Old Testament History and Religion,* 1966; 80–132; K. Barth, "Gospel and Law," in *God, Grace and Gospel,* 1959, 1–27; "The Gift of Freedom," in *The Humanity of God,* 67–96; and *CD* III, 4 ("The Command of God the Creator"); W. Beyerlin, *Origins and History of the Oldest Sinaitic Traditions,* 1965; D. Bonhoeffer, *Creation and Fall,* 1959; and *The Cost of Discipleship,* 1959⁶; G. Bornkamm, *Early Christian Experience,* 1969, 87–104; H. E. Brunner, *The Divine Imperative,* 1937; R. H. Charles, *The Decalogue,* 1923; J. D. M. Derrett, *Law in the New Testament,* 1970; W. Eichrodt, *Theology of the Old Testament,* I, 1961, 70–177; V. P. Furnish, *The Love Command in the New Testament,* 1973; and *Theology and Ethics in Paul,* 1968, 68–111; A. Hunt, "The Great Commandment," *ExpT* 56, 1944–45, 82 f.; A. S. Kapelrud, "Some Recent Points on the Time and Origin of the Decalogue," *StTh* 18, 1964, 81–90; E. Käsemann, "Worship in Everyday Life: a Note on Romans 12," *New Testament Questions of Today,* 1969, 188–95; "The Cry for Liberty in the Worship of the Church," *Perspectives on Paul* 1971, 122–37; G. Kittel, *dogma, TDNT* II 230 ff.; W. Lillie, *Studies in New Testament Ethics,* 1961; T. W. Manson, *Ethics and the Gospel,* 1960; L. H. Marshall, *The Challenge of New Testament Ethics,* 1946; J. Moltmann, "The Understanding of History in Christian Social Ethics", *Hope and Planning,* 1971, 101–29; C. F. D. Moule, "Obligation in the Ethic of Paul," in W. R. Farmer, C. F. D. Moule and R. R. Niebuhr, eds., *Christian History and Interpretation,* 1967, 389–406; E. Nielsen, *The Ten Commandments in New Perspective,* 1968; M. Noth, " 'For All who Rely on Works of the Law are under a Curse'," and "The Laws in the Pentateuch," in *The Laws in the Pentateuch and Other Essays,* 1966, 118–31, 1–107; A. Phillips, *Ancient Israel's Criminal Law: A New Approach to the Decalogue,* 1970; I. T. Ramsey, ed., *Christian Ethics and Contemporary Philosophy,* 1966; L. Schmid, *keleusma, TDNT* III 656 ff.; O. Schmitz, *parangellō, TDNT* V 761–65; R. Schnackenburg, *The Moral Teaching of the New Testament,* 1965; G. Schrenk, *entellomai, entolē, TDNT* II 544–56; J. J. Stamm and M. E. Andrew, *The Ten Commandments in Recent Research,* 1967; H. Thielicke, *Theological Ethics,* I, 1966, 147–297, 609–47; R. de Vaux, *Ancient Israel,* 1961, 143–63; R. S. Wallace, *The Ten Commandments: A Study in Ethical Freedom,* 1965; W. Zimmerli, *The Law and the Prophets,* 1965.

(b). W. Andersen, *Der Gesetzesbegriff in der gegenwärtigen theologischen Diskussion,* Theologische Existenz Heute, Neue Folge 108, 1963; H. Braun, "Röm. 7, 7–25 und das Selbstverständnis des Qumran-Frommen," *ZTK* 56, 1959, 1 ff.; R. Deichgräber, "Gehorsam und Gehorchen in der Verkündigung Jesu," *ZNW* 52, 1961, 119 ff.; H. Diem, "Dogmatik," *EKL* I 947 ff.; M. Elze, "Der Begriff des Dogmas in der Alten Kirche," *ZTK* 61, 1964, 421 ff.; H. Fahlbusch and N. H. Soe, "Ethik," *EKL* I 1166 ff.; H. Flender, "Leben und Verkündigung in den synoptischen Evangelien," *EvTh* 25, 1965, 701 ff.; E. Fuchs, *Die Freiheit des Glaubens,* 1949, 55 ff.; G. Gloege, "Dogma II," *RGG*³ II, 221 ff.; H. Gollwitzer, *Forderung der Freiheit,* 1962; W. Joest and F. Lau, "Gesetz" VI f.; *RGG*³ II 1526 ff.; E. Kamlah, *Die Form der Katalogischen Paränese im Neuen Testament, WUNT* 7, 1964; R. Knierim, "Das erste Gebot," *ZAW* 77, 1965, 20 ff.; K. Koch, "Tempeleinlassliturgien und Dekaloge," *Studien zur Theologie der alttestamentlichen Überlieferungen* (G. von Rad zum 60. Geburtstag), 1961, 45–60; L. Koehler, "Der Dekalog," *ThR,* Neue Folge 1, 1929, 161–84; H. Kremers, "Dekalog," *EKL* I 852 ff.; G. W. Locher, "Glaube und Dogma," *ThSt* 57, 1959; E. Lohse, *Christologie und Ethik im Kolosserbrief, BZNW* 30, 1964; S. Lyonnet, " 'Tu ne convoiteras pas' (Rom. vii 7)," in *Neotestamentica et Patristica: Eine Freundesgabe, Herrn Professor Dr. Oscar Cullmann zu seinem 60. Geburtstag überreicht*, 1962, 157–65; and "L'histoire du salut selon le chapitre VII de l'Épître aux Romains," *Biblica* 43, 1962, 117 ff.; W. Matthias, "Der anthropologische Sinn der Formel Gesetz und Evangelium," *EvTh* 22, 1962, 410 ff.; S. Mowinckel, *Le Décalogue*, 1927; and "Zur Geschichte der Dekaloge," *ZAW* 55, 1937, 218–35; D. von Oppen, "Der Mensch in der offenen Situation," *ZTK* 69, 1962, 315 ff.; H. van Oyen, "Ethik," *RGG³* II 708 ff.; E. Pelletier, "Le vocabulaire du commandment dans le Pentateuque des LXX et dans le Nouveau Testament," *Recherches de Science Religieuse* 41, 1953, 519–24; H. Graf von Reventlow, *Das Heiligkeitsgesetz*, WMANT 6, 1961; and *Gebot und Predigt im Dekalog*, 1962; W. Schrage, *Die konkreten Einzelgebote in der paulinischen Paränese*, 1961; H. Thielicke and H. H. Schrey, *Glaube und Handeln*, 1961²; E. Thurneysen, *Die Bergpredigt*, Theologische Existenz Heute Neue Folge 105, 1963; W. C. van Unnik, *Die Rücksicht auf die Reaktion der Nichtchristen als Motiv in der altchristlichen Paränese*, BZNW 26, 1960, 221 ff; H. Windisch, "Das Problem des paulinischen Imperativs," *ZNW* 23, 1924, 265–81; W. Zimmerli, "Die Frage des Reichen nach dem ewigen Leben," *EvTh* 19, 1959, 90 ff.

Conceive, Apprehend

συλλαμβάνω

συλλαμβάνω (*syllambanō*), seize, conceive, assist.

CL *syllambanō* is a verb compounded from the preposition *syn* (with, together) and *lambanō* (take). From its primary meaning "take with", "collect together", several derived meanings are to be found in secular Gk. literature, e.g. (a) put together, close (as with the eyes and mouth of a corpse – Plato); (b) lay hands on, seize; (c) grasp, apprehend (of the mind); (d) conceive, become pregnant; (e) take part with another, assist.

OT In the LXX, *syllambanō* is very often used to translate Heb. *hārāh*, "conceive", either literally (e.g. Gen. 4:1, 17; 1 Sam. 1:20) or figuratively (Ps. 7:14). Elsewhere it frequently has the meaning "seize" or "arrest". In this latter sense it can describe the physical act of arresting a person or catching an animal (e.g. Num. 5:13; Deut. 21:19; Jdg. 15:4); the capture of a town or place in a military campaign (e.g. 2 Ki. 14:7; Jer. 39:24); or, figuratively, the "snatching away" of sinners before their time by an act of God's judgment (Job 22:16; Ps. 9:16), or the "snaring" of the unsuspecting by the wicked (Jer. 5:26; cf. Eccl. 7:27). It does not carry the meaning of "assist" in the LXX, though the Jewish historian Josephus uses it in this sense.

NT *syllambanō* occurs sixteen times in the NT, and it is used in three distinct ways:
(a) Luke uses it to mean "conceive" in his account of the births of John the Baptist and Jesus (Lk. 1:24; 31, 36; 2:21). *syllambanō* also bears this meaning figuratively in Jas. 1:15; where the imagery of conception, birth and growth demonstrates the close relationship between desire, sin and death.
(b) As in the LXX and classical Gk., *syllambanō* also bears the sense of "seize" or "capture" in the NT. Perhaps because the idea of physical strength is prominent, rather than legal powers of arrest, this is the word used in all four Gospels to describe the seizing of Jesus in the Garden of Gethsemane (Mk. 14:48 par.; Lk. 22:54; Jn. 18:12; cf. Acts 1:16). Luke also employs it in his narrative of the arrest of Peter by Herod (after Herod had "laid violent hands upon some who belonged to the church" – Acts 12:1–3), and again in the account of the attempt by the

343

Jews to lynch Paul outside the temple at Jerusalem (Acts 23:27). In Lk. 5:9 the same word describes a huge catch of fish.

(c) *syllambanō* also appears twice in the middle voice, meaning "take hold of together", "assist" (see CL (e) above). In Lk. 5:7 it carries its usual physical sense, when those in Simon's boat call for help when their nets break under the strain of a miraculous catch; and in Phil. 4:3 Paul uses it to appeal to an unknown church member to "help" Euodia and Syntyche resolve their differences.

→ Birth   D. H. Field

Arndt, 784; G. Delling, *syllambanō*, *TDNT* VII 759–62.

Confess

ὁμολογέω

ὁμολογέω (*homologeō*), promise, confess, declare, praise; *ἐξομολογέω* (*exomologeō*), promise, confess, praise; *ὁμολογία* (*homologia*), confession.

CL *homologeō* (Soph. onwards) and *homologia* (Hdt. onwards) are compounds of *homos*, the same, similar, and *legō*, say, or *logos*, word, speech. Hence *homologeō* means to say the same, i.e. agree in one's statements, and *homologia* means agreement, consent.

The legal connotation is dominant. A man agrees with another's statement, concedes or confesses something (e.g. his guilt before a judge), agrees to something (e.g. another's wish) and so promises. This agreement expresses itself in an act of commitment, promise, or confession in a court or legal contract.

The religious use of the words is probably derived primarily from their use in the language of treaties and the law-courts. The man who binds himself by an oath (*homologeō*) enters into a treaty relationship with the deity. This concept was then transferred from the solemn confession of wrong-doing before a court of law to the confession of sin to the deity. These concepts were used especially in the oriental cults, as may be seen from Lydian and Phrygian expiatory inscriptions. In modern Gk. the concept has come to mean sacramental confession to a priest: *exomologeomai*, I make my confession; *exomologeō*, I hear a confession.

OT 1. In the LXX *homologeō* is used once each to translate Heb. *yāḏâh*, praise (Job 40:14(9)), *nāḏar*, make a vow (Jer. 44:25 (LXX 51:25)) and *šāḇaʿ*, swear (Ezek. 16:8). *homologia* is used occasionally for Heb. *nᵉḏāḇâh*, freewill offering (Deut. 12:17; Ezek. 46:12; Amos 4:5), *neḏer*, vow (Jer. 44:25 (LXX 51:25); Lev. 22:18) and *tôḏâh*, praise, honour (Ezr. 10:11 (LXX 1 Esd. 9:8)). As O. Michel points out, "in transl[ation] the *homologia* group is given less prominence because its legal and commercial sense seemed too profane" (*TDNT* V 204).

Far commoner is the compound *exomologeō*, used *c.* 120 times, mainly as a translation of the Heb. *yāḏâh*, praise, confess. It is sometimes used along with *psallō*, sing praises (cf. 2 Sam. 22:50; Pss. 7:17(18); 18:49(50); 30:4(5)), or *aineō*, thank (cf. 1 Chr. 16:4; 29:13; 2 Chr. 31:2; Ps. 106:47). Hence it means to praise, confess with praise – "among the nations" (Ps. 18:49), worship with song (cf. 2 Chr. 31:2; Ps. 100:4). The same is true of the noun *exomologēsis* (cf. 1 Chr. 25:3; 2 Chr. 20:22; Neh. 12:27; Ps. 147:7). The subject of the praise is God's majesty and power (1

Chr. 29:12 f.), his mighty acts in the history of the people (Ps. 105:1–6), his gracious goodness (Ps. 118:1–4), his saving of men from distress (Ps. 107:1, 8, 15, 21, 31), and his deliverance from enemies (Ps. 9:1(2)). So the word often gains the further connotation of thanks, especially when answered prayer is specially mentioned (Pss. 28:6 f.; 118:21; cf. 106:47).

If we compare it with secular Gk., this usage involves a considerable change in meaning. But the original Gk. meaning of confessing an offence openly was never quite lost. The Heb. *yāḍâh* in hiph. and hith. means both to praise, give glory and confess an offence. This is particularly clear in Jos. 7:19; 1 Ki. 8:33–36; and 2 Chr. 6:24–27, where the glorifying confession of Yahweh's name linked with the acknowledgement of the sin committed is called for. We may compare also Ps. 107:15 with v. 11 and v. 21 with v. 17, where confession of sin and thanks for deliverance are heard together.

For us this association of confession of sin and praise of God is strange. It comes from the fact that in Israel the praise of God is always linked with a definite past action of God, with a saving event in history, or even with an act of judgment. In the last case "in accepting a justly imposed judgment" the one who praises confesses "his transgression and he clothes what he says in the mantle of an avowal giving God the glory" (G. von Rad, *Old Testament Theology* I, 1962, 359). When the one who is praying confesses in his thanksgiving that God is right and so recognizes his own fault and the rightness of the punishment that has followed it, the law-suit against him is closed (von Rad, ibid., 358). This gives a clue to the understanding of passages like Jos. 7:19, where Achan is called on to give glory to God before his execution, and Ezr. 10:11 (LXX 1 Esd. 9:8) with its call to confession by the people.

The combination "call on the name of the Lord, praise . . ." is often expressed by *epikaleō* in the LXX (→ Call).

2. In late Jud. *homologeō, exomologeō*, etc., were used of the confession of sins (cf. Pss. Sol. 9:12(6)). Repentance and confession belong together, and the prayer of repentance developed its own phraseology. Daniel (Dan. 9:3–19), the exiled people (Bar. 1–3), and Tobit (Tob. 3:1–6) confess the sins of their people, humble themselves under God's judgment, confess that he is right, and pray to him to show mercy for his name's sake. Josephus states that confession of sin preserves one from God's judgment (*Ant.*, 8, 4, 6; 8, 10, 3; 8, 13, 8 (129; 256 f.; 362); *War*, 5, 9, 4 (415)). The word-group is also used, as in the Pss., for praise of God and thanksgiving (Sir. 51:1–12). In Josephus *Kaisara despotēn homologein*, to confess Caesar as lord (*War* 7, 418), is parallel to 2 Macc. 7:37, "confess that he (God) is God alone." In the apocalyptic writings the word-group is used for the praise of God in which the elect and the angels of God will unite at the coming of the Judge of the world (cf. O. Michel, *TDNT*, V 204 ff.).

The term *yāḍâh* was particularly important in Qumran. Most of the psalms discovered there (1QH) begin, "I thank Thee, Lord, because . . ." (1QH 2:20, 31, etc.). This is parallel to Matt. 11:25. Confession of faults is often mentioned (1QS 1:24; cf. 1:9 ff.).

NT *homologeō* is found 26 times in the NT (10 times being in John) with a wide range of usage. It stretches from the basic use in secular Gk. via the LXX meanings to those found in the writings of late Jud. This is also partially true of the compound *exomologeō*, which occurs only 10 times. But the noun *homologia* (found 6 times) is confined to the Christian confession (2 Cor. 9:13; 1 Tim. 6:12 f.), and is used with a fixed liturgical connotation (cf. Heb. 3:1; 4:14; 10:23).

1. The secular Hel. usage may be seen most clearly in Matt. 14:7 and Lk. 22:6. Herod promised his step-daughter with an oath to carry out her wish. Judas bound himself with an oath to betray Jesus. In both cases the "confessing" is tantamount to promising or swearing. There is a similar usage in Acts 7:17, for the confession or promise to Abraham was a binding one.

Heb. 11:13 is probably best understood in the light of the secular Gk. usage of confessing and avowing. On the threshold of the promised land the patriarchs had to confess in the presence of death that they were only strangers on the earth. But it may be that we should understand it as a proclamation, as a confession made openly. It could be that the writer deliberately used this word so as to permit both interpretations.

2. *homologeō* in Heb. 13:15 and *exomologeō* in Matt. 11:25; Lk. 10:21; and Rom. 15:9 (quoting Ps. 18:49) have the LXX meaning of praise. Jesus praised God's actions by gladly accepting God's plan. The praise to the glory of God begun in Christ – Ps. 18:49(50) is probably here taken as referring to Christ – is to be taken up and continued by the Gentiles (Rom. 15:9). Heb. 13:15 calls on the church to praise the name of God through Christ, i.e. through his mediation and in his presence.

3. The word-group, however, is used most frequently in the sense of confess, confess openly, state publicly.

(a) Paul made an affirmation before Felix, when he was on trial, which was in fact a confession of Jesus linked with one of God his Father. Similarly, John confessed openly that he was not the one they were awaiting (Jn. 1:20).

(b) Derived from this legal usage, *homologeō* in 1 Jn. 1:9 means the confessing and acknowledgment of sins. The one who makes the avowal faces a fact. He tries neither to hide nor deny it. When someone acknowledges and avows his fault thus honestly, he experiences God's faithfulness and righteousness in the forgiveness of sins. The tradition of the penitential psalms is continued in passages about confession of sins where except in 1 Jn. 1:9 *exomologeō* is used. Confession is a sign of repentance (→ Conversion) and thus a mark of the new life of faith. This is seen particularly clearly in Mk. 1:5 par., where, as in the Pss., public confession of sins means also being set free from them. The same is true of Acts 19:18, where the converts confess their earlier magical practices, and of Jas. 5:16, where James exhorts mutual confession of sins, especially where illness is involved.

(c) The church, or the individual believer, responds to the forgiveness of sins, i.e. to the saving act of God in Jesus Christ, by public confession (cf. 1 Tim. 6:12 which may refer to baptism). In this confession Jesus Christ is acknowledged as → Lord, and testimony is borne that God raised him from the dead for the salvation of his church. "In his 'confession' of faith, the believer turns away from himself, confessing that all he is and has, he is and has through that which God has done" (R. Bultmann, *Theology of the NT* 1 319). So such a confession as an act of faith, even if it bears a formal character, is clearly linked to God's act of salvation in Christ, while the confession of the Pharisees in Acts 23:8 ff. is linked with a point of doctrine, which, though formally true, did not exclude resistance to Jesus. ([Tr.] The

346

implication of this statement may be misleading, for the Jewish confession is for the most part based directly or indirectly on God's saving acts in history.) When belief and confession, heart and mouth, are in unison, there is a promise of justification and salvation for eternity (Rom. 10:8 ff.). It seems certain that a primitive, Christian confessional formula lies behind v. 9. Obedience with regard to the confession (*hypotagē homologias*, 2 Cor. 9:13) is demonstrated in practical loving action (2 Cor. 9:6–13).

An integral part of true faith is the public confession of the incarnate Son of God (cf. Jn. 1:14; 1 Jn. 4:2), for fellowship with God is dependent on it (1 Jn. 2:23; 4:15). It is a mark of true christology in the face of heretical movements, possibly Gnostic, which denied the identity of Jesus with the Christ (1 Jn. 2:22; 4:2 f., 15). John never means isolated teachings, when he writes of confession, but the whole truth which produces fellowship with God. This truth is not a theological proposition but the person of Jesus. In his confession a man indicates that he stands by the fact of Christ and submits his life to it. It becomes a touchstone, a sign which tests the spirits. In his Gospel John relates that anyone openly confessing Jesus as the Messiah was put out of the synagogue (Jn. 9:22; 12:42). He calls on the church to distinguish in its meetings between true and false confessions (cf. 1 Jn. 4:1 f.).

Tit. 1:16 is also an attack on a heretical confession. Since the confession – perhaps one claiming the higher knowledge of the Gnostics – and the life of the one making it contradict one another, it is plain that the confession is false.

When *homologeō* stands in contrast to its opposite *arneomai* (→ deny), it gains a special significance (Jn. 1:20; Tit. 1:16; 1 Jn. 2:23; Matt. 10:32 f.; Lk. 12:8 f.). Since denial is always identical with apostasy from Jesus, the eschatological aspect of the confession is specially emphasized. When someone either places himself on the side of Jesus or separates himself from him in the sight of those who know him, he makes a decision on which God will act in → judgment (Matt. 12:32 f.; Rev. 3:5; cf. Mk. 8:38). The believer is so completely included in fellowship with Jesus, that his confession before man, e.g. before a human court of law during a time of persecution, is regarded as though it had been made before God's judgment seat. In such a context "confession" includes not only what a man says but also his obedience (→ Hear) which has become visible in his whole life. Where this total obedience is not found, where a man is satisfied with his understanding of and knowledge about salvation, it is equivalent to denial, which Jesus will "confess", when he says in judgment, "I never knew you" (Matt. 7:23). At the last every power and might will have to confess Jesus as the Christ, i.e. recognize him and do homage (Phil. 2:11).   *D. Fürst*

(a). G. Bornkamm, "On Understanding the Christ-hymn (Philippians 2:6–11)," *Early Christian Experience*, 1969, 112–22; O. Cullmann, *The Earliest Christian Confessions*, 1949; C. H. Dodd, *The Apostolic Preaching and its Developments*, 1944²; J. N. D. Kelly, *Early Christian Creeds*, 1950; R. P. Martin, *An Early Christian Confession: Philippians II 5–11 in Recent Interpretation*, 1960; and *Carmen Christi: Philippians ii. 5–11*, 1967; O. Michel, *homologeō. TDNT* V 199–220; V. H. Neufeld, *The Earliest Christian Confessions*, 1963; B. Reicke, *The Disobedient Spirits and Christian Baptism: A Study of I Peter 3:19 and its Content*, 1946; H. N. Ridderbos, "The Earliest Confession of the Atonement in Paul," in R. Banks, ed., *Reconciliation and Hope* (Leon Morris Festschrift), 1974, 76–89; J. T. Sanders, *The New Testament Christological Hymns: Their Historical Religious Background*, 1971.
(b). G. Bornkamm, "Homologia," *Hermes* 71, 1938, 377 ff.; and "Das Bekenntnis im Hebräerbrief," *ThBl* 21, 1942, 56 ff.; E. Burnier, *La notion de témoignage dans le Nouveau Testament*, 1939;

H. von Campenhausen, *Die Idee des Martyriums in der Alten Kirche*, 1936; P. Feine, *Die Gestalt des apostolischen Glaubensbekenntnisses in der Zeit des Neuen Testaments*, 1925; K. Fiedler, *Bekennen und Bekenntnis. Hinweise für wahrhaftes Bekennen im Sinne des Evangeliums*, 1943; W. Maurer, *Bekenntnis und Sakrament*, 1939; O. Michel, "Biblische Bekennen und Bezeugen, *homologein* und *martyrein* im biblischen Sprachgebrauch," *EvTh* 2, 1935, 231–45; H. Ott, *Glaube und Bekennen*, 1963; O. Procksch, *Das Bekenntnis im Alten Testament*, 1936; C. Westermann and E. Kamlah, "Bekenntnis," *RGG*³ I 988 ff.

Conscience

συνείδησις

συνείδησις (*syneidēsis*), consciousness, conscience; σύνοιδα (*synoida*), perf. with pres. meaning, be conscious of, have a conscience about.

CL From Aesch. and Hdt. in classical Gk. the verbal form *synoida* is found with the following meanings: (a) to share the knowledge of, be privy to (e.g. as an accusing witness or as one who is able to clear someone); and (b) in the reflexive form *synoida emautō*, to be conscious of (cf. the famous statement of Socrates: "For I know that I have no wisdom, small or great," Plato, *Apol.*, 21b).

From the 1st cent. B.C. *syneidēsis* and *syneidos*, the neut. participle used as a noun, are used synonymously in both pagan Gk. and hel. Jewish writings. *syneidos* is first found in Dem., meaning faculty of memory. *syneidēsis* first occurs in Democ., Frag. 297. According to context, it means consciousness, conscience and conscientiousness.

1. Originally *syneidēsis* appears to focus on knowledge: the capacity to relate to oneself, especially when one looks back at one's own past. This looking back did not stop short with ascertaining facts, but led to evaluations and judgments about the criterion of good and evil. Hence, the word gradually acquired the current moral meaning of conscience. This development began with the Seven Sages (Periander, Bias; according to Stobaeus), and is common in this sense from the 1st cent. B.C., occasionally in the historians Dio, Strabo and Plutarch. Depending on whether a man can justify himself when he looks back on his actions, writers speak of a good (*agathē* or *orthē*) or a bad (*deinē* or *ponēra*) conscience. The usual implication is that the good conscience is at peace, whereas the bad conscience makes itself painfully felt by relentlessly troubling its owner. An example of this is the tragedy of Orestes who is guilty of matricide, and sees conscience as a sickness that destroys him. The description *hē synesis, hoti synoida dein' eirgasmenos* sees conscience as consciousness of evil deeds (Eur., *Or.*, 396). In Gk. literature the Erinyes were a mythical embodiment of the afflictions of an evil conscience.

2. It is striking that pre-Christian Gk. literature speaks almost exclusively of a bad conscience, whereas the Romans often spoke of a *conscientia bona* (good conscience) and even of a *conscientia praeclara* (clear conscience) and a *conscientia optima* (best conscience), especially Cicero. *Conscientia* is a restrospective knowledge of failures and vices which frequently has an accursing, disconcerting character. "But in the ethically robust structure of the Roman officer and lawyer, who knows that his duties are clearly defined and can be discharged, there easily arises the sense of duty done" (C. Maurer, *TDNT* VII 907; cf. Caesar, *Bellum Civile*, 3, 60, 2).

Especially in the Later Stoa (Seneca) the restrospective character of conscience was toned down under the influence of the Pythagoreans. Conscience was seen as a watchman (*epitropos;* Lat. *testis*, witness), bestowed by God upon the individual. Its function was to guide him to live according to nature and to direct his moral progress. "In his conscience he has a reliable direction-sign for his conduct" (M. Pohlenz, *Die Stoa*, I, 1948, 320). Its task was still in the main that of a critical court of appeal in man that passed judgment on what had happened or at best on what was happening. Nevertheless, the ground was prepared for conscience to become a normative guide (cf. C. Maurer, *TDNT*, VII 907).

OT 1. The OT has no special word for the phenomenon of conscience. In the LXX *syneidēsis* occurs only in 3 late passages (Eccl. 10:20; Wis. 17:11; Sir. 42:18). This may be due to a different understanding of human nature from the Greeks'. For the Israelites of the old covenant the problem of man's attitude to himself was less significant than that of his attitude to God. He was more concerned with his accountability before God than with exploring his self-consciousness. Confession was made to God whose law man sought to fulfil in obedience. "Conscience is hearing in the sense of willing adherence" (C. Maurer, *TDNT* VII 908).

This does not mean that the OT knows nothing of the reality of a tormented conscience. But the voice of conscience possesses no intrinsic value. It is the voice of the divine judge, demanding from man an account of his dealings. The function of conscience is attributed to the → heart (Heb. *lēḇ*). Thus the heart of David smote him to remind him of his guilt (1 Sam. 24:6; 2 Sam. 24:10). It summoned him to penitence and regret. Ps. 51:10, which according to its title was a Psalm of David written after his adultery with Bathsheba, contains the plea: "Create in me a clean heart, O God, and put a new and right spirit within me" (51:10). The idea of a clean heart, which is more common in the LXX than in the Heb. Masoretic text of the OT, points forward to the notion of a good conscience in the NT.

2. Where *syneidēsis* occurs in the LXX, an assimilation to the Gk. idea of conscience may be ascertained. This is illustrated by Wis. 17:11 which speaks of a bad conscience in an ethical sense ("for wickedness condemned by its own witness is cowardly, and driven into a pass by conscience it always does what is worst"). Here conscience "takes on the function of the prosecutor and judge in one person" (C. Maurer, *TDNT* VII 909).

3. The correspondence between the OT notion of the heart and the Gk. concept of conscience is still more marked in Philo, who was "the first to think through theologically a doctrine of conscience" (C. Maurer, *TDNT*, 911). Philo heard "its voice just as loud as the Roman Seneca" (M. Pohlenz, op. cit., 377). For him conscience is no mere autonomous court of appeal, but a normative entity shaped by the law of God. Its task is to *elenchein* (convict, reprove, expose), i.e. to bring man consciousness of sin and penitence. "When it (the elenchus native to the soul) is once awakened, it comes forth as an accuser, indicts, charges, and shames; on the other hand it also instructs as a judge, giving correction, advising conversion, and when it persuades it is pleased and propitiated" (*Decal.*, 87). Otherwise, it continues to trouble the sinner. Conscience performs all this in order to drive the sinner into the arms of a merciful God. This relationship with God provides the OT foundation for Philo's doctrine of conscience.

NT In the NT the vb. *synoida* occurs only twice. In 1 Cor. 4:4 it is reflexive: "I am not aware of anything against myself" (RSV); cf. however NEB "I have nothing on my conscience." Acts 5:2 suggests a shared knowledge: "and with his wife's knowledge he kept back . . ." (RSV). On the other hand, the noun *syneidēsis* occurs some 30 times. In addition, it appears in some manuscripts of Jn. 8:9 in the pericope about the woman taken in adultery which is omitted from the best texts of Jn. Apart from this, it does not occur in the Gospels. Apart from two instances in Acts, the passages where it occurs are all in Paul, including the Pastoral Epistles, and in Heb. and 1 Pet.

1. In Rom. 2:15 *syneidēsis* stands alongside *kardia* (→ heart) and *logismoi* (→ thoughts; cf. *dialogismoi*, opinions, Rom. 14:1) as critical organs. They enable the Gentiles to live a life that corresponds to that of the Jews according to the law. Conscience is assigned the role of awakening awareness of the law that is written on the heart. This is shown by the vb. *symmartyrein* (bear witness with; cf. Rom. 9:1 where Paul appeals to his conscience as a witness that he is not lying). Conscience appears – to put it graphically – as a court of appeal which is not able to promulgate any statutes (for only God himself can do this) but is able to deliver judgment on the cases before it. ([Ed.] Rom. 2:14 ff., is often taken to apply to the hypothetical case of Gentiles keeping the law without having heard of the OT law or the gospel. Karl Barth has questioned whether this is Paul's meaning and suggests that Paul is thinking of Gentile converts to Christianity in whom the promise of the new covenant, that the law will be written on their hearts, is fulfilled [*CD*, I, 2, 304; II, 2, 242, 604; IV, 1, 33, 369, 395; cf. C. Brown, *Karl Barth and the Christian Message*, 1967, 96. But see also R. Atallah, "An Egyptian Parallel to Romans 2:15", *Themelios* 10, 3, 1974, 1–7].)

The thought of conscience as a court of appeal is clear in the passages in which Paul deals with the Corinthians' question of the propriety of eating meat that has been sacrificed to idols (1 Cor. 8:7 ff.; 10:25 ff.). Paul makes two points in this connection. On the one hand, he proclaims the Christian's freedom from regimentation by an alien conscience. He is concerned with what Barth calls "the conscience that is freed through the Word of God" (*CD*, I, 2, 788). On the other hand, he calls for regard to the more sensitive conscience of another person.

Paul rejoices in the testimony of his own conscience that has been informed by God (2 Cor. 2:12). Likewise, he hopes that the consciences of others which are open to the sight of God will recognize the sincerity of his missionary life and work (2 Cor. 4:2; 5:11). Thus not only is the avoidance of a bad, accusing conscience (as is mentioned in Jn. 8:9) worth aspiring after. It is even more important to have a good conscience which confirms the agreement of faith and life. Appealing to such a conscience which is in line with the will of God, Paul can also demand obedience to those in authority (Rom. 13:5). A similar thought occurs in 1 Pet. 2:19; 3:16, 21.

Accordingly, Acts 24:16 lays down what is virtually a rule of conduct: "I [Paul] always take pains to have a clear conscience toward God and towards men." Similarly, Paul began his appeal to the council of Jewish leaders: "Brethren, I have lived before God in all good conscience up to this day" (Acts 23:1).

2. The Pastoral Epistles lay great emphasis on a good conscience. They speak of the "corrupt and unbelieving" whose "minds and consciences are corrupted"

(Tit. 1:15), and "liars whose consciences are seared" (1 Tim. 4:2). By contrast, Christians are to hold "faith and a good conscience [*agathēn syneidēsin*]" (1 Tim. 1:19; cf. 1 Pet. 3:16) and "to serve with a clear conscience [*en kathara syneidēsei*]" (2 Tim. 1:3). The good and the clear conscience thus become a characteristic of the Christian, as for him "the verdict of conscience and the verdict of faith coincide" (W. Schrage, *Die Konkreten Einzelgebote in der paulinischen Paränese*, 1961, 152). Alongside a "pure heart [*kathara kardia*]" and a "sincere faith [*pistis anhypokritos*]", 1 Tim. 1:5 names the conscience as the source of love in action. In short, the conscience can be regarded as the place where the "mystery of faith" is to be found (1 Tim. 3:9). That is why "the appeal to God for a clear conscience", which is the essence of baptism (1 Pet. 3:21), is so important. The same passage links it with "the resurrection of Jesus Christ" (→ Resurrection; → Faith).

3. Heb. also stresses the christological basis of the NT understanding of conscience, when it declares that "the blood of Christ" purifies the conscience "from dead works to serve the living God" (Heb. 9:14). Using the symbolism of the Day of Atonement ritual in which the high priest entered the sanctuary once a year, Heb. 10:22 urges believers to enter themselves, drawing near "with a true heart in full assurance of faith, with our hearts sprinkled clean from an evil conscience and our bodies washed with pure water." Late Judaism knew of no complete release from consciousness of sin despite repeated cultic rites (cf. Heb. 9:9; 10:2). It is only because of the high priestly sacrifice of Christ that "we are sure that we have a clear conscience" (Heb. 13:18).

4. In this way the Christian understanding of conscience is transformed by faith in the forgiving power of Jesus Christ. The Greeks saw conscience as something bad operating retrospectively. Christians came to see conscience as being made clean through trust. Its purity lay in the believer's knowledge of his standing in Christ. The fact that it was directed by the Word of God gave the believer heart to serve God in love. *H. C. Hahn*

The researches of C. A. Pierce, *Conscience in the New Testament*, 1955, have shed further light on the background of the whole word-group and have led to a plausible suggestion as to how *syneidēsis* came to feature in the NT epistles. His detailed analysis of the terms in secular Gk. has overthrown the widespread idea that it was a Stoic technical term. At best there are only 3 quotations that can be offered in evidence for the latter idea (op. cit., 13 ff.; see also the tabular analysis of the use of the entire word-group on pp. 132–147). There is little ground for thinking that Paul adopted it from the Stoics. Pierce contends that the term was an everyday Gk. word which in general had the morally bad negative sense of the pain that we feel when we do something wrong.

Pierce suggests that the term came into the NT via the Corinthian church, where conscience was used as a catchword (op. cit., 60 ff.). This explains the absence of the term in the OT and the gospels and its widespread use in the Corinthian correspondence and later epistles. The Corinthians were appealing to conscience to justify their attitudes in the various burning issues of the day, in particular the practice of eating meat that had been offered to idols. Because some claimed that they could do this with a clear conscience, they argued that the practice was permissible. Paul condemns the idea that conscience alone is an invariable and infallible guide. In

351

1 Cor. 4:4 he uses the verbal form *ouden gar emautō synoida* ("I have nothing on my conscience", NEB) to show that that by itself does not acquit him of any wrong that he may have done. A man may have a clear conscience because it is dead or inadequately educated. There are other factors in deciding the rightness and wrongness of actions. At best conscience is a check. Later on in the epistle Paul explains the limitations of conscience in the light of the burning issues at Corinth of the propriety for a Christian to eat meat sacrificed to idols. The weak brother may eat the meat, following the example of the strong brother who knows that idols are nothing. He is weak in the sense that he has no clear principles of conduct settled in his mind. He eats, and is then tormented by conscience (1 Cor. 8:7, 10, 12). The problem here is that of a sensitive conscience which at the same time is imperfectly educated. The way out of the dilemma is not to act out of → "knowledge" (8:1 ff.), or by copying the "strong" brother whose conscience does not pain him, but out of love. "Therefore, if food is a cause of my brother's falling, I will never eat meat lest I cause my brother to fall" (8:13).

In ch. 10 conscience is again given a subordinate role. Again the Christian's motive is to be love (10:23 f.). Indeed, the Corinthians are to avoid referring the matter of conscience (10:27, 28, 29). The question is lifted to the higher plane of concern for the weaker man and his conscience. The believer may eat whatever is sold in the market. It is best to avoid asking questions about its origin, so as to avoid raising questions of conscience. But if the weaker brother says that a piece of meat has been offered to idols, it is best not to eat it. It is a case, not of defiling the eater's conscience or of weakening his spirituality by engaging in dubious practices, but of avoiding inflaming the sensitive man's conscience.

In other words, conscience can be a highly defective guide, if one relies solely on the absence of the pain that we call conscience as a guide to conduct. To function at all, it depends upon knowledge (10:25 ff.). For conscience by itself could not tell where the meat had come from. And it only operates effectively in relation to moral principles outside itself. A clear conscience is no guarantee of being right (4:4). On the other hand, an over-sensitive conscience may lead to tormenting dilemmas that can only be resolved on the other grounds (chs. 8 and 10). The ultimate grounds for action are love and the glory of God (10:31 ff.; cf. 13:1–14:1).

If Pierce is right, conscience came into the NT via the troubles at Corinth. Thereafter, Paul began to find a place for it in his own thinking. Subsequent treatment in the NT amplifies the role assigned to conscience in 1 Cor. The conscience may be seared by constant disregard, and therefore fail to fulfil its function in those who teach false doctrines and practices (1 Tim. 4:2; Tit. 1:15). Conversely, the story of Jephthah in Jdg. 11 appears to be that of a man with an over-sensitive conscience (although, of course, the word is not used). He had made a vow to God which involved the most ungodly consequences. Perhaps his conscience forced him to fulfil the vow, even though human sacrifice was against Heb. religion. To say this, however, does not mean that the NT writers urge that conscience should be ignored. Christ died to make the conscience clean (Heb. 9:14; 10:22; cf. 9:9; 10:2; 1 Pet. 3:21). But the conscience is only part of our moral make-up. Its work is largely negative. As the pain we feel when we do something wrong, it acts like a red warning light. It serves as a sort of moral double-check on our actions. It operates largely on the basis of experience. It needs to be educated and carefully tended.

352

But as such, it is very important (Acts 23:1; 24:16; Rom. 2:15; 9:1; 13:5; 1 Tim. 1:5, 19; 3:9; 2 Tim. 1:3; 1 Pet. 2:19; 3:16; 2 Cor. 1:12).

When we speak of conscience in English, our meaning often seems to oscillate between conscience in the narrow sense as the pain, or the instrument which makes us feel pain, when we transgress the moral law, and the wider sense of moral consciousness. The latter involves the whole person, viewed as a responsible moral being. It is not just a pain which works retrospectively in the light of past actions and which by extension might enable us to forecast what future actions might cause us pain. It includes the power of discernment and rational reflection which enables the mind to analyse situations and actions, to discern moral values and principles, the capacity to hear and apply the Word of God to our lives, and also conscience in the narrower sense. For the Christian, guidance belongs to the realm of moral consciousness in this wider sense which includes *syneidēsis* in the narrower sense, but is by no means confined to it. *C. Brown*

(a). D. Bonhoeffer, *Ethics*, (1955) 1964, 242–48; R. Bultmann, *Theology of the New Testament*, I, 1952, 211–20; R. D. Congdon, "The Doctrine of Conscience," *Bibliotheca Sacra* 102, 1945, 26ff. and 474–89; G. Ebeling, *Word and Faith*, 1963, 407–23; R. Jewett, *Paul's Anthropological Terms: A Study of their Use in Conflict Settings*, 1971, 402–46, 458 ff.; W. Lillie, *Studies in New Testament Ethics*, 1961, 45–56; C. Maurer, *synoida, TDNT* VII 898–919; C. A. Pierce, *Conscience in the New Testament*, 1955; N. H. G. Robinson, *Christ and Conscience*, 1956; R. Schnackenburg, *The Moral Teaching of the New Testament*, 1968, 287–96; J. N. Sevenster, *Paul and Seneca*, 1971; C. Spicq, "Conscience," *EBT* I 131–34; W. D. Stacey *The Pauline View of Man*, 1956, 206 f.. K. Stendahl, "The Apostle Paul and the Introspective Conscience of the West", *HTR* 56, 1963, 199–215; H. Thielicke, *Theological Ethics*, I, 1968, 298–382; M. E. Thrall, "The Pauline Use of SYNEIDESIS," *NTS* 14, 1967–68, 118–25; and "The Meaning of *oikodomeō* in Relation to the Concept of *syneidēsis*", *Stud Ev* IV 1, 1968, 468–72.
(b). P. Althaus, *Paulus und Luther über den Menschen*, 1958; G. Bornkamm, *Studien zu Antike und Christentum*, II, 1962, 111–18; F. Delekat, *Der gegenwärtige Christus*, 1949, 104 ff.; H. G. Drescher, "Das Gewissen," *Das Gespräch* 32, 1961; L. Eckstein, *Stufen der Gewissensbildung*, 1961; *Das Gewissen*, Studien a. d. C. G. Jung-Institut VII, 1958; W. Korff, *Ehre, Prestige, Gewissen*, 1966; W. Loch, "Biologische und gesellschaftliche Faktoren der Gewissensbildung," *Wege zum Menschen*, 1962, 346 ff.; C. von Monakow, *Gehirn und Gewissen*, 1950; C. Maurer, "Glaubensbindung und Gewissensfreiheit im Neuen Testament," *ThZ* 17, 1961, 107 ff.; H. van Oyen, "Über das Gewissen," in F. Karrenberg, ed., *Spannungsfelder der evangelischen Soziallehre*, 1960, 39 ff.; M. Pohlenz, *Die Stoa*, I, 1948; B. Reicke, "*Syneidēsis* in Röm. II, 15," *TZ* 12, 1956, 157–61; W. Ross, "Das Fluch des guten Gewissens," *Wege zum Menschen*, 1962, 138 ff.; G. Rudberg, "Cicero und das Gewissen," *Symbolae Osloenses*, 1955, 96–104; W. Schrage, *Die konkreten Einzelgebote in der paulinischen Paränese*, 1961, 152 ff.; H. H. Schrey, "Gewissen," *Theologie für Nichttheologen*, II, 1964, 33 ff.; O. Seel, "Zur Vorgeschichte des Gewissensbegriffes, im altgriechischen Denken," *Festschrift F. Dornseiff*, 1953; 291–319; C. Spicq, *RB* 47, 1938, 50–80; and *Jahresbericht über die Fortschritte der klassischen Altertumswissenschaft*, 1943, 169 f.; J. Stelzenberger, *Syneidēsis im Neuen Testament*, 1961; G. Wehrung, *Welt und Reich*, 1952, 315 ff.; E. Wolf, "Vom Problem des Gewissens in reformatorischer Sicht," *Peregrinatio*, I, 1954, 81 ff.; and "Gewissen zwischen Gesetz und Evangelium," *Peregrinatio*, II, 1965, 104 ff.

Conversion, Penitence, Repentance, Proselyte

Repentance, penitence and conversion are closely linked. Whenever someone gives his thought and life a new direction, it always involves a judgment on his previous views and behaviour. This process is expressed in the NT by three word-groups which deal with its various aspects: *epistrephō, metamelomai* and *metanoeō*. The first and third both mean turn round, turn oneself round, and refer to a man's conversion. This presupposes and includes a complete change under the influence of the Holy → Spirit. *metamelomai* expresses rather the feeling of repentance for error, debt, failure and sin, and so it looks back. Hence, it does not necessarily cause a man to turn to God. *epistrephō* is probably the widest conception, because it always includes → faith. We often find *pisteuō*, believe, expressly used with *metanoeō*, since faith complements repentance (cf. L. Berkhof, *Systematic Theology*, 1938, 482).

ἐπιστρέφω

ἐπιστρέφω (*epistrephō*), turn, turn around, turn back, be converted; στρέφω (*strephō*), turn, change; ἀποστρέφω (*apostrephō*), turn away from; ἐπιστροφή (*epistrophē*), conversion.

CL From Homer onwards *strephō, apostrephō* and *epistrephō* were used transitively and intransitively by Gk. authors, e.g. Xen., Aristoph., Polyb., and in inscriptions and magical papyri. All three share the meaning of turn, turn to, turn oneself, turn round. They describe a largely intentional turning of the body, or thoughts, to a person or thing. *strephō* is used more in the sense of turn over, turn round, transform, and later turn towards. *epistrephō* means turn towards, turn round, return, both trans. and reflex., and then derivatively be converted, i.e. change one's mind and behaviour. Thus in the classical philosophical literature *epistrephō* and its sub. *epistrophē* mean *inter alia* the turning of the soul to piety or the divine. This concept passed from secular Gk. via the LXX into the vocabulary of the NT. For the compound *anastrephō* → walk.

OT 1. Behind *epistrophē* in the LXX lies the Heb. *šûḇ*, which occurs *c.* 1050 times in the OT and means turn round, return (qal), bring back, restore (hiph.). It appears with its specifically theological meaning *c.* 120 times: turn round, return, be converted, bring back, in the sense of a change in behaviour and of a return to the living God. The LXX translates these passages by *epistrephō, apostrephō, anastrephō*, but not, as in the NT, by *metanoeō*. The theological meaning of *šûḇ* can be clearly traced in the NT.

Turning, or conversion, is described in the OT as turning from evil (Jer. 18:8) to the Lord (Mal. 3:7). Man can, however, be so permeated by evil (Hos. 5:4) that he resists such turning (2 Chr. 36:13). God gives the impulse to conversion; God first moves man (Jer. 31:18; Lam. 5:21). Even when man returns, it is because he has first received (Jer. 24:7). Both individuals (2 Ki. 23:25) and nations (Jon. 3:10) may turn. God uses the prophets to help to bring about conversion (Neh. 9:26; Zech. 1:4). Those who refuse to return to God experience God's wrath in drought (Amos 4:6–8), captivity (Hos. 11:5), destruction (1 Ki. 9:6–9) and death (Ezek. 33:9, 11). He who returns to God receives → forgiveness (Isa. 55:7), remission of punishment (Jon. 3:9 f.), fertility and prosperity (Hos. 14:5 ff. (MT 6 ff.)), and life (Ezek. 33:14 ff.). The historical books of the OT always call for the conversion of Israel as a body, but the prophets, especially Jer. and Ezek., stress that of the individual. They look forward to the new covenant when God will give a new → heart and spirit (Jer. 33:31 ff.; Ezek. 11:19; 18:31; 36:26 f.; 37:14). The conversion of the people as a whole is seen as taking place in the messianic age (Deut. 4:30; Hos. 3:5; Mal. 4:5 f. (MT 3:23 f.)).

2. Rab. Judaism accepted and developed the OT tradition. A prior condition for

354

admittance to the Qumran community was conversion, i.e. turning from all evil and turning to the Law of Moses. The members of the community called themselves "those who had turned from transgression" (cf. Isa. 59:20) or "the converts of Israel". Hel. circles also knew before the Christian era the concept of religious conversion. He who turns to Yahweh is forgiven his sins; he does not continue deliberately in sin but keeps the commandments of God. "Conversion is always an individual and practical problem, never a theoretical and theological one" (K. H. Rengstorf, *RGG*³, I 978). *strephō* and its compounds or their equivalents occur in Test. XII, Eth. Enoch, Sib., Syr. Bar., Josephus and Philo (cf. SB VI 799).

NT 1. *epistrephō* is found 36 times in the NT, and in addition in variant readings in Lk. 10:6(D), Acts 15:16(D), 2 Pet. 2:21(TR) (cf. Arndt s.v.). 18 times it has its secular meaning of turning, returning, turning away, etc. (cf. Matt. 10:13; 2 Pet. 2:22), and 18 times with its theological meaning of conversion especially in Acts and the Epistles (cf. Mk. 4:12 par.; Lk. 1:16 f.; 22:32; Acts 15:19; 2 Cor. 3:16; Jas. 5:19 f.). Here, unlike the LXX, it is often synonymous with *metanoeō*. Only in Matt. 18:3 and Jn. 12:40 is *strephō* used with the meaning of turning oneself (be converted); likewise *apostrephō* only in Acts 3:26. The noun *epistrophē* is found only once in the NT in Acts 15:3.

2. (a) When men are called in the NT to conversion, it means a fundamentally new turning of the human will to God, a return home from blindness and error to the Saviour of all (Acts 26:18; 1 Pet. 2:25). The use of *epistrephō* suggests that we are not concerned primarily with turning from the old life, but that the stress is on the turning to Christ, and through him to God (cf. Jn. 14:1, 6) and so to a new life. Conversion involves a change of → lords. The one who until then has been under the lordship of Satan (cf. Eph. 2:1 f.) comes under the lordship of God, and comes out of darkness into light (Acts 26:18; cf. Eph. 5:8). Conversion and surrender of the life to God is done in → faith, and includes faith in Jesus Christ (Acts 11:21). Such a conversion leads to a fundamental change of the whole of life (Acts 26:20). It receives a new outlook and objectives. God's original purpose in creating man is realized in the new life. The converted man is to serve him alone with a clear conscience in voluntary dependence (1 Thess. 1:9; Acts 14:15; cf. Heb. 9:14). The effect of conversion is the forgiveness of all sins (Acts 3:19; 26:18).

Acts frequently describes the results of the missionary → proclamation by the first Christians. It always speaks of conversion as a once-for-all and self-contained event (Acts 9:35; 11:21). From Acts 15:3 it is clear that the word "conversion" very soon became a technical term that needed no further explanation.

(b) *epistrephō* is used for the conversion of a man which involves a complete transformation (→ Form, Art. *morphē*) of his existence under the influence of the Holy Spirit. *metamelomai*, however, expresses rather the feeling of repentance of sin, which need not involve a true turning of a man to God. *metanoeō* on the other side is much closer to *epistrephō* (→ *metanoia*; cf. Acts 3:19; 26:20). It expresses the conscious turning from → sin, a change of mind (→ Reason, Art. *nous*) and of the whole inner attitude to life, without which true conversion is not possible. *epistrephō* has a wider meaning than *metanoeō*, for it always includes faith, while *metanoeō* and *pisteuō* can stand together and complement each other (cf. L. Berkhof, *Systematic Theology*, 482).   *F. Laubach*

355

| μεταμέλομαι | μεταμέλομαι (metamelomai), change one's mind, regret, repent; ἀμεταμέλητος (ametameletos), not to be regretted, hence irrevocable. |

CL metamelomai is linked with the impersonal melei, it concerns (someone). In classical Gk. metamelomai expressed a changed feeling towards a thing, but it cannot always be clearly distinguished from metanoeō, which implies that in retrospect one thinks differently about a matter (cf. nous → Reason). In secular speech metamelomai is found in Thuc., Diod. Sic. and inscriptions and means feel regret, repent.

OT The Heb. nāḥam (in niph.) is rendered c. 35 times in the LXX either by metanoeō or metamelomai, showing that the LXX distinguished between them no more clearly than did classical Gk. The word is used in Exod. 13:17 and Jdg. 21:6 for purely human regret. In Job 42:6 and Jer. 31:19 it involves humble agreement with God's righteous judgment, for good or ill. When God is said to "repent", there are two possibilities. God can reject men, because they have turned against him in disobedience though he had earlier chosen them (1 Sam. 15:11, 35). However, in spite of his judgment God can also turn again to men in grace and mercy (Jdg. 2:18; 1 Chr. 21:15; Ps. 106:45; Jon. 3:9 f.). When it is clearly stressed that God does not repent (Ps. 110:4; Jer. 4:28), it is the guarantee that God will not deviate from the plan that he conceived at the first.

The tension between God's justice and grace is familiar also in Judaism. As the Almighty, he is simultaneously the Judge and the merciful One.

NT While the word-group metanoeō is frequently found in the NT, metamelomai occurs only in Matt. 21:29, 32; 27:3; 2 Cor. 7:8 (twice); Heb. 7:21, quoting Ps. 110:4; and the adj. ametameletos, not to be regretted, only occurs in Rom. 11:29 and 2 Cor. 7:10. It refers to something of which God (Rom. 11:29) or a man (2 Cor. 7:10) will not repent, and hence means irrevocable.

In Jesus' parable in Matt. 21:28–32 the father asks both of his sons to work in his vineyard. One says Yes, but does not go. The other refuses, but then regrets his answer and goes. In such a context the word can be translated "change one's decision". Jesus applied the parable to the high priests and elders of Israel. The second son had changed his attitude to his father, and so had the tax-collectors and harlots, who had believed John the Baptist's message and had repented. In contrast, the elders of Israel had continued in their disobedience (oude metemelē-thēte).

The example of Judas makes it clear that metamelomai and metanoeō do not have identical meanings in the NT (see above CL and OT). Judas recognized that Jesus had been wrongly condemned. He regretted his betrayal (Matt. 27:3), but he did not find the way to genuine repentance. We find the same differentiation in 2 Cor. 7:8–10. Paul did not regret that he had written a sharp letter to the Corinthians, for the sorrow caused to its recipients had led them to true repentance (metanoia), to an inner turning to God. There is no need to regret such a repentance, for it always serves only our salvation.

The oath which God will never regret (Heb. 7:21, quoting Ps. 110:4; RSV both here and in Ps. 110:4 "change his mind") serves both to guarantee the superiority

356

of Jesus' high-priesthood over that of the OT and to express the unchangeable faithfulness of God. This faithfulness can be recognized also by the fact that God's gracious gifts and call are *ametameletos*, irrevocable (Rom. 11:29). In spite of the disobedience and hardening of men's hearts God will accomplish his purpose of salvation also in his people Israel. *F. Laubach*

| μετάνοια |

μετάνοια (*metanoia*), change of mind, repentance, conversion; *μετανοέω* (*metanoeō*), change one's mind, repent, be converted; *ἀμετανόητος* (*ametanoētos*), impenitent.

CL The word-group is found relatively rarely in classical Gk. literature, the vb. from the sophist Antiphon onwards, the noun from Thuc. onwards. Both words are used more frequently in Koine Gk. The prep. *meta* used with vbs. of motion and of mental activity indicates a change in the meaning of the simple vb. Hence, *metanoeō* is equivalent to the Heb. *niham* (niph.), to be sorry about something. It is so used of God in 1 Sam. 15:29. Hence, if the change of mind involves the recognition that the previous opinion was false or bad, we get the meaning of feel remorse or regret for the vb. and that of a change of mind, remorse, regret for the noun In pre-Biblical Gk. the word-group does not develop the precision which characterizes its use in the NT. Gk. society never thought of a radical change in a man's life as a whole, of conversion or turning round, even though we may find some of the factors which belong to conversion. This shows that the concept of conversion is not derived from Gk. thought, and its origin must be sought elsewhere.

OT 1. We are not helped by the LXX. It does not use the noun. (Prov. 14:15 is not a translation of the Heb. text.) The vb. is used to render *niham* (see above CL), whether of God (cf. 1 Sam. 15:29; Jer. 18:8; Joel 2:13 f.; Amos 7:3, 6), or of men (Jer. 8:6; 13:19). The thought of turning round, preached especially by the prophets and expressed by the Heb. verb *šûb*, is rendered by → *epistrephō* in Gk. (Amos 4:6; Hos. 5:4; 6:1). The prophetic call to turn presupposes that the relationship of the people and of the individual to God must be understood in personal terms. Sin and apostasy disturb and break this personal relationship. Turning means giving a completely new direction to the man as a whole and a return to God. This includes turning away from evil.

2. The Qumran community continued this call to repentance by demanding from its members that they be converted from all evil (1QS 5:1) and return to every commandment of the Law of Moses (1QS 5:8). The members of the community therefore called themselves the converts of Israel (CD 4:2), those that turn from transgression (1QS 10:20; 1QH 2:9, etc.). They called their covenant the covenant of conversion (CD 19:16).

NT 1. The NT does not follow LXX usage but employs *metanoeō* to express the force of *šûb*, turn round. This change in meaning was prepared for by other Gk. translations of the OT and in Hellenistic Jud. (for evidence cf. J. Behm, *TDNT* IV 989). The change in the choice of words – *metanoeō* instead of *epistrephō* – shows that the NT does not stress the concrete, physical concept implied in the OT use of *šûb*, but rather the thought, the will, the *nous*. The ideas of repent, be converted, (and correspondingly repentance and conversion) come to the fore. Correspondingly

357

ametanoētos (only in Rom. 2:5) means impenitent. For all that, the change of words has not merely intellectualized the concept of *šûb*. In fact the predominantly intellectual understanding of *metanoia* as change of mind plays very little part in the NT. Rather the decision by the whole man to turn round is stressed. It is clear that we are concerned neither with a purely outward turning nor with a merely intellectual change of ideas.

2. The closest link with the prophetic call to repentance is undoubtedly found in John the Baptist, who called the people to repentance and to "bear fruit that befits repentance" (Matt. 3:2, 8 par.). Corresponding to the OT pattern, the call was addressed to the whole people (cf. Acts 13:24; 19:4) and also to the pious, who believed that they did not need to repent (Matt. 3:7 ff.). John, like the rest of the NT, based the urgency of his message on a different foundation from that of the → prophets. Motivation in the OT for repentance and returning along the true road of God's → righteousness was linked with the past and its social unrighteousness and idolatry. For John it was that "the kingdom of heaven is at hand" (Matt. 3:2). Hence, there can be only one way for the man wishing to escape judgment. He must repent, so that his whole life is changed and brought into a new relationship with God (Matt. 3:10). John linked his call to repentance with the eschatological sacrament of the → baptism of repentance, as sign of the → forgiveness of sins (Mk. 1:4 par.) having repentance as its goal (Matt. 3:11, *eis metanoian*; cf. Acts 13:24; 19:4). This indicates that repentance is regarded both as an act open to man and as a duty. It is a possibility given to man by God as an eschatological gift of grace, and it is also a duty required of him.

3. According to the Synoptics, the preaching of Jesus resembled that of the Baptist. Matt. 3:2 and 4:17 record the identical call, "Repent, for the kingdom of heaven is at hand." The clear difference between them is that Jesus did not, as did John, look for one to follow him (Matt. 3:11). He saw in his own coming the beginning of God's decisive work (Lk. 11:20; 17:21; Matt. 11:6). Hence the woes addressed to the towns that were not ready to repent (Matt. 11:20–24 par.). That is why the inhabitants of Nineveh will find it better in the day of judgment than will the contemporaries of Jesus. The former repented at the preaching of Jonah, and "behold, something greater than Jonah is here" (Matt. 12:41 par.). Hence, repentance is now no longer obedience to a law but to a person. The call to repentance becomes a call to → discipleship. So repentance, faith and discipleship are different aspects of the same thing (Mk. 1:15, "Repent and believe").

There are many passages in which the term *metanoeō* does not appear, but in which the thought of repentance is clearly present. This helps us to see to what extent Jesus' message was determined by the call to repent in the light of God's sovereign rule, which he himself had brought in. Examples are: "Unless you turn (*straphēte*) and become like children, you will never enter the kingdom of heaven" (Matt. 18:3); "so therefore, whoever of you does not renounce all that he has cannot be my disciple" (Lk. 14:33). It is the spiritually poor, the little ones and the helpless, and those that need our help who receive the promise of the → kingdom of God (Matt. 5:3; 18:10, 14). Jesus came not to call the righteous but sinners to repentance (Lk. 5:32). However absolute the call to repentance, it was a message of joy, because the possibility of repentance exists. Because God has turned to man (Lk. 5:32, *elēlytha* (perf.) I have come), man should, may and can turn to God.

Hence conversion and repentance are accompanied by joy, for they mean the opening up of life for the one who has turned. The parables in Lk. 15 bear testimony to the joy of God over the sinner who repents and call on men to share it. God's gift to men in their conversion is → life. When the parable of the prodigal son pictures conversion as a return to the Father, it can be said of the man who has repented, "This my son was dead, and is alive again" (Lk. 15:24; cf. 32).

4. Primitive Christian preaching continues the call for repentance (cf. Mk. 6:12 and the sermons in Acts). This missionary preaching linked with the call for repentance all the elements we have already met, the call to faith (Acts 20:21; cf. Acts 26:18; 19:4), the demand to be baptized (Acts 2:38), the promise of the forgiveness of sins (Lk. 24:47; Acts 3:19; 5:31), and of life and of salvation (Acts 11:18; 2 Cor. 7:9 f.). Conversion is turning from evil (Acts 8:22; 2 Cor. 12:21; Rev. 2:21 f.) to God (Acts 20:21; 26:20; Rev. 16:9). In Acts 3:19 and 26:20 *metanoeō* and *epistrephō* are placed side by side. This shows that the two concepts are related. In these cases *metanoeō* describes rather the turning from evil and *epistrephō* the turning to God.

5. The fact that this group of words does not occur often in the Pauline writings (only 6 times) and not at all in the Johannine (apart from Rev.), does not mean that the idea of conversion is not present there but only that in the meantime a more specialized terminology had developed. Both Paul and John convey the idea of conversion by that of → faith. Paul speaks of faith as "being in Christ", as the "dying and rising of a man with Christ", as the "new creation", as "putting on the new man". The Johannine literature represents the new → life in Christ as "new birth", as a passing from death to life and from → darkness to → light, or as the victory of → truth over falsehood and of → love over hate.

6. The early church soon began to consider whether it were possible for man to turn repeatedly to God. This arose from experiences in their missionary activity and from certain elements in their tradition, e.g. after Peter had long been following Jesus he was told, "When you have turned again . . ." (Lk. 22:32, where *epistrephō* is used). The present writer believes that Hebrews took the matter to its logical conclusion and sees Heb. 6:4–8 as rejecting the possiblity of a second repentance. On the one hand, in keeping with the view of the rest of the NT, this was done to stress the absoluteness of conversion over against a form of Christian faith that was lapsing into apathy. On the other hand, it showed that conversion was not just a human act but that God must give a "chance to repent" (Heb. 12:17). A man who deliberately sins after conversion incurs God's judgment (Heb. 6:8; 10:26 f.). Such a heavy emphasis on the finality of conversion does not exclude God's all-embracing desire to save. He "does not desire that any should be lost, but rather that all should come to repent" (2 Pet. 3:9). Rather it stresses the absoluteness of his mercy. God saves completely and finally, and thus man's conversion to God must be complete and final.

J. Goetzmann

| προσήλυτος | προσήλυτος (prosēlytos), proselyte; φοβούμενος τὸν θεόν (phoboumenos ton theon), God-fearer; σεβόμενος τὸν θεόν (sebomenos ton theon), God-fearer. |

359

CL *prosēlytos* (from *proserchomai*, approach) occurs only in Jewish and Christian literature. It is a technical term and designates the proselyte, i.e. the non-Jew who has gone over (from paganism) to Judaism.

OT 1. In LXX *prosēlytos* translates *gēr*, stranger, sojourner. In OT the *gēr*, as a non-Israelite settled in the land, is distinguished from the *nokrî*, the stranger only temporarily in the land. He was usually subject to an Israelite master (head of a house, tribe or locality) as a citizen without full rights, but in contrast to the → slave he had his personal freedom. He was not allowed to own or acquire landed property. Thus *gēr* at the first was a sociological concept. But as the *gēr* had a share in the land, he stood not only under the protection but also to a certain extent under the jurisdiction of Israel. Thus he had, for example, to keep the sabbath with Israel according to the directions of the Book of the Covenant (Exod. 23:12; 20:10) and was not to be discriminated against by the Israelites, as his cry would come before Yahweh just as theirs did (Exod. 22:21 ff.; MT 22:20 ff.; cf. 23:9).

Later, when Israel, for the sake of its purity, separated itself more and more from everything non-Jewish, the *gēr*, who after all lived in Israel and already had certain religious duties, was to an increasing degree drawn into its life. He was given a share in the law, as in the sacrifices and the great festivals (Num. 15:15 f., 30; Deut. 16:10, 13 f.). If he accepted → circumcision he could even celebrate the Passover and was then fully integrated into the people (Exod. 12:48). At this point the concept of the *gēr* has already come very close to the later one of the *prosēlytos*.

2. The term acquired its characteristic meaning in Inter-Testamental Judaism. An intensive missionary movement began in the Hel. Jewish Diaspora. On the one hand, it was very effective because of its concept of the transcendent → God who is invisible and incapable of representation by an image. On the other hand, it was limited by → circumcision as an act of complete adherence because of fear of anti-Semitism (K. G. Kuhn, *TDNT* VI 731). Those pagans who identified themselves with the Jews by circumcision were called *prosēlytoi*, corresponding to the OT *gēr*. In this sense the term is also found in Philo. It was taken for granted that proselytes were circumcised.

Only the Damascus Rule among the Qumran texts refers to the *gērîm* (CD 14:3 ff.). In the order of precedence sojourners took the lowest place after priests, Levites and Israelite commoners.

In Palestinian Judaism *gēr* now always referred to the pagan who had been converted to Judaism. According to the Rab. texts, conversion followed on the acceptance of circumcision (in the case of men), baptism and a sacrifice in the Temple. Thereafter the converted pagan counted as a Jew. He was like, it was said, a new-born child. His former pagan life was no longer significant. The greatest possible emphasis was laid on circumcision; without it the convert remained a pagan.

3. Proselytes are to be distinguished from those non-Jews, who took part in synagogue worship and kept the law to some extent, without, however, being converted to Judaism through the acceptance of circumcision. The latter were required only to keep the Sabbath and food laws, together with the moral code, and to acknowledge the one God (E. Lohse, *RGG*[3] IV 972; cf. the so-called Noahic Commandments). The Rabbis called them *yir'ê šāmayîm*, God-fearers, Gk.

phoboumenoi (from *phobeomai*, → fear) *ton theon* or, more freely translated, *sebomenoi* (from *sebomai*, worship; → Godliness) *ton theon*. *sebomenoi* can also stand alone (Acts 17:4, 17). With this concept, too, we are dealing with a technical term (to be distinguished from *theosebēs*; → Godliness, art. *sebomai*).

NT In the NT the terms proselyte (with the single exception of Matt. 23:15) and God-fearer appear characteristically in Acts, the book which sets out to describe the coming into being of the young church on the mission field or among the Jews of the dispersion. As there is little reason for questioning its presentation of Paul's missionary methods of linking up with the synagogues (cf. K. G. Kuhn, *TDNT* VI 744) it is remarkable that the terms do not occur in the Pauline writings (but → Greek).

1. *prosēlytos* occurs only four times:

(a) In Matt. 23:15 among the woes pronounced against the Pharisees. Jesus is not here attacking the missionary zeal of the Pharisees as such, but the fact that they convert their followers to their own legalistic understanding of the law and thus make them "children of hell" (Kuhn, *TDNT* VI 742).

(b) In Acts 2:11 the various national groups are summed up as *Ioudaioi te kai prosēlytoi*, as → Jews by birth and proselytes. But all who had gathered were Jews from the dispersion who had come together for the festival.

(c) In Acts 6:5 Nicolaus, one of the Seven, is called *prosēlytos Antiocheus*, a proselyte of Antioch. In contrast to the others, who were born Jews, he was born a pagan.

(d) Acts 13:43: *sebomenōn prosēlytōn* (gen. pl. "devout converts to Judaism" RSV). This more precise definition is not found anywhere else. Usually we find in Acts alongside the Jews the *sebomenoi*, non-Jews who took part in the synagogue worship. Here, too, *sebomenōn* must have this technical sense, so our text is an inexactitude on the part of Luke or an old gloss (E. Haenchen, *The Acts of the Apostles*, 1971, ad loc.). ([Ed.] Or else it is used to characterize full, worshipping proselytes; there is no MS evidence to support the idea of a gloss (cf. F. F. Bruce, *The Acts of the Apostles*, 1952², 272 f.).)

2. The phrase *phoboumenos* or *sebomenos ton theon* occurs only in Acts. Paul preached in the synagogues before Jews and "God-fearers" (Acts 13:16, 26; on 13:43 see above). The → Greeks of Acts 14:1 and 18:4 must have been also such "God-fearers." It was among them that the apostle found a hearing. Lydia, the seller of purple stuff in Philippi (Acts 16:14) and Titius Justus in Corinth (Acts 18:7) are mentioned by name. It was because Paul did not demand circumcision but faith in Christ that the *sebomenoi* attached themselves to him. As a result he came into conflict with the Jews, who accused him before Gallio of persuading men to worship God contrary to the law (Acts 18:13).

But the same conflict arose even within the Christian community, as is apparent in the story of the centurion, Cornelius (Acts 10:1–11:18). Cornelius is described as *phoboumenos ton theon* (Acts 10:2, 22). In the primitive church the "God-fearer" was regarded, in accordance with the Palestinian-Jewish way of thinking, as a pagan because he was not circumcised (cf. OT 2). Therefore Peter was attacked by the Jerusalem church because he had not avoided contact with the uncircumcised, as was commanded in the law. In the case of the God-fearing women in Acts 13:50 we are probably dealing with women proselytes.   *U. Becker* (a). K. Barth, *CD* IV, 2, 553–84; J. B. Bauer, "Conversion," *EBT* 1, 138 ff.; J. Behm and E. Würthwein, *metanoeō*, *TDNT* IV 975–1008; G. Bertram, *strephō*, *TDNT* VII 714–29; S. H. Blank "The Current Misinterpretation of Isaiah's She'ar Yashub," *JBL* 68, 1948, 211–15; J. Dupont, "The Conversion of Paul and its Influence on his Understanding of Salvation by Faith," in W. W. Gasque and R. P. Martin, *Apostolic History and the Gospel*, 1970, 176–94; W. Eichrodt, *Theology of the Old Testament*, II, 1967, 443–83; E. M. B. Green, *Evangelism in the Early Church*, 1970, 146–65; F. Hahn, *Mission in the New Testament*, SBT, 1965; A. von Harnack, *The Mission and Expansion of Christianity*, (1908) 1962; W. L. Holladay, *The Root šûb in the Old Testament*, 1958; J. Jeremias, *Jesus' Promise to the Nations*, 1958; and *Jerusalem in the Time of Jesus*, 1969, 320–34; K. G. Kuhn, *prosēlytos*, *TDNT* VI 727–44; Moore, *Judaism* I 507 ff.; A. D. Nock, *Conversion*, 1933; Schürer II, ii, 291–327; R. Schnackenburg, *The Moral Teaching of the New Testament*, 1968, 10 ff.; J. Schniewind, "The Biblical Doctrine of Conversion", *SJT* 5, 1952, 267–81; J. N. Sevenster, "Education or Conversion: Epictetus or the Gospels," *NovT* 8, 1966, 247–62; R. J. Thompson, *Penitence and Sacrifice in Early Israel outside the Levitical Law*, 1963; commentaries on *Acts* by F. F. Bruce (1951) and E. Haenchen (1971) on Acts 6:5.

(b). A. Bertholet, *Die Stellung der Israeliten und der Juden zu den Fremden*, 1896; H. Braun, " 'Umkehr' in spätjüd.-häretischer und in frühchristlicher Sicht," *ZTK* 50, 1953, 243–58; and "Spätjüd.-häretischer und frühchristlicher Radikalismus," I, II, *BHTh* 24 I, II, 1957; E. K. Dietrich *Die Umkehr im Alten Testament und Judentum*, 1936; P. Feine, *Bekehrung im Neuen Testament und in der Gegenwart*, 1908; J. Fichtner, K. H. Rengstorf, W. Joest and W. Freytag, "Bekehrung," *RGG*³ I 1976–84; G. Fohrer, "Umkehr und Erlösung beim Propheten Jeremia," *ThZ* 11, 1955, 161–85; H. Hegermann, "Das hellenistische Judentum" in J. Leipoldt and W. Grundmann, *Umwelt des Urchristentums*, I, 1965, 307 ff.; J. Herzog, *Der Begriff der Bekehrung*, 1903; M. Hofer, *Metanoia, Bekehrung und Busse* (Dissertation Tübingen) 1947; A. Hulsbosch, *Die Bekehrung im Zeugnis der Bibel*, 1968; R. Joly, "Note sur metanoia," *Revue de l'histoire des Religions* 160, 1961, 148–56; O. Kietzig, "Bekehrung zum Glauben an Jesus Christus," *TLZ* 11, 1957, 891 ff.; R. Koch, "Die religiöse-sittliche Umkehr nach den drei ältesten Evangelien und der Apostelgeschichte," *Anima* 14, 1959, 296–307; S. Légasse, "Jésus a-t-il annoncé la Conversion Finale d'Israël? (A propos de Marc x. 23–7)," *NTS* 10, 1963–4, 480–7; E. Lerle, *Proselytenwerbung und Urchristentum*, 1960; E. Lohmeyer and W. Schmauch, *Das Evangelium des Matthäus*, KEK 1967⁴, on Matt. 23:15; E. Lohse, "Mission," *RGG*³ IV 971 ff.; M. Meinertz, *Jesus und die Heidenmission*, 1925; W. Pesch, *Der Ruf zur Entscheidung. Die Bekehrungspredigt des Neuen Testaments*, 1964; H. Pohlmann, *Die Metanoia als Zentralbegriff der christlichen Frömmigkeit*, 1938; SB I 162 ff.; K. L. Schmidt, "Israels Stellung zu den Fremden und Beisassen," *Judaica* 1, 1945–46, 269 ff.; J. Schniewind, *Die Freude der Busse*, 1960; and *Das biblische Wort von der Bekehrung*, 1951; and "Was verstand Jesus unter Umkehr?" in H. Asmussen, ed., *Rechtgläubigkeit und Frömmigkeit*, II, 1938, 70–84; E. Sjöberg, *Gott und die Sünder im palästinischen Judentum*, *BWANT* IV, 27, 1939; T. Sorg, *Das biblische Zeugnis von der Bekehrung und unsere Verständigung*, 1962; G. Strecker, "Noachische Gebote," *RGG*³ IV 1500 f.; J. de Vries and F. Horst, "Fremde," *RGG*³ II 1124 ff.; H. W. Wolff, "Das Thema 'Umkehr' in der alttestamentlichen Prophetie," *ZTK* 48, 1951, 129–48.

Council, Sanhedrin

| συμβουλεύω |

συμβουλεύω (*symbouleuō*), advise; σύμβουλος (*symboulos*), adviser; συμβουλία (*symboulia*), advice; συμβούλιον (*symboulion*), advice, council.

CL Words associated with the stem *symboul-* refer to the giving of advice by one person to another. *symbouleuō* means to advise, counsel; middle, to consult with a person, ask for advice. *symboulos* is one who gives advice, advisor, counsellor; it could be used of public officials. *symboulia* is counsel, especially in public affairs, or a "consultation". *symboulion* means counsel or a council.

OT All the words are found in the LXX, but *symboulion* is rare. *symbouleuō* often
translates *yāʿaṣ*, to advise. *symboulos* is used once of a person who might give
advice to God (Isa. 40:13), the thought, however, being the inappropriateness of
attempting to counsel God. God has no need of a heavenly council of advisers.
(On this passage see R. N. Whybray, *The Heavenly Counsellor in Isaiah XL 13–14*,
1971.)

NT The words are mostly employed in secular senses in the NT. *symbouleuō* is used
of the evil plots of the Jews against Jesus and the early church (Matt. 26:4; Jn.
18:14; Acts 9:23), but also of the good advice given by Christ to the church at
Laodicea (Rev. 3:18). *symboulion* can be used concretely of the panel of advisers
(Lat. *consilium*) employed by a Roman governor (Acts 25:12; cf. Jos. *Ant.* 14, 192;
16, 163; cf. Philo's reference to *synedroi*, *Leg.* 244, 254, 350). Matt. uses the phrase
symboulion lambanein, a Latinism equivalent to *consilium capere*, to resolve, with
reference to the machinations of the Jewish authorities against Jesus (12:14; 22:15;
27:1, 7; 28:12). The similar phrase *symboulion didonai* (Mk. 3:6) has the same
meaning. *symboulion poiein* (Mk. 15:1 B *Byz;* UBS) can mean to resolve or to hold
a meeting (the variant *symboulion hetoimazein* (Aleph *pc;* BFBS) means to make a
decision), but the phraseology leaves it uncertain whether a second, morning
meeting of the sanhedrin took place. *symboulos* occurs in a quotation of Isa. 40:13
in Rom. 11:34; the rhetorical question stresses the transcendent and incomprehensible character of God's wisdom. *I. H. Marshall*

| συνέδριον | συνέδριον (*synedrion*), council, sanhedrin.

CL *synedrion* is a Gk. word related to *synedros* (*syn, hedra*), one who sits with
somebody else, sc. in a council, and *synedreuō*, to sit in council. Originally it
meant the place where a council met, then the body of councillors or their actual
meeting. It was used of various official bodies (including courts) and served to
render Latin *senatus* into Gk.

OT The word is used a dozen times in the LXX, but with no fixed significance. Jos.
uses it for various councils and courts, but the most important from the NT
point of view is as a technical term for the supreme Jewish council. The body
which guided Jewish affairs in Jerusalem from an uncertain point after the return
from the exile was an aristocratic council of priests and lay leaders, originally
termed a *gerousia* (Josephus, *Ant.*, 2, 138; Acts 5:21; cf. Moulton–Milligan, 124;
literally, a council of old men). Its rights were curtailed under the Hasmoneans,
and in the reign of Alexandra the scribes of the Pharisaic party gained seats on it.
The earliest use of the term *synedrion* in this sense occurs in a decree of Gabinius
(57–55 B.C.) which mentions five such bodies in different areas of Palestine (Josephus
Ant., 14, 91; *War*, 1, 170). Slightly later the Jerusalem council gained authority
over the whole country and was regularly called *synedrion*, even by the Jews themselves who took the word over in the Hebrew/Aramaic form *sanhedrîn* (hence
English "sanhedrin").

It was composed of 71 members with the high priest as chairman and included
the heads of the chief priestly families (or leading priestly officials), leaders of the

lay aristocracy (the "elders") and a number of scribes; the first two groups stood together as the → Sadducean party, while the third group was → Pharisaic in outlook. The membership appears to have been self-perpetuating. The sanhedrin was essentially a court charged with the maintenance of Jewish customs. It could impose the death sentence, but (except in rare circumstances) the Romans retained the right of actually inflicting the penalty (Jn. 18:31). We do not know how it functioned in NT times, since the rules for procedure in the Mishnah reflect Pharisaic ideals rather than the actual Sadducean practice.

There were also smaller Jewish courts known by the same name outside Jerusalem to exercise jurisdiction among Jewish communities both in Palestine and the Diaspora. The Mishnah lays down a membership of 23 persons for them.

NT In the NT Christians are warned that they may be summoned to bear witness before such local courts and even to be sentenced to scourging by them (Matt. 10:17; par. Mk. 13:9). Jesus said that a person who is angry with his brother (→ Anger) is liable to judgment by the sanhedrin, thus indicating metaphorically that the sin of anger is as culpable as the crime of murder for which a person would be tried by the sanhedrin (Matt. 5:21 f.).

The majority of references to the sanhedrin are in connection with its proceedings against Jesus and the early church. From an early point in his ministry the sanhedrin determined that Jesus must be put away (Jn. 11:47), and it seized the opportunity given by Judas at the passover to arrest Jesus and try him (Lk. 22:66; Mk. 14:55 (par. Matt. 26:59); 15:1). The historical problems raised by this account cannot be raised here (see bibliography). The theological significance of the sanhedrin is that it is seen as the focus of the opposition of the Jewish leadership to Jesus. This opposition continued towards the early church (Acts 4; 5:17 ff.; 6:8 ff.; 22:30–23:10, 20, 28; 24:20), but according to Acts the Pharisees took a more favourable position towards the early church.   *I. H. Marshall*

E. Bammel, ed., *The Trial of Jesus*, 1970; J. Blinzler, *The Trial of Jesus*, 1959 (much fuller: *Der Prozess Jesu*, 1969[4]); D. R. Catchpole, *The Trial of Jesus*, 1971; J. Jeremias, *Jerusalem in the Time of Jesus*, 1969; E. Lohse, *TDNT* VII 860–871; S. Safrai, M. Stern *et al.*, eds., *The Jewish People in the First Century*, I, 1974; E. Schürer, II, 1, 163–195; N. B. Stonehouse, *Paul before the Areopagus*, 1957, 41–69; P. Winter, *On the Trial of Jesus*, (1969) 1974[2].

Courage, Boldness

τολμάω

τολμάω (tolmaō), be brave, dare, risk; τολμηρός (tolmēros), confident, bold, audacious; τολμητής (tolmētēs) arrogant.

CL With a basic sense of doing or bearing that which is fearful or difficult, the vb., adj. and noun are well exemplified classically, embracing the related ideas of patience, submissiveness, courage and daring (in good sense of "brave enough" and in the bad sense of "rash, foolhardy enough").

OT Only the vb. is exemplified in the LXX. Twice in Esther it has the sense of "to have the affrontery to" (1:18; 7:5) and in Job 15:12 (where Heb. uses *lāqaḥ* as in Prov. 6:25 in the sense "to take captive, to enslave, with consequent loss of moral and rational status") it implies "what rashness does your heart suggest?"

NT NT usage is much more varied and flexible than LXX and reflects the wider interests of classical writers. The single occurrence of the noun (*tolmētēs*) is clearly in the bad sense indicated above, the "arrogant" man of 2 Pet. 2:10 who brooks no restriction on self-will and recognizes no authority to which he will be answerable. The single case of the comparative adverb (*tolmēroteron*, from *tolmēros*, Rom. 15:15) is, however, in a good sense: the confidence proper to a person who is sure of his ground. The vb. swings freely between these two points, but for the most part it moves in the realm of the moral rather than the physical. It describes the sheer courage of Joseph in asking the body of Jesus (Mk. 15:43) and the cowardice of those who shrank from joining the early church (Acts 5:13); the true moral propriety of Moses who dared not gaze on God (Acts 7:32) and of Paul who asserted the courage of his convictions in relation to Corinthian opponents (2 Cor. 10:2; cf. Jude 9); and the moral impropriety of questioning the unimpeachable evidence of the resurrection (Jn. 21:12) or of taking a fellow Christian to law (1 Cor. 6:1). Moral and physical courage are both involved in Matt. 22:46 and parallels, a meaning combining both "did not have the face to" and "did not have the gall to". It has the strongest sense of "putting oneself at risk" in Rom. 5:7, and a weak but similar sense in Rom. 15:18; 2 Cor. 10:12; 11:21, where it is little more than a conventional politeness: "to venture to." *J. A. Motyer*

→ Openness, art. *parrhēsia*

G. Fitzer, *tolmaō* etc., *TDNT* VIII 181–6.

Covenant, Guarantee, Mediator

This article examines the terms *covenant, guarantee,* and *mediator* which are all used in the Bible to describe the relationship between God and man established by the covenant.

διαθήκη

διαθήκη (*diathēkē*), covenant.

CL The term *diathēkē* occurs from Democritus and Aristoph. onwards in the sense of a will or testament. It is not thought to be derived from the act. *diatithēmi*, distribute, allocate, regulate, but only from the mid. *diatithemai*, control persons and things (Xen.), and especially dispose of by will (so private legal documents among papyri). It denotes, therefore, an irrevocable decision, which cannot be cancelled by anyone. A prerequisite of its effectiveness before the law is the death of the disposer. Hence *diathēkē* must be clearly distinguished from *synthēkē*, an agreement. In the latter two partners engaged in common activity accept reciprocal obligations. *diathēkē* is found only once with this meaning (Aristoph. *Birds*, 1, 440). Elsewhere it always means a one-sided action.

OT 1. In the LXX *diathēkē* is the commonest rendering (270 times) for Heb. *berît*, covenant. This is the common OT word for a wide variety of agreements.

(a) They include a covenant between two friends (1 Sam. 18:3), which however was regarded as having legal force (1 Sam. 20:8); a covenant between two rulers

365

fixing their spheres of interest (Gen. 21:22 ff.; 26:26 ff.; 1 Ki. 5:12, MT 5:26), or terms of peace (1 Ki. 20:34); the covenant between two kings which, of course, included their peoples. Two tribes could also make a covenant (Jos. 15:9). It is even used for a covenant between Israel and its slaves (Jer. 34:8 ff.). ([Tr.] The natural meaning of the Heb. is that it was a covenant between the king and the slave owners.)

(b) The situation was somewhat different when the king made a covenant with his subjects (2 Ki. 11:4; [Tr.] this was probably a private agreement between Jehoiada and the royal guard); or when by the covenant a man became the subject of the other (1 Sam. 11:1). The covenant made by Abner with David (2 Sam. 3:12 f.) was intended to make all Israel (v. 21) subject to David, not merely Abner.

(c) Yahweh's covenants with Noah (Gen. 6:18), Abraham (2 Ki. 13:23), or David (Jer. 33:21) are similar. Here the covenant extends explicitly to their descendants (Gen. 9:8 ff.; 15:18; cf. 2 Sam. 7:12–16), and becomes a covenant with Israel (Exod. 6:4 f.). But in Jer. 50:5 the covenant can also be interpreted as a covenant of Israel with its God. Ezek. 16:8 speaks of a covenant with Jerusalem. Linguistically the LXX might have used *synthēkē* in the examples under (a) (cf. CL above). But in the latter cases *bᵉrît* is used to denote the one's disposition of the many (Gen. 9:12; 17:7 f.; Jer. 31:31–34, etc.). Hence the LXX translation *diathēkē* has its full force. On the other hand, there are exceptional usages like Yahweh's covenant with day and night (Jer. 33:25), and Jerusalem's with death (Isa. 28:14–18).

(d) Earlier scholars used to distinguish between secular and religious covenants but the variety of covenant conceptions, all using the same terminology, makes this impossible. Moreover, the most secular of covenants presupposes that it has been witnessed by God (Gen. 31:44–50; 1 Sam. 23:18), while in the most religious covenants Yahweh remains comparable with a monarch making a covenant. For the OT a separation between religious and secular is unthinkable.

2. This situation has made many ask whether there was not some original and unambiguous idea of the covenant, from which the others developed. Modern research has produced four answers. (i) J. Pedersen considered that originally the two sides in the covenant stood on an equality. (ii) J. Begrich, on the other hand, maintained that the covenant started as something the stronger granted to the weaker. (iii) G. E. Mendenhall found the religio-historical background in the Hittite suzerainty treaties, and deduced that the treaty element was the most important in the covenant. (iv) M. Noth has drawn attention to the most recent textual finds, which show that the covenant was mediated by a third party between the two sides. It is impossible to prove that any one of these elements was original, or that any came later. God's covenant and the people's covenant are mentioned in Exod. 34; the individual and the royal covenant in 2 Sam. 3. We cannot at present decide on any original form for the covenant.

3. Since all these concepts were expressed by the one term *bᵉrît*, the Jews must have felt some unity behind them. Though neither the relationship of the covenant partners nor the contents of the covenant agreement provided this, it has been shown that there was a common pattern in the making of a covenant (Baltzer, see bibliography). There were 6 vital elements in such a ceremony: (i) the preamble mentioning the names of the partners; (ii) a preliminary history of the relationship

of those entering the covenant; (iii) a basic declaration about the future relationship of the partners; (iv) details of the new relationship; (v) an invocation of the respective gods worshipped by both sides to act as witnesses; (vi) a pronouncement of curse and blessing. Baltzer traced this outline right down to the Qumran documents, and even into and beyond the NT. This shows that at least outwardly the covenant conception is as fundamental an element in biblical thought as it is in the national existence of Israel.

4. When we approach them from the standpoint of the covenant, we see how very diverse elements in OT tradition belong together. The preamble is suggestive of the way in which Yahweh introduces himself (cf. Exod. 20:2, which, as in the covenant formula, is followed by a survey of past events). This seems to be the source of Israel's unique interest in its history, which is seen to be Yahweh's history with it, and hence covenant history and so salvation history. The third section reflects the thought which found its clearest expression in Isa. as proclamation of salvation, the promise of divine faithfulness and peace (Isa. 54:10; 55:3). Since this promise cannot be revoked because of the disobedience of the people, God has proclaimed himself bound and has renounced all arbitrariness. "The basis is thus laid for the Gospel" (G. Quell, *TDNT* II 123). When we compare these covenant promises and those in Jer. 31 with (e.g.) the formula of the Sinai covenant we realize that the details mentioned in 3 (iv) above are not to be understood as a condition to be first fulfilled which would be followed by a reward for achievement. This impression might be given by passages like Lev. 26:15 f. and Deut. 31:20. They are rather the regulations for the new life that is made possible by God's covenant (cf. Gen. 9:9; 15:13–16; Jer. 31:31). As in Deut. 26, Israel's reflection on its past history and the law belong together as instruction for its new life.

5. The relationship of the partners in the covenant is expressed by *ḥeseḏ*, God's covenant loyalty (RSV steadfast love; NEB love, loyalty, constancy). 1 Sam. 20:8 understands it as protective action. Man's remembrance of the covenant expresses itself in action (Ps. 103:17 f.). Both partners – Yahweh and the covenant people, represented only by an individual – face one another in the *bᵉrîṯ*. They are thus in an active and real partnership (Pedersen), and so they both share in the covenant meal (Gen. 31:54; Exod. 24:9 ff.). It goes without saying that this strengthens the → fellowship of those involved. This does not mean to say that the covenant and its renewal were purely cultic acts. It can hardly be denied that it had a place in the cultus (Ps. 50). This seems to have been especially the case in Shechem (Jos. 8:30–35; 23:24). The relationship to Baal-berith or El-berith, formerly worshipped there, has never been satisfactorily explained (Jdg. 8:33; 9:4, 46). Nevertheless, the covenant belongs in the first place to the daily life of the tribes of the covenant people, which it seems to have steadily separated from the cultus. This may be seen in Deut. with its covenant theology and secularization of life. The cultus could not guarantee the continuance of an intact, everlasting covenant. Yahweh alone, as founder of this covenant, could guarantee its continuance and with it the cultus in its true meaning. Only he could renew the covenant broken by human disobedience.

This explains why in many prophets the thought of the covenant virtually vanishes in favour of the call to obedience. The early parts of Isa. avoided – obviously

367

deliberately – the concept of covenant almost entirely, the only exceptions being 24:5; 33:8 and the covenant with death mentioned earlier (28:15, 18). Hosea probably felt the danger of a one-sided appeal to the legal character of the covenant, and so he preferred to describe God's relationship to his people by the picture of marriage. The *bᵉrît* is mentioned only as broken in 6:7; 8:1; in 10:4; 12:1(2) it refers to human agreements. Jeremiah stressed his expectation of a completely new covenant in the place of the one that had been broken (31:31–34). Whatever continuity there may be is created solely by Yahweh. It is completely other in that the direct working of God on human hearts through his Spirit takes the place of the demand for obedience. This shows how deep the break is, and prepares the way for the NT.

([Ed.] There is, however, an essential continuity, for Jeremiah does not speak of the abolition of the law. Rather, he declares: "But this is the covenant which I will make with the house of Israel after those, says the Lord: I will put my law within them, and I will write it upon their hearts; and I will be their God, and they shall be my people" (Jer. 31:33). There is here the same divine upholding of the covenant that is found elsewhere in the OT (see 4, above). The covenant relationship is summed up in the promise, "I will be your God, and you shall be my people" (cf. Exod. 6:7; Lev. 26:12; Jer. 7:23; 11:4; 30:22; 32:38; 2 Cor. 6:16; Heb. 8:10; Rev. 21:3). For Jeremiah, this relationship is to be realized not by setting aside the law but by a more personal application of it.)

6. The standard expression in the OT, *kārat bᵉrît*, to cut, i.e. make, a covenant, is probably to be explained by Gen. 15:9 f., 17 and Jer. 34:18. ([Tr.] It is not the only expression used, and it does not seem to have been essential for the making of a covenant.) It is expressed in the LXX by *diathēkēn diatithemai*, to establish a *diathēkē*. The Gk. understanding of the term *diathēkē* suggests that the covenant was no longer an agreement between two parties with equal rights. It came about as an exclusively divine action, which men can only accept in the form in which it is given to them. However, the LXX is supported by the Heb. expression *hēqîm bᵉrît*, which occurs frequently after the exile, and means "to establish a covenant". The apocryphal books carry this further. Philo worked out an allegorical exegesis of the thought of a will. The rabbis confined the covenant to the concept of an absolute law.

The Qumran community attributed great importance to the covenant. They considered that the promise of the new covenant (Jer. 31:31–34) had been fulfilled in their midst and called themselves "the new covenant in the land of Damascus" (CD 6:19). While the Sinaitic covenant was for the whole people, the Qumran covenanters considered themselves to be its holy remnant, the pure, eschatological community of the age of salvation. This explains their strict rules for receiving new members and their commitment to the "laws of the covenant (i.e. the Law as it was expounded by the community) which characterized the community. The sect's eschatological thinking on the covenant distinguished them especially from the rabbis, who equated the covenant with circumcision and saw its preservation guaranteed by a rigorous keeping of the Mosaic Law, and who expected the fulfilment of Jer. 31:31–34 only in the future. ([Tr.] In fact, probably owing to polemics against Qumran and Jewish Christianity, the new covenant plays virtually no role in Talmudic Jud.)

NT It is noteworthy that while covenant is found almost 300 times in the OT, it occurs only 33 times in the NT. Almost half of these instances come in quotations from the OT, and another 5 clearly look back to OT statements. The few independent cases are almost exclusively in Heb., quite rarely in Paul (never in the Pastorals) and Acts, and never in the Johannine writings.

In accord with this, *diatithemai* (only mid.), order, enact, dispose, is found only twice in the Lukan writings and four times in Heb., each time clearly looking back to the OT. In the 2 cases where the standard Gk. meaning of "will" plays a part (Heb. 9:16; Gal. 3:15) it is easy to recognize the intention of helping the Greeks to understand the OT concept. Paul makes this explicit.

These statistics are, however, misleading. The covenant question in the NT cannot be answered solely from the passages where the word is used. It involves a whole complex of theological ideas including covenant terminology. There are 3 groups of problems: (1) the question of the Lord's Supper; (2) the Pauline question about the relationship of the Christian church to Israel as the people of God; (3) the covenant theology in Heb.

1. In all 4 NT passages dealing with the Lord's Supper *diathēkē* plays an important part: 1 Cor. 11:25; Mk. 14:24; Matt. 26:28; Lk. 22:20 (omitted in some MSS and RSV and NEB). Each time it is in connection with the cup, and only there. Paul and Lk. add the adj. "new". This gives a new stress, which hides to some extent the link with the blood, in contrast with the original formula preserved in Matt., Mk., "the blood of the covenant". The use of this formula together with "shed" or "poured out" makes clear beyond question the reference to the covenant blood of the OT (cf. Exod. 24:5–8) and with it the covenant which Yahweh made with Israel. This means that, in the Christian *kērygma* and witness, the work of Jesus was, according to his own word, a taking up and fulfilling of the covenant statements of the OT. Schniewind is, therefore, fully justified in pointing out that "Jer. 31:31–34 can be heard in every variation of the words over the cup" and that the prophetic promise finds fulfilment here.

If the term covenant (*diathēkē*) does not appear as often as one might expect, the reason is that the underlying thought has been taken over in the sayings about the → kingdom of God. Linguistically we can see this perhaps most clearly in Lk. 22:29 in the phrase *diatithemai . . . basileian*, appoint a kingdom, which exactly expresses the formula *diatithemai diathēkēn* (see above OT 6). The new covenant and the kingdom of God are correlated concepts.

In the OT the common meal followed the completion of the covenant by the sprinkling of the people with blood after its pledge (Exod. 24:8 ff.), because the covenant had been made with a people that was already united. In the NT such a single, united people cannot be presupposed. The new people of God is derived rather from that which until then was no people (Rom. 9:25; 1 Pet. 2:10, quoting Hos. 2:23(25)). It is composed of the "many" who have come to share the atoning power of Jesus' blood through his word and spirit (Matt. 20:28; Mk. 10:45). The fellowship of the early Christians based on the word found expression in the common meal (1 Cor. 10:16b, 17; Acts 2:46), which has its counterpart in the first part of the Lord's Supper.

As in the old covenant curse and blessing played a part, so there is also in the new covenant an indication of the curse (1 Cor. 11:27–32; cf. 12:3). Just as one could keep the old covenant only if one knew its ordinances, so in the Lord's Supper repetition is expressly intended to produce remembrance (*anamnēsis*, 1 Cor. 11:25). Not long after this entire Christian writings like the *Didache* were moulded by the theology of the Lord's Supper and show the structure of the covenant ritual. It is only a development of a connection that is already obvious here.

2. It is not easy to formulate Paul's attitude to the old people of God.

(a) Paul himself can use only the term "mystery" (→ *mystērion*, secret) for the Jewish rejection of Jesus and their enmity to the gospel and the church (Rom. 11:25). He does so in "great sorrow and unceasing anguish" (Rom. 9:2). He was so deeply moved by this subject, that his delineation of the righteousness of God given through Christ (Rom. 1–8) of necessity passed over to a presentation of the inexplicable hardening of Israel, which nevertheless is to lead to salvation in God's will (Rom. 9–11, especially 11:11–16). This account reaches its climax in praise of the unfathomable depths of the divine action (Rom. 11:33–36). In it Paul appeals to the fact that Israel's rejection and unfaithfulness cannot cancel God's covenant. He also knows that there is a fellowship between Israel and the church which cannot be removed, because it is based on the unity of the One who calls. In other words, God's people from now on includes the church and Israel.

(b) In the light of this, Paul considers the fact that a part of Israel has been hardened (Rom. 11:25). The expression "a hardening *has come upon* Israel" (*tō Israēl gegonen*) suggests that it has happened through God's will. God promised Israel in his covenant that sin would be completely blotted out and that all obstacles between God and man would be removed without trace. This is the force of the quotation from Isa. 59:20 f. in Rom. 11:26 f. It is, therefore, obvious that the fulfilment of this covenant promise is still to be awaited, so long as the obstacle of the hardening still exists. Since God's covenant has not reached complete fulfilment or has been cancelled or repented of by him (Rom. 11:29), the promise will be fulfilled with regard to the remnant of Israel.

(c) To make this clearer still, in Gal. 3:15 Paul examined the Gk. concept of a will that could not be annulled. If a human will cannot be annulled, how much less can God's covenant with Israel (3:17), through which it has such incomparable privileges (Rom. 9:4 f.), of which Paul the Christian can boast again and again (Rom. 11:1; 2 Cor. 11:22; Phil. 3:5)?

If God's covenant with Abraham, which consists of the promise, has come into force (Gal. 3:16), something which came in later as an addition to it (Rom. 5:20), the law (Gal. 3:17), cannot narrow this promise or annul it. In the opinion of the present writer, Paul could hardly mean the law which according to OT conceptions belonged to the covenant by its very nature, and thus must be regarded as an ordinance (see above OT 4). Hence it is no more in contradiction with the covenant of grace as the OT is with the NT. Paul is thinking rather of the law as seen by late Jud., and the rabbis and understood as something in its own right and absolute (see above OT 6). This mass of inexplicable regulations, which simply have to be fulfilled, has been annulled by Christ (Rom. 10:4), because it was only a *paidagōgos*, custodian (RSV), tutor (NEB), "until Christ came" (Gal. 3:24). The law of God itself is not evil, but "holy and just and good" (Rom. 7:12). It belongs to the Sinaitic covenant (Gal. 4:24), not to the Abrahamic covenant (Gal. 4:23, the picture of the two women representing two covenants). Hence it cannot bring salvation. The one who clings to it remains a slave child (Gal. 4:25). Christians, on the other hand, are children of the promise (Gal. 4:26 ff.) and hence free, and belong to Christ without any distinctions (Gal. 3:26 ff.).

([Ed.] The identification of the law here with the elaborations of late Judaism is not the most obvious interpretation of the references cited. The argument about circumcision and keeping the law in Rom. and Gal. does not suggest that Paul is arguing against a particular rabbinic interpretation. Rather, he is arguing that man cannot use the ordinances of God to establish his own righteousness. Man is saved by the grace of God through Christ's atoning death. Paul does not attack the ordinances of the law as such, but the assumption that man becomes righteous through conformity with certain tenets. Such an attitude of mind implies that it is in man's power to keep the entire law. It betrays a profound lack of awareness of the deep-rooted character of sin and its seriousness in the eyes of God. The Christian, Paul argues, must not relapse into a legalistic frame of mind, for righteousness is the free gift of God in Christ.)

3. We have been seeing how the covenant concept stands in its relationship to the → Law, the → Promise, and the people of God, but we have to turn to Heb. for a developed covenant theology (*diathēkē* is mentioned 17 times). Since the high-priestly office of Christ is "the prevailing conception of Hebrews' Christology", it expresses the new covenant in a cultic setting, which reflects the author's intense concern for "purification, sanctification, perfection" and also sacrifice, atonement and blood (W. G. Kümmel, *Introduction to the New Testament*, 1966, 277). He clearly contrasts the old and the new covenants. The new is the better covenant (cf. 7:22 *kreittōn*, superior). Its guarantor and mediator is Christ (8:6; 12:24) through his death for the redemption from the sins of the old covenant (9:5). It is against this background of blemish that the prophetic promise of Jer. 31:31–34, twice quoted (8:8–12; 10:16 f.), becomes important and is developed. By the very promise of the new covenant the old has been declared obsolete by God himself, and so it is ready to vanish away (8:13). This does not mean that it has been completely ruled out, but that it has been overtaken and fulfilled by the new. In Christ the pattern (*typos*, 8:5) and "the true form" (*eikōn*, 10:1) of the one covenant concept has become a reality. The new covenant is founded on better promises (8:6; 9:15), but like the old covenant it is a covenant in blood (10:29; 12:24; 13:20). It is not, however, the blood of a sacrificial animal, but the blood of the sacrificer himself, the high priest (9:13 ff.; 10:12 ff.). Hence the death of Christ was essential, for only through the death of the testator does his will become operative in law (9:16 f.; cf. above CL).

Seeing that the forgiveness of sins and renewal of heart promised in Jer. 31:31–34 has become a reality in Christ (Heb. 10:16 ff.), the old covenant is explained as a shadow of that to come. In the new it has been annulled in the sense that it has become "obsolete" and "superfluous". On the other hand, the Pauline tension over the problem of Israel's hardening has disappeared here. That which Paul could only proclaim in his praise of God's mystery (Rom. 11:33–36) is presented in Heb. in an almost rationalistic and comprehensive manner. This can be explained probably only because the author of Heb. faces the old covenant more theoretically, while Paul, in spite of all, knows and confesses that he belongs to it.

([Ed.] Many scholars would dissent from the writer's conclusions here. It is not that the author of Heb. presents everything more rationalistically than Paul. Indeed, he refrains from speculating about the future of Israel and does not discuss the problems that Paul wrestled with. Instead, his warnings against the danger of rejecting Christ come like a refrain throughout his work (3:7–19; 4:1–13; 6:4–8; 10:26 ff., 38 f.; 12:1–29). Conscious of the judgments which befell the rebellious and hardened in Israel, he warns his readers against deliberate, conscious sin. For him there is a point beyond which a man cannot return. That point cannot be defined in advance. The safeguard against falling into condemnation is summed up in the quotation from Ps. 95:7 f., "Today, when you hear his voice, do not harden your hearts" (Heb. 3:7, 15; 4:7).)   *J. Guhrt*

| ἔγγυος | ἔγγυος (*engyos*), guarantor. |

CL & OT *engyos* is derived from the verb *engyaō* pledge, engage. As an adj., it means offering surety, and so becomes a noun meaning guarantee or guarantor. The *arrabōn* pledge (→ Gift) applied to things: *engyos*, surety, guarantee, may be applied to persons. The *engyos* guaranteed that a legal obligation would be carried out. This could lead even to risking his life for another (Sir. 29:15). Metaphorically in 2 Macc. 10:28 reliance upon the Lord is the pledge of victory. In many religions when an oath was taken, a god was called on to act as guarantor (A. Oepke, *TDNT*, IV 603).

NT *engyos* is found in the NT only in Heb. 7:22, though it has an obvious par. in 8:6, where *mesitēs*, mediator (see below), stands instead of it. 7:22 is to be linked with v. 20. Here the usual procedure with an oath (see above CL/OT) has been reversed. For man has not named God as guarantor, but God has placed the man Jesus as guarantor for the new divine dispensation (*diathēkē*), which has the → promise (8:6 *epangelia*) as its content. Paul expresses the fact by saying that the Holy Spirit comes to us on earth, i.e. to the church of Christ, as the heavenly gift and pledge (*arrabōn*) of our redemption (2 Cor. 1:22; Eph. 1:14). Heb. does it by showing that, after Jesus had offered the vicarious sacrifice of himself, he ascended to God in heaven, where he now acts as the guarantor and representative of those who are still on earth awaiting the rest promised to the people of God (4:9). This can hardly be taken to mean that he is a guarantor before God for our faith and obedience. He is rather a guarantee to those who believe God's promise and know that it has been accomplished in Christ, though they do not yet see its fulfilment. This guarantee is anchored as our hope (6:19) in his twofold and unrepeatable work: his offering up of himself (7:27), and his entrance into the sanctuary (9:12). Through it our sanctification (10:10) has been accomplished once for all. In this way he links our future perfection with his already achieved perfection.

O. Becker

| μεσίτης | μεσίτης (*mesitēs*), mediator, intermediary, guarantor. |

CL *mesitēs*, mediator, is a Hel. formation, found from Polyb. on, derived from adj. *mesos*, in the middle (cf. *politēs* derived from *polis*). Hence *mesitēs* means one who finds himself between two bodies or parties. The vb. *mesiteuō*, to function as a mediator, is derived from the sub. (cf. *politeuō* derived from *politēs*).

1. Already in cl. Gk. *mesos* has become a legal term with the meaning of the neutral (cf. Lat. *neuter*, neither of two) place between two parties in conflict, occupied by the arbitrator who seeks to judge and settle (Homer *Il.* 23, 574). "We look for the judge as *mesos* (the man who stands in the middle), and call him *mesidios*" (the later Hel. *mesitēs*) (Aristot. *Eth. Nic.* 1132a, 22 f.). This may be compared with 1 Cor. 6:5: "Can it be that there is no man among you wise enough to decide *ana meson tou adelphou autou*, between his brother," i.e. between one and another of his brothers.

At first there was the ceremonial of coming between the two parties, and this is the origin of the later concept of the mediator stepping in as a neutral third party. This gave *mesitēs* in legal terminology a wide range of meaning. He could be the conciliator or arbitrator in cases that had not yet come before a court of law, so as to prevent this happening. He could be the administrator or trustee for something in dispute. He was also the witness to legal business that had been settled with the responsibility of guaranteeing that the decision would be carried out. He could be a pawnbroker and sometimes a guarantor (→ *engyos*), who guarantees the liabilities of another with his own property.

2. The vb. *mesiteuō* points to another function of a mediator, that of a negotiator, appointed by one side to establish a link with the other side and so negotiate appropriate terms (e.g. in a peace treaty).

OT 1. (a) There is no single term for a mediator in OT, either in Heb. or Gk. The comprehensive Gk. term *mesitēs* is found in the LXX only in Job. 9:33 in an inaccurate rendering. The Heb. *môkîaḥ* (RSV umpire) is rendered here *elenchōn*, the convictor, which is close to the basic Heb. meaning. It was not really a question of arbitrating between the two parties, but of listening to accusation and defence and restoring the infringed law by dealing with the guilty party – unless of course the accusation was rejected. Thus the relationship between the parties was restored. In Israel there was no civil code which would function by upholding a golden mean between conflicting interests. There was only divine law, which bound together the members of the people as fellow-men. It was ultimately God who chastened and judged (cf. Ps. 6:1 (MT 5:2)). Hence there could hardly be any real difference between an arbitrator and an official judge in Israel.

(b) The negotiator, representative, Heb. *mēlîṣ*, probably originally meant spokesman (2 Chr. 32:31). In Gen. 42:23 it means interpreter.

(c) All this means that we cannot find the concept of mediator in the OT. Where the term appears, it means something quite different from the concept in the Gk. world. The → priest and → prophet were mediators between God and his people, though never in the role of a neutral third party. This is less true of the king, for it is only in his future role as Messiah that he is the mediator of salvation for Israel. Two mediators stand out in Israel's history. One comes at the beginning and the other is eschatological. → Moses mediated salvation at the Red Sea (Exod. 14:15–18). He was the mediator of the covenant at Sinai (Exod. 24:4–8) and as such of the → law and of → revelation (Exod. 33:7–11). These thoughts occur again in the eschatological picture of the awaited Servant of Yahweh (→ Son of God) in Isa.

He is the bearer of God's revelation (Isa. 42:1–4). God makes him the bearer of salvation to the nations (Isa. 49:1–6). He takes the guilt of men upon himself and blots it out by his suffering (Isa. 52:13–53:12).

2. In post-biblical Heb. and Aram. *sarsōr* means middle man, negotiator, interpreter. It acquires a theological meaning when applied to Moses who is the mediator *par excellence* of the Torah to the nation (SB III 556). Jewish literature shows, however, surprisingly little interest in the Servant of Yahweh ([Tr.] This, if we may judge from Qumran, is a deliberate counter to Jewish-Christian propaganda.) Philo uses *mesiteuō* to express the activity of the invisible God and of the Logos (→ Word), who is also called *mesitēs*. But this epithet is also applied to the angels and Moses.

3. The concept of mediation belongs to the essential nature of all religions, both in man's relationship to the divine (e.g. priests, sacral kingship, prophets) and in man's relationship to his fellow man (e.g. law, truth, a god called on to act as witness, mediator and guarantor of oaths). Yet both in the ancient world and later we can hardly find a theology which makes the concept of mediation as such central. On the other hand, there were various mediating figures like Mithras in the Persian mystery religions who was a familiar figure for the Hel. world. The concept of mediator became pivotal for Calvin (cf. *Institutes*, II 12–17), but it is already prominent in Thomas Aquinas (*Summa Theologiae*, III QQ 16–26).

NT The vb. occurs only once in the NT (Heb. 6:17) and there it has God as its subject. The noun occurs only 6 times. (a) As applied to Christ, *mesitēs* is qualified by the gen. → *diathēkēs*, of a covenant (of a better covenant, Heb. 8:6; of a new covenant, Heb. 9:15; 12:24), or by the gen. *theou kai anthrōpou*, between God and men (1 Tim. 2:5). (b) It also refers to another figure who once mediated the law (Gal. 3:13 f.).

For us it is a familiar thought that Jesus is the mediator between God and man, but the fact that this concept appears so seldom in the NT raises the question whether we are justified in seeing in Jesus "the fulfilment of the mediator concept as such" (A. Oepke, *TDNT* IV 624).

1. In Gal. 3:19 f. the word *mesitēs* appears to have depreciatory overtones. According to Paul, in company with many rabbis (SB III 554 ff.), the law was not given directly by the one God, but by many cosmic powers (→ Angel). A mediator, Moses, between this multitude and the people was, therefore, necessary. The age of the law, and so of Moses and the powers he represented, was brought to an end by Christ, who had been referred to in the promise given 430 years before the giving of the law. Unlike Moses he is not a mediator, nor a representative of the promise, but its fulfilment. Hence the age of the mediator has passed and that of the Son has come (Gal. 4:4; cf. Jn. 1:17).

2. In Hebrews *mesitēs* has an entirely different meaning. Here we are concerned with "the surety for our attaining the heavenly homeland" (E. Käsemann). The promise which underlies this surety is expressed in the new covenant (*diathēkē*). In Heb. this always denotes the right instituted by God through Christ for liberation from death and sin. *mesitēs*, like *diathēkē*, has a legal function, and describes the one who procures and guarantees that right. On the one hand, this right is "legally secured" (8:6 NEB) by the promise given and, on the other hand, it is the

pre-supposition of the fulfilment of the promise (9:15), which in any case was "guaranteed" by God with an oath (6:17 NEB). *mesiteuō* accordingly does not mean mediate (cf. 7:20 ff., where the office of Jesus as high priest and guarantor are made dependent on this oath). Both from the meaning we have been led to give to *mesiteuō* and from the parallelism of 7:22 to 8:6 (*engyos* with *mesitēs*) we see that we have to give *mesitēs* the meaning of guarantor in Hebrews.

Moreover, *mesitēs* denotes the One who guarantees us salvation, both as its creator and giver. As the ever-present high priest, who has been exalted by his obedience, sufferings, death on the cross, and sacrifice accepted by God, he has by his own blood transformed the right of vengeance (Abel) into the right of forgiveness (12:24). He who believes this promise shares this right (4:3). Just as Heb. uses the terms *mesitēs* and *engyos* to express a legal guarantee for those who believe in Jesus Christ, so Paul uses a similar legal term, *arrabōn*, pledge (→ Gift) for the Holy Spirit.

3. If we should not translate *mesitēs* in Heb. by mediator, there remains only one passage in the NT where Jesus Christ is explicitly called a mediator between God and man, 1 Tim. 2:5. On the one hand, in Rom. 3:30 and Eph. 4:6 the unity of God is used as the foundation for showing the universality of salvation including Jews and Gentiles. On the other hand, in Gal. 3:12–19 and 2 Cor. 5:14 our whole salvation is found in the one man Jesus. The concept of mediator in 1 Tim. 2:4 ff. links the two closely. Just as in Gal. 3:19 f. the importance for salvation of Moses is rejected, because he was only a mediator, so in 1 Tim. 2:5 the importance of Moses and every other figure in salvation history is excluded, because Jesus Christ alone is the mediator between God and all men.

4. If there is then only one passage in the NT where Jesus Christ is called mediator in the full sense of the word, we still must ask whether there are not other passages where the same thought finds expression in other terms. The most obvious is probably Jn. 14:6, "I am the way . . . ." Matt. 11:25–30, especially v. 27, points the same way. But it excludes the thought of a mediator understood as though there were a bridge from man via Jesus to the Father. For the Son, i.e. the secret of the person of Jesus which includes his function as mediator, is known only by the Father.

This may be one reason why the NT is so reticent about the concept of mediation, using it only once in a way that excludes every other possible figure right back to Moses as a mediator between God and man. Where the figure of a mediator like the Servant of Yahweh in Isa., or titles like → priest, → prophet or king are taken over by the NT, Jesus is directly identified with them. This is never done so as to allow us to say that this figure or title tells us who Jesus is. The person and work of Jesus, revealed to us through his resurrection and exaltation, make it possible for us to recognize who is meant by this figure or title. We may express it by a paradox. Because Jesus is a mediator between God and men in this way, he does not fulfil the concept of mediator as generally understood. He has emptied all our preconceived ideas of mediation of their meaning for salvation. *O. Becker*

(a). B. W. Anderson, "The New Covenant and the Old," in B. W. Anderson, ed., *The Old Testament and the Christian Faith*, 1964, 225–42; K. Baltzer, *The Covenant Formulary in Old Testament, Jewish, and Early Christian Writings*, 1971; K. Barth, *CD* II, 2, 7 ff.; IV 1, 22–78; W. Beyerlin, *Origins and History of the Oldest Sinaitic Traditions*, 1965; C. Brown, *Karl Barth and the Christian Message*, 1967, 99–139; L. H. Brockington, *Ideas of Mediation between God and Man in the*

Apocrypha, 1962; G. W. Buchanan, *The Consequences of the Covenant*, 1970; R. E. Clements, *Prophecy and Covenant*, 1965; G. Dalman, *Jesus-Jeshua*, 1929, 86–184; W. Eichrodt, *Theology of the Old Testament*, I, 1961; F. C. Fensham, "The Covenant as Giving Expression to the Relationship between Old and New Testament," *TB* 22, 1971, 82–94; D. R. Hillers, *Covenant: The History of a Biblical Idea*, 1969; J. Jeremias, *The Eucharistic Words of Jesus*, 1966²; J. Jocz, *The Covenant: A Theology of Human Destiny*, 1968; M. G. Kline, *Treaty of the Great King*, 1963; "Dynastic Covenant," *WTJ* 23, 1960, 1–15; and "Law Covenant," *WJT* 27, 1964, 1–20; *The Structure of Biblical Authority*, 1972; D. J. McCarthy, *Treaty and Covenant: A Study in Form in the Ancient Documents and the Old Testament*, Analecta Biblica 21, 1963; and *Old Testament Covenant: A Survey of Current Opinions*, 1972 (extensive bibliography); G. E. Mendenhall, "Covenant," *IDB* I 714–23; and *Law and Covenant in Israel and the Ancient Near East*, 1955; A. R. Millard, "Covenant and Communion in First Corinthians," in W. W. Gasque and R. P. Martin, *Apostolic History and the Gospel*, 1970, 242–47; J. Muilenburg, "The Intercession of the Covenant Mediator (Exodus 33:1a, 12–17)" in P. R. Ackroyd and B. Lindars, *Words and Meanings: Essays Presented to David Winton Thomas*, 1968, 159–82; J. Murray, *The Covenant of Grace*, 1954; and articles on Covenant in *NBD*, 264–68; M. L. Newman, *The People of the Covenant*, 1965; M. Noth, "Old Testament Covenant-Making in the Light of a Text from Mari," and "The Laws in the Pentateuch" in *The Laws in the Pentateuch and Other Studies*, 1966, 108–117, 20–49; A. Oepke, *mesitēs, TDNT* IV 598–624; J. Pedersen, *Israel*, I–II, 1954², 263–310; J. Plastaras, *Creation and Covenant*, 1968; H. Preisker, *engyos, TDNT* II 330 ff.; G. Quell and J. Behm, *diatithēmi, diathēkē, TDNT* II 104–34; J. Schildenberg, "Covenant," *EBT* I 140–46; G. J. Wenham, "Legal Forms in the Book of the Covenant," *TB* 22, 1971, 95–102.

(b). J. Begrich, "Berit. Ein Beitrag zur Erfassung einer alttestamentlichen Denkform," *ZAW* 60, 1944, 1–11 (*Gesammelte Studien zum Alten Testament*, ed. W. Zimmerli, 1964, 55–66); O. Bückmann and W. Kasch, "Bund," *EKL* I, 618 ff.; H. Gottlieb, *To haima mou tēs diathēkēs, StTh* 14, 1960, 115 ff.; J. Hempel and L. Goppelt, "Bund," *RGG*³ I 1512 ff.; P. Karge, *Geschichte des Bundesgedankens im Alten Testament*, 1910; E. Kutsch, *bᵉrît, THAT* I, 339–52; O. Michel, *Der Brief an die Hebräer*, KEK 13, 1957¹⁰; W. L. Moran, "Moses und der Bundesschluss am Sinai," *Stimmen der Zeit*, 170, 1961–62, 120–33 (*Verbum Domini*, 40, 1962, 3–17); H. Graf Reventlow, "Prophetenamt und Mittleramt," *ZTK* 58, 1961, 269 ff.; L. Rost, *Das kleine Credo und andere Studien zum Alten Testament*, 1965; R. Smend, "Bundesformel," *ThSt* 68, 1963; H. W. Wolff, "Jahwe als Bundesvermittler," *VT* 6, 1956, 316–20.

Creation, Foundation, Creature, Maker

The term creation has a number of meanings in current usage. But it always refers to an act by which something which has not previously existed in this form is brought into being. In Gk. there are two groups of words which denote this idea. In both cases the terms can have many different shades of meaning which vary according to context. *katabolē* refers primarily to foundation, and thus can mean beginning, that which gives something direction and determination. *ktisis*, originally foundation, describes in a broad sense rather the process of becoming and coming into being, resulting from a decision of the will. But it also goes beyond the meaning of *katabolē* and denotes the result of such an act, the created thing as an entity. Although both groups of words are represented in the NT, the *ktizō* group is used much more in biblical statements about God's creative activity, both with regard to existence in general and as it concerns faith in particular.

| καταβολή | καταβολή (*katabolē*), foundation, beginning; καταβάλλω (*kataballō*), throw or strike down, found, ground. |

CL The vb. *kataballō* (Homer) derives its basic meaning from its two roots *kata*, down, and *ballein*, to throw. It thus means, to bring from an upright into a horizontal position (e.g. to throw down, fell to the ground, kill, throw away; or, in a fig. sense, to put down, disparage, reject, and also pay down). The meaning with which we are concerned, to lay a foundation, found, originate, is no exception. It is derived from ancient building technique, and refers to the throwing (or stacking) of stones into the foundation trench; or on rocky ground, the rolling, pushing and squaring of the vital cornerstones of the building. This was something more than the merely symbolic laying of a foundation stone today. The rarer and late noun *katabolē*, lit. laying down, chiefly takes up the fig. meaning. It can mean, payment (laying out) of certain sums of money, or the date by which payment must be made; the date of commencement for a building. In medical language it denotes an attack of fever (*pyretou*). Biologically it denotes the depositing of seed (*tou spermatos*) in the ground or mother, i.e. sowing or fertilization (cf. Aristot., *Problemata*, 20, 12).

katabolē refers also to an historical starting-point, e.g. in the phrase *katabolēn tēs staseōs poiein*, to start the quarrel. From Polybius (2nd cent. B.C.) onwards writers use the phrase *apo* or *ek katabolēs kosmou*, since the beginning of the world. Aristeas, 129 (before 100 B.C.), already uses *katabolē* absolutely in the sense of the creation as the totality of created things.

OT 1. The Heb. equivalents of the vb. *kataballō* are of no significance with regard to the concept of creation. In any case, they are lacking in 15 out of the 42 instances in the LXX. They belong chiefly to military language (to fell with the sword, to bring down city walls, etc.). This is also true of the non-canonical books. Only in 2 Macc. 2:13 does it have the sense of to found. Nehemiah is reported to have founded a library by collecting the ancient writings of Israel, i.e. he originated something.

2. The noun *katabolē* is found in the LXX only at 2 Macc. 2:29, in a *pars pro toto* expression. *architektoni tēs holēs katabolēs phrontisteon*, the master builder must be concerned with the whole construction.

3. Among inter-testamental writers Aristeas uses *katabolē* absolutely, as above mentioned. Philo speaks of the begetting of individuals as *tē prōtē katabolē tōn anthrōpōn* (*Op. Mund.*, 132). Josephus uses the noun in reporting an historical date in speaking of the *beginning* of the rebellion (*War*, 2, 260).

NT 1. In the NT only the noun is found: twice in Matt., 3 times each in Heb. and the Johannine literature, once each in Lk., Eph. and 1 Pet. Foundation of the world (*katabolē kosmou*, without art.) and the term foundation, used absolutely (Matt. 13:35 a citation of Ps. 78:2 with *katabolē* for *archē* where TR adds *kosmou*), have become fixed expressions for the point from which historical dates are reckoned (cf. Jewish chronology). When God's free activity is dated before this point in time (*pro katabolēs kosmou*) as in Jn. 17:24 (where the object of God's love is Jesus) and Eph. 1:4 (where the object is the believer), the purpose is to declare the independence of God's providence from the absolute beginning which he himself set and from history. This independence enables him to break into history in his loving purposes and to bring the course of history to its completion, again in his love (cf. also Rab. literature; → art. *ktisis* OT 7).

2. Two points stand out in all the texts which mention the foundation of the world. One is that it is always associated with a statement about man's destiny.

The other is the implied connection between God's → foreknowledge and pre-destination. In particular, Matt. 25:34 and Eph. 1:4 speak of → election. Rev. 13:8 and 17:8 speak of reprobation. Lk. 11:50 (a lamentation of Jesus) and Heb. 4:3 speak of historical failure for which account must be rendered. Finally Matt. 13:35 (quoting Ps. 78:2); Heb. 9:26 and 1 Pet. 1:20 (cf. Jn. 17:24) refer to the unique, central position of Jesus Christ in the history of salvation. He reveals in the midst of history what has been hidden since the foundation of the world, and thus fixes the end of time. The phrase *"before the foundation of the world"* in Eph. 1:4; 1 Pet. 1:20; Jn. 17:24 is foreign to the OT and is probably an attempt to express the independence of the creator from his creation in the face of Hellenism, and thus to make his acts of salvation dependent on him alone.

3. In Heb. 11:11 where the text is dubious, *katabolē* is used in the same way as in Philo (see above OT, 2). It is linked with *spermatos*, and means laying or depositing seed, i.e. begetting. V. 11a should be translated "he also, together with Sarah, received power to beget a child" (cf. O. Michel, *Der Brief an die Hebräer*, KEK 13 10 ad loc.; cf. F. Hauck *TDNT* III 621).

κτίσις

κτίζω (*ktizō*), create, produce; κτίσις (*ktisis*), creation, creature; κτίσμα (*ktisma*), created thing, creature; κτίστης (*ktistēs*), originator, creator.

CL The root *kti* (according to Hofmann, *kpei*; cf. Latin *situs*; Ger. *siedeln*) is found as early as Mycenaean Gk., and has the meaning, to build on, found. The vb. *ktizō* (Homer) originally had the meaning of the root, but then the transf. meaning, to bring into being, set in operation, colonize. (Hence the substantive part. *hoi ktisantes*, the original inhabitants.) The derived sub., *hē ktisis* (Pindar) means (a) the act of creation; (b) the created thing, the result of this act; (c) more rarely, the result of the act of an authority, generally a foundation. The meaning (b) may be compared with *to ktisma* (Polybius). *to ktisma* does not occur before the LXX in this sense of the result of creation. When it does, it is generally synonymous with *ktisis*. It also occurs in the plur. meaning the individual constituents of the creation. *ho ktistēs* (Aristotle) is most often a name for rulers in their function as founders and originators, in particular as restorers of the old order (Plut., *Cimon*, 10, 22). Applied to the deity, it means creator. In the biblical literature, the words are almost exclusively reserved for the incomparable creative activity of God, and its products.

OT 1. LXX has two terms for create: *dēmiourgein*, to work on or with a material, manufacture; and *ktizein* which expresses the decisive, basic act of will behind the bringing into being, foundation or institution of something. Of these, the latter is consciously preferred as a description of God's creative activity (cf. W. Foerster, *TDNT* III 1023 ff.). Nevertheless, the exclusiveness implied by the Heb. *bārā'* (see below) remains largely hidden in the LXX translation of the Pentateuch and Isa., since the general term *poiein*, to make, is used instead of *ktizein* to render it. (Incidentally, this fact gives some insight into the length of time it took for the LXX to be produced, and into the development of theological outlook of the translators; cf. W. Foerster, *TDNT* III 1026.) *ktizein* occurs 66 times in the LXX, and in 39 of these instances without Heb. equivalent. The survey which follows shows the relative frequency of the Heb. equivalents.

(a) Heb. *bārā'* (translated *ktizō* 16 times) is a theological term, whose subject is always God. It is the word used to convey the explicit faith in creation which is expressed in the later chapters of Isa. and the development of the theology of Gen. 1. *bārā'* expresses the incomparable creative activity of God, in which word and act of creation are one (cf. Gen. 1; Ps. 148:5). It refers not only to God's activity in calling the world and individual creatures into being, but also to his actions in history which lie behind election, temporal destiny, human behaviour, and even justification. A simple statistical survey shows the close association which exists between faith in God's government of history and salvation, and the doctrine of creation. R. Rendtorff in "Die theologische Stellung des Schöpfungsglaubens bei Deuterojesaja", *ZThK* 51 1945, 3 ff. and G. von Rad in *The Problem of the Hexateuch and Other Essays*, 1966, 131–143, maintain that the developed doctrine of creation is a late offshoot of the Israelites' doctrine of salvation in history which emerged during the period when their faith was in extreme danger of destruction in the Babylonian exile. It was proclaimed both in attack and defence, and afterwards continued as an inalienable tenet, about which there was complete confidence. This may be compared with the similar situation with regard to the 1st and 2nd articles of the Christian creed, ever since the refutation of Marcion.

Referring to the original creative activity of God, *bārā'* (Ps. 148:5) is used of the creation of the heavens and of the heavenly waters (Gen. 1:1) which were separated on the second day (Gen. 1:7). It is also used of the spreading of the circle of the earth, of North and South (Ps. 89(88):12, par. to *yāsad*, to found the world), the mountains and the wind (Amos 4:13), man upon the earth (Deut. 4:32), and man in his transient nature (Ps. 89:47).

bārā' is also used to express God's new work of creation extending into history, or rather the historical continuation of his creative activity. Thus Ps. 104(103):30, echoing Gen. 2, declares: "When Thou sendest forth Thy Spirit, they are created." In Eccl. 12:1 (lit. "Remember him who created you"; the noun "Creator" is foreign to the MT) the reference is to the creation of the individual (cf. the creation of the King of Tyre, Ezek. 28:13, 15). A people yet to be created will praise God (Ps. 102:18). In the well-known text, "Create in me a clean heart, O God" (Ps. 51:10), *bārā'* is again used in this sense. These last two references in the Pss., like those from the prophets mentioned below reveal the rift that runs through the original creation, which make it necessary for God to intervene on behalf of his chosen people and the individual sinner.

The link between the statements of God's original creation and those concerning his creative work in history becomes clear in the following passages. Yahweh who forms light and created darkness (according to Gen. 1:3–5, light is created by the word, but darkness is not created) also "makes weal and creates woe" (Isa. 45:7). He who has created the weapons which threaten has also created the destroyer of those weapons (Isa. 54:16). The people that God has created nonetheless profanes the covenant (Mal. 2:10).

The later Gk. versions of the OT – Theodotion (1st cent. A.D.), Aquila (2nd cent. A.D.) and Symmachus (3rd cent. A.D.) – consistently use *ktizein* instead of the more general words used to translate *bārā'* in the LXX (see above OT) in passages which

379

they regard as important in Gen., Deut., Isa., and Jer. These include Gen. 1:1, heaven and earth; 1:27, man in God's image; Isa. 40:26, the heavenly host; 41:20, new plant life in the wilderness, as a picture of Yahweh's historical power to save; 43:7, foreign nations from the ends of the world; 65:17 f., the new heaven, the new earth, the new Jerusalem, the new people; Jer. 31:22, a new thing on earth.

(b) qānâh (translated 3 times by ktizō) means to create, produce. Gen. 14:19, 22 speak of God Most High, in blessing and prayer respectively, as he who has made heaven and earth. Wisdom (Prov. 8:22), probably seen here as a heavenly being with a mediatorial role, exists before God's creation of the world. (Jer. 32(39):15 should probably be translated, as against Codex Sinaiticus and Codex Vaticanus, "fields . . . shall be bought (ktēthēsontai)" rather than "created" (ktisthēsontai).

(c) yāṣar (twice rendered by ktizō) means to form, fashion (like a potter), or plan. It is sometimes used of the spontaneous action of God in history. He directs destinies (Isa. 22:11). His planning and doing (poiein) are simultaneous.

(d) kûn (twice the Heb. equivalent of ktizō) is used both of the original creation and of God's working in history. Thus precious stones were prepared (Ezek. 28:13, par. to bārā' see above (b)). Yahweh is the One who has prepared, or established, Israel (Deut. 32:6d).

(e) ktizō is used once for yāsaḏ (niph., to be founded; used of Egypt in Exod. 9:18); once for 'āmaḏ, to stand forth at God's creative word (Ps. 33(32):9; see above 1(a), and the excursus of H.-J. Kraus in BKAT XV 263 f. on the creative power of the word of God). It is also used once for šāḵan, to be situated, established (part.), of the "tabernacle", the tent of meeting (Lev. 16:16) built according to the revealed pattern (Exod. 25:9).

2. In the passages without Heb. equivalent, which belong predominantly to the literature of Wisdom and of legendary history, expression is given to the contemporary priority of the doctrine of creation over the doctrine of redemption. Especially in the latter type of literature, confession, praise, and prayer to the Creator can become the sole basis and content of faith (1 Esd. 6:13; Jud. 13:18; Bel 5; 3 Macc. 2:3, 9). With the exception of Hag. 2:9 (a LXX addition to the MT) and 1 Esd. 5:53, where ktizein describes human acts of foundation, the term is everywhere reserved for divine activity. Traces of Hel. and general thought of the late classical period are linked up with previous Israelite ideas about creation. God has created all things that they might exist (Wis. 1:14), and the world out of formless matter (11:17). He has created man for incorruption in the likeness of his own nature (2:23). He is called "author of beauty" in connection with the creation of the stars (13:3). However, Gen. 1:14 ff. keeps at a cool, demythologizing distance in recounting the creation of the heavenly lights (cf. the LXX addition to Hos. 13:4).

Emphasis on the pre-existence of the hypostasized figure of wisdom as the first created being likewise demonstrates the dehistoricizing of the concept of God. God becomes absolutely transcendent, and exercises only mediate influence on present history. It also dehistoricizes creation (Wis. 10:1; Sir. 1:4, 9 f.; 24:8 f.; the latter passage also speaks of the post-existence of wisdom for eternity). This reverses what happened with the emergence of an explicit doctrine of creation. History must now be seen from the viewpoint of creation in which all is foreseen. From the beginning goodness is determined for the good. Winds, fire, hail, famine and plague are created for punishment; and death, bloodshed, strife, sword, devastation,

380

corruption, hunger and tribulation for the ungodly (cf. Sir. 23:20; 39:21–30; 40:10). Creaturely limitations are retained: pride and anger are not created for man (Sir. 10:18). Man is created from earth (Sir. 17:1; 33:10), and to the earth he will return (Sir. 17:1). The eye is recognized as the greatest possible source of danger to man among created things. This warning is graphically expressed in the question: "What has been created more evil than the eye?" (Sir. 13:13; cf. Matt. 5:29). One of the theological emphases of the wisdom literature is the extension of the doctrine of creation to include joy in the good things that have been made (cf. the hymns and songs of the Baroque period celebrating creation!). Wine has been created to make men glad (Sir. 31:27). Tilling the soil is an ordinance of the Most High, and should not be despised (Sir. 5:15). Men have God to thank for doctors and medicines (Sir. 38:1; 4, 12). Only once is reference made to the direct creative work of God in history, we have to thank God for the glory of famous men (Sir. 44:2).

3. The noun *ktisis* has only 2 Heb. equivalents in the MT, *hôn* and *qinyān*, each occurring twice and meaning possessions, goods, wealth, belongings. In three passages (Ps. 105(104):21; Prov. 1:13; 10:15) we should therefore (and also on grounds of textual criticism) read rather *ktēsis*, possessions. Only in the creation Psalm 105 does *qinyān* have the sense of creatures (Ps. 104(103):24).

Of more interest are the 15 instances in the LXX which have no Heb. equivalent. A number of them underline the doctrine of creation in prayer (see above 2) in the manner typical of this period of Judaism (Tob. 8:5, 15; Jud. 9:12; 16:14; Ps. 74 (73):18; 3 Macc. 2:2, 7; 6:2). Since God is the Creator and everything results from his word, he can be taken at his word and addressed as the Lord of creation (Jud. 16:14b, and the above-mentioned prayers). God's power in history is no longer seen or believed to be direct in its operation, but mediated by his creation. His power to predict and to elect are thus in effect one and the same. He arms the *ktisis*, creation, to bring vengeance on his enemies. It exerts itself to punish sinners, and relaxes for the sake of those who have trust in God (Wis. 5:17; 16:24). Thus the miracle at the Red Sea is not regarded as an incursion by Yahweh into his creation or a sovereign action against it. Rather God creates special new conditions for the creation which then obeys his special commands, to bring about the redemption of his elect (Wis. 19:6). The proper attitude of man to the creation is to marvel at its wonders (Sir. 43:24 f.), praise the Creator (Tob. 8:5, 15), and serve his fellow man (Jud. 16:14). On the other hand, it is despicable to misuse the creation in order to gain purely selfish enjoyment, as the ungodly encourage one another to do (Wis. 2:6). The righteous should not, however, indulge in nihilism because of their own insignificance amid the immeasurable extent of the created order (Sir. 16:17). The answer to the question of the meaning of life is given not by the creation but by the Creator. The context makes clear in each passage which of the two meanings of *ktisis* is intended, creation or creatures.

4. The late noun *ktisma* occurs only in passages without a Heb. equivalent in the sense listed in CL above (6 times, of which 2 are in prayers). In Wis. 9:2 a prayer for wisdom is being made, and wisdom is seen as the instrument of creation, as having something to do with man's commission to have dominion. In Sir. 36:15 a prayer for God's intervention in a historical situation to free Israel is based upon the continuing interest of God in his creation. (It must be left as an open question whether Israel, the patriarchs, wisdom, the Messiah, or his kingdom, all of which

381

belong according to Judaism to the class of things created before the rest of creation, are meant here. This argument from creation corresponds to the argument from eschatology in the same context, where the present activity of God is under consideration.) Wis. 13:5 and 14:11 should be seen as having a direct link with Rom. 1:20 ff. The greatness and beauty of created things enables conclusions to be drawn regarding their Creator, but idols (→ Image; → Man) are an abomination within the created order. With a faintly ironical undertone Sir. 38:34 concludes that artisans maintain the stability of the eternal creation (Jerusalem Bible: "they give solidity to the created world"), but are not in a position to attain wisdom. Ultimately this low estimation of practical work makes it impossible for the service of God in daily life to be regarded as an expression of faith in creation. The result is the emergence of the hierarchy of righteousness which Jesus later sharply criticized. *ktisma* is also used of parts of the eternal, good created order, such as sleep (3 Macc. 5:11): God remains its Lord and causes it to come and go.

5. The noun *ktistēs*, creator, is found only in non-canonical texts. 2 Sam. 22:32 (where the MT has "rock" and only the LXX translates it "creator"), and Isa. 43:15 (where Symmachus has "creator" for the participial form "I who have created" (cf. Eccl. 12:1), while the LXX has "I who have discovered thee") are thus no real exceptions.

The rare use of the noun (only 9 times including 2 Sam. 22:32 and Isa. 43:15 Symmachus) nevertheless gives us a glimpse of the central position occupied by the doctrine of creation in the two centuries before Christ. In confession (2 Macc. 7:23) and confession before non-Jews in persecution the Creator of the universe is invoked (4 Macc. 11:5). To him is committed in prayer the salvation of Israel (2 Macc. 1:24 ff.), and the outcome in holy war (2 Macc. 13:14). The hypostasized figure of wisdom stands as mediator in direct relation to him (Sir. 24:8). The historical association of the Creator with Israel is no longer expressed in terms of action (→ Covenant; → Grace), but ontologically after the manner of the Greeks. He is the one who "feels with us according to his nature" (4 Macc. 5:25).

6. The Qumran sect brought to the doctrine of creation a demonological and anthropological dualism. God has created the spirits of light and of darkness, and based every work upon them (1QS 3:25). Along with his commission to have dominion over the earth, man is assigned spirits of truth and of wickedness (1QS 3:17 f.). The doctrine of double predestination which is bound up with the foreknowledge of God corresponds to this in the case of the historical creation of individuals. Before he created the eternal generations, God knew their works for all eternity (1QH 1:7 f.). He created the righteous and the ungodly (1QH 4:38), the one intended for the day of favour, the other for the day of conflict (1QH 15:14 f., 17). God created breath for the tongue. He knows its words and fixes the fruit of the lips before they appear (1QH 1:27 f.).

In contrast to Gen. 1, this dualistic thinking allows the seas and floods to have been created and not merely separated (1QH 1:13 f.). Like the Priestly writing, 1QM 10:12 emphasizes that God created laws dividing the earth at the same time as he created the earth itself. The basic and final authority of the Creator over the dualistic forces remains a theme of hymns of praise, in which the righteous identify themselves with the side of the victor. (Hence the majority of references to creation occur in the hymns, 1QH.) For the righteous have been created to praise the name of God (1Q34 3, 1, 7). The idea of the new, eternal creation after the break-up of the old is therefore a quite consistent part of the eschatological future envisaged by the righteous (1QH 13:11 f.).

Moreover, monogamy – mentioned in polemic against the bigamous ideas of the false prophet Zaw – is based on Gen. 1:27c interpreted in the singular: "as man and wife he created them" (CD 4:21).

7. In Rab. literature the doctrine of creation is also connected with the doctrine of providence and prescience. God's foreknowledge can either begin with the commencement of his creative work, or be fixed and determined in God's purpose before the beginning of creation (cf. SB I 982; → *katabolē*, NT 2).

8. The history of the OT doctrine of creation is not adequately covered by a mere survey of the meaning of the term *ktizō* with its derivatives and equivalents. It can be mapped out roughly in stages: Gen. 2 – Ps. 104 – Isa. 40 – Gen. 1 – Ps. 33 – and then the non-canonical books of history and wisdom. At every stage we may see a witness to the God of Israel as Lord of creation and as Lord of the world. This shows the ability of Israel to take over every theory of life, and to use it in declaring the creative power and world dominion of her God. The only process of development which can be observed in this doctrine is a movement from an anthropocentric view of creation, which sees the limits of the world only in a horizontal direction (Gen. 2), to a cosmic, total view of creation. It reached its climax by way of the pre-exilic creation psalms in the explicit doctrine of creation in the exilic period when it had an apologetic motive (see above 1(a)). It gained further profundity as existential implications were thought out.

In biblical literature covenant and salvation are closely linked with creation. Karl Barth saw in Gen. 1 "Creation as the external basis of the covenant" and in Gen. 2 "The covenant as the internal basis of creation" (*CD*, III 1, 94–329). But the final phase of development in non-canonical literature led to the isolation and absolute dominance of the doctrine of creation. Here we are no longer allowed to find a basis for the doctrine in the covenant. Creator and creation are held to be perspicuous to all. The Lord of history has now departed into a transcendent realm. He has become the One who at creation has already determined the whole course of history, which is left to unroll according to plan. He is no longer the One who is ready to act on Israel's behalf, and who appears when and where he so chooses in his freedom (cf. Exod. 3:14 ff.).

NT 1. *ktizō*, create, produce, and its derivatives are found 38 times in the NT. Of these there are 14 instances of the vb. and 19 of the noun *ktisis* in the senses mentioned in CL above. Sense (b) may be further subdivided into the total creation and the creature. *ktisma*, thing created, occurs 4 times; *ktistēs*, creator, only in 1 Pet. 4:19. The latter concept is, however, expressed 3 times by a relative clause or a participle, as in the Heb. verbal construction.

The occurrences of this group of words do not, however, exhaust the terminology of creation. The following are also found, though less frequently: *poieō*, to make, *plassō*, to form; and less frequently still *kataskeuazō*, prepare (Heb. 3:4), *themelioō*, found, and *dēmiourgos*, craftsman, shaper. Other terms like *ta panta*, all, *archē*, → beginning (used absolutely in Jn. 1:1), and lists of the separate areas of creation (heaven, earth, sea, etc.) and their inhabitants likewise refer to the doctrine of creation. So too do statements which directly refer to creation events (Rom. 4:17), or repeat phrases from the creation narratives (Matt. 6:26a; 2 Cor. 4:6).

Occurrences of the *ktizō* group of words which apply exclusively to divine activity are divided as follows among the NT writers: Matt. once; Mk. 4 times; the Pauline Epistles 22 times (Rom. 8 times; Eph. and Col. 4 or 5 times; 1 Tim. twice); Jas. once; Heb. twice; 1 Pet. twice; 2 Pet. once; Rev. 5 times.

2. The NT presupposes the OT-Jewish doctrine of creation. To this extent the Christian church is dependent on the primeval narratives of the OT. But the NT gains anew the historical power of faith in the God of creation in its proclamation of God's kingdom being at hand and having its dawn in Christ. A key text here is the passage in the Sermon on the Mount which centres on the prohibition of worry (Matt. 6:24 ff.; cf. esp. v. 33). There is here a return to the original prophetic order, and the vital link between a person's faith in historical salvation ("Seek first. . .") and faith in creation ("all these things shall be added unto you"). The same is true of the Lord's prayer (cf. the first three petitions with the fourth).

In the preaching and actions of the earthly Jesus men are brought into a position of unbroken, healing confidence in the Creator. The Sabbath was *made* for man (*egeneto*, Mk. 2:27 par.). Foods do not defile a man (Matt. 15:11 par.). Fasting is not appropriate in the presence of Jesus (Mk. 2:18 ff. par.; Matt. 11:19), In his service there is no lack of the necessities of life (Lk. 22:35). He gives thanks when breaking bread and observing the feast (at the feeding of the 5000, and the Passover feast). Monogamy and the indissolubility of marriage are expressly based by Jesus on the creation ordinance from the beginning (Mk. 10:6, *ktisis*; in the par. Matt. 19:4, *ktizō*), as against the practice of divorce which arises from selfish hardness of heart. He does not succumb to the temptation arbitrarily to use the creation in opposition to the will of God (Matt. 4:1–11 par.).

Jesus demonstrates his creative power in the so-called nature miracles (the feeding miracles, walking on the water, and stilling of the storm). These give rise to the question, "Who then is this, that . . . ?" (Mk. 4:41 par.). In his exorcisms, healings and raising of the dead, in which new life is created by the liberating word, Jesus' creative power is exercised for the benefit of men who belong to a fallen creation. Thus according to the longer but inauthentic ending of Mk., the whole creation seems to be in need of the gospel of Christ (Mk. 16:15).

3. It is therefore a necessary consequence of the self-revelation of God which has taken place in Jesus of Nazareth, that the post-resurrection confession of faith should include worship of *the ascended One*, who now sits at God's right hand, as the original *mediator of creation* (1 Cor. 8:6; Col. 1:16; Heb. 1:2, 10; Jn. 1:1 ff.). The whole creation was made through him and with him in view (Jn. 1:3; 9–12). It has its basis (Rev. 3:14) and its goal in him (Heb. 1:11 f.).

4. References in the Pauline epistles to the doctrine of creation may be grouped into (a) those concerning the nature of the first creation, and (b) those which have as their subject the new creation, *kainē ktisis*, which has begun in Christ. The latter predominate, and there are many references to the relation between the two groups (e.g. Rom. 8:19 ff.; 2 Cor. 5:17; Gal. 6:15).

(a) The Creator alone is worthy of worship and veneration. The creature is limited by the fact that it is created. The limitation of creaturehood cannot be

384

overcome from man's side. Where worship is nevertheless offered to creatures, God gives up those who have thus transgressed to their own evil ways (Rom. 1:25). Since the creation (*ktisis*) of the world God's invisible nature has been clearly seen and recognized in his works (cf. Wis. 13:5). It follows that all human creatures are without excuse (Rom. 1:20). But all men in their disobedience have failed to make use of this opportunity, and are therefore dependent on God's free gift in the redemptive work of Jesus Christ (Rom. 3:21 ff.). Everything created (*ktisma*) by God is good, and nothing that God has created is to be rejected. This includes foods which are to be received with thanksgiving (1 Tim. 4 3 f., see above 1). However, because of the arrogance and rebelliousness of man, the creation (*ktisis* here means creaturely status) is in danger of becoming a temptation to him and separating him from the love of God firmly assured in Christ (Rom. 8:39). Since man is the goal of the whole creation, the state of the created order is determined by him. It is to man that all the non-human creation looks. All the hopes and longings of every created thing (*ktisis*) are therefore directed to him. With man, who has subjected the created world to himself, it has become subjected to futility, and it sighs and groans in its sufferings (Rom. 8:19a, 20, 22).

In a polemical passage (1 Cor. 11:9), Paul bases his teaching on the behaviour and rôle of women in worship on the principle of the original creation, whereby woman was made for man (Gen. 2:18; → Head). In the central passage, Gal. 3:28, however, he declares equality of the sexes in the unity which exists in the fellowship of Christ. Whilst he ascribes to man an authority which he does not ascribe to woman on the basis of Gen. 2:18, he nevertheless asserts their mutual dependence on each other and their joint dependence on God (1 Cor. 11:11 f.).)

(b) Because of what man has done, all creatures are dependent on the restoration of a right relationship between God and his representative in the created world. This can come about only through God's intervention. This is what Rom. 8:19b means when it speaks of waiting for the revelation of the sons of God. Since their acceptance as sons has already been promised (v. 23c) while they are still in the body (v. 23d), the hope of the final revelation of the sons of God is also hope which looks for the liberation of all creatures from bondage to decay (v. 21). The final realization of sonship lies outside the believer hidden ready in Christ. Christ is identified with the love of God (Rom. 8:39). Paul can therefore speak here and in 2 Cor. 5:17 with complete assurance about the new reality. Where a person belongs to Christ, new creation is a fact. Former things which hitherto determined his life have passed away.

In Christ the old privileges which men use to erect barriers between themselves (circumcision and uncircumcision) are no longer valid. Only belonging to him counts – the new creation. The past has been cancelled by the cross. Therefore the world, as the embodiment of the old creation, is unable to make any claims upon Christ. For his part the Christian is unable to live in dependence on the world: they are dead to each other (Gal. 6:14 f.).

Similarly, in Eph. 2:15 the removal by Christ of the basic distinction among mankind – the distinction between God's people and those who do not belong to it, i.e. between Jews and non-Jews – is regarded as *the* decisive act of reconciliation. *One* new man is created in Christ who now stands before God representing all men. The result of the new creation is here named, in a phrase popular in Eph. and Col., as *the new man.* It is the nature of this new man to see himself totally and unconditionally in the light of God's act of creation in Christ, as his workmanship (Eph. 2:10). The new man can be "put on" as a new self, who no longer has anything to do with the old. Where the old man was characterized by acts which destroy fellowship with God and with other men, the new is marked by a new knowledge, emanating from the will of God. This knowledge allows the new man to become truly an image of his Creator (here referred to in a relative clause) in acts of neighbourly love (Col. 3:10–12). The new man's condition of being "created after the likeness of God" (Eph. 4:24) means therefore that he is created so as to match up to God. He accepts the rightness of his gracious verdict upon us (in righteousness); he is separated for his service (in holiness); and lives in dependence upon him who is the truth, i.e. Christ (in truth). The drive of man to establish himself by his own efforts, even when these efforts are religious in character, belongs to the sphere of the old man. Yet there is a place for good works. For God has not only created the new man. He has created him for good works which he has prepared beforehand that we should live in them (Eph. 2:10).

5. The occasional references in the Catholic Epistles to the old creation and the new are essentially no different from the Pauline ones. Christians are the *first-fruits of God's creatures*, because they are "brought forth by the word of truth", i.e. born again (Jas. 1:18). The soteriological interpretation of this verse is to be preferred to the cosmological one. Heb. emphasizes God's eternal creative power which sees no conflict between his unlimited knowledge of all his creatures and their duty to give account of themselves (Heb. 4:13; cf. Rom. 1:20b; Rev. 4:11; 5:13). Heb. also stresses the infinite superiority of the new covenant over the old. The centre of worship for the old covenant belongs to this, our present created order. It is made with hands. The sphere of operation of the one heavenly high priest, Christ, is not subject to such limitation (Heb. 9:11). 1 Pet. attributes the ability of Christians to put their life at God's disposal for good works, even when this means suffering, to the faithfulness of the Creator (1 Pet. 4:19).

The interpretation of *ktisis* in 1 Pet. 2:13 is debated. In order to avoid the offensive teaching that we should submit to "every human *creature*" (which would be tantamount to making created beings into a god), it has been suggested that the translation should read "every human *ordinance*", or that instead of *ktisei* we should read *krisei*, judgment. The concept of subordination is, however, modified by the teaching, that it is not for the creature's sake, or for our own, but for the Lord's sake. Thus this subordination is seen as a sign of freedom, with the limitation set upon it that a man remains the servant of God.

2 Pet. 3:4 defends the Christian hope of the return of Christ against people who maintain that there is a perpetual continuity "from the beginning of creation", and use it to justify their self-assurance.

6. The language of Revelation depicts a visionary anticipation of the world to come. In hymns and acts of heavenly worship it proclaims what is already true in faith and will one day be objectively true finally, for ever and for all. He who sits upon the throne is worthy to receive glory, honour and power, for he has created all things and they owe their existence to his will (4:11). This worship of every creature (*ktisma*) belongs (5:13) not only to him, but also the Lamb (a metaphor for the crucified and exalted One). The act of praise goes out from heaven, reaching

386

in concentric circles, as it were, the earth, the region under the earth, and the sea, together with the creatures in them (cf. W. Foerster, *TDNT* III 1130 f.). As in 10:6, heaven and all that lives within it, are here seen as something created. But as the central scene of the worship of God it is clearly distinguished from earth and sea. Startling in its applicability to the present day is the vision of the death of a third of the creatures (*ktismata*) in the sea, when a mountain of fire is thrown into it (8:8 f.). The revelation speaks of God's new work of creation as something going beyond the individual to embrace the whole world. It is a new creation of the cosmos (21:1 ff.). But the word used in this context is not *ktizō*, but *poieō*, make (21:5; → Work, art. *poieō*). *H. H. Esser*

| δημιουργός | δημιουργός (*dēmiourgos*), maker. |

CL & OT *dēmiourgos* (originally a "public worker") and associated forms were used in Gk. of magistrates and of workmen, especially skilled handworkers. From Plato onwards they were also used to refer to the activity of God in creating the universe (*Tim.* 28 ff.; *Rep.* 530a). The word group is scarcely used in the LXX; the verb *dēmiourgeō* is used of a potter (Wis. 15:13) and of making altars (2 Macc. 10:2), the noun metaphorically of causing evils (2 Macc. 4:1), and only later in Symmachus is the noun applied to God as creator (Job 37:15; 38:4). But the word group is common enough outside the Bible, being applied to God by Josephus (*Ant.* 1, 155; 7, 380; 12, 23). Philo makes considerable use of the terms, with frequent reference to God as the creator of the universe (*Op. Mund,* 10; *Mut. Nom.,* 29–32); sometimes the term *technitēs* (craftsman) occurs in the same context (*Rer. Div. Her.* 133). From Philo's usage it is clear why the term was scarcely ever used of God in the Gk. Bible or in Rabbinic Judaism (but cf. P. Aboth 4:22): Philo comments that God did not just handle existing material as an artificer (*dēmiourgos*) but was himself its creator (*ktistēs*) (*Som.* 1, 76). In general, however, Philo was influenced by Gk. ideas of God as the fashioner of the world. The Bible prefers to use *ktizō*, a word which better conveys the idea of God's rule over the universe and his power to create out of nothing.

NT Hence the virtual absence of *dēmiourgos* from the NT is not without significance.

In Heb. 11:10 it is used of God as the *technitēs* (Wis. 13:1) and *dēmiourgos* of the heavenly city. The writer here uses a fine, rhetorical phrase to stress the excellence and abiding quality of the heavenly city as one built on firm foundations by God himself; the thought is metaphorical and non-philosophical.

In later Christian writing the word became more common (1 Clem. 20:11; Ep. Diog. 7:2), and it also played a considerable role in Gnosticism, in which the idea of a "demiurge", separate from and inferior to God, was used to explain the origin of the evil, material universe. *I. H. Marshall*

→ Beginning

(a). I. G. Barbour, *Issues in Science and Religion*, 1968; and *Myths, Models and Paradigms*, 1974; I. G. Barbour, ed., *Science and Religion*, 1968; K. Barth, *CD* III, 1–4, *The Doctrine of Creation*; D. Bonhoeffer, *Creation and Fall*, 1959; E. Brunner, *Dogmatics* III, *The Christian Doctrine of*

Creation and Redemption, 1952; R. Bultmann, "Faith in God the Creator," *Existence and Faith*, 1964, 202–16; O. Cullmann, *Christ and Time*, 1951; and "The Connection of Primal Events and End avents with the New Testament Redemptive History," in B. W. Anderson, ed., *The Old Testament End Christian Faith*, 1964, 115–23; W. Dantine, "Creation and Redemption," *SJT* 18, 1965, 129–47; W. D. Davies, *The New Creation*, 1971; A. Ehrhardt, "Creatio ex nihilo," *The Framework of the New Testament Stories*, 1964, 200–33; A. Ehrhardt, *The Beginning: A Study in the Greek Philosophical Approach to the Concept of Creation from Anaximander to St John*, 1968; W. Eichrodt, *Theology of the Old Testament*, I, 1960, 15–228; T. Fawcett, *Hebrew Myths and Christian Gospel*, 1973, 53–70, 237–52; W. Foerster, *ktizō*, *TDNT* III 100–35; J. G. Gibbs, *Creation and Redemption: A Study in Pauline Theology*, 1971; T. C. Hammond, *The New Creation*, 1953; F. Hauck, *katabolē*, *TDNT* III 620 f.; A. Heidel, *The Babylonian Genesis: The Story of Creation*, 1951[2]; A. Hulsbosch, *God's Creation*, 1965; G. W. H. Lampe, "The New Testament Doctrine of Ktisis," *SJT* 17, 1964 449–62; H. McCabe, *The New Creation*, 1964; K. H. Miskotte, *When the Gods are Silent*, 1967; J. Plastaras, *Creation and Covenant*, 1968; G. von Rad, "The Theological Problem of the OT Doctrine of Creation", *The Problem of the Hexateuch and Other Essays*, 1966, 131 ff.; H. Renckens, *Israel's Concept of the Beginning. The Theology of Gen. 1–3*, 1964; N. H. Ridderbos, *Is there a Conflict between Genesis I and Natural Science?* 1957; A. Richardson, *The Bible in the Age of Science*, 1961; P. Schoonenberg, *Covenant and Creation*, 1968; L. H. Taylor, *A Study of the Biblical Doctrine of "Kaine Ktisis" in Pauline Theology*, 1955; G. Trenkler, "Creation," *EBT* I 147–55; C. Westermann, *Creation*, 1974; G. Wingren, *Creation and Law*, 1961.

Commentaries on *Genesis* by U. Cassuto, I, 1961; D. Kidner, 1967; A. Richardson, (1–11) 1953; G. von Rad, 1963[2]; E. A. Speiser, 1964.

(b). G. Altner, *Schöpfungsglaube und Entwicklungsgedanke in der protestantischen Theologie zwischen Ernst Haeckel und Teilhard de Chardin*, 1965; W. Andersen, "Jesus Christus und der Kosmos," *EvTh* 23, 1963, 471 ff.; H. Benckert, "Schöpfung und Geschichte," *EvTh* 20, 1960, 433 ff.; K. H. Bernhardt, "Zur Bedeutung der Schöpfungsvorstellung für die Religion Israels in vorexilischer Zeit," *TLZ* 85, 1960, 821 ff.; F. N. T. Böhl, "Bara als Terminus der Weltschöpfung im alttestamentlichen Sprachgebrauch," *Festschrift Kittel* 1913, 42 ff.; P. Brunner, "Gott, das Nichts und die Kreatur," *KuD* 6, 1960, 172 ff.; F. Buri, "Gott und seine Schöpfung," *ThZ* 19, 1963, 273 ff.; S. M. Daecke, *Teilhard de Chardin und die evangelische Theologie*, 1967; G. Eder, H. Oepen, A. Portmann and G. von Rad, *Naturwissenschaften und biblische Welterkenntnis*, 1 Folge, 1967; C. M. Edsman *et al.*, "Schöpfung," *RGG*[3] V 1469 ff.; A. Feuillet, "La Création de l'Univers 'dans le Christ' d'après l'Épître aux Colossiens," *NTS* 12, 1965, 1–9; H. Fruhstorfer, *Weltschöpfung und Paradies nach der Bibel*, 1927; K. Galling, "Der Charakter der Chaosschilderung in Gen. 1, 2," *ZTK* 47, 1950, 145 ff.; G. Gloege, "Schöpfungsglaube und Weltbild," in *Vom Herrengeheimnis der Wahrheit*, Festschrift H. Vogel, 1962, 158 ff.; F. Gogarten, "Der Glaube an Gott den Schöpfer" *Zwischen den Zeiten* 4, 1926, 451 ff.; S. Herrmann, "Die Naturlehre des Schöpfungsberichtes," *TLZ* 86, 1961, 413 ff.; P. Humbert, "Emploi et portée du verbe bārā' (créer) dans l'Ancien Testament," *ThZ* 3, 1947, 401–22; G. Jacob, *Himmel ohne Gott*, 1960[2]; A. Janssens, "De scripturae doctrina de Creatione mundi," *Coll. Gandaviones* 30, 1947, 95–9; H. Jonas, *Zwischen Nichts und Ewigkeit*, 1963; C. A. Keller, " 'Existentielle' und 'heilsgeschichtliche' Deutung der Schöpfungsgeschichte," *ThZ* 11, 1956, 10 ff.; H.-J. Kraus, "Schöpfung und Weltvollendung," *EvTh* 24, 1964, 462 ff.; W. Kreck, "Schöpfung und Gesetz," *Kirche in der Zeit* 15, 1960, 369 ff.; F. Lämmli, *Vom Chaos zum Kosmos*, I–II, 1962; F. Lau, "Theologie der Schöpfung gleich Theologie überhaupt?" *Luther Jahrbuch* 29, 1962, 44 ff.; H. Lehmann, "Schöpfergott und Heilsgott im Zeugnis der Bibel," *EvTh* 11, 1951, 97–112; G. Lindeskog, *Studien zum neutestamentlichen Schöpfungsgedanken*, 1952; W. Link, "Schöpfung und Versöhnung," *EvTh* 1, 1934–35, 345 ff.; A. F. Loen, *Säkularisation. Von der wahren Voraussetzung und angeblichen Gottlosigkeit der Wissenschaft*, 1965; W. D. Marsch, *Zukunft*, 1969, 57 ff., 69 ff., 139 ff.; F. Merkel, "Die biblische Urgeschichte im kirchlichen Unterricht," in *Studien zur Theologie der alttestamentlichen Überlieferungen*, Festschrift G. von Rad, 1961, 141 ff.; O. Plöger, W. Kasch, and E. Kinder, "Schöpfung, *EKL* III 831 ff.; R. Rendtorff "Die theologische Stellung des Schöpfungsglaubens bei Deuterojesaja," *ZTK* 51, 1954, 3 ff.; H. Rohrbach, *Naturwissenschaft, Weltbild, Glaube*, 1967; K. H. Schelkle, *Theologie des Neuen Testaments*, I, 1968; W. H. Schmidt, *Die Schöpfungsgeschichte der Priesterschrift*, *WMANT* 17, 1967[2]; and *br'*, *THAT* I 335–39; G. Schneider, *Kaine Ktisis. Die Idee der Neuschöpfung beim Apostel Paulus und ihr religionsgeschichtlicher Hintergrund*, 1959; H. Schwantes, *Schöpfung der Endzeit. Ein Beitrag zum Verständnis der Auferweckung bei Paulus*, 1963; P. Stuhlmacher,

"Erwägungen zum ontologischen Charakter der *kainē ktisis* bei Paulus," *EvTh* 27, 1967, 1 ff.; O. Weber, *Grundlagen der Dogmatik* I, 1955, 510 ff.; C. F. von Weizsäcker, *Die Geschichte der Natur*, 1964[6]; V. von Weizsäcker, *Am Anfang schuf Gott Himmel und Erde*, 1963[6] C. Westermann, *Genesis, BKAT* I, 1966; "Zum hermeneutischen Problem des Redens von Schöpfer und Schöpfung," *TLZ* 92, 1967, 243 ff.; *Neuere Arbeiten zur Schöpfung, Verkündigung und Forschung*, 1969; H. Wildberger, "Das Abbild Gottes, Gen. 1, 26–30," *ThZ* 21, 1965, 245 ff., 481 ff; E. Würthwein, "Chaos und Schöpfung im mythischen Denken und in der biblischen Urgeschichte," in E. Dinkler, ed., *Zeit und Geschichte, Dankesgabe an R. Bultmann*, 1964, 317 ff.; W. Zimmerli, *1. Mose 1–11. Die Urgeschichte*, 1943.
On *dēmiourgos* see: Arndt, 177 f.; W. Foerster, *TDNT* II 1025–26; Lampe, 342; R. Williamson, *Philo and the Epistle to the Hebrews*, 1970, 42–51.

Cross, Wood, Tree

The word now normally translated as *cross* denotes in Greek an instrument of torture and execution. It has gained a special significance through its historic connection with the death of Jesus. Two words are used for the instrument of execution on which Jesus died: *xylon* (wood, tree) and *stauros* (stake, cross). *xylon* meant originally wood, and is often used in the NT of wood as a material. Through its connection with Deut. 21:23 (quoted in Gal. 3:13, "Cursed be everyone who hangs on a tree"), *xylon* could virtually be treated as synonymous with *stauros*. In the gospels *stauros* is used in the accounts of the execution of Jesus, and in the theological reflection of the Pauline literature it symbolizes the → sufferings and → death of Christ.

ξύλον

ξύλον (*xylon*), wood, pole, gallows, tree, cross.

CL *xylon* is commonly used in cl. literature for wood or timber, as a building material, fuel, and material from which utensils and cultic objects are made (e.g. Dem. 45, 33; Hesiod, *Works* 808). Cudgels, clubs, instruments of torture and punishment in the form of sticks, blocks and collars for slaves, lunatics and prisoners were called *xylon* (Hdt., 2, 63; 4, 180). *xylon* as a tree is rare. It is first attested in Hdt., 3:46; 7, 65; Euripides, *Cyclops*, 572; and Xen., *Anab.*, 6, 4 5.

OT Wood is mentioned in the LXX as fuel (Gen. 22:3), building material (Gen. 6:14; Exod. 25:10 ff.; 1 Ki. 6:15), and as an instrument of torture (stocks, Job 33:11 RSV). The meaning *tree* is more common than in secular Gk. *xylon* is used to denote fruit trees, cypresses and trees planted by running water (Gen. 1:11; Isa. 14:8; Ps. 1:3). According to Gen. 2:9, "God made to grow every tree that is pleasant to the sight and good for food, the tree of life also in the midst of the garden, and the tree of the knowledge of good and evil." The Garden of Eden represents God's providential care. The tree of life represents the fact that all life comes from God as a gift. The tree of the knowledge of good and evil which is forbidden to man symbolizes the benevolent character of God's commands (cf. G. von Rad, *Genesis*, 1961, ad loc.). God gives and sets limitations at the same time. In setting the tree of knowledge as a limit, he lets man know that he both gives and requires obedience. The motif of the tree of life, to which later Jewish apocalyptic attributed supernatural vital powers in a paradise at the end of time (Eth. En.

389

25:4 f.; cf. Prov. 3:18), already suggests a primeval paradise. (On the trees see U. Cassuto, *A Commentary on the Book of Genesis*, 1961, I, 110 ff.)

Disobedience turns a created thing into a god. The tree becomes a cultic object and the carving an idol. The prophets condemned Israel's apostasy as "adultery with stone and tree" (Jer. 3:9 RSV; cf. Isa. 40:20; 44:13 ff.; Ezek. 20:32).

In the LXX wood is rarely mentioned as an instrument of torture and execution. However, executed criminals were hanged on a stake and exposed to public view. "And if a man has committed a crime punishable by death and he is put to death, and you hang him on a tree, his body shall not remain all night upon the tree, but you shall bury him the same day, for a hanged man is accursed by God; you shall not defile your land which the Lord your God gives you for an inheritance" (Deut. 21:22 f. RSV; cf. Jos. 10:26; Est. 5:14).

NT 1. The NT mentions wood as a weapon (staves) and building material in Matt. 26:47; Mk. 14:43; and Rev. 18:12. Jesus asked figuratively: "For if they do this when the wood is green, what will happen when it is dry?" (Lk. 23:31). If he himself was not spared divine judgment, how much more will Israel burn like dead wood in the fire of judgment? (Cf. J. M. Creed; "if the innocent Jesus [*en hygrō xylō*] meets such a fate, what will be the fate of guilty Jerusalem [*en tō xērō*]?", *The Gospel According to St. Luke*, 1930, 286; cf. SB II 263. There may also be an element of time implied in the contrast between the green wood and the dry: if this happens now, what will happen later?)

In 1 Cor. 3:12 wood is mentioned metaphorically in the context of a series of materials ranging from → gold to straw. There is only one possible → foundation in the church, and that is Christ. But men may build a variety of structures on this foundation which will all be tested by fire. Those which are perishable like wood and straw will be consumed, though the foundation will remain. A man's work may be burned up, but he himself will be saved, but only as through fire.

2. The concepts of the tree and the curse and the "tree of life" are theologically more central. Peter accused the Jewish leaders of killing Jesus "by hanging him on a tree" (Acts 5:30; cf. 10:39). The expression is reminiscent of Deut. 21:23, and stresses the shame of the crucifixion. For as someone hanged on a tree, Jesus stood under the curse of God. Paul drew this inference in Gal. 3:13: "Christ redeemed us from the curse of the law, having become a curse for us – for it is written, 'Cursed be every one who hangs on a tree.' " He has taken upon himself in our place and for our benefit the curse of the law and by his death has destroyed it (cf. 2 Cor. 5:21). Alluding to Isa. 53:4, 12, 1 Pet. 2:24 declares: "He himself bore our sins in his body on the tree, that we might die to sin and live to righteousness." The tree is the place at which Christ's body, laden with our sin, was killed. Through the death of his body sin was annulled. (On Jn. 3:14; Num. 21:9 → Dragon, art. *ophis*.)

The picture of the tree of life reappears in Rev. 2:7: "To him who conquers I will grant to eat the tree of life, which is in the paradise of God." What was forbidden to → Adam and Eve is given in the new creation. In the new → Jerusalem on either side of the river of → life grows "the tree of life with its twelve kinds of fruit, yielding its fruit each month; and the leaves of the tree were for the healing of the nations" (Rev. 22:2). The righteous alone have access to the tree of life (Rev.

22:14, 19). The living tree symbolizes life, and presents a contrast with the cross as the wooden instrument of death. But the significance of the cross is retained. It is the place where God bears and overcomes suffering and death, so that he may give life to a world overcome by sin and death (Rev. 22:14).   *B. Siede*

σταυρός

σταυρός (*stauros*), stake, cross; σταυρόω (*stauroō*), hang upon a cross, crucify; ἀνασταυρόω (*anastauroō*), crucify; συσταυρόω (*systauroō*), crucify with; κρεμάννυμι (*kremannymi*), hang.

CL 1. (a) *stauros* is an upright, sometimes pointed stake. It may serve various purposes, e.g. as fencing (Hom., *Od.*, 14, 11), a foundation (Thuc., 7, 25, 5), and as a palisade (Homer onwards). Similarly, *stauroō* means to drive in stakes, or erect a palisade (Thuc. onwards).

(b) Both the noun and the vb. have a more specific meaning in connection with punishment. But this occurred in a variety of ways. The words do not always have the same precise meaning, and cannot without closer definition be applied to the crucifixion of Jesus.

The vb. is more common in the compound *anastauroō* which has the same meaning. It is virtually interchangeable with *anakremannymi* (Hdt., 3, 125, 3 f.; 7, 194, 1 f.) and *anaskolopizō* (Hdt., 9, 78, 3) meaning to hang up, impale, apparently always in public. These vbs. may have the following possible meanings, depending upon the manner of execution then current: impale (Hdt. 7, 238, 1); hang up, especially as a sign of disgrace (Hdt., 3, 125, 3 f.) as well as a form of execution (see below, 2 (a)); fix to a cross, crucify (see below, 2 (a)).

Corresponding to the vb. which was more common, *stauros* can mean a stake which was sometimes pointed on which an executed criminal was publicly displayed in shame as a further punishment. It could be used for hanging (so probably Diod. Sic., 2, 18, 2), impaling, or strangulation. *stauros* could also be an instrument of torture, perhaps in the sense of the Lat. *patibulum*, a cross-beam laid on the shoulders. Finally it could be an instrument of execution in the form of a vertical stake and a cross-beam of the same length forming a cross in the narrower sense of the term. It took the form either of a T (Lat. *crux commissa*) or of a + (*crux immissa*).

2. The exact technical form and significance of execution are not conveyed by the words *stauros* and (*ana*)*stauroō*, without further definition. In order to determine this, it is necessary to know in what region and under what authority the execution was carried out. It is also necessary to know the standpoint of the writer who uses these terms.

(a) There appears to be a fundamental difference between the East and the West over the question of execution and its means. In the East there was the practice of hanging and impaling bodies which were sometimes decapitated (cf. Polyb., 7, 21, 3). This was an additional penalty. By being exhibited the person executed was put to further shame.

This form of punishment was rejected in the West and not practised (cf. Hdt., 7, 238, 1 f. with 9, 78, 3; 9, 79, 1; Plut., *De Pericle*, 28, 1). Hanging or fastening in some way to a stake, beam or cross was a means of execution of someone still alive (cf. Hdt., 9, 120, 4). A distinction must, however, be drawn between the various modes of execution. A more or less quick death was effected by strangulation. On the other hand, hanging could be long and painful for the victim. This was the intention of fastening the condemned man to the *stauros* while he was still alive. Execution by crucifixion was known in Greece and Carthage. The Romans may even have taken it over from the Carthaginians. Crucifixion in this sense was not developed and practised in the East.

(b) In Judea at the time of Jesus sentencing to crucifixion and execution was entirely in the hands of the Roman authorities. With regard to the procedure followed by the Romans the following may be said. As with the Greeks and probably throughout the East, freemen with Roman citizenship were exempted from crucifixion up to the early imperial period. Apart from a few executions carried out against this generally established right, crucifixion was inflicted on slaves, foreigners and inhabitants of foreign provinces.

As a rule, crucifixion was inflicted on slaves only in cases of serious crimes. It is significant that this form of capital punishment was instituted primarily for offences against the state, such as treason that was potentially dangerous to security. It is understandable that in Palestine it constituted an important punitive weapon in the hands of the Roman occupying power, by which it sought to deal effectively with any resistance to its authority.

Punishment by crucifixion was seen as a disciplinary measure for the maintenance of existing authority, intended more as a deterrent than as a means of retribution. This explains why the instrument of execution was set up in an open place. The public and starkly cruel character of this form of execution also answered to this purpose. Contemporary writers condemned this form of execution as excessively cruel and disgraceful (Cicero, *In Verrem*, 64, 165 and often; Tacitus, *Historia*, 4, 3, 11; Josephus, *War*, 7, 203).

It is certain only that the Romans practised this form of execution. But it is most likely that the *stauros* had a transverse in the form of a crossbeam. Secular sources do not permit any conclusion to be drawn as to the precise form of the cross, as to whether it was the *crux immissa* + or the *crux commissa* T. As it was not very common to affix a *titlos* (superscription, loanword from the Lat. *titulus*), it does not necessarily follow that the cross had the form of a *crux immissa*.

There were two possible ways of erecting the *stauros*. The condemned man could be fastened to the cross lying on the ground at the place of execution, and so lifted up on the cross. Alternatively, it was probably usual to have the stake implanted in the ground before the execution. The victim was tied to the cross-piece, and was hoisted up with the horizontal beam and made fast to the vertical stake. As this was the simpler form of erection, and the carrying of the cross-beam (*patibulum*) was probably connected with the punishment for slaves, the *crux commissa* may be taken as the normal practice. The cross would probably have been not much higher than the height of a man.

According to Roman practice, the procedure of crucifixion would then be as follows. First, there was the legal conviction. Only in extraordinary cases, such as in times of war, did this occur at the place of execution itself. If the execution took place at somewhere other than the place of sentencing, the condemned man carried the *patibulum* to the spot which was usually outside the town. The expression "to bear the cross (*stauros*)" which is a typical description of the punishment of slaves

392

has its origin here. At the place of execution the victim was stripped and scourged. He may also have been previously scourged. This practice was an important part of crucifixion which took place between sentencing and execution. The condemned man was tied with outstretched arms to the cross-beam which was presumably laid upon his shoulders. Nailing is testified to only in isolated instances (Hdt., 9, 120, 4; 7, 33). It is uncertain whether this was done to the feet as well as to the hands. (In the post-resurrection narratives of Jesus' appearances, Jn. 20:20, 25 ff. mentions Jesus' hands, and Lk. 24:39 his hands and feet.) The victim was then hoisted on to the stake with the cross beam. Death came slowly after extraordinary agony, probably through exhaustion or suffocation. The body could be left on the scaffold to rot or provide food for predatory animals and carrion-crows. There is evidence that the body was occasionally given to relatives or acquaintances

It must be remembered that the secular writers of the period did not deign to provide a detailed description of this disgraceful and cruel form of execution. Many questions must be left open. The picture obtained on the basis of secular accounts may not, without more ado, be enlarged or altered by means of the gospel narratives concerning the crucifixion of Jesus.

([F.F.B.] In June 1968 an ossuary was discovered on Ammunition Hill, north of Jerusalem, containing the bones of a young man who had plainly been crucified, about the beginning of the 1st century A.D. One nail had been driven through each of his forearms, and a third, which was still *in situ*, through both his ankles together. His legs had been broken like those of Jesus' two companions in John 19:32 (cf. V. Tzaferis and others, "Jewish Tombs at and near Giv'at ha-Mivtar, Jerusalem", *Israel Exploration Journal* 20, 1970, 18 ff.).)

OT 1. According to the OT, oriental ways of execution (see above CL 2. (a)) were known in Israel and were in part followed. The body of Saul was beheaded by the Philistines and set up on a stake (1 Sam. 31:9 f.). Joseph interpreted the dream of a royal, Egyptian court official. Pharaoh would behead him and dishonour him by leaving his body hanging on a stake (Gen. 40:18 f.). This, however, cannot be taken as certain proof for normal practice in Egypt. According to Ezr. 6:11, Darius made a decree that anyone infringing an edict of king Cyrus should have a beam pulled from his house and be impaled on it. Est. 5:14; 6:4; 7:9 f. 9:13 f. reflect oriental practice. But inferences should not be drawn from these about particular Persian practices. The regulation in Deut. 21:22 f. clearly shows that penal procedure in Israel followed general oriental practice. This is applied here to capital offences, but a specific limitation is also made. The corpse is not to remain on the tree overnight, lest the land be defiled. This regulation corresponds to two accounts of executions under Joshua in which the victims were hanged then buried under stones or sealed in a cave before nightfall (Jos. 8:29; 10:26). Thus according to the OT, Israel did not know of the stake as a means of torture and death or of execution by crucifixion.

2. The LXX never uses the word *stauros*. The vb. *stauroō* occurs only in Est. 7:9 (for Heb. *tālâh*, hang); Est. 8:12 (a LXX addition); and in Lam. 5:13 v.l. The usage alone does not permit an unambiguous interpretation. Est. 8:12 does not admit any firm inferences. The expression in Est. 7:9 *staurōthētō ep' autou* ("Let him be crucified on that") is immediately followed by *ekremasthē* ("he was hanged") which

393

refers to hanging Haman on the gallows. This may, therefore, suggest the oriental custom. Lam. 5:13 v.l. *en xylō estaurōthēsan* (they were hanged on a tree) could imply the execution of a person who was still alive. Ezr. 6:11 is ambiguous. Only the LXX translation of Jos. 8:29 suggests that the author may have thought of actual crucifixion, and even so he avoids using the words *stauros* and *stauroō*. After speaking of *kremannymi epi xylou* (hang upon a tree) he adds *didymou*, i.e. to the twofold tree. This might be taken as a reference to hanging on a cross. ([Ed.] But this may simply indicate a form of gallows, and the king of Ai evidently died much more quickly than was normal at crucifixions.) The Jews of the Hel. dispersion may thus have known of crucifixion as practised in the West, and the LXX translator may just conceivably have depicted this event as a crucifixion.

3. Apart from this, there is record of the Jewish ruler Alexander Jannaeus (103-76 B.C.) ordering a mass execution by hanging men alive on stakes. The violent attack on this form of execution in 4QpNah 1:7 and Josephus (*Ant.*, 11, 261, 266 f.; 17, 295; 20, 102, 129, 161; *War*, 5, 449 ff.) indicates that it was a highly unusual procedure, detested and not normally practised in Judaism.

4. The same picture is presented by rab. sources, where in particular the form of execution in Deut. 21:22 f. is taken as a basis and defined still further. Thus the additional hanging of a blasphemer who has been previously stoned to death becomes a mere legal formality. Someone binds the condemned man first, and someone else unbinds him immediately afterwards (SB I 1034 f.). This, however, is an ideal prescription and not regular practice. From the middle of the 1st cent. B.C. implementation of the death penalty was in practice taken out of the hands of the Sanhedrin. Nevertheless, even these idealistic discussions, which were partly directed against Roman penal practice, show how much the Jews detested the Roman practice of crucifixion which they must have come to know in Palestine. They also show how little crucifixion was legally practised in Judaism or advocated by Jews as a form of punishment.

NT In the NT the words *stauros* (cross), *anastauroō* and *stauroō* (crucify), and *systauroō* (crucify with) occur essentially in two sets of textual and theological complexes. (1) In the passion narratives of the gospels (Mk. 15:1–47; Matt. 27:1 f., 11–61; Lk. 23:1–56; Jn. 18:28–19:24). Here also belong: Matt. 20:19 (the reference to the crucifixion in the third passion prediction); Matt. 26:2 (further prediction of the crucifixion of Jesus); Lk. 24:20; Acts 2:36; 4:10 (statements about the Jews' part in the crucifixion of Jesus); Rev. 11:8 (the identification of the "great city" with Sodom and Egypt "where their Lord was crucified"). (2) In the theological reflection of the Pauline letters (some 20 times). To this may be added because of their content Heb. 6:6; 12:2 and the synoptic sayings about bearing the cross (Mk. 8:34; Matt. 16:24; Lk. 9:23; and Mk. 10:38; Lk. 14:27).

1. *The crucifixion of Jesus as a historical and theological question.*

Paul who was the earliest NT writer speaks of the cross of Christ in numerous places but gives no details at all about the event. 1 Thess. 2:15 f. is, however, important in view of the fact that Paul sees the church threatened by persecution from the Jews in a parallel situation to Jesus. For the Jews "killed both the Lord Jesus and the prophets, and drove us out, and displease God and oppose all men" (2:15). Paul may have been drawing on traditional material in saying this (cf. 1 Cor.

15:1 ff.). Similar in content is the saying: "Therefore I send you prophets and wise men and scribes, some of whom you will kill and crucify, and some you will scourge in your synagogues and persecute from town to town" (Matt. 23:34).

The Jews and their representatives similarly appear in the oldest gospel narrative in Mk. as the driving force behind the crucifixion for which they are virtually alone responsible.

It is at their instigation that Jesus is arrested (Mk. 14:43 ff.), tried and sentenced to death by the Sanhedrin (14:53 ff.). Pilate recognizes their motive, but finds no grounds for condemnation. Finally like a weakling anxious for their favour, he gives in to the people who have been stirred up by the agents of the Jews, violently demanding the crucifixion of Jesus. There is no suggestion of a formal sentence passed by the representative of imperial Rome (15:1–15). The theologically significant insults heaped upon the crucified one come from the lips of passing Jews and those who represent the Jewish nation and its theology: "[29] 'Aha! You who would destroy the temple and build it in three days, [30]save yourself, and come down from the cross!' [31]So also the chief priests mocked him to one another with the scribes, saying, 'He saved others; he cannot save himself. [32]Let the Christ, the King of Israel, come down now from the cross, that we may see and believe' " (15:29–32).

In the narratives of the other evangelists this tendency is less pronounced, partly due to the inclusion of material not found in Mk. Pilate's wife urged her husband: "Have nothing to do with that righteous man, for I have suffered much over him today in a dream" (Matt. 27:19). Pilate washed his hands and declared, "I am innocent of this man's blood: see to it yourselves" (Matt. 27:20, 24 f.). Lk. records the saying, "Daughters of Jerusalem, do not weep for me, but weep for yourselves and for your children" (Lk. 23:28; cf. 23:2, 5, 10, 13 ff., 22b, 25b, 28–31 for Lk.'s account of the events leading up to the crucifixion). For Jn.'s account see Jn. 18:31, 38b; 19:4, 6 f., 12 f., 15b. Lk. expresses the evangelists' typical attitude in the words of Peter addressed to the Jews at Pentecost: "this Jesus whom you crucified" (Acts 2:36; cf. 4:10; Lk. 24:20).

In this there may have been the partial motive of absolving Roman rule of responsibility. But this was in any case secondary. The chief motivation was, as in the early tradition reflected in 1 Thess. 2:15 f., the contemporary debate with Judaism. The persecution and sufferings of the early church have to be taken into account in assessing the form and original context of the narrative traditions of the trial and crucifixion of Jesus.

(a) Any historical reconstruction must be based upon the following facts. In Judaea capital jurisdiction during the period of occupation belonged to the imperial representative alone and was not assigned to the Sanhedrin in any form however restricted. The following may be regarded as historically certain: (1) Pilate's judicial decision for the *stauros* was decisive. (2) Like the death sentence, the execution was carried out by Romans according to Roman practice. (3) Hence, Jesus died on the cross as an instrument of torture, probably slowly through suffocation or exhaustion. (4) Crucifixion according to Roman practice would authenticate the account of the scourging of Jesus (wherever it took place), the removal of his clothing and the guard of Roman soldiers at the place of execution. This would follow from our knowledge of current Roman practice, regardless of whether the accounts rest upon eye-witnesses.

395

The custom of bearing the cross was probably used outside the city (Mk. 15:20b, 21). If the *stauros* was the cross-beam (Lat. *patibulum*), the form of the cross would probably be the *crux commissa* T. One cannot begin with the *titlos*, the superscription on the cross, as a basis for reconstruction. On the other hand, the explicit demand for the crucifixion of Jesus came from the Jews (Mk. 15:6–15; Matt. 27:15–26; Lk. 23:17–25). Some scholars find this difficult to accept in view of the Jewish detestation of this Roman form of punishment (see above OT 4). They also find it difficult to believe that Pilate would have ordered Jesus' crucifixion against his better judgment to meet Jewish demands. They see his action as incompatible with the integrity of Roman rule. In Roman eyes, Jesus would have been condemned and executed according to their standards and legal practices, not as a blasphemer, but an agitator, whatever the justice of the case (see above, CL 2. (b)).

This does not rule out, however, the interaction of interests on the part of the Romans and the upper stratum of Jews in Jerusalem who instigated the affair. It is supported by the striking fact that, as compared with other penal actions by the Romans, only Jesus was arrested, and that by the Jewish temple police. His followers were allowed to escape. On the analogy of other incidents, the intervention of Roman soldiers would have had other consequences (cf. Josephus, *Ant.*, 18, 85 ff.; 20, 97 ff.; 20, 169 ff.; *War*, 2, 2, 261 ff.). On the other hand, there were quite different reasons among the Jews which could have come into play. These concerned the opposition of the Jewish theologians and pious laity to the preaching of Jesus, and are evidenced elsewhere in the synoptic tradition (cf. E. Käsemann, *Jesus Means Freedom*, 1969, 43 ff.). The current abiding dispute between the church and Judaism lead the gospel accounts to focus on the Jewish motivation rather than on the decisive role of the Romans.

(b) Exegetical and theological considerations also demand close critical scrutiny of the historical question. Matt. and especially Lk. exhibit differences from Mk.'s account. Jn. deals with the passion narrative quite differently. In each case theological motives can be clearly seen. This process of shaping the material can be seen elsewhere in the synoptic tradition even before Mk. Thus the oldest tradition of the crucifixion of Jesus used by Mk. shows a definite theological tendency. The events are seen in terms of Ps. 22 (cf. Ps. 22:19; Matt. 27:35; Mk. 15:24; Lk. 23:34b; Jn. 19:24; Ps. 22:7 f.; Matt. 27:39, 43; Mk. 15:29; Lk. 23:35; Ps. 22:9; Matt. 27:43; Ps. 22:2; Matt. 27:46; Mk. 15:34; Ps. 22:22; Heb. 2:12; on this see H. Gese, "Psalm 22 und das Neue Testament", *ZTK* 65, 1968, 1–22). Attempts to harmonize the account should not be allowed to obscure such theological intentions. Passages like Heb. 2:14–18; 3:14; 4:14 f.; and 5:7–10 indicate the early church's interest in the story of the crucifixion and suffering of its Lord. Basic is the church's confession of the crucified one as the one exalted to God in the sense of a cosmic, saving act. When the church saw itself attacked, persecuted and suffering as a consequence of this confession, its interest in the earthly career of its Lord came to the fore. This form of the tradition of the suffering and crucifixion of Jesus shows in anticipation and perspective the church's walk on earth. The saviour leads the way as an obligatory pattern of suffering for his followers. This is how the narrative of the suffering and crucifixion of Jesus is understood, even though its soteriological character is not immediately apparent.

The ground of the opposition to Jesus is stated by Mk. 15:10 and Matt. 27:18

as envy. Jn. presents the actions of Caiaphas as being motivated by expediency: "It is expedient for you that one man should die for the people, and that the whole nation should not perish" (Jn. 11:49). But there was a genuine theological zeal which was present in the Jews' attitude to Jesus and their reaction to the early church. The repudiation of the craving for legitimization of "the word of the cross" by signs (1 Cor. 1:18–25) is reflected in the crucifixion narrative of Mk. 15:29–32; Matt. 27:39–43; Lk. 23:35 ff.

The historical question of responsibility for the crucifixion must be discussed without prejudice. But equally the historical question of guilt transcends the time of Jesus and demands a decision of the Jews as of men in general including Christians. This aspect which transcends time and persons is shown by Heb. 6:6 where those who commit apostasy are said to "crucify [*anastaurountas*, present participle] the Son of God on their own account and hold him up to contempt" (RSV). The question of guilt for the cross of Christ remains a contemporary one, wherever man's righteousness is presented as grounded in the grace of God demanding self-surrender in faith.

2. *The theological significance of the crucifixion of Jesus.*

(a) Paul. The use of these words in this sense occurs most frequently in Paul. They occur altogether 17 times: *stauros* 7 times; *stauroō* 8 times; *systauroō* twice. All these statements refer to something quite distinct from the actual procedure of crucifixion. The cross of Christ is seen as the saving event which radically transforms the world, providing a completely new motivation for action and thought.

The *euangelion* (→ Gospel) is central for Paul. It embraces the *logos tou staurou* (→ word of the cross), i.e. the saving proclamation based on the cross of Christ (1 Cor. 1:17 f.; cf. 2:1 f.; Rom. 1:16; Gal. 3:1; → also Proclamation, art. *kēryssō* for the term *kērygma*, proclamation, preaching). This terminology shows that the cross of Christ is not to be understood purely as an immanent, isolated event in history, but as the act of God. God acts as the cross of Christ is proclaimed as his Word, his liberating and binding message to mankind. In the kerygma of the messengers of Christ, the transcendent action of God is present as the word of the cross. The proclamation of Christ did not paint the historic details of the crucifixion before the eyes of its hearers. Instead, it publicly proclaimed Jesus Christ as the crucified one, portraying him to everyone as God's saving event in terms of the law. This is how Gal. 3:1 is to be understood (cf. H. Schlier, *Der Brief an die Galater*, KEK 7, 1971[14] ad loc.).

The message of the cross brings *sōtēria*, salvation (1 Cor. 1:18, 21; → Redemption, art. *sōzō*). This is indeed only to the *pisteuontes*, believers (1 Cor. 1:21→Faith), those who submit to God's verdict in the cross of Christ (1:19 ff.) on man's self-seeking wordly wisdom which even seeks to justify itself through man's religious experiences (1 Cor. passim). It is for those who let themselves be crucified by the word of the cross (Gal. 6:14; cf. 2:19). This condemnatory and at the same time liberating message of salvation is folly and scandalous not only to the Jews and Greeks (1 Cor. 1:18–25). It is also this to any perverted form of Christianity, whether it is enamoured of its own religious experiences (like the Corinthian church) or whether it falls back into a legalism which effectively denies the cross of Christ (like the Galatians).

This identification of the gospel with the cross of Christ is underlined by Phil. 2:8. Most scholars regard Phil. 2:6–11 as a hymn about Christ's renunciation of equal status with God and humiliation and obedience to death which Paul incorporated into his argument to urge Christians to have the mind of Christ. But Paul was not satisfied merely with the statement in the hymn about the death of Christ. He added the words *thanatou de staurou* ("even death on a cross" RSV). ([Ed.] On this passage see R. P. Martin, *Carmen Christi: Philippians ii. 5–11 in Recent Interpretation and in the Setting of Early Christian Worship*, 1967, 199–228; C. F. D. Moule, "Further Reflections on Philippians 2:5–11", in W. W. Gasque and R. P. Martin, eds., *Apostolic History and the Gospel*, 1970, 246–76.)

This focussing on the theology of the cross coincides with Paul's particular emphases. 1 Cor. 1:13 shows how Paul took over the traditional interpretation of the death of Jesus (cf. 1 Cor. 15:3). In a question that reveals the absurd behaviour of the Corinthians, Paul asks, "Was Paul crucified for you?" Paul has not brought about salvation. The Corinthians were not his property. And so there was no ground for dividing the church as the body of Christ on his account. Paul uses here the preposition *hyper* (for) in connection with *stauroō* in a way which was characteristic of the early church sacrificial and representative theology.

([Ed.] Although this is the only instance where Paul brings the two words *stauroō* and *hyper* together in the sense of being *crucified for*, it would not be true to think that this is the only case where Paul thinks of Christ's death as a representative sacrifice bearing the punishment of sin on behalf of others. The whole argument of Rom. depends upon the fact that God put forth Christ "as a propitiation by his blood, to be received by faith. This was to show God's righteousness, because in his divine forbearance he had passed over former sins; it was to prove at the present time that he himself is righteous and that he justifies him who has faith in Jesus" [Rom. 3:25 f.]. On the term propitiation (*hilastērion*) → Redemption; cf. L. Morris, *The Apostolic Preaching of the Cross*, 1955, 125–85. The preposition *hyper*, meaning for, instead of, in the place of, in the name of, in the interest of, for the benefit of, is used by Paul in connection with the death of Christ in the crucial passages and Gal. 3:13 and 1 Cor. 15:3 (cf. its use in 1 Cor. 15:29; 2 Cor. 5:20; Phlm. 13; 1 Tim. 2:6; Mk. 10:45; Jn. 10:11; 11:50; Rom. 16:4; cf. L. Morris, op. cit., 59). Other passages which stress the sacrificial, penal, representative and substitutionary character of the death of Christ without using the words cross or crucify are Rom. 5:10 f., 18; 8:1 ff.; 1 Cor. 11:24 f.; 2 Cor. 5:19 ff.; Eph. 1:7; 2:13. → Blood, → Reconciliation, → Redemption.)

In addition, Paul's theology of the cross has its own special emphases. Paul saw men as unredeemed, whether they were heathen or Jews who kept strictly to the law. This was not simply because of an uncleanness brought about by the accumulation of individual acts of sin. It was because of man's basic, depraved, self-seeking hostility to God. This appears: (1) in man's religious concern for achievements and in his presumptuous demand that the Word of God should be validated by miraculous proofs; and (2) in his insistence that the gospel of God should conform to → wisdom in both its teaching and form. In Christian terms, this meant that its power (its spiritual *dynamis*) should elevate and exalt the religious man to the realm of the superhuman and divine (1 Cor. 1:22; and cf. the underlying controversies of 1 and 2 Cor.). In all this is manifested nothing but that self-centred ego that rejects with ingratitude and disobedience God's claim on man which would liberate him (cf. Rom. 1:12 f.). Man is not content simply to live by receiving (cf. 1 Cor. 4:6 ff.). Therefore, in effect he judges God and discounts the cross and its proclamation for man's salvation (1 Cor. 1:19 ff., 26–29). Wisdom theology no less than legalistic piety discounts the cross of Christ. Both deprive it of its significance (1 Cor. 1:17).

From the standpoint of his *theologia crucis* (theology of the cross) Paul's teaching can be seen as a unity. On the one hand, Paul opposes the Jewish-Hellenistic view of life and salvation, which was measured in terms of wordly-legalistic and spiritual ecstatic wisdom, by life in Christ. On the other hand, he opposes Judaism with his doctrine of justification which was the consequence of his message of the cross. This is expressed in 1 and 2 Cor. and Gal. in terms of *stauros* and *stauroō*. But in the comprehensive exposition of justification in Rom. only *systauroō* occurs in Rom. 6:6 ("We know that our old self was crucified with him so that the sinful body might be destroyed, and we might no longer be enslaved to sin"). Nevertheless, Paul's doctrine of justification is to be understood on the basis of the cross. For the end of every legalistic theology is Christ who is none other than the crucified one in the sense of the Pauline "word of the cross" (1 Cor. 1:18). (On the parallels of the terminology of 1 and 2 Cor. and the doctrine of justification see H. Braun, *ThV* 49, 1948, 26 ff.) The parallel is also demonstrated by Gal. 2:19 ff. and 6:12. The *theologia crucis* and the doctrine of justification form an inseparable unity and are to be interpreted mutually in terms of each other.

Gal. 6:12 also demonstrates how Paul's doctrine of justification, preached in terms of the cross of Christ, brought with it persecution by the supporters of legalistic theology. (Cf. also Paul's reference to bearing in his body "the marks of Jesus", Gal. 6:17; → Body, art. *sōma* NT 2. (a).) Paul apparently thinks that such persecution provoked by the "offence of the cross", like the opposition provoked by the message of justification of the sinner without prior merit and the implied sacrifice of the intellect, would not occur (Gal. 5:11), if the message of the cross of Christ were turned into another gospel (Gal. 1:6 ff.).

In the case of the erring church it is not enough to speak of "Christ". For "Christ" could be understood as a glorified Christ removed from the world and removing men from the world (see the context of 1 and 2 Cor.). He might also be understood as a perfect Moses (as in Gal.). But Paul sets alongside the word *Christos* the unambiguous *estaurōmenos* (crucified, 1 Cor. 1:23; Gal. 3:1). He speaks with special emphasis in 1 Cor. 2:2: "For I decided to know nothing among you except Jesus Christ and him crucified (*ei mē Iesoun Christon kai touton estaurōmenon*)." This intensification reflects Paul's experience in Corinth and in general (Gal. 3:1). The cross of Christ alone (again the exclusive *ei mē*, Gal. 6:14) is Paul's ground for boasting and confidence. In practical terms, this means that Paul boasted most gladly of his weaknesses (2 Cor. 12:9 f.).

The practical significance of the resurrection is implied in Paul's teaching about the cross. Paul presents Christ crucified as the decisive act of God in salvation. The risen Christ does not simply supersede the crucified Christ. His self-humiliation and obedience in the shame of the death on the cross are not simply cancelled out. Through the exaltation they are justly raised in power as the sign of salvation (Phil. 2:8 ff.). Christ who took upon himself this weakness and was thus crucified, lives by reason of the creative power of God which raises the dead (2 Cor. 13:4). Believers who enter this new level of existence which is determined by the cross live in hope that is founded on the same act of God. This resurrection life which comes from God conquers death in the believers' existence under the cross. It is already manifest in this life for the well-being of others (2 Cor. 4:7–12). This is the ground of the apostle's existence under the cross (1 Cor. 15:30 ff.). This is the power of God grounded in the cross of Christ which is now revealed and active. Without it the apostle's life would be the most pitiable self-deception imaginable (1 Cor. 15:29).

The cross of Christ and the crucified Christ present in the kerygma are alone the → power (*dynamis*) and → wisdom (*sophia*) of God (1 Cor. 1:18–24). This is not the unmitigated power of the Corinthians' theology that would replace it with the world and its high-handed behaviour. But knowledge of the true power of God in the cross and the kerygma substantially forms the basis of Paul's exhortations and practical teaching. Paul reminded the erring churches, each in a specific way, to submit to the message of the cross (1 Cor.; Gal.; Phil. 3). It is not only the sections on the divisions in the Corinthian church (1 Cor. 1:10–4:21) but the whole of 1 Cor. that urges that thought and action should be determined by the cross of Christ. This applies to preoccupation with power, fame, and wisdom that is purely self-seeking and thus divisive of the body of Christ (1:10–4:21). It also applies to re-nunciation of one's rights (6:1–11) and even of one's proper freedom for the sake of others (8:1–11:1). Moreover, Paul refers not only to the crucified Christ himself as present in the word, but also to an astonishing extent to his own mode of life and preaching. They represent almost bodily the way of life controlled by the cross of Christ (1:17, 23; 2:1–5; 3:5 ff.; 4:6; cf. also the exhortations to imitate Paul which occasionally round off the longer sections, 4:16; 11:1).

The fundamental basis here is Christ as the pattern, especially his renunciation of his rights (1 Cor. 11:1; cf. ch. 6 and what follows) and his humiliation to death on the cross for the sake of others (Phil. 2:1 ff.). To this also belongs Heb. 12:2. The afflicted are exhorted to look to Jesus who endured the cross despising its shame "for the joy that was set before him (*anti tēs prokeimenēs autō charas*)." This phrase can be taken to mean: (1) instead of the joy that he could have had; or (2) for the sake of the joy that was set before him. There may be an underlying parallel with Phil. 2:6 which would favour (1). But in the context of Heb. 12, meaning (2) may be more likely, though this thought would be more removed from Paul's thought in Phil. 2.

Paul can even speak of some people as "enemies of the cross of Christ" (Phil. 3:18) in the context of a call to imitate the example of himself and others (Phil. 3:17). These enemies are those who strive after earthly things and whose life is not shaped by the message of the cross (3:18 f.). They are those who have not sought salvation in Christ crucified. They have not, like Paul, left their legalistic existence behind them like refuse, or sought to know the sufferings of Christ, or be conformed to his death (3:7 ff.).

What Paul says about the basis of the church in the preaching of the cross in 1 Cor., about humility in the Christ-hymn of Phil. 2, about the message of justification in Phil. 3, and in all three places about imitation and its practical application, he also develops in relation to → baptism (Rom. 6; cf. Gal. 2:19). Christ has died (Rom. 6:10), and thus Christians have also died (6:2). They have been thereby, like

400

him, freed from the power of sin. "The death he died he died to sin, once for all" (6:10). Baptism into Christ means baptism into his death (6:3). Baptism thus represents the unique and all-encompassing event of Christ's death. Believers are thus crucified with Christ (*systauroō*, Rom. 6:6; Gal. 2:19).

Gal. 2:19 speaks of the crucifixion of the sinful self which is given over to legalism. But behind this, the historical and religious background can still be seen. Rom. 6:6 speaks of "our old self (*ho palaios hēmōn anthrōpos*)" or "our old man" being crucified with him so that "the sinful body might be destroyed." By this means the power of sin over us is broken ("we might no longer be enslaved to sin", 6:6). Gal. 6:14 is a parallel statement on a cosmic scale: "Be it far from me to glory except in the cross of our Lord Jesus Christ, by which the world has been crucified to me, and I to the world." Through the cross of Christ the compelling power of the → world has been crucified for the benefit of the inner self of the believer. On the other hand, the self was delivered to death to the hurt of the world, so that it has lost its basis of operation. Above all, the active formulation of this idea shows that the thought goes beyond the crucifixion of Christ and the cultic background of soteriology (→ Reconciliation). Believers who have become Christ's possession have crucified the flesh with its passions and desires (Gal. 5:24). In this they are not merely passive; it is something that they do themselves.

Two ideas have been critically adopted here: (1) the anthropological idea that salvation comes about through killing the flesh or the external man; (2) the idea of a primeval figure who went just such a way to accomplish salvation into which men of his sort can now enter. Paul uses these ideas to express the radical transformation brought about by the cross of Christ and its continuing decisive role in the life of the believer. In the same way, Paul exhorts Christians to imitate the example of him who gave himself, putting them under an obligation and at the same time giving them hope. He remained the obedient in suffering and shame of the cross. And in all this he gave an eschatological manifestation of God's right in action. This interpretation of the cross must also be set in relation to the message of justification and worked out systematically and critically. This is what is in fact done in an unconscious way in Rom. 6 (cf. the basis for it in 1:18–5:21); Gal. 2:19; 6:14; Phil. 3:10, 17.

(b) Col. and Eph. adopt a different approach from the epistles of Paul already discussed. They mention only the noun (3 times).

Col. continues the earlier Pauline teaching which in Rom. 6 relates dying with Christ to baptism. "For you have died and your life is hid with Christ in God" (Col. 3:3). "And you were buried with him (*syntaphentes autō*) in baptism, in which you were also raised with him through faith in the working of God, who raised him from the dead" (Col. 2:12). Moreover, this liberates man from the enslaving, cosmic elemental powers. "If with Christ you died to the elemental spirits of the universe (*stoicheia tou kosmou*), why do you live as if you still belonged to the world? Why do you submit to regulations?" (Col. 2:20). ([Ed.] Alternatively, *stoicheia* is taken by other interpreters to mean the elementary principles of the world; → Law, art. *stoicheia*.) There is a partial analogy here with Gal. 5:24. The exhortation to the believers themselves to put to death what is earthly in them (Col. 3:5), the particular forms of sin which arise from the → flesh (Col. 3:5–9), is seen as the outworking of the decisive saving event of the death of Christ. Eph., on

401

the other hand, speaks only of the believer's being made alive in Christ, which has already taken place. "And you he made alive, when you were dead through trespasses and sins" (Eph. 2:1; cf. 1:20; 2:6; Col. 3:1). In both Col. and Eph. there is no longer any talk of a crucifixion with Christ that has already taken place. The development of soteriological ideas is correspondingly less rigorous than in the earlier epistles. This may be seen in the way Col. 2:22 urges the readers: "Put off your old nature which belongs to your former manner of life and is corrupt through sinful lusts." This may be compared with the similar exhortation in Rom. 6:6 which is set in the context of a carefully articulated discussion of the death of Christ.

On the other hand, Col. and Eph. develop a theology of the cosmic significance of the Christ-event which is not found in the earlier epistles. Col. 1:19 f. may be based on an already existing hymn: "For in him all the fullness of God was pleased to dwell, and through him to reconcile to himself all things, whether on earth or in heaven, making peace by the blood of the cross." The reconciliation of all things through his exaltation and assumption of authority is grounded in "the blood of the cross." Eph. 2:16 develops this thought in a specific direction, declaring that his purpose was to "reconcile us both [i.e. Jew and Gentile] to God in one body through the cross, thereby bringing the hostility to an end." By "abolishing in his flesh the law of commandments" he creates "in himself one new man in place of the two, so making peace" (Eph. 2:15).

Col. 2:14 f. further develops the cosmic significance of the cross. The decisive conquest of the powers of evil took place on the cross, and this is related to his "having cancelled the bond which stood against us with its legal demands; this he set aside, nailing it to the cross" (v. 14). Two pictures are combined here. (1) There is the picture of debt, drawn from the ancient business world. This represents the ordinances of the Jewish law and the dictates of the false teachers. Its accusing testimony is cancelled. (2) There is also the picture of a public, official decree that has been posted up. This was probably in accordance with the custom sometimes adopted of fastening a *titulus* with the *causa poenae* of the criminal to the cross. Taken together these pictures show that Christ himself made the cross into a public valid declaration, proclaiming the cancelling out of our sins and the end of all claim to legalism.

(c) *The sayings about bearing the cross.*

These occur 5 times in 2 lines of tradition. What may be called Version A (Matt. 10:38; Lk. 14:27) is thought by many scholars to be derived from the Q source. They regard Lk.'s version as being nearer to the original. Version B is common to all three Synoptic Gospels (Matt. 16:24; Lk. 9:23; Mk. 8:34). Most scholars regard Matt. and Lk. as drawing on Mk. Lk. includes the words *kath' hēmeran* (daily); the cross is to be taken up repeatedly without flagging. Scholars think that the saying in the conjectured Q source was formulated negatively and was the more original: whoever does not constantly bear his own cross as a disciple and so follow Christ on the way he has opened cannot possibly belong to the disciples. Mk.'s version speaks positively about entering the way of Christ which is generally described by taking the cross on oneself.

There is considerable debate about the original setting and significance of these sayings. The pictorial way of speaking presupposes that they go back to Jesus. There is no evidence of this way of speaking in contemporary Judaism (SB I 587).

402

Gen. R 56 (36c) declares that, "Abraham took the wood for sacrifice and laid it on his son Isaac, like one who bears the cross on his shoulders" (cf. J. Schniewind, *Das Evangelium nach Markus*, NTD 1 1960[9], 85). But this is no real, historically dependable parallel. Its date is uncertain. The purely hypothetical assumption that Jesus adopted this way of speaking from the Zealots and their disciples (A. Schlatter, *Der Evangelist Matthäus*, 1959[5], 350 f., who also cites Gen. R. 56 and Tanh. 46, 114) is hardly credible. Just as the Roman practice of crucifixion was foreign to the East and was thoroughly detested by the Jews (see above, CL 2), the Jewish world did not know of the expression *bastazein stauron* in the sense of the Lat. *patibulum ferre*. E. Dinkler has made the original suggestion that Jesus was referring to the cultic sign in the form of a cross by means of the letters tau or chi (τ and χ) and that he required this as a seal of the elect in the end-time (*Signum Crucis*, 1967, 55 ff.). But this would mean that the words of Jesus had undergone a thorough transformation of meaning in the church's tradition. Originally they would have had a merely formal significance. The theory appears to be altogether too artificial and arbitrary.

There remains the theory that the sayings are a word from the exalted Christ delivered by an early church prophet to a church fearful of persecution. The church is reminded that, if they will gain life, they too are not exempted from self-renunciation. The way of Christ must also be the way for Christians in this particular way. The sayings about bearing the cross are thus the synoptic equivalent of Paul's theology of the cross. The striking formula of "his" (i.e. the disciple's) cross underlines the theological connection between Christ's way and the Christian's way. It denotes not merely the particular form of punishment by crucifixion, but the implicit renunciation of life that could even mean martyrdom. Lk. 9:23 gives expression to this wider meaning.   *E. Brandenburger*

The contention that the sayings about bearing the cross are the synoptic equivalent of Paul's practical application of the theology of the cross is a valid one. However, there are several objections against regarding these sayings as utterances of prophets speaking in the name of Jesus to the early church. (1) The above argument about the uniqueness of pictorial language and its connection with Jesus would point to the earthly Jesus as the author of these sayings. (2) Their present context suggests that they were understood as such. It remains to be demonstrated that the early church made no sharp differentiation between utterances of the earthly Jesus and those of the ascended Christ. The literary genres that we have in the NT suggest the opposite. (3) If the earthly Jesus did not warn his followers in this way, there is the implication that the followers of Jesus were instructed about the extreme demands of renunciation with the implication of martyrdom only after the death of Jesus. (4) The historical setting indicated by the gospels in the life and ministry of Jesus is coherent in itself. Jesus was aware of the only possible outcome of his mission, given the attitudes of the religious leaders of the day. He would also realize that only the Romans had power of capital punishment and that the form of capital punishment was crucifixion. This was something that he lived with. He would know also of the practice of the condemned man bearing the *patibulum*. Whatever fate, therefore, awaited him would also await those who followed him.

403

The sayings about bearing the cross form part of warning the disciples to count the cost (see the context of Matt. 10:38 and Lk. 14:27). This is coupled with the warning that a servant is not above his master (Matt. 10:24; cf. Lk. 6:40; Jn. 13:16; 15:20). Moreover, the saying common to all three Synoptic Gospels occurs in the context of Jesus' acknowledgment of Peter's confession of him as the Christ. For Jesus the inevitable implication of being the Christ is suffering, death, and the opposition of men. Inevitably, therefore, those who associate with him as the Christ are liable to the same fate.   *C. Brown*

(a). E. Bammel, ed., *The Trial of Jesus*, 1970; G. C. Berkouwer, *The Work of Christ*, 1965; E. Best, *The Temptation and Passion: The Markan Soteriology*, 1965; M. Black, "The Chi-Rho Sign – Christogram and/or Staurogram," in W. W. Gasque and R. P. Martin, *Apostolic History and the Gospel* (F. F. Bruce Festschrift), 1970, 319–27; J. Blinzler, *The Trial of Jesus*, 1959 (fuller: *Der Prozess Jesu*, 1969⁴); S. G. F. Brandon, *The Trial of Jesus of Nazareth*, 1968; R. Bultmann, "New Testament and Mythology," in H.-W. Bartsch, ed., *Kerygma and Myth*, I, 1953, 1–44 (see also the discussion in the remaining essays in the volume); D. R. Catchpole, *The Trial of Jesus: A Study of the Gospels and Jewish Historiography from 1770 to the Present Day*, 1971; J. Daniélou, "Cross," *EBT* I 155 f.; and *The Development of Christian Doctrine before the Council of Nicea*, I, *The Theology of Jewish Christianity*, 1964, 265–92; E. Dinkler, "Comments on the History of the Symbol of the Cross", *Journal for Theology and the Church* I, 1965, 124–45; E. E. Ellis, "Christ Crucified", in R. Banks, ed., *Reconciliation and Hope* (Leon Morris Festschrift), 1974, 69–75; R. S. Franks, *The Work of Christ*, (1918) 1962; E. M. B. Green, *The Meaning of Salvation*, 1965; J. G. Griffiths, "The Disciple's Cross," *NTS* 16, 1969–70, 358–64; E. Käsemann, "The Saving Significance of the Death of Jesus in Paul," *Perspectives on Paul*, 1971, 32–59; W. Künneth, *The Theology of the Resurrection*, 1965, 123 ff., 150 ff.; L. Morris, *The Apostolic Preaching of the Cross*, 1960²; and *The Cross in the New Testament*, 1967; J. I. Packer, "What did the Cross Achieve? The Logic of Penal Substitution", *TB* 25, 1974, 3 ff.; H. Wheeler Robinson, *The Cross in the Old Testament*, 1955; J. Schneider, *xylon*, *TDNT* V 37–41; and *stauros*, *TDNT* VII 572–84; A. N. Sherwin–White, *Roman Society and Roman Law in the New Testament*, 1963; D. Sölle, *Christ the Representative*, 1967; V. Taylor, *Jesus and his Sacrifice*, 1937; *The Atonement in New Testament Teaching*, 1940; and *The Passion Narrative of St. Luke*, 1972; J. L. Teicher, "The Interpretation of the Sign ✕ in the Isaiah Scroll," *VT* 5, 1955, 189–98; P. Winter, *On the Trial of Jesus*, Studia Judaica 1 (1961) 1974².

(b). J. Blinzler, "Kreuzigung," *LTK* VI 621 ff.; G. Bornkamm, "Kreuz," in *Theologie für Nichttheologen*, III, 1965, 5 ff.; J. Daniélou, *Les symboles chrétiens primitifs*, 1961, 143–51; G. Delling, "Der Tod Jesu in der Verkündigung des Paulus," in *Apophoreta*, Festschrift E. Haenchen, 1964, 85 ff.; E. Dinkler, "Kreuzzeichen und Kreuz," *Jahrbuch für Antike und Christentum* 5, 1962, 93–112; "Jesu Worte vom Kreuztragen," in *Neutestamentliche Studien für R. Bultmann*, 1957³, 110 ff. (*BZNW* 21, 1954; *Signum Crucis*, 1967, 77 ff.); "Das Kreuz als Siegeszeichen" *ZTK* 62, 1965, 1 ff. (*Signum Crucis*, 1967, 55 ff.); G. Eichholz, "Paulus im Umgang mit jungen Kirchen. Exegetische Beobachtungen zu 1 Kor. 1:18–25," in *Basileia*, Festschrift für W. Freytag, 1959, 49 ff. (*ThBl* 29, 1965, 99 f.); O. Glombitza, "Das Kreuz. Eine neutestamentliche Studie," in *Festschrift* M. Mitzenheim, 1961; H. Gollwitzer, *Von der Stellvertretung Gottes*, 1967; A. Grillmeier, *Der Logos am Kreuz*, 1956; H. F. Hitzig, "Crux", Pauly-Wissowa IV 1728 ff.; J. Jeremias, *Der Opfertod Jesu Christi*, 1963; E. Käsemann, "Die Gegenwart des Gekreuzigten," in *Protestantische Texte*, 1967, 85 ff.; and "Das Kreuz," in *Christus unter uns*, 1967; B. Klappert, ed., *Diskussion um Kreuz und Auferstehung*, 1968³; W. Kreck, "Zum Verständnis des Todes Jesu," *EvTh* 28, 1968, 277 ff.; K. Latte, "Todesstrafe," Pauly–Wissowa Supplement VII 1599 ff.; H. Lietzmann, "Der Prozess Jesu," *Kleine Schriften*, II, 1958, 251 ff.; E. Lohse, *Märtyrer und Gottesknecht*, 1963²; W. Marxsen, "Erwägungen zum Problem des verkündigten Kreuzes," *NTS* 8, 1961–62, 204 ff.; W. Michaelis, "Zeichen, Siegel, Kreuz", *ThZ* 12, 1956, 505 ff.; K. Müller, "1 Kor. 1, 18–25. Die eschatologisch-kritische Funktion des Kreuzes," *BZ* 10, 1966, 246 ff.; F. J. Ortkemper, *Das Kreuz in der Verkündigung des Paulus*, 1964; C. D. Peddinghaus, *Die Entstehung der Leidensgeschichte*, (Dissertation Heidelberg) 1965; E. Peterson, *Das Kreuz und das Gebet nach Ostern: Frühkirche, Judentum, und Gnosis*, 1959, 15–35; H. Rahner, "Das mystische Tau," *Zeitschrift für katholische Theologie*, 75, 1953, 385–410; SB I 1034 f.; III 792; IV 1121 ff.; V. Schultze, "Kreuz und Kreuzigung," *RE* XI 90 ff.; M. Sulzberger, "Le symbole de la croix," *Byzantion*, 2, 1925, 356–83; F. Viering, *Der*

Kreuztod Jesu, 1969; O. Weber, "Das dogmatische Problem der Versöhnungslehre," *EvTh* 26, 1966, 258 ff.; U. Wilckens, *Weisheit und Torheit. Eine exegetische-religions-geschichtliche Untersuchung zu 1 Kor. 1, 18–2, 16*, BHTh 26, 1959.

Crown, Sceptre, Rod

στέφανος

στέφανος (*stephanos*), wreath, crown; στεφανόω (*stephanoō*), to crown; στέμμα (*stemma*), garland; διάδημα (*diadēma*), diadem, crown.

CL (a) *stephanos* (from *stephō*, surround, encompass) was used originally of anything which encircles, such as a besieging army (Homer) or the wall around a city (Pindar). The usual meaning throughout secular Greek became a "crown" or "wreath" (Homeric Hymns and Hesiod onwards), especially the victor's wreath of leaves at the various athletic games (Pindar etc.). A wreath, often worked in gold, was awarded by Greek states as a high mark of honour (Plato etc.). The *stephanos* in fact played its part in many ancient customs, and bore diverse connotations, of victory, festivity, worship, public office or honour, kingship or royal visitation.

stephanos and the verb *stephanoō* were often used figuratively, especially where "crown" denotes an "object of pride".

(b) *stemma* was used especially of the laurel-wreath of a sacrificing priest. Homer speaks of it as wound around his staff (*skēptron, Il.*, 1, 14–15; → sceptre).

(c) *diadēma* (band, from *diadeō*, bind on either side) was strictly the band round the *tiara* of the Persian king (Xenophon), worn also by Alexander and later kings (Arrian, Plutarch), and so generally "crown" as a badge of kingship.

OT (a) In the LXX *stephanos* mostly represents the Heb. *'aṭārāh*, both of a royal crown (2 Sam. 12:30 etc.), and very commonly figurative, of honour, victory or pride, especially in the poetic books. *diadēma* is applied in Est. to the royal crown of Persia (Heb. *keṭer*), but is more frequent in the apocryphal books, and there often in metaphorical senses otherwise confined to *stephanos* (Wisd. 5:16; Sir. 47:6; etc.).

The Heb. *nēzer* (consecration, crown; cf. *nāzar*, to consecrate, separate), applied regularly to the crown of the kings of Israel and to the headdress of the high-priest, is variably and confusedly rendered in the LXX.

(b) The crown was a frequent image in later Judaism. The future expectation of a "crown of glory" appears in Test. Ben. 4:1. Other references appear to build on the term *nēzer* in passages like Ps. 89:39 and 132:18: the king as well as the priest, was divinely consecrated to his office, and the crown was attributed to the ideal Davidic king. So there were said to be three "crowns", of Torah, priesthood and royalty (Pirqe Aboth 4:17; 6:5; cf. Yoma 72b).

NT (a) In the NT *stephanos* occurs 18 times (8 of them in Rev.), *diadēma* 3 times (all in Rev.) and *stemma* once (Acts 14:13, its only appearance in Biblical Greek).

(b) *diadēma* signifies kingship, of the dragon (Rev. 12:3), of the beast (13:1), and of Christ (19:2).

(c) *stemma* is used only of the "garlands" brought by the pagan priest who would have offered sacrifice to Paul and Barnabas at Lystra.

405

(d) *stephanos* is used of the "crown of thorns" (Matt. 27:29; Mk. 15:17; Jn. 19:2, 5). As a wreath made of a plant it was literally so called. To the soldiers it meant mock royalty: to the evangelists it constituted testimony to the true kingship of Christ over a spiritual kingdom, while perhaps also implying his forthcoming victory over death. The view that *stephanos* could never be used thus of kingship is overstated.

(e) *stephanos* in the NT is often the prize of athletic victory as a metaphor for the eternal reward of the faithful. *stephanos* or *stephanoō* are used thus 1 Cor. 9:25; 2 Tim. 2:5; 4:8; Jas. 1:12 ("crown of life"); 1 Pet. 5:4 ("crown of glory"); Rev. 3:11; 4:4, 10. Cf. also the thought of passages like 1 Tim. 4:8 and Heb. 12:1, where the athletic imagery is very clear. The eternal hope is set against the transience of perishable wreaths (1 Cor. 9:25; 1 Pet. 5:4): in the former case there may be allusion to the use of *withered* parsley for the crown at the Isthmian Games.

Paul refers elsewhere (Phil. 4:1; 1 Thess. 2:19) to the recipient churches as his "crown", his pride or glory. Another line of thought may also sometimes be subtly blended with the athletic metaphor. At the official visit (Gk. *parousia*) of a human potentate it was the custom to present him with a crown as a token of allegiance (Deissmann, *Light*, pp. 368–373; cf. also 1 Macc. 13:37; 2 Macc. 14:4; and the use of the term for a money tribute, 1 Macc. 10:29; Jos., *Ant.* 12, 3, 3 (142)). Perhaps in 1 Thess. 2:19 the Thessalonians are seen as Paul's joyful tribute to the coming Christ. In 2 Tim. 4:8 (cf. 1 Pet. 5:4) this may be combined with the athletic image: Christ at his *parousia*, instead of demanding a crown from his people, will bestow on them the athlete's prize.

(f) The phrase "crown of life" in Rev. 2:10 (cf. Jas. 1:2) is of special interest. The genitive here, as in the parallels, is best taken as epexegetic, of the prize "which consists in life". The term was particularly apposite in Smyrna, where a crown or wreath was a pervasively common numismatic emblem and a constant theme of the rhetorical panegyrics of Aelius Aristides in the following century. Cicero (*pro Flacco*, 31, 75) alludes with emphatic sarcasm to a Smyrnaean custom of bestowing a crown as a posthumous honour to distinguished citizens (cf. the numerous class of inscribed monuments, *CIG*, 3216 ff.). Eternal life, untouched by the threat of spiritual death, shall be the prize of the faithful "athlete" who endures persecution to the suffering of physical death. In that he shall share the experience of him "who was dead, and is alive" (Rev. 2:8). Cf. the common Christian image of the martyr as an athlete, winning his "crown" in the arena: Polycarp, the classic instance, suffered thus at Smyrna.

(g) *stephanoō* is used in Heb. 2:7, 9, in a messianic application of Ps. 8:5. Some have seen here reference to the Transfiguration or the crown of thorns as preceding Christ's death and prefiguring his heavenly glory. Probably the words are not to be pressed in this way, and the reference is to Christ's future glory, as in Phil. 2:9 and elsewhere in Heb.

C. J. Hemer

G. T. Purves, *HDB* I 129–131; W. M. Ramsay, *The Letters to the Seven Churches*, 1904, 251–80; A. Deissmann, *Light from the Ancient East*, tr. L. R. M. Strachan, 1927, 368–373; H. St. J. Hart, "The Crown of Thorns in John 19, 2–5", *JTS* n.s. 3, 1952, 66–75; O. Broneer, "The Isthmian Victory Crown", *American Journal of Archeology* 66, 1962, 259–263.

$\dot{\rho}\dot{\alpha}\beta\delta o\varsigma$	$\dot{\rho}\dot{\alpha}\beta\delta o\varsigma$ (rhabdos), rod, staff; $\sigma\kappa\tilde{\eta}\pi\tau\rho o\nu$ (skēptron), staff, sceptre.

CL *skēptron* (from *skēptō*), to prop, lean), a staff, esp. that borne by kings as a hereditary emblem of authority and by heralds and public speakers (Homer), occurs mostly in older Greek and in poetry. *rhabdos* later tends to replace *skēptron* for a staff of office. Under the Romans *rhabdouchos* (rod-bearer) was used to render the Lat. *lictor*. These officers were the attendants of the consuls or other Roman magistrates and bore the *rhabdoi* (Lat. *fasces*) which were the badge of their authority.

OT (a) In the LXX both *rhabdos* and *skēptron* are common, rendering several Heb. words, but mostly *šēbeṭ* and *maṭṭeh*. *šēbeṭ*, used of a shepherd's club, is often also the badge of authority or chastisement; *maṭṭeh* (cf. *nāṭâh*, spread, incline) may be the traveller's staff, but is also used like *šēbeṭ*. These Heb. words are both also applied to the "tribes" of Israel. In 1 Sam. 2:28 etc. *šēbeṭ* in the latter sense is incongruously rendered *skēptron*.

(b) Several passages containing this word-group were important in later Jewish interpretation. Passages referring to a future ruler of Israel were applied Messianically. Such are Gen. 49:10, where *šēbeṭ* becomes LXX *archōn* (ruler), and notably Num. 24:17 (LXX *anthrōpos*, man), cited thus in Test. Levi 18:3, in Test. Judah 24:1 and in the Qumran literature, where the star and sceptre of this verse are respectively equated with the royal and the priestly Messiah expected by the sect. The same verse underlies the Messianic claim in the title Bar-Kokhba. Again, the Qumran Isaiah commentary applies to the kingly Messiah the term "rod" of Jesse from Isa. 11:1 (Heb. *ḥōṭer;* LXX *rhabdos*).

NT (a) *skēptron* is absent from the NT.

(b) *rhabdos* occurs 12 times in the NT. It is used literally of a traveller's "staff" in Matt. 10:10; Mk. 6:8; Lk. 9:3, each referring to Jesus' sending forth of the Twelve. In two of the Gospels they are to take no staff; in Mk. a staff alone is permitted.

(c) *rhabdos* and its derivatives are also used literally in the NT of a "rod" of authority or chastisement. The *rhabdouchoi* at Philippi (Acts 16:35, 38) were the lictors attendant on the two colonial *stratēgoi* (Lat. *praetores, duumviri*): *rhabdizō* (beat with rods) was used of the flogging inflicted by them (Acts 16:22; cf. 2 Cor. 11:25).

(d) This sense of *rhabdos* may be applied figuratively, as in Paul's threat in 1 Cor. 4:21. In the Rev. some of the OT passages where the "sceptre" or "rod" were already explained messianically in Judaism are applied to Christ Balaam, the seer who uttered the crucial oracle in Num. 24:17, is prominent in the Pergamene letter (→ Nicolaitans), and in the closely related one to Thyatira a messianic application of his "star" is linked with the citation of Ps. 2:9 ("thou shalt break them with a rod of iron") in the conqueror's promise of dominance over the nations (Rev. 2:27–28; on which see Rev. 22:16, and with that cf. Isa. 11:1 above). The same image is used of the man child of 12:5 and of the triumphant Christ in 19:15, where the two symbols of authority in the two letters, "sword" and "rod", are combined. In Thyatira, as at Pergamum, the Christian was helpless before hostile pagan authority: in each case Christ's authority is elevated above that of human tyrannies and represented by a suitable figure derived from the OT. The conqueror, who in obedience to Christ's authority keeps his works to the end, shall himself be delegated that messianic authority over the forces which now oppress him. This reading of the context favours the rendering "rule" rather than "break" for the problematic *poimanei* (Rev. 2:27), whether or not this usage is to be explained simply as a citation from the LXX.

(e) References to *rhabdos* in Heb. illustrate further the theme of the rod or sceptre of authority in the NT exegesis of the OT. Heb. 1:8 cites Ps. 45:6–7. The superiority of the unique Son to angels is enforced by appeal to a series of OT testimonies, again including Ps. 2 and this royal marriage-psalm which invokes the righteous king as "God". Heb. 9:4, in a passage contrasting the temporary character of the OT sanctuary and its furnishings with the eternal new covenant, alludes to the rod of Aaron which budded and was then to be preserved (Num. 17:10), the emblem of the Levitical priesthood, itself now superseded.

In the reference to the faith of Jacob in his blessing of the sons of Joseph (Heb. 11:21) the word *rhabdos* is taken from the LXX of Gen. 47:31, which apparently renders *maṭṭeh* where the MT has the vocalization *miṭṭâh* (bed).   *C. J. Hemer*

C. Schneider, *rhabdos, TDNT.* VI 966–71.

Cry

κράζω

κράζω (*krazō*), cry aloud; ἐπιφωνέω (*epiphōneō*), call out, shout; κέλευσμα (*keleusma*), a call, signal, command.

CL (a) The verb *krazō* has an onomatopoeic derivation, *kr* + vowel + guttural, reflecting the raucous cry of the raven. Post-Homeric, it is found in writers from Aeschylus on, and, among wildlife, not only of the cry of ravens but also of the noise of frogs (Aristophanes). More commonly it is applied to men. Its religious connection is usually in the sphere of the demonic. Lucian uses the verb to describe the invocation of the gods of the underworld by the magus after blood-offering. It can refer to a wailing, inarticulate and mysterious beseeching of the gods (Hippolytus). Witches cry out magical incantations. On the other hand, both the Greeks and the Romans tended to regard the cries of demons themselves as rather vulgar and barbaric (e.g. Juvenal). The verb is also used with a less evil connotation of the hierophant's proclamation of the Eleusinian mysteries (Hippolytus, Plutarch).

(b) In secular Gk. the verb *epiphōneō* is used from the time of Sophocles, and can bear a strong meaning, "call out", "proclaim", "exclaim" (Epicurus) or a weaker sense, "tell of" (Aristaenetus). Plutarch's use, "say with respect to (someone)", carries a denunciatory nuance.

(c) The noun *keleusma* (cf. Lat. loan-word, *celeusma*, a command of the chief oarsman to the rowers) derives from the root *kel* "to impel", and is often found in its older form *keleuma*. Its range of meanings includes a broad spectrum: (1) "a specific command", whether of a man or a god (Sophocles, Euripides, Herodotus); (2) "signal", "summons", "terse order" whose substance is understood by the recipient (Herodotus, Plato, Aeschylus, Xenophon – the latter of the call of the *keleustēs*, chief oarsman who sets the rhythm for the rowers); (3) "inarticulate cry" or "shout" (Aeschylus, Euripides). → Command, art. *keleusma*.

408

OT (a) In the LXX *krazō* occurs most frequently in the perfect and aorist tenses, usually standing for Heb. *ṣāʿaq, zāʿaq,* and *qārāʾ*. Flexible enough to cover the shout of war (Jos. 6:16), the cry of childbirth (Isa. 26:17), the wild call of a raven or the braying of an ass (Job 38:41 and 6:5 respectively), *krazō* becomes especially significant when it translates *qārāʾ*, notably in the Psalms. Men cry to the Lord in individual or national distress, and God hears and delivers (Exod. 22:22 f.; Jdg. 3:9; Pss. 21:5; 33:17; 106:6; etc.). Although Yahweh invites such crying from Jeremiah (40:3 ff. LXX), which cry elicits the proclamation of redemption from Babylon, the coming of the Messiah, and the inauguration of the new covenant, he will not hear the cry of the ungodly (Mic. 3:4). Nevertheless the crying depicted in the Psalms often pulsates with assurance that God will answer (e.g. 4:3; 21:24; 54:16); the idea of relationship with the Almighty is very strong, and in this differs from Hellenistic usage. Two distinctive uses deserve special note: the worshipful crying of the angels who stand in Yahweh's presence (Isa. 6:3 f.), and the quietness of the coming of the Servant of the Lord (Isa. 42:2).

Philo makes little use of the verb (but cf. *De Ebrietate,* 98, a Hellenistic usage). Josephus uses *krazō* in the sense of prophetic proclamation (cf. also *Tanchuma*). The Rabbis refer to "crying" (*ṣwwḥ*) as part of a formula introducing quotations cited by them in support of their views. However, a more OT late-Jewish usage is preserved in apocalyptic (e.g. Eth. En. 71:11).

(b) In the three instances where *epiphōneō* is used in the LXX – and all three are outside the Heb. canon – the idea appears to be of a quasi-liturgical response of the people (1 Es. 9:47; 2 Macc. 1:23; 3 Macc. 7:13).

(c) The noun *keleusma* is found but once in the LXX, of the command to "march" given by one locust to his fellows (Prov. 24:62; MT 30:27). Both Josephus and Philo apply the word in all three senses given above.

NT (a) *Synoptics:* Common in the Synoptics, *krazō* is used primarily for cries of help springing out of need and/or fear (e.g. Matt. 9:27; 14:26 (Mk. 6:49 uses a cognate); 14:30; 15:22 f.), and for the cries of demons, whether articulate (Mk. 1:23; Matt. 8:29, etc.) or inarticulate (Mk. 5:5; Lk. 9:39). It is possible that the latter are magical incantations. An element of praise is introduced by the personification metaphor of Lk. 19:40: the stones themselves would cry out if Jesus were to hush the crowd. But more resonant are the cries of hate demanding Jesus' death (Matt. 27:23; Mk. 15:13 f.; *epiphōneō* in Lk. 23:21, only here in NT outside of Acts) or the release of Barabbas (Lk. 23:18). Jesus himself is quiet; Isa. 42:2 is fulfilled in him (Matt. 12:19, but the verb is the cognate *kraugazō*). When he does cry (Matt. 27:50) it is not an inarticulate sound (cf. Lk. 23:46), but the prayer to his Father which brings his → work on the → cross to its blessed climax.

(b) *John:* The Fourth Evangelist customarily employs *kraugazō* where the Synoptists prefer *krazō* (e.g. 12:13; 18:40; 19:12). In addition, Jesus calls forth (*kraugazō*) Lazarus from his tomb. John's four occurrences of *krazō* bear a distinctive meaning akin to the rabbinic sense of "proclaim". Each refers to some facet of Christ's person or work. Once it is the Baptist who thus proclaims the superiority of Jesus (1:15), while on the other three occasions Jesus himself is the One who cries out his message to the people (7:28, 37 f.; 12:44 ff.).

(c) *Acts:* This book embraces both a Synoptic and a Johannine use of *krazō*.

There are several references to the cries of Christians, e.g. in petition for others (7:60), and in protest (14:14); as well as to public outcry (e.g. 19:28). The verb *epiphōneō* puts in its three other NT appearances. Two of these refer to the incoherent but denunciatory uproar against Paul (Acts 21:34; 22:24), and in the other the people cry in idolatrous (mocking?) worship of Herod (12:22).

(d) *Pauline Corpus:* Paul utilizes *krazō* three times. One occurrence is in the sense of prophetic proclamation (Rom. 9:27); the other two appear to be a NT modification of the calling on the Lord by a righteous man, so common in the Psalms (Rom. 8:15; Gal. 4:6). The difference is that it is the Spirit (of adoption, Rom.; of God's Son, Gal.) which enables the believer to cry "Abba, Father!".

The one use of *keleusma* in the NT is found in 1 Thess. 4:16. The reference is problematical: it is unclear whether the "shout" is the same triumphant noise as the "voice of the archangel" and the "trump of God", or whether the three are to be distinguished or possibly reduced to two sounds. It may well be the authoritative signal which heralds the parousia.

(e) *James:* Injustice, or more explicitly, withheld pay, is personified and cries out to heaven (5:4). The personification is reminiscent of Lk. 19:40; the implicit denunciation, of Acts 16:17; the plea for help, of the Psalms.

(f) *Revelation:* This book puts *krazō* to a variety of uses: a call for help (6:10); a cry of jubilation (7:10); an angelic cry (10:3), command (7:2; 19:17), proclamation (18:2), or call to the Son of Man 14:15); the wail of the woman in childbirth (12:2); and lamentation over fallen Babylon (18:2). The plethora of dramatic cries reinforces the thought that the end comes quickly and cataclysmically.

D. A. Carson

| βοάω | βοάω (*boaō*), call, shout, cry out; ἀναβοάω (*anaboaō*), cry out; βοή (*boē*), cry, shout. |

CL & OT *boaō* occurs in cl. Gk. from Homer onwards and also in inscriptions, the papyri, the LXX, Philo and Josephus. It is used in the sense of crying out (Heb. *qārā'*) in Isa. 36:13; 1 Macc. 13:45; 4 Macc. 6:16; 10:2 and of calling to in Gen. 39:14. But in many contexts in both Testaments it is expressive of the extremities of man's needs and joys. Both *boaō* and *anaboaō* are used in the LXX in the sense of calling out in distress (Heb. *ṣāʿaq*), e.g. Jdg. 10:10; Num. 20:16. The noun occurs in 1 Sam. 9:16 and Exod. 2:23. In each case the cry of God's people in their affliction does not go unheeded by God. Numerous warnings are given against disregarding the cries of the needy (Exod. 22:20 ff.; Deut. 24:15; Job 31:38; Mal. 3:5). There is also an extended use of the idea of crying in the sense of a murder crying out for justice and retribution. In Gen. 4:10 the blood of Abel is said to cry (Heb. *ṣāʿaq*) for vengeance (cf. Job 16:18 ff.; Isa. 26:21; 1 Ki. 21:19 ff.; 2 Macc. 8:3; Eth. En. 7:5–9:3; 22:7, 12; Sl. Enoch 58:6). Both the crime and the victim cry for retribution. If the victim is dead, the deed itself is an accusing witness. Such passages indicate a sense of justice built into the structure of human affairs, which man is expected to heed. But if man does not heed, God remains the ultimate → judge.

Crying is used in the context of the coming salvation promised in Isa. Isa. 40:3 refers to the triumphant return of the exiles from Babylon through the deserts led

410

by the Lord himself: "A voice cries [*qārā'*]: 'In the wilderness [*miḏbār*] prepare the way of the Lord, make straight in the desert ["*rāḇâh*] a highway for our God." The coming of the Lord will be a demonstration to all → flesh of his glory. In the next stanza the prophet is told to cry of the transitoriness of man compared with the → word of God: "A voice says, 'Cry!' And I said, 'What shall I cry?' All flesh is grass and all its beauty is like the flower of the field. . . . The grass withers, the flower fades; but the word of our God will stand for ever" (Isa. 40:6, 8). Isa. 54:1 refers to crying aloud for joy: "Sing, O barren one, who did not bear; break forth into singing and cry aloud [*ṣāhal*], you who have not been in travail! For the children of the desolate one will be more than the children of her that is married, says the Lord." The passage recalls the theme of the increase of the nation despite apparent adverse circumstances (cf. Gen. 12:2; 15:5; 17:4, 5; 18:18; 22:17; 28:14; 32:12; 35:11; 46:3).

NT The same range of reference is found in the NT, where the Isa. passages are seen as finding their fulfilment in events attending the coming of Christ. *anaboaō* is used lit. in Mk. 15:8 *v.l.*; Lk. 1:42 *v.l.*; 9:38 *v.l.* and of Jesus' cry of anguish in Matt. 27:46 (where the parallel in Mk. 15:34 uses *boaō*). This cry from the cross expresses the desolation of the sense of abandonment by God in the words of Ps. 22:1. Taken at their face-value, the words suggest that Jesus experienced the desolation that the people of God experienced throughout their history. But there is a double irony in the situation. For this was *the* Son of God experiencing the desolation, and it was at the hands of the people of God and not merely at the hands of aliens. Many commentators hold, however, that the cry is to be taken in the context of the entire Psalm and see in it "not a cry of despair, but the prayer of a righteous sufferer who still trusts in the protection of God and confidently expects vindication (see Ps. 22:24, 26)" (D. Hill, *The Gospel of Matthew*, 1972, 355; cf. G. H. Dalman, *Jesus-Jeshua*, 1929, 206; see further the discussion in K. Stendahl, *The School of St. Matthew*, 1968², 84–7; R. H. Gundry, *The Use of the Old Testament in St. Matthew's Gospel*, 1967, 63 ff., 203, 210 f.).

boē (Jas. 5:4) is the cry of the oppressed. *boaō* is used of evil spirits when leaving a person (Acts 8:7), of the sick (Lk. 9:38; 18:38), and of the shouts of the crowds in Acts 17:6; 25:24. Crying to God is a form of → prayer which God answers (Lk. 18:7).

boaō also occurs in the quotation from Isa. 40:3 which all four evangelists apply to John the Baptist (Matt. 3:3; Mk. 1:3; Lk. 3:4; Jn. 1:23; cf. Barr. 9:3). The synoptists see it as the → fulfilment of prophecy, and Jn. attributes the quotation to the Baptist's understanding of his own mission. The Baptist himself is the voice which cries, and his message is a christological interpretation of the cry in Isa. 40:3. The preparation of the desert for the coming of the Lord is seen as a type of the preparation of the people for the coming of the Lord in the person of Jesus Christ. (See further C. H. H. Scobie, *John the Baptist*, 1964, 15, 41, 46 f., 126 f., 196; D. Hill, op. cit., 88 f.; K. Stendahl, op. cit., 47 ff.; R. H. Gundry, op. cit., 9 f., 225.)

Isa. 54:1 is applied to the church in contrast with Israel in Gal. 4:27 [cf. 2 Clem. 2:1 f.). The quotation occurs in the context of an argument which contrasts Isaac and Ishmael, Sarah and Hagar, the Jerusalem above with the present Jerusalem, the new covenant with the one from Mount Sinai, and the free-born children with

411

those born in slavery. In each case the latter are characterized by the bondage entailed by the desire to be under the law (cf. v. 21) and the former by promise (cf. v. 28). In so far as believers live by the promises of God, the promise, the freedom, and the joy of Isa. 40:3 applies to them.   *C. Brown*

W. Grundmann, *krazō*, *TDNT* III 898–903; W. Janzen, *Mourning Cry and Woe Oracle*, 1972; E. Käsemann, "The Cry for Liberty in the Worship of the Church", *Perspectives on Paul*, 1971, 122–37; L. Schmid, *keleusma*, *TDNT* III 656–59; E. Stauffer, *boaō*, *TDNT* I 625–28; A. Walde, *Vergleichendes Wörterbuch der indogermanischen Sprachen*, ed. J. Pokorny, 1926, I, 413 f.

Cunning

πανουργία

πανουργία (*panourgia*), craftiness, cunning; *πανοῦργος* (*panourgos*), crafty, cunning, knavish.

CL The word group derives from the two roots *pan-* (→ all) and *erg-* (→ work), giving the basic meaning "capable of all work". Its first appearance is in Aeschylus; and from then on in secular Greek its connotation is most commonly pejorative, an unprincipled "capable of doing anything" (e.g. Aristotle, Lysias). Even as a divine attribute (in Euripides, Artemis applies it to Aphrodite) the connotation is negative. In the few instances where the word bears a positive sense, there is a hint of presumption or perhaps deceptive evaluation (Plato, Plutarch). It is possible that the positive ability implicit in the etymology of the word group never got off the ground because in Gk. thought the very idea of such ability is indicative of an arrogance which soon tinges the *panourgia* with undesirable characteristics.

OT In the LXX, the word group is significantly affected by the Heb. verb '*ārōm* and its cognates, for which it stands seventeen times. The Heb. group can mean "crafty", "sly" (e.g. Jos. 9:4; Job. 5:12), but in Proverbs, where it occurs most frequently, it takes on an unconditionally positive nuance, "prudent", "clever" (1:4; 8:5; 12:16, etc.). The three other occurrences of the *panourgia* group, translating other Heb. words (Prov. 13:1; 21:1; 28:2), are likewise positive. The antithetical Hebrew formulations of ethical behaviour have invested *panourgia* with new meaning, probably due in part to the belief that the man who fears God and is blessed by him can indeed successfully accomplish any task.

Although there are positive uses in the LXX outside the Heb. canon (e.g. Ecclus. 1:6; 6:32; 21:20) nonetheless it is made explicit that *panourgia* derives from wisdom springing from divine revelation. When *panourgia* throws off this presuppositional restriction it degenerates to *panourgia* in the secular sense (Ecclus. 21:12; cf. 19:25). For both Josephus and Philo, the term is consistently negative and heads a long list of vices. The one possible exception is *Leg. All.*, 2, 106 f., where the term refers to an artisan's "manual skill"; but the context reveals that even this "skill" is put to perverted use.

On the other hand, Qumran scrolls use the noun '*ormâh* in a positive fashion akin to usage in Proverbs, while tying the ethical more closely to sectarian covenanting formulations (e.g. 1QHab. 7:14; CD 2:4).

412

NT With this background in mind it is somewhat surprising that in its half dozen
NT appearances *panourgia* is used only negatively. The scribes and the chief
priests are guilty of "trickery" in their question to Jesus (Lk. 20:23); but God
catches the wise in their "craftiness" (1 Cor. 3:19), for man's ability to reason
cannot stand up against divine sovereignty. Opponents of the truth are accused of
"treacherously perverting" the Word of God (2 Cor. 4:2; Eph. 4:14); and therefore
Paul fears that the minds of the Corinthian converts may be led astray from purity
of devotion to Christ, as the serpent by his "craftiness" deceived Eve (2 Cor. 11:3).
The one occurrence of *panourgos* in the NT bears the added weight of irony (2 Cor.
12:16): Paul claims he is "crafty", meaning, of course, that he is not.

D. A. Carson

O. Bauernfeind, *panourgia*, *TDNT* V 722–727.

Curse, Insult, Fool

Under the central word *curse* are included all the terms which carry the sense of
verbal, as opposed to physical, hurt. The evil word stands in contrast to the good,
as with → blessing or praise (→ Thank). Its expressions extend from denial of the
honesty of another through evil slander and deliberate disparagement *kakologeō*,
invective and abuse *blasphēmeō*, *katalaleō*, *loidoreō* to actual damning *kataraomai*,
an action which was originally doubtless accompanied by a corresponding gesture.
To this day as understood in the East, its aim is to destroy the object of the curse,
since it delivers him up to the destructive working of supernatural powers or
brings them into action against him. Also discussed is the swear-word *rhaka* which
stems perhaps from the Aramaic and is used only once in the NT, as is also the
formula of excommunication *anathema*, which was so significant in later dealings
with heretics.

ἀνάθεμα

ἀνάθημα (*anathēma*), votive offering; ἀνάθεμα (*anathema*)
cursed, accursed; ἀναθεματίζω (*anathematizō*), execrate,
to lay a curse on; κατάθεμα (*katathema*), that which is devoted to the deity and
hence accursed thing; καταθεματίζω (*katathematizō*), curse.

CL *anathema*, a Hel. secondary form of the Att. *anathēma*, made up of *ana* (on) and
tithēmi (set, place, lay), means that which is set up. From this the following
meanings have evolved: the consecrated gift, the offering (set up in the temple of the
deity); what is handed over (to the wrath of the gods); what is dedicated (to destruction), and what has fallen under the power of a curse or ban.

OT 1. The LXX uses *anathema* regularly to translate the Heb. *ḥērem*, ban, what is
banned (cf. Num. 21:3; Jos. 6:17; 7:12; Jdg. 1:17; Zech. 14:11 with the original
root meaning to forbid (Arab. *ḥarama*), separate, consecrate, annihilate). What is
banned (persons or things) is directly given up to God and so cannot be redeemed
(Lev. 27:18). To ban is the right of the conqueror (Jos. 11:21; 1 Sam. 15:3 ff.). The
OT recognizes the destruction of what is banned (Lev. 27:19; Deut. 13:16; Jos.

10:28 ff.) or its annihilation (mostly by fire, Deut. 13:17). But also it may be assigned in some instances to the priests for their maintenance or disposal (Num. 18:14; Ezek. 44:29). In Jdg. 21:10 virgins were spared and given in marriage to those who had been wronged.

2. Besides the understanding of the ban as dedication the ban can also be punishment (Lev. 27:29). He who appropriated to himself what has been banned or refuses to accept the *anathema* in all its extent, comes under the power of the ban himself (Deut. 7:26; 1 Ki. 20:42). Likewise when an offence is suspected against the sacred covenant (Jdg. 21:11) or when punishment by God is spoken of (Isa. 34:2, 5; 43:28; Jer. 50:21, 26; Zech. 14:11; Mal. 3:24 and often), *anathema* occurs as punishment.

3. Ezr. 10:8 distinguishes between a ban on all *belongings* and *personal exclusion* from the community. In the OT ban and excommunication are always different measures (F. Horst, *RGG*³ I 861). In excommunication those referred to are exiled from the community and so from the sphere of salvation, but they are not, as in the case of the banned, directly given over to God and destroyed.

4. The occurrence of the word *anathema* on the table of curses from Megara (1–2 cent. A.D.) may well be an indication of Jewish influence. The idea passed into the NT from OT vocabulary. In the time of the Talmud two kinds of punitive ban were known: the simple ban from the synagogue (*niddûy* from *nāḏâh*, to exclude) which could be pronounced by anyone, and the intensified ban from the synagogue (*ḥērem*) which could be decreed only by a court pronouncement.

NT 1. The old form *anathēma* is found only in Lk. 21:5 with the meaning of a consecrated gift. These consecrated gifts offered in the temple are in fact votive offerings which were often costly (cf. 2 Macc. 2:13; Jud. 16:18 f.).

2. Paul takes over a restricted use of *anathema* from the LXX: the cursed thing, what has been dedicated to destruction (cf. J. Behm, *TDNT* I 354).

(a) Paul's Jewish kinship is not abolished by his membership of the church of Jesus Christ. For the salvation of his own people he is even ready to come under the curse (*anathema*), to be annihilated by God, to renounce his association with the Messiah (*apo tou Christou*), and to deliver himself to eschatological judgment, in order to save Israel (Rom. 9:3). Paul speaks here in the prophetic style of late Judaism. The relation of his readiness to the sacrifice of Christ is not the point at issue (cf. on Rom. 9:3 the excellent review of research in O. Michel, *Der Brief an die Römer*, 224–227).

(b) In 1 Cor. 12:3 the issue is to distinguish between → ecstasy which is the work of the Spirit of God and ecstasy which issues from demonic influence. Persons in ecstasy who pronounce the *anathema* on Jesus, who in uttering the ban deliver Jesus to annihilation by God, cannot possibly speak by the Holy Spirit. Such persons have become the mouth and instrument of demonic powers.

(c) As G. Bornkamm has shown convincingly, the curse formula in 1 Cor. 16:22, like the remaining formulae at the end of 1 Cor., stems from the liturgy of the Lord's Supper. The *anathema* calls upon those participating to test their faith – which finds expression in their love to the Lord – before the meal so that before the partaking of it the unworthy may be excluded (cf. 1 Cor. 11:28). The formula *ētō anathema* ("let him be anathema;" RSV "accursed") is not a "disciplinary order" of some human court to prosecute an unworthy person. Rather, it pronounces for a specific case the sentence that comes from God and delivers the offender to the punishment of God. Thereby responsibility rests entirely upon the person addressed and the *anathema* means a call to self-examination (cf. G. Bornkamm *Early Christian Experience*, 1969, 171). Cf. *maranatha* (→ Present) which with its reference to the heavenly Lord further emphasizes the *anathema*.

(d) Paul uses *anathema* in the same sense in Gal. 1:8, 9. He who preaches a false gospel is delivered to destruction by God. Again it is not a matter of an act of church discipline in the sense of excommunication. The curse exposes the culprits to the judicial wrath of God.

3. In this act of being handed over to God lies the theological meaning of the consecrated gift and the ban curse. As the consecrated gift is a sign of acknowledgment (1 Sam. 10:27) and submission (1 Ki. 10:25), of atonement for wounded honour (Gen. 12:16; 20:16) and of reconciliation (Gen. 32:14 f.), so, like a consecrated gift, the person sentenced by the *anathema* is immediately delivered up to the judgment of God. At the same time hope of a last-minute change of mind is not discounted. On the contrary, it is emphasized (cf. 1 Tim. 1:20).

4. *anathema* is also used in association with the vb. *anathematizein*, to bind with an oath or a curse and thus confirm an agreement that has been made (Acts 23:14; cf. Deut. 13:15; 20:27). In the LXX the vb. has as a rule the meaning: to carry out the ban (Num. 21:2 f.; Deut. 13:15; 20:27; Jos. 6:21). But it also may mean: to spread a curse over, to execrate. In Mk. 14:71 it is simply "to curse" with the same meaning as the verb *katathematizein*, used in the parallel passage Matt. 26:74. The noun *katathema* (Rev. 22:3) is not markedly different in meaning from *anathema* and denotes likewise what has been delivered up to God, what has had the ban curse laid upon it.   *H. Aust, D. Müller*

| κακολογέω |

κακολογέω (*kakologeō*), speak evil of, revile, insult, execrate.

CL & OT *kakologeō* is found in secular Gk. from the time of Homer, but is relatively seldom used. It means to speak ill of, to revile; and is used with the aid of both persons and things. In LXX usage *kakologeō* serves to render the Hebrew *qallēl*, to execrate (cf. Exod. 21:16; 22:27, Ezek. 22:7). In 2 Macc. 4:2 it has its original meaning, to speak ill of. The transition to the meaning of execrate has its explanation in the belief in the power of the spoken word. Certainly reviling can also include a curse.

NT *kakologeō* occurs in the NT only in four passages. In Matt. 15:4 and Mk. 7:10 it means to execrate. ([Ed.] RSV, however, translates both passages in the sense of "speak evil of".) The basis here is Exod. 21:16. Jesus takes issue with the Jewish interpretation of the commandments (→ Command; cf. SB I, 709 ff.). This interpretation softened the meaning of the biblical commandments and robbed them of their force (Matt. 15:5, 6). In Mk. 9:39 Jesus forbids his disciples to restrain a strange wonder-worker who wishes to cast out demons in his name. "For no one who does a mighty work in my name will be able soon after to speak evil of me." In Acts 19:9 *kakologeō* is also rendered, speak ill of. The unbelieving Jews speak ill of the "way", the Christian teaching about salvation.

415

καταράομαι

καταράομαι (*kataraomai*), curse; κατάρα (*katara*), curse, malediction; ἀρά (*ara*), curse; ἐπικατάρατος (*epikataratos*), cursed; ἐπάρατος (*eparatos*), accursed.

CL 1. *ara*, curse is current from the time of Homer. From the 5th–4th cent. B.C. there is also the compound *katara* with the same meaning. *kataraomai*, curse someone (dat.) or to execrate him (acc.), occurs in secular Gk. from Homer. Besides the pass. part. *katēramenos* there are found the verbal adjs. *eparatos* (since the time of Thucydides, but not in the LXX) and *epikataratos*, execrated. The latter appears only in the LXX and in post-biblical Gk.

2. In ancient thought the spoken word has intrinsic power which is released by the act of utterance and is independent of it. The person cursed is thus exposed to a sphere of destructive power. The curse works effectively against the person execrated until the power that dwells in the curse is spent. That is clear in the Gk. tragedies, in which men act under the compulsion of the *ara*. Words of malediction and words of benediction are thus more than evil or pious wishes.

OT 1. In the LXX *ara* (Ps. 9:28; 13:4; 56:13 and often) is found as well as *katara*. The latter renders as a rule the Heb. *qᵉlālâh* and is the opposite of *eulogia* → blessing (Deut. 11:26–29; 30:1–19). "I have set before you life and death, blessing and curse" (Deut. 30:19). *kataraomai* usually renders the Heb. *qallēl* with the dat. (e.g.) in Ep. Jer. 65 and the acc. in Gen. 12:3; Num. 22:6–12 and often. It is used as an alternative to the synonymous *araomai* in Num. 22:6, 11 and *epikataraomai* in Num. 22:17; 23:7 and often. In 2 Ki. 9:34 Jezebel is designated *katēramenē*, the accursed one. *epikataratos*, Heb. *'ārûr*, stands in Deut. 27:15 ff. and 28:16 ff. in the threatening of curses at the end of the Torah. The story of Balaam in Num. 22–24 shows that the belief, widespread in the world of religion, that with a curse "fulfilment is implied in the act of cursing" (F. Büchsel, *TDNT* I 449; see above CL, 2), was also lively in Israel. The Moabite king Balak charged Balaam to curse Israel that he might become master of his mighty enemy. But God prevented Balaam from pronouncing the curse. Rather he had to bless Israel against the will of his employer.

The curse decreed by God or his messengers works irrevocably. Jer. 26:6 is here instructive. The punishment with which Jeremiah here threatens Jerusalem consists in her being delivered defenceless to the curse of the heathen (cf. 24:9). Likewise in Mal. 2:2, the divine judgment consists in the blessing of the priests being changed by God into a curse. Only God himself can annul this curse.

2. Maledictions also played a large part in late Judaism. The liturgy of the feast for the renewal of the covenant in the Qumran community contains solemn maledictions upon the hypocritical and the godless who are described as *mᵉqalᵉlîm* and pronounced *'ārûr* (1QS 2:4 ff.).

NT In the NT *ara* occurs only in Rom. 3:14 (LXX citation of Ps. 9:28 [10:7]). It exhibits the sinfulness of men who live under the law (cf. 9:19). Heretics who entice unbalanced souls are "children of the curse", *kataras tekna* (2 Pet. 2:14). Ground which, in spite of rain and cultivation, grows only thorns and thistles is said figuratively in Heb. 6:8 to be near to being cursed. The passage has in mind Christians who, in spite of the spiritual blessing which they have received, fall

416

away from the faith (6:4–10). The vb. *kataraomai* is found in the story of the fig tree which Jesus cursed because he found no fruit on it (Mk. 11:21; → Fruit, art. *sykē*). The curse was fulfilled and the tree withered. Many expositors (including A. Schlatter and J. Schniewind) find in this story a figurative reference to the judgment of God (cf. Lk. 13:6–9). Men should not take an active part in the divine judgment. Therefore, Christians are forbidden to curse (Rom. 12:14, 19). In giving this instruction, Paul is in accord with the word of Jesus. Disciples should love their enemies and bless those who curse them (Matt. 5:44; Lk. 6:28). The warning given in Jas. 3:9 f. points in the same direction.

eparatos, accursed, is found only in Jn. 7:49. In the judgment of the Pharisees people who believe in Jesus are accursed. The cause of this belief can only be ignorance of the law. Here the enmity of the Pharisees against Jesus is clear. But to Jesus the curse also makes evident the finality of the divine judgment. The accursed, *katēramenoi* (Matt. 25:41), are the sinners who are condemned in the last judgment.

The verbal adj. *epikataratos* occurs twice in the NT (Gal. 3:10–13). It is used in the context of expositions in which Paul speaks about the curse of the law and redemption through Christ. The curse of the law signifies being surrendered to the judgment and wrath of God, which includes the whole of sinful humanity (Rom. 1:18; 2:5). The curse affects all who do not abide in the commandments of the law (Gal. 3:10). From Lev. 18:5 and Deut. 27:26 Paul concludes that all action comes under the domain of the law. But Jews and Gentiles who have come under the power of sin are not doers of the law (Rom. 3:19), and so remain under the curse. Jesus, who hung upon the cross as one accursed and died the death of a criminal, took upon himself the curse which lay upon sinful humanity and with it the judgment of God. The proof from scripture is given in Deut. 21:23. Here is found also the idea of substitution which is also often expressed by Paul (Rom. 3:25; 1 Cor. 1:30; 2 Cor. 5:21). Through redemption by Christ the ban curse (see above CL, 2) has been broken. The blessing of Abraham can now come to those who hold to Christ in faith. As the redeemed who are called to divine sonship and have life through belief, they also receive the fullness of salvation which is bound up with the promise of the Holy Spirit (Gal. 3:14; 4:5 ff.). *W. Mundle*

ῥακά	ῥακά (*rhaka*), empty-head, fool.

CL & OT The origin of *rhaka* is uncertain. The variant *rhacha* is sparsely attested.

Derivations from Aram., Heb. and Gk. have been suggested (cf. Arndt. 741).

(a) J. Jeremias (*TDNT* VI 973 f.) and J. Schniewind (*NTD* on Matt. 5:22) regard *rhaka* as the transcription of the Aram. term of abuse *rêqā'*, empty-head, blockhead (cf. Heb. *rîq*, empty in the brain). *rhaka*, instead of *rhēka*, was formed under Syr. influence.

(b) In the Gk. of pre-NT times *rhaka* appears only in a Zeno papyrus (257 B.C.), where it is a cat-call.

(c) Rab. writings present a great number of instances of *rēqā'* (cf. SB I 278, 286,

385; II 586, 714). In personal address *rēqā'* is an expression of angry scorn, perhaps with the meaning mutton-head, ass.

NT In the NT *rhaka* appears only in Matt. 5:22: "But I say to you that everyone who is angry with his brother shall be liable to judgment: whoever shall say to his brother, 'Empty-head' (*rhaka*), shall be liable to the council; and whoever says, 'Fool' (*mōre*), shall be liable to the Gehenna of fire." *rhaka* is here compared with *mōre*, the term of abuse that was most in use (→ Wisdom, Folly). *mōre* is more drastic in meaning and is perhaps to be rendered by idiot or fool (cf. 14:1). In Matt. 5:22 there are thus assembled the two everyday terms of abuse that were most prevalent in Jesus' environment (J. Jeremias, *TDNT* VI 975).

The *egō de legō hymin*, "but I say to you", of Jesus introduces a divine law that is a development of the OT. Not only does actual murder place men under the punishment of death. The heart that has become inflamed with the destructive mental attitude, from which springs the damning word, merits the same judgment. With tremendous sharpness Jesus' word makes it clear that God's judgment on sin is radical and far-reaching. It does not merely cover the accomplished deed; it exposes the motive behind it. Jesus does not simply condition the divine commandment by an overstatement which emphasizes human powerlessness. "He sets together the inevitability of judgment and the reality of new conduct" (J. Schniewind, op. cit., 60). Accordingly in this three-stage development, Jesus sets the sins of thought and tongue (which include the damning of a man) on the same level as physical murder which can be atoned for only by death.   *T. Sorg*

(a). Arndt, 53 f., 103, 398, 418, 741; J. Behm, *anathema*, *TDNT* I 354 f.; S. H. Blank, "The Curse, the Blasphemy, the Spell, and the Oath," *Hebrew Union College Annual* 23, 1950–51, 73–95; G. Bornkamm, "The Anathema in the Early Christian Lord's Supper Liturgy," in *Early Christian Experience*, 1969, 169–79; H. C. Brichto, *The Problem of "Curse" in the Hebrew Bible*, 1963; F. Büchsel, *ara, kataraomai* etc., *TDNT* I 448–57; T. Canaan, "The Curse in Palestinian Folklore," *Journal of the Palestine Oriental Society* 15, 1935, 235–79; F. C. Fensham, "Malediction and Benediction in Ancient Near-Eastern Vassal-Treaties and the Old Testament," *ZAW* 74, 1962, 1–9; and "Common Trends in Curse in the Near Eastern Treaties and Kudurru-Inscriptions," *ZAW* 75, 1963, 155–75; D. R. Hillers, *Treaty Curses and the Old Testament Prophets*, 1964; J. Jeremias, *rhaka*, *TDNT* VI 973–76; G. E. Mendenhall, *The Tenth Generation*, 1973; M. Noth, "For All who Rely on Works of the Law are under a Curse," in *The Laws in the Pentateuch and Other Essays*, 1966, 118–31; J. Pedersen, *Israel*, I–II, 1926, 433–52; J. Scharbert, "Curse", *EBT* I 174–79; J. Schneider, *kakologeō*, *TDNT* III 468. W. C. van Unnik, "Jesus: Anathema or Kyrios (I Cor. 12:3)", in B. Lindars and S. S. Smalley, *Christ and Spirit in the New Testament: Studies in Honour of C. F. D. Moule*, 1973, 113–26; G. P. Wiles, *Paul's Intercessory Prayers*, 1974, 135–55.

(b). H. A. Brongers, "Die Rache- und Fluchpsalmen im Alten Testament," *OTS* 13, 1963, 21–42; L. Brun, *Segen und Fluch im Urchristentum*, 1932; P. Heinisch, *Das Wort im Alten Testament und im Alten Orient*, 1922; J. Hempel, "Die israelitische Anschauungen von Segen und Fluch im Licht orientalischer Parallelen," *Zeitschrift der deutschen morgenländischen Gesellschaft* 79, 1925, 20–110; K. Hofmann, *anathema*, *RAC* I 427 ff.; F. Horst, "Bann," *RGG*³ I 860 f.; and "Segen und Fluch im AT," *RGG*³ V 1649 ff.; J. Kiss, "Der Begriff 'Fluch' im Neuen Testament," *Communio Viatorum* 7, 1964, 87–92; H. Köster, "Segen und Fluch im NT," *RGG* V 1651 f.; E. Lohmeyer, *Das Evangelium des Matthäus*, ed. W. Schmauch, KEK 1967⁴; O. Michel, *Der Brief an die Römer*, KEK 4 1966¹³; S. Mowinckel, *Segen und Fluch in Israels Kult und Psalmendichtung*, 1924; J. Pedersen, *Der Eid bei den Semiten*, 1914; J. Scharbert, *Solidarität in Segen und Fluch im Alten Testament und in seiner Umwelt*, 1958; and " 'Fluchen' und 'Segnen' im Alten Testament," *Biblica* 39, 1958, 1–26; J. Schniewind, *Das Evangelium nach Matthäus*, NTD II, 1968¹²; F. Steinmetzer, "Babylon: Parallelen zu den Fluchpsalmen," *BZ* 10, 1912, 133–42 and 363–69.

Danger, Risk, Peril

κινδυνεύω

κινδυνεύω (*kindyneuō*), be in danger; κίνδυνος (*kindynos*), danger, risk.

CL & OT Both vb. and noun are found widely in Hellenistic Greek from the time of Herodotus onwards. An occurrence of *kindyneuō* is attested in Josephus (*Antiquities*, 4, 188). In the LXX the vb. can be found in Isa. 28:13, where it describes, along with vbs. indicating their fate, the risk run by those who refuse to hear. In Ps. 114:3 (116:3) *kindynos* is used with Hades to describe the predicament from which the Psalmist has been delivered. In Sirach 43:24 *kindynos* is used of the perils faced by mariners.

NT The vb. *kindyneuō* occurs 4 times in the NT. In the Gospel narrative of the stilling of the storm, Luke includes a note, peculiar to his own story, to the effect that the disciples were in danger (Lk. 8:23, contrast Mk. 4:36–41; Matt. 8:23–27), thus adding to the colour and drama of the narrative. In 1 Cor. 15:30 Paul refers to the constant dangers attending his ministry; his argument is that to face these risks is pointless if there is no resurrection. Two further occurrences of the vb. can be found in Acts 19. Both occur in the story of the riot at Ephesus. In 19:27 Demetrius and his fellow craftsmen are concerned at the danger posed to their trade by the activity of Paul; in 19:40 the town clerk warns of the perilous consequences of the rioting.

Paul uses the noun *kindynos* in two places. In Rom. 8:35 peril is one of the series of unpleasant phenomena which cannot separate the Christian from the love of Christ. In 2 Cor. 11:26 he uses it several times to describe the difficulties with which his ministry has been beset. The perils in question include the elements (sea and storm) and the hostility of men (robbers, Jews and Gentiles). In the whole context these reflections are part of Paul's attempt to demonstrate to the Corinthians the authenticity of his apostolic ministry.   *P. J. Budd*

χαλεπός

χαλεπός (*chalepos*), hard, difficult.

CL & OT This word is well attested from Homer onwards both in Hellenistic and Jewish sources. It can be used of words that are hard to bear, or of men and animals that are hard to deal with, and therefore dangerous (cf. e.g. Josephus, *Antiquities* 15, 98). In some authors (e.g. Xenophon) *chalepos* has moral implications meaning bad or evil. In the LXX it is used of a nation (Isa. 18:2), probably in the sense of harsh. In Wis. it has the moral sense, denoting evil and wickedness (3:19; 17:11; 19:13). In Sir. 3:21, however, *chalepos* is used of intellectual difficulty – that which is too hard for the student.

NT In the NT *chalepos* is used on only two occasions. In Matt. 8:28 it indicates the devilish ferocity of the two demoniacs from the country of the Gadarenes. This is a peculiarly Matthaean touch. In 2 Tim. 3:1 it is used in a very different way to denote the character of the last days – times of stress and hardship when self-interest is the decisive factor in human relationships (3:2–4).   *P. J. Budd*

Darkness, Night

What is dark, gloomy, and therefore sinister is the opposite of what is → light. In Gk. the concept is conveyed by the group of words connected with *skotos*, darkness, used literally, physically and also with ethical and religious overtones. Absence of light leaves room for → evil and → sin. In this sense darkness may be described as evil. This double meaning also extends to *nyx*, night. Here admittedly the darkness is no longer absolute. But where *nyx* is used symbolically and not simply as a measure of time, it can have the same range of meaning as *skotia*, darkness.

νύξ

νύξ (*nyx*), night.

CL *nyx* (cf. Lat. *nox*), night, means the period without sunlight which is divided into 3 or 4 watches. In a fig. sense *nyx* means darkness, obscurity, blindness, powerlessness, death. In cl. Gk. *nyx* is only occasionally seen positively (i.e. as the time of refreshment in sleep). Mostly the term has a negative character. Night is ominous and brings fear. In mythology *Nyx*, the goddess of night, appears among other things as the mother of the Furies. *nyx* is also the time for → magic and the moon goddess who favours sorcery.

OT In the OT the word is used as a simple indication of time (e.g. Gen. 7:4; Jon. 1:17). But it is also the hour of terror (Ps. 91:5; Wis. 17:14 f., where Hades is said to be its place of origin), the time of drunkenness (Gen. 19:33), thieves (Jer. 49:9), sexual misdeeds (Jdg. 19:25), murder (Neh. 6:10), and occult practices (1 Sam. 28:8). By night man is particularly prone to worry and to the attacks of the evil one (Job 7:3; Ps. 6:7). But *nyx* is also God's time, when he shows the way by a pillar of → fire (Exod. 13:21), and makes himself known in dreams (Gen. 20:3) and visions (Dan. 7:2; Zech. 1:8). At the last day, on the other hand, when salvation is fulfilled, there will be no more night (Zech. 14:7).

NT In the NT *nyx* occurs 61 times (20 times in the synoptic gospels, 16 times in Acts, 11 times in Paul, 6 times in John, and 8 times in Rev.). *nyx* serves chiefly in the NT as an indication of time. In the fourth watch of the night Jesus walked upon the water (Matt. 14:25). By night he prayed (Lk. 6:12, *dianyktereuō*, pass the night; cf. Matt. 26:36 ff.; and Acts 16:25, *mesonyktion*, midnight). Nicodemus chose the quietness of night for his visit (Jn. 3:2). *nyx* is the hour of escape (Acts 9:25),

420

betrayal (Jn. 13:30), and denial (Matt. 26:34). It is found in formal indications of time (e.g. Matt. 4:2; 12:40). Particularly in Acts, *nyx* appears as the time for the activity of divine powers. It is at night that → angels perform their services (Lk. 2:8 f.; Acts 5:19; 12:7; 27:23; cf. Matt. 12:20; 2:13), that God speaks to man in visions (→ See; cf. Acts 16:9; 18:9; 23:11) and instructs him in dreams (Matt. 2:12, 22).

Metaphorically *nyx* can have the meaning of → *skotia*, darkness, describing, in contrast to *phōs* (→ light), the situation of estrangement from God or Christ (Jn. 11:10; 9:4). In a similar sense Paul uses *nyx* in contrast to *hēmera*, day (→ Present) in connection with the era of salvation which has dawned in Jesus Christ (1 Thess. 5:5–7). Similarly in Rom. 13:12 the contrast of *nyx* and *hēmera* illustrates that between the old aeon (destined to pass away) and the new (just about to break in). He who clings to Christ is no longer under the curse of night (1 Thess. 5:5). He is no longer a sleeper or drunken (1 Thess. 5:7), but is awake (1 Thess. 5:6; cf. 1 Cor. 16:13; 1 Pet. 5:8). After the darkening accompanying the last day which breaks in "like a thief in the night" (1 Thess. 5:2; Lk. 17:34, Rev. 8:12), the heavenly Jerusalem will receive him, and there will be no more night (Rev. 21:25), "for the Lord God will be their light" (Rev. 22:5).   *H. C. Hahn*

σκότος

σκότος (*skotos*), darkness, gloom; σκοτία (*skotia*), darkness, gloom; σκοτόω (*skotoō*), darken; σκοτίζω (*skotizō*), darken; σκοτεινός (*skoteinos*), dark, obscure.

CL 1. From Homer (*Il.*, 5, 47; *Od.*, 19, 389) onwards the masc. noun *skotos*, darkness, gloom, is found in cl. Gk. The fem. form *skotia*, which has the same meaning, is of Hel. origin (Apoll. Rhod., 4, 1698). In addition to these nouns, there are the vbs. *skotoō*, darken (Soph., *Ajax*, 85), which is found only in the pass. in the NT, and the Hel. *skotizō* (Plut., *Adversus Colotem*, 24, 2, 1120e) also meaning to darken. A further derivative which appears in the NT is the adj. *skoteinos*, dark, obscure (Aesch., *Choephori*, 661).

2. In cl. Gk. darkness applies primarily to the state characterized by the absence of → light (*phōs*) without any special metaphysical overtones. The thought is chiefly of the effect of darkness upon man. In the dark man gropes around uncertainly (Plato, *Phaedo*, 99b), since his ability to see is severely limited. Thus the man who can see may become → blind in the darkness, and no longer know which way to turn. Hence darkness appears as the "sphere of objective peril and of subjective anxiety" (H. Conzelmann, *TDNT* VII 424). Since all anxiety ultimately derives from the fear of death, the ominous character of darkness culminates in the darkness of death which no man can escape (cf. Homer, *Il.*, 4, 461). Darkness is therefore Hades, the world of the dead, which already reaches out into our world in the mythical figures of the Eumenides, the children of Skotos and Gaia (Soph., *Oedipus Coloneus*, 40).

Freed from their proper, temporal sense, the words of this group can be used in a metaphorical sense to describe human ways of life and behaviour. Thus they can describe a man's seclusion or obscurity. They can also indicate the secrecy, furtiveness or deceitfulness of his activity, the abstruseness of his speech, lack of enlightenment, insight and knowledge. "The word does not attain to high conceptual rank

421

in philosophy. Mention of darkness serves to set off light; it has no philosophical content of its own" (*TDNT* VII 425 f.).

3. This does, however, happen in Gnosticism. Here the concept of darkness goes beyond the purely relative, to become an independent force, seen as the unlimited ruler of the earthly world. This world is so filled with darkness that even its luminaries are but *skoteinon phōs*, dark light (Corp. Herm. 1, 28). In radical contrast to this world of darkness shines the transcendent world, the priority of which is stressed in Gnostic literature. Man has been endowed with a soul, coming from a spark of light. It is his task by means of *gnōsis* (→ knowledge) to attain to enlightenment. Hence, by contrast with *gnōsis* darkness has the character of *agnoia*, the sphere of ignorance which keeps man from his salvation. The very fact of having a body involves the natural man in this sphere. The contrast between the world of light and the world of darkness results in a call to *metanoia*, repentance (→ conversion), the decision to turn from the darkness of the earth-bound and bodily to the → light and life.

This dualism, calling for a decision between the light which contains salvation and darkness which means death, is developed to its most consistent conclusion in the metaphysical systems of the Mandaeans and of Manichaeism.

ot 1. The key to the OT view of light and darkness is faith in God as Creator who stands above both. He is not only the Lord of light; darkness also has to bow before him. Darkness is first mentioned in connection with the primeval ocean or chaos (Gen. 1:2). God creates both light and darkness (Isa. 45:7). He causes day to follow night (Ps. 104:20; Amos 5:8; cf. Gen. 1:4 f., 18). In his saving activity he can make use of darkness, as when he sent darkness upon Egypt (Ps. 105:28; Exod. 10:22).

The fact that God is Lord over darkness does not automatically diminish the threat of this force hostile to man. As in the Greek world, darkness describes "the whole range of the harmful or evil – in the sense of the threat to life, of what is bad for me, as well as in that of moral evil – or fatal" (*TDNT* VII 428). Hence, the OT depicts darkness as a symbol of limitation, restraint and affliction (Isa. 9:1). Man belongs to this sphere by nature. "They will look to the earth, but behold, distress and darkness, the gloom of anguish; and they will be thrust into thick darkness" (Isa. 8:22; cf. 60:2). It should be noted that here the term darkness is used chiefly in a sense influenced by theological considerations. Darkness is the place where the light of God does not shine. When a person separates himself from God by disobedience, darkness remains (Ps. 107:10 f.). On the other hand, God illumines the darkness for those who fear him. The person who walks through the valley of deep darkness need not fear (Ps. 23:4; cf. 112:4; Isa. 50:10; Mic. 7:8). For darkness is not dark to God (Ps. 139:11 f.) and to those who will be led by him (cf. Isa. 42:7, 16; 49:9).

Although God allows darkness to exercise a certain power even exposing the righteous to its terrors (Ps. 88:6; Job 19:8; 30:26), and although he wraps himself in impenetrable darkness (1 Ki. 8:12; Ps. 18:9 ff.), the promise remains that the people who walked in darkness shall see a great light (Isa. 9:2).

However, there are those who hide themselves from the light of God (Isa. 29:15), as for instance the people who offend against the commandment to love one's parents (Prov. 20:20) and the liars who turn darkness into light (Isa. 5:20). All such are heading for the day when God who sees through all darkness (Job 34:21 f.) will bring the darkness of sin out into the light (Job. 12:22) and hold a terrible judgment (Job 34:23 f.). Hence the prophets proclaim that the day of Yahweh will not be, as the people expect, a day of joy for Israel, but a day of darkness and calamity (Joel 2:2, 10; Amos 5:20; 8:9), unless Israel repents at the last moment (Joel 2:12 ff.). The darkness of the day of judgment will be far worse for the ungodly than the day of natural → death, for eschatological darkness means the final and eternal → destruction of the faithless and disobedient.

2. The concept of eschatological darkness and damnation in the world beyond is emphasized and further developed in later Jewish writings (cf. Jub. 5:14; Eth. Enoch 17:6; 63:6; 108:11 ff.). The purpose of such teaching is to bring about enlightenment and a decision to follow the way of light.

One of the most important themes of the Qumran literature is that of man caught in the tension between light and darkness. Here light and darkness oppose one another as cosmic forces which determine the existence of man. Thus darkness seeks to lead him astray by means of its representative Belial (1QM 13:11 f.; 1QS 3:21–24). Man can extricate himself from the influence of darkness and its ruling power by deciding to enter the → covenant (OT 6). By this means he can be changed from a child of darkness into a son of light for whom is prepared life eternal in everlasting light (1QS 4:7 f.).

NT As in the literature already mentioned, the NT uses this group of words in both the lit. and (as a rule) the fig. senses. It occurs relatively often: *skotos* 30 times; *skotia* 17 times, of which 14 are in the Johannine literature, both terms meaning darkness or gloom; *skotizesthai* (be darkened) 5 times; *skotousthai* (be darkened) and *skoteinos* (dark) 3 times each.

1. It serves as an indication of time and is mentioned in connection with the darkness of night setting in or departing (Jn. 6:17; 20:1). Metaphorically but without any particularly negative allusion attaching to night, *skotia* and *phōs* (light) are used in Matt. and Lk. "What I tell you in the dark, utter in the light" (Matt. 10:27). "Whatever you have said in the dark shall be heard in the light, and what you have whispered in private rooms shall be proclaimed upon the housetops" (Lk. 12:3).

2. The words are given a clearly negative sense in those passages which contrast a sound eye (as the organ which guides) in a body full of light with an evil eye in a body full of darkness (Matt. 6:22 f.; Lk. 11:34–36). By looking in the wrong direction the → body succumbs to the power of darkness. At the arrest of Jesus (Lk. 22:53) and still more in the hour of his death (Matt. 27:45; Mk. 15:33; Lk. 23:44), this power of darkness could give the impression of having won a victory. But at Easter the divine power of → light triumphed once and for all over the Satanic powers of darkness, the world's night and the gloom of death. It is in the light of this victory that darkness is mostly seen and evaluated in the NT.

3. The natural man lives in the domain of darkness. He belongs to the people who dwell in darkness (cf. the Isaiah citation [9:2] in Matt. 4:16). He cannot avoid the darkness of → death (Lk. 1:79). But above all, darkness appears as darkness before God. "Before the encounter with the Revealer the life of all men lies in darkness and sin" (R. Bultmann, *The Gospel of John*, 1971, 159). In this sphere the

"power of Satan" holds sway (Acts 26:18; cf. Eph. 6:12). This impels men to do the evil → works of darkness (Jn. 3:19; Rom. 13:12; Eph. 5:11). Through it the minds of the heathen (Eph. 4:18) or in another phrase, "their senseless → hearts" (Rom. 1:21) are darkened. Through it the Jew who is faithful to the law can become so blinded as to make, for instance, out of → circumcision a system of false security about salvation. So he becomes a blind leader of the blind (Matt. 8:12; 15:14; cf. Rom. 2:19).

In view of the dominating power of darkness – which is to be seen in close connection with the terms → sin, → flesh, and → desire – Paul goes so far as to identify man with this force and say that those to whom he is writing were once darkness (Eph. 5:8). This makes it clear that "it is not merely a supernatural, dark, spiritual power which sets itself up secretly in opposition to Him (God); no, the 'principalities and powers' also assume quite tangible and visible forms in the situations facing both world and church" (W. Lüthi, *Johannes*, 1963, 11).

4. Darkness does not, of course, appear as a power on the same level as God. Bultmann points out: "*skotia* is not an autonomous power existing alongside the *phōs*, but it is only because of the light that there is darkness at all" (op. cit., 47). This is hinted at in the passages which speak of God himself as darkening the eyes of (i.e. hardening) certain people: the citation from Psalm 69:23 in Rom. 11:10; and also Acts 13:11, where God blinds the magician Bar-Jesus by a word of the Spirit spoken by Paul. And just as in creation, God now causes light to shine out of darkness into the hearts of men (2 Cor. 4:6). He is Lord over darkness also.

This Lordship of God is displayed above all in Jesus Christ whom he has sent into the world in order to call his holy people out of darkness into his wonderful light (1 Pet. 2:9), into the kingdom of the son of his love (Col. 1:13). This theme is taken up particularly by John who makes great use of the metaphor of light and darkness. In the prologue of his gospel it is introduced as a principal theme: "The light shines in the darkness, and the darkness has not overcome it" (Jn. 1:5). Light and darkness are set over against each other in the Johannine writings in similar fashion to other pairs of opposites (→ life and → death, → truth and → lie). These opposites are mutually exclusive, as in Paul's rhetorical question, "What fellowship has light with darkness?" (2 Cor. 6:14). A decision has to be made for one or the other, for God or against him who is the light in whom there is no darkness at all (1 Jn. 1:5), or to be more precise, for or against Jesus Christ who described himself as the light (Jn. 12:46; cf. 8:12). It is his person that provides the yardstick. He who rejects him condemns himself by the same act (Jn. 3:18 f.). On the other hand, he who believes him (Jn. 12:46) and follows him (Jn. 8:12) no longer walks in darkness.

5. However, it is not enough merely to confess with one's lips allegiance to the light. It is impossible to have fellowship with God and at the same time to walk in darkness. He who declares the opposite to be true is a liar (1 Jn. 1:6). Unless he has the kind of faith which affects his whole life and being and finds expression in love of the brethren, a man is still in darkness (1 Jn. 2:9). He who continues to hate his brother is behaving like a man of darkness, wandering around without sight (1 Jn. 2:11; cf. Jn. 12:35). He has not yet understood that darkness is passing away, and that the one true light is already shining (1 Jn. 2:8).

For these people who stubbornly reject the light, who refuse to acknowledge

Jesus Christ as Lord and perform the works of darkness – here false teachers come in for special mention (2 Pet. 2:17; Jude 13) – there is coming one day the deepest darkness of all, God's judgment. In this judgment the Lord will "bring to light even the hidden things of darkness and expose the counsels of the hearts" (1 Cor. 4:5). Whereas others will be accepted, these men of darkness will be cast out into the gloomy place of eschatological destruction (Matt. 8:12; 22:13; 25:30; → Destroy). This judgment is expected at the second coming of Christ which, according to the NT records leaning on apocalyptic ideas from the OT, will be accompanied by manifestations of darkness. "The sun will be darkened, and the moon will not give its light" (Mk. 13:24 and Matt. 24:29; cf. Isa. 13:10; Ezek. 32:7; Joel 2:10 f.; Zeph. 1:15; cf. also the quotation from Joel 2 in Acts 2:20; Rev. 3:12; 9:2; 16:10). Therefore Paul can strongly exhort Christians to watchfulness and soberness in the light of the → Parousia which is suddenly to overtake them. "Do not be in darkness, for that day to surprise you like a thief; for you are all sons of the day. We are not of the night nor of darkness. So let us not sleep, as others do" (1 Thess. 5:4–6).

H. C. Hahn

→ Light, → Present, Day and the bibliographies under these articles, → Conceive, Apprehend.

(a). H. Conzelmann, *skotos*, *TDNT* VII 423–45; G. Delling, *nyx*, *TDNT* IV 1123–26; C. H. Dodd, *The Interpretation of the Fourth Gospel*, 1953, 201–12, 345–62; A. R. C. Leaney, *The Rule of Qumran and its Meaning*, 1966, 37 ff.; commentaries on John by C. K. Barrett, 1955; R. E. Brown, 1967; R. Bultmann, 1971; B. Lindars, 1972; J. Marsh, 1968; J. N. Sanders and B. A. Mastin, 1968; L. Morris, 1972; R. Schnackenburg, 1969; and B. F. Westcott, 1958 reprint.
(b). S. Aalen, *Die Begriffe Licht und Finsternis im Alten Testament, im Spätjudentum und im Rabbinismus*, 1951; R. Bultmann, "Zur Geschichte der Lichtsymbolik im Altertum," *Philologus* 97, 1948, 1 ff.; H. W. Huppenbauer, *Der Mensch zwischen zwei Welten*, AThANT 34, 1959; W. Lüthi, *Johannes. Das Vierte Evangelium*, 1963; W. Nagel, "Die Finsternis hat's nicht begriffen (Joh. 1, 5)," *ZNW* 50, 1959, 132 ff.

David

$\Delta\alpha\nu\iota\delta$	$\Delta\alpha\nu\iota\delta$ (*Dauid*), Heb. *dāwīḏ*. David.

OT The origins of kingship in Israel are not as much shrouded in obscurity as beset by problems of detail, interesting in themselves but beyond the scope of this article. One thing, however, must be examined. The contrast between the premonarchic and the monarchic periods must not be drawn in terms of a theocratic and a non-theocratic system. In Israel, judgeship and kingship were two forms of the same theocratic ideal, that Yahweh is both → Judge and → King. Thoughtful examination of the traditions shows that the element of divine rebuke occasioned by the request for a king did not arise from the fact that monarchy as such betokened a decline from the theocratic principle, but from the fact that a permanent institution such as kingship inevitably meant that the people were not walking in absolute confidence that Yahweh would continue to care for them in the provision of timely leadership, as he had done throughout the period of the judges. It was in this sense that they had rejected him from being king (1 Sam. 8:7) and it is to this point precisely that Samuel directs his magnificent farewell speech: that hitherto prayer had sufficed (1 Sam. 12:8, 10) but now, pressed by a new Ammonite threat (v. 12), they wearied of the demands of the way of faith and pressed for the security of an institutionalized system. Yet monarchy, Samuel asserted, left the theocracy and its demands unimpaired: it was still with Yahweh that both king and people had to do (vv. 14 ff.).

It is one of the continuing stresses of biblical theology that divine purposes are fulfilled by an apparent condescension to human needs and failings. Kingship is no exception, but it comes without surprise that what was thus introduced as a seeming accommodation to need (1 Sam. 12:12), failure (1 Sam. 8:1–3) and stubbornness (1 Sam. 8:19) was found to be the highest and best intention of God. This was realized in the person of David whose history is recounted in 1 Sam. 16—1 Ki. 2 and 1 Chr. 11–29.

At this point another group of problems arises. When David became established on his throne, he apparently considered that the time of the Deuteronomic ideal had arrived (cf. Deut. 12:10 with 2 Sam. 7:1) and wished to crystallize national religious aspiration by building Yahweh's house in Yahweh's chosen place. This was forbidden, and in the neatest possible way Nathan's oracle of prohibition was turned into an oracle of hope: far from David building Yahweh a house, Yahweh would build the house of David (2 Sam. 7:11). In some unspecified connection with this oracle, and arising at some time subsequent to it, the Davidic hope began to be cherished in Israel. Nathan did not promise an ideal king in David's line; at most he promised an endless succession of kings who, at least potentially, might come under Yahweh's chastening. Yet, somehow, the vision of the ideal grew and became focused in a single expectation.

At what point did the "honeymoon" view of monarchy and its benefits, as spelled out in the book of Judges, end, to be replaced by the hope that one day a perfect king would arise? And at what point was that perfect king first conceived of as *David redivivus*? There is no sure answer to these questions, though Psalm-study, among other factors, has made the late dating of what we may (even if loosely) call "messianic hope" seem less than realistic. If longing for the ideal arose by contrast with the short-comings of the actual we need not look beyond the days of Solomon for a point of origin. Indeed, in the light of Nathan's oracle, such a hope would more naturally arise while the promised line was still in vital existence (i.e. during the monarchic period) than after the Davidic line had run out into the arid sands of the exile and post-exile.

The Psalms clearly show a hope running beyond the dimensions of any actual king (e.g. 2, 72) and we cannot be far if at all wrong if we see them as taking their origin from the focal points (e.g. coronation, marriage, royal cult ceremonies) of the reign of an actual king but consciously reaching forward to the realization of that which he was failing to be.

The main point of such an expectation were as follows: the qualities of the kingly person and rule (e.g. Isa. 11:1–9), his universal sway (e.g. Isa. 9:7; Ps. 72), the priestly dimension of his kingship (Ps. 110; Zech. 3:8–10; 6:12, 13), even (if we follow the clues of Is. 55:3 and elsewhere and identify the Servant with the Davidic Messiah) that he would himself perform the priestly rite of substitutionary sacrifice (Isa. 52:13–53:12). There is also in the OT what must be called the mystery of the person of the expected king: three examples must suffice: he is a shoot from Jesse's

426

stock, but he is also the root from which Jesse springs (Isa. 11:1, 10); he can be addressed as "God" (the most direct understanding of Ps. 45:6, but see comms.) and yet receive anointing from "God, thy God" (45:7); he is born in David's line and yet entitled "mighty God" (Isa. 9:6,7), he can spring out from a buried, seemingly defunct, root and yet be "the Arm of the Lord" (53:1–3). This mystery finds no solution prior to the NT revelation.

NT Within the NT the life of David is alluded to in Matt. 12:3; Mk. 2:25; Lk. 6:3; Acts 7:45; 13:22; Heb. 11:32; Acts 2:9, 34; 13:36. His authorship of certain psalms is asserted in Acts 1:16; 2:25; 4:25; Rom. 4:6; 11:9; Heb. 4:7. But the main interest in the NT is to be found in those places where Jesus is connected directly with David and where David concepts are applied to Jesus.

The "ancestry theme" is found in Matt. 1:1 ff.; Lk. 1:27, 32 2:4, 11; 3:31; Rom. 1:3; 2 Tim. 2:8. There are two stresses to be discerned. An unequivocally human ancestry secures the reality of the unequivocal humanity of Jesus, so that both the miracle and the power of his resurrection shine out. Theologically, this, in turn, secures the truth so prized in Hebrews, that the values exemplified in the life of the man, Christ Jesus, are those which have been hall-marked by the act of God. Secondly the reality of the descent of Jesus from David makes him the repository of the promises vouchsafed to but never secured by his famous ancestor: Lk. 1:69; Jn. 7:42; Acts 13:34; 15:16.

By the time of Jesus, messianism in Davidic terms had developed to the point where it was common knowledge and could even be trespassed upon by the non-Israelite in hope of securing an Israelite favour (e.g. Matt. 15:22). The general acceptance of the terminology of the Davidic hope is seen in the greetings given (unwittingly) to Jesus: Matt. 21:15; Mk. 11:10; more thoughtfully it reveals itself in the query whether any but the expected son of David could act in such power as to heal a demoniac (Matt. 12:23); with complete assurance, it sounds out in the descriptions of the royal Christ of the book of Revelation, the possessor of Davidic authority (3:8), David's root (5:5), and in one glorious paradox, the whole OT mystery unrolled, David's root and offspring (22:16).

This leads us to the passage wherein most completely the self-consciousness of Jesus on this point stands revealed: his question to the scribes and Pharisees how the expected Messiah could be both David's son and David's lord (Matt. 22:41–45; Mk. 12:35–37; Lk. 20:41–44). This was certainly no mere debating point to be scored and then left, nor is its thrust to be weakened by any specialist hesitations concerning the Davidic authorship of Ps. 110. To Jesus the matter appeared thus: David, the inspired author, saw a descendant upon his throne, appointed by Yahweh, and referred to that descendant as "Lord". How can one and the same person be derivative and therefore dependent and also lord and therefore superior?

It is germane at this point to remind ourselves that Jesus deliberately shunned the ascription of kingship as currently defined. His reply to Pilate (" 'King' is your word", Jn. 18:37, NEB) is most pointed: he could not deny being a king, yet he could not accept the ascription, tainted and deformed as it was by Pilate's and Jewish political ambitions and half-understandings. Therefore, if possible before it is too late, Jesus would have the religious leaders face up to the mystery inherent in the expectations they professed, and facing up to the mystery, learn to reform

427

their thinking, first in the light of the total OT revelation of the Messiah, and secondly in the light of that revelation illumined, explained and fulfilled in Jesus. → Son of David   *J. A. Motyer*

(a). A. Weiser, *The Psalms*, 1962; A. A. Anderson, *The Psalms*, I–II, 1972; F. D. Kidner, *The Psalms*, 1973; H. Ringgren, *The Faith of the Psalmists*, 1963; D. Anders Richards, *The Drama of the Psalms*, 1968; H. Ringgren, *The Messiah in the Old Testament*, 1956; S. Mowinckel, *He That Cometh*, 1959; W. Vischer, *The Witness of the Old Testament to Christ*, 1949; M. Buber, *Kingship of God*, 1967; *NBD*, "Messiah"; B. B. Warfield, "The Divine Messiah in the Old Testament", *Biblical and Theological Studies*, 1952; A. R. Johnson, *Sacral Kingship in Ancient Israel*, 1955; A. Bentzen, *King and Messiah*, 1955; A. T. Hanson, *Jesus Christ in the Old Testament*, 1965; R. T. France, *Jesus and the Old Testament*, 1971; R. E. Clements, *Abraham and David*, 1967; D. F. Payne, *The Rise and Fall of the Monarchy; David and his Heirs*, 1976; O. Eissfeldt, "The Promises of Grace to David in Isa. 55. 1–5," *Israel's Prophetic Heritage*, ed. B. W. Anderson and W. Harrelson, 1962, 196–207; M. Noth, "David and Israel in II Sam. 7," *The Laws of the Pentateuch and Other Studies*, 1966, 250–90; D. C. Duling, "The Promises to David and their Entrance into Christianity – Nailing Down a Likely Hypothesis," *NTS* 20, 1973–74, 55–77; S. E. Johnson, "The Davidic-Royal Motif in the Gospels", *JBL* 87, 1968, 136–50.
(b). A. H. J. Gunneweg, "Sinaibund und Davidbund," *VT* 10, 1960, 335–41; N.-U. Nübel, *Davids Aufsteig in der frühen israelitischen Geschichtsschreibung*, dissertation Bonn, 1959; L. Rost, "Die Überlieferung von der Thronnachfolge Davids," *Das kleine Credo und andere Studien zum Alten Testament*, 1965, 119–253; "Davidsbund und Sinaibund," *ThLZ* 72, 1947, 129–34; A. Weiser, "Der Tempelbaukrise unter David," *ZAW* 77, 1965, 153–68; C. Burger, *Jesus als Davidsshon*, 1970.

Deaf, Dumb

κωφός

κωφός (*kōphos*), deaf, dumb.

CL In classical Greek *kōphos* has the general sense of blunt or dull, but more specifically can mean either deaf (Homer) or dumb (Herodotus). The context gives the sense required.

OT This quality is also present in Jewish usage. With the meaning dumb *kōphos* can be found in Wisdom 10:21, in Philo (*Flacc.* 20) and in Josephus (*Ant.* 18, 135). The meaning deaf occurs in Philo (*Mut. Nom.* 143), and several times in the LXX (cf. e.g. Exod. 4:11; Isa. 43:8; Ps. 37:14). In some contexts *kōphos* can be used of a deaf mute (Philo, *Spec. Leg.* 4:197; Sib. 4:28). A figurative use applied to idols occurs in Hab. 2:18.

NT In the NT *kōphos* is to be found only in the Gospels. These occurrences are found in five distinct incidents, four of which have to do with cures achieved by Jesus. In Mk. 7:32, 37 the word must mean deaf since the text also uses the rare word *mogilalou* (having a speech impediment), and since the miracle includes the gift of hearing (7:35). This narrative is peculiar to Mark's Gospel. In Mk. 9:25 *kōphos* is a peculiarly Markan feature of the story of the possessed boy. Mark, unlike the other Evangelists, has already described the spirit as dumb (*alalos*) (9:17), and now, in addressing the spirit, Jesus also calls it *kōphos*, meaning presumably a spirit of deafness. In Matt. 11:5; Lk. 7:22 deafness is again the meaning in this description by Jesus to the imprisoned John the Baptist of the content of his ministry. Part of the evidence demonstrating Jesus's messiahship is the fact that the *kōphoi* hear.

The use of *kōphos* to signify dumbness is also attested. In Matt. 9:32, 33; 12:22; Lk. 11:14 the criticism that Jesus heals by devilish power is prompted by the healing of a man who is *kōphos* and who now speaks (cf. also the general observation about Jesus' healing ministry in Matt. 15:30–31 which must also refer to dumbness). In Lk. 1:22 Zechariah's vision in the Temple renders him unable to speak, and he remains *kōphos*.

For all three Evangelists this particular aspect of Jesus' ministry is a firm indication of the fulfilment in him of such prophecies as Isa. 35:5–6; 43:8; 61:1–2. It is in particular a ministry of release involving vigorous conflict with spiritual evil (Mk. 9:25), calling for effort (Mk. 7:34), and by its very nature and Israel's hardness of heart open to serious misinterpretation (Matt. 9:34).   *P. J. Budd*
→ Blind, → Heal, → Lame

(a). C. E. B. Cranfield, "St. Mark 9:14–29," *SJT* 3, 1950, 57–67; J. Moffatt, "Matthew 11:5," *ExpT* 18, 1906–7, 286 f.; A. S. Weatherhead, "The Healing of One Deaf and Dumb," *ExpT* 23, 1911–12, 381; R. K. Harrison, "Disease," *IDB* I 847–54; A. Cole, *The Gospel according to Mark*, 1961, 134 f.
(b). F. Fenner, *Die Krankheit im Neuen Testament*, 1930.

Death, Kill, Sleep

In the NT, as in classical literature, a variety of words describe death and dying – those events which remind man that life is something over which he has no ultimate control. In addition to the words related to *thanatos* (death), there are other terms which originally have a quite different meaning. Sleep (*hypnos*) which was used early on as a euphemism for death and dying was used even more in the Christian era. Other related terms are *katheudō* (to sleep), and *koimaomai* (to fall asleep). That which is lifeless, whether it be a corpse or inanimate matter, is *nekros* (dead). *teleutaō* means to come to an end, finish and thus to die. *apokteinō* (kill) indicates a violent extinction of life. The words of the *thanatos* group and *nekros* have particular theological undertones in the NT.

ἀποκτείνω	ἀποκτείνω (*apokteinō*), kill; τελευτάω (*teleutaō*), come to an end, die.

CL 1. The vb. *apokteinō* (Homer), derived from *kteinō*, kill, expresses any kind of violent ending to (someone else's, only later one's own) life. It can thus mean to kill, have put to death, murder, and execute.

2. *teleutaō*, derived from *telos* (→ Goal, End), and attested from Homer onwards, originally had the general meaning of bring to an end (e.g. one's work), to complete; intrans., to come to an end, be fulfilled (e.g. of dreams), and then also to die, lose one's life.

OT 1. *apokteinō*, kill, is found over 150 times in the LXX, chiefly to render the Heb. roots *hāraḡ*, kill, and *mût*, die (especially hiph., cause to die). It can refer to homicide (Gen. 4:8, of Cain), penal execution (Exod. 32:27), or the carrying out of mass killing in the course of a holy war (Num. 31:7 f.; 1 Sam. 15:3). It also occurs in prophetic visions of judgment (Amos 4:10; 9:1; Ezek. 23:10).

2. In about 70 instances in the LXX *teleutaō* is used to render the Heb. *mût*, die, almost always in the sense of expire, end one's life. No distinction is drawn here as to whether the death is from natural causes (e.g. Exod. 1:6; Jos. 1:2), or is sudden and violent (*thanatō teleutēsei*, he will, or shall, die the death, Exod. 19:12; 21:16 f.; Amos 9:10).

NT 1. *apokteinō*, kill, occurs 74 times in the NT, especially often in the four gospels and Rev. (15 times); only 5 instances are found in the (Pauline) epistles. In these passages the vb. nearly always refers to the violent killing of God's messengers, whether in direct narrative (Matt. 14:5, of Herod's intention with regard to John; cf. Mk. 6:19), in parables (Mk. 12:5 ff. and parallels of the labourers in the vineyard; cf. Matt. 23:37 par.), or prophetically with reference to the disciples in the synoptic apocalypse (Matt. 24:9). Its use in the three synoptic passion predictions (Mk. 8:31; 9:31; 10:34; and parallels) is of central significance. The → witness who is to be killed and upon whom the attacks are concentrated is the → Son (cf. 1 Thess. 2:15). In Jn. it is noteworthy that *apokteinō* is almost always combined with *zēteō*, seek, or *bouleuomai*, plan (e.g. 7:1; 19 ff.; 11:53). The disciples also come within the scope of this threat (Acts 21:31; 23:12–14). This is indicated especially in Rev. 6:11 (cf. also 11:7, where the beast kills the two witnesses), though the vb. is there used more often of the execution of God's judgment (by the four riders, Rev. 6:8; cf. 9:15–18; 19:21). In a late interpretation of the meaning of the cross, Eph. 2:16 declares that by his death Jesus has "killed" the hostility, i.e. brought about reconciliation. Paul uses the word twice in a fig. sense. In Rom. 7:11 → sin (*hamartia*), here regarded as a power, is said to kill man by means of the → commandment (*entolē*). It forces man into a conflict which deceives him as to his standing before God and thus brings death. It is really the law which brings death here. In 2 Cor. 3:6 the meaning is the same: there *gramma*, letter, is said to kill in contrast to the life-giving Spirit.

2. *teleutaō* is found only 11 times in the NT, and of these 3 are in quotations from the OT (Matt. 15:4; Mk. 7:10; 9:48). It is noteworthy that in Matt. 9:18 (aor). and Jn. 11:39 (perf. part.) the vb. is used with reference to dead persons who are subsequently raised to life again by Jesus. The evangelists seem here to use the word in order to emphasize the fact that the girl and Lazarus have really died. The use of → *katheudō* or *koimaomai* (sleep, fall asleep) in the same context implies no contradiction of this. The vb. is also used of the death of Herod (Matt. 2:19), in the parable of the brothers who died (Matt. 22:25), and in historical allusions to the deaths of David, Jacob and Joseph (Acts 2:29; 7:15; and Heb. 11:22). The dominant word for die in the NT is undoubtedly *apothnēskō* (→ *thanatos*).

L. Coenen

θάνατος

θάνατος (*thanatos*), death; θανατόω (*thanatoō*), kill; ἀθανασία (*athanasia*), immortality; θνῄσκω (*thnēskō*) die; ἀποθνῄσκω (*apothnēskō*), die; συναποθνῄσκω (*synapothnēskō*), die together, with someone; θνητός (*thnētos*), mortal.

CL *thanatos* (Homer) means the act of dying or the state of death. But it is also used of mortal danger, the manner of death, and the death penalty. Similarly *thanatoō* means to put someone to death, kill, and lead into mortal danger. Living creatures subject to death are described as early as Homer as *thnētos*, mortal. Men are referred to as *hoi thnētoi* (the mortals), in contrast to the gods who possess *athanasia* (immortality). Only in exceptional cases are men elevated as heroes into the number of the immortal gods.

thnēskō, die, and *apothnēskō*, expire (both Homeric) denote the act of dying. Where the reference is to a death shared with others we find the compound form *synapothnēskō*, die together with someone (Hdt.; cf. the Indian custom of burning the widow).

In the Hel. period the terms *thanatos, thanatoō, thnēskō* and *apothnēskō* are also used metaphorically of intellectual and spiritual death.

1. For the Greeks, death meant the end of living activity, the closing of the life-span, the destruction of existence, even if the shade (→ soul) found a place in the realm of the dead (Homer, *Od.* 11, 204–222). Death is the common destiny of man, and its negative side is occasionally made evident, when death appears personified as a demon or monster from the underworld (Eur., *Alcestis* 28 ff.). Since they had no doctrine of creation, death did not pose for them the question "Why?". All men by nature are subject to it, just as immortality is the natural lot of the much-envied gods. Complaints about the mortality of man are frequently expressed (cf. Homer, *Od.* 11, 488). Realization of the inevitability of death found its normal consequence in the demand to enjoy → life (*zōē*) to the full. The maxim cited by Paul in 1 Cor. 15:32, "Let us eat and drink, for tomorrow we die", accords with many expressions of Greek and Roman thought on the matter (cf. Eur., *Alcestis*, 782 ff.). Roman dining rooms of the imperial period sometimes had pictures of a skeleton with the inscription "Know thyself". This is an invitation to make sure not to miss the pleasures of the moment. Where age mars the enjoyment of the plea-sures of life, one might as well die at once (Eur., *Hecuba*, 1104 ff.). The necropoleis of the ancient world lie along the main roads of the city, and are intended to bring near to those who are dead the only life that there is, the life of those who have not yet died. A gentle death after a long life is regarded as a great blessing (Homer, *Od.*, 11, 134 ff.), but comfort is also found in the realization that death is a release from the futilities of life (Eur., *Troades*, 635 ff.).

2. Death itself does, however, present a problem, and the horror of it becomes a subject for reflection. A way of overcoming it is sought, and often the view appears that a man lives on in his children (Mimnermus, *Frag.*, 2, 13 ff.). Epitaphs and great funeral monuments keep alive the memory of the deceased, proclaiming his deeds to posterity and so make death tolerable.

A special characteristic of the Greeks, however, is to make death a part of life by regarding it not as a fate but rather as an act of human achievement. It is important to die gloriously, either in fighting courageously or by facing death without fear (Eur., *Heraclidae*, 533 f.). Where in some such way death can be seen as one of the achievements of life, it is regarded as a fine thing, ensuring that the name of the one who had died will be honoured by those who live on, particularly if he died on behalf of the *polis* (→ People) (Eur., *Heraclidae*, 621 ff.).

(a) For Plato real life consisted of withdrawing from the constraint of purely natural circumstances and living not for the sake of pleasure but for virtue. For the man who lives thus even death loses its terrors. For why should I fear death, whose nature I cannot comprehend, rather than flee from the evils of this life which are well-known to me? The calm with which a person who has this philosophical insight is able to meet death, again turns death into a human achievement (*Phaedo*, 80e), especially since death often provides an opportunity for a direct display of virtue, especially where it could only be avoided – e.g. in battle – at the price of base conduct (*Apology*, 38e–39b).

(b) The Stoics took a similar view. For them death lost its terrors when a person accepted its natural inevitability and regarded himself as one in the process of dying. This enabled the Stoics to feel free with regard to death and to regard his own status as a mortal. He needs no liberation from the power of death. He who is overcome by death and the fear of it is the one who is really dead (Epict., *Dissertationes*, I, 19, 9). This continual, free readiness to die calmly after a virtuous life again turns death into a human achievement (Seneca, *Letters*, 93; 101, 15), which can even be consciously brought about by suicide. "Where one ceases is of no importance. Cease when you wish. It only matters that the end be a good one" (idem, 77, 20),

3. (a) In addition to these attitudes, and occasionally in combination with them, belief is sometimes found in the immortality of the → soul. This originated from the obscure springs of Orphic and Pythagorean mysticism. But Plato was the first to discuss it at any length and give it a philosophical basis as the corollary of a moral view of personality. In death the soul is freed from the → body, the immortal from the mortal, the passionless from the suffering part of man (*Phaedo*, 80c ff.). Since the philosopher's life is completely devoted to the pursuit of pure reason, a wise man can view death, which frees him from a body bereft of reason, only as a goal to be coveted (*Phaedo*, 114a ff.). ([Ed.] The *Rep.*, 10, 614–21, contains a doctrine of the transmigration of souls which is connected with rewards and punishments for actions in life. In the Hel. period such views of immortality became more widespread, but they did not find complete acceptance in popular belief.)

(b) Stoicism in general rejected personal immortality; the individual soul becomes submerged in the divine universal soul, which permeates the cosmos (→ Earth, World).

(c) In the mystery religions coming in from the East, man was elevated from the mortal state he had by nature to a divine state by means of initiation rites. These gave him a share in the life-force of the god concerned.

(d) In Gnosticism (→ Knowledge, art. *ginōskō*) the mild, anthropological body-soul dualism of Plato underwent an intensification, becoming a sharp, antithetical cosmic dualism. The cosmos is regarded as devilish, and the body as a part of the cosmos. The soul, on the other hand, stems from a world of → light and → life which is separate from the cosmos, and has become imprisoned in the body. Real death is life in the body; liberation from the body means victory over death.

(e) In Neo-Platonism, Platonic ideas and Gnostic myths were combined to form a speculative system, in which an important part is played by the journey of the soul and its progressive purification and elevation over the world of the senses.

OT All the words in this group are found in the LXX, except that *athanasia* (immortality) occurs only in late writings influenced by Hellenism (Wis., 4 Macc.). The way in which they are used is not much different from that in classical Gk. literature. The Heb. equivalent for all these terms is, with few exceptions, *māwet* (death), or *mût* (to die, kill).

1. (a) In OT thought death means the final end of man's existence (2 Sam. 12:15). "We are like water spilt on the ground, which cannot be gathered up again" (2 Sam. 14:14). Man has been taken from the ground, and to dust he returns (Gen. 3:19). Once the soul or shade has descended to Sheol (→ Hell, art. *hadēs*), no further life can come to it. This is particularly evident from the frequent complaints that death brings with it separation from Yahweh, the source of life (Ps. 6:5; 30:9; 88:5, 10 ff.; Isa. 38:11). Man has no option but to accept the common lot of death (Gen. 3:19; Sir. 14:18 f.; 41:1–4). If God allows him to die old and full of days, so that he achieves in his life what is possible for man, he may be thankful and content (Ps. 91:16; Gen. 15:15). That is not to say that he will not sigh over the transience and shortness of life (Ps. 90). Where life is marred by sickness and trouble, a man may speak in his prayers of the snares of death and of descent into hell (Ps. 116:3,8), as if death juts out here and there into life. Death, however, does not become in itself an object of fear. What is to be feared is an evil or early death which, according to popular opinion, indicates God's → punishment for human → guilt. For God punishes individuals by death in order to clearse the community of his people of evil-doers. In the same way the community itself condemns individuals to the death penalty, in order to ward off → judgment from the whole people (Deut. 13).

(b) Death itself is not a divine punishment, since it was not part of the intention of creation that man should be immortal. Adam was threatened with *early* death as a punishment for a definite act of disobedience; after the fall had taken place he was punished merely by exclusion from the garden of Eden. Even in Ps. 90, which refers back to the story of the fall and reflects upon the connection between → sin and death, it is never death, but rather the fleeting nature of life, which is attributed to human sin (cf. also Ps. 51; 14:2). Although there is thus mention of the universality of sin and death (the only exceptions being the cases of "translation"), there is in the OT as little mention of inherited death as a consequence of the sin and death of Adam as there is of original sin. Since God's relationship is not primarily with individuals, but with the people (→ covenant; → Israel), death does not represent a threat to faith, and the question "why?" does not arise with regard to death.

(c) Furthermore, since the individual is given his life and can lead it only as a member of the people of Yahweh, the idea does not occur to anyone that death may be seen or brought about as an act of heroism. Even where the individual becomes very keenly aware of the burdensomeness of life, the temptation to commit suicide is outweighed by the fact that this would be a denial of life, or by the desire for a "good" death. When Saul killed himself after the death of his sons and defeat in battle, in order to avoid falling into the hands of the Philistines, there is no suggestion that this is a heroic ending to his life (1 Sam. 31; cf. Ahithophel, 2 Sam. 17:23)

(d) Only occasionally is Yahweh seen as the Lord of Sheol (Ps. 139:8). Here we find that total confidence may be placed in him, even n the face of death (Ps. 73:23 ff.; Job 19:25). It was of such passages that the later doctrine of the → resurrection was able to avail itself.

2. (a) After the Exile the concepts of the → people and the → covenant of Yahweh were given a new meaning. The central position came to be occupied by belief in the Torah, and in a certain sense we may speak of an individualization of

the relationship with God (Jer. 31:29 ff.; Ezek. 18:2). This meant that for the Jews of the last few centuries before Christ, death posed a difficult problem. It was looked upon as something inappropriate to human destiny, and its origin sought in human sin. No longer just untimely death but death altogether is seen as a punishment for sin. The line which in the opinion of some scholars may already be seen in the Yahwistic tradition of the fall narrative, Gen. 2 and 3, is now extrapolated in a heightened form. Adam's sin first brought death into the world: "Thou didst lay upon him (Adam) a single commandment of thine; but he transgressed it. At once thou didst appoint death for him and for his descendants" (2 Esd. 3:7). "From a woman sin had its beginning, and because of her we all die" (Sir. 25:24). Opinions differ as to whether there are or have been sinless men, who have to die only because of the common destiny of death brought about by Adam, or whether all men deserve death on account of their own sins (cf. for example Syr. Bar. 54:19: "Adam is the cause of his own soul, and only his; but we have each become an Adam for ourselves". Further material in SB I 815 f.; III 227 ff.).

(b) Where death is thus regarded not as the natural destiny of man, but as something brought upon him in the course of history, the way is open for reflection upon the possibility that God will overcome sin and death. Thus in Jewish apocalyptic we find the concept of a Kingdom of God at the end of time, in which sin has been conquered and death has lost its power. The hope of a resurrection, first found in Isa. 26:19 and Dan. 12:2, and then formulated with the help of Iranian ideas, further makes possible a faith that even for earlier generations death will be overcome by a divine act of new creation. The righteous will enter into eternal life, the unrighteous into eternal death (2 Esd. 7:31 ff.). The doctrine of → resurrection (art. *anastasis* OT) naturally remained a subject of controversy. The Pharisees defended it, and were opposed by the Sadducees. There were also differing opinions as to whether only Israelites will be resurrected, or also Gentiles, only the righteous or also the unrighteous (the latter to judgment).

(c) Where the ancient Jewish view of death is maintained alongside these ideas of resurrection, the result can be pessimism. "For the fate of the sons of men and the fate of beasts is the same; as one dies, so dies the other. They all have the same breath, and man has no advantage over the beasts . . . all are from dust, and all turn to dust again" (Eccl. 3:19 f.).

(d) There is also an increasing use of the language of death in a figurative sense. In Deut. 30:15 we already find it being said of the commandments and laws of Yahweh, "See, I have set before you this day life and good, death and evil" (cf. Jer. 21:8). Death takes place whenever Israel, or (begininng with Ezek.) the individual Israelite, breaks away from God (Ezek. 18:21 ff., 31 f.). Here it is the breaking off of fellowship with God which is seen as death, just as its enjoyment is seen as → life.

(e) [Ed.] On the possible implications of life after death in Job 19:25 f. see H. H. Rowley, *Job*, 1970, 172 ff.: "For I know that my Redeemer lives, and at last he will stand upon the earth; and after my skin has been thus destroyed, then without my flesh (mg. from my flesh, Heb. *mibbeśārî*) I shall see God" (RSV). Although many commentators see this as Job's faith in vindication in this life, Rowley is inclined to see in these words a hope for vindication after death in view of the fact that in the preceding verses Job sees no hope of vindication in the present life.

3. With the changes of spiritual emphasis which characterized the Hel. period, and the greater importance attached to man-centred categories, strongly dualistic ideas began to find their way into Judaism to a greater or lesser extent.

(a) Thus the → soul came to be regarded as immortal (Wis. 3:4; 4:1; 15:3). It remains in heavenly places awaiting the resurrection (Eth.En. 102 ff.; 2 Esd. 7:88 ff.) except where the concept of resurrection is completely abandoned and an eternal, bodiless existence held to begin immediately after death (4 Macc. 16:13; 17:12).

(b) Another effect of Gk. influence can be seen in the way that Jewish martyrs come to see their death as an heroic deed, so that the death of martyrs is extolled as glorious (4 Macc. 10:1) and virtuous (2 Macc. 6:31).

(c) Philo described the body as an "evil and dead companion" of the soul, and so saw physical death, which separates the soul from the body, as an act of liberation (Leg. All., 1, 107). He sees two kinds of death in this world, adopting a Gk. idea in that he makes light of natural death and regards real death as the state where the body rules the soul and buries it under passions and evil things of every kind (Leg. All., 1, 105 ff.).

(d) Josephus makes the Jewish commander Eleazar produce the usual Hel. arguments when he is encouraging the Jews in the fortress of Masada to choose death rather than surrender to the Romans. If it is impossible to live with honour, one ought to die bravely (War, 7, 341). The choice of a death so fine and free (War, 7, 325 f.) leaves behind it admiration for such boldness (War, 7, 338). He who falls fighting for liberty must be regarded as fortunate (War, 7, 372). Moreover, death bestows upon the soul freedom from the evil of a mortal body – souls fettered to the body are in reality dead – and leads it into its native fields (War, 7, 341 ff.). For the soul possesses immortality (War, 7, 340).

NT In the NT thanatos (death) is found about 120 times: in the gospels mostly with reference to the death of Jesus; in Paul mainly of human death. thanatoō, kill, occurs 11 times in various parts of the NT; thnētos, mortal, 6 times, all in Paul. apothnēskō, die is used 113 times in the NT (and thnēskō 6 times). In the Synoptic Gospels it is rarely used of the death of Jesus. But in Paul, on the other hand, this use is frequent because of the pre-Pauline confessional formula, "Christ died for our sins" (1 Cor. 15:3; Rom. 5:8). synapothnēskō, die together with someone, occurs in Mk. 14:31; 2 Cor. 7:3; 2 Tim. 2:11. Only in the last instance has it a christological reference. athanasia (immortality) is found 3 times. 1 Cor. 15:53 f. speaks of immortality being "put on" in an apocalyptic context. In 1 Tim. 6:16 God is described as the One to whom alone immortality belongs.

1. The NT view of death is in direct continuity with the old Jewish view. The Hel. influences of intertestamental Judaism have had scarcely any effect. For the most part a consistent view is maintained. Whenever the term thnētos (mortal) occurs, it indicates that the mortality of man is taken as a self-evident fact. Man lives in the shadow of death (Matt. 4:16; Isa. 9:1 LXX). God, the source of all life, is the only one to whom immortality belongs (1 Tim. 6:16), whereas man has to live out his whole life in the fear of death (Heb. 2:15). As in Judaism death is always seen as the death of an individual, and the possibility of relativizing death by reference to the continuing life of a community is foreign to NT thought.

435

(a) This being the case, importance is naturally attached to the question of what causes death. The answer to this question is summed up by Paul in a pregnant statement: "The wages of sin is death" (Rom. 6:23). On the basis of this view, the devil (→ Satan) can be regarded as the one who has power over death (Heb. 2:14), although, of course, it is God himself who can destroy both body and soul in hell (Matt. 10:28; Rev. 2:23). For the NT the question as to the cause of death is not a speculative one. Indeed, it is in connection with death that we are made most clearly aware that the NT is not interested in scientific problems. The question must be interpreted in the light of its answer. This way we can see that Paul does not reflect upon death as a biological phenomenon, but as a theological one, in the sense that in the universality of death, the universality of man's guilt and need of redemption become evident. Where man turns his back upon God, "who gives life to the dead and calls into existence the things that do not exist" (Rom. 4:17), he cuts himself off from the root of his life and becomes subject to death. The phenomenon of death reveals, on this interpretation, the objective state of man in his lifetime. Living by what is created, by natural things over which he exercises control, he has cut himself off from the source of true life and thus given himself up to worthlessness. In his "progress" towards death man can catch sight of the basic condition of his life. He lives as a sinner *in* death. Death is thus the power dominating his life, and to that extent a *present* reality. "Spiritual" death and "physical" death, inextricably bound up together, constitute the reality of a life in sin. This leads the sinner to cry: "Who will deliver me from this body of death?" (Rom. 7:24). In the same way the father of the prodigal son calls his son dead (→ *nekros*, Lk. 15:24, 32). In the Fourth Gospel death and life are also present realities of existence, depending on how man responds to Jesus as the divine crisis of his existence (Jn. 5:24; 8:51; 11:25). He who cuts himself off from the church, in which the life-bringing word is proclaimed, is at the point of death (Rev. 3:2).

(b) It is Paul who among the NT writers reflects most on the connection between the guilty state of man and his mortal destiny. After setting out in Rom. 1–4 a number of arguments to provide evidence that all men without distinction have fallen into sin and thus become subject to death, and that they are called to life in Christ, he goes on in Rom. 5:12–21 to develop these themes further with the help of → Adam–Christ typology. The life which has been brought about by Christ is made to form an analogy to the fact that "sin came into the world by one man, and death through sin" (Rom. 5:12; cf. 1 Cor. 15:21 f.). Paul explains that death has spread to all men "because all have sinned", thus guarding against the idea that death as a result of sin is simply a fate we have inherited. He underlines its active character, and the fact that death is a punishment for each man's own sin (cf. G. Bornkamm, *Aufsätze*, I, 84 f.). This does not, however, alter the important statement that all men without exception are subject to sin and death. Hence, salvation and life, that is victory over death, are not to be expected as a result of man's own efforts, but only through an act of God's grace coming from outside man and appropriated by him.

In his rebellion against God, man is always seeking to find life through his own → works, and consequently whenever he avails himself of the law as a means of salvation, he only finds death. For Paul therefore → law, → sin and death are all on the same level. "The sting of death is sin, and the strength of sin is the law" (1

Cor. 15:56). Accordingly, for the man who tries to find life on the basis of law, death becomes a present reality: "When the commandment came sin revived and I died" (Rom. 7:9 f.).

If death is regarded as the historical consequence of human sin, the "natural" association of human death with that of other living creatures raises the question why non-human living creatures are likewise subject to mortality. To this question Paul, in line with contemporary Judaism (Gen. R. 12:5), replies that the → "creation" has been subjected not by its own will, but as a result of human sin, to futility and impermanence. It now waits to be set free from death, together with the "children of God" (Rom. 8:19–22). Thus Paul does not regard even death in the world of nature as a "natural" phenomenon.

(c) From all that we have said it is evident that in the NT death is regarded not as a natural process, but as an historical event, indicating clearly the sinful condition of man. In this historical sense death is seen as a power which enslaves man in the course of this life (Heb. 2:15). Hence it appears sometimes in a quasi-personal form (Rev. 20:14). The possibility of removing the horror of death by means of intellectual insight concerning its inevitability, or through a heroic act of dying, is therefore excluded for NT thought. The effect of the latter means would be rather to intensify sin. For it would mean that a man was trying to earn salvation by his own effort even at the moment of dying, when death itself spells out a definitive condemnation of that whole attitude.

2. Statements about the death of Jesus form the central point of the story of salvation in the NT (→ Cross, art. *stauros* NT, 2). They are nearly always found in the NT in connection with statements about his → resurrection and the justification or new → life of those who believe.

(a) Even in pre-Pauline confessions it is stated "that Christ died for our sins in accordance with the scriptures, that he was buried, that he was raised on the third day in accordance with the scriptures, and that he appeared" (1 Cor. 15:3 ff.), and that he "was put to death for our trespasses and raised for our justification" (Rom. 4:25). Jesus died our human death (Phil. 2:7 f.; Heb. 2:14), and he really died it, as the "buried" of the early confession indicates (1 Cor. 15:3 f.). This death is "for us", i.e. to our advantage (Rom. 5:6 ff.; 1 Thess. 5:10; Heb. 2:9 f.; Mk. 10:45), a teaching which is emphasized in various ways by statements about his resurrection and exaltation (e.g. 2 Cor. 5:14 f.; 1 Pet. 3:18). His death overcomes the law (Rom. 7:4; cf. Gal. 2:21), sin (2 Cor. 5:21; Col. 1:22; → Reconciliation), and our death (Rom. 5:9; 2 Tim. 1:10; Heb. 2:14 f.; Rev. 1:17 f.). It is to make manifest this victory that the death of Jesus, the risen, present and coming One (1 Cor. 11:26; 2 Cor. 5:14 ff.), is proclaimed, in order that his death may not have been in vain (Gal. 2:21).

(b) This gospel of victory over death is expressed in many different kinds of language. A very early and widespread concept is that taken from Isa. 53, the concept of Jesus' death as a propitiatory sacrifice (→ Reconciliation, art. *hilaskomai*), which removes the guilt of sin (Rom. 3:25 f., a pre-Pauline formula; 1 Cor. 11:24 f., pre-Pauline eucharistic words; cf. also Eph. 1:7; 1 Pet. 1:18 f.). Here the OT ideas of the covenant sacrifice (Mk. 14:24; Heb. 13:20) and the passover sacrifice (1 Cor. 5:7) can also find a place. In addition we find the related concept of Christ's death as a substitutionary sacrifice (2 Cor. 5:21). Frequent too is the idea of ransom, a concept originating in the laws of slavery, but strongly metaphorical in its christological use (→ Redemption, art. *lytron;* cf. Mk. 10:45; Gal. 3:13; 2 Pet. 2:1). Another concept is that of the descent of the slain redeemer into Hades, there to defeat the devil and release from death the people in his power (Heb. 2:14 f.; Rev. 1:17 f.; cf. 1 Pet. 3:19 f.; cf. J.N.D. Kelly, *Early Christian Creeds,* 1972², 378–88).

The difficulty of the language borrowed from the cultic and forensic spheres (propitiation, ransom, substitution) is that it expresses only deliverance from the burden of guilt in the past, and from future death as a punishment for the sins which brought that guilt. It does not give full expression to the idea of the present as the sphere of sin or of → righteousness, of death or life.

(c) The Pauline literature therefore uses not only theological expressions drawn from the cultic and forensic sphere, but also the language of the mystery cults and gnosticism, since the categories provided by these religions allow the effect of the death of Jesus on human life to be expressed with particular clarity. ([Ed.] Dr. Schmithals has dealt with the question of gnosticism more fully in *Gnosticism in Corinth,* 1971, and *Paul and the Gnostics,* 1972. A contrary position which sees gnosticism as essentially post-Christian and therefore not decisive in the background has been argued by E. Yamauchi, *Pre-Christian Gnosticism,* 1973; cf. F. L. Cross, ed., *The Jung Codex,* 1955. See also the discussions in U. Bianchi, ed., *Origins of Gnosticism,* 1967. On the mystery religions see G. Wagner, *Pauline Baptism and the Mystery Religions,* 1967; → also art. Baptism.) The language of the mysteries is found especially in connection with the significance of → baptism: "Do you not know that all of us who have been baptized into Christ Jesus were baptized into his death? We were buried therefore with him by baptism into death . . ." (Rom. 6:3 f.). "To die with Christ" thus means to die to the world as the sphere of opportunity for finding life (Gal. 6:14), or to the enslaving powers of the world (Col. 2:20; → Law), to the slavery of the law (Rom. 7:6), to life in sin (Rom. 6:6), or to living "for oneself" (2 Cor. 5:14 f.). Elsewhere there appears to be some relation to Gnostic language, with its assumption of a substantial unity of redeemer and redeemed, e.g. in 2 Cor. 4:10: "always carrying in the body the death of Jesus, so that the life of Jesus may be manifested in our mortal flesh" (cf. also Col. 1:24).

(d) John, in contrast to the Pauline and pre-Pauline tradition, lays emphasis not specifically on the death of Jesus, but on the whole event of his coming (→ Come, art. *erchomai*) into this world of death. Jesus' death on the → cross is the highest expression of the incarnation of the Logos (→ Word). At the same time, when seen as an exaltation, it is a divine token of the general victory over death (Jn. 12:33; 18:32).

(e) The ways in which the death of Jesus is described, in terms of the religious concepts of the period, indicate that the early Christians did not attach importance to it primarily as a biographical event. Jesus' death is regarded neither as the death of a noble man and martyr for a good cause, nor as that of a political rebel or the victim of an error of justice. It is seen rather as a unique, fundamental event of salvation history, and is proclaimed as such (Rom. 6:10).

The various statements of the NT concerning the death of Jesus have in common that they proclaim it as a death "for" (for us, Rom. 5:8; 1 Cor. 15:3; for many, Mk. 10:45; 14:24 par. in Matt. 26:28; Heb. 9:28; cf. Jn. 10:15; for you, 1 Cor.

11:24; cf. Lk. 22:19 f.). The intention here is to declare that God breaks the power of sin by identifying himself with man in the death of Jesus, unmasking the death-bringing power of the → law, ending its validity, and thus robbing death of its power. Since God seeks out man in the place where he is, namely death, and offers his own self as a basis for life, man is freed from compulsion to commit the primal sin of self-righteousness. He is acquitted (justification of the sinner), brought into a proper creaturely status (new creature), and given new life with Christ.

3. In the teaching of the NT especial importance is accorded to this defeat of death (or of law, or sin), already accomplished through the death of Jesus, and to the corresponding promise of life already present. For this purpose particular use is made of statements taken from Gnosticism and the Mysteries.

(a) Compare, for instance, the following statements from Pauline literature. "The death he died he died to sin, once for all, but the life he lives he lives to God. So you also must consider yourselves dead to sin and alive to God in Christ Jesus" (Rom. 6:10 f.). "For I through the law died to the law, that I might live to God. I have been crucified with Christ; it is no longer I that live, but Christ who lives in me; and the life I now live. . ." (Gal 2:19 f.). "If with Christ you died to the elemental spirits of the universe, . . . why do you submit to regulations?" (Col. 2:20).

These passages are saying: where the "scandal" of Christ's death on the cross has been overcome, where a man has given up to death his "old" self, the "old man", i.e. the desire or imagined obligation to find life independently by his own efforts, there Christ is experienced in the here and now as the power and wisdom of God (cf. 1 Cor. 1:23 f.). True life is the life which comes by God's grace, and is free from the obligation to seek autonomously one's own fulfilment. It begins with faith in Jesus Christ.

(b) John expresses the same concept in statements which are given particular emphasis: "Truly, truly, I say to you, if any one keeps my word, he will never taste death" (Jn. 8:51). "Truly, truly, I say to you, he who hears my word and believes him who sent me, has eternal life; he does not come into judgment, but has passed from death to life" (Jn. 5:24). "We know that we have passed out of death into life, because we love the brethren" (1 Jn. 3:14). Freedom from death, in the sense of a death-bringing obligation continually to justify oneself, gives to the man who knows that he has been accepted by God the freedom to give himself without reserve to his neighbour.

(c) In the Synoptic Gospels the fact that death has already been defeated is demonstrated especially by the miracle stories, and in particular the raising of the dead. Faced with death, Jesus says: "Do not fear, only believe" (Mk. 5:36). He can therefore say to his disciples, "Follow me, and leave the dead to bury their own dead" (Matt. 8:22). All these sayings are consistent in viewing freedom from sin as deliverance from the fate of death and the beginning of real life: to live by God's grace is truly to live.

(d) The defeat of death here and now for the Christian has a natural corollary in the final subjection of the unbeliever to death. For the apostle's preaching is "to one a fragrance from death to death, to the other a fragrance from life to life" (2 Cor. 2:16).

4. If by the death of Jesus the power of sin has been broken, and the Christian delivered from the vicious circle of sin and death, so that he already lives as a new

creature (2 Cor. 5:17), the fact that physical death continues to reign over man raises a question in view of the direct connection between sin and death. Although at the outset of NT thinking "spiritual" and "physical" death were not distinguished, since death in every sense had its origin in sin, reflection on the facts of human life resulted in a distinction being drawn. For the believer had been delivered from the power of sin and death ("as men who have been brought from death to life", Rom. 6:13) and yet had to die. During the period when the end was expected at any time, this phenomenon could be overlooked. When it arose, various answers were given.

(a) For Paul the phenomenon of physical death serves to guard against a sense of security with regard to judgment, and the dialectic of "now already" and "not yet" is developed. For if the final defeat of death, as the "last enemy", remains to be accomplished (1 Cor. 15:26), man is not yet removed from danger. He continues to be utterly dependent on the grace of God which never becomes a possession at his own disposal. Thus along with statements about present salvation – "Behold, now is the day of salvation" (1 Cor. 6:2) – we find future expectation. "As in Adam all die, so also in Christ shall all be made alive" (1 Cor. 15:22). The Christian has received the → Spirit as a pledge of eternal life, but he awaits as something future the redemption of his body (Rom. 8:23; 1 Cor. 15:53). The expectation of this future victory over death takes the concrete form of a belief in the resurrection of the dead, which according to Paul has already begun with the resurrection of Jesus from the dead (1 Cor. 15:12 ff.). The fact that physical death is to be expected means that hope in the God who gives life to the dead (Rom. 4:17) becomes an integral part of the faith (2 Cor. 5:1–10; Rom. 5:1–5). Not even the believer can become master of his life and of his death. The assurance that death has yet to be swallowed up in victory (1 Cor. 15:54 f.) therefore appears side by side with the believer's song of triumph. "Thanks to be to God, who gives us the victory through our Lord Jesus Christ" (1 Cor. 15:57).

This thought is developed at the christological level, where the Christian learns to regard his sufferings and death, through an act of faith, as suffering and dying with Christ. For him it is in the very experience of suffering and death that he finds fellowship with God, and thus also assurance of salvation and of eternal life (2 Cor. 4:11 f.; Phil. 1:20; Rom. 8:36 ff.). In this sense Paul can regard death as simply a laying aside of the mortal body. "For to me to live is Christ, and to die is gain" (Phil. 1:21).

Luke develops this idea in a special way when he portrays the death of Jesus as an example of martyrdom, and describes the martyrdom of Stephen in terms modelled on the death of Jesus (Acts 7:54 ff.). His purpose here is to show to the martyrs of his own day a positive way of looking at the death they have to undergo, though he does so of course at the expense of a thoroughgoing *theologia crucis*.

(b) For John the fact that the believer has to die is not a subject for extensive theological consideration. So radically does he emphasize the present tense of salvation, that even the connection between death and the traditional doctrine of judgment and resurrection disappears altogether (except for Jn. 5:28 f.). Since believers have passed through the judgment and already have eternal life, they will not die for all eternity (Jn. 10:28). Hence in Jn. 14:2 f. we read of being taken up into the "mansions" of the Father's house by the returning Son – doubtless a reference to the death of believers.

440

(c) In the later writings of the NT, and even in the Synoptic Gospels, we do not find the same intensive concern with the dialectic of salvation and judgment, life and death, as we do in those of John and the earlier letters of Paul (cf. 2 Tim. 4:7 f.; Tit. 3:7 f.; 2 Pet. 3:11 ff.). The emphasis on present experience of salvation becomes progressively replaced in the later church by a strong moral interpretation of the Christian faith, with the result that physical death ceases to be a problem for the Christian. We must all die on account of our sins, only to find grace at the final judgment: "If we die with him, we shall also live with him" (2 Tim. 2:11). Since the believer will thus stand in the judgment and remain in eternal life, it is easy to understand how the concept arises which we find in Revelation, of a second death for those who are condemned. "He who conquers shall not be hurt by the second death" (Rev. 2:11; 20:13 f.).

(d) At the same time the different traditions have in common the conviction that death does not separate the Christian from God, but rather leads him into fellowship with the suffering and dying Christ, and thus to the source and spring of all life. Thus Paul, especially, delimits the Christian view of death by insisting that on the one side Christian faith cannot go further than this in its teaching about death, but on the other that it must not be content with anything less. "Life or death or the present or the future, all are yours; and you are Christ's; and Christ is God's" (1 Cor. 3:22 f.). "If we live, we live to the Lord, and if we die, we die to the Lord; so then, whether we live or whether we die, we are the Lord's" (Rom. 14:8). "For I am sure that neither death, nor life, nor angels, nor principalities, nor things present, nor things to come, nor powers, nor height, nor depth, nor anything else in all creation, will be able to separate us from the love of God in Christ Jesus our Lord" (Rom. 8:38; cf. Phil. 1:20; 1 Thess. 4:13 f.; Jn. 12:24–26; Rev. 14:13).

W. Schmithals

| καθεύδω | καθεύδω (*katheudō*), sleep; κοιμάομαι (*koimaomai*), sleep, fall asleep; ὕπνος (*hypnos*), sleep. |

CL 1. Whereas *katheudō* in cl. Gk. is used exclusively to mean sleep, the vb.

koimaō, derived from *keimai*, to lie, has as its basic meaning, to lull (oneself), to sink into sleep (Homer, *Il.*, 11, 241). Particularly in its mid. and pass. forms it can be used either of natural sleep, or (with or without an explanatory phrase), of dying. There is no clear evidence that it is used in the sexual sense, to sleep together with.

2. *hypnos* (Indo-Germanic* *supnos*; Lat. *sopor*) is attested from Homer onwards in the sense of natural sleep which refreshes or overcomes man, causing him to forget the burdens of the day. However, the fact that in sleep we are inactive and the body appears to be lifeless causes philosophers and religious thinkers to draw certain conclusions. Inasmuch as life is identified with our waking consciousness in which we are involved with the world around us, sleep inevitably comes to be seen as useless, obstructive, degrading and animal-like (as early as Heraclitus, but particularly in Plato, e.g. *Republic*, 9, 571c; cf. also Epictetus, *Dissertationes*, 3, 22, 95). The similarity between sleep and death led in mythology to the portrayal of *Hypnos* as the twin brother of the god *Thanatos* (Homer, *Il.*, 16, 671 ff.). In early

441

medicine sleep was regarded as an intermediate, physical stage between life and death, the death of the body, not of the soul (cf. Aristotle, *De somno et vigilia*, p 453b 11 ff.). The euphemistic use of the expression in the sense of death hardly appears at all, however, before the 2nd cent. B.C. It is much more frequent altogether in the 1st and 2nd cent. A.D. (cf. the inscriptions collected by E. Peek, *Griechische Grabgedichte*, 1960). This shows the usage to be Hellenistic.

OT 1. (a) In the LXX *katheudō* (36 instances) is used chiefly to render the Heb. *šākab*, to lie down (e.g. 1 Sam. 3:2 ff.). It denotes natural sleep, and is never used to mean to die. The same applies to the noun *hypnos* which generally stands for the Heb. *šēnā'*, sleep, except for Jer. 51:39 (*hypnon aiōnion*, eternal sleep), and Job 14:12, where the context ("will not awake") makes it clear that the noun and the vb. derived from it, *hypnoō*, refer to the state of death (cf. also Ps. 13:3, *hypnōsō eis thanaton*, to fall asleep into death). There are some 80 instances of the vb. *hypnoō*, sleep.

(b) The same cannot be said about the more frequently used vb. *koimaomai* (about 150 instances, again chiefly for the Heb. *šākab*). The act. form is found only in Gen. 24:11 and 1 Ki. 17:19, and means to lay down, or make to lie down. Otherwise it is found only in the mid. (lie down, encamp, lie). Hence it comes to mean sleep (e.g. 1 Sam. 3:9, like *katheudō*). In the Pentateuch especially (*koimaomai meta*, e.g. Gen. 19:32 ff.) it is used of sleeping together. In the later strands of the OT, especially in historical narrative, it acquired the meaning to die, in the sense of an honourable death, when used in the phrase *ekoimēthē meta tōn paterōn autou*, he slept with his fathers (36 instances in 2 Ki. and Chron., e.g. 2 Ki. 14:16 22, 29; 15:7, 22, 38; 2 Cron. 26:2, 23). Hence it came also to be used in this sense without any explanatory phrase (Ezek. 32:19 ff.; Job 14:12; Isa. 43:17; 50:11). In earlier literature the word is used only occasionally in this sense (e.g. Gen. 47:30; Jdg. 5:27).

2. Heb. *šākab*, in the sense of to die, is frequently used by the Jewish Rabbis. But *katheudō* and *hypnos* are used even by Philo and Josephus of sleep in the physical sense only, except where they refer to knowledge and watchfulness. On the other hand, as early as Test.Iss. 9:9 the idea is found of an *hypnos aiōnios*, eternal sleep, i.e. sleep of death, from which the departed are to be awakened (cf. Test.Jud. 25:4, *exhypnizō*). This concept of the sleep of the dead (→ Soul OT), the so-called intermediate state, finds further development especially in Jewish apocalyptic (e.g. Eth.Enoch 91:10; 92:3), and forms the background of NT teaching about death and resurrection.

NT 1. The noun *hypnos*, sleep (only 5 instances in the NT), and the vb. *katheudō*, to sleep, always refer to the literal state of sleep (e.g. Matt. 1:24; Lk. 9:32; Jn. 11:13). However, in the scene in Gethsemane (Matt. 26:40; Mk. 14:37; Lk. 22:45) and in 1 Thess. 5:6 sleep has a negative connotation, in that it indicates a lack of watchfulness. The vb. *koimaomai*, sleep, (only in mid. in the NT) has, on the other hand, in 15 out of 18 instances the meaning, to die. Only at Matt. 28:13; Lk. 22:45 and Acts 12:6 is it used in the lit. sense, to sleep.

It is chiefly Paul who uses the vb. in the fig. sense, emphasizing as it does the close relationship which exists for the observer between a person asleep and one dead. Accordingly he generally uses participial forms to describe the dead. It is noticeable that in 1 Thess. 4:13, 14, 15 and again in 1 Cor. 15:18, 20 these occur in connection with statements about the → resurrection or reawakening by Jesus of the dead. The same is true, both in grammar and in meaning, of Matt. 27:52. Since an ambivalence of meaning between sleep and death is attested as early as Homer and also in the LXX, we should be careful not to exaggerate this connection. Nevertheless, the term is well suited to the purpose of identifying the person who is to be called to a new life with the one who has "fallen asleep" or died.

In 1 Cor. 7:39; 15:6, 51 *koimaomai* is used as an exact equivalent of to die (cf. also Acts 7:60; 13:36; 2 Pet. 3:4 of "the fathers"). John uses the ancient ambiguity of the vb. quite deliberately in Jn. 11:11–14, in the story of the raising of Lazarus, in order to show a misunderstanding on the part of the disciples. Jesus means that Lazarus has died, but the disciples understand him to mean a sleep which will bring healing. Perhaps here too the language is intended to draw attention to Jesus' victory over the humanly invincible power of death. For him who overcomes these powers, *thanatos* is no more than *hypnos*.

2. Only at 1 Thess. 5:10 is *katheudō* used in the sense of having died. At Matt. 9:24 par., where it appears in contrast to *apethanen*, she is dead, it is used in the mouth of Jesus to indicate that for him the child's state is not final and irrevocable.

L. Coenen

| νεκρός | νεκρός (*nekros*), dead, dead person; νεκρόω (*nekroō*), put to death; νέκρωσις (*nekrōsis*), death, deadness. |

CL 1. From the root *nek*- with its basic meaning of trouble, misfortune (cf. Lat. *nex*, murder, death; *neco*, to kill; *noceo*, to harm) are derived both the poetic masc. *nekys*, dead person, corpse, and *nekros*, with the same meaning. As a noun it means a dead person, corpse (e.g. Homer, *Il.*, 6, 71). From Pindar onwards it is found as an adj., dead. At first it is used only to refer to the dead bodies of humans or animals (Pindar, *Fragments*, 203), meaning that which is no longer animated by the *psychē* (→ Soul), i.e. mere matter (Plotinus, 4, 7, 9). The vb. *nekroō*, to kill, put to death, more often used passively, to die, and the noun *nekrōsis*, meaning the process of dying or the state of being dead, are Hel. forms from the medical sphere. They indicate the mortification of a part of the body due to illness (Galen, 11, 265; 18(1), 156). Later the terms were used to refer to frozen things in nature, a tree (*Corpus Medicorum Graecorum*, 1908 ff. V, 9, 1 p 31, 5); the earth (Plotinus, 5, 1, 2), and sometimes even actively of the effect of narcotics (*Corpus Medicorum Graecorum*, V, 9, 1 p 115, 11).

2. Whereas cl. Gk. literature throughout uses *nekros* in the lit. sense, Stoic writers use the word as an adj. especially in a fig. sense. They distinguish three criteria: (a) What is *nekros* is what is not controlled by the *psychē*, soul, or the *nous*, → mind, or spirit, i.e. the world of the senses (cf. M. Ant., 12, 3, 2). (b) Also *nekros* is the physical part of man, i.e. his *sōma*, → body, which the *nous* has to drag around with itself, the part of man which he has in common with the *zōa*, the animal world (→ Life), and which separates him from what is divine (cf. Epictetus, *Dissertationes*, 1, 3, 3; 2, 19, 27; M. Ant., 9, 24). (c) Finally *nekros* is also used to describe that which does not accord with one's own standards of judgment, determined by *nous*, e.g. false teachers or philosophers (e.g. Epictetus, *Dissertationes*,

1, 9, 19; 3, 23, 28). All three definitions are based on the assumption that nothing but the consciousness of the highest and most sublime in us (*nous*) is worthy of being described as alive. Hence, all that does not come under its control is dead.

ot 1. In the LXX the Hel. verbal and substantival forms are not found at all.

nekros, along with participles like *tethnēkōs*, dead, is attested about 60 times, mostly as a noun, but also as an adj. In 28 instances in the Wisdom literature, Tob., Jud. and Macc., there is no Heb. equivalent. But otherwise the word is predominantly used to render the Heb. participle *mēt*, one who has died, a dead person. In Ezek. 9:7; 11:6, 7 it renders *hālāl*, pierced, slain. Occasionally it stands for other words meaning a corpse. It is consistently used literally of people who are in the state of death (e.g. Abraham's wife, Gen. 23:3 ff.; *sōmata nekra*, dead bodies or corpses, 2 Ki. 19:35), whether still visible on earth, or already consigned to the realm of the dead (Deut. 18:11). The dead are buried (Tob. 2:8; 12:12). It is regarded as a terrible punishment if they are left uncovered, to be eaten by the beasts (Jer. 7:33; 19:7; Deut. 28:26). In Num. 19:16 the particular nuance of *nekros* becomes evident. It is here distinguished from the one who has just been slain, where it is the occurrence of death that has the prominence (as with *tethnēkōs*), and from the skeleton. In other words, *nekros* includes recognizable identity, but excludes animation. The same chapter of the Mosaic law draws an absolute boundary between the sphere of death and that of life, which is also that of the cult and of God. He who comes directly or indirectly in contact with the dead is unclean, i.e. separated from Yahweh. The dead know and see nothing (Eccl. 9:5; Isa. 26:14; cf. Ps. 88:4 f.). God has no more dealings with them (Ps. 88:10). They do not praise God (Ps. 115:17). There is no hope for them (Ps. 143:3; Wis. 13:10), and so "a living dog is better than a dead lion" (Eccl. 9:4). All this marks off Israel's religion sharply from the cult of the dead and the oracles of the dead which are so common in the surrounding world. Not until the exile and afterwards do we find the beginnings of a hope of resurrection, arising from the experience of the suffering of the righteous. This hope at first takes the form of a confidence that even death cannot separate from Yahweh (cf. Isa. 26:19; Sir. 48:5; cf. also Ezek. 37:9). On the other hand, only in late literature influenced by Hellenism are idols characterized in a transferred sense as "dead" (Wis. 15:5).

It is worth noting that in Heb. it is quite possible to combine *mēt* with *nepeš*, soul, life. For *nepeš* means the whole man, his total existence, and it is the whole man that dies. In the LXX, however, *nekros* is not combined with *psychē*, soul. By thus accommodating the Gk. concept of a permanent → soul contrasted with a transient body (the soul does not die), the way was prepared for the later infiltration of the doctrine of the soul's immortality.

2. The Heb. literature of Qumran does not depart from the usage of the OT. In Rab. literature, on the other hand, a metaphorical use is occasionally found. The ungodly can be described as dead (SB I 489, on Matt. 8:22). In the Jewish Eighteen Benedictions mention is made of the God "who makes the dead (*hammētîm*) to live". Finally, Philo adopted the figurative usage of the Stoics, and with it the doctrine that the spiritual and intellectual is life, and that all that is subject to the senses is death.

NT 1. In the NT there are 130 instances of *nekros* (dead, a dead person), both as an adj. and as a noun. It is rather more frequent than elsewhere in Acts, Rom. and 1 Cor. 15, and lacking altogether in the Johannine letters, 2 Thess., 2 Pet., Jude and 2 Tim. The vb. *nekroō*, kill, is found only at Rom. 4:19, Col. 3:5, and Heb. 11:12, and the noun *nekrōsis*, death, putting to death, deadness, only at Rom. 4:19 and 2 Cor. 4:10. In Rom. 4:19 Paul makes use of these Hel. terms in order to indicate the ending of Abraham's and Sarah's capacity to beget children (cf. Heb. 11:12 and non-Biblical literature). In 2 Cor. 4:10 the *nekrōsis tou Iēsou*, the "dying of Jesus", which the apostle speaks of carrying about in his own body, is a reference to the symptoms of a loss of strength and suffering marked by death. It is, as it were, a (sacramental?) sharing in the passion of Christ which takes place in this life. Col. 3:5, on the other hand, possibly takes up the language used by opponents who are advocating asceticism. It launches into an attack on this very thing in its outward form, interpreting the *melē*, members, which are to be mortified as the passions which govern the body and its members.

2. The NT use of *nekros* differs both from the normal Gk. usage and from that of the OT. In the NT the state of death is no longer a final state for man. It has to be viewed in the light of the resurrection of Jesus. This can be seen from statistics alone: in no less than 75 places *nekros* is the object of *egeirō*, to awaken, or *anastasis*, (→ resurrection), or other cognate words. In addition to this, there are a number of similar combinations, such as with *zōopoieō*, to make alive (→ life; e.g. Rom. 4:17; Col. 2:13), and *prōtotokos ek*, → firstborn of (e.g. Col. 1:18; Rev. 1:5).

(a) This association of terms gives expression to a set of doctrines underlying them. From the earliest Pauline epistles (1 Thess. 1:10) to the gospels (e.g. Matt. 27:64; 28:7; Jn. 20:9; 21:14) and right through to later texts like Eph. 1:20, 2 Tim. 2:8, and Rev. 1:5, the basis of Christian → proclamation lies in testimony to the fact that God raised Jesus from the dead (see especially the early chapters of Acts, e.g. 3:15; 4:10; 10:40 f.; 13:30, 34), that he is the "firstborn of the dead", and that he is alive (Rev. 2:8). This testimony is most extensively developed in 1 Cor. 15:3 ff.: "Now if Christ is preached as raised from the dead. . . ."

(b) In the OT it was still necessary to say that God is "God not of the dead, but of the living" (see above OT 1). This boundary is still to be seen in the background of the Lukan question: "Why do you seek the living among the dead?" (*meta tōn nekrōn*, Lk. 24:5). When, however, the statement is taken up in the mouth of Jesus at Mk. 12:27 (par. Matt. 22:32; Lk. 20:38), it is put into the context of the expectation of and testimony to the general → resurrection. It is consequently changed in the light of the death and resurrection of Jesus. He is Lord (*kyrieusē*) both of the dead and of the living (Rom. 14:9), or, as Luke has it, "the one ordained by God to be judge of the living and the dead" (Acts 10:42; cf. 1 Pet. 4:5). Death is no longer a realm inaccessible to God and beyond the range of his power. It has been conquered by Jesus. The accounts in the gospels of Jesus raising the dead to life (Matt. 9:23 ff., par.; Lk. 7:11 ff., especially v. 15; Jn. 11; 12:1, 9) provide graphic backing for this assertion, and lead to the claiming of prophetic promises as the background of the fulfilment which has taken place in Christ (Matt. 11:5 par.; Lk. 7:22). Here the formulae of Isa. 35:5 f. and 61:1 ff. are taken up, but are extended by the addition of *nekroi egeirontai*, dead are raised up. Moreover, since the conquest of death is seen as a vital part of the Christ-event, it is natural that a

445

similar promise be applied (together with promises that the sick will recover and → demons be cast out) to the disciples in Matt. 10:8 (cf. Mk. 16:17 ff.), and again that such a miracle be recorded, in the raising of a dead man by Paul (Acts 20:9–12).

Associated with the preaching of the resurrection of Jesus in the NT is that of the general resurrection (Rom. 4:17, 24; again especially 1 Cor. 15:12 ff.; Mk. 12:25 f. par.; Acts 23:6; Jn. 5:21, 25). This was already foreshadowed in Jewish expectation (cf. on this also the saying about John the Baptist, Mk. 6:14 par.). Precedence in this is accorded to those who have died believing in Christ (1 Cor. 15:23; 1 Thess. 4:16; Rev. 14:13).

3. There are only a few places where *nekros* occurs apart from this context in the lit. sense of corpse. Rev. 11:18; 20:5, 12 f. speak of the dead in the final → judgment. Matt. 8:22 and the par. Lk. 9:60 set the word in its lit. sense alongside a figurative usage. "Let the dead bury their dead" puts "those who resist the call of Jesus . . . on the same level as the dead" (R. Bultmann, *TDNT* IV 893). For the true life is found only in following Christ. In Mk. 9:26 (the state of the epileptic boy) and Matt. 28:4 (the state of the guards) *nekros* is used with *hōs*, like, in a simile. Thus strictly speaking the old, literal meaning is present only in Acts 5:10 (of Sapphira).

4. (a) It is a different matter when we come to the fig. sense foreshadowed in the Stoic writers. In the parable of the Prodigal Son, Luke calls the one son "dead" (Lk. 15:24, 32) in the sense that as far as the father is concerned he has left the number of the living. Paul uses the adj. in sacramental language concerning the doctrine of baptism at Rom. 6:11, 13, where he exhorts Christians to consider themselves *nekrous men tē hamartia*, dead to sin, and to give themselves to God as "men who have been brought from death to life." The same probably applies to Rom. 8:10, although the terminology seems dualistic. What we have here is not a pejorative declaration concerning the nothingness of the *sōma*, body; for even the → spirit and → soul of man belong for Paul to the sphere of the *sarx*, flesh. The reference is rather to the fact that man in his independence, man loose from God, man without Christ, is subject to judgment and hence to death. This is shown clearly also by Eph. 2:1, 5 and Col. 2:13, where the state of being *nekros* is seen to be grounded in transgressions (*paraptōmasin*; → Sin).

(b) Typical examples of the fig. use are found in the advanced reflection of Heb. and Jas. In Heb. 6:1; 9:14, *erga* (→ works), i.e. the works-righteousness of man without Christ, are described as *nekros*, dead. Jas. 2:17, 26 goes a step further and characterizes even *pistis* (→ faith) as dead, if it does not result in outward manifestations of life. Here *erga* (works) occurs again, but this time of course in a positive sense. Belief in the conquest of death makes it impossible to allow even the word itself any permanent place in its own right. *L. Coenen*

→ Adam, → Destroy, → Heaven, → Judgment, → Law, → Life, → Resurrection, → Sin, and the attached bibliographies.

(a). H. Balz, *hypnos*, *TDNT* VIII 545–56; F. F. Bruce, "Paul on Immortality", *SJT* 24, 1971, 457–72; R. Bultmann, *thanatos*, *TDNT* III 7–21; and *nekros*, *TDNT* IV 892–95; J. B. Burns, "The Mythology of Death in the Old Testament", *SJT* 26, 1973, 327–40; O. Cullmann, *Immortality of the Soul or Resurrection of the Dead*, 1958; J. Denney, *The Death of Christ*, 1902; J. D. G. Dunn, "Paul's Understanding of the Death of Jesus," in R. Banks, ed., *Reconciliation and Hope*

(Leon Morris Festschrift), 1974, 125–41; R. Martin-Achard, *From Death to Life: A Study of the Development of the Doctrine of the Resurrection in the Old Testament*, 1960; J. D. McCaughey, "The Death of Death (1 Cor. 15:26)," in R. Banks, ed., *Reconciliation and Hope* (Leon Morris Festschrift), 1974, 246–61; A. Oepke, *katheudō, TDNT* III 431–37; J. Owen, *The Death of Death in the Death of Christ*, 1960 reprint, also in reprint of Owen's *Works*, X, 1967; K. Rahner, *On the Theology of Death*, 1961; H. H. Rowley, "Death and Beyond," *The Faith of Israel*, 1956, 150–76; E. Schmitt, "Death", *EBT* I 181–4; E. Schweizer, "Dying and Rising with Christ," *NTS* 14, 1967–68, 1 ff.; R. L. Tannehill, *Dying and Rising with Christ, BZNW* 32, 1966.

(b). C. Barth, *Die Errettung vom Tode in den individuellen Klage- und Dankliedern des Alten Testaments*, 1947; H.-W. Bartsch, "Die Bedeutung des Sterbens Jesu nach den Synoptikern," *ThZ* 20, 1964, 87 ff.; E. Benz, *Das Todesproblem in der stoischen Philosophie*, 1929; E. Brandenburger, *Adam und Christus, WMANT* 7, 1962; G. Braumann, "Leidenskelch und Todestaufe (Mk- 10, 38)," *ZNW* 56, 1965, 178 ff.; J. Choron, *Der Tod im abendländischen Denken*, 1967; H. Conzelmann, E. Flesseman van Leer, E. Haenchen, E. Käsemann, E. Lohse, *Zur Bedeutung des Todes Jesu*, 1967; H. M. Feret, *Das Mysterium des Todes*, 1955; F. Hesse, S. Schulz and H. Engelland, "Tod und Totenreich," *EKL* III 1451 ff.; P. Hoffmann, *Die Toten in Christus, NTAbh* Neue Folge 2, 1966; E. Jüngel, *Tod, Themen der Theologie*, 8, 1971; A. Kassing, "Der Tod im Leben des Christen nach dem Apostel Paulus," *Pro Veritate*, 1963, 7–21; J. Leipoldt, *Der Tod bei Griechen und Juden*, 1942; O. Michel, "Jesu Lehre vom Todeschlaf," *ZNW* 35, 1936, 285 ff.; G. Pfannmüller, *Tod, Jenseits und Unsterblichkeit in der Religion, Literatur und und Philosophie der Griechen und Römer*, 1953; G. Quell, *Die Auffassung des Todes in Israel*, 1925; E. Rohde, *Psyche, Seelenkult und Unsterblichkeitsglaube der Griechen*, (1893) 1925[10]; J. Roloff, "Anfänge der soteriologischen Deutung des Todes Jesu (Mk. x. 45 und Lk. xxii. 27)," *NTS* 19, 1972–3, 38–64; F. Schneider, "Das Problem des Todes in der Biochemie," *Praktische Theologie* 58, 1969, 174 ff.; J. Schreiner, "Geburt und Tod in biblischer Sicht," *BuL* 7, 1966, 127 ff.; A. Schulz, *Der Sinn des Todes im Alten Testament*, 1919; G. Schunack, *Das hermeneutische Problem des Todes. Im Horizont von Römer 5 untersucht, Hermeneutische Untersuchungen zur Theologie* 7, 1967; E. Schweizer, "Die Mystik des Sterbens und Auferstehens mit Christus bei Paulus," *EvTh* 26, 1966, 239 ff.; and "Die Leiblichkeit des Menschen: Leben – Tod – Auferstehung," *EvTh* 29, 1969, 40 ff.; L. Wächter, *Der Tod im Alten Testament, AzTh* II, 8, 1967.

Defile

μιαίνω

μιαίνω (*miainō*), defile; μίασμα (*miasma*); μιασμός (*miasmos*), defilement, pollution; ἀμίαντος (*amiantos*), undefiled, pure.

CL The basic meaning of *miainō* is to colour something by painting or staining it.
In this sense the word is morally and aesthetically neutral. But from Homer on it is also used metaphorically for causing oneself or other people or places to be "stained", i.e. unclean, with defilement that needs deliberate ritual cleansing. And in a broader moral sense *miainō* is used for profaning religion and justice (Aeschylus), sullying one's father's fame (Euripides), and polluting one's soul (Plato). *miasma*, meaning the defilement resulting, and *miasmos*, meaning the defiled state, have a corresponding range of physical, cultic and moral meaning, while *amiantos* signifies freedom from defilement in both the moral and the religious sense.

OT In the LXX, *miainō* frequently renders forms of *tāmē'*, "defile", especially in ritual contexts in Lev., Num. and Ezek. In Lev. 13:3 the meaning of *miainō* is declarative, "to pronounce unclean." Since the OT does not contrast ritual and moral defilement, as modern scholarship tends to do, but rather assimilates the two, seeing both as contraventions of God's revealed will, it is no surprise to find *miainō* used also of the defilement which moral and spiritual transgressions cause

447

(e.g. Isa. 47:6; Ezek. 14:11; Hos. 6:11(10)). Disregard for God's law in general and sexual license in particular are highlighted as sources of defilement in this latter group of passages. In the canonical LXX *miasma* occurs three times, in the apocryphal books *miasma* is found four times, *miasmos* twice, and *amiantos* five times; and each word denotes defilement in both its ritual and its moral aspects, just as *miainō* does.

NT In the NT *miainō* is used of the ritual uncleanness Jews feared from entering Gentile premises (Jn. 18:28), and also of the moral defilement of mind, conscience and flesh (total psycho-physical being) which results from becoming a faithless libertine (Tit. 1:15; Jude 8). Heb. 12:15 expresses the fear that one apostate will defile others, presumably by drawing them to follow his bad example. *miasma* comes only in the phrase "pollutions of (i.e., incurred and communicated by) the (ungodly) world" (2 Pet. 2:20); *miasmos* appears only in 2 Pet. 2:10, in a phrase meaning either "in their foul lust" or "in their lust for filthiness", apparently referring to sexual and perhaps homosexual self-indulgence. *amiantos* is used to express the purity of Christ as High Priest (Heb. 7:27), of our heavenly inheritance (2 Pet. 1:4), of sexual relations within marriage (Heb. 13:4), and of practical religion (Jas. 1:27); what it affirms in each of its applications is the absence of anything that would constitute guilt before God.

The adj. *koinos*, in the sense of common or impure, ceremonially unclean, and the corresponding vb., *koinoō*, in the sense of to make common or impure, defile, profane, desecrate, also occur in the NT. For *koinos* in the sense of common, communal, and other related words → Fellowship, art. *koinōnia*. *koinos*, in the sense of unclean, occurs in Mk. 7:2, 5 (cf. *koinoō* in Mk. 7:15, 18, 20, 23; Matt. 15:11, 18, 20) in the context of Jesus' teaching that it is not dirt or anything external that defiles a man but the thoughts of the → heart. Likewise Paul declared: "I know and am persuaded in the Lord Jesus that nothing is unclean in itself; but it is unclean for any one who thinks it unclean" (Rom. 14:14). The vision to Peter in Acts 10 in which he was commanded to eat unclean creatures (*koinos* in 10:14, 28; 11:8; cf. 1 Macc. 1:62; *koinoō*, in the sense of consider or declare unclean, 10:15; 11:9) symbolized God's acceptance of the Gentiles and their inclusion in the new → covenant. Paul was accused of defiling the temple by introducing Gentiles (Acts 10:28), although in fact he had refrained from giving offence in this way. *koinos* refers to defilement under the old covenant in Heb. 9:13. But Heb. 10:29 speaks of defiling or profaning the blood of the covenant, spurning the Son of God, and thus being worthy of greater punishment than under the old covenant. Rev. 21:27 takes up the concept and applies it in a moral sense, when it declares that, "nothing unclean shall enter" the new → Jerusalem, "nor any one who practises abomination or falsehood, but only those who are written in the Lamb's book of life." (See further F. Hauck, *TDNT* III 789–97; C. E. Carlston, "The Things that Defile (Mk. 7:14) and the Law in Matthew and Mark", *NTS* 15, 1968–69, 75–96.)

| μολύνω, μολυσμός | μολύνω (*molynō*), defile, befoul; μολυσμός (*molysmos*), defilement. |

CL & OT The literal meaning of *molynō* is "besmear, soil", as one does by applying mud or other filth. Metaphorically, it is used in ethical and religious contexts to signify actions which demean and pollute oneself and/or others, especially in sexual matters. The noun *molysmos* has a comparable range of meaning. In the LXX rendering of the canonical OT, *molynō* occurs ten times (for eight different Heb. equivalents!), being used both literally, of dirtying feet and clothes (Gen. 37:31; Cant. 5:3; Isa. 59:3) and metaphorically, of causing defilement before God (Isa. 65:4; Jer. 23:11). *molysmos* occurs once, in a parallel metaphorical sense, in Jer. 23:15.

NT In the NT *molynō* is used in its metaphorical sense three times: in 1 Cor. 8:7, of of a weak conscience that is defiled, i.e. made to feel guilty, through doing things about which one had scruples; and in Rev. 3:4; 14:4, of not lapsing into unfaithful and disobedient ways, pictured in the first reference as dirtying one's clothes and in the second as losing one's virginity. *molysmos* appears once, in 2 Cor. 7:1, signifying the moral and spiritual defilement that comes from embracing the pagan life-style. *J. I. Packer*

F. Hauck, *miainō*, etc., and *molynō*, etc., *TDNT* IV 644 ff., 736 f.; R. C. Trench, *Synonyms of the NT*, 1880[9], 110 f.

Demon, Air, Cast Out

The article on *daimōn* should be compared with that on *pneuma* (→ Spirit), for it is concerned with spiritual, intermediary powers in personal form. Since in the NT it is used only of evil powers, it should be compared also with the article on *diabolos* (→ Satan). It is examined here together with *aēr* (air) and *ekballō* (cast out). For in the NT the air is normally the sphere of the demonic powers, and *ekballō* is theologically relevant only in connection with casting out demons.

ἀήρ	ἀήρ (*aēr*), air.

CL & OT According to cl. concepts the *aēr*, air, filled the space between the earth and the moon. The Greeks distinguished qualitatively between *aēr* as the lower, impure air (vapour), and the upper, pure air, the ether. Since *aēr* was the less pure element, it was the home of the spirits. This idea is already found in Pythagoras (*c.* 500 B.C.). Late Jud. also at times regarded the air as the home of the demons (Sl. Enoch 31; Asc. Isa. 11:23).

NT *aēr* appears 7 times in the NT. It is used (a) for the space above us (Acts 22:23; 1 Thess. 4:17; Rev. 16:17); (b) in idioms: beat the air (1 Cor. 9:26), speak into the air (1 Cor. 14:9); (c) in God's eschatological judgments "the air" is also affected. The smoke from the abyss (→ Hell, art. *abyssos*, underworld) darkens both it and the sun (Rev. 9:12); one of the angels pours his bowl of wrath into the air (Rev. 16:17).

Since the air fills the space between heaven and earth, it is the place where Christ meets the church at the parousia. The church is caught up to meet Christ in the air (1 Thess. 4:17). Satan is the evil spirit who rules in the air (Eph. 2:2; cf. 6:12) and is at work in the godless. Contemporary Jewish concepts are here brought into relationship. The organized evil spirits are under a ruler, a concept modelled on the angels (or lords) of the darkness found in the Qumran writings, from which it may have been derived (→ *daimōn*; → Satan, art. *diabolos*).　　　　*H. Bietenhard*

| δαιμόνιον |

δαίμων (*daimōn*), demon; *δαιμόνιον* (*daimonion*), demon, evil spirit; *δεισιδαιμονία* (*deisidaimonia*), reverence for the divinity, religion, superstition; *δεισιδαίμων* (*deisidaimōn*), superstitious, religious; *δαιμονίζομαι* (*daimonizomai*), be possessed by a demon.

CL *daimōn* is derived from *daiomai*, divide, apportion. It may be connected with the idea of the god of the dead as the divider of corpses. It denotes superhuman power, god, goddess, destiny, and demon.

In Gk. popular belief the world was full of demons, beings between gods and men which could be appeased or controlled by magic, spells and incantations. They were first of all spirits of the dead, especially the unburied (an animistic concept), then ghosts which could appear in varying forms especially at night. There is no essential difference between → gods and demons. The latter lived in the air near the earth. The work of demons could be seen in the disasters and miseries of human fate. Through natural catastrophes they shook the cosmos. Above all they made men sick or mad.

Gk. philosophy was not able to free itself completely from this belief. The world was not a system of abstract forces, but was filled with demons. Offensive myths about the gods were explained away or opposed by using the idea of demon. The problem of divine providence was also approached from this standpoint. In Homer's *Il.*, *daimōn* is still sometimes used for the gods, but in the *Od.*, this was avoided so as not to place them on the same level as lower spirits. In Hesiod during the golden age men became demons after death. As Zeus' representatives they watched over human behaviour, apportioning rewards and punishments at his command. For Empedocles the *daimōn* was a separate spiritual being, not the *psyche* which accompanied a man from birth. Socrates' *daimonion*, his "good spirit", had the same characteristics. It dissuaded, but never advised him (Plato, *Apology*, 31c, 8 ff.). *daimōn* was even equated with the *hēgemonikon* (the authoritative part of the soul, the reason) of the Stoics. In later systems (Neoplatonism, Porphyry) whole hierarchies and courses of demons were drawn up. The demons were mediators between gods and men. Sometimes they supervised men. They could also be considered as one of the stages leading from deity to matter.

daimonion is the adj. of *daimōn*, and is used as a noun as the "divine". It expresses that which lies outside "human capacity and is thus to be attributed to the intervention of higher powers" (W. Foerster, *TDNT* II 8). In popular belief *daimonion* was used as a diminutive of *daimōn*.

Philo and Josephus stood entirely in the Gk. tradition. Philo considered that → angels and demons were of the same nature, but angels kept their distance from the earth and were used by God as messengers. Josephus used *daimonia* especially for evil spirits.

OT 1. Traces of the general popular belief are also to be found in the OT (1 Sam. 28:13; Isa. 8:19). Necromancy was forbidden in Israel (Deut. 18:11; Lev. 19:31;

1 Sam. 28:36), as were sacrifices to evil spirits (Lev. 17:7). Demonic beings are called the *šeʿîrîm* (satyrs, demons, BDB), *šēḏîm* (demons), *lilît* (lilith) and *ʿazāʾzēl* (Azazel) (Isa. 13:21; 34:14; Deut. 32:17; Lev. 16:8, 10, 26; Eth. En. 6:6 onwards). Demons are mentioned in connection with Israel's idolatry. It may be that heathen gods were mockingly called demons (Deut. 32:17; 2 Chr. 11:15; Ps. 106:37).

The general trend in the OT is to exclude belief in demons. An example is the way in which sun, moon and stars in Gen. 1 are simply called "luminaries", while the surrounding nations looked on them as demons and feared and honoured them. Another example is the manner in which calamities and evil are attributed to God (1 Sam. 16:14; 2 Sam. 24:1; → Satan). The mediators between God and man are not demons, but the → angel of Yahweh. The Israelite may not turn to any power other than Yahweh. Above all he had to keep himself from → magic.

In the LXX *daimōn* occurs only in Isa. 65:11. *daimonion* is found 19 times, 9 times in Tob., twice in Bar. Psa. 96:5 is important: all the gods of the peoples are *daimonia* (cf. Deut. 32:17; Psa. 106:37; Isa. 65:3; Bar. 4:7). Heb. *šēḏ* is rendered by *daimonion*, as is *šēʿîr* in Isa. 13:21 and 34:14. The concept in Tob. 6:7, 13 f. is late. It holds that an evil spirit, hostile to a man, can gain power over him and kill him (but cf. Exod. 4:24 ff.). The LXX's use of *daimonia*, rather than *daimōn*, influenced Josephus and the NT, where the evil spirits of popular belief are so named.

2. Judaism. (a) Rab. Jud. abandoned the strict reserve of OT piety. Belief in demons became widespread, though the Jews never felt themselves as strongly threatened by them as did their neighbours. The scribes also were steeped in belief in demons. They had many names for them; *šēḏîm*, powerful ones, lords, demons; *mazzîqîm*, harmers; *meḥabbelîm*, destroyers; *peḡāʿîm*, attackers; *šeʿîrîm*, satyrs; *rûaḥ rāʿāh*, evil spirit; *rûaḥ*, spirit. In the earlier period it was believed that demons were the result of sexual relations between fallen angels and women. This thought is sometimes attributed to Gen. 6:1–4. Others thought that some of the generation of the Tower of Babel were turned into demons, or that they were the result of sexual relations between Adam and Eve and female or male spirits, or that they were a special creation by God.

The demons are spirits, but they have bodily organs such as wings. They need food and drink. They can propagate themselves and appear in human or other forms. They are innumerable and fill the world. They are led by Ashmedai, a figure borrowed from the Parsees who has lesser leaders under him. The demons have access to heaven, where they can discover God's counsels. They live both on the earth and in the air, preferably in deserts, ruins and impure places, especially cemeteries. Though they belong to Satan's kingdom, God gives them authority to inflict the punishments imposed on sinners. Their power began in the time of Enosh (Gen. 4:26) and will end in the days of the Messiah. Their main goal is to lead men into sin. They can also kill. They are the cause of some, but not all, diseases. God and the holy → angels, God's word, the keeping of commandments, amulets, and exorcisms protect men against against them. Traditionally Solomon was the controller of the demons. Among the people, including some rabbis, there was much magic. In contrast to the Gk. world, the demons were not intermediate stages between God and man, nor were they the spirits of the dead. A clear distinction was drawn between angels and demons.

451

(b) Pseudepigrapha. The commonest name for the demons is "spirit" (unclean, evil). Gen. 6:1–4 is important as giving the origin of demons. They are sometimes called Satan's angels. They lead astray to magic, idolatry, war, conflict and bloodshed (cf. Jas. 3:15). They also tempt men to penetrate into hidden secrets. Eth. Enoch 8:1 attributes the gains of culture to them. The heathen worship them (Eth. Enoch 99:7; Jub. 1:11; 22:17). Fallen angels generate giants who lead men astray (Eth. Enoch 7:2 ff.; Jub. 5:1). The angels are already kept incarcerated for judgment. Unclean demons led the descendants of Noah astray (Jub. 7:27; 10:1 ff.). They are bound at the place of condemnation, but a remnant is at the disposal of Mastema, "the Lord of the Spirits", so that he can lead men astray and harm them.

(c) Qumran. The Qumran documents present a cosmological dualism mitigated by monotheism. Two spirits are subordinate to God: Michael, the spirit (angel) of light, and Belial (→ Satan), the spirit (angel) of darkness (cf. 1QS 1:18; 3:17–25; 4:1, 9–11; 1QM 13:11 f.). 1QS 4:9–11 gives a list of the vices of the spirit of darkness, which also applies to the characters of those who belong to his "lot". "Angels of destruction" (1QS 4:12) serve under the evil spirit and execute God's temporal and eternal judgments on evil-doers. Belial seeks to cause evil-doing and create guilt (1QM 13:11 ff.). His angels walk according to the laws of darkness. In these writings we find the concept of a prince of evil, controlling a kingdom of evil spirits. This was probably developed under the influence of Parseeism. In the Qumran community's rites both at men's entry into the covenant and at the covenant renewal ceremonies, the Levites had to recite the transgressions of Israel under the lordship of Belial (1QS 1:23) and to curse all "men of the lot of Belial" solemnly (1QS 2:4 ff.). A man is not freed from responsibility, because he belongs to the lot of Belial. In the final, eschatological battle Belial and his angels fight alongside the enemies of the "sons of light" (1QM 1:10 f., 13–15). After the fight a curse is pronounced against Belial and his angels (1QM 13:1–5).

In the night after Pharaoh had taken Sarah (Gen. 12:15 ff.) God sent a destructive spirit who did all kinds of harm in the palace. Only the prayer of Abraham was effective against him (1QGenAp 20:16 ff., 28 f.).

NT In the NT *daimōn* occurs only in Matt. 8:31 in the plur. Otherwise we always find *daimonion* (63 times) or *pneuma* (→ spirit). There is no belief in the spirits of the dead or in ghosts. Angels and demons appears as opposites. The fear of demons disappears because of faith in the triumph of Jesus Christ.

Since dealings with demons lie behind sorcery (→ Magic), it is rejected (Gal. 5:20; Rev. 9:20 f.; 18:23; 21:8; 22:15). Heathen worship brings men into contact with demons (1 Cor. 10:20 f.), for demons stand behind paganism in general (Rev. 9:20). They will be specially active in this sphere in the last times (1 Tim. 4:1; Rev. 16:13 f.). Demons are active today (Eph. 6:12), and teach their wisdom (Jas. 3:15). Hence it is important to discern the spirits (1 Jn. 4:1; 1 Cor. 12:10). The demonic powers are destined for judgment (Matt. 25:41; 8:29). The idea of the demons being chained and kept for judgment which appears in the Pseudepigrapha is found in 2 Pet. 2:4 and Jude 6.

Demons are subordinate to → Satan, and are his angels (Eph. 2:2; Mk. 3:20 ff., the prince of the demons). They have power to do evil. Above all they cause illness. In Lk. 13:11, 16 the woman who had "a spirit of infirmity" had been bound by

Satan (cf. Acts 10:38; 2 Cor. 12:7). But not all illness is attributed to them. In the gospels we find demon-possessed persons whose personality had been eliminated by the evil spirits who spoke out of them (Mk. 5:5 ff.). Because the kingdom of God was present in Jesus, he broke the power of the demons (Matt. 12:28) through his word of command (→ ekballō). Demons have more than human knowledge. They knew Jesus and their own fate (Matt. 8:29; Jas. 2:19). The reproach was made against Jesus himself that he had a demon (Jn. 7:20; 8:48 f., 52; 10:20 f.). This was the most complete rejection of Jesus because of its religious motivation. Had it been true, no one would have been justified in listening to him. In his answer Jesus claimed that he honoured the Father (Jn. 8:49).

deisidaimonia is compounded of *deidō*, to be afraid, and *daimōn*, and means reverence for the gods, fear of God, superstition, religion. In the NT it is found only in Acts 25:19, where it means religion (so NEB; RSV "superstition"). Festus told Agrippa and Bernice that the Jews had certain disputes about their *deisidaimonia* and a certain Jesus.

deisidaimōn, reverent before gods or God, superstitious, religious, is found only in Acts 17:22. Paul addressed the Athenians as being especially religious. This agrees with other writers who said the same about them.

daimonizomai, "be possessed by a demon" is found 7 times in Matt., 4 times in Mk., once each in Lk. and Jn.   *H. Bietenhard*

| ἐκβάλλω | ἐκβάλλω (*ekballō*), drive out, expel, send out, take out. |

CL & OT *ekballō* is used in secular Gk. and in the LXX (in the latter some 50 times).
    It has the sense of drive out: Gen. 3:24, of man from Eden; Lev. 21:7, lit. "driven away from her husband" hence divorce; Jdg. 6:9 (for *gāraš*) and Exod. 34:24 (for *yāraš*) for forcible throwing out, rejection and driving out of enemies, demons and similarly unwelcome beings from a house. Not until the 1st and 2nd cent. A.D. is it used in the favourable sense of sending out.

NT The 81 cases in the NT illustrate the whole gamut of its range of meanings. The slave-wife is cast out (Gal. 4:30; cf. Gen. 21:10). A disciple of Jesus is cast out of synagogue fellowship (Jn. 9:34 f.). The name of Christ (i.e. the Christian) is despised (Lk. 6:22). While Jesus rejects no one who comes to him (Jn. 6:37), Diotrephes excludes Christians from the church (3 Jn. 10). The taking out of a splinter (Matt. 7:4) and the removal of an eye (Mk. 9:47) still imply the use of force. But other passages like Mk. 1:12 (where the Spirit "drives" Jesus into the wilderness) and Jn. 10:4 (the shepherd "drives" the sheep out) show the transition to the positive sense of sending out reapers (Matt. 9:38 par.), sending away (Acts 16:37, "smuggle out" NEB; Jas. 2:25), leaving out (Rev. 11:2), and bringing out, distributing (Matt. 12:35; 13:52; Lk. 10:35).

The word has a theological bearing only in connection with casting out demons (cf. Matt. 7:22; 8:16 par.; 9:34; 12:26 f.; 17:19 par.; Lk. 13:32). Jesus and the primitive church shared the conceptions of their contemporaries about demons (→ *daimonion*). But while the pagans and Jews of the contemporary world environment tried to drive out the demons by magic, exorcisms and other magical practices,

Jesus needed only his word of command (Matt. 8:16). The driving out of the demons was as much an accompaniment of his proclamation as were his acts of healing (Mk. 1:39). Because Jesus with the authority of God showed himself the stronger (Mk. 1:24 par.), the demon had to yield to him and bow to his power. In his majesty Jesus also gave his disciples authority to cast out demons (Matt. 10:1, 8). His dominion over these powers was a sign that the kingdom of God had come in his person (Matt. 12:22–28).   *H. Bietenhard*

→ Accuser, → Magic, → Satan

(a). Arndt, 19 f., 168 f.; K. Barth, *CD* III, 2, 519–31; B. J. Bamberger, *Fallen Angels*, 1952; G. A. Barton, "Demons and Spirits (Hebrew)," *ERE* IV 594 ff.; H.-W. Bartsch, ed., *Kerygma and Myth*, I, 1953; II, 1962; G. B. Caird, *Principalities and Powers: A Study in Pauline Theology*, 1956; S. Eitrem, *Some Notes on the Demonology in the New Testament*, 1950; W. Foerster, *aēr*, *TDNT* I 165 f.; and *daimōn*, *TDNT* II 1–20; F. Hauck, *ballō* etc., *TDNT* I 526–29; E. Langton, *The Essentials of Demonology: A Study of Jewish and Christian Doctrine – Its Origin and Development*, 1949; R. Leivestad, *Christ the Conqueror: Ideas of Conflict and Victory in the New Testament*, 1954; H. Loewe, "Demons and Spirits (Jewish)," *ERE* IV 612 ff.; J. Michl, "Demon", *EBT* I 191–96; G. H. C. Macgregor, "Principalities and Powers: the Cosmic Background to St. Paul's Thought," *NTS* 1, 1954–55, 17–28; W. Manson, "Principalities and Powers: the Spiritual Background of the Work of Jesus in the Synoptic Gospels," *Bulletin of the Studiorum Novi Testamenti Societas*, 1952; M. Prager, "Possession by evil spirits," *EBT* II 669 ff.; H. Schlier, *Principalities and Powers*, 1961; M. F. Unger, *Biblical Demonology: A Study of the Spiritual Forces behind the present World Unrest*, 1952.

(b). F. Andres, "Daemon," Pauly-Wissowa *Supplement* III 267 ff.; O. Böcher, *Dämonenfurcht und Dämonenabwehr*, 1970 (extensive bibliography); E. Dhorme, "La démonologie biblique," *Hommage W. Fischer*, 1960, 46–54; M. Dibelius, *Die Geisterwelt im Glauben des Paulus*, 1909; A. Dupont–Sommer, "L'Instruction sur les deux Esprits dans le 'Manuel de Discipline' ", *Revue de l'Histoire des Religions* 142, 1952, 5–35; G. Gloege, "Dämonen," *RGG³* II 2 ff.; H. W. M. de Jong, *Demonische ziekten in Babylon en Bijbel*, 1959; H. Kaupel, *Die Dämonen im Alten Testament*, 1930; B. Noack, *Satanas und Soteria: Untersuchungen zur neutestamentlichen Dämonologie*, 1948; F. Nötscher, "Geist und Geister in den Texten von Qumran," *Mélanges bibliques A. Robert*, 1957, 305–15; B. Otzen, "Die neugefundenen Sektenschriften und die Testamente der zwölf Patriarchen" *StTh* 7, 1953–54, 125–57; E. von Petersdorff, *Dämonologie*, I, *Dämonen im Weltplan*, 1956; J. Samain, "L'Accusation de Magie contre le Christ dans les Évangiles," *Ephemerides Theologicae Lovanienses* 15, 1938, 449–90; J. Smit, *De daemoniacis in historia evangelica*, 1913; H. Wohlstein, "Zu den altisraelitischen Vorstellungen von Toten- und Ahnengeistern," *BZ* 5, 1961, 30–38; M. Ziegler, *Engel und Dämonen im Lichte der Bibel*, 1957.

Deny

ἀρνέομαι

ἀρνέομαι (*arneomai*), refuse, deny, dispute, disown, disregard; ἀπαρνέομαι (*aparneomai*), deny, disown, renounce.

CL The primary meaning of *arneomai* (Homer) is to deny. In the context of a demand or challenge the denial becomes definite: to refuse, reject, decline (Hesiod, *Works and Days*, 408; Demosthenes, 18, 282). The opposite is *didonai*, to grant, give (e.g. Hdt., 3, 1, 2). With reference to a matter needing clarification, or to a question, *arneomai* means to dispute, contest, gainsay (Thuc. 6, 60). The opposite is *homologeō*, to agree, assent to (e.g. Hdt., 2:81; → Lie, art. *pseudomai*.). In Hel. literature (e.g. Appian, *Bella Civilia*, 2, 39) and especially the NT *arneomai* has the further meaning of disown, renounce. It is in this sense that the originally intensive form *aparneomai* is mostly used in the NT.

ot Only in Gen. 18:15 does *arneomai* in the LXX have a Heb. equivalent: *kāḥaš* dispute, deny. *aparneomai* occurs only at Isa. 31:7, where it stands for *mā'as*, reject. This is not to say that the concept which *arneomai* expresses is not present in the OT. But in the LXX *kāḥaš* is mostly rendered by *pseudomai*, lie, and *mā'as* usually by *exoutheneō*, despise, reject. In the few places in later Jewish literature where *arneomai* occurs, it has the sense of refuse (Wis. 12:27; 16:16; 17:10), and renounce (4 Macc. 8:7; 10:15). Rab. texts speak of rejecting (*kāpar*)) the commandments (Shabbath 116a) or God (Sanhedrin 102b; cf. SB I 585, II 518).

nt 1. In the NT *arneomai* (32 times) is found chiefly in the gospels and Acts, and occasionally in the Pastorals, 1 and 2 Pet., and Rev. *aparneomai* (12 times) is found only in the synoptic gospels. In addition to the senses of refuse (e.g. Heb. 11:24) and deny (Jn. 1:20), the vb. has the specific sense of disown in relation to Jesus Christ.

2. Denial and rejection of Jesus Christ can be the result of ignorance (Acts 3:13 f., cf. 17). Generally, however, *arneomai* means to fall back from a previous relationship with him into unfaithfulness. This is the meaning of the denial of Peter (Mk. 14:30, 68, 70). The opposite to this denial is "to hold fast" (Rev. 2:13), or "to be faithful" (2:10). Used absolutely, *arneomai* can mean to abandon fellowship with the Lord (2 Tim. 2:12). Instead of the person of Jesus (2 Pet. 2:1; 1 Jn. 2:22 f.; Jude 4), it can be his name (Rev. 3:8) or faith in him (Rev. 2:13) that is denied.

(a) Denial of Jesus is not only a matter of the lips; it is failure in discipleship. The above verses in Rev. show that in the situation of suffering there is particular danger of denying the Lord (cf. also the contrast between denying and dying, or suffering with, Christ, 2 Tim. 2:11 f.). The motive for denial is usually fear of men, anxiety about what others will think, or the thought that to confess faith in the one who was crucified may mean suffering ridicule and persecution.

(b) According to 1 Jn. 2:22, denial consists of disputing that the earthly Jesus is the Messiah. Here an attack is being made on [gnostic?) teaching, which would distinguish the true, spiritual redeemer from the one who has come in the flesh. That would be to separate Jesus from God (v. 23), and to set oneself in opposition to him and hence to God.

3. Denial of Christ is also present where the claims of one's neighbour go unrecognized and unfulfilled (1 Tim. 5:8; 2 Tim. 3:5; Jude 4). Such a denial of God on man's part can only be met by a denial of man on God's part (Lk. 12:9; 2 Tim. 2:12). For denial is a rejection of God's offer of salvation and a conscious renunciation of the grace which has appeared. The only apparent contradiction to this is in 2 Tim. 2:13. In contrast to v. 12, we read here: "He cannot deny himself," i.e. he remains true to his own nature. He holds fast to his commission and his claim, in spite of our faithlessness.

4. To follow him who "emptied himself" (Phil. 2:7) implies "to deny oneself" and "to take up one's cross" (Matt. 16:24; Mk. 8:34; Lk. 9:23). If we interpret this in the light of Peter's denial ("I do not know the man" Matt. 26:70; 72, 74; Mk. 14:68, 70 ff.; Lk. 22:57 ff.; Jn. 18:25 ff.), this means to say no to one's self and to surrender oneself totally. It may be that the thought here is on the necessity, if circumstances demand, of dying a martyr's death. But the connection with Paul's remarks about "being buried with Christ" (Rom. 6:4 f.) and being crucified with

455

Christ so that Christ lives in him (Gal. 2:20), should not be overlooked. "To deny oneself" is not therefore a legalistic demand, but the way forward into life "in Christ."
H.-G. Link, E. Tiedtke

(a). O. Cullmann, *Peter: Disciple – Apostle – Martyr*, 1962²; M. Goguel, "Did Peter Deny his Lord?" *HTR* 25, 1932, 1–27; R. Koch, "Self-Denial," *EBT* III 833–39; G. W. H. Lampe, "St. Peter's Denial", *BJRL* 55, 1972–73, 346–68; H. Riesenfeld, "The Meaning of the Verb *arneisthai*," *Coniectanea Neotestamentica* 11, 1947, 207–19; H. Schlier, *arneomai, TDNT* I 469 ff.; M. Wilcox, "The Denial-Sequence in Mark xiv. 26–31, 66–72," *NTS* 17, 1970–71, 426–36.
(b). E. Dinkler, "Jesu Wort vom Kreuztragen," *Neutestamentliche Studien für Rudolf Bultmann*, 1954, 110–29; A. Fridrichsen, "Sich selbst verleugnen," *Coniectanea Neotestamentica* 2, 1936, 1–8; 6, 1942, 94 ff.; *Sv. exeg. Årsbok*, 5, 1940, 158–62; G. Klein, "Die Verleugnung des Petrus – eine traditionsgeschichtliche Untersuchung," *ZTK* 58, 1961, 285 ff. (= *Rekonstruktion und Interpretation*, *BEvTh* 50, 1969, 49 ff.); J. Lebreton, "La doctrine du renoncement dans le Nouveau Testament," *Nouvelle Revue Théologique*, 65, 1938, 385–412; and "Le Renoncement," *Lumen Christi*, 1947, 171–96; E. Linnemann, "Die Verleugnung des Petrus," *ZTK* 63, 1966, 1 ff. (= *Studien zur Passionsgeschichte*, *FRLANT* 102, 1970, 70 ff.).

Desire, Lust, Pleasure

A whole range of words – desire, longing, greed, craving, lust – expresses man's inner striving for an objective which may be a person, a thing or an experience. They also indicate the sort of action that may follow. The same is found in Gk. The most important word is *epithymia* (desire, lust). *hēdonē* (pleasure) which is familiar in ordinary speech and especially in philosophy is less important. *orexis* (desire) and *epipotheō* (long for, desire) are little used, the latter being somewhat commoner.

ἐπιθυμία

ἐπιθυμία (*epithymia*), desire, lust; ἐπιθυμέω (*epithymeō*), desire, want.

CL Both these words are found already before Socrates, especially in Hdt. From the basic meaning of being excited about something (cf. *thymos*, urge, passion) they already had in secular Gk. the meaning of impulse, desire. The word is first found in literature in a neutral sense. But later it is ethically bad, because *epithymia*, like the other three passions, fear, pleasure and sorrow, results from a false evaluation of the possessions and evils of this life.

OT In the LXX *epithymia* and *epithymeō* each occur about 50 times. They are used in the first place for human aspirations in general, and normally translate Heb. *'āwâh* and *ḥāmaḏ*. They express: (a) a morally indifferent desire (e.g. Deut. 12:20 f., as much as you want); (b) a praiseworthy desire (e.g. Gen. 31:30, the desire for one's father's house; Isa. 58:2, the yearning of the righteous for God); (c) an evil desire, which is opposed to God's will (e.g. Num. 11:4; Num. 11:34; Deut. 9:22 ([Tr.] cf. Kibroth-hatta'avah, graves of craving)). If the tenth commandment (Exod. 20:17) forbids such desire, it is because God desires from men not merely obedience in acts, but also in their words, thoughts, looks, efforts and wishes. He desires love from the whole heart (Deut. 6:5).

NT 1. Apart from Lk., where it is found 5 times, the word-group is not found in the Gospels and is rare in Heb. and Rev. It is quite lacking in 2 Cor. and 2 Thess.

456

Most of the occurrences are found in the other Pauline writings (19 of the 38 cases of *epithymia* and 5 of the 16 cases of *epithymeō*). The noun is found in a neutral or good sense only in Lk. 22:15; Phil. 1:23; 1 Thess. 2:17 and perhaps Rev. 18:14. In all other cases its connotation is bad. Normally the vb. is used in a good sense. Only in Paul and Matt. 5:28 has it a bad connotation. Paul uses *epipotheō* when the desire is praiseworthy.

2. Where the terms are used in a neutral or good sense (cf. CL, OT), they express a particularly strong desire (cf. Matt. 13:17; Lk. 15:16; Phil. 1:23; 1 Thess. 2:17; Heb. 6:11). It is to be noticed that the vb. is more often used in a good sense than the noun, and → *oregomai* can stand parallel to it with the same meaning (cf. 1 Tim. 3:1).

3. Theologically those passages are more important where *epithymia* is used in a bad sense of evil desire or lust.

(a) In the Synoptics this bad sense is found only in Matt. 5:28 (where it refers to sexual desire and lust) and in Mk. 4:19 (where it is used of the desire for all kinds of other goods and values of this world, like riches (→ Possessions)). It is clear from both these passages that Jesus considered *epithymia* as a sin with a highly destructive power. It chokes the word (Mk. 4:19, where it is compared to an exuberantly growing thorn thicket which always tries to spread if it is not prevented). It breaks marriage (Matt. 5:28). In other words, Jesus is far from making little of desire, because it "only" operates in the thoughts and wishes of the → heart, and not in the realm of deeds. For Jesus, evil desires, just like evil deeds, flow out of and betray the evil heart which has separated itself from God.

(b) Paul sees *epithymia* as an expression of the → sin which rules man. He sees in it the driving power in man's → "flesh" (*sarx*), his sinful being which has turned from God. *epithymia* seeks gratification (Gal. 5:16). It urges man to activity. When all is said and done, it expresses the deeply rooted tendency in man to find the focus of his life in himself, to trust himself, and to love himself more than others. Paul equates this tendency with the flesh and the passions (Eph. 2:3), the powers which draw a man away from God. The power of the "old nature" (Eph. 4:22) is seen in *epithymia*.

Desires can find their expression in every direction: sexual desire, material enjoyment, coveting another's possessions (cf. Rom. 1:24; 1 Tim. 6:9; Tit. 3:3; Gal. 5:16–21). By directing a man's attention, they can bring him completely under their domination. The recognition expressed in Rom. 6:12 that anyone who allows himself to be driven by his desires is already under the reign of → sin recurs frequently in the Pauline writings (Eph. 2:3; 2 Tim. 3:6; Tit. 3:3). The desires determine and enslave a man. While he becomes the → slave of their allurements and temptations (Eph. 4:22), his "heart", i.e. the centre of his whole personality (Rom. 1:24), comes under their control. When that happens, all decisions of the will, and even the best and highest impulses and powers of a man are determined by these desires. Only the life that is turned to God's will and regulation and is subject to God and determined by him, presents the opposite picture (Rom. 6:12 ff.; Eph. 4:22 ff.; Tit. 2:12 ff.).

Since there is something primitive and instinctive in human desire, Paul maintains that it is recognized as what it really is when the law speaks to it (as in the commandment, "You shall not covet"). This causes desire to become conscious sin

457

(Rom. 7:7 f.) which flagrantly contradicts God's commandment. Before I know the law, desire is instinctive and not yet a consciously desiring will.

God's anwer to desire is the → Spirit. The man who walks by the Spirit has the power to resist desire (Gal. 5:16; cf. Rom. 8:9 ff.), because the Spirit replaces desire as the determining power in his life (Eph. 4:23).

When Paul speaks of desire and longing in a good sense, he uses *epipotheō* (cf. Rom. 1:11; 2 Cor. 5:2; 9:14), *epipothēsis* (2 Cor. 7:7, 11) and *epipothia* (Rom. 15: 23). This word-group is used 13 times in the NT, 11 of them being in the Pauline writings and always in a good sense.

(c) In the Johannine writings the origin of desire is traced even further back. It does not originate merely in man but in the → "world" (1 Jn. 2:16), and ultimately comes from the devil (Jn. 8:44; → Satan). World here means the sphere of enmity to God and Christ, the sphere in which one recognizes the authority of "the prince of this world". He entices with "the lust of the flesh and the lust of the eyes and the pride of life" (1 Jn. 2:16), i.e. with external allurements appealing to the senses, material in their nature, by which he tries to gain our "love". He awakens the dormant thoughts of hatred in man and his tendencies to lie, for "he is a murderer from the beginning" and "the father of lies" (Jn. 8:44).

Since desire originates "from the world", it is transient like this world. He who builds on it and allows himself and his life to be determined by it will "pass away" with it. Conversely he who is led by God's will "abides for ever" (1 Jn. 2:17).

(d) In the Catholic Epistles the use of *epithymia* is either neutral or shows the same trend as in Paul and John. It represents the "flesh" and its passions (1 Pet. 2:11; 2 Pet. 2:10). It is related to other lusts of the senses in their desire for the material, in revels, drunkenness, carousing (1 Pet. 4:3), and debauchery (2 Pet. 2:18 NEB). It is a power which draws, entices, and lures a man, so as to bring him under its domination (Jas. 1:14; 1 Pet. 1:14; 2 Pet. 2:18). It promises him complete freedom and liberty but in reality abjectly enslaves him (→ Slave). It is always lying in wait within a man, so that at the right moment he may yield his will to it and become subject to it (Jas. 1:14). When that happens it "gives birth" to sinful action, which makes a man guilty before God (Jas. 1:15). And so it leads finally to "death" (Rom. 7:5) and "corruption" (2 Pet. 1:4).

Since *epithymia* is so bound up with man's nature, the Christian needs constantly to be attentive and awake in turning from it. He can conquer it, if he constantly allows himself to be controlled by the Spirit of God and lives "by the will of God" (1 Pet. 4:2). *H. Schönweiss*

| ἡδονή | ἡδονή (*hēdonē*), pleasure; φιλήδονος (*philēdonos*), lover of pleasure. |

CL *hēdonē* is from the same root as *hēdys*, sweet, pleasant, pleasing. Originally it meant something pleasant to the taste, and then pleasant generally. In Hdt. it means the pleasures of the senses. It occurs in an extended sense as feelings of pleasure, enjoyment (already in Homer in the form *hēdos*). Finally, just as with → *epithymia*, it came to mean desire for pleasure (Xen.). When regarded as a gift of nature, *hēdonē* was considered good. Plato called pleasure in the good, true and beautiful *hēdonē*. Aristotle used it as a synonym of *chara*, joy, in expressing pleasure in practising the virtues and for aesthetic pleasure in works of art (*Eth. Nic.* VII 12:1 (1152b 25 ff.)).

In Hellenism a distinction was made between higher and lower *hēdonai*, between those of the mind and soul and those of the body. Then the concept was confined to its ethically bad elements, and it was used in contrast to *chara*, joy, and *aretē*, virtue. In the language of the Cynic-Stoic travelling teachers it meant the pleasure of the senses, of sex, and then the unrestricted passions. The growing pessimism of the late classical period caused the concept to mean man's involvement in his material surroundings, which held down the soul trying to mount up to God. It was considered that the one who let himself be ruled by *hēdonē* had missed the purpose of life.

OT In the canonical books of the LXX the word is only used with a Heb. equivalent in Num. 11:8, where it represents the Heb. *ṭa'am*, (good) taste. In the par. Exod. 16:31 *geuma* is used. It is used first in a good sense, meaning a quality in a thing which gives a man pleasure. It has the same meaning in the three other passages where it is used: Prov. 17:1 (no equivalent in Heb.); Wis. 7:2; 16:20. It is not until 4 Macc. (11 occurrences) and especially Philo, who uses *hēdonē* as the power in revolt against *logos*, that the word is used in the same sense as in Cynic-Stoic teaching. Here *hēdonē* is a root of all evil impulses and can bring only *ponos*, trouble, pain. There are many parallels in Rab. writings. The feeling of pleasure so characteristic of the Gk. concept is hardly mentioned, but there are repeated warnings against the "evil impulse" (*yēṣer hā-rā'*) which makes a man reluctant to study the Torah (cf. SB IV 473 f.).

NT In the NT *hēdonē* is found only 5 times. All are in later books and all have a bad connotation.

1. The desire for pleasure fills the man estranged from God. He thinks that he is living out his own irresistible desire for pleasure, and in so doing he revolts against God and his will, but in fact he becomes the slave of the *hēdonai*. He has become a *doulos* → slave and lives in → sin. He is separated from God, unless God delivers him from this slavery (Tit. 3:3 ff.). 2 Pet. 2:13 ff. give a picture of these people who have given themselves over to their *hēdonai*, showing how they have become the victims of the destructive powers which are in revolt against God.

2. Men estranged from God are not the only ones threatened by the insatiable desires of the impulses (Tit. 3:3). The Christian also remains exposed to this power. Even prayer can be misused as a means to satisfy these passions. Jas. 4:3 shows how vain prayer is under these circumstances. Where unrestricted impulses have their way and *hēdonē* rules the life, man's relationship to God is inevitably threatened, inner → peace is destroyed, and good relationships with one's fellow-man are poisoned. If a man gives way to his desires, he is entangled in perpetual dissatisfaction and finds himself in a chaotic condition (Jas. 4:1). The NT lists of vices picture clearly and in detail the characteristics and results of *hēdonē*. They range from unrestrained sexuality through all the symptoms of lack of self-discipline to a self-centred indifference to one's fellow-man.

3. The dangers which unchecked impulses have for faith are seen most clearly in the interpretation of the parable of the sower. The word is used only in Lk. 8:14,

hēdonai tou biou "pleasures of life" (cf. the par. in Mk. 4:19 and Matt. 13:22). Where *hēdonē* reasserts its mastery, faith dies, choked among the thorns.

4. This process is seen most clearly in false teachers. They entangle themselves in false teaching, lead others astray into it, and become victims of a moral self-destruction. This is described in vivid detail in 2 Tim. 3:1–5 as one of the ways in which "the last days" can be recognized. Here Paul uses the Hel. forms *philēdonoi*, lovers of pleasure, and in contrast *philotheoi*, lovers of God (both NT *hapax legomena*, but used already by Philo).

5. Both in *epithymia* and *hēdonē* the sinister power of the instincts is expressed. It is insatiable and directed against God. It lives in man, threatens his ethical standards and enslaves him. The NT warns the Christian not to be driven by them – even if the *hēdonai* are expressly mentioned only in Tit. 3:3 – and not to neglect watchfulness. *hēdonē* as the drive to self-expression can be conquered only by the power of God.

We must beware of confounding *hēdonē* with the desire for true → joy (*chara*) which is never rejected by the NT. Joy is satisfied rather by communion with God, often even in the midst of suffering and persecution. If G. Stählin (*TDNT* II 926) is correct in seeing the contrast to 2 Pet. 2:13, "They count it pleasure (*hēdonēn*) to revel in the daytime", in Jas. 1:2, "Count it all joy (*charan*) . . . when you meet various trials", then it is clear how paradoxically the Christian's longing for joy finds its fulfilment and goal. *E. Beyreuther*

| ὀρέγομαι |

ὀρέγομαι (*oregomai*), strive; ὄρεξις (*orexis*), desire.

CL *oregomai*, the mid. voice of *oregō* – both forms are found from Homer onwards – is connected with the Lat. *regere* and the Eng. right, and means stretch oneself, stretch out. It is found especially with a metaphorical meaning. Like the noun *orexis* (Plato onwards) it denotes striving (a) of the heart and mind, (b) of bodily desire (relatively seldom). The Stoics gave it the special sense of a striving of the soul, following on a deliberate decision of the will guided by human reason. When the power and discipline of reason are removed the striving becomes desire (→ *epithymia*). The highest ideal of life is striving in conformity with one's own self (*kata physin*). Philo sees in *orexis* the soul's homesickness for the world of ideas.

OT The concept is first found in the post-canonical books of the Bible. It is used in a good sense in Wis. 16:2 f., where God satisfies the desire of Israel in the wilderness with quails. In a bad sense it is found in Sir. 18:30 and 23:6 where Ben Sira warns against perversions at banquets. The influence of Gk. philosophy can be recognized here.

NT *oregomai* is found 3 times in the NT and *orexis* once. In 1 Tim. 3:1 and Heb. 11:16 they are used in good sense; in 1 Tim. 6:10 and Rom. 1:27 in a bad one. In Heb. 11:16 *oregomai* continues the thought of *epizēteō* in v. 14. It speaks of the desire of faith for a better and heavenly homeland, i.e. a home with God. This desire does not come from immanent impulses in man or from his essential nature but from response to God's promise (Heb. 11:9, 13, 15). It manifests itself in utter reliance upon the promise and the obedience of faith (Heb. 11:8, 17). This means that it is no inner emotional feeling divorced from reality. It brings the will into line with a goal given by God which is expressed in the real things of this world. When the goal of desire and striving is not the salvation given by God, we fall victim to destructive powers, such as love of money (1 Tim. 6:10). The same letter praises the desire for office in the church (1 Tim. 3:1).

In Rom. 1:27 *orexis* is used for sexual desire. But Paul is not rejecting physical desire on the basis of Gk. dualism. He is attacking only perverted forms of that desire, e.g. homosexuality, which find their origin in the fact that men have exchanged the truth of God for a lie (Rom. 1:25).   *J. Guhrt*

→ Belly, → Command, → Flesh, → Law, → Sin, → Virtue

(a). F. Büchsel, *epithymia*, *TDNT* III 167–72; J. Gamberoni, "Desire," *EBT* I 206–9; H. W. Heidland, *oregomai*, *TDNT* V 447 f.; G. Stählin, *hēdonē*, *TDNT* II 909–26; P. Tillich, *Systematic Theology* II, 1957, 59 ff.
(b). B. Bartmann, "Die Konkupiszenz, Herkunft und Wesen," *ThG* 24, 1932, 405 f.; A. M. Dubarle, "Le péché originel dans la Genèse," *RB* 64, 1957, 5–34; and "Le péché originel dans les suggestions de l'Évangile," *Revue des Sciences philosophiques et theologiques* 40, 1956, 213–54; K. G. Kuhn, "*Peirasmos-hamartia-sarx* im Neuen Testament und die damit zusammenhängenden Vorstellungen," *ZTK* 49, 1952, 200–22; S. Lyonnet, " 'Tu ne convoiteras pas' (Rom. vii 7)", in *Neotestamentica et Patristica* (O. Cullmann Festschrift), 1962, 157–65; R. Storr, "Das Frömmigkeitsideal der Propheten," *Biblische Zeitfragen* 12, 1926; SB IV 466–83.

Despise

καταφρονέω

καταφρονέω (*kataphroneō*), περιφρονέω (*periphroneō*), despise; καταφρονητής (*kataphronētēs*), despiser.

CL In classical Gk. *kataphroneō* is a common word, used with a single or double gen. or, more rarely, with the acc. in the general sense of acting in a way that shows contempt or disregard for somebody or something, or for somebody on account of something. Whether it is used as a compliment or a censure depends on who or what it is that is being disparaged. *kataphronētēs*, late and rare, means "one who despises", usually in a bad sense. *periphroneō* is used with both genitive and accusative as a synonym of *kataphroneō*, though its primary meaning, both etymologically and in use, is simply to think hard about something.

OT In the LXX, *kataphroneō* usually renders *bûz* and *bāzáh*. Objects of contempt include God (Hos. 6:7), one's father (Gen. 27:12), one's mother (Prov. 23:22), the ways of the law (Prov. 19:16). Such contempt was, of course, profoundly impious. *periphroneō* appears only in 4 Macc., in a good sense, of despising distress (6:9), torments (7:16), and pains (14:1). *kataphronētēs* renders forms of *bāḡaḏ*, which signifies dealing treacherously and unfaithfully, in Hab. 1:5; 2:5; and Zeph. 3:4. In the second of these references the noun is used absolutely; in the first and third the object of contempt is God.

NT In the NT, *kataphroneō* occurs 9 times. In the proverbial saying of Matt. 6:24 = Lk. 16:13 it is morally neutral; its sense is good in Heb. 12:2, where Jesus is said to have despised the shame of the cross; but it is bad in the warnings against despising God's kindness (Rom. 2:4), God's church (1 Cor. 11:22), Christ's little ones

461

(Matt. 18:10), a youthful leader, or a leader for his youth (1 Tim. 4:12; the double genitive can be rendered either way), and Christian masters of slaves (1 Tim. 6:2). So, too, it is bad when Peter censures heretics for despising "dominion" (*kyriotēs*: possibly angelic powers, but more probably the lordship of Christ exercised through church officers) (2 Pet. 2:10, based on Jude 8, where the verb is *atheteō*, reject). *periphroneō* occurs only in Tit. 2:15, which is parallel in sense to 1 Tim. 4:12, cited above. *kataphronētēs* appears only in Paul's citation of Hab. 1:5 (LXX) at the end of his evangelistic sermon to Jews and proselytes in Antioch of Pisidia (Acts 13:41). In the NT, as in the LXX, the common use of this word-group is in contexts dealing with lack of due respect for the words, works, ministers and people of God.

| ὀλιγωρέω | ὀλιγωρέω (*oligōreō*), despise. |

CL Derived from *oligos*, "little", *oligōreō* in secular Gk. means "think little of, make light of, disregard". Like *kataphroneō* and *periphroneō*, it usually takes the gen. (of comparison).

OT & NT In the LXX, *oligōreō* is used only in Prov. 3:11, where a warning is issued against despising God's *paideia* (training, instruction, corrective discipline). This warning is quoted in Heb. 12:5, as an admonition from the heavenly Father to his persecuted children telling them to see their sufferings as a providential means of sanctifying them for the life with God that is in store for them.
→ Abolish, Nullify, Reject   *J. I. Packer*

C. Schneider, *kataphroneō*, *TDNT* III 631 ff.; R. Macpherson, "Despise", *DCG* I 453 f.

Destroy, Perish, Ruin

The terms considered here deal with destruction, annihilation, disaster, ruin and downfall. A distinction may be made between *apollymi* and the related nouns *apōleia* (destruction) and *olethros* (ruin, perdition) which are more strongly associated with physical destruction, and the vb. *phtheirō* which includes moral and religious destruction. Theologically related concepts include → Darkness, → Hell and → Judgment.

| ἀπώλεια | ἀπώλεια (*apōleia*), destruction; ἀπόλλυμι (*apollymi*), destroy; Ἀπολλύων (*Apollyōn*), Apollyon, Destroyer. |

CL 1. The vb. *apollymi* is a compound of *ollymi* (destroy, make an end of, lose).
It is related to the noun *apōleia*, and is found at an early stage in cl. usage both in a trans. form and in an intrans. middle form.
In Homer the trans. form is found with a dual meaning: (a) to lose (e.g. father, spouse, courage, life); and (b) to annihilate (e.g. a crowd of people in war), destroy, kill (*Il.* 5, 758). The mid. can be rendered according to context: (a) to disappear, get lost, be lost (*Od.*, 11, 586); or (b) to die, go to ruin through financial disaster or violence resulting in loss of life (cf. Hdt., 5, 126; Epictetus, *Dissertationes*, 2, 19, 16).

apōleia which is not found until the 4th century (Aristotle, *Eth. Nic.*, 1120a2) means destruction, downfall, annihilation. *apollyōn* is a personification of the Heb. *'ᵃbaddôn*, ruin. It means the destroyer, and contains a pun on the name of *Apollōn*, the god of plagues (Aesch., *Agamennon* 1081). (See below NT 4.)

2. The ideas conveyed by this group of words usually involve injury (of a violent nature), destruction or the final end of earthly existence. Accordingly, at one point in a dialogue of Plato concerning the immortality of the soul, the conclusion is reached that "evil is everything that corrupts (*apollyon*) and destroys (*diaphtheiron*), and good is that which preserves (*sōzon*) and strengthens (*ōpheloun*)" (*Rep.*, 608e). Among the destructive forces mentioned in the passage which follows are sickness for the body, rot for wood, and rust for iron.

OT 1. In the LXX *apollymi* represents 38 different Heb. words. Most frequently it stands for *'ābad*, to be lost, perish, or, to destroy. In non-religious contexts it is used variously of the destruction of a city, a group of people or a tribe (cf. Num. 16:33; 32:39; 33:52). As with the similar concept *apokteinō* (kill, → Death), *apollymi* (often used in the active) threatens the very existence of an individual or group, such as one's enemies. Of great importance are the requirements of the Holiness Code. These warn transgressors of the law, such as those who make child sacrifices to Moloch and those who consult fortune-tellers or the spirits of the dead, that they will be "cut off" from the people of the covenant. In other words, they will be stoned (Lev. 20:3, 5, 6). The exhortations which conclude the book of Deuteronomy confront the whole nation with the alternatives of receiving the blessing of a long life by means of obedience, or the curse of extinction by disobedience (Deut. 28:20; 22:24; 30:18 etc.). Thus *apōleia* involves not only exclusion from belonging to Yahweh, but also destruction and loss of life. The LXX brings out more strongly than Gk. literature the element of guilt in destruction. Although in most of the OT writings destruction is understood in the sense of earthly death and extinction, later texts occasionally link the words of this group with the concepts of *hadēs*, the underworld (→ Hell), and *thanatos*, → death (Prov. 15:11; 27:20; cf. Job 26:6; 28:22). They give to destruction a far-reaching significance, relating to the state after death.

2. In Jewish apocalyptic of the intertestamental and NT period, the idea appears of an eschatological destruction of the world, sometimes conceived in terms of a world conflagration. The ungodly will perish along with the world. Hence in the Qumran texts they are often called "men of perdition" (1QS) or "sons of perdition" (CD).

NT While the simple form *ollymi* is not found in the NT, verbal forms of *apollymi* or *apollyō* occur 90 times, and *apōleia* 18 times.

1. These words occur in the lit. senses already mentioned. Lk. 15:4, 8 tell of the loss of a sheep and a coin. Similarly the mid. is used of the state of being lost in the case of the sheep and the son (Lk. 15:4, 6, 24, 32). *apollymi* is found in the sense of kill, destroy, in Matt. 2:13; 27:20; Mk. 3:6 par.; 9:22; 11:18 par.; Lk. 6:9. In each case it is with reference to a person. On the other hand, the vb. has an impersonal object in the text quoted from Isa. 29:14 in 1 Cor. 1:19, "I will destroy the wisdom of the wise." Again the mid. is found in the sense to die or perish, both with

reference to things (Jn. 6:12, 27 fragments, food; 1 Pet. 1:7 gold; Heb. 1:11 heaven; 2 Pet. 3:6 the world). More frequently it refers to people (Mk. 4:38 par., the disciples' cry for help, "Do you not care if we perish?"; Matt. 26:52 "by the sword"; Lk. 11:51; 13:3, 5, 33; 15:17; 1 Cor. 10:9 f.; 2 Cor. 4:9). Finally, the noun *apōleia* has in most instances the intrans. meaning of ruin, destruction (Matt. 7:13; Rom. 9:22; Phil. 1:28; 2 Pet. 2:1; Rev. 17:8). But occasionally it appears in the trans. sense of waste, squandering (Mk. 14:4 par.).

2. The fig. theological use of these words in the NT follows in part the usage of the LXX. In the three parables of Lk. 15 the human condition of being lost is portrayed. People without God are like lost → sheep (cf. Ps. 119:176), doomed to perish unless rescued by the → shepherd. Jesus is pictured as this shepherd (cf. Jn. 10:11 ff.). He has come "to seek and to save the lost" (Lk. 19:10). He is commanded not to lose those whom the Father has given him (Jn. 6:39; 18:9). It is in relation to him that the question whether a man is lost or saved (→ Redemption) is decided. He who endeavours to secure his life by his own efforts will lose it. But he who loses it for Christ's sake and the gospel's by giving himself to him and following him (cf. Matt. 8:19–22; 16:24) will keep it (Mk. 8:35 par.; Matt. 10:39; Lk. 17:33; Jn. 12:25). For with him is life. In him God reveals his love "that whoever believes in him should not perish but have eternal life" (Jn. 3:16).

3. The specific theological sense of these words in the NT is brought out by Jn. and Paul. Just as *sōtēria* (salvation) and *zōē aiōnios* (eternal life) connote sure and lasting salvation, so *apollymi* and *apōleia* mean "definitive destruction, not merely in the sense of the extinction of physical existence, but rather of an eternal plunge into Hades and a hopeless destiny of death" (A. Oepke, *TDNT* I 396). Besides those who receive eternal life (Jn. 10:28) there will also be those who "perish" (1 Cor. 1:18; cf. 2 Cor. 2:15; 4:3). "As from now on there are only believers and unbelievers, so there are also now only saved and lost, those who have life and those who are in death" (R. Bultmann, *The Gospel of John*, 1971, 155). Over against life with God there stands the terrible possibility of eternal perdition. The NT use of → *olethros* and related words is characterized by the way in which destruction is set in the light of eternity. Perdition is the fate that awaits the man who does not come to repentance (2 Pet. 3:9; cf. Matt. 13:3, 5), who rejects love of the truth (2 Thess. 2:10), who goes on the broad way "that leads to destruction" (Matt. 7:13), or who is one of the enemies of the cross of Christ (Phil. 3:18 f.). Judas (Jn. 17:12) and the → Antichrist (2 Thess. 2:3) are specifically described as "sons of perdition" (see above, OT 2). Perdition can be brought on a person by another who corrupts his soul (Rom. 14:15; Jn. 10:10), or by one commissioned by God (Mk. 1:24; but cf. Lk. 9:56 *v.l.*; cf. also the curse formula in Acts 8:20), or by God himself as → judge (Jas. 4:12; Matt. 10:28; 22:7; Mk. 12:9 par.). God's role as judge appears also in the manifestation of his wrath. Commenting on Rom. 9:22 f., O. Michel writes: "*orgē* and *apōleia* belong together: the future destruction is revealed just as much in the wrath of God as the future glory is revealed in his mercy" (*Der Brief an die Römer*, KEK 4¹², 214).

4. This group of words includes also the substantive part. *Apollyōn* which occurs only once in the NT at Rev. 9:11. It is given as a translation of *'ᵃbaddôn* (cf. Job 26:2; 28:22; Ps. 88:12; Prov. 15:11; Eth. En. 20:2; → above CL 1). Here it refers to the angelic king of the underworld, the prince of the scorpions, describing him

464

as Destroyer, and so illuminating once again the contrast between God's salvation (*sōtēria*) and eschatological ruin (*apōleia*). *H. C. Hahn*

| ὄλεθρος |

ὄλεθρος (*olethros*), destruction, ruin, death; ὀλοθρεύω (*olothreuō*), destroy, ruin; ἐξολεθρεύω (*exolethreuō*), destroy utterly; ὀλοθρευτής (*olothreutēs*), destroyer.

CL *olethros* (Homer, e.g. *Il.*, 22, 325) is related to *ollymi* (destroy), and means destruction, ruin, death. It can also refer to that which brings destruction. *olothreuō* similarly means to destroy (e.g. Philo, *Leg. All.*, 2, 34). The intensive form *exolethreuō* means to destroy utterly, annihilate. *olothreutēs* (only found in Christian literature) means destroyer. In classical Gk. *olethros* often has the connotation of sudden destruction (*olethros aipys*). It especially refers to destruction of life (*olethros psychēs*). But in some cases it can mean the loss of things (e.g. *olethros chrēmatōn*, loss of money, Thuc. 7, 27). The other three words in the group are seldom found in classical Gk.

OT In the LXX, on the other hand, apart from *olothreutēs* these words are found more often. *olethros*, especially in the prophets, often carries the meaning of an eschatological destruction as a result of God's judgment (e.g. Jer. 5:6; 22:7; 25:36; Ezek. 6:14; 14:16; Hag. 2:22). The vb. *exolethreuō* is also used especially in Deut., Jos. and Pss. to describe punishment by God. It expresses his wrath (→ Anger) over the sin of man and the disobedience of his people Israel.

This language continued to be used later, particularly in Jewish apocalyptic and the Qumran texts which frequently refer to the eschatological destruction of sinners.

NT In the NT *olethros* occurs only 4 times, all in Paul. *olothreuō* and *olothreutēs* are found only in Heb. 11:28 and 1 Cor. 10:10, while *exolethreuō* comes only once in Acts 3:23.

In comparison with → *apōleia*, the *olethros* group is used to a much more limited extent. Whereas *apōleia* embraces various points in a wide spectrum of ideas concerned with destruction, including even the loss or extermination of objects, *olethros* – like the three words derived from it – is used in the few places where it occurs in the NT exclusively of persons.

1. *exolethreuomai* is found in Acts 3:23 in connection with a quotation of Deut. 18:15, 18 f. which is actually made more severe by the use of this word. While Deut. 18:19 only says that God will "require" of the sinner his disobedience to the words of the prophet, the actual punishment is now named. He will be "cut off from his people" (cf. Lev. 23:29). This is probably done in order to bring home to the hearers of this sermon the full seriousness of their own situation and the possibility of repentance. The same object may lie behind the use of *olothreutēs* in 1 Cor. 10:10. Here Paul warns his readers in a reference to the plague of serpents in the wilderness (Num. 21:4–9): "we must not . . . grumble, as some of them did and were destroyed by the Destroyer." *olothreutēs* here means something like the "destroying angel" (cf. 1 Chr. 21:12–15). This is likewise the meaning of *olothreuōn*, destroyer, who is mentioned in Heb. 11:28, again in the context of a kind of sermon from OT history (cf. Exod. 12:12 f., 23; Wis. 18:25).

465

2. In 1 Thess. 5:3 *olethros* refers to eschatological destruction suddenly breaking into a situation of apparent security and surprising men like labour pains coming upon a pregnant woman. Special candidates for final destruction are the rich whose end will be *olethros* and *apōleia* (1 Tim. 6:9). They, of course, are only one group among the ungodly, who will all suffer the same punishment of "exclusion from the presence of the Lord," i.e. "eternal destruction" (2 Thess. 1:9; cf. Ps. 37:17).

H. C. Hahn

3. The context of 1 Cor. 5:5 indicates that destruction may even fall within the province of the judgment of the church. The Corinthian church has apparently countenanced a case of gross immorality and Paul urges that it should be dealt with and the offender "removed from among you" (5:2). "For though absent in body I am present in spirit, and as if present, I have already pronounced judgment in the name of the Lord Jesus on the man who has done such a thing. When you are assembled, and my spirit is present, with the power of our Lord Jesus, you are to deliver this man to Satan for the destruction of the flesh, that his spirit may be saved in the day of the Lord Jesus" (1 Cor. 5:3–5).

The passage has been taken to refer to secret execution (J. Klausner, *From Jesus to Paul*, 1944, 553). Later ages have seen in it justification for the torture and burning of heretics. But the similar expression in 1 Tim. 1:20 can hardly mean that, when Paul "delivered to Satan Hymenaeus and Alexander that they may learn not to blaspheme," he had them privately done away with. In discussing baptism and its significance in Rom. 6:6, Paul writes: "We know that our old self was crucified with him so that the sinful body might be destroyed (*katargēthē*), and we might no longer be enslaved to sin." Although a different vb. is used here, the thought is a similar one. Clearly, physical destruction is not envisaged. The thought of 1 Cor. 5:5 suggests rather expulsion from the church into the realm dominated by "the god of this world" (2 Cor. 4:4). If Rom. 6:6 and 1 Cor. 5:5 are comparable, the inference might be as follows: what the man has failed to accomplish through the means of grace within the church, he must now accomplish without them, in the hope that he would be driven back to God in penitence. The offender would thus be excluded from the sphere of grace and its promises, as mediated by the Word and sacraments. This expulsion would take place at a formal meeting of the church which met in the name of the Lord Jesus and with his power (→ Might) (5:4). Paul's recommendations suggest the proceedings laid down in Matt. 18:15–20, where the → church is given power to → bind and loose in heaven and on earth and where the presence of Jesus Christ is made to those who gather in his name. An instance of such an assembly may be the case of Ananias and Sapphira who actually died on being told that they had lied to God and had tempted the Spirit of the Lord (Acts 5:1–11; cf. also 13:11).

The idea of being delivered to an evil power or to death is paralleled outside the Christian community. C. K. Barrett cites the papyrus formula: "Daemon of the dead . . ., I deliver to thee so-and-so, in order that . . ." (*A Commentary on the First Epistle to the Corinthians*, 1968, 126; cf. A. Deissmann, *Light from the Ancient East*, 1910, 304; *London Magical Papyrus* 46. 334 ff.; = K. Preisendanz, *Papyri Graecae Magicae*, I, 192). He also cites Sanhedrin 6:2 where the criminal about to be executed is instructed to say: May my death be an atonement for all my sins.

466

But as Barrett points out, atonement for Paul is not through our death but through Christ's.

Elsewhere in both the OT and the NT, → Satan is seen as one who in the providence of God is permitted to afflict the flesh for the ultimate benefit of man. He is allowed to afflict Job to show that despite every trial, Job retains his faith and integrity (Job 2:3–10). Paul's own "thorn in the flesh" and "messenger from Satan" (2 Cor. 12:7) brings him to the realization that God's strength is made perfect in man's weakness (v. 9). Here, however, the word destruction (*olethros*) and the circumstances of the offence suggest that the case was so serious that the judgment of exclusion from the church and thus from the realm of grace might lead to the person succumbing to physical death, as in the case of Ananias and Sapphira (cf. also those mentioned later who had profaned the Lord's Supper, 1 Cor. 11:30). For Christ alone is the victor over the powers of evil and death (1 Cor. 15:24–27; cf. Phil. 1:10 f.; Col. 2:15). And to be cut off from the → body of Christ (1 Cor. 12:12 ff.) is to be exposed to the reign of evil and death. In the same way, the idolaters and immoral persons in Israel who turned back from Christ were "destroyed by the Destroyer" (1 Cor. 10:10; cf. 10:1–13; see above NT 1). The destruction of God's temple invites destruction by God (1 Cor. 3:17).

At the same time, there is the expressed intention "that his spirit may be saved in the day of the Lord Jesus" (5:5; cf. 1:8; 3:13; 15:22 ff.). Like the hardening of Israel in Rom. 9–11, the destruction here envisaged is not the final and complete outworking of the wrath of God (→ Anger), such as is mentioned in 2 Thess. 1:9 and 1 Tim. 6:9. The → spirit here refers to the man's essential self. The body may waste away, but the self will be clothed in life (2 Cor. 4:16; 5:4) Behind the remark may lie the conviction that, whilst a man's work may be destroyed in the day of judgment, he himself will be saved "but only as through fire" (1 Cor. 3:15). Paul's hope of the man's ultimate salvation may be related to the hope that the judgment will bring about in him the "godly grief" that "produces repentance that leads to salvation and brings no regret" and not the "worldly grief" that "produces death" (2 Cor. 7:10). Paul's remarks in 2 Cor. 2:5–11 about the restoration to fellowship and forgiveness of one who has erred lest "he may be overwhelmed by excessive sorrow" (v.7) and to "keep Satan from gaining the advantage over us" (v. 11) may be an indication that this was in fact what had happened. However, from Tertullian onwards (*De pudicitia* 13–15) there have been those who have held that the two cases were quite distinct on the grounds of Paul's apparent leniency in 2 Cor.

See further C. K. Barrett, op. cit., 124–27; P. E. Hughes, *Second Corinthians*, 1962, 59 ff.; F. F. Bruce, *1 and 2 Corinthians*, 1971, 54 f., 184.; H. Conzelmann, *Der erste Brief an die Korinther*, KEK 5, 1969[11], 117 f.; C. K. Barrett, "*ho adikēsas* (2. Cor. 7, 12)," in O. Böcher and K. Haacker, eds., *Verborum Veritas: Festschrift für Gustav Stählin*, 1970, 149–57.

C. Brown

| φθείρω | φθείρω (*phtheirō*), destroy, ruin, corrupt, spoil; ἀφθαρσία |

(*aphtharsia*), incorruptibility, immortality; ἄφθαρτος (*aphthartos*), imperishable, incorruptible, immortal; διαφθείρω (*diaphtheirō*), spoil, destroy, ruin; διαφθορά (*diaphthora*), destruction, corruption; φθορά (*phthora*), ruin, destruction, perdition, corruption.

CL In classical Gk. from the time of Homer onwards, and also in Philo and the
Test. XII, *phtheirō* means to ruin, corrupt, destroy, kill. The term has various
shades of meaning: to corrupt morally (Aristotle, *Eth. Nic.*, 1103b), to bring down
the state of laws (Plato, *Laws* 958c), to bribe (Dem., *Orationes* 18, 247), to seduce a
woman (Dem., *Orationes*, 45, 79), to defile a virgin (Lucian, *Cataplus sive Tyrannus*
26). In the pass. it means to go to ruin, perish, be corrupted, destroyed; and in the
mid. to destroy oneself (Thuc., 3, 113, 5).

Derived from the word are *phthora*, destruction, corruption (Plato, *Timaeus*, 23c),
and *diaphthora*, destruction (Polybius, 1, 48, 3, 8), murder (Euripides, *Ion*, 617),
which is later used in the sense of corruption, disorder. Later words are *aphtharsia*,
indestructibility, immortality (not before Epicurus, according to Diog. Laert., 10,
123), and *aphthartos*, incorruptible (Aristotle, *De longitudine et brevitate vitae*, 4,
466a 1; cf. also Wis. 12:1; Philo, *Sacr.*, 95).

diaphtheirō can mean, in combination with other terms, to frustrate attempts to
help (Thuc., 3, 113, 5), to change one's mind (Aesch., *Agamemnon*, 932).

OT In the LXX the words of this group are used chiefly to render the Heb. roots
šāḥat (91 times, 51 of these *diaphtheirō*), and much less often *ḥābal*. They can
mean to kill people (2 Sam. 24:16), to lay waste a stretch of country (1 Chr. 20:1), a
city (1 Sam. 23:10), or to destroy weapons (Isa. 54:16). In Gen. 6:11 and Hos 9:9
phtheirō is used to describe a sinful and fallen world. God is the one who can redeem life from destruction (*phthora*, Ps. 103:4). In the cultic sphere a sacrificial
animal which is not free of blemish is described as marred (*phthartos*, Lev. 22:25).

The contrast between *phthartos*, perishable, and *aphthartos*, imperishable, acquired a special significance in the writings of Philo. Man will pass away utterly,
for he is mortal (*Aet. Mund.*, 143), whereas God is immortal (*Leg. All.*, 3, 36). The
man who is good and wise can gain a share in the immortality of the divine world,
if he lives according to the "right *logos*" (→ Word), which is identified with the
→ Law (*Ebr.*, 142).

NT It is interesting that in the NT this group of words occurs nowhere in the gospels
except for Lk. 12:33 (of moths destroying (*diaphtheirō*) clothes). Of the 8
occurrences of *phtheirō*, 5 are in Paul (1 Cor. 3:17; 15:33; 2 Cor. 7:2; 11:3; Eph.
4:22). The others are in 2 Pet. 2:12; Jude 10 and Rev. 19:2. A similar pattern emerges
in the other words of this group. *diaphthora* occurs only in Acts 2:27, 31; 13:34 f.
From this it may be concluded that the words are used mostly within a Hel. environment. As in classical Gk., various shades of meaning are found in the NT. In Rev.
11:18 *diaphtheirō* expresses the extermination of men as a result of divine judgment.

1. (a) In dealing with the shortcomings at Corinth, Paul writes in the emphatic
style of a cultic law: "If anyone destroys (*phtheirei*) God's temple, God will destroy
(*phtherei*) him" (1 Cor. 3:17). The divine penalty is announced in the form of a legal
judgment, though the possibility of avoiding it is left open. In this way God himself protects his church. Paul, for his part, can claim that "we have wronged no
one, we have corrupted (*ephtheiramen*) no one, we have taken advantage of no one"
(2 Cor. 7:2). He is therefore in a position to require the church to make room in
Corinth for himself and his message. He exhorts this church not to be led astray.
He fears that just as Eve was once "deceived" by the serpent, so the church will be
led into rebellion by his opponents and the confusion they sow. Thus "your

thoughts will be led astray (*phtharē*) from a sincere and pure devotion to Christ" (2 Cor. 11:3). And to demonstrate that false teaching and apostasy are not without their effect on human relationships, Paul refers in 1 Cor. 15:33 to a saying which had become proverbial, originating in the lost comedy *Thais* by the Attic poet Menander (342–291 B.C.): "Bad company ruins (*phtheirousin*) good morals." In this context Paul uses the saying to warn the Corinthians not to make common cause with those who deny the resurrection of the dead.

(b) According to 2 Pet. 2:12, heretics are "like irrational animals", born of nature to be caught and killed (*eis halōsin kai phthoran*). They will "be destroyed in the same destruction with them", they will perish like the beasts (cf. also Jude 10). Those who serve Christ, on the other hand, are "to put off the old nature which belongs to your former manner of life and is corrupt (or "being destroyed" [*phtheiromenon*]) through deceitful lusts" (Eph. 4:22). They are no longer enslaved to the "corruption (*phthora*) that is in the world because of passion"; they live a new life in the power of Christ (2 Pet. 1:4). The church is warned therefore not to sow "to the flesh". For as a man sows, so shall he reap (Gal. 6:7 f.).

(c) In the Rev. the harlot Babylon is the epitome of apostasy against God. In the visionary triumph song it is said that she has corrupted (*ephtheiren*) the earth with her "fornication". But now she is judged. In other words, God's victory over the sin of the world has been made manifest (Rev. 19:2).

2. (a) Immortality (*aphtharsia*) is one of the terms used, as in honorific titles for royalty in late Gk. usage, to describe the character of God. In the doxology of 1 Tim. 1:17 the church praises him as "the King of ages, immortal, invisible, the only God" (cf. Philo, *Vit. Mos.*, 3, 171; and Epicurus according to Diog. Laert., 10, 123). The sin of the heathen is that they "exchange the glory of the immortal God for images resembling mortal man" (Rom. 1:23).

(b) Immortality is not however attributed only to God himself; it is also attributed to Christ as the *Kyrios* (→ Lord). In the closing words of Eph. (6:24) peace is pronounced on all those who "love Jesus Christ *en aphtharsia*." RSV paraphrases this as "with love undying". But M. Dibelius takes it to mean "love Jesus in his immortality" (HNT 12, ad loc.). As the exalted One, he shares fully in the immortality of the Father. It is this Christ whom the church confesses, declaring that he has "abolished death and brought life and immortality to light through the gospel" (2 Tim. 1:10). In spite of the delay of the Parousia the church lives in the knowledge that her salvation is something present and already given. She knows that because of the manifestation of Christ she has been taken up into his immortality. Believers are already in possession of the inheritance which is "imperishable, undefiled and unfading" (1 Pet. 1:4). They are called by the apostolic command to love one another, seeing that they have been born again. They are no longer of natural and therefore perishable origin. They have been born of imperishable seed by the living and abiding word of God (1 Pet. 1:23). This should be apparent even in outward things. Gentleness and quietness, not outward adorning of every kind, are the proper, God-given and hence "imperishable jewels" of the Christian (1 Pet. 3:3 f.).

(c) In 1 Cor. 9:24–27 Paul compares the life of the Christian with an athletic contest (cf. Rom. 9:16; Gal. 2:2; 5:7). In both there is a victory to be striven for;

both demand utter dedication and self-denial. But the aim is a high one. The victor is beckoned by the prize (→ Fight, art. *brabeion*), which for the athlete is a perishable one. The glory and honour brought by sport are as passing as the laurel of which the perishable → crown (*phthartos stephanos*) was made. But for the Christian there awaits an imperishable prize, to be with God for eternity (cf. Rom. 2:7).

3. (a) The contrast between mortality (*phthora*) and immortality (*aphtharsia*) is used by Paul in describing the resurrection of the dead (1 Cor. 15:42 ff.). Using the illustration of the seed sown in the ground, he makes it clear that there is no coming to life without a previous dying. It is only when the seed disintegrates in the earth that it becomes changed into a new form (1 Cor. 15:35–42a). It is the same with the resurrection of the dead – and yet it is quite different. All comparisons which can be used are inadequate. "What is sown is perishable, what is raised is imperishable" (1 Cor. 15:42b). A body tied to the "flesh" is sown, but a spiritual → body (*sōma pneumatikon*) is raised (v. 44). Resurrection is a new creation of life by means of total transformation. Paul thus guards against the idea that there is anything intrinsically imperishable about man. Everything passes away, because the whole man is subject to → sin and hence to → death (Rom. 6:23). The "outward nature is wasting away (*diaphtheiretai*)" (2 Cor. 4:16). Resurrection is a new existence, gained by being raised to immortality. Accordingly it is not simply the resuscitation of bodies lying in the grave. "Flesh and blood cannot inherit the kingdom of God", any more than "the perishable [can] inherit the imperishable" (1 Cor. 15:50).

(b) Paul again emphasizes the same truth when he comes to speak of those who will not yet have died at the time of the Parousia. They do not simply continue their life in immortality; they will be changed (v. 52). It is just as true for them as for the dead, that mortality cannot attain immortality. "Once more must the miracle of God step in between corruption and incorruption, so that the latter may inherit the former" (K. Barth, *The Resurrection of the Dead*, 1933, 217). When the end comes, the great transformation will come for all. The illustration is used of putting on new clothes (→ Clothe, art. *dyō*). This idea may be understood in the context of the initiation rites of the Hel. mystery cults. The inward transformation of the initiate would be symbolized by the laying aside of his old garments. New clothes would be put on. The perishable is laid aside; the imperishable, the divine is put on. The initiate was changed into the divine nature, made like the deity (cf. E. Dinkler, "Die Taufterminologie", 183 ff., see bibliography). Similarly here, the perishable puts on the imperishable; out of what is mortal comes what is immortal (v. 54). Thus "death is swallowed up in victory", which is given "through our Lord Jesus Christ" (vv. 54, 57). Cf. also 2 Cor. 5:1–5.

(c) Jesus is the first to have been resurrected by God, and thus is vindicated as → Messiah. "He did not see corruption (*diaphthora*)" (Acts 2:27, 31; 13:35 ff.), a quotation from the LXX of Ps. 16:10 which gives an interpretative translation of Heb. *šaḥat* (pit, grave). The latter word has the same root as the vb. *šāḥat* (destroy). The grave or pit is the place where the body is destroyed.

The defeat of → death through the victory of Christ affects the whole cosmos. Through the → sin of man it has been subjected to mortality, but the → redemption of mankind means also the redemption of the → creation. It will be set "free from its bondage to decay and obtain the glorious liberty of the children of God" (Rom. 8:21).   *F. Merkel*

| ἐξαλείφω | ἐξαλείφω (exaleiphō), wipe away, blot out. |

CL In classical Gk. *exaleiphō*, a derivative of *aleiphō* which means to anoint and rub with oil, and so to polish by rubbing smooth, signifies literally to plaster, whitewash or wash something over, and metaphorically to wipe out, obliterate, cancel or destroy.

OT In the LXX *exaleiphō* carries both these meanings. In the literal sense of "plaster" it appears in Lev. 14:42, 43, 48; in its metaphorical sense, in which it usually renders forms of *māḥâh*, it denotes God's judicial work of wiping out life (Gen. 7:23) and the names and memory of offenders (Exod. 17:14; Deut. 9:14), and of erasing names from the book of life (Exod. 32:32 f.); also it denotes his gracious work of obliterating sins (Ps. 50[51]:9, 108:14; Isa. 43:25).

NT In the NT, *exaleiphō* appears 5 times as a metaphor for obliterating sins (Acts 3:19), erasing names from the book of life (Rev. 3:5), wiping away tears (Rev. 2:14; 7:17), and cancelling a bond of debt, an IOU (Col. 2:14). The image expressed by the verb here and perhaps elsewhere is most probably smoothing the surface of a wax writing-tablet for re-use (cf. "wiping the slate clean"). The bond in Col. 2:14 is our obligation as God's creatures to keep his law on pain of death – a bond which becomes an actual death-warrant as soon as we sin.   *J. I. Packer*
→ Death, → Judgment

(a). G. Harder, *phtheirō, TDNT* IX 93 ff.; A. Oepke, *apollymi, apōleia, Apollyōn, TDNT* I 394–97; J. Schneider, *olethreuō* etc., *TDNT* V 167–71.
(b). E. Dinkler, "Die Taufterminologie in 2 Kor. i 21 f.," in *Neotestamentica et Patristica*, Festchrift for O. Cullmann, 1962, 173–191 especially 183 ff. (=*Signum Crucis*, 1967, 99 ff. especially 109 ff.); H. Köster, "Verdammnis," *RGG³* VI 1260.

Determine, Appoint, Present

Several words are used in the NT to express appointment. The following are dealt with in this article: *kathistēmi, horizō, paristēmi, procheirizō, tassō, tithēmi, prothesmia, cheirotoneō* and *lanchanō*. In addition, *keimai* (lit. lie, recline; fig. be appointed, set, destined) is used in Lk. 2:34 ("this child *is set* for the fall and rising of many in Israel"), Phil. 1:16 ("I *am put* here for the defence of their gospel"), and 1 Thess. 3:3 ("this *is to be* our lot", RSV).

See also the art. on Foreknowledge, Providence, Predestination for the vbs *proginōskō* (know beforehand), *pronoeō* (think of beforehand), *prooraō* (foresee), *proorizō* (predestine), *protithēmi* (plan, intend) and their cognates.

| καθίστημι | καθίστημι (kathistēmi), bring, appoint, put in charge, make. |

CL *kathistēmi* is a compound of *histēmi*, stand, place, set. It has three main meanings which are basic for our understanding of its NT use: (a) lead or bring in; (b) appoint, especially to an office or position; (c) bring it to pass that, and in perf. (intrans.) have become something, appear as. This expresses both the objective fact

471

and also the subjective representation of, or judgment on, a matter (A. Oepke, *TDNT* III 444 f.).

OT The commonest meaning in the LXX is to place somewhere, and appoint to an office (cf. Deut. 17:15; 1 Sam. 8:1; Ps. 105:21).

NT Meaning (a) is found only in Acts 17:15 "those who conducted Paul"; (b) is found in Acts 6:3 of deacons, Tit. 1:5 of elders, Heb. 5:1; 8:3 of the high priest, Matt. 24:45 par. of the controller of a household.

The usage (c) is theologically important, and occurs in Rom. 5:19; Jas. 4:4; and 2 Pet. 1:8. Rom. 5:12–21 is a passage of major theological importance. In it → Adam and → Christ are contrasted. Adam's act of disobedience has binding results for all; they stand there (*katestathēsan*) as sinners. Through Christ's obedience they are to be reckoned (*katastathēsontai*) as righteous. In v. 19 this contrasted pair of facts is thus in each case described by *kathistēmi*. Paul uses this verb to describe God's judgment on man; he draws on the language and ideas of the OT and late Jud. This anthropomorphic way of expressing it presents two contrasting aspects: existence as a sinner and → justification. The decisive event is seen to be Christ's obedience even to death (cf. Phil. 2:5–11). Through it the real possibility is granted to all of standing as righteous before God. Adam here is a representative of "man" used to illustrate the fact of man's being a "sinner" because of his disobedience. ([Tr.] cf. the discussion of Rab. teaching on Adam in W. D. Davies, *Paul and Rabbinic Judaism*, 1955[2], 36–57.) The reality of man under the judgment of God, as seen by faith, is revealed to him above all in the salvation from his lost state which is offered to him. *S. Wibbing*

ὁρίζω

ὁρίζω (*horizō*), determine, appoint; ἀφορίζω (*aphorizō*), separate, set apart, appoint.

CL *horizō* is connected with *horos*, boundary, and *horion*, region. Originally it meant to set bounds, bound, and hence to establish, determine. In the 5th cent. B.C. it is found frequently in Aesch. and Hdt. In Soph. the gods establish laws, and in Eur. they determine human fate. Plato and Dem. transfer the spatial force of *horizō* to temporal relationships. This occurs also later in Josephus. The compound *aphorizō* (Soph. and Plato onwards), has first the meaning, separate, and then choose, determine.

OT *horizō* is found 17 times in the LXX. In its original meaning of setting a boundary it occurs in Num. 34:6; Jos. 13:27; 15:12; 18:20. In Num. 30:3–12 it is used a number of times for '*āsar*, bind oneself by a vow. In Prov. 18:18 it represents *pārad* (hiph.), separate, decide between. In Prov. 16:30 it is used freely as a par. to *logizomai*, think, plan. *aphorizō* is found *c.* 50 times in the LXX. It has no predominant Heb. equivalent, but all the Heb. concepts represented by it have the connotation of separating, cutting off (cf. Gen. 10:5, "the peoples . . . separated" NEB; Deut. 4:41; Lev. 13:4).

NT *horizō* is found 8 times in the NT (6 in Lk.) meaning determine, establish, appoint. *aphorizō* is found 10 times meaning separate, choose for, determine.

1. Jesus' messianic claim and his death on the cross were irreconcilable, self-contradictory opposites for the Jews. Peter wished to counter this offence by showing that it was God's "deliberate (*hōrismenē*) will and plan" (Acts 2:23 NEB) by which Jesus was crucified by blinded Jewry. Similarly in Lk. 22:22 the Son goes the way "determined" by God for him, "but woe to that man by whom he is betrayed". It is this Jesus who is the one "ordained" by God to be the judge of the last judgment (Acts 10:42).

Paul made a similar statement to the Areopagus. After God had "determined" allotted periods and boundaries for the men that he had created so that they should seek him, he "appointed" a man to judge the world on the day appointed for it (Acts 17:26, 31).

It has been suggested that an adoptionist credal form might lie behind the *horizō* of Acts 10:42 and 17:31. But in context the passages must doubtless be understood in sense of a predestination from all eternity.

Heb. 4:7 declares that after the day of testing in the wilderness (3:8) God appointed another day, a new period of salvation, beginning with Christ, which offers the opportunity to turn.

In Rom. 1:3 f. Paul is apparently quoting a primitive Christian creed to show that he is linked with the tradition of the fathers. In this creed the human mode of Jesus' existence ("descended from David according to the flesh") is contrasted with his divine mode of existence ("designated Son of God in power according to the Spirit of holiness"). The word "designated" suggests an advance: Jesus is the Davidic Messiah, but also much more; he is God's Son in power. It also suggests temporal sequence: he was born as a man but designated Son of God by the resurrection. Many German scholars see in this sequence a primitive, adoptionist christology, because "in the earliest Church Jesus' messiahship was dated from the resurrection" (R. Bultmann, *Theology of the NT*, I 1952, 27). We must remember, however, that Paul does not indicate anywhere else that he thought that Jesus was installed as Son first at his resurrection (cf. Rom. 8:3). He holds that Jesus was God's Son from all eternity. That is why K. L. Schmidt maintains that *horizō* does not have the force here of institute or appoint but that of determine beforehand (*TDNT* V 453). O. Michel is no doubt correct when he writes in his commentary on Romans, "Paul is here concerned with a double truth, with understanding Jesus in his human and in his divine aspect" (*KEK* 4[12] 1963, 40).

In one place alone (Acts 11:29) the vb. is not used of God, but of men, as normally in secular Gk. The disciples "determined" to send relief to the brethren in need.

2. The word *aphorizō* is always concerned with separating. The good are separated from the evil (Matt. 13:49; 25:32). The unbelievers exclude the believers (Lk. 6:22), and conversely the church withdraws from unbelief (Acts 19:9; 2 Cor. 6:17). In Gal. 2:12 Paul accuses Peter of separating himself from the common Lord's Supper with the Gentile Christians after Jewish Christians had come from Jerusalem to Antioch. The importance of Peter's step for Paul was that by separating himself he recognized the validity of the old Jewish dietary laws, which were thereby given greater importance than the one body of Christ composed of Jews and Gentiles.

There are passages, however, where the meaning separate can hardly be distinguished from determine, appoint. Thus Paul knows himself to be set apart and

473

chosen for the service of the gospel (Rom. 1:1; Gal. 1:15). He did not appoint himself as an apostle, but God set him apart for the office (Acts 13:2). *G. Dulon*

παρίστημι

παρίστημι (*paristēmi*), place, put at the disposal of, present.

CL *paristēmi* (from the 2nd cent. B.C. also *paristanō*) is a compound of *histēmi* (stand), the root being connected with the Lat. *sistere* (place, stand). Its basic meaning is (trans.) place beside, (intrans.) stand beside, and (mid.) place before oneself. In secular Gk. this was widely developed in various directions but without any fixed connotation. The following are worth mentioning: (a) (trans.) put down, place at someone's disposal, to bring (especially as a technical term in Hel. sacrificial language), bring before (the emperor or the court); (b) (intrans.) approach (the emperor or an enemy), help someone (already in Homer), wait on (of a female servant, Homer, *Od.*, 1, 335), be present (also used of the time of death and of harvest).

OT The word is used in the LXX *c.* 100 times. One third of these represent Heb. *'āmaḏ* and *yāṣaḇ*. The godly watch for God's coming (Ps. 5:3(4)). Foreigners enter his service (Isa. 60:10). When *paristēmi* is used with a prep., in contrast to secular usage, it means stand as a servant before his master which always implies special honour (cf. 1 Sam. 16:21; 2 Ki. 5:25). It is so used of angels (Job 1:6) and martyrs (4 Macc. 17:18) before God. Standing before God expresses the purpose of the choice of the prophet (1 Ki. 17:1) and priest (Deut. 10:8; 18:5, 8 where it is par. to *leitourgeō* → Serve). The word also expresses God's standing by someone to reveal himself (Exod. 34:5), to help (Ps. 109:31), or to charge him with his sins (Ps. 50:21).

NT 1. In the NT only *paristanō* is found in the present. It is used intrans. of standing before Caesar (Acts 27:24), God's judgment (Rom. 14:10), God's support in standing by someone (2 Tim. 4:17), that of the local church (Rom. 16:2), and of the coming of an angel (Acts 27:23). Gabriel stands before God (Lk. 1:19), because according to contemporary Jewish concepts there was no sitting in heaven. Only God sits, as a sign of his uniqueness and grandeur. All that has been created must stand before him.

2. The trans. use is of more importance and is found virtually only in Acts and the Pauline writings. It is used in Lk. 2:22 of Jesus' presentation to the Lord where it carries with it the idea of consecration (cf. Exod. 13:2). (*paristēmi* is used of Jeroboam's "placing" of priests in Bethel in 1 Ki. 12:32 (LXX).)

Those passages where *paristēmi* is used almost in the sense of make, set up, place, are of special theological importance. Col. 1:22 implies that a holy community has been made by the death of Jesus Christ from a humanity until then estranged from God. Since Christ is perfect, the church can also be presented perfect to God (Col. 1:28, RSV, NEB "mature"). Just as Jesus presented himself after Easter to his apostles in various appearances as alive (Acts 1:3), so God will present the believers raised to a new life with Jesus in his presence (2 Cor. 4:14; → Election and above OT). By his self-sacrifice Christ has presented the church in splendour of a bride

(Eph. 5:27; cf. Col. 1:22). Corresponding to this act of God, we should do our best to present ourselves as approved (2 Tim. 2:15, "worthy of God's approval" NEB). Where such a church has come into being through the preaching and pastoral work of the messenger, Paul can picture himself as the match-maker who brings the bride to the bridegroom (2 Cor. 11:2, *parastēsai*).

Neither the supposed freedom of those who consider themselves strong, nor the scrupulous self-denial of those weak in faith will "bring us into God's presence" (1 Cor. 8:8 NEB). Rather the members that were once yielded to impurity are now to be yielded (*parastēsate*) to the service of righteousness. Sin has no longer a right to claim lordship (Rom. 6:13–19), and those who are justified by faith present their "very selves" (NEB) to God as a sacrifice (Rom. 12:1). Hel. sacrificial terminology made Paul's readers familiar with his linguistic usage. *paristēmi* is a sort of codeword for changing the form of one's existence by changing one's lord. The justified recognize that Jesus is *Kyrios*, Lord, and practise submission. Moreover, they live in sanctification in view of his presence and the coming perfection. "He who is dead in sins will hardly say that he places himself at the disposal of sin; but when he is alive, he can place himself at God's disposal" (J. A. Bengel on Rom. 6:13).

K. Munzer

| $\pi\rho o\chi\epsilon\iota\rho\acute{\iota}\zeta\omega$ | $\pi\rho o\chi\epsilon\iota\rho\acute{\iota}\zeta\omega$ (*procheirizō*), determine, appoint. |

CL *procheirizō* is derived from the adj. *procheiros* (from *pro* in front of, and *cheir*, hand), which means (when used of things) handy, ready, ready for use, and (of persons) decided on an action or ready. *procheirizō* consequently means prepare something or someone for a purpose, or keep ready. It is seldom used in the act., and is found especially in the participial forms in the pass. It is used of the benefits which would accrue to the Athenians if peace were made, and which were spoken of in terms which suggested that they had already been prepared and were ready (*prokecheirismena kai hetoima*, Dem. 7, 33).

The mid. is most used with the meanings: (a) prepare for oneself, keep something at one's disposition (e.g. resources in Aristoph., *Ecclesiazusae* 729; troops, Dem., 4, 19). (b) When used in political and military settings, where it is often found, it means determine, nominate, elect. With the acc. of the person it is used for the election of leaders of the people (Isoc., 8, 122) or the appointment of a prosecutor by the general assembly (Dem., 25, 13). With two acc. it is used of the election of a *stratēgos*, general (Diod. Sic., 12, 27, 1) or of a dictator (Dio Cass. 54, 1, 3). It is also used of the allotment of land (P. Cair. Zen. 132, 3) or of legions to a general (Polyb., 3, 40, 14), or of the resolutions of a legislative or executive body; these resolutions are recorded in the infin. (Polyb., 3, 40, 2) or with an acc. and infin (*SIG*[3] 457:15–20, Thespiae). The term is one that belonged at first to the life of classical Athens, but then became common in Hel. writers and the legal language of the inscriptions and papyri.

OT The Gk.-speaking Jewish Diaspora knew both words, but in the LXX *procheiros* is found only in Prov. 11:3, whereas the vb. occurs 6 times. In Jos. 3:12 it represents *lāqaḥ*, but the par. Jos. 4:2 has *lambanō*. In Exod. 4:13 it is linked with *šālaḥ*, send. It is introduced in Dan. 3:22 without any Heb. equivalent. It means the choice and commissioning of someone by God (Exod. 4:13) or men (Jos. 3:12; Dan. 3:22) to carry out a particular task, especially one of a political or military nature (2 Macc. 3:7; 8:9; 14:12). Prov. 8:23 is difficult. Wisdom says *mēʿōlām nissaktî*, I was poured out from eternity (Eng. versions "I was set up"). The Gk. translators varied in their renderings. Symm. (and perhaps also Theod.) has *ap'aiōnos pro-kecheirismai*. He may have thought of wisdom standing at God's disposal from the first, or having been appointed by God for a particular task.

NT The adj. is not found in the NT, but the vb. is found 3 times in Acts, where it must presumably be understood from common Gk. usage. In Acts 26:16 it is used with two acc. in the words of Christ to Paul who is appointed as a minister and witness to what he had seen and would see (cf. Acts 16:9 f.; 22:17-21; 23:11). This appointment which made him the apostle to the Gentiles is made by the risen Christ's words to him. Ananias' words (Acts 22:14) are to be similarly understood. The God of Israel has elected or appointed Paul to know his will, to see that Just One, and to hear a voice from his mouth. Paul's work of witness rested on this seeing and hearing which demanded his response. The determining is presented as something that has come to pass without any mention of → time. The grammatical construction which this interpretation presupposes, viz. linking *procheirizō* with the acc. of the person and the inf. of purpose, is apparently unparalleled at present. So it may be better to take it as an acc. and infin. as in an inscription from Thespiae, dating from the 3rd cent. B.C. (see above CL). In that case it would not mean that God appointed Paul, but that he determined that Paul should know the divine will.

Acts 3:20 urges repentance "that he may send the Christ appointed for you, Jesus" (*ton prokecheirismenon hymin Christon, Iēsoun*). *P. Schmidt*

τάσσω

τάσσω (*tassō*), arrange, appoint; προστάσσω (*prostassō*), command, appoint.

CL & OT *tassō* is common in classical Gk. Its first meaning is military: to draw up troops (or ships) in battle array, and so to post or station them. From this the verb comes to mean to direct or appoint someone to a task, and to arrange, set up and put in order things or plans which would otherwise be indefinite and uncertain. *prostassō* means first to attach someone somewhere, and then simply to command, in which sense it occurs frequently. Both verbs imply an acknowledged authority and power residing in the person from whom the decisions or directives issue. In the LXX both verbs are used for a wide range of Heb. equivalents, with both God and men as the arranging or directing agents.

NT In the NT both verbs appear in their ordinary meanings. Lk. makes more use of them than any other writer. In addition to being used of such things as Claudius' edict banishing Jews from Rome (Acts 18:2), *tassō* denotes God's appointment of "the powers that be" (Rom. 13:1), of a career of service for Paul (Acts 22:10), and of individual persons to attain eternal life through believing the gospel (Acts 13:48). *prostassō*, with its emphatic and rather official sense of "command", is used with the angel of the Lord (Matt. 1:24), Moses (Mk. 1:44), Peter (Acts 10:48),

476

Jesus (Matt. 21:6) and God as its subject. In Acts 10:33 it refers to what God has charged Peter to say, and in 17:26 (where the Received Text has *protetagmena*, "appointed beforehand") to God's determining definite epochs (*kairos*) in human history.   *J. I. Packer*

τίθημι

τίθημι (*tithēmi*), put, place, set, render, appoint. On *protithēmi* → Foreknowledge, art. *protithēmi*.

CL & OT *tithēmi* is the standard and very common Gk. word for "put" in all sorts of connections, both literal (putting something in a place) and metaphorical (putting something into a category, or a plan). With a predicate in apposition *tithēmi* means "cause to be" or "regard as". In the LXX *tithēmi* is frequent, rendering no less than 37 Heb. equivalents.

NT In the NT *tithēmi* occurs 100 times with the wide range of meaning which it has in secular Gk. It has God as its subject on occasion in both its active and middle voices. In the active voice it signifies God's destining someone for something, both in Heb. 1:2 (the Son appointed heir of all things) and also in four major *testimonia* cited substantially from the LXX: Ps. 110(109):1, "until I *make* thine enemies thy footstool" (quoted in Mk. 12:36; Matt. 12:44; Lk. 20:43; Acts 2:35; 1 Cor. 15:25; Heb. 1:13; 10:13); Gen. 17:5, "A father of many nations have I *made* thee [Abraham]" (quoted in Rom. 4:17); Isa. 49:6, "I have *set* thee [Christ the servant] for a light of the Gentiles" (quoted in Acts 13:47); Isa. 28:16, "I *lay* in Zion a stone. . ." (quoted in Rom. 9:33; 1 Pet. 2:6; both times with *tithēmi* as the verb, though oddly the LXX has *emballō*). In the middle voice (which insofar as it differs from the active accentuates the thought of action for the agent's own benefit) God *fixes* times (Acts 1:7), *arranges* parts of the body (1 Cor. 12:18), *sets* gifted men in the church (1 Cor. 12:18), *appoints* presbyters as overseers (Acts 20:28), and Christians to obtain salvation (1 Thess. 5:9), *puts* Paul into ministerial work (1 Tim. 1:12), *making* him a herald and apostle to further the gospel (1 Tim. 2:7; 2 Tim. 1:11), and *placing* the word of reconciliation in his hands (2 Cor. 5:19). The thought of God settling what shall be by sovereign decision runs through all these passages. *J. I. Packer*

προθεσμία

προθεσμία (*prothesmia*), appointed date.

CL & OT Derived from *thesmos*, meaning "law" in the sense of what is laid down, *prothesmia*, a feminine adjective with which *hēmera*, "day", should be understood, signifies a time-limit appointed in advance for the completing of legal, financial or political transactions. It appears in the papyri though not the LXX, and in secular Gk. is found from the fourth century B.C.

NT In the NT *prothesmia* occurs once, in Gal. 4:2, where the words "of the father" seem to envisage, as the matter of the illustration, a special guardianship operating during the father's lifetime rather than the regular guardianship of an orphaned minor, which was ended automatically not by the father's will but by law when the orphan reached the age of 25. (See E. de W. Burton, *Galatians* [ICC], 1921, 212 ff.)   *J. I. Packer*

477

| χειροτονέω | χειροτονέω (cheirotoneō), appoint; προχειροτονέω (procheirotoneō), appoint beforehand. |

CL & OT *cheirotoneō*, from *cheir*, "hand", and *teinō*, "stretch", means to vote or elect by a show of hands, as was regularly done in the Athenian assembly. From this the verb came to mean appoint, and its *pro-* compound means appoint beforehand (or, in some instances, take a preliminary vote). Neither word appears in the LXX.

NT In 2 Cor. 8:19 *cheirotoneō* refers to the churches' appointment of their representative to accompany Paul to Jerusalem to deliver the collection, and in Acts 14:23 it refers to the appointment by Barnabas and Paul of elders in the Galatian churches; from whence, apparently, it became the standard term for ordination in later ecclesiastical Gk. In Acts 10:41 *procheirotoneō* signifies God's appointment of the apostles, prior to Jesus' resurrection, to be witnesses of that event.

J. I. Packer

| λαγχάνω | λαγχάνω (lanchanō), obtain as by lot; draw lots for. |

CL & OT The basic classical meaning of *lanchanō* is to obtain something by lot. At Athens, both political offices and permission to bring suits in the law courts were awarded by lot, and *lanchanō* often appears in these contexts. More broadly, it denotes getting anything as if by lot, i.e. out of the blue, seemingly by luck rather than as a consequence of effort or desert. In the canonical LXX *lanchanō* is used once, of Saul obtaining the monarchy, which he did by God's appointment divorced from any action of his own (1 Sam. [1 Ki.] 14:47).

NT In Jn. 19:24 *lanchanō* appears in the non-classical sense of casting lots for something (Jesus' coat). Otherwise, it indicates divine appointment irrespective of personal quality. In Lk. 1:9 Zacharias obtains by lot the honour of offering incense in the Holy Place of the temple, where the angel meets him. In Acts 1:17 Peter refers to Judas having obtained through Christ's choice a share in the apostolic ministry. In 2 Pet. 1:1 Peter addresses those who have obtained (through God's grace-gift, not by personal merit) "like precious faith with us" – probably meaning by this Gentile believers.

J. I. Packer

→ Elect, → Foreknowledge, Providence, Predestination

(a). L. C. Allen, "The Old Testament Background of (*pro*)*horizein* in the New Testament", NTS 17, 1970–71, 104–8; H. Conzelmann, *The Theology of St. Luke*, 1960, 149–57; G. Delling, *tassō* etc. *TDNT* VIII 27–48; C. Maurer, *tithēmi* etc., *TDNT* VIII 152–58; W. Michaelis, *procheirizō*, *TDNT* VI 862 ff.; A. Oepke, *kathistēmi*, *TDNT* III 444–47; G. Bertram and B. Reicke, *paristēmi, paristanō*, *TDNT* V 837–41; K. L. Schmidt, *horizō* etc., *TDNT* V 452–56; commentaries on *Acts* by F. F. Bruce, 1951; and E. Haenchen, 1971; commentaries on *Romans* by C. K. Barrett, 1965; F. F. Bruce, 1963; J. Murray, 1967; A. Nygren, 1952; W. Sanday and A. C. Headlam, (ICC) 1902⁵; M. Black, 1973.
(b). E. Lohse, *Die Ordination im Spätjudentum und im Neuen Testament*, 1951; O. Michel, *Der Brief and die Römer*, KEK 4 1966¹³; U. Wilckens, *Die Missionsreden der Apostelgeschichte*, 1961, 152 ff.

Dirt, Filth, Refuse

περίψημα, περικάθαρμα

περίψημα (*peripsēma*); περικάθαρμα (*perikatharma*) filth, offscouring.

CL From *peripsaō*, meaning to wipe round, rub clean, and so clean out, *peripsēma* in secular Gk. means (a) that which is wiped off, refuse, scum (and in inscriptions *peripsēma sou* is used, Chinese-style, to mean "your humble servant"); (b) that which effects cleansing – literally, a sweat-rag or bath-towel, and metaphorically an expiatory sacrifice putting away cultic impurity. It was a recurring Gk. custom for communities to placate angry gods by offering a human sacrifice as a scapegoat (citizens might rub their hands on him to impart to him their own uncleanness). For such sacrifices the "scum" of society – criminals under sentence, paupers, deformed persons – were regularly recruited; thus the pejorative sense of *peripsēma* was reinforced. *perikatharma*, a late noun from *perikathairō*, meaning to cleanse all round, is a more intensive form of *katharma*, and is almost synonymous with *peripsēma*: it signifies (a) a guilt-laden expiatory sacrifice, particularly a human one, and (b) a term of contempt for the kind of persons who volunteered as victims – "human rubbish".

OT In the LXX *peripsēma* occurs only in Tob. 5:18, meaning a sacrifice or ransom in virtue of which God will protect Tobias' life (RV and RSV are wrong here in giving it the sense "refuse", "rubbish"). *perikatharma* occurs only in Prov. 21:18, with which cf. 11:8. The thought is that God in providence expends the wicked to preserve the upright (cf. Isa. 43:3 f.); a pattern of procedure which Christ's cross entirely reversed (cf. 1 Pet. 3:18).

NT In the NT, both words occur once only, in 1 Cor. 4:13, as Paul's ironic description of the apostles as men regard them (*peripsēma*, sense (a); *perikatharma*, sense (b)), with the undertone, clear from the context, that by throwing away their lives as they do the apostles are bringing benefit to others (*peripsēma*, sense (b); *perikatharma*, sense (a); see 2 Cor. 4:10 ff., 6:10; Phil. 2:17; Col. 1:24).

ῥύπος

ῥύπος (*rhypos*), dirt; ῥυπαρία (*rhyparia*), filthiness; ῥυπαρός (*rhyparos*), dirty; ῥυπόω, ῥυπαίνω, ῥυπαρεύω (*rhypoō, rhypainō, rhypareuō*), make filthy.

CL In classical Gk. *rhypos* is used of literal dirt, liquid and solid, and *rhypoō* (also *rhypaō*) is used intransitively for being dirty. *rhyparos* and *rhyparia* carry both literal and metaphorical meanings; with *rhypainō* the metaphorical meaning, to "mess up" one's life and character, seems to be primary.

OT *rhypos* appears twice in the LXX for literal dirt (Job 9:31; 11:15) and twice for defilement before God (Job 14:4; Isa. 4:4). *rhyparos* is used twice in Zech. 3:4 f. of dirty clothes. The other words in this group do not appear.

NT In the NT, *rhypos* occurs once, of physical dirt (1 Pet. 3:21); *rhyparia* once, of moral filthiness (Jas. 1:21); *rhyparos* once of dirty clothing (Jas. 2:2) and once of a morally unclean person (Rev. 22:11); and each verb appears in some manuscripts of Rev. 22:11, where the sense is "let him who is defiled continue to be defiled."

479

| σκύβαλον | σκύβαλον (*skybalon*), refuse, dung. |

CL In secular Gk. this depressing word means rubbish and muck of many kinds: excrement, rotten food, bits left at a meal as not worth eating, a rotting corpse. Nastiness and decay are the constant elements of its meaning; it is a coarse, ugly, violent word implying worthlessness, uselessness, and repulsiveness. Gnostics applied the word to the human body to express their low view of it, as the tomb of the soul.

OT *skybalon* occurs once in the LXX, signifying moral uncleanness and defilement (Ecclus. 27:4).

NT The only NT usage is Paul's in Phil. 3:8, where he says of all the natural and religious privileges which once seemed sweet and precious, and all the things he has lost since becoming a Christian, "I count (estimate, evaluate) them as (nothing but) dung." The coarse and violent word shows how completely Paul had ceased to value them.

| κόπρος, κόπριον | κόπρος, κόπρον, κόπριον (*kopros, kopron, koprion*), dung; κοπρία (*kopria*), dunghill. |

CL & OT In classical Gk. and LXX, *kopros* (which is feminine), *kopron* and *koprion* are the ordinary words for dung, and *kopria* the ordinary word for a dunghill. In Ecclus. 27:4 *kopria* is used for dung caught in a sieve.

NT In the NT, *koprion* and *kopria* are each found once, in their literal sense (Lk. 13:8; 14:35), and *kopros* and *kopron* do not appear. This fact has no theological significance. *J. I. Packer*

G. Stählin, *peripsēma*, *TDNT* VI 84 ff.; F. Hauck, *perikatharma*, *TDNT* III 430 f.; F. Lang, *skybalon*, *TDNT* VII 445 ff.

Disciple, Follow, Imitate, After

Men are dependent upon one another and their lives are shaped by each other in many ways. Sometimes it is through a casual relationship, an interested companion or hanger-on. But it may be the more lasting relationship of a pupil or disciple to his master or teacher. In the NT, the words connected with discipleship are applied chiefly to the followers of Jesus and describe the life of faith. *akoloutheō* (follow) denotes the action of a man answering the call of Jesus whose whole life is redirected in obedience. A *mathētēs* (disciple) is one who has heard the call of Jesus and joins him. *mimeomai* (imitate) can be distinguished, in so far as it mainly emphasizes the nature of a particular kind of behaviour, modelled on someone else. The prep. *opisō* (after) is characteristic of the call to follow Jesus.

| ἀκολουθέω | ἀκολουθέω (*akoloutheō*), follow; ἐξακολουθέω (*exakoloutheō*), follow; ἐπακολουθέω (*epakoloutheō*), follow; |

παρακολουθέω (*parakoloutheō*), accompany, understand; συνακολουθέω (*synakoloutheō*), follow.

CL 1. *akoloutheō* is formed from *keleuthos*, a path (Homer onwards), and is used in cl. Gk. from Thuc. onwards. It means (a) go somewhere with someone, accompany; (b) go behind someone, follow, and also (with hostile intentions) pursue. Alongside the lit. meaning there soon grew up a metaphorical one: follow the drift, understand (Plato), follow someone's opinion, agree (Plato), adapt oneself (Thuc.). Substantival forms meaning disciple or discipleship also occur. Compound vbs. are also found: *exakoloutheō*, follow, reconnoitre; *epakoloutheō*, follow, pursue; *parakoloutheō*, accompany, comprehend; *synakoloutheō*, follow closely, accompany; follow (in logic).

2. Among the Stoics *akoloutheō* has religious and philosophical connotations. It is used to refer to the conformity of the wise to the law of the world (→ Reason art. *nous*; → Nature, art. *physis*). To "follow" nature or God is the basic direction of the philosophical life. Following here virtually means identification of one's being through incorporation. Behind this lies the Gk. view of the innate relationship of rational man with God.

OT 1. The corresponding OT phrase is *hālak 'aḥᵃrê*, lit. go behind (in 1 Ki. 19:20 with → *opisō* where Elisha wants to follow Elijah as his servant). It is used contemptuously in the sense of pursue (Hosea 2:7 (LXX v. 5) similarly with *opisō* where Israel is compared to a whore chasing her lovers). On most occasions the words are used with no particular theological force (e.g. Ruth 1:14). There are no OT precedents for the more specific NT usage of *akoloutheō*. Even where other words are used for following, such as *poreuō*, they are applied to Yahweh only with great care (cf. Deut. 13:5 (EVV v. 4) and 1 Ki. 14:8). They never mean becoming like God, but only obeying him. God remains above this world and incomparable even as the → Covenant God. The negative usage of *hālak 'aḥᵃrê* is therefore the dominant one. It is used as a fixed phrase for backsliding into paganism by going after other gods (cf. Jdg. 2:12; Deut. 4:3; Jer. 2:5).

2. In post-exilic Jud. the general OT usage is found (cf. SB I 372). The negative variant survives in the Qumran texts, denoting association with a deceiver. *hālak 'aḥᵃrê* and *akoloutheō* both assume particular significance among the Rabbis. The words describe the relationship of a pupil to a teacher of the Torah. The pupil (the *talmîd*) who chooses to subordinate himself to a Rabbi follows him everywhere he goes, learning from him and above all serving him (→ *mathētēs*). The pupil's obligation to → serve is an essential part of learning the Law. The goal of all his learning and training is a complete knowledge of the Torah, and ability to practise it in every situation. Without this true piety is scarcely deemed possible (cf. SB I 527; → *mathētēs* OT 2).

NT 1. The very nature and restricted use of the NT occurrences of these words is of importance.

(a) *akoloutheō* appears almost exclusively in the gospels: 56 times in the Synoptics and 14 times in Jn.; only 3 times in Acts, once in Paul and 6 times in Rev. In other words, it occurs in the writings that are nearest to the Rab. world. Whereas secular Gk. knew of an abundance of derivative words, only the vb. occurs in the NT and usually in its simple form. The compound vbs. are less used and are not normally applied to people. Except for *synakoloutheō*, accompany (Mk. 5:3–7; 14:51; Lk. 23:49), they hardly occur at all in the gospels.

481

(b) But following does not in every instance involve being a disciple. Where the Synoptics speak in the ind. of crowds of people who followed Jesus (*akoloutheō*; cf. Matt. 4:25; 8:1; 21:9; Mk. 10:32), the word is used in a neutral sense. No particular calling or conviction can be inferred from this.

(c) The word has special significance where it refers to individuals. On Jesus' lips it often appears as an imperative, as when he calls the disciples (Matt. 9:9 par.; 19:21 par.; 8:22 par.; Jn. 1:43; 21:19 ff.; cf. Mk. 1:16 ff. par. with → *opisō*). The response of those called is described as following (e.g. Lk. 5:11). *akoloutheō* is always the call to decisive and intimate discipleship of the earthly Jesus. It always points to the beginning of discipleship. Jn. hints at its spiritual implications for fellowship with the Exalted One (especially 12:26 ff.).

(d) The occurrences in the Pauline letters and in Acts are not theologically significant. In Rev. 14:4 *akoloutheō* denotes those who have shared in the lot of suffering of the slaughtered and exalted → Lamb.

2. For a theological analysis two observations are important.

(a) The simple *akoloutheō* is never used purely metaphorically in the NT. The semi-literal sense of "going behind" remains even in the special sense noted above (NT 1 (c)). On the other hand, *akoloutheō* is always used (except in Jn. 21:19 ff. and Rev. 14:4) with reference to the earthly Jesus. This fact supports the supposition of an affinity with the teacher-pupil relationship of the Rabbis.

(b) Nevertheless, there are characteristic differences between the disciples of Jesus and those of the Rabbis.

(i) Jesus did not wait for voluntary followers. He called men with divine authority as God himself called the prophets in the OT (Mk. 1:16 par.; Matt. 8:22).

(ii) Jesus did not call men to acquire and master traditional modes of conduct. He pointed them to the future dawn of the Kingdom of God (Lk. 9:59 f.). To be a disciple of Jesus was an eschatological calling to help in the service of the "kingdom" which is "at hand" (Mk. 1:15). Those who were called to discipleship shared accordingly in Jesus' authority. They are sent to the same men (cf. Matt. 15:24 with 10:5 f.), with the same message (cf. Matt. 4:17 with 10:7), to do the same mighty deeds (Mk. 3:14 f.). They will sit with him on the throne of the Judge of the world (Matt. 19:28; Lk. 22:30).

(iii) As a rule, one who takes up the new "calling" gives the old one up. It is not an oppressive pre-condition, however. It follows almost self-evidently (Mk. 1:16 ff.; Matt. 9:9), as the figure of the Rich Young Ruler makes clear (Mk. 10:17 ff.). He founders "when confronted with the unheard-of offer of 'eternal life', and turns again to the emptiness of his worldly possessions" (G. Bornkamm, *Jesus of Nazareth*, 148). He could not free himself from the old ties. Even the disciple who is already following Jesus is not thereby exempt from the danger of making new reservations in his discipleship (cf. Matt. 8:21 f. par.). It is a question here of "the repeated demand for a new decision in terms of complete obedience *within* discipleship" (H. J. Held in G. Bornkamm, G. Barth and H. J. Held, *Tradition and Interpretation in Matthew*, 1963, 203).

(iv) Since the disciple cannot expect any better fortune than his Lord (cf. Matt. 10:24 f.), readiness for → suffering becomes a part of discipleship. "If any man would come after me, let him deny himself and take up his cross and follow me" (Mk. 8:34; cf. Matt. 10:38). "To take up the cross" means "to be ready for death"

(G. Delling, *TDNT* IV 6). But readiness to suffer is only made possible through the "self-denial" which consists in freedom from oneself and all forms of personal security. Such self-denial is possible only when man gives himself to God in unconditional discipleship.

(c) John takes over synoptic phraseology (1:43 ff.), but tends to see it less in its particular historical context and more within the framework of his total vision. Jesus appeared as → Light and → Life in the world of death and darkness. Anyone who "follows" him (8:12) walks in the light and is saved. Accordingly following here means believing acceptance of the → revelation. *akoloutheō* means having →faith (cf. Jn. 12:44). In discipleship men's lives find a new settled purpose as they are directed into the true life. To follow the call of the Shepherd (10:4, 27) means both safety in Christ and fellowship in suffering with him (12:26) which in turn means "exaltation" with him (12:32). "But just as for Jesus himself the exaltation on the cross is at the same time his *doxasthēnai*, so also the promise of following him and being where he is means the promise of participating in his *doxa*" (R. Bultmann *The Gospel of John*, 426). The call to discipleship in Jn. has, therefore, the character of invitation (8:12) and promise (13:35 f.).

3. The word *akoloutheō* is essentially restricted to the gospels. In the rest of the NT writings one can sense a struggle to find another terminology to describe the Christian's fellowship with Christ, such as Paul's concept of being "in Christ", or "imitation" of Christ (cf. Phil. 2:5–11 → *mimeomai*) with its ethical overtones.

C. Blendinger

μαθητής

μαθητής (*mathētēs*), learner, pupil, disciple; μανθάνω (*manthanō*), learn.

CL *manthanō* in the pres. tense has already various stages of development behind it when it first appears in Pindar. Homer uses only the strong aorist forms *mathon, emmathes, emmathen*, from the stem *math-*, from which is formed *mathētēs* (first used by Hdt.).

1. (a) In Homer's writings *manthanō* has the sense of adapting oneself, preparing for, growing accustomed to (cf. Homer, *Il.*, 6, 444; *Od.*, 18, 226 f.). In another area of development it comes to mean acquire or adopt (whether through teaching or experience) and learn (cf. Hdt., 7, 208).

(b) *manthanō* denotes the process by which one acquires theoretical knowledge (Heraclitus, Protagoras and others). The word therefore plays an important role in speculative thought from Socrates onwards. Socrates held that, when a man is learning something, he should penetrate deeply into the nature of everything (including his own nature). He should be able to proceed beyond this "insight" to a knowledge of morality so as to be able to act according to ethical principles. See especially Plato's *Dialogues* (e.g. *Tim.*, 88a; *Theaetet.*, 114b, 150b ff.; *Apol.* 33a f.; and Xen., *Mem.*, 1, 4, 17; 4, 7, 1). Plato goes further than Socrates in defining learning (*manthanein*) "as *anamnēsis*, i.e. the recollection of what was known before time" (K. H. Rengstorf, *TDNT* IV 396). There exists in the human soul, albeit unconsciously, a factual knowledge of ideas and truths, known in a previous existence of which people can only be made aware through the process of teaching (Plato, *Phaed.*, 72e; *Meno.*, 86b). In later Gk. philosophy *manthanō* was rationalized and applied to the acquisition of theoretical knowledge. In the mystery religions the use of the word approximates more closely to that of *ginōskō* (→ knowledge).

2. (a) A man is called a *mathētēs* when he binds himself to someone else in order to acquire his practical and theoretical knowledge. He may be an apprentice in a trade, a student of medicine, or a member of a philosophical school. One can only be a *mathētēs* in the company of a *didaskalos*, a master or teacher, to whom the *mathētēs* since the days of the Sophists generally had to pay a fee. An obvious exception to this is when *mathētēs* refers to spiritual dependence on a thinker long since dead. Socrates never wanted to have any *mathētēs* and never regarded himself as a *didaskalos* (Plato, *Laches*, 186e; *Apol.*, 33a). The reason for this was his concern that a man should use the company of his master to enable himself to fathom the nature of things and gain insight independently. This particular kind of communal relationship, in which both the teacher and the one taught felt themselves committed to the same common goal (such as the knowledge of morality) led far beyond the category of "pupil" to that of "disciple". But the word *mathētēs* could no longer be used because of its impersonal and commercial associations. By contrast with the Sophists, Socrates refused any kind of payment from his pupils. From the time of Socrates (for this reason?) the word *mathētēs*, in the sense of a disciple in relation to his master, largely fell into the background among succeeding Gk. philosophers. Alternative words came to be used such as *hetairos*, friend; *gnōrimos*, expert; *akolouthos*, follower.

(b) In a wide range of ancient philosophical schools, including the Pythagoreans and Neo-Pythagoreans, clearly-defined master-pupil relationships grew up where the disciples developed and represented their masters' case. In these schools a principle of tradition is to be found which scholars long believed only existed in the mystery religions (cf. K. H. Rengstorf, *TDNT* IV 425 f.).

OT 1. (a) *manthanō* is used *c*. 40 times as a translation of a Heb. equivalent. It is used 28 times to render Heb. *lāmaḍ*, grow accustomed to, make oneself familiar with, learn. In most of these passages *manthanō* has no special theological emphasis (e.g. "they will not learn war any more" (Mic. 4:3; Isa. 2:4); "he grew accustomed to tearing his prey" (Ezek. 19:3, 6)).

The theologically relevant usage of *manthanō* is particularly clear in Deut., where Israel is in great danger of forgetting Yahweh's goodness, of taking no further notice of Yahweh's will and of forfeiting its election and the divine promises of salvation (cf. Deut. 6:10–12; 8:17; 9:4–6; 11:2). Israel must now learn again to obey and perform the revealed will of God (Deut. 4:10; 14:23; 17:19; 31:12 f.). In each of these cases the object of *manthanō* is *phobeisthai kyrion ton theon*, to fear the Lord God. Learning means the process by which the past experience of the love of God is translated by the learners into obedience to the Torah of God (cf. Deut. 4:14). It means fully understanding the Torah which in Deut. is the whole story of the saving actions of God's will. This understanding is to lead to an inner acceptance of the divine will (cf. Deut. 30:14).

Similarly in Ps. 119(118):7 f., 71,73 (cf. Isa. 1:17; 26:9) the Psalmist prays ("that I may learn") for a right attitude to the Torah which is here understood as an all-embracing guide and direction. H.-J. Kraus sees it as both the canonical law of God and oral instruction from the priest (*Psalmen*, II, 822). The goal of learning is action which corresponds to the word (Ps. 119(118):101). Even in Isa. 1:17 "it is not primarily a question of individual actions or fulfilment of the Law, but of a fundamental re-direction of human existence. Isaiah is not looking for a new 'disposition' but for a completely different basic attitude, which will express itself in practical dealing with all one's fellow men" (H. Wildberger, *Jesaja*, 47). The objects of *manthanō* are, therefore, *phronēsis*, disposition (Bar. 3:14); *synesis*, power of decision, insight (Sir. 8:9); *sophia*, wisdom (Wis. 6:9; 7:13). All these denote qualities and gifts that are needed to do God's will.

(b) *mathētēs* is found in the LXX only in alternative readings of Jer. 13:21; 20:11; 26:9, and is accordingly weakly attested. Even the Heb. noun corresponding to the vb. *lāmaḏ, talmîḏ*, a pupil, which plays such an important part in later Rabbinic usage, is found only in 1 Chr. 25:8. The lack of any OT vocabulary for a learner, such as the teacher-pupil relationship describes, is bound up with Israel's consciousness of being an elect people. What the individual Israelite has to learn in respect of God's will does not make him a "pupil" in relation to his "master", God. For even as a learner the individual always remains a part of the whole chosen people, all of whom encounter in the divine Word the authority of the Electing One. This excludes any possibility of a disciple-master relationship between men, because even the → priest and the → prophet do not teach on their own authority. This is shown, for example, in the fact that the attendants of Moses and the prophets are not called pupils but servants (*mešārēṯ*). Joshua is the servant of Moses (Exod. 24:12; Num. 11:28); Elisha is the servant of Elijah (1 Ki. 19:19 ff.); Gehazi of Elisha (2 Ki. 4:12); Baruch of Jeremiah (Jer. 32:12 f.). "There is no place for the establishment of a master-disciple relation, nor is there the possibility of setting up a human word alongside the word of God which is proclaimed, nor of trying to ensure the force of the divine address by basing it on the authority of a great personality" (Rengstorf, *TDNT* IV 431).

2. (a) The situation is different in Rab. Judaism. Here the *talmîḏ* is someone whose concern is the whole of Jewish tradition. According to Shammai (Shabbath 31a), this was the written Torah (the biblical writings of the OT) and the oral Torah, the *paradoseis tōn presbyterōn* (the traditions of the fathers) which includes the Mishnah, Midrash, Halachah and Haggadah. The *talmîḏ* now, as originally the Gk. *mathētēs*, belongs to his teacher, to whom he subordinates himself in almost servile fashion. It was the distinct casuistic form of Rab. theology, built around emphasis on achievement in the religious thought of developed Judaism, which created the pre-requisites for attributing a value of its own to human authority which previously was entirely unknown in Israel and Judaism. Since the Rabbi's knowledge gives him direct access to the Scriptures which facilitates right hearing and right understanding, he becomes a kind of mediator between the *talmîḏîm* and the Torah. To listen to the Scriptures without the guidance of a teacher is something to be avoided at all costs (cf. B. Berakoth 47b). *lāmaḏ* and *manthanō* still mean to learn, to occupy oneself with the Torah in order to discover God's will in it. But now learning is determined by the authority of the teacher and his interpretation of the Torah – not by a personal and, as far as possible, unbiased study of the Torah. Therefore learning means primarily that the *talmîḏ* appropriates the knowledge of his teacher and examines it critically by comparing it

485

against the Torah. Only one who had studied and served under a *ḥāḵām* (a Jewish scholar) for an extensive period, and had thus concluded his essential study, could later become a *ḥāḵām* with authority to teach his own tradition in his own school. The pupil-teacher relationship of Rab. Jud., in contradistinction to the OT, thus became an important institution for detailed study of the Torah.

(b) Not only the Rabbi, but also the *talmîḏ* originated through Judaism's contact with Gk. philosophy (cf. Rengstorf, *TDNT* IV 437 ff.). The way in which the various scholars (like many Gk. philosophers) regarded their differing methods and doctrinal opinions as possessing absolute validity gave rise to schools in the Rab. world and then to rival circles of disciples grouped around a master. Hel. influence on Judaism led to a simultaneous intellectualism and dogmatism concerning the revelation of the divine will in Israel.

NT The vb. *manthanō* occurs only 25 times in the NT and only 6 times in the Gospels, where one would have expected it most as a mark of discipleship (3 times in Matt., 1 in Mk., 2 in Jn.; Lk. has it only once in Acts). Much more common in the NT is *didaskō*, teach. The noun *mathētēs* occurs 264 times in the NT, exclusively in the Gospels and Acts. It is used to indicate total attachment to someone in discipleship. The secular Gk. usage of the word in the sense of apprentice, pupil or student is not found. Matt. 10:24 ff. and Lk. 6:40 ("the disciple is not above his master") cannot be used as evidence against this, since the issue here is not simply that of the relationship of a pupil to a teacher, but that of a disciple to the *kyrios*, Jesus.

1. *manthanō* means learn, following secular Gk. usage, in Acts 23:27 and Rev. 14:3. In some cases it is debatable as to whether the word is used in an OT or a secular Gk. sense (cf. Gal. 3:2; Eph. 4:11; Col. 1:7). In many passages it is used in the specifically OT sense of *lāmaḏ*, learn the will of God, or learn to direct the whole of one's human existence towards the will of God (cf. OT 1).

(a) This is the case with those usages of *manthanō* which refer directly to the will of God, as it comes to the hearer in Jesus (Matt. 9:13; 11:29; Jn. 6:45; cf. Mk. 13:28 par). Jesus himself is the central point of reference, where alone man can know the will of God (Matt. 11:29). In living and preaching the compassion of God, Jesus does not introduce a new → Law which must be learnt. Instead he restores to the Law its original function of enabling men to recognize the will of God and directs men to it (cf. G. Barth, op. cit., 58–164). Learning here is not appropriation of knowledge. It comes about through "the surrender of one's own judgment" (Bultmann) and keeping oneself open to the word of the Father which leads men to follow Jesus (Jn. 6:45). Learning here includes the OT emphasis on doing God's will. In concrete terms it means putting one's → faith in Jesus and following him in his work of compassion (cf. Matt. 9:13).

(b) *manthanō* has a similar meaning when it is used in the epistles to refer to the message or teaching (→ Teach) of Jesus (Rom. 16:17; Eph. 4:20; 2 Tim. 3:14). To hold to the teaching which the recipients of the letters received means to hold to their faith. For learning is no mere intellectual process by which one acquires teaching about Christ. It implies acceptance of Christ himself, rejection of the old existence and beginning the new life of discipleship in him (cf. Phil. 4:9; 1 Cor. 4:6). It is possible that the unique formulation, "You have not so learned Christ" (Eph.

486

4:20), is a reminder of previous baptismal instruction in which the Ephesians learned that understanding of the teaching is revealed in one's conduct.

(c) The Hel. play on words in Heb. 5:8 is unique. Speaking of Christ himself, it says that he learnt obedience by virtue of his suffering (*emathen aph' hōn epathen*, he learnt through what he suffered). Learning here means recognition of the Father's will in his suffering and affirmation of that will in his acceptance of the suffering.

(d) In the Pastorals one can be fairly certain that there are reminiscences of the Jewish use of *manthanō*. For example, the ref. in 2 Tim. 3:7 to women who let themselves to be lead astray by false doctrines (of a Judaizing syncretistic gnosticism) is most probably an allusion to legalistic instruction about the Law (cf. also 1 Tim. 5:13).

2. The main interest in this word-group in the NT falls on the noun *mathētēs*. The evangelists who, as we saw, are the only ones to use the word probably took it over from Hel. Jud. But despite possible overtones of the figure of the Rab. *talmîd*, it is given a completely new character through its association with Jesus. That they found the word with a wider frame of reference is also clear from the fact that it was used in circles unrelated to Jesus, such as the disciples of John the Baptist (Matt. 11:2 par.; Mk. 2:18 par.; 6:29; Lk. 5:33; 11:1; Jn. 1:35, 37), the disciples of Moses (Jn. 9:28), and the disciples of the Pharisees (Matt. 22:16; Mk. 2:18).

(a) John the Baptist has "a solid group, closed both inwardly and outwardly" (Rengstorf, *TDNT* IV 456). His disciples were not far away when he was in prison (Matt. 11:2 par.). They later buried his body (Mk. 6:29 par.). They had their own form of prayer (Lk. 11:1), they fasted (Mk. 2:18 par.) and become involved in controversy with the Jews (Jn. 3:25). In all these particulars they were no longer "pupils" like those of the Rab. schools. They were adherents of a movement from which it is possible that Jesus himself came. At any rate, Jn. 1:25 ff. reports that Jesus' first two disciples originated from the Baptist's circle of disciples. This probably contains an ancient tradition which has preserved the historical and factual basis of the account. It is probable that later on the Baptist's movement and Jesus' circle came into conflict with one another from time to time, as is reflected in the scene in Jn. 3:22–26 (cf. R. Bultmann, *The Gospel of John*, 1971, 170 ff.).

(b) In Jn. 9:28 the Jews dispute Jesus' authority. They, the disciples of Moses, appeal to the revelation of God's will which he received. They do not comprehend that the miracle of healing reveals Jesus to be precisely the One who does God's will (v. 30).

(c) Finally, there is the mention of the *mathētai tōn Pharisaiōn*, the disciples of the Pharisees (Mk. 2:18 and elsewhere). This formula may have been used as an explanatory term to readers who were not familiar with the original situation. The par. passage Matt. 9:14 does not argue against this. In Matt. too, the Pharisees, like the Scribes, Sadducees and High Priests, are enemies of Jesus, standing typically for the whole nation (→ Israel). Equally, the expression *hoi hyioi hymōn*, your sons (Matt. 12:27; cf. 22:16), is understandable if the words referred originally to the Jews in general, and the Pharisees were mentioned as typical representatives of controversy (cf. R. Bultmann, *History of the Synoptic Tradition*, 52 ff.; →

487

Pharisee). In view of contemporary practice, one might have expected the phrase "disciples of the Scribes" (see above OT 2), but this does not appear.

3. It is indisputable that the earthly Jesus called men to be his disciples and to follow him. But today we cannot draw a completely clear picture of discipleship under the historical Jesus. No doubt, the nature of discipleship of Jesus was determined right from the beginning by his own person to which his disciples bound themselves (→ Jesus Christ). But despite questions and uncertainties, we can set out a list of characteristics of discipleship at the time of the historical Jesus.

(a) Clearly, Jesus came forward like a Rabbi or Scribe. He taught and discussed like one (Mk. 12:18 ff.), and was asked to make legal decisions (Lk. 12:13 f.). Even if he was not recognized by many, because he had not passed through a Rab. school (Mk. 6:2; Jn. 7:15), it was certainly with justice that he was addressed as "Rabbi" by his disciples (Mk. 9:5; 11:21; Jn. 1:38; 4:31) and outsiders (cf. Jn. 3:2). Even at this point one can see a parallel with the Rabbis of Jud., in that Jesus gathered a circle of disciples around him. But at several decisive points Jesus went beyond the recognized limits for a Rabbi, and this gives the disciple-master relationship its own distinctive colouring.

(b) Whereas in Rab. circles and in Gk. philosophical schools a man made a voluntary decision to join the "school" of his master and so become a disciple, with Jesus it was his → call that was decisive (Lk. 5:1–11; cf. Matt. 5:18 ff.). Jesus seized the initiative and called men into discipleship (Mk. 1:17 par.; 2:14 par.; Lk. 9:59–62; Jn. 1:43).

(c) The Gk. pupil and the Rab. *talmîd* bound themselves personally to their master and looked for objective teaching, with the aim of themselves becoming a master or a Rabbi. But Jesus' call to discipleship does not mean that a disciple is put in a learning relationship from which he can depart as a master (cf. Matt. 23:8). Following Jesus as a disciple means the unconditional sacrifice of his whole life (Matt. 10:37; Lk. 14:26 f.; cf. Mk. 3:31–35; Lk. 9:59–62) for the whole of his life (Matt. 10:24 f.; Jn. 11:16). To be a disciple means (as Matt. in particular emphasizes) to be bound to Jesus and to do God's will (Matt. 12:46–50; cf. Mk. 3:31–35). This means that during Jesus' earthly ministry the disciple had quite literally to "follow" Jesus, i.e. to follow behind him (→ *akoloutheō*) and accept the renunciatory lot of wandering about with him (Matt. 8:20 f.; cf. G. Bornkamm, *Jesus of Nazareth*, 146).

(d) Unlike the Rabbis, Jesus broke through the barriers separating the clean and the unclean, the sinful and the obedient. He summoned the tax-collector who stood outside the worshipping community (Mk. 2:14), just as he did the Zealot (Lk. 6:15; Acts 1:13) and the fisherman (Mk. 1:16 ff.). "The very fact that Jesus calls people to follow him, and that he does this with the consequence that they leave boat and toll-office and family, denotes a quite astonishing knowledge of his mission. . . .This holds good to an even greater extent of the breaking through all barriers as in the case of Levi. Grace becomes an event in such calling" (E. Schweizer, *Lordship and Discipleship*, 13 f.). Jesus' call to tax-collectors and sinners to abandon their old associations for discipleship indicates something of his own self-understanding and also the special nature of such discipleship.

(e) It is important for understanding discipleship of Jesus to realize that the call to be a disciple always includes the call to service. According to Mk. 1:17 and Lk. 5:10, the disciples are to be fishers of men. This is a colloquial phrase, meaning that in view of the impending reign of God, the disciples are to catch men for the coming kingdom by preaching the gospel and working in the name of Jesus (cf. Matt. 16:15 ff.). When Jesus sent out the Twelve (Mk. 6:7–13 par.) and the Seventy (Lk. 10:1–13), they were to go out in pairs healing, bringing salvation and peace, and proclaiming the Kingdom of God. We may see from this that the earthly Jesus himself sent out disciples for service of one kind or another.

(f) This service leads the disciple into the same dangers to which his master was exposed (cf. Mk. 10:32). Jesus went before them in suffering (→ Suffer). The disciple can expect no better fortune than his Lord (Matt. 10:24 f.; 16:24 f.; cf. 10:38).

(g) In the gospel tradition we keep coming up against the disciples' lack of understanding. This applies not only to the message itself (Mk. 4:10 f. par.; Matt. 13:36), their activity (Mk. 10:13 ff.; 10:48), and the goal of discipleship (Mk. 10:35 ff.), but above all to Jesus' suffering (Matt. 16:22 ff.; Mk. 14:47; Lk. 18:34; 22:37 f.).

(h) The promised → reward (which must not be understood as something deserved, since the promise exceeds every kind of merit) is fellowship with God through Jesus and thus a share in Jesus' authority. It is also the new and future life (cf. Matt. 16:25; Jn. 14:6).

(i) Who are meant by *hoi mathētai* (the disciples)? *hoi mathētai* are not simply the equivalent of *hoi dōdeka*, the Twelve. This identification can be observed only in some parts of the tradition. The circle of the Twelve was both a symbolic representation of the twelve tribes of Israel, and thus of the whole people of God, and also a section of the larger circle of disciples which Jesus summoned to discipleship from a still wider group of adherents. This is more probable than to suppose that there existed yet another separate circle of apostles alongside the circle of the disciples (→ Apostle NT 2 (c); but cf. Rengstorf, *TDNT* IV 450–55). It is no longer possible today to determine the precise limits of the circle of disciples. But it is clearly not a question with Jesus of an ascetic elite with a distinct ethic which Jesus was able to demand only of a few people. The disciples would have been a circle of immediate followers who were commissioned to particular service (cf. G. Bornkamm, *Jesus of Nazareth*, 147 f.; E. Schweizer, op. cit. 20).

4. (a) As a rule, the individual gospel passages which speak of "following" and of discipleship are already reflections on the meanings of discipleship. Thus Matt. graphically depicts the lot of the disciples, by linking the account of the storm on the lake with an account of calling, and so presents it as a story whose purpose is to illustrate that those who follow Jesus are destined to suffer (Matt. 8:19–26; cf. G. Bornkamm in *Tradition and Interpretation in Matthew*, 52–57). Renunciation (Matt. 23:7 ff.), humility (Matt. 18:1 ff.), poverty (Matt. 19:23 ff.) and readiness to suffer (Matt. 10:17 ff.) can all become characteristics of true discipleship (→ Humility, → Poor).

Decisive in understanding *mathētes* in the gospels, however, is → faith (Mk. 16:16; Lk. 17:5; 22:32) in Jesus himself (Matt. 18:6; esp. Jn. 2:11; and 6:69; 11:44). "Everyone who acknowledges me before men, the Son of man also will acknowledge before the angels of God; but he who denies me before men will be denied before the angels of God" (Lk. 12:8 f.). These words express the whole promise and also the great dangers of genuine discipleship. The disciple's faithfulness to his Lord is crucial. It is, therefore, not accidental that Lk. avoids using the word *mathētēs* from Gethsemane onwards, taking it up again only in Acts 6:1, albeit now in a different sense (see below (b)).

(b) Reflection on discipleship is particularly characteristic of John's Gospel. Not only do the categories of the narrower and wider circles of disciples point quite fundamentally beyond themselves to the Christian community addressed by Jn. (cf. Jn. 6:60; 61:66). *mathētēs* in Jn. is often simply a term for "Christian" (Jn. 8:31; 13:35; 15:8). Moreover, since any word for the church, such as *ekklēsia*, is entirely lacking (→ Church, art. *ekklēsia* NT 5. (b)), the word *mathētai* comes to stand for the gathered community. Or in Johannine terminology, it denotes those who have come out of the sphere of darkness into the sphere of light (3:21; cf. the farewell discourses, chs. 13–17). This also marks a further step. The disciples are now no longer bound to the presence of the earthly Jesus. Instead, their dwelling "in the Word" (8:31) and "in the Spirit" (14:15–17; 15:26 f.) means that they, his disciples, remain in full fellowship with him. This fellowship finds its visible expression in the world in the manner of their service. Everyone is to be able to recognize a disciple of Jesus by his practical love (Jn. 13:34 f.). A disciple's duty does not consist in maintaining and passing on particular teaching about Jesus. The essence of discipleship lies in the disciple's fulfilment of his duty to be a witness to his Lord in his entire life (→ Witness).

This becomes clearer still from the way the word is used in Acts. Luke has taken over certain specific pieces of tradition which show that the use of *mathetēs* remains confined to particular sections of the book. It is lacking, for instance, in the "we"–sections (Acts 16:10–17; 20:5–15; 21:1–18; 27:1–28:16). In these passages, *mathētēs* has the general sense of "Christian", one who believes in Jesus (cf. Rengstorf, *TDNT* IV 457 ff.; cf. Acts 6:1f., 7; 9:1, 10, 19, 25f., 38; 11:26, 29; 13:52; 14:20, 22, 28; 15:10; 16:1; 18:23, 27; 19:1, 9, 30; 20:1, 30; 21:4, 16).   *D. Müller*

| μιμέομαι | μιμέομαι (*mimeomai*), imitate, follow; μιμητής (*mimētēs*) imitator; συμμιμητής (*symmimētēs*), fellow-imitator. |

CL 1. *mimeomai*, used from the 6th cent. B.C. and derived from the root *mi*, to exchange, means: (a) imitate, mimic what one sees someone else doing. According to Aristot. and Democritus, at the beginning of civilization men learnt from animals – weaving and spinning from spiders, and house-building from swallows (cf. W. Michaelis, *TDNT* IV 660); (b) emulate with joy, follow; (c) in the arts (plays, paintings, sculpture and poetry), represent reality by imitation, imitate in an artistic way. By contrast with Plato, Aristot. gives art a positive basis in the imitation or reality. An actor is therefore a *mimos*, a mimer (Aesch. onwards). A *symmimētēs* (Lat. *imitator*) is an imitator, especially a performer or an artist who imitates. When used in a derogatory sense, the words refer to quasi-dramatic "aping" or feeble copying with lack of originality. Very early on (in Democritus of the pre-Socratics) the words were used to express ethical demands made on men. One should take as one's model the boldness of a hero, or one should imitate the good example of one's teacher or parents.

490

2. The words have a central place in Platonic cosmology. The whole of the lower world of appearances is only the corresponding, imperfect, visible copy or likeness (*mimēma*) of the invisible archetype in the higher world of the Ideas (*Timaeus* 38–48). At first the *mimēsis* concept is a purely ontological designation which expresses the analogous relationship of the various levels of Being to each other. The phrase "to imitate God" (*Phaedrus*, 252 f.) here indicates reflection on the image of the Idea which sticks in the memory and the development of this given state of affairs. It does not contain the crucial element for imitation in an ethical sense – personal decision. Only later do Gk. philosophers reflect an increasing ethical influence on these originally purely cosmological ideas.

 or The LXX only attests *mimeomai* and *mimēma* in the Apocrypha (Wis. 4:2; 9:8; 15:9; 4 Macc. 9:32; 13:9). The Rabbis were the first to speak of imitation of God in the sense of developing the image of God in men. In the Pseudepigrapha in addition to the exhortation to imitate men of outstanding character (Test. Ben. 3:1; 4:1) one can also find the thought of the imitation of God (i.e. keeping his commands, Test. Ash. 4:3) and of particular characteristics of God (Aristeas 188, 210, 280 f.).

nt In the NT *mimeomai* is found only 4 times (2 Thess. 3:7,9; Heb. 13:7; 3 Jn. 11); *mimētēs* 6 times (1 Cor. 4:16; 11:1; Eph. 5:1; 1 Thess. 1:6; 2:14; Heb. 6:12); and *symmimētēs* only once in Phil. 3:17. All are used with an ethical-imperative aim and are linked with obligation to a specific kind of conduct.

1. The words are applied to particular persons who are obvious living examples for the life of → faith. When the apostle Paul puts himself forward as such a model (1 Cor. 4:16; 11:1; Phil. 3:17; 2 Thess. 3:7, 9), he does not think of himself as the personal embodiment of an ideal which must be imitated. In fact, prior to the demand to imitate him, he deliberately places a confession of his own imperfection (Phil. 3:12). The *typos*, the example or type (→ Image), is not here a representation of particular qualities, but first conduct which is shaped by a definite goal (Phil. 2:12–15), and secondly the experience of persecution and suffering for Christ's sake – in short it is life in fellowship with Christ. To be an imitator of the apostle accordingly means laying hold of Christ in the consciousness of one's own imperfection and letting one's life be continually re-moulded by Christ in obedience to him (cf. 3 Jn. 11). The full significance of this is clear in 1 Cor. 4:16. When Paul reminds the Corinthians in v. 17 of his ways and his teaching, his demand for imitation means that they are to direct their manner of living in accordance with the instructions and conduct of the apostle. Even if this assumes an apostolic authority which requires implicit respect (cf. W. Michaelis, *TDNT* IV 667 ff.), Paul's language here cannot be reduced to a demand for personal obedience.

2. (a) Paul never intends to bind the demand for imitation to his own person. It is always ultimately to the One whom he himself follows. On two occasions he names Christ alongside himself as the "type" to be imitated in exhortation to self-correction. These examples show how believers share Christ's lot passively in what they suffer (1 Thess. 1:6) and how they may actively imitate him in his love (1 Cor. 11:1). The present writer believes that when Paul refers to Christ, he is not thinking of specific occasions in the earthly life of Jesus, but rather of the authority of the Exalted One present in his word and his Holy Spirit and of the kind of behaviour

that would be consistent with existence in the sphere of the Lordship of Christ. Christ is to be the Subject who fashions the activity and fulfilment of our life, not its Object (W. Elert, *Das christliche Ethos*, 303). He is more than a general human pattern. He is the archetype, not an *exemplum*, but the *exemplar* (Luther, *WA* 2, 518, 16). Paul's appeal to imitate Christ is otherwise conveyed by other phrases (Rom. 15:3, 7; 2 Cor. 5:14; 8:9; 10:1; Phil. 2:5 ff.; Eph. 5:2, 25; cf. Mk. 10:45; Jn. 13:15).

(b) The letter to the Hebrews uses the word-group much as Paul does. The exhortation of Heb. 6:11 precedes the demand for imitation: "We desire each one of you to show the same earnestness in realizing the full assurance of hope until the end". As imitators, however, they do not stand alone. They are numbered in the ranks of the fathers. The attitude of faith of the OT fathers (6:12) and their own teachers (13:7), as an example of those who have finished their course, strengthens the conviction and confidence of those believers who find themselves still *en route*.

(c) Eph. 5:1 is the first place where the thought appears that God should be imitated – not as a metaphysical Being with certain attributes which might serve as ideals for us, but in his nature as graphically revealed in Christ. What is to be imitated is Christ's obedient adherence to the Father's will, shown in love and forgiveness (cf. Matt. 5:48 par.).

3. "Imitation" in the NT is consequently not conceived as the reproduction of a given pattern. It is the way of life of the man who derives his being from the forgiveness of God. It is not the way to salvation through pious achievement, but an attitude of thanks in response to the salvation that has been given to us (cf. H. Conzelmann, *Epheser*, 83). The summons to discipleship can only be fulfilled, when a man is grasped by Christ and undergoes the transformation which existence under the Lordship of Christ involves.   *W. Bauder*

ὀπίσω

ὀπίσω (*opisō*), behind, after; ὄπισθεν (*opisthen*), from behind.

CL *opisō* (from the root *opi*; cf. Lat. *ob*, facing, against) is an adv. of place, meaning behind, to the rear, backwards. *opisthen* also means from behind as well as being equivalent to *opisō*. Both are also used of time and occur as adv., noun and prep.

OT 1. These words translate Heb. *'aḥar* and its derivatives in the LXX. Linked with vbs. of motion, they indicate following behind as in processions after the ark (cf. Jos. 3:3; 6:9); following in war (1 Sam. 11:7); political allegiance (Jdg. 9:3 f.; 2 Sam. 2:10; Ezek. 29:16); following as a prophet's servant (1 Ki. 19:20 f.); devotion to a lover (Ruth 3:10; Jer. 2:5; Hos. 2:7, 15); following after things (1 Sam. 8:3; Ezek. 33:31; Sir. 31:8) and spiritual objects (2 Ki. 13:2; Isa. 65:2; Jer. 3:17); self-giving (Hos. 1:2 *opisthen*; Exod. 34:15 f.); and, in a religious sense, dedication and obedience to a god (1 Ki. 19:21; Jdg. 2:12 f.; Jer. 2:23; 7:6, 9; Ezek. 20:16; of Yahweh, Deut. 13:4; Sir. 46:10). As a movement of the heart, *opisō* can indicate the direction of the whole human personality (1 Ki. 11:1 ff.; Ps. 63:9; Jer. 16:12).

2. In Jud. too, following behind someone is a sign of subservient subordination to a person of respect. As a Rab. expression, it refers to the state of being a pupil, largely with respect to the shared life with the teacher (→ *mathētēs* OT 2 (b)).

492

NT The temporal use is found in the NT (e.g. in Matt. 3:11; Mk. 1:7; Jn. 1:15, 27, 30; cf. in the OT 1 Sam. 24:22; Eccl. 10:14). And OT phraseology indicating attachment is found in Lk. 21:8; Jn. 6:66; 12:19; Acts 5:37; 20:30; 1 Tim. 5:15; 2 Pet. 2:10; Jude 7; Rev. 13:3. However, *opisō* is largely used in the NT with the gen. predominantly of persons. Those passages where the gen. *opisō mou* refers to Jesus (cf. Matt. 10:38; Mk. 1:17 par., 20; 8:34 par.) are particularly significant theologically. *opisō* here takes on the meaning of *akoloutheō*, follow, go "behind" someone (cf. Mk. 2:14). Mk. 1:17 f. has this call to discipleship in its simplest form: "Come after me (*deute opisō mou*), and I will make you to become fishers of men." "Three points appear to be of interest. 1. The call comes from Jesus. That is the beginning of it all. 2. It is a call to service, and Jesus himself creates the possibility of such service. 3. Obedience entails forsaking old ties" (E. Schweizer, *Lordship and Discipleship*, 13). "Going behind" means having a share in the fellowship of Christ's life and suffering (Matt. 10:38 par.; 16:24 par.; cf. *opisthen* Lk. 23:26). Matt. 16:23, which Bornkamm translates "you would lead me astray" (*Tradition and Interpretation in Matthew*, 47), shows that it is precisely the suffering of discipleship that Peter does not understand, because he does not comprehend the way of the Lord himself. The meaning of discipleship is that Jesus goes on ahead and prescribes the way.

Looking back is no more possible for the disciple than it is for someone who flees persecution (Lk. 17:31 f. par.; cf. Gen. 19:17, 26), for the ploughman at his furrow (Lk. 9:62; cf. 1 Ki. 19:20 f.), or for the runner who dares not look back at the ground he has covered but only at the finishing-post (Phil. 3:13). For the disciple of Jesus, there is no looking back at associations and ties that are left behind, no looking back into the past, and no looking back at former achievements.
→ Apostle, → Bishop, → Call, → Confess, → Deny, → Faith   *W. Bauder*

(a). W. Bauer, *Orthodoxy and Heresy in Earliest Christianity*, 1972; E. Best, "Discipleship in Mark: Mark 8.22–10.50", *SJT* 23, 1970, 323–37; W. P. de Boer, *The Imitation of Paul*, Dissertation Kampen, 1962; D. Bonhoeffer, *The Cost of Discipleship*, 1956[6]; G. Bornkamm *Jesus of Nazareth*, 1960; G. Bornkamm, G. Barth and H. J. Held, *Tradition and Interpretation in Matthew*, 1963; R. Bultmann, *Theology of the New Testament*, II, 1955, 203–36; and *History of the Synoptic Tradition*, 1968[2]; H. von Campenhausen, *Ecclesiastical Authority and Spiritual Power in the Church of the First Three Centuries*, 1969; O. Cullmann, *Peter: Disciple – Apostle – Martyr*, 1962[2]; D. Daube, "Responsibilities of Master and Disciples in the Gospels," *NTS* 19, 1972–3, 1–15; S. Freyne, *The Twelve: Disciples and Apostles. A Study in the Theology of the First Three Gospels*, 1968; A. R. George, *Communion with God in the New Testament*, 1953; J. Jeremias, *New Testament Theology*, I, 1971, 203–30; G. Kittel, *akoloutheō*, *TDNT* I 210–16; E. M. Kredel, "Disciple," *EBT* I 209–13; W. Michaelis, *mimeomai* etc., *TDNT* IV 659–74; K. H. Rengstorf, *manthanō* etc., *TDNT* IV 390–61; K. H. Schelkle, *Discipleship and Priesthood*, 1966; R. Schnackenburg, *The Moral Teaching of the New Testament*, 1964; E. Schweizer, *Lordship and Discipleship*, 1960; H. Seesemann, *opisō*, *TDNT* V 289–92; H. Thielicke, *Theological Ethics*, I, 1966; II, 1969; E. J. Tinsley, *The Imitation of God in Christ: An Essay in the Biblical Basis of Christian Spirituality*, 1960; and "Some Principles for Reconstructing a Doctrine of the Imitation of Christ," *SJT* 25, 1972, 45 ff.
(b). H. D. Betz, *Nachfolge und Nachahmung Jesu Christi im Neuen Testament*, *BHTh* 37, 1967; H. W. Beyer, P. Althaus, H. Conzelmann, G. Friedrich and A. Oepke, *Die kleineren Briefe des Apostels Paulus*, *NTD* 8, 1968[11]; E. Dinkler, *Jesu Wort vom Kreuztragen*, *BZNW* 21, 1954, 110 ff. (=*Signum Crucis* 1967, 77 ff.); F. Frerichs, "Nachfolge Christi," *EKL* II 1495 ff.; P. Gaechter, *Petrus und seine Zeit*, 1958; M. Hengel, *Nachfolge und Charisma*, 1968; H. Kahlefeld, *Der Jünger*, 1962[2]; H.-J. Iwand, *Predigtmeditationen*, 1964, 272 ff., 622 ff.; H. Kosmala, "Nachfolge und Nachahmung Gottes: I Im griechischen Denken, II Im jüdischen Denken," *Annual of the Swedish Theological Institute* 2, 1963, 38 ff.; 3, 1964, 65 ff.; H.-J. Kraus, *Psalmen*, I–II, *BKAT* XV, 1966[3];

E. Larsson, *Chistus als Vorbild*, 1962; E. Lohse, E. Kähler, N. H. Søe, "Nachfolge Christi," *RGG*[3] IV 1286 ff.; A. Oepke, "Nachfolge und Nachahmung Christi im Neuen Testament," *Allg. ev. luth. KZ* 71, 1938, 850 ff., 866 ff.; B. Rigaux, "Die 'Zwölf' in Geschichte und Kerygma," in H. Ristow and K. Matthiae, eds., *Der historische Jesus und der kerygmatische Christus*, (1960) 1962[2], 468–86; A. Schlatter, *Die Geschichte des Christus*, 1921; A. Schulz, *Nachfolge und Nachahmen. Studien über das Verhältnis der neutestamentlichen Jüngerschaft zur urchristlichen Vorbildethik*, 1962; A. Schulz and R. Hoffmann, "Nachfolge Christi," *LTK* VII 758 ff.; T. Süss, "Nachfolge Jesu," *TLZ* 78, 1953, 129 ff.; R. Thysmann, "L'Éthique de l'imitation du Christ dans le Nouveau Testament," *Ephemerides Theologicae Lovanienses* 42, 1966, 138 ff.; H. Wildberger, *Jesaja, BKAT* X, Lieferungen 1–3, 1968; G. Wingren, "Was bedeutet die Forderung der Nachfolge Christi in evangelischer Ethik?" *TLZ* 75, 1950, 385–92; E. Wolf, "Schöpferische Nachfolge," *Peregrinatio*, II, 1965, 230 ff.; J. H. Yoder, *Nachfolge Christi als Gestalt politischer Verantwortung*, 1964.

Discipline, Prudence, Immorality, Prostitute

Discipline is a concept that plays a significant part in the philosophical ethics of classical Greece and also in Hellenism. It is striking that the word-groups discussed here are relatively rarely attested in the NT. The life of man in the Bible is determined not so much by self-control in the sense of an autonomous ethic as by the commandments of God. *enkrateia* denotes more the power and control one has over oneself, whereas *sōphrosynē* (in cl. Gk. one of the four cardinal virtues) describes more strongly the proper moderation which does not overstep the set limits. The word-group *porneuō* is treated here as its antonym, because in *porneia* the limits which are willed and set by God (in this case in the realm of sexual ethics) are obliterated. → Marriage, art. *moicheuō*; → Teach, art. *paideuō*.

ἐνκράτεια

ἐνκράτεια (*enkrateia*), self-control, self-restraint, abstinence; ἐνκρατής (*enkratēs*), master of oneself, self-controlled; ἐνκρατεύομαι (*enkrateuomai*), have control over oneself, exert self-restraint, abstain; ἀκρασιά (*akrasia*), licentiousness, lack of self-control; ἀκρατής (*akratēs*), uncontrolled, unbridled; ἀσκέω (*askeō*), practise something, engage in.

CL 1. *enkrateia* and *enkratēs* contain the root *krat-* which means power or control. *enkratēs* accordingly denotes a man who has power in the physical or intellectual sense (the opposite being *akratēs*). *enkrateia* is also used absolutely of having power over oneself. It then means self-control in the sense of perseverance, steadfastness or restraint with reference to sexual matters (the opposite being *akrasia*). From *enkratēs* is derived the vb. *enkrateuomai*, to abstain from something.

2. The idea of *enkrateia* is first introduced into ethics by Socrates as one of the chief virtues (cf. Xen., *Mem.* 1, 54). Plato and Aristotle adopted it in turn. For Plato *enkrateia*, the control of the sensual drives, is basically a popular expression for → *sōphrosynē* (cf. *Phaedr.*, 256b; *Rep.*, 403e). According to Aristotle, the one who is *enkratēs* has strong desires but is able to suppress them, whereas the one who is *sōphrōn* is elevated above all such fierce drives (*Magna Moralia*, 2, 6, 1203b 13 ff.). Among the Stoics, *enkrateia* was taken as a sign of human freedom. It was part of being truly human to moderate one's desires, particularly one's sexual drive and enjoyment of food and drink. The Neo-Pythagoreans developed a dualistic

494

system: the body must be kept in check through asceticism, so that the soul may rise to God. In making one fit for cultic worship, asceticism also played a large part in the ancient world (→ Pure, art. *hagnos*). Philo praised *enkrateia* as transcendence over one's desires and passions (*Spec.Leg.*, 1, 149, 173; 2, 195; 4, 112). The Essenes at the time of Jesus are known to have recommended celibacy, and also to have lived ascetically in various other ways, e.g. in regard to possessions, food and vigils (Josephus, *War*, 2, 120, 138, 150; cf. H. Ringgren, *The Faith of Qumran*, 1963, 139 f., 237 f.). (See further W. Grundmann, *TDNT* II 340 f.)

3. The vb. *askeō* involves a related idea. Originally it meant to exert oneself, to practise, particularly in the sense of technical work and ornamental decoration (Hom.). In Xen. it is employed of physical, gymnastic exercises, so that an athlete can be directly called an *askētēs*. Epict. spoke of systematic intellectual asceticism, the practice of doing good. This reflects the later meaning of the term: the fundamental, in certain circumstances life-long, taming of the passions, especially of sexual desire.

OT In the LXX *enkrateia* occurs only 3 times, exclusively in the Wisdom literature (Sir. 18:15, 30; 4 Macc. 5:34), meaning abstinence from excess. *enkratēs* (11 times, only in apocryphal writings) and *enkrateuomai* (3 times) are not so much special ascetic terms. They chiefly denote that one has gained or is in control of something (cf. Gen. 43:31; 1 Sam. 13:12; Sir. 6:27). *askeō* is found in the LXX only in 2 Macc. 15:4. Systematic asceticism is not known in the OT, apart from → fasting. The Heb. *'innâh nep̄eš*, to humble the soul, occurs in that connection (Lev. 16:12, 31; 23:27, 32; Num. 29:7; 30:14; Isa. 58:3, 5; Ps. 35:13).

NT In the NT the word-group *enkrateia* (including *akrasia* in Matt. 23:25 and 1 Cor. 7:5, and *akratēs* in 2 Tim. 3:3) is attested only 10 times, of which 4 are in Paul (1 Cor. 7:5, 9; 9:25; Gal. 5:23). *askeō* is found only in Acts 24:16 ("I also take pains at all times to have a clear conscience"). In the Gospels the words are entirely lacking apart from Matt. 23:25, where *akrasia*, shamelessness, self-indulgence, rapacity (RSV), occurs in pictorial language.

1. This statistical survey does not, however, compel us to say that there are no traces of asceticism in the Gospels. Lk., in particular, underlines an ascetic trait, especially with regard to one's possessions, without using these words (cf. Matt. 5:3 ff. with Lk. 6:20 ff.; Matt. 25:34 ff. with Lk. 14:14; also 12:33; 14:33; cf. H. von Campenhausen, *Tradition and Life in the Church*, 1968, 90–122). Viewed as a whole, however, asceticism in the sense of renunciation of possessions, sexual activity, and food-restrictions is not generally enjoined by the teaching of Jesus in the Gospels. This does not mean that renunciation by a particular person in a concrete situation is excluded (cf. the story of the rich young ruler, Matt. 19:21). It is only that from such passages (cf. Matt. 11:19; 9:14 ff.; Mk. 2:18 f.; Lk. 5:33 ff.), one cannot deduce a basic ascetic attitude on the part of Jesus, just as one cannot deduce his will for the overall validity of an ascetic ethic. Renunciation is only demanded where something stands in the way of following Jesus.

2. In Acts 24:25 *enkrateia* is found alongside righteousness and judgment as the theme of Paul's proclamation. "Self-control" may here be an allusion to the marriage of the procurator Felix, which was the result of adultery. But it may also

simply be an expression of an ascetic tendency which Lk. continues in Acts (cf. 2:44 f.; 4:23).

3. 1 Cor. 7 shows clearly that Paul affirms sexual asceticism for himself and regards it as desirable for the members of the congregation (v. 1). But Paul does not thus turn marriage and sexual intercourse into a sin (cf. v. 28). "Come together so that Satan may not tempt you on the grounds of your immodesty (*akrasia*)" (v. 5). It is therefore better to remain within marriage than merely to aggravate suppressed drives by compulsory abstinence (v. 9: "but if they cannot exercise self-control" [*enkrateuontai*]). Asceticism for Paul has no redemptive significance. And yet for him marriage is a concession to the constraint of human drives. Celibacy or abstinence (7:7) is preferable for him. In the expectation of the imminence of the end of the world marriage has lost its value for Paul as an ordinance of creation. He would like to preserve the Corinthians from the hardships that being married involves in the final catastrophe (7:26). They are to be free in the service of their Lord: "Every athlete exercises self-control [*enkrateuetai*] in all things" (9:25). Nevertheless, he does not recommend the break up of → marriage which is a picture of the relationship between Christ and the church (Eph. 5:21–33; Col. 3:18 f.).

enkrateia occurs in Gal. 5:23 in a list of the fruit of the Spirit. Self-control or discipline is here obviously the positive behaviour which is set over against the fornication (→ *porneia*), impurity, debauchery and idolatry of vv. 19 f. *enkrateia*, the possibility of fashioning one's life in the way God desires, is never something firmly at one's disposal. It must always be received afresh as the gift of the Spirit in one's commitment to the gospel. Whether *enkrateia* in Gal. 5:23 refers only to the sexual side or is meant more comprehensively is disputed. What one must hold on to, however, is the fact that, despite the high esteem in which Paul holds sexual asceticism, it is never dualistically anchored (see above CL) and never acquires any inherent value.

4. 2 Tim. 3:3 (*akratēs* in a list of vices) and Tit. 1:8 (*enkratēs* in a list of virtues) do not betray an ascetic attitude in the Pastoral Epistles. Rather, the Pastoral Epistles see marriage as a healthy ordinance of life willed by God, in contrast to some of Paul's opponents (1 Tim. 5:10, 14 f.; Tit. 1:16). Part of the intention of the catalogue of vices in 2 Tim. 3:1 ff., with its affirmation of marriage, is to warn against its dissolution and against a false self-gratification in the last days. Equally, the elder of a congregation should be *enkratēs*, chaste (Tit. 1:8), i.e. not a dissolute character, but married to one woman (1:6; cf. 1 Tim. 3:2), which may be a reflection on the social attitudes of the times.

5. *enkrateia* occurs twice in 2 Pet 1:6. In this late writing of the NT canon, yet another attempt is made with a clearly Hel. vocabulary to make faith intelligible in a new situation, which differed from that at the beginning, so that the tension between the past and the eschatological future is restrained. The author characterizes the attitude of Christians in the period following the apostolic preaching to the time of the Parousia (with the attendant danger of weariness) in a chain of virtues: faith, virtue, knowledge, self-control (*enkrateia*), patience, godliness, love for all men. The list exhibits the movement by which faith comes alive and becomes fruitful in love. *enkrateia* is here hardly to be understood in an ascetic sense. The term is used rather in its original meaning of having power over oneself (→ CL, 1),

496

not however on the basis of some supposed self-realization, but on the basis of the knowledge which comes from → faith (vv. 5 and 6). It is the precondition for the patience which the believer needs to prevent him from becoming weary.

H. Baltensweiler

πορνεύω

πορνεύω (*porneuō*), practise prostitution or sexual immorality, commit fornication; πόρνη (*pornē*), harlot, prostitute; πόρνος (*pornos*), an immoral person, a fornicator; πορνεία (*porneia*) unchastity, harlotry, prostitution, fornication.

CL *porneuō* from *pernēmi* (to sell) (Hdt. onwards), means trans. to prostitute. It is usually in the pass. of the woman: to prostitute oneself, become a prostitute. But it is also used of the man, to whore, to fornicate. Derivations include (a) *pornē* (Aristot. onwards), a woman who is for sale, a prostitute, courtesan; (b) *pornos* (likewise Aristot. onwards), the fornicator who has sexual intercourse with prostitutes, but then also an immoral man, i.e. one who allows himself to be misused for immoral purposes for money, a male prostitute; and (c) *porneia* (Dem. onwards, rare in cl. Gk) harlotry, unchastity (also of a homosexual nature).

1. The word-group can describe various extra-marital sexual modes of behaviour insofar as they deviate from accepted social and religious norms (e.g. homosexuality, promiscuity, paedophilia, and especially prostitution).

(a) According to G. van der Leeuw, "the instincts of sex and hunger are the two great impelling factors whereby the will climbs to power and even rises to heaven; in the face of these the consciousness of impotence collapses. Food and drink on the one hand, and on the other sexual intercourse, are therefore not merely the two outstanding symbols of community with the god, but are also the means wherewith human potency sets to work" (*Religion in its Essence and Manifestation*, 1964[2], 230). For this the most varied religious actions and rites are required. These include cultic prostitution as part of the ancient fertility rites. It was believed that performance of sexual intercourse in the sanctuary would ensure the fertility of everything living in the land and prevent the loss of the procreative and generative faculties. Evidence of cultic prostitution is first found in Babylon. Hdt. recounts that once in her life every Babylonian woman had to "sacrifice" herself to the goddess Mylitta by giving her body to a stranger in the temple precincts (1, 199). Similar customs are attested in other areas, including Cyprus.

In the Gk. world cultic prostitution gained acceptance primarily in the great sanctuaries of Corinth, Eryx and Athens. According to the historian Strabo (8, 378), over a thousand courtesans consecrated to Venus lived in Corinth alone (cf. H. Conzelmann, *Korinth und die Mädchen der Aphrodite: zur Religionsgeschichte der Stadt Korinth*, 1967). Religious prostitution played a particular role for Israel in the Baal cult.

(b) In order to be able to understand secular prostitution in Greece, note must be taken of the following facts especially concerning the Ionians: (i) According to a citizenship law of 451 B.C. inhabitants of Athens did not have any citizenship rights if their parents were not both Athenians. For many this meant material disadvantages, so that now non-Athenian women "worked" more and more as prostitutes. Thus began the professional class of *hetaerae*. (ii) The married women were mostly uneducated and were thus regarded as *oikourēma*, a chattel used for looking after the house (thus Eur.) and for bearing children. (iii) Slavery allowed the men to take slave-girls as mistresses (cf. Homer, *Il.*, 8, 284). The following judgment of Demosthenes is interesting and significant: "The *hetaerae* we have for our pleasure, the concubines for the daily care of our bodies, and our wives so that we can have legitimate children and a true guardian of the house" (59, 122). These circumstances led, on the one hand, to an extended and widely ramified system of prostitution. On the other hand, they encouraged the married Athenian women to have sexual relations with the slaves and to indulge in lesbian love. The situation was very different among the Dorians in Sparta. Ancient marriage conditions, which exhibited traits of earlier group marriage, gave less cause for the growth of prostitution. But paedophilia developed there especially, spreading then over the whole of Greece.

2. The Stoics strove for a new sexual ethic. They did not reject sexual pleasure, but they unanimously condemned all adultery and extra-marital sexual intercourse. The Stoic Musonius Rufus also rejected that of the man with slave-girls and *hetaerae*.

OT 1. The word-group *pornē* in the LXX generally stands for Heb. *zānâh*, to commit fornication, whereas *moicheuō*, to commit adultery (→ Marriage), regularly represents *nā'ap*. Both word-groups are therefore to be clearly separated.

2. Prostitution was likewise not unknown in Israel. But at the beginning it was evidently not felt to be a serious moral problem (cf. Gen. 38:15; Jdg. 15:1; 1 Ki. 3:16). In certain circumstances, therefore, both prostitution (only female prostitution, not male, was ever tolerated) and extra-marital intercourse on the part of the man (e.g. with his maid – Gen. 16:1 f.; 30:1 ff.) were sanctioned. This may have been because of the high infant mortality in the East, where there was often great concern for the preservation of the tribe. (For extra-marital intercourse of the women, → Marriage, art. *moicheuō*.)

Prostitution first became a serious problem through confrontation with the fertility cults, in particular the Baal cult. Baal's "relationship to the earth was that of a *hieros gamos* [a sacred marriage]; he is the mythical generative power that fructifies the earth by means of the sperm of the rain. Human beings share in his fertilising power by entering this mystery and imitating it" (G. von Rad, *Old Testament Theology*, I, 1962, 22). This took place through intercourse with a prostitute in the sanctuary, which was supposed to bring man into cosmic harmony. Since this religion was not simply – as has often been falsely assumed – concerned with gross sensuality but with sensuality in a particular "spiritual" form, it had a strong attraction for the educated Israelites. The prostitutes in the sanctuary were respected women. The bitter struggle (e.g. of Hosea) was primarily directed against Israel's belief that they owed the blessings of the land to the rites of the Baal-cult, the spirit of harlotry, which had gained acceptance in the Yahweh-cult. Israel "does not know that it is I who gave her corn, new wine and oil, who lavished upon her silver and gold" (Hos. 2:10 [EVV v. 8]). "Israel, however, misunderstood both the giver and the gifts; she failed to see that she had been brought into a *status confessionis* before Yahweh because of these gifts; rather, she fell victim to a mythic divinisation of husbandry and of its numinous, chthonic origins" (G. von Rad, op. cit., II, 1965, 142). It is thus not primarily the sexual intercourse that shocks the

498

prophets, but the absolute lack of personal faithfulness. The priests have disregarded the tradition of the word of Yahweh and lost their orientation (cf. Hos. 4:4–19). Cultic prostitution, according to the accounts of Jeremiah (cf. 3:1–9; 5:7 ff.) and Ezekiel (esp. chs. 16 and 23), had taken on disgusting forms. It became – as harlotry – a picture of Israel's apostasy from Yahweh, depicting the whole forlorn situation in which Israel found itself before Yahweh. It was out of this struggle against the Baalization of the Yahweh cult that the sharp rejection of any kind of prostitution in Israel arose. "Passages which originally prohibited cultic prostitution through the sacred Law of God became in the later tradition general prohibitions of fornication in Israel. Acc. to Lv. 19:29 the toleration or even the promoting of fornication, e.g. on the part of a daughter of Israel, defiles the whole land and brings it under the threat of God's judgment" (F. Hauck and S. Schulz, *TDNT* VI 585 f.). Quite distinct from immorality was the so-called Levirate marriage, i.e. the obligatory marriage between a childless widow and her brother-in-law to prevent the extinction of the name of the dead man in Israel (Gen. 38:6–30; Deut. 25:5–10; Ruth 1–4; cf. H. H. Rowley, "The Marriage of Ruth", *The Servant of the Lord and Other Essays*, 1952, 161–86).

3. In later Jewish Rab. language, $z^e n\hat{u}t$ (*porneia*) is to be understood as including not only prostitution and any kind of extra-marital sexual intercourse (Pirqe Aboth 2:8) but also all marriages between relatives forbidden by Rab. law (cf. SB II 729 f.). Incest (Test. Rub. 1, 6; Test. Jud. 13, 6; cf. Lev. 18:6–18) and all kinds of unnatural sexual intercourse (e.g. Test. Ben. 9:1) were viewed as fornication (*porneia*). One who surrenders to it shows ultimately that he has broken with God (cf. Wis. 14:27 f.). Thus Jub. can even call *porneia* an unforgivable mortal sin (33:13, 18). In order to avoid fornication, early marriage was recommended. In the so-called "lists of vices" of Hel. Diaspora Judaism, adultery and prostitution are found alongside idolatry, sorcery and murder. Although intercourse with a slave-girl or a concubine is condemned as a grievous sin (cf. Deut. 23:17 f.), and Israel "boasted repeatedly of the purity of its marriages ... in contrast to the pagan environment", this boast requires to be strictly limited (SB III 66 with many examples). Not without reason could R. Hillel have judged: "Many slave-girls – much fornication." Correspondingly the Dead Sea Scrolls give frequent warnings against such fornication (1QS 1:6; 4:10; CD 2:16; 4:17, 20).

NT In the NT the main weight of the word-group (used in all 55 times, of which *porneia* alone accounts for 25) falls clearly in Paul (21 times, of which 1 Cor. and 2 Cor. account for 15) and in Rev. (19 times). From this one realizes that the question of *porneia* comes up for discussion particularly in the confrontation with the Gk. world and in the context of the final judgment (there again linked with a person's relationship with God).

1. There was also prostitution in Israel at the time of Jesus. Whereas, however, according to Jewish law, prostitutes and tax collectors were excluded from the people of God and thus from salvation, Jesus proclaimed to them God's forgiveness on the basis of their faith, and thus the way to salvation (Matt. 21:31 f.; Heb. 11:31; cf. Jas. 2:25). Their faith is held up as an example for the self-confident priests and elders of the people. This in no way softens Jesus' rejection of prostitution (Mk. 7:21 par.). But it does mean that, along with other sins, it is no longer

499

excluded from forgiveness. It is not absolutely clear whether *porneia* in the "exceptive clause" (Matt. 5:32; 19:9) is to be understood simply as extra-marital sexual intercourse in the sense of *moicheia* or as prostitution (→ Marriage; → Divorce). Some exegetes argue that the reason for divorce could only be that during the marriage the woman's earlier activity as a prostitute became known. Most exegetes, however, suppose that *porneia* is to be understood synonymously with *moicheia* as adultery. Whether in Matt., by contrast with Mk. 3:4; 10:2–12 and Lk. 16:18, we have a secondary, mitigating qualification of the prohibition of adultery, and whether the Matt. version goes back to Jesus himself are disputed. G. Bornkamm holds that in the conflict between the various Rab. schools about what constituted sufficient grounds for divorce, Matt. with the secondary "exceptive clause" represents the strict standpoint of the school of Shammai. "The radical prohibition by Jesus, to which the whole line of argument, even in Matthew, in vv. 4 ff. (Mark 10:6 ff.), is aimed, is thereby robbed of its stringency" (G. Bornkamm, G. Barth, H. J. Held, *Tradition and Interpretation in Matthew*, 1963, 26). ([Ed.] John Murray, on the other hand, holds that the clause goes back to Jesus himself, and that Matt. is dealing with a further question which Mk. and Lk. do not enter upon. Matt. 19:9 is just as absolute as Mk. 10:11 and Lk. 16:18 in abrogating the permission implied in Deut. 24:1–4. The Mosaic Law was not concerned with *divorce for adultery* [for death was the prescribed penalty for those found guilty of adultery, Deut. 22:22] and thus it did not enter upon the question of the *right of remarriage* in the event of such a divorce. Murray holds that this is the question that Matt. is treating here [*Divorce*, 1953, 51 ff.].)

2. In the Pauline writings the word-group *pornē* denotes any kind of illegitimate sexual intercourse. Paul's usage of the word-group predominantly in 1 Cor. (14 times) shows that the problem was posed for him in an acute way in this church. Corinth was a town with traditional temple prostitution (see above CL 1). As an important port it was especially open to the syncretism of the ancient world and stamped with sexual licentiousness in the slums around the harbour and in the sanctuaries. But it was from the circles of this harbour proletariat that many members of the Corinthian Church came (cf. 2 Cor. 12:21). In addition a kind of Gnosticism (→ Knowledge) invaded the Corinthian community. The pneumatic who boasted of his freedom ("all things are lawful") believed that in mystic exaltation he has left the limitations of temporality behind him, and was able to live out a life of unlimited freedom within the context of this world. It is against this background that the problem of incest is to be seen (intercourse of the son with his step-mother). Paul deals with this in 1 Cor. 5:1 ff. If the congregation does not separate from such unchaste persons, the whole church is endangered (5:9 ff.), and stands under God's judgment (→ Destroy, art. *olethros*). Since gnostic dualism saw in corporeality something that decayed and perished, sexual needs relating to one's body could be freely and spontaneously expressed. Paul passionately resisted this outlook (1 Cor. 6:9–20). The stomach is meant for food, but the human body is not intended for unchastity (6:13). Human existence cannot be dissected into two realities, a sarkic and pneumatic (v. 15 ff.). From *porneia* as from *eidololatria*, idolatry, one must flee (6:18; 10:14), because *porneia* cannot be secularized in the way the Corinthians hold. It is rather as if a religious and demonic power is let loose in *porneia*. "It is manifestly a different spirit, a *pneuma akatharton* (Matt. 10:1),

a spirit that is incompatible and irreconcilable with Christ, which takes control of man in *porneia* (Iwand, op. cit., p. 615). Because man does not have a *sōma* (→ Body) but is *sōma* (i.e. is conceived as an indivisible totality), he is either a member of the body of Christ with his total reality or equally totally linked to a *pornē* (1 Cor. 6:15–19; cf. Heb. 12:16). Thus Paul has to keep on warning not only this congregation (1 Cor. 7:2; 10:8), but also others (Gal. 5:19; Eph. 5:3; 1 Thess. 4:3) specifically against *porneia*, and with the greatest urgency, because it affects the whole person.

3. In Rev. unbridled sexual excess is mentioned among the chief sins of the pagans (9:21), just as fornicators are mentioned among the obvious sinners who are threatened by the second death. In the figurative sense → Babylon (chs. 17–19), the great whore, the mother of harlotry and of every obscenity on earth is named as the embodiment and personification of enmity to God. It is here a designation of Rome and its public affairs which stand opposed and hostile to God and his people. Harlotry is therefore meant both literally and also with reference to Rome's wooing for political and economic favours.

H. Reisser

| σωφροσύνη |

σωφροσύνη (*sōphrosynē*), prudence, self-control; σωφρονέω (*sōphroneō*), be of sound mind, be reasonable, prudent; σώφρων (*sōphrōn*), prudent, sensible, self-controlled; σωφρόνως (*sōphronōs*), reasonably, with restraint, soberly.

CL 1. The noun *sōphrosynē*, prudence, belongs to the word-group *sōphroneō*, be reasonable, prudent; *sōphrōn*, sensible, prudent. *sōphrosynē* is formed out of *sōphrōn* (*sao-phrōn*) from the component parts *sōs*, safe, sound, and *phrēn*, the heart as the seat of the passions, the place where the activities of the soul are located. The only word of this group that appears in Homer's *Iliad* is *phrenes* (plur. of *phrēn*). From the time of the *Odyssey sōphrosynē* is found, and from the Tragedians onwards the vb. *sōphroneō*. The meaning is given in *Od.*, 23, 10–14, where *sōphrosynē*, prudence, self-control, is an antonym of ignorance and frivolity and has a corresponding positive sense. The eudaemonism which pervades these early ethical ideas – happiness is the greatest good – is consolidated in Plato into the doctrine of the four cardinal virtues (cf. F. Ueberweg, *History of Philosophy*, I, 1888, 128): wisdom (*sophia*), courage (*andreia*), prudence (*sōphrosynē*), and justice (→ Righteousness, art. *dikaiosynē*). Plato did not tie himself down to a definition of *sōphrosynē*. The main emphasis fell on the man-centred doctrine of the state. In the relationship of the three classes to one another the lower ones have to exercise "moderation". This understanding is equally true for the desires. All → virtues count as a unity, but in their differentiation they include the possibility of further subdivision in each individual case.

2. In the school tradition of the Stoics and in popular philosophy prudence (*sōphrosynē*) is encountered in the scale of the cardinal virtues, and expanded in a series of subordinate virtues (discipline, obedience, decency, propriety, modesty, temperance, self-control). The sub-divisions are intended to give precision and concreteness. In Eur., *Medea*, 635, and *Iph. Aul.*, 544, 1159 the meaning of *sōphrosynē*

501

is narrowed down to moderation and control of the sexual instincts and chastity. (See further U. Luck, *TDNT* VII 1098 ff.)

OT As the LXX shows, there is no Heb. equivalent for *sōphrosynē*, prudence. The noun is found chiefly in 4 Macc. In Hel. Judaism it also assumed a special position as one of the four chief virtues. According to Philo, it is by means of prudence that man is to suppress above all his desires. From the perspective of OT tradition virtue is related to the transcendent divine creator of the world: it is a divine gift, manifested in obedience. In Wis. 8:7 *sōphrosynē* is encountered as one of the four cardinal virtues, which are understood as wisdom, grounded in God.

NT In the NT the noun *sōphrosynē*, prudence, self-control, is found only in Acts 26:25 and 1 Tim. 2:9, 15. *sōphroneō*, to be of sound mind, to be reasonable, prudent, *sōphronōs* and *sōphrōn* occur in Mk. 5:15; Lk. 8:35; 2 Cor. 5:13; cf. Rom. 12:3; 1 Pet. 4:8; and the Pastoral Epistles (Tit. 2:6, 12; 1 Tim. 3:2 etc.). It is no accident that no moral philosophy, and therefore also no scheme of the four cardinal virtues can be found in the NT, even though the paraenetical sections have adopted much from their environment and make use of their language and forms. In the face of an obedience which is linked to definite situations the Gk. ideal of virtue is foreign to the NT. In respect of the catalogues of virtues, however, the Pastoral Epistles stand within the tradition of their Hel. environment, and thus adopt the admonition to be prudent in the correspondingly general sense of moral formulae (1 Tim. 3:2; Tit. 1:8; 2:2). *sōphrōn* in 1 Tim. 2:9 and Tit. 2:5, where the women are addressed directly, again has the meaning of chaste, pure. "To the degree that faith is concerned with the life of Christians in the world, the ethical traditions with their developed concepts help to ward off a pneumatic-ecstatic misunderstanding of the faith" (U. Luck, *TDNT* VII 1103). But there are not here any traces of a direct confrontation. Rather, "being prudent" is here encountered as a Christian virtue, which already displays the stamp of early Christian tradition.

The nature and theme of thoughtful and prudent action are to be based neither in an ethic derived from character nor in moral achievement. This is made clear in Rom. 12:3. Paul sees the capability, the deliberate effort towards thoughtful prudence (*phronein eis to sōphronein*), as grounded in faith. In prudence Paul thus appeals for a basic attitude, which seeks to perceive both its own limitations and the other person in his humanity, and determines its action towards him accordingly. Prudence is not a Stoic "given", nor a virtue based on principle, but a necessary element of a love which maintains the tension between commitment and reflective distance. *S. Wibbing*

→Divorce, → Marriage, → Teach, and the literature mentioned there.

(a). J. B. Bauer and J. Gabriel, "Discipline," *EBT* I 213 f.; W. Bauer, *Orthodoxy and Heresy in Earliest Christianity*, 1972; G. Bertram, *paideuō*, *TDNT* V 596–625; H. von Campenhausen, "Early Christian Asceticism," *Tradition and Life in the Church*, 1968, 90–122; and *Ecclesiastical Authority and Spiritual Power in the Church in the First Three Centuries*, 1969; J. Gray, "The Nature and Function of Adult Christian Education in the Church," *SJT* 19, 1966, 457–63; W. Grundmann, *enkrateia*, *TDNT* II 339–42; F. Hauck and S. Schulz, *pornē TDNT* VI 579–95; G. van der Leeuw, *Religion in its Essence and Manifestation*, 1964²; U. Luck, *sōphrōn*, *TDNT* VII 1097–1104; J. A. Muirhead, *Education in the New Testament*, Monographs in Christian Education 2, 1965; V. C. Pfitzner, *Paul and the Agon Motif: Traditional Athletic Imagery in Pauline Literature*, 1967; J. N. Sevenster, "Education or Conversion: Epictetus and the Gospels," *NovT* 8, 1966, 247–62;

M. Thurian, *Marriage and Celibacy*, 1959; H. Windisch, *askeō*, *TDNT* I 494 f.; H. Malina, "Does *porneia* mean Fornication?" *NovT* 14, 1972, 10–17.
(b). A. Adam, "Enkratiten," *RGG*[3] II 494; R. Bohren, *Kirchenzucht im Neuen Testament*, 1952; H. Chadwick, "Enkrateia," *RAC* V 343 ff.; L. Dürr, "Die Erziehungswesen im Alten Testament und im antiken Orient," *Mitteilungen der vorderasiatisch-ägyptischen Gesellschaft* 36, 2, 1932; W. Gabriel, "Was ist Porneia im Sprachgebrauch Jesu?" *Ethik* 7, 1931, 106 ff.; H.-J. Iwand, *Predigt-Meditationen*, 1964[2], 614 ff.; W. Jentsch, *Urchristliches Erziehungsdenken*, 1951; G. Mensching, H. Bardtke, K. G. Kuhn, F. Lau, "Askese," *RGG*[3] I 639 ff.; H. Strathmann, "Askese," *RAC* I 749 ff.; F. Überweg and K. Praechter, *Grundriss der Geschichte der Philosophie*, I, *Die Philosophie des Altertums*, 1953[13]; S. Wibbing, *Die Tugend- und Lasterkataloge im Neuen Testament*, 1959; W. Zeller, "Askese," *EKL* I 228 ff.

Distinguish, Doubt

διακρίνω

διακρίνω *diakrinō*, make a distinction, judge, judge correctly, render a decision; doubt, waver (only in the NT); διάκρισις (*diakrisis*), distinguishing, quarrel; ἀδιάκριτος (*adiakritos*), unwavering, impartial.

cl *diakrinō* (Hom. onwards; a form of *krinō*, to arrange, strengthened by *dia*) has the basic meaning of 1. (a) to judge, make a distinction, distinguish (Hom., *Od.*, 8, 195). From this is developed the meaning 1. (b) to separate, divide (flocks of sheep, Hom., *Il.*, 2, 475). The vb. is chiefly used as a legal technical term. 2. It also means to give a decision, dispense justice (Xen., *Hel.* 5, 2, 10). 3. In the pass. it is used of an issue that has been brought to a decision (Hdt., 9, 58), and with the meaning to be separated (cf. Hdt., 7, 206).

The noun *diakrisis* (pre-Socratics onwards) means separation, division (Plato), as in 1. (b). It can also mean an interval, judgment (as in law, Plato, *Leg.*, 11, 937b; cf. above 1. (a)), distinction, and quarrel, struggle (Polyb., 18, 28, 3; cf. above 3).

ot In the LXX and Judaism *diakrinō* has chiefly the meaning 1. (a) to judge, distinguish, make a distinction (4 Macc. 1:14; cf. Jos., *War*, 1, 27). In particular, *diakrinō* serves to translate Heb. *šāpaṭ* (Exod. 18:16; 1 Ki. 3:9; 1 Chr. 26:29; Ps. 82(83):1; Ezek. 34:17, 20; Prov. 31:9), and more rarely Heb. *dîn* (Zech. 3:7), with meaning 2. dispense justice. The meaning 3. to take issue, to enter into judgment is also attested (Ezek. 20:33, 36; Joel 4:2 = *šāpaṭ* niph.). The meaning to judge can be intensified to mean examine (Job 12:11; 13:10 = *bāḥan*) and choose (Job 14:9; 15:5 = *bāḥar*). In Philo *diakrinō* can even mean to search out (*Op. Mund.*, 137).

diakrisis is found only once in the LXX in Job 37:16, as a translation of the unique OT word *miplāś* (layer [of clouds], Koehler-Baumgartner, 552). Whether the translator was thinking of something similar to Matt. 16:3, or whether there is a mistake in the translation must remain an open question.

nt 1. In the NT *diakrinō* is found 18 times, including 7 times in Paul (Rom., 1 Cor.), 4 times in Acts and 3 times in Jas. The word-group is entirely lacking in Eph., Col., the Pastorals and Johannine writings. It is rare in the Gospels (3 times).

(a) In 3 instances it means to judge: the appearance of the sky, but not the signs of the times (Matt. 16:3); oneself (1 Cor. 11:31); and prophetic words (1 Cor. 14:29). Twice it means to make a distinction: God makes no distinction between Jews and pagans (Acts 15:9; cf. 11:12). The idea of distinguishing in the sense of making differentiating evaluation is found twice: "Who sees anything different in you?" (1 Cor. 4:7 RSV); "For anyone who eats and drinks without discerning the body eats and drinks judgment upon himself" (1 Cor. 11:29 RSV). The meaning CL 1. (b) "to separate" is lacking (but cf. *Ep. Diog.* 8:7, *panta kata taxin diakrinas*, "arranged all things in order"). As a legal technical term (cf. CL 2), *diakrinō* is found only in 1 Cor. 6:5 of dispensing justice between brother and brother (cf. Ezek. 34:17, 20; Sir. 25:18). It is used twice in the mid. in the sense of take issue with, contend with: the circumcision party with Peter (Acts 11:2); and Michael with the Devil (Jude 9).

(b) The vb. *diakrinō* in the NT takes on the further meaning of doubt (8 times). Rejection of the word of God is found in the OT (cf. Gen. 18:12 with Rom. 4:19, 20 and Isa. 7:1–25), but the OT lacks specific terms for the condition of doubt in the promises of God. Of the vbs. used in pre-NT Gk. for doubt – *distazō* (Plato, Arist.), *amphisbēteō* (Plato, Hdt.), *amphiballō* (Polyb., Aelius Aristides) – only *distazō* occurs twice: "Man of little faith, why did you doubt?" (Matt. 14:31); and "some doubted" (i.e. the promise of Matt. 28:7). No significant difference can be posited between *distazō* and *diakrinō*, though *diakrinō* appears to be more comprehensive.

(c) In some NT passages doubt appears as a lack of → faith and thus as sin (Rom. 14:23). Jas. 1:6–8 relates this to intercession: one must ask in faith (*en pistei*); a man who asks in doubt is a divided man (→ Simplicity). He lacks the power of → hope and yet still prays.

Mk. 11:23 and Matt. 21:21 describe faith which does not doubt as a faith with which one can shift mountains. A comparison with Matt. 17:20, where almost the same *logion* is addressed by Jesus to the disciples "on account of . . . small faith", shows that doubt is akin to faint-heartedness.

In Rom. 4:20 f. doubt comes close to disbelief: "He [Abraham] did not doubt God's promise in disbelief, but grew strong in faith as he gave glory to God, fully convinced that God had power to do what he had promised." Faith is not a substitute knowledge of supernatural matters which have remained hidden despite divine → revelation (art. *epiphaneia*) and human research. Faith is always faith in the promises of the God of history. Doubt is thus a lack of trust in the act of God which he has still to perform and which men are to await.

(d) The dogmatic doubt of others which gives rise to theological apologetics is found explicitly only in the disputed and textually difficult verse Jude 22. Here RSV reads "And convince some, who doubt" (cf. NEB mg. "The are some who raise disputes; these you should refute"; cf. also Arndt. 184). According to Acts 10:20, doubt is lack of trust in the Spirit who desired to set Peter on the road to the pagan believer, Cornelius.

2. The noun *diakrisis* is used in the sense of distinguishing or differentiation, of spirits (1 Cor. 12:10), and of good and bad (Heb. 5:14) (cf. above CL 1 (a) and 1 Clem. 48:5). In Rom. 14:1 and Acts 4:32 (Codex Bezae) it means quarrel (cf. Arndt, 184, and above CL 3). The noun is not found at all in the NT in the sense of doubt. The kind of doubt developed by Descartes in his *Discourse on Method* (1637), especially Part 2, para. 7, for the heuristic method of philosophical comprehension of the world, is foreign to the NT. In the NT the doubter sins against God and his promises, because he judges God falsely.

504

The doubter is ultimately a man whose belief and action do not coincide. He therefore ought to doubt himself, i.e. his own credibility (Jas. 2:4, cf. 1:8, *dipsychos* "double-minded"). His behaviour does not fit with God's behaviour, for in God's wisdom there is nothing wavering or conflicting. The wise man is *adiakritos*, un-wavering, impartial (Arndt, 16), "without uncertainty" (Jas. 3:17 RSV).

If the promise is a structural element of the gospel, hope is a structural element of faith. Strictly speaking, doubt in the NT is directed against hope and confidence. Such doubt is an eschatological problem. It always arises in confrontation with the gospel, in that the possibility of doubt only exists where the gospel can be heard or seen. For it is to this that doubt is related. Doubt in the NT is an affair of the believer rather than of the unbeliever, although doubt can certainly lead to unbelief. → Faith, → Judge   *B. Gärtner*

(a). Arndt, 184; K. Barth, *CD* IV, 3, 1, 434–61; F. Büchsel, *diakrinō, TDNT* III 946 ff.; R. David-son, "Some Aspects of the Theological Significance of Doubt in the Old Testament," *Annual of the Swedish Theological Institute* 7, 1968–69, 41–52; P. Tillich, *Systematic Theology*, II, 1957, III, 1966 (see index); O. J. F. Seitz, "Afterthoughts on the Term 'Dipsychos' ", *NTS* 4, 1957–58, 327–34.
(b). H. Blankertz, "Zweifel," *RGG³* VI 1944 f.; E. Bloch, *Tübinger Einleitung in die Philosophie*, I, 1963, 24 ff.; G. Rein, ed., *Dialog mit Zweifel*, 1969; S. E. Rodke, "Zweifel und Erkenntnis", *Lunds Universitets Årsskrift* NF Avd. I, 41, 3, 1945; E. J. von Tessen-Wesierski, *Wesen und Bedeutung des Zweifels*, 1928.

Divorce

ἀποστάσιον

ἀπολύω (*apolyō*), to set free; ἀποστάσιον (*apostasion*) divorce.

CL *apolyō* means to set free, release, free from; it can be used of releasing prisoners or freeing a person from legal charges. It also means to dismiss, e.g. an individual or a group of people such as an army. It is occasionally used of dismissing a wife (Dion. Hal. 2, 25, 7; Diod. Sic. 12, 18, 1). *apostasion* refers to the relinquishment of a property upon sale (e.g. *apostasiou syngraphē*, deed of cession).

OT Both words are rare in the LXX. *apolyō* is used in a variety of senses, including divorce (Deut. 24:1 ff.; 1 Esd. 9:36; cf. Jos. *Ant.* 15, 259). *apostasion* occurs 4 times with reference to a *sēper keritut*, deed of divorce (Deut. 24:1, 3; Isa. 50:1; Jer. 3:8). OT law allowed divorce if "some indecency" was found in a wife, but forbade it to a man who had been compelled to marry a girl whom he had raped (Deut. 22:28 f.). The penalty for a wife who was discovered not to be virgin was death (Deut. 22:13–21), and the penalty for both partners in a case of adultery was death (Deut. 22:22). In general divorce was frowned upon, but cases did occur (Mal. 2:14–16). After the exile Jewish men who had married foreign wives were required to put them away (Ezr. 9–10; Neh. 13:23 ff.).

NT In the NT *apolyō* has its classical Gk. meanings: to release a prisoner (Mk. 15:6–15 par.; cf. Matt. 18:27 of a debtor); set free from disease (Lk. 13:12); acquit (Lk. 6:37); send people away (Mk. 6:36, 45; 8:3, 9); dismiss from the duties of life, allow to die (Lk. 2:29; cf. dismissal from military service [Moulton–Milligan,

505

66 f.]; Gen. 15:2; Num. 20:29; Tob. 3:6, 13; 2 Macc. 7:9). It is especially used of divorcing a wife (Matt. 1:19; 5:31 f.; 19:3, 7–9; Mk. 10:2, 4, 11 f.; Lk. 16:18). *apostasion* means divorce (Matt. 5:31; 19:7; Mk. 10:4).

Divorce was an accepted fact of life in NT times (for Jewish practice, see SB I, 303–321). A husband was at liberty to put away his wife, provided that the proper legal process of granting her a notice of divorce was followed. But the grounds on which a husband might divorce his wife were disputed between the two rabbinic schools of Shammai and Hillel (teachers in first century B.C.) who allowed divorce only for adultery or for marital incompatibility respectively.

The teaching of Jesus in Mk. 10:1–12 affirms that God's purpose in creation was that husband and wife should become one flesh. Therefore men should not separate what God has joined. Nevertheless, it is admitted that Moses allowed divorce to be carried out, provided that proper legal forms were followed. But this concession was either in view of men's obstinacy of heart towards the commandment of God (perhaps so as to prevent even worse situations arising) or in order to bring such obstinacy out into the open. Jesus' teaching would appear to be that divorce is inconsistent with obedience to God's will. What is not clear is how this teaching affects the Christian attitude to legislation in a non-Christian society, or how the church should treat Christians involved in divorce (see, however, Jn. 7:53–8:11).

In the ensuing discussion Jesus explains why divorce is wrong by defining it in terms of adultery. A man who divorces his wife and remarries is committing adultery *ep'autēn*. The traditional rendering is that he is committing adultery *against* the first wife. If, however, the phrase means that he is committing adultery *with* the second wife, the point is unchanged, for in both cases the adultery can only be against the first wife. It is commonly accepted that in saying this Jesus was going beyond the existing Jewish view of adultery as an offence against a husband, whether by his wife or her lover. Jesus here states that the wife is on the same level as a husband, for his intercourse with another woman is adultery against her. The same principle is applied in Mk. 10:12 to a wife who divorces her husband (as was possible in the Roman world, but not among Jews) and remarries. Remarriage after divorce is adultery. Luke 16:18a makes the same point as Mk. 10:11, and Lk. 16:18b stresses that the man who marries a divorcee commits adultery against her first husband, thus stating that the existing Jewish understanding of adultery must be applied to remarriage as well.

Matt. 19:9 agrees with Mk. 10:11, but allows an exception "in case of adultery". This has often been thought to be a modification of Jesus' saying by the early church in order to bring it into line with the ruling of Shammai, and hence presumably to allow a husband to remarry after divorcing a wife guilty of adultery. An alternative view is that the adultery in question is misconduct on the part of a betrothed woman before the consummation of her marriage. In this case Jewish law demanded that the wedding should not be proceeded with. Before Joseph married Mary he discovered that she was pregnant and felt obliged to put her away according to this law, but received a divine command to continue with the wedding since his wife was free from adultery (Matt. 1:18–25).

A further form of Jesus' teaching appears in Matt. 5:32 where he states that a person who divorces his wife (except for the above reason) is responsible for making her and her second husband commit adultery against him. (For further discussion → Discipline, art. *porneuō*.)

Similar teaching is given by Paul. Only after the death of a person's partner is he or she allowed to remarry (Rom. 7:1–3). He repeats the command of Jesus that husband and wife should not separate from each other; if, however, they do separate they should not remarry (1 Cor. 7:10 f.). In cases where only one partner has become a Christian, the Christian should not regard this as a reason for divorce, perhaps because of the fear that there was something unholy about a union between a Christian and a non-Christian. 1 Cor. 6:15 f. might have led some to this false conclusion, but it refers to union with a prostitute. The marriage bond itself is not a cause of defilement, since the unbelieving partner and any children are "consecrated" by the believing partner. However, if the unbelieving partner seeks a separation, the Christian is to allow it. What is not clear is whether in such a case the Christian partner is free to remarry (the so-called "Pauline privilege"). This particular situation is clearly not one of much contemporary relevance, but it does raise the question whether in the analogous situation of the so-called "innocent party" remarriage is allowable. On this point there does not seem to be any clear NT teaching. *I. H. Marshall*
→ Marriage, Adultery, Bride, Bridegroom

(a). D. Daube, *The New Testament and Rabbinic Judaism*, 1956, 71–86; J. D. M. Derrett, "The Teaching of Jesus on Marriage and Divorce," *Law in the New Testament*, 1970, 363–88; R. H. Ehrlich, "The Indissolubility of Marriage as a Theological Problem", *SJT* 23, 1970, 291–311; F. Hauck, *moicheuō, TDNT* IV 729–35; F. Hauck and S. Schulz, *pornē, TDNT* VI 579–95; A. Isaksson, *Marriage and Ministry in the New Temple*, 1965; W. Lillie, *Studies in New Testament Ethics*, 1961, 118–28; T. W. Manson, *The Sayings of Jesus*, 1949, 136 ff.; J. Murray, *Divorce*, 1953; A. Oepke, *gynē, TDNT* I 776–89; R. Schnackenburg, *The Moral Teaching of the New Testament*, 1965, 132–43; E. Stauffer, *gameō, TDNT* I 648–57.
(b). H. Baltensweiler, *Die Ehe im Neuen Testament. Exegetische Untersuchungen über Ehe, Ehelosigkeit und Ehescheidung*, 1967; G. Delling, "Das Logion Markus 10, 11 und seine Abwandlungen im Neuen Testament," *NovT* 1, 1956, 263–74; H. Greeven, "Ehe nach dem Neuen Testament," *NTS* 15, 1968–69, 365–88; B. Schaller, "Die Sprüche über Ehescheidung und Wiederheirat in der synoptischen Überlieferung," in E. Lohse, ed., *Der Ruf Jesus und die Antwort der Gemeinde*, 1970, 226–46.

Dragon, Serpent, Scorpion, Sting

The term *thērion* is a general expression for a wild → animal or beast. It is used in a bad sense in Rev., but is found elsewhere with a neutral or even a good sense. But *drakōn*, found only in Rev., has always a bad sense. In this there is no difference between the NT and other contemporary religious and epic sources. With few exceptions the snake (*ophis*) is also hostile to God and man. It has symbolic and psychological overtones.

| δράκων | *δράκων* (*drakōn*), dragon. |

CL & OT *drakōn* is derived from *derkomai*, look at, and is the animal with the bewitching, crippling look: the dragon, snake, giant sea-snake, or serpent. In many old myths the dragon or serpent is a picture of the primeval power of chaos.

Its defeat at the hands of a god enabled the world to come into being. In other words, the cosmos is made from chaos. Such concepts may also lie behind some passages in the Bible. God killed dragons in the primeval period (Job 26:12 f.; Isa. 51:8; Ps. 74:13 f.). Monsters or dragons live in the sea (Job. 7:12; Ps. 148:7; Amos 9:3). The time will come when God will kill the dragon in the sea (Isa. 27:1). In calling Pharaoh a dragon, as an enemy of God's people, Ezek. 29:3; 32:2 typifies the attitude of the entire OT to the mythological world view. It is not concerned about mythical beings, their power or their peculiarities. It praises the fact that Yahweh has removed all threats to his people in the past, and will continue to do so. That is why the LXX, in the account of the signs by which Moses was to confirm his call, translates serpent (snake) by dragon, so as to give greater glory to God's action (Exod. 7:9–12).

NT In the NT *drakōn* is found only in Rev., where it is used exclusively as a synonym for → Satan. This is made explicit in 12:9; 20:2. It is a clear ref. back to Gen. 3: "ancient serpent" in these vv. is *ho ophis ho archaios* (→ *ophis*). Rev. 12 uses old mythological concepts. The nearest par. is the Gk. myth of the dragon Python which persecuted Leto and was killed by Apollo. In Rev. 12 the dragon has 7 heads and 10 horns (cf. Dan. 7:7 f.). It has power in heaven and its tail sweeps down a third of the stars. → Demons are subordinate to it. It stands by the woman who is to give birth to the man child so that it may devour him, but is defeated by Michael and his forces of → angels and is cast down to earth together with its demons (12:7 ff.). It persecutes the woman and tries to drown her in a flood of water from its mouth (12:13 ff.), which is probably reminiscent of Bab. concepts of the dragon of chaos. On earth it gives its power and its throne to the "beast" (which like the dragon has 7 heads and 10 horns). Through the beast the dragon causes the inhabitants of the world to worship it (13:2, 4). He who worships the state, personified in its ruler, is in fact worshipping the devil. The dragon is thrown into the abyss by an angel for a thousand years (20:2 f.), so that it can no longer deceive the nations. When the thousand years are past (→ Kingdom, art. *basileia*; → Number), it is released again and it collects Gog and Magog for the final battle against the people of God; it is defeated and thrown into the lake of fire (20:8, 10). The consummation of Christ's victory will be the elimination of Satan.

([Ed.] This period of a thousand years is often referred to in Christian thought as the millennium. Since the early church there have been those who believed that the preaching of the gospel would usher in a golden age prior to the final consummation. There are three main schools of thought. The Postmillennialists maintain that the second coming of Christ will follow the millennium. The Premillennialists believe that these verses refer to a time of restoration and widespread response to the gospel following the second coming of Christ. Amillennialists take these verses to refer not to a future time but to the present era. Satan is bound in the sense that the strong man is bound (Matt. 12:29; Mk. 3:27; Lk. 11:21 f.). Just as Jesus was able to plunder Satan's possessions by binding him first, so there is a sense in which Satan is bound "that he should deceive the nations no more, till the thousand years were ended" (Rev. 20:3). Amillennialists take this to refer to the fact that the gospel is now proclaimed to the Gentiles, and is not confined to the Jewish nation as the people of God.)   *H. Bietenhard*

| $ὄφις$ | $ὄφις$ (*ophis*), snake, serpent. |

CL The attitude of people towards the snake has always been ambivalent. On the one hand, it has been regarded as a strange and threatening animal, dangerous to life and full of cunning, deceit and evil. On the other hand, because of its nearness to the earth and the subterranean waters it has been linked with the subterranean gods and their powers to give and renew life. It was also a symbol of the gods who grant healing (Ascl.). So it became a symbol of the earth itself which both gives life and then receives it back.

OT *ophis* is found 32 times in the LXX, in 29 cases as a translation of *nāḥāš*. It appears with theological importance in Gen. 3, where the snake is introduced as an exceptionally clever, rather sly, animal which by an almost playful use of its cleverness ("Is it true that God. . . ?" NEB) led man into disobedience. This recondite figure conveys the mystery of the breaking in of evil into the world which God had created good. Num. 21 gives one of the many accounts of the people's murmuring against God and Moses which is punished by a plague of snakes. But Yahweh turns again in grace to his people. If anyone turned to the symbol of the bronze snake he was saved. Yahweh did not merely grant his help; he linked it with the symbol that he had appointed. ([Ed.] The Heb. word for these snakes is *śᵉrāpîm* (lit. burning ones). The same word is used of the Seraphim in Isa. 6:1, where they have wings and act as God's messengers. Here they are associated by some scholars with snake-demons, as the jinn of the desert often took a serpent form. The point of lifting up the serpent may be to represent symbolically that the object lay under the curse of God (cf. Deut. 21:23; Gal. 3:13). According to 2 Ki. 18:4, the bronze serpent survived until the time of Hezekiah who destroyed it, because the people of Israel had burned incense to it and called it Nehushtan. Later Jewish tradition emphasized that it was not the serpent itself that saved. "For he that turned himself toward it was not saved because of what he saw, but because of thee, the Saviour of all" (Wisd. 16:17). The Mishnah commented: "But could the serpent slay or the serpent keep alive! – it is, rather, to teach thee that such time as the Israelites directed their thoughts on high and kept their hearts in subjection to their Father in heaven, they were healed; otherwise they pined away" (*Rosh ha-Shanah* 3:8). It went on to draw the general rule that, "any on whom an obligation is not incumbent [e.g. a deaf-mute, an imbecile or a minor] cannot fulfil that obligation on behalf of the many." Philo also discussed the incident (*Leg. All.*, 2, 79–81; *Agric.*, 95–9), but does not seem to throw light on Jn. 3:14 (cf. C. K. Barrett, *The Gospel According to St. John*, 1955, 178).)

In late Jud. it was only in later writings that the snake became an instrument of the devil or was identified with him. Occasionally it was identified with the Angel of Death. They contain speculations about the motives that moved the snake in Paradise to attack man, such as envy, sexual desire, desire for world rule.

NT The condemnation in Matt. 23:33 (cf. Matt. 3:7) calls the scribes and Pharisees "snakes" in view of their evil and unwillingness to repent, possibly indicating their link with Satan. It threatens them with the judgment of *gehenna* (→ Hell). In his call to prayer in faith, Jesus stressed that no father would give his son a snake instead of the fish he had asked for (Matt. 7:10; Lk. 11:11), i.e. something evil

509

and dangerous instead of food. How much more would God give that which was good, when asked by the disciples. Gen. 3:1 and Cant. 5:2; 6:9 lie behind the paradoxical exhortation to wisdom and innocence in Matt. 10:16.

Because Satan has been cast down, the disciples have obtained authority to tread upon snakes and scorpions, the instruments of the Evil One (Lk. 10:19; cf. Ps. 91:13). Mk. 16:18 is similar. Because the Messianic age has broken in, snakes can be picked up without danger (cf. Isa. 11:8). ([Ed.] However, this verse in Mk. belongs to the so-called longer ending of Mk. [vv. 9–20] which is not in the best MSS. The whole passage is probably a later composition, reconstructed from other teaching and such events as Paul's handling of the viper in Acts 28:1–6.)

In Rev. 9:19 the horses of the demonic cavalry have tails like snakes by which they do harm. In Rev. 12:9; 20:2 the snake recalls Gen. 3 and is identified with Satan (cf. art. *drakōn*). 2 Cor. 11:3 also recalls the Genesis story. The church is warned against listening to Satan's whispered suggestions and so being led astray from sincere devotion to and trust in Christ. Jn. 3:14 f. looks back to Num. 21:8 f. As there, to look at the bronze snake brought salvation, so faith saves the one who looks to the Son of Man exalted on the cross and on the throne of God.

H. Bietenhard

[Ed.] Later Christian writers treated the serpent in Jn. 3 as a type of Christ (Barn 12:5 ff.; Justin, *Apol.* I, 60, *Dial.* 94, 112; Tert., *Adv. Marc.*, 3, 18). But the main point of Jn.'s comparison is not the serpent but the lifting up (cf. 12:32; C. K. Barrett, op. cit., 178; R. Schnackenburg, *The Gospel According to St. John*, I, 1968, 396). The Gospel also associates the act with the exaltation of Christ in his suffering, the divine purpose, and the role of faith. R. Bultmann thinks that the notions of the gnostic Ophite sect concerning the serpent go back to Num. 21 and that the sect was older than the Fourth Gospel. Nevertheless; he does not think it possible to show any dependence between Jn. and gnosticism at this point. The gnostics made no use of the exaltation of the serpent which for Jn. is the main point of the comparison (*The Gospel of John*, 1971, 152).

| σκορπίος | σκορπίος (*skorpios*), scorpion. |

CL & OT The scorpion belongs to the spider family, and is some four to five inches long. It was known to both Greek and Jews, with references in Aeschylus, Plato, Philo and Josephus, among others. There are at present some ten species in Palestine. The poisonous sting in its tail is painful, and can be fatal to young children.

In the LXX *skorpios* translates the Hebrew *'aqrāḇ*. In Deut. 8:15 it is depicted as a fearsome denizen of the wilderness, one of the perils from which Yahweh protected his people. Elsewhere the word is used figuratively to convey the idea of extreme pain or harm. In Ezek. 2:6 scorpions are the hostile words and attitude of those to whom the prophet will speak. In 1 Ki. 12:11, 14 (cf. 2 Chr. 10:11, 14) they symbolize the increased demands that Rehoboam intends to make of Israel.

NT In Luke's Gospel Jesus uses *skorpios* twice. In Lk. 10:19 the miraculous protection from scorpions experienced by those sent out on mission is a part of the authority he has given them. In Lk. 11:12 he uses a proverbial style to indicate the disposition of a human father to the request of his son as a means of showing how much more ready the heavenly Father is to respond with the gift of the Holy Spirit.

In Rev. 9:3, 5, 10 supernatural locusts with the power and viciousness of scorpions are allowed to torture the faithless. As in Lk. 10:19 they represent demonic power.
P. J. Budd

κέντρον

κέντρον (*kentron*), sting, goad.

CL & OT The word *kentron* occurs in classical Greek from Homer onwards, in Philo, and in Josephus (cf. e.g. *War* 2, 385; *Antiquities* 7, 169). It is often used of the sting of an animal (as in Aristotle). In the LXX it is used figuratively of death (Hos. 13:14). Another meaning frequently attested in classical Greek is goad. This usage also occurs in the LXX (Prov. 26:3).

OT In the NT both meanings occur. The literal sense of sting occurs in Rev. 9:10 in connection with the locusts mentioned above, while the figurative use of Hos. 13:14 is taken over by Paul as a climax in his argument on resurrection (1 Cor. 15:55, 56). Paul's resistance to the claims of Jesus prior to his conversion is described figuratively as a kicking against the goads (Acts 9:5 t.r.; 26:14).
P. J. Budd

(a). G. S. Cansdale, *Animals of Bible Lands*, 1970; J. L. Cloudsley-Thompson, *Spiders, Scorpions, Centipedes, and Mites*, 1958; W. Foerster, *drakōn*, *TDNT* II 281 ff.; and *ophis*, *TDNT* V 566–82; K. R. Joines, "Winged Serpents in Isaiah's Inaugural Vision", *JBL* 86 1967, 410–15; W. S. McCullough, "Serpent," *IDB* IV 289 ff.; H. Pegg, "A Scorpion for an Egg," *ExpT* 38, 1926–27, 468 f.; H. H. Rowley, "Zadok and Nehushtan," *JBL* 58, 1939, 113–41; L. Schmid, *kentron*, *TDNT* III 662–8; D. J. Wiseman, "Flying Serpents?" *TB* 23, 1972, 108 ff.
(b). M. Eliade, "Drache," *RGG³* II 259 f.; E. Fascher, "Drache," *BHHW* I 353.

Dream

ὄναρ

ὄναρ (*onar*), dream.

CL & OT The word *onar* occurs widely in classical Greek from Homer onwards, but not in the LXX where *enypnion* is customary for dream. It is also used by both Philo (cf. e.g. *Flacc.* 164) and Josephus (cf. e.g. *War* 2, 112; *Ant.* 2, 63; 10, 195).

In the OT, in Judaism, in the Greek world, and in the ancient Near East generally dreams were regularly understood to contain messages from God, particularly the dreams experienced by kings and priests. Such communication was sometimes sought intentionally, as in the dream of King Keret in the Ugaritic texts. Though there is no certain example of this deliberate custom in the OT, dreams with divine content often occurred at sanctuaries (cf. e.g. Jacob at Bethel (Gen. 28:12 ff.), Samuel at Shiloh (1 Sam. 3), and Solomon at Gibeon (1 Kings 3:4–15). Elihu bears witness to this generally held view that dreams are an authentic means of divine revelation (Job 33:14–18; cf. also 1 Sam. 28 6). In Genesis dreams are a regular means of such communication alongside the more direct appearances of

511

Yahweh (cf. e.g. Gen. 20:3; 28:12; 31:11). The dream was also a medium by which truth was conveyed to a prophet (Num. 12:6), while the dreams to be dreamed by old men are a part of the universal and immediate contact with God to be experienced in the latter days (Joel 3:1).

In most cases the content of the divine message is conveyed to the dreamer clearly and unambiguously (cf. e.g. Gen. 20:3; 31:10–13; 1 Ki. 3:4–15), but in two cycles of stories the skills of experts or professional interpreters are required. These are the Joseph stories (cf. Gen. 37:5–10; 40:5 ff.; 41:1 ff.), and the Daniel narratives (cf. Dan. 2). These special interpretative skills are God-given (Gen. 40:8; Dan. 2:27–28), and involve an ability to read the pattern of future events in the various symbolic features of the dream. In the Greek world dreams were treated with the same sort of respect, and sophisticated systems of interpretation were developed (cf. A. Oepke, *onar*, *TDNT* V 227).

On the other hand, dreams and their interpretations were not accepted uncritically by all. The polemic against false prophecy in the prose discourses of Jer. contains scathing criticism of lying dreamers (Jer. 23:32; 27:9), and Zechariah offers similar criticism in terms of their emptiness (Zech. 10:2). A dreamer whose word encouraages apostasy is, in the view of the Deuteronomic law, to be put to death (Deut. 13:2–6). Qoheleth's scepticism extends to the dream world (Eccl. 5:7), and some witness to its fleeting insubstantial character is to be found in Job 20:8; Pss. 73:20; 90:5.

In later Judaism this scepticism can be found in Sir. 34:5 ff, but for the most part the strong uncritical belief in dreams dominates (cf. e.g. Esther 1:1 ff; 10:3 ff. (LXX); 2 Macc. 15:11 ff.; Test. Levi 2–5; Test. Naph. 5–7). In Hellenistic Judaism the strong Platonic-Stoic belief in dreams is prominent. For Philo it is through dreams that God gives knowledge of heavenly things to the pure soul (*Aet. Mund.* 2).

NT In the NT interest in dreams is confined almost exclusively to Matthew's Gospel.

The word *onar* is to be found there alone, and on 5 of its 6 occurrences it is to be found in the birth narratives, as follows: to Joseph explaining Mary's pregnancy, through an angel (1:20); to the wise men warning them not to return to Herod (2:12); to Joseph telling him to flee with his family to Egypt, through an angel (2:13); to Joseph telling him to return from Egypt, through an angel (2:19); to Joseph warning him against settling in Judaea (2:22).

Clearly this means of communication and guidance is a very distinctive feature of Matthew's special source in these chapters. It serves to convey God's particular provision for the infant Jesus in the face of various uncertainties and threats, particularly those posed by hostile rulers. The dream is thus highly valued as an illustration of the divine guidance and intervention operative in the life of Jesus from the outset. This serves to enforce a basic Matthaean theme that this Jesus is God's chosen and anointed one. The other occurrence of *onar* is in Matt. 27:19 where, at the trial of Jesus, Pilate's wife reports the disturbance she has suffered in a dream on Jesus's account. The precise content of the dream is unclear.

In the narrative of Acts direction and encouragement is often given to Paul in visions of the night (Acts 16:9; 18:9; 23:11; 27:23–24), but *onar* is not used. In the quotation from Joel (Acts 2:17) Peter uses *enypnion*. P. J. Budd

512

Arndt, 572 f.; A. Oepke, *onar*, *TDNT*, V 220–38; E. D. Ehrlich, *Der Traum im Alten Testament*, *BZAW* 73, 1953; M. M. Bourke, "The Literary Genre of Matthew 1–2," *CBQ* 22, 1960, 160–75. L. Oppenheim, *The Interpretation of Dreams in the Ancient Near East*, 1956; W. Richter, "Traum und Traumdeutung im Alten Testament," *BZ* 7, 1963, 202–19; J. B. Bauer, "Dream", *EBT* I 214 ff. for further literature.

Drunken, Sober

μεθύω

μεθύω (*methyō*), be drunk; μεθύσκω (*methyskō*), cause to become intoxicated; μέθυσος (*methysos*), drunkard; μέθυσμα (*methysma*), intoxicating drink; μέθη (*methē*), drunkenness.

CL These words occur regularly in Hellenistic Greek in connection with intoxication (*methyō* – Homer; *methyskō* – Herodotus and Xenophon; *methysos* – Aristophanes; *methē* – Herodotus and Plato). In Plotinus intoxication with nectar (*methystheis tou nektaros*) is used to describe a state of mystical union with God. In Hellenistic gnosticism drunkenness is often linked with *agnōsia* in opposition to true *gnōsis*. In the Odes of Solomon (11:8) a drunkenness brought about by the water of the *logos* is contrasted with the *methē tēs agnōsias*.

OT In the LXX *methyō* meaning intoxication with wine is familiar enough (cf. e.g. Gen. 9:21; Isa. 19:14; 28:1; Joel 1:5). It can also be used however of the refreshment brought by rain to dry ground (Isa. 55:10; Ps. 64:10). *methē*, meaning drunkenness, occurs in Isa. 28:7; Ezek. 22:33; Prov. 20:1. *methyō* and *methyskomai* are used by Josephus (*War* 2, 20; 6, 196; *Ant.* 8, 376). Sometimes *methyskō* is used figuratively; in Isa. 34:5 the sword of Yahweh drinks its fill, with blood as the intoxicating liquid (Isa. 34:7; 49:26).

Of particular interest in Philo is his treatise entitled *peri methēs* (*De Ebrietate*). He describes *methē* as *dēmiourgos kakōn*, and drunkenness generally as a mark of the blind and foolish man who is a slave to the material world. For the wise drinking has its value, encouraging relaxation and cheerfulness, so that its effects depend very much on the one who drinks. In his *Vit. Mos.* (1, 187) Philo speaks of Israel's drinking from the sweetened spring in Ex. 15 as a sober intoxication. A favourite expression *nēphalios methē* (temperate or sober intoxication) describes the mystical union of the soul with God in the Dionysus cult.

NT In the NT *methysos* and *methē* occur in lists of vices (Rom. 13:13; Gal. 5:21; 1 Cor. 5:11; 6:10). The words *methyō* and *methyskomai* are also used literally, and generally condemnation is involved (but cf. Jn. 2:10). In these contexts drunkenness is seen as an element in the old way of life now abandoned, and as incompatible with Christian living. Typical of the Pauline attitude is 1 Thess. 5:6, 7, where, with an awareness of the imminence of the end, Paul issues a strong warning against the perils of drunkenness. The argument is based on the conviction that Christians now live in the light of Christ's new day. Since drunkenness is a nighttime experience it is incompatible with authentic Christianity. A similar attitude is present in one of the parables (Matt. 24:49; Lk. 12:45), where drunkenness is shown to be inconsistent with the alertness of the faithful servant, who is properly aware of the eschatological dimension of service in the new age (cf. Lk. 21:34).

This incompatibility can also be deduced from the fact that the Christian is

513

Spirit-filled (Eph. 5:18; cf. Acts 2:15), a condition which shows itself not so much in ecstasies or mystical experiences, but in liturgical praise (Eph. 5:18–20), and in ethical commitment (5:21–6:9). The incongruity of drunkenness and Christian experience emerges very clearly in the context of the Lord's Supper (1 Cor. 11:21), so clearly in fact that current Corinthian practice must be declared invalid (11:20). The Dionysus cult, with its stress on religious intoxication, was familiar in Corinth and further afield, and it is reasonable to see within these NT epistolary texts a concern to draw a clear line between all such Hellenistic cults, and the life of the Christian in the Spirit.

A figurative use of this word group is characteristic of Rev. In 17:2 idolatry is vividly depicted as a drunkenness with the wine of whoredom, probably with direct allusion to the intoxicating and orgiastic character of some current cults. In 17:6 the woman, symbolizing power opposed to God within the world, is drunk with the blood of the saints.

paroinos (drunken) occurs occasionally in Hellenistic Greek, and in Jewish literature in Test. Jud. 14:4. In all such cases it is used of persons who are drunken or addicted to wine. It is the distinctive word for drunkenness in the Pastoral Epistles, occurring twice there but nowhere else in the NT. In 1 Tim. 3:3 and Tit. 1:7 it is one of the disqualifying factors for the office of bishop.

kraipalē (intoxication) occurs in a few Hellenistic sources (e.g. Aristophanes), and can also be used of the effects of intoxication – dizziness and staggering. In the NT *kraipalē* occurs only once, and in conjunction with *methē* (Lk. 21:34). The effect of drunkenness is probably intended (thus "dissipation" RSV). The context, as in Matt. 24:49; Lk. 12:45, is readiness for the day of the Lord's coming.

A further word for drunkenness, *oinophlygia*, is attested in Aristotle and in Philo (cf. e.g. *Vit. Mos.* 2, 185). Its only NT attestation is 1 Pet. 4:3 where it occurs in a list of vices which are a feature of the Gentile world, but incompatible with Christian life.

νήφω	νήφω (nēphō), be sober; νηφάλιος (nēphalios), temperate; ἐκνήφω (eknēphō), become sober; ἀνανήφω (ananēphō),

become sober.

CL & OT This word group carries with it the idea of sobriety, the opposite of intoxi-
cation (see *methyō*). In Hellenistic Greek the words can be used literally, of a state of abstinence from wine, but also figuratively indicating complete clarity of mind and its resulting good judgment. Thus for Plato sobriety can mean a preference for moderate possessions rather than many.

For Philo *nēphein* is a precondition for a proper approach to God, and involves the deliberate avoidance of all that would offend him (*De. Ebr.* 131) (see also the reference to "sober intoxication" under *methyō*).

NT For the NT writers, though the literal is often implied, the figurative sense is
also prominent. *nēphō* occurs twice in the argument of 1 Thess. 5:6–8 (dis-
cussed under *methyō*) denoting the alertness required in the light of an imminent parousia, and once in the Pastoral Epistles (2 Tim. 4:5), where it indicates the clarity of mind able to resist the subtle attractions of deviant mythologies.

In 1 Pet. *nēphō* has a generally eschatological setting, pointing to the appropriate frame of mind for an imminent appearance of Jesus (1:13) and for prayer in the end time (4:7). In such days the ferocious hostility of the devil is evident, and an alertness able to resist is essential (5:8).

nēphalios occurs only in the Pastoral Epistles and denotes the abstemious style of life required of bishops (1 Tim. 3:2), women (1 Tim. 3:11) and elders (Tit. 2:2). The main point in these contexts is the self-control necessary for effective ministry. *eknēphō* occurs only in 1 Cor. 15:34 denoting a clarity of mind similar to that required in 2 Tim. 4:5. The context suggests confusion of ideas concerning the resurrection. *ananēphō* occurs only in 2 Tim. 2:26 and indicates the clarity of mind demanded of a teacher if opponents are to be silenced.   *P. J. Budd*
→ Discipline, → Fast, → Feast, → Wine

Arndt, 449, 500, 540, 564 f.; 634; H. Preisker, *methē* etc. *TDNT* IV 545–8; O. Bauernfeind, *nēphō* etc,. *TDNT* IV 936–41.

Dry Up, Wither

| ξηραίνω |

ξηραίνω (*xērainō*), dry up; ξηρός (*xēros*), dried up.

CL In classical Greek *xērainō* is attested from Homer onwards, and *xēros* likewise from Herodotus. The verb generally occurs in the passive though the active form can be found in Thucydides. The usage is normally literal – of plants in particular, or of dry land, but sometimes of human ailments also (cf. e.g. Hippocrates).

OT In the LXX an active form of the verb is to be found in Isa. 42:15 with reference to plants (cf. also Jer. 28:36). The passive is more usual, however, and occurs in connection with trees (Isa. 56:3; Ezek. 17:24; Joel 1:12), with water (Gen. 8:7; 1 Ki. 17:7; Isa. 19:5, 6), and with Jeroboam's withered hand (1 Ki. 13:4). On many occasions *xēros* means dry land (cf. e.g. Gen 1:9), and it can also be used of sea that has been dried up (Jon. 1:9; Hag. 2:21; 1 Macc. 8:23, 32). In Hos. 9:14 it is used of milkless breasts.

Several of these usages can be found in other Jewish texts (cf. e.g. Josephus, *War*, 3, 228; *Antiquities*, 5, 249; Testament of Levi 4:1; Testament of Zebulun 2:7). The use of *xēros* in connection with a diseased condition is particularly noteworthy in Testament of Simeon 2:12.

NT In the NT there is only one active occurrence of the verb in Jas. 1:11. Here *xērainō* is used of the scorching effect of the sun's heat on grass. This effect is likened to the transience of the rich man's wealth.

With the passive form there are three texts which refer to withered trees. The story of the → fig tree (Mk. 11:20, 21; Matt. 21:19, 20) appears to use this illustration of Jesus' power as a word of condemnation against contemporary Judaism – a leafy appearance of righteousness without the fruit. In Matthew the withering takes effect at once; in Mark a lapse of time seems to be envisaged. The idea of condemnation is also central in Jn. 15:6 where the severed and withering branch is fit only for burning. In the peculiarly Lukan word of Jesus (Lk. 23:31), set in the

crucifixion narrative, dry wood (*xēros*) is the symbol of times of testing and difficulty. The saying has some rabbinic parallels, and in context seems to stress the
fearsome fate that will overtake those guilty of the crucifixion in the less propitious
times that are coming.

The parable of the sower uses the verb of plants which lack good roots, and
therefore cannot withstand the heat of the sun (Matt. 13:6; Mk. 4:6; Lk. 8:6).
Here again a judgment motif is central: for the coming of the kingdom does not
meet with universal recognition. In 1 Pet. 1:24, where the verb occurs in a quotation
from Isa. 40:7, the idea of withering is used to stress the fleetingness of human
existence in contrast to the permanence of God's word. In Rev. 14:15 the verb
occurs in a context which seems to demand that it be understood in terms of
ripeness – ready for harvesting (RSV). It is possible that over-ripeness is intended
(RV).

The drying up of the Euphrates (Rev. 16:12) also appears in a prominently
judgmental context; it is a prelude to the final battle between God and his adversaries. In Heb. 11:29 the word is used of the drying up of the Red Sea, while in
Matt. 23:15, Jesus' reference to the proselytizing activity of the Pharisees, *xēros* is
used of land in general.

Several occurrences of both words can be found in connection with the healing
ministry of Jesus. The story of the man with the withered hand (Matt. 12:11; Mk.
3:1; Lk. 6:6) probably refers to some form of paralysis (cf. Jn. 5:3). Mark also
uses forms of the verb to describe the healing of the woman with the flow of →
blood (Mk. 5:29), and the condition of rigidity to which the spirit reduces the
possessed boy (Mk. 9:18).   *P. J. Budd*
→ Fruit, art. *sykē*

J. N. Birdsall, "The Withering of the Fig Tree," *Exp. T.* 73, 1961–62, 191; F. Fenner, *Die Krankheit im Neuen Testament*, 1930; C. W. F. Smith, "No Time for Figs", *JBL* 79, 1960, 315–27.

E

Earth, Land, World

For the Bible the world is not so much a part of the universe as the place where man lives. *gē*, which was originally used to distinguish land and soil from the sky (→ Heaven) and the sea (→ Water), is more particularly used for the area where man lives and works, or for a country as part of it. When the thought is geographical rather than political, *hē oikoumenē* is more often used. This has no special theological significance in the NT. It is seen rather as the area into which the gospel has to penetrate. Both words are clearly concrete in their application in contrast to *kosmos* (world) which has strong philosophical and religious overtones. It may be noted that Eng. idiom often demands the translation "world" for them.

γῆ

γῆ (*gē*), earth, world; ἐπίγειος (*epigeios*), earthly.

CL 1. *gē* is the earth or world; the land in contrast to water; and also, as part of the earth, a piece of land, a field with arable soil. The meaning "land", as the area controlled by a single state, emerged by analogy alongside these natural meanings.

2. In ancient Gk. mythology *gē* and *ouranos*, sky, are among the oldest deities. They were not envisaged like the gods in the Homeric epics. *gē* was a woman, half of whose body extended from the ground. As she received seed and rain, she was the mother from whom all life proceeds.

OT The LXX uses *gē* more than 2,000 times. Neither in the LXX nor the NT is there any thought of divinity about it. The earth is part of God's creation (cf. Gen. 1:1 f.). Heb. *'ereṣ* has very much the same meaning as in CL 1 above, though the thought of its having been created is always strong. All that is said of NT usage applies also to the OT.

NT In NT *gē* is used 248 times, particularly in the Gospels, Acts and Rev. It is first of all the soil in which the sower sows his seed ("since they had no depth of soil", Matt. 13:5). One can sit down on the earth (Mk. 8:6). It stands in contrast to water ("the boat by this time was many furlongs distant from the land", Matt. 14:24). All land taken together has a boundary ("the queen of the south . . . came from the ends of the earth," Matt. 12:42; the witnesses of the risen One were to go "to the ends of the earth", *heōs eschatou tēs gēs*, Acts 1:8). The angels of judgment stood "at the four corners of the earth", controlling "the four winds of the earth" (Rev. 7:1; cf. Matt. 24:31). Christ will be, as was Jonah when he was

517

in the fish in the midst of the water, "in the heart of the earth" (Matt. 12:40). There is also a sphere of life "under the earth" (*katachthonios*, Phil. 2:10; cf. Exod. 20:4). In all these passages the earth is something created. They never go beyond the ideas of the ancient world.

1. The historical use of the term occurs wherever it is used in a political sense, e.g. the land of Judah (Matt. 2:6), the land of Israel (Matt. 2:20), the land of Midian and the land of Egypt (Acts 7:29, 36). It is frequently difficult to decide whether a particular passage is speaking of a particular country, especially the land of Israel, or of the populated earth as a whole (→ *oikoumenē*). With our modern outlook on the world we are inclined to think globally and universally. However, the NT can use "the earth" in a very particularistic way. *pasai hai phylai tēs gēs* (Matt. 24:30; Rev. 1:7) means in the setting of Zech. 12:10–14 "all the tribes of the land". On the other hand, the remarkable expression "from the ends of the earth to the ends of heaven" (Mk. 13:27) means the whole earth, expressed here by joining two OT sentences, Ps. 19:6(7) and Deut. 13:7 (but cf. also Deut. 30:4; Jer. 12:12). According to the classical world, the end of the earth and the end of heaven could coincide.

2. Both earth and → heaven are God's creation. Heaven and earth can and will pass away (Matt. 5:18; 24:35). But in so doing, they will make way for "a new heaven and a new earth" (Rev. 21:1; 2 Pet. 3:13). The passing of heaven and earth means the passing away of the present sinful world order, which must be renewed by passing through God's judgments. Redemption extends to the furthest corner of the physical realm. That the meek will inherit the earth is the promise of Christ (Matt. 5:5) and this earthly kingdom is the same as the kingdom of heaven, the world of the coming age, the coming redeemed creation (Rom. 8:21).

Though, especially in eschatological passages, heaven and earth are brought together as works of the Creator, a distinction is made between them following key passages which reflect OT thought: Isa. 66:1; Matt. 5:34 f.; Acts 7:49. The earth is the scene of the imperfect (Heb. 8:4 f.), of sin (Mk. 2:10; Rev. 17:5), and of death (1 Cor. 15:47). Hence Christians are to set their minds on things that are above, not on things that are on earth (Col. 3:2). And they are to put to death their "members upon the earth" (Col. 3:5 RV).

3. *epigeios* (7 times in the NT) means lit. "on the earth", but it can also be linked with the dualism of heaven and earth and so mean earthly (1 Cor. 15:40; 2 Cor. 5:1; Phil. 3:19). *R. Morgenthaler*

| οἰκουμένη | οἰκουμένη (*oikoumenē*), earth. |

CL *oikoumenē* (understand *gē*) is the pres. part. pass. of *oikeō*, inhabit. It means the inhabited (earth) and was used (a) from Dem. (4th cent. B.C.) on for the world inhabited by Greeks in contrast to those lands inhabited by "barbarians"; (b) from Aristot. (4th cent. B.C.) on for the inhabited world, including the barbarian lands, i.e. settled, as opposed to unsettled, areas; (c) in the Roman period (since the conquest of the East in the 2nd cent. B.C.) for the *imperium Romanum* – the lands under Roman rule. In other words, what had originally been a geographical and cultural concept had become a political concept in the Roman period. The

Emperor Nero was entitled *sōtēr* (saviour) and *euergetēs* (benefactor) of the *oikoumenē* (→ Salvation, art. *sōzō*).

OT The LXX uses the word 46 times, especially in the Pss. (15 times, but *kosmos* is entirely absent here) and in Isa. (15 times). In the Pss. it is often found in expressions of an obviously confessional type: "He will judge the world with righteousness" (Pss. 9:8(9); 67:4(5); 96:13; 98:9); "to the end of the world" (Pss. 19:4(5); 72:8); "the world and those who dwell therein" (Pss 24:1; 98:7; cf. Isa. 34:1); "all the inhabitants of the world" (Pss. 33:8; 49:2(1); cf. Lam. 4:12). In Isa. it appears especially in the oracles against the nations in chs. 13, 14, 23 (10:14, 23 probably belongs to this section also).

Throughout, the word means the inhabited world (see above CL (b)). This is clear in Exod. 16:35 where Israel comes again into an inhabited land, i.e. a settled land in contrast to the wilderness where the nomads roam. In Isa. 62:4 the LXX text differs from the Heb.: "Your land shall be called Inhabited (*oikoumenē*)".

NT *oikoumenē* is found 15 times in NT, mainly in Luke (8 times) and Rev. (3 times). Is it used generally as in Hel. popular speech meaning inhabited world (O. Michel *TDNT* V 157 ff.), or does the political and imperial usage predominate (M. Paeslack, *Theologia Viatorum* 2, 1950, 33 ff.)? The latter is clearly the main one in Lk. 2:1. The Emperor Augustus ordered a census of the whole *oikoumenē*, i.e. the territories over which he ruled. Also in Rev. 3:10; 12:9; 16:14 there is probably a political note. The *oikoumenē* is the inhabited world in the sense that all its population has to suffer under Satanic powers for religious, but mainly political, reasons. Equally in the story of Christ's temptation, the replacement in Lk. 4:5 of *kosmos* by *oikoumenē* suggests a strong political connotation, even though "the kingdoms of the world" prevents a direct identification with the Roman empire. In Lk. 21:26, Acts 11:28 and Rev. 3:10 it is used in apocalyptic prophecies. In Acts 17:6 the preaching of the apostles is attacked as a political crime directed against the Emperor by men "who have turned the *oikoumenē* upside down". Similarly in Acts 19:27 and 24:5 Paul is called a causer of trouble in the *oikoumenē*. In the latter passage he is accused of it before the Roman governor.

Heb. 1:6 uses it in the general Hel. sense. Heb. 2:5 speaks of the coming world as the future *oikoumenē*. In Matt. 24:14 it is also hard to believe that there is any political connotation.

It is striking that the term is not used by Paul except in Rom. 10:18, where he is quoting the LXX Ps. 18:5(19:4). Can it be that Paul still saw the state in a friendlier light than Luke and Rev., and so avoided using for it an expression which had negative overtones for him? We have to agree with M. Paeslack's conclusion, that in the NT *oikoumenē* is "not the fellowship of Christians" – this is rather the *ekklēsia* (→ Church) – "but the world of the heathen Graeco-Roman Empire threatened by the powers of darkness" (op. cit., 47). This does not exclude the *oikoumenē* from being the field where the church is to labour. The *oikoumenē* is the sphere in which the church lives and which she claims for her Lord, who according to Heb. has been brought into the *oikoumenē* as first-born, and who therefore is its legitimate ruler. An inward-looking ecumenical attitude by the Church is therefore a contradiction in terms (W. A. Visser't Hooft, *The Meaning of "Ecumenical"*, 12).   *O. Flender*

ἀγρός

ἀγρός *(agros)*, field; ἄγριος *(agrios)*, of the field, wild.

CL In secular Gk., *agros* is normally used to denote a piece of cultivated land, but it can also mean the countryside as distinct from the town or village. The adjective *agrios* has a similar double reference. Sometimes it describes trees, animals or crops to be found "in the fields", but more often it has the sense of "wild", describing life and terrain to be found outside the conurbations of man. In this latter sense it is frequently applied figuratively to people (savage, fierce), and to things and circumstances (cruel, harsh).

OT Most of the above usages are found in the LXX. Any piece of land under cultivation is an *agros* (e.g. Exod. 8:13; Num. 21:22; Ruth 2:2), whether owned by an individual (Gen. 23:9; 1 Ki. 2:26) or by the community (Lev. 25:34; Ruth 1:1, 2). At the same time *agros* describes the untilled open country beyond the town or village boundary (e.g. Deut. 22:27; 1 Sam. 30:11), where the traveller might expect to meet the bear and the lion, as well as the hind (Hos. 13:8; Jer. 14:51). Such beasts are naturally *agrios*, wild (Job. 6:5; Ps. 79:14). The adj. is not applied figuratively to people in the LXX or other Jewish writings, but it can describe a "malignant" ulcer (Lev. 21:20; Deut. 28:27) or "wild" waves (Wis. 14:1).

NT *agros* occurs 30 times in the Gospels, but only once elsewhere in the NT. On 18 occasions it refers to land under cultivation or destined for it (e.g. Matt. 13:24; Lk. 14:18; Acts 4:37). Otherwise (apart from allusions to the potter's field in Matt. 27:7 f., 10; cf. Zech. 11:13, bought with Judas' betrayal money as a burial ground), the reference is to the countryside (e.g. Mk. 15:21). The adjective *agrios* is used in its lit. sense, "found in the open field" in Mk. 1:6 par.; fig., to describe the "wild" waves of the sea in Jude 13.   *D. H. Field*

χοῦς

χοῦς *(chous)*, soil, dust; χοϊκός *(choikos)*, made of soil.

CL The noun *chous* (deriving from the verb *cheō*, which means "pour" a liquid or "throw up" earth) is used by the classical historians Herodotus and Thucydides to describe excavated or heaped up soil. *choikos*, the adjective, is not found until Philo's time.

OT *chous*, in the sense of "dirt" or "dust", is used extensively in the LXX to translate the Heb. *'āpār*. In similes it often signifies a tiny or worthless object (e.g. Ps. 34:5; Isa. 17:13; cf. Neh. 4:10). Enemies lick up *chous* in humiliation, while the penitent and bereaved pour it over their heads in grief (Jos. 7:6; Lam. 2:10). Significantly, it was out of *chous* that God made man (Gen. 2:7; Ps. 102:14), and it is to *chous* that man returns when he dies (Eccl. 3:20; 12:7). The adj. *choikos* does not feature in the LXX, but Philo uses it once with *konis*, dust.

NT *chous* appears twice in the NT, where it stands for the dust of the road (Mk. 6:11) and for dirt thrown on the head as a sign of mourning (Rev. 18:19). *choikos* occurs 4 times in 1 Cor. 15:47–49, where Paul distinguishes man as God created him (cf. Gen. 2:7) from Jesus, "the second man", whose origin is heavenly, not earthly. Cf. Philo, *Op. Mund.* 134 ff., *Leg. All.* 1, 31 f.; and *TDNT* IX 474 ff.   *D. H. Field*

| κόσμος | κόσμος (kosmos), order (in cl. Gk.), adornment, world; κοσμέω (kosmeō), arrange, put in order, adorn; κόσμιος |

(kosmios), respectable, honourable; κοσμικός (kosmikos), earthly, worldly.

CL 1. The noun *kosmos*, attested from Homer onwards, denoted originally building and construction (e.g. Homer, *Od.*, 8, 492; Hdt., 3, 2). But more especially it denotes order, both generally (e.g. Homer, *Il.*, 2, 214 and often in the phrase *kata kosmon*, duly, in order) and in a specific sense (e.g. the seating position of the rowers, *Od.*, 13, 76 f.; battle array, *Il.*, 12, 225; later the regulation of life in human society, the constitution, Plato, *Leg.*, 8, 846d). It also often means ornament and adornment (esp. of women; e.g. Hom. *Il.*, 14, 187; Hes., *Works* 76; Hdt., 5, 92).

In Gk. philosophy (see below, 2) *kosmos* is the basic term for the world-order, the world-system, the sum total of things preserved by this ordering, the world in the spatial sense, the cosmos, the universe, the earth, and also (in Koine Gk.) the inhabitants of the earth, humanity, the → *oikoumenē*.

The vb. *kosmeō*, corresponding with the basic meaning of *kosmos* as order, is used as a technical term, e.g. to marshal an army, to arrange battle formation (Homer, *Il.*, 2, 554; Xen. *Cyr.*, 2, 1, 26), and also generally to organize, put in order, and very frequently to adorn (e.g. Hesiod, *Works*, 72).

2. The cosmos-concept of Gk. philosophy may be seen against the background of the question: How is it possible that, with all the individual things conflicting with one another (heaven and earth; God, men and living beings), the world is not destroyed? The answer was given that they are held together by an all-embracing order (cf. Anaximander, *Frag.* 9). This world-order is designated by the word *kosmos* which also come to denote the world in the spatial sense. According to Democritus, man is a microcosm (*Frag.* 34). This enables him to perceive the order of the world and praises its beauty (Heracl., *Frag.* 124) and the perfection of its spherical form and circular movement.

(a) Plato was the first to teach that the origin of the cosmos was due to a Demiurge (→ Creation, art. *dēmiourgos*) who formed "the world in accordance with the idea of the perfect living being" (*TDNT* III 875; cf. *Tim.*, 28 ff.). For him the cosmos is an animated body, a rational being and thus a manifestation of God. The cosmos is not creature and not creation, but a copy.

(b) Aristotle's conception of the world, which prevailed in the West for almost 2000 years, is of a spherical earth, surrounded by various layers of heavenly spheres, which rests unmoved in the centre of a spherical cosmos (*Cael.*, 2, 2p, 285a, 32). The cosmos is the sum total of everything linked to space and time. Beyond that is the transcendent world of God which, removed from space and time, leads an unchangeable and thus perfect life. God has not fashioned the world. He is pure → reason (*nous*) meditating on himself. He moves everything, but he himself remains unmoved and does not intervene in world events.

(c) The Stoics linked their cosmology with the thought of eternally returning same-ness, an idea stemming from oriental astrology. The cosmos does not owe its origin to a new beginning, but is the restoration (*apokatastasis*, → Reconciliation) of that which once was. The disappearance of the cosmos in a universal conflagration is not its end. It arises anew in a cosmic rebirth (→ Birth, art. *palingenesia*).

(d) In Neo-Platonism the dualism which one can already find in Plato reaches its climax. The intelligible world (*kosmos ekeinos*, that world) and the world of appearances (*kosmos houtos*, this world) are mutually opposed. Although the empirical world is the beginning of evil, Plotinus can boast of its size, order and beauty; how much more praiseworthy, then, must be the true cosmos, the archetype of this world (*Enneads*, 5, 1, 4; 5, 8; 3, 2, 2 ff.; cf. H. Sasse, *TDNT* III 879).

In Hellenistic times when oriental cosmologies were penetrating the world of Gk. culture, the cosmos became a foreign country. It is no longer a harmonic unity, but falls into two domains: the lower earthly world and the world of the stars. What happens on earth depends on what happens in the world of the stars. Men's dealings are fundamentally meaningless.

In gnosticism there are to some extent conflicting statements about the cosmos. The separation between God and world has become absolute. The cosmos was a creation of demonic powers from the chaos of darkness, with the help of light-elements. It is an imitation of the construction of the world of light. God is that which is not-world, the cosmos has been rid of every element of divinity. It is purely material and fleshly, a → fullness (*plērōma*) of evil (*Corp. Herm.*, 6, 4). It is therefore not only foreign territory, but a prison from which the pre-existent soul of man longs for liberation, for which the heavenly figure of light, the Son of God, gives him help. But the *kosmos* may also be a mythological figure, and is designated *inter alia* "Son of God" (*Corp. Herm.*, 8, 5). It may even be viewed as an animate organism which is the image of God and of which man is the image (*Corp. Herm.*, 10, 11). ([Ed.] The Hermetic writings probably date from the middle of the 1st to the end of the 3rd cent. A.D., see Glossary of Technical Terms.)

OT 1. The LXX uses *kosmos* 7 times to translate Heb. *ʿªḏî*, ornaments (e.g. Jer. 2:32; 4:30), once for *kºlî*, ornaments, jewellery (Isa. 61:10), twice for *tip̄ʾeret̞*, ornament, decoration (Prov. 20:29, Isa. 3:18); also 5 times for *ṣāḇāʾ*, the hosts of heaven (and earth), the stars (cf. Gen. 2:1; Deut. 4:19). Meaning "world", *kosmos* is only found in the later Gk. writings of the LXX (Wis. 19 times, 2 Macc. 5 times, 4 Macc. 4 times). It was probably adopted in this meaning from Gk. linguistic usage under the influence of Hel. Judaism.

2. The OT knows of no word for the world corresponding to the Gk. *kosmos*. It calls the universe "heaven and earth", and only in later writings *hakkōl* (lit. the all), the universe (Jer. 10:16; Ps. 103:19; also without the art. (*kōl*, lit. all), Isa. 44:24; Ps. 8:7). As well as the word, the OT also lacks the Gk. concept of the cosmos. It never regards the world as an independent entity in itself, but always in its relation to God, the Creator (→ Creation). It is true that the account of creation in Gen. 1:1–2:4a is interested in cosmology, in that it speaks of the deep and the waters (the primeval flood and primeval darkness), the firmament, the heavenly ocean and the stars. But its statements have the sole intention of witnessing to God as the Lord over everything including chaos. Its objective is clearly the creation of man which stands at the focal point of the statements in Gen. 2:4b – 25. Man's vocation is to recognize his task in the world as accountable to God and to exercise lordship over the creation (1:26, 28; 2:15, 19; cf. Ps. 18). The first account is not concerned (as the second is) to describe an immanent world-order, but rather to express God's lordship over man, the nations of the world and their history.

When it states that "everything that he had made . . . was very good" (Gen. 1:31), it is not the world as such that is being praised, but God who made it and established his dominion over the world for the salvation of man (cf. Pss. 33; 65; 136; 148; Amos 4:13; 5:8; 9:5 f.).

3. The OT does not give a unique picture of the world which has nothing in common with other pictures. It draws on contemporary oriental ideas which it uses in its own particular way as material or framework for its own proclamation. The world is thus represented as tripartite.

The vault or firmament (*raqîa'*) of → heaven divides the waters above from the waters below (Gen. 1:6 ff.). This vault rests on "pillars" (Job 26:11; cf. Ps. 104:3), and the stars are set in it as luminaries (Gen. 1:14 f., 17).

The earth is sometimes pictured as a disc, whose middle-point is the central sanctuary (Jdg. 9:37; Ezek. 38:12; cf. Eth. Enoch 26:1; Jub. 8:19). It too rests on pillars (Job 9:6; cf. Ps. 104:5; 1 Sam. 2:8), or is suspended over nothing (Job 26:7). The waters above it and below it are restrained by God's providential care (Gen. 1:7; 7:11; 49:25; Exod. 20:4; Deut. 33:13; Prov. 8:27 f.).

The theological pronouncements of the OT made use of this common imagery. Heaven, the dwelling-place of Yahweh (Ezek. 1:22 f.) and the water are (like Tiamat in the Babylonian myth) the abode of beasts (Leviathan in Job 3:8; Ps. 74:14; Isa. 27:1; Rahab in Ps. 89:10; the serpent kept by Yahweh under the sea in Amos 9:3).

The underworld, *š'ôl* (→ Hell) is the kingdom of the dead, from which there is no return (Job 10:21). In complete contrast with contemporary religions, the OT also refuses to engage in speculative embellishment in statements about the underworld.

Nature, cosmic entities and elements are not observed for their own sake but always in their relation to their Creator and Lord. They are only instruments of God. The OT thus assimilates mythical cosmological elements with absolute freedom, but at the same time demythologizes them by co-ordinating them with and subordinating them to theological and soteriological statements.

4. Philo uses the word *kosmos* with strikingly greater frequency than the OT, but in statements which conflict with one another. He distinguishes between a *kosmos noētos*, the world which can only be apprehended by the mind, and the *kosmos aisthētos*, the world which is apprehended by the senses (*Op. Mund.*, 25). He also calls the latter "this world" (*Rer. Div. Her.*, 75) or the "visible world" (*Op. Mund.*, 16). At the same time he says that there is only one cosmos. Philo can speak of the cosmos as a living and animate being. Starting from the picture of God as the Father of the cosmos (*Vit. Mos.*, 2, 134), he can even call it *hyios theou*, son or child of God (*Ebr.*, 30; *Deus. Imm*, 31). These thoughts were taken up and developed by Egyptian Hel. gnosticism.

5. Under the influence of Hel. Judaism the originally temporal understanding of the Heb. word '*ôlām* (age, cf. Aram. '*ālᵉmā*'; long, far off; → Time, art. *aiōn*) acquired the spatial meaning of *kosmos*, world, universe, world of men, *oikoumenē* (from the time of 4 Esd.). Whereas '*ôlām* still has the old temporal meaning in the Dead Sea Scrolls, this spatial meaning of "world" is found increasingly frequently in Rabbinic usage. "Lord of the world" or "King of the world" are favourite titles of God.

This change of meaning took effect particularly in developed Judaism and, together with the Jewish apocalyptic doctrine of the Two Ages (→ Time, art. *aiōn*), conditioned views of the world. "This world", like "this age", is described in Rab. lit. as being under the domination of Satan, sin and death (cf. SB IV 847 ff.). This led to a simultaneous moral depreciation of the existing cosmos. But as Judaism held fast to belief in creation, it never adopted a gnostic dualistic world-view.

NT 1. (a) In the NT, as in secular Gk. and Hel. Judaism, the noun *kosmos* denotes the world. The sole exception is 1 Pet. 3:3, where it means adornment. Of the 185 occurrences of the word 78 come in Jn., 24 in the Johannine letters, 47 in the Pauline letters, 14 in the Synoptics and 22 in the rest of the NT writings. This frequent usage indicates both its theological importance and the area of confrontation. The *kosmos*-concept demands clarification when the gospel comes into contact with Gk. thought.

(b) The adjs. are found rarely and only in the later NT writings: *kosmios*, honourable, virtuous, respectable, only in 1 Tim. 2:9; 3:2; *kosmikos*, earthly, worldly, only in Tit. 2:12; Heb. 9:1.

In the vb. *kosmeō* (10 times) to put in order (Matt. 25:7, trim), decorate, adorn, (e.g. Matt. 12:44; Tit. 2:10) it is still the basic meaning of *kosmos* as adornment or order which counts.

2. The use of the noun *kosmos* in the inclusive sense of "world" exhibits three nuances:

(a) It can denote the universe (e.g. Acts 17:24; cf. also the phrase *ta panta*, (everything, all things) for the world as the sum-total of created things, cf. Jn. 1:3).

(b) It can also mean the world as the sphere or place of human life, the earth, the *oikoumenē*. This usage takes precedence in the Synoptics; thus Mk. 8:36, to gain the whole world; Matt. 4:8, all the kingdoms of the world (cf. Lk. 4:5, all the kingdoms of the *oikoumenē*).

The phrases "to come into the world" (Jn. 1:9; 3:19 etc.), "to be in the world" (e.g. Jn. 1:10; 2 Cor. 1:12 etc.) and "to go out of the world" (e.g. 1 Cor. 5:10) can also be understood in this sense.

(c) Finally it can stand for humanity, the world of men (cf. Jn. 3:19; 2 Cor. 5:19), where, especially in Paul and John, it designates the place and object of God's saving activity.

3. As early as Paul, the term *kosmos* is given a typically anthropological and historical stamp.

(a) The course of the world is determined by → man, through whose → fall → death came into the world and rules over it (Rom. 5:12 ff.). "The whole world" (i.e. of man) has become guilty before God (Rom. 3:19). Even the created world (Rom. 8:20–22; literally "the whole of creation") has been subjected to transience and longs for liberation. The *kosmos* is thus also the whole → creation subject to futility. This understanding of the world primarily finds verbal expression where Paul speaks of this world (*ho kosmos houtos*) analogously to this age (*ho aiōn houtos*, cf. 1 Cor. 3:19; 5:10; Eph. 2:2). God's → judgment is passed on this cosmos (Rom. 3:6), which belongs to the present age (→ Time, art. *aiōn*). The degree to which the word *kosmos* serves to denote the existent world threatened by futility and need can also be seen in the fact that the future redeemed world is never called *kosmos*, but the → "kingdom of God", "a new heaven and a new earth". There is no phrase corresponding to "this cosmos" (*ho kosmos houtos*) such as "the coming", "the future", or "that" cosmos. God and *kosmos* are strictly disparate.

(b) But it is into this world as it is, a world which has fallen into the power of → sin and → destruction, that God has sent his Son in order to reconcile it to himself (2 Cor. 5:19 ff.). And in this cosmos, whose → form is passing away (1 Cor. 7:31) the Christian → church lives as a sign of the presence of Christ (→ Body). Its relationship to the world is therefore dialectically determined. It can be neither unconditional surrender to nor denial of the world. Because Christians live in the cosmos (1 Cor. 5:10; Phil. 2:15), they must have dealings with the world. But it must be as if they had no dealings with it (1 Cor. 7:29 ff.). The church can be assured that everything belongs to them ("whether . . . the world or life or death or the present or the future"), but they themselves belong not to the cosmos but to Christ (1 Cor. 3:21 ff.). The world has thus become the field for obedience and maintenance of faith. Despite all its responsibility to the world and its involvement in it, the Christian church can still stand in the freedom of Christ. For it is also free from the world and its regulations (1 Cor. 7:20 ff.; cf. Matt. 17:24 ff.).

(c) Colossians shows how early Christianity had to get to grips with confronting the *kosmos*. The principalities and powers have been defeated by Christ (2:15). Therefore the elements of the cosmos (2:8, 20a) cannot be the object of ritual celebration or veneration. Christians who through Christ have died to the elements of the cosmos, no longer live "in the cosmos" (2:20b), but have been completely freed from subjection to its precepts and constraints.

4. *John*. R. Bultmann suggests that Jn. has utilized such concepts of gnosticism as the lostness of man in the world, the dualism of light and darkness, God and world, Jesus' descent from heaven, and the response of those in the truth (*The Gospel of John*, 1971, 7 ff.). He presents an individual understanding of the relationship between God and world, and man and world. By contrast with gnosticism, however, Jn. provides no cosmological undergirding for the lostness of the world and of man. The God-world dualism is not traced back to the badness of the cosmos as an innate quality in it, but is recognized as the consequence of the fault of man. Man belongs so much to the world that *kosmos* in Jn. almost always means the world of men. *kosmos* in Jn. can certainly be seen under different aspects, for example, as the world of men separated off from the rest of → creation (as subject 1:10; 15:19; as object of divine action 3:16 ff.; 4:42). Yet it is the world of men that is the determining feature of the whole of creation, notably in those places which speak of sending or coming into the world (3:17, 19; 9:39; cf. Bultmann, op. cit., 55 f. on Jn. 1:10). Out of love for this world (a completely un-Gk. thought!) God sends his Son (3:16), not to judge but to save (3:17; 12:47). As "the Lamb of God" he bears the sins of the world (1:29; cf. 1 Jn. 2:2). But the Son who has come into the world to bring salvation at the same time becomes its judgment (3:19), since it does not know him and is blind to him (1:10). The *kosmos* (understood as the world of men) constitutes a uniform subject which opposes God in enmity, resists the redeeming work of the Son, does not believe in him, and indeed hates him (7:7; 15:18 ff.). It is ruled by the prince of this cosmos (12:31; 16:11), i.e. the Evil One (1 Jn. 5:18). Nonetheless, the Son remains the victor over the world

525

(16:33). This does not lead to the extinction of the cosmos but to the redeemer of the world creating men who are not born "from out of the cosmos" (15:19; 17:14, 16) but of God (1:12 f.) and the Holy → Spirit (3:5). They endure much anguish in the world, but are removed from its domination (16:33).

Even though believers are no longer conditioned by the cosmos, they are not taken out of the world (17:15), but, in that they (as the frequently recurring formula says) remain "in him" (i.e. the Son), they are able to demonstrate in the world the belief and practice of the new commandment to love (13:34 f.; 15:9 ff.). When the Christian church is warned to maintain its distance over against the world (as in 1 Jn. 2:15: "Do not love the world or the things in the world. If any one loves the world, love for the Father is not in him"), we are concerned with the cosmos in its transience (v. 17), *ho kosmos houtos*, this world (cf. 12:31; 16:11). The church is to keep itself free from its seductive power. For anyone who loves this cosmos, i.e., abandons himself to it, does not have any share in the love of God which reaches out to him, and is therefore not capable of love as instructed in the command of the Lord. For as God has devoted his love to the world of men by sending his Son, so the Christian community is sent into the world by the Son (17:18; cf. 20:21) to keep his word and commandment (14:15, 23).　　　　　　　　　　　　　　*J. Guhrt*

→ Beginning, → Creation, → Heaven, → Kingdom, → Time, → Water

(a). Arndt, 13, 156, 44–48; 563 f., 892; A. Auer, "World," *EBT* III 1001–6; G. Bornkamm, "Christ and the World in the Early Christian Message," *Early Christian Experience*, 1969, 14–28; R. Bultmann, "The Understanding of Man and the World in the New Testament and in the Greek World," *Essays*, 1955, 67–89; and *Theology of the New Testament*, I, 1952, 254–59; II, 1955, 15–32; W. D. Davies, *The Gospel and the Land: Early Christianity and Jewish Territorial Doctrine*, 1974; W. Eichrodt, *Theology of the Old Testament*, II, 1967, 93–117; G. Johnston, "*Oikoumenē* and *kosmos* in the New Testament," *NTS* 10, 1963–64, 352 ff.; O. Michel, *oikoumenē, TDNT* V 157 ff.; G. von Rad, *Old Testament Theology*, I, 1962, 296–305; II, 1965 (see index); J. M. Robinson, "World in Modern Theology and in New Testament Theology," in *Soli Deo Gloria, Festschrift* for W. C. Robinson, 1968, 88 ff.; H. Sasse, *kosmeō, kosmos* etc., *TDNT* III 867–98; H. Schlier, *Principalities and Powers*, 1961; W. A. Visser t'Hooft, *The Meaning of Ecumenical* (The Burge Memorial Lecture, 1953), 1953; and "The Word 'Ecumenical' – its History and Use," in R. Rouse and S. C. Neill, *A History of the Ecumenical Movement, 1517–1948*, 1967²; 735–44; E. Schweizer, *choikos, TDNT* IX 472–9.

(b). G. Gloege, "Welt," *RGG*³ VI 1595 ff.; G. Harbsmeier, "Welt," *EKL* III 1756 ff.; G. Hierzenberger, *Weltbewertung bei Paulus nach 1 Kor. 7, 29–31. Eine exegetisch-kerygmatische Studie*, 1967; E. Jenni, "Das Wort '*ōlām* im Alten Testament," *ZAW* 64, 1952, 197 ff.; 65, 1953, 1 ff.; E. Jüngel, "Die Welt als Möglichkeit und Wirklichkeit," *EvTh* 29, 1969, 417 ff.; W. Kranz, "Kosmos," *Archiv für Begriffsgeschichte*, II 1 and 2, ed. E. Rothacker, 1955–57; R. Löwe, *Aiōn und Kosmos*, 1935; K. Lüthi, "Säkulare Welt als Objekt der Liebe Gottes," *EvTh* 26, 1966, 113 ff.; W. E. Mühlmann *et al.*, "Weltbild," *RGG*³ VI 1606 ff.; F. Mussner, *Christus das All und die Kirche*, 1955; and "Kosmos," *LTK* VI 576 ff.; M. Paeslack, "Die 'Oikoumene' im Neuen Testament," *Theologia Viatorum* 2, 1950, 33 ff.; R. Schnackenburg, *Christliche Existenz nach dem Neuen Testament*, II, 1968, 149–85; and "Das Verständnis der Welt nach dem Neuen Testament," op. cit., I., 1967, 157–85; W. Schrage, "Die Stellung zur Welt bei Paulus, Epiktet und in der Apokalyptik," *ZTK* 61, 1964, 125 ff.; J. Sint, "Kosmologie," *LTK* VI 569 ff.; R. Völkl, *Christ und Welt nach dem Neuen Testament*, 1961; E. Walter, *Christus und der Kosmos*, 1948; H. F. Weiss, *Untersuchungen zur Kosmologie des hellenistischen und palästinischen Judentums*, TU 97, 1966; H. E. Wilhelm *et al.*, "Weltbild, Weltanschauung," *EKL* III 1761 ff.

Ecstasy, Astonishment, Distraction, Horror, Madness

The NT uses two different word-groups to express the behaviour of a person who is no longer controlled by his normal reason. *ekstasis* means basically that a person has been brought out of his normal routine and outlook by the experience of a power or experience outside him. This can happen through the power of the Spirit of God. *mainomai*, however, is always used to express a diseased mental condition, normally associated in the ancient world with → demonic powers. *ekplēssō* means amaze, astound.

| ἔκστασις |

ἔκστασις (*ekstasis*), distraction, confusion, astonishment, terror, trance, ecstasy; ἐξίστημι (*existēmi*), trans. drive out of one's senses, confuse, amaze, astound; intrans. lose one's mind, be out of one's senses, be amazed, astonished.

CL *ekstasis* is found in secular Gk. from 5th–4th cent. B.C. Originally it meant a change of location, and then metaphorically confusion, terror, madness. The specific meaning of ecstasy, in which consciousness is partially or entirely non-operative through the work of a divine power, is found especially in Philo. The verb *existēmi* (variant form *existanō*) from 5th cent. B.C. on means confuse, terrify; in the mid. *existamai* (aor. *exestēn*) means lose one's wits. The biblical usage, be terrified, is seldom found in secular Gk.

OT Neither vb. nor noun is used in the LXX in the specific sense of ecstasy. (For such states *prophēteuō*, Heb. *hiṭnabbē'*, is used.) *ekstasis* often means confusion, terror, madness (cf. Jer. 5:30; Zech. 12:4). In 1 Sam. 11:6; 14:15 it means a terror or panic caused by God; in Deut. 28:28 madness. The vb. used in the act. sense is found in Exod. 23:27; Jdg. 4:15; 8:12 with the same force as in secular Gk. The mid. *existamai* means in Isa. 28:7 lose one's wits, but the meaning of be terrified, be frightened is commoner. In Ezek. 26:16; 27:35 etc. it is strengthened by the addition of *ekstasei*, i.e. be terribly frightened (cf. Gen. 42:28; 43:33).

Ecstatic phenomena are found in the OT just as in the Gk. and Hel. worlds. In the early days of Israel there was the ecstasy of the elders in the wilderness (Num. 11:24–29) and the description of the trance condition of Balaam (Num. 24:4). The ecstatic character of the early Israelite prophetic bands is described in 1 Sam. 10:5 f., 10; 19:20–24. When occasionally prophets are said to be mad (2 Ki. 9:11; Hos. 9:7) or drunken (Isa. 28:7; Jer. 23:9), the passages point to the link between prophecy and ecstasy. But false prophets also appeared in Israel and neighbouring countries as ecstatics and visionaries. The prophets of Baal, whom Elijah as the true prophet of God opposed on Carmel, even cut themselves in their prophesying (1 Ki. 18:28). Israelite prophets claimed their own visions as messages from God (cf. Jer. 23:16 f.). Neither ecstasy, visions, nor the claim to an oracle are infallible signs which distinguish the true from the false prophet. Only the message itself will do that. In the intertestamental period prophecy gradually died out. The Jewish apocalyptic works hence claimed ecstatic experiences for pious men in time past, but their descriptions show that such experiences were not entirely unknown (cf. Dan. 4:16 (LXX); Eth. Enoch 71:11 "And I fell on my face, and my whole body became relaxed, and my spirit was transfigured"). In accounts of the Merkabah mysticism among the rabbis ecstatic experiences are described (Hagigah 13 ff.).

527

NT In the NT *ekstasis* and *existasthai* are used to express men's reaction to the wonderful acts of God, as are *thaumazō* and related expressions (→ Miracle, art. *thauma*; cf. Mk. 2:12; 5:42; Lk. 5:26; Acts 3:10). The act. *existēmi* is found in Lk. 24:22 and Acts 8:9, 11 with the meaning terrify, amaze.

The statement of Jesus' relations about him might be understood in the specific sense of ecstasy (Mk. 3:21), which would mean that he was taken to be an ecstatic. We should, however, prefer the interpretation that they were saying he was mad, for there are no ecstatic traits in Jesus' life of faith and prayer as depicted by the evangelists. According to Acts 10:10; 11:5; 22:17, the visions seen by Peter in Joppa and Paul in Jerusalem were in a trance (*ekstasei*). Acts also records speaking in tongues, and recognizes in it the work of the Holy Spirit (Acts 10:44, 46; 11:15, 17; 19:6). But in 1 Cor. 14 Paul clearly regards this phenomenon as ecstatic (cf. v. 23). On the other hand, it is purely a hypothesis when Behm suggests that the historic kernel of the Pentecostal event in Acts 2 was "mass ecstasy on the part of the disciples which includes outbreaks of glossolalia" (*TDNT* I 725). Paul says in 1 Cor. 14:18 that he was no stranger to speaking in tongues. Hence some have seen in 2 Cor. 5:13 a reference to ecstatic speech. In that case the thought would be the same as in 1 Cor. 14:19. It is more probable that Paul is defending himself against the charge of having exaggerated his authority above measure (cf. A. Oepke, *TDNT* II 457 f.). 1 Cor. 14:18 and Acts 22:17 suggest that the visions and revelations of 2 Cor. 12:2 ff., 7 were ecstatic experiences. The same could be true of John (Rev. 1:10; 4:1 f.) who describes his own spiritual experiences in contrast to the Jewish apocalypses. If so, he was seized by the Spirit and carried up to heaven, like Paul in 2 Cor. 12:2, 4. The apostle's reticence in 2 Cor. 12 and his sober evaluation of speaking in tongues in 1 Cor. 14:19 show that one must not overrate the importance of ecstasy for the primitive church. Paul did not regard his initial vision of Christ on the road to Damascus as ecstatic (1 Cor. 9:1; 15:8; Gal. 1:16). The strong spiritual consciousness which meets us in the NT writings is founded on the certainty that the church has been given a new revelation in Christ, transcending all that has gone before. The examples of ecstatic pious experiences are to be seen as a result but not as the cause of this faith. *W. Mundle*

μαίνομαι	μαίνομαι (*mainomai*), rave, be mad, be out of one's mind; μανία (*mania*), madness, frenzy.

CL *mainomai* (already in the Orphic writings) is linked with the Indo-European root *men-*, think, be moved, desire (cf. Lat. *memento*). Gk. used *mainomai* especially for excited thought, being in ecstasy, raving: (a) rage, rave (in Homer for both gods and men); (b) be intoxicated (Homer *Od.*, 21, 298), through an intoxicating drink; (c) the passion of love (Plato, cf. Test. Jos. 8:3); (d) be mad, in opposition to *sōphroneō;* (e) an expression for the madness and enthusiasm of the Bacchantes, be entranced; "A prophet is Dionysus also, for the Bacchus frenzy, the drunken madness, includes in it the prophetic power, for the one quite possessed by the spirit of the god, he makes to rave that he may foretell that which will be" (Eur., *Bacchae*, 260 ff.); "Because such a one stands aloof from human interests, and is rapt in contemplation of the divine, he is taken to task by the multitude as a man demented, because the multitude do not see that he is inspired by God" (Plato, *Phaedrus*, 249 d; cf. Jn. 10:20).

mainesthai is the technical term of the cult of Dionysus and of the inspired "mantic" divination, the best known representatives of which were the Sibyls in the grip of a divine power. At that time Dionysus was the favourite god to whom ecstasy was attributed. *mania* was one of his oldest attributes. At the same time he could free a man of madness and allow him to return to quiet self-consciousness through an act of purification.

OT The LXX renders Jer. 25:16 "be crazed" (of the peoples who have drunk from God's cup of wrath) by *manēsontai*. Yahweh threatens them all with the terror of war as punishment. In Jer. 29:26 (LXX 39:26) "every one who is mad" (*mainomenō*) is placed beside "who prophesies" (*propēēteuonti*) in a context intended to bring Jeremiah's prophetic opponents into discredit. In 4 Macc. 8:5; 10:13 Antiochus Epiphanes considers as madness the loyalty to their faith of the priest Eleazar and his sons, which led to their death as martyrs. Josephus called the building of the Tower of Babel madness (*Ant.*, 1, 116).

NT *mainomai* is found 5 times, and *mania* once in the NT. In Acts 12:15 Rhoda was told "You are mad", when she came with incomprehensible news. Festus (Acts 26:24) believed that Paul was mad and that he had lost his reason in his enthusiasm to penetrate into the ultimate secrets. Paul placed the "sober truth" (*sōphrosynē*) in antithesis to *mania* (v. 25). The elders of Athens had once judged Solon as Festus had judged Paul; "they said that he was mad (*mainesthai*)" (Diog. Laert., 1, 49). In 1 Cor. 14:23 Paul used *mainesthai* to describe the impression that would be made on invited or casual visitors to the church by speaking in tongues.

In Jn. 10:20 the use of *mainetai* is important. The unbelieving among the Jews reacted to Jesus' message by saying, "You have a demon and are mad." One was not allowed to listen to a demon-possessed man. In other words, we have here a strong religiously motivated repudiation of Jesus. While faith recognizes the highest sense in Jesus' message, it becomes madness for unbelief. The use of *mainesthai* reminds us of the madness in the cult of Dionysus in which a man is carried away in *mania* from his own responsible thinking into an ecstasy caused by the deity. Some of his hearers thought that by saying that Jesus had lost his wits through the action of an evil demon (cf. Jn. 7:20; 8:43, 52) they were absolved from the responsibility of listening further. Others, however, saw in the healing of the blind man God's vindication of Jesus' message.   *J. Schattenmann*

| ἐκπλήσσω | ἐκπλήσσω (*ekplēssō*), amaze, astound. |

CL The primary meaning of *ekplēssō* is to strike out or expel. The vb. is found with this sense in classical Gk. (e.g. "enjoyment banishes grief", Thucydides), but it occurs far more frequently with its derived meaning of astound or amaze (i.e. drive out of one's senses by a sudden shock). Among the sources of amazement expressed by *ekplēssō* in non-biblical literature are fear, desire, love, joy and pleasure.

OT Josephus uses *ekplēssō* several times to express amazement or overwhelming fear. The only example the LXX provides of its use is in Eccl. 7:17, where it translates the Heb. *šāmēm*, and means "be appalled" in the strong sense of "be destroyed".

NT *ekplēssō* occurs 13 times in the NT, but only once outside the Gospels. It is always found in the passive (*ekplēssomai*, be amazed). Usually it expresses the astonished reaction of uncommitted onlookers to Jesus' teaching (e.g. Mk. 1:22 par.; 6:2 par.) and – just once – to a demonstration of his healing power (Lk. 9:43). Only Luke names individuals as the subject of *ekplēssomai*: Mary and Joseph are amazed to find the boy Jesus sitting among the temple teachers (Lk. 2:48), and the proconsul Sergius Paulus is "astonished at the teaching of the Lord" (Acts 13:12). *D. H. Field*
→ Demon, → Knowledge, → Holy Spirit, → Prophet, → Revelation, → Word, → Tongue

(a). J. Behm, *glōssa, TDNT* I 719–27; J. D. G. Dunn, *Baptism in the Holy Spirit*, 1970; H. von Campenhausen, "Spirit and Authority in the Pauline Congregation", *Ecclesiastical Authority and Spiritual Power in the Church of the First Three Centuries*, 1969, 55–75; J. C. Hurd, *The Origin of 1 Corinthians*, 1965; A. Oepke, *ekstasis, TDNT* II 449–60; J. Preisker, *mainomai, TDNT* IV 360 ff.; J. P. M. Sweet, "A Sign for Unbelievers: Paul's Attitude to Glossolalia," *NTS* 13, 1966–67, 240–57; S. Tugwell, *Did You Receive the Spirit?* 1971; I. M. Lewis, *Ecstatic Religion*, 1971.
(b). F. Maass, "Zur psychologischen Sonderung der Ekstase," *Festschrift A. Alt, Wissenschaftliche Zeitschrift* Leipzig 3, 1953–54, 167 ff.; and "Ekstase," *EKL* I 1057 f.; E. Rohde, *Psyche*, II 4, 1910, 40 ff., 59 ff.; A. Schimmel, "Ekstase," *RGG*³ II 410 ff.; C. Schneider, *Geistesgeschichte des antiken Christentums*, 1954, 140 ff.

Egypt, Egyptian

Αἴγυπτος

Αἴγυπτος (*Aigyptos*), Egypt; *Αἰγύπτιος* (*Aigyptios*), Egyptian.

OT The Greek word derives from Egyptian *ḥwt-k3-Ptḥ* (pronounced approximately *ḥa-ku-ptaḥ*), a name of Memphis, Egypt's ancient capital (opposite modern Cairo, its successor). The term was extended (by the Greeks?) to include the country as well as its capital, much as in modern Arabic *Maṣr* (strictly Cairo) applies to Egypt. In the LXX, *Aigyptos* translates Hebrew *miṣrayim*, a word of uncertain meaning (connected with "forts" or "borders"?), whose outwardly dual form might possibly reflect Egypt's duality in geography (long valley, broad delta) and institutions (twin origins and forms of pharaonic monarchy and administration).

In the OT (hence also LXX), the significance of Egypt may be surveyed under seven heads.

1. *Part of God's World.* In Gen. 10:6, 13, *miṣrayim* (LXX, *Mesrain*) appears as an ancestral or eponymous figure for Egypt and the Egyptians, securing them their place in God's world among the families of the earth. At the opposite extreme from the Euphrates, the East-Delta arm of the Nile of Egypt was an outermost bound of

530

the lands covenanted with Abraham (Gen. 15:18). Culturally, Egypt was a land of great antiquity (cf. Isa. 19:11), known for luxurious products – fine linen (Prov. 7:16; Ezek. 27:7), or dashing chariots and steeds (1 Ki. 10:28–29; Cant. 1:9). Like Assyria or → Babylon, Egypt was a great Gentile power *per excellence*; but as such, it was still subject to God's summons (Zech. 14:18–19). The sweeping onset of her annual Nile flood was the symbol of devastating judgment on Israel (Amos 8:8; 9:5).

2. *Place of Refuge and Sojourn.* (a) *Of Man's Choice.* After Bethel (cf. Gen. 12:8; 13:3–4), → Abraham pressed by famine sought deliverance not from God but in Egypt (Gen. 12:10–13:1). Thence he brought Hagar, by whom he and Sarah thereafter sought a purely human solution to their childlessness (Gen. 16), though God's promise came not by the "bondwoman" but by his gift (cf. Gen. 17:19; 21:10).

(b) *Of God's Giving.* In due time (cf. Gen. 15:13–14), Egypt was the divinely-provided refuge for Israel's family (Gen. 37; 39–50), through Joseph (Gen. 45:7–8; 50:20), whence Jacob-Israel himself made a funerary "exodus" (Gen. 50:5 ff.) as later did Joseph (Gen. 50:25; cf. Exod. 13:19).

3. *Bondage whence God Delivered Israel.* In OT tradition, Egypt became above all else "the house of bondage" from which God saved Israel by his might and wonders (Exod. 20:1; Deut. *passim*) at the Exodus (Exod. 1–15). This deliverance was recalled in the wilderness (Exod. 23; 32; Lev. 11:45; 25:38; etc.) and impressed Israel's foes (Jos. 9:9; 1 Sa. 4:8; 6:6). Forever after it re-echoed down the centuries as a major starting-point whence God led a rebellious Israel through history – under the judges (Jdg. 2:1, 2; 1 Sa. 8:8; 10:18), Solomon (1 Ki. 8), later kings (e.g. 2 Ki. 17:7) and after the Babylonian Exile (Neh. 9:9, 18). The psalmists sang of it (e.g., Pss. 78:12, 43, 51; 80:8; 106:7, 21), and the prophets swelled the chorus (e.g., Jer. 2:6 and *passim*; Ezek. 20; Dan. 9:15; Hos. 12:9, 13; Amos 2:10; 9:7; Hag. 2:5). Israel came forth as God's "son" (Hos. 11:1).

4. *As Measure of Later Bondage and Deliverance.* God's marvels in delivering early Israel from Egypt are the measure he gives of future acts (Mic. 7:15). Egypt further became a symbol of spiritual bondage, e.g. of servitude to idolatry in future exiles (Hos. 8:13 and 9:3 in context of Assyrian threat), although not again to be the place of exile of the whole Hebrew nation (Hos. 11:5). Future deliverances for Israel were to be measured by the Egyptian deliverance (Isa. 11:11; Hos. 11:11; Zech. 10:10), also in minor key (so Jer. 44:28).

5. *In Later Historical Contexts.* After the Exodus period, Egypt's role in the OT again varies – occasionally an ally (1 Ki. 3:1) or a refuge (1 Ki 11:40; Jer. 26:21 ff.), sometimes an outright foe (1 Ki. 14:25 ff.; 2 Ki. 23:33–34; cf. Ezek. 19:4), but above all as a snare, an object of misplaced confidence for help (e.g., 2 Ki. 17:4; cf. 18:21, etc.). Hebrew trust in Egyptian "strength" rather than in God's provision led to new forms of bondage, political and similar (cf. (e.g.) Isa. 30–31; Jer. 2:18, 36; 37:5, 7; 41:17; 42–44; Ezek. 17:15; 23; Hos. 7:11, 16; 12:1).

6. *Object of Judgments.* Judgment was pronounced on Egypt by the word of the Lord through Isaiah (19; 20), Jeremiah (46), Ezekiel (29–32) and even Joel (3:19), because of pride, self-assertion, and attacks on the covenant people.

7. *Object of Blessing.* But Egypt was also to know restoration and divine healing.

531

With Assyria and Israel Egypt too was to become "his people" (cf. Isa.19:19–25),but not again to be a snare or exalted over other nations (cf. Ezek. 29:13–16).

NT In the NT, Egypt's roles correspond in outline to those in the OT.

1. *Part of God's World.* At Pentecost, among so many others, Egyptians heard God's works proclaimed in their own tongue (Acts 2:10). An Egyptian is mentioned as one who had sought violent means to solve political problems (Acts 21:38; cf. Jos. *War*, 2, 261; *Ant.* 20, 169 ff.).

2. *Bondage from which God Delivered Israel.* In the NT, deliverance from Egypt at the Exodus remains a paradigm example of God's saving power (Acts 7; 13:17); and Israel's subsequent unfaithfulness, of human sin (Acts 7:39; Heb. 3:16; 8:9; Jude 5).

3. *Refuge from which God called His Son.* As of old the patriarch Israel and his people were divinely sustained in Egypt (Gen. 45:5, 7), whence God later called forth Israel as his "son" (Hos. 11:1), so the infant Jesus was taken into refuge in Egypt by divine command (Matt. 2:13), and thence came forth in final fulfilment of Hosea's words (Matt. 2:15, 19). → Fullness, art. *plēroō.*

4. *Symbol of Man's Materialism and Earthbound Law.* In the gallery of faith, Moses is seen to have rejected Egypt's blandishments of rank and material treasures in favour of God's call to lead his people to deliverance (Heb. 11:24–27). This antithesis of rebel worldliness in opposition to God finds focus also in Rev. 11:8, where the bodies of faithful slain lie in the street of a city called "Sodom and Egypt", in character with earthly pharisaic Jerusalem and idolatrous Rome. Finally, Paul draws from Gen. 16 (cf. OT 2 (a) above) the example of Hagar/Ishmael and Sarah/Isaac to illustrate human legalistic devising and divine promise and fulfilment, and to make clear the distinction between law and grace. The one is born of human self-will, under law; the other is the heir of promise, God's gift from above (Gal. 4:21–31). *K. A. Kitchen*

The following works provide bibliographical aids: I. A. Pratt, *Ancient Egypt, Sources in New York Public Library*, 1925; I. A. Pratt, *Ancient Egypt* (1925–41), 1942; W. Federn in *Orientalia* 17–19 (1948–50) for 1939–46; thereafter J. M. A. Janssen, Heerma van Voss and J. J. Janssen, *Annual Egyptological Bibliography*, 1948– (for 1947 onwards); and from 1971 by the quarterly lists, B. J. Kemp, ed., *Egyptology Titles.*
On monuments history and geography see: B. Porter, R. L. B. Moss *et al., Topographical Bibliography of Ancient Egyptian Hieroglyphic Texts, Reliefs and Paintings*, I–VII (1927–51) 1960–²; H. Kees, *Ancient Egypt, a Cultural Topography*, 1961; A. Gardiner, *Egypt of the Pharaohs*, 1961; É. Drioton and J. Vandier, *L'Égypte*, 1962⁴; the relevant chapters of the *Cambridge Ancient History*, I–II, 1961–, 2nd ed. in fascicles, 1970–³ bound; K. A. Kitchen, *The Third Intermediate Period in Egypt (1100–650 B.C.)*, 1972; S. Herrmann, *Israel in Egypt*, 1973 (but on this see the critical review by K. A. Kitchen, *TSF Bulletin* 71, 1975, 24 f.).
On culture, literature, language and religion see: G. Posener, S. Sauneron, J. Yoyotte, *Dictionary of Egyptian Civilization*, 1962; C. Aldred, *The Egyptians*, 1961; A. Erman, tr. A. M. Blackman, *Literature of the Ancient Egyptians*, 1927, with new introduction by W. K. Simpson as *The Ancient Egyptians, A Sourcebook of their Writings*, 1966; R. O. Faulkner, E. F. Wente, W. K. Simpson, *The Literature of Ancient Egypt*, 1972; J. B. Pritchard, ed., *Ancient Near Eastern Texts Relating to the Old Testament*, (1950) 1969; J. H. Breasted, *Ancient Records of Egypt*, I–V, 1906–7; A. H. Gardiner, *Egyptian Grammar*, 1957³ and reprints; R. O. Faulkner, *A Concise Dictionary of Middle Egyptian*, 1962 and reprints; J. H. Breasted, *Development of Religion and Thought in Ancient Egypt* (1912) 1959; H. Frankfort, *Ancient Egyptian Religion*, (1948) 1961; S. Sauneron, *The Priests of Ancient Egypt*, 1960; P. Montet, *L'Égypte et la Bible*, 1959; K. A. Kitchen, Art. "Egypt" in *NBD* 337–54; and "Egypt, Land of" *ZPEB* II 225–58; J. R. Harris, ed., *The Legacy of Egypt*, 1971².

Elect, Choose

Two groups of words are used in the NT to describe the act of judgment or decision by which preference is given to one of several possibilities, people or groups. They are *haireomai* and *eklegomai* in their various forms. The second group is much more frequent than the first, although neither occurs particularly often. Both are capable of expressing not only human choice, but the electing activity of God in a specifically theological sense. In the great majority of cases, however, it is clear that the latter meaning is intended. When the sense is that of commission to a particular task, giving the person concerned what is in effect a special position, *kaleō* and its derivatives (→ Call) are used. For the definition of the limits of such a task, the word is *horizō* or *prohorizō* (→ Determine, Appoint). Where it is a matter of appointment to a particular office or to a function within a certain order of precedence, *kathistēmi, paristēmi* (→ Determine, Appoint) or *tassō* (→ Place, Put) are also found.

αἱρέομαι

αἱρέομαι (*haireomai*), choose; αἵρεσις (*hairesis*), sect, school, party, group; αἱρετικός (*hairetikos*), factious, heretical, heretic; αἱρετίζω (*hairetizō*), choose; διαιρέω (*dihaireō*), distribute, divide; διαίρεσις (*dihairesis*), allotment, division.

CL 1. *haireō* (act.) is found frequently in cl. Gk. from Homer onwards (also Philo, Josephus), in the senses of take, seize, grasp, gain, understand. But the mid. *haireomai*, take for oneself, seize for oneself, gain for oneself, choose for oneself, decide in favour of something, is also in common use. The noun *hairesis* (Aesch., Hdt.), formed from the vb. *hairein*, denotes in cl. Gk. (a) taking, acquisition, conquest; (b) choice, opportunity to choose; (c) aspiration, desire for something, inclination; and (d) purposeful decision or resolve. Thus it always contains an element of action and personal decision.

The adj. *hairetikos*, used as a noun in cl. Gk., describes someone who is capable of choice, able to choose. *hairetizō* (Hippocrates) is an intensive form of *haireomai* meaning to make someone *hairetos* (Hdt.), eligible, i.e. to choose him. Finally, the derivative *dihaireō* (Homer) means to take apart, tear asunder, divide, in order to differentiate; i.e. to distinguish, separate, distribute; then also allocate. The noun *dihairesis* (Hdt.) similarly means dissection, dividing, distribution, allocation, and also classification, distinction. As in the case of *hairesis*, the emphasis is on the action, and only secondarily on the effect.

2. In the late classical writers, and especially in Hel. Gk., the two nouns *hairesis* and *dihairesis* have a specific meaning. *hairesis* here has its meaning objectified and denotes the teaching or the school of a particular philosopher with which a person identifies himself by his own choice. A school of philosophy, which gathered around the authoritative figure of its teacher, was defined by dogmas (→ Commandment, art. *dogma*) to which the followers assented and by a communal set of rules governing their style of life. *dihairesis* is used by Plato as a term for dialectic method, as employed for the purpose of classifying words (cf. *Pol.* 258c ff.).

OT 1. In the LXX this group of words – in contrast to → *eklegomai* or *boulomai* (→ Will) – is not particularly frequent. This may be due to the character of the

OT concept of election which was not, of course, based upon the pattern of free, political choice or that of complete freedom to choose a set of teachings or an outlook on life. Of the 11 texts in which *haireomai* occurs, in 4 it represents *bāḥar*, choose, choose out, prefer (e.g. 2 Sam. 15:15; Jer. 8:3). Otherwise, it stands *inter alia* for *hāpēṣ*, delight in (1 Sam. 19:1; → Please). *hairesis* is found only 5 times altogether, and only in Lev. 22:18, 21 as a direct translation (*nᵉḏāḇâh*, free-will offering) of a Heb. equivalent. It has the meaning choice in the phrases *ex haireseōs* (Gen. 49:5) and *kata hairesin* (Lev. 22:18, 21), of free choice. Rather more frequent is the intensive form *hairetizō* (to choose) which usually stands for *bāḥar*. It is often used together with *eklegomai* for God's act of choice (cf. 1 Chr. 28:4, 6, 10; Ps. 25:12; 119:30). In some examples (Hag. 2:23; Mal. 3:17) the sense of adoption is also present. Matt. 12:18, the only place where *hairetizō* occurs in the NT, is a quotation from Isa. 42:1, where the meaning is "choose" in parallelism with *eudokein* ("be well pleased", though Matt. is not following the LXX but another translation here).

dihaireō is used for various forms of *ḥālaq*, divide, share, take possession of, and *ḥāṣâh*, to divide, and also for *bāḥar* (Gen. 15:10) and other words. It is found chiefly in the sense of classify, apportion (cf. Gen. 32:7; Jos. 18:5; 1 Chr. 24:3 ff.; Ezek. 37:22). The noun *dihairesis* usually represents the Heb. *maḥᵃlōqeṭ*, division, and means distribution, part, division (e.g. 1 Chr. 27:1 ff.), or even clan (Jdg. 5:15).

2. The writings of Philo and especially those of Josephus contain a specific development of these nouns. *hairesis* is used to describe both Gk. schools of philosophy and the religious groups within Judaism, the Essenes, the Sadducees and the Pharisees. The Heb. equivalent in Rab. Judaism is *mîn*, which however denotes a member of a sect (*hairetikos*) rather than the sect itself. At this point the meaning of the word underwent a decisive change. Used at first quite generally for the parties within Judaism, it came to be used more and more for a heretical sect in the bad sense. This change, which came around A.D. 100, finally caused *mîn* by the end of the 2nd cent. A.D. to be used no longer to distinguish between groups within the Jewish community, but for people of other faiths, e.g. Christians or Gnostics. These stood outside the believing community and were thus altogether outside the sphere of salvation.

NT 1. In the NT *haireomai* occurs in only 3 places, always in the mid. voice. At Phil. 1:22 and Heb. 11:25 it has the weakened meaning, prefer. This corresponds to its frequent use in cl. Gk. with or without *mallon*, rather (*mallon haireisthai . . . ē . . .*), or with the accusative. Here it overlaps in meaning with *thelō* and *boulomai* (→ Will). However, *thelō* expresses more a sovereign decision with clear, resolute intent, while *boulomai* means a wish and desire based on asserted authority.

In 2 Thess. 2:13 *haireomai* has a specialized biblical meaning not found in cl. Gk., elect someone to something (here God's election of the church to salvation). In this sense of God's elective decision, it is to be distinguished from *eudokeō*, have good pleasure (→ Please) which expresses his sovereign choice, and *klēroō* which promises to the chosen, as those called, their appointed destiny (→ Inheritance, art. *klēros*). *eklegomai*, on the other hand, emphasizes the selective aspect of the choice, and *dechomai* acceptance and reception on the ground of God's good pleasure.

534

2. The NT meaning of *hairesis* follows the usage in Hel. Gk. and Jud. In Acts, where 6 of the 9 examples are found, it refers to the parties of the Pharisees and Sadducees as groups within the Jewish community: *hairesis tōn Saddoukaiōn*, the sect of the Sadducees (Acts 5:17); *hairesis tōn Pharisaiōn*, the sect of the Pharisees (Acts 15:5; cf. 26:5). From the Jewish point of view, the Christians too are described as belonging to a *hairesis: prōtostatēs tēs tōn Nazaraiōn haireseōs*, ringleader of the sect of the Nazarenes (Acts 24:5; cf. Acts 24:14; 28:22).

Because of its universal character, the Christian *ekklēsia* (→ Church) could not be content to regard itself as a *hairesis*. All Christians belong to the church, "the lawful public assembly of the whole people of God" (H. Schlier, *TDNT* I 183), while the term *hairesis* suggests the private, unauthorized character of a school or party. Hence in Gal. 5:20 *haireseis* are listed as one of the *erga tēs sarkos*, works of the flesh. Justification for this is provided in 1 Cor. He who splits the church or breaks it up into parties is dividing Christ, whose body is the church (1 Cor. 1:10 ff.; 11:18 f.; cf. 12:27). A distinction is drawn in 1 Cor. between *haireseis* and *schismata*. Whereas *schismata* means "splits in the church caused by personally motivated disputes" (H. Schlier, ibid.), *haireseis* add to the division an eschatological aspect. "*haireseis* are the results of the *schismata*" (H. Lietzmann, 1 *Kor.*, *HNT*, 56). The ruinous *haireseis* are brought about by the activities of false teachers (*pseudodidaskaloi*; → Teach) who deny Christ (cf. 2 Pet. 2:1).

In complete contrast to its use in cl. Gk. (where it means able to choose), *hairetikos* is used in biblical Gk. for the adherents of a *hairesis*, a heretic. In Tit. 3:10 we see the church's procedure for disciplining heretics, following Matt. 13:15 ff. and 2 Jn. 10.

In the early church *hairesis* became a technical term for a body opposing the *ekklēsia* understood in eschatological terms. This is especially true in Ignatius and Justin (Ign., *Eph.* 6:10; *Tral.* 6:1; Justin, *Dial.*, 51:2). But Origen returns to the old meaning of *hairesis*, using it to refer to different schools within Christianity (*Contra Celsum*, 3, 12).

3. In the list of the *erga tēs sarkos*, works of the flesh (Gal. 5:19 ff.), between *eritheiai*, quarrels (→ Anger), and *haireseis* there is mention of *dichostasiai*. This word is used in cl. Gk. to mean dispute, disunity, strife, in general, and also political opposition, revolt, rebellion. It is warned against in Rom. 16:17 together with the creation of stumbling-blocks (*ta skandala*). In some MSS of 1 Cor. 3:3 it is listed together with *zēlos* and *eris* and declared to be "fleshly" behaviour (*kata anthrōpon*). If it is here a matter of disunity and dissensions in the church, the political meaning in 1 Clem. 46:5 is unmistakable.

4. *dihaireō* should be translated in the NT, to distribute. Lk. 15:12: "And he divided his living between them". 1 Cor. 12:11 speaks of the distribution of spiritual gifts which the Spirit apportions to the various members of the church as he will (→ Body).

The noun *dihairesis* occurs in the NT only in 1 Cor. 12:4 ff., where the reference is to the manifold nature of the gifts of the Spirit and their *distribution* among many members in the unity of single grace of God, bearing witness to God's revelation. This use of the word led later to the appearance in the Fathers of *dihairesis* as a term for the distinctions in the relationship between the persons of the Trinity (H. Schlier, *TDNT* I 185).   G. Nordholt

ἐκλέγομαι

ἐκλέγομαι (*eklegomai*), pick out for oneself, choose (out); ἐκλεκτός (*eklektos*), chosen (out); ἐκλογή (*eklogē*), picking out, election, selection.

CL 1. *eklegomai* (Hdt.) is the mid. of *eklegō*, pick out, choose out a person or thing (from a sizeable number). The act. form does not occur at all in the NT and only occasionally in the LXX. It is derived from *legō*, count, collect, read (→ Word). The verbal adj. *eklektos*, which is sometimes used absolutely (attested since Plato), denotes the person or thing upon whom the choice has fallen. The noun *eklogē*, derived from the vb. (likewise Plato) and originally meaning exclusively the act of choosing, can be used with the vbs. *lambanō*, take, *poieomai*, do, or *ginomai*, here in the sense of arrive at. The words of this group are used in various contexts, but wherever they are found, it is evident that certain things common to them all are implied. First, there are several objects from which to choose; secondly, the person making the choice is not tied down by any circumstances which force his hand, but is free to make his own decision. Thirdly, the person making the choice – at least at the moment of choosing – has the person or thing to be chosen at his disposal. Moreover, the act of choosing (and thus the words of this group) includes a judgment by the chooser as to which object he considers to be the most suitable for the fulfilment of his purpose. It is not of vital importance whether it be objective criteria, or subjective feelings and considerations which are paramount in making the decision.

2. Although these words originate in military vocabulary, by the time of Plato *eklegomai* and *eklogē* are already in use in a political sense (referring to elections). In every case it is a matter of electing people to perform a certain task, or administer a certain office. These include in the political sphere the *presbytai*, → elders, for the administration of the *polis* (Plato, *Rep.*, 536c; Polybius, 6, 10, 9), the *archontes* (Plato, *Rep.*, 414a, → Beginning, art. *archē* NT 4), or other officials and people with public responsibilities (Plato, *Laws*, 802b). *eklogē*, however, is also used of the general conscription of men for military service (Polybius 5,63,11), and the selection of individuals from the whole army for a particularly difficult or glorious mission (Polybius 9, 13, 9). Prudence and experience, appropriate standing in society or sufficient wealth, courage and suitability constitute the conditions necessary in each instance, if a person is to be considered for election. But it is the election itself which makes it possible for him to take up his function and which at the same time lays an obligation upon him. For election, whether of individuals or of a group, is regarded as a distinction (very occasionally it is used in a negative sense, implying especial severity). It is usually conducted in a manner in keeping with the concept of an aristocratic élite. It is always, however, accompanied by some kind of obligation or task concerned with the well-being of all the other members of the community of which the one elected forms part. Through its proper organs, the *polis* gives the individual who has special gifts the opportunity to develop these for the benefit of all.

3. At the same time, the words may be applied to objects. *eklegomai* is used of the choice of certain places (Plato, *Tim.*, 24c), deciding in favour of what is intellectually or aesthetically good (*Symposium*, 198d), or selection of especially treasured passages from literature in general or from the work of a certain author (Athenaeus, 14, 663c; Polybius, 1, 47, 9). *eklogē* can also refer to the requisition of material

536

(e.g. ships), or the levying of official tribute and taxes (Athenaeus 6, 235b). The words express in every case the idea that a part has been claimed from a greater quantity, by an independent act of decision for a particular purpose, and that the remainder has been passed over.

4. It is not until the Stoic writers that we find a change in meaning of the words of this group, approximating to what we have said about *haireomai. eklogē* can now be used, no longer with reference to a special dignity, but in an individual sense, to mean a single person's free decision between two or more possibilities with respect to his manner of life, livelihood or use of his material goods. Epictetus (*Dissertationes*, 2, 10, 6) produces the maxim that such a choice must be in favour of that which is fitting to the nature of the case.

OT 1. (a) The first thing to be noticed in the LXX is that the Gk. noun *eklogē* is completely lacking. This is due to the fact that there is no Heb. word for it to translate, since abstract concepts are generally foreign to the Heb. language. The fact that only verbal forms are found automatically results in an emphasis, not so much on the action itself (see above CL, *eklogē*), as on the person who chooses and the one chosen (*eklektos*) in each instance. The act. form *eklegō*. which has the same meaning and syntax, occurs only 10 times, especially in the books of Kings and Chr. The mid. *eklegomai* nearly always renders forms of the Heb. vb. *bāḥar*, choose, select, prefer. Only in exceptional cases is *bāḥar* translated by *epilegō*, a related word of the same meaning (cf. Exod. 17:9; Num. 16:5), *haireomai* (cf. 2 Sam. 15:15; 1 Chr. 28:6), *hairetizō* (cf. Ps. 119:30), *areskō*, to have good pleasure in (Deut. 23:17), and *bouleuomai*, to prefer.

bāḥar, however, has in fact roughly the same range of meanings as the Gk. vb. For instance, in Isa. 40:20 it describes the choice of a suitable material (wood for an idol); in Gen. 6:2 the carefully considered choice of a wife, at the same time motivated by liking and desire; in Gen. 13:11 Lot's choice of the part of the land which seemed to him most favourable. In Prov. the niph. is used to portray an object as especially desirable in comparison to another. Understanding, fear of God, and wisdom, in short a devout and obedient life before God is to be preferred to gold and silver (Prov. 8:10, 19; 16:16). The vb. is also found in the sense of election by the people (cf. the Gk. election of *archontes*) of a king (1 Sam. 8 18). The participial forms *bāḥūr* and *bāḥîr* (again like the Gk.) can be used to describe specially chosen élite troops (cf. Jdg. 20:15 f.; 1 Sam. 24:2; 2 Chr. 25:5), or particularly suitable material (Exod. 14:7, chariots). *eklegomai* can even be used in the sense of a considered choice between several possibilities (the punishment to be imposed, 2 Sam. 24:12; or the promised reward, 2 Sam. 19:39). Finally it is used of the basic religious decision between Yahweh and other gods (Jos. 24:15), or between life in God's temple and life in the world of evildoers (Ps. 84:10).

(b) Besides *bāḥar*, *eklegomai* is also used to translate the rare vb. *bārar*, set apart, select, purge (e.g. 1 Chr. 16:41, of the dedication of priests for service before the ark; Ezek. 20:38, of the separation of rebels from the rest of the people). *eklektos* also appears a number of times for Heb. roots connoting loveliness, preciousness (Jer. 3:19; Hag. 2:7), or excellent condition (e.g. the cows in Gen. 41:2, 4). Here the adj. does not express the fact of being chosen, but in a wider sense factors already present which make choice likely.

537

(c) In the majority of cases where *bāḥar* (and thus *eklegomai*) is found, it is not man, but God, who does the choosing. Yahweh is the subject, the one who chooses. This is true particularly in Deut., the books of Samuel, Ki. and Chr., some of the Pss., and Isa. As the object of God's choice, the picture is as follows. In Deut., besides the people which God has singled out for a special mission (Deut. 4:37; 7:7; 14:2), it is above all the one place (Heb. *māqôm*; Gk. *topos*) excluding all others which God has appointed for his people as a centre for worship and the performance of his sacrifices (cf. Deut. 16:6 f.; 18:5 f.; 26:2). In 1 Ki. (cf. 11:13, 32; 14:21) and 2 Chr. (cf. 6:34, 38; 12:13) this is defined more closely as the city of David (→ Jerusalem on the choice of Zion). David is himself likewise described as chosen in this context (1 Ki. 8:16; 11:34). In the cultic sphere we also find the choice of the priests (Deut. 18:5; 1 Sam. 2:28; 1 Chr. 15:2; 16:41, also including Levites). Saul and David are regarded as having been chosen as kings (1 Sam. 10:24; 16:8–10; and especially 2 Sam. 6:21; but note the contrast between this and 1 Sam. 8:18). Finally, in the later chapters of Isa., the Deuteronomic statements about the election of the people (see above) are applied to the servant (Isa. 43:10), Jacob and Abraham (41:8), as representatives of the people.

2. The linguistic observation, that in the use of the Heb. and Gk. terms the emphasis is totally on the action of God, is strengthened still more by the fact that the part. *bāḥûr*, which points rather to the quality of the object, is not used of Israel as the chosen people. Theologically, this means that the OT – obviously quite consciously and consistently – is concerned to avoid the temptation of drawing attention to the importance or status of the nation. Rather it is to be directed to God's free acts of grace which indeed run counter to all human concepts of merit. For this reason the other participial form *bāḥîr* is used, although this is not apparent in the Gk. of the LXX (*eklektos* is used for both). *bāḥîr* (cf. 2 Sam. 21:6; Ps. 105:43; Isa. 42:1; 65:22) indicates that the purpose of the choice is some commission or service, and can only meaningfully retain its validity in its fulfilment. The whole Deut. outlook, as well as Isa., sees in this activity of God the creation among the nations of a new, quite different type of community. Its purpose is to show in Israel in the midst of world history God's sovereign acts, his grace, and the seriousness of his demands. The doctrine of election is thus an indissoluble part of the knowledge of God's holiness, uniqueness, and unconditioned sovereignty. It expresses the total claim he makes in keeping with these aspects of his nature. This line of thought reaches its climax in the passages of Isa. which speak of God's servant (→ Son of God, art. *pais theou*), where the latter appears as God's agent in the redemption of all mankind. God's election is not tied to and is certainly not based upon human qualifications. Nor does it create a position of privilege. Hence, it can only be meaningfully maintained, where it leads to a response to the love of God, to obedience, and to the kind of life which is presupposed by the commission and the → commandments. It is not a goal already reached, but a beginning which has to be confirmed. Therefore, we find at the same time a warning that God may reject again those whom he has drawn to him in this way (cf. 1 Sam. 16:1; Jer. 14:19).

The concept we are here considering is, however, elsewhere sometimes spoken of by means of other terms and metaphors, e.g. in language about the → covenant, the → love of God, God's knowledge (Amos 3:2), and the (new) creation (Deut. 32:6). From this it can be seen that Israel's consciousness of being chosen has its roots in the patriarchal tradition (→ Abraham) and that of the exodus (→ Moses), but that it was more explicitly worked out during the exile and later. It was in the break-up of Israel's national existence that her religious and political boundaries were overcome and the way opened up into the wider world outside.

3. There is, however, a danger of thinking and speaking of those who are chosen, their qualifications and the difference between them and other people, as if man could dispose over election as an established fact. This is unavoidable, when the idea creeps in of an élite who deserve preference over the rest by reason of their struggles, sufferings, their stricter discipline or their greater self-sacrifice. Rab. theology, and even more so apocalyptic (→ Secret, art. *mystērion* OT), effected such a transformation in the interpretation of suffering in connection with the servant passages in Isa. It similarly saw proof of election in unyielding resistance in times of affliction (the infiltration of Hellenism, and the Jewish war). Thus the utmost im-portance came to be attached to the possession and knowledge of the Torah as a basis for belief in election, giving Israel an advantage over others (cf. 4 Ezr. 5:23 ff.). This was expressed particularly in thoughts of vengeance which also influenced this line of thought (cf. Eth. Enoch 62:11–15). Election thus became a status and privi-lege which can be recognized and achieved by means of dubious merits (cf. 1QM 10:9 f.). It is only a continuation of these ideas when the OT teaching about the difference between the true spiritual Israel and mere political and physical member-ship of the people, especially in the context of resistance to Hellenistic "infiltration", led the devout to separate themselves off into exclusive groups. Inevitably this brought the concept of individual election further to the fore (cf. 1QH 9:29 f.). This is especially apparent in the Qumran texts (e.g. 1QS 4:22; 8:1–15) in which conscious-ness of being chosen leads not only to a feeling of superiority over other nations, and over the ungodly in their own (the chosen are seen as judges, 1QpHab 5:4 ff.), but also to a direct hatred for those who have been rejected (1QS 1:4). Certain aspects of Pharisaic piety, e.g. their contempt for the common people (*'am hā'āreṣ*), are also expressive of such an attitude (→ Pharisee).

NT 1. In the NT, the vb. *eklegomai* and the part. *eklektos*, used as a noun, occur relatively seldom in comparison with the LXX (each 22 times). The noun *eklogē*, not found in the LXX (only in Aquila and Theodotion), is found 7 times, chiefly in Paul.

(a) Matt. and Mk. (except for 13:20) use only the part. in the plur. in the context of eschatological sayings. This use is clearly in the same sense as Jewish tradition, according to which the object of election (→ Redemption) is a body of people, even though it is spoken of as many individuals. (This is also made explicit in 1 Pet. 2:9, *genos eklekton*.) This rule applies in other instances of the word as well, though exceptions stand out. The sing. is applied to Jesus Christ in Lk. 23:35 (which corresponds to the verbal form in 9:35), Jn. 1:34 (*v.l.*), and 1 Pet. 2:4, 6. On the other hand, it is used only on one occasion (Rom. 16:13) of an individual church member. It occurs also in 2 Jn. 1 and 13 with *kyria* or *adelphē*, but the reference is hardly to individual persons, but rather to churches.

(b) Of the 22 instances of the vb., always mid., the majority occur in the writings of Luke. Otherwise, it occurs 5 times in Jn., 3 times in the same context in 1 Cor. 1, and once each in Eph., Jas. and Mk. 13 (along with part.). As far as the subject of *eklegomai* is concerned, we may group the instances under four heads. (i) In 4 places in Acts (6:5; 15:22, 25; and possibly 1:24) the vb. indicates appointment by the church to a particular office (see above CL 2; cf. also the par. words under → Call, → Determine, Appoint, → Hand). (ii) Lk. 14:7 describes the self-esteem in which men indulge when they choose special seats at table (see above CL 3). (iii) In Lk. 10:42 Mary's decision to devote herself exclusively to the words of Jesus, to receive something rather than to be occupied with her own exertions, is described by saying that she has chosen the good part (see above CL 3 and 4; cf. 1 Sam. 15:22). (iv) In all other cases, it is used in connection with God's or Christ's work of election. Only one of the NT writers, however, John, consistently represents Christ as the agent of election (6:70; 13:18; 15:16, 19). Otherwise, there is only one instance, when Luke speaks (Lk. 6:13) of the selection of the Twelve (→ Apostle).

(c) The noun *eklogē* is used unambiguously and exclusively for God's act of election: in Rom. 9:11; 11:5, 7, 28, each time with reference to → Israel; in 1 Thess. 1:4 and 2 Pet. 1:10, where the church is reminded that God's election is the basis of her existence; and in Acts 9:15, the only case in which the meaning is slightly different, where Paul is described in the words of the exalted Lord as a *skeuos eklogēs*, vessel of election, i.e. an instrument by means of which God operates and makes effective his choice.

2. If we set aside as irrelevant to theological discussion those examples of the vb. in the writings of Lk. where it is used in the same way as is normal in classical Gk., we may concentrate our attention first on what is said about the circumstances and purpose of God's elective activity, and secondly on the unique position given to Christ or attributed to him in the thought of the biblical witnesses. It is necessary to speak in these terms, because all the statements about election arose as a result of reflection on the part of these witnesses to God's work after they had encountered him and been added to the church. It was then that they began to face the question of where the fundamental starting-point lay on their own road to → faith, and of what was the foundation of a → church which was able to survive temptation and persecution. In other words, they were asking themselves whether faith and → discipleship were the fruit of human temperament and human decision, or whether the secret lay elsewhere of how a response of obedience came to be made to the → call which went out through the → preaching of the → gospel, the word of the → cross. Statements about election are thus an attempt to express the truth that the existence of people of God can be explained only on the basis of God's plan (→ Foreknowledge), → will, and action, not from a series of human resolves. The problem is presented most clearly in Matt. 22:14 (in some MSS also at Matt. 20:16), where we find added to a parable the epigrammatic saying: "Many are called (*klētoi*), but few are chosen (*eklektoi*)." Here we may detect the surprise occasioned by a consideration of historical experience, which shows that evidently not all to whom God shows favour actually arrive at the goal of this call. This saying of Jesus directs attention to two facts: first, that between the first stage and the last God is active in relation to man; and second, that arrival at this goal is based solely on God's gracious choice.

3. In Rom. 9–11 Paul, whose whole outlook on life has been shaken to the roots, wrestles with this problem as it related to Israel's position before God in view of her → rejection of Christ. He comes to the conclusion that → Israel is counted as

God's chosen people because of a free decision of God, dependent not on any conditions, but solely on the One who elects. The nation continues to enjoy God's love in election not because of blood-descent, but because of his promise (Rom. 9:11 f.; 11:28). Since election was a free act of God's grace, not all have in fact reached the goal (cf. the Matthaean epigram above). But although the majority have gone astray, there remains a → remnant (Rom. 11:5, 7). Even God's elect, Israel, can for a time become enemies of God and of his message. But he does not abandon his aim, even though for the time being all seems lost. The interval during which Israel rejects God's purpose serves rather to extend the horizon of God's grace (Rom. 11:28 ff.). It means that (for the time being!) he shows favour to the Gentiles.

In one of the speeches of Paul in Acts (13:17), Lk. likewise draws attention to the choice of Israel through the patriarchs. He also gives expression to the Pauline thought of Rom. 11 in the address of Peter in Acts 15:7. This is the only passage in which *ta ethnē*, the nations or Gentiles (→ People), are expressly named as the object or the sphere of operation of God's elective activity. The barrier is now broken down; salvation (→ Redemption) has become universal. This does not mean, of course, that the mystery of God's electing grace has been fathomed. It is based on a plan, and yet it is not an automatic process which one could predict. It is the action of God in history which is always open to modification.

4. Is there any discernible reason for this activity of God in picking out those whom he chooses? Again it is Luke who hints at the answer in his gospel. When in the story of the transfiguration the heavenly voice bears witness to the greatness of Jesus (Lk. 9:35), Lk. substitutes for *agapētos* in the par. passages in Matt. and Mk. the word *eklelegmenos*, chosen. This is to show that the whole elective activity of God reaches its culmination in him, the Son, who abstains in his behaviour from every attempt to assert himself (cf. the mocking words of the rulers, Lk. 23:35). The use of the same title, which a few MSS put into the mouth of the Baptist at Jn. 1:34, is unlikely to be original. Jesus is God's chosen One. The ultimate goal of all previous election was to prepare the way for him to be revealed. If we add to this the teaching of 1 Pet., we find that through him is revealed also the lack of understanding among men, and even among his own people. The possibility of recognizing the work of God in and through him is closed to them. It is the One rejected and cast out by men (cf. 3 above) whom God makes his chosen cornerstone (*lithon eklekton akrogōniaion*, 1 Pet. 2:4, 6; cf. Ps. 118(117):22; Isa. 28:16 → Stone). The consequences of being God's chosen one becomes apparent in his life.

5. It is upon this cornerstone, Christ, that God builds up his church from the nations. At the same time the continuity of the → covenant is assured in him. As men are called by election, the church comes into being as the → body of Christ, the new *genos eklekton* (1 Pet. 2:9), the chosen race. Wherever we read of the election of the church (e.g. 1 Thess. 1:4), the underlying thought is that of the basis of its existence in Christ. It is significant how seldom this is in fact mentioned. Generally its existence is attributed directly to the → grace of God. However, in the "little apocalypse" (Mk. 13 par.) and Lk. 18:7, the church is spoken of as the elect (*eklektoi*). This is in the context of the → persecution which, as the "final gleanings of God" (Schrenk), they are to endure, the → suffering which they are to bear in the course of discipleship, and the protection which they will be given by

God, who entirely for their sake will go so far as to shorten the time (*koloboō*, Mk. 13:20 par.). Again, it is nothing but the fact that they belong to Christ that will protect the church's members from → judgment and condemnation (Rom. 8:33). With direct reference to the apostles but as an example of what is true of disciples generally, John shows Christ as the One who chooses and puts God's election into effect. In Jn. 6:70; 13:18; 15:16, 19, Jesus is the explicit subject (with an emphatic *egō*, I) of *eklegomai*. Lk. 6:13 likewise refers to the choice of the apostles, and so in its context does Acts 1:24. The chosen One of God is God's agent of choice. In Christ God's favour has already been bestowed upon man, and it comes to him effectively in the call which goes out and invites him through Christ.

6. If it be asked what are the principles which underlie God's choice, the only positive answer that can be given is that he bestows his favour upon men and joins them to himself solely on the basis of his own free decision and his → love which is not dependent on any temporal circumstances. This is probably the deeper meaning of Eph. 1:4, where *pro katabolēs kosmou*, before the foundation of the world, is surely not to be understood in a purely temporal sense. Rather it refers to a decision rooted in the depths of God's nature, like his *prognōsis* (foreknowledge) or *prothesis* (purpose). (Cf. here the chain of verbs in Rom. 8:29 f., whose tense suggests that all these actions are already past.) In any case, what is revealed of God's work of election runs right across all the usual human standards. With majestic independence he passes by those who are worthy of respect (or have they scornfully rejected his call?), and presents as his elect the poor (Jas. 2:5), the weak, the foolish and the despised of this world (1 Cor. 1:27 f.). Does this result in a pure *corpus electorum*, a community of the elect? As far as their character in God's eyes is concerned, yes, certainly. But the question attributed to Jesus in Jn. 6:70 gives food for thought. Among the company of the elect there is a devil! Is it possible to fall from grace? Certainly the assurance of election must never be allowed to turn into a false sense of security. As early as 1 Thess. 1:4, but stated more clearly in Col. 3:12 and 2 Pet. 1:10, we find the reminder of the manifestation of God's grace linked with an imperative, an exhortation also to live in it, to prove oneself as one whom God has sanctified (→ Holy). For it is only if and when faith is lived out, that election is evident (cf. Tit. 1:1). We can only really speak of election, when we also give due weight to what Jn. in particular emphasizes, but which is always implicit: the commission to fruit-bearing service, obedience and a God-fearing and God-trusting life. *L. Coenen*

→ Covenant, → Determine, → Foreknowledge, → Hard

(a). K. Barth, *CD* II, 2, 3–506; G. C. Berkouwer, *Divine Election*, 1960; M. Black, "The Interpretation of Rom. 8:28", in *Neotestamentica et Patristica* (*Festschrift* for O. Cullmann), 1962, 166–72; L. Boettner, *The Reformed Doctrine of Predestination*, 1932; C. Brown, *Karl Barth and the Christian Message*, 1967, 100–39; J. Calvin, *Institutes of the Christian Religion*, 3, 21, ed. J. T. McNeill and F. L. Battles, 1961; and *Concerning the Eternal Predestination of God*, ed. J.K.S. Reid, 1961; C.E.B. Cranfield, "Romans 8:28", *SJT* 19, 1966, 204–15; F. Davidson, *Pauline Predestination*, 1946; J. Farrelly, *Predestination, Grace and Free Will*, 1964; K. Grayston, "The Doctrine of Election in Rom. 8:28–30", *StudEv*, II, 1964, 574–83; J. Jocz, *A Theology of Election: Israel and the Church*, 1958; M. Luther, *The Bondage of the Will*, ed. J. I. Packer and O. R. Johnston, 1957; *Luther and Erasmus: Free Will and Salvation*, ed. E. G. Rupp and B. Drewery, 1969; H. H. Rowley, *The Biblical Doctrine of Election*, 1950; J. Munck, *Paul and the Salvation of Mankind*, 1959, 247–81; G. Quell and G. Schrenk, *eklegomai*, *TDNT* IV 144–92; H. Schlier, *haireomai*, *TDNT* I 180–85; C. Spicq, "Predestination," *EBT* II 694–700; B. B. Warfield, *The Plan of Salvation*, reprint 1955.

(b). E. B. Allo, "Versets 28–30 du *c.* VIII ad Romanos," *Revue des Sciences théologiques et philosophiques* 7, 1913, 263–73; and "Encore Rom. 8:28–30," op. cit. 13, 1924, 503 ff.; J. B. Bauer, "Röm. 8:28," *ZNW* 50, 1959, 106–12; A. Feuillet, "Le plan salvifique de l'Épître aux Romains," *RB* 57, 1950, 336–87 and 489–529; F. Hesse, *Das Verstockungsproblem im Alten Testament*, 1955; K. Koch, "Zur Geschichte der Erwählungsvorstellung in Israel," *ZAW* 67, 1955, 205 ff.; W. Kreck, "Die Lehre von der Prädestination," O. Weber, "Die Lehre von der Erwählung und die Verkündigung," E. Wolf, "Ehrwählungslehre und Prädestinationsproblem," in *Die Predigt von der Gnadenwahl, Theologische Existenz Heute* Neue Folge 28, 1951; R. Liechtenhan, *Die göttliche Vorherbestimmung bei Paulus und in der Posidonianischen Philosophie*, 1922; P. Maury, *La Prédestination*, 1957; J. Munck, *Christus und Israel. Eine Auslegung von Röm. 9–11*, 1956; F. Nötscher, "Schicksalsglaube in Qumran und Umwelt," *BZ* 3, 1959, 205–34, and 4, 1960, 98–121; E. Schweizer, "Zur Herkunft der Präexistenzvorstellung bei Paulus," *EvTh* 66, 1959; C. Schedl, "Bund und Erwählung," *ZTK* 80, 1958, 493 ff.; K. Stürmer, *Auferstehung und Erwählung*, 1953; T. C. Vriezen, *Die Erwählung Israels nach dem Alten Testament*, *AThANT* 24, 1953; H. Wildberger, *Jahwes Eigentumsvolk. Eine Studie zur Traditionsgeschichte und Theologie des Erwählungsgedankens*, 1960; G. E. Wright, E. L. Dietrich, J. Schneider, W. Pannenberg, "Erwählung," *RGG*³ II 610 ff.

Elijah

'Ηλίας

'Ηλίας (*Hēlias*), Elijah (Elias, Vulg., AV); Heb. *'ēlîyyâhû* or *'ēlîyyâh* (Yah(u) is God, BDB, 45).

OT 1. The OT account about Elijah is found in 1 Ki. 17 – 2 Ki. 2. Elijah came from Tishbe (so LXX, RSV, NEB) in Transjordan, and was active as a prophet in the Northern Kingdom of Israel in the first half of the 9th cent. B.C. The Carmel area became Israelite through his activity. He prepared for Jehu's revolution, which destroyed the dynasty of Omri which favoured absolutism and Canaanite culture and religion. Elijah took a stand on the position that in Israel Yahweh's claims alone should be recognized and faith in Yahweh should remain free from all Canaanite influences, and thus remain practical monotheism. Elijah was "jealous" for Yahweh (→ Zeal). He fought that the old faith in Yahweh should be maintained even under the changed conditions of a settled culture.

Elijah preached that it was Yahweh who guided the fortunes of men and nations. The forces of nature, e.g. the drought in 1 Ki. 17, for which the Baal cult had no explanation, were also under Yahweh's sovereignty and served to carry out his purposes. Yahweh demanded the rule of law and justice, and watched over the ethical and legal norms for life, to which the king also was subject. Yahweh, not Baal, had the power over life and death. Yahweh was the giver of rain and in addition of all the good things of settled life. He did not intervene merely at critical times in the affairs of the people. From this he deduced Yahweh's claim to sole obedience from his people. Yahweh revealed his character not merely in catastrophic expressions of his rage but also in the silence (cf. "a still small voice" [1 Ki. 17:12]). He worked quietly, hardly recognizable behind events (cf. "the waters of Shiloah that flow gently" [Isa. 8:6]). Elijah cast the old faith in Yahweh in a new mould and placed it on a new foundation. This justifies the tradition that places him beside Moses. Mal. 4:5 f. (MT 3:23 f.) presents Elijah as a figure of the Messianic age. He prepares the way for God, purifies the priests and creates peace.

2. In Inter-Testamental and Rab. Jud. three parallel concepts of Elijah's return were developed: (a) Elijah belonged to the tribe of Gad; he would prepare the way

for God and deliver Israel in the last days. (b) Elijah belonged to the tribe of Benjamin: he would be the forerunner of the Messiah. (c) Elijah belonged to the tribe of Levi: he would be the high-priest of the Messianic age.

In his life Elijah was sinless and so he obtained eternal existence. It was assumed that Elijah was the intercessor for Israel in heaven. He was also the one who rescued from greatest need. In post-NT times we find the idea that he was the heavenly scribe who made a record of the acts of men and especially that he kept a register of Israelite marriages. He accompanied the souls of the dead into the other world. Later Talmudic accounts tell how he had appeared to individuals, especially rabbis, in the form of a man or angel. (As with much Rab. haggadah it is questionable how much of this speculation was meant to be taken seriously.)

Sir. 48:10 expects that Elijah will have the task of restoring the tribes of Israel which in Isa. 49:6 is one of the tasks of the Servant of the Lord. Elijah thus receives a messianic function. It was widely believed that Elijah was a forerunner of the Messiah who proclaimed the coming days of salvation, fought against the Antichrist, introduced the Messiah, and sometimes anointed him. Since Mal. 3:1; 4:5 f. (MT 3:23 f.) were combined with 2:4, the expectation was reached that Elijah would be the eschatological high-priest. According to Mal. 4:6 (MT 3:24), Elijah is to reconcile men. He would restore pure doctrine and a pure community. He would clear up controversies in doctrine, law and difficult passages of Scripture. Hence many points in Jud. were left open. One awaited the coming of Elijah who would decide the matter. According to the Targum, God would gather the diaspora through Elijah and Moses. The Midrash on Ps. 43 says there are two deliverers, Elijah of the tribe of Levi and the Messiah of the house of David (cf. the expectation at Qumran that in the Messianic age there would be a priestly Messiah beside the Messiah from the tribe of Judah). Some thought that Elijah had been Phinehas, the son of Aaron (Exod. 6:25). According to R. Phineas b. Jair, Elijah would be involved in the resurrection of the dead (Sot. 9:15).

NT Elijah is mentioned 29 times in the NT (30 if *v.l.* in Lk. 9:54 is included). Lk. 4:25 f.; Jas. 5:17; and Rev. 11:6 refer to the historical details of his life. The statement in Jas. 5:17 that the drought lasted $3\frac{1}{2}$ years is based on Palestinian tradition (a legitimate deduction from the OT story). Lk. 4:25 f. is a threat by Jesus, that it may please God to offer salvation to the Gentiles to the exclusion of Israel. Jas. 5:17 stresses the power of prayer by quoting the example of Elijah. Lk. 9:54 refers to 2 Ki. 1:10, 12; cf. Sir. 48:3 (the reading "as Elijah did" is found already in the 2nd cent. in Marcion). Jesus rejected the suggestion that he should act like Elijah, for it was incompatible with his task to save and help.

In Mk. 15:34 f. and Matt. 27:46 ff., Jesus prayed in the words of Ps. 22:1(2) on the cross. This prayer was misunderstood by those standing by as a call to Elijah to help, since Elijah was the helper in need. Since Elijah did not intervene Jesus' Messianic claim could be considered a failure (A. Schlatter, *Der Evangelist Matthäus*, 1963[6], 783). The NT does not know the concept of Elijah as helper in need, but only Jesus as such.

According to the NT, some expected Elijah to come before the dawn of the end (Mk. 9:11; Matt. 17:10). Some wondered whether John the Baptist was Elijah (Jn. 1:21, 25); others thought that Jesus himself was Elijah who had returned

544

(Mk. 6:15 par.; 8:28 par.). Mk. 9:11 expresses the Jewish expectation of Elijah as forerunner of the Messiah and restorer. Rev. 11:3 shows that it was expected that the restoration would come by the preaching of repentance. This expectation was based on Scripture, "first Elijah must come" (Mk. 9:11). The argument of the scribes was that since he had not come, Jesus could not be the Messiah. This was also the belief of the disciples. By stressing that Elijah had not yet come they wanted to refute Jesus' prophecy of his sufferings.

Jn. 1:21, 25 states that John the Baptist refused to accept that he was the eschatological Elijah. We have no grounds for doubting this, for it is an isolated statement contrasting with the more common affirmation that the appearance of John had fulfilled the expectation of the coming of Elijah. Mk. 9:11 ff. par. and Matt. 11:10–14 par. give this as Jesus' verdict on John. Matt. 11:14 ("if you are willing to accept it") shows that this was a new and unusual verdict. His statement meant that there was to be no pure, direct embodiment of Elijah in person, but also that the promise was fulfilled. It meant also that Jesus did not take the restitution in a political or national sense, but in a religious one through repentance and forgiveness. In addition Jesus saw his own fate foreshadowed in that of the Baptist (Mk. 9:13). The primitive church accepted Jesus' verdict and thereby confessed Jesus' Messiahship (Mk. 1:2; Lk. 1:16 f., 76).

Elijah appeared with → Moses at Jesus' transfiguration (Mk. 9:4 f. par.). Apocalyptic but not Rab. tradition knew of two forerunners of the Messiah (Eth. Enoch 90:31; 2 Esd. 6:26), normally Enoch and Elijah both of whom were raptured. But in Rev. 11:3–6 they are Moses and Elijah. When Moses and Elijah appear at Jesus' transfiguration, it is an announcement of the beginning of the end time. According to Mk. 9:12 f., Rev. 11:3 ff., and also non-canonical literature, Elijah is a suffering figure. That he appears at Jesus' transfiguration points to Jesus' coming sufferings and confirms his prediction of suffering (Mk. 8:31 f.; Lk. 9:31).

There is a tension between Rev. 11:3 ff. and the idea that John the Baptist was the fulfilment of the expectation of Elijah, for one of the two who preach repentance and are killed by the beast is Elijah, for the power "to shut the sky" (v. 6) refers back to 1 Ki. 17:1.

Paul refers to the OT story in Rom. 11:2 ff. He had gained the conviction from 1 Ki. 19:10, 14, 18 that also in Elijah's time God had separated for himself an elect, holy remnant, viz. those Jews who believed on Jesus as their Messiah.

H. Bietenhard

→ Messiah, → Moses, → Redemption

(a). G. H. Boobyer, *St. Mark and the Transfiguration Story*, 1942; C. E. Carlston, "Transfiguration and Resurrection," *JBL* 70, 1961, 233–40; D. Daube, *The New Testament and Rabbinic Judaism*, 1956, 20–26; J. Jeremias, *El(e)ias*, TDNT II 928–41; J. A. T. Robinson, "Elijah, John and Jesus", *Twelve New Testament Studies*, 1962, 28–52; H. H. Rowley, *Men of God*, 1963, 37–65; B. L. Smith, "Elijah," *NBD*, 363 f.; M. Thrall, "Elijah and Moses in Mark's account of the Transfiguration," *NTS* 16, 1969–70, 305–17; R. S. Wallace, *Elijah and Elisha*, 1957.
(b). H. Baltensweiler, *Die Verklärung Jesu*, AThANT 33, 1959; G. Fohrer, *Elia*, AThANT 31, 1957; W. Gerber, "Die metamorphose Jesu, Mark. 9, 2 f. par.," *ThZ* 23, 1967, 385–95; SB IV 764–98, Exkursus "Der Prophet Elia nach seiner Entrückung aus dem Diesseits"; A. Schlatter, *Der Evangelist Matthäus*, 1963⁶, 783; P. Volz, *Die Eschatologie der jüdischen Gemeinde im neutestamentichen Zeitalter*, 1934, 195 ff.; C. A. Keller, "Wer war Elia?", *ThZ* 16, 1960, 298 ff.

Empty, Vain

The word empty refers to things, but it may be applied metaphorically to people. In the first instance, *kenos* means lit. empty (e.g. an empty well or house). When applied to people, it means devoid of sense, foolish, senseless. A life may be empty in the sense of being worthless or ineffective. The word *mataios* and its derivatives have an essentially more personal application. It is used in the sense of empty, useless, worthless, and futile. It denotes a person who falls short of God's standard and human norms. His life is illusory, motiveless, aimless, scandalous and foolish

κενός

κενός (*kenos*), empty, and thus fig. without content, basis, truth or power, without result or profit; κενόω (*kenoō*), to empty, and thus destroy, render void; κενοδοξία (*kenodoxia*), vanity, conceit, illusion, delusion, error; κενόδοξος (*kenodoxos*), conceited, boastful.

CL 1. *kenos*, found frequently from Homer onwards, means empty, as opposed to *plērēs* (full). It is thus used mostly lit. of things (e.g. an empty jug, pit [cf. Gen. 37:24], or house). But it is also occasionally used of persons (e.g. with empty hands [cf. Gen. 31:42]).

When used metaphorically in connection with things, *kenos* means either lacking content (e.g. *kenoi logoi*, empty words [cf. Plato, *Lach.*, 196b]), or a missing effect (especially in the expression *eis kenon*, in vain [*The Flinders Petrie Papyri*, II, 37, 1b, 12; Josephus, *Ant.*, 19, 96]). With people, *kenos* means hollow, shallow, lacking in judgment (*tou nou kenos*, empty in mind [Soph., *OC*, 931]), and also in the ethical sense of ineffectual, vain (Soph., *Ant.*, 709).

2. The vb. *kenoō* occurs from Herodotus onwards, meaning to empty, in the sense of either to plunder (Aesch., *Supp.*, 660; cf. Phil. 2:7) or to bring to nothing (Vettius Valens, II, 22p, 90, 7).

3. *kenodoxos* means vain-glorious, conceited. It denotes the man who has acquired an unfounded reputation (*kenē doxa*, vain repute, or glory, cf. Polyb., 27, 6, 12).

4. *kenodoxia* means either vanity, conceit, the futile thirst for glory (Polyb., 3, 81, 9) or error, delusion (Epictetus, p. 78, 7).

OT 1. Heb. has no exact equivalent to Gk. *kenos*. This is indicated by the fact that the LXX translates 19 different Heb. words by *kenos*. The most common of these is *rîq*, empty, worthless, vain. The commonest occurrence is in the prophets (especially Isa. and Jer.) and the later writings (especially Pss., Job, Sir.).

2. *kenos* is used mostly in the lit. sense of empty (e.g. Jer. 14:3, vessels; Exod. 3:21 and Deut. 15:13, empty-handed). But it also has a distinctive metaphorical sense. Jdg. 9:4 and 11:3 speak of *andres kenoi*, worthless men, who are not counted among the people of Yahweh and who are ready and willing to perform any kind of deed, even murder. The prophets spoke of turning away from Yahweh as giving oneself to vanity. The help that Israel sought from the Egyptians was worthless and empty (Isa. 30:7). Israel has forgotten Yahweh and offers sacrifice to vanity or nothing, i.e. the idols (Jer. 18:15). The idea of emptiness was sharpened in the message of the prophets as a deceptive power upon which no reliance can be placed (Isa. 29:8). It is unmasked as senselessness. Only Yahweh can help. The Lord's chosen ones shall not toil in vain (Isa. 65:23).

3. The term is found most frequently in the cries of Job. He resents the vain words (Job 27:12) and the empty comfort (21:34) of his friends. He sees not only the things around him but his own life sink into nothing. He laments the months of emptiness (7:3) and vain hope (7:6). He cries out: "Leave me alone! For my life is nothing" (7:16). He sees himself delivered to the curse of nothingness without reason. Unless Yahweh rescues him, he can only perish.

NT *kenos* occurs almost exclusively in the Pauline literature. It is very rare in the synoptics. The vb. *kenoō* occurs only in Paul.

1. *kenos* occurs in the parable of the vineyard, when the tenants send back the master's servants empty, i.e. empty-handed (Mk. 12:3; Lk. 20:10 f.; but not the par. in Matt. 21:35 f.). But Paul gives it a distinctive sense, especially in the negative expression *mē eis kenon*, not in vain. If in the LXX the idea denotes emptiness, vanity and nothingness, now the accent is on fruitlessness and inefficacy. Paul uses it to suggest that under certain circumstances certain things would be pointless, fruitless, or in vain. He can apply it to grace (2 Cor. 6:1), preaching (1 Cor. 15:14), missionary work (1 Thess. 3:5), and his own activity as an apostle (Gal. 2:2; Phil. 2:16). In all these cases the basic question is the power and effectiveness of Paul's mission. As the work of God, it is wrought in power in contrast to the empty, ineffective words of paganism (Eph. 5:6). For the apostle, the power of divine grace is put to the proof in the effectiveness of his preaching. Hence, neither his missionary work, nor grace, nor the kerygma are in vain.

2. With the vb. *kenoō*, on the other hand, the emphasis falls on emptying and making void. Significantly, Paul uses it again negatively and also passively. He speaks of certain things that cannot be made empty, i.e. made void. Among them are faith (Rom. 4:14), the cross of Christ (1 Cor. 1:17), and his boasting as an apostle (2 Cor. 9:3). The cross and faith form the central subject matter of the gospel and thus constitute its power. Hence, the offence of the cross which both condemns and saves should not be made void by word of worldly wisdom (1 Cor. 1:17). The saving way of faith should not be made void by justification through the law (Rom. 4:14).

3. The precise significance of *heauton ekenōsen* (Phil. 2:6) has been much discussed. The words mean lit. "he emptied himself." Most scholars regard Phil. 2:6–11 as a pre-Pauline hymn about Christ which Paul quotes in the course of his argument in order to illustrate his point, that Christians should be unselfish, humble and outgoing in their relationships, and thus have the mind of Christ. E. Käsemann (*Exegetische Versuche und Besinnungen*, I, 1950, 71 ff.) adopts the same approach as A. Oepke (*TDNT* III 661). He sees it against the Hel. background of a gnostic heavenly redeemer, involving the incarnation of the pre-existent Christ. He emptied himself in the sense that he freely exchanged his pre-existent, divine mode of being (v. 6) for common, human, earthly existence. According to Oepke, "What is meant is that the heavenly Christ did not selfishly exploit his divine form and mode of being . . . , but by his own decision emptied Himself of it or laid it by, taking the form of a servant by becoming man." He sees 2 Cor. 8:9 as the best commentary: "though he was rich, yet for your sake he became poor, so that by his poverty you might become rich."

A different view is taken by E. Lohmeyer (*Kyrios Jesus*, 1928) and J. Jeremias (*TDNT* V 711). They see the passage against the background of the early Palestinian church and Isa. 53. Jeremias points out that the expression "is not attested elsewhere in Gk., and is grammatically extremely harsh, [and] is an exact translation of *he*ʿ*râh . . . napšô*" (Isa. 53:12). Thus the passage should be translated: "he poured out his life" (Isa. 53:12). The passage would then refer, not to the incarnation as such, but to Jesus' self-surrender and the giving of his life on the cross. The former interpretation is, however, favoured if the passage is taken as a progression: v. 7 speaks generally of his becoming a man, and v. 8 of his humiliation and obedience to death on a cross.   *E. Tiedtke, H.-G. Link*

Phil. 2:7 has played an important part in the discussion of christology. It has given rise to the doctrine of *kenōsis*, according to which Christ emptied himself or did not make use of some at least of his divine attributes during the period of his earthly life. Thus, he was not omnipresent, omniscient or omnipotent in his incarnate state. Scholars appealed to the gospels to show that Jesus was tired and had other bodily needs. He also disclaimed omniscience (Mk. 13:32). They then explained this in terms of a self-emptying of divine attributes which they found implied in Phil. 2:7.

The Lutheran *Formula of Concord* condemned the idea if not in name (Epitome VIII, Affirmativa 3–11, Negativa 20). A kind of kenoticism found devotional expression in the writings of Count Zinzendorf and in Charles Wesley's lines, "Emptied himself of all but love, And bled for Adam's helpless race." It was taught by Ernst Sartorius and W. F. Gess. But the most significant exponents of *kenōsis* in the 19th cent. were Gottfried Thomasius in Germany and Charles Gore in England.

In *Christi Person und Werk* I–III (1853–61) Thomasius endeavoured to state a doctrine of the incarnation which would answer the charges of radical critics like D. F. Strauss that the orthodox picture of Christ as divine and human was that of a historically inconceivable hybrid. Thomasius's answer was designed to show how Jesus could be thought of as God and yet at the same time living a life that was fully human. His reply was thus a restatement of dogmatic ideas to meet the exigencies of historical criticism. It may be noted, however, that whereas more liberal and radical attempts to restate who Christ was simply cut the knot and said that he was a man inspired by God comparable with the prophets, kenotic christology was an attempt to preserve the two-natures doctrine of Christ. Whereas the radicals said that Jesus was not divine, *kenōsis* replied that he was divine, but he did not possess or use all the divine attributes. For he deliberately accommodated himself to the common conditions of mankind. (For Thomasius see C. Welch, *God and Incarnation in Mid-Nineteenth Century German Theology*, 1965, 31–101.)

In *Lux Mundi* (1889) Gore appealed to *kenōsis* to reconcile liberal, critical views of the OT with the acceptance of Jesus' authority as a teacher. He explained that Jesus' views were at variance with modern criticism partly because he sometimes deliberately accommodated his teaching to his hearers and partly because Jesus himself was subject to the limitations of his time. In later writings Gore saw *kenōsis* as an expression of the divine humility in general in the way in which God deliberately limits himself in his dealings with mankind. In developing this teaching,

Gore, like Thomasius, was endeavouring to adapt a traditional orthodox christology to meet certain needs without surrendering altogether the divinity or humanity of Christ. (On Gore see C. Brown, "Charles Gore" in P. E. Hughes, ed., *Creative Minds in Contemporary Theology*, 1966, 354 ff., 367 ff.)

Kenotic christology has been questioned on two levels: (1) the theological questions that it raises; and (2) whether kenoticism is really implied by Phil. 2:7.

(1) The attributes of omniscience, omnipotence and omnipresence are in fact essential attributes of divinity. God would not be God without them. If Christ be divested of essential divine attributes, it is difficult to see how the doctrine of his divinity could still be maintained, as both Gore and Thomasius want to maintain it. It would make him, as the Arians believed, something less than God, but more than man. A further question which all orthodox christologies have to face is: What became of the cosmic functions of the divine Word (cf. Jn. 1:1 ff.; Col. 1:17; Heb. 1:3) during the period of the incarnation? Did the Word abandon them (as *kenōsis* seems to imply)? Or was it rather that the divine Word which sustains the universe was both in him, living out the divine life in this human life, and also outside him (as the doctrine of the *extra Calvinisticum* teaches)?

To resolve this dilemma the suggestion has been made there may be some analogy between the conscious mind's relation to the unconscious mind and Jesus' relationship with the divine Word. The conscious mind is only partly aware of its own workings, yet nevertheless it continues to work unconsciously. In a similar way, perhaps Jesus was aware only of what he needed to be aware of as the son and servant of man (cf. W. Sanday, *Christology and Personality*, 1911, 135 ff.).

(2) Neither the gospels nor Phil. 2 present the picture of the abandonment of any divine attributes. They do, however, show Jesus clearly accepting the status and role of a servant (Phil. 2:7; Mk. 10:45; Lk. 22:27; Jn. 13:4–16; 15:20; Matt. 10:24). The motive and guiding principle in all Jesus' actions was love, humility and obedience to the Father, as Phil. 2 shows (cf. Matt. 3:15; Jn. 5:19; 7:16; 15:10; 17:4; Gal. 4:4). As a servant, Jesus accepted the limitations that were the Father's will. Phil. 2 sees Christ as having a pre-existent state, the state of humiliation as a servant in his life and death, and a state of exaltation in which he is universally acknowledged as Lord. It is usual to take the various descriptions in vv. 7 and 8 as involving successive acts. But the emptying, the taking the form of a servant, and being born in the likeness of men were clearly not successive acts, for the birth is mentioned last. Similarly, the humbling and obedience were not stages which followed each other until they were replaced by the cross. Rather, these descriptions each apply to the whole of Christ's life, all of them culminating in the cross. It would seem that Phil. 2 does not demand that we should choose between the interpretations of Oepke and Jeremias, to the exclusion of one of them. Rather, the imagery of the passages makes use of both the picture of the pre-existent Christ and Isa. 53. The emptying of v. 7 is the outpouring of himself in life and also on the cross.

C. Brown

μάταιος

μάταιος (*mataios*), empty, fruitless, useless, powerless, worthless, futile; ματαιότης (*mataiotēs*), emptiness, futility, worthlessness; ματαιόω (*mataioō*), render futile; μάτην (*matēn*), in vain,

549

to no end; ματαιολογία (*mataiologia*), useless talk, empty prattle; ματαιολόγος (*mataiologos*), idle talker.

CL *mataios*, derived from *matē*, folly, fault, and *matia*, vain effort, means null as both cause and effect. Hence it means both fallacious, fictitious, groundless, and in vain, ineffectual, aimless.

In Gk. literature *mataios* and its cognates have as their background certain set values, moral standards, religious realities, recognized truths and facts. The conduct of anyone who ignores them wittingly or unwittingly, or disregards and transgresses them, falls under the judgment of being *mataios*. A man's life thus becomes a deceptive appearance. *kenos* which is also applied to such circumstances stresses the emptiness of things and people, who are thus empty, worthless or vain. The idea is especially common in the tragedies. Creon, blinded by lust for power and hate, feels himself duped by fortune and finally declares himself to be an *anēr mataios* (Soph., *Ant.*, 1339). Lit. this means an "empty man", but it amounts to being a "fool" or even a "criminal". For he has despised the divine warning and misused his freedom. The Gk. world counselled reflection and prudence to guard against such aberrations.

To check *mataiotēs*, Aeschylus coined the counter-idea *mē mataion* (*Suppl.*, 197 f.) which manifests itself in *sōphrosynē* (→ Discipline, Prudence). But surprisingly the idea receded in the later Gk. world. Gk. antiquity allowed itself to be carried away neither by scepticism into a thorough-going relativism, nor by nihilism. On the other hand, the gods did not possess the power effectively to overcome negative *mataiotēs*. Evidently the conflict between *mataios* and *mē mataion*, between man's mere appearance and his being, slackened off in a later age.

OT The LXX used *mataios* and *matēn* etc. to translate various Heb. words which denote different aspects of nothingness. The most frequent are: *hebel* (breath, vanity, nothingness), *šāw'* (worthless, in vain, unfounded, deception), *kāzāb* (deception, imposture), *tōhû* (lit. desert, hence emptiness, unreality; adv. in vain), *hinnām* (in vain), *'āwen* (trouble, wickedness; also used for idolatry).

These words all denote the various ways in which man can resist the reality of God in his revelation and claims on him. The diversity of these Heb. words is an indication of the fact that the OT can express these truths in a much more varied and also more radical way than the Gk. tragedies. An example of Yahweh's uncompromising confrontation with vanity is the Third Commandment: "You shall not take the name of the Lord your God in vain" (Exod. 20:7). G. von Rad suggests that the original term here (*šāw'*) may originally have signified magic, adding that even in Israel it is conceivable that people were at times liable to use Yahweh's name for sinister purposes (*Old Testament Theology*, I, 1962, 183).

mataios occurs in the OT chiefly in 3 contexts: (1) as a designation of the lying words of false prophets; (2) in condemnation of the idols of foreign nations; (3) in statements about men and their lives.

1. Prophets who speak without being commissioned and utter the revelations of their imaginations as the Word of God speak vanity. Their words are lies and deception. They fall under the judgment of God. Anyone who follows them falls prey to vanity. He experiences it in the magisterial judgment of God which gives the lie to the words of the false prophets (Ezek. 13:6 ff.; Zech. 10:2; Lam. 2:14; Jer.

23:16 ff., the latter being the sole occasion when *mataioō* is used actively). Zeph. 3:13 promises the cessation of lies and vanity in the eschatological future.

2. *mataios* is often used as a designation of the idols, the making of idols, and of their worship. *ta mataia* (the empty things or vain things) is often used as a translation for the names of gods of foreign peoples (Isa. 2:20; 2 Chron. 11:15). They are "nothings", "nonentities" or "worthless gods" (cf. G. von Rad, *Old Testament Theology*, II, 1965, 340; cf. Lev. 17:7; Jer. 2:5; 8:19; 10:15; 51:18; Jon. 2:9; in each case for Heb. *hebel*).

3. The godly man in the OT is not unaware of the futility and vanity of human life (Ps. 103:14 ff.; Job 14:1 ff. and often) and thought (Ps. 94:11). But in Eccles. this awareness is intensified to the point of extreme scepticism. "All is vanity" (Eccles. 1:2; cf. 2:1 and often). *mataiotēs* occurs more than 30 times for Heb. *hebel*. The Preacher's scepticism can understand neither God's government nor the meaning of his own life. There remains only the resignation of tragic existence which has no message but only lamentation for the vanity of existence. This may be partly explained by the distance in time from the mighty acts of God in history and the absence of God's intervention in the course of the world in the present. Nevertheless, he is held back from plunging into nihilism by such affirmations of life as Eccles. 2:25; 3:13; 7:14; 9:7 ff. There are overtones of resignation in the following passages which speak of the vanity of work and effort: "In vain have I smitten your children, they took no correction" (Jer. 2:30); "I have laboured in vain, I have spent my strength for nothing and vanity" (Isa. 49:4); "You have said, 'It is vain to serve God' " (Mal. 3:14). Each of these cases concerns the relationship between God and man.

NT *mataios* and its cognates occur in the NT only 11 times. They are absent from the Gospels, and occur only in Acts, the Pauline l terature and Catholic Epistles. This may be compared with the frequent use of *mataios* in the prophets in contrast to the historical books of the OT. *mataios* in the NT means mostly empty, futile, vain. With the same sharpness as in the OT, the judgment *mataios* is passed upon everything that is opposed to God and his → commandments. It falls on: (1) the presumption of human thought (1 Cor. 3:20; Rom. 1:21); (2) pagan idolatry (Acts 14:15); (3) a deceitful way of life (1 Pet. 1:18; Jas. 1:26).

1. In 1 Cor. 3:20 Paul contends against Christian pseudo-wisdom. The cross of Jesus makes those who would be clever foolish before God and man. Paul finds confirmation of this in Ps. 94:11. The Lord "knows the thoughts of man that they are but a breath." The "Christian" → wisdom of the wise stands in contrast to the foolishness of the cross which is God's wisdom for those who believe (1 Cor. 1:24; Rom. 1:21 see below). The cross appears foolishness, weakness and vanity to natural thinking. In 1 Cor. 15:17 Paul describes as vain a faith which denies the reality of the risen Christ. It is still under the power of sin. It would remove the basis of the kerygma, the message of Christ. It would be empty, just as faith in such a message would be empty. 1 Cor. 15:14 uses *kenos* twice. However, because the resurrection of Jesus actually happened as the act of God, faith is no "illusion" (*mataia*, v. 17).

2. The prophetic attack on idols is continued in missionary preaching (Acts 14:15). The revelation of God in Christ does not permit foreign gods, men or

images to be worshipped as divine. The gospel causes men to turn from these non-entities (Zeus and Hermes who were thought to be personified in the figures of Barnabas and Paul) to the living God.

3. 1 Pet. 1:14–18 contrasts the church's sanctified way of life with the pagan way. Christ's sacrificial death brings about redemption from the futile way of life inherited from their fathers (1:18). The Gentile Christian would understand *mataios* here as the worship of idols which is the root of his former unrestrained way of life. According to Jas. 1:26, a man's religion is vain when he is outwardly pious but at the same time deludes himself as to his real godless state by his unrestrained prattle (cf. 2 Pet. 2:18). The Catholic Epistles understand *mataios* as powerless life which denies the bodily obedience of Christian existence. It is this that they are contending with.

4. *mataiotēs*, vanity, is a recurring expression in the OT, especially in Eccles. In Rom. 8:20 Paul likewise sees the whole creation subject to vanity. It is in bondage to decay (v. 21). But this corruptibility also passes, because it is not self-elected but imposed upon it by the creator, so that he may reveal to it its future splendour. Thus there is not only sighing (v. 22), but a well-founded waiting for redemption from vanity (v. 19).

According to Eph. 4:17, *mataiotēs* is the characteristic of the pagan way of thought and life. In ingratitude man forsakes God, the fountain of life. In his thought he takes counsel only for himself, and in carrying out his vain thoughts he thwarts himself and the world he lives in.

5. In the NT *mataioō* occurs almost entirely in the passive in the sense of being given over to vanity (cf. Jer. 2:5). Rom. 1:21 speaks of men being responsible for this (cf. the discussion of 8:20 above, where the transitoriness of creatureliness is imposed by God). But man is given over to vanity because he ungratefully denies God the honour that is justly God's. It destroys his thinking, planning and action.

matēn, in vain, occurs in Matt. 15:9; Mk. 7:7; cf. Isa. 29:13. *mataiologia* (1 Tim. 1:6) means empty prattle, "vain discussion" (RSV). This comes about when men do not keep to what God has appointed for them: "love that issues from a pure heart and a good conscience and sincere faith" (1:5; cf. 2 Pet. 2:18). There are many "empty talkers" (*mataiologoi*, Tit. 1:10) and deceivers especially among the circumcision party. *E. Tiedtke*

→ Jesus Christ, → Fullness, art. *plēroō*, → Serve

(a). D. M. Baillie, *God was in Christ*, 1948; O. Bauernfeind, *mataios*, *TDNT* IV 519–24; G. C. Berkouwer, *The Person of Christ*, 1954, 27–31; H. W. Boers, *The Diversity of New Testament Christological Concepts* (Dissertation, Bonn), 1962, 114 ff.; G. Bornkamm, "On Understanding the Christ-hymn (Philippians 2.6–11)," *Early Christian Experience*, 1969, 112–22; A. B. Bruce, *The Humiliation of Christ*, 1900[5]; L. Cerfaux, *Christ in the Theology of St. Paul*, 1959; O. Cullmann, *The Christology of the New Testament*, 1963[2]; E. R. Fairweather, "The 'Kenotic' Christology," in F. W. Beare, *A Commentary on the Epistle to the Philippians* (BNTC), 1959, 159–74; W. Foerster, *harpagmos*, *TDNT* I, 472 ff.; J. Harvey, "A New Look at the Christ Hymn in Philippians 2:6–11," *ExpT* 76, 1964–65, 337 ff.; J. Jeremias, *pais theou*, *TDNT* V 711 ff.; H. Johnson, *The Humanity of the Saviour*, 1962; R. P. Martin, *An Early Christian Confession: Philippians II. 5–11 in Recent Interpretation*, 1960; *Carmen Christi: Philippians ii.5–11 in Recent Interpretation and in the Setting of Early Christian Worship*, 1967; and *The Epistle of Paul to the Philippians*, 1959; W. R. Matthews, *The Problem of Christ in the Twentieth Century*, 1950; I. H. Marshall, "The Christ-Hymn in Philippians 2:5–11," *TB* 19, 1968, 104–27; E. L. Mascall, *Christ, the Christian and the Church*, 1946, 23–47; C. F. D. Moule, "Further Reflections on Philippians 2:5–11," in W. W. Gasque and R. P. Martin, eds., *Apostolic History and the Gospel, Biblical and Historical Essays presented to*

F. F. Bruce, 1970, 264–76; A. Oepke, *kenos*, *TDNT* III 659–62; J. A. T. Robinson, *The Human Face of God*, 1973, 206 ff.; P. Schoonenberg, "The kenosis or Self-Emptying of Christ", *Concilium* I, 2, 1966, 27–36; L. B. Smedes, *The Incarnation: Trends in Modern Anglican Thought*, 1953; E. Schweizer, *Lordship and Discipleship*, 1960; S. W. Sykes and J. P. Clayton, eds., *Christ, Faith and History: Cambridge Studies in Christology*, 1972; C. H. Talbert, "The Problem of Pre-Existence in Philippians 2:6–11," *JBL* 86, 1967, 141–53.

(b). G. Braumann, *Vorpaulinische christliche Taufverkündigung bei Paulus*, *BWANT* 5, 2, 1962, 56 ff.; A. Feuillet, "L'hymne christologique de l'épître aux Philippiens," *RB* 27, 1965, 352 ff., 418 ff.; D. Georgi, "Der vorpaulinische Hymnus, Phil. 2:6–11," in E. Dinkler, ed., *Zeit und Geschichte, Dankesgabe an Rudolf Bultmann*, 1964, 263 ff.; E. Haenchen, "Die frühe Christologie," *ZTK* 63, 1966, 152 f.; P. Henry, "Kénose," *Dictionnaire de la Bible*, Suppl. V, 1957, 56 ff.; J. Jeremias, "Zur Gedankenführung in den paulinischen Briefen," *Studia Paulina*, Festschrift J. de Zwaan, 1953, 152 ff. (= *Abba*, 1966, 269 ff.); and "Zu Phil. 2, 7," *NovT* 6, 1963 182 ff. (= *Abba*, 1966, 308 ff.); L. Krinentzki, "Der Einfluss von Jes. 52, 13 ff. auf Phil. 2, 6 ff.," *ThQ* 139, 1959, 157 ff., 291 ff.; E. Lohmeyer, *Kyrios Jesus. Eine Untersuchung zu Phil. 2, 5–11*, (1928) 1961²; O. Michel, "Zur Exegese von Phil. 2, 5–11," in *Theologie als Glaubenswagnis*, Festschrift Karl Heim, 1954, 79 ff.; W. Schmauch, *Beiheft zu E. Lohmeyer, Die Briefe an die Philipper, Kolosser und an Philemon*, *KEK* 9, 1964¹³, 19 ff.; and "Das Heilsgeschehen in Christo Jesu. Zur Interpretation von Phil. 2, 5–11," in "... *zu achten aufs Wort.*" *Aufsätze*, ed. W.-C. Schmauch, C. Grengel and M. Punge, 1967, 37 ff.; G. Strecker, "Redaktion und Tradition im Christus-Hymnus Phil. 2, 6–11," *ZNW* 55, 1964, 63 ff.; K. Wegenast, *Das Verständnis der Tradition bei Paulus und den Deuteropaulinen*, *WMANT* 8, 1962, 83 ff.; K. Wengst, *Christologische Formeln und Lieder des Urchristentums* (Bonn Dissertation), 1967, 137 ff.

Enemy, Enmity, Hate

When our relationships with others rise above absolute indifference, they are conditioned by basic attitudes which may be positive or negative in character. The NT describes an inward attitude which is directed positively towards the well-being of another as → love or friendship, and the esteem which derives from such an attitude as → honour. The opposite concepts are enmity and hatred.

miseō, hate, originally denoted the resentment which arises when someone feels himself injured by the behaviour of another (→ Suffer). This meaning is also broadened to include an active element (→ Persecution, art. *diōkō*). *echthros* and its cognates, on the other hand, derive from the Gk. *echthos*, hatred, and convey rather the fixed idea of irreconcilable, deep-rooted enmity. An *echthros* is someone from whom one can expect only harm and danger, or at least from whom one imagines that this is what one should expect. → also Foreign.

| $\dot{\epsilon}\chi\theta\rho\acuteος$ | $\dot{\epsilon}\chi\theta\rho\acuteος$ (*echthros*), hostile, hated, enemy; $\ddot{\epsilon}\chi\theta\rho\alpha$ (*echthra*), enmity; $\dot{\alpha}\nu\tau\acuteιδικος$ (*antidikos*), enemy, opponent. |

CL *echthros* in the pass. sense, hated, hateful (Homer); in the act. sense, hostile, enemy, opponent (Hesiod). *antidikos* is originally an opponent, standing over against one in a trial (Xen.), hence, enemy, adversary.

OT In the LXX *echthros* occurs more than 450 times, usually to translate '*ôyēb*, but also *ṣar*. *echthroi* are enemies in military conflicts, the nations with which one is in a state of war (1 Sam. 29:8; Nah. 3:11, 13), and also a man's personal enemies (Exod. 23:4; Num. 35:23; Ps. 5:8; 13:3). In the case of Israel's enemies it is not a matter merely of national enemies in the normal sense. Since Israel is God's people, its enemies are also God's enemies (Exod. 23:22; Jos. 7:8; 2 Sam. 12:14 LXX). When the people fall away from God, God's enemies are to be found within Israel itself (Isa. 1:24). The ungodly man is the enemy of the righteous (Ps. 5:8 ff.; 55:3) and of God (Ps. 37:20). Hope for the future centres upon deliverance from enemies and their destruction (Mic. 5:9; Isa. 62:8; Num. 24:18; Ps. 110:1 f.; 132:18). In the Pseudepigrapha → Satan is occasionally described as the "enemy" (Test. Dan 6:3 f.; Apc. Mos. 2, 7, 25; Gr. Bar. 13:2).

NT In the NT *echthros* occurs 32 times (of which 16 are in the Synoptic Gospels, and 9 in Pauline writings), *echthra* only 6 times (4 times in Pauline writings), and *antidikos* 5 times.

1. *echthros* is first of all someone's personal enemy (Rom. 12:20; Gal. 4:16). OT usage is taken up in the idea that the coming of the era of salvation implies deliverance from enemies (Lk. 1:71, 74). In the prophecies concerning Jerusalem, it is said that enemies will besiege and destroy the city (Lk. 19:43). Enemies rise against the two eschatological witnesses (Rev. 11:5, 12). The enemies of the cross of Christ will come to grief (Phil. 3:18; Acts 13:10). Enemies of Christ are referred to again in those passages where Ps. 110:1 is cited as a prophecy of Christ (Matt. 22:44; Mk. 12:36; Lk. 20:43; Acts 2:35; 1 Cor. 15:25; Heb. 1:13; 10:13). In 2 Thess. 3:15 the reference is to an enemy of the church, with whom fellowship is to be broken off. Satan, too, as in certain pseudepigraphical writings, can be described as *echthros* (Matt. 13:24 ff.; Lk. 10:19) and even *antidikos* (1 Pet. 5:8). Possibly here the thought is that of → accuser in the final judgment, for *antidikos* is found otherwise in the NT only in the sense of opponent in the lawcourt (Matt. 5:25; Lk. 12:58; cf. 18:3).

Since the natural man rebels against God in his thought and action, he is an *echthros* in relation to God (Rom. 5:10; Col. 1:21). According to Rom. 11:28, those Jews who do not yet believe are "enemies" for the Gentiles' sake. Because of the stubbornness and unbelief of the Jews, the gospel, God's salvation, comes to the Gentiles.

When in Matt. 5:43 f. the command to love one's neighbour is contrasted with a call to hate one's enemy, the reference can scarcely be to any OT passage (cf. Ps. 31:6a; 139:21f.). It may well be more to the point to compare certain regulations of the Qumran community. Those who belong to this community undertake to "love all that he (God) has chosen, and hate all that he has rejected" (1QS 1:3); and further, to "love all the sons of light, each according to his lot in God's community, and hate all the sons of darkness, each according to his guilt, in God's vengeance" (1QS 1:9 f.). The Levites curse "all the men of the lot of Belial" (1QS 2:4–9), a group to which all ultimately belong who are not members of the Qumran community. Josephus also reports that the Essenes had to swear to hate the unrighteous and to support the just (*War* 2, 8, 7(139)). It is highly possible that in Matt. 5:43 f. Jesus was dissociating himself from the regulations of a contemporary sect, and that it was with such ideas in mind that he introduced the commandment to love one's enemies.

2. *echthra*, hate, enmity, existed between Herod Antipas and Pilate (Lk. 23:12), but as a result of their common action against Jesus this turned into friendship. In the catalogue of sins in Gal. 5:19 ff. *echthra* is explicitly named as one of the

"works of the flesh" (v. 20). The "mind set on the flesh" is *echthra* against God (Rom. 8:7, RSV "hostile to God"). Christ, however, has brought peace, in that he has removed the hostility between God and man and the hostility between Jews and Gentiles through his cross (Eph. 2:14, 16). *H. Bietenhard*

| μισέω | μισέω (*miseō*), hate. |

CL *miseō* (etymology uncertain) attested since Homer, means hate, abhor, reject.

The vb. connotes not only antipathy to certain actions, but also a permanent and deep-seated human hostility towards other men or even the deity. It is further used of the gods' abhorrence of the base aspects of man's nature (Eur., *Or.* 708 f.), and divine hatred of unrighteous men who are the objects of divine punishment (especially Aesch.; cf. *TDNT* IV 683 f.).

OT 1. The Heb. equivalent of the LXX *miseō* is nearly always *śānēʾ*. This can mean:

(a) Hate, as an emotional impulse. Joseph's brothers hated him because he was the favourite (Gen. 37:2 ff.). Wisdom teaches that hatred stirs up strife, but love covers all offences, *peśāʿîm* (Prov. 10:12). All a poor man's brothers hate him; indeed, even his friends are far from him (Prov. 19:7 LXX). Yahweh however forbids hatred against a member of Israel and commands that love be extended to him as to oneself (Lev. 19:17 f.).

(b) The pass. *miseomai*, especially the part. *misoumenē*, can also be used of a wife who is not loved (Gen. 29:31, 33; Deut. 21:15 ff.; 22:13 ff.; Isa. 60:15). The transformation of strong desire into utter loathing is portrayed in 2 Sam. 13.

(c) The term haters is often a synonym for enemies (Deut. 7:15; 30:7; 2 Sam. 22:18; Ps. 18:17); also where the reference is to enemies of God (Num. 10:35; Ps. 68:1; 139:21). Similarly one's enemies are those whom one hates oneself (Ezek. 16:37; 23:28). It does not make sense to love those who hate one and to hate those who love one (2 Sam. 19:6 f.).

(d) Those who hate God are also those who are disobedient to him (Exod. 20:5; Deut. 5:9; 7:9–11). They hate anyone who reproves them in the name of Yahweh (1 Ki. 22:8; Amos 5:10; cf. Ps. 50:17; Prov. 5:12). They hate right knowledge (Prov. 1:22, 29), the righteous (godly) man (Ps. 34:21; 69:4; 9:13; 69:14; Prov. 29:10) and the man of discretion (Prov. 14:17).

(e) God hates wickedness (Jer. 44:3 f.; Zech. 8:17; Mal. 2:16, divorce) and the man who does it (Hos. 9:15; Jer. 12:8; Ps. 5:5, an aphorism; Prov. 6:16 ff.). Israel therefore is also to hate wickedness (Amos 5:15; cf. Ps. 119:104, the way of lying; 26:5, the company of evildoers; Ps. 139:21 f., those who hate God).

(f) To hate oneself is folly. He who despises correction hates himself (*napśô*, lit. "his soul", Prov. 15:32; cf. 29:24).

2. Ancient Judaism recognized the destructive power of hatred. Baseless hatred destroyed the second temple, for hatred is more serious than immorality, idolaery and the shedding of blood put together (*Yoma* 9a). At the same time there is a hatred which is commanded. "Hate the Epicureans [free-thinkers], those who seduce and mislead, and likewise those who betray" (Ab. R.N. 16; cf. Ps. 139:21 f.). "It is forbidden to harbour feelings of anger and revenge against the sons of the people [sc. and fully-fledged proselytes], but not against others" (Siphra on Lev. 19:18;

555

cf. SB I 358 on Matt. 5:43 f.). The Qumran community spoke in similar vein. Its members were to "do what is good and righteous before Him [God] as He commanded by the hand of Moses and all His servants the Prophets ... [to] love all the sons of light, each according to his lot in God's design, and hate the sons of darkness, each according to his guilt in God's vengeance" (1QS 1:2 f., 9–11; cf. 9:21–23).

NT *miseō* occurs 39 times in the NT (20 times in the Johannine writings alone).

1. According to the preaching of Jesus, God now accepts his enemies as sons (Matt. 5:43 ff.; Lk. 15:11 ff.). Hence it no longer makes sense for the righteous to hate "the sons of darkness" (1QS 1) and wayward spirits (see above OT 2). Rather, in the name of God Jesus demands: "You have heard that it was said, 'You shall love your neighbour and hate your enemy.' But I say to you, Love your enemies" (Matt. 5:43 f.); "Do good to those who hate you" (Lk. 6:27). It is of course right for the Christian church, as for "the Son" (Heb. 1:9), to hate evil and evil deeds (Rev. 2:6; cf. also Jude 23 "hating even the garment spotted by the flesh", probably to be understood, in view of Zech. 3:3 f., as a metaphor for *anomia*, lawlessness, of the wearers, who have fallen into a heresy, probably with libertine teachings; cf. Rev. 3:4). Within the church, however, "He who says he is in the light and hates his brother is in darkness still" (1 Jn. 2:9). "Anyone who hates his brother is a murderer" (3:15; cf. 4:20). In the last days there will be hatred even within the church (Matt. 24:10). But this is really the mark of non-Christian humanity (Tit. 3:3).

2. Jesus' radical command to love one's enemies brings the disciples into line with God's action towards good and evil men (Matt. 5:45 ff.; Lk. 6:35). But Jesus could also say: "If anyone comes to me and does not hate his own father and mother and wife and children and brothers and sisters, yes, and even his own life, he cannot be my disciple" (Lk. 14:26; cf. Jn. 12:25). Like God himself (Deut. 13:6 ff.), Jesus thus requires that obedience to God must take precedence over all human obligations. God's own action and demands are represented in him, Jesus. The world, however, like everyone who does evil, hates the light (Jn. 3:20). It hates the Revealer without cause (Jn. 15:25), because he bears witness that its works are evil (Jn. 7:7). This hatred is directed also against Jesus' disciples (Matt. 10:22; Mk. 13:13; Lk. 21:17; Jn. 15:18 ff.; 17:14; 1 Jn. 3:13). They are counted blessed when men hate them (Lk. 6:22) for the Revealer's sake (Matt. 5:11). Those, on the other hand, who do not reckon themselves separated from the world (the brothers of Jesus) are not hated (Jn. 7:7).

3. Paul uses *miseō* in two difficult passages. (a) In Rom. 7:15 he says of man under the → law. "I do not understand my own actions; for I do not do what I want, but I do the very thing I hate." The reference is not to man's inability to become righteous in terms of God's law (as Phil. 3:6 shows), but his inability to discern what is the outcome of his endeavour to fulfil the law. For he does not attain to life, as he wants, but to death which he hates, since sin is able to make use even of the law for its own ends and cannot therefore be restrained by the law.

(b) In Rom. 9:13 Paul cites from Mal. 1:2 f.: "Jacob I loved, but Esau I hated". This means that even before the two sons of Isaac could give any grounds for acceptance or rejection, God chose the younger one, Jacob, as the heir of his promise, and rejected Esau, the older brother, in order to show that his salvation rests on his promise (*epangelia*) alone, and not on natural descent or similar prerogatives (cf. Rom. 9:7 f., 11 f. Gen. 25 and 28; → Israel).

4. *miseō* is used in a sense completely in line with OT usage at Lk. 1:71 (of enemies) and Rev. 18:2 (of unclean → birds, loathed by God).　　*H. Seebass*
→ Brother, → Love

(a). G. W. Anderson, "Enemies and Evildoers in the Book of Psalms", *BJRL* 48, 1965–66, 18 ff.; H. Birkeland, *The Evildoers in the Book of Psalms*, 1955; A. Carr, "The meaning of 'Hatred' in the New Testament," *The Expositor* VI, 12, 1905, 153–60; B. S. Childs, "The Enemy from the North and the Chaos Tradition," *JBL* 78, 1959, 187–98; W. D. Davies, *The Setting of the Sermon on the Mount*, 1964, 211 ff., 245 f., 405 ff.; W. Foerster, *echthros*, *TDNT* II 811–16; O. Michel, *miseō*, *TDNT* IV 683–94; J. Scharbert, "Enemy", *EBT* I 220–24; M. Smith, "Mt. v 43. Hate thine enemy," *HTR* 45, 1952, 71 ff.; F. L. R. Stachowiak, "Hatred," *EBT* I 351–55; E. F. Sutcliffe, "Hatred at Qumran," *Revue de Qumran* 2, 1959–60, 345–56; O. J. F. Seitz, "Love your Enemies," *NTS* 16, 1969–70, 39–54; commentaries on the *Psalms* by A. Weiser, 1962; and A. A. Anderson, I–II, 1972.
(b). W. Bleibtreu, *Paradoxe Ansprüche Jesu*, 1926, 15–35; P. Jedzink, *Das Gebot der Nächstenliebe im Evangelium*, 1916; H.-J. Kraus, "Die Feinde des Einzelnen," in *Psalmen*, I, 1960, 40 ff.; J. Nikel, *Das Alte Testament und die Nächstenliebe*, 1913; A. F. Puukko, "Der Feind in den Psalmen," *Oudtestamentische Studien* 8, 1950, 47–65; J. Ridderbos, *De Psalmen*, I, 1955, 382–408; SB I 353–68; H. Schmidt, *Das Gebet des Angeklagten*, 1928.

Envy

| $\phi\theta o\nu\acute{\epsilon}\omega$ |

$\phi\theta o\nu\acute{\epsilon}\omega$ (*phthoneō*), be envious; $\phi\theta\acute{o}\nu o\varsigma$ (*phthonos*), envy.

CL In secular Gk., *phthoneō* can mean to bear ill-will of a general kind, but more often it is used specifically to express the envy which makes one man grudge another something which he himself desires, but does not possess. The noun *phthonos* is used in a similar way. Frequently it appears with *zēlos*, jealousy, but several classical writers are careful to distinguish between these two apparent synonyms. Aristotle, for example, defines *zēlos* as the desire to have what another man possesses, without necessarily bearing a grudge against him because he has it; while *phthonos* is concerned more to deprive the other man of the desired thing than to gain it. "The envious are those who are annoyed only at their friends' successes" (Xenophon).

OT Neither *phthoneō* nor *phthonos* appears in the canonical literature of the LXX, though the idea is apparent in such verses as Prov. 14:30, and the noun is found in the apocryphal writings of I Maccabees and Wisdom (where the coming of death into the world is attributed to the devil's *phthonos*, Wis. 2:24).

NT In the NT *phthoneō* is found only once (in Gal. 5:26, where "envying one another" is set in sharp contrast to "living by the Spirit"). *phthonos* occurs nine times in all: (a) In the Epistles it features in several lists of bad qualities which characterize the unredeemed life. It is one of the "works of the flesh" which are opposed to the "fruit of the Spirit" in Gal. 5:19–24. It marks out those whom God has given up to a "base mind" (*adokimon noun*, Rom. 1:29). It is a feature of life before conversion (Tit. 3:3), to be "put away" by those who "grow up to salvation"

(1 Pet. 2:2). And it is symptomatic of pseudo-Christian teaching which trades on controversy and wordy dispute (1 Tim. 6:4).

(b) The phrase *dia phthonon*, "because of envy", describes the evil motives of those who delivered Jesus to Pontius Pilate (Mk. 15:10 par.). The same expression reappears in Phil. 1:15 (bracketed with *eris*, "strife" and contrasted to *eudokia*, "good will") to expose the motivation of those who preached the gospel from a desire to undermine Paul's evangelistic reputation, rather than share his gift.

(c) Jas. 4:5 may provide the only example of *phthonos* used in a good sense, but the translation of this verse in notoriously difficult. Following RSV, God "yearns jealously (*pros phthonon*) over the spirit which he has made to dwell in us". The description of God as the jealous lover who cannot brook a rival is prominent in the OT, but the Gk. word used to translate the Heb. *qin'âh* in this context is *zēlos*, not *phthonos* (cf. Zech. 1:14). Thus NEB (e.g.) prefers to take the (human) spirit as the subject of the sentence in Jas. 4:5, giving *phthonos* its more usual bad sense of envy. *D. H. Field*

R. C. Trench, *Synonyms of the New Testament*, 1880, 86 ff.; W. Barclay, *Flesh and Spirit*, 1962 44 ff.; S. S. Laws, "Does Scripture speak in vain? A reconsideration of James iv. 5," *NTS* 20, 1973–4, 210 ff.

Escape, Flee

φεύγω

φεύγω (*pheugō*), escape, flee, avoid; ἀποφεύγω (*apopheugō*), flee from, avoid; φυγή (*phygē*), flight.

CL The *pheugō* word group derives from Indo-European *bheug-* (cf. Lat. *fugere*). From the time of Homer, its most common meaning is "flee", "take flight", whether absolutely, or from someone or something (Homer, Plato, Herodotus, etc.). The present and imperfect tenses often express only the purpose or endeavour to get away. Hence the compounds *apopheugō, katapheugō, ekpheugō,* or *propheugō* may be added to the participle *pheugōn* in a sentence to denote the escape itself. The accusative (and occasionally the genitive) with *pheugō* specifies that which is being "shunned", "escaped from", or "avoided" – whether death and war (Homer), evil (Demosthenes), or the consequences of murder (Euripides). Metaphorically reins may "escape from" the hands of the charioteer. Because a person may flee his country, the articular participle refers to "the exile(s)" (Homer, Xenophon, Thucydides); and since such people may well have been banished, by a natural extension the active verb itself takes on the quasi-passive force of "be banished", "be expelled" (Herodotus, Xenophon, Dinarchus). Similarly *phygē* comes to mean "exile", "banishment". In Attic Greek, both *pheugō* and *apopheugō* occur as law-terms. The *pheugōn* is the defendant, as opposed to the *diōkōn*, the prosecutor; and *pheugein graphēn* (or *dikēn*) means "to be put on trial", while an added genitive (e.g. *phonou*, murder) specifies the charge. To escape the prosecutors (*apopheugein tous diōkontas*) therefore means "to be acquitted".

OT In the LXX the *pheugō* word group represents eight different Heb. roots, the most important of which are *nûs* (flee, escape, depart, take flight, fly to the attack) and *bāraḥ* (go through, flee, hasten quickly). Unlike the secular literature, the LXX does not yield examples of a legal idiom, but offers more instances of flight in a moral context: e.g. flight from an unbearable friend (Sir. 22:22), or from sin (Sir. 21:2); flight to the Lord or to the altar (3 Ki. 2:29), or flight based on fearful ungodliness (Prov. 28:1). The Jewish background is also revealed by a pedantic translation of Heb. idiom, e.g. the large number of times the Israelites "flee to their tents". Cf. also the stilted idiom of 2 Ki. 18:3; Job 27:22. On the whole *pheugō* is avoided when the Heb. original means something less than rapid flight: e.g. in Cant. 2:17; 4:6 the Heb. verb *nûs* is used for the "departing" shadows of night; but *pheugō* is not used. Contrast Cant. 8:14. The noun *phygē* always means "flight" or "escape", although in Ps. 141:4 the thought is close to "refuge". In Philo and Josephus the word-group is more restricted to the concepts of physical "flight" and "escape" than in the LXX.

NT (a) In the most literal sense, Joseph was ordered to flee to Egypt with Mary and the infant Jesus (Matt. 2:13); and the disciples when persecuted in one city were to flee to the next and continue their ministry (Matt. 10:23). Similarly there is no shame in the flight of the sheep from false shepherds (Jn. 10:5), nor in the escape from the sword accomplished by men of faith (Heb. 11:34). Indeed, the believers in Jesus' day were commanded to flee to the mountains when Jerusalem appeared in danger (Matt. 24:16 = Lk. 21:21; cf. Matt. 24:20, the only occurrence of *phygē* in the NT). On the other hand, fear is attached to the flight of the swine-herds (Mk. 5:14 par.) and to the escape of Moses (Acts 7:29); cowardice to the hirelings (Jn. 10:12); irresponsibility and unbelief to the sailors manning the boat which conveyed Paul towards Rome (Acts 27:30); and shame to the total aban-donment of Christ by the disciples in the Garden (Mk. 14:50, 52 par.). Jesus himself is never said to flee, unless we accept the weaker *v.l.* of Jn. 6:15. The devil, however, will flee from men if he is resisted (Jas. 4:7).

(b) Both John the Baptist and Jesus warn men to flee from the wrath to come, from the judgment of hell, in contexts urging tangible evidence of genuine repen-tance (Matt. 3:7 = Lk. 3:7; Matt. 23:33). Repentance thus becomes evidence of such flight.

(c) Related to this is the epistolary exhortation to flee from moral evil. The Corinthians are told to avoid fornication (I Cor. 6:18) and idolatry (10:14); Timothy to flee youthful lusts (2 Tim. 2:22) and assorted vices (I Tim. 6:11), and pursue such virtues as righteousness, godliness, faith, love, etc. 2 Pet. 1:4; 2:18, 20 use *apopheugō* in the sense of "escape", rather than "flee", the escape being from the corruption of the world. If one successfully escapes such defilements and then returns to them, the end depravity is incomparably worse than the first entanglement.

(d) *pheugō* is used metaphorically in the majestic apocalyptic panoramas of Revelation. The woman flees to the desert (12:6). When men seek death, it flees from them (9:6). The islands flee and the mountains disappear in God's fierce wrath (16:20); indeed, before the face of his majesty, heaven and earth flee away (20:11).   *D. A. Carson*

Eunuch

εὐνοῦχος

εὐνοῦχος (*eunouchos*), eunuch; εὐνουχίζω (*eunouchizo*), castrate.

559

CL The Greeks themselves explained *eunouchos* as a compound of *eunē*, bed, and *echō*, hold. Hence it meant a holder or guardian of the bed. There is, however, the view that it is really a Sem. loan word. Primarily it meant a guardian of the harem. This office was normally carried out by those who had been castrated, and so the word came to mean eunuch, as we understand the term. Sometimes when the term is used of a high official of state (cf. Acts 8:27), it is no longer clear whether we are to take it literally, or whether "eunuch" has become a mere title. The term is used fig. of castrated animals and of plants that do not bear seed. The vb. *eunouchizō*, found only twice in classical literature, is used only for the act of castration.

OT Almost half the OT occurrences are in Est. Where no stress seems intended, we must take *sārîs* as a court official without our being able to affirm whether or not he was castrated (cf. Gen. 39:1, Potiphar; Gen. 40:2, Pharaoh's chief butler and baker; 1 Sam. 8:15 and in Kings generally). Etymologically *sārîs* has nothing to do with castration. If it acquired the meaning of a eunuch, it was because many court officials fell into this class. It is purely a title. The eunuch was excluded from the community of Israel (Deut. 23:1). This separated Israel from the fertility cults of its neighbours which found their climax not merely in the *hieros gamos* and sacred prostitution, but also in self-castration to the glory of the deity. This latter is attested in the cults of Cybele, the Magna Mater, in Asia Minor, of Attis, and of the Ephesian Artemis. In the last days the eunuch who had been excluded will find a place in God's salvation (Isa. 56:3 ff.).

Rab. Judaism, like the OT, rejected castration. It differentiates, however, between those who are sterile because of physical malformation and those who have been made eunuchs by men. The reason is basically the command to marry which was deduced from Gen. 1:28. Probably as a result of Hel. influence a certain laxness had come in the NT period. Josephus tells us that Herod had eunuchs at his court (*War*, 1, 488).

NT In the NT the treasurer of Queen Candace is called a eunuch (Acts 8:27), but perhaps it should not be taken literally. It could mean no more than a high court official. If he really was a eunuch his conversion could be seen as a fulfilment of Isa. 56:3 ff. Since the resurrection of Jesus the age of salvation and of the Messiah was dawning, and so such persons could be received into the community of salvation. The treasurer would have been a semi-proselyte; as a eunuch he could not be a full proselyte. So the previous barriers were doubly breached. The gospel was offered to the half-proselyte and to one who was until then excluded from the community of salvation (→ Conversion, art. *prosēlytos*).

The vb. *eunouchizō* is found twice linked with *eunouchos* in Matt. 19:12, where three types of eunuchs are described: (a) those who are such from birth, due to corporal malformation, (b) those who have been made such by men, (c) those who made themselves eunuchs "for the sake of the kingdom of heaven".

Jesus is clearly speaking not merely of celibacy, but also of unfitness for marriage. He is dealing only with the physical, without considering other causes that might prevent marriage. Under the first two headings Jesus adopts the division accepted by the rabbis. Only the third category, those who are eunuchs for the kingdom of heaven's sake, presents something new, showing that the real stress falls here.

Physical inability by nature or castration is intended in the first two, but this is improbable in the third. There were those who took it lit. in the early centuries of the church, and there were rare cases of self-castration, e.g. Origen (cf. Eusebius, *HE*, 6, 8; cf. Justin, *Apol.* I, 29; Canons of Nicea, 1). Later, however, Origen clearly rejected a lit. understanding of the passage (*Commentary on Matthew*, 15, 3).

It could be that Jesus is here reacting against a slander spoken against him and his disciples. Because he was unmarried he was perhaps accused of being a eunuch (cf. the charge in Matt. 11:19, "a glutton and a drunkard"). Jesus answers by referring to the kingdom of God. One's joy in it can be so great, that one is prepared for the sake of the kingdom to renounce everything else, under some circumstances even marriage.

We can also approach it from a comparison with Matt. 5:29 f., plucking out an eye and cutting off a hand. Measured by the standards of the kingdom of heaven even things necessary to life are unimportant, and must be surrendered where there is a conflict.
H. Baltensweiler

→ Discipline, → Marriage

(a). D. Hill, *The Gospel of Matthew*, 1972, 278–82; A. Isaksson, *Marriage and Ministry in the New Temple*, 1965; J. Schneider, *eunouchos, TDNT* II 765–68.
(b). J. Blinzler, *Eisin eunouchoi, ZNW* 48, 1957, 254 ff.; SB I 805 ff.

Evil, Bad, Wickedness

The two main NT terms for expressing the shortcomings or inferiority of a thing (i.e. bad) and the ethically negative and religiously destructive character of a person or thought (i.e. evil) are *kakos* and *ponēros*. In the NT *kakos* occurs 50 times and the linguistically later *ponēros* 78 times, though the LXX uses it only 50 times compared to the 300 cases of *kakos*. Unlike the terms dealt with under → Good, it is impossible to show any difference between these two terms. Both are used even for the personification of evil in the devil or men.

κακός	κακός (*kakos*), bad, evil; ἄκακος (*akakos*), guileless, innocent; κακία (*kakia*), badness; κακόω (*kakoō*),

harm, embitter; κακοποιέω (*kakopoieō*), do wrong, harm; κακοποιός (*kakopoios*), evil-doer; κακοῦργος (*kakourgos*), evil-doer, delinquent; ἐγκακέω (*enkakeō*), become tired, lose heart; φαῦλος (*phaulos*), bad, evil.

CL *kakos* is found from Homer on in a large variety of associations. It means bad in the sense of lacking something, always in contrast to *agathos*, → good. Secular Gk. has 4 main uses: (a) negligible, unsuitable, bad; (b) morally bad, evil; (c) weak, miserable; (d) bad, harmful, unfavourable. *to kakon* and the plur. *ta kaka* mean evil, suffering, misfortune, ruin.

In the Gk. world the question of the meaning and origin of evil was answered in many different ways in the course of the centuries. There were, however, two basic concepts around which thinking constantly circled. (a) Evil was seen as a metaphysical principle, e.g. among the Pythagoreans and in Plato's later writings. (b) Man's ignorance is the source of all evil, e.g. in Democritus, Socrates, Plato. An unenlightened and ignorant man does evil involuntarily, and this is the basis of all ruin and corruption (Plato). Enlightenment leads to knowledge and frees him from evil, causing him to do good and so creating the moral man.

Plato reached a synthesis of these two basic concepts by developing a metaphysical dualism of spirit and matter, with its ethical expression in a dualism of soul and body. The cause leading to evil lies in the material and physical. In his old age Plato went a step further and assumed the existence of an evil world-soul.

In Hel. thought evil was understood as imperfection. Plotinus held this to be in the very nature of matter, which in the last analysis stands in contrast to the highest good and the light from which all has been derived. Here too evil is lack of light, i.e. of knowledge.

Whichever cause is regarded as the basis of evil, even when it is seen as *hamartia* (→ Sin), it must not be regarded as personal guilt, for it is not the result of a free and responsible personal decision but of a lack. It may be the lack of knowing the divine providence (Socrates), or of the working of a cosmic power.

OT 1. In the LXX *kakos* is used predominantly for Heb. *ra'* and *rā'âh* (227 times), which are also rendered by → *ponēros* 226 times. There is a similar balance in the use of the verbs *ponēreuomai* (22 times) and *kakoō* (21 times).

(a) *kakos* is primarily the evil which objectively hurts one's existence. (i) It is predominantly looked on as God's punishment (Deut. 31:17) which normally corresponds exactly to the preceding sin. The evil which men set in motion is brought back on their heads by Yahweh. Hence Amos 3:6b can say, "Does evil befall a city, unless Yahweh has done it?" (cf. Homer, *Od.*, 4, 236 f.). (ii) On the other hand, God grants protection in the midst of all evil (Ps. 23(LXX 22):4). When the pious find themselves threatened by evils, they can turn to God, for the purpose of his punishments is not evil. God's "plans [are] for welfare and not for evil" (Jer. 29:11). (iii) Behind the evil lies God's gracious purpose of visitation. His final purpose is "to give you a future and a hope" (Jer. 29:11c). (iv) The OT reaches the climax of its search for the origin and purpose of evil when faced with God's all-sovereign goodness. For here all questioning is silenced. In Job the three friends seek to link Job's suffering with his sins. Job never denies his sinfulness, but the work as a whole makes no direct connection between his sinfulness and his sufferings. Suffering is not necessarily the result of sin. It may be training in faith and hence testing (Job 5:17 f.). Ps. 73(LXX 72) in particular shows us the pious man who wins his way to the "Nevertheless" of faith (v. 23), without having discovered and understood the reason for his suffering. Where evil attacks on every side, man can only seek for still closer links with God through prayer.

(b) Evil is also an aspect of moral behaviour (cf. Mic. 2:1; Jer. 7:24; Pss. 28:3; 34:12 ff. (MT 13 ff.)). It is to be noted that the OT very seldom speaks theoretically of evil. It describes it concretely and concentrates on the case in hand. Hence evil is not abstract.

(c) The OT has no comprehensive theory of evil. Does it derive from the fact of being a creature? The serpent in Gen. 3 was after all a creature of God (cf. 2:9). In Gen. 3:5, 22 → *ponēros* is used in connection with the tree of the knowledge of good and evil. Is evil sent by God himself (1 Sam. 16:14)? The concept of an evil power opposed to God is found only late in Israel (cf. 1 Chr. 21:1 with 2 Sam. 24:1). (→ Dragon, Serpent.)

2. In Zoroastrianism the question of the origin of evil found an answer in a consistent dualism. Two opposed principles have been in conflict from the first, the good power, Ahura Mazda, and the evil power, Ahriman. Men belong to the one or the other power according to their moral behaviour, and will inherit after death either eternal bliss or eternal darkness. Ultimately evil will be conquered and destroyed in a final battle. Zoroastrianism is of special interest because of a number of parallels with Christian eschatology, but it is mythology in the former, history in the latter.

3. Zoroastrian dualism found its way into Qumran, and there are strong reminiscences of it in the Dead Sea Scrolls. According to the teaching of Qumran, God created at the beginning two spirits, the good spirit, the spirit of light, and the evil spirit, the spirit of darkness (Belial). According to God's eternal decree, all men belong to one or other of these spirits, and this is revealed by their good or evil deeds (1QS 3:13 ff.). The dualism in the Qumran texts (light-darkness, truth-wickedness) is the closest parallel in the history of religions to the dualism we find in Jesus' teaching, e.g. God's kingdom – Satan's kingdom (Mk. 3:22–30), especially the dualism in the Johannine writings (light-darkness, truth-lie), and also the dualism in some of Paul's writings (cf. Rom. 13:11–14; 2 Cor. 6:14–18).

4. Philo clearly attributes the origin of good to God and evil to man. But man has the possibility of choosing the good, just as he chooses between good and bad clothes. For Philo, evil is a reality opposed to God, but not a person opposed to him. Gk.-Hel. philosophy does not personify evil as the devil, but regards it as inadequate good. By so doing it makes evil harmless and offers no real help for conquering it.

NT 1. *kakos* is used in the NT with the meaning evil, bad, destructive, damaging, unjust. It is found 50 times, 26 of these being in Paul (Rom. 15 times, but only 7 times in the Synoptics). Its derivative *akakos* means without suspicion, simpleminded (Rom. 16:18), guiltless, untouched by evil (used of Christ in Heb. 7:26).

The noun *kakia* is often used synonymously with the neut. adj. *kakon* as evil, badness, wickedness, and denotes the source of the behaviour of a *kakos*, an evil person, or *kakopoios*, evil-doer (cf. Acts 8:22; Rom. 1:29; 1 Cor. 5:8). In Matt. 6:34 it means trouble, hardship, or misfortune.

The vb. *kakoō* means do evil, cause damage, handle badly or harm (1 Pet. 3:13, and often in Acts), stir up, embitter (Acts 14:2, RSV poison); and *kakopoieō* behave badly, do wrong (1 Pet. 3:17; 3 Jn. 11), harm (cf. Mk. 3:4 par.) A change in meaning is observable with *enkakeō*. It no longer means behave badly, but become tired or careless (in prayer, Lk. 18:1, RSV "lose heart"; 2 Thess. 3:13, be weary in doing good), lose heart (2 Cor. 4:1; Eph. 3:13). Weariness here is not physical but spiritual.

kakos and its derivations are of less importance in the NT than in the OT. The NT prefers → *ponēros* and *hamartia* (→ Sin) to express evil and personal guilt.

2. (a) Though numerous dualistic notes may be heard in the NT (see above OT 3), one can never find a dualism in which evil has the same power as good. Equally the thought is rejected that the root of evil could lie in God; "for God is untouched [lit. cannot be tempted] by evil" (Jas. 1:13, NEB). Evil comes rather from a man's heart in the form of evil thoughts which find expression in acts (Mk. 7:21 f. par.;

563

cf. Matt. 15:19 → *ponēros*), e.g. love of money (1 Tim. 6:10), misuse of the tongue (Jas. 3:6–10; 1 Pet. 3:10).

(b) The question of justifying God's ways does not arise, or is answered in another way. Evil (e.g. Lk. 13:1–5) is either God's righteous punishment and only repentance can save from further experience of it, or it can be borne and conquered by the experience of the love of God in Christ (Rom. 5:5; 8:35, 37 ff.).

(c) *kakos* is used attributively and as a noun of persons (Matt. 21:41; 24:48; Phil. 3:2; Tit. 1:12; Rev. 2:2) and attributively of things (Mk. 7:21; Rom. 13:3; 1 Cor. 15:33; Col. 3:5; Rev. 16:2). Otherwise it is always a neut. noun meaning evil or the evil in the sense of a misfortune, wrong, suffering (cf. Lk. 16:25; Acts 16:28; 28:5), or an evil act, a sin (cf. Matt. 27:23 par.; Acts 23:9; 3 Jn. 11), especially in Paul (cf. Rom. 7:19, 21; 12:21; 13:4; 16:19).

(d) For Paul, the problem of evil (*kakos* appears 26 times in his letters) lies in the fact that a man often does evil against his will (Rom. 7:15, 17 ff.), that it rules in him like a strange law (Rom. 7:21, 23), and yet it is an expression of his existence and nature. His evil nature which shows itself in his evil acts, separates him from God and brings him under judgment. Since a man constantly does the evil instead of the good he wants to do, and therefore achieves death and not life, every hope of conquering evil by his own strength is blasted. The solution of this problem is not to be found, therefore, in a human struggle, but in Christ's victory over evil in his cross and resurrection. This solution is seen in Paul's shout of salvation, "Thanks be to God through Jesus Christ our Lord!" (Rom. 7:25).

(e) We must understand the many apostolic exhortations to conquer, lay aside, and shun the evil against this background of evil's being stripped of its power (Rom. 12:17, 21; 16:19; 1 Cor. 10:6; 1 Pet. 3:11; Col. 3:5). Though every governing authority (Rom. 13:1, 3 f.; *exousia* → Power) should hold down evil as God's representative, the problem of evil is solved only by justification and sanctification. The one who has been justified is in the sphere of influence of the One who has conquered evil and gives the Spirit. Hence he does not face the powers of evil without strength (Rom. 13:10; 1 Cor. 13:5; 2 Cor. 13:7).

3. *phaulos* (6 times in the NT) is used as a synonym of *kakos* and means evil, bad. In Tit. 2:8 it is used in a judgment on people. Otherwise it is used for actions (Jn. 3:20; 5:29; Rom. 9:11; 2 Cor. 5:10; Jas. 3:16 (RSV "vile")). Its opposite is *agathos* (→ Good).

4. In two passages in the NT we find *kakourgos*, evil doer. In Lk. 23:32, 33, 39 it is used for the criminals crucified with Jesus. In 2 Tim. 2:9 Paul uses it with reference to his imprisonment "like a criminal." *E. Achilles*

πονηρός

πονηρός (*ponēros*), in a poor condition, sick, bad, evil, wicked; πονηρία (*ponēria*), evil, badness, wickedness.

CL *ponēros*, sub. *ponēria*, is derived from *ponos*, work, toil, and *poneō*, to be involved in work, labour (→ Burden). They are often used as synonyms of → *kakos* and *kakia* and their derivatives. The original vb. was *penomai*, take pains, be poor, with its derivatives *penia* (not in the NT), poverty, and *penichros* (in the NT only Lk.

21:2), poor, in want (→ Poor). *ponēros* is not found in Homer, but it is used by Hesiod and Thuc. as well as by inscriptions and papyri, all with pass. force in the sense of laden with toil, full of suffering, unfortunate, to be pitied, unfit, miserable. The act. force is also found in the sense of bad, causing disaster, dangerous, especially in the political and social arena where it describes an enemy of the state. This leads to the moral concept of ethically reprehensible, bad.

OT 1. In the LXX *ponēros* represents Heb. *ra'* (→ *kakos*, OT 1), evil, bad, of little value, unusable; of animals, food, land and persons (e.g. 1 Sam. 25:3). When used of animals it can mean dangerous, harmful (Gen. 37:20). It can also mean damaging to a person's reputation (e.g. Deut. 22:14) or, very often, evil in relation to the human spirit (e.g. 1 Sam. 16:14 ff.). In Neh. 2:2 it means sad looking. Ethically *ponēros* means evil, bad, worthless, depraved, corrupt, whether used of persons (cf. Gen. 13:13; Isa. 9:17(16); Sir. 25:25) or of things (cf. Isa. 3:9). Like → *kakos*, *ponēros* has not merely a moral but also a religious connotation. It implies separation from God, opposition to God and his will (Amos 5:14 f.). In contrast to the NT, it is never used to denote the devil. The expression "good and evil" (Gen. 3:5, 22), in which *ponēros* is used, means in the widest sense "everything." "What the serpent's insinuation means is the possibility of an extension of human existence beyond the limits set for it by God at creation . . . power over mysteries that lie beyond man" (G. von Rad, *Genesis*, 1961, 87). Such knowledge renders man autonomous, for it and not God is exalted to the guiding principle of his life. ([Tr.] In a passage like Deut. 1:39 it means the knowledge brought by maturity rather than omniscience.)

The noun *ponēria* shares many of the meanings of the adj. In addition, it means the harm or calamity which God brings on man (Jer. 2:3) or man brings on his fellow man (Gen. 26:29).

2. For various uses in late Jud. see *kakos*, OT 2 ff.

3. In the pseudepigrapha *ponēros* and *ponēria* are used almost exclusively in ethical and religious contexts and are virtually synonymous with → Sin. The same is true of Philo and Josephus, though they frequently use *kakos* and *kakia*.

NT *ponēros* is used 78 times in the NT, 26 times in Matt., 13 in Lk., 13 in Paul, 8 in Acts, 8 in Jn. *ponēria* occurs 7 times.

1. It is used physically of the eyes in Matt. 6:23 and Lk. 11:34 as bad, sick. It cannot be established with certainty whether it was intended here in an ethical sense (so Jülicher), but the final exegesis will be little affected by our answer, for even if the ref. is to sickness of the eye rather than to evilness the parable means us to understand it in a metaphorical sense (so, e.g., Schlatter). In Matt. 18:32 it refers to worthless servants. It is used of trees and their fruit in Matt. 7:17 f. as spoilt, useless. ([Tr.] Note that the word applied to the tree is *sapros*.)

2. It is used ethically in the sense of being opposed to God. (a) Jesus used it as an adj. of men in general, whom he called evil (cf. Matt. 7:11 par.). God alone is good, in contrast to them (Mk. 10:18). The Pharisees were evil in the sense of being hardened (Matt. 12:34), just as the Jews were the evil generation (Matt. 12:39; 16:4; Lk. 11:29), who showed their character in their opposition to Jesus. So too anyone is evil who decides against Jesus (cf. 2 Thess. 3:2; 2 Tim. 3:13). Out of the

evil treasure of his heart he brings forth evil (Matt. 12:35 par.). It is used in a social sense in Acts 17:5 (NEB, "low fellows").

Thoughts also can be evil (Matt. 15:19). In Jas. 2:4 the *dialogismōn ponērōn* mean the evil reflections by which judges may be led astray (NEB, "you. . .judge by false standards"). In Col. 1:21 and 2 Tim. 4:18 it is used with *ergon* to denote human actions (the RSV "from every evil" is inadequate in the latter; cf. NEB "from every attempt to do me evil"). *ponēros* can also be used in connection with boasting, words, insults, conscience, the name of Christian (Lk. 6:22, the verdict of unbelievers), the present age (Gal. 1:4), and the present day (Eph. 6:13). Jn.'s contrast of *ponēros* with God's light, work and word is particularly striking (Jn. 3:19; 17:15; 1 Jn. 2:13; 3:12; 5:18 f.; 2 Jn. 11; 3 Jn. 10).

(b) When used as a noun, *ponēros* has a double meaning. (i) A bad man. This is so even in Matt. 22:10, where many have wanted to give it a social sense, e.g. someone in rags. In fact, it is the man who has rejected the gospel. In Matt. 5:39a we should, as in RSV and NEB, understand it of the evil person, for this is the inference to be drawn from the 2nd half of the verse. Matt. 13:49 f. declares that in the final judgment the *ponēroi* will be separated out by God and condemned (cf. Matt. 22:13 f.). The church should exclude the evil man (1 Cor. 5:13). But the goodness of God is available even for the evil as long as they live on earth. Hence Christians should show them love (Lk. 6:35).

(ii) *ho ponēros*, standing absolutely, is the evil one (→ Satan). This is clear in Matt. 13:19, for the par. Mk. 4:15 has Satan, and Lk. 8:12 the devil. The same is true of Eph. 6:12, *ta pneumatika tēs ponērias*, where Phillips has "spiritual agents from the very headquarters of evil"); Jn. 17:15; Eph. 6:16; 2 Thess. 3:3 (RSV mg, NEB). It is used noticeably often in 1 Jn. (cf. 2:13, 14; 3:12; 5:18, 19). It is debatable whether we should understand *tou ponērou* in Matt. 13:38 as masculine (i.e. the evil one) or neuter (i.e. evil). G. Harder (*TDNT* VI 560 f.) decides for the latter. But this is not completely certain, for the source of the evil is said in v. 39 to be the devil, and this prevents us giving any weakened meaning to evil (v. 38). The history of theology shows that efforts to avoid the personifying of evil in the devil have led to a depersonalizing of God and Christ.

Translators and expositors are divided over the meaning of Matt. 6:13b. RSV follows the traditional rendering: "But deliver us from evil." But RSV mg and NEB suggest that the prayer is for deliverance from → Satan by rendering it "the evil one." G. Harder rejects the personal interpretation on the grounds of impersonal rab. parallels, the impersonal use elsewhere in Jesus' teaching, and the fact that rescuing in the NT is never applied to the devil (*TDNT* VI 561). He sees it as a prayer for eschatological deliverance (cf. Col. 1:13; Lk. 1:74; Rom. 7:24; 1 Thess. 1:10). W. Lüthi regards the prayer as a petition for the passing away of the evil world (*The Lord's Prayer*, 1961, 68). E. Lohmeyer sees the words "from evil" as summing up all the last dangers, external and internal, as expressions of the naked power of Satan (*The Lord's Prayer*, 1965, 227). It is clear that *tou ponērou* must be read in the light of the first half of the verse. J. Jeremias maintains that "temptation" does not refer to small, everyday temptations but to the great temptation of the last days, which is at the door and will involve the whole world (*New Testament Theology*, I, 1971, 202; *The Prayers of Jesus*, 1967, 104 ff.). He thinks of the revelation of the mystery of evil and the Antichrist, of the abomination of desolation,

Satan in the place of God, the final persecution and the testing of God through false prophets and false saviours. If 6:13a is so clearly a petition for help against the devil, then we must understand *ponērou* in v. 13b. as masc. It is a prayer to be snatched out of this power (cf. K. G. Kuhn; see bibliography). J. A. Bengel, *Gnomon*, ad loc., considers the 6th and 7th petitions to be closely linked, a positive and negative formulation of the same matter, which are therefore considered one petition by some. He quotes Hiller on Matt. 6:13, "The evil one has not changed his purpose since Adam's temptation. He remains the evil one, and he is the enemy of God and of Christ, and of all who believe on God and Christ."

(iii) *ponēros* is also used as a neut. noun (*to ponēron*), Lk. 6:45b; Rom. 12:9; 1 Thess. 5:22; Matt. 5:11; Acts 5:4 (*v.l.*); 28:21). It should be remembered, however, that several passages in the NT trace evil to the devil. When in Matt. 9:4 Jesus accuses the scribes, and in Matt. 12:35 the Pharisees, of evil thoughts, *ponēros* is also to be linked with the devil. Elsewhere (Jn. 8:44) Jesus called them children of the devil. There is no neutral zone between God and the devil, where evil as something purely neutral could find its home.   *E. Achilles*

→ Demon, → Fall, → Satan, → Sin

In the following list * denotes works dealing with the more philosophical implications of evil.
(a). M. B. Ahern, *The Problem of Evil*, 1971*; K. Barth, *CD*, III 3. 289–368; G. C. Berkouwer, *The Triumph of Grace in the Theology of Karl Barth*, 1956; G. Bornkamm, "Sin, Law and Death (Romans 7)," *Early Christian Experience*, 1969, 87–104; R. Bultmann, "Christ the End of the Law," *Essays*, 1955, 36–66; A. Farrer, *Love Almighty and Ills Unlimited*, 1961*; W. Grundmann, *kakos, TDNT* III 469–87; A. T. Hanson, "The Conquest of the Powers," *Studies in Paul's Technique and Theology*, 1974, 1–12; G. Harder, *ponēros, TDNT* VI 546–66; J. Hick, "The Problem of Evil",* in P. Edwards, ed., *The Encyclopedia of Philosophy*, III, 1961, 136–41; and *Evil and the God of Love*, 1966*; J. Jeremias, *The Prayers of Jesus*, 1967; and *New Testament Theology*, I, 1971; C. E. M. Joad, *God and Evil*, 1943*; C. S. Lewis, *The Problem of Pain*, 1940*; E. Lohmeyer, *The Lord's Prayer*, 1965; W. Lüthi, *The Lord's Prayer*, 1961; H. Meynell, *God and the World*, 1971, 64–83*; G. von Rad, *Genesis*, 1963²; W. Temple, *Mens Creatrix*, 1917*; F. R. Tennant, *Philosophical Theology*, II, 1929*; Y. Yadin, *The Scroll of the War of the Sons of Light against the Sons of Darkness*, 1962.
(b). G. Baumbach, *Das Verständnis des Bösen in den synoptischen Evangelien*, 1963; J. Becker, *Das Heil Gottes*, 1964; W. Krötke, *Sünde und Nichtiges bei Karl Barth*, 1971; K. G. Kuhn, *Achtzehngebet und Vaterunser und der Reim*, 1950; W. Lüthi, *Gott und das Böse*, 1961; G. Mensching, *Gut und Böse im Glauben der Völker*, 1950; S. Wibbing, *Die Tugend- und Lasterkataloge im Neuen Testament und deren Traditionsgeschichte unter besonderer Berücksichtigung der Qumrantexte*, 1959.

Exhort, Warn, Console, Rebuke

Teaching has primarily to do with imparting intellectual insight and knowledge, and education (as it concerns the whole man) is often thought to be limited to a person's formative years. But to exhort means to exert influence upon the will and decisions of another with the object of guiding him into a generally accepted code of behaviour or of encouraging him to observe certain instructions. Exhortation always presupposes some previous knowledge. It consists of reminding a person of this with the intention that he should carry it out. To exhort is to address the whole man. Originally at least knowledge, emotion, and will are all involved. In NT Greek, with one exception, only Paul uses the vb. *noutheteō* (8 times altogether, the noun 3 times) to express this concept. Elsewhere the broader term *parakaleō*, is employed, denoting anything from urgent pressure to comfort and encouragement.

νουθετέω

νουθετέω (*noutheteō*), to warn, advise; *νουθεσία* (*nouthesia*), admonition, warning, instruction.

CL *noutheteō* (tragic poets) and the noun *nouthesia* (Aristophanes), derived from *nous* (mind) and *tithēmi* (put) (Liddell-Scott), describe the exertion of influence upon the *nous*, implying that there is resistance. By means of admonition, advice, warning, reminding, teaching and spurring on, a person can be redirected from wrong ways and his behaviour corrected. In contrast to *didaskō*, which is concerned with the development and guidance of the intellect, *noutheteō* has to do with the will and the feelings of a man. Its meaning is more restricted than that of *paideuō* and *paideia* (→ Teach), which refer to the education of a child, with all the appropriate means which are used to guide it into the world of adults. *paideuō* is always used with reference to minors who must be treated with strictness and severity. In the case of *noutheteō*, however, the meaning chastise is only secondary and does not occur in the NT at all. *kolazō* (punish) and *kolasis* (punishment) refer to → punishment, as the reaction and answer to evil deeds, not as a means of education. Punishment in this sense can at the most serve as a deterrent and warning to the outsider.

OT The LXX uses *noutheteō*, with the exception of 1 Sam. 3:13 (correct), only in the Wisdom Literature: Wis. 11:10; 12:2, 26, warn; similarly the noun, in the LXX only at Wis. 16:6, means warning – the plague of serpents during Israel's wilderness wanderings was God's "warning" for the people. In the book of Job the vb. has the active sense of instruct (Job 4:3). But it can also be used in a negative sense. "The least of men treat me like schoolmasters, one after another" (Job 30:1 LXX). The more unusual passive meaning, to let oneself be taught, let someone tell one something, gain insight, understand, is also found in Job (23:15; 36:12; 37:14; 38:18).

NT In the NT *noutheteō* is found only in the letters of Paul and Acts 20:31, where Luke is reporting a speech of the apostle; the noun only at 1 Cor. 10:11; Eph. 6:4; and Tit. 3:10.

In Ephesus the apostle worked as a faithful and exemplary church leader with constant zeal for the continued life of the church, taking trouble over every individual and "admonishing him with tears" (Acts 20:31). Likewise he "admonishes" the church leaders in Corinth as his "beloved children" (1 Cor. 4:14). Even if he has to write to them in a correcting and critical vein, it is done out of his love for them and for their own good.

In Col. 1:28 and 3:16 *noutheteō* is coupled with *didaskō*, in reference to the proclamation of Christ. Warning and → teaching belong inseparably together, as the constant counterpart of knowledge and action. The aim of this teaching and warning ministry is "maturity in Christ" (1:28).

It is an important task of apostles, church leaders and elders to admonish the members of the church. It is for the church to accept and recognize this ministry in love (1 Thess. 5:12). Admonition as a form of spiritual counselling is also the task of the whole church towards one another (Col. 3:16), provided that it is spiritually fit to do so like the church at Rome (Rom. 15:14). Individual members too, when disobedient, must be corrected by the church, in order that they may be made aware of the wrongness of what they are doing and won back again (1 Thess. 5:14; 2 Thess. 3:15). Failure to respond to such admonition can under certain circumstances lead to total rejection of the one who has been warned (Tit. 3:10; *nouthesia*).

According to Eph. 6:4, the right way to bring up children is *en paideia kai nouthesia* ("in discipline and correction"). It is not determined by the use or nonuse of certain educational helps, but by whether it is directed towards the Lord. With this as the guiding principle, the means to be employed may be chosen in freedom and yet out of a sense of duty. The two terms used are here more or less identical in meaning (cf. G. Bertram, *TDNT* V 624; H. Schlier, *Die Zeit der Kirche*, 282 f.). It is not the educational method, but the purpose for which it is used, that characterizes Christian upbringing. In 1 Cor. 10:11 *nouthesia* is used as in Wis. 16:6 in the sense of warning. The list of punishments, which befell the people because of their sins, should serve as a warning to the readers.   *F. Selter*

παρακαλέω

παρακαλέω (*parakaleō*), summon, invite, exhort, encourage, implore; παράκλησις (*paraklēsis*), encouragement, exhortation, appeal, comfort, consolation.

CL *parakaleō* means to call in (e.g. Xenophon, *Anab.* 3, 1, 32: *ton stratēgon parekaloun*, "they called in the general"). From this follow the other meanings which are often hard to distinguish from one another: to ask (e.g. *BGU* 846, 10: *paraka(l)ō soi, mētēr, d(i)alagēti moi*, "I beg you, mother, be reconciled to me"), sometimes used of invocation of the gods (e.g. *kai gar peri toutou parakalesa ton theon*, "And concerning this I besought the god," cf. A. Deissmann, *Light from the Ancient East*, 1911², 311; Moulton–Milligan, 484); to exhort, request (e.g. Xenophon, *Anab.*, 5, 6, 19: *bouletai gar Xenophōn kai hēmas parakalei*, "for Xenophon wants to and is encouraging us (to join him)"); and, although examples are rare, to speak consoling words especially in cases of bereavement, the consolation always containing a note of exhortation (e.g. an encouragement to maintain one's proper behaviour even in sorrow). On the origin of the word → Call, art. *kaleō* CL).

OT In the LXX *parakaleō* is chiefly used for the Heb. *nāḥam* (especially the niph. and piel), be moved to pity, comfort, usually in the latter sense (cf. Ps. 119:50, *hautē me parekalesen en tē tapeinōsei mou*, "this has comforted me in my humiliation"; Gen. 37:35, concerning mourning for the dead, *kai ēlthon parakalesai auton, kai ouk ēthelen parakaleisthai*, "and they came to comfort him, but he would not be comforted"). It is part of the prophet's task to bring comfort (cf. Isa. 40:1, *parakaleite parakaleite ton laon mou*, comfort, comfort my people). Similarly *parakaleō* is used in Test. Rub. 4:4 ("And yet my father comforted me and prayed for me to the Lord"); Test.Jos. 17:4; 2 Esd. 10:19; and often.

parakaleō can however stand for *nāḥam* (niph. and hith.), where the sense is to be sorry, have compassion, e.g. Ps. 135:14 ("the Lord has compassion on his servants"; cf. Deut. 32:36), and Jdg. 2:18 ("the Lord was moved to pity by their groaning"). This use of the word is found only in the LXX.

Where *parakaleō* is used for other Heb. equivalents, it also means to encourage, strengthen (Deut. 3:28; Job 4:3), lead astray (Deut. 13:6), or lead along, guide (Exod. 15:13).

In 1st century Jud. the "consolation of Israel" (cf. Lk. 2:25) is spoken of and means "the fulfilment of the Messianic hope" (SB II 124). "For if ye endure and persevere in His fear, and do not forget His law, the times shall change over you for good, and ye shall see the consolation of Zion" (Syr. Bar. 44:7).

It is striking that in the Hel. world more is heard of asking and exhortation, while the emphasis is on comfort where the influence of the OT is felt. One may ask whether this is coincidental, or whether it expresses the comfortlessness which burdened Hellenism and the consolation hoped for in the world of the OT (cf. G. Stählin, *TDNT* V 787 f.).

NT *parakaleō* occurs 109 times in the NT and means: (a) summon, invite, ask, implore; (b) exhort; (c) comfort, encourage. The noun *paraklēsis* means exhortation, encouragement, appeal, request, comfort, consolation. The words are not found in the Johannine literature, Jas., or 2 Pet.

1. The sense of summon (or ask) is found in Acts 28:20. In Acts 28:14 it should be translated in the special sense of invite. In all the strands of the synoptic tradition *parakaleō* means to ask, implore, in the context of needy people who come with their requests to Jesus (in the "Q" passages Lk. 7:4 = Matt. 8:5; Mk. 5:12 = Matt. 8:31 = Lk. 8:32; and also Lk. 15:28; Matt. 18:29). Only at Matt. 26:53 is it said of Jesus himself, that he could ask his Father for angelic assistance. In Acts 16:9 f. (cf. also 8:31; 13:42) the reference is to a request for missionary ministry.

2. Obviously even before Paul, exhortation had its place in the life of the church, especially as the task of the early Christian prophets. In 1 Cor. 14:30 f. Paul sees the need of requiring the (charismatic and gnostically-inclined) prophets to speak one after another in order, so that all may be exhorted. In Acts 15:32 the prophets Judas and Silas are said to have exhorted the brethren. Exhortation is an almost stereotyped part of the church's life (cf. Acts 16:40). Paul encourages the Philippians to exhort one another (Phil. 2:1). He sends Timothy, among other things, to exhort the church (1 Thess. 3:2; cf. Rom. 12:8). This ministry of exhortation, attested as it is from the earliest Christian period, is probably the setting (*Sitz im Leben*) for the paraenetic passages found particularly at the end of the Pauline letters. Paul sees it as his duty to follow the normal custom of the early church and to exhort the community (1 Thess. 4:1; Phil. 4:2; Rom. 12:1). Theologically, however, Paul gives to exhortation a specific basis. He does not give his readers direct moral instruction, but addresses them "through" (*dia*) God or Christ, so that the apostle thinks of his admonition as mediated "by the mercy of God" (Rom. 12:1; cf. v. 3), "by our Lord Jesus Christ and by the love of the Spirit" (Rom. 15:30); "by the name of Jesus Christ" (1 Cor. 1:10, → baptism, so that here the interpretation "by invocation" may be correct, cf. O. Michel on Rom. 12:1); "by the meekness and gentleness of Christ" (2 Cor. 10:1; W. G. Kümmel, ad loc., sees here a possible allusion to the earthly Jesus and to Matt. 11:29). May this also be the explanation of *di' hēmōn* in 2 Cor. 5:20? In this case it would mean that God

makes use of our mediation (H. Lietzmann, ad loc., by our mouth), and himself warns (or asks?). The same idea is behind 1 Thess. 4:1; and 2 Thess. 3:12, *parakaloumen en kyriō*, we exhort "in" the Lord (cf. also Phil. 4:2).

Consideration of the special basis for exhortation in Paul leads us, however, to the fundamental and much wider problem of ethics and the imperative in Paul. This imperative can only be properly understood, when it is viewed in the light of the indicative. "If the whole being of the man who is justified is determined by *charis*, so also is the imperative under which he stands. For it is a part of the life of the justified to stand under the imperative. The believer can understand this life only as the gift of God. So just as the moral demand expressed by the imperative is for him the commandment of God, the attitude of obedience towards the command is also the gift of God, worked by the *pneuma*, although this does not mean that the demand loses its imperative character" (R. Bultmann, *ZNW* 23, 1924, 140). Similarly Paul exhorts the Corinthians not to receive the grace of God "in vain" (2 Cor. 6:1). For that would be the case if they did not prove themselves in their lives. The apostle can describe himself as their example in view of his "ways in Christ" (1 Cor. 4:16 f.; cf. 1 Thess. 2:12; 4:1, 10; 5:11).

For Luke the present era gains in importance (because of the delay of the Parousia, or because of the persecution affecting the church?). Hence there is an added emphasis on the demand for right conduct in this life. Now is the time when it is important to prove oneself. Therefore, John the Baptist, Judas, Silas, and others exhort people to → walk aright (cf. Lk. 3:18; Acts 15:32). It is necessary to warn them to → remain faithful to the Lord (Acts 11:23), to continue in the faith (Acts 14:22), and to save themselves (Acts 2:40). The necessity of mastering the present leads further in Eph. 4:1, the Pastoral Epistles, Heb. and 1 Pet. to the exhortation to → "walk worthy", and similar expressions. In some passages the translation "exhort" is questionable, and we should possibly in some cases render it "comfort" (cf. Rom. 12:8; 1 Cor. 14:31; 2 Cor. 13:11; 1 Thess. 4:18; 5 11; but see above).

3. The sense of "comfort", which connotes friendly speech as much as exhortation (e.g. Acts 16:39), is found in various writings of the NT and with especial frequency in 2 Cor. 1:3 ff. Here Paul sets consolation over against tribulation, suffering and death, identifying his own sufferings with those of Christ, and at the same time sharing in Christ's comfort. This line of thought is carried further by the application of the apostle's suffering and his experience of comfort to the situation of his readers. In 2 Cor. 7:4 ff. the tribulation and comfort theme is again taken up. Paul is now comforted by Titus and what he has to tell of the situation in Corinth (cf. also 1 Thess. 3:7). The comfort promised to the mourners in Matt. 5:4 is paralleled by the woes promised to the rich in Lk. 6:24. According to Matthew (as in Paul), suffering is met by God's consolation. Luke presents the alternative: he who is rich in this life cannot expect the consolation of God in the life to come (cf. also Lk. 16:25). Finally, comfort (along with hope, Rom. 15:4; 2 Thess. 2:16) is part of Christian experience in this world (Heb. 6:18; 12:5). The suggestion that an allusion to the name Barnabas (cf. Acts 4:36, where it is interpreted as meaning "son of consolation") is intended also in Heb. 13:22 (*logos tēs paraklēseōs*), as Bornhäuser and others have thought, has nothing to support it in the text. For *paraklētos* → Advocate.   *G. Braumann*

| ἐπιτιμάω | ἐπιτιμάω (*epitimaō*), rebuke; ἐπιτιμία (*epitimia*), censure. |

CL The vb. is found in secular Greek from Herodotus to the 3rd cent. A.D., meaning to honour, censure, penalize and raise in price. The noun, also found until 3rd cent. A.D., can mean penalty, value, honour and respect.

OT In the LXX, Jewish Apocrypha, Damascus Document and pseudo-Philo men rebuke (e.g. Gen. 37:10) but should not do so (Ruth 2:16), unless they have authority, judicial, paternal or fraternal (Ecclus. 11:7; Prov. 17:10 Aquila, Theodotion; Jubilees 11:19). But God does have the right to rebuke, not only men or his enemies (Pss. 75:6; 9:5) but also the created order (Pss. 105:9) and → Satan (Zech. 3:2). The noun means punishment (Wis. 3:10).

NT The vb. is found frequently in all three Synoptic Gospels, implying disapproval, but not exaction of a concrete penalty. The sense "censure", "rebuke," will suit all instances, but more precise definition is possible. (1) People rebuke one another as a sign of disapproval, the disciples rebuking those who presented children to Jesus (Mk. 10:13 par.), the crowd rebuking the blind man who sought Jesus (Mk. 10:48 par.), Peter rebuking Jesus for his passion prediction (Mk. 8:32 par.) and the Pharisees asking Jesus to rebuke the disciples (Lk. 19:39). In each instance Jesus disapproves of the rebuke, but he himself is free to deliver a rebuke (to Peter, Mk. 8:33; to the Sons of Thunder, Lk. 9:55). It is conceivable that Jesus objected to men rebuking one another on the principle of Matt. 7:2, regarding it as his own right *in loco Dei* (cf. Yahweh in Ps. 75:6). However, both the rebuke by the penitent thief and the situation of one brother rebuking another do not receive adverse comment (Lk. 23:40; 17:3). E. Schweizer, *The Good News according to Mark*, 1970, accounts for each rebuke by Jesus one by one, seeing the ground not in general terms but in the particular context. (2) Sometimes Jesus rebukes in order to repress, when he casts out demons (Mk. 1:25; 9:25; D. E. Nineham, *Saint Mark*, 1963, 75, claims that *epitimaō* is a common term in exorcism formulae), dispels a fever (Lk. 4:39), or stills a storm (Mk. 4:39). Jesus is here depicted as Lord of all on the model of Yahweh (Ps. 105:9; E. Schweizer, op. cit., 109) and as bringer of salvation, for demons flee at his command (J. Jeremias, *New Testament Theology*, I, 94 f., 253-4). (3) At Mk. 3:12; 8:30 and parallels, Jesus does not censure what is happening or has happened, but he rebukes in the sense of forbidding what might happen, when the disciples or cured demoniacs were likely to publish his deeds as Lord of all. He was reluctant for "the proclamation of the demons, the healed, or even the disciples, however exact it may be, can only do harm until Jesus' path to the cross makes it possible for men to follow and even makes that following an irrevocable requirement" (Schweizer, op. cit., 56; → Christ). Otherwise, the vb. appears in 2 Tim. 4:2, where rebuking is a function of the authoritative Christian teacher alongside preaching, convincing and exhorting in "the teaching"; also at Jude 9, where the archangel Michael upbraids Satan with "the Lord rebuke you", recalling Zech. 3:2.

The noun *epitimia* appears only in the NT at 2 Cor. 2:6, where it refers to censure or even punishment meted out by the church in congregational discipline.

G. T. D. Angel

→ Advocate, → Command, → Conscience, → Discipline, → Teach

(a). J. Behm, *noutheteō, TDNT* IV 1019–22; G. Bertram, *paideuō, TDNT* V 596–625; G. Bornkamm, "The Edification of the Congregation as the Body of Christ," *Early Christian Experience*, 1969, 161–69; E. Brunner, *The Divine Imperative*, 1937; C. E. B. Cranfield, *A Commentary on Romans*, 12–13, *SJT Occasional Papers* 12, 1965; A. Deissmann, *Light from the Ancient East*, 1911²; R. N. Flew, *Jesus and his Way*, 1963; K. H. Rengstorf, *didaskō, TDNT* II 135–148; O. Schmitz and G. Stählin, *parakaleō, TDNT* V 773–99; R. Schnackenburg, *The Moral Teaching of the New Testament*, 1965; E. Stauffer, *epitimaō, TDNT* II 623–6.

(b). C. J. Bjerkelund, *Parakalō. Form, Funktion, und Sinn der Parakalō-Sätze in den paulinischen Briefen*, 1967; R. Bultmann, "Das Problem der Ethik, bei Paulus," *ZNW* 23, 1924, 123 ff.; A. Grabner-Haider, *Paraklese und Eschatologie bei Paulus*, 1968; W. Flitner, "Erziehung," *RGG*³ II 631 ff.; E. Kamlah, *Die Form der katalogischen Paränese im Neuen Testament*, 1964; W. G. Kümmel, "*paresis* und *endeixis*, ein Beitrag zum Verständnis der paulinischen Rechtfertigungslehre," *ZTK* 49, 1952, 154 ff.; E. Lohse, "Paränese und Kerygma im 1. Petrusbrief," *ZNW* 45, 1954, 62 ff.; M. Müller, "Freiheit. Über Autonomie und Gnade von Paulus bis Clemens von Alexandria," *ZNW* 25, 1926, 177 ff.; W. Mundle, "Religion und Sittlichkeit bei Paulus in ihrem Zusammenhang," *ZSTh* 4, 1927, 456 ff.; T. Ohm *et al.*, "Strafe," *RGG*³ VI 392 ff.; H. von Soden, *Sakrament und Ethik bei Paulus*, 1931; S. Wibbing, *Die Tugend- und Lasterkataloge im Neuen Testament*, 1959; H. Windisch, "Das Problem des paulinischen Imperativs," *ZNW* 23, 1924, 265 ff.

Explain, Interpret, Tell, Narrative

ἐξηγέομαι

ἐξηγέομαι (*exēgeomai*), explain, expound, interpret, tell; ἐξήγησις (*exēgēsis*), narrative, explanation, interpretation; ἐξηγητής (*exēgētēs*), interpreter; διήγησις (*diēgēsis*), narrative, account; διηγέομαι (*diēgeomai*), tell, describe.

CL 1. (a) In classical writers *exēgeomai* may mean to lead or to govern (e.g. Thucydides, 1, 76; Plato, *Rep.* 474c). But this use of the term is not strictly relevant to the NT (unless we accept M.-E. Boismard's interpretation of Jn. 1:18 discussed below).

(b) *exēgeomai* also means to dictate or to prescribe, as when Plato speaks of "what the law prescribes" (*Rep.*, 604b). (c) The use of the word to mean to expound or to interpret (Herodotus, 2, 49; Plato, *Cratylus*, 407a) is more important from the viewpoint of NT study. Lysias (6:10) speaks of unwritten laws which the Eumolpidae, priests of Eleusis, follow in their exposition (*exēgountai*). Plato speaks about expounding (*exēgoumenous*) the intentions of the lawgiver (*Laws*, 802c), and also about expounding the poets (*Cratylus*, 407a). Hence the adj. *exēgēmatikos* means having a gift for exposition, whilst the noun *exēgēma* means explanation. (d) In such authors as Herodotus, Aeschylus, Xenophon and Thucydides, *exēgeomai* may also mean simply to tell, to relate, or to relate in full. Thus Thucydides (5, 26, 6) proposes to relate (*exēgēsomai*) the course of hostilities after the first ten years of war.

2. The noun *exēgēsis* may mean either statement, narrative (Thucydides, 1, 72; Polybius, 6, 3, 1), or else explanation, interpretation, as when Plato (*Laws*, 631a) speaks of "your exposition of the laws".

3. This brings us to questions about the technical meaning of *exēgētēs* in Greek religion, which some scholars take as a point of departure for examining *exēgēsis* in Jn. 1:18. Herodotus (1, 78, 2) gives this title to a college of diviners at the Telmessian oracle in Lycia. From about the fourth century B.C. Athens had official *exēgētai* who expounded its sacred and ancestral laws. They were custodians of the

573

unwritten law, but also pronounced on related questions in secular and domestic life (cf. J. H. Oliver and O. Kern, see bibliography). Plato speaks of "the interpreters" in the sense of official exponents of sacred law (*Laws*, 759c, e, 775a), and also describes the Delphic Apollo as "the interpreter (*exēgētēs*) of the religion of their fathers" (*Rep.*, 427c). By about A.D. 132 we find the combination of the offices of priest and *exēgētēs* in the Oxyrhynchus Papyri (III 477); and N. Hohlwein investigates the use of the term in the Roman imperial era to designate certain local officials in Egypt (*L'Égypte romaine*, 1912, 224–6). In the 2nd cent. A.D. it occurs in the technical sense of communicating divine secrets in Pollux, 8, 124.

4. *diēgēsis* means narrative or narration, sometimes perhaps, as J. H. Moulton and G. Milligan believe, with the added idea of fullness of detail (*The Vocabulary of the Greek Testament*, 1930, 161). In Gk. rhetoric it sometimes means statement of the case, but also describes the device of inserting a story of some detail into a speech (cf. "*diēgēsis* in Public Speeches" in S. Trenker, *The Greek Novella in the Classical Period*, 1958, 154–62). *diēgeomai* means simply to describe or tell, sometimes perhaps, again, with the force of setting out something in detail.

OT 1. In the LXX *exēgeomai* mainly translates the Hebrew verb *sāpar* when this occurs in the piel, in the sense of recount, tell, or declare. Thus it is used of telling a dream (Jdg. 7:13), of describing a miracle (2 Ki. 8:5), and of declaring the Lord's glory among the nations (1 Chr. 16:24). Once it translates the hiphil form of *yāḏâh*, to speak out, to confess: "he who confesses his fault shall be loved" (Prov. 28:13). Once or perhaps twice it translates the hiphil form of *yārâh*, to show, to point out, to instruct (Lev. 14:57). *exēgēsis* translates *mispār*, from the verb *sāpar*, in Jdg. 7:15, although Codex Alexandrinus has *diēgēsis*. Corresponding roughly to CL 3 above, *exēgētēs* translates the technical term *ḥarṭummîm* (found only in the plural), scribe, Egyptian wise man, writer of hieroglyphics (Gen. 41:8, 24). In Prov. 29:18 it stands for the Hebrew *ḥāzôn*, prophetic vision, oracle ("where there is no prophetic vision, the people cast off restraint"; although the NEB renders the phrase "no one in authority", referring to the role of prophets or sages).

2. *exēgeomai* also occurs in 1 Macc. 3:26 in the sense of telling the story of a battle, and in 2 Macc. 2:13 in the sense of reporting events. In Sirach (Ecclus.) 21:16 *exēgēsis* means simply speech or talking, the talking of a fool. However, in Josephus and in Philo we return to the meaning of interpretation or exposition. Josephus speaks of two rabbis who give expositions of the laws (*exēgoumenous*, *Jewish War*, 1, 649) or who are "interpreters of the ancestral laws" (*exēgētai*, in the parallel account *Jewish Antiquities*, 17, 149; cf. also 11, 192 and 18, 81). Philo describes how expositions (*exēgēseis*) of holy Scripture treat an inner or allegorical meaning (*On the Contemplative Life*, 78). The Old Testament expositor is an *exēgētēs* (*On the Special Laws*, 2, 159). Philo also uses *exēgeomai* in the sense to describe, to relate, or to report.

3. In the LXX *diēgeomai* occurs many more times than *exēgeomai* as the regular translation for *sāpar* in the piel, meaning to tell, to recount, to declare (see above). Thus Abraham's servant tells Isaac all that he has done (Gen. 24:66); Jacob tells Laban of his family (29:13); and Saul is told about the men of Jabesh (1 Sam. 11:5). On 4 occasions *diēgeomai* stands for the Heb. *sîaḥ*, to talk, to sing, or sometimes to complain, as in telling God's wonderful works (1 Chr. 16:9; Ps. 105:2; 145:5), or

574

in complaining to him (Ps. 55:17). *diēgēsis* occurs less frequently in the LXX. Once it translates *ḥîḏâh* in the sense of telling a parable against someone (Hab. 2:6); once in Codex Alexandrinus it translates *mispār* (Jdg. 7:15, see above). It occurs 7 times in Sirach (Ecclus.) in the sense of godly discourse (6:35; 27:11), speech or conversation (9:15; 38:25), or a story (22:6) or a saying (39:2). It is used at the beginning and end of the Letter of Aristeas to describe the narrative which the book tells. Similarly in Philo *diēgēsis* primarily means story or narrative (e.g. *Embassy to Gaius*, 223). In view of questions about to be raised concerning Jn. 1:18, we must also note the occurrence in Sirach (Ecclus.) of *ekdiēgeomai*: "Who has seen him (God) and can describe (*ekdiēgēsetai*) him?" (43:31).

NT 1. In the NT *exēgeomai* occurs once in Jn., and 5 times in Lk.–Acts. Jn. 1:18 has considerable theological importance: "No one has ever seen God; the only Son who is in the bosom of the Father, he has made him known" (*ekeinos exēgēsato*). (a) M.-E. Boismard has suggested that the verb retains its classical meaning of "lead", "lead the way". Thus he emends the text to read "No one has even seen God except (*ei mē*) the only-begotten: to the bosom of the Father he has led the way" (cf. "Dans le sein du Père, Jn. 1:18", *RB* 59, 1952, 23–39). But although the resulting idea may harmonize well with Johannine thought, there are no adequate grounds for emending the text to place *ei mē ho* before "only-begotten", and omitting *ho ōn* before "in the bosom of". Moreover, as we have seen, *exēgeomai* does not, it seems, have this meaning in first-century Gk. (b) A second interpretation, advocated by R. Bultmann, C. K. Barrett, J. N. Sanders, and many others, depends on understanding *exēgeomai* as "a word which from earliest times was used in a technical sense for the interpretation of the will of the gods by professional diviners, priests, and soothsayers, but which can also be used of God himself when he makes known his will" (R. Bultmann, *The Gospel of John* 1971, 83). This interpretation probably began with Wettstein, and gives the verb some such meaning as "reveal". As we have seen, Plato uses the term in this way of the Delphic Apollo, and especially the noun *exēgētēs* is used of priests explaining the oracles. Nevertheless we have also seen that this usage often retains the added idea of interpretation or exposition (it is usually the oracles, rather than the gods themselves, that are revealed or expounded). Further, this is not necessarily the most frequent use of the term in the 1st century. We cannot then conclude with certainty that this background contributes decisively to the meaning of Jn. 1:18. Perhaps the most that can be said is to point out, with J. Marsh and Barnabas Lindars, that Jn. uses a word which is *both* a technical term in Judaism for making known interpretations of the law (see above), *and* a term in Gk. religion for making known divine truths (Marsh, *The Gospel of St. John*, 1968, 112). The incarnate Word brings from the heart of God a revelation both for Jew and for Greek. (c) J. H. Bernard understands *exēgēsato* to mean "it is he who interpreted the Father" (*Gospel according to St. John*, (ICC) 1928, I, 33). The Logos declared the Father with a precision which could only be exhibited by one whose dwelling was in the bosom of the Father. Similarly E. C. Hoskyns writes that "Jesus and the rabbis are bound together as 'exegetes' of the mysteries of God" (*The Fourth Gospel*, 1947², 153); and Leon Morris considers it a "suggestive thought" that Christ is the exegesis of the Father (*Gospel according to John* 1971, 114 n. 122). It is true that, as A.

Schlatter urges (*Der Evangelist Johannes*, 1960³, 36) and as we have seen, *exēgeomai* frequently means to expound or to interpret. This suggestion cannot therefore be ruled out. But it is impossible, again, to be certain that the word bears this more specialized meaning here. (d) Leon Morris believes that the phrase "does point to the adequacy of the revelation made in Christ" (loc. cit.). Christ is "a full and authoritative revelation of the divine being". It may well be that this is implied in the thought of Jn.'s prologue as a whole; but it would be precarious to argue that *exēgeomai* must mean "relate in full" in this verse. (e) Probably, as R. Schnackenburg suggests, the force of the verb in Jn. 1:18 is simply that of "speaking of things hidden in God, tidings of the divine glory" (*The Gospel according to St. John*, I, 1968, 279). The Logos speaks of, makes known, declares, the invisible God. As F. Büchsel points out, Jn. 1:18 is like an intentional answer to the question of Sirach (Ecclus.) 43:31 (above, OT 3). That this is in fact an accurate, clear, and full revelation of God emerges not from the meaning of *exēgeomai* in lexicography, but from the contribution of the wider context of Johannine thought (cf. also Heb. 1:1, 2).

2. In Lk.–Acts *exēgeomai* always means to relate or to tell. Cleopas and his companion relate what happened on the road to Emmaus (Lk. 24:35), and Cornelius relates his vision to his servants (Acts 10:8). In the remaining 3 passages in Acts men relate what God has done (15:12, 14; 21:19). In this last passage Paul relates God's acts "in detail" (*kath' hena hekaston*). The noun *exēgēsis* does not occur in the NT.

3. *diēgeomai* occurs 8 times in the NT, meaning to tell, to describe, or to declare. Witnesses tell what happened to a demoniac (Mk. 5:16); the apostles tell Jesus what they have done (Lk. 9:10; cf. Mk. 9:9; Acts 8:33; 9:27; 12:17; Heb. 11:32). The demoniac who is cured is to declare how much God has done for him (Lk. 8:39). Once (Acts 8:33) the word occurs in a quotation of the LXX of Isa. 53:8, to mean declare or describe.

4. The noun *diēgēsis* is used in the sense of narrative or account in the much-discussed prologue of Lk. (1:1). Lk. has predecessors whose work he describes as attempts *diēgēsin anataxasthai*, and thus the meaning of *diēgēsis* is thought by some to be relevant to questions about Gospel origins. G. E. Lessing argued that, since the term occurred in the singular, Lk. was referring to an original single narrative, which was composed by the apostles, and which Lessing identified as the Gospel of the Nazarenes. He was then obliged to take *anataxasthai* to mean "re-arranged" rather than "drew up". More recently W. R. Farmer has also urged that *diēgēsis* refers to a single narrative, namely the Gospel of Matthew (*The Synoptic Problem*, 1964, 221–3). The "many" are then compilers who are not eye-witnesses. More often, however, it has been argued that Lk.'s predecessors are Mk. and Q, and that little else can be said. J. Bauer has urged that Lk.'s reference to "many" cannot be pressed ("Polloi, Lk. 1:1" in *Novum Testamentum* 4, 1960, 263–6). It is also likely that *diēgēsis* refers to a narrative-unit much larger than the usual pericopae of form criticism. Apart from this, we must conclude, however, that the meaning of *diēgēsis* itself offers no substantial help towards solving problems of Gospel origins.

| ἐπιλύω | ἐπιλύω (*epilyō*), explain, interpret, settle, solve, release; ἐπίλυσις (*epilysis*), explanation, interpretation. |

CL 1. In classical Gk. (e.g. in Xenophon, Plato, and Theocritus) *epilyō* may mean
to loose, to untie, or to release. This meaning does not occur in the NT, but
appears again in the second century A.D. and later (e.g. in Lucian). *epilysis* is used
in Aeschylus (*Septem contra Thebas*, 134) to mean release from fear. In the papyri
the word is used for the "discharge" of an account.

2. In later authors *epilyō* or *epilyomai* comes to mean to explain, to interpret, or
to solve a problem, occurring mainly in writers of the 1st and 2nd centuries A.D.,
and usually in the middle or passive (e.g. Athenaeus, 10, 45; Vettius Valens, 259,
4). But it may also mean to confute an accusation (Lucian, *Bis Accusatus*, 30). The
noun *epilysis* often, but not always, means interpretation. It is used of the interpretation of an oracle (Heliodorus, 4, 9) or the interpretation of dreams (1, 18), but
also of the exposure of sophisms (Sextus Empiricus, *Pyrrhonic Elements*, 2, 246).
Probably most often it means the explanation of something obscure (e.g. in
Athenaeus and especially in Hermas, see below), although in the specialized
contents of medicine and magic it can mean a change of dressing or a magic spell.

OT *epilyō* and *epilysis* occur in Aquila's version of the LXX to mean the interpretation of dreams (Gen. 40:8; 41:8, 12). Josephus uses the verb in the sense of
solving a problem: Solomon grasps the problems set by the Queen of Sheba, and
solves them (*epelyeto*) quickly (*Jewish Antiquities*, 8, 167). Similarly Philo describes
how the president of the community discusses questions arising from Scripture
and solves one (*epilyetai*) that someone had raised (*On the Contemplative Life*, 75).
But Philo also uses the word to mean exposing fallacies (*On Husbandry*, 16). (On
lysis in Eccl. 8:1, see below.)

NT In the NT the verb *epilyō* occurs twice (Mk. 4:34; Acts 19:39), and the noun
epilysis occurs once (2 Pet. 1:20). 1. The very broad meaning of *epilyō* (active)
in Mk. 4:34 seems to be clear: Jesus explained or expounded the parables privately
to his disciples. But if *epilyō* means to make plain what was obscure, does this imply
that the parables represent only esoteric teaching for the initiated? (a) A. Jülicher
saw a contradiction here between the intentions of Jesus and the view of Mk.
(*Die Gleichnisreden Jesu*, I, 1899²). The parables, he urged, were self-explanatory;
but the evangelists misconceived their purpose and changed them, partly by alle-
gorizing them, into puzzling, concealing stories, which needed interpretation. Thus
Jesus gives a private "explanation" to the disciples. But Jülicher's arguments rest
on too clear-cut a contrast between simile and metaphor, and on too uniform a
view of the category of "parable". Sometimes the application of a parable is left
open-ended in order to let the hearer arrive at its truth *for himself* (cf. the interpretations of E. Fuchs, R. W. Funk, and others). (b) Mk. himself seems to give
content to *epilyō* in terms of the "explanation" of the Parable of the Sower in
4:14–20. This use of the verb would accord perfectly with its repeated reference in
Hermas, *The Shepherd* (Parable 5.3:1, 2; 5.4:2; 5.5:1; 5.6:8; 8.11:1; 9.11:9 (*tas
epilyseis tōn parabolōn*). Nevertheless the meaning of Mk. 4:34 may be broader.
Questions about the parables and their *epilysis* are more far-reaching than questions about how to translate the symbols of a semi-allegorical example of parabolic
teaching. Jesus was not simply concerned about de-coding an allegory. If it were
not for the word "all" (*panta*) in this verse, we might suggest that he is offering
only a sample exposition of *one* parable, whilst allowing the disciples, as well as the

crowd, to arrive at truth for themselves on subsequent occasions. Vincent Taylor insists that there is no suggestion that the parables · were spoken only for the multitudes (*The Gospel according to St. Mark*, 1959, 271). But in addition to the problem of *panta*, Mk. 4:11 seems to suggest a different conclusion. (c) C. E. B. Cranfield rightly sees the importance of "the secret (*to mystērion*) of the kingdom" in 4:11. Whilst the crowds, he suggests, already understand that Jesus is talking about the → kingdom, Jesus' *epilysis* to the disciples concerns the relation of the kingdom to his own person (*The Gospel according to St. Mark*, 1963, 172). The idea that Jesus brings the eschatological crisis here and now would also accord well with notions at Qumran about the "interpretation" of divine secrets (*rāzîm*). Whilst this interpretation has much to commend it, it must be asked whether *epilysis* now has a different content in the intention of Jesus from that understood by Mk. (d) Perhaps the simplest explanation is that *epilyō* refers to the translation of parabolic speech into straightforward discourse, of which Mk. 4:14–20 furnishes only one kind of example. As E. Schweizer points out, the important principle is "as much as they could understand" (*The Good News according to Mark*, 1971, 106). Jesus is not dispensing with indirect communication where it is needed. But whilst in the case of the crowd he was mainly concerned with initial *response*, in the case of the disciples Jesus was also concerned with *instruction*.

2. In Acts 19:39, *epilythēsetai* means to solve a problem or to settle a dispute. The immediate linguistic context is decisive for this meaning: a question can only be "settled", and a problem can only be "solved". Thus the town clerk tells the men of Ephesus that the regular or statutory (*ennomos*) assembly will "settle" any further question which is raised. We have already noted the meaning of "solving a problem" in Josephus or Philo; and to solve a problem is thereby to settle a question.

3. The meaning of *epilysis* in 2 Pet. 1:20 ("No prophecy of Scripture is a matter of one's own interpretation") is controversial. (a) F. Spitta understood *epilysis* to mean "dissolution", and interpreted the verse as "no prophecy of Scripture is of such a kind that it can be annulled". But although in classical authors it can mean "release", this is forcing the meaning of the word, and meets with no general acceptance. (b) Several older commentators (H. Alford, A. T. Robertson, R. H. Strachan) understood *epilysis* to refer to the activity of the Biblical prophet himself; to what was in his mind as he wrote. The word usually translated "is" (*ginetai* with the genitive) means "comes from", denoting origin. The meaning of the verse would then harmonize with a passage in Philo in which Balaam says that he speaks nothing of himself (*idion; Life of Moses*, 2, 125). It also anticipates the thought of the next verse that "it was not through any human whim that men prophesied of old, but ... they spoke the words of God" (2 Pet. 1:21). The difficulty of this interpretation is that, as J. B. Mayor insists, it is not in harmony with the ordinary force of *epilysis*. Further, C. Bigg maintains that *ginetai* cannot possibly mean "comes from." (c) Most commentators take *epilysis* to mean "interpretation." But does *idias epilyseōs* mean "private" in contrast to Spirit-inspired, or "private" in contrast to that of the Christian community? A. R. C. Leaney argues that it is not so much a warning to accept the authority of the church as a reminder about the believer's need of the Spirit (*The Letters of Peter and Jude*, 1967, 117). The passage, together with 3:16, makes it clear that certain false teachers had been guilty of

misusing OT prophecy. It may be that the author is saying: just as the prophets themselves were led by the Spirit (2 Pet. 1:21), so no reader can "interpret" prophecies without the guidance of the Spirit. (d) Traditionally, however, "private interpretation" is understood to mean arbitrary exegesis on the basis of personal whim, without reference to others in the Christian community. J. N. D. Kelly goes as far as to maintain that "the notion of an official Church as the appointed custodian of Scripture is evidently taking shape" (*Commentary on the Epistles of Peter and of Jude*, 1969, 323–4). Perhaps the most that can be said, with C. Spicq, is that the author condemns arbitrary exegesis (*Les Épîtres de S. Pierre*, 1966, 224–6). Whether (c) or (d) is the correct explanation cannot be concluded with absolute certainty, but the use of *idias* ("private" or "one's own") might be said slightly to favour (d).

ἑρμηνεύω	

ἑρμηνεύω (*hermēneuō*), explain, interpret, translate; ἑρμηνεία (*hermēneia*), interpretation, translation; ἑρμηνευτής (*hermēneutēs*), interpreter, translator; μεθερμηνεύω (*methermēneuō*), translate; διερμηνεύω (*diermēneuō*), translate, interpret, explain; διερμηνεία (*diermēneia*), interpretation, translation; διερμηνευτής (*diermēneutēs*), interpreter, translator.

CL 1. In classical Gk. *hermēneuō* may often mean to explain, expound, or interpret.

But of the standard passages cited by lexicographers in which the word is said to have this meaning, a number suggest, on closer examination, little more than "to speak", to "to speak plainly" (e.g. Plato, *Rep.*, 5, 453c; Sophocles, *Oedipus Coloneus* 398, where *hermēneue moi* means either "explain to me" or "tell me plainly"). Even in the case of the well-known example in Plato that good poets "interpret" to us the utterances of the gods, J. M. Robinson suggests that *hermēneuein* means only "act as spokesman for", just as Hermes was spokesman for the gods (*New Frontiers in Theology: II The New Hermeneutic*, 1964, 2). Similarly, the noun *hermēneia* often means interpretation (Plato, *Theaetetus*, 209a), but sometimes means little more than communication or speech (Plato, *Rep.*, 7, 5246). The noun *hermēneus*, found in classical authors but not in the NT, means interpreter (e.g. Pindar, *Olympian Odes*, 2, 85). But *hermēneutēs*, found mainly in later Greek, means either interpreter (Plato, *Laws*, 907d, "a statement [*logos*] to serve as the law's interpreter"), or else, again, spokesman, as in the passage in which Plato speaks of priests or diviners as spokesman (just possibly interpreters) of the gods (*hermēneutai . . . para theōn*, *The Statesman*, 290c). The adjective *hermēneutikos* describes one who possesses the art of the interpreter (*The Statesman*, 260d).

2. Closely related to the meaning of "speech" in general, *hermēneuō* and *hermēneia* are used in the quasi-technical sense of "articulation" or "expression" of thoughts in words. Thus Xenophon refers to the "power of expression" which makes teaching and the formulation of laws possible (*Memorabilia*, 4, 3, 12). Plato speaks of expressing (or perhaps expounding) the laws in word (*Laws* 966b); whilst Aristotle describes how the tongue provides capacity for speech (*On the Soul*, 420b, 20; *On Breath*, 476a, 20).

3. The other main meaning of *hermēneuō* is to translate. It occurs in this sense in Xenophon, but is mainly characteristic of later writers. In the 1st century B.C.

Dionysius of Halicarnassus refers to translating "council" into Gk. (2, 12, 3). *hermēneus* appears in 3rd century A.D. papyri with the meaning "court interpreter", and *hermēneutes* means "translator" in Xenophon. The verb *diermēneuō* occurs in Polybius in the first century B.C. ("translate as accurately as possible," 3, 22, 3). *Methermēneuō* occurs in Polybius (6, 26, 6), in Dionysius of Halicarnassus (4, 76, 2), and in Diodorus Siculus ("the names are translated into Greek . . .", 1, 11, 2).

OT 1. In the LXX the usual meaning of *hermēneuō* is to translate. In Ezra 4:7 it represents the Hebrew *targēm:* a writing is made in Aramaic and also "a translation" (*graphēn . . . hērmēneumenēn = meṭurgām*). In Esther 10:3(2) (LXX) it also means "translate". In Job 42:18 (also LXX only) *hermēneuetai* means simply "described as", but refers to a description in "the Aramaic book". *hermēneutēs* occurs only in Gen. 42:23, of Joseph's use of an official interpreter, where it translates the Hiphil form of *lûṣ* or *lîṣ*. In the prologue to Sirach (Ecclus.), 14, *hermēneia* refers to a translation from Hebrew into Greek, although in 47:17 it refers to "interpretations" alongside songs, proverbs, and parables. *diermēneuō* occurs only in 2 Macc. 1:36, where it should probably be translated "means", or "means in effect"; whilst *methermēneuō* occurs only in the prologue to Sirach (Ecclus.) in the sense of "translate" (14).

The use of these words to mean "translate" occurs in Josephus (*Jewish Antiquities*, 12, 7, to translate the LXX) and in Philo (*On Noah's Work as a Planter*, 38). But *hermēneutēs* also means an interpreter of dreams (*Jewish Antiquities*, 2, 72), and *hermēneia* is used in Philo in the quasi-technical sense of articulating thoughts in words. Thus he speaks of putting something into language (*hermēneian, On the Cherubim*, 105); of reproducing something in actual words (*diermēneuein autolexei, On the Embassy to Gaius*, 353); of literal language in which thought is expressed (*On the Contemplative Life*, 28, 31); of beauty of expression (*The Worse Attacks the Better*, 79); and of how the image of the divine word articulates (*diermēneusantos*) the invisible light (*On the Creation*, 31). In one passage about Moses and Aaron, *hermēneia* occurs twice: on the one hand, Aaron is to be Moses' "spokesman"; on the other hand, God will give to Moses the capacity to express thought in words (*The Worse Attacks the Better*, 39).

2. A purely lexicographical study of *hermēneuō* could not take account of the term *miḍrāš* in Judaism. However, a broader discussion of the *concepts* or "field" relating to "explain", "interpret", would not be complete without at least briefly mentioning it, together with other related terms in Jewish hermeneutics. According to M. Gertner (see bibliography), the "meaning of *miḍrāš*, combining interpretation and narrative, is paralleled in the corresponding Greek and Latin terms *hermēneia, exēgēsis, expositio*, and *interpretatio*" (loc. cit., 11). *miḍrāš* in Judaism represents both the procedure and the result of interpretation. It thus involves, firstly, investigation (*dāraš*, e.g. Ezra 7:10, Greek *zēteō*), analytical study, midrashic interpretation, and exposition; and then, secondly, the conveying of the results arrived at, in what amounts to the beginning of a tradition. In midrashic literature, interpretation may sometimes proceed by means of specific hermeneutical rules (*middôṭ*) such as the seven rules formulated by Hillel (*c.* 30 B.C.). The first of these concerned inferences *a minore ad maius*; the second concerned analogies and comparisons (*gezerâh šāwâh*); and so on (see B. Rosensweig in bibliography). By the second

century Rabbi Eliezer ben Jose the Galilean had expanded these rules until they numbered thirty-two. Originally *miḏrāš* meant little more than "narrative" (2 Chron. 24:27), but as it came increasingly to mean "interpretation", the term *haggāḏāh* was coined to mean narrative. Other related terms of hermeneutical importance include: *pāṭaḥ*, to begin, set out, open, explain; *pāraš*, to specify, pronounce explicitly, explain, interpret; *targēm*, to translate or to elucidate (see above); *pāšar* (*pēšer*, translated as *lysis* in Eccl. 8:1, LXX) and *pāṭar*, to interpret; and *pāšaṭ*, to elucidate, make clear by removing difficulties or obscurities.

NT 1. More than half of the 20 or so occurrences of *hermēneuō* and related words in the NT mean "translate" in a fairly straightforward sense. In the passive *methermēneuomai* always means "is translated", or "means". Thus Emmanuel means "God with us" (Matt. 1:23); the Aramaic transliteration *'Talitha, koum'* (*ṭeliṭā' qūm*) means "Little girl, get up" (Mk. 5:41); Golgotha means a skull (15:22); Messiah means → Christ (Jn. 1:42); rabbi means a teacher (1:38); and so on (Mk. 15:34; Acts 4:36; 13:8). *hermēneuomai* can be used in the same way (Jn. 1:43; 9:7; Heb. 7:2), as also can *diermēneuomai* (Acts 9:36). An interesting point arises, however, in connection with Jn. 9:7 and Heb. 7:2. Siloam does not strictly *mean* "sent", although the word in the Hebrew (*šilōaḥ*, Isa. 8:6) is related to the word for "send" (*šālaḥ*). The word may have been arrived at originally because water was "sent" into the pool by a channel (although some derive it from the Akkadian *siliḥtû*, basin of a canal). But *šilōaḥ* is still not a passive participle, like the Greek *apestalmenos*. Thus *hermeneuetai* means something broader than "is translated". Siloam conveys the thought expressed by "sent", which is an important key word for Jn. There is no justification for insisting on the idea of "means etymologically". Jn. is not primarily interested in bad linguistics. The same can be said of Heb. 7:2. Melchizedek "means" king of righteousness (Heb. *ṣeḏeq*, righteousness; *melek*, king) only in the broad sense that the name expresses the thought inspired by the language. We have already noted this kind of meaning for *hermēneuō* in other writers, especially Philo. The main point about most of the passages in which *hermēneuō* means "translate", however, is the concern of the evangelists that this language should be intelligible to outsiders or non-Jews.

2. In Lk. 24:27 *diermēneuō*, means to expound or to interpret. Beginning with the Pentateuch and the prophets, Jesus expounded the OT in terms of his own person and mission. Lk.–Acts suggests that this would have involved especially such passages as Isa. 53:7–12 (Lk. 22:37; Acts 8:32, 33; cf. Mk. 9:12). This "expounding" is parallel to Christ's "opening" (*diēnoigen*) the Scriptures in Lk. 24:32, which probably corresponds to the use of *pāṭaḥ* in Jewish hermeneutics (see above). In the light of Christ's finished work, OT passages which hitherto had expressed only promise could now be "interpreted" in terms of fulfilment. The OT is seen not simply as an end in itself, but also as a tradition of conceptual and historical paradigms of God's acts which reach their climax in the coming of Christ (cf. 1 Cor. 10:11, "for our benefit"). Thus whilst the OT interprets the coming of Christ, Christ also interprets the OT. Hence the Christian interpretation of Isa.53, for example, can never remain merely "Jewish".

3. The remaining 7 uses of *diermēneuō*, *diermēneutēs*, and *hermēneia* all relate to the interpretation of speaking in tongues (1 Cor. 12:10, 30; 14:5, 13, 26, 27, 28).

It is tempting to imagine that this takes the form of "translating" otherwise unintelligible speech. But if speaking in tongues is, as Paul seems to imply (14:14), subrational and pre-conceptual, it does not provide communicable concepts which may then be "translated" into the native language of the community. Conversely, if glossolalia were already rational and conceptual, it is difficult to see why the speaker could not always "interpret" his own utterances to the church. In at least four places, however, Paul makes it clear that often, although not always, the interpreter is a different person from the one who speaks in tongues (1 Cor. 12:10; 14:5, 13, 28). Further, ecstatic utterance is usually addressed to God rather than to the congregation (14:2; cf. 14:16; although cf. also the reference to "different kinds of tongues", in 12:10). It is therefore doubtful whether any light is shed on this passage by Plato's reference to prophets assessing the ecstatic utterances of seers (*Timaeus*, 72a). Presumably, then, *hermēneia* in these verses is an intelligible description of the pre-conceptual mood or attitude which is expressed in tongues. If this is so, it is perhaps just conceivable that Paul's injunction to the ecstatic to pray for the capacity to "interpret" his own utterance is tantamount to short-circuiting the place of tongues in public worship altogether (14:13). At very least, Paul certainly views tongues as being primarily a private affair between man and God (14:2–6, 16, 19, 23, 28) but by way of concession allows a maximum of two or three ecstatic utterances in public on condition that someone is present who can interpret them (14:27, 28). The basic principle expressed in these passages is the importance of rationality and intelligibility in public worship. Only that which is intelligible can build the church up (14:1–6, 19, *et passim*; cf. further, J. P. M. Sweet, "A Sign for Unbelievers: Paul's Attitude to Glossolalia", *NTS* 13, 1966–7, 240–57; and commentaries on 1 Cor., ad loc.).

4. One famous use of *hermēneutēs* occurs in early Christian literature in Eusebius, *HE* 3, 39. Papias says that Mk., "who had been Peter's *hermēneutēs*, wrote down carefully as much as he remembered, recording the sayings and doings of Christ . . ." Many have taken the term to mean "translator" here, but recently it has been argued that it means something more like "private secretary" or "aide-de-camp" (cf. R. P. Martin, *Mark: Evangelist and Theologian*, 1972, 52; and E. Stauffer, see bibliography).

5. In the history of Christian thought up to the present, the study of hermeneutics has taken two distinct forms.

(a) Traditionally hermeneutics has involved the attempt to formulate general rules for the interpretation of Biblical texts. But this approach encounters two difficulties. Firstly, it has become increasingly recognized in the light of Biblical criticism that different types of Biblical literature require particular methodologies of their own. For example, methods used in the interpretation of the parables of Jesus will be different from those employed in interpreting Hebrew poetry or parts of the Pauline epistles. The few general principles which can be universally applied to all types of Biblical literature tend to be so basic as to be obvious: for example, the need to pay due attention to the linguistic context, the historical situation, the literary genre, and the purpose of the writer. Secondly, nowadays it is also more widely appreciated that the process of understanding a text is, as Schleiermacher insisted, not simply a matter of observing certain hermeneutical rules. The observance of such rules may admittedly constitute a necessary pre-condition for the correct interpretation of a text; but they do not of themselves create or initiate genuine understanding. It is the recognition of this latter difficulty that leads to a second and more adequate understanding of the task of hermeneutics.

(b) If the interpreter is to understand a text adequately and correctly, due account must be taken of his own subjectivity. His own presuppositions, cultural orientation, and psychological capacities will shape his understanding of the text. Some of these presuppositions may act as a barrier to understanding; yet it is more important to note that they also serve as an indispensable point of contact with the subject-matter of the text, at least at the commencement of the ongoing process of understanding. This point was stressed by Schleiermacher, and has connections with Bultmann's conception of pre-understanding (*Vorverständnis*). One special aspect of the problem of the relation between the interpreter and the text is that of historical distance. This aspect was explored especially by Dilthey, and has been sharpened as a two-way problem of "historicality", or historical relativity, in Heidegger, Gadamer, and Pannenberg. Both the text and the interpreter are to some extent conditioned by their particular place in history.

This problem can be illustrated with reference to Bultmann's proposals about demythologizing. He contends that belief in miracles is bound up with a first-century world-view. But it is also possible to argue that the attitude of the modern secular man towards miracles equally reflects his own historicality, as the product of a materialistic science-orientated culture in the twentieth century. The problem of historicality therefore is a two-way issue, and concerns the horizons of the modern interpreter as well as those of the text.

In practice the task of hermeneutics is first to recognize and accept the problem of "distance" between the interpreter and the text, and to allow him to disentangle what the text actually says from his own presuppositions about what at first it merely *seems* to say in the absence of due critical reflection. The interpreter must not merely read his own ideas into the text. Next, the horizons of the interpreter and the horizons of the text must be brought into a relationship of active engagement and dialogue, until the two sets of judgments, or of questions and answers, become eventually fused into one. The two principles, the negative and the positive, are carefully explored by Gadamer in his *Wahrheit und Methode* in the sections on historical distancing and the merging of horizons (*Horizontverschmelzung*). A useful discussion of them is also undertaken by Richard Palmer, and a brief popular approach has been worked out by Walter Wink.

In the writings of Ernst Fuchs this crucial area of shared understanding is described under the key category of *Einverständnis*, often translated as "common understanding", but sometimes also as "empathy". He illustrates what is meant by citing the "common understanding" which exists within a close-knit family, whereby what is said within the home is "understood" by all the members of the family. Understanding rests on shared experiences and attitudes. In particular, Fuchs believes that the parables of Jesus create a "world" into which the hearer is drawn, and is at home. But the content of the parables challenges him, as a new reality. The word of Jesus becomes a language-event, the hearer is grasped deep down, and his own "world" is extended, as it were, from within. To understand the parable is thus not merely to have certain ideas explained, but to enter a new world or reality together with Jesus, so that he hears the word anew. The final goal

583

of hermeneutics, according to Fuchs, is not so much that the interpreter should interpret the text, as that the text should interpret him.

The new hermeneutic, as represented by Fuchs and Ebeling, endeavours to take full account of the subjectivity of the interpreter, but without losing sight of the primacy of the text itself. Admittedly the interpreter's understanding of a text is shaped by his own questions and pre-judgments. But the text, in turn, speaks back to the interpreter, so that his initial questions and pre-judgments are re-shaped. The term "hermeneutical circle" may be misleading, for in the hermeneutical movement between text and interpreter, genuine progress will be achieved towards a fusion of horizons, provided that there is both critical reflection and also a humble listening to the text. It is clear that the hermeneutical problem is a genuine and important one, and it would be a mistake to avoid it by arguing that the interpretation and application of Scripture is exclusively the work of the Holy Spirit. The same might be said about the need for any theological study.   *A. C. Thiselton*

(a). P. J. Achtemeier, *An Introduction to the New Hermeneutic* 1969; J. Behm, *hermēneuō, TDNT* II 661–6; F. Büchsel, *hēgeomai, TDNT* II 908 f.; R. Bultmann "Is Exegesis without Presuppositions Possible?" *Existence and Faith*, 1964, 342–51; and "The Problem of Hermeneutics," *Essays Philosophical and Theological*, 1955, 234–61; G. Ebeling, *Word and Faith*, 1963; and *God and Word*, 1967; and *Theology and Proclamation*, 1966; E. Fuchs, *Studies of the Historical Jesus*, 1964; and "The Hermeneutical Problem," in J. M. Robinson, ed., *The Future of our Religious Past*, 1971, 267–78; R. W. Funk, *Language, Hermeneutic and Word of God*, 1966; M. Gertner, "Terms of Scriptural Interpretation: A Study in Hebrew Semantics," *BSOAS* 25, 1962, 1–27; M. Heidegger, *Being and Time*, 1962; E. D. Hirsch, *Validity in Interpretation* 1967; Licdell-Scott, 593; J. H. Oliver, *The Athenian Expounders of the Sacred and Ancestral Law*, 1950, 122 ff.; R. E. Palmer, *Hermeneutics, Interpretation Theory in Schleiermacher, Dilthey, Heidegger, and Gadamer*, 1969; and "*Hermēneuō* and *Hermēneia*", *Hermeneutics*, 1969, 12–32; W. Pannenberg, *Basic Questions in Theology*, I, 1970; J. M. Robinson and J. Cobb, eds., *New Frontiers in Theology: II, The New Hermeneutic*, 1964; B. Rosensweig, "The Hermeneutic Principles and their Application," *Tradition* 13, 1972, 49–76; A. C. Thiselton, "The Parables as Language-Event. Some Comments on Fuchs's Hermeneutics in the Light of Linguistic Philosophy", *SJT* 23, 1970, 437–68; "The Use of Philosophical Categories in New Testament Hermeneutics," *The Churchman* 87, 1973, 87–100; and "The New Hermeneutic" in I. H. Marshall, ed., *New Testament Interpretation* (forthcoming); W. Wink, *The Bible in Human Transformation* 1973.

(b). A. M. Denis, "Foi et Exégèse: Réflexions sur les Fondements Théologiques," *NTS* 20, 1973–4, 45–54; E. Fuchs, *Hermeneutik* 1970[4]; *Marburger Hermeneutik*, 1968; *Zum hermeneutischen Problem in der Theologie*, 1959; H.-G. Gadamer, *Wahrheit und Methode, Grundzüge einer philosophischen Hermeneutik*, 1965[2]; M. Heidegger, *Unterwegs zur Sprache*, 1960; O. Kern, *exēgētai*, Pauly-Wissowa VI 1583–4; E. Stauffer, "Der Methurgeman des Petrus," in J. Blinzler, ed., *Neutestamentliche Aufsätze*, Festschrift J. Schmid, 1963, 282 ff.

F

Face

πρόσωπον

πρόσωπον (prosōpon), face; προσωπολημψία (prosōpolēmpsia), partiality, bias; προσωπολημπτέω (prosōpolēmpteō), show partiality, give a biased judgment; προσωπολήμπτης
(prosōpolēmptēs), biased, taking sides; ἀπροσωπολήμπτως (aprosōpolēmptōs),
unbiased.

CL prosōpon, face. Originally it probably meant that which struck the eye (pros
towards, and ops eye), that which one looks at. In secular Gk. it meant face,
death-mask, actor's mask, then (fig.) the part played by the actor. When used of
things it meant surface, either the top one, or the one facing the observer. It is
occasionally used for the face of the gods. When used as a part representing the
whole, it meant the figure. The meaning person (not found before Polyb.) is a
borrowing from Lat. usage.

OT prosōpon is found c. 900 times in the LXX, mostly as a translation of pānîm.
    1. It is used: (a) For man's face (Gen. 31:2), his appearance (Gen. 4:5), as a
paraphrase for the whole man (Deut. 7:10). The frequent expression to turn the
face means to greet respectfully. It is sometimes also used for the faces of animals
(Ezek. 1:10). (b) For the side turned to the observer, e.g. the face of the earth
(Gen. 2:6). (c) It is also used with various prepositions to express relationships,
e.g. before the face of, before, into, in front of, opposite.
    2. It is used above all for the face of God: (a) As the aspect of God that concerns
man. Where the LXX speaks of the face of God, it is often referring to some relationship of God to man, e.g. his gracious turning to him, or his disappointed turning from him. If God lifts up or causes his face to shine upon Israel, it receives peace
(i.e. salvation) thereby (Num. 6:25 f.). When God hides or turns away his face, it
implies the withdrawal of grace (cf. Ps. 13:2; 104:29). Actions and reactions of
God which either bring the good fortune of fellowship with God (Ps. 25:25) or an
abiding under God's wrath (Lev. 17:10) are expressed by such anthropomorphic
pictures. The possibility of seeing God's face is mentioned as the most exceptional
possibility (Gen. 32:30, Peniel, the face of God; cf. also Gen. 16:13; Exod. 24:9 ff.;
Deut. 4:12; Jdg. 6:22 f.). It is always stressed how dangerous this experience is.
If a sinful man sees the holy God, he must die (Exod. 33:20; cf. Isa. 6:5). →
Blessing.
    In Exod. 33 three different traditions – Yahweh sends an angel as guide; a link
with Yahweh through the Tent; Yahweh's pānîm accompanies the people – are
linked together by the basic thought of the leading of the people after the departure
from Sinai. In the third strand of tradition pānîm (Exod. 33:14 f.) appears uniquely

hypostatized as a manifestation of Yahweh to Israel. This has led to divergent attempts at interpretation. Some understand "my *pānîm*" as "I myself", i.e. an emphasis on the personal presence of Yahweh. Others maintain that this passage justifies us in claiming that the priest used a mask in the cultus. Others interpret it to mean that in the cultus at the sanctuaries the face of Yahweh was present, i.e. the aspect of him turned manward. No single, certain interpretation can be offered.

(b) When God's face is mentioned in connection with the temple, the language is cultic. Extra-Biblical usage may have had an influence here. Among the nations surrounding Israel the face of the deity was seen and worshipped in that of the temple image. Since there was no image used in Israel's worship, the phrase could be used only in a metaphorical sense, when it was said that the worshipper sought God's face in the temple (Ps. 24:6; 42:2 (MT 42:3); Zech. 8:21 f. (MT and LXX); Mal. 1:9 (MT)). The gracious presence of God is meant, his turning to men which the Israelite sought especially in the temple. So to seek the face of God in the OT means to come near to God in → prayer. Finally, quite apart from the cultus, it has the general meaning of seeking fellowship with God. The psalmist urges Israel to do this "continually" in Ps. 105:4.

The literal meaning of shewbread (Exod. 25:30) is "bread of face" ("bread of the Presence", RSV). Such loaves were known in the heathen cults, where they served as food for the deity (cf. Jer. 7:18). When Israel took over the custom, the → bread (art. *artos*) was put with frankincense on the special table as a gift, not as food, before the face of God. See further Exod. 35:13; 39:36; Num. 4:7; 1 Sam. 21:6; 1 Ki. 7:48; 1 Chron. 9:32; 23:29; 28:16; 2 Chron. 2:4; 4:19; 13:11; 29:18; Neh. 10:33; Matt. 12:4; Mk. 2:26; Lk. 6:4; Heb. 9:2; Josephus, *Ant.*, 3, 6, 6; 3, 10, 7.

(c) In Rab. Judaism man's highest hope is to see the face of God or of the *šekînâh*, either in the hour of death and in the world to come after the days of the Messiah or even according to some opinions during the days of the Messiah. In the reflection of the divine light the face of the righteous will shine like the sun (cf. Dan. 12:3), but the godless will receive their punishment before the face of God. Contrast, however, R. Johanan b. Zakkai's fear on his deathbed (SB I 208; ML 478).

NT NT follows the OT usage, and *prosōpon* is used as follows:

1. (a) Lit. of man's face (e.g. Matt. 6:16 f.; 2 Cor. 11:20). (b) In various metaphorical expressions, e.g. "to fall on one's face" as a sign of respect and subjection (Matt. 17:6; Lk. 5:12; 1 Cor. 14:25), or "he set his face to go to Jerusalem" (Lk. 9:51) which expresses Jesus' immovable decision to go to Jerusalem. For Luke this marks a new period in Jesus' life.

(c) Face can stand for the whole person (2 Cor. 1:11; Gk. "many faces"), especially in the sense of respect of persons (Mk. 12:14 par.).

(d) Combined with prepositions – mostly in literal reproductions of Sem. expressions – e.g. "before thy face" (Mk. 1:2), "in the presence of" (Lk. 2:31).

(e) Face is used to refer to the surface of the earth (Lk. 21:35; Acts 17:26), the appearance of the sky (Matt. 16:3), and of plants (Jas. 1:11).

2. It is further used of the face of God and of Christ. The NT continues Rab. thought when it speaks of seeing God in the heavenly world. The angels of the "little ones" (Matt. 18:10) see the face of God. This is a circumlocution for God's

care for the humble. In the heavenly sanctuary Christ appears for us before the face of God (Heb. 9:24). Thereby the heavenly sanctuary replaces the earthly temple and cultus. The NT reflects Heb. modes of thought and speech, in that it does not describe the appearance of anyone and so not that of Jesus.

For the believer the glory of God (→ Glory, art. *doxa*) has appeared in the face of Christ (2 Cor. 4:6). This verse is linked with the story of the transfiguration (in Matt. 17:2 Jesus' face "shone like the sun"). But Paul writes of the glorified, not the earthly Lord. Hence *prosōpon* is not the outward appearance, nor does it stand only for the person. It recalls the "face" of God in the OT. Christ "is the likeness of God" (2 Cor. 4:4; Jn. 12:45; 14:9), God's turning to us and his final revelation. The reference of the whole context to Exod. 34 makes this certain. The glory on Moses' face, derived from his meeting with God, was transient (2 Cor. 3:13). Hence he covered his face with a veil. Paul expands the picture to cover the whole OT. The veil which hid Moses' transient glory covers the whole OT, where Israel is concerned, so that they cannot see the glory of the promise and fulfilment in Christ (2 Cor. 3:14 f.). Otherwise Moses would serve them as a (negative) witness to Christ. Only when there is faith in Christ is the veil removed (2 Cor. 3:16). Here "face" stands for man's innermost being (as "heart" in 4:6, and "mind" in 3:15; 4:4). In spite of that, all knowledge by faith is only an imperfect anticipation of the future knowledge, "face to face" (1 Cor. 13:12). The servants of God will not see his face till they are in the new Jerusalem (Rev. 22:4; cf. Matt. 5:8).

3. *prosōpon* is also used in the compound words *prosōpolēmpsia*, *prosōpolēmptēs*, *prosōpolēmpteō* which are all compounded with a form of the verb *lambanō* (lit. take). This translates the Heb. *nāśā'*, lift up the face of the one who has bowed humbly in greeting, i.e. to acknowledge him. God does not allow himself to be influenced by appearances or respect of persons (Deut. 10:17, in LXX *thaumazō*, esteem). Equally the earthly judge must refrain from all partiality (Lev. 19:15; Deut. 1:17; 16:19; cf. in the NT Mk. 12:14; Jude 16; Gal. 2:6). *prosōpolēmpsia* which first occurs in the NT means partiality or bias (Rom. 2:22; Eph. 6:9; Col. 3:25; Jas. 2:1). In Jas. 2:9 *prosōpolēmpteō* means to show partiality. These passages warn against common preferences (e.g. of the rich), pretences (eyeservice, Col. 3:22), self-deceit (Col. 3:25), disdain (e.g. of slaves), special religious claims (e.g. by the Jews). They are always based on the fact that God is impartial (*ou prosōpolēmptēs*, Acts 10:34) and acts impartially (*aprosōpolēmptōs*, 1 Pet. 1:17), and shows to all one and the same grace. *E. Tiedtke*

(a). Arndt, 728 f.; E. Lohse, *prosōpon*, *TDNT* VI 768 ff.; Moulton–Milligan, 553; Commentaries on 2 *Corinthians* by J. Denney, 1894, and P. E. Hughes, 1962, on 3:7–18; 4:6.
(b). H. Preisker, "Angesicht," *BHHW* I 93 f.

Faith, Persuade, Belief, Unbelief

The words dealt with here are basically concerned with that personal relationship with a person or thing which is established by trust and trustworthiness (including their negation). If this relationship comes about through persuasion or conviction, the vb. *peithomai* is used. The perf. tense *pepoitha* expresses the firm conviction and confidence that has come about. The words of the *pistis* group are derived from the same verbal stem. They denoted originally the faithful relationship of partners in an agreement and the trustworthiness of their promises. In a broader sense they came to denote the credibility of statements, reports and accounts in general, both sacred and secular. In NT Gk. they gained a special importance and specific content through their application to the relationship with God in Christ: the trusting acceptance and recognition of what God has done and promised in him.

<hr>

πείθομαι

πείθω (*peithō*), convince, persuade; πείθομαι (*peithomai*), obey, believe; πέποιθα (*pepoitha*), be convinced, trust; πεποίθησις (*pepoithēsis*), trust, confidence; πειθός (*peithos*), persuasive; πειθαρχέω (*peitharcheō*), obey; πεισμονή (*peismonē*), persuasion; ἀπειθέω (*apeitheō*), be disobedient; ἀπειθής (*apeithēs*), disobedient; ἀπείθεια (*apeitheia*), disobedience; πιθανολογία (*pithanologia*), persuasive speech, art of persuasion.

CL 1. The stem *peith-* (*pith-*, *poith-*) has the basic meaning of trust (cf. Lat. *fido*, *fides*). The same stem is also the basis of the formations with *pist-* (→ *pisteuō*). Trust can refer to a statement, so that it has the meaning to put faith in, to let oneself be convinced, or to a demand, so that it gets the meaning of obey, be persuaded. The original intrans. act. *peithō* (trust) became trans., to convince, persuade (already in the time of Homer), first through the pass. (be convinced, persuaded). The meaning to trust was taken over with both the above-mentioned branches from the mid. pass. *peithomai*. Only the 2nd perf. *pepoitha* retains in the act. the original intrans. meaning (strictly, to have taken hold of trust with the effect continuing into the present). It has the present meaning of trusting firmly, relying upon. The mid. pass. of the 1st perf. *pepeismai* (strictly, to have been convinced, or to have convinced oneself) likewise means to be convinced. The noun *pepoithēsis* (trust, confidence), derived from *pepoitha* is late Gk.

2. The adj. *peithos* (persuasive), derived from *peithō* is found nowhere in Gk. except 1 Cor. 2:4, where another reading has the noun *peithō* (art of persuading, see under 4) which is common in Gk. but does not occur elsewhere in the NT. From the same stem as *peithō* comes *pithanos* (convincing, trustworthy) and from it *pithanologia* (persuasive speech, art of persuasion) for persuading through appearances in contrast to *apodeixis* (proof, cf. Plato, *Theaet.*, 162e; 1 Cor. 2:4). The earliest and in the NT sole occurrence of *peismonē* (persuasion, persuasiveness) is Gal. 5:8. The vb. *peitharcheō* (obey) is current from the time of Sophocles, and is derived from the adj. *peitharchos* (obeying a superior, the government, or an authority [*archē*]).

3. *apeitheō* (be disobedient) and *apeitheia* (disobedience) are derived from *apeithēs* (disobedient) also in classical Gk.

4. The active meaning convince, persuade, is especially characteristic of Gk. thought. It is significant that Peitho (art of persuading, see above 2) is regarded as a goddess. But *peithō* can also extend the meaning of persuade to include lead astray, corrupt. The mid. pass. meaning of trust, rely on, can also refer to God in secular Gk. From the meaning to allow onself to be convinced comes the variant to have faith (in another). From the meaning let oneself be persuaded comes the use in the sense of follow (another), be obedient, obey (Plato, *Apol.*, 29d: "I will obey God rather than you"). On *pepoitha* cf. Aeschylus, *Eum.*, 826, where Athene says to the chorus of the Eumenides: *kagō pepoitha Zēni* ("I too rely upon Zeus").

OT 1. In contrast to Gk., Heb. has no word for persuade, convince. In the few places, where tenses other than the perf. of *peithō* and *peithomai* occur in the LXX (chiefly in 2 and 4 Macc. and Tob.), there is no Heb. equivalent.

2. It is otherwise in the case of the perf. *pepoitha* which occurs about 80 times for the Heb. *bāṭaḥ*, trust, rely upon. This Heb. word and its derivatives are translated almost as often by *pepoitha* as by the vbs. *elpizō* and *epelpizō* and the noun *elpis* (→ hope). On the other hand, *pepoitha* is used to translate several other Heb. words (especially *ḥāsâh*, seek refuge, which in fact is translated twice as often by *epelpizō*. *pepoitha* serves to draw attention to the object and ground of Israel's hope, especially in Isa. 10:20, Jer., proverbial wisdom and (together with the more common *elpizō*) in the Pss. expressing trust (cf. Pss. 24[25]:2; 56[57]:1). This lies in God's → covenant fidelity, → election and → promise. It is to be distinguished from trust in men, idols and material goods (cf. Isa. 17:7 f.; 32:3; 36:6; Jer. 7:4; Ps. 117[118]:8). The noun *pepoithēsis* occurs in the LXX only once for the Heb. *biṭṭāḥôn*, trust (derived from *bāṭaḥ*), in 1 Ki. 18:19.

3. The noun *pithanologia*, persuasive speech, art of persuasion, which corresponds to *peithō* does not occur at all in the LXX. And the vb. *peitharcheō*, obey, does not occur apart from 1 Esd. 8:94; Sir. 30:38 (33:28) and Dan. 7:27. On the other hand, *apeitheō*, and in one instance *apeithēs*, are used to characterize the people who disobey God, especially in Deut. and Isa. It translates various Heb. vbs. including *mārâh* (Deut. 1:26; 9:23 f.; Isa. 3:8; cf. Philo. *Spec. Leg.*, 5, 741d: "they punish him who is not only disobedient [*ton apeithounta*] to the law but also to God").

NT In the NT *peithō*, *peithomai* and *pepoitha* are quite common; they occur most frequently in Paul (22 times) and Acts (17 times). But they are absent from Mk., Jn., 1 and 2 Pet., Jude and Rev. as well as 1 Cor., Eph., Col., 1 Thess., 1 Tim. and Tit. Examination of the passages shows that Paul – like the LXX – used the active forms only rarely (twice), but the perf. forms of *pepoitha* quite frequently. Otherwise these occur only in quotations in Matt. and Heb. and twice in Lk. The noun *pepoithēsis* is found 6 times in Paul. *peitharcheō* occurs only in Acts (3 times) and Tit. 3:1.

The negative forms are relatively rare. Whereas the vb. *apeitheō* occurs 13 times (5 times in Rom., and 4 times in 1 Pet.), the noun and the adj. are each found only 6 times. Apart from Rom. 1:30, the adj. occurs only in the Pastoral Epistles, Lk. and Acts. *apeitheia* occurs twice each in Rom., Eph. and Heb.

1. The range of meaning of the vb. may be ascertained by looking at its tenses with regard to the beginning, end and duration of the action concerned.

(a) The act. form of *peithō* in the aor. (e.g. *epeisan*, Matt. 27:20; cf. Acts 12:20; 14:19; 19:26) always has the meaning of persuade, induce, and even to mislead or corrupt. But it has no special theological significance.

By contrast, the imperfect expresses the attempt to influence a person to adopt a particular attitude or action. It is characteristic that Acts uses the vb. to describe Paul's preaching to the Jews of the synagogue (→ Church, art. *synagōgē*) and the → Greeks (→ Conversion, art. *prosēlytos*). Here Paul was not trying to evince faith in the one God, but to persuade them of the newly given grace in Christ (Acts 13:43) through teaching (18:4; → Think, art. *dialogizomai*). The same applies to the pres. part. Acts 19:8 describes how Paul argued for three months in the synagogue attempting to convince the Jews of the kingdom of God (cf. 28:31, where his activity is also described as "teaching about the Lord Jesus Christ").

(b) The pres. ind. denotes not only the duration of the action but the fact that it is taking place at the present time. Here the context determines the meaning. In 3 passages the meaning is disputed (Acts 26:28; 2 Cor. 5:11; and Gal. 1:10). E. Haenchen translates Acts 26:28: "Soon you will convince me to play the Christian" (*The Acts of the Apostles*, 1971, 689). The Gk. text reads *en oligō me peitheis Christianon poiēsai*, lit. "In a little you persuade me to make a Christian." Here the vb. *poiēsai* is a technical theatrical term, used of playing a part. These words of the Jewish King Agrippa are not to be taken ironically. They show how he came within a hair's breadth of conversion. He was a Jew, and this suggests that *peitheis* is used here in the sense of 1 (a) above. On the other hand, the expression chosen here indicates just how far he was from taking the step. Some manuscripts have *genesthai* (become) instead of *poiēsai*, but these are inferior. The better manuscripts do not speak directly of the possibility of Agrippa becoming a Christian. F. F. Bruce translates the passage: "In short, you are trying to persuade me to act the Christian" (*The Acts of the Apostles*, 1952², 449). Agrippa sees himself in a dilemma. If he says that he rejects the prophets (v. 27), his reputation for orthodoxy is gone. But if he agrees with Paul's reasoning, he realizes that he is being manoeuvred into a position of public agreement with Paul. For other interpretations, see R. Bultmann, *TDNT* VI 2, n. 4, and Arndt, 645.

2 Cor. 5:11 and Gal. 1:10 are the only instances in Paul of the act. use. They probably do not refer directly to persuasion to accept the gospel. Paul had to defend himself against the claims of spurious authorities, who were working against him. In 2 Cor. 5:11 he says: "Therefore, knowing the fear of the Lord, we persuade men." In Gal. 1:10 he asks: "Am I now trying to persuade [RSV "seeking the favour of"] men or God?" In these passages he is stressing the fact that he strives to convince men by argument, not because it was necessary for his personal authority, but for the sake of the gospel that he proclaimed.

(c) The fut. act. comes very close to the aor. in meaning to persuade. It also means to reassure. Perhaps there is the thought of corruption in the background of Matt. 28:14 (cf. RSV, Arndt. "satisfy"). In 1 Jn. 3:19 ("By this we shall know that we are of the truth, and reassure [*peisomen*] our hearts before him" RSV) it is a question of true self-knowledge. The point is a double one. On the one hand, it is a question of being in the truth or not, and this is shown by whether love is shown in action. On the other hand, it is a question of whether God will condemn us. These two points are not simply parallel. Someone who is merely of the truth could still condemn himself before God, although this does not inevitably follow (cf. v. 21). If his heart drives him to it, he may still reassure it before God. For God knows better than ourselves not only about our guilt, but also that which he has newly created in us.

2. The mid. and pass. deponent *peithomai* corresponds to the act. voice and stresses the result and outcome of the influence. This applies to the aor., imp., and fut. which occur only in the Lucan writings in the NT.

(a) The aor. occurs 3 times. Acts 17:4 shows the success of Paul's teaching in the synagogue (cf. v. 2; see above 1 (a)). Acts 5:39 (RSV v. 40 "So they took his advice [*epeisthēsan de autō*]") refers to the council of Jewish leaders being persuaded by Gamaliel. It is characteristic of Acts that it uses the same form of the vb. in both passages, as also in Acts 23:21 where warning is given (though without theological significance) against being influenced by false advice. The dat. following the vb. refers to the person who is exerting influence. The following are possible meanings: to be persuaded by someone, to follow someone, to yield to (cf. Acts 23:21 RSV), to listen to someone in the sense of hearken and obey.

(b) Similarly, the imp. means to heed, to pay attention to someone's words, attitudes or actions, so that one is influenced by them. According to Acts 27:11, the centurion "paid more attention [*mallon epeitheto*]" (RSV) to the captain and owner of the ship than to Paul. Again, with reference to the behaviour of the Roman Jews, Acts 28:24 expresses a contrast: "And some were convinced [*epeithonto*] by what he said, while others disbelieved [*ēpistoun*]" (RSV). *peithomai* here has the meaning of believe (Paul's words). Thus the vb. can also come to denote following a leader, as in the case of Theudas and Judas the Galilean (Acts 5:36 f.).

(c) In the only passage in the fut., Lk. 16:31, where it follows the conjunction *ean* (if) denoting a hypothetical or possible fut. act, the vb. means to be convinced. "If they do not hear Moses and the prophets, neither will they be convinced if some one should rise from the dead." In Acts Paul seeks to convince the Jews by arguments which any Jew must accept. Lk. 16:31 expresses the corollary. Where agreement to such argument is refused, a man will not be convinced even though someone should rise from the dead.

(d) The pres. has no particular theological significance in Acts 21:14 and 26:26, where it means to be persuaded, and Heb. 13:18 ("we are sure" RSV). In other places it means to obey or follow (Gal. 5:7; Heb. 13:17; Jas. 3:3). In Rom. 2:8 disobedience (→ *apeitheō* below) to the truth is seen as being grounded in subjection to unrighteousness. This is abolished by faith. But where there is a renewed regard for the law, disobedience to the truth necessarily follows (cf. Gal. 5:7; → *peismonē* below).

(e) The perf. always denotes a situation in which the act of examining and weighing up has been concluded, and where a firm conviction has already been reached (cf. Lk. 20:6; Rom. 8:38; 14:14; 15:14; 2 Tim. 1:5, 12; Heb. 6:9). This can refer to convictions concerning facts or people (e.g. that John was a prophet, Lk. 20:6), as well as to the all-embracing, unshakeable certainty that has been attained in faith (Rom. 8:38).

3. The 2nd perf. *pepoitha* with the prep. *epi* always means to depend on, trust in, put one's confidence in. It indicates a conviction as the basis for further thought and action. Thus it can refer to one's trust in one's own righteousness (Lk. 18:9; negatively in 2 Cor. 1:9; cf. the addition in the variant reading in Mk. 10:24; and Lk. 11:22). But it can also refer to the trust in a good sense which can be placed in someone. Thus Paul expressed confidence in the church (2 Cor. 2:3; 2 Thess. 3:4, "in the Lord"; cf. Gal. 5:10; Phil. 2:24). However, in both the former passages the vb. can be understood in relation to the following *hoti*, so that, as in other passages, *pepoitha hoti* can be translated to be confident that. *epi*, like *eis* in Gal. 5:10, means "in view of." Thus the confidence would refer not so much to the persons as to the circumstances brought about by God in which Paul trusts "in the Lord", such as God's faithfulness in completing the work that he has begun. The

trust is ultimately in the Lord himself. At the same time this expresses a hope in the future, a fact indicated by the use of *pepoitha* in the LXX and also Phil. 1:25 and 2.24. Here Paul expresses his conviction that he will survive for the sake of the work, and will come again to Philippi. *pepoitha* is followed by the prep. *en* (in) only in Phil. 3:3 f., where it is set in contrast to glorying in (*en*) Christ Jesus. Here, as with the construction with *epi*, the meaning is to have confidence in. Paul disclaims all confidence in the flesh; rather, he glories in Christ.

Confidence is also expressed by forms of *pepoitha* followed by the infin. "If anyone is confident that he is Christ's [*ei tis pepoithen heautō Christou einai*], let him remind himself that as he is Christ's, so are we" (2 Cor. 10:7; cf. Rom. 2:19). When followed by the dat., the vb. means simply to trust, believe *in* (Phil. 1:14, but see RSV; Phlm. 21). The entrusting of oneself to God that is characteristic of the Pss. finds direct expression only in OT quotations that are applied to Jesus. Matt. 27:43 and Heb. 2:13 (cf. Isa. 8:17) suggest that the personal attitude and hope of the OT prayer is fulfilled in him. Trust in God now coincides with faith in Jesus Christ. This also applies to 2 Cor. 1:9, where trust in God who raises the dead comes from faith in the risen Christ.

4. The noun *pepoithēsis*, confidence (Phil. 3:4), has the same meaning as the vb. in vv. 3 f. It is likewise connected with *en sarki*, "in the → flesh", and refers to the self-confidence that grows out of observance of the law. On the other hand, 2 Cor. 3:4 refers to the confidence that grows out of the apostolic commission (cf. vv. 5 f.). The latter leads Paul to describe the Corinthian church as his letter of commendation written by the Spirit of God on hearts of flesh (v. 3). Confidence in men (2 Cor. 8:22, where the preposition *eis* is used for "in"; cf. Gal. 5:10) is set in the context of confidence in God (*pros ton theon*, 2 Cor. 3:4). The confidence expressed in 2 Cor. 1:15 is to be understood in the light of the → hope spoken of in vv. 13 f. The confidence of 2 Cor. 10:2 is grounded in Paul's commission as an → apostle (see above 2 Cor. 3:4), which enabled him to risk coming into violent conflict with certain people. In Eph. 3:12 this boldness is further defined by the words "and confidence of access [*kai prosagōgēn en pepoithēsei*]" in which the *kai* (and) is epexegetic.

5. On the adj. *peithos* (persuasive) and the noun *peithō* (persuasiveness) it may be said that the meaning of 1 Cor. 2:4 remains the same, whether it is read as *en peithois sophias logois* ("in persuasive words of wisdom") or *en peithoi sophias* ("with the persuasiveness of wisdom", cf. Arndt, 644; to which some manuscripts add *logois* or *logōn*, i.e. through words). On the textual difficulties see C. K. Barrett, *The First Epistle to the Corinthians*, 1968, 62, 65, who thinks that Paul himself was largely responsible for the problem by coining the word *peithos* meaning persuasive from the vb. *peithō* (persuade). In either case it is clear that the Corinthians did not come to faith through human → wisdom and its ways of persuading. The latter are described in Col. 2:4 as *pithanologia* ("beguiling speech" RSV; "persuasive speech", "art of persuasion", "plausible [but false] arguments", Arndt, 663), by which people are deceived.

6. The noun *peismonē* in Gal. 5:8 ("persuasion" RSV) may be understood actively in relation to *peithō*. But there may be here a play on words with *peithesthai* in the preceding verse which means to obey: "Who hindered you from obeying the truth? This persuasion is not from him who called you." The result of this persuasion

which did not come from God would thus be that the Galatians would no longer allow themselves to be persuaded by the truth. The play on words is not reflected by the Eng. tr. R. Bultmann prefers to translate v. 8 by "This following, or obedience, does not come . . ." (*TDNT* VI 9) which would thus preserve the play on words. But on this see H. Schlier, *Der Brief an die Galater*, 1952[12], 236; E. D. Burton, *Galatians*, ICC 1920, 282 f. The text is uncertain. Some manuscripts read: "Who has hindered you? Obey no one in not obeying the truth" (cf. R. Bultmann, *TDNT* VI 4, n. 11; cf. Funk § 488 1 (b)).

7. The vb. *peitharcheō* (obey) is used for obedience both to God (Acts 5:29; cf. above CL 2 on *peithomai*; 5:32) and to men (Acts 27:21 = *peithomai*, v. 11). In Tit. 3:1 it is identified with being submissive to rulers and authorities.

8. (a) *apeithēs* (disobedient) occurs in Acts 26:19 in the form of a double negative designed to stress Paul's obedience: "Wherefore, O King Agrippa, I was not disobedient to the heavenly vision." In Rom. 1:30 and 2 Tim. 3:2 it occurs in the catalogues of vices in connection with disobedience to parents.

(b) In all other passages, where *apeithēs*, the noun *apeitheia* (disobedience) and the vb. *apeitheō* (be disobedient) occur, the context suggests disobedience to God, mostly in contrast with faith. This is the sense of the LXX (cf. Lk. 1:17 which speaks of Elijah being sent to turn "the disobedient to the wisdom of the just"; cf. Mal. 4:5). It is exemplified by Jn. 3:36; Acts 14:2; 19:9 (of disbelieving Jews; see above NT 1 (b) on *peithō* and *peithomai*); Rom. 15:31; Eph. 2:2; 5:6 (with the contrast between the "sons of disobedience" [non-Christians] and "sons of the light", v. 8); and Tit. 1:16. 1 Pet. presents a distinctive usage in the way it qualifies disobedience as disobedience to the → word or to the → gospel (1 Pet. 2:8; cf. v. 7 *v.l.*; 3:1; 4:17; on Rom. 2:8 see above 2). It also speaks of the defective obedience of men before the flood despite the patience of God (1 Pet. 3:20).

Heb. 3:18 and 4:6 hold up to Christians (cf. v. 11) the behaviour of the generation in the wilderness as a warning example. The man will come to grief who looks back, or stops his ears to God's instructions for the present time, and is not ready to receive the future from the hands of God in utter trust. Because of her faith Rahab the harlot was unlike the latter, and she did not meet with the destruction which came upon the disobedient inhabitants of Jericho (Heb. 11:31). The Gentile Christians were themselves once likewise disobedient (Rom. 11:30; cf. Tit. 3:3). But *now* through the *apeitheia* of Israel in which God's covenant people did not as a whole wish to enter the new covenant in Jesus Christ (cf. Rom. 10:21), they have received mercy. Israel's disobedience is *now* intensified through their opposition to the mercy that has come upon the Gentiles (11:31). But in turn they may through all this *now* receive mercy. (This third *now* has been changed to "later" or omitted altogether in some manuscripts.)

The climax of the argument of Rom. 9–11 shows that this lack of trust, obedience, faith, and acceptance of God's will is the normal situation of man (Rom. 11:32). Only God himself can save man by having mercy on him and granting him faith.

O. Becker

πίστις	πίστις (*pistis*), faith; πιστεύω (*pisteuō*), believe; πιστός (*pistos*), pass. trustworthy, faithful, act. trusting, believing;

593

πιστόω (*pistoō*), rely, convince; ἀπιστία (*apistia*), unbelief; ἀπιστέω (*apisteō*), disbelieve; ἄπιστος (*apistos*), unbelievable, faithful, unbelieving.

CL 1. (a) In classical Gk. literature *pistis* means the trust that a man may place in men or the gods (Hesiod, *Works*, 372; Soph., *OT*, 1445), credibility (Soph., *OC*, 611), credit in business (Dem., 36, 57), guarantee (Aesch., Frag. 394), proof (Democ., 125), or something entrusted (*IG* 14, 2012 A 23). Similarly, *pisteuō* means to trust something or someone (Hdt., 1, 24; Aesch., *Pers.*, 800 ff.). It can refer to and confirm legendary tales (Hdt., 4, 96) and mythical ideas (Plato, *Grg.*, 524a). In the construction *pisteuō tini ti* it means to entrust something or someone to someone (Xen., *Mem.*, 4, 4, 17). With reference to people, *pisteuō* means to obey (Soph., *OT*, 625). The pass. means to enjoy trust (Xen., Anab., 7, 6, 33). The adj. *pistos* means trusting (Theognis, 283), trustworthy (Hom., *Il.*, 2, 124). *to piston* means dependability or the faithfulness of those bound through an agreement (Aesch., *Ag.*, 651; Xen., *Anab.*, 2, 4, 7). The vb. *pistoō* has the meaning of binding someone or oneself to be faithful (Soph., *OC*, 650). In the pass. it means to be sure, to trust (Hom., *Od.*, 21, 217 f.). The *pistis* word-group has a special colouring, where it refers to believing *doxa* (opinion). In such a case dependability is limited (cf. Plato, Phd., 107b).

apistia means mistrust (Theognis, 831), unreliability (Soph., *OC*, 611), and incredibility (Hdt., 1, 193). *apisteō* means to be mistrustful to disbelieve (Hom., *Od.*, 13, 339), and particularly to be disobedient (Soph., *Ant.*, 219, 381 f.). *apistos* means distrustful (Hom., *Od.*, 14, 150), undependable (Thuc., 1, 120, 4).

(b) Originally the word-group denoted conduct that honoured an agreement or bond. It had a social orientation, and its use indicated misconduct by implication. In order to obtain a pause in battle, it was necessary to make agreements pledging fidelity (Hom., *Il.*, 2, 124: *horkia pista*). Disappointed confidence led to the accusation: "There is nothing trustworthy in women" (Hom., *Od.*, 11, 456). The critical situation revealed fidelity. Hence, experience of faithfulness and unfaithfulness belongs to the idea of faith from the beginning.

(c) The idea had religious overtones at a very early date. The gods vouch for the validity of an alliance or treaty (Hom., *Il.*, 2, 115 ff.; note the importance of the oath). The words can also be applied directly to the divinity in cases of the trustworthiness of an oracle. The *pistis* word-group plays an important part in questions of the power of the gods to save in face of threatening danger (Aesch., *Sept.*, 211 f.), the unfathomable sovereignty of God ("He who hears the word of God and does not obey is out of his mind," Eur., *Iph. Taur.*, 14, 75 f.), and the power of God to direct a man's fate against his will (Soph., *OT*, 1445). In such case unquestioned obedience to the will of God is required of men.

(d) Faith is given unique expression in the enthusiastic piety of Empedocles of Agrigentum (5th cent. B.C.). He appeared as an immortal god, pointing the way of salvation (Frag. 112), demanding faith in the sense of assent to divine revelations, in his teaching on cosmology and metempsychosis (Frag. 114 ff.). Faith and recognition of the authoritatively proclaimed revelation were the same (Frag. 4, 5).

To the end of the classical era belong the inscriptions of the temple of Asclepius in Epidaurus which received their present form between 350 and 300 B.C. Here too faith is called for, in particular in the miraculous power of God (cf. R. Herzog, *Die Wunderheilungen von Epidauros*, 1931).

2. (a) In the Hel. period during the struggle with scepticism and atheism *pistis* acquired the sense of conviction as to the existence and activity of the gods. It took over the place of the older *nomizō* (deem, hold, believe that; cf. Plut., *De super-stitione*, 11; *Pericles*, 32; *Amatorius*, 13). The didactic element now emerged as the general and basic meaning. *pistis* as faith in God stood for theoretical conviction. But stress was laid on the belief that life was constituted in accordance with this conviction. To that extent *pistis* could assume the practical features of the older *eusebeia* (piety; cf. Plut., *De sera numinis vindicta*, 3; *De Pythiae Oraculis*, 18). The tension between the visible and invisible, the physical and spiritual world likewise left behind it clear traces in discussion. The result was a materialized concept of faith which in the philosophically articulate doctrinal system of Neo-Platonism called for a definite, intellectualistic conviction, conditioned by tradition (Plotinus, *Enneads*, 1, 3, 3; 5, 8, 11; Porphyry, *Ad Marcellam*, 21 ff.).

(b) The Stoic understanding of *pistis* is particularly important. Here the philo-sopher expressed his recognition of the divine ordering of the world, the centre of which was himself as an autonomous moral person (Epict., 2, 14, 11–13). *pistis* reveals the essence of man (Epict., 2, 4, 1). Man's fidelity to his moral destiny leads to fidelity towards others (Epict., 2, 4, 1–3; 2, 22).

(c) In the mystery religions faith denotes abandonment to the deity by following his instruction and teaching, and by putting oneself under his protection (Apul., *Met.*, 11, 25–28; P. Oxy., 11, 1380, 152). In the *Corpus Hermeticum* of syncretistic, Platonic revelations of the 2nd and 3rd centuries A.D., faith is a higher form of → knowledge. It thus belongs to the realm of *nous* (→ Reason, Mind). In a mystical way man is led out of the realm of the Logos, until his spirit comes to rest in the knowledge of faith. He thus participates in the divine (*Corp. Herm.*, 9, 10; *Ascl.*, 29). Besides Judaism and Christianity, the mystery religions stand cut in their demand of faith in their divinities, and the revelations and teaching delivered by them (e.g. the cult of Isis and Osiris). In this way salvation (which in the mystery religions was equated with divinization) was promised to the believer. To the back-ground of Judaism and Christianity probably belong the "divine sons" (→ Child, art. *hyios*) who appeared with express claim to revelation and who thus presented an alternative to Christianity. All had the same demand to hand: "Believe, if you would be saved, or begone" (Origen, *Contra Cels*, 6, 11).

3. In secular Gk., therefore, this group of terms represents a broad spectrum of ideas. It is used to express relations between man and man, and also to express relationship with the divine. The particular meaning is determined by the prevailing philosophical and religious influences. Originally it had to do with binding and obligations. But Stoicism made out of it a theoretically based law of life which brought the individual man into harmony with the cosmos. There was also a dangerous development in which *pistis* was demanded in response to a claim to revelation which was not subject to any control.

OT 1. *The Concept of Faith.* (a) In Heb. the root *'āman* in the niph. means to be true, reliable, faithful. It can be applied to men (e.g. Moses, Num. 12:7; servants, 1 Sam. 22:14; a witness, Isa. 8:2; a messenger, Prov. 25:13; prophets, 1 Sam 3:20).

But it can also be applied to God himself who keeps his covenant and gives grace to those who love him (Deut. 7:9). Particular stress is laid on the word of God (or men) preserving its dependability and being confirmed by subsequent action (1 Ki. 8:26; 1 Chron. 17:23 ff.; in the case of men, Gen. 42:20). In many passages the niph. acquires the meaning of to be entrusted with (Num. 12:7; 1 Sam. 3:20; Hos. 12:1). In an ancient strand of tradition which goes back to an original promise (2 Sam. 7:8 ff.), the Davidic dynasty is called "an established house." This state of being confirmed does not rest upon the qualities of the members of the dynasty or upon human measures, but upon the action of God which is initiated by his promise (2 Sam. 7:16; 1 Sam. 25:28). The niph. of 'āman thus gives expression to an unalterable fact that future generations could – and must – reckon with, despite every change of fortune in history.

A related idea is expressed by the root bāṭaḥ (LXX *pepoithenai; elpizō* → hope) with the meaning to trust, rely upon. The negative evaluation of such action is dominant: men trust in false security (Hab. 2:18), or set their hope on something false (Hos. 10:13). But it was also early on applied to Yahweh, the true ground of security (Jer. 39:18; 2 Ki. 18:30).

(b) Later the root bāṭaḥ was assimilated in meaning to the root 'āman. Basic for the OT idea of faith are the statements of Exod. 4:1–9, 27–31. The question is how will Moses assert his authority as the one sent by God before the people. In reply to Moses' objection that they will doubt his commission, God promises three miracles through which he confirms his authority, whereupon the people believe in Moses' mission and the coming redemption. Faith is here related to a mission which is expressly confirmed by divine authentication. Faith in the word is inseparable from the attitude assumed to the envoy.

(c) The absolute use in Isaiah is pointed. In the confrontation with Ahaz in view of the political threat, Isaiah dares to say: "If you will not believe, surely you shall not be established" (Isa. 7:9). The survival of the people lay alone in firm trust in the eternal God. Political action was called for which corresponded to this trust. Isa. 28:16 contains the saying about Zion's foundation: "Behold, I am laying in Zion for a foundation a stone, a tested stone, a precious cornerstone, of a sure foundation: 'He who believes will not be in haste' " (RSV). In the coming catastrophe only the believer will be sure of divine protection. The prophet himself is an example of believing trust: "I will wait for the Lord, who is hiding his face from the house of Jacob, and I will hope in him" (8:17). The tense hope in Yahweh (here linked with other vbs.) is directed to the future. Moses was a leader to a salvation the way of which was the way of faith. The prophets stood in the midst of national catastrophe as spokesmen for the God who had placed them in an almost hopeless situation. The faith which is set before the people is the way of deliverance from catastrophe to a future beyond the disaster.

(d) Besides the above passages from Isa., Gen. 15:6 is important for the connection between the OT and the NT (cf. Rom. 4:3, 9, 22 f.; Gal. 3:6; Jas. 2:23). The passage speaks of Abraham's faith as his readiness to lay hold of the rich promises of God. He made the word of God his security and base. The "reckoning" of faith constituted a declaratory act, which was formerly customary with the priests. God treats this trust of Abraham as the behaviour appropriate to the covenant relationship. In fellowship with God there lies a claim which man fulfills when he trusts.

The statement in Gen. 15:6 does not describe Abraham's entire relationship with God. But in view of a particular situation God s gracious, overarching judgment was pronounced over him. G. von Rad holds that the text originated at a time in which the question of faith was already known (*Genesis*, 1961, 179 f.; *Old Testament Theology*, I, 1962, 170 f., 379 f.).

(e) For Jewish and Christian tradition, the prophetic context of Hab. 2:3 f. is important. The vision granted by God is expressly confirmed. It is preserved for the end, and will not fail to appear. The "arrogant man" is expressly condemned by God's word; but life is promised to the "righteous" in view of his faithfulness. It is understood that the "arrogant man" stands on the side of the hostile world power and the "righteous" on that of the people of Judah. But textual criticism of the process of tradition has shown that already very early the divine sentence was applied to the devout individual (see further K. Elliger, *Studien zum Habakuk-Kommentar vom Toten Meer*, 1953). "Faithfulness" and "faith" stand here close together in the Heb. term *'emûnâh*. The idea is that of unwavering hold of the word of God against all contrary appearances. The sense is changed by the promise in the LXX translation: "the righteous will live by my faithfulness [*ek pisteōs mou*]."

(f) In a later stratum of the OT which expressly rivets the confession of the devout man to the Torah, the trustworthiness of the commandments is firmly underlined (Ps. 117:7; 119:66). The godly man is instructed by the commandments in the will of God; he knows that he receives wisdom and knowledge from them. In the temptations of life he can – as the servant of God (→ Son of God, art. *pais theou*) who directs his life in accordance with God's word – rely upon the trustworthiness of the → commandments. Post-exilic Torah-piety cannot be called legalistic without qualification. Torah (→ Law) and *dābār* (→ Word) were at the time living entities which were received by the godly in obedience and trust, and praised with thanksgiving and testimony. Stress on insight and knowledge of God points to an understanding of salvation in the wisdom tradition which in turn assigns a somewhat different role to faith (H.-J. Kraus). To sum up, it may be said that *he'emîn* and *'emûnâh* describe a living act of trust in the OT, and also the dimension of human existence in a historical situation. The group of words does not step outside the realm of the personal. Special stress is laid on the future goal. The past was the starting-point but not the goal of trust. The whole emphasis falls on overcoming the opposition of the ungodly and the realization of the divine purpose. Above all, it is clear in the prophets that faith must pass through extreme need and judgment, before it attains its goal in the salvation that lies in the future. In the first instance, faith in the OT is concerned with the fate of → Israel, although time and again the conduct of the individual can be decisive (cf. Gen. 15:6). The LXX translates the Heb. root *'āman* uniformly by *pisteuō* and attempts to include in it the wealth of the OT group terms.

2. *The Influence of the Terms in later Judaism.* (a) In later Jud. the main emphasis fell on the behaviour of the individual. Sotah 48b preserves an aphorism of R. Eliezer b. Hyrcanus: "If anyone has bread in his basket and says, what shall I eat tomorrow? he belongs to those who are small in trust." He knows that faith is frugal (Prov. 30:8), and must overcome anxiety about having more than enough. "Small in faith" has become a deprecatory word-picture which represents failure. According to Taanith 8a, R. Ami taught: "Rain comes only on account of the

people of faithfulness" (referring to Ps. 85:12). The term "men of faithfulness" (*'anšê 'ᵃmānâh*) in rab. literature is the mark of particular, definable, exemplary conduct. Complaint is made of its absence (Sotah 12b). Both the language and the way of thinking are different from the older strata of the OT. Faith is taught and inculcated in the manner of the wisdom writings. Because of its identity with faithfulness, faith remains the most important feature of → righteousness. The celebrated "Song of Faith" in Mek. Exod. 14:31 begins with the words: "Great is faith." It is concerned with the interpretation of Exod. 14:31: faith in God and his servant Moses. The man who believes in the shepherd of Israel believes in God himself who spoke and called the world into being. There follows praise of faith and its reward in the style of the wisdom literature. The "reward" is understood as the holy → Spirit who praises the saving acts of God in hymn and confession (Exod. 14:31; 15:1). Compared with the underlying OT text, the fact of the faith of the people stands in the foreground. There is a hope in the future, but the whole is lacking in enthusiasm.

(b) In the Qumran tradition the basic passage Hab. 2:4 was interpreted of "all doers of the law," and thus of the members of the community. God will save them from the house of judgment on account of their suffering and their faithfulness to the teacher of righteousness (1QpHab 8:1–3). The doing of the law is here the supreme and decisive idea. Faithfulness to the teacher, on the other hand, means holding to the knowledge revealed to him.

(c) The idea of faith played a particular role in later apocalyptic literature, because expectation of the future made a radical demand of faith. The doing of the law and the setting forth of the apocalyptic expectation began to be distinguished (2 Esd. 9:7; Syr. Bar. 57:2). Yet the close connection continued (Syr. Bar. 54:5, 21). The revelation of eschatological truth was at the same time the requital of obedience and disobedience. "For assuredly he who believes will receive reward" (Syr. Bar. 54:16). In these apocalyptic circles the concept of faith was used to help draw a dividing line between the true community and their opponents. In so doing, the ecstatic element receded behind the wisdom teaching tradition.

(d) In Hel. Judaism, faith as the confession of the OT revelation stood in opposition to the surrounding pagan world. It served to distinguish the difference with paganism and the gulf between them. At the same time, it raised the question of the roots of human knowledge in the area of common culture, life-style and wisdom. The contrast between the "godless" and the "righteous" and their differing views of life is typical of wisdom literature (Wis. 2:1 ff.; 3:1 ff.). Faith in wisdom belongs to the teaching about righteousness and wisdom (1:2; 3:9). It is expressed in fixed formulae: *hoi pepoithotes*, those who trust (→ *peithomai*); *hoi pistoi*, the faithful; *hoi eklektoi*, the elect (→ Elect, art. *eklegomai*). Faith stands in a fixed tradition; knowing and proving one's worth constitute the authentic testimony. 4 Macc. 15:24; 16:22; and 17:2 also contain a given element as a foundation (*hē pros theon pistis*, the faith in God). Faith enters the realm of philosophical interpretation and becomes an outlook and a virtue.

In Philo too faith in God can be trust, and the presupposition of all human existence and conduct. In his relation to God the wise man is the "believer"; for his part God bestows trust through his promises (*Abr.*, 268 ff.; 272 ff.). As formerly in Judaism at large, faith is regarded as the source and sum of every other attitude.

As in 4 Macc., faith for Philo can also be taught and learnt. One can learn to distinguish between what changes and what does not (*Leg. All.*, 2, 89). Josephus sets beside each other statements about the right view of God (*orthē doxa*) and trust in God (*hē peri tou theou pistis*), thus giving expression to the Hel. didactic and the OT traditions (*Ap.*, 2, 169, 256). In the description of the messianic tempter, use of the *pistis*-group of words is naturally lacking.

(e) Samaritan religion stressed the meaning of faith more strongly than Judaism, as is shown by the role of Haggadah, teaching and confession. [On the Samaritans see further J. Macdonald, *The Theology of the Samaritans*, 1964.]

NT *pistis* in the NT and the call made to man in the name of God involve a renunciation of existing cult piety and rab. teaching. It was also the special mark of primitive Christian missionary preaching in the Hel. world (R. Bultmann, *TDNT* VI 203 ff., 208 f.). Nevertheless, there are several stages in the early Christian tradition which may not be overlooked. The preaching of John the Baptist set repentance at the centre with a resolute one-sidedness. The earliest preaching of the kingdom of God was also subordinate to the demand of repentance (Matt. 3:2; 4:17). It is impossible to demonstrate a demand for faith in the passages concerning John (cf. A. Schlatter, *Der Evangelist Matthäus*, 1963⁶ 52–85; see also bibliography). And yet his overthrow of all contrived security (Matt. 3:9) is reminiscent of the tension between 'āman and false bāṭaḥ. Moreover, the mission of the Baptist raises the question of its legitimacy and thus also of faith (expressly in Matt. 21:25, 32). Nevertheless, despite all the implied elements of faith, neither Qumran, nor John the Baptist, nor yet the ancient zealot movements made any explicit demand of faith. Only in the post-Easter situation of the primitive Christian mission was the programme developed: "Repent and believe the gospel" (Mk. 1:15). The gospel became a fixed tradition of teaching which laid legitimate claim to be received by every hearer. The call to repent in the Baptist's preaching (Mk. 1:4) was taken up into the faith-preaching of the Hel. Christian tradition. It is this development that is to be examined in the following survey.

The NT use of the *pistis/pisteuō* word-group involves in the first instance the further development of the OT and Jewish tradition and the questions peculiar to it. The frequent use of *pisteuō eis*, believe in (e.g. Gal. 2:16; Jn. 1:12; 3:18), in the vocabulary of mission, is a striking departure from ordinary Gk. and the LXX. *hoti*-sentences (believe *that* . . .) which relate faith to a particular event in the history of Jesus (1 Thess. 4:14; Rom. 10:9), or to a christological statement (Jn. 20:31), are significant for the linguistic usage of the Hel. church. They involve the incorporation of a specific, historical content into the christological confession. "Repentance from dead works" and "faith in God" were important elements in the teaching of the primitive Christian catechism (Heb. 6:1). More important is the pointed use of *pistis* in the context of Pauline theology to denote the reception of Christian → proclamation and the saving faith which was called forth by the gospel (Rom. 1:8; 1 Thess. 1:8). For Paul *pistis* is indissolubly bound with proclamation. Early Christian missionary preaching thus brought faith into sharp focus.

1. *Jesus and the Synoptic Tradition.* The miracle stories often contain reference to the faith of the sick person or those around him (Mk. 2:5; 5:34, 36; 10:52; Matt. 8:10). What is meant is trust in the mission of Jesus and his power to deliver

from trouble. These saving acts are performed in the service of his commission and are intended to confirm an existing faith. The question of faith is clearly bound up with these miracle stories. Jesus did not only seek to deliver people from physical need, but to make men witnesses of his saving work. It is not a matter of making a condition upon which he will act. Rather, he is concerned with the goal beyond the physical process. His intention was not to be a mere "healer", but to be a helper in God's name. He was therefore more concerned to ask for faith than to demand it. Man's trust presents the possibility for God to do his work. It is thus only a start and a first step to what was to be declared later by the Hel. church.

Mk. 6:5 f. contains an account of the opposition in Nazareth, Jesus' home town. Refusal to believe was so strong that he could perform no "mighty works". He confined himself to helping a number of sick individuals. If his saving work was bound up with faith, refusal to believe likewise brought conflict with him. The evangelists did not intend to convey the impression that it was absolutely impossible for Jesus to do "mighty works" here because of the unbelief of the Nazarenes. The accounts of Jesus' teaching contain several sayings which appear to go beyond the specific situation in which they occur (Mk. 9:23; 11:22 ff.; Lk. 17:5 f.; Matt. 17:20). The distinctive feature of these sayings about faith consists in the fact that they present the believer with unlimited possibilities, and that Jesus expressly summons his disciples to this boundless faith. Despite all the external similarities with rab. parallels, these sayings of Jesus stand isolated in the tradition. Their emphatic, confessional tone is at once apparent. Jesus himself lived by faith. He submitted to its possibilities, and encouraged men to follow his example (cf. J. Schniewind, *Das Evangelium nach Markus*, (1931) 1968, 120). The pictures of faith moving mountains (Mk. 11:23) and uprooting the fig tree (Lk. 17:6) confirm the word of power that is able to transform the created order. The instructions to the disciples in Mk. 11:24 f. show the connection in the teaching between the promise that rests upon the word of power and supplication. The supplication is the prerequisite of the word of power.

Faith in God means for Jesus being open to the possibilities that God presents (cf. Mk. 11:22: *echete pistin theou*, have faith in God). It also involves a reckoning with God which is not simply content with the thing given and the events that have come about. Expressions like *echein pistin theou* (to have faith in God, Mk. 11:22) and *prostithenai pistin* (increase faith, Lk. 17:5) show how Jesus' teaching on faith was subsequently understood. There was a special kind of faith in God or Jesus-faith. The antithesis between small and great (Lk. 17:6; Matt. 17:20) presents a contrast between the human attitude and the greatness of the promise. What takes place in man is small compared with the greatness that comes from God. However, Jesus spoke of a boundless faith as if of something new. He did not build on something that was already there, but upon something new. Yet his teaching was quite distinct from wild enthusiasm, because it was not divorced from constant wrestling with God and speaking with him. It stood within the circle of trust (Heb. *biṭṭāḥôn*) and knowledge (*da'at*). Jesus turned to the individual, because his people as a whole were summoned to the decision of faith (Lk. 19:42). Statements about faith in the synoptic tradition are always qualified. One might see here later influences (cf. the imperative *metanoeite*, repent, in the light of the reception of the message of salvation). But it must not be forgotten that every summons and statement of Jesus contained the elements of faith, trust, knowledge, decision, obedience and self-direction. The preaching of Jesus cannot be understood apart from the many-sided aspects of faith (Heb. *'emûnâh*) and trust (Heb. *biṭṭāḥôn*). The faith of Jesus was directed towards reality. It was deeply involved in the act of living, and was on a completely different plane from hypothetical abstractions.

2. *Paul and the Pauline Tradition*. Paul's teaching presupposes a continuity with the teaching of the Palestinian Jewish and the Hel. church. His calling by the risen Lord led him to grapple with the particular questions raised by the churches. He addressed his readers as "believers" (*hoi pisteuontes*, Rom. 1:16; 3:22; 4:11; 1 Cor. 1:21). Their turning to God is described as "believing" (*pisteuein*, 1 Cor. 15:2, 11). "Faith" means receiving the message of salvation and conduct based on the gospel (*hē pistis*, Rom. 1:8; 1 Cor. 2:5; 15:14, 17). It is explicitly a saving faith, based on the → cross of Jesus and his → resurrection (1 Cor. 15:3–4:11). The unique event is the divinely appointed norm which determines every theological statement and every aspect of Christian conduct. This is shown by the debate with the Jews and Judaism. Both started from the validity of the old → covenant and the → law. Both misunderstood the point of eschatological existence. It is also shown by the conflict with Hel. enthusiasm and gnosticism which misconstrued the future and eschatology. The → righteousness received by faith (*ek pisteōs, dia pisteōs, eis pistin*, of faith, through faith, in faith) is a gift of → grace. It contradicts all human boasting and undermines any attempt to base man's relationship with God on doing the law (Gal. 3:10 ff., 23 ff.; Rom. 3:27–31). The new → covenant supersedes the old both in its historical form and its effect on men (Gal. 3:23 ff.; 4:21–31; 2 Cor. 3:6). Faith recognizes the eschatological saving event which was anticipated in the call of → Abraham (Rom. 4:9 ff.; Gal. 3:17 ff.); it finds its goal in the Gentile mission (Rom. 4:17 ff.; Gal. 3:26–29). In the debate with Hel. enthusiasm and gnosticism which were based on a speculative understanding of baptism and the gift of the Spirit, Paul stressed historical facts and also his eschatological goal (2 Cor. 5:7). Since faith contains the element of being sustained (Heb. *'āman*), as well as trust (Heb. *bāṭaḥ*), it merges into hope (Rom. 8:24; 1 Cor. 13:13).

Of special importance is the way Paul's teaching links together the triad of faith, hope and love (1 Thess. 3:5, 8; 1 Cor. 13:13; Col. 1:4 f.). It is not a matter of calling upon men to adopt Hel. virtues. Faith, hope and love are different aspects of the Christian life, derived from the kerygma, which form the basis of the life of the church. It is questionable whether non-Christian lists may be traced behind the Pauline triad (cf. however the fourfold list in Porphyry, *Ad Marcellam*, 24). If the gnostics were inclined to have "lists", the unspeculative character of the Pauline triad is all the more striking. The transforming eschatological prospective reveals the difference: faith and → hope come to fulfilment; → love alone determines the new aeon (1 Cor. 13:13; → Time, art. *aiōn*). The Pauline triad must not be regarded as charismatic gifts, for they are quite distinct from the latter. They are the practical application of the gospel itself and are obligatory for all members of the church without exception. Charismatic gifts have a structure different from the Pauline exposition of the triad (→ Grace, art. *charis*). On the other hand, Paul's endeavour to set out the fullness of gifts in his doctrine of the Spirit led him to include faith as a gift along with the others (1 Cor. 12:9). Justifying faith is not meant here. Nor

601

perhaps is it the "all faith" that can remove mountains (1 Cor. 13:2). What is clear is that it is distinct from "the utterance of wisdom" and "the utterance of knowledge" which are mentioned previously (1 Cor. 12:8).

There is a tension between the invisible that cannot be seen (*ta mē blepomena*) and the visible. This points to the fact that we do not have the future at our disposal. There is a contrast between what is accessible to men and what is accessible to God alone (2 Cor. 4:18; 5:7). The invisible is not the Platonic immaterial world, but the goal of Christian existence perceived in faith and trust. The → cross of Christ is always the focal point of attack against legalism (Gal. 2:21) and speculative wisdom (1 Cor. 1:17). The resurrection opens the way to the gift of a new existence through baptism (Rom. 6:4; 2 Cor. 5:17).

Gal. 5:6 suggests a fixed formula: "For in Christ Jesus neither circumcision nor uncircumcision is of any avail, but faith working through love" (cf. 6:15; 1 Cor. 7:19). Through → baptism a new law has come into operation which transcends all previous differences. The will of God which was expressed in the demands of the law finds its eschatological fulfilment in love. This solution which Paul stresses heavily places faith in the context of eschatological transformation. It thus corresponds directly with Paul's doctrine of the → Spirit. His teaching on faith and the gift of the Spirit are brought together in baptism.

Another important aspect of Paul's teaching is his understanding of the life of faith, characterized by the tension between indicative and imperative (cf. R. Bultmann, *Theology of the New Testament*, I, 1952, 332 f.). The justified believer who has been baptized finds himself in a struggle between the → Spirit and the → flesh (Rom. 8:4 ff.; Gal. 5:16 ff.). He is called upon not to evade the tasks of the Spirit. Without obedience to the tasks of the Spirit, faith does not gain the power required in the conflict (1 Cor. 2:4).

The notion of being "weak" in faith (Rom. 14:1) introduces a particular discussion. It is bound up with making critical judgments. Paul does not evade this. For there is such a thing as growth in faith (2 Cor. 10:15), steadfastness in faith (1 Cor. 15:58), and self-critical examination as to whether one's own attitude springs from faith (cf. the important statement in Rom. 14:23). All these exhortations starkly show how faith is not only exposed to critical judgment, but submits itself repeatedly to it. The fact that the gospel finds its ultimate expression and foundation in the cross of Christ means that faith must constantly measure itself by this norm. Faith is dynamic movement which involves adjustment and self-adjustment. In this respect also the situation corresponds to the doctrine of the Spirit.

Eph. 4:3 calls for the maintenance of "the unity of the Spirit". The exhortation moves in a direction which was subsequently to prove momentous. Despite diversity of groups and differences of opinion, post-apostolic tradition endeavoured to maintain a general outlook. Eph. 4:5 speaks of "one faith" (*mia pistis*) together with "one Lord" and "one baptism", as if this triad reflected the baptismal act. The common outlook conferred by baptism is a process directed towards a goal (Eph. 4:13). It is guided by Christ himself.

3. *The Johannine Tradition.* Here, as in the Heb., the vb. comes to the forefront. The noun is found only occasionally in the epistles (1 Jn. 5:4) and Rev. (2:13, 19; 13:10; 14:12). The adj. *pistos* (the opposite of which is *apistos*) can be applied to Jesus, his witnesses and the church (Rev. 1:5; 2:10; 31; 1 Jn. 1:9; 20:27). The link

with Semitic thought is clear especially in Rev. Faith, and the act of believing, assume the character of fidelity. Rev. also contains didactic lists of qualities and actions in which "works" (*erga*) predominate (2:2, 19), *pistis* here comes close to being the motive of faithfulness (2:19). It is basic for the Johannine tradition that the attitude of faith should be modelled on and formed by the testimony recognized by the church. This testimony is also important for the Gospel, where testimony is based on historical witness.

The thought-forms are different from elsewhere in the NT. Faith arises out of testimony, authenticated by God, in which signs also play a part. It is addressed to all men (Jn. 1:7). The claim to be true and truthful (→ Truth) underlines the fact that it is authenticated by God. Hence, the man who is of the truth hears this call of God (Jn. 18:37). Faith and knowledge (Jn. 6:69), knowledge and faith (Jn. 17:8; 1 Jn. 4:6), are not two processes distinct from each other, but instructive co-ordinates which speak of the reception of the testimony from different stand-points. Faith alone which receives the testimony possesses knowledge; he who knows the truth is pointed to faith. The co-ordination of knowledge and faith is anti-gnostic and anti-speculative. The hearer should understand that both are involved in salvation: acceptance of the testimony as well as personal response and reformation that conforms to the testimony. The distinction in Jn. 4:42 is important.

Faith and life are intimately connected. He who believes in the Son has the promise that he will not perish but have eternal life (Jn. 3:16 ff.; 11:25). The → promise points to a → fulfilment that lies already in the present. The enmity of the world towards God is not a metaphysical one; it is a reaction to the one sent by God (Jn. 3:20; 7:7; 15:18, 23). Even the disciples are drawn into it. The believer is able to endure this conflict with the world through no longer being subject to its motive power and by seeking the will of God (1 Jn. 2:15 ff.). The tension between the believer and the → world is not therefore seen in a speculative manner. The blessing pronounced on those who believe, even though they have not seen, belongs to the complex of questions raised by the Easter tradition. This is not intended as a criticism of the apostolic Easter tradition preserved in the synoptic gospels. Rather, it gives to later generations the same access to the joy of Easter. R. Bultmann takes the opposite view (*The Gospel of John*, 1971, 696).

The original saving event belongs in the past. A new set of problems arises with each new generation to whom are addressed the two sayings: "who have not seen and yet believe" (Jn. 20:29) and "without having seen him you love him" (1 Pet. 1:8). The double application to Jesus in 1 Pet. 1:8 ("without having seen him you love him; though you do not now see him you believe in him with an unutterable and exalted joy") suggests contact with the Johannine tradition. In general, however, the series of exhortations, in which faith and love are presented together in various Hel. contexts, come later (cf. 1 Tim. 2:15; 4:12; 6:11; 2 Tim. 2:22). But here too we do not have the simple appropriation of Hel. virtues. Rather, they represent further instruction for new situations in life which developed out of baptismal teaching.

4. *The Understanding of Faith in the Rest of the NT*. The linguistic usage of Acts frequently points back to formulae and expressions drawn from the terminology of mission. People come to faith in God (16:34), or in the Lord (5:14; 18:8).

Exhortations to faith are directly connected with the promise of eschatological salvation (16:31). There is also a new trust in Christian circles in "what is written" (24:14; 26:27). There thus grew up a way of looking at salvation history analogous to Jewish Hel. piety (cf. the continuity expressed in 2 Tim. 1:5).

Heb. represents an independent tradition of teaching. It makes extensive use of OT motifs, and draws upon the history of the patriarchs in connection with words of the *pistis*-group. In its exhortation, Heb. takes up the promise of faith and the warning against unbelief (Heb. 10:37 f. = Hab. 2:3 f.). Above all, Heb. 11:1 presents an instructive definition which combines OT and Hel. motifs: "Now faith is the assurance of things hoped for, the conviction of things not seen" (RSV). This is not a comprehensive summary of all the elements in faith, but of those which were fundamental for a church under persecution: assurance of what is hoped for and conviction of being led by what cannot be seen. The future and what is hidden from view are here closely connected. This definition introduces the survey of patriarchal history in ch. 11 and the picture of the NT church in 12:1–11. Jesus Christ appears as the "pioneer and perfecter of our faith" (Heb. 12:2). He has been made perfect by God and can now bring the struggle for perfection to its conclusion. As those given the promise, the people of God are charged with acting upon faith. The next world is the goal promised by the word of God. The tension between the here and now and the beyond which characterized Hel. tradition thus finds new expression.

The essence of Paul's thought reappears in the Pastoral Epistles. But it is restated in a context that is opposed to wild enthusiasm and gnostic false teaching. 1 Tim. 1:5 puts forward the thesis: "the aim of our charge is love that issues from a pure heart and a good conscience and sincere faith" (RSV). A tendency opposed to enthusiasm may be detected here. The command to love is reformulated so as to include faith. Soundness in faith (Tit. 1:13; 2:2) sets a new standard that distinguishes the Christian life from all false teaching. The overtones of philosophy and wisdom strengthen the self-awareness of a church that is consolidating itself.

As in the paraenetic tradition elsewhere, Jas. is conscious of the need to prove faith (1:3; cf. 1 Pet. 1:7). He demands renunciation of all conduct that conflicts with living faith and confession (1:6 ff.). For him, faith and obedient conduct are indissolubly linked. Faith understood merely as trust and confession is not able to save. Only through obedience (→ Hear, art. *hypakoē*) and conduct which fulfills the commandments of God does faith come to completion (Jas. 2:22). The opponent that Jas. has in mind does not attack faith but exempts himself from obedience.

([Ed.] Some scholars hold that James's teaching stands in conflict with that of Paul, especially on the question of → justification. It would seem that Jas. is replying to those who have taken Paul's doctrine of justification by faith out of context, assuming that Paul's repudiation of works as the ground of justification relieved them of the need for good works and a changed life. Thus they may have taken Rom. 4:3 and Gal. 3:6 (= Gen. 15:6) and ignored Rom. 6:1 ff.; 12:1 ff.; Gal. 5:15–26. It is striking that Jas. also quotes Gen. 15:6 in Jas. 2:23. He also illustrates his argument by referring to the example of → Abraham. But whereas Paul appeals to Abraham's belief in the promise of God which was the occasion of the verdict of justification in Gen. 15, Jas. appeals to the story in Gen. 22 which shows Abraham's willingness to sacrifice Isaac. Jas. 2:22 draws the conclusion: "You

604

see that faith was active along with his works, and faith was completed by works."
It may be said that for both Paul and James "justify" means to *declare righteous*.
In the case of Paul, it is God who declares the believer righteous. In the case of Jas.,
it is a man's works which declare him righteous by showing that he is a man of
faith. For the thesis which Jas. wishes to argue is that "faith by itself, if it has no
works, is dead" (2:17).)

5. *The Act, Structure and Content of Faith.* Christianity is a unique faith-event. The
act of faith, together with the thought-forms and structures bound up with it and
the relevant relations and norms (the gospel, the kerygma, the word of God), have
a special significance in Christianity. It is striking that in the early church there
were other thought-forms which were originally autonomous (e.g. which started
from the Spirit or from knowledge) and which continued to exist in tension with
the faith-event. Christianity came to be seen as a faith-event, because this gave the
most powerful expression to its understanding of the historical situation and its
outlook in view of the claims of the gospel. It is only in relation to the gospel and
the claims of the word of God that faith can declare what it has to say. The Christian knows that he has received grace and is summoned to follow a particular path
towards a goal. The saving act of God goes before him. The basis of faith is God's
revelation of himself. Faith remains subordinate to knowledge; but knowledge
belongs to the substance of faith. *O. Michel*

→ Law, → Works

(a). J. B. Bauer and H. Zimmermann, "Faith," *EBT* I 237–43; G. Bornkamm, "Faith and Reason
in Paul," *Early Christian Experience*, 1969, 29–46; R. Bring, "Paul and the Old Testament. A
Study of Election, Faith, and Law, in Paul, with Special Reference to Rom. 9:30–10:30," *StTh*
25, 1971, 21–60; M. Buber, *Two Types of Faith*, 1961; R. Bultmann, *Theology of the New Testa-
ment*, I, 1952, 314–29; II, 1955, 70–92; and *peithō, TDNT* VI 1–11; J. Burchill, "On Faith in Paul,"
The Bible Today 53, 1971, 296–304; C. E. B. Cranfield, "*Metron pisteōs* in Rom. xii. 3," *NTS* 8,
1961–2, 345–51; and *A Commentary on Romans 12–13*, *SJT* Occasional Papers 12, 1965; C. H.
Dodd, *Gospel and Law*, 1951; and *The Interpretation of the Fourth Gospel*, 1953, 179–86; G.
Ebeling, *The Nature of Faith*, 1961; and *Word and Faith*, 1963; D. Evans, "Faith and Belief",
Religious Studies 10, 1974, 1–20; G. Foley, *Christ and Faith: Their Relationship in Contemporary
Theology*, 1971; V. P. Furnish, *Theology and Ethics in Paul*, 1968, 181–94; E. Fuchs, "Jesus and
Faith," *Studies of the Historical Jesus*, 1964, 48–64; W. H. P. Hatch, *The Pauline Idea of Faith
in its Relation to Jewish and Hellenistic Religion*, 1917; and *The Idea of Faith in Christian Litera-
ture from the Death of St. Paul to the Close of the Second Century*, 1926; P. Helm, *The Varieties
of Belief*, 1973; J. Hick, *Faith and Knowledge*, 1966²; J. Hick, ed., *Faith and the Philosophers*, 1964;
W. F. Howard, *Christianity according to St. John*, 1943, 151–73; H. Ljungman, *Pistis: A Study
of its Presuppositions and its Meaning in Pauline Use*, 1964; P. S. Minear, *The Obedience of
Faith*, 1971; J. Munck, *Paul and the Salvation of Mankind*, 1959, 196–209; E. D. O'Connor,
Faith in the Synoptic Gospels: A Problem in the Correlation of Scripture and Theology, 1961;
J. Painter, "Eschatological Faith in the Gospel of John," in R. Banks, ed., *Reconciliation and
Hope*, (Leon Morris Festschrift) 1974, 36–52; J. J. O'Rourke, "Pistis in Romans," *CBQ* 35, 1973,
188–94; P. Stachin, "The Concept of Faith in the Johannine Writings," *Logos* 22, 1971, 115–30;
T. F. Torrance, "One Aspect of the Biblical Conception of Faith," *ExpT* 68, 1956–7, 111–14; A.
Weiser and R. Bultmann, *pistis* etc., *TDNT* VI 174–228.
(b). H. Binder, *Der Glaube bei Paulus*, 1968; M. E. Boismard, "La foi selon S. Paul," *Lumière et
Vie* 22, 1955, 65–89; A. M. Denis, "Foi et Exégèse: Réflexions sur les Fondements Théologiques,"
NTS 20, 1973–74, 45–54; C. Dietzfelbinger, *Paulus und das Alte Testament*, ThEH 95, 1961; G. Eich-
holz, *Glaube und Werk bei Paulus und Jakobus*, ThEH 88, 1961; E. Grässer, *Der Glaube im Hebräerbrief*, 1965; R. Gyllenberg, *Pistis*, I–II, 1922; H.-W. Heidland, *Die Anschauung des Glaubens zur
Gerechtigkeit*, BWANT 4. Folge 18, 1936; J. Huby, "La connaissance de foi dans S. Jean," *RSR* 21,
1931, 385–421; W. G. Kümmel, "Der Glaube im Neuen Testament, seine katholische und

reformatorische Deutung," *Heilsgeschehen und Geschichte*, 1965, 67 ff.; W. Künneth, *Glaube an Jesus? Die Begegnung der Christologie mit der modernen Existenz*, 1962; O. Kuss, "Der Glaube nach den paulinischen Hauptbriefen," *Theologie und Glaube* 46, 1956, 1–26; C. Maurer, "Glaubensbindung und Gewissensfreiheit im Neuen Testament," *ThZ* 17, 1961, 107 ff.; O. Michel, "Grundfragen der Pastoralbriefe auf dem Grunde der Apostel und Propheten," *Festschrift T. Wurm*, 1948, 83 ff.; W. Mundle, *Der Glaubensbegriff des Paulus*, 1932; U. Neuenschwander, *Glaube. Eine Besinnung über Wesen und Begriff des Glaubens*, 1957; F. Neugebauer, *"In Christus." Eine Untersuchung zum paulinischen Glaubensverständnis*, 1961; F. Nötscher, *Zur theologischen Terminologie der Qumrantexte*, 1956; E. Pfeiffer, "Glaube im Alten Testament. Eine grammatische lexikalische Nachprüfung gegenwärtigen Theorien," *ZAW* 71, 1959, 151 ff.; C. H. Ratschow *et. al.*, "Glaube", *RGG*³ II 1586 ff.; A. Schlatter, *Der Glaube im Neuen Testament*, (1905) 1963; T. Soiron, *Glaube, Hoffnung, Liebe*, 1934; P. Stuhlmacher, "Glauben und Verstehen bei Paulus," *EvTh* 26, 1966, 337 ff.; C. Thomassen, *Der Glaube nach Paulus dargestellt an den Hauptbriefen des Apostels*, 1970; P. Valloton, *Le Christ et la foi: Étude de théologie biblique*, 1960; H. Waldenfels, *Glauben hat Zukunft. Orientierungspunkte*, 1970; E. Walter, *Glaube, Hoffnung und Liebe im Neuen Testament*, 1940; H. Wildberger, *'mn, THAT* I 177–209; E. Wissmann, *Das Verhältnis von PISTIS und Christusfrömmigkeit bei Paulus*, *FRLANT* 23, 1926.

Fall, Fall Away

ἀφίστημι

ἀφίστημι (*aphistēmi*), trans. cause to revolt, mislead; intrans. go away, withdraw, depart, fall away; ἀποστασία (*apostasia*), rebellion, abandonment, state of apostasy, defection; ἀποστάσιον (*apostasion*), bill of divorce.

CL *aphistēmi* (Homer), derived from *histēmi*, means trans. to put away, remove:
(a) in a spatial sense; (b) from a condition or relationship; (c) from association with a person. It also means to turn someone (either privately or politically) against a person, to cause to revolt (Herodotus). Intrans. it means to remove oneself, go away; to stand aloof, withdraw from, cease, give up; recoil, separate oneself; to fall away. From it are derived the nouns *apostasis*, revolt (first found in cl. Gk., from the time of Thuc., 1, 122); *apostatēs*, deserter, political rebel (e.g. "against the king", "against the country"; a later term found in Polybius); *apostasia*, a late form of the classical *apostasis*, meaning, state of rebellion or apostasy (e.g. "from Nero"; "from the Romans"); and *apostasion*, a legal term for handing over at purchase, conveyance, and used of a bill of divorce (Deut. 24:1, 3; Matt. 5:31; 19:7; Mk. 10:4; → Divorce).

OT 1. In the LXX words of this group are found more than 250 times, rendering about 40 different Heb. words, but most frequently *hēsîr* (hiph. of *sûr*), to remove (about 65 times). It is of especial interest theologically when used to translate forms of *mā'al*, to act unfaithfully, contrary to duty, or against the law (2 Chr. 26:18; 28:19, 22; 29:6; 30:7; 33:19); *pāša'*, to rebel, transgress (2 Chr. 21:8, 10; Jer. 33:8; Ezek. 20:38); *mārad*, to rebel, revolt (Gen. 14:4; Num. 14:9; Jos. 22:16 ff.; 2 Chr. 13:6; Ezr. 4:12, 15, 19; Neh. 2:19; 6:6; 9:26; Ezek. 17:15; Dan. 9:5, 9); → Sin, art. *paraptōma*.

The meaning of *aphistēmi* and its Heb. equivalents is like that in classical Gk.: removal in a spatial sense (Gen. 12:8), separation of persons (1 Sam. 18:13; Ps. 6:8), withdrawal from a relationship (Num. 8:25) or from a state (Prov. 23:18; Isa. 59:9); political revolt (Gen. 14:4; 2 Chr. 21:8, 10; Ezek. 17:15). This is the most frequent meaning of the word and underlies most of the substantival forms.

A meaning not found in cl. Gk. is the use in religious contexts: God departs from men (Jdg. 16:20; 2 Ki. 17:18; 23:27; Ps. 10:1; Ezek. 23:18) and withdraws his gifts (Num. 14:9, protection; Jdg. 16:17, 19, strength; 2 Sam. 7:15, steadfast love; Isa. 59:11, 14, salvation and righteousness). The underlying cause is man's own wilful departure from God (Deut. 32:15; Jer. 2:19; 3:14; 17:5, 13; Sir. 10:12), and scorn of God's gifts (Num. 14:31, the land; Neh. 9:26, the law). This rebellion expresses itself in the cultic worship of other gods (Deut. 7:4; 13:10, 13; Jos. 22; Jdg. 2:19; 2 Chr. 29:6; 1 Macc. 2:19), and in ethical behaviour constituting disobedience towards God (Isa. 30:1; Ezek. 33:8; Dan. 9:9–11; Sir. 48:15; 2 Macc. 5:8). It is against this background that we should understand the exhortations to keep aloof from sin (Exod. 23:7; Ps. 119:29; Isa. 52:11; Tob. 4:21; Sir. 7:2; 23:12; 35:3).

2. At Qumran the act of turning away from the community and its rules is fundamentally condemned as apostasy. The literature of the sect sets down a two-year period of repentance for the apostate member who is willing to return (1QS 7:18 ff.); but anyone who has belonged to the community for more than 10 years is completely excluded if he becomes guilty of apostasy (1QS 7:22 ff.).

NT 1. In the NT this group of words is found only in Luke (*aphistēmi* 10 times and twice in *v.l.*; *apostasia* Acts 21:21), Paul (*aphistēmi* 3 times, and 1 Tim. 6:5 *v.l.*; *apostasia* 2 Thess. 2:3), and Heb. 3:12. Apart from Acts 5:37, only the intrans. sense is found. On *apostasion* → Divorce.

2. *aphistēmi* occurs in the spatial sense in Lk. 2:37 ("she did not leave the temple"). More often it refers to the separation of people: holding back from carrying out a punishment (Acts 5:38; 22:29); the withdrawal of Mark from helping Paul in his work (Acts 15:38); the departure of the Christians from the Jewish synagogue (Acts 19:9); the disappearance of supernatural beings from human presence (Lk. 1:38 *v.l.*; 4:13; 24:51 *v.l.*; Acts 12:10; 2 Cor. 12:8). In Lk. 13:26, 27 (citation of Ps. 6:8) believers are warned against unfruitful discipleship. By having set before them in this parable the possibility of being too late, they are called away from their speculative enquiry (v. 23) to face a genuine decision that affects them in their total existence. The man who fails to recognize and grasp the present hour of grace may one day find himself separated for ever from the Lord: *apostēte ap' emou*, depart from me (v. 27).

In 2 Tim. 2:19 *aphistēmi* refers to moral behaviour: "Let everyone who names the name of the Lord depart from iniquity." Acts 5:37 mentions political defection.

3. Of theological importance is falling away in the religious sense. In Acts 21:21 (cf. 2 Macc. 5:8; Jas. 2:11 *v.l.*) Paul is accused of leading the Diaspora Jews astray by teaching them to disregard the OT law. The absolute use of *apostasia* in 2 Thess. 2:3 is a common expression in Jewish apocalyptic, with its prophecy of a period of apostasy shortly before the appearance of the Messiah (Eth. En. 5:4; 93:9). Paul locates this event in an anti-Christian period directly preceding the return of Christ. 1 Tim. 4:1 describes "falling away from the faith" in the last days in terms of falling into false, heretical beliefs. Lk. 8:13 probably refers to apostasy as a result of eschatological temptation. Here are people who have come to believe, who have received the gospel "with joy". But under the pressure of persecution and tribulation arising because of the faith, they break off the relationship with God into

which they have entered. According to Heb. 3:12 (cf. Heb. 6:6 → *piptō* below; → Sin, art. *paraptōma*), apostasy consists in an unbelieving and self-willed movement away from God (in contrast to Heb. 3:14), which must be prevented at all costs.

aphistēmi thus connotes in the passages just mentioned the serious situation of becoming separated from the living God after a previous turning towards him, by falling away from the faith. It is a movement of unbelief and sin, which can also be expressed by other words (cf. the par. to Lk. 8:13 in Matt. 13:21; Mk. 4:17; → Offence, art. *skandalon*). Expressions equivalent in meaning to the warning in 1 Tim. 4:1 include *nauageō*, suffer shipwreck, 1:19; *astocheō* miss the mark, 1:6; 6:21, 2 Tim. 2:18; cf. also *aperchomai*, go away, Jn. 6:66; *apostrephō*, turn away; *arneomai*, deny; *metatithēmi*, change, alter; *mē menein*, do not abide, Jn. 15:6; → art. *piptō*; → Lead Astray, art. *planaō*; and the pictures of defection in Matt. 24:9–12, and Rev. 13. As can be seen from a consideration of the Heb. words in the LXX corresponding to *aphistēmi*, it emphasizes strongly, like *parapiptō* (Heb. 6:6), the part played by the human → will in the loss of → faith.

πίπτω

πίπτω (*piptō*), fall; ἐκπίπτω (*ekpiptō*), fall off or from, lose one's way; καταπίπτω (*katapiptō*), fall down; παραπίπτω (*parapiptō*), fall beside, fall away; περιπίπτω (*peripiptō*), fall into, among; πτῶμα (*ptōma*), that which has fallen, corpse; πτῶσις (*ptōsis*), falling, fall.

CL *piptō* (root *pet*, to fall, fly, reduplicated; cf. Lat. *peto*, fall upon, attach, beg) has the basic meaning to fall, drop from a height or from an upright position; of men, to fall in battle, but also, to fall into life, i.e. to be born (Homer, *Il.*, 19, 110). It is also used of falling intentionally, to throw oneself down. In a fig. sense *piptō* means to fly into a rage, to fall into misfortune, shame, etc., to fall by the wayside (but not implying guilt in the sense of a moral lapse); also to fall utterly, be ruined.

The noun *ptōsis*, act of falling, and *ptōma*, that which has fallen, signify fall, collapse, and fig. misfortune, disaster, destruction. *ptōma*, like *piptō*, has the special meaning of that which has fallen of a living being, i.e. a corpse, especially of one killed violently.

ekpiptō means to fall out of something, to go out of something, e.g. to lose the way, to give up hope; in the pass. sense, to be driven out, excluded, or to lose something. As a technical naval term it means to be driven off course, to drift, to be cast ashore, because of inability to follow the course on which one has set out.

peripiptō, to fall around, fall in. It is also used of events which befall one. *parapiptō* means lit. fall beside, befall, go astray, err.

OT The LXX mostly uses *piptō* to translate forms of *nāpal*, which is almost exactly equivalent in meaning. The group of words exhibits here the same broad range of meaning as it does outside the Bible. *piptō* has a fig. meaning for the most part in the OT Wisdom Literature: to have a mishap through no fault of one's own (Ps. 37:4; Prov. 24:16; Eccl. 4:10); to go to ruin, be destroyed (e.g. Job 18:12,
608

ptōma; Prov. 24:17; Sir. 5:13, *ptōsis*). The mode of expression remains concrete even in metaphorical use: "the ungodly fall into unrighteousness" (Prov. 11:5; cf. Isa. 8:14; Jer. 8:4; Mic. 7:8). The NT sense of to lose one's salvation has no parallel in the OT. The most that one can say is that it is foreshadowed in Prov. 11:28; Sir. 1:30; 2:7. The meaning to → sin, is found only where *parapiptō* is used (Ezek. 14:13; 15:8; 18:24; 20:27 = Heb. *mā'al*; Wis. 6:9; 12:2).

NT 1. In the NT the words of this group are found most often in the literal sense: of the collapse of buildings (Heb. 11:30 = Jos. 6:5, 20; Lk. 13:4; cf. Isa. 30:25); of things falling flat or falling down (Matt. 15:27; 13:4–8 par.; Jn. 12:24), especially the falling off of dead flowers as an image of the shortness of life and speedy change (1 Pet. 1:24 and Jas. 1:11 = Isa. 40:7; cf. Job 14:2; 15:33), the falling of → animals (Matt. 10:29; cf. Amos 3:5; Matt. 12:11; cf. Exod. 21:33), and the unintentional falling of → men (Matt. 15:14; cf. Isa. 24:18; Jer. 48:44; Acts 20:9; Mk. 9:20; Matt. 17:15).

2. Even abstract things like fear and darkness can be said to fall on someone. The word here conveys the idea of suddenness and inescapability. Generally it is a heavenly vision or some other manifestation of God which brings this about (Lk. 1:12; Acts 13:11; 19:17; Rev. 11:11, cf. Gen. 15:12; Exod. 15:16; Job 13:11; Ps. 55:5). In the same way it is said that God's Spirit "falls" upon people, i.e. the Spirit of God comes with irresistible power, as a divine intervention which silences all opposition and doubt (Acts 10:44; 11:15; cf. 8:16; 1 Sam. 18:10, Ezek. 11:5).

3. The words appear in idiomatic sayings found also outside the Bible. When a person's love is aroused, he has the urge to "fall on someone's neck" (Lk. 15:20; Acts 20:37; cf. Gen. 45:14; 46:29). The "falling" of the lot indicates a decision having nothing to do with human choice, a divine verdict (Acts 1:26; cf. Ps. 16:6; Jon. 1:7). "Not a hair shall fall from your head" means "No evil will befall you" (Acts 27:34; cf. 1 Sam. 14:45; 2 Sam. 14:11). "To fall into the hands of" means to be given up to (Heb. 10:31; cf. Jdg. 11:18; 2 Sam. 24:14; Sir. 2:18; 8:1). The phrase "to fall into a snare" (in the OT Prov. 12:13; Sir. 9:3; Tob. 14:10) is derived from the language of hunting: snares are set and hidden, and an animal gets caught. It is the same with the devil's snare (1 Tim. 3:7; 6:9; cf. Jas. 1:2). "To fall into condemnation" (1 Tim. 3:6; Jas. 5:12) means to give grounds for accusation later resulting in a verdict of guilty.

4. Like the OT (Jos. 21:45; 23:14; 1 Sam. 3:19; 2 Ki. 10:10), the NT says that God's word does not "fall to the ground", but retains its validity and efficacy (Lk. 16:17, of the law; Rom. 9:6, of God's promises; cf. 1 Pet. 1:24). Love will not "fail" either (1 Cor. 13:8), since faith, hope and love form the three unchanging gifts of God's grace which, in contrast to all the others, alone have permanence (v. 13).

5. "To fall on one's face" (usually intentionally) before someone (in the OT, for instance, Gen. 17:3, 17; 44:14; Ruth 2:10; 2 Sam. 1:2; Ps. 95:6; Ezek. 11:13) is an expression of deferential greeting (Jn. 11:32). Thus slaves indicate in this way their subjection to their master (Matt. 18:26). It emphasizes a request (Matt. 18:29; Mk. 5:22; 7:25; Lk. 5:12), or thanksgiving (Lk. 17:16). It is the humblest posture for prayer (Matt. 26:39), and the attitude of self-abasing reverence (before a king, Matt. 2:11; a supernatural being, 4:9; Acts 10:25; Rev. 19:10; 22:8; God and

609

Christ, 1 Cor. 14:25; Rev. 4:10). It can be the effect of a revelation of God (Matt. 17:6; Lk. 5:8; Acts 9:4; 16:29; cf. Mk. 5:33; Jn. 18:6; Rev. 1:17; in the OT, 1 Ki. 18:39; Ezek. 1:28; Dan. 8:17; 10:9). → Prayer, arts. *gonypeteō* and *proskyneō*.

6. *piptō* can also mean to fall down dead, to be killed (Lk. 21:24; Acts 5:5, 10; 28:6; 1 Cor. 10:8; Heb. 3:17; Rev. 17:10). *ptōma*, corpse (in the OT, Jdg. 14:8; Ps. 110:6; Ezek. 6:5), is used of human corpses (Matt. 14:12; Mk. 15:45; Rev. 11:8 f.) and perhaps also animal carcasses in Matt. 24:28. It marks the place where the vultures gather (→ Bird). The connection with v. 27 is perhaps to be found in the sense that just as certainly as the carcass does not remain hidden from the vultures, so at the end everyone will see the coming Messiah. ([Ed.] But in the context of judgment on Israel and Jerusalem a human body may be meant.)

7. The words are used in a number of ways in the portrayal of apocalyptic horrors of the end-time. Everything that is makeshift will collapse in a flood-like catastrophe (Matt. 7:25, 27). Great parts of cities (Rev. 11:13), indeed whole cities (16:19), will become heaps of ruins. The great world-power, hostile to God, will be overthrown (Rev. 14:8; 18:2; cf. Isa. 21:9; Jer. 51:8). In their terror at the desolation of the last days, men will cry out in their longing to die for a great earthquake which will make mountains with their rock faces fall upon them (Lk. 23:30; Rev. 6:16; cf. Hos. 10:8; Ezek. 38:20). In a cosmic upheaval the stars will fall from heaven like meteorites (Matt. 24:29; Mk. 13:25; Rev. 6:13; cf. Isa. 34:4). The stars can also stand for political powers. In Isa. 14:12 the expression is used of the fall of a powerful ruler. The fall of great stars from heaven makes the water on which life depends unusable, and unleashes the powers of darkness (Rev. 8:10; 9:1). The picture of Satan's fall from heaven in Lk. 10:18 is intended to show that the end has come for the devil's dominion. The mighty ruler who up till now has terrorized the world has lost his power and his position as accuser before God in a fall as rapid as a flash of lightning.

8. The fig. sense peculiar to the NT, to lose salvation, and so, to go to eternal destruction, is found in the Gospels, Paul, Heb. and Rev.

(a) It lies in the background of images like that in Matt. 7:25, 27 of total human downfall; of the blind leaders of the blind in Matt. 15:14; Lk. 6:39; and in those passages where Christ is spoken of as the "stone". In Lk. 2:34 he is the → rock on which many will meet their doom. Lk. 20:18 describes the annihilating effect of this stone on everyone who rejects the claim and the person of Jesus. Either they will fall over the stone (i.e. stumbling against it leads to destruction, v. 18a; cf. Isa. 8:15), or the stone will fall upon them (i.e. Christ will crush and shatter his enemies, v. 18b; cf. Dan. 2:34, 44).

(b) Paul uses the metaphor of standing and falling (cf. Prov. 24:16; Jer. 8:4; Amos 5:2; 8:14) in Rom. 14:4. He alludes to the ancient law whereby a slave is subject to his master's jurisdiction which alone decides whether his performance of a task is satisfactory, or whether he must be condemned because of bad work. In the same way the Christian is responsible to no one but his Lord, who alone decides whether he has done well or failed. The same idea is present in 1 Cor. 10:12, with its warning to guard against false security. As long as the eschatological tribulation with its Satanic power has not run its full course, the possibility of falling must not be forgotten (*piptō* here echoes v.8).

610

(c) "To fall from grace" is an expression arising from the concept of grace as the new sphere of life given to the Christian, to which the believer has "obtained access" (cf. Rom. 5:2 RSV). Those who depart from it deny God's unconditional mercy, the redeeming work of Christ (Gal. 5:4). What Christians must do is to abide in this state of grace, and not fall prey to any false teaching (2 Pet. 3:17). In Rom. 11:11, 22 *piptō* is again used of falling into destruction. The fall of Israel – despite God's gracious desire not to give up his people – demonstrates the severity of God's judgment. In Heb. 4:11 falling is the result of disobedience, and means apostasy (cf. 3:17 for *piptō* in the sense of dying under divine judgment). According to 10:31, the apostate faces a terrible future. Cf. also art. *aphistēmi*.

(d) Rev. 2:5 reminds a church of the love in which it stood at first. But it has moved quickly downwards, and fallen a long way. A return is nonetheless still possible, for the corruption has not yet gone too far. Apart from Rev. 2:5 and probably Rom. 11, the thought behind all these passages where *piptō* is used is of the incurring of guilt and the consequent loss of salvation, rather than of a mere failure from which recovery can be made. It is a catastrophic fall, which means eternal ruin. If it were not so, all the warnings against falling would lose their threatening urgency. To fall into sin and guilt, as an expression of a total attitude, is to plunge into irrevocable misfortune.   *W. Bauder*

→ Guard, Keep, → Hard, → Sin

Arndt, 126, 664 f.; I. H. Marshall, *Kept by the Power of God: A Study of Perseverence and Falling Away*, 1969; H. Schlier, *aphistēmi*, *TDNT* I 512 ff.; W. Michaelis, *piptō*, *TDNT* V 161 ff.; E. D. Starbuck, "Backsliding", *ERE* II 319 ff.; V. Taylor, *Forgiveness and Reconciliation*, 1961; H. Windisch, *Taufe und Sünde im ältesten Christentum bis auf Origenes*, 1908.

Fast

νηστεύω

νηστεύω (*nēsteuō*), to fast; *νηστεία* (*nēsteia*), fasting, fast; *νῆστις* (*nēstis*), not eating, fasting.

CL *nēstis* (probably derived from *nē-*, particle of negation, and *edō*, eat, i.e. not eating) means, having an empty stomach. From it are derived *nēsteuō*, fast, and *nēsteia*, fasting. The vb. and noun can also have the more general meaning, not to eat, abstain from food, or, to be without food, starve. These words are, however, more frequently used in the sense of a religious ritual.

To fast is to abstain for a limited period from any kind of food. (Total and permanent abstinence from particular, "forbidden" foods is a quite separate matter.) What is the real motive for fasting? In the pagan religions of the ancient world, it was clearly fear of demons and the idea that fasting was an effective means of preparing oneself for an encounter with the deity, since it created the right kind of openness to divine influence. For this reason it belonged in the mystery religions to the ritual of initiation for novices. In magic and with the oracles fasting was also often regarded as a preparation necessary to success. The custom of fasting following a death was widespread. While the soul of the dead person is still near, there is danger of demonic infection in eating and drinking. Fasting was also required, for instance, in certain fertility rites. Thus at Athens *hē Nēsteia* is the name given to the fast-day in the women's fertility festival in the month of sowing (October). Abstinence, here including particularly sexual abstinence, makes a person readier to receive the divine powers of fertility.

In practice, fasting in the setting of religious rites and as a defence against trouble was common in the whole of the ancient world, but not fasting for ethical motives (asceticism).

OT 1. In the LXX the Gk. words represent the Heb. *ṣûm*, fast. Along with this the MT has *'innâh nep̄eš*, afflict oneself (lit., humble one's soul), referring to a purification rite in which fasting played a part (Lev. 16:29, 31; 23:27, 32; Num. 29:7; Isa. 58:3; Ps. 35:13). Frequently too we read simply of "eating no bread and drinking no water" (e.g. Exod. 34:28).

The forms and purposes of fasting are many. Fasting is practised is Israel as a preparation for converse with God (Exod. 34:28; Deut. 9:9; Dan. 9:3):

(a) It was practised by the individual, when oppressed by great cares (2 Sam. 12:16–23; 1 Ki. 21:27; Ps. 35:13; 69:10).

(b) It was practised by the nation in imminent danger of war and destruction (Jdg. 20:26; 2 Chr. 20:3; Est. 4:16; Jon. 3:4–10; Jud. 4:9, 13); during a plague of locusts (Joel 1 and 2); to bring success to the return of the exiles (Ezr. 8:21–23); as an expiatory rite (Neh. 9:1); and finally in connection with mourning the dead (2 Sam. 1:12).

Fasting and prayer go constantly together (Jer. 14:11–12; Neh. 1:4; Ezr. 8:21, 23). Fasting usually lasts from morning to evening (Jdg. 20:26; 1 Sam. 14:24; 2 Sam. 1:12), although Est. 4:16 tells of a 3-day fast. In the description in Ps. 109:24 the torments of fasting during the period of accusation are at the same time a reflection of the inward torments suffered by the suppliant.

The Israelite law ordained fasting only on the day of atonement (Lev. 6:29–31; 23:27–32; Num. 29:7). After the destruction of Jerusalem (587 B.C.) four fast-days were laid down as days of remembrance (Zech. 7:3–5; 8:19).

2. In the course of time the deeper meaning of fasting, as an expression of man's humbling of himself before God, was lost for Israel. Increasingly it came to be regarded as a pious achievement. The struggle of the prophets against this de-personalization and emptying of the concept (cf. Isa. 58:3–7; Jer. 14:12) was without success. By the time of Jesus those who were earnest about their religion, especially the Pharisees, were required to keep two fast-days each week (cf. SB II 242 ff.). The disciples of John had a similar rule (cf. Mk. 2:18).

NT In the NT *nēsteuō* occurs 20 times, all in the Synoptic Gospels (Matt. 8 times, Mk. 6 times, Lk. 4 times) and Acts (twice). *nēsteia* occurs 5 times (3 times in Lk. and Acts, twice in Paul), and *nēstis* twice (Matt. and Mk.). The words of this group thus do not occur at all in John or (with the two exceptions noted above) in the epistles.

1. The entirely new view brought by the NT to the question of fasting is most clearly expressed in the words of Jesus, "How can the wedding guests fast while the bridegroom is with them?" (Mk. 2:19 par.). The irruption of the kingdom of God, the presence of the Messiah, the good news of salvation not dependent on good works – all this means joy which is something excluded by fasting in the Jewish

612

sense (see above OT 2). In the light of the Messiah-centred preaching of Jesus, such fasting is a thing of the past, belonging to a bygone era. In the Gospels the answer to the question about fasting is linked to the parables of the new patch on the old garment and the new wine in the old bottles (Mk. 2:21 f. par.). We must take this as an indication that fasting has been superseded by Jesus. In fact, there is no evidence from the 1st century that Christians voluntarily imposed fasting on themselves (cf. J. Behm, *TDNT* IV 933). The epistles of the NT make no reference to it, and even in those passages which concentrate on the ascetic tendencies of some (Rom. 14 and Col. 2), fasting remains unmentioned.

2. There are however a number of passages which raise questions about the consistency of this picture:

(a) According to Matt. 4:2, Jesus himself fasted for 40 days and 40 nights before beginning his public ministry. (It might be argued, on the other hand, that this was something which happened "on the threshold" of the coming of salvation.)

(b) In Matt. 6:16–18 Jesus does not condemn fasting as such, but ostentatious fasting. Fasting is not to be practised before the eyes of men, but before God who lives in secret and "sees into the secret place". (Here it could be pointed out that this word is addressed not to the community of his disciples, but to the Jews.)

(c) According to the words of Jesus in Matt. 17:21, there are certain conditions of demonic enslavement from which a man can only be released "through prayer and fasting". (Here it may be observed that this verse is lacking in good MSS and that in the par. Mk. 9:29 prayer alone is mentioned.)

(d) In Acts 13:3 and 14:23 we read that in the Christian church prayer was backed up by fasting (cf. *Did.* 1:3: "fast for those who persecute you").

We may thus conclude that the idea that fasting has a value in its own right was abandoned, but that the primitive Christian church in Palestine still retained the practice of fasting in order to demonstrate that their prayers were in earnest (cf. Acts 13:3; 14:23). In the Hel. churches, as evidenced by the total absence of the terms in the epistles, particularly in those of Paul (for the two instances in 2 Cor. 6:5 and 11:27 are both autobiographical) and in Heb., the practice of fasting does not seem to have existed at all.   *F. S. Rothenberg*

→ Bread, → Hunger

(a). I. Abrahams, *Studies in Pharisaism and the Gospels*, I, 121–28; R. Arbesmann, "Fasting and Prophecy in Pagan and Christian Antiquity," *Traditio* 7, 1949–51, 1–72; J. Behm, *nēstis, TDNT* IV 924–35; D. E. Briggs, *Biblical Teaching on Fasting*, 1953; H. von Campenhausen, "Early Christian Asceticism", *Tradition and Life in the Church*, 1968, 90–122; J. Gamberoni, "Fasting," *EBT* I 257–60; H. H. Guthrie, "Fast, Fasting," *IDB* II 241–44; J. A. Montgomery, "Ascetic Strains in Early Judaism," *JBL* 51, 1932, 183–213; Moore, *Judaism*, II, 55 ff., 257 ff.
(b). H. J. Ebeling, "Die Fastenfrage (Mk. 2, 18–22)," *ThStKr* 3, 1937–38, 387 ff.; M. S. Freiberger, *Die Fasten im alten Israel*, 1929; K. Fruhstorfer, "Fastenvorschriften und Fastenlehren der Heiligen Schrift des Alten Bundes," *Theologisch-praktische Quartalschrift* 69, 1916, 59–72; P. Gerlitz, *Das Fasten im religionsgeschichtlichen Vergleich*, (Dissertation Erlangen) 1954; A. Guillaumont, "*Nēsteuein ton kosmon* (P Oxy I, verso, 1:5–6)," *Bulletin de l'Institut Français d'Archéologie Orientale*, Cairo, 61, 1962, 15–23; K. E. Koch, *Fasten und Beten*, 1963; P. Rohleder, "Die Übung des Fastens", *Quatember* 19, 1954–55; SB IV 77–114; K. T. Schaeffer, " '. . . und dann werden sie fasten an jenem Tage' (Mk. 2, 20)", *Synoptische Studien: Festschrift A. Wikenhauser*, 1953, 124–47; F. Schmidt-Clausing, "Fasten," *RGG*³ II 882 ff.; J. Schümmer, *Die altchristliche Fastenpraxis*, 1933; R. Taut, "Askese tut Not!" in F. S. Rothenberg, ed., *Christsein Heute*, I, 1958, 65 ff.; H.-D. Wendland, "Evangelium und Askese", *Quatember* 19, 1954–55, 65 ff.

Father

In the patriarchal societies of antiquity, the father figure is endowed with two particular characteristics. On the one hand, the father rules as head of the household and the person to whom most respect is due, having absolute authority over his family. On the other hand, he has the responsibility of guarding, supporting and helping the other members. Both these characteristics are also present when a deity is described or addressed as father. Whereas the word *abba*, which is borrowed from the Aramaic, occurs only in the NT and there only in the context of addressing God in prayer as "Father", *patēr* covers the full range of meaning of the Eng. *father*. It can be used both as a description and as a form of address, either in a secular or a religious sense. The religious use of the image of a father "is one of the basic phenomena of religious history" (G. Schrenk, *TDNT* V 951). Biblical theology is concerned with the particular figure to which this phenomenon points in the OT and NT.

ἀββά

ἀββά (*abba*), father.

CL & OT *abba*, father, is an Aram. word, occurring in the NT only in 3 places: Mk. 14:36; Rom. 8:15; Gal. 4:6. In each case it is used in calling on God in prayer. In the other Gk. literature of early Christianity it is found only in quotations of these passages.

1. In Aram. *'abbā'* is originally, like the feminine equivalent *'immā'*, a word derived from baby-language. When a child is weaned, "it learns to say *'abbā'* (daddy) and *'immā'* (mummy)" (Ber. 40a; Sanh. 70b; cf. Tg. Isa. 8:4). Even in the pre-Christian era the word underwent a considerable extension of meaning. It came to replace not only the older form of address common to biblical Heb. and Aram., *'ābî*, my father, but also the Aram. descriptive terms for "the father" and "my father", i.e. the noun in the emphatic and the form with the 1st person sing. suffix. The effect of this widening of meaning was that the word *'abbā'* as a form of address to one's father was no longer restricted to children, but also used by adult sons and daughters. The childish character of the word ("daddy") thus receded, and *'abbā'* acquired the warm, familiar ring which we may feel in such an expression as "dear father".

2. Nowhere in the entire wealth of devotional literature produced by ancient Judaism do we find *'abbā'* being used as a way of addressing God. The pious Jew knew too much of the great gap between God and man (Eccl. 5:1) to be free to address God with the familiar word used in everyday family life. In the literature of Rab. Judaism we find only one example of *'abbā'* used in reference to God. It occurs in a story recorded in the Babylonian Talmud (Taanith 23b): "When the world had need of rain, our teachers used to send the schoolchildren to Rabbi Chanin Hanechba [end of the 1st cent. B.C.], and they would seize the hem of his cloak and call out to him: 'Dear father (*'abbā'*), dear father (*'abbā'*), give us rain'. He said before God: 'Sovereign of the world, do it for the sake of these who cannot distinguish between an *'abbā'* who can give rain and an *'abbā'* who can give no rain' " (cf. SB I 375, 520). It would certainly be reading too much into this text to conclude from it that in ancient Judaism God was described, still less addressed, as *'abbā'*.

Rabbi Chanin is here simply taking up the children's cry of *'abbā'* in order to appeal to God's fatherly mercy; he himself on the other hand uses the respectful invocation "Sovereign of the world."

NT 1. It is clear from the Gospel tradition and moreover indirectly confirmed in Rom. 8:15 and Gal. 4:6 (see below, 2), that Jesus addressed God in his prayers as "My Father". In so doing, he made use of the warm, familiar term *'abbā'* used in the everyday life of the family. The only exception is the cry of dereliction from the cross (Mk. 15:34 par.) which appears to be a quotation from Ps. 22:1 (→ God, art. *theos*, NT 6 (d)).

(a) The invocation *'abbā'* is expressly attested in the Markan text of the prayer in Gethsemane (Mk. 14:36). But in the other prayers of Jesus recorded by the evangelists (→ *patēr* NT 2(a)) it is again the Aram. *'abbā'* that underlies, either directly or indirectly, the various Gk. versions of his invocation of the Father. In the Gk. account of the prayers of Jesus the words used to address the Father vary between the voc. *pater*, the use of the nominative with the art., *ho patēr*, in a vocative sense (unusual in Gk. usage, but found as a Hebraism, cf. Funk § 147), and the voc. form with the 1st person sing., *pater mou*. These variations are to be explained by the fact that we have here to do with variant translations (cf. J. Jeremias, *The Prayers of Jesus*, 1967, 56). These result from the fact already mentioned, that in Palestinian Aram. of the 1st cent. A.D. *'abbā'* was used not only as a form of address (vocative), but also for the nom. with the art., and for the form with the 1st person sing. pronominal suffix.

(b) The entirely new, and for Jews unheard of, use of the childish and familiar term *'abbā'* in prayer is an expression of the unique relationship of Jesus to God. It expresses not only his attitude of trust and obedience towards the Father (Mk. 14:36 par.), but also his incomparable authority (Matt. 11:25 ff. par.).

2. The early church took over the use of *'abbā'* in prayer. This is shown by the two passages Rom. 8:15 and Gal. 4:6, where Paul may have been thinking of the Lord's Prayer. In the oldest versions of this prayer (Lk. 11:2 ff.), the invocation reads *pater*, (dear) Father, and indicates *'abbā'* as the Aram. original. This means that when Jesus gave his disciples the Lord's Prayer, he gave them authority to follow him in addressing God as *'abbā*,' and so gave them a share in his status as Son (→ Son, art. *hyios tou theou*). Accordingly, Paul sees in the invocation "Abba", dear Father, clear evidence of our adoption through Christ as sons, and of the eschatological possession of the Spirit (Rom. 8:14 ff.; Gal. 4:4–7). The fact that the church, like Jesus, may say "Abba" is a fulfilment of God's promise: "I will be a father to you, and you shall be my sons and daughters" (2 Cor. 6:18; a free citation of 2 Sam. 7:14; cf. also Jub. 1:24 f.).

| πατήρ | πατήρ (*patēr*), father; πατριά (*patria*), family, clan; πατρίς (*patris*), fatherland, homeland, home city, one's |

own part of the country; ἀπάτωρ (*apatōr*), fatherless.

CL 1. *patēr*, father, like *mētēr*, mother, a word of Indo-European origin, is used in classical Gk. of a lit. father (Homer, *Od.*, 1, 94), of the patriarch of a family (Josephus, *Ant.*, 14, 255), or in the plur. of forefathers and ancestors generally

(Homer, *Il.*, 6, 209). In a fig. sense the word is used as a title of honour for, or as a respectful means of addressing, a venerable old man (Homer, *Il.*, 24, 362), and also to indicate spiritual or intellectual fatherhood. Thus a philosopher may be called the "father" of his followers (Epictetus, *Dissertationes*, 3, 22, 81 f.), and in the mystery religions the one who conducts the ceremony of initiation can be described as "father" of the newly initiated (Apuleius, *Metamorphoses*, 11, 25, 7).

Derived from *patēr* are the words *patria*, lineage, clan (indicating descent from the same father and ancestral patriarch; in the NT only at Lk. 2:4; Acts 3:25; Eph. 3:15); *patris*, fatherland (in the NT e.g. Jn. 4:44; Heb. 11:14), or home city (e.g. Matt. 13:54; Lk. 4:23); and *apatōr*, fatherless (in NT only at Heb. 7:3). The latter term is used in classical Gk. of orphans, foundlings, children born out of wedlock, outcasts and outlaws (examples in *TDNT* V 1019 ff.; for similar usage in Jewish literature, see ibid. and SB II 693 f.). Where gods are described as "fatherless", the term is intended to indicate their miraculous origin (see *TDNT* ibid.). In the Hel. period *apatōr* is found also – often in combination with *amētōr*, motherless – as an attribute of God. It describes God's divinity and eternity (in Orphism, the mystery religions, and gnosticism). This is the sense of the term in Apoc. Abr. 17:9, where we find the invocation "Fatherless, motherless, unbegotten One." We may compare with this an Egyptian hymn to the god Ptah, which contains the words: "Thou hast no father, who has begotten thee...; thou hast no mother who has borne thee."

2. (a) The use of the name father for *God* in the religions of the ancient orient and classical Greece and Rome is always based upon mythical ideas of an original act of begetting and the natural, physical descent of all men from God. Thus the god El of Ugarit is called "father of mankind", the Babylonian moon-god Sin is "father and begetter of gods and men", and in Greece Zeus (from Homer onwards) is called "father of men and gods". In Egypt the Pharaoh is regarded in a special way as the son of God in a physical sense. The name of father expresses above all God's absolute authority, demanding obedience, but at the same time his merciful love, goodness and care. The appropriate attitude of man for his part is a double one: on the one hand, "recognition of his own powerlessness and total dependence on the deity", and on the other, "the attitude of childlike trust and love towards the deity" (G. Mensching, *RGG*³ VI 1233).

(b) The idea of the fatherhood of God is given a philosophical interpretation in Plato and the Stoics. Plato, in his cosmological elaboration of the father idea, emphasizes the creator relationship of God, the "universal father", to the entire cosmos (*Tim.*, 28c, 41a, and often). According to Stoic teaching, God's authority as father pervades the universe: he is "creator, father, and sustainer" of men, who are his children, related to him (Epictetus, *Dissertationes*, 1, 9, 7; cf. Cleanthes' famous hymn to Zeus).

(c) In the ancient mystery cults the regeneration and deification of the initiate is seen as an act of begetting by the deity; hence the latter is invoked in prayer as "Father" (examples in *TDNT* V 953 f.).

(d) The gnostics too describe the supreme God as the father, or first father (see especially the Gospel of Truth from Nag Hammadi; cf. K. Grobel, *The Gospel of Truth*, 1960, 32 ff. and passim). Here, however, the personal relationship between God and man disappears altogether. The sparks of light emanating from God,

616

which have become locked in the human body, are to the first Father like drops of water to the sea.

OT The OT uses the word father (Heb. '*āb* = LXX *patēr*) almost exclusively (*c.* 1180 times) in a secular and only very occasionally (15 times) in a religious sense. As in the case of the OT, so in the literature of ancient Palestinian Judaism, we may note a marked reserve in the use of the word in a religious sense. Not until the literature of Diaspora Judaism do we find more frequent use of the name "Father" in reference to God.

1. *Secular usage.* (a) Physical fatherhood is the gift and command of the Creator (Gen. 1:28). As bearer of the divine blessing (cf. Gen. 27), the father is head of the family, his → house (cf. Jos. 24:15b), and an authority which must be respected under all circumstances (Exod. 20:12; 21:15, 17; Prov. 23:22). Not only is it his task to feed, protect, and educate his family, but, more important still, he is the family priest (Exod. 12:3 ff.) and teacher (Exod. 12:26 f.; 13:14 ff.; Deut. 6:7, 20 ff.; 32:7, 46; Isa. 38:19; for references in Rab. literature, see SB III 615). He is responsible for seeing that family life is in accordance with the covenant, and that the children receive religious instruction. Even servants may address a master as "my father" (2 Ki. 5:13).

(b) Earlier generations of Israel are called "the fathers" (Ps. 22:4; 106:7), as are outstanding men of God of previous ages (Sir. 44:1 ff.), and particularly the patriarchs Abraham, Isaac and Jacob, the bearers and mediators of the covenant promises of God (Jos. 24:3; 1 Chr. 29:18; Rab. references in SB I 918 f.).

(c) Father is used as a title of honour for a priest (Jdg. 17:10; 18:19), and for a prophet (2 Ki. 6:21; 13:14). In 2 Ki. 2:12, on the lips of the prophet's disciple, it also expresses spiritual relationship. In Rab. Judaism, where the title of father was frequently used of respected scribes (SB I 918 f.), the metaphor of father and child is occasionally applied to the relationship between a teacher of the Torah and his pupil (SB III 340 f.).

2. *Religious usage.* (a) God as Father in the Old Testament. Apart from comparisons with an earthly father (Ps. 103:13; Prov. 3:12; cf. Deut. 1:31; 8:5), the word father is used of God only 15 times in the OT, 13 times as an epithet and twice directly in prayer.

The description of God as Father refers in the OT only to his relationship with the people of Israel (Deut. 32:6; Isa. 63:16 twice; 64:8; Jer. 31:9; Mal. 1:6; 2:10) or to the king of Israel (2 Sam. 7:14 par. 1 Chr. 17:13; 22:10; 28:6; Ps. 89:26; cf. 2:7). It never refers to any other individual (on Ps. 68:5 see below), or to mankind in general. The basic difference between this and the views of the fatherhood of God held by Israel's neighbours is that in the OT God's fatherhood is not understood in a biological or mythological sense, but in a soteriological one. To be a child of God is not a natural state or quality; rather it grounded in the miracle of divine → election and → redemption (cf. also Exod. 4:22; Deut. 14:1 f.; Hos. 11:1 ff.). Even where, in connection with God's fatherhood, the language of creating (→ Creation) and begetting (→ Birth) is used, the reference is to the historical, elective action of God towards a people, or king, who existed already in the biological sense. When God, the One who elects and redeems, is described as Father, expression is given both to his merciful, forgiving → love (Jer. 31:9, 20; cf. Hos. 11:8),

617

and to his claim to respect and obedience (Deut. 32:5 f.; Jer. 3:4 f., 19; Mal. 1:6). Because the Israelites share in being children of God, they have a special obligation to be loyal to one another (Mal. 2:10). If the individual sees God as his Father, it is because of his status as a member of the people and because he has experienced the work of God in a way corresponding to his redemption of Israel (Ps. 68:5 in the context of verses 4–10).

The vocative "my father" is found only at Jer. 3:4, 19, and here significantly not on the lips of an individual, but as a prayer of the chosen people.

(b) God as Father in Palestinian Judaism. As in the OT, so in Palestinian Judaism of the pre-Christian period the description of God as Father is rare. In the Apocrypha and Pseudepigrapha, as far as writings of Palestinian origin are concerned, it is found only very occasionally (Tob. 13:4; Sir. 51:10; Jub. 1:24 f., 28; 19:29), while the Qumran texts provide but a single example (1QH 9:35 f.). In Rab. Judaism of the 1st cent. A.D. the use of the name of Father became more widespread, but it was still far less frequent than other descriptions of God. God is known as "Father in heaven" (examples in J. Jeremias, *The Prayers of Jesus*, 1967, 16 ff.). The addition of "in heaven" indicates the distance between God and man. The new element as compared with OT usage is that in Palestinian Judaism the individual worshipper too speaks of God as his "Father in heaven" (J. Jeremias, op. cit., 21). The texts emphasize, however, that the indispensable condition for this personal relationship of child to father is obedience to God's commandments (cf. Sir. 4:10).

As an invocation of God, we find in the 1st cent. A.D. the expression "our Father, our King". But this is only in liturgical prayers of the whole congregation, not in the normal spoken Aramaic, but in the Heb. language of worship (cf. the "Ahaba rabba" prayer and the New Year litany "Abinu malkenu" in W. Staerk, *Altjüdische liturgische Gebete*, 1930², 6, 27 ff.; cf. J. Jeremias, op. cit., 24 f.). It is to be observed that this expression draws attention to the fatherhood of God and to his majesty at the same time. The invocation "our Father in heaven", which is occasionally to be found in later Jewish prayers, is likewise attested in the 1st cent. A.D. by Matt. 6:9. On the other hand, we have yet to find an example of an individual addressing God as "my Father". Sir. 23:1, 4 appears in the Gk. text as "Lord, my Father", but the Heb. original has, as it does in 51:1, "God of my father" (cf. Exod. 15:2).

(c) God as Father in Diaspora Judaism. The Greek-speaking Jews of the Diaspora were more frequent and less reserved than the Jews of Palestine in their use of the term father as a description of God (3 Macc. 5:7; Wis. 2:16 ff.; Tob. 13:4). Philo (*Op. Mund.*, 89; *Spec. Leg.*, 1, 96; 2, 6 and often) and Josephus (especially *Ant.*, 7, 380) reveal clearly the influence of the Gk. concept of the universal father.

In the Diaspora the invocatory use of "Father" occurs, under Gk. influence, even in the prayers of individuals (3 Macc. 6:3, 8; Wis. 14:3; Apocryphon of Ezek. Frag. 3 = 1 Clem. 8:3).

NT The range of meaning of *patēr*, father, in the NT corresponds to that of '*āḇ* and
  patēr in the OT. In contrast to the OT, which uses the name of Father only very occasionally for God, the number of examples of *patēr* in the religious sense in the NT (245 times) far exceeds the number of those in a secular sense (157 times).

1. *The secular use of patēr*. (a) According to the synoptic tradition, Jesus specifically emphasized the binding validity of the commandment to honour one's parents (Mk. 7:9–13 par.; 10:19 par; cf. Exod. 20:12). Even more important, however, than the tie to father and mother is the obligation that Jesus makes to follow him (Matt. 10:37; Lk. 14:26; cf. Mk. 10:29 f. par.). The family rules laid down in Eph. and Col. again underline the commandment of obedience towards father and mother, but they also point to the human and spiritual responsibility of the father towards his children (Eph. 6:1–4; Col. 3:20 f.).

(b) The close connection between Israel and the church, which receives extended treatment in Rom. 9–11, is the basis of Paul's words in 1 Cor. 10:1, when he speaks of God's people of the Old Testament as "our fathers" even though he is addressing Gentile Christians (cf. also Rom. 9:10; Heb. 1:1; 1 Clem. 4:8; 31:2; 60:4).

(c) The idea of spiritual fatherhood appears in 1 Cor. 4:14 ff. and also indirectly where spiritual sonship is mentioned (Phlm. 10; 1 Tim. 1:2, 18; 2 Tim. 1:2; 2:1; Tit. 1:4; 1 Pet. 5:13). The apostle is regarded as "father" of those Christians who owe their faith to his preaching. Matt. 23:9 forbids the use of the name of father as a title of honour.

(d) Among the derivatives of *patēr*, *apatōr* (without father, Heb. 7:3), deserves special mention. The author of Hebrews describes → Melchizedek as "without father or mother or genealogy, (having) neither beginning of days nor end of life." The writer arrives at this remarkable conclusion with the help of the Rab. principle, "What is not mentioned in the Torah does not exist." In the silence of the OT (Gen. 14:18 ff.) about the descent, parentage, birth and death of Melchizedek he finds a cryptic reference to the miraculous, heavenly origin of the priest-king and to his eternal priesthood. As a heavenly being (cf. 11Q Melchizedek), Melchizedek is superior to the Levitical priests, for whom priestly descent is an absolute precondition for service (Neh. 7:63 f.; Lev. 21:13 ff.; cf. F. Schröger, *Der Verfasser des Hebräerbriefes als Schriftausleger*, 1968, 140 ff.). Hence he is for the writer of Heb. a type and prophetic prefiguring of the pre-existent Son of God and eternal High Priest Christ, who is similarly not descended from the tribe of Levi (Heb. 7:13 f.).

2. *God as Father*. The concordance alone tells us that in the concept of the fatherhood of God we see one of the central ideas of primitive Christian theology. This is confirmed when we consider the meaning of the terms (cf. art. *abba*; also → Child, art. *hyios*).

(a) Jesus' use of the name Father for God. Jesus' use of the name Father as a description of God is attested 3 times in Mk., 4 times in the sayings-source used by Matt. and Lk., 4 times in Lk.'s special material, 31 times in the remaining parts of Matt., and 100 times in Jn. This analysis suggests to some scholars that Jesus himself did not often describe God as Father, and that in the period of the early church there was an increasing tendency to put the name on his lips. Two things are of significance about Jesus' own usage. He evidently never called God the Father of Israel. He spoke of God as his Father ("my Father") and as the Father of the disciples ("your Father"). But he never joined with them together in a common "our Father" (the Lord's Prayer is a prayer for the disciples to use!).

When Jesus called God his Father, this is based upon a unique revelation of God given him from above and on his incomparable status as Son (Matt. 11:25–27 par. Lk. 10:21 f.). On the question of authenticity and for a detailed exposition of these passages, see J. Jeremias, op. cit., 45–52; cf. *New Testament Theology*, I, 1971, 59 ff.). In the mission of Jesus, in whose word and works the coming → Kingdom of God is dawning, God reveals himself as Father. God's fatherhood, revealed in the Son, is therefore an eschatological reality (cf. E. Lohmeyer, *The Lord's Prayer*, 1965, 42 ff.).

The expression "your Father" is found only in the words of Jesus to his disciples. This means that Jesus did not teach the idea that God is the Father of all men. Rather, he linked the fatherhood of God to men's relationship to himself. God shows himself to be the Father of the disciples in his mercy (Lk. 6:36), goodness (Matt. 5:45), forgiving love (Mk. 11:25) and care (Matt. 6:8; 6:32 par. Lk. 12:30). He gives them the gifts of the age of salvation (Matt. 7:11) and is preparing for them full salvation at the close of the age (Lk. 12:32). The disciple's experience of the fatherly love of God places him under a special obligation in the way he conducts himself with his fellow men, as is expressly stated in e.g. Matt. 5:44 ff. and Lk. 6:36.

According to the accounts in all the Gospels (with the exception of the cry of dereliction in Mk. 15:34, par. Matt. 27:46, where the words "My God" were present in Ps. 22:1 which is being quoted), Jesus always addressed God in his prayers with the words "(my) Father" (Mk. 14:36 par. Matt. 26:39, 42 and Lk. 22:42; Matt. 11:25 f. par. Lk. 10:21; Lk. 23:34, 46; Jn. 11:41; 12:27 f.; 17:1, 5, 11, 21, 24 f.). "This constancy of the tradition shows how firmly the address 'Father' was rooted in the tradition of Jesus, quite apart from the question of the authenticity of the individual prayers themselves" (J. Jeremias, *The Prayers of Jesus*, 55). When we consider that the personal invocation "(my) father" was something totally new in Palestine (cf. above ОТ, 2 (b)), it must have seemed nothing short of outrageous that Jesus should make use of the completely unceremonious Aram. word '*abbā*' (→ art. *abba*).

(b) The use of name of Father for God by the NT witnesses. The NT witnesses, especially Paul (including Eph. and Col.) and John (Jn. and 1 & 2 Jn.), are unanimous in making the fatherhood of God rest upon a basis of christology and soteriology.

In the Pauline letters the description of God as Father occurs 40 times, normally in liturgical formulae (blessings: Rom. 1:7; 1 Cor. 1:3; 2 Cor. 1:2; doxologies: Rom. 15:6; 2 Cor. 1:3; Eph. 1:3; creeds: 1 Cor. 8:6; Eph. 4:6; prayers: Eph. 5:20; Col. 1:12). When Paul uses, in addition to "God the Father" and "God our Father", the phrase "the God and Father of our Lord Jesus Christ", as he frequently does (e.g. Rom. 15:6; 2 Cor. 1:3; 11:31), he is emphasizing that God has revealed himself as Father in Jesus Christ and can hence be recognized as such only in him. The fatherhood of God is not a fact of nature, but an eschatological miracle (cf. Rom. 8:14–17; Gal. 4:1 ff.).

John who uses the word Father almost as a synonym for God stresses Jesus' unique relationship to the Father (Jn. 6:57; 10:30; 14:10 f.). As the Son who has been accorded a complete knowledge of God (3:35; 10:15a; 16:15a), Jesus reveals the Father (1:18; 8:26–29; 12:49 f.; 14:7, 9). He thus imparts to his own the status of children of God, a status which can only be attained through him (14:6; 17:25 f.) and can only be received as a gift of divine love (1 Jn. 3:1 f.).

There are only 3 occasions in the NT where a concept of God's fatherhood appears which is without a christological anchor. In Eph. 3:14 f God in his capacity as creator of the world is called "the Father . . . (of) every family (*patria*) in heaven and on earth." In Heb. 12:9 in his capacity as the creator of men's souls he is called "Father of spirits." In Jas. 1:17 as creator of the stars, he is called "Father of lights" (cf. Apc. Mos. 36:3). It is possible that in these passages we see a trace of the Gk. concept of the universal fatherhood of God.

The invocatory use of the term Father for God by the Christian church is attested in Matt. 6:9 par. Lk. 11:2; Rom. 8:15; and Gal. 4:6 (→ *abba* NT, 2). 1 Pet. 1:17 may be an allusion to the invocation of God as Father in the Lord's Prayer (cf. the Coptic Sahidic translation: "If you address him as 'Our Father' who . . ."). With the privilege of calling God "Father" in prayer goes the obligation to live a holy life. *O. Hofius*

→ Adam, → Child, → God, → Man, → Son, → Woman

(a). P. A. H. de Boer, *Fatherhood and Motherhood in Israelite and Judean Piety*, 1974; G. Dalman, *The Words of Jesus*, 1902, 184–94; F. Hahn, *The Titles of Jesus in Christology*, 1969, 307–17; J. Jeremias, *The Central Message of the New Testament*, 1965, 9 ff.; *The Prayers of Jesus*, 1967; *New Testament Theology*, I, 1971, 36 f., 61 ff.; G. Kittel, *abba*, TDNT I 5 f.; G. W. H. Lampe, " 'Our Father' in the Fathers", in P. Brooks, ed., *Christian Spirituality. Essays in Honour of Gordon Rupp*, 1975, 9–31; E. Lohmeyer, *The Lord's Prayer*, 1965; J. Lowe, *The Lord's Prayer*, 1962; W. Lüthi, *The Lord's Prayer*, 1961; T. W. Manson, *The Teaching of Jesus*, (1931) 1959³, 89 ff.; H. G. May, "The God of my Father: A Study of Patriarchal Religion," *JBL* 60, 1941, 155 ff.; H. W. Montefiore, "God as Father in the Synoptic Gospels," *NTS* 3, 1956–57, 31 f.; Moore, *Judaism*, II 201 ff.; G. Quell and G. Schrenk, *patēr* etc. TDNT V 945–1022; H. Ringgren, *'āb*, TDOT I 1 ff.; A. Stöger, "Father," *EBT* I 260–65; T. M. Taylor, " 'Abba, Father' and Baptism", *SJT* II, 1958, 62–71.
(b). W. Bousset and H. Gressmann, *Die Religion des Judentums im späthellenistischen Zeitalter*, 1926³, 377 ff.; J. Carmignac, *Recherches sur le "Notre Père"*, 1969, 55 ff.; W. Grundmann, "Matt. xi, 27 und die Johanneischen 'Der Vater-Der Sohn'-Stellen'," *NTS* 12, 1965–66, 42–49; R. Gyllenberg, "Gott der Vater im Alten Testament und in der Predigt Jesu," *Studia Orientalia*, 1, 1926, 3–140; P. Gutiérrez, *La paternité spirituelle selon S. Paul*, EB 1968; E. Haenchen, "Der Vater der mich gesandt hat," *Gott und Mensch*, 1965, 68 ff.; E. Hübner, "Credo in Deum Patrem?" *EvTh* 23, 1963, 646 ff.; E. Jenni, *'āb*, THAT I 1–17; J. Jeremias, *Abba. Studien zur neutestamentlichen Theologie und Zeitgeschichte*, 1966; J. Jeremias and W. Jannasch, "Vaterunser," *RGG³* VI 1235 ff.; G. Kittel, *Die Religionsgeschichte und das Urchristentum*, 1932, 92 ff.; K. G. Kuhn, *Achtzehngebet und Vaterunser und der Reim*, WUNT 1, 1950; W. Marchel, *Abba, Père! La prière du Christ et des chrétiens. Étude exégétique sur les origines et la signification de l'invocation à la divinité comme père, avant et dans le Nouveau Testament*, Analecta Biblica 19, 1963; G. Mensching, H.-J. Kraus, and J. Jeremias, "Vatername Gottes," *RGG³* VI 1232 ff.; O. Michel, *Der Brief an die Hebräer*, KEK 13, 1966¹², 261 ff. (on *apatōr*); K. H. Rengstorf, *Mann und Frau im Urchristentum*, 1954, 32 ff.; SB I 392 ff.; W. Schmauch and K. Kulp, "Vaterunser," *EKL* III 1610 ff.; W. Schmauch, "Vatername Gottes," *EKL* III 1608 ff.; F. Schröger, *Der Verfasser des Hebräerbriefs als Schriftausleger*, 1968, 136 ff. (on *apatōr*); H. Schürmann, *Das Gebet des Herrn*, 1957, 17–26; W. Staerk, *Altjüdische Gebete*, (1910) 1930²; H. W. Wolff, *Was sagt die Bibel von Vater und Mutter?* (1959) 1966³; T. Zahn, *Der Brief des Paulus an die Römer*, (1910) 1925³, 393 ff.

Fear, Awe

φόβος

φόβος (*phobos*), terror, fear, alarm, fright, reverence, respect, awe; φοβέομαι (*phobeomai*), to be afraid, fear, have reverence, respect for; φοβερός (*phoberos*), fearful, terrible, frightful.

CL *phobos* means panic, fright, fear, awe, reverence. Like the vb. *phobeō*, to be frightened, it is already found in Mycenean Gk. (Linear B). Sometimes these words denote fear of the gods, holy awe. But in general, the attitude of reverence before the deity is denoted by *sebomai* (fear, feel awe, reverence, worship) and the related words *eusebeia* (which can denote reverence towards the gods and one's parents) and its opposite *asebeia* (ungodliness, impiety). (On the latter terms → Godliness, art. *sebomai*; → W. Foerster, art. *sebomai*, *TDNT* VII 168–96.)

OT 1. In addition to the above meanings, *phobos* in the LXX can also mean someone or something that is to be feared. Here the Heb. vb. is *pāḥaḏ* (tremble). It may even be applied to God as one who is to be feared (Gen. 31:42, 53; Isa. 8:13). The Gk. vb. *phobeomai* is used in the LXX and the NT only in the middle (apart from Wis. 17:9). It is used intransitively with the preposition *apo* in the sense of "to be afraid of" (Lev. 26:2; Deut. 1:29). It is used transitively with a personal or impersonal object meaning "to fear" (Num. 14:9, a foreign people; Prov. 13:13, a command; Lev. 19:3, parents; Prov. 24:21, the king). The adj. *phoberos* (fearful, terrible, frightful) was used in secular Gk. from the 5th cent. B.C. It was applied especially to God in his works (e.g. Ps. 66:5 [LXX 65:3]). The rare noun *phobētron* (also *phobēthron*) meaning horror, terror, is found in Isa. 19:17 LXX, Justin, *Apol.*, 2, 8, 7, and once in the NT in Lk. 21:11 where it means terrible sight, event or horror (Arndt, 871, "there will be *dreadful portents* and signs").

2. There is a characteristic difference between Israel's relationship with God and the religious attitude of the Greeks. The Israelite can stand before God in fear and love. God is great, mighty and terrible (Deut. 10:17 f.; cf. 1 Chron. 16:25). Nevertheless, he is gracious to man (Deut. 6:5, 13). Thus we can understand the frequent address to man which passes right on into the NT: "Fear not" (Gen. 15:1; Jdg. 6:23; Isa. 44:2 and often). God's grace and favour do not abolish the solemnity of the address. It demands man's total obedience (Amos 5:6 f.; Hos. 6:6). For love is not mere feeling. It has to be proved in action, just as God's love is proved (Isa. 41:13 and often). Nevertheless, the motive of fear predominates. The fear of God is the first essential motive in the laws of the Pentateuch (Lev. 19:14, 32; Deut. 13:11; 17:13 etc.). It is the decisive religious factor in OT piety, especially in the Pss., Prov. and Sirach (cf. Ps. 103:11, 13, 17; Prov. 1:7; 23:17; Sir. 1:11 ff. and often). On the other hand, the man who trusts in God does not need to fear enemies, adversity or danger (Pss. 27 and 46, and often).

Compared with the frequency of *phobeomai* and its cognates, the LXX uses *sebomai* and *eulabeomai* comparatively rarely, although their meanings are similar. This presents a contrast with secular Gk.

NT 1. The use of these words in the NT follows that outlined in CL and OT. Objects of fear are: the appearance of angels (Lk. 1:12; 2:9; Matt. 28:4); the catastrophes at the end-time (Lk. 21:26); death (Heb. 2:15); rulers (Rom. 13:3); and the Jews (Jn. 7:13; 20:19). Fear in the sense of anxiety is denoted by the expression *phobos kai tromos*, fear and trembling, which occurs already in the LXX (Exod. 15:16 and often; cf. 1 Cor. 2:3; 2 Cor. 7:15; Phil. 2:12; cf. also Mk. 5:33). Similarly, *phobos* and *deilia* (timidity, despondency) are combined in Sir. 4:17. The noun *deilia* occurs in 2 Tim. 1:7, and the vb. *deiliaō* (to be afraid, despondent) in Jn. 14:27 (cf. Deut. 1:21; 3 Macc. 6:19 and often).

phobos and its cognates are used in the sense of fear, awe and reverence before God (e.g. Acts 9:31; 2 Cor. 7:1; Col. 3:22; cf. Eph. 5:21 where the object is Christ). Reverence should be shown to masters (Eph. 6:5; 1 Pet. 2:18), husbands (1 Pet. 3:2), and those outside the church (1 Pet. 3:16). *phobeomai* (fear) may be followed by *apo* (Matt. 10:28; Lk. 12:4 and often). But it may also be used transitively with a person or a thing as its object (Matt. 14:5, the people; Heb. 11:23, the king's edict). In such cases the object of fear is some power behind the immediate object. The vb. is used in the weakened sense of "to be afraid that" in Acts 23:10 and Gal. 4:11.

The term *phoboumenos ton theon*, a God-fearing man (Acts 10:2, 22; 13:16, 26), is a designation for a non-Jew who has connections with the synagogue (→ Conversion, art. *proselytos*). The adj. *phoberos* (fearful, terrible, frightful) occurs in Heb. 10:27, 31; 12:21.

2. Fear and reverence of God, and also of Christ (Eph. 2:21), provide both the motive and manner of Christian conduct (Lk. 18:2, 4; Acts 9:31; 1 Pet. 2:17; Rev. 11:18). Jesus himself impressed upon the disciples the absolute necessity to fear God who can destroy both body and soul in → hell (*geenna*) (Matt. 10:28; Lk. 12:5). "It is a fearful thing to fall into the hands of the living God" (Heb. 10:31; cf. v. 27). Jesus' warning, like the teaching of the apostles (2 Cor. 5:11; 1 Pet. 1:17) points unambiguously to the prospect of judgment. Paul could exhort the Philippians to "work out your own salvation with fear and trembling" (Phil. 2:12). But this is only one side of the motivation. For he immediately adds: "for God is at work in you, both to will and to work for his good pleasure" (2:13).

3. This fear that overtakes men when they encounter God or his messengers may be seen in the accounts of the → miracles of Jesus and the → apostles and also in the appearances of Christ and the → angels. But here, as in the OT, we repeatedly find the command, "Fear not!" It occurs in the accounts of Jairus's daughter (Mk. 5:36; Lk. 8:50), Peter's draught of fishes (Lk. 5:10), the appearance of the angels to Zechariah and Mary (Lk. 1:13, 30), Paul's visions (Acts 18:9; 27:24), John's vision on Patmos (Rev. 1:17), and the prophecy fulfilled on the first Palm Sunday (Jn. 12:15; cf. Isa. 41:10, 13; Zech. 9:9 f.). It occurs in the plur. in the nativity story (Lk. 2:10), Jesus' walking on the water (Matt. 14:27; Mk. 6:50), the transfiguration (Matt. 17:7) and the angel's and Jesus' words at the empty tomb (Matt. 28:5, 10).

4. The exhortation not to fear is also found frequently with regard both to men and the world. The disciples need not fear those who only kill the body (Matt. 10:26, 28; Lk. 12:4 f.). The little flock need not fear want (Lk. 12:32). Christians need not fear their opponents (Phil. 1:28) or suffering (1 Pet. 3:14; Rev. 2:10). For fear of men is taken away from them by security in God (Matt. 10:30 f.; Heb. 11:23, 27; 13:6).

5. The NT letters clearly present the real ground for overcoming fear. Christ has appeared to "deliver all those who through fear of death were subject to lifelong bondage" (Heb. 2:15). Those who are led by the Spirit of God have received the Spirit of sonship which enables them to cry "Abba! Father!" (Rom. 8:15; cf. Gal. 4:6). "God did not give us a spirit of timidity but a spirit of power and love and self-control" (2 Tim. 1:7). "There is no fear in love, but perfect love casts out fear. For fear has to do with punishment, and he who fears is not perfected in love"

623

(1 Jn. 4:18). It is not fear of punishment but this love which provides the motive and power to keep his → commandments (1 Jn. 5:3).

6. The Christian is constantly confronted by the task of overcoming the motive of fear by that of love. Over and above the motive of fear, faith which is active in love appears at the nerve-centre of Christian conduct in the NT (Gal. 5:6). The NT presents a tension between fear and love. In a paradoxical way they exist together. We are not, therefore, justified in ascribing fear of God and judgment entirely to the influence of the Jewish synagogue and dismissing it as a remnant of Jewish thought.   *W. Mundle*

(a). H. Balz and G. Wanke, *phobeō* etc., *TDNT* IX 189 ff.; W. Beilner, "Fear," *EBT* I 265–69; R. Bultmann, *Theology of the New Testament*, I, 1952; II, 1955 (see index); W. Eichrodt, *Theology of the Old Testament*, II, 1967, 268–77 and see index; W. Foerster, *sebomai, TDNT* VII 168–96; R. Otto, *The Idea of the Holy*, 1931; S. J. deVries, "Note concerning the Fear of God in the Qumran Scrolls," *Revue de Qumran* 5, 1965, 233 ff.
(b). J. Becker, *Gottesfurcht im Alten Testament, Analecta Biblica* 25, 1965; H. Cremer and J. Kögel, *Biblisch-theologisches Wörterbuch der neutestamentlichen Grazität*, 1923[11], 1115 ff.; L. Koehler, "Die Offenbarungsformel 'Fürchte dich nicht' im Alten Testament," *SThZ* 36, 1918, 33 ff.; W. Lütgert, "Die Furcht Gottes," *Theologische Studien für M. Kähler*, 1905, 163 ff.; S. Plath, "*Furcht Gottes.*" *Der Begriff "Furcht" im Alten Testament*, 1963; K. Romaniuk, "La crainte de Dieu à Qumran et dans le Nouveau Testament," *Revue de Qumran* 4, 1963, 3–10; A. Strobel, "Furcht, wem Furcht gebührt. Zum profangriechischen Hintergrund von Röm. 13, 7," *ZNW* 55, 1964, 58 ff.

Feast, Passover

Festivals and feasts belong together and denote the passage of time, marking the high points and breaks in the rhythm of life in the ancient world. Nearly always they are religious in origin. The comprehensive Gk. term *heortē* contains both this religious element and the idea of a pause from normal work. The festivals which were important for the biblical writers and the world around them are dealt with in the first and more general article. Because of its particular significance in the passion narrative, the *pascha*, the Passover, is dealt with separately in the second article.

ἑορτή

ἑορτή (*heortē*), festival, feast; ἑορτάζω (*heortazō*), celebrate a festival.

CL 1. *heortē* has the basic meaning of performance, fulfilment (for the benefit of a deity). In its usual meaning of festival it is attested since Homer (*Od.*, 20, 258 f.).

2. Among the Greeks a great many events were elevated by means of festivals out of the common run of daily life: the change of the seasons and the high points of the year's work from seed-time to harvest (fertility festivals); family events and the relationship between the individual and the community (family and tribal festivals). In later times especially, these festivities were practically always associated with certain deities and named after them. In addition to many festivals of local significance, there was an increasing number which were general throughout Greece. The list of these "legally sanctified portions of time" (Plato, *Definitiones*, 415a) produced a well-filled calendar of feasts which covered the whole year (in Roman times about a third of the total number of days in the year!) and every area of human life. It was not until later that important political events were also given

festivals (memorial feasts), e.g. the battle of Marathon and the victory of Salamis. In these festivals the whole family, or clan, or all members of the tribe or nation would take part, depending on the nature of the festival. But later the number was limited (in the secret rites, or mysteries) to the community of believers and initiates.

Spanning the whole realm of nature, every kind of occupation, and every special situation in life, numerous gods were honoured with a festival. Processes that were natural in origin were not only continued, but exaggerated to excess by celebrations involving immoderate indulgence in wine-drinking and love (especially in connection with the cult of Dionysus; cf. also the practice of *hieros gamos*, sacred marriage, → Marriage). Preparation for such feasts included fasting, washings and changes of clothing. The festival itself was celebrated with prayer and song, music and dancing, processions, sacrifice, sport, games and competitions. Markets and fairs were also part of the festival, and hostilities were usually interrupted. Gods appeared and entertained or were entertained by their worshippers. They gave counsel and help, allowed men to join in their mourning and rejoicing, to suffer, die and rise again with them. They gave victory to the spirit over the flesh, and bestowed eternal life in the world of the dead. But for all the individualization and spiritualization which these ceremonies underwent, they were in the end all variations of a fertility religion, which, under the symbols of an ear of corn and the phallus, sought by magical means to further the processes of conception, growth and life in plants, animals and human beings.

OT 1. The ancient farming and city culture of Canaan possessed a wealth of religious cults honouring the gods El, Dagon, Baal, the goddesses Asherah, Astarte-Anath and others, and later Egyptian and Babylonian deities also. These cults were full of fertility rites, which attributed to sexual processes a religious potency (sacred prostitution of men as paederasts and of women as $q^e\underline{d}\bar{e}\check{s}\hat{o}\underline{t}$). The constant temptation of Israel arising from the fascination of these cults is witnessed in particular by the books of Kings. But on the whole Israel, unlike Greece, which in this respect inherited the traditions of the Orient (see above CL), withstood the temptation.

The immigrant shepherd tribes of Israel had to take over a considerable amount from the religion of Canaan in order to be able to live in the land to which that culture belonged. But in order to be able to live before God as the chosen people, they also rejected a great deal (see e.g. the prohibition of religious prostitution, Deut. 23:18 f.; the law forbidding priests to have anything to do with the dead, and the requirements of abstinence from alcoholic drink and women during their service). All sexual activities were separated from the ritual, and reckoned as part of the created order. God himself was also regarded as transcending sexual differences. What was taken over from Israel's neighbours was, moreover, radically altered.

2. Some scholars think that Israel's forebears brought two festivals with them from the steppe-land into the land where they settled. These were the *šabbāṭ* (→ Sabbath), a day on which important decisions and work were avoided, and the Passover (→ art. *pascha*) which had the purpose of protecting the herds from harmful demons. In the land of Canaan Israel found and took over at once the calendar of agricultural festivals which belonged to that land, and divided up the cycle of the farmer's year: *maṣṣôṯ*, at the beginning of the wheat harvest, the Feast

625

of Weeks at the end of it, and the Feast of Tabernacles at the end of the wine harvest. With the combination of the Passover and the *maṣṣôṯ*, the Passover too became a feast of pilgrimage (Deut. 16:1 ff.) without increasing the total of three (Exod. 23:14–17; 34:18, 22 f.).

Ancient festal customs remained. There is a detailed calendar in Lev. 23, Deut. 16:1–16, and the appropriate sacrifices are listed in Num. 28:9–29:39. But the recipient now was quite clearly the God of Israel. Sabbaths and feasts of pilgrimage were "to the Lord" (cf. Exod. 16:23, 25). Israel associated the ancient festivals which were based on the cycle of nature with the events of her great history. Thus the *pesaḥ-maṣṣôṯ* was early associated with the salvation from Egypt, the Feast of Weeks with the making of the covenant and the giving of the commandments on Sinai, and the Feast of Tabernacles with the journey through the wilderness (Exod. 12:12, 17; 19:1; Lev. 23:43). To preserve this historical link, which underlined the ethical content of the festivals, and to prevent Israel from relapsing into mere ritual and heathenism in its feasts, was the task of the prophets who struggled and remonstrated with the people on God's behalf because of their love and the ties of kindred. By threatening (Amos 8:10; Mal. 2:3) and scolding (Amos 5:21; Isa. 1:13 f.), they aimed to make room for God's commandments and their fulfilment along with and indeed within the sacrificial rites. Voluntary abandonment of sacrificial worship was never demanded. But whenever it became impossible for the people to carry on the sacrifices which God had ordained, the → sabbath became the most important festival for Israel, representing both a witness to outsiders and a sign of the covenant (Exod. 31:12–18).

3. The Heb. equivalents for the term *heortē* in the LXX are *ḥaḡ* (about 52 times), with the basic meaning derived from *ḥgg*, to dance (the cycle of dances – the cycle of the year), and *mô'ēḏ* (about 29 times), from the root *y'd* with its primary meaning of appoint, designate. *ḥag* is a general term for festival, and is used for the three festivals of pilgrimage and especially the Feast of Tabernacles. It denotes perhaps also procession, or festal dance. *mô'ēḏ* means appointed time, festal assembly (also festal sacrifice and location).

There were also individual and family celebrations (→ circumcision, → marriage and burial), national ones (accession and victory celebrations), local festivals, and occasions like a festival of sheep-shearing. In addition to sabbath days, importance was attached to celebrating the new moon, when a day of rest was kept and special sacrifices were offered. Two further important religious festivals were held in the autumn (which are attributed by some scholars to the Holiness Code): the New Year on the 1st and the Day of Atonement on the 10th of the month Tishri (Num. 29:1–11; Lev. 23:32–32). There may also have been at the New Year a festival of renewing the covenant (cf. Jos. 24; Exod. 19–24), and even, according to Mowinckel, the enthronement of God. After the exile there arose in the Eastern diaspora the "feast of lots (Purim)", associated with the book of Esther. The Apocrypha tell of the desecration of the feasts and the temple (1 Macc. 1:39, 45; 2 Macc. 6:6 f.), the reconsecration of the temple and the establishment of the feast, Hanukkah, the feast of dedication, to commemorate this event (1 Macc. 4:36–41; 2 Macc. 10:1–8). Tobit (1:6), Judith (8:6; 10:2) and Jesus ben Sirach (33:8; 43:7; 47:10) also tell of the observance of festivals in obedience to God's commandment.

4. In looking for the roots of the Christian attitude to feasts within Jud. we must first consider Philo. He mentions over ten festivals by name (*Spec.Leg.*, 1, 169–89; 2, 41), of which the sabbath is of prime importance as the birthday of the world and to which nature itself points (*Op.Mund.*, 89; *Praem*, 153). Only God himself can celebrate the festivals properly (*Cher.*, 90:85 f.), but he allows the righteous to take part in his celebrations, so that the whole life of the faithful is one continuous feast (*Spec.Leg.* 2, 42–55).

Even Gentiles are impressed by the holiness and seriousness with which, in keeping with Jewish customs, the worshippers can bridle their lusts as with perfect virtue they approach God's sanctuary for prayers and sacrifice (*Congr.*, 161 ff.; *Vit.Mos.*, 2, 20–24; cf. Josephus, *Ap.*, 2, 282). Josephus too records a calendar of feasts (*Ant.*, 3, 237–254) in which he mentions not only those known to Philo, but others like the festival of wood-carrying (*War*, 2, 425), the Festival of Lights in memory of the re-establishment of the temple worship under Judas Maccabaeus (*Ant.*, 12, 323–325), and the celebrations to mark the completion of the Herodian temple (*Ant.*, 15, 421).

5. Philo and Josephus give us an idealized picture of the festivals which were celebrated by the Jews in their time. In fact, Jewish groups have always celebrated the same festivals, but each in their own way and often too at their own particular time. There were even independent festivals, which were of importance only to a particular group, or were directed against other groups. Examples are the days observed by Pharisees of the Shammaite and Zealot schools to celebrate the victory of Pharisaic theology and jurisdiction over that of the Sadducees, and the political victories over the Seleucids and the Romans. Among the Essenes of Qumran there were the Feast of Weeks and the Feast of Renewal of the Covenant, an oil festival, and quarterly intercalary days which served as harvest festival, summer festival, sowing festival and green grass festival. These festivals belonging to isolated groups also differed in content, particularly in regard to the particular group's attitude to the temple or the Messiah figures. The Essenes were so critical of the temple worship that they took no part in the animal sacrifices.

A special cause of differences was provided by the dates of the festivals, since there was no general agreement on the calendar, and the dates observed, for instance, by the Pharisees and the Essenes, differed from one another, as did nominally even the sabbath dates (Jub. 6:32–38; 4QHos. 2:15; Men. 65a–66a). The Pharisees reckoned their calendar according to the lunar cycle, and brought it where necessary (later by calculated rules) into line with the solar year by adding an extra month. The Essenes, on the other hand, reckoned by the sun. Since the law of time illustrates the harmony of heaven and earth, the commandment demands that the days and hours appointed by God should be observed, and that all activity should be ordered by them (1QS 9:13 f.; 10:1–8; 1QHab 7:13 f.; 1QH 12:4–11). Hence at Qumran importance is attached to the exact study of the instructions and of the stars, and to the special revelation concerning the proper times for festivals (CD 6:18 f.; 1QS 1:9; 3:10). The Qumran calendar may be reconstructed from Jub. 6:23–32 and Eth.Enoch 72:7–32; four seasons of equal length $(3 \times 30 + 1$ day $= 91$ days $= 13$ weeks) make up a year of 364 days $= 52$ weeks (cf. also the liturgy of the heavenly sabbath sacrifice, found at Herod's fortress Masada). This meant that every feast was always celebrated on the same day of the week, and that none of the main festivals could fall on a sabbath. A fragment of a calendar found in Cave 4 (called "Mishmarot"), which lays down the periods of duty for the divisions of priests, shows on which days of the week the chief feasts fall (Passover on a Tuesday, offering of sheaves and Feast of Weeks on a Sunday, New Year on a Wednesday, Day of Atonement on a Friday, and the Feast of Tabernacles on a Wednesday).

NT Early Christians found themselves in a tension between the various Jewish communities. Thus in the question of the festival calendar too, they had to face disagreements with other groups. And since their members were drawn from the different "parties", this happened even within their own ranks.

1. In the early Christian church the propriety of celebrating the festivals together with the whole of the Jewish people was never questioned, so that it needed no special mention. Only occasionally is it stated that Jesus or Paul went to the synagogues on the sabbath, in order to pray, read or to teach (cf. Mk. 1:21; Lk. 4:16; Acts 16:13), or that the disciples and the churches took part in the pilgrim festivals. It is thus not surprising that the Jewish festival liturgy finds its way into the literature of the NT. The readings and actions used at the New Year and at the Day of Atonement form, for example, the basis for the liturgical interpretation (homiletic midrash) of Hebrews. A warning like that of 1 Cor. 5:1–8 had as its original setting a celebration during the *pesaḥ-maṣṣôṭ* week (similarly Gal. 5:9). The confessional formula about the one God through whom are all things (1 Cor. 8:4–6) reminds us of the first pericope of the cycle of Bible readings. Pagans who had to give up their form of festival celebrations in order to become Christians, could be taken along to the widely known Jewish festivals, whose historical background was in agreement with the spiritual and moral values which pervaded them.

2. What in the Synoptic Gospels is tacitly assumed rather than explicitly stated, becomes in the Fourth Gospel a main theme: Jesus is not merely a Jew among Jews; he represents rather the true Israel. Therefore, he demonstrates in his life, suffering and death the proper festal celebration. Through him the meaning of the traditional festivals returns with a new, final significance and is offered afresh to the Jews in this renewed form. The Jesus of the Fourth Gospel speaks in the style of the Pesikta (midrashim, sermon-like expositions of bible texts which were read at festivals and important sabbaths, probably in a three-year cycle). Woven into, as it were, the fabric of the recurring festivals of Israel, he presents himself with his discourses as their secret, and yet revealed, centre and climax. In each case the discourse centres on the "I am" words. The significance of this for the structure of John is even shown statistically by the fact that 15 of the total of 25 occurrences of the word *heortē* in the NT are found in this gospel. The prologue of the gospel is related to the liturgy of the Nisan cycle of festivals. With 1st Nisan in the spring, the Jewish festal year began (Rosh ha-Shanah 1:1), and this date was widely regarded as the anniversary of the creation of the world (ibid. 10b–11a; 12). Hence in some Jewish circles the reading of Gen. 1, the first of the series of pericopae, was appointed for Nisan, and Jn. 1:1–18 may well be a homiletic midrash arising from such a reading. The exegesis of the passage underlines the connection between the beginning and the new creation, while the rhythmic form of this → *archē* hymn indicates liturgical associations (similarly Col. 1:15–18).

The temporal statements of Jn. 1:29 ff. enable us to recognize a period of about two weeks, i.e. from 1st Nisan to the Passover festival on 15th Nisan (Jn. 2:13). From 2:13 (23), the cycles of feasts spread through the whole gospel. Probably three years are intended, provided that in 5:2 we read "a" feast, which will then no doubt refer to the Feast of Tabernacles. The second cycle accordingly begins at 6:4, and goes on through the Feast of Tabernacles to the Dedication of the Temple. After initial refusal Jesus goes, when the *kairos* (→ Time) has come, once more to the Feast of Tabernacles (ch. 7), in order to reveal after the fashion of a *pēšer* at Qumran the hidden meaning of the festal customs (the water procession, the great illuminations, Sukkah 5:2 ff.) by his own exposition of them (see Jn. 7:37; 9:7, 5). In the same year Jesus' presence in the temple for the Feast of Dedication is recorded (Jn. 10:22–29; cf. 1 Macc. 4:36–59). The third cycle begins in 11:55. The Passover of the trial and death, which is the only one mentioned by the synoptics, receives in John's record the most extensive treatment.

In all three Passover feasts which he mentions John makes use of a few of the chief characteristics of this festival, which after the destruction of the temple was the easiest one to preserve, since it was a festival of the family and of the laity. The vivid re-enactment of the historical events made redemption a concrete reality in memory, experience and hope, and reached its climax in the messianic hope with which this time was filled. At Passover time multitudes of people thronged together, seeking, and here and there finding, bringers of salvation, messiahs. Many appeared in and around Jerusalem, on the Mount of Olives, or by the Jordan (Josephus, *Ant.*, 20, 169 ff., 97 ff.). Occupation forces, moved from Caesarea to Jerusalem especially for the feast (Josephus, *Ant.*, 20, 106 f.), watched over their movements and prevented them from carrying out their intentions by scattering the communities and killing their leaders. But messianic pretenders also arose far from the temple in Samaria, Galilee, and in the wilderness. Wherever they arose, they inspired the hope that with the dawning of the end-time the early days of Israel would return, e.g. the wilderness period with the miraculous feeding of Israel with bread from heaven.

The Passover at the beginning of John's Gospel, with its record of the cleansing of the temple (2:12–22), already sounds the note of messianic hope. In the second Passover (Jn. 6) the bread motif is emphasized: the bread of slavery becomes the bread of freedom. The chapter is a *pēšer*, an actualizing exposition, on the words bread and flesh. The Christian sacrament of a meal (→ Lord's Supper) is a substitute for the passover sacrifice in a form which had a long history in Judaism and after A.D. 70 became universal practice. In the account of the third Passover (Jn. 12 ff.) the messianic motif is again stressed at the start, and in contrast to his attitude at the feast of the previous year Jesus now accepts the acclamation of the people (12:12–15; cf. 6:15). His ceremonial entry occurs on the very day on which the passover lambs were selected to be slaughtered the day before the evening of the festival. Thus the whole Johannine account of the trial points with unmistakable symbolism to the fact that Jesus is in truth the Lamb of God who will be sacrificed for Israel. He dies on the day and at the hour when Israel kills the lambs, and (in contrast to those crucified with him, but like the passover Lamb, according to the regulation of Exod. 12:46) no bone of his body is broken (Jn. 19 14, 32–36; cf. also 1:29–36; Rev. 5:6, 9, 12; 12:11; 1 Cor. 5:7; 1 Pet. 1:19). This lamb symbolism

629

in Jn. 12 and 19 forms a setting for the passion discourses, in which themes from the Song of Solomon, which was read in the services of Passover week, appear in midrash form (exhortations to unity in love, Jn. 13:31 ff.; 14:15 ff.; 15:9 ff.; question of the way, seeking and finding, 16:5).

In the Johannine account of the Passover of the trial, traces may be discerned of a Passover celebration according to the Essene rites, behind the elements of the Pharisaic tradition. The indication of time in Jn. 12:1 indicates that the framework with which the gospel closes is concentrated, as it were, within a festival week. (The synoptics also show signs of such a reckoning.) The end of the world corresponds to the creation (seven-day cycles of this kind originated and were handed down in priestly circles, cf. Gen. 1; Exod. 24:16). The first day (12:1 ff.) in Bethany is Sunday; the second (12:12 ff.) is Monday with the acclamation of Jesus as Messiah. The next indication of time is indefinite (13:1): "before the feast of the Passover". This introduces the foot-washing and the Last Supper, and because of the many events still to follow occurs as early as possible. The Tuesday would be the exact date for the Passover meal among the Essenes, their 14th Nisan. The discourse on bread in Jn. 6 also takes place shortly before the (Pharisaic) Passover feast. According to this account, Jesus and his party celebrated their feast on the Tuesday evening. Chief importance is attached to the change of clothes and the washing, while the eating of the lamb, which was the most important part of the Pharisees' celebration of the Passover, is given as little attention in John's account as it is in that of the synoptics. All the NT accounts are alike in making it resemble what we know of the Essene feast, which was eschatological in emphasis and probably involved no sacrificial lamb (see the description of their daily meal in Josephus, *War*, 2, 129–131; 1QS 6:4 f.; the eschatological feast, 1QSa 2:17–22; also Gos. Heb. according to Epiphanius, *Haer.*, 30, 22, 4, where Jesus says in answer to his disciples after the Passover meal, "Do you think I desire to eat meat with you at this Passover?"). Towards the morning, i.e. early on Wednesday, the betrayal and arrest take place (18:1 ff.; on Tuesday and Wednesday, Syrian Didascalia 21). This would leave sufficient time on this and the following day to carry out what is recorded in 18:13, 24, 28 without a breach of the law. (For instance it is forbidden, according to Mishnah *Sanhedrin* 4:1, to hold a trial by night or during a festival, or to pass a death sentence at the first hearing.) The impression conveyed by the accounts as they now stand is due to the fact that they are interested in other themes besides strict chronology.

The Pauline tradition does not necessarily contradict this chronology, for the "night when he was betrayed" (1 Cor. 11:23) does not have to be identical with the night before he died. Later church tradition associated (on the ground of Did., 8:1) the Christian practice of fasting on Wednesdays with the arrest of Jesus on this day, and the Friday fast with the crucifixion. The fifth day is again fixed (Jn. 19:14): a Friday, according to Jn. the day of preparation for the Passover, i.e. the 14th Nisan of the Pharisaic calendar (so too Sanhedrin 43a; according to the synoptic tradition the first day of the feast). The sixth day, a sabbath, is only hinted at. For non-Christian Jews it was always a day of pleasure, but here it is a day of quiet mourning on account of Jesus' burial. In contrast to this is the "first day of the week" (20:1 ff.), the day of Jesus' resurrection and thus the symbol of the dawn of a new world. ([Ed.] In 1 Cor. 5:8 Paul sees the Christian life in terms of the Passover:

"Let us, therefore, celebrate the festival [*heortazōmen*]. not with the old leaven, the leaven of malice and evil, but with the unleavened bread of sincerity and truth" [RSV].)

This taking up of the Jewish festivals, which in John's Gospel appears in a thoroughly conservative and biblical form, had the effect of causing the Christian festivals to retain the biblical and historical emphasis, and thus averted the danger of a pagan, erotic form of celebration.

3. In spite of the fact that the Christian festivals were thus rooted in Jewish tradition, differences and conflicts soon appeared. Paul's polemics are particularly severe against feast days which imply recognition of astral and other natural powers instead of the one God which were celebrated in the old spirit (Gal. 4:8–11; Col. 2:8–17; Rom. 14:5 ff.). Moreover, for Paul the significance of all feasts, whether Jewish or pagan, has been superseded by Christ. He does not reject all celebrations as such, but he requires celebration of the right kind.

A similar situation is found in the → sabbath controversy of the Gospels. Jesus took part in the debates of the schools on the question of keeping the sabbath rightly. The catalogue of weekday work which was forbidden had not yet been finalized. The learned scribes were concerned on the one hand to preserve the law, but on the other to preserve humanity. Jesus was criticized by those who held stricter views, and in answer justified his actions in the manner of his times on biblical grounds (cf. Matt. 12:1–12 par.). If in the Fourth Gospel the debate seems to be more intense than in the Synoptics, this intensification of the conflict is not to be seen as the cause of the division between Christians and (what was now) orthodox Judaism, but rather as its immediate result.

4. Along with the general adoption of the Jewish festivals by the early Christian communities with differences of detail, special Christian festivals also began to develop. But in the NT we find only the beginnings of these. In addition to the sabbath services, the Christians had their special gatherings on the first day of the week in memory of the redemption brought about by the resurrection of the Lord (1 Cor. 16:2; Acts 20:7). Towards the end of the 1st cent. it came to be called the "Lord's day" (Rev. 1:10). However, the fact that the two days followed one another soon led to a conscious contrasting of the two (Ign., *Mag.* 9:1; Barn. 15:9; Did. 14:1). In the following centuries, when the days of the week came generally to be given the names of the ancient pagan planet-gods, the name "Lord's day" was changed to "Sunday", which earned for the Christians the accusation that they were sun-worshippers.

It was not until the end of the 2nd cent. that Passover became the Christian Easter, and 100 years later still that the Feast of Weeks became the Christian Whitsuntide. But Jesus who gives new meaning to these feasts points the church back to their Jewish origin. In the course of the 4th cent. Ascension was introduced between them as a purely Christian festival. The last of the great Christian festivals to appear is Christmas around A.D. 335 in Rome. Of the many dates suggested, 25th December prevailed. The purpose was that it should be celebrated in opposition to the sun-cult, but with it were adopted solstice celebration customs from various nations. It is worthy of note, however, that the date is not far removed from that of the Jewish Hanukkah festival. Both were in part known as a Festival of Light.

Christians in every age have celebrated festivals, for the celebration of festivals draws attention to historical realities. It has its basis in an appreciation of time and the refusal simply to accept continuous repetition without a break. Like the commandments, the festivals of Israel were also at first accepted without question by Jewish Christians. In the end they had to be forcibly excluded as heretics, since for them Jesus Christ had become increasingly the real meaning of the ancient feasts, and it was through him that they regarded themselves as permanently linked to all Israel.

Gentile Christian churches also celebrated their festivals in accordance with the Jewish calendar, although in a certain contra-distinction to them. The determination to break free from the fortunes of the Jewish community led them, however, to adopt new pagan elements as well. In the lively controversy which resulted we can see the permanent link between the old community and the new.   *R. Mayer*

πάσχα

πάσχἀ (*pascha*), Passover.

ot *pascha* is the Gk. transliteration of the Aram. *pashā'* which corresponds to the Heb. *pesaḥ*. The meaning is not completely clear. Exod. 12:13, 23, 27 indicate a connection with the Heb. *pāsaḥ 'al*, leap over, spare, but some scholars think that this is a popular explanation. The Gk. pronunciation of the Aram. *pashā'* has in origin nothing to do with *paschein*, suffer, although a kinship between them was postulated in the patristic age.

1. In OT and Jewish literature the word is used in various senses. It can mean (a) the Passover festival (Exod. 12:11; Num. 9:2) which took place between 14th and 15th Nisan (Ezek. 45:21, conjectured reading; Lev. 23:5); (b) the animal killed at this feast (Exod. 12:5, 21; Deut. 16:2); and in Judaism (c) the seven-day festival of *pesaḥ-maṣṣôṭ*, made into a single festival at the time of the exile at the latest (Lev. 23:6–8; cf. *heortē* ot 2).

2. The Passover festival goes back to an ancient nomadic custom, which may have been connected with the annual change of pasture in the spring, and may have had the purpose of protecting the flocks from demons. In the OT tradition, however, it is associated solely with the events of the exodus from Egypt (Exod. 12:21–23), and is dedicated to be a memorial of this in the history of God's salvation of Israel (Deut. 16:1; Exod. 12:11–14). The way in which it was observed underwent various changes in the course of time, the most radical of which was in connection with the religious reforms of Josiah (621 B.C.). These meant that the celebration of the festival, which had originally been undertaken by the individual clans each in its own locality, was now confined to Jerusalem and linked with the temple worship (Deut. 16:1–8; 2 Ki. 23:21–23). Consequently the feast took on the character of a pilgrim festival like that of Pentecost and the Feast of Tabernacles (→ *heortē* ot).

3. (a) In the NT times it was the chief festival of the year, for which thousands of pilgrims from the whole Jewish world streamed to Jerusalem (cf. Lk. 2:41; Jn. 11:55). The actual feast, the Passover meal, used to take place in the houses, and, because of the great number of those taking part (more than 100,000; cf. J. Jeremias, *The Eucharistic Words of Jesus*, 1966², 42), partly on the roofs and in the courtyards. It was held in small groups of at least 10 persons, and began in the evening at or

after sunset (15th Nisan). The killing of the lambs in the inner forecourt of the temple, which was carried out by representatives of the individual groups (the only duty of the priests was the sprinkling of the blood of the lambs on the altar of burnt offering), and the preparation of the Passover meal took place on the previous afternoon (14th Nisan). The meal itself was eaten reclining. (i) To begin with, the head of the household spoke a word of dedication over a first cup of wine, from which he and after him all the members of the household drank. Then a preliminary dish was eaten (various herbs with a sauce of fruit purée). After this the main meal (passover lamb, unleavened bread, bitter herbs and purée, together with wine) was brought in, and a second cup of wine poured out. Neither of these was yet touched, however, for the next event was (ii) the Passover liturgy. The most important part of this was the Passover *haggaḏâh,* in which the head of the family related the story of the exodus from Egypt according to Deut. 26:5–11, and explained the meaning of the special items in the meal (the lamb, the unleavened bread, and the bitter herbs). Then followed the communal singing of Ps. 113 or 113 and 114 (the first part of the Passover *Hallēl*). Not until then was (iii) the main meal eaten, the head of the family introducing this with a prayer over the unleavened bread and ending it with a prayer over a third cup of wine. The end of the feast (iv), which was not allowed to continue beyond midnight, was formed by the singing of Pss. 114–117 or 115–118 (the second part of the Passover *Hallēl*), and the blessing pronounced by the head of the family over a fourth cup of wine.

(b) This feast served in ancient Judaism as a reminder of the redemption of the people from the slavery of the Egyptians and the joy over the freedom thus attained. This is its meaning in the OT also. But in addition to this it was an occasion for looking forward to the coming redemption to be brought by the Messiah. Passover time, particularly during the Roman occupation of Palestine, was always a time of increased Messianic expectation (Lk. 13:1–3; Mk. 15:7 par.; Jn. 6:15; cf. A. Strobel, *ZNW* 49, 1958, 187 ff.).

NT In the NT *pascha* has the same range of meanings as in contemporary Jud. Its chief use is for the Feast of the Passover including the Feast of Unleavened Bread (*maṣṣôṯ*; Matt. 26:2; Lk. 2:41; 22:1; Acts 12:4; Jn. 2:13, 23; 6:4; 11:55; 12:1; 13:1; 18:39; 19:14). But it can also refer to the Passover proper (Mk. 14:1; Matt. 26:18; Heb. 11:28) or the Passover lamb (Mk. 14:12; 14, 16; Matt. 26:17, 19; Lk. 22:7, 8, 11, 13, 15; Jn. 18:28; 1 Cor. 5:7). The expressions "to prepare the Passover" and "to eat the Passover" could also refer to the entire main part of the feast.

1. (a) The only reference made in the NT to the Passover of the exodus from Egypt is at Heb. 11:28. It is interpreted as evidence of the faith of Moses, in that he believed God's promise to spare the people on the ground of the Passover blood, and showed his faith by keeping the Passover.

(b) The Passover background plays a special part in the passion narrative. All four Gospels record that the Last Supper of Jesus, his arrest, trial and condemnation took place at Passover time (Mk. 14; Matt. 26, 27; Lk. 22, 23; Jn. 18, 19). According to the synoptic gospels, Jesus' Last Supper was itself a Passover meal (Mk. 14:12–26 par.), and he was arrested, tried and condemned on the Passover night and crucified the next day. According to John, on the other hand, all these

633

events happened 24 hours earlier (cf. Jn. 18:28; 19:14), so that the death of Jesus took place at the time when the Passover lambs were killed, on the afternoon of the 14th Nisan. Many regard this as a later alteration of the date, probably occasioned by the comparison found elsewhere in the NT (1 Cor. 5:7; 1 Pet. 1:19; Jn. 19:36; cf. Rev. 5:6, 9, 12; 12:11) of Jesus with the Passover lamb. ([Ed.] However, the chronological schemes of the Gospels and the contemporary systems of reckoning are subjects of intense discussion, see bibliography.) The objections which have been raised, particularly against the identification of Jesus' Last Supper with a Passover meal, do not carry much weight. Not only the setting (Mk. 14:12 par.; Lk. 22:14), but also the words of explanation, in which Jesus compares himself to the Passover lamb (Mk. 14:22–24 par.; Lk. 22-19 f.), surely point us to this context (the interpretation of the elements of the feast by the head of the family; cf. J. Jeremias, *The Eucharistic Words of Jesus*, 1966[2], 41–84).

2. In the early church the Passover continued to be celebrated (Jn. 2:13; 6:4; 11:55 imply this; cf. Acts 20:6). As in Judaism, the feast took place on the evening following 14th Nisan and in expectation of eschatological redemption. This cannot be ascertained directly from the NT, but it may be deduced, in particular, from the records we have of the Passover festival of the Quartodecimans (cf. B. Lohse, see bibliography), a Christian community in Asia Minor and Syria which retained in this respect the customs of the earliest church. As we can see from 1 Cor. 5:7–8 (which may be an early Christian Passover *haggaḏâh*) and 1 Pet. 1:13–19, the primitive church regarded itself as the people of God redeemed in the eschatological Passover. The baptized are exhorted, like those involved in the first Passover, to live holy lives in readiness to depart (1 Pet. 1:13, 17), as those redeemed "with the precious blood of Christ, like that of a lamb without blemish or spot" (1 Pet. 1:19, cf. 1 Cor. 5:7 "Christ our Passover"). The church receives the call to keep the feast (*heortazōmen*) and cleanse itself from the old leaven, "that you may be a new lump" (1 Cor. 5:7 f.). The eschatological Passover feast has begun with Good Friday, and its fulfilment in the return of Christ is awaited at any time in the Passover night.

3. This form and interpretation of the Passover festival disappeared early in the history of the church. During the 2nd cent. the celebration of Easter on a Sunday became general, with its emphasis on remembering the sacrificial death of Jesus, the true Passover lamb. This process gives clear expression both to the break between Judaism and Christianity and to the decline of eschatological expectation within the early Christian church. *B. Schaller*

→ Lord's Supper, → Pentecost, → Resurrection, → Sabbath

(a). J.-J. von Allmen, *Worship: Its Theology and Practice*, 1965; J. Bowman, *The Gospel of Mark: The New Christian Jewish Passover Haggadah*, 1965; H. Cazelles and J. Michl, "Passover", *EBT* II 642–47; R. E. Clements, *God and Temple*, 1965; O. Cullmann, *Early Christian Worship*, 1953; G. Delling, *Worship in the New Testament*, 1962; G. Fohrer, *History of Israelite Religion*, 1973; A. S. Herbert, *Worship in Ancient Israel*, 1959; A. J. B. Higgins, *The Lord's Supper in the New Testament*, (1952) 1960; A. Jaubert, *The Date of the Last Supper*, 1965; J. Jeremias, *The Eucharistic Words of Jesus*, 1966[2]; and *pascha*, *TDNT* V 896–904; H.-J. Kraus, *Worship in Israel*, 1966; C. F. D. Moule, *Worship in the New Testament*, 1961; A. R. Johnson, *Sacral Kingship in Ancient Israel*, 1955; H. H. Rowley, *Worship in Ancient Israel: Its Forms and Meaning*, 1967; W. Rordorf, *Sunday*, 1968; E. Ruckstuhl, *Chronology of the Last Days of Jesus*, 1965; J. C. Rylaarsdam, "Feasts and Fasts," *IDB* II 260–64; and "Passover and Feast of Unleavened Bread," *IDB* III 663–68; H. Schauss, *The Jewish Festivals*, 1938; J. B. Segal, *The Hebrew Passover from the Earliest*

Times to A.D. 70, London Oriental Series 12, 1963 (extensive bibliography); M. H. Shepherd, *The Paschal Liturgy and the Apocalypse*, 1960; N. H. Snaith, *The Jewish New Year Festival: Its Origin and Development*, 1947; R. de Vaux, *Ancient Israel: Its Life and Institutions*, 1961, 484–518 (literature on individual feasts, 552); A. Guilding, *The Fourth Gospel and Jewish Worship*, 1960; L. Morris, *The New Testament and the Jewish Lectionaries*, 1964 (reply to Guilding); J. D. M. Derrett, "The Parable of the Great Supper," *Law in the New Testament*, 1970, 126–55; G. Ogg, "The Chronology of the Last Supper," *Historicity and Chronology in the New Testament*, *SPCK Theological Collections* 6, 1965, 75–96.

(b). On *heortē*: E. Auerbach, "Die Feste im alten Israel," *VT* 8, 1958, 1–18; L. Deubner, *Attische Feste*, reprint 1956; I. Elbogen, *Der jüdische Gottesdienst*, 1924²; A. Jaubert, "Jésus et le calendrier de Qumrân", *NTS* 7, 1960–61, 1–30; H.-J. Kraus, "Gottesdienst im alten und neuen Bund," *EvTh* 4–5, 1965, 171 ff.; H. Lietzmann, *Der christliche Kalender*, 1935; G. Loeschke, *Jüdisches und Heidnisches im christlichen Kult*, 1910; R. Mayer, *Der Babylonische Talmud*, 1965² (selections, see on feasts); S. Mowinckel, *Das Betronungsfest Jahwes und der Ursprung der Eschatologie*, 1921; M. P. Nilsson, *Griechische Feste von religiöser Bedeutung, mit Ausschluss der attischen*, reprint 1957; B. Reicke, *Diakonie, Festfreude und Zelos in Verbindung mit der christlichen Agapenfeier*, 1951; L. Rost, *Weidewechsel und altisraelitischer Festkalender*, 1951; P. Volz, *Das Neujahrfest Jahwes*, 1912.

On *pascha*: J. Carmignac, "Comment Jésus et ses contemporains pouvaient-ils célébrer la Pâque à une date non officielle?" *Revue de Qumran* 5, 1964, 59 ff.; L. Le Déaut, *La Nuit Pascale*, 1963; P. Grelot and J. Pierron, *La Nuit et les Fêtes de Paques*, 1956; N. Flüglister *Die Heilsbedeutung des Pascha, Studien zum Alten und Neuen Testament* 8, 1963; H.-J. Kraus, "Zur Geschichte des Passah-Massotfestes im Alten Testament", *EvTh* 18, 1958, 47–67; E. Kutsch, "Erwägungen zur Geschichte der Passahfeier und des Massotfestes," *ZTK* 55, 1958, 1–35; B. Lohse, *Das Passahfest der Quartadezimaner*, *BFChTh* 54, 1953; J. Pedersen, *Passahfest und Passahlegende*, 1933; J. Schildenberger, "Der Gedächtnischarakter des alt- und neutestamentlicher Paschas," in B. Neunheuser, ed., *Opfer Christi und Opfer der Kirche*, 1960, 75–97.

Fellowship, Have, Share, Participate

The following article deals with words which have to do with having, sharing and participation and fellowship. The two key words that are examined together with their associated ideas are *echō* (have), and *koinōnia* (communion, fellowship).

ἔχω

ἔχω (*echō*), have; μετέχω (*metechō*), share, participate in; μετοχή (*metochē*), sharing, participation; μέτοχος (*metochos*), partaking, sharing, participating, a partner, companion.

CL *echō* means to have or hold in wide range of senses: possess, keep, have, hold; aor. acquire, take into possession; intrans. keep, hold oneself. Thus the connection between the subject and object of *echō* can denote a similar wide range of personal, material and metaphorical meanings. Sometimes the subject and object can exchange places. In Gk. one may say "he has a sickness" or "a sickness has him." Moreover, the word can denote entry into any one of these conditions: to attain to, get hold of, come by.

This great breadth of meaning evidently made it possible for Aristotle to take *echō* into his teaching about categories. In view of its content it is clearly regarded as a genuine category (*Cat.*, 15). Elsewhere, however, he felt free to omit it with *keisthai* (posture, attitude, *Cat.*, 2) altogether or to group it with another category (cf. F. Ueberweg, *History of Philosophy*, I, 188, 154). In his later *Metaphysics* it is again counted among the 30 categories discussed there. It means to have or to hold

635

in the following senses: (1) to treat a thing according to its own nature or impulse (e.g. a fever has a man; people have clothes); (2) to be present in (e.g. "the body has a disease" means that a disease is present in the body); (3) to contain or hold (e.g. the vessel holds the liquid); (4) hindering a thing from acting according to its natural impulse (e.g. a pillar holds that which it supports).

metechō means to share or participate. Its object is always in the gen. The noun *metochē* means sharing, participation, and the adj. *metochos* likewise means sharing.

Two aspects of these words are theologically significant. There is the rational and material sense of having (as in Aristotle), and there is the enthusiastic sense of having, as being possessed, or mystical sharing. The latter sense found expression in Homer, Plato, Plotinus and other writers who spoke of the *daimonion echein* (having a demon or a demon having one) which acted in people and which a man could have. Later the idea broadened out into the pantheistic and mystical having of the divine One in Plotinus. In later philosophy the *nous* (mind) became the world-soul which no longer had personal characteristics. It was no longer said that man had *nous* or *logos* (reason). Instead he was said to participate (*metechō*) in them. Plato used *metochē* (participation) to express the relationship of particular things to the Idea or → Form. The lower and relative participates in the higher and absolute. Out of this there arose in the course of philosophical development a cosmic hierarchy of all existents which leads in an unbroken line of participation to a higher world (on Plotinus see *TDNT* II 830). The theological aspect of this idea of cosmic participation found classical expression in Origen's Platonic restatement of the doctrine of creation (cf. J. N. D. Kelly, *Early Christian Doctrines*, 1968[4], 128 ff.).

OT Heb. has no special word for *echō*. What is expressed by *echō* in Gk. is expressed in Heb. by the dat., a pronoun, a preposition or a circumlocution, such as saying that someone or something is in the hand or hands of someone ('*al yaḏ* or *biyḏê* etc.). *echō* is found 12 times in the LXX for these expressions. In all, it is used to translate over 50 different Heb. expressions. *echō* occurs more than 500 times in the LXX. But a large number of these instances come in passages which have no Heb. original.

It is the same with the compounds *metechō*, *metochē*, and *metochos* as with → *koinōneō* etc. The words appear only in the later writings of the OT. *metechō* is used to translate expressions which in Heb. use only prepositions. *metochē* and *metochos* mostly translate words connected with the root *ḥāḇar* (tie, unite).

The words are used in these passages in basically the same sense as in earlier Gk. literature. Their theological significance is not, however, to be derived from the Gk. but from Heb. usage against its OT background.

At the heart of the OT message stands the confession that God has chosen his people. It is his possession. The reverse is also true. He is his people's God (Pss. 33:12; 144:15; cf. Hos. 2:21–25; → Covenant). Therefore, there shall be no other gods beside him (Exod. 20:2 f.). Because Yahweh is the God of his people, he is strength, rock, fortress and saviour of the individual (e.g. Pss. 18:3; 27:1). God is the → inheritance of the Levites (Deut. 10:9; Ezek. 44:28; and often). Hence, Israel's confession: "Our God is a God of salvation" (Ps. 68:20; cf. 73:25). Esther prayed: "I have no helper beside you" (Est. 4:17t LXX). For similar expressions in Maccabean and post-Christian literature see *TDNT* II 817, 822 f.

The word *echō* does not in fact appear in any of these OT passages apart from the late reference in Est. On the other hand, the relationship described there which God guarantees to his people through the → covenant provides the basis for what the NT describes in its theological use of the idea of having. Paul, for example, clearly refers to this when he wrote that Israel had the → law and boasted of it (Rom. 2:20, 23). Israel had a zeal for God (Rom. 10:2) and much more. Israel had "the sonship, the glory, the covenants, the giving of the law, the worship, and the promises . . . the patriarchs, and of their race, according to the flesh . . . the Christ" (Rom. 9:4 f.). But Israel did not have the fulfilment of all this in Christ. The NT is the first to testify to this.

NT The distribution of *echō* in the NT varies considerably in different writings·

But it has the same broad range of meaning as in secular Gk. and the LXX· The following aspects are theologically significant.

1. *echō* is used as an expression for possession and relationship. The phrase *daimonion echein* (to have a demon) which occurs in secular Gk. also occurs in the Synoptics (Matt. 11:18; Lk. 5:33). But the demon is only mentioned in the context of Jesus' lordship over it. For that reason the reproach that he had Beelzebul (→ Satan), i.e. that he was possessed by him, is absurd and blasphemous (Mk. 3:22, 30; cf. Jn. 7:20; 8:48; 10:20 f.). It may be compared with the expression *akatharton pneuma echein*, to have an unclean spirit (Mk. 7:25; Lk. 4:33; and often; cf. 13:11).

The NT has also such statements as to have children, sons, brothers, a wife etc. *echō* is used absolutely for sexual intercourse (Matt. 14:4). The prayer of Esther mentioned above corresponds to the words of the lame man at the pool of Bethesda: "I have no man to put me into the pool" (Jn. 5:7). Similarly Paul: "I have no one like him" (Phil. 2:20; cf. 1:7).

Having is used in a theologically significant way in those passages in which relationship with God is involved. The Jews claimed to have God as their father (Jn. 8:41). "Masters, treat your slaves justly and fairly, knowing that you also have a Master in heaven" (Col. 4:1). This relationship between God and man is further defined by Christ. Believers have him as their advocate with the Father (1 Jn. 2:1) and as high priest (Heb. 4:14; 8:1; 10:21). He who despises him already has a judge (Jn. 12:48).

2. As in the OT, this having fellowship with God is characterized, not by man's striving, but by God's promises and gift. This was also the ground of salvation in the OT. To have salvation is to have it through Jesus Christ. "He who hears my word and believes him who sent me has eternal life" (Jn. 5:24). This thought is stressed by Heb., Paul and especially Jn.

Jn. does this in his own special way. "He who has the Son has life; he who has not the Son has not life" (1 Jn. 5:12). "Anyone who goes ahead and does not abide in the doctrine of Christ does not have God; he who abides in the doctrine of Christ has both the Father and the Son" (2 Jn. 9). A man can know of God, talk about him, and even claim to have him, like the false teachers, and still not have him. Here *echō* is the expression for genuine fellowship with God and true faith in its fullest and deepest sense. To "have fellowship" with one another and with Christ (1 Jn. 1:6 f.) is to "know" him (1 Jn. 2:3) and to "abide" in him (v. 6). These polemically intended words all refer to the same thing which is most tersely expressed by *echō*. The same applies to those passages which speak of having eternal → life (Jn. 3:15 f., 36), → peace (16:33), and the → light (8:12; 12:35 f.).

John's opponents see this fellowship with God as a mystical mastering of God. For John it is possible only through the Son of God who has become flesh. It comes though the witness of the Holy Spirit whom Christians have (1 Jn. 2:20, 27; 5:10). Those who do not have the witness of the Father and his word living in them do not know God and have no life (Jn. 5:38 ff.). But those who stand in a personal relationship to the historical Jesus through the Spirit have the Father and life (1 Jn. 1:1–3; 4:13 ff.). To this also belong → confession (1 Jn. 4:2, 15; 2 Jn. 7), abiding in the doctrine of Christ (2 Jn. 9), and keeping his word and commandments (1 Jn. 2:3 ff.).

In this way John takes up the prophetic, eschatological message of John the Baptist which saw the promised time of salvation break in with Christ. This is a theme which links Jn. with the Synoptics and Paul. Behind it is the thought of late Jewish apocalyptic that the present is void of salvation. For salvation is revealed only to a few gifted visionaries; it is to be expected in its fullness only in the future. However, Jn. and the other NT writers reject this idea. For here and now in the present believers have peace with God (Rom. 5:1), redemption through his blood (Eph. 4:7; Col. 1:14), and access to God's gracious purpose in salvation (Eph. 3:12). Now is the day of salvation (2 Cor. 6:2). Life as full salvation in Christ (Jn. 3:16, 36) is entered into now.

3. This is strongly emphasized by Paul in a different way. To participate in salvation is to be in Jesus Christ through his → Spirit. It is a spiritual having. "Anyone who does not have the Spirit of Christ does not belong to him" (Rom. 8:9). The Spirit of Christ, his *nous* (mind, 1 Cor. 2:16), gives Paul the authority to summon the church to obedience and imitation of Christ (→ Might, art. *exousia*). To have the Spirit means to be led by the Spirit (Rom. 8:14). The believer is no longer his own (1 Cor. 6:19; cf. 3:16). He is Christ's → slave (Rom. 1:1; 1 Cor. 7:22). This also means that to have the Spirit and to be bound to this Lord is to have this treasure in earthen vessels (2 Cor. 4:7) and to bear continually in our bodies the dying of Jesus (2 Cor. 4:10 ff.). Because the Spirit is the pledge and first fruits (→ Gift, art. *arrabōn*; Rom. 8:23; 2 Cor. 1:22; 5:5), the believer remains on this side of the barrier of death which Christ has already broken through. But as the pledge of future resurrection glory he gives us the certainty (Rom. 8:11) that one day our earthly house will be destroyed (2 Cor. 5:1) and we shall participate in this glory. To have in this age is to have in hope (Rom. 5:2; Phil. 3:8 ff.; cf. *TDNT* II 824).

Here lies the point of contrast between Paul and the gnostics. The enthusiasts in Corinth claimed that they had already the resurrection glory (1 Cor. 4:8, 10; 15:12). Paul opposed this with the gospel of the cross (1 Cor. 1:17, 23). In opposition to the self-seeking grandeur of "knowledge" which destroys, Paul stressed love which builds up (8:1). Love is also opposed to libertinism (10:23 f.; 13:2). For the sake of the gospel Paul had to bear much suffering and strife. It even meant

638

bearing the dying of Christ in his own body (2 Cor. 4:10). But in this suffering he also received great strengthening and → comfort (2 Cor. 1:5).

4. This having is to be understood neither as a permanent possession nor as absolution from obedience. This is underlined by the use of *metechō* in Paul and Heb. To share in *dikaiosynē* (righteousness, justification) puts the whole of a man's life under obligation, and excludes *anomia* (lawlessness, 2 Cor. 6:14). To be in Christ leaves no room for sin. Participation in the Lord's Supper rules out participation in pagan sacrifices and vice versa (1 Cor. 10:17, 21). *metechō* is used virtually as a synonym for → *koinōneō*. In Heb. the concern is above all with sharing in the sufferings and → patience of Christ. The *metochoi Christou* (those who "share in Christ", Heb. 3:14; cf. 6:4) are called upon to patient endurance in persecution and holding fast to the true faith, so that they may not lose their share in future glory. To be *metochoi paideias* (participants in chastisement, 12:8) is in fact a sign of being a true → child, for the Lord disciplines those whom he loves (12:6; cf. Prov. 3:12).

5. Just as all spiritual having comes under the lordship of the present and coming Lord, so is also the possession of all material goods. "What do you have that you did not receive?" (1 Cor. 4:7). For all earthly goods God has to be asked in the right attitude (Jas. 4:2). Their use has to be seen in the light of eschatology. Paul is one who has nothing and yet possesses all things (2 Cor. 6:10). Therefore, he urged the Corinthians to have as if they did not have (1 Cor. 7:29 ff.). It is not only for the sake of future glory that they are to break loose from all possessions. They are to work to acquire possessions so that they may have in order to give to those in need (Eph. 4:28). Everything that the NT has to say about having and participating is a testimony to the act of God in Jesus Christ with a view to future glory. But participation is now already a fact through the Holy Spirit who establishes us in sonship, obedience, love and hope. *J. Eichler*

κοινωνία

κοινός (*koinos*), common, communal; κοινόω (*koinoō*), make common or impure, defile, profane; κοινωνέω (*koinōneō*), share, have a share in, participate in; κοινωνία (*koinōnia*), association, communion, fellowship, participation; κοινωνικός (*koinōnikos*), giving, sharing, liberal; κοινωνός (*koinōnos*), companion, partner, sharer; συγκοινωνός (*synkoinōnos*), participant, partner; συγκοινωνέω (*synkoinōneō*), participate in with someone, be connected with, share.

CL 1. *koinos* is found from Mycenean Gk. onwards. When applied to things, it means common, mutual, public. Hence, *to koinon* means the community, common property, in the plur. public affairs, the state. When applied to people, *koinos* means related, a partner, impartial. The corresponding vb. *koinoō* means to have a share in, unite, communicate, and also to profane. *koinōneō* means to possess together, have a share, join oneself to; *koinōnia* communion, participation, intercourse. As an adj., *koinōnos* means common; as a noun, companion, partner.

In the Gk. and Hel. world *koinōnia* was a term which meant the evident, unbroken fellowship between the gods and men. Even Philo spoke of "the sublime fellowship [of Moses] with the father and creator of the universe" (*Vit. Mos.*, 1,

158). But the word was not used in the LXX to denote the relationship between God and man.

koinōnia also denoted the close union and brotherly bond between men. It was taken up by the philosophers to denote the ideal to be sought. The life-tie which united the Pythagoreans was called *hē tou biou koinōnia* (lit. the fellowship of life). *koinōnia* has thus virtually the sense of brotherhood, and is a standing expression for the way social life is constituted. The Stoic doctrine of the state opposed the ethical atomism which was breaking up Hel. society. It went back ultimately to the *zōon koinōnikon* (Aristot., *Eth. Eud.*, 7, 10, which denoted belonging to a society; cf. *TDNT* II 809). The philosopher was regarded as the educator of the nations and his teaching was to provide the basis for political life. A remarkable example of this development is the inscription on the tomb of Antiochus Philopappus of Commagene, a highly important piece of evidence for Hellenism in the first century B.C. The word *koinos* occurs seven times. The term is not only a witness of a religious syncretism which depicted gods from four different cultures reigning together. It also testifies to an ever increasing cosmopolitanism.

2. Plato's *Republic* and *Laws* sketched the ideal of a communistic utopia. His attempt with Dionysius in Syracuse to translate his vision into reality suffered shipwreck. So too did the social revolution of Aristonicus at Pergamum (133–132 B.C.). Impulse to revolutionary ideas came from the fervently religious poetry of Hesiod (*c.* 700 B.C.). To the people groaning under the oppression of the aristocracy his *Works and Days* proclaimed the myth of a golden age, in which dreams of happiness, equality, justice and brotherliness were transposed into a shining primeval period. The doctrine of common property had a primeval aspect. Early Athens was seen as a model. Plato took up the same theme. "Neither had any of them anything of their own, but they regarded all that they had as common property; nor did they claim to receive of the other citizens anything more than their necessary food" (*Critias*, 110). But whereas this looked back to a golden age, the sharing in the early church at Jerusalem is to be understood in the light of its eschatological experience. The Stoics declared that friends must share and possessions are the common property of friends. But they too based their demands on an ideal picture of a golden age, which was now lost for ever in its original pure form. The NT, on the other hand, does not look backwards but forwards. The new age must break into the present, lost world.

OT 1. In the primeval history of Gen. the rupture of fellowship with God was followed by the loss of unity among men. But God's activity in forgiving, saving and preserving did not cease. Instead, it found new ways (Gen. 8:21 f.; 12:3). Abraham and after him the people of Israel stood in a saving relationship to Yahweh, the goal of which was to bridge the gulf between God and man.

God dealt with Israel as a community and fulfilled his promises to it. He gave Israel the land as an inheritance which in the last analysis belonged to himself (Lev. 25:23). The tribes, families and especially the individuals were only tenants of the portions allocated to them. They had therefore no right to dispose of them. The judicial murder of Naboth (1 Ki. 21) should be judged in this light. Its background is the clash between the ancient Israelite right to land described above and the Canaanite royal right which Ahab wished to exercise.

From here a line can be drawn to the attitude of the prophets in general. Just as Elijah denounced the breach of the ancient right, the prophets were opposed to all land speculation (cf. Isa. 5:8), and stood up for the interests of the community.

This obvious solidarity of God, the nation and the land continued into the NT period. Israel could not envisage faith in God without entering the community and receiving the covenant sign. (On the significance of *qāhāl* for Israel → Church; and on the → covenant sign → Circumcision.)

2. The theological motif of broken fellowship with God (as in primeval history), the problem of preserving the community in the order which is according to God's will (cf. Isa. 5:8), and the role of the community in the ultimate, universal picture of salvation (cf. Gen. 1:23; Isa. 49:6), play a large part in the OT. It is therefore all the more striking that the *koinōnia* word group occurs almost exclusively in the later writings (Eccl., Prov., Wis., 1–4 Macc.), usually to translate words connected with the Heb. root *ḥābar* (unite, join together). It is doubtful whether the absence of this term in the earlier OT writings is due to dislike of abstractions. In the OT stress was laid on the covenant and the individual's membership of the people. These were communal ideas. But in contrast to the quasi-egalitarian idea of *koinōnia*, these ideas stressed the unilateral role of Yahweh as the founder and guarantor of the community and its members. Where *koinōnia* etc. occur in the LXX, they are used in a general sense: "It is better to live in a corner of a housetop than in a house shared with a contentious woman" (Prov. 21:9; 25:24); "he who is joined with all the living has hope" (Eccl. 9:4); "who goes in company with evildoers" (Job 34:8). 1 Macc. 1:47 has *koinos* in the sense of profane, ceremonially defiled. This was the sense it often had later (cf. Acts 21:28; Rev. 21:27).

3. According to Josephus (*War*, 2, 119–161) and Philo (*Omn.Prob.Lib.*, 12 f.), the communal life of the Essenes was based on the idea of the equality of all the members. This is emphatically supported by the evidence of the Dead Sea Scrolls for the Qumran community. Each member was required to renounce his possessions (1 QS 1:11 f.; cf. 3:2; 6:19 f.; cf. H. Ringgren, *The Faith of Qumran*, 1963, 142 f., 210, 236; Millar Burrows, *More Light on the Dead Sea Scrolls*, 1958, 81, 116, 383). He had to hand over his entire possessions to the estate of the community. The principal motive for this was not as in ancient Greece the ideal of brotherly communal possession, but the idea that possession of money was tainted with sin. Money was the possession of ungodliness, stained with uncleanness. It was for this reason that the Essene parted with his private property.

According to Philo (*Vit. Cont.*, 25), there was a band of Jewish men and women that lived in a communal life of monastic seclusion, possessing no private property, which was devoted to the study of scripture. The word *monastērion* (monastery) occurs here for the first time. The Christian communities of the 4th cent. A.D. continued the tradition of ascetic, monastic life, sharing common property.

In the tractate Pesahim 7, 3a, 13a *ḥᵃbûrâh* (fellowship) means the Passover fellowship: "One day the Holy[God] . . . will prepare a feast for the devout." At the heavenly table David will distribute the chalice with wine. This eschatological meal recalls Lk. 22:19 and Did. 9:2.

NT *koinōnia* is absent from the synoptics and Jn. But it occurs 13 times in Paul and is a typical Pauline term. The same is true of the vb. *koinōneō*. The use of *koinos* and *koinōnia* in Acts 2 and in general in Lk.'s picture of the primitive church requires special attention. Elsewhere, *koinos* (Matt. 15:11, 18; Mk. 7:15; Acts 10:14) and the vb. *koinoō* (Mk. 7:18; Acts 10:15; 21:28) mean respectively unclean and to defile. *koinōnos* (Lk. 5:10; 2 Cor. 8:23; Phlm. 17) means partner, companion, sharer. In most cases, however, it is to be translated as an adj., sharing, participating in, or by a verbal phrase. *koinōnikos* occurs only in 1 Tim. 6:18, where it means liberal. *synkoinōnos* (participant, partner) and *synkoinōneō* (participate in with someone, be connected with, share) occur only in Paul and Rev. 1:9; 18:4.

1. Acts 4:32 ff. gives a picture of the communal sharing of goods which was practised for a time in the early church. This "religious communism of love" (Troeltsch) in the primitive church was the expression of an enthusiastic love. But it presupposed the continuance of private earning and the voluntary character of sacrifice and giving to the needy. There is no hint of either communal production or communal consumption. It was not organized, and is not to be seen in economic categories. It rose out of the untramelled freedom from care that Jesus preached and from his lofty scorn of goods (Matt. 6:25–34). It is to be seen as the continuance of the common life that Jesus led with his disciples (Lk. 8:1–3; Jn. 12:4 ff.; 13:29). The idea of equality is completely lacking. The extraordinary action of Barnabas (Acts 4:36) and that of Ananias and Sapphira (Acts 5:1–11) were singled out for mention. But this does not mean that the community of possessions was general. This would not have been possible for the great majority of church members. Mention of the house of Mary (Acts 12:12) indicates that private ownership continued. Lk.'s general account of the Jerusalem church reflects the attitude of love which was intensified by an acute expectation of the end.

The *koinōnia* in Acts 2:42 can be taken in an absolute sense as an essential part of the life of worship: "And they devoted themselves to the apostles' teaching and fellowship, to the breaking of bread and the prayers" (Acts 2:42). There were thus four main aspects of this way of life (cf. B. Reicke, *Glauben und Leben der Urgemeinde*, 1957, 56). In this case, *koinōnia* could be translated "communion" or "liturgical fellowship in worship." But *koinōnia* expresses something new and independent. It denotes the unanimity and unity brought about by the Spirit. The individual was completely upheld by the community. The Hellenist Luke clearly had in mind the Pythagoreans and the Essenes. The educated reader would have got the impression that here the Greek ideal of society had been realized.

The early church doubtless had financial cares. The fishermen and peasants that had migrated from Galilee would find earning a living difficult in the capital city. Moreover, the economic state of Palestine deteriorated through famine and continued unrest. The impoverishment of the early church was not a consequence of the sharing of possessions. The collections that Paul brought to Jerusalem were a tangible expression of fellowship in the churches. The collection has a religious overtone in 2 Cor. 9:13: "by the generosity of the fellowship (*koinōnias*, RSV "contribution") for them and for all others." For it arises out of the one gospel that unites Jew and Gentile, and belongs to the same spiritual and material giving and taking of which Paul speaks in Rom. 15:26. There was real need in Jerusalem. The poor among the saints at Jerusalem were in the majority. The stream of "spiritual gifts" which flowed from Jerusalem was answered by a counter-stream of "earthly gifts."

642

The example of the early church remained isolated. Copying its example was neither demanded nor acted upon. The integrity of private property was regarded as a matter of course in all the churches. Christianity brought a new outlook, not a new order of society. At the Evangelical Social Conference in 1895 Friedrich Naumann said: "It is not possible to come to a system of economics from the standpoint of religion." On the other hand, Ernst Troeltsch pointed out that there is an independent revolutionary element in Christianity but no will to instigate revolution (*The Social Teaching of the Christian Churches*, I, 1931, 39–69).

2. In Paul *koinōnia* and the associated words have a central significance. Close analysis of the term shows that Paul never used *koinōnia* in a secular sense but always in a religious one (H. Seesemann, *Der Begriff koinōnia im Neuen Testament*, 1933, 99). It is never equated with *societas*, companionship or community. It is not a parallel to *ekklēsia* and has nothing to do with the local congregation. Nor does it correspond with the Jewish *ḥᵃbûrâh* (fellowship, union). It is not, as in the Stoa, a group of individuals united by a common idea. Hence *koinōnia* is to be sharply distinguished from both Gk. ideas and Judaism.

(a) The idea of an earthly society grounded in human nature is foreign to Paul. For him *koinōnia* refers strictly to the relation of faith to Christ: "the fellowship of his Son" (1 Cor. 1:9), "the fellowship of the Holy Spirit" (2 Cor. 13:13), "fellowship in the gospel" (Phil. 1:5), "fellowship of faith" (Phlm. 6). In each case the object is in the gen. The "right hand of fellowship" (Gal. 2:9) given to Paul and Barnabas by James, Peter and John was not just a handshake over a deal but mutual recognition of being in Christ. Similarly, *koinōnia* in 1 Cor. 10:16 means "participation" in the body and blood of Christ and thus union with the exalted Christ. This fellowship with Christ comes about through the creative intervention of God. It happens through the transformation of man to the very roots of his being. It is birth into a new existence, and can be expressed by the contrast of life and death. This new existence is not a divinization in the sense of mysticism and the mystery religions, but incorporation in Jesus' death, burial, resurrection and glory. It is not the elimination or fusion of personality but a new relationship based on the forgiveness of sins. Paul expressed this in paradoxes, new expressions that he coined and mixed metaphors which he used to present *koinōnia* and guard against mystical misunderstanding. These include: *syzēn*, to live with (Rom. 6:8; 2 Cor. 7:3); *sympaschein*, to suffer with (Rom. 8:17); *systaurousthai*, to be crucified with (Rom. 6:6); *synegeiresthai*, to be raised with (Col. 2:12; 3:1; Eph. 2:6); *syzoō-poiein*, to make alive with (Col. 2:13; Eph. 2:5); *syndoxazein*, to glorify with (Rom. 8:17); *synklēronomein*, to inherit with (Rom. 8:17); *symbasileuein*, reign with (2 Tim. 2:12). The suffering of the apostle which is a part of the total suffering of Christ (Phil. 3:10; Col. 1:24) gives him the prospect of glory (cf. Phil. 3:10 with with Rom. 8:17; 1 Thess. 4:17).

(b) Apart from in Matt. 23:30, where the Pharisees reject the charge that they had a share in the blood of the prophets, and those passages where it means fellow worker or companion, *koinōnos* belongs to this area of Pauline usage. To eat meat that has been sacrificed to idols means to be a sharer in pagan sacrifice and fellowship with demons which excludes one from fellowship in the Lord's Supper and fellowship with Christ (1 Cor. 10:18). 2 Cor. 1:7 and 1 Pet. 5:1 refer to the sharing by the apostle and the church in the suffering and glory of the risen Lord. Anyone who suffers oppression and persecution through following Christ may rest assured that he will like his Lord attain life through temptation and death. In the same connection, Heb. 10:33 speaks of being partners with those who are ill-treated and exhorts its readers to patience. According to 2 Pet. 1:4, believers are made "partakers of the divine nature", "through the knowledge of him who called us to his own → glory" (v. 3) and patient endurance. Thus he has already a share in the divine nature which is superior to all mundane existence. The same applies to passages where *synkoinōneō* and *synkoinōnos* occur. Participation in evil is rejected (Eph. 5:11; Rev. 18:4). But one can participate in suffering (Phil. 4:14) and the gospel and its hope (1 Cor. 9:23; Phil. 1:7). According to Rom. 11:17, the Gentiles who are like branches grafted in to the olive tree of Israel now share in its election and promises.

3. *koinōnia* in 1 Jn. 1:3, 6, 7 does not refer to a mystical fusion with Christ and God, but to fellowship in faith. It is basic in the apostolic preaching of the historical Jesus, walking in the light, and the blood of Jesus which cleanses from all sin. It thus excludes the sectarian pride which denies the incarnation and misrepresents the character of sin. *J. Schattenmann*

→ Avarice, → Body, → Church, → Deny, → Disciple, → Love, → Possessions

(a). M. Burrows, *More Light on the Dead Sea Scrolls*, 1958; J. Y. Campbell, *Three New Testament Studies*, 1965; O. Cullmann, *The State in the New Testament*, 1957; W. R. Farmer, *Maccabees, Zealots and Josephus*, 1956; A. R. George, *Communion with God in the New Testament*, 1953; D. R. Griffiths, *The New Testament and the Roman State*, 1970; H. Hanse, *echō, TDNT* II 816–32; F. Hauck, *koinos, TDNT* III 789–809; W. Lillie, *Studies in New Testament Ethics*, 1961; K. F. Nickle, *The Collection: A Study in Paul's Strategy*, 1966; A. Richardson, *The Political Christ*, 1973; R. Schnackenburg, *The Moral Teaching of the New Testament*, 1965; E. Troeltsch, *The Social Teaching of the Christian Churches*, I–II, 1931.
(b). F. Hauck, *Die Stellung des Urchristentums zu Arbeit und Geld*, 1921; J. L. Leuba, *Institution und Ereignis*, 1952; F. Meffert, *Der "Kommunismus" Jesu und der Kirchenväter*, 1922; R. von Pöhlmann, *Geschichte der sozialen Frage und des Sozialismus in der antiken Welt*, 1925; B. Reicke, *Glauben und Leben in der Urgemeinde*, 1957; H. Seesemann, *Der Begriff koinōnia im Neuen Testament*, 1933.

Fight, Prize, Triumph, Victory

Struggle for superiority can be a contest or fight, *agōn* (not only a sporting contest), or an armed conflict or battle, *polemos*, with the thought of eliminating one's opponent. *polemos* is a large-scale combat carried on by whole groups, as opposed to *machē*, a personal fight or quarrel. It appears in the NT not only in its usual neutral sense, but also especially in the synoptic apocalypses and in Rev. as the work of demonic powers. The noun and vb. (only Jas. and Rev.) are therefore scarcely used for the behaviour of Christians. On the other hand, *agōn* which generally does not have the connotation of → enmity, is frequently used to describe the Christian life as is also *brabeion*, the victor's prize in sport. Victory, *nikē*, is the aim of every fight. *thriambeuō* has special significance as an expression of the triumph of God.

ἀγών

ἀγών (*agōn*), fight; ἀγωνίζομαι (*agōnizomai*), fight; ἀνταγωνίζομαι (*antagōnizomai*), fight against; ἐπαγωνίζομαι (*epagōnizomai*), fight for; καταγωνίζομαι (*katagōnizomai*), conquer, defeat;

συναγωνίζομαι (*synagōnizomai*), fight along with, help; ἀγωνία (*agōnia*), agony, anxiety.

CL 1. *agōn*, from *agō*, drive, lead (both Hom. on; same root as Lat. *ago*), means: (a) gathering, (b) gathering place, e.g. of the gods on Olympus or of ships in a harbour; and (c) the fight itself, even the sporting contest (*agōnes gymnikoi, hippikoi, mousikoi*), for the → *brabeion*, the prize. It also means fight in war, politics or law (a contest between parties, a case).

The vb. *agōnizomai* (attested from Hdt. onwards) has the same shades of meaning even when compounded with *ant-, ep-, kat-, syn-*, as the noun. Similarly *agōnia* (Pindar onwards) which occurs only in higher style ranges in meaning from effort to anxiety.

The word group *athlēsis, athleō, synathleō*, attested in the case of the vb. from Hom., is used for sporting contests (cf. 2 Tim. 2:5: *athlein nomimōs*, compete fairly). It may, however, be used metaphorically of any effort. On the other hand, the word group *machomai, machē* etc. (from Hom.), originally meant hand to hand combat, first of all in war, but then also in sport. It has also in addition the neutral sense of to quarrel, wrangle, contend.

2. In the Cynic and Stoic diatribes in particular the whole outlook and terminology of the stadium is used for exercise in virtue and for life's moral struggle, in complete contrast to OT Judaism to which this range of concepts is completely alien. It is so alien that in his Heb. version of the NT F. Delitzsch is forced to translate 1 Cor. 9:25, "Every athlete exercises self-control in all things", by "Everyone who devotes himself to wrestling is a Nazirite in all things."

OT 1. In the LXX *agōn* occurs only in the Apocrypha (particularly in 2 and 4 Macc., altogether 15 times) and never stands for a Heb. word. The same is true of the vb. *agōnizomai*, and the compounds are altogether absent. Although in 2 Macc. 4:18 the noun denotes the Tyrian games and in Wis. 4:2 moral striving, it otherwise stands predominantly for military conflict. Heb. denotes this by *milḥāmâh* which the Gk. renders, however, almost always by *polemos* (more than 250 times). On the other hand, for a legal battle (Heb. *rîḇ*) the LXX employs a variety of equivalents, ranging from *dikē* to *machē*. It is not until the late Hel. Jewish period that ideas and expressions appear whose origins lie in Hel. sporting terminology. The word for Jacob's wrestling (Gen. 32:24 f.) is *palaiō* (Heb. *'āḇaq*).

2. For Philo, as in the diatribes, the struggle of life is the place in which the hero of virtue can accomplish ascetic achievements in order to overcome lusts and wickedness. Similarly, Macc. speaks of the struggle for → virtue (*aretēs*; 4 Macc. 12:14) and Sir. 4:28 of the struggle for → truth. The suffering of the martyrs which frequently (cf. 2 Macc. 4:11) took place in the hippodrome (circus) is also described in Macc. in the imagery of the stadium. Expressions like *agōn theios*, divine struggle, or *hieroprepēs*, holy struggle (4 Macc. 17:11; 11:20), indicate that, just as the games were held in honour of a deity, the sufferings and deadly combats of the martyrs were considered to be to the glory of God. These ideas had a powerful influence on primitive Christianity, especially in Heb. and Rev.

3. The patient Job in the Test. Job takes something of a middle position between these two meanings: he does not fight against lust (*epithymia* → Desire) nor against a tyrant, but against → Satan. "Like a boxer who bears hardship and distress he

waits for the prize with patience and endurance (*hypomonē kai makrothymia*)"
(Test. Job 4). In his wrestling with and for God the way is prepared for the NT's
wrestling in prayer.

4. The Gk. idea of conflict is foreign to the Qumran community too. Where
fighting is mentioned here, especially in 1QM (e.g. 6:1–6; 16:3 ff.; 10 ff.), it refers
to the holy war which the elect of God, the sons of light, enter upon against the
wicked, the sons of darkness. Their aim is to inflict a military defeat upon them and
thus by their victory usher in the kingdom of God – a concept which is expressly
rejected in the NT.

NT 1. (a) In the gospels *athleō*, to contend, does not occur at all and *agōnizomai*
only twice: Jn. 18:36, of the servants who would fight for Jesus with weapons,
and Lk. 13:24, "Strive to enter [the kingdom] by the narrow door." The remaining
words occur predominantly in the Pauline writings, above all those connected with
agōn (*athleō* only twice in 2 Tim.). The technical terms from the stadium are used
by Paul, who hailed from a Hel. city.

The compounds of *agōnizomai* are only used occasionally, but without any
change of meaning (Heb. 11:33; 12:4; Jude 3; Rom. 15:30). On the other hand,
agōnia (Lk. 22:44 hapax legomenon) which could mean effort, excitement, alarm,
anxiety, as early as Aristotle, stands for fear in Philo and Josephus, as in the Apocrypha. ([Ed.] RSV has "agony", and Arndt gives "agony", "anxiety".) Thus
Lk. 22:44, the Gethsemane passage (cf. Heb. 5:7), should not be translated "as he
fought with death" but, with Schlatter and Karrer, "being afraid". The translation,
struggle with death, which has conditioned the meaning of the loan-word agony,
imports an element not in the original. Stauffer interprets Jesus' *agōnia* in Lk. 22:44
as due not to "fear of death, but concern for victory in face of the approaching
battle on which the part of the world depends" (*TDNT* I 140).

(b) Of the four NT passages which contain forms of *athleō* (2 Tim. 2:5; *synathleō*
Phil. 1:27; 4:3; *athlēsis* Heb. 10:32), three are connected with → suffering. In the
Heb. passage the accompanying *theatrizomenoi* indicates the crowd of spectators
who are present at the abuse and torture, just as in 4 Macc. 17:14 ff. In early
Christendom the image of the *athlētēs*, contestant, found such favour that the word
was taken over into the vocabularies of the Latin and Coptic churches. The
seventh of the books in Codex II of the 12 codices discovered at Nag Hammadi,
which is still unpublished, bears the title, "The Book of Thomas the Athlete" (see
A. K. Helmbold, *The Nag Hammadi Gnostic Texts and the Bible*, 1967, 77 f., for a
summary; cf. also E. M. Yamauchi in R. N. Longenecker and M. C. Tenney, eds.,
New Dimensions in New Testament Study, 1974, 56 f.), and in the Acts of Thomas
(39) Christ is called "our athlete."

(c) Throughout the NT in contrast to secular Gk. and late Hel. Jewish usage,
the word group *machē* is never used in a neutral sense. Nor is it ever used positively
of the struggle demanded of the Christian (contrast *strateuomai*, engage in war
service, 2 Cor. 10:3; 2 Tim. 2:4; used pejoratively in Jas. 4:1; 1 Pet. 2:11). Every
machesthai is rejected (cf. 2 Tim. 2:24) as an expression of readiness to quarrel and
wrangling contentiousness. Not only a bishop (1 Tim. 3:3) but every Christian
(Tit. 3:2) is to be *amachos*, peaceable, *theomachos*, contending against God, rare in
Hellenism and in the LXX, was perhaps chosen by Lk. in Acts 5:39 (the only

passage) as he recalled the *Bacchae* of Eur., which depicts fatal opposition to the triumphal procession of the god Dionysus.

2. The transforming power of the → faith of a Christian shows itself also in his language, which reverses in a positive sense realities like the → cross and slavery which seem completely negative to the natural man. *doulos Christou*, → slave of Christ, becomes a title of honour! It also draws into its range of imagery things essentially foreign to the Christian, like military conflict (cf. Eph. 6:10 ff.: "spiritual armour" and "contending against principalities and powers"). Apart from Paul it is in the later writings, the Pastoral Epistles (not necessarily non-Pauline), Heb. and Lk., in which the image of the fight found a place. Three groups of ideas can be distinguished:

(a) *agōn* emphasizes the conscious application of one's powers for the achievement of a goal. Lk. 13:24 indicates this by its version of our Lord's words, *agōnizesthe eiselthein. agōn* and the related vbs. are connected grammatically with *eis* and *hina*. The apostle's work is not merely the fulfilment of an obligation but an *agōn*, which is linked with toil (*kopos*, → Burden) and hardship (*ponos*, Col. 1:29; 1 Tim. 4:10). What matters is the highest, imperishable and only rewarding goal, the → *brabeion* (cf. from the point of view of content, without the imagery of contest, the parables of the pearl and the treasure in the field, Matt. 13:44 ff.). Therefore, not only supreme effort but also supreme renunciation are demanded. 1 Cor. 9:24–27 (*pas ho agōnizomenos panta enkrateuetai*, everyone who competes exercises self-control) does not mean a kind of asceticism, which keeps the body in submission out of contempt. Rather, the *hypōpiazō mou to sōma kai doulagōgō*, I pommel my body and subdue it (v. 27), is the expression of the contestant's manly discipline (→ Beat). He has his body under control and directs it towards a goal in accordance with his own will. For this, moderation (2 Tim. 4:5) and exercise (1 Tim. 4:7) are necessary. This is the race, the good fight, which, according to the Pastoral Epistles, Paul has completed (2 Tim. 4:7) and which he also recommends to Timothy (1 Tim. 6:12).

(b) The object of this *agōn*, however, is the spreading of the → gospel. It is not primarily a question of striving for the perfection of the individual (although, of course, that is not a matter of indifference, → Holy), a private salvation, but of the salvation of the elect of God, "that we may present every man mature in Christ" (Col. 1:28). So we are always dealing with an *agōn hyper*, a struggle for, on behalf of, others (Col. 2:1 f.; 4:12; Rom. 15:30). It takes place above all in → prayer. "In prayer there is achieved unity between the will of God and that of man, between human struggling and action and effective divine operation" (E. Stauffer, *TDNT* I 139). In prayer a man can intercede for someone else and make this cause and his suffering his own (Rom. 15:30; Col. 4:3; 1 Thess. 5:25; 2 Thess. 3:1; Heb. 13:18).

The proclamation of the divine message leads to conflict with opponents (Heb. 12:3 f.; 2 Cor. 7:5). But in the last analysis the adversaries are not men (*haima kai sarx*, blood and flesh) but "the supernatural principalities and powers, the dark rulers of this world, the spiritual hosts of wickedness" (Eph. 6:12).

(c) This struggle through suffering which reaches its climax in martyrdom is particularly expressed in the prep. *syn*. The compounds *synagōnizomai* and *synathleō* (Rom. 15:30; Phil. 1:27; 4:3) do not just convey the bearing of the same

647

conflict as the apostle (Phil. 1:30), but a suffering with Christ while looking up to him (Heb. 12:1–4), to "share his sufferings" (Phil. 3:10), being "poured out as a libation upon the sacrificial offering (Christ)" (Phil. 2:17; cf. Tim. 4:6), completing "what is lacking in Christ's afflictions for the sake of his body, that is, the church" (Col. 1:24; cf. esp. A. Schweitzer, *The Mysticism of Paul the Apostle*, 1931, ch. 7, "Suffering as a Mode of Manifestation of the Dying with Christ"). Therefore, the *agōn* with all its sufferings brings joy to the Christian, the joy of the team which is indebted to its captain for the victory. *A. Ringwald*

βραβεῖον

βραβεῖον (*brabeion*), prize; βραβεύω (*brabeuō*), award prizes, judge, rule; καταβραβεύω (*katabrabeuō*), decide against, condemn.

CL The noun *brabeion*, victor's prize, is to such an extent a technical term from sport that it is rare even in secular Gk. *brabeuō* denotes the function of the umpire, but was also frequently used metaphorically and then meant to lead, determine, rule.

brabeion embraces as an additional concept – synonymous with *athlon*, which does not occur in the NT but is frequent in secular Gk. – the prizes of the *agōn thematikos* (fixed money prizes; oil, barley, shields as gifts of the deity; money and accompanying rights throughout the home cities) and also the prizes of the *agōn stephanēphoros* (wreath made, according to the sanctuary, of olive, laurel, ivy, pine or flowers, and also of silver or gold; palm branches, *phoinikes*, as in Rev. 7:9 and myrtle, *tainia* to be worn on the head or arm and honours from the herald; → *agōn*; → *nikaō*). Not only the victor but also any ruler who was present was crowned. Originally the wreath was a sign of exaltation by the deity (Pauly-Wissowa, ad loc.). Just as *brabeus*, umpire, can have the meaning of prince, *brabeion* is also used with the sense of sceptre. In addition, *athlon* denotes the prize that is awarded, as seen from the viewpoint of the giver, whereas *brabeion* is used almost without exception for the prize received. Hence, the NT's use of the latter term may not have been accidental.

OT Heb. altogether lacks the idea of the prize. Delitzsch's Heb. NT translates *brabeion* in both NT passages by *seḵar ha-niṣṣāḥôn*, recompense or reward of victory. Despite its use of the imagery of the fight, the LXX does not make use of *brabeion* which does not occur until the Hel. Jewish period, in Gr. Bar. and Philo. Tertullian took it over into Lat. as a loan word, *brabium* (it appears in the form *bravium* in the Vulg. and some pre-Vulg. versions of the NT). *brabeuō* appears in the LXX only in Wis. 10:12 where Wisdom was the umpire at Jacob's struggle with the angel (Gen. 32:24 ff.).

NT To be accurate, *brabeuō* (only in Col. 3:15) should be translated: "let the peace of Christ decide as umpire in your hearts." It is striking that Paul also uses in Col. the word *katabrabeuō*, withhold the victor's prize (Col. 2:18). It stands as an alternative to the *krinein* (judge) of Col. 2:16.

In the two exclusively Pauline passages in which *brabeion* occurs extraordinary emphasis is placed upon the determination with which the contest is to be pursued. *ouk adēlōs*, not hesitantly, in 1 Cor. 9:24 ff. which qualifies *trechein*, run, is followed by a ten-fold "in order to/that." In Phil. 3:10–14 it is underlined by the vbs. *katantaō*, arrive at, *katalambanō*, grasp, *epekteinomai*, stretch out for, *diōkō*, pursue, press after. The *brabeion* is the victor's prize which the Christian obtains only with effort and perhaps the sacrifice of his life (Phil. 2:16–17 in the context of the imagery of a race; cf. *agōn* as the martyr's struggle), and through *koinōnia*, sharing in the → suffering of Christ (cf. Phil. 3:10). This has nothing to do with ethical perfection. Christians have entered the race (1 Cor. 9:24), *teleioi* (Phil. 3:15), having been made Christ's own (v. 12), "not having a righteousness of their own but the righteousness from God that depends on faith" (v. 9). Phil. 3:14 means participation in the resurrection of the dead, not, of course, in the general resurrection of the good and evil, but, "as always in Paul's letters, the resurrection which is revealed to all the children of God to whom has been granted the life-giving Spirit of the glorified Christ, a blessed experience of being with him (1 Thess. 4:17), and reigning with him (cf. *brabeion* as sceptre) in his kingdom" (Rom. 5:17; 1 Cor. 6:2 f.) (Klöpper; → Resurrection). Perhaps we should think of the so-called first resurrection at Christ's return on the clouds before his thousand year reign (1 Thess. 4:14–17; Rev. 20:6; 1 Cor. 15:23; similarly perhaps also 1 Cor. 9:24). In any case the *brabeion*, the victor's prize, does not by any means go to all who were once called Christians.   *A. Ringwald*

| θριαμβεύω | θριαμβεύω (*thriambeuō*), lead to a triumphal procession.

CL & OT The vb. *thriambeuō* is derived from the noun *thriambos*. *thriambos* means the hymn which was sung at the ceremonial processions in honour of the god Dionysus, and so originates in the cult of Dionysus. At a later period this resulted in Dionysus receiving the name *thriambos*. The noun passed by way of Etruscan into Lat. as *triumphus*, with the sense of triumph. *thriambeuō* first attested in Polybius (2nd cent. B.C.), is the Gk. neologism based on Lat. *triumphare* and means (a) intrans: to celebrate a triumph, (b) trans: to lead someone in a triumphal procession. All the meanings of *thriambeuō* go back to the content of the Lat. vb. *triumphare*, right up to Anastasius Sinaita (5th cent. A.D.): the public display of a criminal to shame.

In the Hel. environment of the NT *thriambeuō* meant the triumphal procession of a ruler which his defeated enemies had to follow. "He led both kings and governors in triumph" (Plutarch, *Romulus* 33, 4). The prisoners provided a spectacle laid on by the victor. Censers were also carried in the triumphal processions and spread a festive perfume.

This word group does not occur at all in the LXX.

NT *thriambeuō* only appears twice in the NT: Col. 2:15 and 2 Cor. 2:14, on both occasions in the trans. sense, to lead in a triumphal procession.

1. Col. 2:15 presents God as the triumphant victor: Jesus' journey to the cross is God's triumphal procession. Through Jesus' death and resurrection the authorities (→ Might) and powers opposed to God have been disarmed and defeated. God as the *imperator mundi* (world ruler; cf. G. Delling, *TDNT* III 160) leads them in his triumphal procession like prisoners put on show.

2. 2 Cor. 2:14 reads: "But thanks be to God, who in Christ always leads us in triumph and through us spreads the fragrance of the knowledge of him everywhere." Here Paul himself is led in triumph as one whom God has defeated, who as the → slave (*doulos*) of Jesus Christ is at all times and in all places a part of God's triumphal procession. The apostle understands his missionary task as the work of a slave who puts the power of the divine victor on show and by his proclamation spreads the perfume of the knowledge of God, the one for → life, the other for → death (cf. the context 2 Cor. 2:14–17).   *K. Dahn, H.-G. Link*

νικάω

νικάω (*nikaō*), be victorious; νῖκος (*nikos*), victory; νίκη (*nikē*), victory.

CL From Hom. on *nikaō* is frequently used in Gk. literature and means to be victorious, both in military and legal combat. The vb. expresses visible superiority in the natural rivalry which takes place among men. But it is also applied to the realm of the gods. It can also be translated surpass, overcome, be stronger. It presupposes achievement in physical or spiritual combat. The corresponding noun is *nikē*, victory, or the power that confers victory. *Nikē* is also the name of a Gk. goddess who is often represented in art as a symbol of personal superiority. The gods assist men in their conflicts and give the victory to the side of their choice. In the mystery religions man binds himself cultically to the superior deities who are worshipped as victorious powers.

to nikos, first attested in the LXX, is synonymous with *nikē. hypernikaō*, attested from Hippocrates on but rarely used, strengthens the basic meaning of the simple vb.

OT In the LXX *nikaō* and *nikē* do not occur particularly frequently. The vb. appears about 25 times, and the sub. about 10 times. Of these only a few instances occur in the late books of the Heb. OT (Prov.; Chr.), whereas by far the majority are to be found in Macc. and render the Heb. *nāṣaḥ*, to defeat, have control of, or *nēṣaḥ*, splendour, endurance.

The OT is familiar enough with the phenomenon of human rivalry (cf. the conflict between Hagar and Sarah, Gen. 16; Joseph and his brothers, Gen. 37), but *nikaō* is used in the LXX almost exclusively to denote victory over hostile powers. The real victor is God, who has power over his own enemies and those of his people and of the righteous (1 Chr. 29:11; cf. Ps. 51:6). The people's victory does not primarily depend upon the strength of their soldiers but upon whether God has delivered the enemy into the hands of the Israelite armies (Jdg. 7; 1 Macc. 3:19). For this reason the rallying cry for the "Holy War" in Maccabaean times was "Victory with God!" (2 Macc. 13:15). Finally, the faith of Israel waits and prays for the time when God will defeat all the enemies of the people. In the wisdom literature the word victory acquired a spiritualized metaphorical meaning. The wise man does not allow himself to be conquered by the beauty of an adulteress (Prov. 6:25), but rather reason overcomes instinct (4 Macc. 3:17; 6:33).

NT NT usage of the word group almost always presupposes the conflict between God or Christ and opposing demonic powers. *nikaō* occurs most frequently in

650

Rev. and in the Johannine letters. *nikē* occurs only in 1 Jn. 5:4; *hypernikaō* only in Rom. 8:37. The terms occur seldom in Paul, but nevertheless, when they do, have particular theological significance.

1. In the synoptic tradition the word group appears only in Matt. 12:20 in a quotation from the first Servant Song (Isa. 42:1–4: "he brings justice to victory") and in Lk. 11:22. Here the stronger man overcomes the armed strong man (the synoptic parallels Matt. 12:29 and Mk. 3:27 have "binds"), disarms and despoils him. The metaphor explains Jesus' superiority over the demonic powers. "If it is by the finger of God that I cast out demons, then the kingdom of God has come upon you" (Lk. 11:20). The earthly Jesus demonstrates by his actions that he is the hidden victor over the forces opposed to God, whilst it is not until the resurrection that he achieves the final victory over sin, death and the devil.

2. Rom. 8 and 1 Cor. 15 are the chapters in which Paul speaks most forcibly about overcoming the world and death through the redemptive work of Jesus Christ. Jesus' death on the cross and his resurrection are the reason that no power in the world can finally have the victory. "Death is swallowed up in victory. O death, where is thy victory?" (1 Cor. 15:54 f.). As children of God, believers are included in this victory. Their victory is not an achievement or reward, but is "given" them (1 Cor. 15:57). They are thereby placed in a position in which they themselves can overcome evil (Rom. 12:21). Now they are oppressed by trouble, anxiety, danger, persecution and hunger. But these forces have lost their controlling power. The believer's struggle against the rule of these demonic forces is conducted under the promise of victory and thus takes on the character of overcoming: "No, in all these things we are more than conquerors through him who loved us" (Rom. 8:37).

3. John sums up the forces opposed to God in the term *kosmos* (→ world). Jesus' coming, suffering and return to the Father signify victory over the world. This victory is expressed in the perfect tense (Jn. 16:33). The evil one, the ruler of this world, has had his power restricted by Jesus Christ, in that Jesus, as the stronger man, has freed his people from the dominion of the evil one. The battle has thus been decided, even if it is not yet over. By faith Christians participate in this victory and are thus placed in a position to overcome the world for themselves. Faith is the victory over the world (1 Jn. 5:4 f.; 2:13 f.; 4:4 f.).

4. The seven letters of Rev. (chs. 2 and 3) are directed to troubled Christian churches in Asia Minor suffering under persecution. Each letter concludes with a call to overcome, introduced by the formula *ho nikōn* or *tō nikōnti* (2:7, 11 etc.). The conflict and the trials of this present life in the world and in the church are not final. The church's anticipated victory has its foundations laid in the victory already won by Jesus. The promise of an inheritance is to those who overcome (cf. Rev. 21:7). The end, however, will be preceded by the apocalyptic conflict between God and the demonic powers. This is the theme of Rev. The world powers often gain victories in this conflict (Rev. 6:2; 11:7; 13:7) but their victories are fleeting ones. In the end it is the ultimate victory of the Lamb that will remain. Christians have followed him and have poured out their blood in martyrdom (Rev. 11:7:12). In the middle of the picture of the plagues and the wrath of God John sees the victors standing, singing a hymn of praise (Rev. 15:2 ff.). Thus the victory which the Lamb has won and which he has promised to his people is already secure, despite all confrontations with the demonic powers, for the Lamb is the King of all

kings and the Lord of all lords (Rev. 17:14). This is the origin of the Christian symbol of the Lamb with the banner of victory.   *W. Günther*

→ Caesar, → Crown, → Discipline, → Soldier, → War, → Weapon

(a). O. Bauernfeind, *nikaō*, *TDNT* IV 942–45; and *polemos*, *TDNT* VI 502–15; G. Delling, *thriambeuō*, *TDNT* III 159 f.; H. Gross, "War," *EBT* III 958–61; G. H. C. Macgregor, *The New Testament Basis of Pacifism*, 1953²; J. Pedersen, *Israel: Its Life and Culture*, III–IV, 1926, 1–32; V. C. Pfitzner, *Paul and the Agon Motif: Traditional Athletic Imagery in the Pauline Literature*, 1967; G. von Rad, *Old Testament Theology*, I, 1962; II 1965 (see index); and "Deuteronomy and the Holy War," *Studies in Deuteronomy*, 1953, 45–59; L. E. Toombs, "War, ideas of," *IDB* IV 797–801; E. Stauffer, *agōn*, *TDNT* I 134–40; and *brabeuō*, *TDNT* I 637 ff.; R. de Vaux, "Military Institutions," *Ancient Israel*, 1961, 213–67 (bibliography 535 ff.); J. W. Wevers, "War, methods of," *IDB* IV 801–5; L. Williamson, "Led in Triumph: Paul's Use of *thriambeuō*", *Interpretation* 22, 1968, 317–3; Y. Yadin, *The Art of Warfare in Biblical Lands*, 1963.
(b). H. Fredriksson, *Jahwe als Krieger*, 1945; G. von Rad, *Der Heilige Krieg im Alten Israel*, 1958³; F. Schwally, *Semitische Kriegsaltertümer*, I, *Der heilige Krieg im alten Israel*, 1901.

Fire

The importance which has been attached to fire from the earliest days of human civilization is reflected in the common root which may be traced behind the words used for it from Iceland (*fyrr*) far into the Orient (Hittite *pahhur*, Armenian *hur*). As well as the Gk. word *pyr* we must discuss here the group of words connected with *kauma*, heat. While *pyr* refers primarily to the power contained in fire, or to the fire-place (whether in the temple or at home), with the significance attaching thereto, *kauma* indicates rather the process of burning, scorching, and the effect which this has on the senses (light, heat, etc.). Both groups of words are used in the NT in connection with the activity of God.

καῦμα

καῦμα (*kauma*), heat, burning; καυματίζω (*kaumatizō*), burn, scorch.

CL *kauma* (Homer) means burning, heat, especially sunburn or heat of the sun; and in a transferred sense, fever heat, ardour of love, frostbite. *kaumatizō*, not attested before the NT but later in Plutarch and Arrian, means dry up by heat; and by extension in the mid. form to suffer from fever.

OT 1. In the LXX *kauma* serves most frequently as a translation of *ḥōreb* or *ḥōm* (each 4 times) in its original sense of the heat of the sun, burning sun (cf. Gen. 31:40; Sir. 43:3; Jer. 43(36):30 LXX), but also in the transferred sense of fever heat (Job 30:30). Its use is, however, illuminating as can be seen from the context in each case.

2. (a) Even in Jer. 43(36):30 (LXX) the context should be noted. The fact that the body of Jehoiakim is to be exposed to the heat of the sun and the frost of night is a sign of divine judgment upon him because of his guilt. The same idea is conveyed by the complaint of Job, "My bones burn with heat" (30:30). He sees in this a sign that God has become a cruel enemy (30:21).

(b) The word is also used as a parable for affliction and trouble. Thus in Jer. 17:8 the man who trusts in the Lord "is like a tree planted by water, that sends out its roots by the stream, and does not fear when heat comes, for its leaves remain

652

green." Similarly in Sir. 14:27 the man who meditates on wisdom "will be sheltered by her from the heat." Looking forward to the coming reign of peace, Isaiah prophesies: "Glory will be spread over all as a covering and a canopy, a shade from the heat by day, a refuge and a shelter from rain and tempest" (Isa. 4:5 f. NEB).

NT 1. In the NT the noun and the vb. occur only 6 times; 4 times in Rev., twice in the Gospels. The OT usage outlined in OT 2 above is taken up and continued.

2. (a) Rev. 16:8, 9 speaks of divine judgment and wrath. The fourth bowl of wrath is poured on the sun, "and it was allowed to scorch (*kaumatisai*) men with fire; men were scorched (*ekaumatisthēsan*) by the fierce heat (*kauma*)."

(b) Matt. 13:6 and Mk. 4:6 tell of the seed which fell on rocky ground and was scorched by the sun. The parable here refers to those who take offence at God's word, when tribulation and persecution arise. In Rev. 7:16 it is said of the members of the church, who have come through great affliction and martyrdom and have been raised to the heavenly glory: "They shall hunger no more, neither thirst any more; the sun shall not strike them, nor any scorching heat." *S. Solle*

| πῦρ |

πῦρ (*pyr*), fire; πυρόω (*pyroō*), to set on fire, burn; πύρωσις (*pyrōsis*), burning, being burnt; πύρινος (*pyrinos*), fiery, of fire; πυρράζω (*pyrrazō*), be red; πυρρός (*pyrros*), flame-coloured, red; πυρά (*pyra*), pile of combustible or burning material; πυρετός (*pyretos*), fever; πυρέσσω (*pyressō*), suffer with a fever.

CL *pyr* (related etymologically to the Eng. word *fire*) is attested from Mycenaean Gk. onwards.

1. The history of religion and culture shows fire as something to which great importance has been attached in human life both in a positive and in a negative sense, as a life-giving and as a life-destroying force. On the one hand, it is regarded as a force coming to man from nature, giving him life, but unpredictable and to be held in awe. On the other hand, it is viewed as a human accomplishment, kindled and kept alive by the genius of man (cf., for example, the double birth of fire in the Indian Agni cult). It is "used" by man at the centre of his home (the hearth, which is therefore, like sacrificial fire, regarded by many people as something holy; cf. for instance Hestia, Vesta). It is seen as a protection against evil influences (e.g. the burning of corpses in India; the fire baptism of the Mandaeans, cf. Matt. 3:11; the fire on the altar at Delphi, cf. Plutarch, *Aristides*, 35). It is also used as a weapon in fighting and war.

As far as the environment of the OT and Jud. is concerned, the fire cult of the Persian religion is of particular importance. Fire and a serpent represent the contraries truth and falsehood in the Mazda teaching of Zoroastrianism. In the conflict between the good and evil basic principles, man should place himself on the side of the good to which fire belongs. The body of Mazda is always represented as fiery, as a blazing, uncreated flame. Since fire is revered in this way as the element of purity, it must not be allowed to become contaminated, for instance, by contact with dead bodies. Hence, the burning of corpses is regarded as a terrible sin. In the final judgment fire will be the means employed for the last test. Good and evil are to be separated in a stream of fiery metal, and in the end everything, including hell

653

itself, will be purified by fire. Fire is the protector of the good, divine order of life.

2. In the Greek world fire is used in both secular and religious spheres. Metaphorically it can describe the most diverse human experiences, such as intensity of passion, wickedness, or the heat of battle. At the same time situations of anarchy can be illustrated by the image of fire.

In Gk. religion fire is used as a means of ritual cleansing (e.g. purificatory offering after childbirth or after a death, and the various feasts of purification). Although corpses were burned in funeral rites, it was believed that the soul could not be affected by the fire or cut off from its future existence. Among the gods, Hephaestus and Hestia have a special connection with fire. Prometheus and Hermes are said to have brought fire to men. On the holy, national hearth in the Prytaneion there burned a fire which never went out (F. Lang, *TDNT* VI 931). From it colonists took a flame for the hearth of the daughter-city that they were going out to found. Fire, regarded as one of the various tokens of the gods, accompanies the appearance of a deity. There are fire and rivers of fire in the underworld. Occasionally we find the idea that the soul is purified by fire. Fire plays an important part in the mystery religions, both for purposes of purification and in the representation of the divine (cf. A. Dietrich, *Eine Mithrasliturgie*, 1923³, 8:17 ff.; *TDNT* VI 932) and of the new nature of the initiated. Generally speaking, the Greeks attached a positive value to fire.

In Gk. philosophy fire is one of the four (or five) elements. According to Heraclitus of Ephesus, fire is the basic element of all things: the world is a movement of fire, which is undergoing a constant process of change and is identical with the deity (or *logos*). "As the original fire is endowed with reason and is the cause of all world government ([Diels-Kranz] *Frag.* 64 [I, 165, 1 ff.]), so the soul of man consists of fire" (*TDNT* VI 930). In this pantheistic system, God, the fiery universe, universal reason and the human spirit are all regarded as one. Heraclitus holds that a great world era comes to its end when everything is burned up and so returns to the primal fire; then the world is produced anew out of the primal fire. These ideas were later taken up again by the Stoics who likewise see fire as the active world principle, the world soul which guides everything according to purpose, holding all things together and controlling them by law and reason. The world originates by a transformation of the primal fire, and then by a process of general combustion (*pyrōsis* from Theophrastus onwards; hence the Stoic concept of the *ekpyrōsis*, an end of the world brought about by fire) it returns to the original state, whereupon the world cycle begins again. The human soul is part of the Godhead, and therefore fiery in nature, and it too returns to primal fire when the world disappears in flames.

ot 1. In the OT *pyr* is used in over 350 places to translate the Heb. *'ēš* (altogether 490 times in the LXX). Fire is used for several purposes in the home (Exod. 12:8; Isa. 44:15; Jer. 7:18; 2 Chr. 35:13), and also in craftwork, especially metal work (Isa. 44:12 ff.; Jer. 6:29; Sir. 38:28). In war it is a means of destruction (cf. Deut. 13:16; Jdg. 20:48; Amos 1:4). No fire may be kindled on the sabbath (Exod. 35:3). Among natural phenomena, lightning is the "fire of God" (cf. 1:16; 2 Ki. 1:12). In a metaphorical sense, fire stands for various human activities: slander and quarrelling (Prov. 26:20 f.), anger (Sir. 28:10 f.), the shedding of blood (Sir. 11:32; 22:24), the passion of love and debauchery (Sir. 9:8; 23:16), adultery (Job 31:12; Prov. 6:27 ff.).

Fire also serves in the OT as a means of purification (cf. Lev. 13:52; Num. 31:32; Isa. 6:6). The only corpses which are burned, however, are those of criminals (Gen. 38:24; Lev. 20:14; 21:9; Jos. 7:15). This is done in order that they may have no place in the grave of their fathers.

In worship the sacrificial fire is used for burning gifts upon the altar, and incense in the censer (Lev. 1:7 ff.; 3:5; 6:9 ff.; 16:12 f.). No sacrifice may be offered by fire that does not come from the altar (Lev. 10:1; Num. 3:4). Heathen customs are forbidden: the burning of children for Molech (Lev. 20:2; Deut. 12:31; 18:10), i.e. "making one's son or daughter pass through the fire" (2 Ki. 17:17; 21:6). But this was practised under Ahaz and Manasseh under foreign influence (2 Ki. 16:3; 21:6; Jer. 7:31). We remain, however, completely in the dark as to the purpose and nature of this custom, and the extent to which it was practised.

Since Yahweh is present among his people as the Judge, who brings deliverance as well as punishment, the fire which accompanies him becomes the expression of two different aspects of his activity. First, it is the mark of divine judgment (Gen. 19:24; Exod. 9:24; Lev. 10:2; Num. 11:1; 16:35; 2 Ki. 1:10; Amos 1:4, 7). But secondly, it is also a sign of Yahweh's grace, in that he displays by means of fire his acceptance of a sacrifice (Gen. 15:17; Lev. 9:23 f.; Jdg. 6:21; 1 Ki. 18:38; 1 Chr. 21:26; 2 Chr. 7:1). Moreover, fire is also a sign of divine guidance (cf. the pillars of cloud and of fire, Exod. 13:22; Num. 14:14). Yahweh speaks out of the fire (Deut. 4:12, 15, 33). Especially elect persons can be taken to him with fiery manifestations (2 Ki. 2:11).

Yahweh himself is a devouring fire (Deut. 4:24; 9:3; Isa. 33:14). This is not to say that he is a personification of an element (cf. CL above), but that he watches over obedience to his will with fiery zeal. His word can also be described as a devouring fire (Jer. 23:29).

From the concept of the theophany which has its root in the covenant cultus and in the idea of judgment, it may be seen that when Yahweh appears, he is accompanied by fire (Gen. 15:17; Exod. 3:2 f.; 19:18; Jdg. 6:21; 13:20; Num. 14:14; Isa. 4:5; Ezek. 1:27). This does not mean, however, that he is thought of as the god of fire or the god of the volcano. For Israel drew a distinction between Yahweh himself and the phenomena which accompany his appearance. Fire is one of Yahweh's "servants", an instrument in his hand (1 Ki. 19:11 f.; Ps. 50:3; 104:4). Fire is a symbol of Yahweh's holiness as judge of the world, and also of his divine power and glory (Exod. 24:17; Isa. 6:1–4; Ezek. 1:27 f.). According to Dan. 7:10, a stream of fire issues from beneath the throne of Yahweh, a concept which plays an important part in Jewish and Christian cosmology and apocalyptic.

In the post-exilic period it was expected that Yahweh would appear to bring history to its consummation, and fire is the token announcing the day of Yahweh (Joel 2:30). The enemies of Yahweh will be destroyed by fire and the sword (Isa. 66:15f.; Ezek. 38:22; 39:6; Mal 4:1). According to Isa. 66:24, the effects will be far-reaching: those condemned in the judgment will be continuously tormented by fire.

2. In Jewish apocalyptic fire becomes the mark of the heavenly world. The house in which Yahweh lives in heaven consists of and is surrounded by fire (Eth. Enoch 14:9–22 and often). Fire is the means of punishment in hell (Eth. Enoch 91:9;

100:9; 2 Esd. 7:38; Syr. Bar. 44:15 and often). The final judgment is a judgment by fire (Eth. Enoch 102:1; Syr. Bar. 37:1; 48:39; 2 Esd. 13:10 f.; Jub. 9:15; 3:10). The community of Qumran also expected the ungodly to be judged by fire in the final judgment (1QS 2:8; 4:13; 1QH 17:13). Under Stoic and Persian influence the doctrine of the world conflagration also found its way into Judaism (Sib. 2:186 ff., 238 ff. and often). This is also found in the Qumran texts in the "little apocalypse" (1QH 3:25 ff.).

Rab. speculation concerned itself with the origin of fire, and several states of fire are distinguished. It is said that the Torah originated from fire: letters of black fire were written on white fire. This lies behind the frequent reports of fiery manifestations when Rabbis study the Torah. The fiery place of punishment for the ungodly is called Gehenna (→ Hell). To this is added in the 2nd cent. A.D., as a result of Persian influence, the doctrine of an intervening purgatory.

NT In the NT *pyr* occurs 71 times. It is part of everyday life: Mk. 9:22; Lk. 22:55; Acts 28:5; Heb. 11:34 (torture); Rev. 17:16; 18:8 (in war). It appears in a fig. sense in Jas. 3:5 f. (the tongue as a devouring fire) and Lk. 12:49 (the fire of discord). Similarly the vb. *pyroō*, burn, be inflamed, is used of the heat of emotions: in 1 Cor. 7:9 (of sexual desire); in 2 Cor. 11:29 (of indignation over another's hurt). Several derivative words also occur in the NT: *pyressō*, suffer with a fever (Matt. 8:14; Mk. 1:30); *pyretos*, fever (Lk. 4:38; Acts 28:8); *pyra*, pile of combustible material (Acts 28:2 f.; Lk. 22:55 *v.l.*); *pyrrazō*, be fiery red in colour (Matt. 16:2 f.); *pyrros*, fiery red in colour (Rev. 6:4), also a proper name (Pyrrhus in Eng. versions) in Acts 20:4; *pyrōsis*, the process of burning (Rev. 18:9, 18), and fig. as a fiery test or ordeal (1 Pet. 4:12; cf. Prov. 27:21; Did. 16:5).

Fire has particular theological significance:

1. As a sign of heavenly, divine glory. The exalted Christ has eyes like flames of fire (Rev. 1:15; cf. Ezek. 1:27; Rev. 2:18; 19:12). The angel in Rev. 10:1 has legs like pillars of fire. Before God's throne there burn seven torches of fire (Rev. 4:5; 15:2). The Holy Spirit, being of heavenly origin, appears in tongues as of fire (Acts 2:3, cf. Jn. 3:8), and fire accompanies the appearance of God (Acts 7:30, referring to Exod. 3:2; Heb. 12:18 ff., especially v. 29; cf. Exod. 19:12 ff.).

2. In metaphorical expressions. In the proverbial sayings in 1 Pet. 1:7 (cf. Prov. 17:3), just as gold is tested in fire, so faith is tested by suffering in this world. Sufferings are a *pyrōsis*, burning, which comes upon Christians in order to test or prove them, and is a sign of the end-time (1 Pet. 4:12; cf. v. 7). The image reappears in a way similar to that in 1 Pet. 1:7, at Rev. 3:18: gold refined by fire (*pepyrō-menon*) represents true Christian faith which will stand the test. In the passage about the spiritual armour of the Christian (Eph. 6:16), the shield of faith serves to ward off all the fiery (*pepyrōmena*) darts of the wicked one. Clearly a dualistic thinking (cf. the addition of *tou ponērou*, → Evil) is in the background here, with the idea that the faithful, as children of light, are engaged in battle with the forces of darkness. (Cf. the parallels to this in the Qumran literature: "They have surrounded me with all their weapons of war; arrows destroy, without any to heal, and the spear-point is in a fire which devours trees", 1QH 2:25 f.)

3. (a) As a picture of divine judgment in Matt. 3:10; 7:19; Lk. 3:9; Jn. 15:6. Here images from the farmer's life are used to illustrate the eschatological judgment

of God. Rev. 9:17 f. depicts horses coming out to execute judgment, with smoke and sulphur issuing from their mouths. This marks them out as a scourge, bringing destruction with them. Similarly the rider's breastplates, "the colour of fire" (*pyrinos*), point to the dawning of the judgment. Even in this age God can use fire as a means of judgment. The sons of Zebedee want Jesus to give them permission to call down fire on the inhospitable Samaritan village (Lk. 9:45; cf. 2 Ki. 1:10, 12). The final powers to array themselves against God, Gog and Magog, will be destroyed by divine fire (Rev. 20:9). Lk. 17:29 recalls Gen. 19:24; and Rev. 8:7 recalls Exod. 9:24. (Is the reference to a volcano or to a star?) The two witnesses in Rev. 11 are able to destroy their enemies with fire (cf. v. 5): God's power of judgment is at their disposal (cf. 2 Sam. 22:9). As a sign of the deceiving powers of Satan, the false prophet calls down fire from heaven (Rev. 13:13). An angel is given power over fire (Rev. 14:18). The riders of Rev. 6:1–8 remind us of the horses in Zech. 1:8; 6:2 ff. The rider of the red (*pyrros*) horse brings war and bloodshed. In Rev. 12:3 the red colour signifies that the dragon, i.e. → Satan, is bellicose and murderous. (→ Black, White, Red.)

(b) In Lk. 12:49 f. the mission of Jesus is presented as a fulfilment of the Baptist's prophecy – but now in the sense that he who baptizes in spirit and fire must himself suffer. His way of bringing the judgment is to take it upon himself, and so the eschatological judgment is taken up in the present, historical sufferings of Jesus. In Mk. 9:49 salt and fire are linked together in a riddle. Salt has power to purify, preserve and give flavour, and fire is an image of the divine judgment. He who would find fellowship with God must give up the old man to judgment, by denying himself. If a man will not do that, he is liable to the eschatological judgment of wrath. 1 Cor. 3:13 depicts the traditional notion of an eschatological judgment by fire, in which every man's work will be tested (see above NT 2). Bad workmanship will be burned up, but the builder himself will narrowly escape, like a stick pulled out of a burning wood-pile. In 2 Thess. 1:8 the Parousia is described in OT terminology (cf. Exod. 3:2; Isa. 66:15). In Rom. 12:20 Paul cites Prov. 25:12 f., making the metaphor refer to the final divine judgment. Only in one passage in the NT, 2 Pet. 3:7, 10, 12, does the ancient doctrine of the world conflagration appear, combined with a recollection of the flood catastrophe recorded in the OT.

(c) Fire appears in Matt. 13:42; 18:8 f.; 25:41 par. and Mk. 9:43, 45, 47 as the opposite of the "Kingdom of God" (→ Kingdom, art. *basileia*) and → life (art. *zōē*). The "hell of fire" (→ Hell) in Mk. 9:48 recalls Isa. 66:24. Contemporary Jewish ideas of the present punishment by fire of the people of Sodom and Gomorrah are suggested by Jude 7. Fire and brimstone indicate eternal damnation in hell at the end of time (Rev. 14:10; 19:20; 20:10, 14; 21:8).   *H. Bietenhard*
→ Anger, → Hell, → Holy, → Punishment

(a). J. B. Bauer, "Fire," *EBT* I 269 f.; O. C. de C. Ellis, *A History of Fire and Flame*, 1932; J. G. Frazer, *Myths of the Origin of Fire*, 1930; E. M. Good, "Fire," *IDB* II 268 f.; F. Lang, *pyr* etc. *TDNT* VI 928–52 (bibliography 928); P. D. Miller, "Fire in the Mythology of Canaan and Israel," *CBQ* 17, 1965, 256–61; M. P. Nilsson, "Fire Festivals in Ancient Greece," *Journal of Historical Studies*, 43, 1923, 144–48; A. D. Nock, "Cremation and Burial in the Roman Empire," *HTR* 25, 1932, 321–59.
(b). C. M. Edsman, "Le baptême de feu," *Acta Seminarii Neotestamentici Upsaliensis* 9, 1940; "Ignis divinus. Le feu comme moyen de rajeunissement et d'immortalité: contes, légendes, mythes et rites," *Skrifter utgivna av Vetenskaps-Sozieteten i Lund*, 34, 1949; and "Feuer," *RGG³*

II 927 f.; S. Eitrem, "Die vier Elemente in der Mysterienweihe," *Sym. Osl.* 4, 1926, 39–59; 5, 1927, 39–59; F. Lang, *Das Feuer im Sprachgebrauch der Bibel, dargestellt auf dem Hintergrund der Feuervorstellungen in der Umwelt*, (dissertation Tübingen) 1950; R. Mayer, "Die biblische Vorstellung vom Weltbrand," *Bonner Orientalische Studien*, Neue Folge, 4, 1956, 79–136; J. Michl, "Gerichtsfeuer und Purgatorium, zu 1. Kor. 3, 12–15," *Stud. Paul.*, 1963, 395–401; E. Pax, EPIPHANEIA, *Münchener Theologische Studien*, I 10, 1955; K. Reinhardt, "Heraklits Lehre vom Feuer," *Hermes* 77, 1942, 1–27; F. Stolz, *'ēš, THAT* I 242–46.

Firm, Foundation, Certainty, Confirm

The life of individual people or of the community is often described in the NT under the metaphor of a building (→ House). The durability and toughness of a building depends on the quality of its foundations, and the same is true of human life. *themelios* connotes this basis, usually not immediately obvious to the observer, which upholds, supports and affects the whole edifice. Another word used in the same sense is *hedraiōma*, although this is derived from a different range of concepts. *hedraios* originally refers to the state of standing steady on the ground; then, to the human sitting position. The *bebaios* group, on the other hand, is concerned with that which is based, or still to be fixed or anchored to a foundation, assumed to be unshakeable. Hence *bebaios* becomes a predominantly legal term, used to refer to a position or guarantee which is subject to no risk of alteration (see also → Seal).

βέβαιος

βέβαιος (*bebaios*), sure; βεβαιόω (*bebaioō*), confirm; βεβαίωσις (*bebaiōsis*), confirmation.

CL *bebaios*, from *bainō*, means fit to tread on (having a firm foundation). In classical Gk. from the 5th cent. B.C. it acquires the meaning of firm, durable, unshakeable, sure, reliable, certain; and in the legal sphere, valid, legal. *bebaioō* similarly means make firm, strengthen, confirm; and also, guarantee. *bebaiōsis* means establishing, confirmation, or (in legal language) guarantee (legally valid confirmation of a legal act).

OT In the OT (LXX) this group of words occurs only rarely, e.g. in Ps. 119:28 in the sense, to strengthen. Where it occurs, it has generally the same meaning as in classical Gk.

NT In the NT the words under consideration occur in all 19 times (8 times in Heb. alone). They connote first validity, i.e. the confirming evidence of the divine word (Mk. 16:20; Heb. 2:2 f.), of the gospel (Phil. 1:7), etc. Here the NT has adopted the technical sense that the words had already acquired in the legal sphere (see above CL). Secondly, they are used in the original sense to denote that a thing is firm, reliable, because it has a firm foundation. Thus the hope and confidence of man is firmly secured as by an anchor, when the object of trust is the word of God, which he has legally confirmed with an oath (Heb. 6:16, 19).

1. (a) The → promises of God, the → word of God, and the → gospel will be fulfilled with absolute certainty, because they have been legally confirmed by God, and so form the foundations of the faith. Thus God's promise stands secure. Because of its legal validation it is a reliable and absolutely sure foundation, on

658

which the believer may depend. The promise has been given "from grace" by God to faith, not on the basis of the law (Rom. 4:16). It thus depends for its validity and efficacy on God alone, not on man. It is this that makes it sure Hence it applies to the man who lives totally "from grace", i.e. the believer. It is he who possesses, through the promise, God's future, and not the person who founds his standing before God on the law and his obedience to it. If the validity of God's promises were dependent on that, we should never be able to have assurance about them.

Another reason for the "confirmation" (legal validation) of God's promises to the fathers is given in Rom. 15:8: Jesus Christ has himself given them this legal validation. His whole life was one of "service" to the Jews and to the Gentiles, in order to make God's promises sure for them. He showed them how all the promises of God were fulfilled in him, and thus proved to be true. Thereby he made evident "God's truthfulness" and faithfulness, which form the ultimate and most profound basis for confidence and certainty about the foundations of faith. Heb. 6:16 ff. states that in order to confirm and vouch for his promises, and thus for the impregnable nature of his will, God has even gone so far as to swear an oath. If even in human relations an oath serves to confirm a promise (*eis bebaiōsin* is a recognized Gk. legal term for a guarantee), and excludes any contradiction or any further objection, how much more so when God vouches for his word with an oath! This terminology is also confirmed by its use in Heb. 9:17. God's promise (v. 15) is compared with a will which comes into force when the person who issued it dies. This throws a special light upon the death of Jesus.

(b) Rather than God's promise, it is often the *logos*, the word (of God), which is described by these terms as trustworthy. Heb. 2:2 states that, if the message declared by angels (i.e. the OT law) was sure, impregnable and valid, so that "every transgression or disobedience received a just retribution," how much more is the word of the Lord who is so much "superior to angels" (Heb. 1:4). For God himself has borne witness to that word, and has confirmed it by "signs and wonders and various miracles" (Heb. 2:4). "Behind the *bebaios logos* stands the covenant of God (*diathēkē*), which guarantees that the word will be carried out. It is not the fact that the message is delivered by angels, but that the word is undergirded by the covenant of God on Sinai, that gives it its impregnability and legal validity" (O. Michel, *Der Brief an die Hebräer*, 63; → Covenant). In Mk. 16:20 (not in the best MSS [Ed.]), the validity of the word (of the disciples) is confirmed (*bebaiountos*) by "signs following". These signs are an indication that the living Lord himself is speaking and working through his witnesses, and that their witness is therefore true and reliable. If God's truthfulness and faithfulness are the primary basis for the validity of God's word and therefore for the whole of the Christian's assurance concerning his faith, then these signs are for the Christian a not unimportant subsequent confirmation of his confidence with regard to God's promises. According to 2 Pet. 1:19, we have "the prophetic word made more sure", because it has been confirmed by divine actions and manifestations from the heavenly world, namely at the transfiguration of Jesus. These experiences (like the Easter experiences) strengthened the disciples' confidence in the absolute reliability and validity of the word of God.

(c) This use of the term leads also to the sense of witnessing and witness (to the gospel), as in 1 Cor. 1:6; Phil. 1:7; and Heb. 2:3. Here there is also the idea that

659

God's word is so sure and reliable that it must be believed when it is preached. Thus the idea drawn from the legal sphere, that God's word is here and now made valid by the witness which is borne to it, is often present (cf. H. Schlier, art. *bebaios*, *TDNT* I 603; see above CL). At the same time man's responsibility towards it is emphasized.

2. (a) It is on this basis of the legal foundation and validity of God's word and promise (see above NT 1 (a)) that the believer's assurance about his salvation is to be understood. Often the two meanings are directly related to one another (cf. Heb. 6:16 and 6:19; 1 Cor. 1:6 and 1:8; 2 Pet. 1:10 and 1:19). The certainty of the believer's hope is inextricably rooted in the legal validity of God's word. This is worked out very impressively in Heb. 6:19. Since God's promise is unchangeable and his oath (v. 16) valid (God does not lie!), the believer's hope is firm and assured like a ship which is firmly anchored. The writer of Heb. uses here the formula *asphalē kai bebaian*, an expression common in the Gk. world also. *asphalēs*, safe, can here scarcely be distinguished in meaning from *bebaios* (cf. O. Michel, ad loc., 157). Since the church on earth is always subject to temptation and is therefore in danger of losing its unique confidence (*parrhēsia*, → Openness), it is necessary for the church to show itself unshaken in its trust in God and its expectation of the future, i.e. in its assurance of salvation and that it should be ready to withstand every attack (Heb. 3:6, 14). This is indeed the very condition we must fulfil, in order to belong to "Jesus' house" and be his children and "partners" (v. 14 NEB).

(b) Because of this, the whole position of the Christian gains an element of assurance and certainty. It is God himself who establishes, makes firm, the believer in Christ (2 Cor. 1:21; similarly 1 Cor. 1:8), and seals him with the Holy Spirit. Such a person is "established in the faith" or "through faith" (Col. 2:7). 1 Pet. 5:9 has in the same sense *stereoi tē pistei*, "firm" or "solid" "in the faith", "rooted" (*rhizoomai*, parallel term to *bebaios*) in Christ and "built" on him. He has a "heart established through grace." He is secure just because he looks away from all efforts of his own and stands entirely upon what lies outside himself! In a very similar sense we find *stērizō* in 2 Thess. 2:17, and 1 Pet. 5:10, where it is used alongside *themelioō*. *H. Schönweiss*

θεμέλιος

θεμέλιος (*themelios*), foundation; θεμελιόω (*themelioō*), lay the foundation, pass. be founded; ἑδραῖος (*hedraios*), firm, steadfast; ἑδραίωμα (*hedraiōma*), foundation.

CL *themelios* was probably intended originally as an adj., which went with *lithos*, stone; but this cannot be verified from literature. It is used in the masc. and neut., without any difference in meaning. The word is attested from Homer onwards (there in the form *themeilia*, or *themethla*), and it is linguistically connected with the vb. *tithēmi*, place, stand, lay down. Hence it means that which lies beneath, foundation (stone), base, both in the lit. sense (e.g. foundations of a house, city, or building) and in a transf. sense (e.g. in legal correspondence to describe the right of possession to a building, or in philosophical thought, where the term means the basis of a system). Similarly the vb. *themelioō* means to lay the foundation (attested from Xen. onwards).

A similar meaning is conveyed by the adj. *hedraios* (derived from *hedra*, seat, chair, abode, place), which originally was used by men in the sense of sitting, sedentary, and then more generally for firm, unshakeable, stable. Thus *hedraios* is used in much the same way as *themelios* in questions about absolute certainty and the ultimate basis of all existence (especially by Plotinus). The reference is always to something secure and permanent in itself. The substantival form *hedraiōma*, foundation, is not found in classical Gk.

OT 1. There are various Heb. equivalents to *themelios*, mostly from the root *yāsaḏ*, to lay a foundation; but in the pre-exilic prophets frequently *'armôn*, citadel, palace; cf. Amos' prophecies against the nations. When the CT speaks of a basis and foundation it is never in the Greek, philosophical sense of ultimate, self-sufficient existence. The OT speaks of the foundations of houses (1 Ki. 7:9 f. [LXX 7:45 f.]; Jer. 51:26) and cities (Amos 1:4 ff. especially 2:5), and also of the mountains (Deut. 32:22; Ps. 18:7), the earth (Isa. 24:18; Mic. 6:2; Prov. 8:29) and the heavens (2 Sam. 22:8). Even in the last examples, foundations are here certainly to be understood in a lit. sense, in keeping with the ancient conception of the universe. The important point is that these foundations are not secure in themselves, but are laid by God (Prov. 8:29; Isa. 14:32; cf. Job 9:6) and are capable of being destroyed again (Deut. 32:22; Lam. 4:11; Ps. 18:7). The stability of this world is not an immanent possession of her own, but results from an act of foundation which is wrapped in mystery and so remains a gift from God. Hence the foundations of all things can tremble at the theophany in Ps. 18 (vv. 7, 15), which calls in question at the same time the permanence and stability of the earth's foundations.

Of particular importance for the theological meaning of the term *foundation* is Isa. 28:16 (cf. 54:11). Here Yahweh himself will lay the foundation and cornerstone for Israel in Zion. The image of a new building is certainly not intended to point to a future great new city, but to the establishment in the city of God of a people of God which lives by faith. Zion is to become a centre of pilgrimage for the nations (cf. Isa. 2:2 f.; Mic. 4:1 f.). Not until much later (cf. Eph. 2:20; 1 Pet. 2:4 ff.) is the foundation stone (Isa. 28:16) seen to refer to the Messiah (Christ).

2. In late Jewish literature the use made of the concept in the Qumran texts is striking. Here the Heb. words *sôḏ* and *yᵉsôḏ* are used interchangeably in the sense of foundation. The community is often regarded as the eschatological temple or the eschatological city of God. In such contexts mention is often made of its foundations, Isa. 28:16 being interpreted as referring to the community (1QS 8:5 ff.; 9:3 and often).

NT The NT use of *themelios* extends throughout the NT (in all it occurs 16 times), and does not differ from cl. Gk. usage in its meaning. The vb. is used 5 times. *hedraios*, on the other hand, is used only 3 times by Paul (1 Cor. 7:37; 15:58; Col. 1:23), and *hedraiōma* occurs only in 1 Tim. 3:15 (in the same sense as *themelios*). Luke uses *themelios* only in the lit. sense of the foundations of a building (6:48 f.; 14:29; Acts 16:26). In Heb. 11:10 and Rev. 21:14, 19 it refers to the foundations of the future city of God. Paul, on the other hand, uses the noun and vb. only in a fig. sense.

In discussing the theological significance of these terms, we may ignore all the passages which use them in the lit. and concrete sense, so that apart from Heb. 6:1 and 1 Pet. 5:10 our discussion is confined to the Pauline passages.

1. The image of a → house and house-building (*oikos*, *oikodomē*) is occasionally used in the NT as a picture of how a man governs and orders his life, as he founds and builds it (Matt. 7:24 f.). If he has the words of Jesus as the foundation, he is securely based. This also applies particularly to the Christian community, the church. It is a "spiritual house" (1 Pet. 2:5; Eph. 2:20–22; 1 Tim. 3:15) which Jesus himself plans to build (cf. Matt. 16:18) by his Spirit and his word. Just as the foundation is of decisive importance in building a house, so it is with the church. This foundation is Jesus Christ (1 Cor. 3:11). "Everything that has to be regarded as the reality and truth of justification and faith and their mutual relationship begins in Him and derives from Him" (K. Barth, *CD* IV 1, 637). On this foundation Paul has set the church (v. 10), and on this foundation the further building must proceed (vv. 12 ff.). But whatever is built, Christ must remain the basis (cf. v. 15). Insofar as this foundation only comes to men through the proclamation of the apostles and prophets, they can themselves be described as *themelios*, "Christ Jesus himself being the cornerstone" (Eph. 2:20). In the same way in Matt. 16:18 Peter is called the rock on which the church will be built. The church thus lives from that which God has done in Jesus and caused to be proclaimed by the apostles. She is no longer the church, if she allows other things beside to be regarded as fundamental such as blood or race (→ Rock, Stone).

2. Where the church rests on such a foundation, she can herself conversely be described as the foundation of the truth (1 Tim. 3:15; *hedraiōma*). For it is she who protects and preserves the truth in her confession (v. 16) in the fight against enemies within and without. Similarly in 2 Tim. 2:19 the foundation is formed not only by God's act in Christ, but arising out of this, the fact that the church puts away from herself all unrighteousness (cf. v. 20 f.).

3. As is evident from the simile of building a house, Paul makes a fundamental distinction between two separate tasks of the preacher. The first is to lay the foundation (missionary proclamation, evangelism); the second is to build up the church (1 Cor. 3:10). He believes himself above all called only to the first of these tasks (Rom. 15:20; cf. 2 Cor. 10:16), and is not prepared merely to build further where someone else has already laid the foundation.

4. In addition to these ecclesiological uses, *themelios* can also be applied, like *hedraios*, to the individual Christian. The steadfastness to which he is called (1 Cor. 15:58) depends entirely upon his relationship to his Lord which is grounded in faith (Col. 1:23) and love (Eph. 3:17). There may, however, be an allusion here too to the church, for in both contexts it is mentioned, as the body of Christ or by the expression "in Christ" (Col. 1:18; Eph. 3:21).

5. A completely different use is found in Heb. 6:1, where *themelios* means the basic doctrines of the Christian faith. The distinction made here is between the groundwork, which every Christian has to know, and further insights which come to those who are prepared to study the scriptures in greater depth. *themelios* is thus used here rather to distinguish between the relative importance of various items of Christian teaching, than to refer as in Paul to the relationship of a person to Christ.

J. Blunck

(a). H. Schlier, *bebaios*, *TDNT* I 600–3; K. L. Schmidt, *themelios*, *TDNT* III 63 f.; E. Stauffer, *hedraios*, *TDNT* II 362 ff.

(b). K. Heim, Glaubensgewissheit, 1923; H. J. Rothert, *Gewissheit und Vergewisserung als theologisches Problem*, 1963; K. T. Schäfer, "Über Eph. 2, 20," *Neutestamentliche Aufsätze*, Festschrift J. Schmid, 1963, 218 ff.

| ἀσφάλεια | ἀσφάλεια (*asphaleia*), firmness, certainty, security; ἀσφαλής (*asphalēs*), firm, sure, safe, secure; ἀσφαλίζω |

(*asphalizō*), guard; ἀσφαλῶς (*asphalos*), securely.

CL *asphaleia* occurs in cl. Gk. with the following meanings: security against stumbling (Thuc., *History*, 3, 22), assurance from danger (Aeschylus onwards), caution (in post-Christian writings), assurance, certainty (Thuc. *History*, 2, 11), the certainty or convincing nature of an argument (Xenophon, *Memorabilia*, 4, 6, 15), and as a security, bond or pledge as a technical law term (Arrianus, *Epicteti Dissertationes*, 2, 13, 7; *BGU* 1149, 24; P. Teb. 293, 19; *The Amherst Papyri*, 78:16).

The adj. *asphalēs* occurs from Homer onwards in the sense of immovable, steadfast, unshaken, unfailing both lit. and in the case of friends etc., and safe both lit. and fig. The vb. *asphalizō* is used in the sense of secure, safeguard and, in 1st cent. B.C. literature, arrest.

OT *asphaleia* occurs 19 times in the LXX as a translation of 6 different nouns. In Lev. 26:5 and Deut. 12:10 it is used of the security (Heb. *beṭaḥ*) which the Lord promises his people (cf. Prov. 8:14; 11:15; 28:17 where the Heb. equivalents are all different). In Ps. 103(104):5 it is used of the foundations of the earth. It is found in Isa. 8:15; 18:4; and 34:15. But most instances occur in 2 Macc. (3:22; 4:21; 9:21; 15:1, 11 where it means security, cf. also Jos., *War* 3, 398).

asphalēs occurs in Prov. 3:18 (*v.l.*); 8:28; 15:7 but in each case there are differences between the Heb. and the Gk. and the Eng. tr. does not give a lit. rendering of the Gk. It is also found in Tob. 5:15 (*v.l.*); Wis. 4:3; 7:23; 14:3. The adv. *asphalos* translates Heb. *beṭaḥ* in Gen. 35:25 (they "came upon the city unawares" RSV). It has the meaning of surely, certainly or safely in Wis. 18.6; Bar. 5:7; 1 Macc. 6:40; 3 Macc. 7:6; Aristeas 46.

The vb. *asphalizō* translates *ḥāzaq* in Neh. 3:15 (RSV "repaired the Fountain Gate"). It is used in Isa. 41:10 (Heb. *tāmak*) which RSV translates "I will uphold you with my victorious right hand." In Wis. it means keep safely (4:17), guard (10:12) and make fast (13:15). It has the meaning of guard in P. Teb. 283, 19 (1st cent. B.C.; cf. *Catalogue of the Greek Papyri in the John Rylands Library, Manchester*, 68, 19).

NT *asphaleia* is used in a physical sense in Acts 5:23 ("we found the prison locked in all security"). It is used fig. of the "certainty" or "truth" (RSV) of the things in which Theophilus has been instructed (Lk. 1:4). It denotes security in 1 Thess. 5:3 where Paul is warning against a false sense of security. *asphalēs* means "safe" in Phil. 3:1, i.e. a safe course. The adv. *asphalos* means securely in the sense of being securely guarded in Mk. 14:44 and Acts 16:23. It is used fig in the sense of "certainly", "assuredly" (RSV) in Acts 2:36. *asphalizō* means to guard or make secure (of the tomb of Jesus) in Matt. 27:64 ff.; to guard in Acts 16.30D; and to fasten in Acts 16:24. *C. Brown*

Arndt, 118; Hatch-Redpath, 174; A. J. B. Higgins, "The Preface to Luke and the Kerygma in Acts" in W. W. Gasque and R. P. Martin, eds., *Apostolic History and the Gospel*, 1970, 78–91; Liddell-Scott, 266; J. H. Ropes, "St Luke's Preface: *asphaleia* and *parakoloūthein*", *JTS* 25, 1924, 67–71; K. L. Schmidt, *asphaleia*, *TDNT* I 506; F. Vogel, *Neue kirchliche Zeitschrift*, 44, 1933, 203 ff.

κυρόω

κυρόω (*kyroō*), confirm, ratify, make valid; προκυρόω (*prokyroō*), establish, confirm beforehand.

CL & OT *kyroō*, from *kyros*, meaning authority or validity, expresses the thought of ratifying and making firm in all sorts of contexts. *prokyroō*, a regularly-formed compound meaning confirm beforehand, only appears twice in secular Gk., though *kyroō* is common from Herodotus and Aeschylus on. In the canonical LXX *kyroō* appears twice, both times in the passive voice of confirming possession (Gen. 23:20; Lev. 25:30). In the papyri it appears several times as the legal word for the confirming of transactions and appointments.

NT In Gal. 3:15, 17 both *kyroō* and *prokyroō* appear in connection with the ratifying, i.e. the actual formal making, of a will. In 2 Cor. 2:8 Paul uses *kyroō* in his plea to the Corinthians to "confirm" or perhaps "reaffirm, re-establish" their love towards the errant brother. *J. I. Packer*

First, Firstborn

The word "first" denotes priority within an order. This implies the consequent dependence or secondary status of other persons or things. The existence of such secondary persons or things is demanded by the distinction between *prōtos* (first) and *heis* (→ one) or *monos* (only), since these words exclude any comparable entity. In the NT the term *prōtotokos*, firstborn, which is derived from *prōtos*, has been given particular importance by its use as a title of Christ.

πρῶτος

πρῶτος (*prōtos*), first; πρωτεύω (*prōteuō*), be first; πρότερον (*proteron*), beforehand; πρωτοκαθεδρία (*prōtokathedria*), seat of honour; πρωτοκλισία (*prōtoklisia*), place of honour, best seat; πρωτοκαθεδρίτης (*prōtokathedritēs*), one who occupies a seat of honour, church leader.

CL 1. *prōtos* is the superlative of *pro*, before, and the ordinal number corresponding to *heis*, one. Hence in late Koiné Gk. it is used for *proteron* (earlier) also. It is used first as an adj. or noun meaning first; then in the neut., *prōton*, as an adv. meaning first, at first (so also the proper adv. *prōtōs*, Arist., but lacking in biblical Gk.). *prōtos* is attested from Homer in (a) a spatial, (b) a temporal sense. It further connotes (c) order or succession, and (d) rank and worth. In cl. Gk. these basic meanings give rise to 25 different senses or nuances.

2. In Gk. philosophy *ta prōta* means the elements (Empedocles, 38, 1); in logic, the primary, unprovable propositions; *prōtos syllogismos* is an original, normal, typical conclusion (Aristot., *Rhet.*, α 2, 1357ᵃ 17). In Aristot. *prōtē philosophia* means

that which is of the highest order (i.e. metaphysics); or alternatively, the philosophy of the ancients (i.e. the Pre-Socratics). In mathematics the prime numbers are called *prōtoi arithmoi*. As a title of rank and honour, the Ptolemaic court used the phrase *tōn prōtōn philōn*, one of the first friends (P. Teb 31, 15; cf. W. Michaelis, *TDNT* VI 865; Liddell–Scott, 1939).

3. Hel. religions. Among the followers of Orpheus Zeus is known as "first and last, head and centre" (*prōtos kai eschatos, kephalē kai messa*). Here the phrase *prōtos kai eschatos* denotes the majesty of the Ruler of All (Ps. Aristot., *Mund.* 401a 28; cf. 401b 5; → *basileus*, king; → *archōn*, ruler).

OT 1. In the LXX *prōtos* (*c.* 240 times) usually represents, as does *archē* (→ beginning), the Heb. *rō'š* (including *ri'šôn* and similar related words, 125 times). It is also frequently used for *ḥad, 'eḥād* (17 times), first, one; and *qeḍem* (9 times), forward. Generally speaking, the meanings correspond to those in classical Gk., though they are confined to the four basic senses mentioned above. Even when an order or succession is not directly specified, it is there in the background.

(a) In the spatial sense: in front, towards the East (the first in rank of the directions, "towards the sunrise", Num. 2:3 for *qeḍem*); the furthest town (Jos. 15:21); in the front, above (1 Sam. 9:22); nearest, next (Est. 1:14).

(b) In the temporal sense (the most frequent use): first (Deut. 13:9, here the basic implication of a succession is easiest to discern); first (kindness) (Ruth 3:10); in earlier times, in those days (2 Sam. 16:23); first of all (Tob. 5:10 Symmachus); as a noun in neuter plur., beginning (Job 8:7); former things, in contrast to later (Eccl. 1:11).

(c) As an ordinal number to denote order or succession: first (Gen. 32:17; Exod. 12:18; 1 Sam. 14:14; 1 Chr. 24:7; Dan. 7:4; 2 Macc. 7:7).

(d) To denote rank and worth: (i) of persons, the first, chief priest, the high priest (1 Ki. 2:35); the king's counsellors (1 Chr. 18:17); *prōtos philos*, closest friend (1 Chr. 27:33); the first singer, leader of the choir (2 Esd. 22:46 = Neh. 12:46); *prōteuō* similarly means to be the first, most noble (Est. 5:11); (ii) of things: the most valuable (1 Sam. 15:21), most precious (Amos 6:6); (iii) God is the first (*prōtos*): this is the special characteristic of the preaching and theology of Isa. (cf. 41:4; 44:6; 48:12). He is *prōtos* as the Creator; he is also the last. The whole creation, both man and world, is directed towards his acts. It is true that the temporal sense is present here as well, since the Creator is the Eternal One before (and after) all creation. But in the first instance *prōtos* here expresses the position of God as the Lord of the world.

2. Hel. Jud. and Rab. Jud. In interpreting Gen. 2:7, Philo distinguished two kinds of men. The "first" is from heaven and spiritual; the "second" is → Adam, the forefather of the human race (H. Lietzmann, *HNT* 9, 85; cf. on Rab. ideas, SB III 478). Paul reverses the order: "the first Adam became a living soul, the last Adam a life-giving spirit" (1 Cor. 15:45; cf. C. K. Barrett, *From First Adam to Last*, 1962, 1–21). Occasionally God is called *prōtos kai monos*, the first and only one. Both terms express the uniqueness of God (→ One, art. *monos*; cf. *TDNT* VI 865). In Rab. writings "first" occurs as a title for the Messiah, interpreting Isa. 41:27 (SB I 65). Moreover, besides Adam the Torah is described as "the first" or "first-born" (→ *prōtotokos;* cf. E. Lohmeyer *Der Kolosserbrief*, 1930[8] on 1:15).

NT 1. In the NT *prōtos* occurs altogether 152 times (92 as adj. or noun, 60 as adv.), being relatively frequent and evenly distributed in the Synoptic Gospels (Matt. 23 times; Mk. 17 times; Lk. 20 times) and Acts (16 times), Rev. (18 times) and Heb. (10 times). In Paul the word is important chiefly in Rom. (7 times) and Cor. (8 times). In Jn. it occurs only 13 times. Otherwise is found only here and there. It is used in much the same way as it is in the LXX.

(a) In a spatial sense (Acts 12:10; Heb. 9:2, 6, 8).

(b) In a temporal sense: first, first of all, to begin with, previously (Matt. 5:24 followed by *kai tote*, and then; Lk. 9:59, 61); for *proteron*, beforehand (Matt. 12:29; Jn. 1:15); in the pair of opposites *ta prōta - ta eschata*, beginning – end (Lk. 11:26). An element of evaluation is contained in the contrast, typical for Heb., between *hē prōtē* and *hē kainē diathēkē*, the first and the → new → covenant (Heb. 8:7, 13; cf. 8:8 and 8:6, *kreittōn diathēkē*, better covenant). The first, earlier, → old covenant has been superseded by the new and is no longer valid (in 2 Cor. 5:17 and 2 Pet. 2:5 *archaios* is used; in 2 Cor. 3:14, *palaios*).

(c) In a succession or order, *prōtos* means the first in a series, followed possibly by *deuteros*, *tritos*, second, third, or else by *heteros, heteros*, the other, the third (Matt. 22:25; Lk. 14:18); sometimes in contrast to the last (Matt. 20:8 ff.); or when there are two, *ho prōtos - ho allos*, the one – the other (Jn. 19:32). It is used adverbially as the first, first (Jn. 20:4); and without any idea of continuing the series (Lk. 2:2); the first, best (fish) (Matt. 17:27).

(d) As a designation of rank and office, *prōtos* stands alongside *megistanes* and *chiliarchoi* as a title (Mk. 6:21). It draws attention to the value of a special garment (Lk. 15:22). In the *prōtoi* and *eschatoi* of Matt. 19:30 there is an element of evaluation: the *prōtoi* are those who have been accepted, the last those who are rejected. Used adverbially in this sense, it denotes priority perhaps to the exclusion of others (Mk. 7:27); in the first place (Rom. 1:16; 29:9, 10); so too probably in 1 Tim. 1:16, where Paul as the first is "the typical representative of mercy" (H. Conzelmann, *HNT* 13, 25). Possibly Rev. 2:4 comes under this heading as well: the most important kind of love, namely love of the brethren (cf. E. Lohse, *NTD* 11, 22). Rank and office are also implied by *prōtoklisia*, the seat of honour at a feast (next to the host) (Mk. 12:39 par.; Lk. 14:7, 8), and *prōtokathedria*, the chief seat in the synagogue or its equivalent (Matt. 23:6). On the basis of this the leader of a church came later to be called *prōtokathedritēs*, lit. one who occupies the first seat (Hermas, *Vis.*, 3, 9, 7) and *prohēgoumenos*, president (cf. Arndt, 712, 732; → Bishop). *prōteuō* also denotes privilege: to take the first place, be pre-eminent (Col. 1:18; on this verse → art. *prōtotokos*, and E. Käsemann, "A Primitive Christian Baptismal Liturgy", *Essays on NT Themes*, 1964, 157 f.).

2. The frequent occurrence of *prōtos/prōton* in the NT as an expression of order or sequence (69 times) demonstrates the significance of → order in God's revelation, however important the free, unpredictable Spirit may be. This is partly accounted for by the influence of the OT and Jud. and the importance they attached to a devout, believing, well-ordered life (Lk. 11:38; Jn. 7:51 referring to the orderly process of justice; cf. SB III 469 f.). Jesus insisted on priorities in his new, Messianic order: before bringing your sacrifice, first be reconciled to your brother (Matt. 5:24); seek first the kingdom of God (Matt. 6:33); first take the beam out of your

666

own eye, then see to it and remove the splinter from your neighbour's (Matt. 7:5; cf. Lk. 14:28, 31). For the opposite see Lk. 9:59, 61 (cf. *TDNT* VI 869). God has even ordered the course of the world up to its end in the final judgment (Mk. 9:11 par.; Lk. 17:25; 2 Thess. 2:3; f. Lk. 21:9; 1 Thess. 4:16; 1 Pet. 4:17; *TDNT* VI 869).

The church drew inferences from the divine ordering of events which it applied to the ordering of worship (1 Cor. 14:30; cf. vv. 33 and 40), and the ordering of offices in the church (1 Cor. 12:28). Paul insisted that the freedom of the Spirit is not anarchy (→ Love, art. *agapē*). On the other hand, the order of the church of Jesus Christ must not be made into a hierarchy. To be the first is not, and never becomes, an institution. It always remains a function: he who would be first in the church, let him become your slave and so follow the example of Jesus. He is the only servant (*diakonos*) in the full sense, and hence the only one who is "first" (Matt. 20:27 f.). God made Jesus the Lord of this order by making him the *protos kai eschatos* (a title of God, Isa. 44:6; 48:12; cf. Rev. 1:17; 2:8; 22:13; cf. Acts 26:23). As the First and the Last, he is also the unique One (→ One, art. *monos*). His mission is unique and unrepeatable (→ One, art. *hapax*). Hence Jesus alone has the authority to make the last first and the first last (Matt. 20:16). Thus he confirms Israel's abiding pre-eminence (Mk. 7:27; cf. Rom. 1:16; 2:9 f.; 11:2; but see also Matt. 8:11 and Lk. 13:28–30). And yet for the moment he gives the Gentiles preference over his own people (to be understood literally in the temporal sense, cf. Rom. 11:25 ff.), in order to make them jealous and move them to return to him.   *K. H. Bartels*

| πρωτότοκος |

πρωτότοκος (*prōtotokos*), firstborn.

CL & OT *prōtotokos* is a late derivative from *prōtos* (first) and the aorist root *tek-* (born). The active form *prōtotokos* means, bearing one's firstborn; the pass. form *prōtotokos*, firstborn, is first found in the LXX, about 130 times, almost always for Heb. *bᵉkôr*, firstborn. The *tekein*, i.e. bearing element in the word, sometimes takes a secondary place or disappears in the transferred sense, since *bākar* is related neither to *ri'šôn*, first, nor is it used as a vb. meaning to give birth (see below 2; *TDNT* VI 871 ff.).

1. In the LXX *prōtotokos* is used (a) in its lit. sense both of man and of beast, often as a noun in the neuter sing. with the accompanying phrase "which opens the womb" (*dianoigon tēn mētran*) (e.g. Exod. 13:2). The following expressions are confined to humans: *prōtotokos hyios*, firstborn son (cf. Gen. 25:25 (Esau); Exod. 4:22 (Israel)), and *prōtotokos* as a noun joined to the proper name (cf. Num. 3:2). The idea held generally in the ancient orient that firstborn inherits his father's strength (cf. Gen. 49:3) gives him a special position in law (cf. Deut. 21:15 ff.). For this reason it is normal for him to receive his father's special love (cf. *TDNT* VI 874). (b) In a transferred sense, *prōtotokos* is used to express a special relationship with the father, especially with God. Here the two roots from which it is derived, *prōtos*, first of several, and *tekein*, denoting physical descent, birth, no longer play any part in the meaning. See, for example, Exod. 4:22. In Ps. 89:27 ff. the thought

667

is of "adoption", i.e. the bestowal of special legal rights and honours. It is to be noted that while *prōtotokos* is used in the OT as a title of honour for the chosen, those who have received grace, it is not found in an eschatological or soteriological sense.

2. In Rab. Judaism the Torah is described in a comment on Prov. 8:22, 23 as the first created thing, the firstborn of the way of Yahweh, and the earliest of his works. The same description is applied to the sanctuary with reference to Jer. 17:12. In both cases the term is used in a figurative sense to express the special love of God for the Torah and the sanctuary (SB III 256; → *prōtos*).

NT *prōtotokos* appears 8 times in the NT.

1. In the lit. sense, e.g. Lk. 2:7. "This is the only instance in the NT where, through the paronomastic use of *tiktein*, *prōtotokos* refers unequivocally to the process of birth, and this in the natural sense" (W. Michaelis, *TDNT* VI 876). "Firstborn" possibly conveys the implication that Jesus was the first of several children (cf. Mk. 6:3). Or it may emphasize, in view of the mention in Lk. 1:27, 34 of her virginity, that Mary had borne no previous children. In any case, however, *prōtotokos* does not preclude further children of Mary (cf. ibid.; → *monogenēs*).

2. In the fig. sense, as a title of honour for Jesus, *prōtotokos* is comprehensible only as translation of LXX Gk., with *bākar* in the background (see above OT 2). This must not be forgotten when we encounter shades of meaning for *prōtotokos* in the NT which go beyond its use in the LXX.

(a) As a title for the mediator of creation, it is used in Col. 1:15, as is demonstrated by parallel sayings in v. 16, "in him all things were created . . . all things were created through him and for him," and v. 17, "He is before all things, and in him all things hold together." Both supporters and opponents of the suggestion that *prōtotokos* in Col. 1 echoes Hel., mythical ideas agree that the statement is a confession of the supreme rank of the pre-existent Christ as the mediator in the creation of all things (cf. E. Käsemann, op. cit., 154 ff.; W. Michaelis, *TDNT* VI 879 f.).

(b) It is used in a eschatological sense in Heb. 1:6 to qualify *hyios*, son (v. 5), as a title given to Jesus at his ascension, i.e. the heavenly enthronement of the risen Lord (E. Käsemann, *Das wandernde Gottesvolk*, 1957, 58 f.). According to Ps. 2:7 cited in Heb. 1:5, it follows that, "The exaltation of Christ represents the *teleiōsis* of Jesus and thus the first attestation given by God, to be followed by others when the redeemed are made perfect" (Käsemann, ibid., 73). Michaelis interprets the passage otherwise, seeing v. 6a as a reference to the incarnation of the pre-existent Christ, although he also considers the possibility of a reference to the enthronement of the exalted Christ at the parousia (*TDNT* VI 880). Since the exalted Christ is one step ahead of his followers (in chapter 2 likewise called *hyioi*, sons) on the way to consummation, he is already *prōtotokos*, "Lord and *archēgos* of the redeemed community" (Käsemann, ibid.). Rom. 8:29 refers to the "eschatological transfiguration", when those who have been foreknown and chosen out are made like him (by the resurrection of the dead). As the *prōtotokos*, he will "be like them but above them in rank and dignity, since He remains their Lord" (*TDNT* VI 877). Col. 1:18 and Rev. 1:5 connect the title *prōtotokos* with the resurrection: Jesus is the first to be raised by God (→ *prōtos*, Acts 26:23), with the purpose "of being first in all things" (cf. Acts 3:15; 5:31; Heb. 2:10: the pioneer (founder) of life or salvation).

As a title of honour for Jesus, *prōtotokos* expresses more clearly than almost any other the unity of God's saving will and acts: "the firstborn of all creation", "the firstborn from the dead" (Col. 1:15; 18), "the firstborn among many brethren" (Rom. 8:29; cf. Heb. 12:23). Creator and Redeemer are one and the same, the all-powerful God in Jesus Christ "the first and the last", "the beginning and the end", who binds his own to himself from all eternity, and is their surety for salvation, if they abide in him. This goes beyond the limits of what can be logically asserted: the man Jesus of Nazareth (Lk. 2:1–2) is the mediator of creation; he who was executed on the cross as a criminal is the first to experience resurrection, and the one who leads us into life. This would have been reason enough for the NT witnesses to look back to the language of myth, in order to overstep the limitations of the OT and orthodox Judaism, and to express the inexpressible in the form of a confession (cf. the hymn-like style of Col. 1; so Käsemann, 149 ff.; E. Norden, *Agnostos Theos*, 1923, 241, 253). For in Jesus God has in fact made the impossible true. In the man Christ Jesus, the *prōtotokos*, God has brought his divine power and glory to its climax (Col. 1:19 f.), and has given a share in this to the church.

3. The plur. *prōtotokoi* is used with reference to the church. Should Heb. 12:23 ("the assembly of the firstborn who are enrolled in heaven") be taken literally? This would mean that Christians are here set directly alongside Christ, in an unparalleled and almost dangerous manner. Doubtless the author sees the Son and the sons (chs. 1 and 2), the *hagiazōn*, sanctifier, and the *hagiazomenoi*, those being sanctified, as very closely related. They are *ex henos pantes*, "all of one origin" (2:11). Käsemann refers here to gnostic myth (*syngeneia* teaching; *Das wandernde Gottesvolk*, 92 f.), but is careful to emphasize that the naturalism which characterizes gnostic myth has been abandoned. "The union of Christ and his followers, like the whole process of redemption, cannot be understood here except in terms of God's purpose of salvation" (ibid., 94). This is why Heb. 2 10 stresses *eprepen autō*, it was fitting for him to "make the pioneer [*archēgos*] of their salvation perfect through suffering". The *prōtotokoi*, as "brothers" of Christ, are enrolled in heaven. They do not possess the rank of firstborn as an inalienable right (as in the gnostic myth), but expect it like heirs, on the ground that Christ is the *prōtotokos* and as such their → *archēgos*, pioneer (→ Beginning; cf. *arrabōn*, first instalment, 2 Cor. 1:22, → Gift; cf. Rom. 8:17; *aparchē*, first-fruits, Rom. 8:23; → Sacrifice). *K. H. Bartels*
→ Adam, → Abraham, → Election, → Fruit, → Image, → Jesus Christ, → Lord, → Son of God, → Sacrifice

(a). A. T. Hanson, "Christ the First Fruits, Christ the Tree," *Studies in Paul's Technique and Theology*, 1974, 104–25; E. Käsemann, "A Primitive Christian Baptismal Liturgy," *Essays on New Testament Themes*, 1964, 149–68; V. H. Kooy, "First-born," *IDB* II 270 ff.; W. Kornfeld, "First-fruits (firstborn)," *EBT* I 271 ff.; I. Mendelsohn, "On the Preferential Status of the Eldest Son," *BASOR* 156, 1959, 38 ff.; W. Michaelis, *prōtos*, *TDNT* VI 865–82; J. Morgenstern, "First Fruits", *IDB* II 270; R. de Vaux, *Ancient Israel*, 1961 (see index).
(b). M. Albertz, "Die 'Erstlinge' der Botschaft des Neuen Testaments," *EvTh* 12, 1952–53, 151 ff.; E. Brunner, "Der Ersterschaffene als Gottes Ebenbild," *EvTh* 11, 1951–52, 298 ff.; J. Henninger,

"Menschenopfer bei den Arabern," *Anthropos* 53, 1958, 721 f., 776 f.; E. Käsemann, *Das wandernde Gottesvolk*, 1959³; W. Kornfeld, "Der Moloch," *Wiener Zeitschrift für die Kunde des Morgenlandes* 51, 1952, 287–313; W. Michaelis, "Die biblische Vorstellung von Christus als dem Erstgeborenen," *ZSTh* 23, 1954, 137 ff.; E. Norden, *Agnostos Theos*, (1923) 1960; C. H. Ratschow and A. Wendel, "Erstlinge," *RGG³* II 608 ff.

Fish

ἰχθύς

ἰχθύς (*ichthys*), fish; ἰχθύδιον (*ichthydion*) diminutive of foregoing, little fish; ὀψάριον (*opsarion*), fish for eating (with bread); κῆτος (*kētos*), sea-monster.

CL In cl. Gk. *ichthys* (with a variety of compounds, e.g. *ichthyophagos*, "fish-eating") was in general use. It appears as a metaphor for a "foolish man" in Plut., *Moralia*, 975 B.

Classically, *kētos* is specifically a sea-monster, of the whale kind (Aristotle), a cetacaean. Adj. *kēteios* is used in the general sense "monstrous". *kētos* is also the constellation, and the supposition that sea-monsters inhabited the deep gave rise to *kētos* in the sense "gulf". Possibly derived from *keiō*, to lie outstretched.

OT In the LXX, *ichthys* describes all created life living in the water (e.g. 1 Ki. 4:29 (33); Job 12:8), whether fresh (Exod. 7:18; Ezek. 29:4) or salt (Hos. 4:3) water. Fish are involved in the subservience of creation to the Creator (Ezek. 38:20) and by the Creator's will are under human domination (Gen. 1:26; 9:2; Ps. 8:9[8]). Their commercial value is implied in Neh. 13:13 and by the provision of a "fish-gate" (Neh. 3:3). With the rest of creation, fish fall under divine judgments on man (Exod. 7:18; Ps. 104[105]:29), illustrate divine providential interventions (Isa. 50:2) and figure in the ideal future (Ezek. 47:9). The angler's art aptly denotes man's inhuman treatment of man (Hab. 1:14). Religiously, it is forbidden to make fish-like representations of the divine nature (Dt. 4:18), a prohibition much to the point in the light of Assyrian representations of Ea in fish-form and the fish-costume of exorcist priests (cf. Tob. 6:1 ff.). In all these references LXX OT translates Heb. *dāḡ*, *dāḡâh*, or *dᵉḡat-hayyām*, i.e. the general OT designation of sea-creatures.

kētos is used by the LXX to translate *tannînîm gᵉḏōlîm* (Gen. 1:21), *liwyāṯān* (Job 3:8) and *rahaḇ* (Job 9:13). In the last two it has clear mythological overtones. Otherwise it is only used of the sea-monster (*dāḡ gāḏôl*, and *haddāḡâh*) in Jon. 2:1 [1:17], 11[10].

NT The NT use of *ichthys* reflects much of the OT background. The whole Galilee narrative of the Gospels implies commerce in fish, but neither here nor throughout the OT is there any stress on different species of fish, nor are any particular varieties named, even though Galilee abounded in many sorts. The vocabulary of the LXX is increased by the occasional use of *opsarion* for fish prepared for or designed as food (Jn. 6:11; 21:9). The word does not necessarily mean "small" fish, as Jn. 21:9 ff. indicates. 1 Cor. 15:39 offers the sole NT observation on zoology, but its interest is clearly theological, the subservience of all creation to the Creator's will and design and it is this truth which receives vivid illustration in the nature miracles of Jesus, the two feedings of the multitudes (Matt. 14:17; 15:36, with parallels), the tribute money (Matt. 17:27) and the miraculous catches of fish (Lk. 5:6; Jn. 21:6). The single thread of truth linking these narratives is that by the mere exercise of his will Jesus subdues creation to his plan throughout in works of mercy for the well-being of people, and thus is manifested as the incarnate Creator.

kētos makes its only appearance in Matt. 12:40 with reference to the "great fish" (*dāḡ gāḏôl*) of Jonah. Both the LXX and NT have clearly made the correct choice of word here in the light of total usage, a sea-monster of undefined nature but undoubted size. *J. A. Motyer*

→ Animal, → Bird, → Jonah

G. S. Cansdale, *Animals of Bible Lands*, 1970; J. D. M. Derrett, "Peter's Penny," *Law in the New Testament*, 1970, 247–65; W. S. McCullough, "Fish," *IDB* II 272 f.; J. A. Thompson, "Fish, Fishing," *NBD* 424 f.; C. U. Wolf, "Fishing," *IDB* II 273 f.

Flesh

σάρξ

σάρξ (*sarx*), flesh; σάρκινος (*sarkinos*) consisting of flesh, fleshly; σαρκικός (*sarkikos*), after the manner of the flesh, belonging to the domain of the flesh, fleshly; κρέας (*kreas*), flesh, meat.

CL *sarx*, in Homer nearly always in the plur. (the only exception is in *Od.*, 19, 450), means the flesh of a man as distinct from his bones, sinews etc. From Hesiod onwards it means also the flesh of an animal, and in a wider development (also used now in the sing.) the flesh of fishes and small animals, as well as of fruits. The → body (*sōma*) consists of bones, blood, sinews, flesh and skin (Plato, *Phaedr.*, 98 c.d); or of hair, flesh, bones (*Symp.*, 207d). Occasionally *sarx* denotes the whole physical body which can be old (*sarki palaia*, Aesch., *Ag.*, 72) or young. A typical expression is *hai sarkes kenai phrenōn* (Eur., *El.*, 387), by which men are meant who are without understanding and so mere flesh.

Transitoriness is a particularly characteristic mark of *sarx*. When vital energy (*psychē* → soul) and desire (*thymos*) pass away, flesh and bones disappear (*Od.*, 11, 219–222). Unlike men and animals, the gods have no *sarx*, but are *nous* (mind), *epistēmē* (insight), *logos* (→ word, reason) (Epict., *Diss.*, 118, 2). Accordingly, man's imperishable nature is increasingly contrasted with his perishable flesh. The *onkos sarkōn* (body of flesh), which is buried, is not our own real being (Plato, *Leg.*, 959c; cf. "the strange garment of the flesh", Emp., *Frag.*, 126). Epicurus, however, gave a new turn to this idea. Disappearance is only a dispersion of atoms; but this does not leave behind it any remainder. Accordingly, the start and root of all good is well-being, the *hēdonē* (→ desire) of the belly (*Frag.* 409). When flesh cries out, "Do not hunger, do not freeze, do not thirst", the soul heeds this reminder (*Frag.* 200). Since the *dianoia* (understanding) knows the end and limit of the *sarx*, Epicurus certainly does not invite men to a life of luxury, but on the contrary to one that is utterly controlled and temperate. For not only present but also future *hēdonē* is essential to good fortune (*Frag.* 68).

These ideas were much debased and popularized in a form that was depicted as favour of evil desire, especially by their opponents of the Platonic school. According to them, the cravings and lusts of the body defile the → soul which has a share in the divine. Epicurus was obliged to defend himself against the imputation of

671

approving appetite, bodily desire, fornication, and intemperance (*Frag.* 414). The anti-Epicurean polemic was widely spread in Hellenism and it penetrated deeply into Judaism.

OT The Hebrew equivalents of *sarx* (LXX) are *bāśār* and *š^e'ēr*; *bāśār* is by far the more frequent (266 times against 17 times). *kreas* also renders *bāśār* some 50 times, denoting mostly flesh as an item of food. *sarx* has a wider meaning. It can even denote humanity (Isa. 40:5 f.).

1. (a) *bāśār* denotes flesh as the food of men (1 Sam. 2:13, 15; the flesh of quails, Num. 11:33; of swine, Deut. 14:8; of cows, Gen. 41:2). Flesh and wine are food for good times (Dan. 10:3). → Animal, → Bird.

(b) Likewise, *bāśār* also denotes human flesh. God took one of the ribs of the man and closed up its place with flesh (Gen. 2:21). Daniel and his friends remained, in spite of a reduced diet, *b^erî'ē bāśār*, "fatter in flesh", and therefore in good bodily condition (Dan. 1:15).

Ezek. 37:6, 8 mentions together sinews, flesh, skin and → spirit (*rûaḥ*), and Job 10:11 skin, flesh, bones, sinews. In a specific sense the penis is called the naked flesh (Exod. 28:42), the flesh of the foreskin (Gen. 17:11 ff.; Lev. 12:3), and also simply flesh (Lev. 15:2 f. [LXX *sōma*]; Ezek. 16:26; 23:20; 44:7, 9).

(c) *bāśār* can also denote the human body in its entirety, specifying the part for the whole. "Ahab . . . rent his clothes, put sack-cloth upon his flesh and fasted" (1 Ki. 21:27). When in deep sleep a word from Yahweh is heard, the hair of the flesh stands up (Job 4:15). The flesh is, however, not merely the body but the whole, man as a person. "O God, thou art my God, I seek thee, my soul thirsts for thee my flesh longs for thee" (Ps. 63:2; cf. 54:3). Here the flesh denotes man's own self. ([Ed.] Job 19:25 f. declares: "For I know that my Redeemer lives, and at last he will stand upon the earth; and after my skin has thus been destroyed, then without (mg. from) my flesh (Heb. *mibb^eśārî*) I shall see God." The natural reading of the grammar would suggest that "from" would be the more likely translation, but many commentators are reluctant to ascribe to Job belief in resurrection or life after death. See further H. H. Rowley, *Job*, 1970, 172 ff. Whilst recognizing the textual and grammatical difficulties of the verse and the fact that many commentators see in it a hope for vindication in this life, Rowley is inclined to see here a hope for vindication after death in view of the fact that in the preceding verses Job sees no hope of vindication in the present life.)

(d) The self does not stand alone, however. A relative is "my bone and my flesh" (Gen. 29:14). Accordingly, Gen. 2:23 means: woman is for man, as it were, the place in the world where he is at home. Her intimate relationship creates his home. A brother is "our flesh" (Gen. 37:27). Still more comprehensively all flesh means all mankind. "If he should take back his spirit . . . all flesh would perish together and man would return to dust" (Job 34:15; cf. Ps. 56:6, 12). Similarly, "all flesh" means "everyone" "All flesh shall come to worship, says Yahweh" (Isa. 66:23). Finally the phrase can include humanity and the animal world as in Gen. 6:17 ff.; 9:11 f.

(e) From the meanings that have been adduced it is already clear that, although the obvious starting point is the same for the OT and Gk. literature, the anthropological consequences differ. In the OT flesh denotes man as a whole; man is flesh in his essence. According to the Gk. conception, on the other hand, man has flesh but is *not* flesh. This holds good also for Epicurus, who understood the needs of the flesh as the actual reality which must by all means be satisfied. For *dianoia* (discernment) is necessary, so that future good fortune be not sacrificed to present super-abundance. The raptures of the soul, just as its griefs, are greater than those of the flesh (*Frag.* 445; Diog. Laert., 10, 137).

The same distinction shows itself in the understanding of transitoriness. In the OT the flesh denotes man in his transitoriness as one who suffers sickness, death, fright etc. It is not his desire as such, which is rather expressed by other terms, such as heart (Gen. 8:21). Thus Isaiah says: "All flesh is grass, and all its beauty is like the flower of the field. The grass withers, the flower fades" (Isa. 40:6, 8). Senna-cherib's Assyrian horde is called "an arm of flesh", which is puny compared with God (2 Chr. 32:8). God "remembered that they (Israel) were but flesh – a wind that does not return." Therefore he forgave their iniquity (Ps. 78:39). On the other hand, Jer. 17:5 declares: "Cursed is the man who trusts in man and makes flesh his arm, whose heart turns away from Yahweh."

2. *še'ēr* (Accad. *šîru* flesh, body; Phoen. *š'r* flesh) seems to be the more ancient word and means: flesh to eat (Exod. 2:10; Ps. 78:20, 27); human flesh (Mic. 3:2 f.; Jer. 51:34 f.); a blood relation (Lev. 18:6; 20:19; 25:49; Num. 27:11; in LXX *oikeios* or *oikeia*, related person, kin). For the sake of its meaning Ps. 73:26 may be mentioned: "My flesh and my heart may fail [i.e. if I pass away; cf. Prov. 5:11], but God is the rock of my heart and my portion for ever."

3. Judaism in its various forms closely connected man's carnality with his sin, but without interpreting the flesh as the actual cause of sin. It referred to OT statements which describe dependence on the flesh not merely as folly but also as sin (Isa. 31:3). "All flesh" is mankind, and to strive after evil is inherent in man (Gen. 8:21). There must then be a relation between the flesh and dependence on the flesh.

(a) The Qumran teaching that man "is in iniquity from the womb" (1QH 4:30) fully accords with the OT (Ps. 51:5). But in 1QS 11:12 the elect one speaks other-wise about himself: "If I stagger because of the sin of flesh my justification shall be by the righteousness of God which endures for ever." This probably means that man, in so far as he is merely flesh, belongs to the community of wickedness. For a little earlier (11:9) it is said, "I belong to wicked mankind, to the com-pany of ungodly flesh." And in 1QH 15:16 f.: "Thou alone didst create the just . . . thou wilt raise up his glory from among flesh; but the wicked thou didst create for the time of thy wrath." The righteous man thus receives his life (righteousness) from God; it is no longer derived from the flesh. The counterpart to flesh is not, how-ever, → spirit. For side by side with the spirit of holiness there is also found the spirit of wickedness and of the flesh (1QS 4:20 f.; 1QH 13:13 f.). It is always God or his justifying righteousness that stands over against the flesh.

(b) Rab. usage shows two characteristic departures from the OT. Man in his transitoriness is now called "flesh and blood" (instanced for the first time in Sir. 14:18). Even more important is the frequent replacement of the OT *bāśār* by *gûp* (originally perhaps "cavity", Arab. *ǧauf*, cf. on this *TDNT* VII, 116). Behind this there doubtless stands a new anthropological conception of the body as a vessel which at any time can be possessed by a different spirit. In this way the body is not devalued, since in the final judgment God will fetch the soul and place it in the body and judge the two together (*Sanh.* 91a). But the body no longer denotes man as a whole. "All creatures which are made from heaven derive their soul and body from heaven, and all creatures which are made from the earth derive their soul and body from the earth. Man is the sole exception: his soul is derived from heaven, his body from the earth. If then man obeys the law and does the will of the heavenly Father, then he is as the higher creatures . . . but if he does not fulfil the law and do the will of the heavenly Father, then he is as the lower creatures" (*Siphre Deut.* 305, 233, 2). A Hel. oriental influence is to be found here. But beside it, the OT usage may still be found (cf. SB I 581).

(c) Hel. Judaism showed its peculiarity in two characteristic alterations made in the LXX as compared with the MT. In Ezek. 10:22 it does not speak of the flesh of the cherubim, and in Num. 16:22; 27:16 it translates the Heb. phrase "God of the spirits (*rûḥôṯ*) of all flesh" by *theos tōn pneumatōn kai pasēs sarkos*, "Lord of the spirits and of all flesh". Here, as in Rab. Judaism, there is a considerable separation of heaven and earth. But for the rest, the appraisal of flesh is quite different. According to Eth. En. 17:6, Hades is the place whither no flesh goes. According to Paralipomena Jeremiae 6:6, the *sarx* will have incorruptibility. In the Apocalypse of Elias 35:7 f.; 42:12 f. it is said that the physical flesh is discarded but that a spiritual flesh (*sarkes pneumatos*) is put on, whilst according to Life of Adam 43:4 and 2 Esd. 7:78, 100, the soul in death detaches itself from the body.

Statements inclining in the direction of cosmological dualism are found in Philo. For him God is a being without flesh or body. Accordingly, he can be perceived only by a soul that is without flesh or body (*Deus Imm.* 52–56). For the soul the body (the flesh) is a burden, servitude, a coffin and an urn. Freedom from the flesh through asceticism is thus important, for otherwise the soul is hampered in its upward flight. Guilt begins with the soul's steadfast continuance in the flesh (cf. *Leg. All.* 3, 152). Philo is correspondingly aware that the soul has *aloga pathē*, passions that war with reason, and beget evil when it is overcome by the flesh (*Deus Imm.* 52). For the body with its passions incites men to commit sin. On the other hand, it remains conceivable that the *onkos sarkinos*, fleshly body, may be taken into service as sandals under the feet (*Sacr.* 63).

NT Just as in Hel. Judaism, the different authors of the NT vary in their appraisal of the flesh. The division can be shown statistically. 91 of the 147 instances of *sarx* are found in the Pauline writings, above all in Rom. and Gal. The adjectives *sarkikos* (7 times) and *sarkinos* (6 times) also occur only in Rom. and 1 and 2 Cor., apart from one exception each in Heb. and 1 Pet. In the non-Pauline writings the occurrences are few in comparison. In Jn. the noun is found only 13 times (in Rev. and 1 Pet. 7 times, elsewhere only sporadically). *kreas* occurs in the NT only twice in Paul in the sense of flesh as an item of food.

1. Paul uses *sarx* so frequently that only the most essential passages for its understanding can be discussed.

(a) As mere *flesh* (of men, → animals, → birds, → fishes), *sarx* occurs only in 1 Cor. 15:39. Occasionally it denotes the *human body* (as in 2 Cor. 12:7, a thorn in the flesh probably means sickness (cf. Arndt, 763 f.); Gal. 4:13, infirmity of the flesh, probably again sickness; Gal. 4:14, my flesh means Paul's sick body). But

674

it also denotes man generally. According to 2 Cor. 7:5, "our flesh" (= we) had no rest because there were fightings without and fears within (about the stability of the church). In marriage the flesh suffers troubles (1 Cor. 7:28), because now it is the last time and persecutions threaten (1 Cor. 7:29 ff.). When Paul says that before he began to preach the gospel he did not confer with flesh and blood (Gal. 1:16), he means he did not confer with men. If flesh and blood will not inherit the kingdom of God (1 Cor. 15:50), it means that, according to OT anthropology (Prov. 5:11), in death the whole man must disappear and a new *sōma* come into existence (→ Body).

(b) *sarx* also denotes relationships which have a merely temporary significance. Thus according to the flesh, Jesus is a son of David (Rom. 1:3), but only from the resurrection onwards is his divine sonship manifest according to the spirit of holiness (Rom. 1:4). "Israel after the flesh" (1 Cor. 10:18) is the whole people descended from the patriarch (Rom. 4:1; cf. 11:14). From him Paul's brethren are descended, his kinsmen according to the flesh (Rom. 9:3; cf. "near of kin", *šeʾēr beśārô*, flesh relation, Lev. 18:6). From him comes the Messiah (Rom. 9:5, 8). *sarx* means common humanity in Phlm. 16, when Paul says that the slave Onesimus is Philemon's brother "both in the flesh and in the Lord". But Paul uses "all flesh" for "mankind" only in the fundamental expression of his theology, "All flesh cannot [i.e. no flesh can] boast before God" (Rom. 3:20; cf. Gal. 2:16; 1 Cor. 1:29).

(c) *sarx* is used not only to indicate physical kinship; it can be used also generally in reference to what is human. Thus "the wise after the flesh" are the wise according to human standards (1 Cor. 1:16; cf. 2:6, "wisdom of this age"). The weapons which Paul uses in his campaign are no longer of human invention, but are made effectual by God (2 Cor. 10:4). In contrast to him stand those who wish to make themselves agreeable to the church by human means (Gal. 6:12), so that in human ways they might be able to glory in the → circumcision of a Christian → church (v. 13). But the circumcised, like the uncircumcised, stand under the condemnation that they fall short of the glory of God. Paul might have every reason to glory in descent, in circumcision, in zeal for the law. But that would be to have confidence in a human reckoning (the flesh) which does not count with God (Phil. 3:3 f.). For with God only the → righteousness of Christ, received by faith, is of any consequence (vv. 8–11).

(d) This leads to the use of the phrase *kata sarka*, according to the flesh. Even though Paul lived as a man "in the flesh", he did not carry on his fight in the light of human considerations ("after the flesh" 2 Cor. 10:2 f.; cf. 1:17). To glory in Christian visions is just as foolish as to glory in circumcision (2 Cor. 11:18). For even if one knew the religious capabilities of Jesus, that would merely be to know him after the flesh. "From now on, therefore, we regard no one from a human point of view (*kata sarka*); even though we once regarded Christ from a human point of view (*kata sarka*), we regard him thus no longer" (2 Cor. 5:16 RSV). Similarly, the Christian is no longer in the grip of the self-centred, self-justifying standards of secular man. He → walks "not according to the flesh (*kata sarka*) but according to the Spirit (*kata pneuma*)" (Rom. 8:4). Thus the new life in the Spirit is paralleled by a renunciation in principle of human efforts at self-justification.

(e) The flesh, i.e. man's existence apart from God, has therefore a drive that is opposed to God. It not only occasions sin but also becomes entangled in it.

Accordingly, Paul can draw up a catalogue of vices which he characterizes as "works of the flesh" or "desires of the flesh" (Gal. 5:16, 19; cf. Rom. 13:14). Above all, in Gal. 5:17 he is able to say, "The desires of the flesh are against the Spirit and the desires of the Spirit are against the flesh, for these are opposed to each other to prevent you from doing what you would." This is not the flesh of the anti-Epicurean polemic, but man himself, in so far as he gives himself up to his own aims in opposition to God's. Hence, the → law also is weak through the flesh, because it can be used by it as a means of self-assertion against God (Rom. 8:3). Therefore, God sent his Son in the likeness of a human being determined by sin that in this most Godlike of all men he might bring sin (self-justification before God on the basis of human achievements) into judgment, so that after his death only God's achievement might remain. The believer is thus already dead in respect to the ambitions and drives that mould life apart from God. In this sense he is no longer in the flesh (Rom. 8:8 f.). Moreover, he now lives according to God's life; "for I know that nothing good dwells within me, that is in my flesh" (Rom. 7:18). For man, indeed, desires to achieve what is good, i.e. the true life. But actually he achieves the evil which he does not desire, namely death, because he does not allow God to care for him, but desires to care for himself. "So then, I of myself, serve the law of God with my mind (*noï*), but with my flesh (in actuality) I serve the law of sin" (Rom. 7:25b). Though Paul adopts here a typically Gk. manner of speaking, his understanding of man is completely different. Even the *nous*, the rational power of mental comprehension, is unable to find out what is good, since the true meaning of life remains hidden from it by sin.

(f) On the one hand, Paul can say that the believer no longer lives in the flesh (Rom. 7:5; 8:8 f.; Gal. 5:24). But on the other hand, as a believer, Paul still lives in the flesh (2 Cor. 10:3; Gal. 2:20; Phil. 1:22–24). The contradiction is resolved in Phil. 1:22–24. To be in the flesh is for him something that has been so vanquished, that for him it is all one whether he lives or dies. Life is to exist in and for Christ, and no longer by one's own abilities. Even death, as departure and being with Christ, is much better. But for the sake of the future of the kingdom of God it is more important for him to remain in the flesh.

In the combination *sōma tēs sarkos* Col. seems to show considerable Hel. influence. *sarx* is here the material of which the body (*sōma*) is composed (1:22; 2:11). In the Qumran texts the corresponding Heb. phrase *gᵉwiyyaṭ bᵉśārô* means "physical body" (1Qp Hab. 9:2). Hence, "the uncircumcision of the flesh" in 2:13 means the time before the putting off in baptism of the body of the flesh (2:11). *sarx* is not corporality but the understanding of oneself as flesh. Its meaning is shown in 2:18. "The mind of the flesh" or "sensuous mind" (RSV), Gk. *nous tēs sarkos*, is preoccupied with angelic powers to whom as *sarx* man seems to be in subjection. But the believer holds fast to the head (2:18), in whom the whole fullness of deity dwells bodily (2:9). Thus, living in the flesh, he is not in subjection to these powers, but in his flesh he already shares in the life of Christ (1:24).

Eph. pursues a related thought. In its desires the flesh is open to the powers and influences of this world, which themselves are not flesh and blood (2:2 f.; 6:12). In 2:11 f. *sarx* appears as what is temporary. The wall of partition that existed between circumcision in the flesh and uncircumcision in the flesh Jesus broke down by his death in the flesh, abolishing the law of commandments and ordinances.

676

([Ed.] Flesh in the passage in 1 Tim. 3:16 which appears to be an early credal formulary means human life: "Great indeed, we confess, is the mystery of our religion: He was manifested in the flesh, vindicated in the Spirit, seen by angels, preached among the nations, believed on in the world, taken up in glory.")

2. (a) The non-Pauline uses of *sarx* are, as might be expected, quite different. From the OT heritage comes Matt. 16:17, where flesh and blood, i.e. men, are contrasted with God. The same holds good for Acts 2:31 (cf. Ps. 16:10). Christ was not left in Hades and his flesh did not see corruption, for here "flesh", being parallel to Christ, stands for the whole man. In Lk. 24:39 the Risen One makes it known that he is not a spirit because he has flesh and bones (the expression "to have flesh and bones" appears to be Hellenistic). The saying in Mk. 14:38 that "the spirit is willing but the flesh is weak" is not an OT quotation and is thought by some to be Pauline or to come from Hel. Wisdom literature. But V. Taylor sees it anticipated by Num. 27:16; Isa. 31:3 (*The Gospel according to St. Mark*, 1952, 555). On the other hand, Jude 7 refers to the unnatural lust of the men of Sodom and Gomorrah (Gen. 19) which anticipates contemporary perversions. In 2 Pet. 2:10 there is the more Heb. thought, that one should not in any way hanker after the flesh, because such hankering brings defilement.

In the same way 1 Pet. 2:11 speaks of the fleshly (*sarkikos*) desires which wage war against the soul. Christ has suffered in his flesh. Only the man who suffers in the flesh in the same spirit as Christ is free from sin (4:1–3) and escapes the depravities of the flesh (4:4 f.). On the other hand, Christ was indeed put to death in the flesh, but he was made alive in the spirit (3:18). Accordingly, one interpretation of 1 Pet. 4:6 declares that the gospel was preached to the dead so that like all men in the flesh, they might receive their sentence. In their case, since they were already dead, this has already come about. But, behind this there is the intention that they might live according to the will of God in the spirit. Hence baptism also serves not for the cleansing of the flesh, but for that of the spirit in a good conscience (3:21). ([Ed.] Alternative interpretations of 1 Pet. 4:6 suggest that it refers to the proclamation of the gospel by the preincarnate Christ to men in OT times which might also be related to 1 Pet. 3:20 (cf. 1 Cor. 10:4), or that it refers simply to those in the present age who have received the gospel and since died. The verse would then mean that, although they share the common destiny of sinful mankind in death, nevertheless they live now in the spirit. On the interpretation of Christ's "descent into hell" see E. G. Selwyn, *The First Epistle of St. Peter*, 1947², 313–62; J. N. D. Kelly, *Early Christian Creeds*, 1972², 378–88; and *A Commentary on the Epistles of Peter and Jude*, 1969, 172–75.)

Heb. makes use of flesh as the human nature which Christ assumed. Christ for a while was made lower than the angels and so shared in flesh and blood (2:14). These were "the days of his flesh" (5:7). Through his flesh he made for us a way into the heavenly sanctuary; for the sphere of flesh is the curtain which separates us from it, and by death Jesus passed through it (10:20). He cleanses the conscience, and not just the flesh as do the offerings of rams and bulls (9:13 f.). The *dikaiōmata sarkos* (regulations for the flesh, 9:10) are therefore statutes for the purification of the flesh.

sarkinos (Heb. 7:16) refers to the physical descent of the Levitical priesthood as contrasted with the priesthood of Melchizedek and Christ.

sarx mia (Matt. 19:5b) has a special significance as the translation of the Hebrew *bāśār 'eḥāḏ* (one flesh) of Gen. 2:24. The union of man and woman (→ Marriage) creates a new relationship. "One flesh" does not in the first instance mean sexual intercourse, though it includes it. It signifies the coming into being of a unitary existence, a complete partnership of man and woman which cannot be broken up without damage to the partners in it. That does not mean that every marriage is automatically such a complete partnership. Rather, this complete partnership is the promise of marriage which should be claimed. It is the meaning of marriage granted by God (19:6). This phrase serves to show the positive character of marriage for mankind rather than deny the possibility of divorce by state law.

(b) In many respects, John appears to stand near to the OT. He speaks of "all flesh" in the OT sense (17:2; but cf. also Matt. 24:22). The declaration that men should not judge Jesus according to the flesh (8:15), "by appearances" (7:24) is in accord with Matt. 16:17. One should judge him not by his human circumstances but by his mission. For that which is born of the flesh is flesh, and that which is born of the spirit is spirit (3:6). That which is born of the flesh comes from itself or from the world, but that which is born of the Spirit is a completely new humanity in so far as it comes from God (1:13). It is not surprising, therefore, that the flesh profits nothing. It is the spirit indeed that gives life (6:36). Men cannot comprehend Jesus on a merely human level. But they may do so by seeing him return to where he was before (6:62), and receiving his words which are "spirit and life".

But alongside all this, there is another fact for Jn.: the Word, which was *theos* and was in the beginning with God, became flesh (1:14). The world closes its mind to the → Word. The latter is not merely a communication of divine truth as in gnosticism. The entry of the Word as flesh among all flesh reveals how estranged it is from the Word and so from the true life, which it does not have. Jn. 6:51–58 should be understood against this background. If the believer eats the flesh of the Revealer, he confesses not merely that only the coming of the Word in the flesh can redeem him (so *TDNT* VII 139 f.). He also confesses that there is nothing in the flesh (i.e. the world) to help. In receiving the incarnate Word he is in the world as one who is not of the world.

In the Johannine Epistles the confession that Jesus is come in the flesh separates belief from unbelief (1 Jn. 4:2; 2 Jn. 7). John's opponents no longer wished to associate the Revealer with the flesh that they had rejected. Moreover, it asserts the historicity of the incarnation. A typically Hel. note is struck when in 1 Jn. 2:16 the desire of the flesh is spoken of as parallel with the desire of the eyes.   *H. Seebass*

Since the meaning of *sarx* varies radically from context to context, several distinct points must be made about the hermeneutics of the term.

1. In some contexts, especially in the OT, *sarx* calls attention to man's *creatureliness and frailty;* to the fact that he is fragile, fallible, and vulnerable. Thus "all flesh is grass, and its glory is like the flower of the grass. The grass withers, the flower fades" (Isa. 40:6–8; cf. 1 Pet. 1:24). However promising and flourishing it appears at first sight, it holds out no certain promise of being able to withstand pressures which are brought against it. Like the grass before the winds, man is vulnerable to forces which threaten him, whether these are physical, psychological, or spiritual in form. Physically, a relatively small change in the atmosphere or in

the cells of the brain deprives him of that optimum margin of conditions which are necessary for his life. Psychologically, man is at the mercy of pressures which can arise from loneliness, loss of self-respect, fantasies of his own making, or the need to adjust to the verdicts of the crowd or to a "normal" environment. Spiritually, he may have to wrestle with forces which are more than mere "flesh and blood" (Eph. 6:12; cf. 2 Cor. 10:3).

The biblical writers draw at least four distinct lessons from this basic datum of man's weakness and frailty. (a) They give a warning against any false hope and consequent disillusionment brought about by putting undue confidence and trust in man as a fallible and frail creature (Jer. 17:5; cf. Phil. 3:3 f. discussed below). Further, as against a false type of "enthusiasm," Paul warns us that even Christians remain fallible, since believers still live "in the flesh" (Gal. 2:20; 2 Cor. 10:3, on which see especially R. Jewett, *Paul's Anthropological Terms*, 1971, 129; Phil. 1:23; cf. 1 Cor. 3:1–3). (The apparent contradictions of Rom. 7:5 and 8:9 arise only because these uses of flesh belong under 4(a) below; see also above NT 1 (f).) (b) The Bible also calls attention to man's creatureliness before God, and distance from him in his otherness and transcendence (Gen. 6:3; Job 10:4; Dan. 2:11; 1QpHab. 4:29). As "flesh and blood", man has no natural right to the kingdom of God (1 Cor. 15:50), and stands in need of the Holy Spirit (Jn. 3:6; 6:63). (c) In at least one passage man's very weakness is a ground of God's loving compassion and restraining patience: "he restrained his anger . . . he remembered that they were but flesh" (Ps. 78:38, 39). (d) In times of oppression or persecution, the believer is encouraged not to fear an enemy who is mere flesh: "with him is an arm of flesh, but with us is the Lord our God" (2 Chr. 32:8); "in God I trust without fear; what can flesh do to me?" (Ps. 56:4; cf. Isa. 31:3).

2. In other contexts *sarx* is used quite simply to denote the *physical* part of man, and does not offer an evaluation of man as a whole. "Infirmity of the flesh" (Gal. 4:13) is physical illness; and flesh in 1 Cor. 15:39 means the physical substance appropriate to a given physical environment. The NT asserts the importance of the physical as over against ideas which later developed into gnosticism. (a) Especially in Johannine thought this relates to the incarnation: "the word became flesh" (Jn. 1:14; cf. 6:51–56); the test of whether a spirit is of God hinges on the confession "that Jesus Christ has come in the flesh" (1 Jn. 4:2, cf. 2 Jn. 7). God's spoken word was not merely an inner or psychological reality. Word and deed became one and mutually interpreting, and God entered upon the stage of history in the costliness of an act which involved physical consequences. Thus other NT writings besides John stress that Christ suffered "in the flesh" (1 Pet. 4:1), or that God was "manifested in the flesh" (1 Tim. 3:16; cf. Lk. 24:39; Rom. 8:3; Eph. 2:15; Heb. 5:7).

(b) Similarly the physical nature of *sarx* has positive significance in terms of the bodily obedience of the Christian. Paul is far from endorsing the verdict of Seneca, his contemporary, that the flesh is "useless" (*Epistulae Morales* 92:10, cf. 65:22). The life of Jesus is to be manifested "in our mortal flesh" (2 Cor. 4:11) Here Paul's use of flesh overlaps with that of *sōma*, body (2 Cor. 4:10). The believer still lives "in" the flesh (*en sarki*) although not "according to" the flesh (2 Cor. 10:3). To remain in the flesh is necessary (Phil. 1:24) and of positive value (Col. 1:24). For the fact that man has physical existence as part of the physical world brings home to him his responsibility for his thoughts and actions in terms of visible and tangible consequences. Physical flesh is the raw material which reveals good or bad thoughts and attitudes for what they are, so that belief involves commitment to action and can never be a merely inner or private affair which has no consequences for the individual. What a man chooses to do with his one life becomes indelibly clear, and has permanent repercussions both on himself and on others with whom he interacts.

3. To assess a truth or a phenomenon "in accordance with the flesh" (*kata sarka* or *kata tēn sarka*) is to reach a verdict on the basis of purely *human, external, or natural considerations.* [See above, NT 1 (b)–(d).] It is an assessment which leaves spiritual dimensions out of account. Thus Paul admits that very few of the Corinthian congregation are wise in the "ordinary" sense of the term (1 Cor. 1:26). Jesus warns the Pharisees that they are almost certain to misunderstand him, because they judge his testimony in purely human terms alone (Jn. 8:15). It is parallel to judging "by appearances" only (*kat' opsin*, Jn. 7:24). Paul insists that it is both wrong and misleading to judge either the person of Jesus Christ or even a fellow Christian in purely human terms (2 Cor. 5:16), for this viewpoint leaves out of account the fact that a Christian is God's new creation (5:17). Yet judgment "according to the flesh" is not always wrong or irrelevant. Whatever their spiritual relationship, slaves have those who are their masters on an ordinary human level (Col. 3:22).

It is important to note that Paul is not contrasting some "gnostic" means of insight as over against rational thought. For "mind" (*nous*) and rational argument have a prominent and often positive place in his epistles. The point is, rather, that to understand truths relating to God and his dealings with men, man who is flesh needs the Holy Spirit and a frame of reference instructed by Scripture (1 Cor. 2:10–16; 15:3). The same phenomenon can be seen from different viewpoints, and the viewpoint "according to the flesh" is limited so radically that in many cases it can lead to misunderstanding and error. Nevertheless, what is seen from such a viewpoint is not necessarily dismissed as irrelevant in every single case. Its relevance depends on what is under consideration. This explains why the tone of 1 Cor. 1:26 and Col. 3:22 is so different from that of Jn. 8:15 and 2 Cor. 5:16.

4. A quite different use of *sarx* appears in the major theological passages in Paul such as Rom. 8:5–8, which concludes, "those who are in the flesh cannot please God". In this passage the mental outlook of the flesh (*to phronēma tēs sarkos*) is hostile to God. "Flesh" here evaluates man as a sinner before God. The outlook of the flesh is *the outlook orientated towards the self, that which pursues its own ends in self-sufficient independence of God.*

(a) It is most striking, as R. Bultmann and R. Jewett have rightly pointed out, that Paul explicitly speaks of the "fleshly" outlook in connection with the law and circumcision. The fleshly mind in Gal. above all implies "shifting one's boasting from the cross of Christ (Gal. 6:14) to the circumcised flesh (6:13)" (R. Jewett, op. cit., 95). It represents the desire to secure one's righteousness independently of God's grace in Christ by means of the law. Thus in Jewett's words, "*sarx* for Paul is not rooted in sensuality but rather in religious rebellion in the form of self-righteousness" (p. 114). As Bultmann expresses it, flesh represents "trust in oneself as being able to procure life . . . through one's own strength and accomplishment" (*Theology of the NT*, I 1952, 239) Thus Paul's crucial question, "Having begun with the Spirit, are you now ending with the flesh?" (Gal. 3:3) clearly refers to reliance on obedience to the law rather than on God's grace in Christ. This is precisely the issue also in Phil. 3:3–7, where Paul explains his language about "confidence in the flesh" with reference not just to physical descent but also to "righteousness under the law" (3:6). To be found in Christ, rather than trusting in the flesh, is "not having a righteousness of my own based on law" (3:9). Similarly, Rom. 8:5–9, 12, 13 is closely parallel to the main point in Gal. 3 and 4. The mental outlook of the flesh is both hostile to God and also incapable of genuine obedience to the law (Rom. 8:7). For the very desire to use the law as a means of justification before God makes obedience for its own sake impossible. That is why to live in accordance with the flesh is incompatible with living according to the Holy Spirit (8:4, 5, 9). Fleshly man puts himself at the centre, trusting in his own ability to secure life even, if need be, by cultivating "religion". Man under the Spirit casts himself on God as his father (8:15; cf. Gal. 4:6), abandoning all self-reliance, in complete dependence on God.

(b) At the same time, *sarx* admittedly also characterizes man as a sinner in his rejection of the law [see above NT 1 (e)]. The "works" of the flesh include immorality, licentiousness, idolatry, enmity, strife, and anger (Gal. 5:19–21). The criterion which establishes that the Corinthian Christians are still "fleshly" is the continued presence of jealousy and strife within their community (1 Cor. 3:3, 4). In contrast to the use of *sarx* discussed under heading 1, the point about "flesh" in Gal. 5:19–21 is not that it weakens man's will to do the good, but that it lures him to substitute his own good for God's. Jewett believes that the meaning here is almost the same as in (a) above, namely that both legalism and lawlessness are "fleshly" in so far as they both hold out a false promise of life on the basis of man's own efforts. Thus jealousy, for example, is a by-product of seeking life in popularity; ill-temper arises from frustration in seeking life in comfort and quiet. But it may well be that Jewett sees a closer connection than is actually there. *sarx* functions as a polymorphous concept, the actual content of which varies from case to case. Sometimes it may be used simply as a general value-judgment of disapproval, just as the term "spiritual", to which "fleshly" stands in opposition, may also function as a term of approval, the content of which needs to be defined in a given case (cf. A. C. Thiselton in *SJT* 26, 1973, 204–28). The nearest that we can go towards finding a "general" meaning for this particular category is to say that fleshly life is life lived in pursuit of one's own ends, in independence of God or of the law of God, in contrast to living in accordance with the direction of the Holy Spirit. This can take as many different concrete forms as being "selfish" or "self-centred".

(c) In at least two passages Paul outlines the close relationship between flesh and death: "if you live according to the flesh you will die" (Rom. 8:13); "he who sows to the flesh will from the flesh reap corruption (*phthoran*)" (Gal. 6:8). Here death is the inevitable fruit that grows out of a fleshly way of living. At this point, if not at others, the existentialist interpretation of the NT becomes relevant and convincing. If man is simply what he makes of himself (man as *sarx*), he lives in a world of vanishing possibilities. Each decision that he makes about his own life limits the future possibilities which are still left open to him; he is moulded and restricted by the fruits of his own decisions. By contrast, the Spirit in the NT enables a man to go beyond what his own past has made him, giving him new desires, new capacities, new horizons. If "life" is understood in the dynamic sense which it often has in the

Biblical writings, to live according to the flesh is to travel into the cul-de-sac which ends in death; to live according to the Spirit is to enter life.   *A. C. Thiselton*

→ Body, → Heart, → Soul, → Marriage, → Spirit

(a). W. Barclay, *Flesh and Spirit*, 1962; R. Batey, "The *mia sarx* Union of Christ and the Church," *NTS* 13, 1966–7, 270–81; R. Bultmann, *Theology of the New Testament*, I, 1952, 232–46; E. De Witt Burton, *Spirit, Soul and Flesh*, 1918: W. D. Davies, "Paul and the Dead Sea Scrolls: Flesh and Spirit," in K. Stendahl, ed., *The Scrolls and the New Testament*, 1957, 157–82; J. Jeremias, "Flesh and Blood Cannot Inherit the Kingdom of God," *NTS* 2, 1955–56, 151–59; R. Jewett, *Paul's Anthropological Terms*, 1971; W. G. Kümmel, *Man in the New Testament*, 1963; W. Mork, *The Biblical Meaning of Man*, 1967, 19–32, 146–50; R. E. Murphy, "*Bsr* in the Qumran Literature and *Sarx* in the Epistle to the Romans," *Sacra Pagina* 2, 1959, 60–76; J. A. T. Robinson, *The Body*, 1952, 11–33; J. P. Sampley, '*And the Two Shall Become One Flesh*': *A Study of the Traditions in Ephesians 5:21–33*, 1971; E. Schweizer, *sarx, sarkikos, sarkinos*, *TDNT* VII 98–151; C. Ryder Smith, *The Biblical Doctrine of Man*, 1951, 153–65; W. D. Stacey, *The Pauline View of Man*, 1956, 92 f., 154–80; A. C. Thiselton, "The Meaning of *Sarx* in 1 Cor. 5:5: A Fresh Approach in the Light of Logical and Semantic Factors," *SJT* 26, 1973, 204–28.
(b). E. Brandenburger, *Fleisch und Geist. Paulus und die dualistische Weisheit*, 1968; J. Fichtner and E. Schweizer, "Fleisch und Geist", *RGG*[3] II 974 ff.; W. Gutbrod, *Die paulinische Anthropologie*, 1934; H. W. Huppenbauer, "Fleisch in den Texten von Qumran," *ThZ* 13, 1957, 298 ff.; E. Käsemann, *Leib und Leib Christi*, 1933, 100–118; N. Krautwik, "Der Leib im Kampf des 'pneuma' wider die 'sarx'," *Theologie und Glaube* 39, 1949; K. G. Kuhn, "*peirasmos, hamartia, sarx* im NT und die damit zusammenhängenden Vorstellungen," *ZTK* 49, 1952, 200 ff.; O. Kuss, *Der Römerbrief*, 1959, 506 ff.; N. P. Bratsiotis, *Anthrōpologia tēs Palaias Diathēkēs*, 1967; A. Sand, *Der Begriff "Fleisch" in den paulinischen Hauptbriefen*, 1967; W. Schauf, *Sarx: Der Begriff "Fleisch" beim Apostel Paulus unter besonderer Berücksichtigung seiner Erlösungslehre*, *NTAbh* 11, 1924; W. Schmidt, "Anthropologische Begriffe im Alten Testament," *EvTh* 24, 1964, 374 ff.; E. Schweizer, "Die hellenistische Komponente im neutestamentlichen *sarx*-Begriff," *ZNW* 48, 1957, 237 ff.

Flow

ῥέω

ῥέω (*rheō*), flow, stream; ῥύσις (*rhysis*), a flowing river, stream; παραρρέω (*pararrheō*), flow past, drift away, let slip.

CL Although words for "flow" commonly derive from words for "run", *rheō* is a notable exception: it reflects the Indo-European root *sreu* with the specific meaning "flow" (cf. Sanskrit *sru*). Frequently this root survives in its numerous non-verbal derivatives, the most important of which is *rhysis*.

Occurring widely from the time of Homer, the word group commonly refers to the flow of a stream or river; but it can be applied to the run-off from melted snow (Herodotus), the "running" of milk and honey, equivalent to prosperity (Theocritus), or, with respect to blood, a haemorrhage (Hippocrates, Dioscorides). Homer, Hesiod, and Aeschylus apply it to a stream of glib words; Homer to darts. A city or an area may stream with men (Herodotus, Euripides, Aristophanes) or gold (Herodotus). Solid objects liquefy and "melt away" (Sophocles) – even stone (Aristotle). Hence it is not surprising that the word group takes on the meaning of "fall", "drop off" – of hair (Homer, Hesiod, Theocritus), or ripe fruit (Polybius). An individual may be "given to" something, "inclined" to it (Isocrates, Plato): it is easy to imagine how such an idiom would develop.

OT The LXX reflects an equally wide variety of usage. The word group most often stands for Heb. *zûb* (flow, gush), especially as applied to the promised land which flows with milk and honey (Exod. 3:8; 13:5; Lev. 20:24; Num. 14:8; Deut. 6:3; 26:9; Jos. 5:6; Jer. 11:5; Bar. 1:20; etc.) or to some discharge or haemorrhage (notably in Lev. 15). Further, water flowed from the smitten rock (Ps. 77:20; 104:41; cf. Isa. 48:21, LXX with future tense). The Heb. word group next most likely to be represented by *rheō* is *nāzal* (and synonym *rāʿap*; trickle, drip), usually in connection with the descent of precipitation at the divine command (Job 36:28; 38:30; Ps. 147:18; Prov. 3:20; cf. Job 38·25), but also with the falling of tears (Jer. 9:18) and wafting by the wind of perfume (Cant. 4:16). Joel twice uses *rheō* to translate the diversely-used Heb. verb *hālak* with reference to the flow of water and milk from Judea's hills when the Spirit of the Lord is poured out and blessings abound (3:18 *bis*). A more ominous use of the verb is made by Zechariah, who pictures flesh decaying and eyes "melting out" of their sockets, fitting retribution for those who war against Jerusalem (14:12; Heb. *māqaq*, fester, rot). Simile is invoked to liken the disappearance of the hope of ungrateful people to the "running away" of water and the melting of hoar frost. (Wis. 16:29). Men are warned not to trust in wealth even if it should "flow in" (Ps. 62:10; Heb. *nûḇ*, bear fruit).

Both Philo and Josephus utilize the word group with similar diversity, the latter applying it on one occasion to the stream of memory which "runs down" through the ages, recalling the noble sacrifice of Jeconiah (*War* 6, 105).

NT The verb *rheō* occurs but once in the NT: "from his innermost being shall flow rivers of living water" (Jn. 7:38). Some commentators run 7:37b and 7:38a into one sentence: "If any man is thirsty, let him come to me, and let the one who believes drink." In that case "his" innermost being refers to Christ, who alone provides "living" water (cf. Jn. 4:10). It is more likely correct to see a sentence division at the end of 7:37, making the believer the one from whose being the water (= Spirit) flows. The believer is thus viewed as a channel for the outflowing of the Spirit to others (cp. 15:26 f.).

The 3 NT occurrences of *rhysis* are all in connection with "flow of blood" = haemorrhage (Mk. 5:25 = Lk. 8:43 f.), endured by one woman for twelve years.

([F. F. Bruce] The compound *pararrheō*, lit. "flow past", is used figuratively in Heb. 2:1 with reference to "what we have heard" (i.e. the gospel), "lest we drift away from it" (RSV; cf. RV, NEB). AV, "lest . . . we should let them slip", follows another sense of the vb., e.g. of letting a ring slip off one's finger [Plut., *Amatorius* 754a].)

D. A. Carson

Arndt, 627, 742; W. K. Hobart, *The Medical Language of St. Luke*, 1882, 15 f.; Liddell-Scott, 1322 f., 1568; Moulton-Milligan, 489, 563.

Foreign, Alien, Dispersion, Stranger

Under this heading are grouped together various terms and ideas which have deep roots in the ancient world and particular significance in the OT and NT. The key terms discussed below are: *allotrios* (strange, alien, hostile), *diaspora* (dispersion), *xenos* (strange, an alien), *parepidēmos* (stranger, exile, sojourner), and *paroikos* (stranger, alien).

683

| ἀλλότριος |

ἀλλότριος (*allotrios*), adj., belonging to another, strange, alien, hostile; noun, a stranger; ἀλλοτριόω (*allotrioō*), estrange, alienate; ἀλλογενής (*allogenēs*), foreign; ἀλλόφυλος (*allophylos*), alien to the race, hence from a Jewish standpoint a Gentile, heathen.

CL *allotrios* (derived from *allos*, another, cf. Lat. *alius*) means another, strange, foreign, what belongs to another, alien to the people or the land, and hence unsuitable and even hostile. *apallotrioō* means to alienate, estrange, exclude. *allogenēs* is compounded from *allos* (another) and *genos* (race), and means foreign, strange. *allophylos* is compounded from *allos* and *phylē* (tribe), and means alien to the race, alien to the people, strange.

OT In the LXX, *allotrios* occurs frequently as a translation of Heb. *nokrî*, foreign, alien (Gen. 31:15; Deut. 14:21; 15:3; and often). It also occasionally translates *zār*, strange, foreign (Lev. 10:1; Deut. 32:16). But usually the LXX translates *zār* by *allogenēs* (Exod. 29:33; Num. 16:40; Lev. 22:10; Joel 3:17; and often). The sojourner is in Heb. *gēr* or *gûr* (LXX *prosēlytos*, Exod. 22:20; Lev. 17:12–15; → Conversion) or *tôšāb* (LXX → *paroikos*, e.g. Gen. 23:4). The sojourner is still a foreigner (Exod. 12:43 ff.), but he has certain rights and duties in the community.

NT 1. *allotrios* occurs parabolically in Matt. 17:25 in the discussion of the propriety of paying the half-shekel temple tax (cf. Exod. 30:11–16; 38:26). Jesus asked whether kings took tribute "from their sons or from others [*apo tōn allotriōn*]." Peter replied that it was from others, to which Jesus replied, "Then the sons are free." However, he counselled payment of the tax to avoid giving offence. The incident implies that the disciples are "sons of God", and that the Jews are in fact "others". In Lk. 16:12 *allotrion* (another's) stands parallel to the "unrighteous mammon" (v. 11). Money and possessions belong to another. The implication is that they do not belong to the disciple who is nevertheless a steward. "If then you have not been faithful in the unrighteous mammon, who will entrust to you the true riches? And if you have not been faithful in that which is another's, who will give you that which is your own?" (→ Possessions, art. *mamōnas*). In Jn. 10:5 the stranger and strangers are not known by the sheep who belong to the shepherd whose voice they know and follow. The implication is that Jewish (and other would-be) teachers are strangers disowned by the true flock of God, whereas Jesus is the true shepherd known and followed by the true people of God.

In Acts 7:6 (referring to Gen. 15:13) the *gē allotria* ("a land belonging to others" RSV) is the foreign land (Egypt), whereas Palestine is the homeland of Israel. But for → Abraham even the promised land was a foreign country (Heb. 11:9), because it was not his true, heavenly home. Therefore, he dwelt in tents, and by it testified that he was a stranger in this world.

The Christian is the slave of Christ. Therefore, he has not to judge others (Rom. 14:4). Paul refused to boast of the work or methods of others (2 Cor. 10:15 f.), because he would not adorn himself with borrowed plumage. He would not even preach in a place where others had already been at work, refusing to build on a foundation laid by someone else (Rom. 15:20). Timothy was warned not to be hasty in laying hands on a man and entrusting him with a ministry. Otherwise, he might participate in another man's sins and be called to account for it (1 Tim. 5:22). The Jewish high priest entered the Holy Place with *en haimati allotriō*, "with another's blood" (Heb. 9:25). Unlike Jesus on the cross, he did not bring his own blood as a sacrifice. In Heb. 11:34 the word occurs in the expression "put foreign armies to flight."

2. *apallotrioō* occurs only in Eph. 2:12; 4:18; and Col. 1:21, in each case as the passive participle meaning "alienated", "estranged". Before their conversion, the readers were not citizens of Israel, the chosen people of God. They stood – like the heathen now – outside God's covenant and promises, and were thus subject to wrath. They did not know God, and lived in sin. Since they have now become Christians, they are not to return to their sinful state.

3. *allogenēs* occurs only in Lk. 17:18. The grateful Samaritan who returned to give thanks after being healed of his leprosy is called one of another race, a foreigner, for he was not a Jew. *allophylos* occurs only at Acts 10:28. The Jew is forbidden to have fellowship with an *allophylos*, "one of another nation" (RSV). For the heathen was ceremonially unclean, and he would make the Jew likewise unclean. Only in Christ were these barriers of the → law abolished. *H. Bietenhard*

| διασπορά | *διασπορά* (*diaspora*), dispersion. |

CL *diaspora* (derived from *diaspeirō*, disperse) means dispersion. The word was first used in the LXX, and occurs almost entirely in Jewish and Christian, literature. In cl. Gk. it is found in Plutarch, *Non posse suaviter vivi secundum Epicurum*, 27.

OT 1. *diaspora* occurs 12 times in the LXX. In 3 instances it translates Heb. *niddaḥ*, what is scattered, dispersed, outcast (Deut. 30:4; Neh. 1:9; Ps. 147:2). In the other cases it stands as a rather free translation of *za'awâh*, trembling, terror (Deut. 28:25; Jer. 34:17 [41:17 LXX]); *hašḥît*, destruction (Jer. 13:14); *mizreh*, pitch-fork (Jer. 15:7); *neṣûrê*, the preserved (Isa. 49:6). It also appears without any Heb. equivalent in Ps. 139 [LXX 138] as a title; Dan. 12:2; 2 Macc. 1:27; Jud. 5:19.

The Gk. word has 3 different meanings: (1) the event or state of the dispersion of the Jews among the heathen nations (Deut. 28:25; Jer. 34:17–41:17 LXX); (2) the community of those so dispersed among the Gentiles (Isa. 49:6; Ps. 147:2; 2 Macc. 1:27; Pss. Sol. 8:28); (3) the place or country where the scattered Jews now live (Jud. 5:19; Test. Ass. 7:2).

2. Although *diaspora* virtually became a technical term for the scattering of the Jews, it is remarkable that it is never used to translate the corresponding Heb. terms *gōlâh* and *gālût* which denote the leading away into captivity, the exile, and the exiles. To translate these words the LXX has *aichmalōsia*, captivity (21 times); *apoikia*, exile (19 times); *apoikesia*, captivity (7 times); *metoikesia*, captivity (7 times); *apoikismos*, settlement of a colony (twice); and *paroikia*, sojourning in a foreign land (once). The LXX appears to prefer the hard, negative ideas, suggesting captivity in a foreign country, doubtless out of loyalty to the Heb. original. *diaspora* which made its way into Hel. Jud. is more neutral.

This historical change of usage reflects a historical evolution. After wars of conquest foreign rulers deported masses of Jews, in order to break their military strength. The first large Jewish *diaspora* was in Babylonia, where Nebuchadnezzar had deported a section of the vanquished (2 Ki. 24:14 ff.; 24:11–21) and where the majority of Jews remained even after the edict of Cyrus allowing them to return. Following the great prophets, the deportation and exile were seen as God's punishment (Jer. 17:1–4; Ezek. 12:15). But this outlook gradually dissipated, and out of the exile there grew up minority communities of the Jews of the dispersion who lived there of their own volition. Through the preaching of the exilic and post-exilic prophets a positive attitude to the new situation emerged (cf. Isa. 60; Hag. 2:6 ff.; Zech. 8:20 ff.). Through the dispersion of Israel God intends to bring all nations home to himself. This new approach was powerfully developed in Isa. 40–66. It provided the motivation for the almost worldwide missionary activity of late Judaism.

NT   In the NT *diaspora* occurs only 3 times (as does the vb.). It is always in the traditional sense. Jn. 7:35 speaks of the *diaspora tōn Hellēnōn*, i.e. the dispersion among the Greeks. Acts 8:1, 4 and 11:19 refer to the scattering of the church. Jas. 1:1 and 1 Pet. 1:1 are theologically more significant. If these letters were written to Gentile Christian churches, the word *diaspora* has here a special theological significance. The apostles see in the fact of the "dispersion" a parallel to the Jewish dispersion. The true homeland of the disciples of Christ is not the place where they happen to live. It is in heaven (cf. Phil. 3:20). It is the Jerusalem that is above (cf. Gal. 4:26). On earth they are always strangers, living as → *paroikoi*, sojourners. They are like God's seed that is sown far and wide. Its fruit will only be apparent at the great ingathering (cf. Matt. 24:31).   *F. S. Rothenberg*

ξένος

ξένος (*xenos*), adj., strange, foreign; noun, stranger, alien; φιλοξενία (*philoxenia*), hospitality; φιλόξενος (*philoxenos*), hospitable; ξενοδοχέω (*xenodocheō*), show hospitality.

CL   *xenos* occurs from Mycenean Gk. and Homer onwards. Its root is connected with Lat. *hostis*, stranger, enemy, and Ger. *Gast*, Eng. guest. The following points stand out in the history of religion and culture.

1. In primitive society the stranger is basically an enemy, because he is unknown and therefore sinister. Mutual fear and resistance are characteristic of the attitude of the foreigner and the people round him. Foreigners were often outlawed and put to death, or driven away cowed by magical practices. The stranger never had rights. At a later stage a pattern of relationship with strangers emerged which originally developed out of fear. The stranger was seen as a messenger of the gods. Out of fear of the gods the stranger was given a helping hand and hospitality. The stranger thus came under the protection of religion and the law.

2. Among the Greeks the stranger or foreigner was originally one who did not belong to one's own community, whether it was large or small. In Homer the stranger and the beggar come from Zeus (*Od.*, 6, 207 f.). Hence one must treat them with respect. For the Greeks it was a sign of barbarity, when strangers were

treated as if they had no rights and people did with them what they pleased. Above all, Athens showed an open attitude to the stranger (cf. Soph., *OC*, 560–68, 631–41). But in religion the use of objects from foreign parts was universally avoided, and strangers were excluded from participation in the cult. Sparta was particularly hostile to strangers as a consequence of the puritanical reforms instituted in the period following 600 B.C. and the regulations about strangers that were bound up with it. Otherwise strangers stood under the protection of *Zeus hikesios*, Zeus the protector of suppliants, and also the Dioscuri. Anyone who injured a stranger was subject to the wrath of the Erinyes. The converse was also true. Those who honour the gods also honour strangers. Hence temple and altar assume the role of an asylum for the stranger who desires refuge there or seeks the protection of the priests. The first hospices for strangers sprang up in the vicinity of holy places in the fourth century. Worshippers came from far and wide, and needed to be housed and fed.

3. Through close contact with non-Gk. cities and nations from the time of the Persian wars change set in. The foreigner was simply someone who did not belong to one's own cultic community or *polis*. This did not prevent agreements from being made with strangers. But now, as before, banishment remained a punishment. The situation in religion was ambivalent. On the one hand, people were opposed to all "new" and "strange" gods, since they did not belong to the nation and they endangered morals. On the other hand, the doors were opened wide to innumerable foreign cults.

4. In Rome up to the imperial period the stranger was in theory without rights. Here too he was excluded from the cult. Only if he had a *patronus*, did he have any chance of lodging and the protection of the law. The expulsion of a troublesome alien was always a possibility. From 241 B.C. there was a *praetor peregrinus*, an official in charge of legal disputes between citizens and strangers.

5. Since Homeric times there was a system of regular hospitality. The custom persisted into late antiquity. The motive of both the Greeks and the Romans was not only fear of the gods but also love of man. In ancient catalogues of vices injustice to foreigners is ranked immediately after godlessness and want of reverence to parents (→ Godliness, art. *sebomai*). The ethics of popular philosophy exhorted everyone to show friendship to the stranger. The resident alien had obligations towards the state, such as payment of tax on aliens and military service.

6. Gk. philosophy from the 4th cent. onwards developed the thought of being a stranger. The soul was seen as a stranger in the world, since its true home lay beyond the material sphere. Being a stranger became an anthropological category. The thought was prepared for by the idea of banishment in tragedy. The → body of man, like the → world, is only a temporary lodging for the → soul.

OT 1. *xenos* occurs in the LXX 21 times, mostly as a translation of Heb. *nokrî*. Other words for stranger are → *allotrios*, → *allogenēs*, and → *paroikos*

(a) In the OT, hospitality was also a self-explanatory practice and duty (Gen. 18:1 ff.; 19:1 ff.; 2 Sam. 12:4; Job 31:32). Jael's action was a serious breach of the right of a guest (Jdg. 4:17 ff.) which could only be justified by the extremity of the people of God in their struggle for survival. Among the godless the stranger was entirely at their mercy (Gen. 19:9; Jdg. 19:22). Israel's law forbad the affliction of strangers, because the nation itself was a stranger in Egypt (Exod. 22:21; 23:9; Deut. 24:14). The stranger enjoyed the sabbath rest like the Israelite (Exod. 20:10). Yahweh loves and protects him (Deut. 10:18). At the consecration of the temple Solomon interceded for strangers that would come to honour Yahweh, that he should hear them (1 Ki. 8:41 ff.).

(b) The people of Israel were themselves visitors and strangers in the land of Canaan (Lev. 25:23). The land did not belong to them. It was Yahweh's property and could not be sold. But since the Israelite was God's stranger (*paroikos*), he too enjoyed his protection (Ps. 39:13; 61:5; 119:19; 1 Chron. 29:15). Because Israel is God's people, it is ultimately a stranger in the world (Est. 3:13; but cf. already Num. 23:9). This goes back to the recognition that Yahweh himself is not an immanent power in the world. As its Creator and Lord, he stands over it. It also goes back to the realization that he has chosen his people as his own possession. Hence the acts of Yahweh can be "strange" and "alien" (Isa. 28:21).

(c) It was a misfortune whenever foreigners conquered the land that God had given Israel as a dwelling place (Lam. 5:2). It was seen as the punishment of Yahweh when the Israelites were led away into foreign countries out of the land that God had given them (Jer. 5:19; Deut. 29:28; and often).

(d) The protection afforded to the person of a stranger in Israel was not extended to strange religions. Foreign cults were condemned and punished as idolatry in Israel (1 Ki. 11:4 f.; Jer. 5:19; Jos. 24:23; Deut. 4:25 ff.; and often).

(e) Yahweh is God over all the nations (Amos 9:7). Hence the exilic and post-exilic prophets could speak of the coming proclamation of the glory of God among the heathen (Isa. 42:6 ff.; 66:19) and promise the turning of the heathen to Yahweh (Isa. 14:1; 45:14 ff.; 56:1–8; Zech. 14:16; Ezek. 47:22 f.). The godless heathen were threatened with annihilation (Jer. 46:51; Ezek. 25–32). In practice after the exile there was a strict segregation from the heathen (Neh. 13:1–10). Mixed marriages were prohibited and dissolved (Ezra 9 f.; Neh. 13:23 ff.).

2. Rab. Jud. held hospitality in high esteem. The man who practised it was promised a rich reward in the age to come. On the other hand, the duty of hospitality was restricted to fellow Jews. Some Gk. practices penetrated into Judaism through the Hel. diaspora: regular hospitality (Tob. 5:6; Josephus, *War*, 3, 436 and often), and the establishment of inns (Lk. 10:34). The Essenes kept hospices in every city for strangers. *xenos*, its derivatives, and other terms became loanwords in Heb. and Aram.

3. For part of the Hel. period there was considerable danger of Israel being swamped by foreign practices even in the sphere of religion (1 Macc. 1:11–15). The Maccabean reaction and revolt were directed against this. Those who were loyal to the law restricted trade with the heathen. They refused fellowship and marriage with them. They were afraid of entering Gentile houses for fear of defilement. On the other hand, the rabbis zealously took up missionary work, sometimes with considerable success in making proselytes (cf. Matt. 23:15 and the term "God-fearer" which crops up in Acts; → Conversion, art. *prosēlytos*). Philo and Josephus strove to refute the charge of hostility to strangers which was levelled against Jews. Above all, Hel. Jud. engaged with zeal in propaganda and apologetics. From A.D. 135 conversion to Judaism was prohibited by the Romans. (See further G. Stählin, *TDNT* V 13.)

688

4. It is of great significance for subsequent ages that the LXX never (apart from Job 31:32) translated the Heb. *gēr* (stranger) by the corresponding Gk. word *xenos*, but almost always by *prosēlytos* (proselyte, convert). *(paroikos* is also found 11 times for *gēr*, but only 3 times in the legislation of the Pentateuch.) This may be an indication of a change that had already taken place. But it also led to the OT regulations and commandments concerning strangers being applied only to full proselytes in rab. Jud. (cf. SB I 353 ff.).

NT *xenos* occurs in the NT 14 times, including 5 in Matt., and twice each in Eph. 2, Acts 17, and Heb.

1. Four of the five places in Matt come in Matt. 25:31–46. Care of the *xenos* is care of Jesus Christ himself; refusal to provide hospitality to the stranger is to exclude Jesus himself. According to Matt. 27:7, the high priests bought with the "blood money" flung down by Judas the potter's field for the burial of strangers, i.e. non-Jews.

2. The gospel records show Jesus as the frequent recipient of hospitality in his. public ministry (Mk. 1:29 ff.; 2:15 ff.; Lk. 7:36 ff.; 10:38 ff.; and often). Hospitality figures in the parables of Jesus (Lk. 10:34 f.; 11:5 ff.; and often). God's summons to his kingdom is depicted as a banquet (Lk. 13:29; 14:16 ff.; → Lord's Supper). Jesus sent out his disciples to proclaim the kingdom, expecting that they would enjoy hospitality in the towns and villages (Matt. 10:11 ff.; Lk. 10:5 ff.). Similarly in Judaism hospitality was urged especially towards the rabbis.

3. In the missionary work of the early church missionaries enjoyed hospitality (Acts 10:6; 16:15; and often). In Rom. 16:23 Gaius appears as a *xenos*, i.e. as Paul's host. In 3 Jn. 5 another Gaius is praised for what he has done for brethren from abroad.

4. On occasion, the idea of God as alien or strange occurs without the word *xenos* actually being used (Jn. 8:19; cf. Acts 17:23). Christ is "not of this world", and so is alien in this sense (cf. Jn. 8:14; 25 ff.; 9:29 f.).

5. Before their call to faith in Christ, the Gentile Christians were *xenoi* (strangers) and → *paroikoi* (aliens). As heathen, they had no part in Israel's call to be the people of God, and were excluded from the promises. But now in Christ they are fellow citizens with the saints, i.e. Jewish Christians, and members of the household of God (Eph. 2:19; cf. the whole argument of Eph. 2:11 ff.). As Christians thus become citizens in God's sight, they have their citizenship in heaven (Phil. 3:20; cf. Gal. 4:26; Eph. 2:6; Heb. 11:15 f.; 12:22 f.; 13:14). The patriarchs already provide the pattern for this. They did not receive the promises, but saw them from afar, thereby showing that they lived as *xenoi* (strangers) and *parepidēmoi* (exiles) on the earth (Heb. 11:13). Christians are thus put under a new divine law of life which shields them from the vices of the heathen who regard them as strange (*xenizontai*, 1 Pet. 4:4).

6. The Athenians supposed that Paul wanted to preach foreign deities (Acts 17:18). They themselves and the resident aliens were eager for what was new (Acts 17:21). But Paul preached "strange things" (*xenizonta tina*) to their ears (17:20). On the other hand, the church is warned in advance against being led astray by "strange teachings" (Heb. 13:9). The sufferings which befall the church are not something "strange", but belong to the Christian's lot (1 Pet. 4:12).

7. *philoxenia* (hospitality) is expected from the whole church (1 Pet. 4:9). It is recommended as a virtue to Christians (Rom. 12:13; Heb. 13:2). It is even connected with a promise. Because some practised hospitality (*xenisantes*), they entertained angels unawares (cf. Gen. 18:3; 19:2 f.). In the ancient world many a door was opened to a messenger of the new covenant and the host was thus blessed. Cornelius received Peter, and Publius took in Paul and his companions (Acts 10:23; 28:7). Paul requested Philemon to have a guest room (*xenia*) ready for him (Phlm. 22). The Pastoral Epistles indicate the importance set by hospitality in the young church. It is not only the → bishop who should be hospitable (*philoxenos*, 1 Tim. 3:2; Tit. 1:8). Even the widow was reminded to show hospitality to strangers (1 Tim. 5:10).   *H. Bietenhard*

παρεπίδημος

παρεπίδημος (*parepidēmos*), adj., staying for a while in a strange place; noun, a stranger, resident alien, exile, sojourner.

CL & OT *parepidēmos* is derived from *dēmos* (people) and is found only twice in the LXX (Gen. 23:4; Ps. 38[39]:12). It means someone who lives for a short while in a foreign place as a stranger or alien.

NT It occurs in the NT 3 times. In 1 Pet. 1:1 and 2:11 believers are called *parepidēmoi* ("exiles", RSV). The word stands in parallel to *paroikoi* ("aliens", RSV), pointing back to Gen. 23:4 and Ps. 39:13. Because their true home is in heaven (cf. Phil. 3:20), God's election has drawn them out of all their natural ties and relations. They now live on earth as exiles. This call and vocation gives rise to the warning to abstain from the lusts of the flesh (1 Pet. 2:11). They are to live according to the decrees and laws of their true homeland. Heb. 11:13 depicts → Abraham and the patriarchs as patterns for the Christian. Abraham looked towards the future city (11:10). Hence he and the fathers lived as strangers and exiles on the earth.   *H. Bietenhard*

πάροικος

πάροικος (*paroikos*), stranger, alien; *παροικέω* (*paroikeō*), inhabit as a stranger, live beside; *παροικία* (*paroikia*), the stay or sojourn of someone who is not a citizen in a strange place.

CL *paroikos* is a compound of *para* (by) and *oikos* (house). It was originally an adj., but was later used as a noun meaning neighbouring, the neighbour, the non-citizen, one who lives among resident citizens without having citizen rights yet enjoying the protection of the community. The vb. *paroikeo* means to live beside, to inhabit as a stranger. The noun *paroikia* means sojourning. It became a loan-word in ecclesiastical Lat. *parochia*, denoting the charge of a bishop and later of a priest, as in Eng. parish.

OT 1. In the LXX *paroikos* occurs over 30 times, especially to translate *gēr* and *tôšāḇ*, both words meaning a sojourner or stranger. *paroikeō* occurs over 60 times, especially as the equivalent of *gûr*, to sojourn. *paroikia* is found 16 times. *paroikoi* and various forms of the vb. *paroikeō* are used to designate non-Israelites who live in Israel (2 Sam. 4:3; Isa. 16:4). The Israelites had definite obligations to the resident alien. An adequate living should be made possible for him (Lev.

690

25:35 ff.). He is allowed to share the food of the sabbath year (Lev. 25:6). He had the right of asylum (Num. 35:15). Like widows and orphans, he stood under the protection of the law (Exod. 22:21). But he too had obligations. He was required to keep the sabbath (Exod. 20:10). He was not allowed to eat of the Passover lamb (Exod. 12:45) or the sacrificial gift (Lev. 22:10). Ezek. 47:22 f. promises the equality of Israelites and resident aliens. Above all, repeated stress was laid on the fact that the patriarchs were sojourners (Gen. 12:10; 17:8; 19:9; 20:1; 23:4; 35:27; 47:4; Exod. 6:4). Moses was a sojourner in Midian (Exod. 2:22) and the whole nation of Israel in Egypt. The attitude towards sojourners was motivated by this fact (cf. Exod. 22:21; 23:9; and often). In one sense the Israelites were always sojourners, even when they lived in the promised land (1 Chron. 29:15; Pss. 39:13; 119:19, 54; 120:5; 3 Macc. 7:19; and often). The earth and soil of Palestine, as indeed the whole earth (cf. Ps. 24:1), belongs to Yahweh. The Israelites are only sojourners on it. For this reason the land cannot be sold (Lev. 25:23). On the other hand, the devout sojourner may dwell in the tent of Yahweh (Pss. 15:1; 61:5) and so experience fellowship with God.

2. For Philo, the godly man is a *paroikos*, for he lives far off from his heavenly home. Philo combined the ancient world's denial of the world with OT ideas. (On Philo and Judaism see K. L. and M. A. Schmidt, *TDNT* V 843 ff.) The rabbis required sojourners, resident in the land of Israel, to keep the so-called Noahic commandments as a condition of living together (cf. SB III 737; Moore, *Judaism* I 274 f., 453, 462; R. Meyer, *TDNT* V 850). But this may only have been a matter of theory. → Noah.

NT The words are found only in Acts, 1 Pet., Lk., Heb. and Eph.: *paroikos*, 4 times; *paroikia*, twice; *paroikeō*, twice. Each passage contains a quotation or reference to the history of Israel (cf. Acts 17:6 with Gen. 15:13; cf Acts 7:29 with Exod. 2:15). In Acts 13:16 ff. Paul recalls Israel's *paroikia* in Egypt (cf. Exod. 6:16). Heb. 11:9 f. stresses that Abraham lived as a sojourner in the promised land as in a foreign country, since by faith he was a citizen of the heavenly city. The same thought occurs in the use of → *xenos* and → *parepidēmos* in Heb. 11:13 (cf. Ps. 39:13). In Jesus Christ the Gentile believers are no longer *xenoi* and *paroikoi*, but fellow citizens with the saints and members of the household of God. For the promises made to Israel and the call to the kingdom of God are also valid for them (Eph. 2:19). From this point of view, Christians are also in a new sense *paroikoi* and *parepidēmoi* here on earth. Hence the warning to abstain from fleshly lusts (1 Pet. 2:11). They are to live in their time of sojourning in the fear of God (1 Pet. 1:17). *paroikeō* means "dwell" only in Lk. 24:18. Perhaps even here the thought is that the stranger is a member of the Jewish dispersion living at Jerusalem, or that he is a pilgrim attending the feast who is only spending a few days in the city.

H. Bietenhard

→ Brother, Neighbour, → Church, → Circumcision, → Conversion, → Covenant, → Greek

(a). F. Büchsel, *allos*, *TDNT* I 264–67; A. von Harnack, *The Mission and Expansion of Christianity*, (1908) 1961; M. Hengel, *Judaism and Hellenism*, I–II, 1974; Moore, *Judaism* I–III (see index); J. A. Sanders, "Dispersion," *IDB* II 854 ff.; K. L. Schmidt, *diaspora*, *TDNT* II 98–104; K. L. Schmidt, M. A. Schmidt and R. Meyer, *paroikos*, *TDNT* V 841–53; G. Stählin, *xenos*, *TDNT* V 1–36.

(b). H. Braun, "Die Diaspora und ihre Verheissung im Neuen Testament," *Die evangelische Diaspora* 35, 1965, 97 ff.; R. Gyllenberg and B. Reicke, "Fremder," *BHHW* I 498 f.; K. L. Schmidt, *Die Polis in Kirche und Welt*, 1940; A. van Selms, E. L. Rapp and F. Lau,"Diaspora,"*RGG*³ II 174ff. J. de Vries and F. Horst, "Fremde," *RGG*³ II 1124 ff.

Foreknowledge, Providence, Predestination

This group of articles brings together words which denote human or divine foreknowledge, predestination and predetermination of future events. Their common characteristic is the prefix *pro-*, before, in both spatial and temporal significance. The temporal component is strongest in the vb. *proginōskō*, know beforehand, and in the noun *prognōsis*, foreknowledge. On the other hand, the vb. *protithēmi*, set before, plan, propose and the noun *prothesis*, setting forth, plan, purpose have spatial overtones. But when they denote a previously determined resolution they have assimilated a temporal sense. Approximating somewhat to these is the vb. *prohorizō*, predestine, which likewise expresses definite planning and care. *pronoeō*, consider beforehand, plan carefully, and the noun *pronoia*, foresight, forethought, care, are by contrast with the surrounding Gk. Hellenistic world attested in the NT only very rarely.

| προγινώσκω | προγινώσκω (*proginōskō*), know beforehand, know in advance; πρόγνωσις (*prognōsis*), foreknowledge. |

CL The composite *proginōskō*, formed from the prefix, *pro-*, before, and the vb. *ginōskō*, perceive, be acquainted with, understand, know, is attested from Euripides onwards (*Hippolytus*, 1072) and means to know or perceive in advance, to see the future (→ Knowledge, art. *ginōskō*). The corresponding noun *prognōsis* (attested as a medical technical term since Hippocrates) denotes the foreknowledge which makes it possible to predict the future. The early Gks. understood this as non-verbal foreknowledge of a dream-like kind which can however be apprehended and communicated by those who were clever enough. It belongs to the realm of destiny. It is often both hidden from men and open to them. It is capricious like the gods themselves. Both gods and men are subject to it. Its power controls the rise and fall of gods and nations. Hel. thinkers, especially the Stoics, transformed the concept and understood it in a pantheistic way as an expression of the purposefully creative order of the divine world-force which includes both nature and men. Fate itself is subjected to this order, and can be a factor in the order itself. Divinity, destiny, order and necessity become identical. Everything is arranged rationally and harmoniously, or at least in the direction of a development towards a harmonious consummation.

OT The vb. *proginōskō*, foreknow, is found in the LXX only 3 times, always without any Heb. equivalent. Two of these occurrences concern *sophia* (→ Wisdom), conceived in personal terms: Wisdom knows in advance those who desire her (Wis. 6:13); Wisdom has foreknowledge of signs and wonders (Wis. 8:8). The other reference concerns the foreknowledge which the Israelites in Egypt were given of the destruction of the Egyptian first-born (Wis. 18:6). The noun *prognōsis*,

692

foreknowledge, is found only twice in the LXX (Jud. 9:6 of God's foreknowledge decreeing the fall of the Egyptians; Jud. 11:19 of prophetic foreknowledge).

NT 1. In the NT the vb. *proginōskō*, foreknow, know beforehand or in advance, choose beforehand, is found 5 times. Two occurrences are in Paul (Rom. 8:29; 11:2). Acts 26:5 speaks of a human "having known long since" (similarly 1 Pet. 1:20; 2 Pet. 3:17). The noun *prognōsis*, foreknowledge, is attested in the NT only in Acts 2:23 and 1 Pet. 1:2.

2. In Paul the vb. *proginōskō*, foreknow, choose beforehand, demonstrates the character of God's activity among men. It assumes the aspect of a personal relationship with a group of people which originates in God himself. Rom. 8:29 declares that those whom God "foreknew he also predestined to be conformed to the image of his Son" (RSV). In Rom. 11:2 the vb. expresses God's election and love of Israel which opposes the idea of a final rejection of Israel.

3. 1 Pet. 1:20 says that Christ was "foreknown" or "destined (*proegnōsmenou*) before the foundation of the world" (RSV). The noun *prognōsis* denotes in 1 Pet. 1:2 the foreknowledge of God, which is said to be for the Christians in the Diaspora the ground of their → election. Membership of the community in a completely differently orientated and partly hostile environment is accordingly grounded in the relationship which God takes up with men as their → Father.

2 Pet. 3:17 speaks of the foreknowledge or advance knowledge of believers. They are aware that the parousia is coming despite the delay. The point at issue here is the misunderstandings and disagreements over statements of Paul (cf. 3:15 f.). They are, therefore, urged to watchfulness to counteract the danger of apostasy (→ Fall). Human *proginōskein* thus gains here a theological stress in paraenesis.

4. In Acts 2:23 *prognōsis*, foreknowledge (much as in 1 Pet. 1:20) characterizes the events surrounding Jesus of Nazareth before and up to his execution. Jesus was "delivered up according to the definite plan and foreknowledge of God [*tē hōrismenē boulē kai prognōsei tou theou ekdoton*]" (RSV).

5. Thus in the few relevant passages both the vb. and the noun speak chiefly of God's action towards Christ or towards men, and witness to his activity as planned and directed. Any interpretation in terms of an impersonal constraint (such as destiny, fate or doom), or of an autonomy which removes itself from the normal course of world events, would contradict the NT use of these words.

| προνοέω |

προνοέω (*pronoeō*), perceive beforehand, foresee, provide, think of beforehand, take care for, take thought for; πρόνοια (*pronoia*), forethought, provident care.

CL 1. The vb. *pronoeō* (from *pro* and *noeō*, observe, notice; → Reason, art. *nous*) means initially to observe in advance, notice beforehand, foresee (e.g. Hom. *Il.* 18, 526, of a deception). But in most cases it has the meaning of to care, to see to it that, make provision for, attend to (e.g. Xen. *Cyr.* 8, 1, 1, caring for children). With the noun *pronoia*, attested since Aeschylus (*Ag.* 648), much as with the vb., the temporal meaning of foresight or foreknowledge is rare. The predominant meaning is foresight in the sense of forethought, intention, care, providence.

2. From Hdt. (3, 108, 2) onwards the noun serves to designate divine providence and a generation later in Xen. (e.g. *Mem.*, 1 4, 6) and Plato (e.g. *Tim.* 44c, cf. 30b)

693

it is a philosophical technical term. In Stoic philosophy, in particular a few generations later again (e.g. Zeno, *Frag.* 174, 176, in J. von Arnim, *Stoicorum veterum Fragmenta*, 1921, I, 44) it became an important concept for describing the emanation of the purposeful operations of a world-force possessing divine status and working for the benefit of mankind as well as the perfection of nature. *pronoia*, providence, thus gained a religious significance and became an expression of religious piety. In fact, among the Stoics, it was raised to the level of an indisputable dogma. Chance is ruled out, because everything runs its course according to an implanted divine law of development which is itself divine.

The characteristics of this understanding of providence are twofold. First, providence is implanted as a law, as the divinity of nature, humanity and history. The imperative is understood as an indicative. Secondly, everything evolves automatically in line with this providential power; everything repugnant is excluded. The legacy of this conception of providence was, after its rediscovery in the Renaissance, taken over in the development of the history of ideas from rationalism right up to speculative idealism and romanticism. It was also partly expressed in Christian and biblical terms, with the result that the diversity of categories in Gk. and biblical ideas was overlooked.

OT. 1. In the LXX the vb. *pronoeō*, see in advance, care for, and also see, is attested only 10 times: once for the Heb. *bîn*, note, understand (Dan. 11:37); twice for Heb. *šûr*, look, catch sight of (Num. 23:9 and Job 24:15); all the other refs. are found in the apocryphal literature (Wis. 6:7; 13:16; 1 Esd. 2:28; 2 Macc. 14:9; 3 Macc. 3:24; 4 Macc. 7:18). Only in Wis. 6:7 is the vb. used of God: "He provides for all (small and great) alike."

2. The noun *pronoia*, care, foresight, is found only 9 times, almost exclusively in the Apocrypha. 2 Macc. 4:6 speaks of the hoped-for human assistance of King Seleucus IV. All the other passages speak either of God's care: God's care steers the ship (Wis. 14:3); by God's provision the jaws of the lions remain shut (Dan. 6:19 LXX; cf. 3 Macc. 5:30; 4 Macc. 9:24); of the eternal (Wis. 17:2), omniscient (4 Macc. 13:19), or divine providence (4 Macc. 17:22). Of theological importance is the thought in the final reference, that the divine providence redeems the nation through the blood of the martyrs (the seven brothers), as a way of propitiation (→ Reconciliation, art. *hilaskomai*).

3. The term for providence has, therefore, no corresponding equivalent in the Heb. of the OT. Similarly, the idea of providence did not take on any distinctive didactic stamp in the OT. Rather, the idea itself and its didactic expression stem from Gk.-Hellenistic thought. It was there and in Hel.-determined Latin that it gained conceptuality in the notion of *providentia*.

4. The acceptance of the Hel. idea of providence into Jewish thought becomes particularly evident in Philo and Josephus. The attestations for *pronoeō*, care for, and *pronoia*, care, foresight, are numerous. God's providence and provision become clear in the ruin of a persecutor of the Jews (Josephus, *War*, 7, 453) and in the example of Abraham (Josephus, *Ant.*, 11, 169). God cares for the world (Philo, *Op. Mund.*, 171), for the creation as a whole and in particular (Philo, *Spec.Leg.*, 3, 189). Like the early Stoic Chrysippus, Philo wrote a book *peri pronoias* (*Concerning Providence*).

694

NT In the NT the vb. *pronoeō*, take thought for, be intent on, care for, aim, is found only in Rom. 12:17 and 2 Cor. 8:21. Significantly, both instances refer to human endeavour in goodness, honesty and sincerity (probably with ref. to the LXX wording of Prov. 3:4). The noun *pronoia* (Rom. 13:14) also means concern, solicitude, provision. In this case it refers to the body (→ Flesh). In Acts 24:3 the advocate Tertullus praises the provisions of Felix. Vb. and noun are not used of God's caring activity. The fact that the word *pronoia*, in the sense of a divine wisdom of the world, does not appear in the NT despite its representation of one of the central and basic concepts of the surrounding world is not accidental. It is a sign that the NT speaks an equally eloquent language by avoiding some Hel. concepts, as it does by accepting and re-coining others (e.g. *agapē*, → Love).

| προοράω | *προοράω* (*prohoraō*), see previously, see in advance, foresee (the future), know already, take care that. |

CL The vb. *prohoraō* (from *pro*, in front, before, and *horaō*, → see, notice) is attested in the spatial sense of seeing in front of one since Homer (*Od.*, 5, 393), and in the sense of foreseeing or knowing the future in advance, first in Pindar (*Nem.* 1, 27).

OT 1. In the LXX *prohoraō*, and all the forms of *proidein*, are found only in Ps. 138 (139):3 ("thou seest all my ways (before)") of God's forward-reaching sight and knowledge, in Ps. 15(16):8 of a man keeping the Lord before his eyes, in Gen. 37:18 of Joseph's being seen from a distance by his brothers, and in 1 Esd. 5:63 of those who had seen the former house of God.

2. Philo used the word largely in the temporal sense of foreseeing dangers (*Praem.*, 72) and in combination with → *pronoia*, the providence of God (*Deus.Imm.*, 29), by which God in contrast to men foresees what is coming. In Josephus we find in addition the meaning to make provision for (e.g. *Ant.*, 16, 378).

NT In the NT *prohoraō*, see before, is attested 4 times. In Gal. 3:8 Paul says, with ref. to Gen. 12:3, that the → Scripture (here personalized) foresaw "that God would justify the Gentiles by faith." The three other passages are in Acts and mean to have in front of one's eyes (2:25, quoting Ps. 16:8), to have seen already before (21:29), and – similarly to the Pauline ref. – to foresee or foreknow (2:31, with ref. to Ps. 16:10: David spoke with foresight or foreknowledge of the resurrection). The vb. is thus not used in the NT – any more than *pronoeō* and *pronoia* – to describe the activity of God.

| προορίζω | *προορίζω* (*prohorizō*), decide upon beforehand, predestine. |

CL & OT The compound *prohorizō* (formed from *pro*, in front, before and *horizō*, to ordain, → determine) is only used from the 4th cent. B.C. onwards (Demosth., 31, 4), and means to preordain. It is not found in the LXX.

NT The NT uses *prohorizō*, preordain, 6 times to speak exclusively of God's decrees.

1. Paul uses the vb. in Rom. 8:29 together with → *proginōskō*, foreknow, and → *prothesis*, plan, decision, in order to ground the → call of God in his prior

decree. In v. 30 the vb. is taken up again, in order to specify the end to which these dealings of God with men are directed, namely to justify those who are called and to give them a share in his → glory (art. *doxa* NT). 1 Cor. 2:7 speaks of the → Wisdom (art. *sophia*) of God which he himself "predestined" (JB), "ordained" (AV), "decreed" (RSV), "for our glory" (JB). God's predestination is thus described as an activity of his with men directed towards their fellowship with him. (See further C. E. B. Cranfield, "Romans 8:28", *SJT* 19, 1966, 204–15; A. R. C. Leaney, "Conformed to the Image of His Son", *NTS* 10, 1963–64, 470–9; K. Grayston, "The Doctrine of Election in Rom. 8:28–30", *StudEv*, II, 1964, 574–83; M. Black, *Romans*, 1973, 124 f.; → Elect.)

2. Essentially on the same lines is the statement in Eph. 1:5, which describes sonship shared in Christ as grounded in the predetermining love of God. In Eph. 1:11 the vb. is again used with → *prothesis*, plan, decree, in order to characterize the inheritance which Christians themselves are and which Christ has made possible. This all derives from the will of God who accomplishes all things according to the counsel of his will.

3. In Acts 4:27 f. expression is given to the conviction that Herod, Pontius Pilate, the nations and peoples are only able to do to Jesus that which God has previously established or determined. *prohorizō* is thus here intended to underline that even men's sinful actions are drawn into the realization of the divine plan of salvation.

προτίθημι

προτίθημι (*protithēmi*), mid. display publicly, plan, propose, intend; act. set before as a duty; πρόθεσις (*prothesis*), setting forth, presentation, display, exhibition, plan, purpose, resolve, will. On *tithēmi* → Determine, Appoint, Present, art. *tithēmi*.

CL The vb. *protithēmi* (a compound of *pro*, in front, before, and *tithēmi*, set, place, lay, insert, make into) is attested early on. It possesses a basic local meaning, to set before (Hes., *Theog.*, 537, set food before), but also means to resolve (e.g. Plato, *Phaedr.*, 259e), propose, determine, put forward openly.

The noun *prothesis* can denote the public lying in state of the dead (Plato, *Leg.*, 12, 947b), public announcements (Aristot., *Pol.*, 6, 8, p. 1322a 9), and later an intention (Polyb., 5, 35, 2). See further C. Maurer, *tithēmi*, *TDNT* VIII 164 f.

OT In the LXX the vb. *protithēmi* is used 5 times in the sense of laying before or laying on (e.g. Exod. 40:4 of the showbread). Altogether it is used 19 times; of which 11 render a total of 6 Heb. equivalents, 6 are in the apocryphal writings, and 2 have no correspondence in the MT. In Ps. 54(53):3 and 86(85):14 it renders Heb. *śîm* (set, place, lay) in the sense of keeping God before one's eyes. It thus describes a conscious turning to God or a refusal to do so (cf. also Ps. 101[100]:3 and 3 Macc. 2:27). The noun *prothesis* (used 17 times of which 7 are in 1, 2 and 3 Macc.) is 13 times a technical term for the showbread (e.g. Exod. 39:36), and is thus to be translated ordering, presentation. Meaning intention, purpose, plan, it is found only in 2 Macc. 3:8; 3 Macc. 1:22; 2:26; 5:12, 29. These words, then, do not have any particular theological emphasis in the OT.

NT 1. In the NT the vb. *protithēmi* is found 3 times. It means to resolve in Rom. 1:13 (cf. Paul's intention to visit Rome), and to put forward in Rom. 3:25 (God put Christ forward as a propitiation; → Reconciliation, art. *hilaskomai*, NT 4), and to set forth in Eph. 1:9 (God has set forth his purpose in Christ).

The noun *prothesis*, display, exhibition, plan, intention, (previously made) decision, is attested 12 times, 4 of which refer to the showbread. Human objectives are mentioned in Acts 11:23; 27:13 and 2 Tim. 3:10 (RSV "aim in life").

2. By contrast with the non-theological use of the word in the LXX, Paul uses the noun twice in order to describe the primal decision of God (*TDNT* VIII 166). In Rom. 8:28 God's *prothesis*, resolve, decision, or purpose, is stated to be the foundation of the → call of the Christians. The → hope and certainty of a Christian are based on and upheld by God's previous activity, and not by any human capacity for decision-making. Paul uses the word similarly in Rom. 9:11 (cf. Gen. 25:23). The election of Jacob is already laid down in God's resolve even before the birth of the twins. Here too the word *prothesis* serves to characterize God's activity among men as free and grounded in his → will alone. It is thus independent of human prerogatives. The accomplishment of the promise is always God's free act both in Israel and the church.

3. Similarly, in Eph. 1:11 the existence of the church is described as the result of a decision made by God. This decision of God is both in time and in all aspects a *preceding resolve*. Here as in Rom. 8:28 ff. there is an accumulation of words which emphasize the priority of the → will of God. In Eph. 3:8 ff. it is the realization of God's saving plan in Christ (→ House, art. *oikonomia* NT 2) which is under discussion. The word *prothesis*, plan, in v. 11 serves to characterize God's activity in Christ as the fulfilment of an eternal purpose. It is one in which men do not have a say, either in time or in its intentions. 2 Tim. 1:9 is concerned with the redeeming (→ Redemption, art. *sōzō*) and calling activity of God among men. Its assumptions do not lie in the area of prior human achievement but of God's own decision.

→ Determine, → Elect, → Fullness, → Promise   *P. Jacobs, H. Krienke*

(a). K. Barth, *CD* III 3, 3–57; J. Behm, *pronoeō*, *TDNT* IV 1009–17; G. C. Berkouwer, *The Providence of God*, 1952; R. Bultmann, *Primitive Christianity in its Historical Setting*, 1956 (see index); W. Eichrodt, *Theology of the Old Testament*, II, 1967, 167–85; J. Jeremias, *Jesus' Promise to the Nations*, 1955; C. Maurer, *protithēmi*, *TDNT* VIII 164–68; R. Pesch, "Providence," *EBT* II 722–25; K. L. Schmidt, *prohorizō*, *TDNT* V 456; M. Wiles, ed., *Providence*, *SPCK Theological Collections* 12, 1969.
(b). W. Eichrodt, "Vorsehungsglaube und Theodizee im Alten Testament," *Procksch Festschrift*, 1934, 45 ff.; F. Nötscher, *Gotteswege und Menschenwege in der Bibel und in Qumran*, *Bonner Biblische Beiträge* 15, 1958; W. Wiesner, "Vorsehung," *EKL* III 1705 ff.

Forgiveness

ἀφίημι

ἀφίημι (*aphiēmi*), let go, cancel, remit, leave, forgive; ἄφεσις (*aphesis*), release, pardon, cancellation, forgiveness; πάρεσις (*paresis*), letting pass, passing over.

CL *aphiēmi* (derived from *apo*, from, and *hiēmi*, to put in motion, send), attested since Homer, means the voluntary release of a person or thing over which one has legal or actual control. In addition to the vb., the noun *aphesis*, discharge, setting free, is used from Plato onwards. In its fig. use *aphiēmi* overlaps in meaning with *pariēmi* (Homer), lit. to let drop, let by; fig., to let pass, allow (the noun *paresis*, since Hippocrates).

1. *aphiēmi* is used in classical Gk. both in a lit. and in a fig. sense:

(a) With a personal object, to send forth, send away (of a woman, to divorce; of a meeting, to dissolve, end), to let go, to leave, dispatch; with an impersonal object, to loose (e.g. a ship into the sea), to discharge (e.g. arrows), to give up.

(b) In the fig. sense the vb. means to let alone, permit, let pass, neglect, give up (taking trouble, etc.); in Josephus, *Ant.*, 1, 12, 3, to lose one's life, die. The legal use is important: to release from a legal bond (office, guilt, etc. and also, a woman from marriage, e.g. Hdt., 5, 39), to acquit (e.g. cancellation of criminal proceedings, Plato, *Laws*, 9, 86, 9d), to exempt (from guilt, obligation, punishment, etc.; e.g. Hdt., 6, 30). Similarly the noun *aphesis* (e.g. Demosthenes, 24, 45) means release, pardon, or remission, etc. All these meanings apply from Homer onwards only to human relationships; they are not found in a religious sense.

2. The same fig. meaning is found frequently with *pariēmi*, to let by, relax (e.g. of slackening a sail, Plato, *Laws*, 11, 931d); but also to let go unpunished, to allow, in the sense of personal leniency or indulgence (e.g. Hdt., 7, 169, 2), and the cognate noun *paresis*, letting pass.

OT The LXX uses *aphiēmi* in such classical Gk. senses as to let go (Jdg. 3:1), leave, give up (Jdg. 9:9, 11, 13), leave behind (2 Sam. 15:16; 20:3), allow (2 Sam. 16:10 f.), leave over (Ps. 17:14), release in the year of release (Deut. 15:2). It is used relatively seldom in the sense to forgive. Where it is, it usually renders the Heb. *nāśā'*, to release from guilt or punishment (Gen. 18:26; Ps. 25:18; 32:1, 5; 85:2; Isa. 33:24), or *sālaḥ*, to forgive, pardon (Lev. 4:20 ff.; 5:6 ff.; Num. 14:19; 15:25 f.; Isa. 55:7). Sometimes it stands for *kippēr*, to cover, make atonement (Isa. 22:14). The one who forgives is God (but cf. Gen. 50:17). Through the act of forgiveness, the relationship between God and man which has been disturbed or destroyed by sin is reconstituted.

Of the 50 or so instances of *aphesis* in the LXX, 22 are found in Lev. 25 and 27 (for Heb. *yôḇēl*, year of jubilee) and 5 in Deut. 15:1–9 (for Heb. *šāmaṭ*, release from debts in the year of jubilee). In general, it is more often used of the release of captives and slaves (Isa. 61:1; Jer. 34:8, 15, 17; Ezek. 46:17). Only once does *aphesis* appear in the sense of forgiveness (Lev. 16:26), and there it is without Heb. equivalent, used as an interpretation of Azazel. [F. F. Bruce suggests that in Lev. 16:26 LXX *aphesis* has the simple sense of "sending away" – an attempt at a lit. translation of *ʿz'āzēl*, as though from the root *'āzal*; cf. Lat. *caper emissarius*.]

The occurrence of *aphiēmi* and *aphesis* thus indicates that they are not the words chiefly used in the LXX to convey the concept of forgiveness. Israel experienced God's grace in forgiveness largely in the context of the cultus (cf. OT, 1), so that all kinds of terms from the language of the cultus come to be used to express the idea (washing, cleansing, covering, etc.).

1. *Forgiveness in the OT*. It is clear that Israel was aware before the exile that God can forgive sin (cf. Isa. 6). The part played by the forgiveness of sins in the faith and worship of that period depends on the date ascribed to the Pentateuch. A remarkable example is to be found in a number of pre-exilic Psalms (cf. Pss. 25:11;

698

65:3; 78:38; 79:9) which show a degree of reflection on the consciousness of sin and forgiveness of sins unparalleled in the early writings of the OT. The guilt here does not, however, arise from individual acts of moral transgression, but from "the opposition of the two wills, the divine and the human" (G. van der Leeuw, *Religion in Essence and Manifestation*, 1938). Sin is here opposition to God, grounded in the inmost part of man's nature. It can only be brought to an end by a new, gracious gift of God (cf. Ps. 65:5 ff.). In "Sühne and Vergebung um die Wende von der exilischen zur nachexilischen Zeit" (*EvTh* 26, 1966, 217 ff.) to which the following points are indebted, K. Koch has argued that those passages which speak of God's compassion in response to prophetic intercession (Amos 7; Exod. 32:12, 14; Jer. 26:19; cf. Mic. 7:18) mean that God passes the sinner by (*'ābar*). He is forbearing and avoids entering "the circles of the man laden with guilt." "Where such pardon is extended, punishment is also lightened, but never in the pre-exilic period cancelled" (K. Koch, op. cit., 221). The final punishment of Israel by Yahweh, in the prophetic forecasts of doom, is only comprehensible against a background of a fatal and disastrous act which renders God's forgiveness, in the sense of a removal of guilt, impossible. God can no longer pass by the sin of the people (→ Reconciliation, especially art. *hilaskomai*).

Earlier prophetic writings also speak of the forgiveness of sins, but it is Koch's opinion that the recognition that God forgives sin has been introduced at a later date by editorial additions (cf. Ezek. 36:29, 33; Isa. 4:3 f.; Mic. 7:19). The question whether sin was forgiven through cultic sacrifice prior to the exile depends on the view taken of the date of the sacrificial ordinances in the Pentateuch. According to Koch, it was in the exilic and post-exilic periods that Israel discovered "God's readiness to forgive: forgiveness is seen to be brought about by cultic acts and priestly pronouncements, and deliverance from sin is experienced" (op. cit., 227; cf. G. von Rad, *Old Testament Theology*, I, 1962, 262 ff.). On the other hand, the passages in the law which deal with sacrifice and forgiveness quoted above locate the institution of these ordinances in the time of → Moses and the exodus. The Israelite did not think of → sin (*hamartia*) in the abstract, but as a localized sphere arising out of transgression. It could not simply be forgotten. The only way that it could be forgiven was by expiatory ritual by which God broke through the continued outworking of the act and, as in Lev. 16:20 ff., pass it on to the animal and so remove the guilt (Lev. 16:20, 22; 17:11). This puts certain prophetic allusions (cf. Isa. 1:16, 18; 6:7) and passages in the Psalms (Pss. 25:11; 65:3; 79:9) into a new light. The essential point is that God alone is the one who frees and forgives in all acts of atonement.

However, it is not every sin that can be atoned for, and so forgiven, by rites of atonement (e.g. offences against the law of circumcision, Gen. 17:14; and against the laws of the Sabbath and the Passover, Exod. 12:15; Num. 9:13).

Isa. 40–55 goes beyond these ideas, particularly those of the priestly literature. The prophet recognizes that atonement by means of the blood of animals (→ Blood, art. *haima*) is not enough. Moreover, he sees that in the situation of the exile expiatory ritual simply disappears. In the coming servant of God he heralds the one on whom the sin of Israel and of the other nations will be laid, and through whom God will bring about an all-embracing atonement and forgiveness of sin (Isa. 53; cf. 55:6–13).

To sum up, it may be said that from the exile onwards Israel sees her history as upheld by the forgiving activity of God. This is also evident in the significance which is attached to the second → temple. It is the place where the Day of Atonement is celebrated, the festival whose rites bring forgiveness of sins to every Israelite (cf. Sir. 50; 1 Bar. 1:10 ff.).

2. *Judaism*. *aphiēmi* and *aphesis* are found as terms for forgiveness in Josephus (*Ant.*, 6, 92) and Philo (*Vit. Mos.*, 2, 147; *Spec. Leg.*, 1, 190). However, a tension appears between this and the forgiving goodness of God which in the OT is associated with his righteousness (cf. Ps. 143:11). This is especially apparent in Josephus. The idea of man's working together with God, on the one hand, and God's *dikē* (the central concept of his theology), on the other, cause him to turn forgiveness into leniency on God's part. Where there is confession of sin and a change of mind, God is ready to be reconciled (*War*, 5, 415) and hence to remit punishment (*Ant.*, 9, 214; 11, 114). But this kind of forgiveness does not mean that evil is overcome and sin removed.

Rab. Judaism developed a thoroughgoing system of casuistry, in which God's forgiveness is catalogued. A distinction is made between (a) forgiveness of sins in this world by virtue of repentance and propitiatory sacrifices, e.g. on the great Day of Atonement (cf. T. Yoma 5:6 ff.; cf. SB I 636); (b) forgiveness of sins in the world to come by means of expiation in the fire of Gehenna, or by means of divine grace (cf. SB I 637); and (c) forgiveness of sins, or preservation from sins, in the Messianic age. In connection with the latter it is said of the Messiah that he will gain forgiveness for Israel on the grounds of his intercession and sufferings (Tg. Isa. 53:4 ff.), but there is nowhere a reference to the Messiah forgiving men's sins by virtue of his own authority. God alone has the right to forgive sins. As in the OT, however, there are unforgivable sins (e.g. blasphemy against the → name of God).

3. *Qumran*. There are a number of passages, especially in the Community Rule (1QS), the Damascus Rule (CD) and the Scroll of Hymns (1QH) which speak of God's forgiveness (1QS 3:6–12; 11:3; CD 2:3 f.; 3:18; 1QH 4:37; 7:18; 30, 35 and often). In addition to a strong consciousness of election and mission, every single member of the community had a very marked sense of sin and worthlessness (cf. 1QH 1:5–39). This awareness of the worthlessness and creatureliness of man and at the same time of election by God was emphasized by a strong insistence on sin and forgiveness and with it a confession of utter dependence upon God's grace (1QH 10:21; 11:9; and often). Forgiveness at Qumran is not tied to bloody rites of propitiation; forgiveness is obtained by the man who sees the error of his way and turns from it in humility and a right spirit (cf. 1QH 14:24; 1QS 3:7 ff.: "His sin is atoned for"). He who does not repent sincerely, but clings to Belial (Satan), excludes himself from forgiveness and thus from the new covenant (1QS 2:8, 26).

NT 1. *aphiēmi* is attested 142 times in the NT. Of these examples 47 are found in Matt., 34 each in Mk. and the Lucan writings, and 14 in Jn. This leaves only 13 examples in the whole of the rest of the NT. Oddly enough *aphiēmi* occurs only 45 times in the sense to forgive (17 times in Matt.; 8 times in Mk.; 14 times in Lk. – Acts; twice in John; and only once in Paul!). It is used occasionally in a secular sense (Matt. 18:27, 32), but usually in the religious sense of forgiveness (absolutely in Matt. 12:32 par., etc.), or forgiveness of sins (aphienai hamartias, Mk. 2:5, 7, par.; Lk. 7:47 ff., etc.), debts (opheilēmata, Matt. 6:12), trespasses (paraptōmata, Mk. 11:25 f.; Matt. 6:14 f., etc.). In most cases, however, the NT uses aphiēmi in the original senses of to let (Mk. 1:34; 5:19, 37 par.; Acts 14:17, etc.); to dismiss, divorce, release (Matt. 13:36; 1 Cor. 7:11–13, etc.); to leave (Mk. 1:20; 10:28 par., etc.); to leave behind (Mk. 1:18 par., etc.); and to abandon (Mk. 7:8; Rom. 1:27, etc.).

The use of aphesis is in contrast to this. Of 17 examples in the NT, 15 have the sense of forgiveness (cf. Mk. 1:4 par.; Matt. 26:23; Lk. 1:77; Acts 2:38; Heb. 9:22), and two, release from captivity (Lk. 4:18). It is notable that of these 17 examples, 5 are found in Luke and Acts, 2 in Heb. and 2 in Mk., whereas aphesis is totally lacking in Paul, apart from Eph. 1:7 and Col. 1:14. This suggests that it was not used in the early period.

paresis, passing over, letting go unpunished, occurs only at Rom. 3:25. There are, in addition, further circumlocutions for forgiveness (some of them echoing OT ritual language), such as kalyptō, to cover (→ Hide), airō, to take away, cancel (Jn. 1:29, etc.), apolouomai, to get oneself washed (→ Baptism, art. louō).

In Paul the idea is expressed in more precise theological terms: dikaioō, to justify (→ Righteousness, art. dikaiosynē), and katallassō, to reconcile (→ Reconciliation).

2. (a) Just as the fact that man is a sinner has destroyed his relationship with God (→ Sin, art. hamartia; → Man, art. anthrōpos NT), so forgiveness takes the central place in Christian proclamation as the means whereby this relationship is restored. It stands as the action of God in the face of the sinful behaviour of man, and is based on Christ (Col. 1:14; Eph. 1:7), whose power to forgive sins is made known in preaching (Lk. 24:47; Acts 10:42 f.; 13:38), → baptism (cf. Acts 2:38; Mk. 1:4 f. par.; Rom. 6:1 ff.), and the → Lord's Supper (Matt. 26:28; cf. Jn. 6:53 ff.). The OT proclamation of forgiveness is here taken up and preached afresh as the fulfilment in Christ of what was promised of old (Jer. 31:34; 33:8) in the eschatological present (cf. Lk. 1:77; 4:18 ff.). The Synoptic Gospels and Acts often use parallel to the vb. (see above, 1) the fixed formula aphesis hamartiōn, forgiveness of sins (cf. Mk. 1:4 f. par., Matt. 26:28. Acts 5:31). The terms preferred by the other NT writers like → redemption (apolytrōsis), → reconciliation (katallagē), justification (dikaiōsis or the vb. dikaioō; → righteousness, art. dikaiosynē NT, 1), concentrate more upon the work of Christ (but cf. also Col. 1:14 and similarly Eph. 1:7).

(b) According to Mk. 10:45 par., the preaching of Jesus reached its climax in the forgiveness brought by him (Lk. 4:18–21; 15:11 ff.; Matt. 18:21 ff.). It appears as the activity appropriate to him (Mk. 2:7, 10 par.; Lk. 7:49). In Mk. 2:1–12 par. (the healing of the paralytic) we see forgiveness taking, despite all the objections, the place it is to occupy in the activity of Jesus as the one proper essential work he has come to do. Jesus' attitude to notorious sinners underlines his preaching by action (Lk. 7:36–50; 19:1–10).

(c) Forgiveness includes making of no account the sin which has been committed (Mk. 2:5 par.; cf. Jn. 8:11), and the acceptance of the sinner (Lk. 15:20 ff.; cf. also Col. 1:13 f.: deliverance from the dominion of the powers and transference to the kingdom of Christ), to whom a new life is given and with it the promise of eternal life (Lk. 23:43; Matt. 5:43–48; Jn. 14:19b). Early Christian

701

preaching shows that this acceptance is at the same time an acceptance into the church. It therefore includes a share in the forgiveness which is continually pronounced there, because it is continually needed (Matt. 18:18; cf. 16:19; Jn. 20:23; cf. also 10:42 f.; 13:38). Forgiveness is closely associated with the death of Jesus on the cross (in addition to general references like Mk. 10:45 par. and Jn. 3:16; cf. Heb. 9:22 and Rom. 8:32). As the "Lamb of God", he takes away the sin of the world (Jn. 1:29; cf. 1 Pet. 2:21–24). In the → Lord's Supper reference is made to the reconciling effect of the death of Jesus in the words "blood of the covenant . . . poured out . . . for the forgiveness of sins" (Matt. 26:28). In 1 Cor. 15:17 it is linked to the → resurrection of Jesus (cf. Rom. 4:25; 14:9; 2 Cor. 5:15b; Lk. 24:46 f.; cf. also Acts 5:31).

(d) Repentance (*metanoia*, → Conversion) and confession of sins (Mk. 1:15; Acts 2:38; 5:31; 1 Jn. 1:9; Heb. 6:1, 6; Jas. 5:16) are not "works" offered up to God. Rather, they are the acceptance, brought about by God himself, of his verdict upon the "old man", and an openness to his word of deliverance (cf. Acts 19:18). Nor can the readiness of a man to forgive, with which the divine declaration of forgiveness is closely linked (Matt. 6:12 par.; 14 f.; cf. 5:23 f.; Mk. 11:25; Lk. 6:37), be regarded as a meritorious precondition. It belongs to the new life which has been given. Where this has been received, it is the natural, daily sign of the forgiven sinner's gratitude. This is demonstrated negatively by the example of the wicked servant (Matt. 18:32–35). The passages cited from the Sermon on the Mount are also directed at those who have already received God's forgiveness, in whom gratitude is to be expected as a consequence, showing itself in the following or imitation of Christ and his forgiveness (cf. Col. 3:13; Eph. 4:32). Man's forgiveness of his debtor (Matt. 6:12 par.) and even of his enemy (Matt. 5:38–48; Rom. 12:19 ff.) comes about as the consequence of God's forgiveness in Christ.

(e) In Paul the terms *aphiēmi* and *aphesis* virtually disappear. (Rom. 4:7 in an OT quotation from Ps. 32:1 has *aphiēmi* in the sense of forgive; and Rom. 3:25 *paresis* in a similar sense.) This is because the proclamation of forgiveness appears in Paul's writings as a thought-out and systematized doctrine. The fact that forgiveness is not merely a remission of past guilt, but includes total deliverance from the power of sin and restoration to fellowship with God, is expressed by Paul in his doctrine of justification (→ righteousness; cf. Rom. 3:21 ff.; 4:22, 25; Gal. 3:6–9) and of → reconciliation (of the sinner, Rom. 5:10 f.; 2 Cor. 5:18; of the world, Rom. 11:15; 2 Cor. 5:19) with God. This has taken place in Christ (Rom. 5:10 f.) as God's own free act (2 Cor. 5:18 f.) and is the centre of the gospel. Forgiveness takes place because God gives himself completely in the sacrifice of his Son (2 Cor. 5:21; Rom. 8:32), and so gives man a share in his own righteousness (Rom. 3:21–28). Thus "in Christ" man becomes a pardoned sinner (Rom. 8:1) and a "new creature" (2 Cor. 5:17). This teaching represents a summary and theological consolidation of the early Christian preaching of forgiveness.

(f) The task of proclaiming the forgiveness which has been brought about by Christ is given to the → church. This task is carried out in preaching, in the personal declaration of forgiveness to individuals, and also in the proclamatore rites of baptism and the eucharist. It is not a case of mere reference to and repetition of something past. Each time it is a fresh act of proclamation, coming from Christ himself to the concrete situation of the present. Its validity is grounded in the authority given by Christ to the church (Matt. 18:18; cf. 16:19; Jn. 20:23; cf. also 1 Jn. 5:16; Jas. 5:15 f.), and always remains conditional on obedience to him.

This comes about through renewed realization of forgiveness in the real situations of everyday life, with their call to decision, and not in some timeless application. This is shown by the commission to retain along with the commission to forgive (*krateō*, as opposed to *aphiēmi*, Jn. 20:23; cf. Matt. 18:18; 16:19; → Bind). Without this, forgiveness would be in danger of being trivialized. In this connection see 1 Cor. 5:1–5; Matt. 12:30 ff. par.; Acts 5:1–11; 1 Jn. 5:16 f.; Heb. 6:4; 10:26 f. These passages deal with the live issue of apostasy and renewed repentance, a question later taken up again by the Shepherd of Hermas.   *H. Vorländer*
→ Baptism, → Blood, → Conversion, → Cross, → Grace (for *charizomai*, graciously forgive), → Judgment, → Reconciliation, → Redemption, → Sacrifice, → Sin, → Slave, Servant, → Son

(a). R. Bultmann, *aphiēmi*, *TDNT*, I 509–12; J. D. M. Derrett, "The Anointing at Bethany and the Story of Zacchaeus," *Law in the New Testament*, 1970, 266–85; W. Eichrodt, *Theology of the Old Testament*, II, 1967, 380–95; O. E. Evans, "The Unforgivable Sin," *ExpT*. 68, 1956–57, 240–44; F. C. Fensham, "The Legal Background of Mt. 6, 12," *NovT*. 4, 1960, 1 f.; J. M. Ford, "The Forgiveness Clause in the Matthaean Form of the Our Father," *ZNW* 59, 1968, 127 ff.; E. M. B. Green, *The Meaning of Salvation*, 1965; J. Jeremias, *The Prayers of Jesus*, 1967; E. Lohmeyer, *The Lord's Prayer*, 1965, 160–90; J. Lowe, *The Lord's Prayer*, 1962, 37–42; W. Lüthi, *The Lord's Prayer*, 1962, 46–52; H. McKeating, "Divine Forgiveness in the Psalms", *SJT* 18, 1965, 69–83; I. H. Marshall, *Kept by the Power of God: A Study of Perseverance and Falling Away*, 1969; R. P. Martin, "Reconciliation and Forgiveness in Colossians," in R. Banks, ed., *Reconciliation and Hope* (Leon Morris Festschrift), 1974, 104–24; E. B. Redlich, *The Forgiveness of Sins*, 1937; K. Stendahl, "Prayer and Forgiveness," *Svensk Exegetisk Årsbok* 22–23, 1957–58, 75 ff.; V. Taylor, *Forgiveness and Reconciliation*, 1941; W. Telfer, *The Forgiveness of Sins*, 1959 H. Thyen, *BAPTISMA METANOIAS EIS APHESIN AMARTIŌN*, in J. M. Robinson, ed., *The Future of Our Religious Past, Essays in Honour of Rudolf Bultmann*, 1971, 131–68; J. G. S. S, Thompson, *The Praying Christ*, 1959.
(b). H. Dee "Vergebung der Sünden," *EvTh* 26, 1966, 652 ff.; H. Gollwitzer, ' Zu H. Dee 'Vergebung der Sünden,' " *EvTh* 26, 1966, 652 ff.; W. Koch, H. Bienert, P. Jacobs, "Vergeltung und Vergebung," *EKL* III 1636 ff.; K. Koch, "Sühne und Sündevergebung um die Wende von der exilischen zur nachexilischen Zeit," *EvTh* 26, 1966, 217 ff.; H. Thyen, *Studien zur Sündenvergebung im Neuen Testament und seine alttestamentlichen und jüdischen Voraussetzungen*, *FRLANT* 96, 1969; T. C. Vriezen et al., "Sündenvergebung," *RGG*³ VI 507 ff.

Form, Substance

The distinction is commonly drawn between outward form and essential substance. Whilst this distinction is also found in Gk., the Gk. idea of form does not imply that every kind of form is a mere outward appearance. The following article examines three words which may be translated as form: *eidos*, *morphē* and *schēma*. It also examines *hypostasis* which, among other things, may be translated as substance, essential nature, essence and actual being, as well as assurance, confidence.

| εἶδος | εἶδος (*eidos*), form, outward appearance, sight. |

CL The noun *eidos* is connected with the vb. *eidō, see (cf. Lat. *video*). It occurs from Homer onwards and denotes appearance, visible form, stressing the link between the visible appearance and reality. Hdt. could speak of praising the *eidos* of a woman (1, 8), meaning not only her outward beauty but her true character. The word is used in Plato for the Forms or Ideas which are the existing realities behind our world (*Phaedo*, 75, 102; *Rep.*, 6, 508–11; cf. 7, 514 ff.). The modern distinction between the external and the internal, the visible and the invisible, the husk and the kernel, and between outward form and essential content is inappropriate and foreign to this aspect of Gk. thought. Although Aristotle distinguished between *eidos*, → *morphē* and *hylē* (matter), he was not thinking of two different materials. The *eidos* was the expression of the essence in visible form.

OT The LXX uses *eidos* to translate *mar'eh* (sight, appearance, vision) and *tō'ar* (form). Here too the outward appearance of the whole being is meant (cf. Gen. 29:17; Isa. 53:2 f.), and not merely the outer shell behind which something quite different might be supposed. God conversed *en eidei* with Moses (Num. 12:8). This means that Moses saw the glory of the Lord.

NT 1. *eidos* occurs only 5 times in the NT (twice in Paul and Lk., and once in Jn.).
   1 Thess. 5:22 goes back to Job 1:1, 8: "Abstain from every form of evil." G. Kittel thinks that *eidos* here means a "mint" and that the verse may reflect a saying of Jesus concerning money changers preserved in the early church (*TDNT* II 375). But Arndt (220) prefers to translate it as "kind".
   2. 2 Cor. 5:7 declares that "We walk by faith and not *dia eidous* [by sight, RSV]." The interpretation is difficult, because *eidos* does not normally mean "sight" but the visible form. There is also the question of the subject of the verse. In the first half it is the 1st person plur. "we". If "we" is also to be understood as the subject of "not by sight", the verse might then imply a contrast of the present time as the sphere of faith with the coming future time in which we shall have a visible form.
   On the other hand, v. 7b may be taken to refer to the visible form of the Lord. We now walk by faith (*dia pisteōs*), but the Lord does not walk in visible form. Against this view is the fact that it requires a sudden, implicit change of subject.
   There is, however, a third possibility that Paul simply means that we now live by faith and not by sight.
   3. In his account of the baptism of Jesus, Lk. says that the Holy Spirit descended upon Jesus in bodily form (*sōmatikō eidei*) like a dove (Lk. 3:22; cf. Mk. 1:10; Matt. 3:16). The account intends to stress the reality of what happened. Similarly, Lk. also uses *eidos* in his account of the transfiguration. "And as he was praying, the appearance of his countenance (*to eidos tou prosōpou autou*) was altered" (Lk. 9:29; cf. Matt. 17:2; Mk. 9:2). But no special tendency in Lk.'s writing can be deduced from this.
   4. Jn. 5:37 contains the statement: "His voice you have never heard, his form (*eidos*) you have never seen." This is contrasted with the first half of the verse: "And the Father who sent me has himself born witness to me" (cf. also v. 38). It was part of the OT witness that God cannot be seen in visible form (cf. Deut. 4:12). But this is never intended as a reproach. Similarly, Jn. 5:37 cannot be interpreted in this way. It means rather that they have not given heed to God (cf. v. 38). ([Ed.] However, there may be the further implication that Jesus has in fact heard the voice of the Father and seen his "form" and thus has an authority and relationship with the Father which no other man has ever had [cf. the whole argument in Jn. 5:17–47].)

G. Braumann

| μορφή |

μορφή (morphē), form, outward appearance, shape; σύμμορφος (symmorphos), having the same shape, similar in form or appearance; συμμορφίζομαι (symmorphizomai), be conformed to, take on the same form as; συμμορφόομαι (symmorphoomai), take on the same form; μεταμορφόομαι (metamorphoomai), be transformed; μόρφασις (morphōsis), embodiment, formulation, outward form, appearance; μορφόω (morphoō), form, shape.

CL 1. (a) *morphē* is instanced from Homer onwards and means form in the sense of outward appearance. Aeschylus speaks of seeing neither voice nor form of man (*PV*, 21 f.). It can also mean the embodiment of the form, the person in so far as it comes into view. "The spirit of misfortune . . . has robbed me in sending to me dust and a vain shade instead of your most loved form" (Soph., *El.*, 1156 ff.). Gk. philosophy was concerned with the question of matter and form. Plato presents Socrates as saying that an exact description of the nature of the soul will enable us to see "whether she be single and the same, or, like the *morphē* of the body, multiform. That is what we should call showing the nature of the soul" (*Phdr.*, 271; cf. 103, 104). Aristotle worked out a more precise set of concepts. He distinguished matter (*hylē*) from form (*morphē*, → also *eidos*). Matter has within itself a great number of possibilities for becoming a form and thus becoming manifest as a form. See further Aristot., *Met.*, 990b, 9; 1029a, 29; 1057b, 7; *Phys.*, 187a, 18; *Cat.*, 2b, 7.

These concepts do not imply that form and matter are separable like husk and kernel. Rather they represent different principles and ways of looking at the same object. The outward appearance cannot be detached from the essence of the thing. The essence of the thing is indicated by its outward form.

(b) Similarly, *morphōsis* means embodiment, receiving form; *symmorphos* having the same form; *symmorphizomai* and *symmorphoomai* to take on the same form; and *metamorphoomai* to be transformed (cf. Arndt, 513, 530, 786).

(c) Of special interest is the use of the word in the literature of gnosticism and the Hel. mystery religions. In the first instance, these texts are not to be compared with the accounts of the appearance of the gods in various forms (e.g. Jupiter in mortal form, *specie mortali*, Ovid, *Metamorphoses*, 8, 262). For it is not so much the question of the transformation of the deity into human form (though cf. Phil. 2:6), but that of men into divine form. It is not merely the external appearance that is changed. Rather, the change of the *morphē* involves a change of essential character. According to *Pistis Sophia*, c. 66, one of the emanations changed itself into the form of a great serpent, whilst another changed itself into the form of a basilisk. The meaning of external appearance can even recede behind that of essential character. There is a place where there is neither man nor woman nor even forms, but a perpetual, ineffable light (*Pistis Sophia*, c. 143). "All the very mournful forms he [Uriel] will lead to judgment" (*Sibylline Oracles*, 2, 230). The external appearance is undoubtedly meant not as an antithesis to the essential character, but as the expression of it.

Thus the Hel. mystery religions contain a great number of stories about transformations. The initiate is transformed by dedication and rites into divine substances and so is deified. "I passed into an immortal body, and now I am not what

I was before but am born again in *nous* [mind]" (*Corp. Herm.*, 13, 3). The whole man is affected and not just a part or something in him.

OT 1. *morphē* occurs only rarely in the Gk. translations of the OT. Altogether it appears 9 times for various Heb. or Aram. words: *t^emûnâh* (Job 4:16), *taḇnîṯ* (Isa. 44:13), *ṣ^elēm* (Dan. 3:19). (See further J. Behm, *TDNT* II 749; E. Lohmeyer, *Der Brief an die Philipper*, KEK 9, 1930[8], 91 f.)

The OT spoke of God in anthropological terms. But inevitably men have to speak of God in this way (cf. K. Barth, *CD*, II, 1, 222 f., 264, 286, 369 f.). According to Gen. 18:1 ff., God appeared to Abraham in the form of three men. However, the LXX never used *morphē* to speak of the form of God.

2. Jewish apocalyptic expected in the future a transformation of the present world. But the transformation did not take place in the present. It was something that lay in the future. According to Syr. Bar. 51:1, when the appointed day has passed, the appearance of sinners is transformed. Those who have acted righteously then appear glorified.

NT *morphē* and its cognates occur only rarely in the NT. *morphē* itself in fact occurs only twice. It is remarkable that, apart from Matt. 17:2, Mk. 9:2 and 16:12, the words are confined to the Pauline writings.

1. It is a matter of debate whether Phil. 2:6–11 forms a single unit and whether Paul incorporated into Phil. an already existing hymn. (For a review of this discussion see R. P. Martin, *Carmen Christi: Philippians ii. 5–11 in Recent Interpretation and in the Setting of Early Christian Worship*, 1967, 15–95.) Nevertheless, it can hardly be questioned that these verses do constitute a hymn about Christ in which the expressions *morphē theou* (form of God) and *morphē doulou* (form of a servant, → Slave) occur. Christ is said to have been *en morphē theou* (in the form of God, v. 6). The *en* does not mean that the essential nature of Christ was different from the form (cf. Lohmeyer), as it were an outer shell or a part played by an actor. Rather it means that the essential nature of Christ is defined as divine nature which, by analogy with the Hel. mystery religions is thought of as existing "in" divine substance and power (cf. E. Käsemann, *Exegetische Versuche und Besinnungen*, I, 1960, 51 ff.). Christ is said not only to have been surrounded by divine glory and to have had the same form as God (cf. O. Cullmann, *The Christology of the New Testament*, 1959, 177). "Outside his human nature Christ has no other manner of existing apart from being divine" (L. Cerfaux, *Christ in the Theology of St. Paul*, 1959, 387). Whether this is to be understood in a gnostic sense is doubtful (cf. O. Michel, "Zur Exegese von Phil. 2, 5–11" in *Theologie als Glaubenswagnis, Festschrift Karl Heim*, 1954). It is said of this divine mode of existence that Christ existed in it in the past (*hyparchōn*, being, v. 6). It refers to his pre-existence prior to the incarnation. *en morphē theou* characterizes, therefore, his existence before his earthly life, but not his existence in that earthly life. For he emptied himself (*heauton ekenōsen*, v. 7) taking the "form of a servant" (*morphēn doulou*). This form replaces the "form of God". It is not to be thought of like clothing put over the previous form or as an addition to the pre-existing form. Christ's mode of being was essentially changed. ([Ed.] For other interpretations of this passage → Empty, art. *kenos*, NT 3.)

Christ's mode of existence in his earthly life is described as that of a servant. This has been interpreted in various ways. Lohmeyer and Jeremias see it as a title of

706

honour corresponding to the Servant of the Lord in Isa. 53 (→ Son of God, art. *pais theou*; → Empty, art. *kenos*). E. Schweizer sees it as a picture of righteous suffering (*Lordship and Discipleship*, 1960). In the opinion of the present writer, G. Bornkamm is right when he says that Christ entered upon a mode of existence which is under bondage and serfdom to the rule of cosmic powers and the elements of the world ("On the Understanding of the Christ-hymn (Philippians 2:6–11)", *Early Christian Experience*, 1969, 112–22).

According to G. Friedrich, the Christ-hymn does not contain "great speculations and profound reflections" from which dogmatic formulations can be proved (*Die Kleineren Briefe des Apostels Paulus: Der Brief an die Philipper*. NTD 8, 1962[9], 109). Käsemann sees it simply as the narrative of a continuous succession of events from the pre-existent divine mode of being which Christ gave up to an earthly existence of which the essential character was *douleia* (servitude).

2. Phil. 3:21 is to be understood in a similar way: "who will change [*metaschē-matisei*] our lowly body to be like [*symmorphon*] his glorious body, by the power which enables him even to subject all things to himself." The terms used here recall Phil. 2:6 ff. (cf. G. Strecker, "Redaktion und Tradition im Christushymnus Phil. 2, 6–11", *ZNW* 55, 1964, 63 ff.; E. Güttgemanns, *Der leidende Apostel und sein Herr*, 1966). Possibly it also contains a pre-Pauline tradition. The thought is not that of clothing in the sense of covering the essential character (→ Clothe), but that of the essential transformation of the lowly → body into a completely different one which is a glorified body. *symmorphos* does not mean becoming like, similar or equal. Rather it signifies an existence in Christ whose own mode of *sōma* permeates us without dissolving our own persons (cf. E. Güttgemanns, op. cit.; J. Jervell, *Imago Dei*, 1960). Christ and ourselves are not sharply separated individuals according to the modern understanding of personality. We have our existence in the realm of the power of Christ (→ *schēma*).

Rom. 8:29 declares that, "those whom he foreknew he also predestined to be conformed to the image [*symmorphous tēs eikonos*] of his Son, in order that he might be the firstborn among many brethren." The passage presupposes that Christ is the → image of God. In Christ God is really present. Again *symmorphos* means that we shall not only be similar to or like Christ but that we shall come into the same realm of power as he. We shall be identified with the same substance as he, and enter into the same essential nature as Christ. One might even speak in the same vein as the Hel. mystery religions and speak of a "divinization" or "Christening" (the objection of J. Behm, *TDNT* IV 758, is not fully convincing). Nevertheless, within this relationship Christ retains separate identity ("the firstborn among many brethren", cf. also 2 Cor. 3:18).

Phil. 3:10 relates *symmorphizomai* to the death of Christ: "that I may know him and the power of his resurrection, and may share his sufferings, becoming like him in his death [*symmorphizomenos tō thanatō autou*]." Again the thought is not that of a way of becoming like in the sense that the apostle might through martyrdom become like Jesus on the cross. Rather the apostle in his suffering sees the death of Christ becoming a reality in his own death. The death of Christ acquires a *morphē* in the death of the apostle. The death of Jesus is not simply a historical datum of the past for Paul. It is a present event. Nevertheless, here too Paul and Christ remain two separate personalities. (→ Like.)

3. In Gal. 4:19 Paul speaks of being "in travail until Christ be formed [*morphōthē*] in you." The thought is not that of having correct teaching in contrast to the erroneous teaching of the Galatians (cf. R. Herrmann, "Über den Sinn des *morphousthai Christon en hymin* in Gal. 4, 19," *TLZ* 80, 1955, 713 ff.). It is rather that of coming into the world as a child comes into the world through conception and → birth. Christ himself is to be formed in them in the reality of his being.

Rom. 12:2 declares: "Do not be conformed to this world [*mē syschēmatizesthe tō aiōni toutō*] but be transformed by the renewal of your mind [*alla metamorphousthe tē anakainōsei tou noos*], that you may prove what is the will of God, what is good and acceptable and perfect." This is no mere change of mind or adoption of a new moral outlook. It is a complete transformation and change, a thorough renewal of the whole man. "What is meant is not a theoretical relearning, but the renewal of the will" (R. Bultmann, *Theology of the New Testament*, I, 1952, 211; → Reason, art. *nous*).

4. Rom. 2:20 refers to the Jew as "a corrector of the foolish, a teacher of children, having in the law the embodiment of knowledge and truth [*tēn morphōsin tēs gnōseōs kai tēs alētheias*]." Perhaps this is a reference to a Jewish work of propaganda which contained the word *morphōsis* in its title (cf. O. Michel, *Der Brief an die Römer*, KEK 12, 1963, 88). Knowledge and truth are contained in the law and are really present in it.

5. If the above passages may be understood primarily against the religious background of gnosticism and the mystery cults, other explanations are more probable in the case of the remaining passages. 2 Tim. 3:5 speaks of those "holding the form of piety [*morphōsin eusebeias*] but denying its power." Here the meaning is more of "appearance." The heretics are not really pious; they are only apparently devout.

6. In the longer ending of Mk. Jesus is said to appear "in another form [*en hetera morphē*]" (Mk. 16:12). The question is not raised whether the risen Christ could be recognized as the one he was before his death.

7. The transfiguration narrative (Mk. 9:2 ff.) follows on from Peter's confession of Christ (Mk. 8:27 ff.). It is presented as a divine confirmation of the preceding human confession. Both man and God confess Jesus. The word for "transfigured" in Mk. 9:2 is *metemorphōthē* (cf. Matt. 17:2). Lk. expresses it differently and says that "the appearance of his face became different [*egeneto . . . to eidos tou prosōpou autou heteron*], and his raiment became dazzling white" (Lk. 9:29). Mk. mentions his snow-white clothing, and Matt. his countenance and clothes.   *G. Braumann*

σχῆμα

σχῆμα (*schēma*), outward appearance, form, shape; μετασχηματίζω (*metaschēmatizō*), change the form of, transform, change; συσχηματίζω (*syschēmatizō*), mould, form after; pass. be formed like, be conformed to.

CL *schēma* means: (1) form, shape, figure; (2) appearance, as opposed to reality; (3) bearing, air, mien; (4) fashion, manner; (5) character. Gk. thought did not sharply distinguish between the external and the internal. *schēma* denotes the form that is seen. It could thus denote the role played by an actor which includes its essential character (Plato, *Leg.*, 11, 918e). But the outward form can also be deceptive, and appearance become a sham. *schēma* can thus mean mere appearance as opposed to reality. It can also mean a dancing figure (Plato, *Ion*, 536c), bodily attitude or bearing (Eur., *Medea*, 1039), clothing (Xen., *Cyr.*, 5, 1, 5), and occasionally semblance (Theophrastus, *Historia Plantarum*, 3, 12, 7).

In studying the Gk. word, one has to beware of the modern outlook which would relate *schēma* merely to external things, implying that the essential character was something different. To the Gk. mind, the observer saw not only the outer shell but the whole form with it.

syschēmatizō means not only to conform to the external form, but (from Aristotle onwards) to assume the form of something, to identify oneself essentially with someone else. In the NT it occurs only in the pass.

metaschēmatizō indicates the process by which an object or a person is thoroughly transformed and changed.

ot Jer. 3:17 is the only passage in the LXX where *schēma* has a Heb. equivalent. It refers to the proud bearing of women. 4 Macc. 9:22 uses *metaschēmatizō* to describe the transformation of martyrs at death to immortality. On the other hand, in 1 Sam. 28:8 it means disguise. Saul made himself unrecognizable. The words occur with various shades of meaning in Philo and Josephus (cf. J. Schneider, *TDNT* VII 955 f.).

nt *schēma* occurs only twice in the NT, both instances being in Paul. *syschēmatizō* likewise occurs only twice (once in Paul and once in 1 Pet.). *metaschēmatizō* occurs only in Paul (5 times in the Corinthian correspondence and Phil. 3).

1. On Phil. 2 → above on *morphē* NT 1, and → Empty, art. *kenos* NT 3. Phil. 2:7 declares that: he "emptied himself, taking the form of a servant [*morphēn doulou labōn*], being born in the likeness [*schēmati*] of men." This does not refer to the moral character of this earthly life (Lohmeyer), or to the appearance of Jesus (Dibelius), or to the fact of his humanity, but to the way in which Jesus' humanity appeared (Käsemann), as anyone could see. This is the force of *heuretheis* ("being found").

2. (a) 1 Cor. 7:31 shows how real the *schēma* was for Paul when he declared: "The form of this world is passing away."

(b) Phil. 3:21 depicts the eschatological transformation which comes over Christians. *metaschēmatizō* does not refer to a gnostic identification of the believer with Christ (cf. Güttgemanns), but real participation in the glorified body of Christ (→ *morphē*, NT 2).

(c) Rom. 12:2 (→ *morphē*, NT 3) is not concerned merely with making various concessions to this age, or coming down to the same level. It warns against being absorbed by it, surrendering oneself to it, and falling prey to it. To do so is to yield oneself to its power (cf. 1 Pet. 1:14).

(d) In 1 Cor. 4:6 Paul says: "I have applied [*meteschēmatisa*] all this to myself and to Apollos for your benefit" (RSV). J. Schneider takes the vb. here as expressing "something in another than the expected or customary form" (*TDNT* VII 958). Arndt, however, paraphrases: "I have given this teaching of mine the form of an exposition concerning Apollos and myself" (515).

3. In 2 Cor. 11:13 ff. the thought is not that pseudo-apostles had transformed themselves into apostles, but that they had appeared as apostles and were regarded by some as such. At this time people did not sharply define what constituted an apostle. Paul's opponents called themselves apostles and earnestly presented themselves as such. In the eyes of many, these opponents really were apostles. It was Paul who first called them false apostles. Various forms of *metaschēmatizō* occur 3 times in vv. 13–15. In each case RSV translates it as "disguise." However, the meaning may rather be that Paul ironically describes them as transforming themselves into apostles. The pseudo-apostles really did assume the form of an apostle. They identified themselves with them. They were apostles – but false apostles.

The same applies to Satan. He not only disguises himself as an angel of light and plays at being such. He really identifies himself with an angel of light, and assumes the character. The fact that it is only an appearance is disclosed in v. 15. But this is not due so much to the vb. *metaschēmatizō* as to the insertion of the word *hōs* (as). The servants of Satan present themselves "as" servants of righteousness. *metaschēmatizō* has the same meaning in these passages as it has elsewhere in Paul.

G. Braumann

| ὑπόστασις |

ὑπόστασις (*hypostasis*), (1) substantial nature, substance, essence, actual being; (2) confidence, conviction, steadfastness.

CL 1. The noun is the substantival form of the vb. *hyphistēmi* (to place under), reflexive *hyphistamai* (to stand under). It has a wide range of meanings in both secular Gk. and the LXX.

(a) It is used concretely for what stands under, the basis of something (Sextus Empiricus, *Adversus Mathematicos*, 8, 161, 183; 10, 335); the bottom under water on which one can get a foothold (Aristotle, *Hist. An.*, 551b, 29); the economic basis, the value of property or land (so frequently in the papyri, cf. F. Preisigke, *Wörterbuch der griechischen Papyruskunden*, II, col. 672); treasure, *substantia bonorum operum* (4 Esd. 8:36); life's starting point, the sidereal hour of birth, a military outpost (Nah. 2:7 LXX; 1 Sam. 13:23), garrison (Hdt. 8, 91), seat (for *enedra;* Socrates, *Historia Ecclesiastica*, 3, 7), substance (Pss. 88:48; 138:15 LXX); material substance (Chrysippus, *SVF* II, 503; Arius Didymus, *SVF* II, 163 f., 8 f.); essence (Ps. Sol. 17:24); stock, perhaps even source.

(b) As a human attitude *hypostasis* means putting oneself between, holding one's ground, enduring (Polyb. 4, 50, 10); *anhypostata*, what one cannot withstand (Polyb. 4, 8, 10), e.g. the endurance of torment (Josephus, *Ant.*, 18, 24); a bold venture, enterprise (together with *hormē* [impulse, assault], Aelianus, *Frag*, 56; Diodorus 16, 33, 1) venturing, pledging oneself (Hdt., 9, 34, 2; Eur., *Iph. Aul.*, 360); entering upon a risky undertaking (Diodorus 1, 3, 7; 16, 32, 3; Hdt., 3, 127, 2); constancy (Aristotle, *Metaph.*, 382b, 14). It is also related to hope, confidence (Ez. 19:5 LXX; Ruth 1:12; Polyb., 6, 55, 2; together with *tolma* [boldness, recklessness], resistance, Thuc., 1, 144, 5; 7, 66, 2) and strength to resist (Polyb., 6, 55, 2).

(c) In the physical realm *hypostasis* denotes what sets itself below, dregs (Aristotle, *Part. An.*, 671b, 20; *Metaph.*, 358a, 8; Menander in Socrates, *Historia Ecclesiastica*,

3, 7); residue, sediment (Hippocrates, *Aphorismi*, 4, 69); the sediment in the process of smelting (Polyb., 34, 9, 10 f.; Strabo, 3, 10).

(d) In philosophy *hyphistamai* can mean to be obvious, to show up against, to come into view. It denotes the transition from the latent to the manifest actualization (cf. Wis. 16:21), realization, being a substance, matter, or an object (Plut., *De Communibus Notitiis*, 50, 1085e). It then denotes the immanent Logos (→ word) in matter giving it form. Here the *hypostasis* is to be distinguished from the *hypokeimenon*, the basic primary matter which has not yet been formed. Thus God, as the world-logos, is the *hypostasis* of the world. In Neo-Pythagorean thought → number fulfilled this function (Sextus Empiricus, *ad Math.*, 7, 93). *hypostasis* can thus mean the realization of an intention (Diodorus, 1, 3, 2; Josephus, *Ap.*, 1, 1), the entering into a relationship of matter and quality, without which there can be nothing empirical and no real being. It can also thus mean the actualization of a body (Arius Didymus, *Fr.Phys.*, 2, in H. Diels, *Doxographi Graeci*, 1879, 448, 12.)

2. In view of the above the following basic elements in the word emerge: (a) that which is permanently constituted; (b) the enduring relationship of the particular thing to reality; (c) virtually the same as essence (*ousia*), realization (cf. Aristotle, *Top.*, 2, 4p, 161, 30), especially among the Stoics. *hypostasis* is substantial, concrete being between the merely actual but contingent and the realities that are merely mental.

epinoia (thought) and *emphasis* (appearance) do have *hyparxis* (existence), but not *hypostasis* (reality) (*SVF* III, 26; Diog.Laert., 7, 135; *SVF* III, 267, 3; Seneca, Letter 58; cf. Boethius, *SVF*, II, 332). This distinction evidently originated with Posidonius (*c.* 135–51 B.C.), cf. also the *Oneirocriticus* of Artemidorus (3, 14) in the 2nd cent. A.D.

Reality and appearance were thus opposed (Diog.Laert., 9, 91; Posidonius in Aetius 3, 5 [Diels, op. cit., 371, 27]; Aristotle, *Mund.*, 4, 395a, 30). Time was thought of as *noēma* (thought, concept) and *metron* (measure) but not as *hypostasis* (Antiphon 10, 9; Aetius 1, 22, 6; cf. Diels, op. cit., 3, 18b, 22). Here too belongs Philo who said that the *augē* (light) of fire had no reality or *hypostasis* of itself (*Aet.Mund.*, 88; cf. 92). In the Middle Platonists (*c.* 50 B.C.–A.D. 250) *hypostasis* means the manifestation of the world spirit or world soul. According to Albinus (10, 2p; 167, 17 ff.), there is a *hypostasis* which belongs to being. For the Peripatetics *hypostasis* meant that which gives stability to the concrete, individual thing. It was thus not far removed from *substantia*.

OT The LXX shows how in the Hel. period a complex word like *hypostasis* had become a fashionable term comparable with the word "existence" today. The 20 instances represent 15 different Heb. equivalents, which in itself is something rare. In the 1st and 2nd centuries B.C. *hypostasis* was already a current philosophical term. This may explain its use for so many Heb. words which differ considerably in meaning.

1. In a more general sense it is used as follows: for *mā'ᵃmād*, ground under water on which one can stand (Ps. 68:3 [69:2]); *y*ᵉ*qûm*, living being (Deut. 11:6); *heleḏ*, duration of life (Pss. 38:6 [39:5]; 88:48 [89:47]); *miḥyâh*, food, sustenance (Jdg. 6:4); *kᵉnā'âh*, load, pack (Jer. 10:17); *maṣṣāḇ*, outpost (1 Sam. 14:4); *maṣṣēḇâh*,

pillar (Ezek. 26:11); *ruqqamtî*, lit. I was (when an embryo) woven (Ps.138[139]:15); *tᵉḵûnâh*, arrangement (Ezek. 43:11).

2. It is used in a more philosophical sense for *sôḍ*, council, group of intimates (Jer. 23:22); *maśśā'*, burden (Deut. 1:12); *tôḥeleṭ*, expectation, hope (Ps. 38[39]: 8); and *tiqwâh*, hope (Ezek. 19:5). These last two Heb. equivalents give the term *hypostasis* a new meaning within the compass of scripture. The elements of hope and confidence are important for understanding NT usage.

NT *hypostasis* occurs in the NT only 5 times. The reason for this may well be that, up to the author of Heb., the NT writers were not interested in philosophical trains of thought.

1. 2 Cor. 9:4 says "lest if some Macedonians come with me and find that you are not ready, we be humiliated – to say nothing of you – for being so confident [*en tē hypostasei tautē*, lit. in this *hypostasis*]" (RSV). This interpretation follows that of A. Plummer, *The Second Epistle of St Paul to the Corinthians*, ICC 1915, 255; cf. P. Bachmann, *Der 2. Brief an die Korinther*, 1922⁴, ad loc. H. Lietzmann takes it to mean confidence (*An die Korinther I,II*. HNT 9 1949⁴, 137). Both Lietzmann and Plummer appeal to Ruth 1:12; Ps. 38[39]:8; Ezek. 19:5; Heb. 3:14; 11:1. This meaning is, however, rare. RSV translates *en tautē tē hypostasei tēs kauchēseōs* (2 Cor. 11:17) as "in this boastful confidence." But it may be asked whether the meaning in both passages should not be "enterprise" or "venture".

2. Compared with Paul, the use of *hypostasis* in Heb. is more theologically significant.

(a) The term is important in christology in Heb. 1:3: "He reflects the glory of God and bears the very stamp of his nature [*charaktēr tēs hypostaseōs autou*], upholding the universe by the word of his power" (RSV). H. W. Montefiore translates this as "the exact representation of God's being" (*A Commentary on the Epistle to the Hebrews*, 1964, 35). J. Héring comments: "He is not merely like the Father, He is of the same essence, although subordinate to the Father" (*The Epistle to the Hebrews*, 1970, 5). F. F. Bruce comments: "Just as the glory is really in the effulgence, so the substance (Gk. *hypostasis*) of God is really in Christ, who is its impress, its exact representation and embodiment. What God essentially is, is made manifest in Christ. To see Christ is to see what the Father is like" (*Commentary on the Epistle to the Hebrews*, NLC 1964, 6). He holds that *hypostasis* here means "substance" or "real essence" in contrast to what merely appears to be.

(b) RSV translates Heb. 3:14: "For we share in Christ, if only we hold our first confidence [*tēn archēn tēs hypostaseōs*] to the end." Some manuscripts have *tēn archēn tēs hypostaseōs autou*. This suggests that the copyists of these manuscripts understood the word in the same sense as in Heb. 1:3 and that the thought they intended was to hold to Christ's essential being. The phrase might thus be translated "the basis, his substance." One manuscript, perhaps referring to v. 6 and 1 Tim. 5:12 replaces *hypostaseōs* by *pisteōs* (faith). But the thought of the passage is that of confidence (cf. 1 above; F. F. Bruce, op. cit., 67). The thought is similar to that of patience (6:12) and perseverance (12:1).

(c) From the instances cited so far, it may be seen how different are the uses of *hypostasis* in Heb. The meaning in Heb. 1:3 and 3:14 is not necessarily determinative for Heb. 11:1: "Now faith is the *hypostasis* of things hoped for, the conviction [*elenchos*] of things not seen." The following alternative translations may be considered:

(i) Confidence, expectation, confident trust in what is hoped for. The gen. would thus be understood as an objective gen. This interpretation is adopted by B. Weiss, *Der Brief an die Hebräer*, KEK 1897; E. Riggenbach, *Der Brief an die Hebräer*, 1913; J. Moffatt, *The Epistle to the Hebrews*, ICC 1924; and H. Windisch, *Der Hebräerbrief*, HNT 1931. In favour of this interpretation is Heb. 10:38, where faith and shrinking back are contrasted ("but my righteous one shall live by faith, and if he shrinks back, my soul has no pleasure in him").

(ii) Pledge, security, guarantee, assurance. C. Spicq takes it as the "guarantee of what is hoped for" (*L'Épître aux Hébreux*, II, 1953, 337). Montefiore sees it as "certainty concerning what is hoped for" (op. cit., 185). ARV translates it: "Now faith is assurance of *things* hoped for, a conviction of things not seen" (cf. F. F. Bruce, op. cit., 277). "Faith is confident assurance of the things we hope for" (Arndt, 854). RSV has "assurance."

(iii) Realization, actualization (cf. H. Dörrie, "HYPOSTASIS: Wort- und Bedeutungsgeschichte", *Nachrichten der Akademie der Wissenschaften in Göttingen, philologisch-historische Klasse*, 1955, No. 3; cf. Vulg. *sperandarum substantia rerum*, so also various fathers). Héring takes it as "essence" or "substance" as in 1:3 "In hyperbolic language, which highlights the Christian's absolute certainty that the divine promises will be fulfilled, the writer declares that faith already grasps the substance of what is promised" (op. cit., 98 f.). Riggenbach rejects the idea of a literal realization, however, on the grounds that, "The thought that faith gives a present existence to things hoped for in the future . . . brings faith very close to illusion" (ad loc.).

In support of (i) above, H. Windisch refers to the context, especially the preceding verse, and sees *hypostasis* as a confident reliance in contrast to the idea of shrinking back (*hypostolē*). There, however, the contrast is between *pistis* (→ faith) and *hypostolē*. Heb. 11 proceeds to pile up a series of examples. Faith does not only grasp an event, an act of God like the creation (11:3); it also shows itself in events. The more pleasing sacrifice and walk of Abel, the construction of the ark, the saving of Noah, Abraham's obedience in going forth and life as a sojourner, the sacrifice of Isaac, the blessing of the patriarchs, Moses' severance with the Egyptians, the saving of the firstborn of Israel by the Passover blood, the crossing of the Red Sea, the conquest of Jericho, and the rescue of Rahab – these were all events, saving acts, the history of the people of God, something new and unique on earth. Admittedly, the goal of all the hope still lay ahead. What is reported is not the *komizesthai*, the obtaining, the actual fulfilment of the promises. The people in the account are guarantees of their ultimate realization for the people of God. For this reason those addressed are exhorted not to neglect meeting together (10:25), and to remain with the people of God, in whom faith brings about a new reality and through whom God's deeds are wrought.

It is to be noted in 11:1 that *elenchos ou blepomenōn* ("a proving of [or conviction about] unseen things," Arndt, 248) stands in parallel. This could not be said of mere confidence. The question may be asked, whether *hypostasis* is not to be interpreted in the light of *elenchos*.

Since Heb. 11 follows the pattern of early Jewish enumeration of examples (cf. Wis. 10; Sir. 44–50; 4 Macc. 16:16–23), it must be asked, whether its concept of faith does not come near to that of Judaism. In Judaism a distinction was drawn between $z^e\underline{k}\hat{u}\underline{t}$ *tôrâh* and $z^e\underline{k}\hat{u}\underline{t}$ *'emûnāh* (the righteousness of the law and the righteousness of faith). Both were, therefore, known. Paul gladly made use of the terminology. However, he understood righteousness by the law to be formal, external behaviour, corresponding to the demands of the law. Righteousness by faith likewise corresponded to the divine requirement, but it was characterized and made possible by faith.

It may be noted that throughout Heb. 11 faith is qualified by the instrumental dat. ("by faith . . ."). This faith is seen as the relationship to the commands and promises of God which made possible the acts and behaviour of the person concerned. It is that by which what is hoped for becomes a reality piece by piece in the contemporary world. According to Dörrie, faith brings about things which are not yet there or which are *para physin* (against nature). "Faith bestows on that which we hope for the full certainty of future realization. Faith bestows on what we do not see the full certainty of proof." The word *elpizomenōn* in the expression "things hoped for" is not an objective gen., as if the thing hoped for became real. Rather it is a subjective gen. The thing hoped for works through faith and produces action and attitudes. Thus Abraham hoped for a future city and therefore chose the life of a sojourner. *G. Harder*

→ Empty (for exegesis of Phil. 2), → Image

(a). J. Behm, *morphē*, *TDNT* IV 742–59; G. Bornkamm, "On the Understanding of the Christ-hymn (Philippians 2.6–11)," *Early Christian Experience*, 1969, 112–22; O. Cullmann, *The Christology of the New Testament*, 1963²; G. Kittel, *eidos*, *TDNT* II 373 ff.; D. M. MacKinnon, "Substance in christology – a cross-bench view," in S. W. Sykes and J. P. Clayton, eds., *Christ, Faith and History*, 1972, 279–300; I. H. Marshall, "The Christ-Hymn in Philippians 2:5–11," *TB* 19, 1968, 104–27; R. P. Martin, *Carmen Christi: Philippians ii. 5–11 in Recent Interpretation and in the Setting of Early Christian Worship*, 1967; and *Philippians*, 1959; C. F. D. Moule, "Further Reflections on Philippians 2:5–11," in W. W. Gasque and R. P. Martin, eds., *Apostolic History and the Gospel* (F. F. Bruce Festschrift), 1970, 264–77; J. Schneider, *schēma*, *TDNT* VII 954–58; D. H. Wallace, "A Note on *morphē*," *ThZ* 22, 1966, 19 ff.; R. I. Witt, *"Hypostasis"*, *Amicitiae Corolla* (Festschrift R. Harris), 1933, 319 ff.; commentaries on *2 Corinthians* by A. Plummer (*ICC*), 1915; and P. E. Hughes (*NLC*), 1962; commentaries on *Hebrews* by J. Moffatt (*ICC*), 1924; B. F. Westcott, 1892²; H. W. Montefiore (BNTC) 1964; F. F. Bruce (*NLC*), 1965; J. Héring, 1970.
(b). C. Arpe, "Substantiae," *Philologus*, 1940, 65 ff.; P. Bachmann, *Der 2. Brief an die Korinther*, 1922⁴; H. Cremer and J. Kögel, *Biblisch-theologisches Wörterbuch der neutestamentlichen Gräzität*, 1923¹¹ (s.v. *hypostasis*); M. Dibelius, *An die Philipper*, HNT 11, 1937³; R. Deichgräber, *Gotteshymnus und Christushymnus in der frühen Christenheit*, 1967; H. Dörrie, *Hypostasis. Wort- und Bedeutungsgeschichte*, Nachdrücke der Akademie der Wissenschaften, Göttingen, 1955, 35 ff.; and "Zu Hebr. 11, 1," *ZNW* 46, 1955, 196 ff.; E. Grässer, *Der Glaube im Hebräerbrief*, 1965; E. Güttgemanns, *Der leidende Apostel und sein Herr*, 1966; J. Hempel, *Gott und Mensch im Alten Testament*, 1936; J. Jervell, *Imago Dei*, 1960; E. Käsemann, "Kritische Analyse von Phil. 2, 5–11," *ZTK* 47, 1950, 313 ff. (= *Exegetische Versuche und Besinnungen*, I, 1960, 51 ff.); E. Lohmeyer, *Der Brief an die Philipper*, KEK 9, 1930⁸; W. F. Otto, *Die Götter Griechenlands*, 1929; R. Reitzenstein, *Die hellenistischen Mysterienreligionen*, 1927²; E. Riggenbach, *Der Brief an die Hebräer*, 1922³; A. Schlatter, *Der Glaube im Neuen Testament*, 1927⁴, 614 ff.; and *Paulus, der Bote Jesu*, 1938⁴; C. Spicq, *L'Épître aux Hebreux*, II, 1953; G. Strecker, "Redaktion und Tradition im Christushymnus Phil. 2, 6–11," *ZNW* 55, 1964, 63 ff.; H. F. Weber, *Eschatologie und Mystik im Neuen Testament*, 1930; B. Weiss, *Der Brief an die Hebräer*, KEK 13, 1897⁶; H. Windisch, *Der Hebräerbrief*, HNT 14, 1931².

Freedom

ἐλευθερία

ἐλευθερία (*eleutheria*), freedom, liberty; ἐλεύθερος (*eleutheros*), free, independent, not bound; ἐλευθερόω (*eleutheroō*), to free, set free; ἀπελεύθερος (*apeleutheros*), freedman.

CL The noun *eleutheria* is derived from the adj. *eleutheros*. O. Schrader derives it from the Indo-Germanic **leudh-*, belonging to the people, and thus not subject. It is connected with Lat. *liber* (free), and Schrader links it with Old High German *liut*, Modern German *Leute*, people (*Reallexikon der indogermanischen Altertumskunde*, II 1929², 454 f.; but cf. Liddell–Scott, 532). In so far as a man belongs to the people, he is a free citizen as contrasted with a slave or foreigner. *eleutheria* thus means freedom, independence, in the sense of being independent of others, being able to dispose. This way of speaking arose originally in contrast to the bondage of → slaves. Similarly, the adj. *eleutheros* means free, not bound, of free birth. It also indicates someone who is his own master. Later the noun and the adj. could occasionally be used to denote the mental attitude which makes use of freedom. It could be used (as it mostly was) in the good sense of noble, being in control of oneself, magnanimous, generous. But it could also be used in the less frequent and bad sense of being reckless, or unrestrained. The adj *apeleutheros* follows the original sense and denotes a freedman, one who is not free by birth. This was basic to the Gk. idea. The corresponding vb. *eleutheroō* means to free, to set free, but not exclusively in relation to slaves. It could also refer to freeing someone from any bond which prevented them from acting freely.

1. In secular Gk. *eleutheros* has primarily a political sense. The *eleutheros* is the full citizen who belongs to the *polis*, the city state, in contrast to the slave who did not enjoy full rights as a citizen. Freedom consists in his right to participate fully in public debates over civic matters. It is the right of free speech, *parrhēsia* → openness, boldness, frankness. He can decide about his own affairs within the *polis*. On numerous occasions, Aristotle spoke of the Gk. *polis* as the community of the free. He considered freedom to be the essential good of the *polis*. But in order to preserve this freedom, the → law (*nomos*) is required as the principle of order. Freedom and law are thus not contradictory opposites. They belong together and qualify each other. The constant danger is rejection of the law in the name of a misconceived freedom which is purely arbitrary, because it is willing to grant itself more freedom than it is willing to grant to others. This idea of freedom was naturally applied to relations between states which gave rise to the idea of sovereignty. (See further H. Schlier, *TDNT* II 487–92.)

2. In Stoic philosophy this political idea of freedom was transformed through the collapse of the *polis* and the corresponding idea of society. Freedom was understood in a philosophical and religious sense. For the Stoic, man in the last analysis was not in control of external things, like the body, money, honour, and political freedom. *eleutheria* therefore means rather withdrawal from the apparent reality of this world. It signifies an asceticism not found in the NT. It is a deliberate surrender to the law and rule of the cosmos, or the deity that rules the cosmos. This means that man must free himself from whatever binds him too closely to the world: his passions (such as anger, anxiety and pity) and the fear of death. Freedom means that a man must be so adjusted and detached that he lives in complete

715

harmony with the cosmos or the gods (Epict., *Dissertationes*, 4, 1, 89 f.). He thus masters himself completely and transcends the cosmos in his inner self. This freedom must be perpetually renewed through constant struggle and unending effort. (See further H. Schlier, *TDNT* II 493–96.)

3. The mystery religions had their own answer to the question of freedom. Through the cultic rites, the initiate was freed from this hopeless world and obtained a part in the destiny of the deity (→ Knowledge, art. *ginōskō*; G. Wagner, *Pauline Baptism and the Pagan Mysteries*, 1967).

OT 1. In the LXX, *eleutheria* and its cognates are used only in the context of → slavery (Exod. 21:2, 5, 27; Lev. 19:20; Deut. 15:12 f.; and often), prisoners of war (Deut. 21:14), and once with reference to exemption from obligations (1 Sam. 17:25). It is striking that it is not found in connection either with the liberation of Israel from Egypt or the return of Israel from exile. The political use of *eleutheria* is apparently foreign to the LXX. Saul's proclamation of rewards to the victor over Goliath included making "his father's house free in Israel" (1 Sam. 17:25). The *ḥōrîm* were "nobles" (RSV) and are called *eleutheroi*, free (1 Ki. 21:8, 11; cf. Neh. 13:17; Jer. 36[29]:2). These references indicate that under the monarchy the Israelites were not free subjects, but were the king's slaves (1 Sam. 8:10–18). Only a few privileged men stood out as free. Everything here belongs to the general context of slavery.

The question of slavery in Israel is to be understood in the context of Yahweh's lordship over his people. Through the ordinances that he has given to his people, Yahweh protects the helpless and weak, including the slaves. Deut. 15:13 ff. relates Yahweh's intervention on behalf of slaves to the liberation of Egypt from Israel. An enslaved Israelite could never become a person's property in Israel. After six years he was to be set free without payment (Ex. 21:2 ff.). According to Deut. 15:12 ff., the owner was even under obligation to make material provision for him as he went. Jer. 34:8 ff. (see especially v. 11) indicates that there were those in Israel who wanted to follow the pattern in the surrounding nations of keeping slaves for life. Because of these social injustices, Jeremiah derisively proclaimed to Israel "liberty to the sword, to pestilence, and to famine" (34:17; cf. Amos 2:6–16; 8:1 ff. etc.).

2. However, the conclusion should not be drawn from the narrow range of meaning of these words that the problem of freedom did not exist for Israel. Rather, Israel's freedom, and that of its individual members, was not considered as a subject separate from the redeeming and saving acts of God. Freedom for Israel meant being set free by Yahweh, as e.g. from bondage in Egypt (Exod. 20:2; Deut. 7:8). Thus it was identical with → redemption. It was not given by nature, but was always experienced as the gracious gift of God.

The fact that Israel, even as a political entity, existed on the basis of this act of liberation has several consequences.

(a) The gift of freedom remained bound to the giver. Desertion of Yahweh had the necessary consequence of loss of freedom. This is shown by the era of the judges which was an age of falling away from Yahweh, slavery, repentance and liberation (Jdg. 2:1 ff.). The history of the northern and southern kingdoms was similar. The Assyrian conquest was the consequence of the godlessness of the

716

northern kingdom (2 Ki. 17:7–23), just as the Babylonian captivity was the consequence of the godlessness of the southern kingdom (2 Ki. 21:10–15; 22:19 f.; 23:25 ff.). The end of Israel's political freedom found intensely moving expression in the Lamentations of Jeremiah.

(b) The acts of God are fundamental to communal human life. "According to the Decalogue, freedom belongs, like life (Exod. 20:13), marriage (20:14), honour (20:16) and possessions (20:17), to the basic rights of man which Yahweh gives to, and maintains for, his covenant-people; for Exod. 20:15 originally forbad kidnapping" (E. Fahlbusch following A. Alt in *EKL* I, 1374). This high regard for freedom was extended to the stranger (Exod. 22:20–23:9; Lev. 19:33 f.) and to the slave (see above 1). The escaped slave was even to be afforded protection from his former master (Deut. 23:15 f.).

(c) The struggle to preserve this freedom, wrought by Yahweh and bound to him, played a repeated and significant role in the message of the prophets who developed it in their own particular ways (Isa. 1:23; 10:1–4; Jer. 7:5 f.; Amos 2:6 f.; 4:1 ff.; 5:7, 11 ff.; Mic. 3:1–3; 7:3; cf. G. von Rad, *Old Testament Theology*, II, 80 ff.). Enslavement by the nobility of whole strata of society which were originally free is a breach of divine law. The promise is given to those that are bound that the Messiah will come "to proclaim liberty to the captives and the opening of the prison to those that are bound" (Isa. 61:1).

3. In later Judaism and at the time of Jesus freedom was understood predominantly in an external, political sense (cf. the typical misunderstanding in Jn. 8:33). Freedom movements with a religious basis were repeatedly formed with the intention of implementing the promised freedom by force against the pagan secular authorities. The best known of these were the Maccabaeans in the second century B.C. who wanted to ensure religious freedom by political freedom, and the Zealots at the time of Jesus (cf. Acts 5:37; 21:38).

NT 1. (a) In the NT *eleutheria* occurs 11 times (7 in Paul and twice each in Jas. and the letters of Pet.), *eleutheros* 23 times (16 in Paul, twice in Jn., 3 times in Rev. and once each in Matt. and 1 Pet.), *eleutheroō* 7 times (5 in Paul and 2 in Jn.), and *apeleutheros* only at 1 Cor. 7:22. The words are thus found chiefly in Paul (especially in Rom. 6–8; 1 Cor. 7–10; and Gal. 2–5) and Jn. 8:32–36. They are entirely absent from the synoptic vocabulary, apart from Matt. 17:26.

(b) NT usage exhibits some interesting nuances. *eleutheria* is never used in the secular sense of political freedom. From this it may be inferred that the recovery of Israel's political freedom no longer played any part in the thinking of the NT writers. Jesus was no political messiah. The NT also dissociates itself from the idea of freedom as power to do with oneself and one's life whatever one wants. *eleutheria* is to be seen in the light of "the glorious liberty of the children of God" (Rom. 8:21). It is present "where the Spirit of the Lord is" (2 Cor. 3:17). The term means "the freedom which we have in Christ Jesus" (Gal. 2:4), the freedom for which "Christ has set us free" (Gal. 5:1). When Jas. 1:25 and 2:12 speak of "the law of freedom", *eleutheria* means the new way of life in which man lives in accordance with the will of God. Even the vb. *eleutheroō* is used in the NT exclusively for the act which occurs or has occurred through Jesus: "The truth will make you free" (Jn. 8:32), "having been set free from sin" (Rom. 6:18, cf. 22).

On the other hand, *eleutheros* has mostly the secular sense of being free in contrast to being a slave (Gal. 3:28; Eph. 6:8; Col. 3:11; Rev. 6:15), or being independent with regard to a law (Rom. 7:3). Gal. 4:22 f. is thus used with a double meaning and leads in Gal. 4:26, 31; 5:1 to the specifically NT idea of being free in Christ. The characteristic of this free man is not the contrast with the slave but the fact that, as a free man, he is at the same time the slave of Christ (1 Pet. 2:16; 1 Cor. 9:19; cf. Paul's self-designation in Rom. 1:1; Phil. 1:1). The *apeleutheros kyriou* (freedman of the Lord) is at the same time the *doulos Christou* (slave of Christ) (1 Cor. 7:22).

2. (a) What does freedom mean? In contrast to the secular Gk. mind, the NT sees man as basically unfree (Rom. 6:20; 2 Pet. 2:19; Jn. 8:39). It denies him all possibility of being able to free himself and order his life, as if he were not in bondage. Man's perennial efforts to take himself in hand, however he attempts it, lead to the greatest bondage in which man misses what he was meant to be (Matt. 16:25; Jn. 12:15). Man's true freedom does not consist of the unfettered power to direct his life, either in a political or in a Stoic sense. It lies in life with God, lived as it was originally intended by God for man (Rom. 6:22; Gal. 5:1, 13; 1 Pet. 2:16). He only gains this as he denies himself (Matt. 16:24). Paradoxically, the free man does not belong to himself (1 Cor. 16:19; 9:19; 1 Pet. 2:16). He belongs to him who has set him free (Rom. 6:18, 22; Gal. 5:1), "who for their sake died and was raised" (2 Cor. 5:15). The NT idea of freedom thus follows on from the OT. The gift of freedom is bound to the giver. "For all things are yours . . . and you are Christ's and Christ is God's" (1 Cor. 3:21, 23). This subjection is at the same time an alliance. Its realm even extends to the supernatural powers and rulers which are robbed of their absolute authority, because they have been conquered by Christ and can no longer separate man from Christ (Rom. 8:38; Gal. 4:3, 9; 1 Cor. 15:24). The impenetrable horizon becomes transparent in the light of this freedom.

(b) What is man freed from? Man is bound in that he is subject to the powers of this age (→ Time, art. *aiōn*; cf. Eph. 6:12; Matt. 17:18; Lk. 13:16; 1 Pet. 5:8). The NT idea of freedom goes far beyond that of the OT in that it sees freedom as liberation from the manifold powers which suppress true humanity: sin (Rom. 6:18–22; 8:2 ff.; Jn. 8:31–36); → Satan (Matt. 12:22; Lk. 13:16; Eph. 6:12); the → law (Rom. 7:3–6; 8:3; Gal. 2:4; 4:21–31; 5:1–13); and → death (Rom. 6:20–23; 8:21). It is a liberation from the → "old man" (Rom. 6:6; Eph. 4:22; Col. 3:9).

Sin in the NT is not a single act which with time may pass and disappear. It has a permanent and irrevocable bondage as its consequence for the man who once lends himself to it (2 Pet. 2:19). He is no longer free to serve God; he is compelled to sin. Man is meant to be free from this compulsion. But there is no magical insurance against sin. The believer is called to a constant struggle with sin (Rom. 6:12, 19; 1 Cor. 6:18 f.; Eph. 6:10 ff.; and often). He is even exposed to the tempter (2 Cor. 2:11; 1 Thess. 3:5) and remains sinful. Side by side with the indicative statement that "we have died to sin" (Rom. 6:2) there is the imperative to give no room to sin (6:12) and to live in Christ to God (6:11). These statements are not in contradiction. The imperative follows on from the indicative.

As liberation from the compulsion to sin, *eleutheria* (Rom. 6:14, 18) opens up the hitherto impossible possibility of serving God (cf. Jas. 1:25; 2:12). What previously separated God and man, and thus stood in the way of true humanity, is removed.

The OT law declared to man God's irrevocable intention of leading him to life in fellowship with God (Rom. 7:10; 10:5). But in fact it had the opposite effect, because it prompted man more than ever to sin (Rom. 7:7–13) and revealed his profound godlessness (Rom. 5:20; Gal. 3:19). Hence, there is no one just who can stand before God's law (Rom. 3:19 ff., 23). What was to serve as man's way of salvation became a curse to him (Gal. 3:10; Rom. 7:10). Christ has freed man from this curse (Gal. 3:13). However, the fact that man may be free from the law does not mean that the law is completely set aside (Rom. 3:31; 6:15; Matt. 5:17). It remains for the believer the expression of God's holy will (Rom. 7:12, 14; Matt. 5:18 f.), which is now to find its fulfilment in love (Jn. 13:34 f.; Gal. 5:13 f.). But it is no longer the impossible way to life. As a way of salvation, the law had its end in Christ (Rom. 10:4). Man who lives in servitude under the law (Gal. 4:3) can through Christ (v. 5) live as a son and heir (v. 7). Therefore, anyone who tries to resurrect the law as a way of salvation by trying to fulfil its demands stands under a curse (Gal. 1:8 f.; 2:18 f.; 3:1–5; 5:11 ff.).

Death is the harvest which man reaps from his life under sin and the law (Rom. 6:21, 23; 7:10 f., 23 f.; 1 Cor. 15:56). Death has a double meaning in that it denotes death in time and in eternity (Rom. 8:6). Just as Rom. 6 presents freedom from sin, and Rom. 7 freedom from the law, Rom. 8 follows the sequence by presenting freedom from death (cf. 1 Cor. 15:26). The thought here, as in the case of these other powers, is not their utter abolition, but liberation from the inevitability of their compulsion and claim. Christians must also die. But for them the sting of death is removed (1 Cor. 15:55), because they know of the resurrection of Christ as the pledge of their own resurrection. Freedom from death means that man is promised and assured of a future which lies in Christ beyond himself and his own death. The certainty that nothing more can stand between him and God (Rom. 8:38 f.) and that death in all its finality is overcome can liberate man from the fear of death. It is no longer the utter annihilation of his existence.

(c) The means of freedom. The liberation of man does not lie within the realm of his own capacities. It does not come about by man's reflection on himself, an act of the will, or by any deed of this sort or that. For this reason there is in the NT no summons to contend for freedom. It is already given in what Christ has done for us (Gal. 5:1). Only the son can open up the possibility of existence in *eleutheria* (Jn. 8:36). It is realized by him in the event of the cross (Gal. 3:13). But for man it only becomes a present reality, when he opens his life to the call of the gospel (2 Cor. 5:20 f.). This comes about when proclamation leads to faith and to an abiding bond to Christ and his word (Jn. 8:31 f.; Rom. 10:14 ff). The Christian message of Christ's liberating act on the cross summons man from the only possible way of life open to him *kata sarka*, after the flesh, i.e. according to human standards and thinking. It calls him to live now *kata pneuma*, according to the → Spirit (Rom. 8:12 f.; Gal. 6:8). True freedom exists only where the Holy Spirit works in a man, becoming the principle of his life, and where man does not block his working (2 Cor. 3:17; Rom. 8:1 ff.; Gal. 5:18).

(d) The goal of freedom. This freedom can be misused as "a pretext for evil" (1 Pet. 2:16). This occurs where freedom is misunderstood in the Gk. sense of man

719

being the master of all his decisions. This leads to libertinism or antinomianism instead of serving one's neighbour (Gal. 5:13 f.). The man who is truly free shows his freedom in being free for the service of God (1 Thess. 1:9), → righteousness (Rom. 6:18 ff.), and his fellow man (1 Cor. 9:19; Jas. 1:25). "For the love of Christ controls us" (1 Cor. 5:14). The man who is free is a *doulos Christou*, a slave of Christ (1 Cor. 7:22; Rom. 1:1; Phil. 1:1). As Luther put it, "A Christian is a perfectly free lord of all, subject to none. A Christian is a perfectly dutiful servant of all, subject to all" (*The Freedom of a Christian* [1520], cf. J. Dillenberger, ed., *Martin Luther: Selections from his Writings*, 1961, 53). This service can take many forms (Gal. 5:22; 1 Cor. 9:19 ff.). The ultimate decisive factor is that it should be done in love (1 Cor. 13). The deeper a man penetrates into the "law of liberty", the more free he becomes for such action (Jas. 1:25; 2:12).

(e) The political demand for freedom. Strangely enough to modern man, political freedom plays a quite subordinate role in the NT. Jesus unambiguously swept aside all misunderstanding here. He and his kingdom do not live by this external freedom. Otherwise, it would not have been so readily abandoned (Jn. 19:36). Even in those places where Jesus stressed his earthly authority (Matt. 28:18), no conclusions were drawn about claims for political freedom. He disappointed all the late Jewish expectation of a political messiah. His teaching had a quite different aim. The kind of freedom he preached was that which comes through returning to the Father – not freedom with regard to men (Matt. 4:17; Lk. 24:47; Jn. 8:34 ff. and often).

For the Christian, freedom is no longer a highest good (Heb. 13:14) which, if need be, is justified by resort to war and force. He knows of a freedom in Christ in which he can live even while the world and mankind remain unchanged, although it is often hidden among sufferings (Jn. 8:31, 38; Rom. 8:18–23).

At the same time, the fact cannot be ignored that within the church, as with the prophets, there was a move towards freedom in the sense of equal rights for all. The old distinctions which reflected the environment of the ancient world between the free man and the slave (cf. Phlm.), and the behaviour of men and women (1 Cor. 14:34 following on from OT law), still remained. Yet in the last analysis such distinctions are invalid (Gal. 3:28; 1 Cor. 12:13; Col. 3:11). The freedom granted by God was given to operate above all in the communal life of the people of God. For the Christian → church is the community of free men (Gal. 4:21–31).

J. Blunck

→ Courage, → Election, → Openness

(a). K. Barth, *CD* III, 4 (dealing with "The command of God the Creator" in relation to various aspects of freedom); S. G. F. Brandon, *Jesus and the Zealots*, 1967; R. Bultmann, *Theology of the New Testament*, I, 1952, 330–52; and "The Significance of the Idea of Freedom for Western Civilization," *Essays*, 1955, 305–25; H. von Campenhausen, *Ecclesiastical Authority and Spiritual Power in the Church of the First Three Centuries*, 1969; *Concilium* 6, 10, 1974 (whole volume devoted to "Liberation and Faith"); O. Cullmann, *The State in the New Testament*, 1957; C. H. Dodd, *The Gospel and the Law of Christ*, 1947; W. Eichrodt, *Theology of the Old Testament*, II. 1967 (see index); R. Guardini, *Freedom, Grace and Destiny*, 1961; M. Hengel, *Was Jesus a Revolutionist?*, 1971; *Victory over Violence*, 1973; and *Judaism and Hellenism*, I–II, 1974; C. Johansson, *Concepts of Freedom in the Old Testament*, 1965; E. Käsemann, *Jesus Means Freedom*, 1969; and "The Cry for Liberty in the Worship of the Church," *Perspectives on Paul*, 1971, 122–37; J. Kosnetter, "Freedom," *EBT* I 280–86; H. Küng, *The Church and Freedom*, 1965; Martin

Luther, *The Freedom of a Christian* (1520) in *Luther's Works*, 31, 1957, 327–77 (also in other editions); J. Moltmann, *Theology and Joy*, 1973; J. C. Murray, *The Problem of Religious Freedom*, 1965; G. von Rad, *Old Testament Theology*, II, 1965 (see index); K. Rahner, "Freedom in the Church," *Theological Investigations*, II, 1963, 89–107; and *Free Speech in the Church*, 1959; A. Richardson, *The Political Christ*, 1973; H. Schlier, *eleutheria*, *TDNT* II 487–502; Schürer I (see index); H. Thielicke, *Theological Ethics*, I, 1968; II, 1969 (see indexes).

(b). K. Barth, *Das Geschenk der Freiheit*, 1953; O. Betz, *Gefährliche Freiheit*, 1961; G. Bornkamm, "Christliche Freiheit," *Paulus Studien*, BEvTh 16, 1952, 133 ff.; W. Brandt, *Freiheit im Neuen Testament*, 1932; H. von Campenhausen and G. Bornkamm, *Bindung und Freiheit in der Ordnung der Kirche*, 1959; E. Dinkler, "Zum Problem der Ethik bei Paulus (1. Kor. 6, 1–11)," *ZTK* 49, 1952, 167 ff.; R. Egenter, *Von der Freiheit der Kinder Gottes*, 1949; E. Fahlbusch, "Freiheit," *EKL* I 1371 ff.; E. Fuchs, *Die Freiheit des Glaubens, Röm. 5–8 ausgelegt*, BEvTh 14, 1949; and "Freiheit," *RGG*[3] II 1101 ff.; H. Gollwitzer, *Forderungen der Freiheit; Aufsätze und Reden zur politischen Ethik*, 1964[2]; E. Grässer, "Freiheit und apostolisches Wirken bei Paulus," *EvTh* 15, 1955, 333 ff.; M. Hengel, *Die Zeloten*, 1961; W. Joest, *Das Problem des Tertius Usus Legis und die neutestamentliche Paränese*, 1951; H. Jonas, *Augustin und das paulinische Freiheitsproblem*, 1930; E. Käsemann, *Exegetische Versuche und Besinnungen*, I, 1964[3], 263 ff.; S. Lyonnet, *Liberté chrétienne et loi nouvelle selon S. Paul*, 1954; C. Maurer, "Glaubensbindung und Gewissensfreiheit im Neuen Testament," *ThZ* 17, 1961, 107–17; O. Michel, "Der antike und der christliche Freiheitsbegriff," *Universitas* 1, 1946, 1–17; J. Michl, *Freiheit und Bindung: Eine zeitgemässe Frage im Lichte des Neuen Testaments*, 1950; M. Müller, "Freiheit," *ZNW* 25, 1926, 177 ff.; K. Niederwimmer, *Der Begriff der Freiheit im Neuen Testament*, 1966; F. Nötscher, "Schicksal und Freiheit," *Biblica* 40, 1959, 446–62; and "Schicksalsglaube in Qumran und Umwelt," *BZ* 3, 1959, 205–34; H. Ridderbos, "Vrijheid en wet volgens Paulus' brief aan de Galater," *Arcana Revelata* (F. W. Grosheide Festschrift), 1951, 89–103; K. H. Schelkle, "Erwählung und Freiheit im Römerbrief nach der Auslegung der Väter," *ThQ* 131, 1951, 17–31 and 189–207; K. Stalder, *Das Werk des Geistes in der Heiligung bei Paulus*, 1961; C. Spicq, *Charité et liberté dans le Nouveau Testament*, 1961; and *Théologie morale du Nouveau Testament*, II, 1965, 623–64; R. Zorn, *Das Problem der Freiheit*, 1952.

Fruit, Fig, Thorn, Thistle

	καρπός (*karpos*), fruit; καρποφορέω (*karpophoreō*),
καρπός	bear fruit; ἄκαρπος (*akarpos*), unfruitful, fruitless.

CL In secular Gk. *karpos* (cf. Lat. *carpo*, pluck) is used especially of the fruit of the ground (Homer), but also often of the offspring of animals (Xenophon). It is also found in an extended sense for the result of an undertaking, whether good or ill: the outcome, consequence (Philo, Marcus Aurelius).

OT In the LXX *karpos* stands chiefly for the Heb. *perî* which in the OT is used for the fruit of plants (e.g. Deut. 1:25; Mal. 3:11), but also for the fruit of the body, posterity (e.g. Gen. 30:2; Deut. 7:13; Mic. 6:7; Ps. 21:11). Finally it is used metaphorically for the fruit of an action (e.g. Hos. 10:13; Jer. 6:19; 17:10).

This last use was taken over especially in late Judaism. The righteous man brings forth good fruit; the unrighteous brings forth bad fruit. Commercial language utilized *perî* and *karpos* in the sense of interest (as the fruit of a transaction), as also did theology with its growing emphasis on belief in the beyond. Thus in discussing sin, a distinction was drawn between the original stock or capital (so-called original sin; Heb. *qeren*) and interest (individual sins). Punishment of the former was reserved for the beyond; the latter was punished here and now, partly through giving birth to ever new sins to plague mankind.

721

NT 1. *Primary Meaning.* (a) *karpos* occurs in the NT 66 times, mostly in Matt. and hardly at all in the Pastoral and Catholic Epistles except Jas. It has its primary, simple meaning as the fruit of plants (Matt. 21:19 par.; 13:8 par.; Lk. 12:17) or the produce of the earth (Jas. 5:7, 18; cf. Lk. 20:10). Passages like Jas. 5 make it clear that man can prepare for and encourage the growth of fruit by his labours, but he can expect and receive it only as a gift. The → seed and harvest are bestowed upon him. To what extent the growth of fruit is removed from human will-power is also shown by the fact it ripens at its appointed time (→ *kairos*) (Matt. 21:34). Its form is not optional, but is determined from the first by the seed (cf. 1 Cor. 15:35 ff.), so that one may reason back from the fruit to the plant (Matt. 12:33 par.; cf. 7:16, 20). This applies not only to the species but to quality. Matt. especially contrasts good fruit (*karpous kalous*) with bad fruit (*karpous ponērous*) (Matt. 3:10; 7:17–19) or rotten fruit (*karpon sapron*) (Matt. 12:33; cf. Lk. 6:43). The point is to show that fruit which does not come up to expectation is useless and that which bears it (the tree, Matt. 7:19; Lk. 3:9; 13:6 ff.) is designated as unusable.

(b) *karpos* in the sense of fruit of the body, offspring, is found only in the Lucan writings (Lk. 1:42; Acts 2:30).

2. *Extended Meaning.* The passages under 1 (a) are not concerned with the picture of the processes of nature but with man before God. This applies even more to the remaining passages in which the idea of fruit is applied to man's life. These are often connected with the verbs *poiein* (do) and *pherein* (bear, bring forth). The verbal compound *karpophorein* (bear fruit) occurs 8 times in the Synoptics and Paul.

(a) When, according to the Synoptics, John the Baptist demanded good deeds from men as fruit of repentance (Matt. 3:8 par.), the use of the term fruit expressly indicates that it is not a question of deliberate, self-determined action on man's part. Rather it is that "fruit-bearing" which follows from his turning to God and the power of the Spirit working in him. When Jesus taught that true disciples are recognized as such precisely by their fruits (Matt. 7:16 ff.) which they bear in true discipleship, the meaning is that their faith shows itself alive in their love. In receiving divine love, they will love; in receiving forgiveness, they will forgive. In short, the sanctification which has come to them and is going on in them is expressed by their giving God the honour. At the same time they put at the disposal of others the benefit of the divine working in them through what they do and say. The graphic pronouncement, that every tree without fruit will be condemned in the judgment of God (Matt. 3:10; 7:19; Lk. 13:6), also raises the question of the outworking of faith in the man who has received the word. Those who check the growth of fruit or even hold back others from enjoying it have their deserts set before them.

(b) In Jn. the expression *karpon pherein* (bear fruit) is used especially in Jn. 15:2 ff., where Jesus' disciples' close fellowship with the Lord is seen as the secret of the power to bear fruit. His death is the soil out of which rich fruit grows (Jn. 12:24); his death on the cross brings about redemption for men. As the vine (i.e. here the tree of life), he sends through his branches that life-giving power which is the prerequisite and means of faith. Man can indeed accomplish moral and technical achievements by his natural gifts. But the "fruit of the gospel" (Luther) – that which God expects from man – can grow only from the soil of obedience, which

722

essentially consists in recognition of the bond between creator and creature, established by the death of Christ. He no longer needs to consider his own achievements. Freed from the anxiety of failure, he is capable of the highest endeavour ("more fruit", Jn. 15:2, 5 8). Because the source of his capacity to bear fruit lies outside himself, the yield is certain. It counts and abides for eternal life (Jn. 4:36; 15:16).

(c) Paul recognizes the good deed as the fruit of faith, righteousness (*karpos dikaiosynēs*, Phil. 1:11; so too Heb. 12:11; Jas. 3:18) and light (*tou phōtos*, Eph. 5:9), produced by God himself, Jesus Christ or the Holy Spirit. Paul sharply distinguishes it from man's own striving to attain salvation (Gal. 5:22; Col. 1:10). The term *ergon* (→ work) which comes from the world of techniques and craftsmanship, signifying what man produces by his own efforts, is used comparatively seldom in a positive sense. On the other hand, *karpos* which comes from the realm of natural growth signifies that which grows as a matter of course, drawing on the life-giving power of the tree or soil (cf. *automatē*, of itself, Mk. 4:28). But this growth (→ Grow) as a sign of → life does not lie at man's disposal. In using this term, Paul wishes to stress that in those who have been received into the body of Christ, in whom the Spirit of Christ is active and who have a share in the gifts of this living fellowship, the outworking – the fruit – appears naturally, because it is not something manufactured. While believers in Christ thus bring their fruit to God and live for him, the power of sinful desires can only bear fruit for death (Rom. 7:4 f.).

(d) Where fruit is lacking, the NT uses – apart from its metaphorical use in Jude 12 – the adj. *akarpos*, unfruitful, fruitless, barren, unproductive (e.g. Mk. 4:19 par.; Tit. 3:14; 2 Pet. 1:8). *akarpos* is used to describe the works of darkness (Eph. 5:11) and also the state of the mind when prayer is made in tongues (1 Cor. 14:14).

(e) While *karpos* is widely used to express the outworking of faith in the witness and conduct of the individual and the church (→ Walk), Paul uses it in a further sense for the results of his own missionary work (Rom. 1:13; Phil. 1:22). It can even be understood in the sense that the apostles and, in particular, missionaries who are building up the churches by their labours "live by their fruits". They have a claim on maintenance by the churches (1 Cor. 9:7; 2 Tim. 2:6). In these passages – as in Matt. 21:41 ff.; Lk. 20:10 – fruit is seen as wages (cf. also Jn. 4:36).

(f) *karpos* occurs twice in Rev. 22:2. The picture of the tree of life, bearing fruit each month, represents the fullness of God's pervading presence in the new world, where shame and sin are overcome and all hindrances to the activity of the divine Spirit are removed. *R. Hensel*

| συκῆ | συκῆ (*sykē*), fig, *Ficus Carica*, both the tree and the fruit. |

CL The forms *sykea* and *sykē* are both found, and can refer to the resin of the pine or fir, as well as to the fig tree.

OT *sykē* is widely used in the LXX for the Heb. *tᵉēnâh* for the tree, its fruit and its leaves (Gen. 3:7; Num. 13:24), especially as characteristic of the fruitfulness of the promised land (Deut. 8:8). *sykē* has wide parabolic (cf. Jdg 9:10) and figurative extensions. It is figurative of ease and prosperity (cf. 1 Ki. 4:25) especially in the messianic age (Mic. 4:4; Zech. 3:10); it affords comparisons for that which is intrinsically desirable (Hos. 9:10), for renewal (Joel 2:22), that which fades (Isa. 34:4), and is easy to capture (Nah. 3:12). It is also a description of disappointed hopes (Hab. 3:17). Its destruction, like that of other trees and crops, is a picture of judgment (Hos. 2:12; Isa. 34:4; Jer. 5:17; 8:13; Joel 1:2–12). In Hos. 9:10 and Jer. 24 (cf. 29:17) it symbolizes the nation which otherwise is generally pictured as a vine. Mic. 7:1–6 depicts the corrupt state of the nation which is full of bitterness, mutual hostility and bloodshed, in terms of the absence of the fig when sought: "Woe is me! For I have become as when the summer fruit has been gathered, as when the vintage has been gleaned: there is no cluster to eat, no first-ripe fig which my soul desires" (v. 1). In Rab. circles the passage was sometimes applied to times of national crisis (Sotah 9:9, 15).

NT The reference to Jesus seeing Nathanael under the fig tree (Jn. 1:48, 50) is presumably literal (for speculations about its significance see C. F. D. Moule, *JTS* New Series, 5, 1954, 210 f.; R. E. Brown, *The Gospel according to John*, I, 1966, 83). The remaining references in the NT all have figurative and symbolic aspects.

Particular problems attend the interpretation of the cursing of the fig tree (Matt. 21:18–22; Mk. 11:12 ff.). As it stands, it is not only the sole miracle of destruction in the ministry of Jesus, but it also contains statements which at first sight place it beyond the bounds of credibility. T. W. Manson's view, classing it as "ill-tempered" and "incredible" ("The Cleansing of the Temple", *BJRL* 33, 1951, 271–82) and C. E. B. Cranfield's acceptance of the early notion that in an acted parable Jesus "used the fig tree to set forth the judgment which was about to fall on Jerusalem" (*The Gospel according to St. Mark*, 1959, 356) set the limits of interpretation. Undoubtedly Cranfield is right, but it is hardly enough for him to outflank the strong-point in Manson's position by saying that for Jesus to seek figs, where he knew there could be none, supplies the element of the incongruous which calls attention to the presence of a parable. Examination of the crucial sentence, "For it was not the season of figs", goes far to relieve the problem. First, "season" (*kairos* → Time) is to be understood as in Mk. 12:2 of the time of ingathering. Jesus is thus reported to have come by the tree when, by its show of leaves it ought to be in fruit, and, inasmuch as the harvest had not been gathered, the fruit should be showing on the tree. Secondly, the explanatory clause "for the time" (*ho gar kairos*, Mk. 11:13) should not be attached to the foregoing words, "he found nothing but leaves" (this is the root of Manson's incredibility), but to the words before that again, "if haply he might find anything." An explanatory clause of exactly this structure occurs in Mk. 12:12, where *egnōsen gar* ("for he knew") belongs to the preceding clause but one. R. H. Hiers sees a parallel with Lk. 19:40; cf. Matt. 21:15 f.: "If stones should now cry out to greet the Messiah, surely a fig tree might bear fruit out of season! For in the messianic age, should not all fruit be continually in season?" (" 'Not the Season for Figs' ", *JBL* 87, 1968, 400). He points out that the incident follows Jesus' entry into Jerusalem on the first Palm Sunday which he sees as the inauguration of the messianic age. A. de Q. Robin draws attention to the OT precedents for the association of the destruction of fig trees with judgment and the symbolic representation of Israel under the figure of figs ("The Cursing of the Fig Tree in Mark xi. A Hypothesis", *NTS* 8, 1961–62, 276–81). But in particular he sees Mic. 7:1–6 as "an appropriate summing-up of the attitude of the Jewish hierarchy to Jesus and to the impending treachery of Judas as the crisis of the Passion became imminent" (op. cit., 280). The spiritual state of the nation and its leaders was uppermost in Jesus' mind at this period (cf. Mk. 11:1; Lk. 19:41 ff.). It may be added that Jesus' allusion to the language of Mic. 7:6 in Matt. 10:21, 35 f.; Mk. 13:12; and Lk. 12:53 indicates that he saw the times in terms of the passage. The cursing of the fig tree is, therefore, not an isolated, incidental event, but an integral part of the symbolic acts of Jesus' final visit to Jerusalem, beginning with the entry on the ass (→ Animal) on the first Palm Sunday. It symbolizes judgment on the nation for its barren state, and is of a piece with the cleansing of the → temple which occurred at the same time.

Lk. does not record the cursing of the fig tree but contains a parable which presents a counterpart and which is placed some time before the time of the cursing. In Lk. 13:6 the fig tree symbolizes Israel which, despite tending, has so far failed to produce fruit. The master in the parable has sought fruit for the past three years (the period of Jesus' ministry?). But the vine-dresser asks for it to be spared one more year to give it a final chance to bear fruit. If not, he will cut it down. The context of Lk. 13:1–8 refers to disasters which have befallen people, with regard to which Jesus warns his hearers: "Unless you repent you will all likewise perish" (v. 5). The time of sparing corresponds to the time in which Israel is spared the final calamity of judgment, so giving it a final chance to bear fruit.

In Matt. 24:32 f., Mk. 13:28 and Lk. 21:29 the growth of the fig tree is seen as a sign of the approaching summer, the climax of which will be the time when the figs are ripe for gathering. This is the time when the Son of man will gather the elect (Mk. 13:27; cf. Matt. 24:31; Lk. 21:28), and come to take account (Mk. 13:34–37; cf. Matt. 24:36 ff.; Lk. 21:34 f.). If the references to the fig tree in the ministry of Jesus are connected, then the fig tree in Matt. 24:32 f., Mk. 13:28 and Lk. 21:29 is also a picture of Israel as it moves inevitably to the time when fruit will be sought and none found, reminiscent of the fig tree that was cursed.

Expectation of fruit also underlies Jas. 3:12, where the picture is one of expected natural (and thence, moral) consistency. In Rev. 6:13, as in the LXX, the picture suggests that which falls easily in judgment. *J. A. Motyer*

| ἄκανθα | ἄκανθα (*akantha*), thorn; ἀκάνθινος (*akanthinos*), thorny, of thorn. |

CL In general classical use for a thorn tree or bush, also for any prickle, whether of plant, animal (e.g. porcupine) or fish. Likewise, the adj. means thorny, made of thorn-wood, and is even used of "thorny questions".

OT The LXX uses the word with literal reference in Exod. 22:6; Cant. 2:2; Jdg. 8:7, 16. But the symbolic is never far away. Literal and symbolic combine in Gen. 3:18 where the growth of thorns symbolizes the new perversity of nature consequent upon the sin of man. The main figurative uses are for affliction (Ps. 31[32]:4, LXX only; Ezek. 28:24), that which is hazardous, full of difficulty (Prov. 15:19), painful or out of place (Prov. 26:9). "Thorns for grapes" typifies disappointed and blighted hopes (e.g. Isa. 5:2, 4, LXX only) and looks back to

Gen. 3:18 as its origin. Thorns are the wild growth when cultivation ceases (Isa. 5:6), not only physically but spiritually and religiously (e.g. Isa. 34:13; Hos. 10:8).

NT Literal blends with symbolic in the "crown of thorns" (Matt. 27:29) or "thorny crown" (Mk. 15:17; Jn. 19:5): Jesus is not only in intense suffering but bearing the fruit of the curse of Gen. 3:18. Thorns are the enemy of growth (Matt. 13:7) and spiritually are specified as the anxious care typical of this world, the deceptive allure of riches and all manner of desires (Matt. 13:22; Lk. 8:14). Spiritually, thorns evidence failure to respond to the word of God and reveal an unregenerate heart (Heb. 6:8). For botanical discussion see H. L. and A. N. Moldenke, *Plants of the Bible*, 1952. *J. A. Motyer*

τρίβολος

τρίβολος (*tribolos*), thistle.

CL The root idea is "three-pointed", and *tribolos* is first a weapon with three spikes, then a spiked water plant, the water-caltrop, then a similar land plant, or a burr. It was metaphorically transferred to "sharp" tastes like vinegar, and sharp instrument, like threshing machines.

OT It appears in LXX in Gen. 3:18 with → *akanthai*; in 2 Sam. 12:31 "iron *triboloi*" are "harrows". In Prov. 22:5 *triboloi* makes the way of the wicked hazardous. On Hos. 10:8 cf. on *akantha*.

NT Occurring twice only in the NT, once (Matt. 7:16) it illustrates consistency in nature, applied figuratively to the moral life, and once in Heb. 6:8 as illustrative evidence of an unchanged heart, cf. on *akantha*. *J. A. Motyer*

σκόλοψ

σκόλοψ (*skolops*), thorn.

CL The word *skolops* which is translated in 2 Cor. 12:7 as Paul's *thorn* in the flesh only occurs here in the NT and is not very common in secular Gk. It means something pointed, and is probably connected with *skallo*, hack. Originally it meant a pointed stake, used in defence (Homer, *Od.*, 7, 45; *Il.*, 8, 343) or upon which the head of any enemy could be stuck (Homer, *Il.*, 18, 176 f.). It was used in a similar sense to *stauros*, → cross. But it is also found in the sense of a thorn or splinter in Aesop's *Fables* (279, 11), and this sense is well attested.

OT The meaning *stake* is not found in the LXX. *skolops* is found in Num. 33:55 ("But if you do not drive out the inhabitants of the land from before you, then those of them whom you let shall be as pricks in your eyes and thorns in your sides, and they shall trouble you in the land where you dwell") and Ezek. 28:24 ("As for the house of Israel there shall be no more a brier to prick [*skolops pikrias*] or a thorn to hurt [*akantha odynēs*] them among all their neighbours who have treated them with contempt. Then they will know that I am the Lord God"). See also Hos. 2:8 and Sir. 43:19.

726

NT In 2 Cor. 12 Paul refers to his own "visions and revelations" (v. 1) in evident reply to those at Corinth who vaunted their own spiritual experiences and decried Paul's foolishness and weakness (11:16 ff.). Whereas his opponents made much of power, Paul refrains from → boasting, "so that no one may think more of me than he sees in me or hears from me" (12:6). He then refers to his own experience. "And to keep me from being too elated by the abundance of revelations, a thorn was given me in the flesh, a messenger of Satan, to harass me, to keep me from being too elated" (12:7). Various theories have been put forward as to what this thorn was. For discussions and literature see Arndt 763 f.; G. Delling, *skolops, TDNT* V 411 ff.; P. E. Hughes, *Paul's Second Epistle to the Corinthians, NLC* 1962, 442–58; C. K. Barrett, *The Second Epistle to the Corinthians, BNTC* 1973, 314 ff. It has been suggested that it was a temptation to hate or covet. Some scholars take → flesh in the widest sense as the sphere of physical existence, and thus Paul need not refer to a physical ailment. He may refer to opponents or Satan behind his opponents. Physical ailments are not implied in the OT uses of the word. However, the context suggests weakness or hardship (12:9 f.; cf. 11:23–30). Epilepsy and some form of eye trouble are possible explanations, if the expression refers to a bodily ailment. In support of the latter some commentators refer to Gal. 4:13–15, where Paul refers to a "bodily ailment" and where he reminds the Galatians that formerly "you would have plucked out your eyes and given them to me." The theory of eye trouble may be supported by the reference to the "large letters" written with his own hand (Gal. 6:11). The reference to bearing in his body "the marks of Jesus" (Gal. 6:17) may refer to some physical illness or to afflictions suffered in the course of preaching the gospel. Luke the physician's attendance on Paul may have been due to his ailments. The fact that Paul was able to travel so much and endure great hardship does not by itself prove that he was in robust health; the whole context of 2 Cor. 11–12 is a celebration of triumph over disability and hardship.

The exact nature of the thorn in the flesh remains obscure. It is perhaps significant that Paul deliberately uses this apparently trivial expression in contrast with the → cross of Christ. Elsewhere he speaks of being crucified with Christ (Gal. 2:20). Here, however, the affliction which may have been severe is seen to be ultimately trivial. The case illustrates the the role of intercessory prayer. Paul did not regard it as wrong to pray for himself for alleviation. But in answer to his prayer the Lord said to him, "My grace is sufficient for you, for my power is made perfect in weakness" (v. 9). Paul does not see the Christian life as one which is spared all weakness and hardship. In response he declares: "I will all the more gladly boast of my weaknesses, that the power of Christ may rest upon me. For the sake of Christ, then, I am content with weaknesses, insults, hardships, persecutions, and calamities; for when I am weak, then I am strong" (vv. 9 f.).   *C. Brown*

(a). R. Bultmann, *The Gospel of John*, 1971, 532 ff.; A. T. Hanson, "Christ the First Fruits, Christ the Tree," *Studies in Paul's Technique and Theology*, 1974, 104–25; F. Hauck, *karpos, TDNT* III 614 ff.; R. H. Hiers, " 'Not the Season for Figs'," *JBL* 87, 1968, 394–400; H. N. and A. L. Moldenke, *Plants of the Bible*, 1952; T. Y. Mullins, "Paul's Thorn in the Flesh," *JBL* 76, 1957, 299–303; G. F. Post, *Flora of Syria, Palestine and Sinai*, 2nd ed. I, 1932, II, 1933; A. de Q. Robin, "The Cursing of the Fig Tree in Mark xi, A Hypothesis," *NTS* 8, 1961–62, 276–81; N. S. Smith, "The Thorn that Stayed: An Exposition of II Corinthians 12:7–9," *Interpretation* 13, 1959, 409–16; J. C. Trever, "Fig Tree, Fig," "Fruit (Products)," "Thistle, Thorn," *IDB* II 267, 320, IV 630 f.;

W. Walker, *All the Plants of the Bible*, 1957; M. Zohary, "Flora," *IDB* II 284–302; C. W. F. Smith, "No Time for Figs," *JBL* 79, 1960, 315–27; J. N. Birdsall, "The Withering of the Fig Tree," *ExpT* 73, 1961–2, 191.

(b). G. Dalman, *Arbeit und Sitte in Palästina*, I–II, 1928; I. Loew, *Die Flora der Juden*, I, 1928; II–III, 1924; IV, 1934.

Fullness, Abound, Multitude, Fulfil, Make Room

The words grouped together under this heading cover a wide variety of ideas. They are connected by the thought, suggested by their etymologies, of occupying, filling and even overflowing a given space. However, in some instances context and usage supersede etymology. *perisseuō* (be more than enough, be present in abundance, abound) and its cognates suggest being present in a way that the given space is unable to contain. *plēthos* means a quantity, a number or multitude, hence a crowd, assembly, population, and the whole body of a church. The cognate vb. *plēthynō* means to increase, multiply, grow. *plēroō* (like the less common *pimplēmi*) means to fill, fulfil. The noun *plērōma* means that which fills, fullness, fulfilling, and is also used as an eschatological technical term for the fullness of time and the fulfilment of the will of God. *chōreō* means to make room, go, have room for, hold, contain. The corresponding noun *chōros* means a place. Also treated in this article are *gemō* (to load, be full) and *chortazō* which is used of filling with food.

περισσεύω

περισσεύω (*perisseuō*), be more than enough, be left over, be present in abundance, be abundant, abound, excel; περισσός (*perissos*), exceeding the usual number or size, extraordinary, abundant, profuse, superfluous, unnecessary; περισσότερος (*perissoteros*), greater, more; περισσοτέρως (*perissoterōs*), adv. more; περισσῶς (*perissōs*), exceedingly, beyond measure, very; ὑπερ[εκ]περισσῶς (*hyper[ek]perissōs*), beyond all measure; περισσεία (*perisseia*), surplus, abundance; περίσσευμα (*perisseuma*), abundance, fullness.

CL *perisseuō* is used intrans. from the time of Hesiod in the sense of to be over and above, go beyond, outflank, be more than enough, remain over, abound. The adj. *perissos* means beyond the regular number or size, out of the common, extraordinary, strange, more than sufficient, superfluous, excessive, extravagant. The adv. *perissōs* means extraordinarily, exceedingly. Formations with *hyper-* are late Gk. and rare. *hyperekperissōs* and *hyperekperissou*, beyond all measure, belong to NT Gk.

OT *perisseuō* and its cognates are not common in the LXX. Normally they translate the vb. *yātar*, remain over; cf. the noun *yeter*, remainder, excess.

1. (a) *perisseia* occurs only in Eccles., usually in the sense of gain, advantage. "What does a man gain by all the toil at which he toils under the sun?" (Eccles. 1:3). The wise man like the fool (2:14b; 6:8), man like the beast (3:19), must go hence and be forgotten. God is a free Lord who bestows earthly goods (6:2). Therefore, man should enjoy them in gratitude and not haggle with God over the place that has been allotted to him (6:9 f.). Such wisdom which recognizes the freedom of the creator is real gain (7:12, 19; cf. 2:13 f.; 12:13).

(b) *perisseuō* means to have precedence (1 Macc. 3:30), posterity (1 Sam. 2:33, 36), but elsewhere to have abundance (Sir. 11:12). According to Sir. 19:24, the man who is too sure of his wisdom stands in greater danger of transgressing the law.

(c) *perissos* denotes what is over, the remainder (Exod. 10:5; 2 Sam. 25:11), what is superfluous and useless (Prov. 2:15). But it also denotes what is extraordinary and outstanding (Dan. 5:12, 14), advantage (Prov. 14:23).

2. Late Judaism expected in the end-time an abundance and blessed profusion of all desirable goods: numerous offspring, possessions, superabundant crops (Eth. En. 10:17 ff.; Syr. Bar. 29:5-8; cf. SB IV 886 f), as well as joy (Eth. En. 51:5 f.), righteousness and wisdom (Eth. En. 48:1), and spirit (or breath) from God (Sib. 4:46, 189).

NT In the NT the words of this group occur relatively frequently: *perisseuō* 39 times; *perissos* and its comparative and adverbial forms 37 times; *perisseuma* 5 times; *perisseia* 4 times; and the forms with the prefix *hyper-* 6 times. All the words occur predominantly in the Pauline writings, and next to them the Gospels. In all the words there is the element of excess and fullness that overflows the set bounds. In this process of overflowing, the existing standards and rules are transcended, and what was comparable becomes incomparable.

1. (a) In the Gospels *perisseuō* and its cognates are found with the primary meaning to have abundance, to have many goods. Mk. 12:44 tells of the widow who gave all that she possessed, whereas others gave of their abundance. Lk. 12:15 warns of misplaced trust in the abundance of possessions. The proverbial utterance in Matt. 12:34 declares: "For out of the abundance of the heart the mouth speaks." The more Jesus commanded men not to tell of his healing work, the more (*mallon perissoteron*) they proclaimed it (Mk. 7:36). The secret of his person exerted pressure on men to proclaim it openly in view of his mighty acts. The crowd was astonished beyond measure (*hyperperissōs*, Mk. 7:37) and likewise the disciples were utterly astounded (*lian ek perissou en heautois existanto*, Mk. 6:51).

(b) As the one who prepared the way for Jesus, John was more than a prophet (Matt. 11:9). But the victorious breaking in of the kingdom with Jesus showed that he still stood at the threshold. With a unique authority Jesus called the weary to him to refresh themselves (Matt. 11:28). This is brought out in the accounts of the feeding of the four thousand (Matt. 15:32-39; Mk. 8:1-10) and the five thousand (Matt. 14:13-21; Mk. 6:30-44; Lk. 9:10-17; Jn. 6:1-13). All the accounts mention the quantities of bread that were left over (12 baskets full of what remained [*perisseumata*], Mk. 8:8; cf. *to perisseuon tōn klasmatōn*, the broken pieces left over, Matt. 15:37; cf. Jn. 6:13). Jesus is seen as performing more through his Father's enabling than Moses in the desert. He gives more than food for the day (cf. Exod. 16:18). Those who belong to him have life and have it abundantly (*perisson*, Jn. 10:10). The prodigal son reflected that his father's servants had bread enough and to spare (Lk. 15:17). All this shows that the father has abundant grace which he holds out to the lost.

(c) Corresponding to the offer of abundant grace is the requirement that the disciples' righteousness must exceed greatly (*perisseusē ... pleion*) that of the scribes and Pharisees (Matt. 5:20; cf. 5:47). The perfection of the disciples is to

729

correspond to that of the Father (Matt. 5:48). This radical demand raises the anxious question as to who then can be saved (Matt. 19:25; Mk. 10:26; Lk. 18:26). The NT precludes all self-security, riches in their widest sense (Matt. 19:24), and Pharisaic casuistry (Matt. 5:37; 15:4 f.). Faith should rely on the fact that with God all things are possible (Matt. 19:26), and therefore God can make obedience possible to faith.

The two great commandments to love God and to love one's neighbour as oneself are the basis of the teaching of the law and the prophets. There are no commandments greater (*perissoteron*) than these (Mk. 12:33). By contrast, those who devour widows' houses and for a pretence make long prayers will receive the greater (*perissoteron*) condemnation (Lk. 20:47; Mk. 10:40). Those who know so much of God's electing love as Pharisaic Judaism and can still reject it in Christ will receive greater condemnation. "Every one to whom much is given, of him will much be required; and of him to whom men commit much they will demand the more [*perissoteron*]" (Lk. 12:48; cf. Matt. 13:12). The parables show how this applies to man's relationship with God.

2. (a) Paul uses *perisseuō* and its cognates in Rom., when he speaks of the justifying → grace of God. No one and nothing is beyond its reach. God is rich to all who call upon him (Rom. 10:12). "Law came in, to increase the trespass; but where sin increased, grace abounded all the more [*hypereperisseusen*]" (Rom. 5:20 RSV). The splendour of the law now seems to have no splendour because of splendour which surpasses it, inasmuch as the dispensation of condemnation is surpassed by the dispensation of righteousness (2 Cor. 3:9 f.). As sin gained dominance in Adam, so grace abounded (*eperisseusen*) in Christ (Rom. 5:15; cf. 10:4). Because the abundance (*perisseia*) of grace cannot be exhausted, there can be no place for reliance on fulfilling the law (Rom. 3:20). The advantage (*perisson*) of the Jew (Rom. 3:1) consists in the fact that the Jews were entrusted with the oracles of God. But their denial cannot hinder the victorious course of grace. Rather, it brings about the fact that whatever man does it abounds to God's glory (Rom. 3:7). Moreover, it means that God's grace has now come to the Gentiles (Rom. 11:11).

Jew and Gentile alike are utterly dependent upon grace. "God has consigned all men to disobedience, that he may have mercy upon all" (Rom. 11:32). In view of this, Paul prays: "May the God of hope fill you with all joy and peace in believing, so that by the power of the Holy Spirit you may abound in hope [*eis to perisseuein hymas en tē elpidi*]" (Rom. 15:13). Eph. 3:20 declares that "by the power at work in us [God] is able to do far more abundantly [*hyperekperissou*] than all that we ask or think." Eph. 1:7 ff. defines the riches of his grace which he lavished (*eperisseusen*) upon us as "redemption through his blood, the forgiveness of our trespasses" which he has revealed to us as part of his plan to unite all things in himself. Knowing Christ and being rooted and built up in him, believers should live in him, "abounding in thanksgiving [*perisseuontes en eucharistia*]" (Col. 2:7).

(b) Just as the Apostle Paul was exceedingly (*perissos*) zealous in the persecution of the church (Acts 26:11) and the traditions of the law (Gal. 1:14), he pursued with the same zeal the saving work of Christ in the building up and sanctification of the churches (cf. 1 Cor. 15:58; Phil. 1:9, 26; 1 Thess. 3:12; 4:1, 10; in each case the vb. *perisseuein* appears). In 1 Thess. 3:10 Paul says that he prayed earnestly (*hyperekperissou*) day and night that he might be with the Thessalonian church to supply what was lacking in their faith (cf. 2:17). He urged the Corinthians to use their gifts for building up the church, so that they might abound (1 Cor. 14:12). With regard to meat offered to idols, Paul urged the "strong" not to make use of their freedom, because it brought no advantage. "Food will not commend us to God. We are no worse off if we do not eat, and no better off [*perisseuomen*] if we do" (1 Cor. 8:8 RSV).

The apostle knows how to be abased (*tapeinousthai*) and how to abound (*perisseuein*), according to whether the former is commanded or the latter given (Phil. 4:12; cf. 4:18). He has striven more and suffered more (*perissoterōs*) (1 Cor. 15:20; 2 Cor. 11:23; 12:15). He had more cause for boasting than his opponents (2 Cor. 1:12; 10:8). But his way is to be satisfied with the power that proves itself in weakness (2 Cor. 12:9). Hence, imprisonment and suffering arouse in him more courage to bear witness (Phil. 1:14; cf. Lk. 12:4).

(c) *perisseuō* is featured in a particular way in connection with the collection for Jerusalem in 2 Cor. Paul is concerned with more than the money that is brought in. It is a test of love for the churches which shows whether it corresponds to Christ's self-sacrifice (2 Cor. 8:8 f.). For this reason, he praises the churches of Macedonia, "for in a severe test of affliction, their abundance of joy [*hē perisseia tēs charas autōn*] and their extreme poverty have overflowed [*eperisseusen*] in a wealth of liberality on their part" (8:2 RSV). The apostle expresses his conviction that: "God is able to provide you with every blessing in abundance [*perisseusai*], so that you may always have enough of everything and may provide in abundance [*perisseuēte*] for every good work" (9:8). (Perhaps a play on words is intended by introductory remark: "Now it is superfluous [*perisson*] for me to write to you about the offering for the saints".) The collection represented a key link between the Jerusalem church and the Gentile churches. "For the rendering of this service not only supplies the wants of the saints but also overflows [*perisseuousa*] in many thanksgivings to God" (9:12). It is thus for Paul a recognition of God's gracious work among the Gentiles.

3. Heb. warns the church, threatened by persecution, to keep its eyes on its goal and to pay closer (*perissoterōs*) attention to the teaching it has been given (Heb. 2:1). When God desired to "point out even more clearly [*perissoteron*]" (6:17; cf. Arndt, 657) to the heirs of promise his unchangeable character, he interposed with an oath. The character of Christ's priesthood becomes "even more [*perissoteron*] evident" (7:15 RSV; cf. Arndt, 657) in view of the testimony of Ps. 110:4 to being a priest for ever after the order of → Melchizedek.

The expression *perisseia kakias* (Jas. 1:21) is translated fig. by RSV as "rank growth of wickedness." Arndt takes it to mean "all the evil prevailing [around you]" (Arndt, 656). The thought is not that of *perisseia* in the sense of a surplus or abundance of evil as yet uncommitted, but evil in the way that it abounds so freely if it is not firmly dealt with. It is this that James urges his readers to put away and receive with meekness the implanted word that is able to save their souls.

T. Brandt

| πλῆθος | πλῆθος (*plēthos*), number, multitude, crowd, throng, assembly, people, populace, population, sometimes used |

731

for the community or assembly of the church; πληθύνω (*plēthynō*), increase, multiply, grow.

CL The noun *plēthos* is attested from Hom. onwards. It is connected with the root
plē-, meaning fullness, and means a crowd or multitude, in contrast to a small number or an individual. It can also denote what is too big to count. The vb. *plēthynō* (in which the ending *-ynō* means make) means to make full, to fill; intrans. to be full.

The noun is used: (a) as a general term denoting a great number of things, and, in connection with time, duration; (b) with persons, a multitude, crowd; as a military term, a mass of troops; from a sociological and derogatory standpoint, the mass which lacks culture and moral understanding; in a democracy, the total number of voters or the majority that turns the scales in political decisions; people, population; the assembly (e.g. of the citizens of Athens); in religious communities, the body of members, the whole group, the congregation. The plur. can be used to give emphasis (crowds, flocks). Otherwise, an adj. can be added to give emphasis. *plēthos* can also be used as an adj., many (the comparative, more, the great majority; and the superlative, most). The meaning of the vb. corresponds to that of the noun: trans., increase, enlarge, multiply; in the pass. and intrans., to increase in number, grow, fill, be full.

OT In the LXX *plēthos* is found nearly 300 times, and *plēthynō* about 200 times.
Most often it translates forms of the root *rābâh*, be or become much, many, great; cf. the noun *rōb*, multitude, abundance, greatness. The various forms are used to describe the abundant fullness of God's giving: in the blessing of creation (Gen. 1:22, 28); in the promise to the patriarchs and the people of God of great posterity (Gen. 17:2, 4; 22:17; Exod. 1:7, 20; 32:13); in the bestowal of rich blessings (Deut. 28:11) and salvation (Pss. 5:7[8]; 31:19[20]; 51:1[3]; of the king of salvation Ps. 72:7[71:7]; in a greeting, LXX Dan. 3:31; 6:26). God's fullness of → glory (*doxa*; Exod. 15:7) and majesty (*megalōsynē*, Ps. 150:2) is to be praised. Man, on the other hand, has no cause to trust *en plēthei ischyos*, in the abundance of his strength (Ps. 32:[33]:16), nor the people in the multitude of their warriors (Hos. 10:13) or of their sacrifices (Isa. 1:11; cf. G. Delling, *TDNT* VI 276). Man stands before God in his greatness and majesty with an abundance of guilt (Gen. 6:5; Amos 4:4; Sir. 5:6; 23:3, 16).

The noun *rōb*, which corresponds to the Gk. *plēthos*, is also frequent in the Qumran writings. It is used to denote the assembly of the community's members (1QS 5:2, 9; 6:19). It is also often used to strengthen a term used in connection with salvation: e.g. fullness of grace, fullness of mercy, fullness of salvation.

NT *plēthos* occurs 31 times in the NT, of which 24 instances (and one *v.l.*) are in the
Lukan writings. *plēthynō* occurs 11 times, including 5 instances in Acts.
The words can serve to describe the fullness of God's giving. This is illustrated by passages citing the OT which refer to the growth of the people of God in fulfilment of the divine promises (Acts 7:17 = Exod. 1:7; Heb. 6:14 = Gen. 22:17; Heb. 11:12 = Gen. 15:5; → People, art. *laos*; → Grow, art. *auxanō*). *plēthynō* also occurs in the formula of greeting offering the prayer that grace and peace (1

Pet. 1:2; 2 Pet. 1:2), and mercy, peace and love (Jude 2), may be multiplied to the readers.

Jas. 5:20 and 1 Pet. 4:8 (= Prov. 10:12) declare that the love that brings back a sinner from the error of his ways and the mutual love that is practised in the community cover a multitude of sins. The expression *plēthos hamartiōn* (cf. the MT of Prov. 10:12: "love covers all offences") is not so much concerned with the number of sins committed, as if they were counted up in some divine book-keeping, but with the effect of love which shows itself to be all the greater in undoing sin. 2 Cor. 9:10 (cf. Isa. 55:10; Hos. 10:12) promises that God will see to it that no gift of love will make a person poor, but will multiply rich blessings.

Luke frequently uses the words to describe the great impact made by Jesus and the gospel exciting the populace (Lk. 8:37; Acts 14:4; 21:36) and causing a number to follow him (Lk. 6:17 par. Mk. 3:7; Lk. 23:27; Acts 5:14, 16; 14:1; 17:4). Peter's apostolic missionary work and the harvest of the gospel among the Gentiles is anticipated by the great draught of fishes (Lk. 5:6; Jn. 21:6). The vb. especially is used to indicate the increase of the church through the spreading of the Word of God (Acts 6:17: 9:31; 12:24; reminiscent of the OT account of the creation and of the increase of the people of God as a sign of blessing).

Lk. also makes a literary use of *plēthos* to focus attention on a small group of people alongside the anonymous multitude: the priest and the multitude (Lk. 1:10); the angel of the Lord and the heavenly host (2:13); the disciples and the people (6:17); the Twelve and the great body of the church (Acts 6:2, 5). It means company or assembly in Acts 4:32; 14:4; 23:7, and underlines the corporate character of the action of the group concerned in Lk. 19:37; 23:1; Acts 4 32; 25:24.

In Lk. *plēthos* can also mean a religious assembly: participants in worship (Lk. 1:10; Acts 19:9); the company of believers (Acts 4:32); the great body of the church (Acts 6:2, 5; 15:12, 30; 21:22 *v.l.*).

Matt. 24:12 speaks of the end-time: "And because wickedness is multiplied, most men's love will grow cold." The disciples are not to lose their zeal under the pressure of events, especially when anti-Christian forces gain control even in the church and the widespread rejection of God's law makes life unbearable.

W. Bauder

πληρόω

πληρόω (*plēroō*), fill, complete, fulfil, accomplish, carry out; πλήρης (*plērēs*), full, filled, complete; πλήρωμα (*plērōma*), that which has been completed, fullness; ἀναπληρόω (*anaplēroō*), fill up; πληροφορέω (*plērophoreō*), bring in full measure, fulfil, accomplish, persuade, assure, satisfy fully; πληροφορία (*plērophoria*), fullness, full assurance; πίμπλημι (*pimplēmi*), fill, complete, fulfil; ἐμπίμπλημι (*empimplēmi*), fill full, fill up, satisfy.

CL 1. *plērēs* and its derivatives are to be found in Gk. literature from Aesch. onwards, and *pimplēmi* from Homer. *plērophoreō*, on the other hand, is a late formation and is found once in Ctesias, otherwise in the 2nd cent. B.C. The majority of meanings of all these words are derived from the common root *plē-*, full, fullness. *plēroō*, as well as *empimplēmi*, means lit. to fill a vessel, so that the result can be described by *plērēs* or *plērōma*. It can be applied, for instance, to the manning of a ship. It is used in an extended sense of fulfilling a wish, hearing a prayer, stilling wrath and anger, satisfying a desire, meeting obligation and carrying out work. It has the further sense of bringing to full measure, delivering a reward or tribute, filling a gap, enlarging (also as an alternative *anapleroō*). It is used in a temporal sense in the pass. of expiring, coming to an end, e.g. a full (*plērēs*) year, a full number (*plērōma*) of years.

2. Just as a person can be full of pain, joy, love, and virtue, he can also be said to be filled with God (*plērēs theou;* Pollux, *Onomasticon,* 1, 15), i.e. possessed and inspired by God (ibid., 1, 16). The Pythian priestess was said to be filled by the spirit of God when she uttered an oracle (Origen, *Contra Cels.,* 7, 3). This mantic filling by God is to be distinguished from the thought that God permeates the universe and fills it (so Zeus Sarapis in Aelius Aristides, *Orationes,* 45, 21). This need not be taken in a pantheistic sense, as can be shown from Philo's use of such expressions (*Leg. All.,* 3, 4; cf. 1, 44; *Sacr.,* 67; *Vit. Mos.,* 2, 238; *Conf. Ling.,* 134 ff.). Despite Stoic influences, his idea of the God who fills the universe is that of a transcendent God (as in Platonic) dualism who fills the universe by his presence and working (as in the OT).

OT 1. *plēroō* and *pimplēmi* are almost equally common in the LXX. Together with derivatives, they translate chiefly the Heb. *mālē'*, and less frequently *ṣāḇaʿ*, *tāmam,* and *šālēm*. There is the same range of meaning as in CL above: the lit. sense (2 Ki. 4:4; Gen. 21:19; 42:25; Ps. 96:11 and 98:7 in the expression "the sea and all that fills it"); of the divine ordinance to fill the earth (Gen. 1:28; 9:1; cf. the earth and what fills it, Ps. 24:1). In an extended sense, *plēroō* and its derivatives are used of hearing prayers (Ps. 20:6), finishing work (1 Ki. 7:51), paying tribute (2 Macc. 8:10, *ekplēroō*), confirming the words of someone else (1 Ki. 1:14), bringing a punishment to full measure (Wis. 19:4, *prosanaplēroō*).

2. *plēroō* is used frequently (*pimplēmi* less so) in connection with expressions of time: to make a time full, mainly in the pass. in the sense of expiring, coming to an end. The idea implies a definite amount of → time that must inevitably come to an end, because nature (e.g. Gen. 25:24), a vow (Num. 6:5), the law (Lev. 8:33) or God's word (cf. the 70 years in Jer. 25:12; 2 Chron. 36:21) decree or determine it. Tob. 14:5[7] is interesting in this connection. Tobias has said that Israel would be devastated for a time (*mechri chronou*), but God would bring back the exiles (Tob. 14:4[6]). The house of God would also be rebuilt, but not with the former appearance. Yet this inferiority would be merely temporal. It will last until "the time of the aeons" ["the time of the times", Codex Sinaiticus] are fulfilled. Behind all this lies the idea that God has fixed a limit for the times of man (cf. Dan. 12:13 LXX). In the same way the OT speaks about the filling up of sins. Here again there is the idea of a measure to be filled up, though not in so many words. Thus, Gen. 15:16 speaks of the iniquity of the Amorites being not yet complete. The attainment of the full measure of their sins means the end of the dominion of the four godless kingdoms (Dan. 8:23). The perspective of 2 Macc. 6:12–16 is very instructive. The misery of the people of Israel is but God's temporary chastisement which has come about as a warning (v. 12). For God desires to spare sinners from ultimate punishment (v. 13). They know that: "In the case of other nations, the sovereign Lord in his forbearance refrains from punishing them till they have filled up their sins to the

734

full, but in our case he has determined otherwise, that his vengeance may not fall on us in after-days when our sins have reached their height" (v. 14).

3. There is a specific OT use of the term, when the word of God spoken by the prophets is said to be fulfilled (cf. 1 Esd. 1:57 [*anaplērōsis*]; 1 Ki. 2:27; 2 Chron. 36:21 f. [*plēroō*]). It is Yahweh himself who executes that which has been prophesied in his name (1 Ki. 8:15, 24).

4. There are numerous references to being filled (*empimplēmi*) by the Spirit of God. It is the distinguishing mark of the prophets (Sir. 48:12), and can be transmitted by the laying on of hands (Deut. 34:9). Skilled craftsmen are also said to be filled by a spirit, viz. that of knowledge and craftsmanship (Exod. 28:3; 31:3). Being filled by the Spirit is also given to those who seek the Lord and study the → law (Sir. 39:8), so that they instruct others (vv. 9 f.). He who keeps a bridle on his tongue is filled by the Spirit (Prov. 15:4 LXX).

The statement of Wis. 1:7 that "the Spirit of the Lord fills the world" is not to be understood in a pantheistic sense any more than in Philo. It is a confession that God hears and knows everything, and that he punishes sin (see the context). Similarly, the rhetorical question of Jer. 23:24, "Do I not fill heaven and earth?" means that God sees all things. The statement that God's → glory (Heb. *kābôd*; Gk. *doxa*) fills the earth (cf. Ps. 72:19; Isa. 6:3; Num. 14:21) means that God will reveal himself in full measure. Originally this glory was confined to the → tabernacle (Exod. 40:34 f.), the first (1 Ki. 8:10 f.; 2 Chron. 5:14; 7:1) and second (Hag. 2:9) temples, and was perceived by only a few. But in the end-time, "the earth will be filled [*plēsthēsetai*] with the knowledge of the glory of the Lord, as the waters cover the sea" (Hab. 2:14).

5. The Qumran writings mainly use the Heb. *mālē'* to denote the completion of a period of time (cf. 1QS 7:20, 22) and also in the pregnant eschatological sense, that all existence and events are fulfilled according to a firm plan that is already fixed by God (1QS 3:16; cf. 1QM 17:9). In the time of salvation expected at the end God will fill his land with the rich bounty of blessing and all the wealth of the nations will be brought together at Jerusalem (1QM 12:12 ff.; cf. 14:4)

NT The NT usage of these terms has much in common with what has been said under CL and OT. *pimplēmi* and the compound *empimplēmi*, neither of which is very common, remain close to the lit. meaning. Both are used chiefly by Luke.: the former to denote endowment by the Spirit which is pictured in a rather physical and visual manner, the latter to denote satisfying and filling again conceived in a somewhat physical way (Lk. 1:53; 6:25). *plēroō* is more significant, not only because it is more frequent (86 times), but also because it is virtually a technical term used in connection with the fulfilment of scripture and also a designation of the fulfilment of → time in an eschatological sense. It has thus a special theological significance. *plērēs* is used lit. in the Synoptic Gospels. It is also applied to people in the Lucan and Johannine writings. A man can be full of the Holy → Spirit, full of → faith, or full of good → works (cf. Acts 6:3, 5; 9:36). *plērophoreō* and *plērophoria* (in all 10 times) come close in meaning to the vb. → *perisseuō*, though they are translated in various ways. In 2 Tim. 4:5, 17 the vb. means to carry out the ministry of preaching. The noun *plērophoria* can mean lit. fullness and also full assurance, conviction. It is difficult to determine whether *plērōma* focuses on the process of filling or the fact of being filled. The term occurs especially in Paul. There are only a few references to the word in its original sense (*plēroō*, Jn. 12:3; Acts 2:2; *pimplēmi*, Lk. 5:7; cf. the compound *symplēroō*, Lk. 8:23). Attention will therefore be confined to the more theological uses of these terms.

1. *Fulfilment of OT Scripture.* (a) The NT church was conscious of its living continuity with the OT. It found its strength in the OT, not only in the use it made of the OT in authenticating its apologetic and mission vis-à-vis Judaism. Right from the beginning going back to Jesus himself, the church felt the need to base its life on the OT. The OT was appealed to with a sometimes surprising self-confidence in a manner characterized by the key concept of fulfilment. The usual term here was the vb. *plēroō*, but *anaplēroō* and *pimplēmi* both occur once in this connection.

(b) The fulfilment is often introduced by the conjunctions *hopōs* and *hina*, so that . . . (especially in Matt. and Jn.). This is particularly true of those fulfilment-quotations which have their origin in the church's understanding of its faith (e.g. Jas. 2:23), or episodes in the life of Jesus which were seen as the fulfilment of the divine plan of salvation revealed in the OT. In this sense writers speak of the fulfilment of the → scriptures (*graphai*, Mk. 14:49), and of all that is written (Lk. 21:22). The thought is perhaps that of the whole OT (Lk. 24:44: Moses, the prophets, Psalms), but in particular of the prophetic writings (Matt. 26:56). Most often a particular passage is in mind which is introduced by the expressions "what was spoken" (*to rhēthen*, 10 times in Matt., e.g. Matt. 4:14), "the word" (*ho logos*, Jn. 12:38; 15:25), "the scripture" (i.e. the scripture passage, *hē graphē*, Mk. 15:28; Jn. 13:18; 17:12; 19:24, 28, 36; Acts 1:16; Jas. 2:23; cf. Lk. 4:21). The source of the quotation is often the prophets. Hence, writers may speak of the fulfilment of prophecy (Matt. 13:14, *hē prophēteia*), and of the words of the prophets (Acts 13:27).

Sometimes the prophets are named whose words are cited as scripture (Isaiah in Matt. 3:3; 4:14; 8:17; 12:17; 13:14, 35 *v.l.*; 15:7; Mk. 1:2; 7:6; Lk. 3:4; 4:17; Jn. 1:23; 12:38 f., 41; Acts 8:28, 30; 28:25; Rom. 9:27, 29; 10:16, 20; 15:12; Jeremiah in Matt. 2:17; cf. 16:14; 27:9; 2 Chron. 36:21). Sometimes the reference is simply to "the prophet" (Matt. 1:22; 2:5, 15; 21:4). Matt. expressly characterizes their activity as a subordinate one by his use of the preposition *dia*, through ("through the prophet," 10 times). Behind the scripture and the particular passage stands the true author for Matt., God himself (note the use of *hypo*, by, in the expression "what the Lord had spoken by the prophet", Matt. 1:22; 2:15). It is God himself who has declared it beforehand (Acts 3:18).

(c) Just as God is the originator, he is also the fulfiller of the word spoken by him. This finds expression in the frequent circumlocution using the semitic pass. *to be fulfilled*. Acts 13:33 and 3:18 make it clear it is God who brings about fulfilment. However, this does not preclude human participation. By their failure to understand the utterances of the prophets the inhabitants of Jerusalem fulfilled scripture (Acts 13:27).

The NT also speaks of the fulfilment of the words of an angel (Lk. 1:20) and of Jesus (Jn. 18:9, 32). In evaluating scripture proof, it is to be noted that the process starts from the eschatologically understood present and reaches back to the OT scripture, and not the reverse (cf. the frequent *kathōs gegraptai*, as it is written, e.g. Mk. 1:2; Lk. 2:23 and often). Generally it is the wording of the LXX and not the Heb. text that is referred to. Certain passages are understood as mysteriously presaging the present advent of the final events (→ Secret; → Revelation, art. *apokalypsis*). Faith discovers in the OT the promise of the salvation that is now coming to pass. In the endeavour to discover the greatest number of mysteries (cf. Jn. 5:39: "You search the scriptures"), a form of scripture proof emerged which can be seen in Matt. But even here there is a striking freedom in dealing with the wording of the OT, as compared with Judaism. Jesus' attitude to the wording was already discriminating (cf. Matt. 5:17; Mk. 10:2 ff.). Paul also distinguished between the → Spirit and the letter (2 Cor. 3:7 ff.). Sometimes he expounded the OT in an allegorical manner (1 Cor. 9:9; cf. Deut. 25:4). This may be compared with the interpretation given to the parables (cf. Mk. 4:13–20). Heb. takes the form of a homily in which a connected string of OT passages is expounded step by step.

([Ed.] It is sometimes suggested that the apologetic interest of the NT writers has caused them to wrest OT passages out of their original context in order to give them a christological interpretation. Thus the quotation of Hos. 11:1 ("Out of Egypt have I called my son") by Matt. 2:15 appears in context to have nothing to do with the infant Jesus returning from Egypt. Rather, it refers to the original exodus of the people of Israel. Similarly the Emmanuel prophecy of Isa. 7:14 quoted by Matt. 1:23 appears to lose its point for Isaiah's time, if the fulfilment was not to occur until the birth of Jesus. The slaughter of the innocents at Bethlehem by Herod does not seem to have been the original point of Jer. 31:15, quoted by Matt. 2:18. If these and other OT quotations are regarded as direct predictions of events which did not happen until Jesus, then the NT writers cannot be exonerated of taking texts out of context for apologetic purposes, displaying ignorance of or indifference to the original meaning of the text. But as R. Schippers has pointed out above (NT 1 (c)), these NT passages are understood from the standpoint of an eschatological present. The OT passages are not treated as mere predictions but as anticipations. From the standpoint of the Jew living at the time of the original prophetic utterance, the utterance was about something significant in the history of the Jewish people. It was something that had happened or was happening in history. Matt.'s idea of fulfilment says, in effect, that the event that the Jews thought was significant turns out to be only an anticipation of an event of a similar kind but ultimately more significant in God's purposes for the salvation of mankind. It is in this sense that the latter fulfills the former.)

2. *The fulfilment of* → *time*. (a) In a general sense, the fulfilment of time refers to coming to an end, expiring. It is always pass. in the NT. The following vbs. are used: *pimplēmi* (Lk. 1:23, 57; 2:6, 21 f. in the birth narratives); *teleō* (Lk. 2:43); and *plēroō* (Acts 7:23, 30; 9:23; 24:27; cf. 19:21). Days (5 times) and years (3 times), and a point in time (Lk. 1:57) are all said to have been fulfilled, or to have come. Perhaps *plērophoreō* in Lk. 1:1 has also a temporal aspect ("the things that have been accomplished among us" RSV).

(b) The idea of fulfilment in Lk. 21:24 is more significant. The execution of judgment on Jerusalem will go on "until the times of the Gentiles are fulfilled" (cf. Tob. 14 under OT 2, above). There is more emphasis here than under (a) on the thought that God determines the times and seasons. In these passive constructions God is the implied subject. Time (→ art. *aiōn*) has a function in the plan of salvation. Lk. 9:51 and Acts 2:1 use the composite *symplēroō* in the pass. The former speaks of the days of his reception being fulfilled (*en tō symplērousthai tas*

737

hēmeras tēs analēmpseōs). The latter speaks of the day of Pentecost being fulfilled (*en tō symplērousthai tēn hēmeran tēs Pentēkostēs*), when correspondingly the Spirit was given.

(c) According to Mk. 1:15, Jesus' first public preaching began with the words, "The time is fulfilled [*peplērōtai ho kairos*]." The time appointed by God and awaited by Israel has come. This may be compared with Jesus' declaration in the synagogue at Nazareth after reading from Isa. 61:1 f. (Lk. 4:18 f.): "Today this scripture has been fulfilled in your hearing" (Lk. 4:21). By contrast, Jesus declares in Jn. 7:8, "My time is not yet fulfilled [*ho emos kairos oupō peplērōtai*]." Although the time of God's intervention in Christ has already come, the events of Jesus' earthly life are still fully in the hands of God. No man, not even Jesus himself, can control them (cf. Jn. 2:4; 7:30; 8:20). The time is only revealed to Jesus later (Jn. 12:33; 13:1; 17:1).

(d) In this connection, Paul makes use of the noun *plērōma*: "But when the time had fully come [*hote ēlthen to plērōma tou chronou*], God sent forth his Son, born of woman, born under the law, to redeem those who were under the law, so that we might receive adoption as sons" (Gal. 4:4 f.). This does not mean only that a particular time has expired, or that an appointed time has come. Rather, it means that in the divine economy of salvation human time has reached its full measure. In Eph. 1:10 Paul links the *oikonomia* (administration, → House; RSV "plan") with the *plērōma* (fullness) of times (*kairōn*). He wishes to stress that the Christ-event does not lie in the realm of human factors and possibilities but in the counsel of God (v. 9).

3. *The fulfilment of God's will.* (a) Discussion of fulfilment of the → Law in the NT is always concerned with the basic thought that "love is the fulfilling of the law [*plērōma oun nomou hē agapē*]" (Rom. 13:10). "For he who loves his neighbour has fulfilled [*peplērōken*] the law" (Rom. 13:8). In Gal. 5:14 Paul says that, "The whole law is fulfilled in one word, 'You shall love your neighbour as yourself'" (quoting Lev. 19:18; cf. Matt. 22:39; Jn. 13:34). Concretely, this can mean: "Bear one another's burdens, and so fulfil [*anaplērōsete*] the law of Christ" (Gal. 6:2).

(b) In the Sermon on the Mount Jesus said that he had not come to abolish the law and the prophets (i.e. the scriptures in which God has made his will known) but to fulfil them (Matt. 5:17). However one attempts to resolve the tension between vv. 18 ff. and 21 ff., it is clear that fulfilment is not to be understood in a formal way. Here too the basic motive is love. Jesus has shown this love from the first in fulfilling "all righteousness" (Matt. 3:15).

(c) The righteous demand of the law still remains, but the sting of death is removed. Through the righteous act (*dikaiōma*) of Christ righteousness has come to us (Rom. 5:18). The sending of God's Son and the condemnation of sin in the flesh (Rom. 8:3) effect what the law could not do, "in order that the just requirement of the law might be fulfilled in us, who walk not according to the flesh but according to the Spirit" (Rom. 8:4).

4. *Being filled with the Spirit.* In this connection *pimplēmi* and *pleroō* are used only in the pass. God is always thought of as the giver. The adj. *plērēs* also occurs. The thought is specifically Lucan. Paul develops his doctrine of the → Spirit in a quite different way.

(a) In Lk. 1:15 John the Baptist is said to be "filled [*plēsthēsetai*] with the Holy Spirit" from his mother's womb. Likewise, his parents Elizabeth (v. 41) and Zechariah (v. 67) are full of the Holy Spirit in their prophesying.

(b) Lk. 4:1 records that Jesus returned from his baptism "full of the Holy Spirit." From the parallel passage in Mk. 1:12 it is apparent that the older tradition contained another view which was more dynamic and related to the OT. The Spirit drives (*ekballei*) Jesus into the desert as a personal power (cf. the temporary endowment by the Spirit of the charismatic leaders in the Book of Judges, e.g. Jdg. 6:34; 11:29; 14:19). Lk., on the other hand, presents the idea of a special act of bestowing the Spirit in baptism which endows the recipient with an enduring, miraculous power.

(c) What until Pentecost, the decisive date for the universal church, was the privilege of only a few individuals, is from that day forward the most important characteristic of the Jewish and subsequently (cf. Acts 10) the Gentile church. According to Acts 2:4, all were "filled with the Holy Spirit." This was manifest in the gift of tongues. The connection between being filled (*pimplanai*) and speaking also comes out in Acts 4:8 and 4:31 (cf. 13:9). It signifies that the filling is not an end in itself, but the condition for speaking with boldness in the missionary situation (cf. especially Acts 4:31). Although being filled with the Spirit appears to be a mark of the Christian in general, it is specially stressed in the case of certain individuals, such as Stephen (Acts 6:5, 10; 7:55), Paul (9:17) and Barnabas (11:24).

(d) Acts 6 shows that various gifts were apparently bestowed together with the gift of the Spirit: wisdom (vv. 3, 10), faith (v. 5), grace and power (v. 8). "Full of grace [*plērēs charitos*]" is a specifically Lucan expression (8 times in the Gospel; 17 times in Acts). → Grace, art. *charis*. On Acts 13:52 → Joy, art. *chairō*.

Without the Spirit one can be filled with bad qualities: wrath (Acts 19:28; Lk. 4:28), fury (Lk. 6:11), jealousy (Acts 5:17; 13:45), vices which are normally connected with *pimplēmi*. Peter, filled with the Spirit, unmasked their originator as Satan (Acts 5:3; 13:9). There is evidently no neutral position for a man between Christ and → Satan (Lk. 11:23 ff.).

(e) Paul saw men as standing between these two alternatives. A man either brings forth "the → fruit of the Spirit" or he does "the works of the → flesh" (Gal. 5:19, 22). This is also made clear by Phil. 1:11, where Paul exhorts the Philippians to sanctification by being "filled with the fruits of righteousness which come through Jesus Christ." Here, however, Paul's quite different doctrine of the Spirit comes into the open. To be filled with the power of the Spirit means to "live by the Spirit [*zōmen pneumati*]" (Gal. 5:25), or to be "in Christ", to "have the mind of Christ [*noun Christou echein*]" (1 Cor. 2:16), and thus to have the fullness of the gifts of grace flow through one as a member of the → body of Christ.

5. *The fullness of Christ.* A few passages in the NT speak of being filled by Christ. The noun *plērōma* is used in this connection. It is not easy to attribute a single, unambiguous meaning to it. In Rom. 11:12 it means "full inclusion" (RSV) and in Rom. 11:25 "full number" (RSV). It means "fullness" in Rom. 15:29 and fulfilling in the act. sense in Rom. 13:10.

(a) Jn. 1:16 says that the incarnate → Word possesses a fullness, which has already been referred to in v. 14, where the Logos is described as being "full of grace and truth." This fullness is not a gnostic mystery of the heavenly world, but (like the → glory [*doxa*] in v. 14) revelation. Men can see it and have a part in this glory.

(b) According to Col. 2:9, "the whole fullness of deity dwells bodily [*katoikei pan to plērōma tēs theotētos sōmatikōs*]" in Christ. This fullness which is described in Col. 1:15–18 is entirely related to Christ's cross (v. 20), death (v. 22), and resurrection (v. 18). For this reason believers also have this fullness in him (2:10). By his cross, death and resurrection they are reconciled through faith (2:12 ff.), renewed, and made to participate in his triumph. ([Ed.] Some scholars see in Col. 2:1–15 Paul's answer to the specifically gnostic features of the Colossian heresy [cf. R. N. Longenecker, *The Christology of Early Jewish Christianity*, 1970, 56 f.; and the discussions in C. F. D. Moule, " 'Fullness' and 'Full' in the New Testament", *SJT* 4, 1951, 80; and R. McL. Wilson, "Gnosis, Gnosticism and the New Testament" in U. Bianchi, ed., *Le Origini dello Gnosticismo*, 1967, 518 ff.]. *plērōma* was certainly a technical term in later Valentinian gnosticism. But as both Moule and Wilson point out, the expression in Col. 2:9 cannot possibly be equated with the gnostic's hierarchy of beings lying between God and the world. It must mean deity, Godhead, entirely, the sum total of divine attributes. Wilson suggests that certain elements of later gnostic speculation [such as Jesus as the perfect fruit and star of the *plērōma*] appear to originate in Col. 1:19, 2:9, and Eph. 4:13. He concludes that the term should not be claimed to be specifically gnostic, nor should a gnostic interpretation be put upon it at all costs. On the other hand, a sweeping rejection of any relation to gnosticism would be equally erroneous. The whole complex of ideas in Eph. and Col. suggests that we have to deal with something here that was already in process of developing into what we know as second-century gnosticism. But the obscurity of the situation requires the greatest caution in drawing conclusions.)

(c) Believers "have come to fullness of life in him" (Col. 2:10). But the fact of salvation does not exclude their own contribution to this fullness. Eph. 3:19 contains the prayer that the readers may "know the love of Christ which surpasses knowledge, that you may be filled with all the fullness of God" (RSV). This knowledge is not given automatically. It depends upon the building up of the church as the body of Christ. Christian service must contribute to the realization of the unity of faith and the knowledge of the Son of God. This in turn leads "to the measure of the stature of the fullness of Christ" (Eph. 4:13), in which believers are no longer carried about by every wind of doctrine (v. 14). This faith-knowledge is assured by Christ and is given to the church "which is his body, the fullness of him who fills all in all" (Eph. 1:23).

6. *The filling up of the measure of sin.* It was seen above (section OT) that the filling up of the measure of sin in the OT was applied to the Gentile nations. Tob. 14:5 restricts it to them and argues that God will protect the people of Israel against it. But in Matt. 23:32 Jesus says expressly to the Jewish leaders: "Fill up, then, the measure of your fathers [*plērōsate to metron tōn paterōn hymōn*]." This implies that they sin just as much as their fathers, or that they fill out what was still lacking in sins. Paul also turns the expression against the Jews in 1.Thess. 2:16: they have killed the Lord Jesus and the prophets "and drove us out, and displease God and oppose all men" (v. 15), "by hindering us from speaking to the Gentiles that they may be saved – so as always to fill up the measure of their sins [*eis to anaplērōsai*

autōn tas hamartias pantote]. But God's wrath has come upon them at last [*eis telos*]" (RSV; cf. RSV mg. "completely" or "for ever").

7. *Filling a need.* In the Pauline letters the vbs. *anaplēroō* (1 Cor. 16:17; Phil. 2:30), *antanaplēroō* (Col. 1:24) and *prosanaplēroō* (2 Cor. 9:12; 11:9) are linked with *hysterēma*, lack (both in sing. and plur.), in the sense of to fill a lack which someone has. Thus, the coming of Stephanas, Fortunatus and Achaicus made up for being separated from the Corinthian church (1 Cor. 16:17). Epaphroditus served Paul as the representative of the Philippian church in their stead (Phil. 2:30). Perhaps he even completed what was still lacking. In Col. 1:24 Paul declares: "Now I rejoice in my suffering for your sake, and in my flesh I complete what is lacking in Christ's afflictions for the sake of his body, that is, the church." There are still afflictions of Christ (→ Persecution, art. *thlipsis*), for the sufferings of the church are not to be separated from those of Christ. Not all persecution fell to the historical Jesus; a part remains for the members of the → body of Christ, the → church. Paul, the servant (Col. 1:23, 25) felt that the great suffering that was his lot was in a certain measure → suffering for the body of Christ. He can thus rejoice in his own suffering, because he thereby diverts the suffering of the church. ([Ed.] J. B. Lightfooot distinguished between sufferings which made satisfaction and those which were edificatory. Christ's sufferings were the former; Paul's were the latter in that they came about through the work of building up the church [*Saint Paul's Epistles to the Colossians and to Philemon*, 1879³, 164 f.].)

8. *Complete joy.* In Jn. and the Johannine letters there is a frequent connection between → joy (*chara*) as a subject and the vb. *plēroō* in the pass., to be filled. This joy is the joy of Jesus (Jn. 15:11; 17:13) which he brings through his coming (3:29), his words (15:11; 17:13), and his return (16:22) to his disciples (15:11; 17:13). It replaces the sorrow that fills their hearts (16:16, 20). Thus Christ's joy becomes their joy (15:11; 16:24; cf. 1 Jn. 1:4). This joy characterizes the life of the disciples in their walk with Jesus; it becomes complete (Jn. 3:29; 15:11; 16:24; 17:13; 1 Jn. 1:4; 2 Jn. 12). The pass. underlies the fact that it is God who completes this joy.

R. Schippers

| χωρέω | χωρέω (*chōreō*), make room, give way, go, go out, go away, reach, have room for, hold, contain. |

CL *chōreō* is a verbal derivative of *chōros* or *chōra*, an open space, a land, country, region.

1. Intrans. it means to give room, to be in motion from one place to another. (a) When applied to persons, it means: to give ground in battle (Hom., *Il.*, 17, 533); with preps. in an extended sense, to tackle and carry out something, e.g. to start a rebellion (Appian, *Bella civilia*, 5, 4, 30); to come to regret an action (Plut., *De Fluviis*, 9, 2). (b) When applied to things, its meaning includes: to move things, e.g. the fluid content of a body (Aristot., *Problemata*, 1, 55); to spread news or commands (Xen., *Institutio Cyri*, 3, 3, 62; Plato, *Epistolae*, 7, 338b); to take course, of a process or undertaking, e.g. a war (Thuc., 1, 82, 6; without specifying whether a successful outcome was reached, Plut., *De Galba*, 10, 1).

2. Trans. it means: (a) to be able to take up, hold (of cavities, vessels, Diod. Sic., 13, 83, 3); (b) in an extended sense, to be able to put up with someone (of a city,

741

Dem., 21, 200); in the post-Christian era (cf. OT 2 (b)) also of intellectual and spiritual capacities (Plut., *De Catone Minore*, 64, 3).

OT 1. *chōreō* is rare in the LXX. In the 6 instances where there is a Heb. equivalent, it translates 5 Heb. roots. It is used in connection with the capacity to hold of cultic vessels (e.g. 1 Ki. 7:38; cf. Jn. 2:6; see below NT 2 (a)).

2. In the literature of Hel. Judaism outside the LXX *chōreō* is relatively common: (a) intrans. of war spreading (Jos., *War*, 6, 130); of human wickedness increasing and spreading (Test. Iss. 1:11); (b) trans. often of man's incapacity to grasp the knowledge of God presented to him (Philo, *Spec. Leg.*, 1, 44) or to bear the word of God (*Post. C.*, 143).

NT 1. *Intransitive use.* The expression *pantas eis metanoian chōrēsai* (2 Pet. 3:9, "that all should reach repentance" RSV) corresponds to the use of *chōreō* in the sense of tackling something and carrying it out. The thought is probably that of a single act that is possible, because God is delaying the last judgment. The phrase *eis tēn koilian chōrei* (Matt. 15:17 "passes into the stomach") corresponds to the description of physiological processes in medicine (see above, CL 1 (b)). It expresses a certain independence of the natural processes of the mind and the will (→ Heart, art. *kardia*). *chōreō* in Jn. 8:37 means to spread or make progress. It is applied to the failure of Jesus' word to make progress in the hearts and minds of his Jewish opponents. The assumption is less likely that *en* (in) is used in the sense of *eis* (into), giving the meaning that the word of Jesus finds no access. If the context of Jn. 8:30 is to be understood, Jesus is speaking to Jews who have heard his teaching with approval yet without letting it take effect. On the other hand, there is a tension between Jn. 8:31 and v. 37. The underlying thought is that of a process through which man is freed from the bondage to sin (8:32, 34).

2. *Transitive use.* (a) *chōreō* is used to denote the capacity to hold of water jugs (Jn. 2:6), of a place (Mk. 2:2, "so that there was no longer room for them, not even about the door"), and the world (Jn. 21:25). (b) It means to receive or embrace the apocalyptic teaching of Jesus (Matt. 19:11 f., contained in vv. 9 or 10). The meaning corresponds to understanding and grasping the teaching of the parables (cf. Matt. 13:11, 16 f., 19, 23). In both instances Matt. stresses the understanding of the disciples. *chōreō* appears to go beyond understanding and points to the capacity to receive and act upon the teaching. Matt. 19:12 contains a form of apocalyptic warning found elsewhere in primitive Christianity. It exhorts a group of people who have been given an insight or a gift for something to make use of it, and thereby marks off this group from others. Paul's plea, "Make room for us [*chōrēsate hēmas*]" (2 Cor. 7:2), takes up his earlier plea to extend themselves (6:13), and corresponds to the assurance that, "You are not restricted [*stenochōreisthe*] by us, but you are restricted [*stenochōreisthe*] in your own affections" (6:12). The Corinthians are to recognize Paul in his apostolic ministry as he has given himself to be known by them (2 Cor. 1–6), so that they can be proud of each other on the day of the Lord Jesus (2 Cor. 1:14). *P. Schmidt*

γέμω

γέμω (*gemō*), to load, be full; γεμίζω (*gemizō*), to load; γεμιστός (*gemistos*), laden.

CL In secular Gk. *gemō*, used only in pres. and imp., and *gemizō* were properly used of loading a ship (Herodotus, Thucydides), animals (Posidonius), and of being full, e.g. a harbour with craft (Plato). They are found in an extended sense also: full of truth (Aeschylus); full of evil (Euripides); of over-boldness, of disproportion and ugliness (Plato).

OT In the LXX *gemō* and its cognates are used only 6 times (omitting a mistaken use in Job 32:19) and translate the Heb. *nāśā'*, in the sense of bearing spices, gold (Gen. 37:25; 2 Chr. 9:21); *ṭā'an*, loading beasts (Gen. 45:17); *mālē'*, adj. full (Ps. 10:7; Amos 2:13).

NT Of the 20 occurrences of the vbs. in the NT, most convey the sense of filling an object with something, the root idea of "loading", used originally in exaggeration, having been forgotten. In the other instances the filling is with something intangible and usually uncomplimentary: full of wickedness (Matt. 23:25; Lk. 11:39); of cursing and bitterness (Rom. 3:4); of God's wrath (Rev. 15:7); of possessions (Rev. 17:3); of abominations (Rev. 17:4); of seven plagues (Rev. 21:9).

χορτάζω

χορτάζω (*chortazō*), to feed, fatten; *χόρτασμα* (*chortasma*), used mostly in plur., fodder; *χόρτος* (*chortos*), enclosed pasturage, fodder.

CL In earlier Gk. *chortazō* was used uniformly of animals but in the exaggeration of comedy was applied to men feasting. Under the influence of colloquial use, it lost its strong sense and became virtually the equivalent of *esthiō*. It used at least twice in this sense by Eubulus. *chortos*, feeding place, fodder for animals, implies primarily grass or hay for horses and cattle, but as early as the 6th and 5th centuries B.C. it was being used in poetry for food in general (Hipponax, Euripides).

OT In the LXX *chortazō* translates the Heb. *śāba'*, to be sated with. While the basic idea is that of satisfying with food (Pss. 37:19; 59:15; 132:15), the ground is satisfied with rain (Job 38:27), the trees with sap (Ps. 104:13), and the earth with the fruit of God's works (Ps. 104:13). On two occasions disillusion is expressed (Jer. 5:7; Lam. 3:15, 29), but more often the depth of satisfaction goes beyond that of mere food to that of seeing and knowing God (Pss. 17:15; 81:16; 107:9).

chortasma 4 times translates *mispô'*, provender (Gen. 24:25, 32; 42:27; 43:24; Jdg. 19:19), and once *'ēśeb*, grass (Deut. 11:15). *chortos* translates a variety of words for grass, plants, among which are *'ēśeb*, which includes human food (e.g. Gen. 1:29; 2:5; 3:18); *deše'*, grass (Ps. 37:2; Is. 15:6); *ḥāṣîr*, grass (Isa. 15:6; 44:4; 51:12); *šāmîr*, thorns (Isa. 32:13). Because grass grows in Palestine only during the period of the winter and spring rains and withers immediately the heat comes, it is a ready illustration of the brevity of human life, used especially in the poetical books (Job 13:25; Pss. 37:2; 102:4, 11; 103:15), and in Isaiah (37:27; 40:6, 7).

NT In the NT *chortazō* is used almost invariably to mean to eat or to satisfy with food, as in the accounts of the feeding of the five and four thousand (Matt. 14:20; 15:33; Mk. 6:42; 8:4, 8; Lk. 9:17; Jn. 6:26). The evangelists all laid stress on the fact that the crowds not only ate but were satisfied, so taking up the sense of *chortazō* in the LXX of the Psalms, and Jesus promises the same in the Beatitudes (Matt. 5:6; Lk. 6:21). That all distinction between this vb. and *esthiō* has vanished is clear from Mk. 7:27, 28, where *esthiō* is used for the pet dogs and *chortazō* for the children. For this reason it is probably incorrect to say that Paul allows himself a vulgarism in Phil. 4:12 (Nägeli, 58, quoted in Moulton and Milligan). The only other occurrences of the verb are in Lk. 16:21, Jas. 2:16 and Rev. 19:21. *chortasma* occurs once only in the sense of food (Acts 7:11). *chortos* is used of growing plants (Matt. 13:26; Mk. 4:28), of hay as an insubstantial building material (1 Cor. 3:12), and of grass in general, commented upon because only at certain seasons was there green grass (Mk. 6:39), much grass (Jn. 6:10; cf. Matt. 14:19). The short life of the grass of the field is used by Jesus as an *a fortiori* argument that God will clothe his children (Matt. 6:30; Lk. 12:28). James and Peter quote from Isa. 40:7, 8 (Jas. 1:10, 11; 1 Pet. 1:24), emphasizing the shortness of human life. In the only other occurrences of the word it is used literally of grass (Rev. 8:7; 9:4).   *J. G. Baldwin*

(a). B. W. Anderson, ed., *The Old Testament and Christian Faith*, 1964; P. Benoit, "Body, Head and *Pleroma* in the Epistles of the Captivity", *Jesus and the Gospel*, II, 1974, 51–92; F. F. Bruce, *This is That: The New Testament Development of Some Old Testament Themes*, 1968; F. F. Bruce, ed., *Promise and Fulfilment: Essays Presented to Professor S. H. Hooke*, 1963; R. Bultmann, "Prophecy and Fulfilment," *Essays*, 1955, 182–208; W. D. Davies, "Matthew 5:17, 18," *Christian Origins and Judaism*, 1962, 31–66; G. Delling, *plērēs, plēroō*, etc., *TDNT* VI 283–309; W. Eichrodt, *Theology of the Old Testament*, I, 1961, 381–7; C. H. Dodd, *According to the Scriptures*, 1952; E. E. Ellis, *Paul's Use of the Old Testament*, 1957; R. T. France, *Jesus and the Old Testament*, 1971; L. Goppelt, *typos* etc. *TDNT* VIII, 246–59; R. H. Gundry, *The Use of the Old Testament in St. Matthew's Gospel*, 1967; F. Hauck, *perisseuō*, *TDNT* VI 58–62; W. G. Kümmel, *Promise and Fulfilment: the Eschatological Message of Jesus*, 1961²; B. Lindars, *New Testament Apologetic*, 1961; W. Lock, "Pleroma," *HDB* IV 1 f.; B. J. Roberts, "Bible Exegesis and Fulfilment in Qumran," in P. R. Ackroyd and B. Lindars, eds., *Words and Meanings: Essays Presented to David Winton Thomas*, 1968, 195–208; C. F. D. Moule, "Fulfilment," *IDB* II 327–330; and " 'Fulness' and 'Fill' in the New Testament," *SJT* 4, 1951, 79–86; and "Fulfilment-Words in the New Testament: Use and Abuse", *NTS* 14, 1967–68, 293–320; G. von Rad, *Old Testament Theology*, II, 1965, 357–87; J. A. Robinson, *St. Paul's Epistle to the Ephesians*, 1903, 255–59; K. Runia, "The Interpretation of the Old Testament by the New Testament," *Vox Reformata*, 5, 1965; J. Schildenberger, "Fulfilment," *EBT* I 289–95; K. Stendahl, *The School of St. Matthew*, 1968²; R. Yates, "A Re-examination of Ephesians 1:23," *ExpT* 83, 1971–72, 146–51.
(b). F. Baumgärtel and W. G. Kümmel, "Weissagung und Erfüllung," *RGG*³ VI 1584–88; H. Berkhof, *Die Katholizität der Kirche*, 1964; P. Bläser, "Erfüllung der Schrift," *LTK* III 983 f.; H. Gross, "Zum Problem Verheissung und Erfüllung," *BZ* 3, 1959, 3–17; P. Ketter, "Nicht alle fassen das Wort," *Pastor Bonus* 49, 1938–39, 311 ff.; H. Ljungmann, "Das Gesetz erfüllen," *Lunds Universitets Årsskrift*, New Series I, 30, 1954; W. Rothfuchs, *Die Erfüllungszitate des Matthäusevangeliums*, 1969; J. Schildenberger, "Weissagung und Erfüllung," *Biblica* 24, 1943, 107–24 and 205–30; and *Vom Geheimnis des Gotteswortes*, 1950, 181–204; A. Schlatter, *Paulus, der Bote Jesu. Eine Deutung seiner Briefe an die Korinther*, 1934; H. Schlier, *Christus und die Kirche im Epheserbrief*, *BHTh* 6, 1930; R. Steiger, *Die Dialektik der paulinischen Existenz*, 1931; A. Suhl, *Die Funktion der alttestamentliche Zitate und Anspielungen im Markusevangelium*, 1965.

Indexes

Index of Hebrew
and Aramaic Words

Index of Greek Words

757

General Index

(chief references in **bold figures***)*

Aaronic blessing 98, 211, 212
Aaron's rod 408
Abandon 455, 488, 513, 526, 541, 549, 606, 613, 681, 701, 720
Abandonment 51, 411, 559, 595
Abase 731
Abba 286, 289, 410, 614, 623
Abdomen 169
Abhor 555
Abide 166, 282, 338, 458, 608, 611, 637, 638, 669, 723
Abiding 73, 469, 719
Ability 248, 278, 481, 676, 681, 731
Ablution 144, 149, 150, 152, 153
Abode 523, 661
Abolish 73, 368, 414, 462, 469, 591, 622, 676, 685, 738
Abolition 719
Abomination 109, 142, 225, 382, 448, 743
Abomination of Desolation 74–75, 125, 566
Aborted 182
Abound 683, 728–744
Above 518, 665
Abraham 76–80, 159, 286, 311, 531, 539, 601, 604, 640, 669, 684, 690, 693
Abraham's bosom 78, 240
Abroad 689
Abrogate 500
Absence 598, 724
Absent 466
Absolute 500, 522, 616, 636, 718
Absolution 639
Absolutism 543
Absolve 529
Absorb 709
Abstain 261, 494, 541, 611, 690, 691, 704
Abstemious 515
Abstinence 494–496, 514, 611, 612, 625
Abstract 450, 537, 562, 609
Abstraction 601, 641
Abstruse 421
Absurd 637
Abundance 727–732
Abuse 183, 264, 413, 418, 646
Abyss 449, 508
Accede 320, 322
Accept 110, 112, 368, 375, 414, 425, 483, 484, 486–488, 556, 568, 578, 590, 629, 666, 695
Acceptable 235, 675, 708
Acceptance 534, 588, 593, 603, 655, 701, 702
Access 223, 324, 390, 485, 592, 603, 611, 638, 742

Accessible 602
Accession 177, 626
Acclamation 122, 629, 630
Accommodate 548
Accompany 322, 480, 481, 585
Accomplish 696, 733, 737
Accomplishment 653, 680, 697
Account 56, 378, 386, 573, 577, 588, 725
Accountability 349, 522
Accursed 265, 390, 413, 414, 416, 417
Accusation 82–84, 281, 373, 402, 577, 594, 609, 612, 631
Accuse 82–84, 349, 350, 410, 473
Accuser 82–84, 454, 554, 610
Accustomed 483, 484
Achievement 398, 431, 432, 485, 492, 493, 502, 612, 645, 647, 650, 651, 676, 697, 722, 723
Acknowledge 265, 489, 549, 587
Acknowledgment 415
Acquaint 692
Acquire 482–484, 635, 639
Acquisition 533
Acquit 205, 352, 439, 505, 558, 698
Action 207, 484, 504, 505, 552, 556, 564, 585, 589–591, 600, 603, 639, 679, 680, 693, 697, 702, 713, 714, 721, 722, 741, 742
Active 400, 605, 624
Activity 489, 491, 595, 627, 655, 686, 693, 695–697
Actor 706, 708
Actual 710, 711
Actualization 711, 713
Adam 71, 73, 77, 84–88, 179, 327, 390, 434, 436, 440, 446, 451, 472, 548, 567, 621, 669, 730
Adapt 481, 483
Add 540
Addict 514
Address 66, 285, 286, 488, 582, 614–617, 620, 622
Adequacy 576
Adequate 690
Adherent 487, 489, 535
Adjuration 97, 98
Adjustment 602, 679, 715
Administer 536
Administration 192, 738
Administrative 198
Administrator 190, 198, 373
Admiration 99, 435
Admit 680
Admonition 110, 319, 462, 502, 568, 569

Force 453, 508, 543, 651, 653, 678, 679, 692, 694, 717, 720, 733
Forearm 393
Forebear 287
Forecast 699
Forecourt 633
Forefather 280, 285, 324, 615, 665
Foreign 305, 505, 522, 550, 551, 553, 622, 655, **683–692**
Foreigner 308, 392, 474, 715
Foreknowledge 273, 278, 378, 382, 383, 471, 477, 478, 540, 542, 668, **692–697**
Forensic 438
Forerunner 125, 150, 544, 545
Foresee 471, 693, 695
Foreshadow 115, 158, 266, 290, 545
Foresight 692–694
Foreskin 307–309, 672
Foretell 528
Forethought 692, 693
Forfeit 240, 484
Forget 441, 484, 546, 570, 728
Forgiveness 86, 87, 97, 110, 146, 148, 155–158, 191, 216, 222–225, 301, 303, 317, 327, 328, 333, 346, 351, 354, 355, 358, 359, 371, 375, 467, 492, 499, 500, 545, 643, 673, **697–703**, 722, 730
Forgiving 617, 620, 640
Form 50, 66, 71, 204, 234, 299, 355, 371, 380, 525, 547, 636, 678, **703–714**, 722, 737
Form-criticism **57**, 58, 67, 68, 576
Form history 57
Formal 664, 714, 738
Formality 394
Former 665
Former Prophets **66**
Formless 380
Formulation 579, 705
Fornication 106, 233, 469, 496–501, 559, 672
Forsake 493, 552
Forsaken 113, 174
Fortress 636
Fortunate 215
Fortune 208, 435, 482, 489, 543, 585, 596, 671, 673
Fortune-teller 463
Forward 665
Foul 110, 114
Found 376, 377, 383
Foundation 244, 279, 302, 327, 329, 375, **376–389**, 390, 391, 540, 542, 543, 596, 598, 602, **658–664**, 684, 693, 697
Founder 168, 641, 669
Foundling 616
Fountain 151, 552
Fox 118, 173
Fracture 302
Fragile 678
Fragment 464
Fragrance 122, 439, 650
Frailty 678, 679
Frankincense 586
Frankness 329, 715

Fraternal 572
Free 120, 223, 275, 310, 346, 371, 401, 432, 439, 452, 470, 482, 506, 525, 526, 529, 534, 536, 537, 540, 542, 562, 572, 632, 651, 666, 677, 684, 697, 699, 702, **715–721**, 723, 728, 742
Free will (→ Will, Free)
Free-will offering 344, 534
Freeborn 411, 715
Freedmen 297, 715, 718
Freedom 54, 62, 79, 81, 148, 219, 238, 248, 286, 289, 298, 310, 360, 383, 386, 400, 412, 435, 439, 447, 458, 475, 483, 494, 500, 525, 534, 569, 629, 633, 642, 667, 674, **715–721**, 728, 731, 737
Freeman 299, 392
Freethinkers 62, 555
Freeze 671
Frenzy 528
Friend 77, 206, 215, **254–260**, 270, 284, 365, 484, 555, 557, 559, 571, 640, 663, 665
Friendship 338, 553, 554, 687
Fright 621, 673
Frighten 226, 328, 527
Fringes 254
Frivolity 501
Frog 114, 408
Front 665
Frost 652
Frostbite 652
Frozen 443
Fructify 498
Frugal 597
Fruit 77, 85, 87, 112, 139, 178, 181, 187, 228, 240, 297, 358, 382, 389, 390, 417, 496, 515, 540, 557, 565, 633, 669, 671, 681–683, 686, **721–728**, 739, 740, 743
Fruit-bearing 542
Fruitful 180, 211, 214, 496
Fruitfulness 723
Fruitless 263, 547, 549, 721, 723
Frustration 468, 681
Fuel 389
Fulfil 99, 178, 216, 289, 322, 335, 337, 349, 352, 367, 369, 409, 417, 492, 509, 545, 556, 596, 604, 640, 658, 674, 711, 713, 719, **728–744**
Fulfiller 303
Fulfilment 72, 95, 117, 138, 170, 175, 214, 223, 228, 243, 251, 290, 305, 311, 329, 339, 368, 370, 372, 374, 375, 411, 416, 428, 429, 439, 445, 460, 485, 492, 532, 536, 538, 545, 560, 570, 581, 587, 592, 601–603, 615, 624, 626, 634, 637, 647, 657, 697, 701, 719, 736, 737
Full 546, 732
Fuller 151
Fullness 93, 95, 171, 237, 238, 323, 402, 417, 522, 532, 552, 601, 638, 676, 697, 723, **728–744**
Function 128, 129, 133, 188–190, 193, 194, 196–198, 219, 230, 231, 237, 280, 300, 302, 336, 349, 352, 373, 375, 378, 486, 533, 536, 544, 549, 572, 648, 667, 681, 711, 737

795

797

807

813